THE WORKS

OF

HUBERT HOWE BANCROFT

THE WORKS

OF

HUBERT HOWE BANCROFT

VOLUME XXII.

HISTORY OF CALIFORNIA
VOL. V. 1846-1848

979. 4
B
v. 5
c. 1

PRINTED IN FACSIMILE FROM THE FIRST AMERICAN EDITION

PUBLISHED AT SANTA BARBARA BY WALLACE HEBBERD

To

DORIS MARION WRIGHT

A Valley White Oak   drawing by John Gorham

THE WORKS

OF

HUBERT HOWE BANCROFT.

THE WORKS

OF

HUBERT HOWE BANCROFT.

VOLUME XXII.

HISTORY OF CALIFORNIA.

Vol. V. 1846–1848.

SAN FRANCISCO:
THE HISTORY COMPANY, PUBLISHERS.
1886.

CONTENTS OF THIS VOLUME.

CHAPTER I.

OPERATIONS OF FRÉMONT AND GILLESPIÉ.

January–May, 1846.

CHAPTER II.

POLITICAL AND MILITARY.

January–June, 1846.

CHAPTER VI.

CHAPTER VII.

CHAPTER VIII.

CHAPTER IX.

PRELIMINARIES OF THE CONQUEST.
1846.

CHAPTER X.

CONQUEST BY THE UNITED STATES—SLOAT'S RULE.
July, 1846.

CHAPTER XI.

THE CONQUEST—STOCKTON'S RULE—OCCUPATION OF THE SOUTH.
August, 1846.

CHAPTER XII.

CHAPTER XIII.

CHAPTER XIV.

CHAPTER XV.

THE CONQUEST COMPLETED BY STOCKTON AND FRÉMONT.

January, 1847.

CHAPTER XVI.

STOCKTON'S CONTROVERSY WITH KEARNY.

January–February, 1847.

CHAPTER XVII.

FRÉMONT'S CONTROVERSY WITH KEARNY.

March–May, 1847.

CHAPTER XVIII.

THE MORMON BATTALION.

1846-1848.

PAGE

CHAPTER XIX.

NEW YORK VOLUNTEERS AND ARTILLERY COMPANY.

1846-1848.

CHAPTER XX.

PIONEERS—DONNER PARTY—THE MORMONS.

1846-1848.

CHAPTER XXIV.

LOCAL ANNALS OF THE NORTH.

1846–1848.

HISTORY OF CALIFORNIA.

CHAPTER I.

OPERATIONS OF FRÉMONT AND GILLESPIE.

JANUARY–MAY, 1846.

EXPLORERS IN THE TULARES—FRÉMONT AT NEW HELVETIA, YERBA BUENA, AND SAN JOSÉ—VISIT TO LARKIN AND CASTRO AT MONTEREY—EXPLANATIONS TO THE PREFECT—PERMISSION TO RECRUIT HIS MEN ON THE FRONTIER—THE WALKER-TALBOT-KERN PARTY—IN CAMP AT FISHER'S RANCHO—FRÉMONT BREAKS HIS AGREEMENT—INSULT TO ALCALDE PACHECO—OVER THE SANTA CRUZ MOUNTAINS—IN CAMP AT ALISAL— ORDERED TO DEPART—DEFIANCE—THE STARS AND STRIPES ON GAVILAN PEAK—LARKIN'S EFFORTS—CASTRO'S MILITARY PREPARATIONS—FALSITY OF CURRENT VERSIONS—FRÉMONT RUNS AWAY—HIS BLUNDER—PROCLAMATIONS AND REPORTS—IN THE SACRAMENTO VALLEY—LETTER TO CLYMAN—TO THE OREGON BORDER—A NIGHT ATTACK BY INDIANS— BACK TO CALIFORNIA—GILLESPIE'S ARRIVAL AND INSTRUCTIONS—UP THE RIVER BY BOAT—SUTTER'S WARNING TO CASTRO.

THE present volume is devoted to the annals of 1846–7, including also 1848 in all matters not directly connected with the great event of that year, the discovery of gold. The period is by far the most eventful in Californian history. The volume may be termed a History of the Conquest. It includes, however, besides developments pertaining to the change of flag and Mexican war, the earlier operations of American filibusters constituting what is known as the Bear Flag revolt, and the later interregnum of military rule. Here I record the last petty quarrels under Mexican auspices of north and south, of the military and civil authorities, of Castro and Pico. Here I chronicle the foolish interference of Frémont and his explorers, the diplomatic efforts of Larkin and Stearns to secure a change of sovereignty by pacific methods, the revolutionary blunders of Ide and his associate settlers, and the raising of the stars and stripes by Sloat and Montgomery of the navy. Next are presented the achievements of the California battalion, Stockton's rule, the commodore's unwise policy and energetic struggles to put down the resulting revolt, the final efforts of the Californians under Flores and Andrés Pico to shake off the foreign yoke, the coming of Kearny and his dragoons across the continent, their disaster at San Pascual, and the closing campaigns of the war ending in the occupation of Los Ángeles and the treaty of Cahuenga. Then follow politico-military controversies of Stockton, Kearny, and Frémont under the new régime, reënforcements by land and sea for garrison service, Cooke and his Mormon battalion, Tompkins, Sherman, Ord, and Halleck with the artillery company, Stevenson and the New York volunteers, the peaceful rule of Mason as military governor, and news of a national treaty making California a permanent possession of the United States. In this volume are given also institutional annals of 1846–8, a commercial and maritime record, mission and ecclesiastical affairs under new conditions, the immigration of three years, with the tragic experiences of the Donner party, and several chapters of local annals. Finally, I here complete the alphabetical Pioneer Register and Index of all who came to the country before 1849. All is brought down to the dawn of a new era, that of gold and 'flush times,' to be treated in the following volume.

At the beginning of 1846 Frémont's exploring expedition was encamped in the region now known as Fresno and Kern counties. Frémont with fifteen men had entered California by the Truckee route, and had hastened from Sutter's Fort southward with fresh supplies for the relief of his companions, whom he expected to find on Kings River. Meanwhile the main body of about fifty, under Talbot, Kern, and Walker, had entered the country by Owens River and Walker Pass, and were waiting for the captain on Kern River. The double error in locating the rendezvous has been already explained.[1] At this time the explorers had no intention of meddling with political or military affairs; nor did the Californian authorities know anything of their presence in the country, beyond the bare fact that the smaller party had arrived at New Helvetia in December.

His supplies being nearly exhausted, and Walker's men not making their appearance, Frémont left his camp January 7th and returned to Sutter's Fort, where he arrived on the 15th, after having had, perhaps, some trouble with Indians on the way.[2] He was again warmly welcomed by Sutter, who gave a grand dinner for his entertainment and that of Vice-consul Leidesdorff and Captain Hinckley, who had lately come up the river; and after a stay of four days, with eight of his own men Frémont sailed on Sutter's launch for the bay.[3] From Yerba Buena he sailed with Hinckley on a visit to San José and the newly discovered mine of Almaden;[4] but he was back again before January 24th, on which date he wrote to his wife of past hardships and of the 'good time coming,' when his explorations would be completed and he

[1] See *Hist. Cal.*, vol. iv., chap. xxiv., this series. In a letter of Larkin— that of March 27th, to be noted later—a 'second place of rendezvous' is mentioned, but it was probably New Helvetia.

[2] *Fremont's Geog. Mem.*, 19, 30; Jan. 20th, Larkin to Sutter. Would be glad to see Frémont at Monterey. *Larkin's Off. Corresp.*, MS., i. 73. Tho Ind ian troubles rest on Carson's statement in *Peters' Life of Kit Carson*, 250–1, not a good authority.

[3] *N. Helvetia Diary*, MS., 30–1; *Sutter's Diary*, 6–7.

[4] *Lancey's Cruise of the 'Dale'*, 35–6. This author says that at S. José Frémont learned that Walker's party were encamped on the S. Joaquin, and sent Carson to guide them to S. José; but this, as we shall see, cannot have been so at this time, though he may have sent a man to search for them. In *Peters' Life of Carson*, 251–2, Carson is said to have gone out in search of the other party, whom he found and brought back—which is not true.

might return.[5] On the same day he set out with
Leidesdorff by land for San José and Monterey,
where they were received by Consul Larkin on the
27th.[6]

It is fair to suppose that Frémont's business with
Larkin and Leidesdorff was not only to make arrangements for obtaining fresh supplies, but to talk over
the political situation and prospects in their relation
to the policy of the United States; but while we know
nothing of the conferences in this respect, it is certain
that no hostility or annoyance to the Californians was
proposed, because Larkin, as we shall see later, was
engaged, in accordance with instructions from Washington, and with much hope of success, in efforts to
conciliate the people and prepare the way for a peaceable annexation. At any rate, the explorer became
acquainted with the exact state of affairs. On the
29th, Prefect Castro, as was his duty, addressed to
Larkin a note, asking to be informed respecting the
purpose for which United States troops had entered
the department, and their leader had come to Monterey. Frémont's explanation, transmitted on the same
day through the consul, was that he had come by
order of his government to survey a practicable route
to the Pacific; that he had left his company of fifty
hired men, not soldiers, on the frontier of the department to rest themselves and their animals;[7] that he
had come to Monterey to obtain clothing, and funds
for the purchase of animals and provisions; and that
when his men were recruited, he intended to continue

[5] Jan. 24th, Frémont's letter, in *Niles' Reg.*, lxx. 161. He is now going to
see some gentlemen on the coast—on business; and then will complete his
survey as soon as possible.

[6] Jan. 24th, Sub-prefect Guerrero to prefect. Announces departure of Frémont and Leidesdorff. *Castro, Doc.*, MS., i. 311. Arrival on Jan. 27th. *Doc.
Hist. Cal.*, iii. 86. Lancey tells us that they spent the three nights of the
journey at the ranchos of Francisco Sanchez, Antonio M. Suñol, and Joaquin
Gomez. Wm F. Swasey says that Frémont's men, Godey and others, were
left at Yerba Buena, and went with the writer a little later to S. José by
water. *Swasey's Cal. in 1845-6*, MS., 4.

[7] As a matter of fact, Frémont had at this time no knowledge of his company's whereabouts; for all he knew, they might have perished in the mountains; but it was safe enough to say he had left them 'on the frontier.'

his journey to Oregon. This explanation—repeated at a personal interview between the parties named, in presence of the alcalde, Colonel Alvarado, and General Castro, and also duly forwarded to Governor Pico and the supreme government—was satisfactory, at least to such an extent that no objection was made; and Frémont was thus tacitly permitted to carry out his plans. Pico made no objection, but directed that a close watch be kept on the explorer's movements, with a view to learn if he had any other design than that of preparing for a trip to Oregon.[8]

It should be noted particularly here that the only license given to Frémont at this time was a tacit, or implied, permission to recruit his men on the frontiers, away from the settlements, after obtaining the necessary funds at Monterey. That is, Castro did not order Frémont to quit the country at once, thus indirectly authorizing him to remain. This rests not on the statements of Castro, but of Larkin and Frémont.[9] The current version given by Tuthill, Lan-

[8] In one instance Frémont, *Court-Martial*, 372, claimed that his plan (and Castro's license) was to explore southward to the Gila; but there is no other evidence in this direction, and the difference has no important bearing on what followed. Jan. 29th, prefect to Larkin. The date in the original blotters being Jan. 28th, but changed to 29th; L. to prefect in reply. Originals in *Doc. Hist. Cal.*, MS., ii. 86, 89; *Castro, Doc.*, MS., i. 316; official copies in *Larkin's Off. Corresp.*, MS., i. 76; ii. 146; copies in *Sawyer's Doc.*, MS., 1–2; and printed in *Niles' Reg.*, lxxi. 188. Same date, prefect to gov. *Doc. Hist. Cal.*, MS., iii. 90, 121. Same date, Id. to sup. govt. *Dept. St. Pap.*, MS., vi. 107. Feb. 18th, Pico's reply. *Castro, Doc.*, MS., ii. 15.

[9] L. mentions the interview in his letter of March 4th. *Frémont's Cal. Claims 1848*, in *U. S. Govt Doc.*, 30th cong. 1st sess., Sen. Repts, no. 75, p. 64; *Niles' Reg.*, lxxi. 188–9. Also in the letter of March 9th, in which he says that F. 'informed them of his business; and there was no objection made.' *Frémont's Cal. Claims*, 65; *Larkin's Off. Corresp.*, MS., ii. 44–5. To his office copy of the letter of Jan. 29th, he appends this note: 'The general was at his own request officially informed by Capt. Frémont of his motives in coming here; which motives were accepted by Gen. Castro in not answering the letter.' *Id.*, i. 76. Benton, in his letter of Nov. 9th, *Niles' Reg.*, lxxi. 173, and in his *Thirty Years in U. S. Senate*, ii. 688, states that F. asked and received verbal permission to recruit his men 'in the valley of the San Joaquin,' or 'in the uninhabited parts of the valley of the S. Joaquin.' This is also the version given by the sec. of war in his report of Dec. 5th, 29th cong. 2d sess., H. Ex. Doc. 4, p. 50; and *Cutts' Conq. of Cal.*, 143–4. Frémont himself, *Court-Martial*, 372, says: 'I explained to Gen. Castro the object of my coming into Cal. and my desire to obtain permission to winter in the valley of the S. Joaquin, ... where there was plenty of game, ... and *no inhabitants to be molested by our presence.* Leave was granted,' etc.

cey, Phelps, and others, that Castro gave his word of
honor, and on being urged to put his permission in
writing indulged in some bluster about the 'word of
a Mexican officer,' is pure invention.   All agree, however, that it was in the San Joaquin Valley that the
foreigners were to recuperate their strength.   Naturally anxious about the fate of his companions, Frémont left Monterey a few days later.   Larkin says
it was "well known that he was to return when he
collected his men;"[10] but it is doubtful that this was
known to the authorities, and certain that he was not
expected to bring his men with him.   His route lay
over the mountains to the Santa Clara Valley.[11]

Walker, Talbot, and Kern, with the main body of
explorers, remained on Kern River, waiting for Frémont, until January 18th, when they broke camp and
started northward.   On the 26th they reached Kings
River, mistaking it for the San Joaquin; and in
attempting a cut-off across a supposed 'big bend' of
this stream, they floundered for a day or two in the
tule marshes, but reached the real San Joaquin on the
30th, and February 6th camped on the Calaveras.
From this point Walker with one companion started
out in quest of tidings from Frémont, and met 'Le
Gros' Fallon, the old mountaineer, who reported the
captain to be at San José.   Thereupon Walker went
to the pueblo, while the company returned to the San
Joaquin ford to await orders, hunting grizzly bears
with much success in the mean time.   On the 11th
they were joined by Carson and Owens; and on the
15th, having met a party with fresh horses, they
passed through the town, and at noon rejoined their
captain and companions at the Laguna farm, or
Alvirezs' rancho, or Fisher's—near the historic battle-

[10] Letter of March 27th.   *Larkin's Off. Corresp.*, MS., ii. 45–6.
[11] Feb. 5th he was in the mountains; and Feb. 13th in the valley, probably at Fisher's rancho. *Frémont's Geog. Mem.*, 36.

field of Santa Teresa. The united force amounted to about sixty men.[12]

After remaining about a week in camp, Frémont started with his whole company across the valley and up into the Santa Cruz Mountains by way of Los Gatos, that of the modern railroad—not the most direct route to Oregon, as it seemed to the Californians. His trip across the mountains, past the big trees, took four days; and then, on February 25th, he descended to the coast at a point near Santa Cruz; was delayed for some days by the prevalent rains and fogs; but finally resumed his march on March 1st, following the bay-coast southward, thence turning inland up the Salinas Valley, and encamping on the 3d at Hartnell's rancho, or Alisal.[13] By the very act of permitting his men to enter the Santa Clara Valley, Frémont had broken his agreement with the authorities, and had forfeited every right conferred by Castro's promise, even if that promise had been as direct and definite as any one has ever claimed. His march to the coast without receiving or even asking permission was, under the circumstances, an insult and a menace to the Californian authorities, who, in view of prevalent rumors and fears of war and foreign invasion, would have been justified in manifesting a greater degree of alarm and anger than they did at seeing an armed force of sixty men marching

[12] *Kern's Journal*, 484–6; *Frémont's Geog. Mem.*, 19, 30–1; *Martin's Narr.*, MS., 10–11. Feb. 15th, Marsh writes from Alvirezs' rancho, where he had come to see Frémont. *Larkin's Doc.*, MS., iv. 39.

[13] *Frémont's Geog. Mem.*, 36–7; Larkin's letter of March 27th. *Id.*, *Cal. Claims*, 67. In his letter of March 4th, *Id.*, 64, Larkin says of F.: 'He is now in this vicinity surveying, and will be again at this consular house during this month. He then proceeds for the Oregon, returns here in May, and expects to be in Washington about September.' It should be noted that F.'s movements were but slightly more consistent with a plan of exploring southward to the Colorado and Gila, as he claimed was his plan in one document only—*Frémont's Court-Martial*, 372—than with the trip to Oregon; Yet he says, *Id.*, 'I commenced the march south, crossing into the valley of the Salinas,' and was soon ordered to quit! In his *Memoir*, Frémont gives considerable attention to the big trees—the largest seen by him being 14 feet in diameter. The big-tree grove is now a popular pleasure resort, and one of its standard traditions is to the effect that Frémont spent a night in the hollow tree still shown to every visitor—as indeed he may have done, though he does not mention it.

through the country under the command of a United States officer.

Besides Frémont's return to the coast, a step that seemed utterly inconsistent with his previously announced designs, there were two other matters, not important in themselves, but which nevertheless tended to foment the prevalent alarm and feeling against the strangers. While the explorers were encamped in the San José Valley, Sebastian Peralta claimed some of their horses as his own. Frémont refused to give them up, and ordered Peralta rather unceremoniously out of camp. Complaint was made to Alcalde Pacheco of San Jose, who sent Frémont an official communication on February 20th. The captain's reply of the next day is extant. In it he explained that all his animals, with the exception of four obtained from the Tulares Indians, had been purchased and paid for; and that the one claimed had been brought from the states. "The insult of which he complains," Frémont continues, "and which was authorized by myself, consisted in his being ordered immediately to leave the camp. After having been detected in endeavoring to obtain animals under false pretences, he should have been well satisfied to escape without a severe horse-whipping... Any further communications on this subject will not, therefore, receive attention. You will readily understand that my duties will not permit me to appear before the magistrates of your towns on the complaint of every straggling vagabond who may chance to visit my camp. You inform me that unless satisfaction be immediately made by the delivery of the animals in question, the complaint will be forwarded to the governor. I would beg you at the same time to enclose to his Excellency a copy of this note."[14] Alcalde Pacheco simply forwarded the correspondence to the prefect, with a recommendation of

[14] Feb. 21st, Frémont to Pacheco, from 'camp near road to Sta Cruz,' printed from original then in possession of Manuel Castro, in *S. Francisco Alta*, June 15, 1866. Original Spanish translation by Hartnell, in *Castro, Doc.*, MS., ii. 28. The letter has been frequently reprinted from the *Alta*.

Peralta as an *hombre de bien*.[15]   Whatever may have been the merit of Peralta's claim, it is evident that Frémont's refusal to obey the summons of the legal authorities was altogether unjustifiable, and the tone of his refusal most insolent.

From the southern camp in the early days of March three of Frémont's men visited the rancho of Angel Castro.   One of the men under the influence of liquor behaved rudely to Don Angel's daughter, insisting on her drinking with him, and was ordered out of the house by the angry father.   He was ejected by his companions, though making resistance and drawing a pistol.   A fine of ten dollars was paid for the offence. This is the version given by Larkin, and there is no reason to doubt its accuracy.   The affair reflects no discredit upon Frémont; but naturally exaggerated reports were circulated, by no means favorable to the Americans.[16]

From his camp at Hartnell's rancho, Frémont wrote to Larkin the 5th of March, thanking him for news, declining his invitation to visit Monterey at present, announcing his hope of passing the spring pleasantly among the Californian flowers before proceeding northward, and stating that he would that night move his camp to the banks of the Salinas River.[17]   Before night, however, a Californian officer arrived with the following order from General Castro: "This morning at seven, information reached this office that you and your party have entered the settlements of this department; and this being prohibited by our laws, I find myself obliged to notify you that on the receipt

[15] Feb. 23d, Pacheco to prefect, in *Doc. Hist. Cal.*, MS., iii. 120.

[16] Larkin's letter of March 27th, in *Larkin's Off. Corresp.*, MS., ii. 46. This part of the letter is omitted in *Frémont's Cal. Claims*, 68.   Osio, *Hist. Cal.*, MS., 458–9, makes the insult offered a much more serious one, presenting a vivid picture of the old man Castro defending his daughter from outrage.

[17] March 5th, F. to L., in *Larkin's Doc.*, MS., iv. 61.   Larkin's letter, not extant, is said to have awakened some memories which made Frémont's occupations less interesting, but the allusion is not intelligible.

of this you must immediately retire beyond the limits of the department, such being the orders of the supreme government, which the undersigned is under the obligation of enforcing." A similar order was issued by the prefect in behalf of the civil authority. Both orders were communicated to the supreme government, to Larkin, and by the latter to the government of the United States.[18] It was understood by Larkin at the time that Castro claimed to have just received special orders from Mexico not to permit Frémont's entry; and certain Californians have confirmed this view of the matter; but it is nearly certain that Castro neither received nor pretended to have received any such instructions. General orders, with which the reader is familiar, were more than sufficient to justify Castro's measures in the eyes of the national government; while Frémont's actions afforded ample justification from a legal and equitable point of view.[19]

Frémont not only did not obey the orders of the authorities, but he did not even vouchsafe a written reply in explanation of his past action or present determination. He merely sent back a verbal refusal to

[18] March 5, 1845, José Castro to Frémont; Prefect Castro to Frémont, both transcribed to Larkin; L. to U. S. sec. state, with copies—all English translations not agreeing verbally with each other—in *Larkin's Off. Corresp.*, MS., ii. 42–4, 147; *Niles' Reg.*, lxxi. 189. Later correct translation by Hittell of the prefect's order in *S. F. Alta*, June 15, 1866, and from that source copied in *Lancey's Cruise*, 38; *Yolo Co. Hist.*, 14; and various newspapers. Castro's original blotter I have in *Hittell, Papeles Históricos de 1846*, MS., no. 2. This is a collection of half a dozen originals pertaining to the Frémont affair, presented to my Library by John S. Hittell, a most important contribution. The order in question is as follows: 'I have learned with much displeasure that you in disregard of the laws and authorities of the Mex. repub. have entered the pueblos of this district under my charge, with an armed force, on a commission which the govt of your nation must have given you to survey solely its own territory. Therefore, this prefecture orders you as soon as you receive this communication, without any excuse, to retire with your men beyond the limits of this department; it being understood that if you do not do it, this prefecture will adopt the necessary measures to make you respect this determination.' This was also sent to Larkin, with the following note on the same sheet: 'On this date I say to Capt. Frémont, etc. [as above]; and I have the honor to transcribe it to your honor for your knowledge, and in order that so far as it may pertain to you, you may demand of Capt. Frémont compliance with what is ordered in the said note.' Yours, etc.

[19] In *Lancey's Cruise*, 38; *S. José Pioneer*, March 24, 1877, a rumor is mentioned that a man named Green warned Castro that F. was plotting to unite with the foreigners and take the country; but this has no support.

obey, which was virtually a challenge. Then he moved his camp to the summit of the Gavilan Peak, hastily erected fortifications, and raised over his fort the flag of the United States. It was a hasty, foolish, and altogether unjustifiable step.[20] On March 6th, the same day that Frémont began the construction of his log fort, General Castro stated the case very fairly in a report to the minister of war, as follows: "This man presented himself at my headquarters some days ago, with the object of asking permission to procure provisions for his men, whom he had left in the mountains—which was given him. But two days ago I was much surprised at being informed that he was only two days' journey from this place. Consequently I at once sent him a communication, ordering him, on the instant of its receipt, to put himself on the march and leave the department. But I have received no answer, and in order to make him obey in case of resistance, I sent a force to observe his operations, and to-day I march in person to join it and to see that the object is attained."[21] On the same day Larkin wrote to the general and prefect, not criticising their orders, but urging caution in selecting an officer to command the force to be sent to Gavilan, so as to avoid a possibly needless conflict growing out of false rumors and deceptive appearances. Evidently the consul did not

[20] The only possible excuse for the step—one never made, so far as I know, by Frémont or any of his friends—might be found in a statement of Alvarado, *Hist. Cal.*, MS., v. 159, etc., that Lieut Chavez, who was sent by Castro to the camp, did not deliver the written order, but a verbal one instead, in very violent and insulting terms. This statement is not, however, supported by any other testimony.

[21] March 6th, Castro to min. of war. Translation in *Lancey's Cruise*, 39; *Yolo Co. Hist.*, 14–15. There are added to what I have quoted the usual assurances of patriotic determination, etc., *á lo Mejicano*. This communication is referred to in a later one of April 1st, in *Monitor Republicano*, May 10, 1846; *Niles' Reg.*, lxxi. 187–8, in which Castro says: 'This officer, failing in the respect due to the laws of the republic and the authorities of the country, introduced himself into the midst of the population of the department, with a respectable force, under the pretext of coming with a scientific commission from his govt; and treating with contempt the notice referred to, he took possession of the heights of the sierra, having made only a verbal reply... that he would remain on that spot prepared to resist any force that should attack them.'

quite comprehend Frémont's movements, but thought
either that Castro's orders had not been clearly understood, since he now sent copies and translations of
those orders, or that the captain had secret instructions from his government.[22]

On the 7th there was no correspondence to be noted
except an unimportant note from the general to the
prefect.[23]   Next day the prefect, in a reply to Larkin,
maintained that his orders to Frémont had not been
founded on 'false reports or appearances,' as implied,
but on the laws and oft-repeated instructions from
Mexico; complained that the consul, instead of ordering Frémont to depart, had to a certain extent defended his entry; and urged him to impress on the
captain the necessity of submitting at once if he would
avert the consequences of his illegal entry—whether
it had been from malice or error.[24]   Larkin enclosed
this letter to Frémont with one of his own in which
he warned that officer, without venturing to criticise
his policy, that Castro would soon have at least 200
men in arms against him.   "It is not for me to point
out to you your line of conduct," he wrote; "you have
your instructions from the government; my knowledge of your character obliges me to believe you will
follow them; you are of course taking every care
and safeguard to protect your men, but not knowing
your actual situation and the people who surround you,

[22] March 6th, Larkin to the Castros. *Castro, Doc.*, MS., i. 151; ii. 32–3;
Larkin's Off. Corresp., MS., i. 79; *Hittell, Pap. Hist.*, MS., no. 4; *Niles'
Reg.*, lxxi. 188; *Sawyer's Doc.*, MS., 4–5.   Same date, L. to Frémont, with
copies of the orders. *Id.*, 4.

[23] Mar. 7th, José to Manuel Castro from Tucho rancho. 'Capt. Frémont
came down this morning with 40 men in search of La Torre's party, advising
some rancheros not to join either side. It is a declaration. If you can move
some force, take the Pájaro road to S. Juan. If not, join Narvaez, to whom
I send an order to quarter all the men he can in the govt house, securing the
artillery.'   Yours, etc.   Original in *Hittell, Pap. Hist.*, MS., no. 3.

[24] Mar. 8th, C. to L.   *Doc. Hist. Cal.*, MS., iii. 286; *Larkin's Off. Corresp.*,
MS., ii. 148; *Hittell, Pap. Hist.*, MS., 4; *Sawyer's Doc.*, MS., 5–7; *Niles'
Reg.*, lxxi. 188.   On an original translation, Larkin notes that Castro has mis-
interpreted his note.   In *Sawyer's Doc.*, MS., 26, there is a copy of a procl.
by Gen. Castro on Mar. 8th.   The first part is almost literally the same as
that of Mar. 13th, to be noted later, and with which Sawyer confounds it.
The last part is a call to arms with a view to 'lance the ulcer,' etc.   Its genuineness may be doubted.

your care may prove insufficient...Your encamping so near town has caused much excitement. The natives are firm in the belief that they will break you up, and that you can be entirely destroyed by their power. In all probability they will attack you; the result either way may cause trouble hereafter to resident Americans...Should it be impossible or inconvenient for you to leave California at present, I think, in a proper representation to the general and prefecto, an arrangement could be made for your camp to be continued, but at some greater distance; which arrangement I should advise if you can offer it."[25] This letter was not forwarded till the 9th, when one copy was intrusted to a Californian and another to an American courier.[26] On the same day Larkin wrote to John Parrott at Mazatlan, enclosing with copies of past correspondence an explanation of the critical situation of affairs, and a request that a man-of-war be sent to California with the least possible delay. These despatches, with another to the secretary of state, were sent to Santa Bárbara to overtake the *Hannah*, which had a few days before left Monterey for Mazatlan. The result was to hasten the coming of the *Portsmouth*, which arrived in April.[27]

Larkin's communications to Frémont, sent by an American whose name does not appear, were inter-

<hr>

[25] March 8th, L. to F. *Larkin's Off. Corresp.*, MS., i. 80; *Sawyer's Doc.*, MS., 8–11; *Niles' Reg.*, lxxi. 188. L. offers to visit the camp.

[26] L.'s letter of March 27th, in *Frémont's Cal. Claims*, 67, and elsewhere. March 8th, L.'s instructions to the couriers. They were to show their despatches to any official who might demand to see them; but if forcibly deprived of their papers, to note who took them and tell Frémont of what had occurred, warning him also to beware of treachery or attack by night, and not to expect regular warfare. The couriers were to start the next day (Monday). *Larkin's Off. Corresp.*, MS., i. 72; *Sawyer's Doc.*, MS., 7–8.

[27] March 9th, L. to sec. state. *Larkin's Off. Corresp.*, MS., ii. 44; *Niles' Reg.*, lxxi. 189; *Frémont's Cal. Claims*, 65. In this despatch, L. complains: 'Having had over half of my hospital expenses of 1844 cut off, and know not why, and even my bill for a flag, I do not feel disposed to hazard much for govt, though the life of Capt. Frémont and party may need it. I hardly know how to act.' March 9th, L. to the commander of any U. S. ship-of-war at Mazatlan or S. Blas. *Larkin's Off. Corresp.*, MS., i. 82–3; *Sawyer's Doc.*, MS., 13–16. March 9th, L. to Parrott. *Frémont's Cal. Claims*, 65; *Lancey's Cruise*, 39–40.

cepted by Castro, and a little later sent to Mexico.[28] Prudencio Espinosa, however, succeeded in reaching the explorers' camp with the duplicates; and he came back at 8 P. M. on the 9th with a note in pencil from Frémont—his only communication from the camp on the Cerro del Gavilan—which was as follows: "I this moment received your letters, and without waiting to read them, acknowledge the receipt, which the courier requires instantly. I am making myself as strong as possible, in the intention that if we are unjustly attacked we will fight to extremity and refuse quarter (!), trusting to our country to avenge our death. No one has reached my camp, and from the heights we are able to see troops—with the glass—mustering at St John's and preparing cannon. I thank you for your kindness and good wishes, and would write more at length as to my intentions did I not fear that my letter would be intercepted. We have in no wise dong wrong to the people, or the authorities of the country, and if we are hemmed in and assaulted here, we will die, every man of us, under the flag of our country. P. S.—I am encamped on the top of the sierra, at the head waters of a stream which strikes the road to Monterey at the house of Don Joaquin Gomez."[29]

[28] April 4th, Prefect Castro to min. of rel., enclosing the captured letters. *Doc. Hist. Cal.*, MS., iii. 157. He sends them as proof of bad faith on the part of both Larkin and Frémont.

[29] March 9th (the original bears no date, and most of the printed copies are dated on the 10th, but on an original translation in *Hittell, Pap. Hist.*, MS., 6, Larkin certifies that the note was received 'last night at 8 o'clock,' and that he has allowed a translation to be made at request of Alcalde Diaz, to prove that he, the consul, had no improper correspondence with Frémont, and also in hopes to 'mitigar la sensacion actual'), F. to L., in *Larkin's Off. Corresp.*, MS., i. 62-3; *Niles' Reg.*, lxxi. 188; *Frémont's Cal. Claims*, 65-6; *Cutts' Conq.*, 149-50; *Sawyer's Doc.*, MS., 11-12; *Lancey's Cruise*, 40; *Yolo Co. Hist.*, 15, etc. March 10th, receipt of Espinosa for $27.50 for carrying the despatches. *Monterey, Consulate Arch.*, MS., ii. 14. March 10th, Alcalde Diaz to Manuel Castro. Espinosa was told by us to present himself to you before carrying the despatches. All of us think that by means of a conference all differences with Frémont might be settled. *Castro, Doc. Hist. Cal.*, MS., ii. 37. The phrase 'refuse quarter' in Frémont's note was translated by Hartnell 'will not give quarter' (sin dar cuartel), and was naturally not pleasing to the Californians. March 19th, Larkin asks Stearns to correct the alleged error in the governor's copy, the true meaning being 'will not accept quarter.' *Larkin's Off. Corresp.*, MS., i. 90.

Espinosa had carried the despatches under a passport from Alcalde Diaz, and on his return, at the request of that official, Larkin furnished translations of those despatches and of Frémont's reply, taking occasion to suggest to the authorities the importance of holding a conference with Frémont before resorting to force.[30]   Meanwhile Castro had continued his military preparations, about which we know little beyond the fact that he collected about two hundred men at San Juan.   I have statements from several Californians who were with the army; but except some petty details and personal incidents—more interesting than accurate as a rule—they add nothing to our knowledge of the campaign.   Most of them agree that Castro was less eager for an attack than some of his subordinates, for which he was unfavorably criticised.[31]   As a matter of course, General Castro did

[30] March 10th, Alcalde Diaz to Larkin, asking for a translation of Frémont's letter, hoping it may contribute to allay the present excitement. *Sawyer's Col. Doc.*, 16.   Same date Larkin to Diaz with the translation (already referred to as in my possession), and suggesting an hour's conversation between Castro and Frémont. *Larkin's Off. Corresp.*, MS., i. 86; *Vallejo, Doc.*, MS., xii. 188; *Sawyer's Doc.*, MS., 17–18; *Niles' Reg.*, lxxi. 190.   L. says he knows not if F. will approve his act in giving up the letter, and that he has no authority over that officer, but is anxious to prevent a useless shedding of blood. Same date (11th by error), Diaz to Castro, forwarding the note obtained from Larkin. *Doc. Hist. Cal.*, MS., iii. 134.   Also a private note from Diaz to Castro, urging that a conference could do no harm, all at Monterey thinking it might prevent hostilities. *Hittell, Pap. Hist.*, MS., 5.   Same date, L. to F., with information of what he had done.   'My native courier said he was well treated by you—that 2,000 men could not drive you.   In all cases of couriers, order your men to have no hints or words with them, as it is magnified; this one said a man pointed to a tree and said, "There's your life."   He expected to be led to you blindfolded; says you have 62 men,' etc. *Larkin's Off. Corresp.*, MS., i. 84; *Niles' Reg.*, lxxi. 190.   According to Phelps, *Fore and Aft*, 279–80, Godey, one of Frémont's men, had come in to Monterey; and if this was so, he doubtless was the messenger who took Larkin's letter.   Phelps was there at the time, and says he also wrote to Frémont, offering any assistance in his power, and telling him that if driven to any point on the coast he would take him and his party on board his vessel.   It is strange, however, that Godey, if he was at Monterey on the 10th, had nothing to say about Frémont's retreat.

[31] *Alvarado, Hist. Cal.*, MS., v. 159–71; *Rico, Mem.*, MS., 17–19; *Torre, Remin.*, MS., 137–44; *Castro, Rel.*, MS., 165–72; *Escobar, Camp.*, MS., p. 2–7; *German, Sucesos*, MS., 6–9, 17–18.   Also narratives by Californians not personally engaged in the campaign, in *Vallejo, Hist. Cal.*, MS., v. 97–106; *Fernandez, Cosas*, MS., 123–7; *Carrillo, Narr.*, MS., 9–10; *Osio, Hist. Cal.*, MS., 457–60; *Ord, Ocurrencias*, MS., 138–9; *Guerra*, in *Doc. Hist. Cal.*, MS., iv. 1003–4; *Pinto, Apunt.*, MS., 99–100; *Botello, Anales*, MS., 130–1; *Larios, Convulsiones*, MS., 24; *Ezquer, Mem.*, MS., 21; *Gomez, Lo Que Sabe*, MS.,

not wish to attack Frémont.   A much braver man than he would have hesitated to lead his men up the steep sides of the Gavilan Peak against a force of sixty expert riflemen, protected by a barricade of logs—especially when there was no necessity for such a foolhardy movement.   Castro had ordered Frémont to quit the country, and he hoped that a show of military preparation, together with Larkin's influence, would induce him to obey.   His cause was a just one, his policy was prudent, his orders—up to this point at least—were moderate and dignified in style, and his plans were successful.   He was not very brave himself, nor were his men efficient soldiers; but it was their good fortune not to have their valor and efficiency put to the test on this occasion.   Revere, Phelps, Tuthill, Lancey, and to greater or less extent most others whose writings on the subject have appeared in print, have exhausted their vocabulary of ridicule and abuse in picturing the treachery and cowardice and braggadocio of Castro's actions in this affair.   Their versions are amusing from a dime-novel standpoiñt; but Castro's brilliant evolutions in the plain, his boastful challenges to combat, his desperate charges up the hill just out of rifle-range, like the patient waiting of Fremont's gallant band day after day in the vain hope of an attack by the foe—have no foundation more substantial than the lively and patriotic imagination of the writers cited.[32]   Of the two, Frémont made by far the greater fool of himself.

276–80; *Garnica, Recuerdos*, MS., 10–11; *Amador, Mem.*, MS., 165.   Though the Californian narratives add nothing to what we learn from contemporary corresp. on the events of March 1846, yet many of them give a very fair and unprejudiced version of those events.

Martin, one of Frémont's men, *Narrative*, MS., 11–12, gives a very inaccurate account of the operations around Gavilan.   Wm F. Swasey, *Cal. '45-6*, MS., 5–7, tells us that from S. José John Daubenbiss was sent by Weber to the north for aid, while the writer was sent to Frémont's camp to tell him what was being done for him.   Swasey and Julius Martin were, however, captured by Castro near S. Juan, and were unable to carry out their mission.   He learned at Gomez rancho that F. had left his camp.   Mention of the Gavilan affair in *Bidwell's Cal. 1841-8*, MS., p. 155–6; *Belden's Hist. Statement*, MS., 45–6.   Bidwell disapproves Frémont's actions.

[32] *Revere's Tour*, 46-8; *Phelps' Fore and Aft*, 277–84; *Tuthill's Hist.*

Early on the 10th, Prefect Castro sent out a summons to the people of the north, calling upon them to join the force at San Juan, and aid in the work of repelling invasion and vindicating the national honor.[33] The response did not come until the occasion for alarm was past, which was indeed but a few hours later; for before noon of the same day, Castro learned through his scouts that the camp on the Gavilan had

Cal., 163–5; Lancey's Cruise, 39–43. Of each of these works there is much to be said in praise, as will be seen elsewhere; but in this matter they have given themselves up entirely to patriotism, prejudice, and burlesque. Thomas H. Benton, in his letter of Nov. 9, 1846, Niles' Reg., lxxi. 173–4, struck the key-note of the abuse showered upon Castro ever since. Benton, however, made an absurd blunder, though excusable at the time, through his ignorance of Californian geography. Castro, according to this writer, gave Frémont permission to winter with his troops in the S. Joaquin Valley, but no sooner had F. brought his men 'to that beautiful valley' than Castro prepared to attack him on the pretext that he was exciting Americans to revolt! The sec. of war in his report of Dec. 5th takes a similar view briefly. H. Ex. Doc. no. 4, p. 50, 29th cong. 2d sess.

Other printed accounts of Frémont's operations—besides the documentary ones so often cited in Niles' Reg., lxxi. 188–90, and Frémont's Cal. Claims, 1848—are found in Cutts' Conq., 142–52, with some documents; Soulé's Annals, 91; Bigelow's Memoirs of Frémont, 136; Upham's Life of Frémont, 211–16; Hall's Hist. S. José, 142–3; Ripley's War with Mex., i. 286–92; Möllhausen, Tagebuch, 289–90; Walpole's Four Years, ii. 206–7; Honolulu Friend, iv. 153–4; Frignet, Cal., 68.

[33] March 10th, prefect to sub-prefect of Yerba Buena, and by him transcribed to the com. of the northern line. Vallejo, Doc., MS., xii. 189; Castro, Doc., MS., ii. 39. March 10th, Alcalde Diaz to prefect. All tranquil at Monterey. Citizens anxiously awaiting news. Id., ii. 37. March 11th, same to same. No signs of outbreak among the foreigners. Id., ii. 47. March 11th, Andrés Castillero at Sta Clara to Vallejo. The writer will at once join Castro. Lancey's Cruise, 40. March 12th, Sub-prefect Guerrero at Yerba Buena to the receptor, asking for funds to buy war material for the men who march to the defence of country and laws, 'sufocados por una fuerza armada estrangera.' Pinto, Doc., MS., ii. 227. March 14th, a courier sent by Marsh announced Frémont's position at Sutter's Fort. N. Helv. Diary, MS., 39; but 17th according to Sutter's Diary, 7. March 14th, Guerrero from Sierra Morena to prefect, narrating the preparations under his orders. He had raised 52 men, including some naturalized foreigners and Englishmen; Estudillo had raised 38 men (in Contra Costa?), and they had marched to S. José. Now that Frémont had retreated, the men would like at least to go to the Alto del Gavilan to raise the Mexican flag. All were ready in case of new alarms. Castro, Doc., MS., ii. 49. March 14th, Com. Sanchez to corporal in command at S. Rafael. He must come with all his men to join the force at S. Juan. Vallejo, Doc., MS., xii. 193. March 14th, 15th, Vallejo at Sonoma to authorities of S. Rafael, and to the people of the north. A stirring appeal to rally for the defence of Mexican sovereignty. Vallejo, Doc., MS., xii. 185, 188–9, 195–6. March 15th, Alcalde Pacheco of S. José to Castro, on the patriotism and warlike spirit of the people of his town, who now have been permitted to retire to their farms, etc. Hittell, Pap. Hist., MS., 7. March 17th–21st, Clyman, Diary and Note-Book, encamped at the head of Napa Valley, heard of the Frémont affair and of the call upon all citizens to assemble at Sonoma for defence. On the 22d he heard of Frémont's flight.

been abandoned in the night—that of March 9th–
10th; and still later in the day it was ascertained that
Frémont had moved off eastward and fortified another
camp. Next morning, John Gilroy is said to have
been sent by Castro with a message, but to have
found the second camp also deserted, its occupants
having continued their retreat to the San Joaquin.[34]
Naturally the Californian chiefs were jubilant at Frémont's flight, which they, somewhat pardonably under
the circumstances, regarded as a great victory for
themselves. The citizen soldiers were dismissed to
their homes, with instructions to hold themselves in
readiness for action should the attempted invasion be
renewed; and the leaders, in their proclamations to
the people and reports to their superiors announcing
results, indulged rather freely in the gasconade deemed
an essential part of such documents. It is fair to
state, however, that this feature of the documents in
question has been most grossly exaggerated, writers
having gone so far even as to print imaginary despatches—some of them "signed with gunpowder on
the field of battle." The purport of the genuine documents—of which I translate in a note the one that

[34] March 10th, Prefect Castro to Alcalde Diaz, acknowledging receipt of
letter of same date with copy of Frémont's note, and announcing that the fort
had been abandoned. *Doc. Hist. Cal.*, MS., iii. 132. Larkin in his report of
March 27th, *Niles' Reg.*, lxxi. 189, etc., states that in a postscript to a letter
written on the evening of the 10th, Gen. Castro said 'that Capt. Frémont had
crossed a small river, and was then about three miles distant from them.' L.
also mentioned Gilroy's mission. In later years a rumor has gained currency
that Gilroy was sent to suggest an arrangement by which the forces of Frémont and Castro were to unite, declare Cal. independent, and march against
Pico! It would require the strongest of confirmatory proofs—and there exists
not the slightest evidence—to outweigh the inherent absurdity of this rumor,
though it has been advanced as a fact by Lancey and others. Gilroy was sent
to F., if at all, either in accordance with Larkin's recommendation in favor of
a conference (see note 30), or merely as a spy to learn F.'s position and intentions. Another current rumor among the Californians, which seems to have
but little foundation in fact or probability, is to the effect that Capistrano
Lopez, Castro's scout, revealed to F. the preparations that were being made
against him, receiving gold for the information. The exact locality of F.'s
second camp—somewhere in the hills east of S. Juan—is not known to me.
In his map, with *U. S. Govt Doc.*, 31st cong. 1st sess., H. Ex. Doc., 17, two
crossings are indicated, one by the Pacheco Pass, and another by the S.
Juan Pass farther south. Pinto, *Apunt.*, MS., 99, says the route was by Tres
Pinos and Carrizalito; he adds that many foolish people have tried to find the
a large sum of money which Frémont by tradition had been forced to bury.

gave most offence—was that certain audacious adventurers, who had dared to raise a foreign flag on Californian soil, had been induced to flee ignominiously at the sight of two hundred patriots resolved to defend their country, leaving behind a part of their camp equipage—for Frémont had abandoned in one of his camps a few worn-out articles not worth removing.[35]

[35] March 12th, Gen. Castro to alcalde of S. José. Frémont has fled. Men to be disbanded with thanks. *S. José, Arch., Loose Papers,* 35. Prefect Castro to same effect. *Id.,* 25. March 14th, similar communication. *Id.,* 36. March 13th, Gen. Castro's proclamation to the people (see below), in *Vallejo, Doc.,* MS., xxxiv. 186. This was posted in the billiard-saloon, and Larkin tried without success to get a copy of it. *Larkin's Off. Corresp.,* MS., i. 87; *Niles' Reg.,* lxxi. 190; *Sawyer's Doc.,* MS., 25–6. Sawyer copies a translation of an earlier proclamation as the one posted in the billiard-room. March 14th, Prefect Castro to Gov. Pico. A report of the whole affair, enclosing past corresp., etc. *Doc. Hist. Cal.,* MS., iii. 150; *Dept. St. Pap., Ben. Pref. y Juzg.,* MS., ii. 88–90. March 14th, Sub-prefect Guerrero to Vallejo, announcing Frémont's flight 'en virtud de haber visto el entusiasmo de los hijos del pais.' *Vallejo, Doc.,* MS., xii. 194. March 19th, Leidesdorff to Larkin. The news is that F. has run away, leaving a green cloak, 3 or 4 axes, some cash(!), and cooking utensils. *Larkin's Doc.,* MS., iv. 72. No date, Rico to Castro. Rumor that F. was coming back to renew the struggle. He had told the rancheros to remain neutral or the devil would carry them off. *Castro, Doc.,* MS., i. 129.

Later communications, in which events of the Gavilan are narrated, and which I have had occasion to quote already, are as follows: March 27th, Larkin to sec. state, in *Larkin's Off. Corresp.,* MS., ii. 45–7; *Niles' Reg.,* lxxi. 189; *Frémont's Cal. Claims,* 66–8; *Cutts' Conq.,* 145–6. The writer takes some pains in this and other letters to show that F. moved away leisurely, and not from fear of Castro. April 1st, Gen. Castro to min. of war, from *Monitor Republicano,* May 10th, in *Niles' Reg.,* lxxi. 187–8, criticised by Benton in *Id.,* lxxi. Castro writes: 'Having organized a force of 150 men, I went to the vicinity of the sierra where Frémont had intrenched himself under the American flag. I was prepared to attack him in the night of the 10th, when he, taking advantage of the darkness, abandoned the fortification, doubtless precipitately, as we found there the next day some iron instruments and other things; and in trying to find the trail to know what direction they took, it was impossible on account of their having withdrawn in complete dispersion. This obliged me to stay for some days, until by some persons from the Tulares I was informed that the adventurers were taking the road by the river to the north.' April 2d, Larkin to sec. state. Similar in purport to that of March 27th. Thinks that F., who had been in no real danger, has gone to Sta Bárbara. *Larkin's Off. Corresp.,* MS., ii. 48–9; *Niles' Reg.,* lxxi. 189–90. April 4th, Prefect Castro to min. of rel. *Doc. Hist. Cal.,* MS., iii. 157. April 18th, L. to sec. state. Castro and the rest state, and writer is inclined to believe, that the Californians had no intention of attacking F., but acted solely for effect in Mexico! *Larkin's Off. Corresp.,* MS., ii. 51.

Castro's proclamation of March 13th, the original of which is in my possession, may be literally translated as follows: 'Fellow-citizens—a party of highwaymen who, without respecting the laws or authorities of the department, boldly entered the country under the leadership of Don J. C. Frémont, captain in the U. S. army, have disobeyed the orders of this comandancia general and of the prefecture of the 2d district, by which said leader was notified immediately to march beyond the bounds of our territory; and without replying

Frémont's act in defying the Californian authorities and raising the stars and stripes over his Gavilan camp had been, as we have seen, a most unwise and unjustifiable one. He had taken the step under a rash impulse of the moment, strengthened by the advice of irresponsible followers. As a United States officer, he had put himself in a false and compromising position—and this even if it be admitted that he had been unfairly treated by Castro, which was by no means true. A little reflection made clear to him the error he had committed. Having once taken the step, nothing remained but to retreat, or to raise the standard of revolt in favor of independence, and call on resident foreigners to support him. What he saw with his field-glass at San Juan indicated that he must decide promptly; and Larkin's communication threw additional light on the real state of affairs. Frémont was not yet prepared to declare himself openly a filibuster; and though it was a severe blow to his pride, he was obliged to run away. Larkin's letter arrived late in the afternoon of March 9th, and in the darkness of the same night the brave explorers—for their bravery is unquestionable, despite their retreat and the absurd fame of dime-novel heroes accorded them by many writers—left their famous camp on the Gavilan.[36] Frémont's method of excusing his blunder was to say very little about it in detail, to allude to

to the said notes in writing, the said captain merely sent a verbal message that on the Sierra del Gavilan he was prepared to resist the forces which the authorities might send to attack him. The following measures of this command and of the prefecture, putting in action all possible elements, produced as a result that he at the sight of 200 patriots abandoned the camp which he occupied, leaving in it some clothing and other war material, and according to the scouts took the route to the Tulares. Compatriots, the act of unfurling the American flag on the hills, the insults and threats offered to the authorities, are worthy of execration and hatred from Mexicans; prepare, then, to defend our independence in order that united we may repel with a strong hand the audacity of men who, receiving every mark of true hospitality in our country, repay with such ingratitude the favors obtained from our cordiality and benevolence. Headquarters at San Juan Bautista, March 13, 1846.'

[36] Martin, *Narr.*, MS., 12, tells us that they left the fort on receipt of orders from Larkin. This suggests the idea that Frémont may very likely have put the matter in that light before his men, who were naturally not pleased with the retreat, and who knew little of a consul's powers.

Castro's broken promise, and to imply rather than state directly—the rest being left to enthusiastic friends—that he acted in self-defence, Castro having raised the whole country in arms against him. The reader knows, however, not only that Castro broke no promise, but that he made no threats of attack except in case his order to quit the district should be disobeyed — an order which Frémont could have obeyed quite as well on the 6th as on the 10th of March. In a letter to Mrs Frémont, written a little later, the captain says: "About the middle of next month, at latest, I will start for home. The Spaniards were somewhat rude and inhospitable below, and ordered us out of the country after having given me permission to winter there. My sense of duty did not permit me to fight them, but we retired slowly and growlingly before a force of three or four hundred men and three pieces of artillery. Without a shadow of a cause, the governor suddenly raised the whole country against us, issuing a false and scandalous proclamation. Of course I did not dare to compromise the United States, against which appearances would have been strong; but though it was in my power to increase my party by many Americans, I refrained from committing a solitary act of hostility or impropriety. For my own part, I have become disgusted with everything belonging to the Mexicans. Our government will not require me to return by the southern route against the will of this government; I shall therefore return by the heads of the Missouri."[37] To what extent these statements are true or false, the reader can judge.

Descending into the great valley, perhaps by the Pacheco Pass, on March 11th, Frémont crossed the San Joaquin in boats on the 13th, reached the Stan-

---

[37] April 1st, F. on the Sacramento to Mrs F. *Niles' Reg.*, lxxi. 190. Hittell, *Hist. S. F.*, 99, etc., gives briefly a correct view of Frémont's operations. He seems to be the only prominent writer who has not been led astray in this matter. Gilbert, in *Yolo Co. Hist.*, also takes a correct view of the matter, as do a few other writers in similar publications.

islaus the 16th, and arrived at New Helvetia the 21st,
pitching his camp just across the American River.
Three days later he moved on up the valley, visiting
Keyser's rancho on Bear River, Cordua's on the Yuba,
and Neal's on Butte Creek, and arriving at Lassen's
on Deer Creek the 30th of March. The company
remained here until April 5th; and after a week's trip
up the valley to Cow Creek and back, they encamped
again at Lassen's on April 11th–14th.[38]

While in the Sacramento Valley, Frémont sent
Talbot down the river to obtain supplies at Yerba
Buena.[39] He also sent out men in various directions
to buy horses from the Indians, a transaction that
appears not to have given entire satisfaction to the
former owners of the stolen animals. Testimony on
this subject is, however, not of the best.[40] Carson and
Martin relate that while at Lassen's, the explorers
were called upon by the settlers for aid against the
Indians, who were threatening a general attack. The
result was a raid in which the Indians were defeated
at their village, a large number being slain in the
battle.[41]

Yet another episode of the stay in this region was a

[38] *Frémont's Geog. Mem.*, 20–7, 57; *Sutter's Diary*, 7; *Martin's Narr.*, MS.,
12; *Lancey's Cruise*, 43–5. One of F.'s men arrived at Sutter's on the 20th.
N. Helv. Diary, MS., 39. Sutter, *Personal Remin.*, MS., 138, etc., describes
Frémont's actions at this time as having been very mysterious and suspicious.

[39] *Phelps' Fore and Aft*, 283. Talbot left Sutter's on the launch on March
26th. *N. Helv. Diary*, MS. He returned April 9th. *Id.* April 16th, Leidesdorff writes that he is daily expecting a draft from Frémont on account of
money and supplies furnished since he left S. Juan. *Doc. Hist. Cal.*, MS.,
iii. 172.

[40] Martin, *Narr.*, MS., 12-13, tells us that Godey and himself were sent
to the Tulares, and purchased 187 animals very cheap. Sutter, *Person. Remin.*,
MS., 145–8, mentions the purchase of horses in the valley, and says he wrote
to F. at Lassen's, urging him to leave the stolen animals behind, a letter
which was not answered, and the writing of which F. never forgave. This
story is probably true, as Sutter made a similar statement, and enclosed a copy
of his letter in a communication to Castro of May 31st. 21 horses that had
been stolen from settlers had been taken away to Oregon. *Castro, Doc.*, MS.,
ii. 41.

[41] *Peters' Life of Kit Carson*, 254; *Martin's Narr.*, MS., 13–14. Carson
tells us that the Ind. were preparing to attack the rancheros. 'probably at the
instigation of the Mexicans'! Martin says that more than 175 Ind. were slain
in less than three hours, they having been attacked while engaged in a war-
dance. Lancey, *Cruise*, 44, locates the fight on Reading's rancho.

grand fiesta, or barbecue, given by Frémont's men to a party of immigrants who were encamped in the valley, having come from Oregon the year before, and being now engaged in preparations for a return trip, some to Oregon, others to the States. The feasting and dancing—there were women in the immigrant company, though border men could dance without female partners upon occasion—lasted two days; and an Indian servant who was present carried south the sensational report that the assemblage was one of two hundred armed foreigners, whose purpose was to fall upon Monterey as soon as Indian reënforcements could be obtained from Oregon![42] Clyman, one of the immigrants who proposed to quit the country, though not apparently one of those present at the barbecue, desired to unite his company to that of Frémont for the return trip—or, as he claims, for a movement against the Californians—but his proposition was declined.[43]

Leaving Lassen's on or about April 14th, Frémont proceeded northward to Oregon.[44] On May 8th,

[42] May 6th, sub-prefect to prefect. *Castro, Doc.*, MS., ii. 79; *Dept. St. Pap., Ben. Pref. y Juzg.*, MS., ii. 85. May 31st, Sutter to Castro. *Castro, Doc.*, MS., ii. 41. See also *Martin's Narr.*, 14–15. The Indian was an ex-neophyte of S. José named Antolino, who was at work for Francis Day.

[43] *Clyman's Note Book*, MS., 18, 26–7. A letter from Frémont is copied from the original in Clyman's possession. In the copy it is dated, 'Camp on Feather River, Dec. 19, 1845,' but this of course is all wrong. The letter, if genuine, which there is no other reason to doubt, must have been written in March or April 1846. Clyman and party started for the states at the end of April from Johnson's rancho. I quote the letter as showing, in connection with that of April 1st to Mrs Frémont, the captain's feelings and plans. 'Your favor of the 21st ult. has been received through the kindness of Mr Flint...I am placed in a peculiar position. Having carried out to the best of my ability my instructions to explore the far west, I see myself on the eve of my departure for home confronted by the most perplexing complications. I have received information to the effect that a declaration of war between our government and Mexico is probable, but so far this news has not been confirmed. The Californian authorities object to my presence here, and threaten to overwhelm me. If peace is preserved, I have no right or business here; if war ensues, I shall be outnumbered ten to one, and be compelled to make good my retreat, pressed by a pursuing enemy. It seems that the only way open to me is to make my way back eastward, and as a military man you must perceive at once that an increase of my command would only encumber and not assist my retreat through a region where wild game is the only thing procurable in the way of food. Under these circumstances, I must make my way back alone, and gratefully decline your offer of a company of hardy warriors.'

[44] *Frémont's Geog. Mem.*, 31–2, 57–8; Frémont's map in *U. S. Govt Doc.*,

having passed up by the western shore of Klamath
Lake, he encamped near the north end of that body
of water.   Late that evening two horsemen, Samuel
Neal and William Sigler, rode into camp with the
news that a United States officer was two days behind with despatches, protected by a small escort and
probably in great danger.   Next morning Frémont
took nine of his men, Carson, Maxwell, Godey,
Owens, Lajeunesse, and four Delawares, hastened
back with Neal and Sigler, and after a ride of some
twenty-five miles—not sixty miles as was claimed at
the time and has been often repeated—he met at
nightfall Lieutenant Archibald H. Gillespie.   This
officer, of whose arrival I shall have more to say
presently, had reached Sutter's April 28th, and Lassen's the 1st of May.   From that point, with only
five companions, Lassen, Neal, Sigler, Stepp, and a
negro servant named Ben, he started May 2d on
Frémont's trail.   On the 7th the two men were sent
in advance, and the others encamped at the outlet of
Klamath Lake, unable to ford the river, and having
nothing to eat for forty hours.   On the morning of
the 9th, a party of Indians made their appearance,
who in great apparent kindness gave the travellers a
fresh salmon for food, and ferried them over the
water in canoes.   After a day's journey of some
thirty miles, Gillespie met Frémont at sunset, as related, at a stream named from the events of that
night Ambuscade Creek.[45]

31st cong. 1st sess., H. Ex. no. 17.   The route is indicated by the following
stations: Deer Creek, April 14th; Mill Cr., Antelope Cr., Nozah Cr. (opposite
Cottonwood Cr.), April 25th; Brant's Cr., 26th; Campbell's Cr., 27th; Upper
Sacramento (Pit River) above Fall River, 29th; same, upper end of Round
Valley, 30th; Rhett Lake, eastern shore, May 1st; McCrady's River, 4th;
Denny's branch, 6th; Ambuscade Cr., 7th; north end of Klamath Lake, 8th,
9th—and returning—Corral Cr., Torrey River, Wétowah Cr. (all running
into the east side of Klamath Lake), 11th, 12th, 14th; Russell's branch, 19th;
Poinsett's River, 20th; Myers' branch, 21st; and Deer Cr., or Lassen's, May
24th.
    [45] Frémont's testimony in *Frémont's Cal. Claims*, 12; Gillespie in *Id.*, 30-
1; Gillespie to Larkin from Lassen's May 24th, in *Larkin's Doc.*, MS., iv.
134; May 24th, Frémont to Benton. *Niles' Reg.*, lxxi. 190; *Sutter's Diary*, 7;
Yolo Co. Hist., 15-16; 151-2; *Lancey's Cruise*, 45-8; *Bidwell's Cal. 1841-8*,

The sixteen tired travellers retired early after the two parties were united on May 9th, and were soon sleeping soundly—Frémont sitting up later than the rest to read his despatches and letters from home. The Indians were deemed friendly, and no watch was kept. Just before midnight the camp was attacked by savages. Basil Lajeunesse and a Delaware were killed as they slept, by blows from axes. The sound of these blows aroused Carson and Owens, who gave the alarm; when the Indians fled, after killing with their arrows a Delaware named Crane, and leaving dead a chief of their number, who proved to be the very man from whom Gillespie had that morning been furnished with food and aid farther south. Next morning they started northward to join the main body, burying the bodies of their slain comrades on the way. The whole party started on the 11th down the eastern side of the lake, wreaking terrible vengeance on the innocent natives along the route, if we may credit the statement of Kit Carson, who played a leading part in the butcheries. They reached Lassen's rancho on their return the 24th, and a few days later moved their camp down to the Buttes.[46] Gillespie's arrival had little to do with the alleged motive of Frémont's return from the north, which motive was the

MS., 157–60. Sutter, in his *Personal Remin.*, MS., complains that Gillespie borrowed his favorite $300 mule and brought it back wind-broken. In *N. Helv. Diary*, MS., 46, G.'s arrival at Sutter's is recorded, and it is stated that Stepp and Downing went on with him next day.

[46] See, besides most of the citations of the preceding note, *Peters' Life of Kit Carson*, 255–69; *Abbott's Kit Carson*, 249–55. Carson goes very fully into details of Indian fights on the return trip, noting the burning of one large village after many of its people had been slain; also the gallant manner in which his (Carson's) life was saved on one occasion by Frémont. Several writers speak of a curious wooden coat-of-mail worn by one of the Ind. warriors; and all speak of the bravery shown by these natives. Accounts or mentions of the affair also in *Martin's Narr.*, 16–21; June 1st, Larkin to sec. state. *Larkin's Off. Corresp.*, MS., ii. 56; *Smucker's Life Frémont*, 23–6; *Tuthill's Hist. Cal.*, 166–7; *Honolulu Friend*, iv. 154; *Vallejo, Hist. Cal.* MS., v. 109; *Osio, Hist. Cal.*, MS., 461–3. Several mention the absurd suspicion that the Klamaths were instigated to attack Frémont by Castro's agents! Sutter, *Diary*, 7; also *N. Helv. Diary*, MS., 49–50, notes Neal's arrival from the north on May 25th, and Gillespie's on May 30th. Capt. Phelps, *Fore and Aft*, 285–6, succeeds in condensing many errors into a small space. See also *Möllhausen, Tagebuch*, 288–9; *Frignet. Californie*, 68–9.

difficulty of crossing the mountains into Oregon on account of the snow. The captain had nearly determined—so he said—to change his route before he heard of Gillespie's approach; and he still announced, late in May, his intention to return homeward by a southern route.[47] I shall have more to say on certain phases of this topic in another chapter.

A letter from Buchanan to Larkin dated October 17, 1845, has already been quoted in this history, being a most important document, never before made public.[48] It contained a clear statement of the policy of the United States respecting California; appointed Larkin a confidential agent of the government to aid in carrying out that policy; and contained also the following passage: "Lieutenant Archibald H. Gillespie of the marine corps will immediately proceed to Monterey, and will probably reach you before this despatch. He is a gentleman in whom the president reposes entire confidence. He has seen these instructions, and will coöperate as a confidential agent with you in carrying them into execution." Gillespie left Washington early in November 1845. He carried

---

[47] May 24th, F. to Benton. 'I have but a faint hope that this note will reach you before I do...I shall now proceed directly homewards by the Colorado.' *Niles' Reg.*, lxxi. 191. In his letter of July 25th, he says: 'Snow was falling steadily and heavily in the mountains, which entirely surrounded and dominated the elevated valley region into which we had penetrated. In the east and north and west, barriers absolutely impassable barred our road; we had no provisions; our animals were already feeble, and while any other way was open, I could not bring myself to attempt such a doubtful enterprise as a passage of these unknown mountains in the dead of winter. Every day the snow was falling; and in the face of the depressing influence exercised on the people by the loss of our men, and the unpromising appearance of things, I judged it inexpedient to pursue our journey farther in this direction, and determined to retrace my steps and carry out the views of the govt by reaching the frontier on the line of the Colorado River.' *Id.*, lxxi. 191. Larkin wrote on June 1st, 'Frémont now starts for the States.' *Larkin's Off. Corresp.*, MS., ii. 56. May 24th, Gillespie wrote: 'There was too much snow upon the mountains to cross. He now goes home from here.' *Id.*, *Doc.*, MS., iv. 134. In his testimony of 1848 Frémont says that 'his progress farther north was then barred by hostile Indians and impassable snowy mountains, and he was meditating some change in his route when' Gillespie came, etc. *Frémont's Cal. Claims*, 12. It was the idea of Carson and others of the men that it was Gillespie's despatches which prompted the return.

[48] *Buchanan's Instruc.*, MS. See long quotation in chap. xxv. of vol. v.

with him a duplicate copy of the document just cited, which he destroyed on the way, after having committed its contents to memory, in fear that it might fall into the hands of the Mexicans.[49] He carried also letters of introduction from Buchanan to Larkin and to Frémont;[50] and a packet containing private correspondence from Senator Thomas H. Benton addressed to Frémont, his son-in-law.[51] The exact purport of Benton's letters has never been made public; whether, as supplemented by Gillespie's oral communications, they went further in their political significance than the official written instructions, is a question that has always been wrapped in mystery, and one that may be more intelligibly and profitably considered a little later, when I come to narrate Frémont's subsequent acts.

Gillespie went under his true name, but in the assumed character of an invalid merchant travelling for his health. He was delayed for a time at the city of Mexico in consequence of the Paredes revolution; but finally reached Mazatlan and sailed on the U. S. man-of-war *Cyane*, Mervine commander, via Honolulu for Monterey, where he arrived April 17th, a month later than he had anticipated at his departure from the States. Entering at once into communication with Larkin, he remained at Monterey two days, as did the *Cyane* also to take back the consul's despatches.[52]

[49] Gillespie's testimony of 1848, in *Frémont's Cal. Claims*, 30. He states: 'Early in Nov. 1845, I received orders from the president and secretary of the navy, Mr Bancroft, to proceed to Cal. by way of Vera Cruz, and the shortest route through Mexico to Mazatlan, with instructions to watch over the interest of the U. S. in Cal., and to counteract the influence of any foreign or European agents who might be in that country with objects prejudicial to the U. S.' Gillespie's written instructions, if they were put in writing, are not extant, but of course they were substantially the same as those to Larkin.

[50] Nov. 1, 1845. 'I take pleasure in introducing to you the bearer hereof, Mr Archibald H. Gillespie, as a gentleman of respectability and worth. He is about to visit the north-west coast of America on business, and should he stop on his way at Monterey, allow me to bespeak for him your kind attention. You will find him to be in every respect worthy of your regard. Yours very respectfully, James Buchanan. To Thomas O. Larkin, Esq.' Original in *Larkin's Doc.*, MS., iii. 362. This letter is not mentioned in Gillespie's testimony. That addressed to Frémont was doubtless of the same purport.

[51] Gillespie's testimony; also Frémont's deposition in *Frémont's Cal. Claims*, 12.

[52] April 17th, G. on board the *Cyane* to L. 'Confidential. Enclosed I send

Gillespie's true character as an officer—if not as a confidential agent, or 'spy' as the Mexicans would somewhat plausibly have termed him—was suspected from the first by the Californians; but he was not hindered from starting on the 19th for Yerba Buena on his way to find Frémont, after having been entertained at a grand ball given by Ex-governor Alvarado, or at least at his house. It is stated, however, that the lieutenant had to depart secretly in the night while the ball was in progress, so great was the suspicion of the authorities, strengthened as some say by a warning which David Spence had received from Mazatlan.[53] He left San Francisco April 25th in a boat furnished by Leidesdorff, to whom he seems to have announced the certainty of war with Mexico, representing that to be the nature of his message to Frémont.[54]

you a letter of introduction, which I doubt not you will understand, and as I have an important despatch for you, as also other sealed packages, I will be obliged by your coming on board as early as possible.' *Larkin's Doc.*, MS., iv. 91. April 17th, L. to Mervine, requesting him to remain until the 19th for despatches. Same date, Mervine consents. *Id.*, iv. 92; *Id.*, *Off. Corresp.*, MS., i. 92.

[53] April 19th, Capt. Mervine and his officers cannot attend the dance. *Larkin's Doc.*, MS., iv. 94. Same date, Larkin to Leidesdorff, introducing Gillespie as a friend in ill health, who 'wishes to travel through your part of the country to enjoy the climate,' etc. 'I believe he has some personal acquaintance with Capt. Frémont, and may wish to see him if the trouble and expense is not too much.' Furnish all needed aid, etc. *Id.*, *Off. Corresp.*, MS., i. 93. June 1st, L. writes to sec. state, 'Mr G. was at once known here as an officer, or fully supposed to be so, and could not pass for a merchant...In fact, so long as it is not correctly known, I prefer that he should be supposed to be what he actually is.' *Id.*, ii. 50, 56.

Vallejo, *Hist. Cal.*, MS., v. 106–9, says that Spence received by the *Cyane* a box of quinine, which under a false bottom contained a letter of warning against Gillespie. The same letter or one of similar purport was addressed to 13 other men in the north. Castro tried to make him drunk at the ball, but he kept his head, and left about midnight with horses and guides furnished by Larkin. Vallejo was in Monterey at the time, and was not in favor of allowing Gillespie to depart; but no proofs could be brought against him. Alvarado, *Hist. Cal.*, MS., v. 172–8, tells a similar story, but says Spence did not reveal his secret, except perhaps that his wife, an old flame of the general, may have dropped a hint to him. Alvarado says that Gillespie pretended to speak Spanish very badly, though able to speak it fluently. See also *Ord, Ocurrencias*, MS., 140–1; *Torres, Peripecias*, MS., 46–8.

[54] April 25th, Leidesdorff to Larkin. Gillespie to start in a few hours. 'Glorious news for Frémont! I think I see him smile. By your letters it appears that this news was not generally known; however, they must have some news here, as the sub-prefect is busily despatching couriers,' etc. *Larkin's Doc.*, MS., iv. 104. On April 23d, Larkin sent Gillespie a letter on arrival

Arriving at New Helvetia on the 28th, the confidential agent hurried on up the valley, overtook Frémont, and returned with him, as I have already related, at the end of May. Before I proceed with the record of the two officers' subsequent operations in June, there are other important matters to be disposed of. I may note here, however, that Sutter warned Castro that, despite Gillespie's pretence of being an invalid with private letters for Frémont, he was really, as Sutter suspected, an officer of the U. S. army and the bearer of important despatches—indeed, he had admitted himself to be an officer, though claiming to be on the retired list.[55]

of the *Portsmouth*, etc. It was not received until G. had returned from the north. *Lancey's Cruise*, 41. April 30th, Thomas Cole gets $40 from Larkin for carrying the said letter. *Monterey, Consulate Arch.*, MS., ii. 14.

[55] May 31st, Sutter to Castro. Original in *Castro, Doc.*, MS., ii. 41, 98. Of course it was Sutter's duty as a Mexican official to give this warning; but the act does not exactly accord with some of the captain's later pretensions of favor to the U. S. On Gillespie's mission—including his supposed secret instructions, to be noticed later—see also *Frémont's Cal. Claims, Report*, 817 (30th cong. 1st sess., H. Report); *Cooke's Conquest*, 203–5; *Swasey's Cal.*, MS., 45–6; *Jay's Mex. War*, 150–4; *Gleeson's Hist. Cath. Church*, ii. 159–60; *Clark's Speech on Cal. Claims; U. S. Govt Doc.*, 36th cong. 1st sess., H. Rept. Court of Claims, no. 229, vol. iv.; *Price*, in *Cal. Ass. Pioneers, 1875*, p. 18–19; *Tuthill's Hist. Cal.*, 166–8; *Dunbar's Romance*, 31–2.

CHAPTER II.

POLITICAL AND MILITARY.

JANUARY–JUNE, 1846.

A FRUITLESS CONTROVERSY—ALVARADO AS CONGRESSMAN—CASTAÑARES AND TELLEZ—COVARRUBIAS AS PICO'S AGENT—MISSION OF CASTILLERO—AFFAIRS IN MEXICO—INIESTRA'S EXPEDITION—TELLEZ AND MORALES—CAMBUSTON AND CASTRO—VALLE AND TREASURY TROUBLES—ASSEMBLY—GUERRA SENT TO MONTEREY—RETURN OF J. A. CARRILLO—PICO AS CONSTITUTIONAL GOVERNOR—MILITARY JUNTA AT MONTEREY—ADHESION TO PRESIDENT PAREDES—MEASURES FOR DEFENCE—PICO'S PROTESTS—VALLEJO'S POSITION—GUERRA SENT TO ANGELES—CONSEJO GENERAL DE PUEBLOS UNIDOS AT SANTA BÁRBARA—CASTRO'S PROTESTS—MARTIAL LAW—THE ASSEMBLY DEPOSES CASTRO—PICO AND HIS ARMY MARCH NORTH AGAINST CASTRO—WARLIKE PREPARATIONS FOR DEFENCE OF ANGELES—COÖPERATION OF FOREIGNERS—BANDINI AND CASTRO—AFFAIRS IN THE NORTH.

THE topics that make up the political annals of 1846 are bound together by two parallel or intertwined threads. One is the fear of foreign invasion; the other, with the disentanglement of which I have chiefly to do in this chapter, is the controversy between Castro and Pico; between the military and civil authorities; between the north and south; between comandante general with custom-house and treasury, at Monterey, and governor with the assembly, at Los Angeles. The quarrel was continuous, undignified, and fruitless. All admitted the deplorable condition of California, and attributed it largely to internal dissensions, as well as to Mexican neglect. As a matter of fact, nothing that was being done or left undone, had upon the future of the country any

(30)

other effect than the indirect one of so disgusting a part of the people that they were ready to welcome any change. Yet each faction pretended to believe that with the coöperation—that is, the entire submission—of the other faction, the country might be saved. Pio Pico had little doubt that from the patriotic wisdom of himself and the southern assemblymen, the true representatives of the popular will, a plan might be evolved for salvation—would General Castro but recognize that wisdom, let the revenues alone, keep the Indians in check, and use his military force exclusively to carry out measures dictated by the political authorities. José Castro, on the other hand, maintained that the protection of the country was purely a military duty, since the chief danger was that of invasion, and that until the danger should be past, it behooved the governor and the assembly not to interfere with the general's prerogatives, but humbly to furnish such aid as might be asked for. Each entertained, personally, feelings of jealousy, distrust, and hostility toward the other; and each exaggerated the other's hostility. Each thought at times of using force to overthrow the other, doubting not the other was devoting his constant energies to similar ends. Each appealed sometimes to the other to forget past dissensions for the country's sake; mutual friends interfered more or less injudiciously and unsuccessfully; and the foolish quarrel dragged its slow length along. I have to note the controversy in some of its petty phases and results; but I have no historic lens so powerful, no balance so nicely adjusted, as to assign to either side a preponderence of blame.

Alvarado, diputado-elect to congress for 1846–7, did not go to Mexico to take his seat, because there were no funds for his expenses, much as Pico desired his absence. Alvarado no longer had charge of the custom-house, but he was regarded by the abajeños as being at the bottom of all Castro's political in-

trigues.[1] Though Don Juan Bautista did no go to
Mexico, California was still represented there by the
brothers Castañares;[2] and two other comisionados
were sent early this year. The first was the governor's secretary, José María Covarrubias, who was despatched by Pico, and sailed from San Pedro February 14th on the *Juanita*. His mission, fulfilled in
Mexico in April, was the old one of explaining California's peril and absolute lack of resources, and of
suggesting methods of relief. Whether an attempt
was made to strike a blow at Castro is not known, as
Covarrubias' instructions are not extant. Some of his
special suggestions, such as the acquisition of Sutter's
Fort and of Stephen Smith's lands at Bodega, and the
appointment of a diplomatic agent at the Hawaiian
Islands, were deferred for additional investigation; but
Pico was assured that the government had already
taken steps to secure the safety of the department,
counting on the patriotic zeal of all Californians to
aid in the good cause.[3] The second was Andrés

[1] Feb. 18, 1846, Pico to Alvarado, urging him to start soon for Mexico.
Dept. St. Pap., MS., vi. 71.   March 1st, A. to P. Is ready to start as soon
as means shall be supplied. Needs $4,000 at least. His health is not good.
Thinks this may be the last service he can render Cal. *Id.*, vii. 117. A strange
communication from A. appears in *Id.*, viii. 96–7, in which he announces his
return from Mexico after performing his duties as deputy, and asks payment
of his expenses!
[2] They took part in the junta of Jan. 3d, voting for a president ad. int.
Mexico, Mem. Relaciones, 1847, p. 86–8; *Bustamante, Nuevo Bernal Diaz*, i.
109.   Aug. 8th, Col. Tellez wrote to Castro: 'Unfortunately there are among
us some selfish people, who, being unworthy of the trust reposed in them,
only seek their own advantage; for example, the Messrs Castañares, representatives of the Californias. These two personages have only endeavored to
draw private advantages from the commission intrusted to them; and perhaps they would have already gone to that department to collect the fruits
of their perfidious machinations, if I who know them and feel an interest in
that country had not prevented them as much as possible, as I shall continue
to do; and I assure you that if the revolution in which I find myself plunged
triumphs, the Californians can trust they will not have the sorrow again to
see on their shores those wicked men, or any others that may resemble them.'
U. S. Govt Doc., 31st cong. 1st sess., H. Ex. no. 70, p. 43, and so in Col.
Tellez California had another representative and protector! April 3d, Manuel Castañares to Vallejo. Has done his best to make congress understand
California's needs and risks. *Vallejo, Doc.*, MS., xi. 201.
[3] Feb. 18th, March 2d, Pico announces Covarrubias' departure. *Castro,
Doc.*, MS., ii. 22; *Olvera, Doc.*, MS., 15. Sailing recorded in *Lancey's Cruise*,
37.   Pico, *Hist. Cal.*, MS., 135, tells us that through C. he urged the govt
to accept his resignation. April 23d, min. of rel. to Pico, in reply to the com-

Castillero, who sailed on the *Don Quixote* early in April, being sent by Castro with a warning against the Americans, and not improbably with complaints against Pico, in consequence of Frémont's operations in March. Nothing appears respecting the reception and labors of Don Andrés in Mexico.[4]

The result of all appeals to Mexico in 1846 was that the national government sent back a brief series of warnings, of exhortations, of 'ample faculties' to defend the country, and even of promises to render material aid—which, as in the past, never came.[5] As to the Iniestra expedition, the exact date when its failure became a certainty does not clearly appear. The scheme seems to have been partially revived, even after the confiscation of the stores and men provided at Acapulco by Álvarez, the revolutionist; but Iniestra died early in the spring. In February or March a force was sent to Mazatlan for California, apparently under the command of Colonel Tellez; but this leader chose to engage in a revolution, and did not proceed beyond Sinaloa. In August an expedition under General Morales is mentioned as about to start. The record of all these projects is, however, exceedingly vague and unsatisfactory.[6]

mission. *Dept. St. Pap., Ang.*, MS., viii. 72–5; *St. Pap., Miss. and Colon.*, MS., ii. 411–14.

[4] *Doc. Hist. Cal.*, MS., iii. 157; *Larkin's Off. Corresp.*, MS., i. 91; *Niles' Reg.*, lxxi. 188, 190; *Davis' Glimpses*, MS., 223, 336.

[5] Jan. 14th, American families on the frontier must not remain in the repub. while peaceful relations are interrupted. *Sup. Govt St. Pap.*, MS., xviii. 25. March 10th, war certain to break out. The pres. orders a vigorous defence. Aid will be sent, and much confidence is felt in Cal. patriotism. The gov. and com. gen. are given ample powers. *Pico, Doc.*, MS., ii. 171–2 (original); *Hayes' Mission Book*, i. 364, etc. It is under this order that Pico's sale of certain missions was supported in later litigation; but the plea was not sustained by the U. S. courts. *Hoffman's Opinions*, 12–13, etc. April 4th, decree of pres. that four armed schooners be stationed on the coast, one of them at S. Diego. *Pinart, Doc. Hist. Mex.*, no. 788. April 7th, acknowledgment of receipt of despatch of Feb. 19th, announcing the irruption of immigrants. April 23d, preparations made for occupation of Cal. *Willey*, in *Sta Cruz Sentinel*, June 3, 1876. July 4th, gov. of Cal. authorized to raise resources for defence. *Mexico, Mem. Relaciones*, 1847, 9. Aug. 6th, election decree. The two Californias to form one department and have one diputado. *Pinart, Doc. Hist. Mex.*, no. 810.

[6] May 11th, Mott and Talbot of Mazatlan to Larkin. 'You need not fear any expedition from this coast to your quarter. Iniestra is dead, and the

About the middle of January Henri Cambuston, a French teacher at Monterey, on the occasion of a ball at the house of Dr Stokes, became involved in a personal quarrel with Prefect Castro, and came to blows with Captain Narvaez, a friend of Don Manuel. The Frenchman, on being ordered under arrest, refused to recognize Castro's authority, on the ground that he was not old enough to be prefect legally; but he was put in prison, and a successor was appointed to take charge of his school. The matter was investigated before the alcalde, and submitted to the governor, who decided that both parties merited a reprimand. Meanwhile the French consul, Gasquet, had interfered, and had demanded from General Castro the prisoner's release, with heavy damages for his arrest. The general declined to interfere with the prerogatives of the political authorities; but he seems to have disapproved Don Manuel's conduct, much to the latter's displeasure. The prefect was also displeased at Pico's attitude in the matter. The quarrel had no other political significance, so far as can be known; neither is its result definitely recorded; but I have introduced the affair here because of the high position of the parties involved, the interference of a foreign consul, the local excitement caused by the quarrel, and the bulky correspondence to which it gave rise, as shown by the archives.[7]

There is but little in the records of January and

ships engaged to take the troops have been paid the false freight and discharged.' *Larkin's Doc.*, MS., iv. 115. See also *El Tiempo*, Jan. 26, May 7, 1846. Feb. 9th, the expedition about to start, but delayed by Iniestra's illness. *Bustamante, Mem. Hist. Mex.*, MS., iv. 54. March 5th, the exped. has started for Mazatlan; but it is not believed it will reach its destination. *Id.*, iv. 83. Exped. under Morales. *Id.*, v. 82. Guerra, *Apuntes*, 371, says that Tellez reached Mazatlan in April with a force, but revolted against Paredes. We have seen that Tellez wrote from Mazatlan in Aug., while engaged in a revolt.

[7] The quarrel occurred on Jan. 18th. Investigation in the alcalde's court Jan. 21st, etc.; resulting corresp. between the Castros, Cambuston, Gasquet, Pico, and others, extending to March, in *Castro, Doc.*, MS., i. 293–303; *Dept. St. Pap., Ben. Pref. y Juzg.*, MS., ii. 4–8; *Doc. Hist. Cal.*, MS., iii. 57, 64, 66, 91; i. 497. March 9th, 10th, Pico to prefect and to Gasquet, trying to hush up the matter, which he fears may lead to serious complications. *Fernandez, Doc.*, MS., 61–3; *Dept. St. Pap.*, MS., vii. 109, 111.

February to throw light on the condition of public affairs or on the troubles of the rival chieftains;[8] but I have to note another unsuccessful attempt by the governor to gain control of the revenues. Failing to remove the treasury to Los Angeles, he had sent Ignacio del Valle to take possession of the office at the end of 1845; but General Castro had prevented the transfer. Early in February Valle came again to Monterey, Pico having agreed not to move the office, but declining to appoint a northern man in the place of Ábrego. Castro, however, still continued his opposition, on the grounds that Pico had no authority to appoint a treasurer, and that any change in such critical times was inexpedient. Ábrego professed to be willing to surrender the office, but received positive orders from Castro not to do so; and Don Ignacio had to content himself with the management of that small portion of the country's revenues which found its way to the south.[9] Subsequently Pico re-

[8] Jan. 16th, several Sta Bárbara officers resign their military rank, including Valentin Cota, José Carrillo, H. García, and José Lugo. *Dept. St. Pap., Ben. Pref. y Juzg.*, MS., ii. 61. Jan. 24th, Feb. 27th, Rafael Sanchez to Pico. Complains that Mexicans are insulted constantly, that officers of the old battalion are not receiving the treatment guaranteed by the treaty of Cahuenga, while Castro's 'auxiliary and permanent drunkards' receive pay while rendering no service. Alvarado and Castro should be accused before the sup. govt. *Dept. St. Pap.*, MS., vii. 102, 108–9. Jan. 26th, Pablo de la Guerra to his father. The time is passed when the laws ruled. Now circumstances are the rulers, and it is necessary to yield in non-essentials. *Doc. Hist. Cal.*, MS., iv. 1168. Jan. 29th, Pico to Bandini. Will close the port of Monterey in case of expected infractions of order. *Bandini, Doc.*, MS., 65. Feb. 15th, Francisco Arce to Vallejo, on the unfortunate state of affairs. Begs V. to come to the country's rescue by joining the party of Castro against Pico, whose conduct is ruining all that is good. He does nothing but build up Los Angeles and plunder the missions. *Vallejo, Doc.*, MS., xii. 184. Feb. 20th, Prefect Castro to Pico. Has toiled hard, but foes are in league against him. His resignation not yet accepted. The country in a deplorable state, all on account of dissensions between gov. and gen., of which foreigners take advantage. Thinks Pico's presence in the north very desirable. *Doc. Hist. Cal.*, MS., iii. 116.

[9] Jan. 1st, 15th, Ábrego to Pico, explaining his difficulties. He is blamed by Montereyans for his willingness to give up the office. Advises that the funds be paid directly from the custom-house to the general, and not to him; or that a northern man be appointed as treasurer. He is tired of being denounced and insulted as a 'Mexican.' *Dept. St. Pap.*, MS., vii. 96–9. Jan. 22d, Pico to Castro, with Valle's appointment. *Valle, Doc.*, MS., 50–1. Jan. 24th, Rafael Sanchez and Juan Bandini to Pico, complaining of scandalous irregularities in the distribution of public funds, the real govt being kept in a state of beggary. *Dept. St. Pap.*, MS., vii. 102–3. Feb. 10th, 12th, Castro to

newed the financial controversy by trying to enforce
a recent Mexican law, which provided that the departments should receive two thirds of all revenues, the
national government—that is, the military branch so
far as California was concerned—retaining only one
third. Pico ordered the administrator of customs,
therefore, to pay over the two thirds to the prefect, as
representative of the civil authority. General Castro
would not submit to any such reduction—from two
thirds to one third—of the funds at his disposal. He
held that his orders from Mexico to defend the country conferred the right to use the country's revenues
for that purpose; insisted that the distribution must
be continued on the former basis; and his orders were
obeyed.[10]

At the beginning of March the assembly met at
Los Angeles, and I append in a note an abstract of
legislative proceedings for the year, though some of
the matters treated will require to be noticed more
fully elsewhere.[11] The members—all abajeños, though

Valle, refusing his consent to the change; Feb. 11th, 16th, Valle to Ábrego
and replies. *Valle, Doc.*, MS., 50-3; *Dept. St. Pap.*, MS., xiii. 18-22. No
date, Valle to Castro, accusing him of disturbing the public peace by ignoring
the gov. *Id.*, vii. 4. March 1st, Castro to Pico. The change deferred until
an interview can be held. *Id.*, vii. 41-2. March 18th, Valle's report to Pico
after his return. Will hold no further relations with general or treasurer.
Id., Ben., iii. 136-9, 85. See also mention in *Valle, Lo Pasado*, MS., 38-9;
Botello, Anales, MS., 125-6; *Arce*, in *Vallejo, Doc.*, MS., xii. 184.

[10] April 15th, Pico to administrator and to prefect. *Doc. Hist. Cal.*, MS.,
iii. 166; *Dept. St. Pap.*, MS., vi. 79-80; *Id., Ben.*, iii. 139. April 16th, 18th,
All direct taxes, etc., must also be paid to the dept. govt. *Id., Angeles*, ix.
57; *Pico, Doc.*, MS., i. 26. May 9th-15th, corresp. between gen., prefect, and
admin. *Unbound Doc.*, MS., 206-10; *Doc. Hist. Cal.*, MS., iii. 224. June
16th, admin. declares that payment to the prefect would be illegal. *Dept. St.
Pap., Ben.*, MS., iii. 86. May 28th, Gen. Castro orders Receptor Diaz to
pay over directly to a military officer the duties collected from an English
ship. *Guerra, Doc.*, MS., v. 192. May 11th, Castro authorizes Vallejo to
raise a loan for defence. *Vallejo, Doc.*, MS., xii. 205.

[11] Sessions of assembly March 2 to July 24, 1846, in *Leg. Rec.*, MS., iv.
315-71. English translation in *U. S. vs Bolton, Appellant's Brief, in U. S.
Sup. Court*, p. 221-53. March 2d, the new members, Bandini and Argüello,
admitted. Gov.'s opening message read, and committees appointed. (The
message in full is found in *Olvera, Doc.*, MS., 13-19.) Bandini's motion for a
'consejo general de pueblos unidos' referred to a com. Ayunt. of Angeles
wants funds for schools. March 4th, Ábrego sends excuse of sickness for his
absence. (Pico to Ábrego, in *Dept. St. Pap.*, MS., viii. 120.) Sta B. producers
ask for exemption from double taxation. Citizens ask for a grant of S. Gabriel

they do not seem to have indulged in any legislation of a violently partisan and revengeful nature—were Figueroa, Guerra, Botello, Bandini, and Argüello;

for a town. Botello granted leave of absence. Argüello not present. March 6th, Angeles wants a police force supported by contributions from men of means. March 9th, Guerra granted leave of absence to go as a commissioner to Monterey. Land grants. March 13th, Alvarado desires instructions as to his duties in congress, but gets none. American traders wish to be relieved of the annual tax of $600 for each vessel. Isaac Williams proposes to build a fort in the cajon if allowed to introduce $25,000 in goods free of duties. March 16th, land grants. March 18th, lands. Sec. Olvera granted leave of absence. (Olvera to Pico. *Dept. St. Pap.*, MS., viii. 96.) March 23d, S. Gabriel cannot be granted for a pueblo. Bandini's prop. on sale of missions. Argüello sec. pro tem. March 30th, Bandini's mission prop. adopted. April 8th, Abrego sends certificates of illness, and is exempted, a suplente being summoned. April 15th, Pico's appointment as constitutional governor received; also the Montesdeoca doc. of Nov. 14th on mission sales; also other unimportant Mex. decrees. Castro's report of March 17th on the Frémont affair received. Bandini denounces the general's disregard of law. April 18th, special session. Pico sworn in as gov. Olvera acting as suplente. (April 17th, assembly to Olvera. Summons. *Dept. St. Pap.*, MS., viii. 121; *Olvera, Doc.*, MS., 20–1.) April 24th (?), no record. April 29th, matter of the com. gen. to be discussed in secret session. Figueroa's act to repress Ind. hostilities passed. May 8th, more certificates of illness from Abrego. 45 land grants submitted. (May 2d, assembly decrees that interrupted sessions shall continue? *Dept. St. Pap.*, MS., viii. 127.) May 11th, report of Guerra on his mission to Mont. and Castro's bad faith. Pablo de la Guerra introduced as a commissioner from Castro. Speech of Bandini against Castro. Pico desires permission to leave the capital should he deem it necessary. May 13th, Mex. order on missions. Munic. matters. Bandini's proposition of March 2d for a consejo general passed. Guerra not allowed leave of absence. May 15th, Sta B. taxes. Lands. June 3d, hide regulations. Lands. Figueroa's prop. to establish a fort in the cajon against Ind. Warning from Castro of Frémont's hostile intentions. The consejo general not to be held as ordered on May 13th. The gov. to take steps to defend the country. June 10th, land grants and hide regulations. June 15th, munic. affairs. Figueroa presiding. Pico absent in the north. Botello present and acting as sec. pro tem. July 1st, communications from Pico at Sta B., enclosing others from Castro on startling events at Sonoma (details elsewhere). Assembly declines to go to Sta B., as Pico desires; and refuses to bear any responsibility for consequences. (Illness of members alleged by Botello as a reason for not going to Sta B. *Moreno, Doc.*, MS., 27–8.) July 2d, unimportant reference to business of the last session. A weekly courier to be established. July 3d, vague reference to business of last sessions. July 6th, communication from Pico on the McNamara colonization scheme. July 7th, com. report on McNamara grant approved. July 8th, land grants. Bandini says he must go home on account of illness. Argüello is going home because Bandini's departure will leave no quorum. Pico presiding. (July 8th, Botello to Moreno. Assembly dissolves, owing to Bandini's illness. This is the last session. *Moreno, Doc.*, MS., 18.) July 24th, extra session. Pico submits Sloat's proclamation, etc. Members express 'patriotic fervor.' The people to be called upon for services. An auxiliary military force to be organized. (Nothing more in the *Legislative Records*.) Aug. 10th, session presided by Pico. Olvera, sec. Castro writes that he cannot defend the country, and is going to Mexico. Pico sees no better way than to go with Castro. The assembly to be dissolved, so that the invaders may find no legal authorities. Blotter record in *Olvera, Doc.*, MS., 32–6. Oct. 26th, 27th, 30th, Dec. 5th, sessions under the administration of Gov. Flores.

Pico presiding and Olvera acting as secretary. Ábrego, the only northern member elect, was absent on account of illness and perhaps his duties as treasurer. Pico in his opening message indicated the question of foreign relations—including that of immigration and the reported approach of 10,000 Mormons—as a most urgent one, that should receive exclusive attention until fully disposed of. The department was represented as being from every point of view in a most unfortunate condition. Education was utterly neglected; as was the administration of justice, largely on account of the fact that justices of the supreme court had declined to accept their appointments. The missions were so burdened with debt that the governor had been able to sell or rent only a few of them. The army was totally disorganized, soldiers enough for the protection of Monterey only being kept under arms by the general, while the rest of the department was left defenceless. Of financial matters, the writer had been able to learn but little, but was sure that most of the revenues had been wasted. Of course much was expected from the wisdom of the assembly, though its president had no definite suggestions to offer.

Early in March Pico sent Francisco de la Guerra as a commissioner to Castro, presumably to suggest some basis upon which the two chiefs might work in harmony, and perhaps to urge a conference at Santa Bárbara; though the exact nature of his instructions is not known.[12] Neither does it appear that his

Members present, Figueroa, Botello, Guerra, and suplentes Olvera and Joaquin Carrillo. Details of measures against the Americans will be given later. Fragmentary records in *Id.*, 39–56; *Carrillo (D.)*, *Doc.*, MS., 44; *Castro, Doc.*, MS., ii. 150; *Janssens, Doc.*, MS., 32–3; *Soberanes, Doc.*, MS., 326.

[12] March 9th, Guerra sent with verbal instructions. He was to use the good offices of influential persons. *Guerra, Doc.*, MS., vi. 14–15. Appointment, and license from assembly. *Dept. St. Pap.*, MS., viii. 129; *Leg. Rec.*, MS., iv. 320–1. March 16th, Padre Duran to Gen. Castro, urging him to look favorably upon Pico's propositions, it being of great importance that the two should unite on some plan of internal policy. *Pico, Doc.*, MS., ii. 69–70. March 2d, Rafael Sanchez to Pico. Urges him to come to Monterey and sustain his authority—else he will soon be gov. only of Los Angeles. Complains that neither Pico nor Castro has shown good faith to the Mexicans

efforts as a conciliator were successful. He made a report, however, of what he had accomplished, or failed to accomplish, and gave the document to Castro, to be forwarded to the governor; but the general, curious perhaps, as we are, to know its contents, kept the report.[13] About the same time that Pico's commissioner left Los Angeles, Castro sent to the capital his report of the troubles with Frémont, coupled with the announcement of his intention to defend the country—acting by virtue of his own authority and instructions from Mexico, in case the governor would not come to Monterey as he was urged to do. He also announced the return of José Antonio Carrillo from his exile in Sinaloa, and requested Pico not to prosecute him further, as his services were needed.[14] These communications on being laid before the assembly produced a commotion. The danger of invasion was lost sight of in view of the fact that Castro had dared to issue a proclamation to the people, the prefect's share in the proceedings being ignored by the irate southerners. The defence of the country was unimportant in comparison with the thought of undertaking that defence without consulting, or rather without awaiting the coöperation of, the political chief. Juan Bandini made a speech, denouncing Castro's abuse of his powers, and called upon Pico to "reply to him with decorum, and at the same time with that firmness and energy which a proceeding so

under the treaty of Cahuenga. *Dept. St. Pap.*, MS., vii. 106–8. March 2d, 4th, Prefect Castro to Pico. Also urges him to come north and make up his differences with the general. *Id.*, vii. 110.

[13] So Guerra reported to the assembly on May 11th. *Leg. Rec.*, MS., iv. 337. April 14th, Castro to Pico. Believes that he will be convinced of the rectitude of writer's intentions and of the force of the reasons that prevent him from acceding to his request. *Dept. St. Pap.*, MS., vii. 52. May 5th, Guerra to Castro, a letter of reproaches for his conduct in not forwarding the report. *Id.*, vii. 55. May 8th, G. to P. The most Castro would promise was to try to come to Sta B. after the meeting of a military junta. *Id.*, vii. 56.

[14] March 17th, C. to P. *Dept. St. Pap.*, MS., vii. 48–9. This communication as reported in the assembly was to the effect that 'as Pico had not come north, Castro would proceed,' etc.; but in the original Castro still urges Pico to come. March 25th, Prefect Castro writes to the min. of rel. on the needs of Cal. *Doc. Hist. Cal.*, MS., iii. 142.

scandalous demanded."[15]   And Pico did write what
was probably intended to be such a reply, but what
was in reality an absurd exhibition of petty suspicion
and weakness.[16]

But Don Pio, thus insulted by Castro's presumption and threats to defend the country, was at the
same time comforted by the receipt of his appointment as constitutional governor of the Californias.
This appointment was issued by President Herrera
September 3, 1845, in accordance with the assembly's
recommendation of June 27th, and in consideration of
"the patriotism and commendable qualities which
make you worthy of the confidence of the supreme
government."[17]   The document was communicated to
the assembly April 15th, and on the 18th, before that
body and in presence of a large concourse of citizens
and officials, Pico took the oath of office, delivering
an address, and subsequently assisting with all the
authorities at the usual religious te deum.[18]   On the
same day the governor's speech was issued in substance
as a proclamation to the people.   It contained the
usual expressions of patriotic zeal, lack of self-confi-
dence, flattery for the people, and trust in God; and

[15] Session of April 15th. *Leg. Rec.*, MS., iv. 330–1.   April 14th, Castro
to Pico.   Has never doubted the purity of his intentions.   Cannot leave the
north, but hopes P. will come. *Dept. St. Pap.*, MS., vii. 115–16.   April 17th,
P. to Prefect Castro, complaining that no full reports have come from him on
the Frémont affair. *Doc. Hist. Cal.*, MS., iii. 174.   April 24th, a friend to
Bandini.   The new plan of reform, in preparation since Carrillo's arrival,
will cause a great transformation.   Mexicans are to be expelled.   This alone
will raise the devil. *Bandini, Doc.*, MS., 70.

[16] No date, P. to C. *Doc. Hist. Cal.*, MS., iii. 289.   By what right does the
gen. venture to issue proclamations, and to alarm the people with whom, not
being soldiers, he has nothing to do?   He must have forgotten that there is a
govt; or does he desire to overturn all order? or does he flatter himself he has
power over free and enlightened citizens?   How would he like it if the gov.
should usurp military functions or alarm the soldiers? etc.   Suspects that
Castro's orders from Mexico, which nobody has seen, are ample enough to
allow him to do as he pleases, etc.

[17] Sept. 3d, min. of rel. to Pico. *Doc. Hist. Cal.*, MS., iii. 165; *Pico, Doc.*,
MS., ii. 167; *Dept. St. Pap., Ang.*, MS., xi. 171.

[18] April 15th, 18th. *Leg. Rec.*, MS., iv. 329–32; Pico to Ábrego. *Dept. St.
Pap.*, MS., xiii. 15.   May 4th, Larkin congratulates Pico. *Larkin's Off.
Corresp.*, MS., i. 98.   May 16th–17th, publication of the appointment at
Monterey. *Dept. St. Pap., Mont.*, MS., iii. 123.   Pico, *Hist. Cal.*, MS., 135,
claims to have kept back the appointment for several months after it was re-
ceived, hoping to be relieved of so burdensome and difficult a position!

concluded of course with a call upon all Californians to be united for the common welfare. "With honor and law as our emblems, victory will be ours."[19]

Besides reporting Frémont's movements, inviting the governor to a conference, despatching Castillero to Mexico for aid, and announcing his determination to resist invasion, either with or without Pico's coöperation—Castro also convoked a junta of military men at Monterey to deliberate on the condition of the country, and to advise him as to the best policy to be pursued.[20] The junta met at the end of March, and its first recorded act was to declare on April 2d its adhesion to the 'plan regenerador of San Luis Potosí,' and its recognition of Paredes as president ad interim of Mexico.[21] This pronunciamiento was not made public for over a month, during which time the number of signatures was increased from the six or eight of the junta proper to twenty-nine. On May 7th it received the adhesion of the Monterey ayuntamiento, and was officially communicated to the prefect, being also indorsed next day by the officials of the custom-house, and a little later by the local authorities of San José, and probably by those of other northern towns. Prefect Castro refused his approval of the act in all its phases, suspecting that it was intended as an attack on the political authority represented in the north by him. Not only did the Mon-

[19] April 18th, Pico's proclamation on assuming the proprietary governorship. Original in *Doc. Hist. Cal.*, MS., iii. 178, 181; *Guerra, Doc.*, MS., i. 161–3.

[20] March 16th, Castro to Vallejo, who is summoned in the name of the country to come immediately to Monterey. *Vallejo, Doc.*, MS., xii. 197.

[21] April 2d, pronunciamiento in favor of Paredes, signed by the following officers: Gen. José Castro, Col. J. B. Alvarado, Com'te J. A. Carrillo, Capt. Mariano Silva, Capt. Joaquin de la Torre, Lieut Fran. Arce, Alf. Bautista Castro, Col. M. G. Vallejo, Lieut-Col Victor Prudon, Treasurer José Ábrego, Capt. Pedro Narvaez, Lieut Macedonio Padilla, Sub-lieut Ign. Servin, Manuel R. Castro, José Mª Soberanes, Lieut A. M. Somoza, Rafael Sanchez, Capt. Juan Castañeda, Capt. José M. Flores, Lieut Fran. Limon, Lieut Valentin Gajiola, Sub-lieut Juan Soberanes, Capt. Eug. Montenegro, Mariano Villa, Lieut Man. Marquez, Lieut Fran. Eguren, Sub-lieut Man. Garfias, Capt. Gabriel de la Torre, Alf. Guad. Soberanes. *Doc. Hist. Cal.*, MS., iii. 153; *Vallejo, Doc.*, MS., xxxiv. 193.

terey officers approve the new plan, and recognize the
new president, but they protested against the acts of
the late administration; and as one of these acts had
been the confirmation of Pico as governor, it was
feared that this was the objective point of the whole
movement. Respecting the reception of this act of
the junta by Pico and the assembly early in June, I
shall have something to say later.[22]

After having performed its supposed duties toward
the nation, the junta of Monterey turned its attention
to affairs at home, and the decision reached on April
11th was as follows: 1st, that Castro's presence was
indispensable in the northern towns, which must be
fortified and defended; 2d, that Pico should be
invited to come to Monterey and take part in the
salvation of the department; 3d, that if, as was
improbable, Pico should not accept the invitation,
the general might act as seemed best, and establish
his headquarters at Santa Clara; 4th, that this
arrangement should last until the coming of the orders
and resources solicited from Mexico through Castillero.[23] The governor's reply to this act was a
violent protest against it, as "an assumption of patriotism for the purpose of paralyzing the administration
and disturbing the peace." He also expressed great
displeasure at the part taken by the prefect in this
scandalous subversion of order and law.[24] He continued his protests in a private letter to Vallejo,

[22] May 7th, action of Monterey ayunt. Doc. Hist. Cal., MS., iii. 201–2.
May 7th, Gen. Castro to prefect. Castro, Doc., MS., ii. 81, 84. May 8th,
action of custom-house officers. Doc. Hist. Cal., MS., iii. 204. May 8th,
9th, prefect to Gen. Castro. Id., iii. 203, 205; May 9th, prefect to juez of S.
José. S. José, Arch., Loose Pap., MS., 58. May 12th, 13th, prefect vs
general. Doc. Hist. Cal., MS., iii. 209; Castro, Doc., MS., ii. 94. May 13th,
Gen. Castro to Pico, urging him to accept the plan. Dept. St. Pap., MS., vii.
52–3. May 16th, 17th, juez of S. José to prefect. Doc. Hist. Cal., MS., iii.
219, 225. See also Alvarado, Hist. Cal., MS., v. 130–2; Castro, Rel., MS.,
175–6.

[23] April 11th, acta of junta de militares in Monterey. Dept. St. Pap., MS.,
vii. 50–1. Signed by Castro, Vallejo, Alvarado, Prudon, Carrillo, and
Manuel Castro.

[24] April 30th, Pico to the Castros. Doc. Hist. Cal., MS., iii. 190. He begs
Gen. C. to desist from his project, and to unite with him in the country's
defence.

insisting that the junta had merely called upon the people to join Castro in a struggle against the legitimate authorities, and had ignored not only the governor, but the assembly, and even the whole south. He regretted deeply that so true a patriot as Vallejo should have been induced to take part in a measure so ruinous to his country; and he even carried his flattery so far as to say that the junta ought to have made Vallejo general in the place of Castro, and to hint at rewards for the colonel's favor in the final distribution of mission property.[25] Vallejo's reply was to point out in a long and friendly letter the groundless nature of Pico's suspicions. He maintained that the danger of foreign invasion in the north was real and imminent; that the junta had acted in good faith and with no partisan views whatever; that neither the council of officers nor Castro in this instance had in any respect exceeded their legitimate powers; and that it would be an absurdity to require a comandante general to consult a governor two hundred leagues away in a case of emergency. Vallejo made it very clear, in language forcible but friendly, that Pico at this stage of the quarrel had allowed his prejudice to get the better of his reason, and had assumed a position utterly untenable.[26]

At the end of April, apparently before receiving Pico's protests, Castro addressed to the governor a letter in support of the measures decided upon, urging that only by working in accord was there any hope of averting calamity, and that the time had now come when all personal and local differences should be put aside. Pablo de la Guerra was sent as commissioner to Los Angeles to explain the situation,[27] and to obtain at the least an interview between the two chiefs at San Luis Obispo.[28] Guerra was introduced, and Cas-

[25] May 2d, P. to V. *Vallejo, Doc.*, MS., xxxiv. 196; xii. 204.
[26] June 1st, V. to P., in *Vallejo, Doc.*, MS., xii. 219.
[27] April 27th, 28th, C. to P. *Doc. Hist. Cal.*, MS., iv. 1178–80; *Dept. St. Pap.*, MS., vii. 53.
[28] May 10th, 11th, letters from both José and Manuel Castro to Pico, urg-

tro's communication was read, to the assembly at the session of May 11th; but the only result—when Guerra had explained his business, and Juan Bandini had made a speech bitterly denunciatory of Castro's acts in general, and of his present assurance in venturing to instruct the governor and assembly on the true condition of the department—was that Pico was granted permission, should he deem the matter of sufficient importance, to leave the capital.[29]

It was probably the holding of a junta at Monterey, as just recorded, that prompted the southern politicians to organize a somewhat similar meeting of their own. Early in March, Juan Bandini had proposed a 'consejo general de pueblos unidos de la Alta California;' but the scheme, after some discussion in April, had not met with much favor, and had been, perhaps, practically abandoned.[30] It was revived, however, on the arrival of Pablo de la Guerra, and, as the latter claimed, at his instigation, in accordance with the ideas of Castro and his friends in the north; but it seems certain, from preceding and subsequent circumstances, that such could not have been the origin of the plan.[31] Everything points to it as a phase of the quarrel between governor and general, designed as a southern measure to counterbalance the junta of Monterey.

ing him to consent to a conference at San Luis, to lay aside personal resentments, and not to add the danger of civil war to that of foreign invasion. *Doc. Hist. Cal.*, MS., iii. 206; *Dept. St. Pap., Ben. Pref. y Juzg.*, MS., ii. 86–8. May 25th, alcalde of S. José to prefect, on military preparations. People here have as yet taken no part with Gen. Castro. He seems to hint that there is some concealed plan in connection with the preparations. *Doc. Hist. Cal.*, MS., iii. 233.

[29] May 11th. *Leg. Rec.*, MS., iv. 337–41. It was at the same session that Castro's treatment of Francisco de la Guerra was reported, a fact that did not put the abajeños in a very friendly mood.

[30] March 2d, April 22d, 29th. *Leg. Rec.*, MS., iv. 317–18; *Dept. St. Pap.*, MS., viii. 96, 99–104, 122–5.

[31] Pablo de la Guerra, in an original blotter letter without date—but probably written in his own defence in later years—says that he suggested to Castro the idea of independence, which was favored also by Vallejo and Alvarado; and he was sent south to advance the scheme, and succeeded in obtaining the call for a consejo—but on his return found that Castro had changed his mind. *Doc. Hist. Cal.*, MS., iv. 1299–1300. As Guerra's mission to Angeles is otherwise clearly accounted for, and his cool reception by the assembly recorded, I cannot place much reliance on this version of the matter.

On May 13th the assembly took up and approved the committee report of April 22d, on Bandini's proposition of March 2d; and on the same day it was published in a bando by Pico. In a preamble the condition and prospects of California were presented in the darkest colors; and two important questions were suggested respecting emergencies likely to arise: 1st, what are the means of defence if a foreign invasion precedes the coming of aid from Mexico? and 2d, should troops come from Mexico without provision for their support, what would be the consequences to Californians? The decree provided that a *consejo general*, composed of eighteen delegates to be elected on May 30th—four each from Los Angeles, Santa Bárbara, and Monterey; two each from San Diego and San José; and one each from Sonoma and San Francisco—together with the six vocales of the assembly as speaking and voting members, and with such ecclesiastical and military representatives, not exceeding five each, as the respective authorities might deem proper to admit—should meet at Santa Bárbara June 15th, under the presidency of the governor—twelve elected delegates to constitute a quorum—with the object of "determining all that may be deemed best to avoid the fatal events impending at home and abroad."[32]

Elections were held as ordered in the north, though most of the delegates chosen declined to serve, either on account of one or another disability, or because they did not approve the objects of the council.[33] Doubtless elections were also held in the south,

[32] *Consejo General de Pueblos Unidos de California, Bando de 13 de Mayo, 1846,* MS. Details of the 10 articles, on elections and petty matters of organization and routine, etc., are omitted as of no importance. May 13th, Pico to both José and Manuel Castro, urging the importance of the proposed consejo. *Dept. St. Pap.,* MS., vii. 2–3; *Castro, Doc.,* MS., ii. 89–90.

[33] The delegates chosen were, for Monterey, Manuel Castro, Rafael Gonzalez, Francisco Rico, and Rafael Sanchez; for S. José, Antonio Suñol and Jesus Vallejo; for Yerba Buena, Benito Diaz; and for Sonoma, Victor Prudon. *Doc. Hist. Cal.,* MS., iii. 229, 238–47; *Castro, Doc.,* MS., ii. 73, 100; *Vallejo, Doc.,* MS., xii. 210, 216; xxxiv. 197, 201; *Fernandez, Doc.,* MS., 13. Rico, Vallejo, Suñol, and Prudon declined—the latter declaring it would be treason to accept; while Gonzalez and Sanchez referred the matter to Gen. Castro, which was equivalent to declining.

though I find no records.   The missionary prelate was
invited to name the ecclesiastical delegates, but declined for want of padres, and because he questioned
the propriety of their taking part in politics.[34]   Castro
refused to appoint the military delegates, or to have
anything whatever to do with a project which he denounced, in terms even more violent than those applied by Pico to the action of the Monterey junta, as
ruinous, treasonable, illegal, preposterous, and 'liber-
tycidal'! He protested, in the name of God, the country, and his armed force, against the holding of the
consejo and all acts that might emanate from such a
body. He besought the governor to retrace his steps
while there was yet time, announced his purpose to
defend the country at all hazards, and finally declared
the department in a state of siege and under martial
law.[35] He did not condescend to give any definite
reasons for his opposition; but in reality he opposed
the consejo mainly because he and his friends could
not control it, the south having a majority of the elec-
tive delegates, besides the members of the assembly,
who were all abajeños. Vallejo in a letter to Pico
based his opposition openly on that ground, declaring
the whole scheme a very transparent trick against the
north, and pointing out the injustice of giving San
Diego two delegates, while San Rafael, Sonoma, and
New Helvetia combined were to have but one.[36]

[34] *Arch. Arzob.*, MS., v. pt ii. 68–9. P. Duran was applied to, but he was
ill, and P. Gonzalez replied instead.

[35] May 28th, Castro's protest.   Original in *Soberanes, Doc.*, MS., 316–20.
June 8th, more to same effect. *Bandini, Doc.*, MS., 73; *Dept. St. Pap.*, MS.,
vii. 21–4. 'I see with astonishment the libel aborted in the govt house at
Angeles on May 13th, under the title of decree.   Never could the insane
hydra of discord have ejected a more destructive flame than that of this
abominable paper.   Are its authors Mexicans?'

[36] June 1st, V. to P. *Vallejo, Doc.*, MS., xii. 219.   Osio, *Hist. Cal.*, MS.,
456, thinks Castillero's influence prevented the meeting, that officer fearing
that it might result in a reconciliation between Castro and Pico.   Vallejo,
Hist. Cal., MS., v. 92–3, is of opinion that had the junta been held Pico would
have tried through its agency to raise troops and funds for an attack on Castro.
May 30th, Manuel Castro urges José Castro to appoint military delegates to
the junta, and to have an interview with Pico. *Soberanes, Doc.*, MS., 322–5.
May 30th, 31st, Gonzalez and Sanchez, delegates elect, ask advice of Castro,
and express suspicion as to the purpose of the junta. *Vallejo, Doc.*, MS., xii.
211, 214.

The purposes of Pico and his friends in convoking
the council of Santa Bárbara were doubtless somewhat vague, the only definite phase of the matter being a determination that whatever was done for the
salvation of the country must be done under southern
control. It was believed, however, that an influence
would be brought to bear in favor of independence
from Mexico; and it was also suspected that certain
men would go so far as to urge an English or French
protectorate. This suspicion, not altogether without
foundation, will be noticed more fully in the next
chapter. Whatever may have been its object, the consejo never met, the decree of May 13th having been
suspended by the assembly the 3d of June.[37] No definite reason was assigned for this action; but at the
same session was announced the declaration of the
Monterey junta in favor of Paredes;[38] and a communication from Castro was also read, in which he announced the imminence of an attack by Frémont, and
urged the governor to come north. Moreover, the refusal of the northerners to take part in the consejo
rendered it impossible to obtain a quorum according
to the terms of the call.

Pico and his advisers regarded the acts of the Monterey junta in favor of Paredes and against Herrera,
in connection with the refusal of the arribeños to
assist in the consejo, as virtually a declaration of war
against the south, and especially against the civil authorities; and they gave little or no credence to the
rumors of impending invasion by Frémont, regarding

[37] *Leg. Rec.*, MS., iv. 352-3; *Dept. St. Pap.*, MS., vii. 20. Doc. in *Pico,
Acont.*, MS., 83-4; *Coronel, Doc.*, MS., 243-5. The southern delegates were
ordered not to go to Sta Bárbara.
[38] June 12th, Abel Stearns writes to Larkin: 'The asamblea by act have
deferred the junta that was to take place at Sta B. on the 15th. The cause
of this was the act passed by the said-to-be junta de guerra held at Monterey,
in which they declare the decrees and acts of the govt of Sr Herrera relative
to Cal. to be null; thus indirectly declaring against the gov. of this dept, and
other acts or decrees of the general govt favorable to the civil list, which probably does not very well coincide with the interest of the military gentlemen
your way.' *Larkin's Doc.*, MS., iv. 151.

them, and also the efforts to secure the governor's
presence in the north, as mere pretexts on the part of
Castro, whose plan was to depose Pico by the aid of
the force raised ostensibly to resist Frémont. These
fears, greatly exaggerated if not altogether without
foundation, were doubtless real on the part of the
abajeño chiefs. They at once resolved to assume the
offensive instead of awaiting an attack, using both
force and stratagem. Pico was to adopt Castro's own
devices; to raise a military force with which ostensibly to resist foreign invasion; to march northward in
pretended compliance with the general's invitation;
but eventually to forcibly remove that officer from the
command. In the session of June 3d, besides deferring
the meeting of the Santa Bárbara council, the assembly authorized the governor to take such steps as
might be necessary to "save the country." This in
open session; but in secret session that body passed a
decree formally suspending General Castro until public tranquillity should be restored.[39]

In pursuance of the scheme just noted, Pico took
steps to raise funds by methods closely resembling
forced loans. He called on Sonoran and New Mexican visitors to unite with Californians in support of
so holy a cause, and wrote to Juan Bandini, soliciting
his presence and coöperation at Angeles. The 16th
of June he left the capital with a military force.
Three days later he was at San Buenaventura with
eighty men, expecting to be joined by thirty more at
Santa Bárbara, where he arrived on or before June
21st, and where two days later he was destined to receive some startling news from Sonoma. Pico's letters of these times describe himself and his men as
enthusiastic and confident of success. They are filled
with denunciations of Castro's treachery and lack of
patriotism, and announce as certain Castro's intention

[39] This action is not recorded in the *Leg. Rec.*, as now extant; but is mentioned in an original letter of Pico to Bandini on the same day, June 3d,
Bandini, Doc., MS., 72; and it is indirectly confirmed, as will be seen, in
subsequent records.

to invade the south at the head of an army, urging
upon citizens and legislators the necessity of active
measures, military and political, for sectional, departmental, and national defence.[40]

Pico had left the capital in charge of the ayuntamiento, the duties of which body were not very arduous

[40] May 26th, Pico to Bandini, urging his presence as member of the as-
semby. He declares that Garfias, Eguren, and other officers in the south
were summoned north, not, as pretended, to serve against Frémont, but to
sign the *acta* of the junta. *Bandini, Doc.*, MS., 71. May 30th, sub-prefect
of Sta B. refuses to recognize Capt. Cota's *fuero militar*, in spite of Castro's
orders. *Cota, Doc.*, MS., 19–20. May 30th, assembly (or ayunt.?) decrees
that traders in the capital shall furnish $3,000 within 5 days. *Dept. St. Pap.*,
MS., viii. 135. Gov. wants a loan from Figueroa, Temple, and Vignes. *Id.*,
vii. 25. No date, assembly not being in session, the sub-prefect with Pres.
Figueroa takes measures for protection of the capital, in view of Castro's
communications. *Id.*, viii. 141. June 3d, Pico calls upon Sonorans to aid
against Americans. *Id.*, viii. 135. June 3d, Pico to Bandini. Will start
on the 12th; hopes to meet him before that date. *Bandini, Doc.*, MS., 72.
June 3d, Wilson to Bandini. All recognize him (B.) as the only man who can
save the country from a foreign yoke. *Id.*, 81. June 12th, comandante principal at Angeles to Capt. Andrés Pico, transmitting gov.'s official note of
same date. Dept in danger from quasi invasion by U. S. Asks that all
army officers be placed at his disposal, to command the troops about to march
to the north. *Pico, Doc.*, MS., 97–100. June 12th, Pico to 1st judge of S.
Luis Obispo. Will start at once for the north to restore order and defend the
country. Asks for coöperation of all good citizens. *S. Luis Obispo, Arch.*,
MS., 12. June 13th, Comandante Eguren to Capt. Andrés Pico. Orders him
to proceed to Mont. under the gov.'s orders. *Pico, Doc.*, MS., ii. 81. June
13th, Eguren to Pico, announcing his orders to Andrés. *Dept. St. Pap.*, MS.,
vii. 58. June 13th, Wilson, from Jurupa, to gov. Sends 10 New Mexicans,
all he can find. *Id., Ben. Pref. y Juzg.*, ii. 46. June 16th, Pico sold city
lands for $200 to raise money for his expedition. *Los Angeles, Ayunt. Rec.*,
MS., 16. June 16th, Anast. Carrillo advises Pico not to go north. *Dept. St.
Pap.*, MS., vii. 119. June 16th, Pico to start to-day. *Id., Angeles*, xi. 175;
Los Angeles, Arch., MS., v. 349. June 16th, ayunt. regrets his departure.
Dept. St. Pap., Ben. Pref. y Juzg., MS., iv. 54. June 19th, Pico from S.
Buenaventura to Bandini. Has just received a despatch from Castro, whose
conduct he pronounces as 'insulting, profane, and outrageous.' He must be
denounced and punished. Come to Angeles at once to aid in the good work,
and bring Argüello with you. *Bandini, Doc.*, MS., 76. June 19th, Pico to
the assembly, transmitting Castro's despatch of June 8th—his protest against
the consejo, and threat to declare the dept in a state of siege and under martial law—protesting and urging the assembly to protest against such arbitrary
and outrageous proceedings, to which he proposes to put a stop immediately.
Dept. St. Pap., MS., vii. 25–6, with Castro's despatch. *Id.*, vii. 21–4. June
21st, Pico's sec. to sub-prefect. The gov. doubts not Castro's seditious intentions, nor that he is now on his march to invade Angeles; but will crush
the hydra. *Id.*, vii. 27. Some general accounts and remarks on the controversy between Pico and Castro, adding nothing to the contemporary corresp.
Nearly all agree that down to the last each was resolved to overthrow the
other. *Castro, Rel.*, MS., 173–5, 181–4; *Alvarado, Hist. Cal.*, MS., v. 129,
150–6; *Pico, Hist. Cal.*, MS., 139–48; *Botello, Anales*, MS., 134–8; *Coronel,
Cosas*, MS., 122; *Bidwell's Cal. 1841–8*, MS., 147–9; *Tuthill's Hist. Cal.*, 151.

for the first few days;[41] but on June 20th there came
a report through Juan Gallardo that Castro was coming to attack the town within three days at furthest;
and formidable preparations for defence were at once
made—on paper. The alarm was abated next day,
when it was learned that Castro was at least much
farther away than had been reported;[42] but it was renewed with all its terrors on the 22d, when Pico's
letter was received, with Castro's protest and declaration of martial law, and a report, brought by an English vessel, that Castro had been in Monterey on the
14th with seventy men, but had disappeared the next
morning, presumably on his way to Angeles. The
sub-prefect, Abel Stearns, at the invitation of President Figueroa of the assembly, convoked a junta of
the citizens, native and foreign, at his house; and a
committee of that junta proceeded to prepare a series
of resolutions strongly condemnatory of Castro's arbitrary attempts "to erect an absolute dictatorship to
the prejudice of all guaranties," expressive of a preference "to perish under the ruins of the *patria* rather
than let it become the sport of evil-disposed persons;"
and, what was more to the point, declaratory of their
purpose to resist by force Castro's entry into the
city.[43] The resolutions were approved by about eighty
citizens, of whom twenty-five were foreigners; and the
methods of defence were left to the ayuntamiento.
This body on the 23d issued regulations organizing
the citizens into three companies, one of artillery
under Miguel Pryor, another of riflemen under Benito

[41] June 16th, session of the ayunt. A list of respectable citizens to be
formed, and other measures to be adopted for the preservation of order. *Los
Angeles, Arch.*, MS., v. 349-50.
[42] *Los Angeles, Arch.*, MS., v. 353; *Dept. St. Pap.*, MS., vii. 4-6; *Id., Ben.
Pref. y Juzg.*, ii. 161.
[43] June 22d, Stearns to foreigners. *Dept. St. Pap.*, MS., vii. 6. Report of
the committee, consisting of Requena, Figueroa, Botello, Temple, and Workman, with a long list of signers, in *Dept. St. Pap.*, MS., vii. 62-5; *Id., Ben.
Pref. y Juzg.*, ii. 163-5; *Los Angeles, Arch.*, MS., iii. 31-6. Stearns to Pico,
with the resolutions. *Dept. St. Pap., Ben. Pref. y Juzg.*, MS., ii. 162-3.
Id. to ayunt. *Los Angeles, Arch.*, MS.. iii. 16-17; *Dept. St. Pap., Ang.*, MS.,
xi. 175-8.

Wilson, and a third of cavalry under Jorge Palomares. Next day Julian Workman was chosen comandante principal of all the forces.[44]

Juan Bandini, despite his illness, came up to the capital from San Diego to join his voice to the current denunciations of Castro, as "a man who under pretence of saving California seeks to tyrannically subdue and trample on her."[45] He also seems to have devoted his energies to the preparation of an elaborate address to the people, intended to be published by the assembly at the proper time as a defence of its action in deposing Castro. This document—never issued so far as I know, but the original blotter of which in Don Juan's handwriting exists in my collection—was a long, fierce, and declamatory denunciation of all that the general had done. It was filled with the most bitter abuse of Castro in respect not only of his public acts, but of his private character. The conclusion reached was that the assembly could no longer recognize the authority of so vicious and ignorant and incapable and tyrannical a monster, trusting that all patriotic citizens would approve that determination. The violence of this effusion was as absurd as that of Castro's protest against the consejo—which is saying a good deal.[46]

Of Castro's operations in June little can be definitely known, beyond the fact that he was at Santa Clara and San Juan, visiting also Monterey and Sonoma, engaged in not very successful efforts to raise men for the alleged purpose of resisting foreign invasion, and greatly annoyed by Pico's refusal to coöper-

---

[44] June 23d–24th, regulations by ayunt., and Workman's election. 50 men are also to be sent to reënforce Pico. *Dept. St. Pap.*, MS., vii. 7–8; *Los Angeles, Arch.*, MS., v. 354. June 26th, S. Diego sends approval of the action against Castro. *Dept. St. Pap.*, MS., vii. 85, with a similar approval from the sub-prefect of Sta B., dated June 27th.

[45] June 23d, B. to Pico. *Bandini, Doc.*, MS., 80.

[46] No date. *Bandini, Doc.*, MS., 58. In *Id.*, 101, is an undated decree of the assembly, ignoring Castro's authority, and authorizing the use of force against him and his men if they would not lay down their arms. This may be the decree already referred to, or it may be a supplementary one proposed by Bandini.

ate with him. The records are meagre, and do not
show either the number or organization of the forces
under his command; neither do they throw much light
on his real plans. In his despatch of June 8th, after
an absurdly violent protest against the proposed consejo, the general proceeded to urge upon the governor
the importance of coming north to aid in the work of
defence, and concluded as follows: "I have notified
you over and over again of the risk which the country runs, and of the necessity of taking steps for its
defence; but, with regret that I cannot count on your
coöperation for that sacred object, and as the integrity of this part of the republic is exclusively intrusted
to me, I shall be absolutely compelled to declare the
department in a state of siege, and the martial law in
full force—a legal resource employed in such circumstances by all the peoples of the universe."[47] All this
was reasonable enough on its face, and afforded no
cause for the ridiculous ravings of Pico and Bandini;
yet these gentlemen believed that Castro was devoting his whole attention, with the aid of Alvarado and
others, to plots against the civil government, regarding his preparations against foreign aggression as a
mere pretence. It is difficult to determine what were
Castro's plans at this time. He was not a man in
whose favor much could be said at any stage of his
career, or in whose good faith much reliance could be
placed. If in the latest phases of the controversy he
showed to better advantage than his rival, it was due
more to circumstances and to Pico's folly than to any
merit of his own. It is certain that he hated Pico,
and would not have scrupled to use force against him.
Had Pico come north in response to his invitation,
Castro would probably have arrested and deposed, if
he could not control him. Yet it would have been
difficult to obtain men for a successful attack on the
governor or the capital, and I do not think the general thought of such an expedition in June, if he had

[47] June 8th, C. to P. from Sta Clara. *Dept. St. Pap.*, MS., vii. 24.

before. Moreover, his fears of foreign invasion were by no means a pretence at this time, after Frémont's operations in March, and his return from Oregon at the end of May.[48]

I have thus brought the political annals of 1846, that is, the controversy of Pico versus Castro, down to the dates on which the capture of Sonoma by the Americans was made known to the different factions: to the citizens of Angeles on June 24th, when they were valiantly arming to resist an attack from a foe hundreds of miles away, with no intention so far as can be known of coming nearer; to Pico at Santa Bárbara on June 23d, when he was nearly ready to march northward with his army against the general; and to Castro at Santa Clara on June 15th, when he was preparing to resist whatever foes might present themselves, native or foreign. The effect of the startling news on the actions of the hostile chieftains must be told in later chapters.

[48] There were suspicions of some hidden purpose on Castro's part, even in the north, as appears from Dolores Pacheco's communications to the prefect, in *Doc. Hist. Cal.*, MS., iii. 251–2. Com. Carrillo writes of pasquinades posted at Sta Clara against Castro and other leaders. *S. José, Arch., Loose Pap.*, MS., 4. June 8th, Castro sends some miltary orders to Angeles, and asks Pico's coöperation. *Dept. St. Pap.*, MS., vii. 57–8.

CHAPTER III.

FOREIGN RELATIONS—UNITED STATES AND ENGLAND.

JANUARY–JUNE, 1846.

LARKIN AS U. S. CONFIDENTIAL AGENT—HIS INSTRUCTIONS—CORRESPOND-
ENCE—FEARS OF INVASION—TREATMENT OF FOREIGNERS—FRÉMONT'S
OPERATIONS IN MARCH—LARKIN'S EFFORTS AND HOPES—MONTEREY
JUNTA—IMAGINARY SPEECHES FOR ENGLAND, FRANCE, AND THE U. S.—
STEARNS, LEESE, AND WARNER—SUTTER'S POLICY—CONSEJO GENERAL
AT SANTA BÁRBARA, AND ITS BEARING ON FOREIGN SCHEMES—VIEWS OF
STEARNS AND LARKIN—PICO'S INTRIGUES—EXAGGERATIONS ON ENGLISH
INTERFERENCE—TESTIMONY OF GILLESPIE AND MINOR—POSITION OF
FORBES AND SPENCE—STEARNS AS SUB-AGENT OF THE U. S.—CONDITION
OF AFFAIRS IN JUNE—GENERAL CONCLUSIONS.

YET once again have I to go over the early months
of 1846 before describing the revolt which in June
served as a prelude to the downfall of Mexican
rule. It will be my purpose in this chapter, largely
by extracts from correspondence of the time, to show
what was done and said, what was feared and hoped,
in California respecting an anticipated change of flag;
and I shall also notice as an important phase of the
same general subject the feeling and policy of native
citizens and authorities toward foreign residents and
immigrants.

Thomas O. Larkin was a very prominent man in
connection with the matters to which I have just referred, being constantly engaged in active efforts to
secure California for the United States and to defeat
the schemes, real or imaginary, of European nations
supposed to be intriguing for the same prize. In
October 1845 Larkin had been appointed a confi-

dential agent of his government for the critical period believed to be approaching. His instructions, prefaced by a definite statement of the administration's policy, were, in brief, to report fully and often on the country, its resources and condition, the character and influence and political disposition of its leading citizens, and on the general progress of events; to warn the people against the evils of European interference, which would be disastrous to their true interests, and would not be permitted by the United States; to impress upon the Californians the advantages of liberty as enjoyed under the stars and stripes, assuring them that, could they but assert and maintain their independence from Mexico, they would be welcomed as a sister republic or as a component part of the great union; and finally, to do all this with such prudence and skill as not to awaken suspicion or the jealousy of the men who represented other powers.[1] Whatever view may be taken of President Polk's general policy respecting California, it must be admitted that this peculiar appointment conferred upon a foreign consul, when regarded from the highest standpoint of international honor, reflected no credit upon the government at Washington; and it is not surprising that the act has never been made known to the public.

Larkin did not receive or know of his appointment until April; but he acted much as he would have done had he received it earlier. On the 1st of January he transferred his mercantile business to Talbot H. Green;[2] and thereafter devoted much of his time to

---

[1] *Buchanan's Instructions of the Secretary of State to Thomas O. Larkin as Confidential Agent of the United States Government, Oct. 17, 1845.* Original MS. 'In addition to your consular functions, the president has thought proper to appoint you a confidential agent in Cal.; and you may consider the present despatch as your authority for acting in this character. The confidence which he reposes in your patriotism and discretion is evinced by conferring upon you this delicate and important trust. You will take care not to awaken the jealousy of the French and English agents there by assuming any other than your consular character.' Larkin's compensation was to be $6 per day; and Gillespie was to coöperate with him. See quotations from this document in chap. xxv. of vol. iv., and chap. i. of this vol.

[2] Jan. 1, 1846, contract between L. and G. The latter was to take charge

his consular duties, and in a quiet way to the work of conciliating Californian sentiment and of watching the other consuls, there existing naturally no definite record of his earliest efforts in this direction. Nor were there any important developments or even rumors connected with foreign relations in January and February; though I may notice a warning sent to the supreme government by Prefect Castro respecting the dangerous increase of immigration; some complaints of local authorities about the freedom with which some of last year's immigrants moved about the country under passes from Sutter; a few vague items that may relate to intrigues for English intervention; and a letter of a prominent Californian, in which he alludes to Hastings' book, and says: "The idea of those gentlemen is that God made the world and them also; therefore, what there is in the world belongs to them as sons of God"![3]

of store, warehouses, etc., and $10,000 worth of goods; and to conduct the business for three years, receiving one third of the profits. *Larkin's Doc.*, MS., iv. 1.

[3] Jan. 24th, Sub-prefect Guerrero to prefect. Has tried to get the book— in which the Californians are said to be abused—but has not succeeded, though offering $20. *Castro, Doc.*, MS., i. 311. In Feb., however, he got a copy and sent it to Castro. *Doc. Hist. Cal.*, MS., iii. 95. Jan. 2d, G. to Larkin, asking him to cause his countrymen who have entered illegally to retire, if he has jurisdiction in such matters. *Larkin's Doc.*, MS., iv. 5. Jan. 8th, Gov. Pico calls upon the prefect for a report on the immigrants of the past year. *Doc. Hist. Cal.*, MS., iii. 21. Jan. 22d, Guerrero to prefect. What shall he do with the strangers coming from the Sacramento? Thirty arrived yesterday. Can Sutter issue passports? *Doc. Hist. Cal.*, MS., iii. 77. More arrivals. *Castro, Doc.*, MS., ii. 12. Jan. 29th, 30th, prefect to sup. govt. and to gov. Speaks of the 200 armed foreigners who had entered illegally, and of the much larger number expected this year; has no doubt the intention is to take possession of the country, the intrusion being probably instigated by the U. S.; speaks of the general's permission to the immigrants to remain through the winter; sends some statistics and names; and urges the necessity of protective measures. *Doc. Hist. Cal.*, MS., iii. 90, 121; *Dept. St. Pap.*, MS., vi. 105–6. Feb. 18th, Pico in reply agrees with the prefect's views, and recommends a strict watch. Understands that Castro's promise was only conditional, and will 'order' that officer to coöperate. It is important to satisfy the national govt. that we are doing all we can. *Castro, Doc.*, MS., ii. 15. Feb. 15th, Francisco Arce writes to Vallejo that the continual irruption of foreign adventurers will end, if no check can be put to the abuse, in the country falling into the hands of those audacious people who, not content with the generous hospitality extended to them, 'advance more and more in their design to destroy our political system and deprive us of our native country.' *Vallejo, Doc.*, MS., xii. 184. In Guerrero's letters of Jan.–Feb. to Manuel Castro, he alludes in a somewhat mysterious way to Consul Forbes in connection with the departure of Pico's comisionado, Covarrubias, for Mex-

The Californian authorities were naturally alarmed
at the presence of so many armed Americans in the
north at a time when war was regarded as imminent;
and they felt impelled as Mexican officials to exhibit
more alarm than they really felt.   Moreover, the governor and prefect were disposed to criticise the permission accorded to the immigrants of 1845, simply
because it was Castro that granted it.   But it is noticeable that no practical steps were taken, and no
real disposition was shown, either to oppress foreign
residents, or even to enforce the going of the new-
comers who had promised to depart in the spring if
required to do so.   In the records of these two months
we have nothing but the old hackneyed official expressions of the evils likely to arise from the increase of
American immigration; and in the following months
no change in this respect was observable.[4]

ico, seeming to indicate, though there is nothing clear, an understanding
with Forbes respecting a scheme of some importance in connection with Covarrubias' mission. *Castro, Doc.*, MS., i. 262, 313; ii. 12.   This may possibly
have a bearing on the traditional English schemes of this year, in connection
with Pio Pico's statement, *Hist. Cal.*, MS., 136-7, that Covarrubias was instructed to apply to the commander of some English vessel for protection if
he could get no aid from Mexico.   Pico claims also that he made many efforts
to secure a conference with Castro, with a view to declare the country's independence, a step that was prevented by the general's jealous fears!

[4] March 2, 1846, Pico to the assembly.   Complains that through the 'tol-
erance or dissimulation' of certain parties—that is, Castro and the military
authorities—Mexican orders and his own instructions to prevent the illegal
entry of overland immigrants have not been carried out. *Olvera, Doc.*, MS.,
13-14.   March 4th, Justice Bolcof of Sta Cruz laments the injury done by
foreign lumbermen, who refuse to pay taxes.   April 5th, Justice Pacheco at
S. José complains at great length of the foreigners who, just because they
have married and obtained naturalization, put themselves on a level with and
even above the natives.   See the Sainsevain mill affair in the local annals of
S. José. *Doc. Hist. Cal.*, MS., iii. 158.   Complaint that the true faith has
been insulted by Sutter and Forbes. *Dept. St. Pap.*, MS., viii. 127.   April
17th, Sub-prefect Guerrero again wants to know what to do with the foreigners who swarm at Yerba Buena.   Their number is continually increased by
deserters, who do not mind the penalty of public works, eating more than
they earn. *Doc. Hist. Cal.*, MS., iii. 176.   April 17th, order to sub-prefects,
etc., that foreigners not naturalized cannot hold lands, no matter how acquired, that alcaldes must enforce this, and make the foreigners understand
it, and also that they are liable to be expelled from the country whenever the
govt may see fit to require it. *Id.*, iii. 175.   Same sent to Larkin by sub-prefect on April 30th. *Larkin's Doc.*, MS., iv. 109.   Same to Leidesdorff April
30th. *Sawyer's Doc.*, MS., 36-7.   This is the nearest approximation to the
order, mentioned by many Bear Flag men, expelling all Americans from the
country, and causing them to rise in self-defence!   May 25th, Vallejo to Castro.   Learns that in July 2,000 American families will arrive.   Something

Frémont's operations in March, as detailed in a
former chapter, had no other effect than to stir up ill
feeling between the Californians and Americans; the
former being surprised and offended by so grievous an
outrage coming from an officer of a government in whose
paternal solicitude for their welfare and earnest desire
for their favor they were being urged by Larkin and
others to trust; while the latter, in certain sections, by
distorted and false versions of the affair, were made
to believe, or obtained a pretext for asserting, that
Castro and his men were determined to drive Americans from the country.   This was a serious obstacle
to Larkin's plans.   He could but disapprove Frémont's
policy, yet as consul, not knowing under what instructions that officer was acting, he afforded him all possible aid, and prepared for possible contingencies by
sending down the coast for a man-of-war; but after
Frémont had been brought to his senses by reflection
and the consul's advice and Castro's military preparations, Larkin did not yet despair of success and hastened to assure his government that there was no real
hostility on the part of the Californians, who were in
their turn asked to believe that all had been an error,
which should cause no interruption of friendly feelings.
To the secretary of state he wrote that Castro's acts
against Frémont had been intended chiefly for effect
in Mexico, and that for the same purpose a commissioner was to be sent with the unfounded reports that
Frémont's men were joining the Indians for an attack
on the farms, that the settlers were about to take
possession of a northern town, and that Hastings was
laying out a town for the Mormons at New Helvetia.
Yet notwithstanding the excitement growing out of
the Frémont affair, "the undersigned believes that
the flag, if respectfully planted, will receive the good-
will of much of the wealth and respectability of the

should be done to prevent it. *Dept. St. Pap.*, MS., vii. 57.   June 11th, Diaz
to Castro.   Belden has arrived and reports no new arrivals of *estrangeros* at
the Sacramento. *Doc. Hist. Cal.*, MS., iii. 133.

country. Those who live by office and by the absence of law, and some few others, would faintly struggle against a change. Many natives and foreigners of wealth are already calculating on the apparent coming change."[5]

The action of the military junta at Monterey in April has been fully noticed. Its avowed purpose was to devise means of defence against foreign aggression; and there is nothing in the contemporary records of its acts and discussions to indicate any ulterior motive or sentiment of disloyalty to Mexico on the part of its members. There is a tradition, however, somewhat widely published, that the junta took into consideration, not only a scheme of independence from Mexico, but also of a foreign protectorate or annexation, the failure of the scheme being due chiefly to the inability of members to agree whether California should be intrusted to the protection of the United States, England, or France.

Lieutenant Revere, who arrived at Monterey while the junta was in session, was "favored by an intelligent member" with what purported to be the substance of two speeches delivered by Pio Pico and M. G. Vallejo, the former in favor of annexation to France or England, and the latter an eloquent plea in behalf of the United States. Revere published these speeches in his book in 1849, with the explanation that "the arguments of Vallejo failed to carry conviction to the majority, but the stand taken by him caused a sudden sine die adjournment of the junta, without arriving at any definite conclusion upon the weighty matter concerning which they had met to deliberate." Va-

[5] April 3d, 18th, L. to sec. state. *Larkin's Off. Corresp.*, MS., ii. 49–51. To the U. S. min. in Mexico he expressed his confidence that there was no danger of invasion by Americans. *Id.*, i. 71. Yet L. had just received a letter from Hastings, in which that gentleman predicted great things for Cal. from the immense immigration; and announced that a business firm—really under a confidential arrangement with the govt, made for reasons that L. will readily understand—was to despatch two ships each year, bringing immigrants free of charge! *Larkin's Doc.*, MS., iv. 55.

llejo, after writing to Pio Pico a letter embodying his views, left Monterey for Sonoma to await the issue. Revere's account, founded on information obtained, not at the time—when he knew nothing "except the notorious facts that two parties existed, and that General Vallejo was supposed to be the leader of the American party, while Castro was at the head of the European movement"—but subsequently, and doubtless after the conquest, has been repeated by Lancey and others, with the additional information that the junta met at San Juan! Of course, as the reader knows, Pico took no part in the meeting, being at Los Angeles at the time; nor is Revere's explanation— that J. A. Carrillo "reflected the views of Pico, officiated as his especial mouth-piece," and might even have made the speech attributed to Don Pio—calculated to throw much light on the subject, as Carrillo was politically a bitter foe of the governor.[6]

Colonel Vallejo was perhaps the source of Revere's information, and at any rate, he has become chief sponsor for the events as described in later years. In 1866, John W. Dwinelle, after a consultation with Vallejo, reproduced the speeches, which he stated to have been put in writing at the time of delivery by Larkin.[7] Finally, Vallejo himself, in his manuscript

[6] *Revere's Tour*, 24–32; *Lancey's Cruise*, 51–4; *Marin Co. Hist.*, 62–5; *Mendocino Co. Hist.*, 62–8. Revere adds that in a private conversation Castro asked a few weeks later 'whether the govt of the U. S. would give him a brigadier general's commission in case he decided to pronounce for the establishment of their authority.' 'He spoke apparently in jest, but I could perceive that the promise of such an appointment would have had its effect.' C. E. Pickett, in *Shuck's Repres. Men*, 229–30, gives a very muddled account of this junta in connection with that convoked at Sta Bárbara.

[7] *Dwinelle's Address, 1866*, p. 21–7. He describes the meeting as an informal one, held at the house of Castro at Monterey; does not name Pico as author of the first speech, since he is 'now a loyal citizen of Cal.;' and he speaks of the action of this meeting as having made useless the holding of that at Sta Bárbara, though as a matter of fact the latter was not called until May, long after the former was held. In a memorandum for Dwinelle's use, Vallejo, *Doc.*, MS., xxxiv. 197, says Pico's speech was made at Los Angeles; and names consuls Larkin and Gasquet as having been present at the Monterey meeting. Swasey, who was at Monterey at the time, says, *Cal. '45–6*, MS., 8–9, and in conversation, that such a meeting was held, at which Vallejo prevented the success of a plan to put the country under English protection; but he does not claim to have known anything of the matter beyond a current report of the time.

history, gives a detailed account of the whole matter, which is more or less fully confirmed by Alvarado.[8] His version is that Castro convoked the junta ostensibly to devise means of defence, but really to gain the support of leading citizens against Pico, whom he proposed to overthrow in favor of some man who would take part in his own schemes for a French protectorate.   Vallejo was summoned to attend the junta, and was joined on his way dy Sanchez and Alvires at Santa Clara.   The meeting was held on the 27th of March, at the house of Larkin, and was presided by Castro, who in an opening speech, that accredited by Revere to Pico, made an argument in favor of annexation to France.[9]   Castro's proposition caused some surprise, as he had been supposed to favor absolute independence.   David Spence then urged the advantages of England as a strong nation, which, though protestant, afforded equal protection to her catholic citizens. Rafael Gonzalez made a speech in favor of "California, libre, soberana, y independiente"! and was followed by Prudon and Sanchez in behalf of the United States, by Pablo de la Guerra[10] and Juan Alvires for independence, by Hartnell for England, and by Cambuston for France.   Finally, Vallejo made his famous speech in favor of annexation to the United States;[11] and Prudon immediately called for a vote on Vallejo's proposition.   Castro objected, with satirical allusion to the "gentlemen of the frontier" who were present only by condescension of the south and centre, representing the wealth and intelligence of the coun-

[8] *Vallejo, Hist. Cal.*, MS., v. 61-92; *Alvarado, Hist. Cal.*, MS., v. 133-46.
[9] The speech is given in full.   Vallejo tells us that to Castro's final clause, 'I propose annexation to France,' Hartnell, the official reporter (?), an Englishman, added: ' or England,' etc.—words really spoken by Spence, though Castro favored France decidedly, on account of her religion, as he said.

[10] Except by this author Guerra is supposed with much reason to have been a partisan of England.   Alvarado says that he should have favored independence.

[11] The speech in substance as given by Revere.   Vallejo says that many delegates were present from the south, all in favor of England except Bandini and A. M. Pico, who favored the U. S.   Bandini certainly was not there, and probably no southern delegate was even invited to come.

try, and insisted that a vote must be taken on his own proposition. Prudon replied, but the feeling of the assembly was manifestly against him, and Vallejo barely succeeded in having a vote postponed until after a recess. During this recess, realizing that his party was outnumbered by the opposition, which would doubtless unite in favor of England, Vallejo and his friends decided to quit Monterey and to return to their homes, which they did, leaving the junta without a quorum, and thus defeating temporarily all schemes of European intervention![12]

A desire to be strictly accurate, the leading motive of all my historical researches, compels me to state that I believe all that has been said of this meeting, including the eloquent speeches so literally quoted, to be purely imaginary. No such meeting was ever held, and no such speeches were ever made. My belief in this respect is founded on the absence of any contemporary corroborative evidence, under circumstances which would certainly have produced allusions to such extraordinary schemes and discussions; especially on the silence of Larkin, who assuredly would have known and written about a matter so particularly interesting and important to himself; and on the many inherent discrepancies and errors that have been pointed out in the testimony extant. There is no reason to doubt that Vallejo was disposed in 1846 to favor annexation to the United States, or that others looked with more favor on European nations for protection; and it is not unlikely that some of the leaders may have expressed their preferences to one another and guardedly to foreigners; but in thus recording a formal meeting, with deliberate discussion of propositions to deliver their country to a foreign power,

---

[12] It is to be noted that Vallejo makes the date of the junta March 27th, while its action of April 11th, abundantly recorded, is not mentioned at all by him. He speaks of Pico's letter disapproving of his speech, and of the junta's action, though most of the members had assembled by Pico's order, with instructions to vote for England! but Pico's letter and Vallejo's reply are extant, as already noted, and they contain no reference to foreign relations.

I am very sure that General Vallejo's memory has been greatly aided by his imagination.

On April 17th, the day of Gillespie's arrival with news of Larkin's appointment as confidential agent, Larkin wrote letters to Abel Stearns, Jacob P. Leese, and John Warner, to whom he communicated news brought from Mazatlan by the *Portsmouth*, to the effect that war was believed to have been declared, or at least that it would not long be delayed. In the event of war, he writes, "I believe the stars would shine over California before the Fourth of July! blessing those who see them and their posterity after them." This, he believes, would be most advantageous to the people, though probably not to himself and other merchants. "As a trader, I prefer everything as it is; the times and the country are good enough for me." After painting in bright colors the benefits of annexation to the United States, the writer urges the gentlemen addressed to disseminate his views with diligence and secrecy, reporting promptly all that they could learn of the popular feeling in their respective sections. Especially were the people to be warned against the evils of European interference. In their distress, "some look to England, some to the United States, and a few to France as a *dernier ressort*. Those who look to Europe know nothing of a European colonist's life, or of the heavy tax and imposition he suffers. The idea of independence is from his mother's breast implanted in every native of the American continent. Then where should he look for assistance but to the United States of America? He will there find a fellow-feeling with those who can participate in all his ideas, and hail him as a republican and citizen of the land of freedom. Be all this as it may, from the time of Mr Monroe, the United States have said that no European government should plant colonies in North America. Mr Polk reiterates this position, and his government will make it good; and the day that European colonist by purchase, or European soldier by war, places his foot on Californian soil, that day shall we see the hardy sons of the west come to the rescue."[13]

At or about the same time Larkin prepared another letter, expressing views similar to those just noted, but in language almost identical with that used by Buchanan in his instructions. This document without signature was translated into Spanish, and was intended to be shown to different Californians, but only as embodying Larkin's private opinions.[14] To the secretary of state the consul wrote, that while the leaders would prefer to rule the country under Mexico, and were inclined to vacillate in their ideas of foreign protection, yet he believed they would not oppose annexation to the United States if their offices and salaries could be secured to them.[15] To Gillespie Larkin wrote: "I have said, as my opinion, to Castro, Carrillo, and Vallejo, that our flag may fly here in thirty days. The former says for his own plans war is preferable to peace, as affairs will at once be brought to a crisis, and each one know his doom. I answered that without war he could secure to himself and his friends fame, honor, and permanent employ and pay. He and others know not what to do or say but wait advices from Mexico...I have had many of the lead-

[13] April 17, 1846, L. to Stearns, Leese, and Warner. *Larkin's Off. Corresp.*, MS., i. 77–9. This letter might be shown to Californians, but neither original nor a copy must be allowed to fall into their hands.

[14] No date, Larkin's circular letter. Copy in *Sawyer's Doc.*, MS., 18–24, with a note by L. explaining the circumstances under which it was written— in Feb. he says, but this must be an error, perhaps of the copyist. I have not found the original, but Sawyer saw it among L.'s papers before they came into my possession. In this document the Californians are clearly informed that the U. S. will not permit European intervention, but will welcome Cal. as a sister republic or as a part of the American union.

[15] April 17, 1846, L. to sec. state. *Larkin's Off. Corresp.*, MS., ii. 52–4. He says Castro talks of going to the Sacramento in July to prevent the entry of expected immigrants. He is probably not in earnest, but if he does go it will only hasten the crisis. Larkin thinks Castro will soon overthrow Pico; represents Forbes and Gasquet as men not very influential or likely to meddle much in politics; and he thanks the president for his appointment as agent, promising to do his best to give satisfaction.

ers at my house to inquire into the news, and I believe they are fast preparing for the coming event."[16]

Respecting the policy of Sutter in these days, so far as foreign relations are concerned, little is known. He was not in 1846, as he had been to some extent before, one of those to whom Larkin confided his political plans. In a communication to Castro, written in April or May—the same in which he warned that officer against Gillespie as an agent of the United States with important despatches for Frémont, whom he perhaps intended to recall from the northern frontier—Sutter wrote: "I recommend you to station a respectable garrison at this point before the arrival of immigrants from the United States, which will be about the middle of September. According to reports, they may number some thousands, though not ten thousand, as has been said. Believing that the government will buy my establishment, I shall put every thing in the best order. I am putting a new story on the large new building which you have seen, and will make it ready as soon as possible, containing quarters for two or three hundred soldiers, with sufficient parade-ground within the fort for the troops. I have also written to Prudon about this matter."[17] The only comment to be made on Sutter's warning against Gillespie, and on his recommendation to garrison New Helvetia against American immigrants, is that these acts were much more consistent with his duty as a Mexican citizen and officer than with his later pretensions of American partisanship.

On May 13th was issued the call for a 'consejo general de pueblos unidos,' to deliberate on the future destiny of California. I have already noticed this con-

[16] April 23, 1846, L. to G. *Larkin's Off. Corresp.*, MS., i. 73-5.

[17] No date (about 3 weeks after Frémont's visit), Sutter to Castro in Spanish. *Castro, Doc.*, MS., 98, 41. For the letter to Prudon, see chap. xxv., this vol. Sutter's preparations were soon to be utilized, as will be seen, but not by a Mexican garrison, as he had intended.

sejo as a phase of the controversy between Pico and Castro, and explained that the opposition of the latter and his friends prevented its success.   It has been believed from that time to this, that the promoters of this council intended in it to urge the scheme of independence from Mexico, involving probably an appeal to some other nation for protection.   The wording of the call,[18] together with the correspondence of such men as Stearns and Larkin, indicates that the belief was well founded; though little contemporary evidence exists from Californian sources.[19]   I have no doubt that the consejo would have discussed the questions to which I have alluded; that among the members would have appeared advocates of loyalty to Mexico, of absolute independence, of annexation to the United States, and of an English or French protectorate; and that on a vote the parties would have stood numerically in the order just indicated.   Friends of the United States might very likely have united with the advocates of independence, since, in the event of no war with Mexico, independence would have been less embarrassing to the government at Washington than annexation, though practically and eventually amounting to the same thing.   But all the other factions would have united in behalf of Mexico, and California would almost certainly have maintained its former status, so far as the consejo could affect it.

Larkin was not alarmed at the rumors that the consejo was to be controlled by advocates of European interference.   He proposed to visit Santa Bárbara in person; and he had no doubt of his ability, with the aid of Vallejo, Bandini, and Stearns, all of whom he urged to attend as members, to prevent any triumph of foes to the United States, though he did not expect a positive decision in favor of his own plans.

[18] See chap. ii. of this vol.
[19] May 30, 1846, Manuel Castro to José Castro.   Mentions the rumor that the southern delegates will favor independence; at which the writer is indignant, and urges the gen. to take part in the consejo, with a view to prevent the success of such a scheme. *Soberanes, Doc.*, MS., 322–5.

Stearns thought the proposed meeting would consider foreign relations only as a secondary question, the quarrel between Pico and Castro being of primary importance; but he believed that the United States had more friends in the south than any European nation, and that a majority would favor annexation, could they be assured of immediate protection against Mexico.[20]

The importance of the proposed consejo, as a scheme designed to put the country under the protection of England, has been grossly exaggerated, as indeed has all that pertains in any way to English interference. It has been asserted that Pico and other promoters of the council had so arranged its membership as to insure a decision in favor of Great Britain. Many native Californians have taken this view of the mat-

[20] May 14, 1846, Stearns to Larkin, announcing the convocation of the consejo. He says: 'The idea among the Californians for independence has for a long time been cherished here at the south; more so than at the north. Such a measure I have always been opposed to, and think it a wild scheme. Other plans have been spoken of by some—such as to ask protection of England or the U. S. The desire for some kind of a change is almost universal, as it is certain that no protection can be expected from Mexico in her present revolutionary state.' *Larkin's Doc.*, MS., iv. 119. May 21st, L. to S. *Id.*, *Off. Corresp.*, MS., i. 80. May 24th, L. to Leese. Asks him to urge Vallejo to attend the consejo. *Id.*, i. 81. June 1st, Stearns to L., explaining his ideas as to the object of the meeting. *Id.*, *Doc.*, MS., iv. 151. 'I often hear the most respectable people say, "Ojalá que tome esta los Americanos"! They appear to be inclined to any kind of a change that will free them from Mexico. The govt men are of the same opinion generally.' June 1st, L. to Gillespie. Does not believe the junta will have a quorum. 'I have no reason to suppose that this junta is more than to do something for the benefit of Cal.; what that may be the members themselves do not exactly know...I as a private person told Forbes, Castro, Vallejo, and Prudon that if they were confident that Mexico would do nothing for Cal., to make one more effort and present from a large junta a respectable (sic) memorial representing the state of Cal.; and if Mexico cannot afford protection, let them humbly offer their advice of selling the country. Forbes told me he could not mention such a thing. I told him I would, and my govt could displace me if they saw proper; as I had no pay (!), there would be no risk or loss; that as a private man and land speculator I would agitate questions for my private ends, benefit, and account. To do this he wished me to be there '—at Sta Bárbara. *Id.*, *Off. Corresp.*, MS., i. 87–9. June 1st, L. to sec. state, announcing the proposed holding of the consejo by the gov. and assembly, 'from a dread of something, they hardly know what.' *Id.*, ii. 56. June 18th, L. to Mott and Talbot, Mazatlan. Thinks the scheme will fail. *Id.*, *Doc.*, MS., iv. 165. Castro, *Relacion*, MS., 177–80, says that Pico's motive in convoking the consejo was to forestall Gen. Castro in his supposed scheme of a foreign protectorate—a most ridiculous enterprise. The gen. had really sent Guerra (so G. claimed also) to urge Pico to join him in such a scheme.

ter, especially certain arribeños, who have thus accounted for their opposition to the scheme, with a view to magnify their services in behalf of the United States.[21] Another fruitful source of exaggeration was the congressional investigation of a few years later respecting California claims on the treasury, on which occasion it became important for certain interests to magnify the importance of services rendered by revolutionists to the United States. Many witnesses were brought forward to prove that California had been on the point of being surrendered to England by the authorities, the transfer being prevented—as was Pico's prodigal distribution of lands among his English friends —by the prompt action of American settlers on the northern frontier. The absurdity of this claim will be shown later; and I introduce the matter here only to show the origin of a popular idea, that California was in imminent danger of being handed over to England. The testimony cited was that of those who merely repeated the rumors current among a class who had the least opportunities of knowing the facts; and they paid but little attention to the chronology of such rumors, confounding those that followed with those that preceded the raising of the American flag in July.[22]

[21] Vallejo, *Hist. Cal.*, MS., v. 41, 93; *Id.*, *Doc.*, MS., xxxiv. 192, is positive in his statements to this effect, declaring also that Forbes was active in promoting the scheme. Alvarado, *Hist. Cal.*, MS., v. 109–10, 146–50, expresses the same opinion, so far as Pico's designs are concerned; but he thinks the governor's following was not numerically strong, and he names David Spence as the most prominent English agent. Osio, *Hist. Cal.*, MS., 457, confirms the statement that Pico was intriguing with Forbes and other agents of England. Rafael Pinto, *Apunt.*, MS., 106, claims to have started for the south with Pablo de la Guerrra, who was sent by Castro and Alvarado to confer with Pico, and urge a scheme for an English protectorate. Manuel Torres, *Peripecias*, MS., 72–4, tells us that Dr Stokes was one of the most active partisans of the English cause; but that Forbes and Richardson held aloof. See also, on Pico's schemes, *Juarcz*, *Narr.*, MS.; *Carrillo*, *Narr.*, MS., 6–10; *Sanchez*, *Notas*, MS., 22. John Bidwell, *Cal. in 1841–8*, MS., 141–2, says it was generally understood that Pico and other prominent men were agitating the question of English protection, and he thinks there was some foundation for the idea. Juan Forster, *Pioneer Data*, MS., 28–9, also thinks there was an understanding between English agents and the Californian authorities. See also *Lancey's Cruise*, 54. Hepworth Dixon, *White Conquest*, i. 40, names Vallejo as an advocate of English schemes! See also *Hall's Hist. S. José*, 143, and many newspaper articles.

[22] *Frémont's Cal. Claims* (30th cong. 1st sess., Sen. Repts no. 75); *Dix's*

The truth of the matter is simply that Pico and half a dozen other somewhat prominent men, including Pablo de la Guerra and Juan B. Alvarado, were inclined, through various motives of personal ambitions, dislikes, and friendships, to favor European intervention as a means of keeping their country from the United States. Popular sentiment was not strong in their favor, and they could not have controlled the consejo in behalf of England, even had they acted together, as they were not likely to do. The theory that Pico had so planned the meeting as to control it absolutely in this respect, or in any other respect except that of opposition to Castro and the northern clique, was one developed in later years from the imagination of Vallejo and his friends. Larkin and Stearns, the men best qualified to judge in the matter, had no fear of results so far as the action of Californians was concerned, their only apprehensions, much less troublesome than in former years, being founded on what England might accomplish in Mexico. Had England sent a force to take California, together with guaranties of office or emolument to Pico and Castro, then the attitude of those officials would have assumed an importance that it did not possess under any other circumstances. What were the plans of the English government it is no part of my present duty to consider.

It is not easy to determine what steps were taken by Forbes and David Spence to encourage Pico and his friends in their purpose of appealing to England. The correspondence of the time naturally touches this

Speeches, i. 278–80; *Hartmann's Brief*, 61–75. Lieutenants Gillespie and Minor were the witnesses that spoke most positively about the Sta Bárbara junta, the former getting his information from Leese chiefly, and the latter— who represented the junta as having actually decided in favor of England— from Pedro C. Carrillo. 15 or 20 other witnesses testified to the general belief that Pico was granting the public lands as fast as possible to Englishmen. The chief absurdity to which I have alluded in my text was in the claim that the action of the northern revolutionists, in the middle of June, had any effect to check Pico's grants. Most of the witnesses mention the McNamara grant, which will be fully noticed later, and of which nothing was known in northern California before the end of June.

topic but vaguely.[23]   Forbes always denied having
been concerned in any intrigues whatever in behalf
of his government.   In conversation with Larkin in
1846, he gave him to understand that he had once
been reprimanded by his government for having
introduced the subject of California politics in some
of his communications; that he believed the rumors
of English negotiations with the authorities to be
false, though England would not regard with satisfaction the interference of any other nation; that his
individual preference was in favor of the United
States, though his official position did not permit an
open expression of this preference; and finally, that
his policy would be to say nothing, not to meddle in
politics, and to acquire some lands in anticipation of
the coming change.[24]   It is not by any means necessary to place implicit confidence in the literal accuracy

[23] March 17th, Forbes writes to Bandini: 'You being in my opinion a man
whose intelligence penetrates the designs of California's foes, and not being
able at present to enter into particulars, I have authorized Henry Dalton to
propose to you a certain method of frustrating those designs in a manner
honorable and beneficial to this country.   Please write to me if you find it
necessary in order to forward the desired object.' *Bandini, Doc.*, MS., 68.
Don Juan's reply, *Id.*, 69, was dated April 21st.   It was long—Bandini never
wrote a short communication—and somewhat vague and mysterious.   The
danger was no secret to him, he said, and he seems to approve the plan proposed; but 'unfortunately we are in a country where everything cannot be
told, and where a good result cannot be expected if the few men capable of
treating so serious a subject do not dedicate themselves exclusively to it.'
It is necessary to use great caution, to dissemble, and to await an opportunity,
carefully avoiding premature action, etc.   He also alludes vaguely to commercial topics.   This corresp. may or may not have a political significance.
Forbes seems to have addressed Pico, asking an explanation respecting Frémont's motives; for Pico, on April 22d, replied that he did not know what
those motives were, but assuring Forbes that the govt does not admit the
protection of any foreign power. *Dept. St. Pap.*, MS., viii. 128.
[24] May 21, 1846, L. to Stearns. *Larkin's Off. Corresp.*, MS., i. 80–1.
May 24th, same to same. *Id.*, i. 81–3; *Id.*, *Doc.*, MS., iv. 133.   May 26th,
same to same. *Id.*, *Off. Corresp.*, MS., i. 83.   'It is possible that the gov.
may obtain sufficient from Mr Forbes to give up any idea of looking to England.'   June 1st, L. to Gillespie. *Id.*, i. 87–9.   June 1st, L. to sec. state.
Id., ii. 56–8.   The same idea is clearly expressed in all these letters.   Stearns
had written on the 14th of May that he knew positively that English agents
were at work; and L. had been somewhat alarmed at the news until he had
talked with Forbes and Spence.   McKay, *Recollections*, MS., 4, arriving at
S. F. in March, says he found the air thick with rumors on account of Frémont's operations.   The Englishmen there seemed to take sides with the
Americans, though they blamed the English govt for not taking prompt
action to secure the country for the British crown.

of these statements of Forbes and Spence; but it is well to note that evidence against them is exceedingly slight, and that Larkin, the man best qualified and most interested to learn the truth, as well as the one who had in former years been most suspicious of English interference, was inclined to credit those statements.

In May Larkin appointed Abel Stearns his confidential agent for Los Angeles and southern California, implying, though not stating clearly, the nature of his own relations to the administration at Washington.[25] At the end of the month he wrote to Frémont, and said in answer to the latter's offers to be of service to him at Washington: "I have neither demands nor favors to ask of our government, nor 'odds,' to use a western expression. What time may require, time must bring to light. You are aware that great changes are about to take place in a country we are both acquainted with; to aid this I am giving up business, holding myself in readiness for the times to come, and the results; thus drawing myself into the political vortex. This in time may bring my name too prominently forward, so that I may be assailed. Should this ever happen, you may render me service."[26] The same sentiments respecting the country's prospects are expressed to Buchanan in a letter of June 1st, in which Larkin suggests that he would be will-

[25] May 23, 1846, L. to S. *Larkin's Off. Corresp.*, MS., i. 84. The following paragraph illustrates one trait of the writer's character: 'You are aware I have been for some time in public employ without any pecuniary remuneration, and therefore cannot offer you any. I can only say the offer cannot be of much trouble or expense to an active and energetic man like yourself, who would find a pleasure in what others would call laborious business. I cannot even promise you that my offer holds out any future inducement to you or your interests, but I believe that both may be advanced at some future day not far distant. Therefore the end may justify the means, at least in the result. You must only look for recompense at present in an extended knowledge of affairs.' Nothing of Larkin's $6 per day! L. also wrote in these times letters for the *N. Y. Herald* and *Sun*, as appears from corresp. with Bennett and Beach in *Larkin's Doc.*, MS., iv. 124, 129. These editors valued the letters highly, and offered pay, but L. would accept nothing, unless possibly protection in case of future slanders.

[26] May 31, 1846, L. to F., in *Larkin's Off. Corresp.*, MS., i. 86.

ing to undertake a secret diplomatic mission to Mexico on the pretext of collecting sums due him personally; and also suggests that he has at Washington a relative, Eben L. Childs, who might be utilized as special messenger to California, or who might be employed to write secret despatches without signature, as his handwriting was known to Larkin.[27]   This idea arose from the delay of the important despatch of October 17, 1845, of which Larkin had as yet received only a copy written from memory of the duplicate intrusted to Gillespie.   The original arrived, however, before the 15th, on which date Larkin renewed his thanks for the honor, describing his zealous efforts in the past, urging the necessity of an increased salary, and forwarding carefully prepared sketches of California, its condition, institutions, and people.[28]   About this time he obtained from General Castro, in an interview, a general assent to his political scheme, in the form of a written plan of a movement of independence to be undertaken as soon as the number of foreign settlers should be deemed sufficient to insure success.[29]

[27] June 1, 1846, L. to sec. state. *Larkin's Off. Corresp.*, MS., ii. 56-8. June 1st, receipt of Narciso Botiller for $40 from L. for carrying a mail from Sta Clara to Monterey. *Monterey, Consulate Arch.*, MS., ii. 15. Phelps, *Fore and Aft*, 283-4, tells us that being at Los Angeles early in June, when despatches arrived announcing that war would soon be declared, he was assured by Pico that in spite of orders from Mexico, American trading vessels on the coast should not be molested.

[28] June 15th, L. to sec. state. *Larkin's Off. Corresp.*, MS., ii. 63-4; 94-116. The sketches sent I quote elsewhere as *Larkin's Description of California;* and *Id.*, *Notes on the Personal Character of Californians.* In the former he states that in a popular cause, Pico and Castro could bring into the field 800 or 1,000 men to serve without pay for a month or more; to aid Mexico in expelling foreigners they could raise perhaps 300 or 400. There is continual dread of a Mexican general coming with an army to depose the present rulers. Many in office are convinced that a 'favorable change' would so enhance the value of their lands as to render salary a secondary consideration. Only such as thrive by absence of law can prosper in the present state of things. It would be well to pension off or give sinecures to men of influence and position, as they would then quietly draw others with them. June 17th, Forbes writes to Bandini that the *Juanita* is expected to bring news of war. *Bandini, Doc.*, MS., 74. June 19th, Pico tells Bandini that the English corvette brought news of war, but he knows nothing officially. *Id.*, 76.
On allusions more or less accurate to the efforts and hopes of Larkin and others, see *Dunbar's Romance*, 30-1; *Pacheco, Contra Costa Gazette*, Dec. 21, 1867; *Willey's Thirty Years*, 13; *Hyde's Statement*, MS., 6-7; *Torres, Peripecias*, MS., 49; *Pinto, Apunt.*, MS., 104; *Leese's Bear Flag Mem.*, MS., 9; *Sanchez, Notas*, MS., 21-2.

[29] Larkin to sec. state, July 10th. *Off. Corresp.*, MS., ii. 77.

From a careful study of the correspondence and other evidence cited in this and the two preceding chapters, I reach the following conclusions respecting the condition of Californian affairs in the early weeks of June 1846: All classes of the inhabitants realized that a political change was imminent. There was little hope that Mexico would or could afford protection or relief by sending money and an army; nor was it expected that without such aid the country could much longer maintain its status as a Mexican dependency. The anticipated change must naturally be either a declaration of absolute independence, or annexation in some form to a foreign power. The United States or England might get the country either by conquest, purchase from Mexico, or voluntary action of the Californians. There were prominent men among the natives disposed to favor each of the schemes proposed, though not yet openly or actively; while their parties were not clearly defined, the masses being for the most apathetic and indifferent. Notwithstanding the strong prejudice against Mexico, affinities of race, language, religion, and association were still potent in favor of loyalty; yet on the other hand many were beginning to speculate on the prospective increase in the value of their lands under a new régime. With personal interests in conflict with the old prejudices, the ultimate issue was wellnigh certain. The chief authorities, political and military, while protesting their loyalty to Mexico and their determination to resist foreign invasion, were in reality lukewarm in this respect, being thoroughly in earnest only in their opposition to each other. In their minds the controversy between Pico and Castro outweighed all questions of national allegiance, and was second only to personal and ambitious interests. Any foreign nation taking a decided stand could have obtained the cöoperation of either Don Pio or Don José, if not of both. Had it been practicable to bring the question of the political future to a voting test among representative men, loyalty to Mexico would have temporarily won the day, mainly through the inability of other factions to combine their forces.

While not yet sufficiently numerous or zealous to effect an immediate change in their own favor against all the others, the American party was beyond all comparison the strongest. It really included the independents, since a declaration of independence was in certain contingencies quite as favorable to the United States as an appeal for annexation. Americans were more numerous, and collectively more influential, than foreign residents of any European nation. A large increase of immigration was expected in the early future. The Californians were republicans, with but little sympathy for monarchical institutions. Not only was the American party aided by delay and by the general tendency of events, but more active agents were at work. Larkin, as a secret confidential agent of the administration at Washington, was working zealously to advance the cause. He was authorized not only to conciliate the favor of leading Californians, and to urge the advantages of annexation, but also to promise welcome to a new 'sister republic,' and, what was still more effective, to state that his government would use force to prevent European interference. He was confident, as were other leading Americans, and not without good reasons, that he was making rapid progress, notwithstanding the drawbacks occasioned by Frémont's blunders. It was believed that in the event of war California might be occupied without any serious opposition from the people; and that if there was no war, the Californians would soon by declaring their independence start voluntarily on the way to ultimate annexation. The imminence of war was in itself, of course, a favorable circumstance, as it could hardly fail to result in an American occupation, not likely to be merely temporary.

The only obstacle that could seriously impede the

progress of American plans was armed interference by a European power. This was understood in California, and there were a few leading men, including Pico, who were in favor of an appeal for protection to England. These men and their followers were influenced not so much by a preference for a European system of government as by their personal ambitions, their friendships for resident Englishmen, and their quarrels with individual Americans. They knew that English holders of Mexican bonds, as well as English travellers, had recommended the acquisition by their government of Californian territory. They were encouraged in their ideas of a British protectorate by British residents; and they adopted the current American idea that England had set her heart upon acquiring the country. There is no evidence that they received any official encouragement from the British government or its agents, and no proof that Forbes and Spence were intriguing with Pico in favor of an appeal to England. Pico and his friends had a right to entertain their preference, which was by no means a criminal or unreasonable one, as it has been the fashion among excessively American writers to imply; but as a matter of fact, they were never very deeply in earnest, never had much strength as a party; and the popular idea that they were likely to control the destinies of California has been an absurd exaggeration. So far as negotiations or intrigues in the country were concerned, the scheme of European interference was a most shadowy myth. The only danger to be apprehended by the United States was that England would obtain a cession of California from Mexico, and would attempt a forcible occupation, securing the governor's coöperation as a pretext of popular approval. This danger was also a slight one; but I shall have occasion to speak again of it.

Finally, we have found no disposition on the part of Californian officials or the Californian people to molest foreign residents. Pico and Castro, in accordance with their routine duty as Mexican officials, talked of resisting invasion, and even of preventing the entry of the thousands of immigrants expected over the mountains in the autumn; but they had no thought and made no threats of expelling those in the country. Americans were treated quite as well as Englishmen or other foreigners. The immigrants of 1845 were not even notified to leave the country, as they had promised to do if required. The popular prejudice against foreigners, fomented by personal intercourse with individuals, and still more by reports from Mexican sources of what had been done in Texas, was naturally stronger against Americans than others; but considering the imminence of war and other unfavorable circumstances, the toleration and kindness manifested were remarkable, and in themselves afforded evidence that Larkin's hopes of success in his conciliatory policy were not without foundation.

CHAPTER IV.

CAUSES OF THE SETTLERS' REVOLT.

JUNE, 1846.

An Unexpected Outbreak—Its Alleged Motives—Self-defence and Resistance to Oppression—Mere Pretexts—Current Rumors—The Insurgents Classified—Adventurers—American Enthusiasts—Ambitious Politicians—Real Motives of the Leaders—Frémont's Policy—Gillespie's Mission—Ambition and Revenge—A Bold Resolution—Overmuch Caution—Nature of Frémont's Coöperation—Ide's Theories and Statements—A Filibustering Scheme—Needless, Unjustifiable, Productive of No Good—Not a Part of the Conquest—Serious Responsibilities of the Insurgent Leaders—A Fortunate Ending.

THE condition of affairs being as described in the preceding chapter, there broke out in June a revolt of American settlers in the Sacramento and Napa valleys, who with the support of Frémont's men seized the town of Sonoma, captured several leading Californians, and proclaimed the country independent. The action was startling to all but participants. It was so unexpected, so utterly inconsistent with the policy by which agents of the United States believed themselves to be making progress toward voluntary annexation; the time was so strangely chosen, when news of war, involving a legitimate military occupation, was expected from day to day; and indeed, the affair was apparently so ill-timed, ill-advised, and extraordinary in all its phases, that it becomes necessary to study the motives that led to the outbreak before proceeding to narrate in detail its stirring scenes.

I begin with the alleged motives, which were by
no means mysterious or complicated, and to illustrate
which I introduce in the appended note a somewhat
extended list of quotations.[1]   Long as it is, the list

[1] In *History of the Bear Flag Revolt*, by *a Committee of Citizens*, published in
1847, we read: 'The American and other foreign portion of the people of Upper California learned in May 1846 that the govt had determined upon their
expulsion from the country, and were making preparations to seize or kill all
foreigners, and send such as should be made prisoners to the city of Mexico.
A large body of horses were collected, and some 500 or 600 men were ordered
under arms by Gen. Castro for that purpose.   Information was received by Mr
W. B. Ide on June 8th, brought by an Indian runner, that 200 mounted Mexicans were on their march up the Sacramento River, with the design of destroying the crops, burning the houses, and driving off cattle belonging to the foreigners.'   Ide proceeded to warn and organize the settlers, but 'it was quite
apparent that further and more decisive action was necessary to secure the
lives and property of the immigrants; and it was determined to seize the fort
of Sonoma.' Wm B. Ide was probably the writer of the preceding.   In *Ide's
Biog. Sketch*, 48, Mrs Healy (Miss Ide) says: 'We had not been there long [on
Belden's rancho in April] before a young man, Mr L. H. Ford, came to tell father
that Gen. Don Castro was on his way to drive all Americans from the country.'
On p. 51–2 we read: 'Soon after his arrival he was confronted with the solution of an important problem regarding the rights and privileges of himself
and his fellow-emigrants. . . He supposed he had conformed to all the legal conditions entitling him to all the privileges, etc., of a citizen(!). . .The question
was, whether he should be forcibly ejected from his humble abode and driven
back to the states, or whether he would unite with his fellow-emigrants in resisting the threatened war of extermination as put forth in a proclamation of
the then reputed governor of the country. . .He had seen the proclamation of
Gen. Don Castro warning the emigrants to leave the country or they would
be driven into the mountains or made prisoners, or be shot in case of resistance.'   p. 62.   The 'inhuman and arbitrary exaction' of taxes from foreigners is mentioned on p. 90.   In his remarkable letter to Senator Wambough,
which fills a large part of the volume, regretfully omitting Ide's ingenious arguments, we read, p. 106: 'Imagine the disappointment of those brave men
who had conquered the difficulties of the pathless Sierra, etc. . . . when by the intervention of a self-constituted government, heated to madness by jealousy,
excited by designing emissaries, we were forbidden the usual hospitalities of
the country and ordered to return!'   On p. 108–9, after a sharp blow at Larkin and Frémont, Ide writes: 'Immediately after [about the first of April],
Gen. José Castro, naturally humane and generous, caused to be issued and
posted up at Sonoma and various other places a proclamation ordering 'all
foreigners whose residence in the country was less than one year to leave the
country and their property and beasts of burden, on pain of death.'   This danger was temporarily averted in a way not clearly described, though a large
party was frightened away to Oregon; when Gillespie came and went after
Frémont.   When Frémont came he soon circulated the following: 'Notice is
hereby given that a large body of armed Spaniards on horseback, amounting
to 250 men, have been seen on their way to the Sacramento Valley, destroying the crops, burning the houses, and driving off the cattle.   Capt. Frémont
invites every freeman in the valley to come to his camp at the Buttes immediately.'   The letter to Wambough is repeated in *Ide's Who Conquered Cal.?*
   The following statements are from men who took part in the revolution,
or at least were in Cal. at the time.   Henry L. Ford, *Bear Flag Revolution*,
MS., 3, tells us that a meeting of Mexican officers at Sonoma 'resulted in
Gen. Castro issuing his edict for all Americans to leave the country.'   Wm
Hargrave, *Cal. in '46*, MS., 3, says the hostility of the natives was very bit-

might be made longer, even if restricted to original
authorities; and it might be extended almost without
limit if made to include accounts of later writers in

ter, and foreigners became convinced that in bold action lay the only prospect of safety. According to Benj. Dewell, in *Napa Reporter*, Oct. 12, 1872,
'the Spaniards became very troublesome in the spring.' James Gregson,
Statement, MS., 3, has it that Sutter received a proclamation ordering all
Americans to quit the country, which he read to the settlers, asking them to
stand by him. Marshall, *Statement*, MS., 1, says one cause of the alarm was
the knowledge that Castro wanted to purchase New Helvetia. Belden says
there was some talk of preventing further immigration, and even of getting
rid of those already in the country. *Hist. Statement*, MS., 44–5. Semple,
Hesperian, iii. 387–8, says that during the winter Castro issued several proclamations, to the effect that all foreigners not naturalized must leave the
country; but the people remained quiet, believing that the order could not
be enforced; and paid but little attention to an order read at Sonoma for all
Americans to depart forthwith; but were finally alarmed by Castro's military preparations—really against Pico.

In the *Monterey Californian*, Sept. 5, 1846, we read: 'Each man having
felt the oppression of the then existing govt, and the certainty of an increase
of those oppressions, with a clear sense of their danger, their rights, and
their duty, they rushed to the rescue with one impulse and one object. The
watchword was equal rights and equal laws, and they nobly sustained their
principles.' And in the same journal of May 23, 1847: 'In this state of things
Gen. Castro issued one proclamation after another, ordering foreigners to leave
the country; but the people, knowing the character of Castro, remained quiet
until the time was ripe for action.'

Frémont, in a letter of July 25, 1846, to Benton, writes: 'I had scarcely
reached the Lower Sacramento when Gen. Castro, then in the north at Sonoma, declared his determination immediately to proceed against the foreigners settled in the country, for whose expulsion an order had just been
issued by the gov. of the Californias. For these purposes Castro immediately assembled a force at the mission of Santa Clara...Castro's first measure
was an attempt to incite the Indian population of the Joaquin and Sacramento valleys, and the neighboring mountains, to burn the crops of the foreigners,
and otherwise proceed immediately against them.' In his testimony in 1847
Frémont says: 'Information was received that Gen. Castro was then raising
forces and exciting the Indians both against the settlers and my party, upon
the unfounded pretext of an intended insurrection by them against the Mexican govt in California.. The movement was one of self-defence.' *Frémont's
Cal. Claims*, 12–13. Gillespie testifies: 'So soon as it became known to the
settlers that Capt. Frémont had returned, they came to the camp, bringing
us the information that the Indians were leaving their rancherías, or wigwams,
and flying to the mountains. In some places they had shown a very hostile
feeling, and certainly had been aroused by some foreign emissiary...On the
90th I was informed by Capt. Sutter that it was positively true that Gen.
Castro had excited the Indians to a revolt and to join the Californians in ex-
terminating the settlers; that the Indians had been bribed to burn the wheat
then nearly dry; and that it was Gen. Castro's intention to attack and cut off
Capt. Frémont's party if he possibly could...On June 7th I learned (at S. F.)
that Castro had gone to Sonoma to hold a council with the Vallejos and to
procure horses to commence his operations, which he endeavored to disguise
under the rumor of making an attack upon the gov., Don Pio Pico, who had
disapproved of Castro's want of good faith in making his first attack upon
Capt. Frémont in March' (!). May 28th, 'a courier was received from Capt.
Sutter, informing Capt. Frémont and myself that "two Spaniards had been
sent by Gen. Castro amongst the different tribes of Indians, and that this was

books and newspapers, who have generally accepted without question the testimony of the contemporary witnesses. The testimony is clear and to the point. It is to the effect that the revolt was purely a movement of self-defence on the part of the American settlers; that General Castro had published a series of proclamations ordering all Americans not naturalized to quit the country before a specified date, under penalty of being forcibly expelled; that he had collected a large military force with which to enforce his orders; that he had started to attack the settlers, having meanwhile instigated the Indians to destroy the Americans' crops; and that the settlers had simply to choose whether they would fight in defence of their homes and families, or, abandoning their property, flee to almost certain destruction in the moun-

the cause of their flying to the mountains, they having been excited against the settlers.''' 'An Indian had been taken prisoner who had received a musket from Gen. Castro for the express purpose of killing Capt. Sutter' (!). *Id.*, 25–6, 29.   Samuel Hensley testifies: 'I returned to Sutter's a few days after seeing Vallejo,' who had told him of the English scheme.   'Capt. Sutter informed me that there was great excitement among the Indians; that he had sent for the Seguamme chief who had recently been among the Californian settlements...On his arrival Sutter examined him as alcalde.   The chief stated that he had seen Castro, and that Castro had made him great promises on condition that he would excite Indians to burn all the wheat crops of the American emigrants, as he intended to drive all the Americans out of the country in a short time.'   Then Hensley went to Frémont's camp to report and to give it 'as my opinion that American residents would have to leave the country or fight for their homes; at the same time saying I was sure we would not leave the country.' *Id.*, 33–4.   Richard Owens said: 'We found the people expecting an attack from the Californians...The report was, and it was generally believed, that Castro had instigated the Indians to rise and burn the crops of the settlers.   Proclamations had been sent out ordering the Americans to quit the country or they would be driven out by a certain time. It was known that troops had been collected at Sta Clara, and that Gen. Castro had come into Sonoma for the purpose of raising a body of Spaniards and Indians to come out against the emigrants and Capt. Frémont's party.' *Id.*, 38.   Wm N. Loker said, besides confirming the statements of Hensley and Owens: 'Just before his [Frémont's] return there was a meeting of the principal men at Monterey.   They then thought it advisable to order all foreigners to leave the country, and published a bando to that effect...Women and children were included in the banishment...The bando was translated and sent up the valley; and I put one of them up at Sutter's Fort.' *Id.*, 39– 40.   June 1, 1846, Sutter wrote to Vallejo that the Moquelumnes had risen, and he was about to march against them before they could set fire to his wheat, as they had been advised to do by persons at S. José, and before Eusebio could kill him with a gun which the same persons had given him for that purpose. *Vallejo, Doc.*, MS., xii. 220.   In his *Diary*, p. 7, Sutter also tells the story of Castro's inciting the Indians against him; and he describes the campaign against them which began June 3d.

tains and deserts of the overland route. Driven, however, to fight for self-protection, it is not denied that they took a certain patriotic pride in conquering new territory for freedom, in opening new fields for Anglo-Saxon enterprise, in overthrowing an inefficient and antiquated system, and in rescuing even their oppressors from Mexican tyranny! It is a grand and thrilling picture, and one that has been more than once brilliantly portrayed—that of a little band of heroic men who defied the power of a nation, and resolved to die rather than be driven like dogs from the homes to which they had been invited, and to secure which they had crossed a continent! What a pity to go behind the scenes and expose the stage effect!

As is well known to the reader, the revolting settlers were men who had been hospitably received in a land which they had entered in defiance of its laws. The political and military authorities had given their national superiors just cause of offence by their toleration of the strangers in spite of positive orders. They had not threatened or oppressed Americans, notwithstanding the imminence of war and their peculiar position. General Castro did not issue the proclamations imputed to him; did not order the settlers to quit the country; did not organize an army with which to attack them; and did not instigate savages to destroy their crops. That he could have done any of these things without its reaching the knowledge of anybody south of San Francisco Bay is improbable; but such acts would also have been in direct opposition to the spirit shown in all correspondence of the time. The Americans of the Sacramento had nothing to fear from the Californians; and this must have been almost as well known to the leading spirits of the revolt as to us. The alleged motives, so far at least as the leaders were concerned, were assuredly not the real ones. They were but pretexts of designing men, used at the time to secure unanimity of action, and after success to justify that action.

I am disposed to think, though I cannot prove it, that certain men went so far as to circulate forged translations of edicts purporting to emanate from Castro.

For it cannot be doubted that rumors of impending hostility and expulsion were current in the northern valleys, or that they were credited by many, even of those who required no such incentive to revolt. There were many who did require such an incentive. I do not attempt to name them. Let it be hoped they constituted a majority of all. They had been but few years in the country; were fitted by education to believe anything that was bad respecting a man who had Spanish blood in his veins; did not approve the Mexican methods of life or government; could hardly understand the justice of requiring of a free American citizen any formalities of passports or naturalization; and they were firm believers in the destiny of their nation to possess this western land. But at the same time these men were lovers of peace and law. They had a dim perception of the right of a people, even Mexicans, to govern their own country in their own way; and only by fear of actual oppression, and as a measure of self-defence, could they be induced to engage in a filibustering scheme involving the shedding of blood, especially if the objects desired were likely to be accomplished legitimately by a little delay.

The support of these men was essential to success, and the circumstances were all favorable for the revolutionists. The American settlers of the northern frontier formed an isolated community, coming but rarely and indirectly into contact with the natives, and knowing but little of what was actually occurring south of the bay. News was eagerly sought, and the wildest rumors found ready listeners. Larkin's efforts and prospects were naturally but vaguely known, if at all, to the majority. Long delay in the declaration of war by Mexico had caused fears on the

part of some that there would be no war, and that
for a long time no aid was to be expected from the
naval forces of the United States. The troubles of
March between Castro and Frémont were known in
the north mainly through false reports of the latter
and his men; and it was widely believed that Castro
had arbitrarily and treacherously driven Frémont out
of the country after having promised hospitality.
Castro was known to be organizing a military force
at Santa Clara. This organization, with Castro's announcements as a Mexican officer of a determination
to defend California against the expected invasion in
case of war—an invasion with which he naturally and
with much real alarm connected Frémont's return
from Oregon at the bidding of an official messenger
from Washington—as intrepreted in the north, was
readily confounded with hostile preparations against
the settlers. That Castro in reality feared Pico and
his southern allies much more than he did the Americans was not generally understood by the immigrants; and some of the revolutionists had the assurance even to attribute Pico's hostility to his disapproval
of Castro's opposition to Frémont and to the foreigners! Finally, just at the most opportune moment for
the plans of the filibusters, Castro sent a party of
armed men, as will be narrated presently, to bring a
large number of horses from the north; and this
movement was fully utilized to remove any lingering
doubts that yet remained as to the necessity of
defensive aggression. That the revolution was to
prevent English occupation of the country, and especially to prevent the success of the McNamara
colonization scheme, was entirely an invention of
later times; but the tenure of lands was a subject on
which the settlers were very sensitive, and there are
some indications that among the current rumors were
some to the effect that the Californian authorities
were making hurried grants of all public lands in
anticipation of a political change.

Eliminating that element which engaged in the revolt honestly as a measure of self-defence, whose fears of danger to life and property though unfounded were to some extent real, we shall find among the remaining filibusters, including most of the leaders and many of the followers, some diversity of motive. There was a class—among the overland immigrants, deserters from vessels who had come up to New Helvetia from the bay, and Frémont's men—composed of adventurers pure and simple. Reckless, daring, and unprincipled men, with nothing to lose, they were eager for a fight with the Californians, partly for the mere excitement of the thing, just as they were always ready for a fight with the Indians. In the turmoil of a revolution, something might occur to their advantage; at least, they could gratify certain personal dislikes; and especially did they have an eye on the herds of the native rancheros. Of another stamp were political adventurers, whose reward was to be, not plunder in the vulgar sense, but glory and office and wealth, under a reformed political system. Some were enthusiastic Americans, who believed in the manifest destiny of their nation to possess this land, and had no doubt of their right to raise the stars and stripes anywhere in America, without regard to the wishes of the natives. They looked upon the Californians as an inferior people, who must be taught by force the beauties of freedom, and who had no right to resist what they chose to regard as their own superior civilization. They regarded independence as but a step to annexation, and they were proud to aid such a cause, even in a struggle which should involve the shedding of blood, and utter disregard of national, departmental, or individual rights. Some of the leaders looked forward to official prominence in an independent Californian republic; others looked further, to the contracting of debts, the issuance of bonds, and to future profitable negotiations with the United States; while still others looked upon the movement as but the beginning of war in favor of the United States, from the government and people of which nation they expected great honor, and in which war they hoped to secure a more prominent position than if they waited for the naval forces to begin hostilities. They were all mere filibusters, and were entitled to none of the sympathy or honor which the world accords to revolutionists who struggle against oppression.

The revolution broke out soon after Frémont's return from Oregon; and it would not have broken out at all had it not been for the presence and coöperation of that officer and his hardy followers. Consequently his movements and motives have great interest in this connection; and they have been the subject of much speculation and comment in later years. An impression has been prevalent that Frémont engaged in the revolt by reason of secret instructions from the United States, conveyed to him by Gillespie either in writing or verbally, or indirectly through private letters from Senator Benton. Frémont has never stated that he received such instructions: having of course no right to do so even if it were true. On the contrary, he has often denied it more or less directly. But in his testimony and that of Gillespie in 1847–8 room was left, designedly I think, for an inference that they could say more if at liberty to do so; and the spirit of this testimony, given at a time when it was sought to legalize against the United States certain claims for supplies taken by Frémont's men, together with the secrecy observed by the government respecting the written instructions to Gillespie, Larkin, and Frémont, originated, as I suppose, the current theory to which I have alluded, but which, for reasons that will presently appear, I regard as without foundation in fact.[2]

[2] Frémont testified that Gillespie 'brought me a letter of introduction from the sec. of state. and letters and papers from Sen. Benton and his family. The letter from the sec. was directed to me in my private or citizen capacity, and though importing nothing beyond the introduction, accredited the bearer

The story of Frémont's return from Oregon has
been told in an earlier chapter.   The reasons that he
gave for that return were the dangers of further advance northward, arising from the depth of snow, lack
of supplies, and hostility of the Indians—and the nature of the communications received from Gillespie.

to me as coming from the sec. of state, and, in connection with the circumstances and place of its delivery, indicated a purpose in sending it which was
intelligibly explained to me by the accompanying letter from Sen. Benton,
and by communications from Lieut Gillespie.   This officer informed me that
he had been directed by the sec. of state to find me, and to acquaint me with
his instructions, which had for their principal objects to ascertain the disposition of the California people, to conciliate their feelings in favor of the U.
S., and to find out, with a design of counteracting, the designs of the British
govt upon that country.' *Frémont's Cal. Claims*, 12.   And again, in *Frémont's
Court-martial*, 373: 'One of the letters from him [Benton], while apparently
of mere friendship and family details, contained passages enigmatical and obscure, but which I studied out, and made the meaning to be that I was required by the govt to find out any foreign schemes in relation to the Cal. and
to counteract them.'   Gillespie said his instructions were 'to watch over the
interests of the U. S. in Cal., and to counteract the influence of any foreign or
European agents who might be in that country with objects prejudicial to the
U. S.   I was the bearer of the duplicate of a despatch to the U. S. consul at
Monterey, T. O. Larkin, Esq., as also a packet for J. C. Frémont, Esq., and
a letter of introduction to the latter gentleman from the Hon. James Buchanan; the former I destroyed before entering the port of Vera Cruz, having
committed it to memory.   The packet and letter of introduction I delivered
to Capt. Frémont upon the 9th of May, in the mountains of Oregon...I was
directed to confer with and make known to him my instructions.   It was desirable that we should act in concert, and great vigilance and activity was expected of both...I made him acquainted with the wishes of the govt, which
were the same as stated above for my own guidance...In answer to the first
inquiry of the honorable committee, "Were you charged with any verbal instructions or communications?" etc., I have to state that I was directed by
Mr Buchanan to confer with Col. Frémont, and make known to him my own
instructions...I was also directed to show to Col. Frémont the duplicate of the
despatch to Mr Larkin.   In answer to the 2d inquiry, "You have said that
you communicated the wishes of the govt to Col. Frémont; state particularly
what you did communicate to him as the wishes of the govt," I beg leave to
state that the answer above contains, as near as I can recollect, what I communicated to Col. Frémont; telling him at the same time that it was the wish
of the govt that we should conciliate the feelings of the people of Cal., and
encourage a friendship towards the U. S.' *Id.*, 30–3.

That the testimony cited was regarded at the time as evasive and incomplete, is shown by the following quotations from the report of the house committee in Aug. 1848, denying the validity of all claims contracted before the
U. S. flag was raised, on the ground that Frémont and the rest acted without
any known authority from the U. S: 'What the purpose was in sending an
officer of the U. S. in search of Col. Frémont, with a simple letter of introduction, "which was intelligibly explained by the accompanying letter of Sen.
Benton," is left to conjecture, except so far as is disclosed by the language of
Col. Frémont as quoted; but the effect was to turn Col. Frémont with the
men under his command from their exploring expedition to Oregon back into
Cal., where they at once "joined the settlers" (or the settlers joined them),
and engaged in a revolutionary movement against the authorities of Cal...
Up to this time there was and could have been no knowledge in Cal. of the

These communications, as both officers stated, required them "to ascertain the disposition of the Californian people, to conciliate their feelings in favor of the United States, and to find out, with a design of counteracting, the designs of the British government upon that country." These reasons, even if the former was

existence of war between Mexico and the U. S. Whether the purpose of the sec. of state, acting as it must be supposed under the direction of the president, and so "intelligibly explained" by the letter of Sen. Benton, was developed by the conduct of Col. Frémont consequent therefrom, must be entirely a matter of surmise until that "intelligible explanation" shall have been presented to the public; but it is very manifest that much yet remains to be told of this as yet dark and mysterious proceeding.' Thus the operations were 'undertaken either upon individual responsibility and without the authority of the govt or any of its departments, or such authority being given, it is not only not disclosed, but studiously withheld from the public eye.' *Frémont's Cal. Claims* (House Rept no. 817), 1–5. I do not refer here to all the govt reports on the Cal. claims, and on Frémont's court-martial, though all of them contain more or less repetition of the testimony and comments cited.

Senator Clark, in his speech of April 25, 1848, *Clark's Speech on Cal. Claims*, p. 3–14; also in *Cong. Globe*, 30th cong. 1st sess., appen., p. 569; see also, in *Id.*, speeches of other senators on the subject—made a strong argument for the payment of the claims, on the ground that the U. S. govt had undoubtedly instructed Frémont through Gillespie to act as he did, though the speaker by no means approved the policy of the govt. 'Whilst the U. S. were professing to be governed by a spirit of justice and love of peace upon the eastern border of Mexico, different indeed was her course in regard to those states in the west, as shown by the mission of Gillespie early in Nov. 1845, with secret instructions to the consul in Cal., and to call from scientific pursuits an officer to foment rebellion and aid in revolutionizing the govt.'

Jay, *Mexican War*, 150–4, takes a similar view, and after citing the evidence, remarks: 'It is impossible to resist the conviction that Frémont was given to understand, but in a way not to compromit the govt, that the abandonment of the exploration in Oregon for the purpose of exciting and aiding an insurrection in Cal. would not expose him to censure.' Edmund Randolph, in his *Oration*, says: 'But resentment and anticipation of evil were not the sole cause of this movement. There cannot now be a doubt that it was prompted, as it was approved, by the govt of the U. S.; and that Capt. Frémont obeyed his orders no less than his own feelings...What Frémont's instructions were is a well kept cabinet secret, which will probably not be divulged, at least in our time.' *Dwinelle's Address, 1866*, p. 19–20. 'There is reason to believe that he was instructed to feel the geographical pulse of the natives as well as the mountain passes.' *Wise's Los Gringos*, 41. 'There were some expressions in a letter from Col. Benton that the old senator's son-in-law studied with extraordinary diligence. No doubt the oral communications of Gillespie helped to draw from them a deeper significance than the words conveyed on the first reading...Frémont determined to become the pursuer rather than the pursued, to turn upon the faithless foe, and revolutionize the govt. This would have been a hazardous course,...unless, either in his secret instructions before starting or in the advices conveyed by Lieut Gillespie, he was assured that a successful indiscretion of this sort would be acceptable to his govt. As to the precise plan he adopted, there is no doubt that he consulted his own judgment alone. But there is abundant circumstantial evidence that he was given to understand that any defensible method of gaining

somewhat exaggerated as is probable, were amply sufficient to account for and justify his action in turning back, though he well knew—as the government did not—that his services as a conciliator were not likely to be very effective in California. There is no need of secret instructions in favor of filibusterism to account for his actions so far. Yet were that all, and did the nature of the communications rest solely on the testimony of Frémont and Gillespie, the theory of such secret instructions would perhaps be as fascinating for me as it has been for others; but there is other evidence which I deem conclusive. Secretary Buchanan's secret instructions to Larkin as confidential agent—the nature of which has been a matter of surmise to other writers; which are represented to have been in purport identical with Gillespie's instructions; which he was directed to show to Frémont; a duplicate of which he destroyed after committing its contents to memory; but the original of which is in my possession—confirm entirely the cited testimony of the two officers, though not all the inferences they desired to be drawn from that testimony; and contain no encouragement, direct or indirect, for any revolt except by the Californians themselves. Had this document been one written to be seen with intent to mislead those into whose hands it might fall, it would prove nothing in this connection; but its existence, on the contrary, was intended to be kept, and has been kept until now, a profound state secret. It contains a clear presentment of the policy of the United States

Cal. to the Union would be acceptable...A hint was enough for one so ambitious as Frémont, and if he was not instructed he was most fortunate in his instincts. A different issue might have overwhelmed him with reproach. As it resulted, he had the perfect and flattering indorsement of the sec. of state.' *Tuthill's Hist. Cal.*, 167–8. As early as 1847, F. D. Atherton, in a letter from Valparaiso to Larkin, expressed grave doubts that Frémont had been turned back by the snows in June. *Larkin's Doc.*, MS., v. 58.

I might easily extend these citations to show the prevalence of the idea that Frémont acted under secret instructions; but those given are sufficient. Nor do I deem it necessary to cite the opinions of numerous Mexican and native Californian writers to the same effect, because they had in reality little opportunity of knowing anything about Frémont's motives, most of them taking it for granted that he acted as a secret agent of the U. S.

—to take possession of California in the event of war with Mexico; to prevent, by force of arms if necessary, any occupation by a European power; but meanwhile to conciliate by every possible means the good-will of the natives, with a view that the occupation in case of war might be without opposition, or, if there were no war, that the people might voluntarily seek annexation a little later. This policy, from an American standpoint, was essentially a sound and prudent one. I have already expressed my opinion that the means adopted to carry it out were not in certain respects honorable from an international point of view; but I am by no means willing to charge the administration at Washington with an action so stupidly inconsistent as to have sent on the same date and by the same confidential messenger, to two different agents in California, two radically different and utterly irreconcilable sets of secret instructions. I think there can be no possible room for doubt that Frémont's instructions were identical with those issued to Gillespie and Larkin; and I believe that no doubt would ever have arisen on the subject had the document which I have cited been known to previous investigators.

Assuming, then, that Frémont engaged in a revolutionary movement, not in accordance with, but in disobedience of his orders from Washington, what were his motives? He claimed to act at the entreaties of the American settlers in defence of their lives and rights. I need not repeat that this on his part, as on that of other leaders, was a mere pretext, Frémont most certainly not being one of those who really believed the settlers to be in danger. I cite in a note his letter to Benton in explanation of his action.[3] Clearly

[3] 'You will remember how grossly outraged and insulted we had already been by this officer [Castro]; many in my own camp and throughout the country thought that I should not have retreated in March last. I felt humiliated and humbled; one of the main objects proposed by the expedition had been entirely defeated, and it was the opinion of the officers of the squadron (so I was informed by Mr Gillespie) that I could not again retreat consistently with any military reputation...My animals were in such a state that I could not get out of the valley without reaching the country which lies on the west (?)

the retreat from Gavilan in March had been a severe
blow to the captain's pride, and the wound still smarted
as irritated by the taunts of bold and irresponsible
comrades and of filibustering settlers.   Yet there can
be no doubt that Frémont's strongest incentive was
personal ambition.   He confidently counted upon an
immediate declaration of war between the United
States and Mexico; and he believed that by commencing hostilities he might gain for himself a large share
of credit for the conquest, which would otherwise fall
to the naval commanders.   The prevalent rumors
among the settlers afforded him a plausible pretext for
an action that also offered a remedy for wounded military pride.   Should he err in his expectations of war,
there would yet remain a chance of prominence in an
independent Californian republic.   Young and adven-
turous, he resolved to take the risks.   From the standpoint of a purely personal ambition, he decided wisely.
The result probably surpassed his most sanguine expectations.   His decision made him subsequently a
popular hero, a senator of the United States, a candidate for the presidency, a millionnaire ad interim, a
major-general; in fact, it gave him greater prominence
than has perhaps ever been attained in the United
States by any other man of no greater ability.   He
was essentially a lucky fellow.

Our admiration for Frémont as a filibustero chieftain—the only admiration due him in this connection
—would be vastly increased had he acted with some-

side of them in an entirely destitute condition.   Having carefully examined my position, and foreseeing, I think, clearly, all the consequences which
may eventuate to me from such a step, I determined to take such active and
anticipatory measures as should seem to me most expedient to protect my
party and justify my own character.   I am well aware of the grave responsibility which I assumed; but I also determined that, having once decided to do
so, I would assume it and its consequences fully and entirely, and go through
with the business completely to the end. . .On the 6th of June I decided on
the course which I would pursue, and immediately concerted my operations
with the foreigners inhabiting the Sacramento Valley.'   Frémont to Benton,
July 25, 1846, in *Niles' Reg.*, lxxi. 191.   I have already, in note 1 of this chapter, quoted this letter on Castro's hostile preparations; and I shall have occasion to refer to it again.

what less of caution after deciding to engage in the revolt, or had he been somewhat more modest in his subsequent claims. I have already stated that but for his presence and support the revolt would not have occurred. The departure of Hastings and Clyman for the east, and of others for Oregon in April, shows that there was then but little hope of a successful rising. But as to the exact nature of his coöperation there has been some difference of opinion. William Baldridge attributes the movement of the American settlers, of whom he was one, to Frémont's direct encouragement, believing—though this of course was an afterthought—that that officer's true purpose was to provoke a declaration of war by Mexico;[4] and William B. Ide had some theories on the subject, which will be noticed presently; but the weight of evidence, direct and circumstantial, goes to show that Frémont, while holding himself somewhat aloof from the masses, secretly conspired with a few leaders to bring about an outbreak, and promised the full support of himself and his party in case it should be needed, though as an officer of the United States he desired to abstain from open participation as long as possible. The settlers had no fear of any force the Californians could muster north of the bay; but if Castro were to send soldiers from the south, they might require assistance. This assistance Frémont promised, and, as we shall see, proffered later. This was the sum and substance of his coöperation. In the few stirring events of the revolution he personally took no part. He merely held himself in readiness to act when the necessity should arise, and marched against the foe after others had won a victory. Yet in the letter to Benton he clearly gave that gentleman, and through him the people of the United States, to understand that in all that had occurred he had taken an active part, and had been personally in command. In this

[4] *Baldridge's Days of '46*, MS., passim.

he was guilty of selfish and dishonorable misrepresentation.[5]

There is another version of Frémont's part in the revolution which merits attention on account of its author's prominence in the movement, if for no other

[5] In his letter to Benton, already cited, *Niles' Reg.*, lxxi. 191, Frémont says: 'On June 6th I decided on the course which I would pursue, and immediately concerted my operations with the foreigners.' A few days later, etc., going on to mention the capture of Arce's horses, taking of Sonoma, capture of Gen. Vallejo, etc., and continuing: 'These enterprises accomplished, I proceeded' (from where?) 'to the American settlements on the Sacramento and Rio de los Americanos to obtain reënforcements'—thus leaving it to be inferred that he had taken an active part in all the events narrated, instead of remaining in camp at Sutter's Fort. Then he was called to Sonoma by news of a threatened attack by Castro, and in his narrative of what followed makes no effort to distinguish between his own acts and those of others, implying very clearly that all was done by him, with the coöperation of Gillespie, and continuing: 'We reached Sonoma again on the evening of July 4th, and in the morning I called the people together and spoke to them in relation to the position of the country, advising a course of operations which was unanimously adopted. Cal. was declared independent,' etc. I do not quote more fully, because the events have to be narrated in the next chapter; but I do not exaggerate in saying that Frémont deliberately conveyed the impression that he was in active command throughout the revolution. Benton so understood it, or at least wished it to be so understood; and he repeated Frémont's version in language similar but more positive in a letter of Nov. 9, 1846, *Niles' Reg.*, lxxi. 173, to the president, who, like the sec. of war, repeated the version substantially in public documents; and thus the ambitious captain obtained much popular credit and admiration which by no means belonged to him, even if credit or admiration had been due to anybody for such actions. In his *Court-martial*, 374, Frémont says: 'In concert and in coöperation with the American settlers, and in the brief space of about 30 days, all was accomplished north of the bay, and independence declared on July 5th.' In August 1856, Thompson of New Jersey—*Speech on the Conquest of California*, Wash. 1856, 8vo, 16 p.; also in *Congress. Globe*, 1855–6, p. 2006–9—made a forcible protest in the U. S. senate against the claim of Frémont to be considered the conqueror of Cal., showing in a clear light the misrepresentations made by and in behalf of that officer, though he had to rely mainly for evidence on the document already cited as *Hist. Bear Flag Revol.*, and signed as it appears by Ide, Nash, and Grigsby. Thompson says: 'In these letters it will be found that Frémont recites various successful military actions. He does not say that he participated in them, but states them in such a way as to leave the inference irresistible that he did so. Mr Benton and Mr Marcy both take such for granted, and so indeed would any one on reading the artful connection in which they are stated. Besides, there are no documents on file in the department from which the sec. could have made up the statement in his report, except the letters of Col. Benton and Mrs Frémont. The facts relate to the time when Frémont joined the movement, . . . to two actions in which the Californians were defeated, and the taking of Sonoma. The sec. relates these events so as to produce the impression (no doubt on his own mind) that Frémont was among the first to countenance the independent movement; that he took part in the defeat of the Mexicans and the capture of Sonoma. But we have positive proof showing that Frémont had nothing to do with these several events.' And this was true, though in certain respects Thompson overestimated the value of his proofs, Ide, Grigsby, and Nash being interested persons, like Frémont, and coloring their version accordingly.

reason. It is that given by William B. Ide in his
letter to Senator Wambough, and subsequently confirmed to some extent by Ide, Grigsby, and Nash in
their narrative. According to Ide, the American
merchants, Larkin and others of his class, "failed
not in the genuine spirit of Yankeedom to direct and
profit by those political impositions, change of administration, and continued increase of tariff duties by
which during ten years of increasing distress and
ruin the main body of the people were made misera-
bly poor," therefore refusing support to the oppressed
settlers; then "Frémont came among us, who, after
having provoked the assumed authorities of the country, left us to experience the wrath and retaliatory
vengeance his acts had engendered;...next came Gillespie, who failed not to give cautionary advice in
relation to a state of preparedness on the part of all
of United States origin, but dissuaded from any kind
of organization," suggesting, however, that after Frémont's return his camp would be the means of temporary protection. Finally, after a month of suspense
and terror on the part of the settlers in view of Castro's proclamations and military preparations, Frémont returned from the north, and soon in writing
summoned "every freeman in the valley to come to
his camp at the Buttes immediately," announcing at
the same time the approach of Castro's forces. To
Ide and a few others, not named, Frémont made
known his plan of conquest as follows: "First, select
a dozen men who have nothing to lose but everything
to gain. Second, encourage them to commit depredations against General Castro the usurper, and thus
supply the camp with horses necessary for a trip to
the States. Third, to make prisoners of some of the
principal men, and thus provoke Castro to strike the
first blow in a war with the United States. This
done, finish the conquest by uniting the forces and
marching back to the States." This scheme was denounced by Ide and his comrades as dishonorable and

treacherous, whereupon Frémont in anger broke up the interview. "Thus ended all intercourse on our part with Captain Frémont until June 25th." Subsequently, however, King, inviting the visitors to another tent, asked, "Suppose the men succeed in taking the horses, what will you in that case propose to be done?" The reply was, "When the breach is once made that involves us all in its consequences, it is useless to consider the propriety of the measure. We are too few for division. In for it, the whole man! Widen the breach, that none can stand outside thereof. Down on Sonoma! Never flee the country, nor give it up while there is an arm to fight or a voice to cry aloud for Independence. But let truth and honor guide our course."

Ide continues: "Several persons, among whom was Kit Carson, begged of Frémont their discharge from the service of the exploring expedition that they might be at liberty to join us. This was peremptorily refused. Frémont, in my hearing, expressly declared that he was not at liberty to afford us the least aid or assistance; nor would he suffer any of his men to do so; that he had not asked the assistance of the emigrants for his protection; that he was able, of his own party, to fight and whip Castro if he chose, but that he should not do so unless first assaulted by him; and that positively he should wait only for a supply of provisions, two weeks at furthest, when he would, without further reference to what might take place here, be on his march for the States." That same night the captured horses arrived, and next day the expedition to Sonoma began; many embarking in it with the idea that they were only carrying out Frémont's plan of provoking hostilities.[6]

[6] *Ide's Biog. Sketch*, 107–19, confirmed in the *Hist. Bear Flag Revolution*, by the statement that at the interview in question Frémont 'advised immediate organization and resistance on the part of the foreigners, but declined any action on his part or that of the men under his command,' stating that he expected to leave for the States in two weeks; and by the further statement that Frémont at Sonoma later declared 'that he had determined to pursue and take José Castro, whom he considered but an

Ide's version will be found on close examination to confirm rather than contradict what I have said respecting Frémont's policy. That gentleman wrote under a strong feeling, amounting almost to a mania, that he had been robbed by Frémont of the honor of having been at the head of the revolution, a feeling that strongly colored all his remarks, and led to many exaggerations; but though prejudiced and fanatical, Ide was not a man to tell a deliberate falsehood, and I have no doubt that his account of the interview is substantially correct. All goes to show that Frémont, though one of the original plotters of the revolt, had a direct understanding with but few of the leaders, of which number Ide was not one, to whom he promised active coöperation when it should be required. To the rest he spoke guardedly, inciting them indirectly to revolt, but cautiously avoiding re-

usurper in Cal., being unauthorized by the govt of Mexico,...that although he could not and would not intermeddle in the internal affairs of Cal.,' yet, if they would make certain pledges, 'he would not only aid them with his advice, but that he would volunteer his whole force against Castro, and that he would stand by them at least until Castro shall have been subdued.' In connection with the last phrase cited, I may note that Folsom, in a letter of Nov. 30, 1847, to Vallejo, speaks of an interview in which Frémont told Prudon that he was merely acting in aid of Pico against Castro. *Vallejo, Doc.*, MS., xii. 321.

Wm Hargrave, *Cal. in '46*, MS, 4–11, tells us that after much discussion among the settlers of Napa at the writer's camp, he, Kelsey, Swift, and another went to consult with Frémont, being joined by others on the way. At the interview on Feather River, Kelsey being spokesman, Frémont seemed very cautious, though willing enough to resume active operations. ' He preferred to see for himself how far the settlers of Napa and Sonoma were ready to go in shaking off the Mexican yoke. At any rate, he peremptorily refused to take any responsibility for sudden action on our part, and endeavored to delay or frustrate our efforts. Whether he expressed himself differently when he spoke to Kelsey alone later in the day I cannot say.' Hargrave says he later heard Frémont ridicule Ide's proclamation. Fowler, *Bear Party*, 2, also mentions the mission of Hargrave and Kelsey. Both imply that the rising would not have taken place at that time but for a popular belief that Frémont would in some way coöperate. Some favored action without regard to the captain's plans, but this was opposed by a majority. Baldridge, *Days of '46*, MS., passim, is confident that the settlers would not have risen but for Frémont's indirect promptings and promises. The writer and Thos W. Bradley were in Berreyesa Valley when John Grigsby and Wm Elliot came up with the news. 'Grigsby says Frémont prompted them to take up arms, telling them that it would not do for him to commence the affair, as he was in the employ of the U. S., but for them to seize on some place which they would be able to hold, and then he would discharge all his men, and with them would join us as volunteers. He also said he wanted to start on an active campaign as soon as it was possible to get men enough together to do so.'

marks and promises which might in certain contingencies be used to his disadvantage later. There is no reason to doubt that with his men he would have fought bravely, had circumstances required it, in defence of the cause he had espoused; though, as we have seen, he was mean enough in the hour of success to appropriate to himself the credit for actions in which he really took no part.

In thus presenting the real causes which led to the revolt of June 1846, I have of course condemned the movement. An armed insurrection involving loss of life is justifiable in the eyes of the civilized world only as a measure of self-defence in resistance to gross oppression. In this case there was no oppression or other than imaginary danger, to say nothing of the fact that the revolutionists, with few exceptions, had entered Mexican territory in defiance of the country's laws. There is, however, much more to be said in condemnation of this revolt. In spite of our theorizing, the world is prone to approve practically, after all is over, a movement, whatever its causes, which leads to beneficial results. Californian affairs under the Mexican régime were in a sad state, and not improving. An occupation of the country by a progressive nation could not fail to, and did, produce a marked improvement in every respect; and the tendency has been, even among those who could not justify the revolt, to give its promoters credit for the good that resulted from the change. They are entitled, however, to no such credit. The revolution was in no sense a part of the conquest of California, neither leading to nor in any way promoting that movement. Before the revolt, the government of the United States had ordered the occupation of the country on account of war with Mexico; and the occupation would have been effected in the same manner and at the same date had no revolt taken place.[7]

[7] We shall see later that it was claimed in behalf of Frémont that his ac-

Two specific claims, closely connected with the general one of having commenced the conquest, which have been quite generally but very carelessly allowed in favor of the revolutionists, are that their acts kept California from falling into the hands of England, and that they checked Governor Pico in his work of granting the public lands to his own personal friends and to enemies of the United States. The absurdity of the first claim should be apparent. If England had any intention of taking California, she certainly would not have been deterred by the armed settlers of a single section. On the contrary, the revolt would have served as a most plausible pretext for the Californians to seek and for England to grant a protectorate. As to the second claim, I may remark that the McNamara land grant, on which most stress is laid in this connection, did not come up for action in California, and was probably unknown to every one of the filibusters until after the revolt was far advanced; that theoretically the rising must have tended, not to check, but to hasten Pico in granting lands; that as a matter of fact it did have that effect so far as it had any; and that the United States government did not subsequently make June 14th but July 7th the chronologic limit of legitimate grants.

That the revolt was unjustifiable, uncalled for, and not productive of good results, is not by any means all that is to be said against it. Its promoters were morally responsible for all the blood shed in battle, as well as for outrages committed by both sides on persons and property before the raising of the stars and stripes; and not only this, but for a bitterness of feel-

tions, presumably in accord with instructions from Washington, by confirming Commodore Sloat in his belief that war had been declared, influenced that officer to raise the United States flag. It is probably true that the somewhat irresolute commodore derived much comfort from the reports of Frémont's operations, as confirming the news of war obtained at Mazatlan; and that had his exploit proved premature, like that of Jones in 1842, he would have urged those reports in his own defence; but it is hardly credible that they caused him to perform an act which he had come from Mazatlan expressly to perform in accordance with his orders, and with very positive news that war had begun.

ing between the two races in California which lasted
for many years.   Not only did the insurgents not contribute to the American occupation of the country,
but they absolutely retarded it, and increased its difficulties.   They were largely accountable for all the
blood that was spilled throughout the war.   The men
who had given the subject most attention and were
best qualified to understand the true state of affairs
believed with some reason that the change of flag
might have been accomplished without resistance or
bloodshed, had it not been for the outbreak at Sonoma,
and the hostility engendered by that affair.[8]   However this may be, whether or not Larkin, Stearns, and
Leese were correct in their expectation of a peaceable
occupation, whether or not the land owners with the

[8] In a letter of July 20, 1846, Larkin said to the sec. of state in substance
that Cal. would in a few years have come under the U. S. flag of her own accord; that he is inclined to regret the action of the Bear Flag party, and of
Com. Sloat, as the people now deemed themselves coerced and injured, especially by the Bear party.   Frémont and Gillespie should have consulted
with him and others south of the bay before beginning hostilities.   Castro had
assured him personally that he intended to declare the country independent
as soon as there were enough foreigners to insure success. *Larkin's Off. Corresp.*, MS., ii. 75-7.   In another letter of Jan. 7, 1847, L. wrote: 'It has been
my object for some years to bring the Californians to look on our countrymen
as their best friends.   I am satisfied very many were of that way of thinking,
and more were becoming so.   Gen. Castro from 1842 to 1846 made every demonstration in our favor, and opened plans for future operations, granting passports to all the Americans whom I presented to him.   At the same time he
made some foolish proclamations, supposing they would only be believed in
Mexico.   The sudden rising of the party on the Sacramento under the Bear
Flag, taking Californians' property to a large amount, and other acts completely frustrated all hopes I had of the friendship of the natives to my countrymen, and of Gen. Castro through fear of his people, to come into the arrangements I expected.   On the arrival of the war squadron this came to my
knowledge more and more fully.'   Quoted from original in the *S. F. Alta Cal.*,
July 7, 1867.   And on June 30, 1847, he wrote to the same effect. 'The Bear
Flag party have broken all friendship and good feeling in Cal. toward our
government.' *Larkin's Off. Corresp.*, MS., ii. 118.   The views of Larkin,
Stearns, and others on this matter have been more fully cited in an earlier
chapter.   Leese, *Bear Flag Revolt*, MS., p. 12, says that Castro, when at Sonoma a few days before the outbreak, said he was in favor of the U. S. taking
possession.   Alfred Robinson, *Statement*, MS., 21, tells us that the Bear
movement greatly imbittered the hostile feeling aroused by Frémont's previous actions.   Capt. Folsom on Nov. 30, 1847, wrote that 'well disposed
Californians were driven into hostility by the ill-advised, injudicious, and dis-
honest conduct of our own agents, and that the country has been constantly
agitated and much of the time in open hostility to the American cause in consequence.' *Vallejo, Doc.*, MS., xii. 321.   I might multiply evidence in the
shape of such opinions.   The Californians almost without exception express
the same views, sometimes in most extravagant language.

coöperation of Vallejo and other influential citizens and officials would have been able so far to control their countrymen as to prevent armed resistance, at least there can be no possible doubt that the revolt did materially intensify the hostility of the natives, and thus prolong the struggle.

We must go yet further, and besides the evils enumerated which were caused by the outbreak, we must hold the participators in that affair responsible for other and far more serious evils that were averted, not by their foresight, but by sheer good luck. Frémont and his companions had, it is true, reasons to believe that war would be declared between the United States and Mexico; but they had no means of knowing the date at which hostilities would begin; and some of them did not reckon on or care for the declaration of war at all. Let the reader consider what would have been the result had war not been declared, or had the declaration been made some months later. The filibusters had no understanding with foreign settlers south of the bay. They would have maintained their position in the north, and would probably have conquered central California; but meanwhile Americans in the latter region must unquestionably have suffered at the hands of the angry natives before they could have organized and joined the insurgents at some central point. In the south yet greater disaster could have been avoided only—as it very likely would have been—by southern foreigners joining the Californians, temporarily at least, against the insurgents. In any event, and whatever the ultimate result, the country would have been devastated by a guerilla warfare in which a large amount of property must have been destroyed, and much blood have been shed, all to no purpose.[9] Fortunately, and no thanks to the insur-

---

[9] It should be stated here that there are some exceptions among the writers who have approved the revolt of June 1846, and treated it as a part of the conquest. Notably John S. Hittell, both as editor of the *Alta California*, June 15, 1866, July 7, 1867, and in his *History of S. F.*, 102–3, has expressed briefly but accurately the true nature of the movement. Some participants,

gents, these results were averted, and the insurrection was nipped in the bud by the action of the United States.

like Baldridge, *Days of '46*, MS., 18–20, disapprove the action, and say they only joined in it as a choice of evils. The general tenor of John Bidwell's views, *Cal. 1841–8*, MS., is against the revolt. Lieut Wise, *Los Gringos*, 42, denounces the operations of the filibusters in language much too severe. Dunbar, *Romance*, 34–6, points out the evil effects of the outbreak. During the political campaign of 1856 much was said against the Bear Flag leaders; but chiefly from a spirit of opposition to Frémont, rather than from any proper understanding of the merits of the case. Of those who have eulogized the insurgents as heroes in books and newspapers, a long list might be presented.

Just as this volume goes to press there appears *Royce's California*, 1846–56,' an admirable work of the 'American Commonwealths' series, a long chapter of which, on 'The American as conqueror; the secret mission and the Bear Flag,' is devoted to an elaborate study of certain topics here treated. I am pleased that the conclusions of so able a thinker and writer as Dr Royce—founded to some extent on original evidence in my Library, for the use of which the author makes most hearty and satisfactory acknowledgment—do not differ materially from my own. New data obtained by Royce include a statement from Frémont, which throws light, if not on the general's acts of 1846, on his character as a witness, and shows that I had taken too favorable a view of his veracity, since he now affirms what he had before wisely left to be inferred. It seems proper to state that this volume as now given to the public was in stereotype before the date of Royce's investigations in my Library.

Another book appearing too late for present use is the *History of California* by *Theodore H. Hittell*. Here I can only note the existence of this work, remarking that it contains nothing to modify any view or record of this or earlier volumes, and expressing a hope that it may prove helpful in later investigations, as I shall have occasion to cite both Royce and Hittell in volumes vi. and vii.

CHAPTER V.

BEAR FLAG REVOLT—TAKING OF SONOMA.

JUNE, 1846.

FRÉMONT'S RETURN FROM OREGON—HENSLEY'S MISSION—A SUMMONS TO
REVOLT—FRÉMONT CAUTIOUS—ALL READY—CAMP MOVED TO BEAR
RIVER—CASTRO AT SANTA CLARA—HIS VISIT TO SONOMA—ARCE'S CA-
BALLADA—MERRITT SENT BY FRÉMONT TO BEGIN HOSTILITIES—SEIZ-
URE OF HORSES ON THE COSUMNES—THE FILIBUSTERS REËNFORCED IN
NAPA VALLEY—NAMES—OCCUPATION OF SONOMA—VALLEJO A PRISONER
OF WAR—NEGOTIATIONS—WRITTEN GUARANTIES—BROKEN BEFORE THE
INK WAS DRY—INCIDENTS OF THE MORNING—THE INSURGENTS UNMAN-
AGEABLE—AGUARDIENTE—A CONTROVERSY—JOHN GRIGSBY DECLINES
THE COMMAND—WILLIAM B. IDE CHOSEN—JOURNEY OF THE PRISONERS
TO FRÉMONT'S CAMP—LOCKED UP IN SUTTER'S FORT.

IT was on May 24th that Frémont and party, returning from the Oregon frontier, reached the region
of Lassen's rancho in the upper Sacramento Valley.
In a letter to Benton written on that date he announced his intention to proceed directly homeward
by way of the Colorado, giving a brief account of his
trip northward and return.[1] At the same time Gillespie wrote to Larkin, narrating his experience since
leaving Monterey, asking for news, especially about
the men-of-war, enclosing a note for the commodore,
if there, but to be carefully locked up if not, announcing that Frémont would now proceed homeward, and
that the writer would at once start for Yerba Buena
in quest of supplies.[2] The letters were intrusted to

---

[1] May 24, 1846, F. to B. *Niles' Reg.*, lxxi. 191.
[2] May 24, 1846, G. to L. *Larkin's Doc.*, MS., iv. 134. F. and G. were at
Lassen's; the rest were 15 miles above.

Samuel Neal, who hastened down the valley.[3]   The
explorers camped at Lassen's two days, and one day
at the farm of Neal and Dutton on Deer Creek, thence
moving down to the Buttes.   Before they reached
that point Gillespie left the party, reached Sutter's on
the 30th, and went down to San Francisco on the
launch, arriving on June 7th, and obtaining from Captain Montgomery of the *Portsmouth* a boat-load of
supplies, with which he reached New Helvetia a week
later, accompanied by several naval officers.[4]   Before
his return some startling events had happened.

It is not to be believed that Frémont had any intention of proceeding immediately homeward, as announced in the letters cited.   It is reasonably certain
that revolutionary plans had already been developed
to some extent by him and his associate, though it is
of course impossible, as it is comparatively unimportant, to fix the exact stage of development at this
time.   The instructions from Washington which had
chiefly caused his return from the north would not
permit him now to go east.   Gillespie had told him
on the frontier not only of the impending war, but of
the growing revolutionary spirit among the settlers.
On his first arrival at the ranchos he found abundant
evidence of discontent.   The Indians were said to be
on the war-path at Castro's instigation; and Frémont was asked to join in a raid upon the foe.   He
declined, though offering protection to the settlers.[5]
It is to be presumed that he had already considered

---

[3] Neal reached Sutter's May 25th, and went on, but came back next day on
account of high water, starting again on the 27th via Sonoma. *New Helvetia
Diary*, MS., 49.

[4] G.'s testimony, in *Frémont's Cal. Claims*, 26–7; *New Helvetia Diary*, MS.,
50.   June 7th, G. to L. *Larkin's Doc.*, MS., iv. 144.   He arrived at Sutter's
June 12th, and was joined by Frémont on the American Fork next day.
Lieut Hunter, Purser Watmough, and Asst Surgeon Duvall accompanied him
in the ship's launch.

[5] Gillespie's testimony, in *Frémont's Cal. Claims*, 26, 29.   Upham, *Life of
Frémont*, 231–2, tells us that his hero did march against 600 of the savages,
routing them, dispersing five villages. and breaking up the great combination
against the settlers!   June 1st, Sutter writes to Vallejo that Frémont has arrived above, and will probably await on the American River orders per the
Congress. Vallejo, Doc., MS., xii. 220.

the project, which at any rate he soon fully adopted, of promoting a revolt of the settlers, whose pretext should be imminent danger of an attack from the Californians, and in whose behalf he would interfere on pretext of protecting Americans as soon as such interference should be either politic or necessary.

There was a strong element among the settlers, as already explained, ready and eager to meet the filibuster more than half-way. The news that Frémont was returning fanned into new life the fire that had hardly smouldered. At every hunter's camp the topic was discussed; at every rancho a political junta of neighbors and rovers was in daily session. The revolutionists recognized their opportunity to prevail over what had been a somewhat unmanageable minority. The old rumors of Castro's hostile preparations were revived, and new ones invented; new appeals to American patriotism were made; men were urged from love of life, of family, of liberty, from ambition, from greed of gain, from whatever motive was likely to be most potent with each, to shake off the tyrant's yoke. Especially was Frémont's return presented as a significant and auspicious circumstance. He would not return at all, it was urged, were not an outbreak of hostilities from some cause expected. The settlers' attention was thus turned with anxiety toward the explorer. From all directions delegations were sent to learn his purposes, and soon the roving population of the valley had established itself in considerable numbers near the camp at the Buttes.

It took but a few days for the settlers to convince themselves that Frémont desired a revolt, and would join it eventually should the necessity arise, though he would not openly take an active part in beginning it. Naturally we know but little of the many interviews in respect of persons, dates, and other details. Two or three are however on record. We know the results; and it is evident that only to a few did Frémont make definite promises, others receiving them

at second-hand through trusty agents sent out by the
few.   Samuel J. Hensley, during a trip to the bay,
had learned from Vallejo and others some facts and
more rumors respecting the junta at Monterey, the
project of an appeal to England, Castro's preparations at Santa Clara, and points of the general situation.   Returning, he arrived at New Helvetia May
28th.   From Sutter he learned that the Indians were
threatening serious trouble; and a chieftain was conveniently found to testify that the savages were acting at the instigation of Castro.   On June 3d, Sutter
started on a campaign against the Indians; while
Hensley on the 4th hastened up the valley to make
Frémont acquainted with the impending dangers.   At
about the same time Neal returned from below with
opportune confirmation of alarming rumors.   It was
on the 6th that Frémont, after consultation with Hensley, decided on the course to be pursued; and two
days later Hensley and Neal returned to Sutter's, from
that point sending out trusty agents to summon the
settlers in all parts of the district.[6]   If we may credit
Ide, a written summons was circulated in Frémont's
name, though not signed by him.   Ide and others
made haste to obey the summons, which they received
on the 8th; but, not being filibusters of a radical
type, were much troubled that Frémont's plan, so
far as he would condescend to make it known to them,
was not one of independence, but rather one to provoke Castro to begin hostilities through outrages to
be committed by persons who had nothing to risk
either of property or reputation.[7]   This was on the
10th; and before that Kelsey, Hargrave, Swift, and
others had come as representatives of the Napa Valley settlers, they like Ide not being able to obtain
from Frémont any definite promise of aid.[8]   All was

    [6] Hensley's testimony, in *Frémont's Cal. Claims*, 33–4; Frémont to Benton.
Niles' Reg., lxxi. 191.   The dates are fixed and confirmed by the *New Helvetia Diary*, MS., 49–51; and also to some extent by *Sutter's Diary*, 7–8, where
the campaign against the Moquelumnes is described.
    [7] *Ide's Biog. Sketch*, 111–19.
    [8] *Hargrave's Cal. in '46*, MS., 4–11; *Fowler's Bear Party*, 2.

ready, however; the train was laid; new occurrences were exceptionally favorable; and steps had already been taken to apply the match. On the 10th the first act of hostility was committed. About the same time Frémont moved his camp from the Buttes to the Feather River, and then down to Bear River, near its junction with the Feather.

General Castro was striving to organize at Santa Clara, under the immediate command of José Antonio Carrillo, a force of militia with which ostensibly to resist the invasion threatened by the United States, and especially to resist Frémont, whose return could be interpreted only as a threat. Castro had really some fear of Frémont, though probably no hope of defeating him; but his chief purpose was to resist Governor Pico, who was believed to be preparing for a march northward. Not much can be known of the general's success; but though funds were scarce, and public sentiment not enthusiastically patriotic, he doubtless raised about a hundred men, whom he had great difficulty in keeping together, arming, and mounting. At the beginning of June he made a trip to San Rafael and Sonoma in quest of supplies, and to consult with Colonel Vallejo. Victor Castro was directed to be ready with his boat on the 5th, to bring back the general, with such munitions as he might obtain.[9] Respecting the nature and success of Castro's demands upon Vallejo, we know only that he obtained from the latter and through his influence about 170

[9] June 6, 1846, Alcalde Pacheco of San José to Prefect Castro, mentioning the general's departure and instructions to Victor Castro. It was also expected that Vallejo might come over on the boat. The writer speaks of the campaign of Sutter, 'now allied with Castro' against the hostile Moquelumnes. He alludes to troubles between citizens and civil authorities on one side and the military officers on the other, displays considerable bitterness, implies that Castro's preparations are really to overthrow the civil authority, and urges the prefect to warn the govt. *Doc. Hist. Cal.*, MS., iii. 251-2. The spirit of this letter shows where the filibusters obtained some of their reports of Castro's instigating the Indians, etc. Lancey, *Cruise of the 'Dale,'* 49, says that the general went by way of Yerba Buena, and was absent four days, which is likely accurate, though no authority is given.

horses, belonging part to the mission Indians of San
Rafael and part to private citizens.[10]   Francisco Arce,
the general's secretary, and also a militia lieutenant,
had crossed the bay with Castro, and was now sent
with Lieutenant José María Alviso and an escort of
eight men to conduct the horses by the Sacramento
to Santa Clara.[11]   Crossing the river at William
Knight's place, now known as Knight Landing, the
party arrived at the fort June 8th, and next day continued their journey, camping for the night at Murphy's rancho on the Cosumnes.[12]

The approach of Alviso and Arce from Sonoma was
made the foundation of the rumor, said to have been
brought by an Indian, that Castro's force was advancing up the valley, destroying the crops and committing
other outrages.   It has also been said, and it is not
impossible the statement was remotely founded on
fact, that Arce told Knight or his wife at the crossing
that the horses were to be used by Castro for a campaign by which the settlers were to be driven out,
after which a fort was to be established to prevent the
entrance of any more immigrants by the Bear River
pass.   This report was carried by Knight in all haste
to Frémont's camp.[13]   It may be that Don Francisco,

[10] Vallejo, *Hist. Cal.*, MS., v. 110–11, says that the horses were 200 belonging to the govt and 100 to the mission of San Rafael; and that all were being
pastured by Castro's orders on the Cosumne River.   This, though confirmed
by Alvarado, *Hist. Cal.*, MS., v. 156–9, and Fernandez, *Cosas de Cal.*, MS.,
130–1, is not accurate.

[11] By an official report of Gen. Carrillo it appears that Alviso was really in
command, Arce having been detailed to assist him.   Arce in his report also
named Alviso as in command.   Arce's statement of the number of the escort
agrees with the entries in the diaries kept at Sutter's, and is doubtless correct,
though the force has often been represented as much larger by those who
wished to magnify the exploit of the insurgents.   José Noriega, Blas Alviso,
and Blas Piña were of the number.

[12] *N. Helvetia, Diary*, MS., 51; *Sutter's Diary*, 8; *Arce, Mem.*, MS., 52–4.
The river is also called Tahualmes and Macasomy.   Sutter, *Personal Remin.*,
MS., 138, etc., implies that a few horses were added to the band at his place.

[13] This version seems to rest on the authority of Semple.   It first appeared
in the *Monterey Californian*, Aug. 29, 1846, and subsequently with slight variations in the *Hesperian*, iii. 387–8; *First Steamship Pioneers*, 171–3; *Bryant's
What I Saw in Cal.*, 287–8; *S. F. Alta Cal.*, Aug. 2, 1866; *Lancey's Cruise*,
49–50, etc.   Semple was in a sense an excellent authority, but he was also a
prominent conspirator, and one of those who knew well that the settlers were
in no danger.   Ford, *Bear Flag*, MS., 4–5, gives a confused version to the

a somewhat talkative young man, did make some
foolish and boasting remarks as represented; but it is
more likely that the story was invented for effect, as
other similar ones are known to have been. At any
rate, the opportunity was too good a one to be lost by
the filibusters. In the forenoon of the 9th, eleven or
twelve started in pursuit of Arce from the vicinity of
Frémont's camp. Hensley states that they were sent
by Frémont;[14] and there can be no doubt that the
movement was instigated and planned by that officer.
It was during the absence of this party that Ide had
an interview with Frémont, as already narrated, the
latter urging the importance of a raid on Castro's
horses, and King being anxious to know what the settlers would do if the horses were taken.[15] It was also
at this time that the camp was moved to Bear River.
Ezekiel Merritt commanded the pursuing party, the
exact composition of which is not known. Semple
seems to have been a member, as probably were Granville P. Swift and Henry L. Ford, and possibly one
or two of Frémont's men. Most were of the roving
immigrants and hunters who had been for a week assembling near the Buttes, men of the class described
by Frémont as having nothing to risk.[16]

Merritt and his men were joined by two others at
Hock farm. They crossed the American River at
dusk, supped at the rancho of Allen Montgomery,
who with another joined the force. They encamped
at night within two or three miles of where the Cali-

same general effect, representing that Arce made his boasts while on the way
to Sonoma after the horses, and that Knight was a spy sent out by Frémont.

[14] Hensley's testimony in *Frémont's Cal. Claims*, 33. Frémont himself says
'they were surprised by a party from my camp.' Letter to Benton. *Niles'
Reg.*, lxxi. 191.

[15] *Ide's Biog. Sketch*, 111-19.

[16] Bidwell, *Cal.*, 1841-8, MS., 161-4, who was at Sutter's at the time,
thinks there were no permanent settlers in the party, but chiefly hunters
whom Frémont sent out, using Arce's expedition as a pretext for a beginning
of hostilities. Martin, *Narr.*, MS., 21-2, says Frémont called for volunteers
among his own men, of whom the writer was one, and that 15 started under
Swift; but Martin is not good authority. Baldridge, *Days of '46*, MS., 27,
also names Swift. One account names Neal and Knight as members of the
party.

fornians were camped, guarding their horses in **Murphy's corral.**[17]   At early dawn on the 10th, they surprised Arce and his companions, requiring them to give up their arms, which of course was done without resistance.[18]   Subsequently, however, after a certain amount of threatening bluster from Merritt and his fellow-filibusters, the arms were restored, with a horse for each man, and also a few horses claimed as private property by Alviso, who concealed his real position as leader of the party; and the prisoners were dismissed with a message that if Castro wanted his horses he might come and take them, and with the announcement of a purpose to take Sonoma and New Helvetia, and to continue the war.[19]

The filibusters returned with the captured horses by the same route they had come, slept that night at Nicholas Allgeier's rancho, and reached Frémont's new camp in the forenoon of the 11th, after an absence of forty-eight hours.   Arce and his men made haste to San José and reported their mishap to Car-

[17] Ford, *Bear Flag*, MS., 6–7, gives the most complete description of the expedition.   See also *Lancey's Cruise*, 56.

[18] Frémont in his letter to Benton, *Niles' Reg.*, lxxi. 291, gave the date incorrectly as June 11th, and the error was repeated in Sec. Marcy's report of Dec. 5th—29th cong. 2d sess., H. Ex. Doc. no. 4, p. 51, and from this source in *Smucker's Life of Frémont*, 28; *Cutts' Conq.*, 152–3; and many other accounts.   Most writers have taken pride in representing the number of Merritt's men as 12 and of Arce's party as larger.   Larkin's letters make the force 12 on each side.   Semple spoke of 18 prisoners, and Ford of 23!   Some miscellaneous references on the capture of Arce's horses are: *Tuthill's Hist. Cal.*, 169–70; *Hist. Bear Flag Revol.*; *Piña, Narr.*, MS., 3–5; *Tinkham's Hist. Stockton*, 89; *Willey's 30 Years*, 9; *Mendocino Co. Hist.*, 60; *Marshall's Statement*, MS., 1–2; *Belden's Hist. Statement*, MS., 43; *Honolulu Friend*, iv. 169; *Sta Cruz Sentinel*, June 12, 1869.

[19] The announcement of a purpose to take Sonoma is proved by the fact that it was announced in the official reports before Sonoma was taken.   Arce, *Memorias*, MS., 52–4, says it was at first the intention to kill him and his companions, and that they were saved only by the intercession of Murphy and his wife.   Of course there was no intention of killing them; but Merritt was a rough man, who may have tried to make them think so.   In one of Larkin's letters, *Larkin's Off. Corresp.*, MS., i. 131, the story was told as a report that on Arce's complaining that he had been taken by surprise, Merritt proposed to repeat the operation, the Californians armed and mounted to choose their distance and give a signal for the attack!   This has been often repeated, and may or may not have had some foundation in fact.   Noriega, one of Arce's men, disappeared after the affair, as appears from corresp. of the time; and he turned up at Sutter's 9 days later, coming from Murphy's.   *N. Helvetia Diary*, MS., 52.

rillo and Castro, who in their correspondence represented the affair in its true light, as an outrage committed by a band of irresponsible highwaymen at the
instigation of Frémont. They regarded it as the pre-
cursor of invasion, and made an earnest appeal to the
prefect, as representing the civil authority, to forget
all past dissensions, and join the military in the country's defence. Consul Larkin volunteered his assistance in recovering the stolen animals, or punishing
the offenders, if any feasible method of action could
be pointed out.[20]

Merritt and his party had announced at the Cosumnes their plan to take Sonoma. Such a plan may
or may not have been definitely formed before they
had started in pursuit of Arce; but if not, it was
formed immediately on their return to camp on the
11th. It was manifestly important, having once begun hostilities, to leave the Californians no rallying-
point north of the bay. Without delay the company
was increased to twenty men, and, still under Ezekiel
Merritt's leadership, left Frémont's camp on Bear
Creek in the afternoon of the same day. Crossing
the Sacramento probably at Knight's, supping at Gordon's on Cache Creek, and crossing the hills by night,

[20] June 13th, Arce to Mayor Gen. Carrillo, and Carrillo to Gen. Castro by
a 'violento extraordinario,' forwarded the same day from 'El Rio' to Prefect
Manuel Castro. *Castro, Doc.*, MS., ii. 103, 105. June 13th, Sub-prefect
Guerrero at Yerba Buena to prefect. *Id.*, ii. 112. Same to juez of S. José.
S. José, Arch., Loose Papers, MS., 24. Same date, Carrillo to S. José al-
calde. *Id.*, 51. All agree that the filibusters claimed to be acting under
Frémont's orders, and threatened to continue their depredations. Lancey,
Cruise, 49, tells us that Gen. Castro received the news on June 12th, on the
Salinas River, hastening back to Monterey and dictating a letter—as he could
only paint his signature!—the same day to Manuel Castro calling for aid.
June 14th, Larkin to Gen. Castro, original in *Arce, Doc.*, MS., 13. June
14th, L. to Manuel Castro, original in *Doc. Hist. Cal.*, MS., iii. 257; copies
Larkin's Off. Corresp., MS., i. 113; *Sawyer's Doc.*, MS., 49. June 15th, Alcalde Pacheco to prefect. Has seen one MacGuinsé (McKenzie?), who was
with Arce, and says that none of the filibusters belonged to Frémont's party.
He recognized only Merritt, and says that they claimed to fear that Castro
intended to use the horses to drive the settlers away. Noriega has not been
heard of. *Doc. Hist. Cal.*, MS., iii. 259. Larkin gave a brief account of the
affair in letters to the sec. state on June 18th, 24th, and in a 'circular to
several Americans' on July 8th. *Larkin's Off. Corresp.*, MS., i. 131; ii. 65;
Sawyer's Doc., MS., 55.

they arrived in Napa Valley in the forenoon of the 12th. They remained there two days, and their number was increased to 32 or 33, whose names, so far as they can be known, for no list has ever been made until now, are appended in a note.[21]   About midnight they started again over the range of hills separating the valleys; and just before dawn on Sunday, June 14th, were at the town of Sonoma.[22]

[21] Ezekiel Merritt, Wm B. Ide, John Grigsby, Robert Semple, H. L. Ford, Wm Todd, Wm Fallon, Wm Knight, Wm Hargrave, Sam. Kelsey, G. P. Swift, Sam. Gibson, W. W. Scott, Benj. Dewell, Thos Cowie, Wm B. Elliott, Thos Knight, Horace Sanders, Henry Booker, Dav. Hudson, John Sears, and most of the following: J. H. Kelly, C. C. Griffith, Harvey Porterfield, John Scott, Ira Stebbins, Marion Wise, Ferguson, Peter Storm, Pat. McChristian, Bartlett Vines, Fowler, John Gibbs, Andrew Kelsey, and Benj. Kelsey.

[22] There is no doubt about the date of arrival at Sonoma; but there is a possibility that they did not leave Bear Creek until the 12th. Lancey, *Cruise*, 56, etc., takes that view of it. Ford, *Bear Flag*, MS., 7–10, says they started at 3 P. M. on the 10th, which, like all those given by this writer, is an impossible date. Ide, *Biog. Sketch*, 120, etc., says it was at sunrise on the 11th, which is equally impossible. These two authorities, however, are the best extant on details of the march; and as they seem to agree that one whole night was spent in Napa Valley, I have little doubt that the start was at 3 P. M. of the 11th. This is partially confirmed by the statement of Baldridge, *Days of '46*, MS., 21, etc., 35–8, that Grigsby and Elliott made a tour through the valley to enlist the settlers the day before the attack was to be made. Yet Semple, *Hesperian*, iii. 388–9, gave the date of starting as the 12th. The date of taking Sonoma was incorrectly given by Frémont as the 15th, Letter to Benton in *Niles' Reg.*, lxxi. 191; and the error has been often repeated. Newspaper discussions on this date in recent years will have to be noticed presently in another connection; they have been further complicated by Ford's error in making the date of the capture June 12th.

There is also a discrepancy about the composition of the party. Ide says 13 men left the Sacramento, and were increased to 32 in Napa Valley, though he implies later that the whole number was 34. Ford makes the number 20 at first, increased to 33 at Napa. Most authorities content themselves with stating that there were 33 men at last. The *West Shore Gazeteer, Yolo Co.*, 12–13, followed by Lancey, says that 12 men out on an Indian expedition with Armijo, a Mexican, learned at Gordon's of Merritt's movement, and marched en masse to join him. It is noticeable that these 12 men added to Ford's 20 make up Ide's total of 32. There is no agreement respecting the place of rendezvous in Napa Valley. Grigsby's, Kelsey's, and 'Major Barnard's' are mentioned.

Baldridge, *Days of '46*, MS., 5, says that while Merritt was nominally the leader, Grigsby had entire control of the affair. Sutter, *Pers. Remin.*, MS., 147–50, says the 'band of robbers' were Frémont's men, implying that the captain went with them, and that some of Sutter's workmen and Indians went along. He confounds this with later events. Martin, *Narr.*, MS., 24, tells us that Frémont's men were disbanded, and immediately volunteered to take Sonoma under command of Swift! Pat. McChristian, *Narr.*, MS., 1–5, claims that the company was organized according to previous notice, in the hills near Salvador Vallejo's rancho. Boggs, *Napa Register*, April 6, 1872, copies an order sent in advance as follows: 'Mr. Geo. Yount: please deliver to the Republic of California 1,000 bbls of flour—signed Wm B. Ide, gover-

In narratives of the time, and later, it was customary to magnify the exploit of June 14th, by speaking of Sonoma as a Californian stronghold, a fort, a garrisoned town, taken by surprise, or even by a "gallant charge" without shedding of blood, so skilfully was the movement planned. There was, however, no garrison at Sonoma. The soldiers formerly in service there had been discharged some years before, during the Micheltorena troubles. Some of the citizens even were absent from the town, and there was no thought of even posting a sentinel. It is true, there remained as relics of the old military régime nine small cannon, a few of them still mounted, and over 200 muskets in the *cuartel*, with a small quantity of ammunition. All was technically public property, though in reality belonging to Colonel Vallejo, who had not seen fit to deliver it to the general on his late visit. Two men residing there held commissions in the Mexican army; otherwise, a more peaceful burg than this stronghold of the Frontera del Norte on that Sunday morning it would be difficult to find.

At daybreak Vallejo was aroused by a noise, and on looking out saw that his house was surrounded by armed men. This state of things was sufficiently alarming in itself, and all the more so by reason of the uncouth and even ferocious aspect of the strangers. Says Semple: "Almost the whole party was dressed in leather hunting-shirts, many of them very greasy; taking the

---

nor;' and gravely tells us that the flour was delivered! Of course this is pure invention. The same writer says that on reaching the Sonoma Valley, a Californian was found encamped, and was arrested to prevent his giving an alarm. The wheels of this man's cart stood for years unmoved, marking the spot. Ide, *Biog. Sketch*, 120–1, informs us that Gordon and 'Major Barnard,' at whose places they stopped, were liberal with their hospitality, but not willing to join the party. At Napa, 11 P. M., on the 13th, 'sleep and drowsiness were on the point of delaying if not defeating our enterprise.' Ford and Lancey speak of an address by Semple before the departure from Napa. John Fowler, Wm Baldridge, T. W. Bradley, and others, according to their own statements, did not immediately join the company, which was regarded as amply strong. Thos Knight, *Early Events*, MS., 7–11, speaks, like Boggs, of the arrest of a native before reaching the town. Ide says the captain of the guard was arrested a little way out, perhaps referring to the same occurrence.

whole party together, they were about as rough a looking set of men as one could well imagine. It is not
to be wondered at that any one would feel some
dread in falling into their hands." And Vallejo himself declares that there was by no means such a uni-
formity of dress as a greasy hunting-shirt for each man
would imply.[23] Vallejo's wife was even more alarmed
than her husband, whom she begged to escape by a
back door, but who, deeming such a course undignified as well as impracticable, hastily dressed, ordered
the front door opened, and met the intruders as they
entered his *sala*, demanding who was their chief and
what their business. Not much progress in explanation was made at first, though it soon became apparent
that the colonel, while he was to consider himself a
prisoner, was not in danger of any personal violence.
Lieutenant-colonel Prudon and Captain Salvador Vallejo entered the room a few minutes later, attracted by
the noise, or possibly were arrested at their houses
and brought there; at any rate, they were put under
arrest like the colonel. Jacob P. Leese was sent for
to serve as interpreter, after which mutual explanations
progressed more favorably.

Early in the ensuing negotiations between prisoners
and filibusters, it became apparent that the latter had
neither acknowledged leader nor regular plan of operations beyond the seizure of government property and
of the officers. Some were acting, as in the capture
of Arce's horses, merely with a view to obtain arms,
animals, and hostages—to bring about hostilities, and
at the same time to deprive the foe of his resources;
others believed themselves to have undertaken a revolution, in which steps to be immediately taken were
a formal declaration of independence and the election
of officers, Merritt being regarded rather as a guide
than captain. All seemed to agree, however, that
they were acting under Frémont's orders, and this to

[23] Semple, in *Monterey Californian*, Sept. 5, 1846; *Vallejo, Hist. Cal.*, MS.,
v. 111, etc.

the prisoners was the most assuring feature in the case. Vallejo had for some time favored the annexation of California to the United States. He had expected and often predicted a movement to that end. There is no foundation for the suspicion that the taking of Sonoma and his own capture were planned by himself, in collusion with the filibuster chiefs, with a view to evade responsibility; yet it is certain that he had little if any objection to an enforced arrest by officers of the United States as a means of escaping from the delicacy of his position as a Mexican officer. Accordingly, being assured that the insurgents were acting under Frémont, he submitted to arrest, gave up keys to public property, and entered upon negotiations with a view to obtain guaranties of protection for non-combatants.

The guaranties sought were then drawn up in writing and signed by the respective parties. The originals of those documents are in my possession, and are given in a note.[24]

[24] No. 1. An exact copy, except that as the duplicates do not exactly agree in orthography and contractions, I have written each word correctly and in full.

'Conste por la presente que, habiendo sido sorprendido por una numerosa fuerza armada que me tomó prisionero y á los gefes y oficiales que estaban de guarnicion en esta plaza, de la que se apoderó la expresada fuerza, habiendo la encontrado absolutamente indefensa, tanto yo como los señores oficiales que suscriben comprometemos nuestra palabra de honor de que estando bajo las garantías de prisioneros de guerra no tomaremos ni á favor ni contra la repetida fuerza armada de quien hemos recibido la intimacion del momento y un escrito firmado que garantiza nuestras vidas familias é intereses y las de todo el vecindario de esta jurisdiccion mientras no hagamos oposicion.   Sonoma, Junio 14 de 1846.   M. G. Vallejo, Victor Prudon, Salvador Vallejo.'   In English the document is as follows: 'Be it known by these presents, that, having been surprised by a numerous armed force which took me prisoner, with the chief and officers belonging to the garrison of this place that the said force took possession of, having found it absolutely defenceless, myself as well as the undersigned officers pledge our word of honor that, being under the guaranties of prisoners of war, we will not take up arms for or against the said armed force, from which we have received the present intimation, and a signed writing which guarantees our lives, families, and property, and those of all the residents of this jurisdiction, so long as we make no opposition.'

No. 2.   'We, the undersigned, members of the republican party in California, having taken Gen. M. G. Vallejo, Lieut-col. Victor Prudon, and Capt. D. Salvidor Vallejo as prisoners, pledge ourselves that in so doing, or in any other portion of our actions, we will not disturb private property, molest themselves, their families, or the citizens of the town of Zanoma or its vicinity, our object alone being to prevent their opposition in the progress of the

It was naturally to be expected, under the circumstances, that the arrested officers would be released on parole. Such was evidently the view taken on both sides at first. Ford says there were some who favored such a course. Leese, who had the best opportunities for understanding the matter, and who gives a more detailed account than any other writer, tells us that such a decision was reached; and finally, the documents which I have presented, Nos 1 and 2 being to all intents and purposes regular parole papers, leave no doubt upon the subject. But now difficulties arose, respecting some phases of which there is contradictory testimony.

Thus far only a few of the insurgent leaders had entered, or at least remained in the house; and the negotiations had in reality been conducted by Semple and Leese very much in their own way. Ide testifies that Merritt, Semple, and Wm Knight, the latter accompanying the expedition merely as an interpreter, were the first to enter the house, while the rest waited outside; that presently hearing nothing, they became impatient, determined to choose a captain, and elected John Grigsby, who thereupon went in; and that after waiting what appeared an age, the men again lost patience and called upon the writer,

en[ds?] of the liberation'. . . .—one or two words perhaps at the end, and the signatures, if there were any, are torn off.

No. 3. 'We, the undersigned, having resolved to establish a government of on (upon?) republican principles, in connection with others of our fellow-citizens, and having taken up arms to support it, we have taken three Mexican officers as prisoners, Gen. M. G. Vallejo, Lieut-col. Victor Prudon, and Capt. D. Salvador Vallejo, having formed and published to the world no regular plan of government, feel it our duty to say that it is not our intention to take or injure any person who is not found in opposition to the cause, nor will we take or destroy the property of private individuals further than is necessary for our immediate support. Ezekiel Merritt, R. Semple, William Fallon, Samuel Kelsay.'

These important papers are found in *Bear Flag Papers*, MS., 19–20, 60–1. They were given me by Gen. Vallejo. There are two signed originals of no. 1, one in the handwriting of Salvador Vallejo, and the other in that of Victor Prudon. In *Vallejo, Doc.*, MS., xii. 226, is another incomplete and unsigned blotter copy. Nos 1 and 3 were printed in *Marin Co. Hist.*, 68–9, and *Sonoma Co. Hist.*, 100–1, from copies furnished by me to Gen. Vallejo. The English document is probably the work of Semple, but possibly of Merritt, as indicated by spelling and grammar.

Ide, to go and investigate the causes of delay. Now the discrepancies in testimony begin. Ide describes the state of things which met his view as follows: "The general's generous spirits gave proof of his usual hospitality, as the richest wines and brandies sparkled in the glasses, and those who had thus unceremoniously met soon became merry companions; more especially the merry visitors. There sat Dr S., just modifying a long string of articles of capitulation. There sat Merritt, his head fallen; there sat Knight, no longer able to interpret; and there sat the new-made captain, as mute as the seat he sat upon. The bottles had wellnigh vanquished the captors"![25] Leese also states that brandy was a potent factor in that morning's events; but according to his version, it was on the company outside that its influence was exerted, rendering them noisy and unmanageable, though an effort had been made by his advice to put the liquor out of reach.[26] I do not, however, deem it at all likely that the leaders drank more than it was customary to drink in a Californian's parlor, or more than they could carry; but that some of the rough characters in the company became intoxicated we may well believe.

At any rate, disagreement ensued; the men refused entirely to ratify the capitulation made by their former leaders, insisting that the prisoners must be sent to the Sacramento; some of them were inclined to be insubordinate and eager for plunder; while the lawless spirits were restrained from committing outrages by the eloquence of Semple and the voice of the majority; yet the leaders could not agree. Captain Grigsby declined to retain the leadership that had been conferred upon him. So William B. Ide was chosen in his stead; and the revolutionists immediately took possession of all public property, as well as of such horses and other private property as they needed, at the same time lock-

[25] *Ide's Biog. Sketch*, 123-5.
[26] *Leese's Bear Flag Statement*, MS., 6-12. Vallejo, *Hist. Cal.*, MS., v. 113, says that the Canadian Beaulieu gave the men a barrel of aguardiente, which caused all the trouble.

ing up all citizens that could be found.[27]   It would seem that the second of the documents I have presented was torn, and the third drawn up and signed at an early stage of the disagreements, after it became apparent that it might be best to send the prisoners to the Sacramento, the signatures showing that it could not have been later.   Vallejo, though not encouraged

[27] Leese, *Bear Flag*, MS., 6–12, says that after the capitulations were all completed he left the house; but returning half an hour later, he found all in confusion; Ide insisted that the prisoners must be sent to Frémont's camp; Semple admitted that he could not fully control the men, and said it would be better to yield; Fallon and 'English Jim' notified Vallejo that they must have 80 horses in half an hour; others insisted on searching Vallejo's house and took all the arms and ammunition they could find; and finally they took 60 horses belonging to the writer, refusing his request to leave two that belonged to his children.   So great did the excitement become, and so freely were some of the men drinking, that the writer feared personal violence.   Leese mentions the fact that Merritt, having once been struck by Salvador Vallejo, insisted at first on putting him in irons, but was persuaded to forget his private grievances.   This story in a more dramatic form has often been repeated.   'With all the keen resentment of a brave man, Mr Merritt suddenly found this man in his power, the blood rushed to his cheeks and his eyes sparkled; he leaned forward like a mad tiger in the act of springing upon his prey, and in an energetic and manly tone said: "When I was your prisoner you struck me; now you are my prisoner, I will not strike you"'! is the way Semple tells it in the *Monterey Californian*, Sept. 5, 1846.   Don Salvador and Merritt were both men more likely to quarrel than to select so magnanimous a method of revenge.

Another statement of Semple, Id., has been very popular.   'A single man cried out, "Let us divide the spoils," but one universal, dark, indignant frown made him shrink from the presence of honest men, and from that time forward no man dared to hint anything like violating the sanctity of a private house, or touching private property; so far did they carry this principle that they were unwilling to take the beef which was offered by our prisoner'! 'Their children in generations yet to come will look back with pleasure upon the commencement of a revolution carried on by their fathers upon principles high and holy as the laws of eternal justice.'   Vallejo, *Hist. Cal.*, MS., v. 114–15, thinks that it was only by the zealous efforts of Semple, Grigsby, Kelsey, and a few others that indiscriminate plunder was prevented.   Many Californians talk of plunder and other outrages that never occurred.   Ide says, *Biog. Sketch*, 128: 'Joy lighted up every mind, and in a moment all was secured; 18 prisoners, 9 brass cannon, 250 stands of arms, and tons of copper shot and other public property, of the value of 10 or 1200 dollars, was seized and held in trust for the public benefit.'   Baldridge, *Days of '46*, MS., 5, 43–5, who was not one of those who took Sonoma, gives a remark of Prudon, 'Boys, you have been a little too fast for us, we were going to serve you in the same way in just 10 days'!   He also quotes Grigsby to the effect that some sailors announced their determination to have the money which they knew to be in the house, but obeyed Grigsby's order to desist, especially when two rifles were levelled at them.   Martin, *Narr.*, MS., 24–6, gives an absurdly incorrect account of the taking of Sonoma, in which he pretends to have assisted; talks of 18 loaded cannon with matches burning which faced the attacking party! etc.   Salvador Vallejo, *Notas*, MS., 101–17, tells a little truth about the affair, mingled, as usual in his testimony, with much that is too absurdly false to deceive any one.

at seeing that the leaders were not permitted by their
followers to keep their promises, was not very much
displeased at being sent to New Helvetia. He was
assured that the insurgents were acting by Frémont's
orders; his own views were known to be favorable to
the schemes of the United States; and he had no reason to doubt that on meeting Frémont he and his companions would at once be released on parole.

Before the departure of the prisoners and their escort a formal meeting of the revolutionists was held.
That Semple, secretary, made a speech counselling
united action and moderation in the treatment of the
natives, and that William B. Ide was chosen captain,
is all that is known of this meeting,[28] except what we
may learn from Ide's narrative. The leaders differed
in their ideas, not only respecting the disposition to be
made of the prisoners, but about the chief object of
the movement. Evidently there had been no definitely arranged plan of operations. Frémont had succeeded in bringing about a state of open hostility
without committing himself. Some of the men regarded their movement as merely intended to provoke
Castro to make an attack on Frémont; or at least they
dreaded the responsibility of engaging in a regular revolution, especially when it was learned that no one
could produce any definite promise from Frémont in
black and white to support such a movement. Others
were in favor of an immediate declaration of independence. That such differences of opinion did exist as
Ide states, is in itself by no means improbable; and
it is confirmed to some extent by the fact that Grigsby
did resign his leadership, and by the somewhat strange
circumstance that three such prominent men as
Grigsby, Merritt, and Semple should have left Sonoma
to accompany the prisoners. Ide writes that when
Grigsby heard that no positive orders from Frémont
could be produced, his "'fears of doing wrong' over-

[28] *Semple*, in *Hesperian*, iii. 388–9; and in *First Steamship Pioneers*, 174–5.
See also *Lancey's Cruise*, 57.

came his patriotism, and he interrupted the speaker by saying: 'Gentlemen, I have been deceived; I cannot go with you; I resign and back out of the scrape.   I can take my family to the mountains as cheap as any of you'—and Dr S. at that moment led him into the house.   Disorder and confusion prevailed.   One swore he would not stay to guard prisoners; another swore we would all have our throats cut; another called for fresh horses; and all were on the move, every man for himself, when the speaker [Ide] resumed his effort, raising his voice louder and more loud, as the men receded from the place, saying: 'We need no horses; saddle no horse for me; I can go to the Spaniards and make freemen of them.   I will lay my bones here before I will take upon myself the ignominy of commencing an honorable work and then flee like cowards, like thieves, when no enemy is in sight.   In vain will you say you had honorable motives.   Who will believe it?   Flee this day, and the longest life cannot wear out your disgrace!   Choose ye this day what you will be!   We are robbers, or we must be conquerors!'   and the speaker in despair turned his back upon his receding companions.   With new hope they rallied around the desponding speaker, made him their commander, their chief; and his next words commanded the taking of the fort."   Subsequently "the three leaders of the party of the primitive plan of 'neutral conquest' left us alone in our glory."   I find no reason to doubt that this version, though somewhat highly colored, is in substance accurate; that Merritt, having captured horses and prisoners, was content to rest on his laurels; that Grigsby was timid about assuming the responsibility of declaring independence without a positive assurance of Frémont's coöperation; that Semple, while in favor of independence, preferred that Sacramento should be the centre of operations, unless—what Vallejo and Leese also favored—Frémont could be induced to establish his headquarters at Sonoma; or finally, that Ide and his associates influenced the majority to complete their revolutionary work and take no backward steps. I think, however, that Ide and all the rest counted confidently on Frémont's support; and that Semple and Grigsby were by no means regarded as abandoning the cause when they left Sonoma.

It was about 11 A. M., on June 14th, when the three prisoners, accompanied by Leese as interpreter at their request and that of the captors—not himself a prisoner as has been generally stated—and guarded by Grigsby, Semple, Merritt, Hargrave, Knight, and four or five others,[29] started on horses from Vallejo's herds for the Sacramento. It will be most convenient to follow them before proceeding to narrate later developments at Sonoma. Before starting, and on the way, Vallejo was often questioned by Californians as to the situation of affairs; but could only counsel them to remain quiet, announcing that he would probably .return within four or five days. His idea was that Frémont, after releasing him and his companions on parole, might be induced to establish his headquarters at Sonoma, an idea shared by Semple, Grigsby, and Leese. Relations between captives and captors were altogether friendly, except in the case of some hostile feeling among a few individuals against Don Salvador.[30] They encamped that night at Vaca's rancho. No special pains was taken to guard the prisoners, who with Leese slept on a pile of straw near the camp. Vallejo had desired to travel all night; but the men declined to do so, having had no sleep the night before. Before dawn on the morning of the 15th, a

[29] Lancey names Kit Carson as one of the guard, falling into the error from the fact that Carson accompanied Merritt from Frémont's camp to Sutter's Fort. There were probably none of Frémont's men in the party that took Sonoma. Ide says the guard contained 10 men; Leese says about 12 men. Both Ide and Ford state that the force left behind was 24 men, which would indicate that the guard numbered 9.

[30] Several writers state, without any foundation in fact, that Don Salvador was arrested, not at Sonoma, but at his Napa rancho on the way to Sacramento.

Californian succeeded in reaching the captives, and informed Vallejo that a company of his countrymen had been organized to effect his rescue, and only awaited his orders. The colonel refused to permit such an attempt to be made, both because he had no reason to fear any unpleasant results from his enforced visit to the Sacramento, and because he feared retaliation at Sonoma in case an attempt to escape should bring harm to any of the guard.[31]   On the 15th the party reached Hardy's place on the Sacramento.   Here Merritt left the others, intending to visit Frémont's camp and return next morning; but as he did not come back, Leese with one companion started in the forenoon of the 16th also in quest of Frémont.   Arriving at Allgeier's place, they learned that the captain had moved his camp to American River; and starting for that point, they rejoined their companions before arrival.   Here Grigsby presented an order from Frémont for Leese's arrest, for which, so far as known, no explanation was given.[32]

Late in the afternoon they reached the camp, and the prisoners were brought into the presence of Frémont.   That officer's reception of them was very different from what had been anticipated.   His words and manner were reserved and mysterious.   He denied, when Vallejo demanded for what offence and by what

[31] *Leese's Bear Flag*, MS., 8–9. This writer thinks that Vallejo's course saved the lives of all the guard, as the surprise would have been complete, and there were some desperate characters among the rescuers. Revere, *Tour of Duty*, 65, heard a similar version from a person who was present, and that the Californians were under the command of Juan Padilla, who was also the messenger. Also *Lancey's Cruise*, 57. Vallejo, *Hist. Cal.*, MS., v. 126–7, and Cayetano Juarez, *Narrative*, MS., and in *Savage, Doc.*, MS., i. 39–40, tell us that Juarez posted himself at the Portezuela with a small force, sending his brother disguised as a woman to notify Vallejo of his design to effect a rescue, if permitted. By Boggs, *Napa Register*, April 6, 1872, we are informed that 60 or 70 of Castro's men sent to drive out the settlers intercepted the guard near Higuera's rancho, but were kept off by Vallejo's shouts that he was in danger of being shot if they came nearer! And in the *Sacramento Record-Union*, March 15, 1876, we read of the attempted rescue at Napa, which failed by reason of Grigsby's coolness in threatening to shoot the prisoners!

[32] Leese's account is confirmed by a letter written by Vallejo while in prison, to be noticed later.

authority he had caused their arrest, that he was in any way responsible for what had been done; declared that they were prisoners of the people, who had been driven to revolt for self-protection; refused to accept their paroles; and sent them that same night, under a guard composed in part if not wholly of his own men—Kit Carson and Merritt being sent in advance— to be locked up at Sutter's Fort.[33]

[33] Vallejo, *Hist. Cal.*, MS., v. 122-8, thinks that Frémont was not un-friendly, but that he dared not oppose the popular feeling of the rough trap-pers and settlers. Leese, on the other hand, very angry of course that no explanation was given of his own arrest, except that he was 'a bad man,' blames Frémont exclusively, describing his words and actions as arbitrary and offensive in the extreme. The arrival of Carson and Merritt, and that of the prisoners later, are recorded in *N. Helvetia Diary*, MS., 52; *Sutter's Diary*, 8.

CHAPTER VI.

BEAR FLAG REVOLT CONTINUED—AFFAIRS AT SUTTER'S FORT AND SOUTH OF THE BAY.

JUNE-JULY, 1846.

SUTTER'S POSITION—THE PRISONERS—THEIR TREATMENT—CORRESPONDENCE OF THE CAPTIVES—EVENTS AT NEW HELVETIA—SOUTH OF THE BAY— ROSA SENT BY VALLEJO TO MONTGOMERY—MISROON'S MISSION—OFFICIAL AND PRIVATE CORRESPONDENCE—CASTRO'S PROCLAMATIONS—MILITARY PREPARATIONS—THREE DIVISIONS TO RETAKE SONOMA—TORRE SENT ACROSS THE BAY—MANUEL CASTRO'S MISSION—INSURGENTS AT SAN FRANCISCO—WEBER'S ARREST—MONTGOMERY'S POLICY—PICO AT SANTA BÁRBARA—THE ANGELINOS NOT WARLIKE—FOREIGNERS OFFENDED—THE ASSEMBLY—PICO AND LARKIN—PICO MARCHES NORTH —MEETS CASTRO—EMBRACE OF GOVERNOR AND GENERAL.

CAPTAIN SUTTER was still nominally in command at the fort. The turn affairs were taking sadly interfered with his plans of selling the establishment, though he was not without hopes that the revolt might in one way or another be made to advance his personal interests. Had his plans in this respect, and especially his recent advice to Castro to garrison the fort against Americans, been fully known to the insurgents, he also would have been put under arrest. As it was, while he was not fully trusted, neither was he much feared. He doubtless gave to Hensley and others assurances of secret support, and was therefore excused from active participation, though he was closely watched the while. It is well known, being also admitted by himself, that his relations with Frémont were not friendly.[1] What understanding had

[1] Sutter, *Person. Remin.*, MS., 140-50, in a very inaccurate sketch of these times, claims to have been acting in good faith as an ally of the U. S., renounc-

(122)

been reached at the time of Carson's arrival or earlier
is not known; but when the prisoners arrived, Sutter
simply obeyed Frémont's instructions, and they were
locked up in one of the rooms of the fort, to pass the
night in not very agreeable meditations on their unfortunate condition, mingled at times with regret that they
had not availed themselves of a favorable opportunity
to escape. Vallejo states further that their room contained no furniture except some rude benches; that
no blankets were furnished for that first night; and
that they were without food or water till 11 A. M. next
day, when an Indian was sent in with a pot of soup
and meat which they were free to eat as best they
could without spoons or dishes. "Doubtless God had
decreed," writes the general, "that June 1846 was
to be the black month of my life." With a view to
render all safe, and to guard against the effects of any
possible sympathy of Sutter for his brother officers, E.
M. Kern was stationed at New Helvetia with a small
detachment of Frémont's men to guard the captives.[2]

Having once opened hostilities, the filibusters are
not to be blamed for seizing Sonoma or for arresting
the Mexican officers; and having once arrested them,
it was perhaps for the best to send them to the Sacramento; or at least, it is not strange that the leaders
could not control their rough associates and were

ing his allegiance to Mexico by opening his gates to Frémont! He admits that F. acted suspiciously, was 'shy' of him, and had him closely
watched, the men he finally left at the fort being really spies rather than a
garrison. He attributes F.'s dislike to the affair of the stolen horses just before the capt. went to Oregon. S. claims also to have earnestly disapproved
the outrage on Vallejo and his companions. Bidwell, *Cal. in 1841-8*, MS.,
164-7, tells us that Sutter had denounced the taking of Arce's horses, which
greatly displeased Frémont, so that when he came down to the fort he told
S. that if he did not like what was being done he might go and join the
Mexicans.

[2] About Kern's command at the fort there is not much information extant. Possibly he was not stationed there until Frémont started for Sonoma.
Hensley, however, testimony in *Fremont's Cal. Claims*, 34, states that it was
before his own departure for the south, that is, on the 16th; and Leese represents that the prisoners were delivered to Kern at first. There are frequent
references to the fact of his being in command in later correpondence. Sutter speaks of the garrison of spies left at Frémont's departure. The *Diaries*
contain no intimation of any other authority than Sutter's.

forced to break a solemn agreement.   But once at
Sutter's, for Frémont and his fellow-revolutionists to
put the captives in prison, and keep them there, disregarding past pledges, demands for justice, or explanations, and especially Vallejo's rank and well known
sympathies and honorable character, as well as Leese's
nationality, was a gross and inexcusable outrage.   It
was a severe blow to Vallejo's pride, and a most un-
generous return for his many acts of kindness to
American settlers, his influence in behalf of annexation to the United States, and the ready confidence
with which, counselling his countrymen against resistance, he had given his parole, and intrusted himself
to the protection of a man whom he regarded as an
officer and a gentleman.

The Sonoma prisoners remained in confinement at
New Helvetia until August, being released, under
circumstances to be noticed later, after the revolution
was at an end, and the conquest by the United States
had begun.   José Noriega and Vicente Peralta, making their appearance at the fort shortly after the outbreak, were added to the number; and Julio Carrillo,
Vallejo's brother-in-law, coming later from Sonoma
under a passport to assure the colonel of his family's
safety, shared the same fate.   Respecting the prisoners' experience and treatment during their confinement, evidence is meagre and contradictory.   I attach
but little importance to the complaints of later years,
coming from the prisoners themselves, and exaggerated by their friends, complaints involving gross ill-
treatment and cruelty; nor on the other hand do I
credit the statement of Sutter that the captives "were
placed in my best rooms, and treated with every consideration; took their meals at my table, and walked
out with me in the evening; their room was not
guarded night or day, nor did any guard accompany
them when they walked."   There is no reason, however, to doubt that Sutter himself was disposed to
treat them kindly, or perhaps that he was chided by

Frémont for his kindness.[3] The truth is, that Vallejo
and his companions were kept in close confinement for
nearly two months, in rough and inconvenient quarters.   They were fed with coarse food, and were allowed no communication with friends or families.
The few letters allowed to pass from the prison were
closely examined by Frémont's men; not the slightest
attention was paid to their appeals for justice; and
they were occasionally insulted by an irresponsible
guard.   This was the sum and substance of their
grievance, and it was indeed a serious one.   Their
mental sufferings arising from anxiety for family and
property, as well as from wounded pride, were greater
than those of the body resulting from hunger or hard
beds.   Vallejo had never been in all respects a popular man in California; and now there were not wanting among his countrymen those who expressed a
degree of satisfaction that the 'autocrat of Sonoma'

[3] *Sutter's Pers. Remin.*, MS., 148, etc. He says that after Frémont's first
complaint, the prisoners were put in charge of Loker, and later of Bidwell,
who treated them not much less kindly than Sutter himself. He did not
cease his visits and care for them until warned through Townsend that he
would be himself arrested. He ignores Kern altogether. In his *Diary*, 8, he
says: 'I have treated them with kindness and so good as I could, which was
reported to Frémont, and he then told me that prisoners ought not to be
treated so; then I told him if it is not right how I treat them, to give them in
charge of somebody else.' Revere, *Tour of Duty*, 74–5, says they were rigor-
ously guarded, the jailers being suspicious and distrustful, going so far as to
threaten to shoot Sutter for the crime of being polite. Marshall, *Statement*,
MS., 2, who was there at the time, says that Sutter allowed the prisoners to
walk about on parole, until Frémont threatened to hang him should any escape. Leese, *Bear Flag*, MS., 16, says also that Sutter called often to encourage them, until Frémont threatened to hang him if he continued his visits.
Vallejo, *Hist. Cal.*, MS., iv. 387–91; v. 128–64, 183, 199–200, speaks of
'Charles,' who was one of the guards at the prison. He had been greatly
befriended by Salvador Vallejo the year before, but 'gratitude has no place in
the Missourian heart.' On one occasion, loaves of bread from Sonoma were
admitted, each of which had a coin in its centre. 'Blue Jacket,' one of the
worst of the guards, died soon after of hydrophobia from the bite of a skunk.
Chas E. Pickett arrived from Oregon during the captivity, and gained Vallejo's life-long friendship by his sympathy and kindness. I have no doubt
that Vallejo exaggerates the cruelty with which they were treated. His
charges are general and indefinite; and those of others are as a rule absurd.
Salvador Vallejo is somewhat more moderate on this topic than on most
others. What troubled him most was the coming of the sentinel each day to
see if the 'damned greasers' were still safe. Hargrave, *Cal. in 1846*, MS., 7,
11, says Vallejo had no cause for complaint, and was very comfortably lodged
at the fort. Osio, *Hist. Cal.*, MS., 465, says Vallejo was treated as he had
treated his southern prisoners at Sonoma—that is, very badly.

was reaping the rewards of long 'coquetting' with the Americans. I have some of the letters written by the captives, which I cite briefly in a note. To the Californians they wrote that all was well with them, urging submission rather than resistance; to others they spoke only of their arbitrary and unjust imprisonment, demanding release or a specification of the charges against them. The absence of complaints of personal ill-treatment has perhaps no significance, as such complaints would not have been allowed to pass. Further correspondence relating to their release will be noticed in due time.[4]

Before returning to Sonoma, let us glance briefly and in chronologic order, first, at events on the Sac-

[4] June 28th, Prudon to José de la Rosa. He and the rest still held. Does not know how long it is to continue. Not allowed to communicate with any one. *Vallejo, Doc.*, MS., xii. 228. July 6th, Vallejo to his brother, José de Jesus V. They are not dead as has been reported. Robt Ridley is named as one of the prisoners. Their situation is not very bad, but indispensable for the new order of things. There is reason to believe there will be an entire change founded in justice, which will raise the country from its miserable condition. They will all be eternally grateful to Sutter for kindness shown. They have been solemnly promised that their persons, property, and families shall be respected. The writer charges his brother to make all this public. *Vallejo, Doc.*, MS., xxxiv. 216. July 6th, W. A. Bartlett, Sonoma, to Vallejo, at whose house he and Dr Henderson are. Mrs V. as cheerful as could be expected. All hoping for his early return. *Id.*, xii. 229. July 10th, V. to Frémont, complaining that F. had not come to see him as he promised. Our imprisonment, 'as you know, has been made more severe, with absolute incommunication since June 16th.' Is it to end now that the U. S. flag is flying over the fort?—insuring as he hopes a prosperous future for his country. Blotter in *Bear Flag Papers*, MS. July 23d, Prudon to Larkin from the 'Prison of the Sacramento,' complaining of an 'unjust, severe, and prolonged imprisonment,' and asking L. to use his influence for their liberation. 'Our situation is most lamentable, and its horrors are augmented by our absolute incommunication, so that we could not know what was passing outside, or others what we were suffering within. I have written a journal, which at the proper time will come to light.' They have received Larkin's letter of the 16th; and they send a representation for Com. Sloat, who is doubtless not aware of their iniquitous treatment. *Larkin, Doc.*, MS., iv. 221-2. July 23d, Vallejo to Larkin of same general purport. Cannot understand why they are still detained now that he has seen the U. S. flag flying. Alludes to the written guaranties given on June 14th, which are still in his possession, and which were violated 'before the ink of the signatures had time to dry.' Their cattle have been driven off during their imprisonment. Spanish, and translation, in *Larkin's Doc*, MS., iv. 219, 223. No date (July 23d?), Vallejo to (Sloat?) giving a brief and clear narrative of their capture and unjust confinement. This account confirms Leese's narrative in all essential parts, though less complete. The writer puts his wrongs in a very strong light, and cannot believe that those wrongs are continued with the knowledge of U. S. officers. Blotter in *Bear Flag Papers*, MS., 63-6.

ramento, and then at occurrences south of the bay during the whole revolutionary period, though some of them have been or will be noticed more fully elsewhere. It was on June 10th that Arce's horses were taken on the Cosumnes. On the 11th Hensley and Reading arrived at the fort from up the river; and this afternoon or the next Merritt and his men left camp for Sonoma. On the 12th or 13th[5] Gillespie arrived from Yerba Buena in the *Portsmouth's* launch, accompanied by several officers of the navy, and bringing a boat-load of supplies for Frémont, proceeding with Hensley in the launch to the American River. Frémont came down with a part of his force, as Gillespie states, on the 13th, encamping near the mouth of the American; while the main body encamped on the 15th, eight or ten miles farther up that stream. The captives taken at Sonoma on the 14th reached Frémont's camp in the afternoon of the 16th. Carson and Merritt started at once for Sutter's, while Hensley and Reading were despatched ostensibly on a hunting tour, but really to talk politics with Marsh, and learn the situation south of the bay.[6] The prisoners were locked up in the fort at nightfall, as we have seen. On the 17th, the supplies having been delivered, Gillespie and Frémont went up the American to join the main body, while the *Portsmouth's* launch started for Sauzalito. The supplies in question were furnished by Montgomery, on the requisition of Frémont as an officer of the United States. It was on its face a perfectly legitimate transaction; and I know of no reason to suppose that Montgomery was informed by Gillespie of the revolutionary project on foot.[7] This same day, the 17th, three men,

---

[5] In *N. Helvetia Diary*, MS., 51, and *Sutter's Diary*, 8, the latter date is given; the former in Gillespie's testimony. *Frémont's Cal. Claims*, 26–7.

[6] The dates, etc., are fixed by the diaries; the motive by Hensley's testimony. *Frémont's Cal. Claims*, 34.

[7] In his letter to Benton, *Niles' Reg.*, lxxi. 191, Frémont says he wrote to Montgomery by the returning launch, 'describing to him fully my position and intentions, in order that he might not by supposing me to be acting under orders from our govt unwittingly commit himself,' etc.

Wise, Ferguson, and Stebbins, arrived at the fort from Sonoma, presumably with news, as they started at once for Frémont's camp. On the 18th a courier came from Sonoma with a letter from Captain Montgomery. Frémont with twenty men visited the fort on the 19th; and José Noriega, a Spaniard from San José, made his appearance and was detained; and next day Vicente Peralta, coming back from a visit up the river, shared the same fate. It was also on the 20th that Hensley and Reading returned from below, hastening to Frémont's camp with the report that Castro was preparing for a hostile movement, a report confirmed by John Neal, who brought news that a force was crossing the bay to attack Sonoma. It was on or about this date that Julio Carrillo arrived and was imprisoned. On the 21st Frémont arrived near the fort; and next day, leaving a small garrison —his company being reënforced by Hensley, Reading, and many trappers and settlers—he marched for Sonoma.[8] On the 23d a party, including Bidwell, was sent toward the Cosumnes to learn whether any foes were approaching from below, and to make arrangements for a watch to be kept by the Indians. Friday the 26th was marked by the arrival of Lieutenant Revere and Dr Henderson of the *Portsmouth*, who came up from Sauzalito on the ship's launch;[9] and also by that of a small party of immigrants from Oregon. Next day Henderson departed for Sonoma with a small party; on the 28th Lieutenant Bartlett and Dr Townsend arrived from Yerba Buena; and on the 29th Bartlett started with Bidwell for Sono-

[8] In his letter to Benton, Frémont, says he broke camp on the American Fork on the 23d. This may mean that after leaving Sutter's he camped at the mouth of that stream and started next morning for Sonoma. Lancey, *Cruise*, 64, confirms this, and speaks of Harrison Peirce coming into camp on the 23d with news of great alarm at Sonoma.

[9] Revere, *Tour of Duty*, 66-75, gives no dates and few details of occurrences from his own observations on this trip. He had an interview with Vallejo, ' which it was easy to see excited a very ridiculous amount of suspicion on the part of his vigilant jailers, whose position, however, as revolutionists was a little ticklish, and excited in them that distrust which in dangerous times is inseparable from low and ignorant minds.'

ma;[10] while Revere returned down the river by boat. It was on July 8th that Robert Ridley was sent up from below and was added to the number of prisoners. It was on July 10th, the day of Frémont's arrival from Sonoma, that news came of the raising of the stars and stripes at Monterey; and next day that flag was raised over Sutter's Fort, of which event more anon.

South of the bay, as we have seen, public attention was directed mainly on the 13th and 14th of June to the taking of Arce's horses; next day came the news that Sonoma was in the hands of American insurgents, and that Vallejo with other officers were prisoners. I find four written records of this news, bearing date of June 15th. The first is a communication from Sub-prefect Guerrero to the prefect. He had received the tidings at Yerba Buena verbally from Joaquin Carrillo, the second alcalde of Sonoma, who had run away when he saw the arrest of Berreyesa, the first alcalde.[11] The second was sent by Justice Estudillo at San Leandro to Alcalde Pacheco at San José. He obtained his information from Rafael Félix, whom Vallejo had despatched as a messenger to his brother Don Jesus, and who had arrived at 11 P. M.[12] The third record is that of an interview on the *Portsmouth* at Sauzalito between Captain Montgomery and José de la Rosa, Lieutenant Bartlett serving as interpreter and secretary. Rosa had been sent by Vallejo—just before the latter started for the Sacramento, though he had not been able to leave

[10] In *Sutter's Diary*, 8, it is stated that Bartlett 'organized the garrison,' which is unintelligible. After Bidwell's departure the diary at New Helvetia was practically suspended until May 1847.

[11] June 15, 1846, Guerrero to Castro. *Castro, Doc.*, MS., ii. 115. The party that took Sonoma was composed of 70 men under the 'Doctor of the Sacramento,' and another man whom Salvador Vallejo knew from once having had a quarrel with him (Merritt).

[12] June 15, 1846, Estudillo to Pacheco, in *Doc. Hist. Cal.*, MS., iii. 258. He wrote also to the prefect at the same time. This report was that the prisoners, guarded by 12 men under Merritt, had passed the rancho of Cayetano Juarez en route for Feather River.

Sonoma until 3 P. M.—to inform Montgomery of what
had occurred, "and to ask of him to exercise his
authority or use his influence to prevent the commission of acts of violence, inasmuch as they seemed to
be without any effectual head or authority; and to
this end he hoped for an officer to be sent to the
place, or a letter that would have the effect of saving
the helpless inhabitants from violence and anarchy."
The captain's response, which Rosa promised to deliver to Vallejo at the earliest possible moment, was
to disavow in the most explicit terms any knowledge
of or authority for the movement on the part of the
United States, of himself, or even of Frémont; to declare that he could not officially interfere in any manner with local, political, or criminal affairs in no way
concerning his government; but to proffer personal
sympathy and express his willingness to exert his
individual influence for the protection of innocent
persons.[13]

Besides the message sent back by Rosa, Montgomery decided to send an officer as requested. He
selected Lieutenant John S. Misroon for the mission,
and his instructions given on the evening of the 15th,
with a supplement next morning, form the fourth of
the records to which I have alluded. Misroon, being
fully informed respecting Rosa's report and the reply
that had been given, was directed to visit the insurgent leader; to make known the "state of apprehen-
sion and terror" into which the Californian people had
been thrown by the late movement; to "request from
me that he will extend his protecting care over the
defenceless families of their prisoners and other inoffensive persons of Sonoma;" to impress the minds of
those in power "with a sense of the advantages which
will accrue to their cause, whatever its intrinsic merits
may be, from pursuing a course of kind and benevolent

[13] June 15, 1846, record of interview. Copy of original by Bartlett.
Rosa said there were 80 men in the party; otherwise his version was a very
accurate one. Montgomery in his reply expressed a belief that there was
no danger of violence to non-combatants. *Bear Flag Papers*, MS., 46–9.

treatment of prisoners" and of the Californians generally; and finally, to explain his mission fully to the civil
authorities of Sonoma, conveying to them such assurances as he might have obtained from the insurgents,
but avoiding any discussion or remarks respecting the
merits of the revolt.[14]   The lieutenant was conveyed
across the bay in the ship's boat, reached Sonoma late
on the 16th, remained until the next noon, and at sunset of the 17th was back at the ship.   Of his experience
at Sonoma I shall have more to say later; but his report was most reässuring, being to the effect that the
insurgents intended no violence to the persons or property of non-combatants; that the "utmost harmony and
good order prevailed in camp;" and that Vallejo was
held merely as a hostage.[15]   Before Misroon's departure William L. Todd had arrived as a courier from
Ide direct to Montgomery; and he went back in the
same boat with Misroon.

The tidings from the north of course spread rapidly in the next few days, and were the topic of many
communications, both among natives and foreigners.[16]

[14] June 15th, 16th, Montgomery's instructions to Misroon.   Bartlett's original copy in *Bear Flag Papers*, MS., 50–2.
[15] June 18, 1846, Misroon's report to Montgomery. *Bear Flag Papers*,
MS., 53–7.   The report included a copy of Ide's proclamation, and described
the *flag*.
[16] June 16, 1846, Capt. Montgomery to Larkin, giving a brief account of the
affair at Sonoma, as reported by Rosa and Todd. *Larkin's Doc.*, MS., iv. 158.
Prefect Castro to alcaldes.   Tells the news, and orders a meeting of ayunt.,
that the people may be called to arms. *Castro, Doc.*, MS., ii. 117.   Gen.
Castro to alcalde S. José.   Is adopting measures to resist the foreign invasion which has begun. *S. José, Arch., Loose Papers*, MS., 47.   Gen. Castro
to his soldiers.   Refers to the Sonoma outrage.   Trusts they will march enthusiastically to break the chain that is being wound about them. *Dept. St.
Pap.*, MS., vii. 58–9.   June 17th, Leidesdorff at Yerba Buena to Larkin.
Gives no details, as Montgomery has written.   Gillespie will probably be
back in a few days.   Castro is at Sta Cruz preparing to go up the Sacramento
and put things right.   The writer is very bitter against Capt. Hinckley, who
is a Mexican at heart, and who has said 'the Californians are fools if they do
not at once take the same number of Americans prisoners.'   (Hinckley died a
few days later.) *Larkin's Doc.*, MS., iv. 160.   Same day, Leidesdorff's receipt
for $36.25 from U. S. consul for a messenger giving the news. *Monterey, Con-
sulate Arch.*, MS., ii. 19.   Fran. Arce to Manuel Castro from Sta Clara.
The hour of the country's suffering has now arrived.   They are invaded on
all sides. *Castro, Doc.*, MS., ii. 122.   Prefect Castro to min. of rel.   Invasion of the northern frontier by Frémont, aided by the commander of the
Portsmouth.   All that is possible being done for defence.   Hopes Mexico will
not abandon Cal. *Id.*, ii. 121.   June 18th, Larkin to sec. state.   Does not

The current ideas of what had happened were, as a rule, tolerably accurate. It was understood that Frémont was at the bottom of the movement; and this led many of the Californians to believe erroneously that he acted under instructions from the government at Washington, and that Montgomery, especially as he had just sent a boat-load of supplies to Frémont, was also in the plot. The reported raising of a strange and unheard-of flag by the insurgents was alarming to many of the natives, but much less so than if it had not been supposed that the bear and star were but a temporary substitute for the stars and stripes. Even Americans were disposed to think that Frémont was acting under instructions, else their surprise would have been much greater.

The first measure of defence, naturally from a Mexican standpoint, was a patriotic proclamation. General Castro issued two of them on June 17th from his headquarters at Santa Clara. I reproduce them in a note.[17] The first was an appeal to the Californians to

know if the reports are true or not. Frémont and Gillespie suspected of being at the root of the matter. Many believe the U. S. consul has known of the plans all along. *Larkin's Off. Corresp.*, MS., ii. 65-6. June 19th, Leidesdorff to Larkin. Gives an account from 'the only authentic sources.' No disorders at Sonoma. Full guaranties. All property taken paid for, etc. *Id.*, *Doc.*, MS., iv. 167. June 20th, Montgomery to Leidesdorff. Is surprised to learn by his letter that 200 men have been collected to oppose the insurgents. The launch has returned from Frémont. The prisoners were taken to his camp by the request of Vallejo. Frémont's neutral position did not allow his taking charge of them, so they were removed to Sutter's, where they are detained as hostages. Sutter has joined the insurgents. The insurgent force must have increased considerably. Doubts that they can easily be surprised. The men know how to use their arms. 'My position, you know, is neutral. I am a mere observer of passing events...I know no way consistently with this view of doing what you name, but feel not much concerned on that account, for reasons before stated.' Shall move to Yerba Buena (from Sauzalito) next week, if it be found expedient.' *Fitch, Doc.*, MS., 394.

[17] The original of the first is found in *Dept. St. Pap.*, MS., vii. 239, apparently in Arce's writing with Castro's signature. In respect of style, grammar, and orthography, it is very bad, defying literal translation. I have found no original or Spanish copy of the 2d proclamation. Three sets of translations are extant: one, inaccurate in some respects, in the *Monterey Californian*, Sept. 12, 1846; and *S. F. Californian*, June 5, 1847; another, slightly corrected, in *Bryant's What I Saw in Cal.*, 293-4, followed with slight changes in *Lancey's Cruise*, 62-3; *Marin Co. Hist.*, 77-8, and other local histories; and a third was that made for Larkin from the original, more nearly literal than the others, in *Larkin's Off. Corresp.*, MS., ii. 70-1; *Sawyer's Doc.*, MS., 52,

fight in defence of their country; and the second a promise of protection to all foreign residents taking no part in the revolt. Both documents were of the type usually employed in such cases by officers of Latin race—and by many of other races—to arouse the patriotism of those under their command, and to 'save their responsibility' with superiors. They were in substance what circumstances required, and by no means so absurdly bombastic as it has been the fashion to regard them. It is true that the outrage at Sonoma was attributed to the 'contemptible policy' of the United States; but Castro had every reason to suppose Frémont to be acting under instructions, and had this been so, the policy, in connection with the recent acts and utterances of Larkin and other agents of their government, would have been indeed 'contemptible.'

60–1. The following version varies slightly here and there from either of the three:

'The citizen José Castro, lieut-col. of cavalry in the Mexican army, and comandante general ad interim of the department of Californias. Fellow-citizens: The contemptible policy of the agents of the government of the U. S. of the north has induced a number of adventurers, regardless of the rights of men, to boldly undertake an invasion, by possessing themselves of the town of Sonoma, and taking by surprise the military commander of that frontier, Col. Don M. G. Vallejo, Lieut-col. Don Victor Prudon, Capt. Don Salvador Vallejo, and Mr Jacob P. Leese. Fellow-countrymen: The defence of our liberty, of the religion of our fathers, and of our independence impels us to sacrifice ourselves rather than lose these inestimable blessings. Banish from your hearts all petty resentments; turn and behold those families and children unfortunately in the hands of our foes—snatched from the bosoms of their fathers, who are prisoners among foreigners, and who loudly call on us for succor. There is yet time for us to rise en masse, irresistible and just. Doubt not that divine providence will guide us to glory. Nor should you doubt that in this headquarters, notwithstanding the smallness of the garrison, the first to sacrifice himself will be your fellow-citizen and friend, José Castro. Headquarters at Sta Clara, June 17, 1846.'

'The citizen José Castro, etc. All foreigners residing among us, occupied in their business, may rest assured of protection from all authorities of the department so long as they take no part in revolutionary movements. The comandancia in my charge will never proceed lightly against any person whatever, neither will it be influenced by mere words without proofs; declarations shall be taken, proof exacted, and the liberty and rights of the laborious, ever commendable, shall be protected. Let the fortune of war take its chance with those ungrateful persons who with arms in their hands have attacked the country, forgetting that in former times they were treated by the undersigned with his characteristic indulgence. Impartial inhabitants of the dept are witnesses to the truth of this. I have nothing to fear; duty leads me to death or victory. I am a Mexican soldier, and I will be free and independent, or die with pleasure for those inestimable blessings. José Castro,' etc.

Prefect Manuel Castro coöperated with the general in his efforts to prepare for defence, as did the different alcaldes to some extent; but the response on the part of the people was not a very hearty one. With considerable difficulty Castro succeeded in increasing his force to about one hundred and sixty in ten days; a force organized in three divisions under the command of J. A. Carrillo, Joaquin de la Torre, and Manuel Castro respectively.[18]   It was his inten-

[18] Castro in a letter to Pico on June 25th gives 160 as the total of his force. *Castro, Doc.*, MS., ii. 127.   There is no other definite contemporary record on the subject.   I give the following résumé of correspondence:
June 17, 1846, Gen. Castro to Pico.   An earnest appeal for P.'s coöperation.   All resentment should be dropped.   Let us act together, and give an example of patriotism.   *Dept. St. Pap.*, MS., vii. 60–1, 119.   June 17th, bando posted by Alcalde Escamilla of Monterey.   All subordinate local officials must call upon the citizens to rise.   Every one having horses must contribute them by 10 o'clock to-morrow, also supplying arms, etc., as they can.   A record to be kept of all contributions and receipts to be given.   *Dept. St. Pap., Mont.*, MS., iii. 121–2.   June 17th, Sub-prefect Guerrero to alcalde of S. José, describing the 'bear flag,' and warning against dangers at S. José.   *S. José, Arch., Loose Pap.*, MS., 37.   June 19th, Manuel Castro leaves Monterey with citizens for S. Juan to take part in the campaign.   *Dept. St. Pap.*, MS., vii. 29.   June 21st, Castro to Pico, urging him to come north with all the force he can raise.   If he will not do it, let him say so at once, so that time and men may not be wasted in sending despatches.   *Id.*, vii. 56–7.   Leidesdorff to Larkin.   Sutter has joined the rebels.   'I am told that some of the Californians have driven all their horses off to the coast, so that Castro will not get them.'   *Larkin's Doc.*, MS., iv. 171.   Larkin to U. S. consul at Honolulu. Sends his wife and children for protection.   The Californians talk of seizing him; and at any rate, war has broken out.   *Id., Off. Corresp.*, MS., i. 116. June 22d, Prefect Castro to alcalde of S. José.   Is coöperating with the general.   The citizen who makes excuses is a traitor.   Volunteer companies of 50 men may choose their officers.   Our homes must be defended.   *S. José, Arch., Loose Pap.*, MS., 28.   June 23d, same to same.   Let the men march to Sta Clara at once.   *Id.*, 59.   Let fire-arms be collected at the ranchos.   *Id.*, 26. To Pedro Chaboya.   Let a list be sent him of those making excuses.   *Id.*, 35. June 24th, Larkin to sec. state.   Castro has 200 men at Sta Clara; got but few from Monterey.   No news of any increase in Ide's forces.   Castro will probably not go north.   *Sawyer's Doc.*, MS., 55–7.   June 24th, a messenger paid $65 for carrying expresses from Monterey to S. José and to Leidesdorff and to Montgomery.   *Monterey, Consulate Arch.*, MS., ii. 15.   Same date, letter to the *Honolulu Friend*, iv. 169–70, from a Yerba Buena correspondent, giving a very good account of what had occurred, including Castro's proclamation, and Misroon's visit to Sonoma.   He says that Ide and Castro are said to have each about 150 men.   Forty or 50 of Castro's men crossed the bay to-day (or perhaps on the 23d), and a fight will soon occur.   June 25th, Manuel Castro to Pico, 'en route for Sonoma.'   Has been to Sta Cruz to get horses and stir up the people.   Second division organized and on the march.   Urges Pico to render aid.   *Dept. St. Pap.*, MS., vii. 10.   Same date, Gen. Castro to Pico, 160 men moving on Sonoma.   He is marching in the rear and organizing a reserve force to guard against a repulse.   Frémont with 400 (!) riflemen on his way to protect Sonoma.   Pico has now a chance to immortalize his name if he will but listen to Castro's advice.   *Castro, Doc.*, MS., ii. 127; *Dept.*

tion to send the three divisions across the bay to attack Ide's garrison.   To this end Torre with his fifty or sixty men did cross from San Pablo to Point Quintin probably in the evening of June 23d, employing for that purpose the launch belonging to the owner of the rancho.   The other divisions under Carrillo and Castro also followed a day or two later as far as San Pablo, but did not attempt to cross.   Why not, is not altogether clear.   Lack of boats is given as the reason by some, and by others cowardice on the part of the leaders.   Either of these motives would certainly have been quite as strong in the case of Torre as in that of the others.   The truth is apparently that the crossing, to be followed by a combined attack on Sonoma, was to take place either on a fixed day, or on a day to be fixed by Torre; but before the arrival of the day, or before any communication from Don Joa-

St. Pap., MS., vii. 67.   Rafael Pinto ordered to report for duty at headquarters.   Id., Ben. Cust.-H., vi. 679.   June 26th, prefect to alcalde.   All citizens must at once become soldiers.   S. José, Arch., Loose Pap., MS., 26.   June 30th, Leidesdorff to Larkin.   If the Portsmouth were not here, he would have to run away, since Hinckley has advised his arrest.   H. and Ridley are 'more Mexicans than the Mexicans themselves.   However, they will get their just due one of these days.'   Larkin's Doc., MS., iv. 189.   June 30th, Larkin to U. S. consul at Honolulu.   Has received a letter from Pico, who blames him; 'but the most I could do would be to act like his Excellency and issue a proclamation....I am dreaming of trying to persuade the Californians to call on the commodore for protection, hoist his flag, and be his countrymen, or the Bears may destroy them.'   Id., Off. Corresp., MS., i. 125.   June 30th, Leidesdorff to Larkin.   S. Rafael taken; 150 insurgents there and 50 at Sonoma. Castro was to have crossed yesterday from S. Pablo.   If he did, it is 'all up with him.'   Torre was also to have attacked Sonoma yesterday.   Bidwell in command at Sutter's.   Reading, Hensley, and all the rest are coming to join the force.   Id., Doc., MS., iv. 189.   June 30th, Gen. Castro to Pico.   Back at Sta Clara; and reports Torre's retreat and that of the other divisions (as explained in my text).   A council of war has decided to send Manual Castro as a comisionado to the gov.   A new plan of operations must be formed.   The insurgents are being rapidly reënforced.   Blotter in Castro, Doc., MS., ii. 131. Same document, dated July 1st.   Dept. St. Pap., MS., vii. 67–8.   July 2d, Castro (Sta Clara) to Ábrego.   Must try to negotiate a loan, pledging lands of S. Juan, S. José, and Sta Clara.   Id., xiii. 14–15.   July 2d, Montgomery to Larkin.   The insurgents have come to Yerba Buena and taken Ridley prisoner.   The country is undoubtedly theirs without much more trouble.   In 15 days they will be in your midst.   A letter from Castro to Torre was intercepted, directing him to kill every American and Englishman that fell into his hands.   The men are very bitter against Castro.   Larkin's Doc., MS., iv. 192.   July 4th, L. to U. S. consul at Honolulu.   Explains Castro's former plan of campaign—that is, to join his three divisions with the natives north of the bay and to surprise Ide's garrison.   Id., Off. Corresp., MS., i. 125.

quin could be obtained, that officer himself recrossed
the bay in retreat, reporting that the insurgent force
was too strong to be attacked with any hope of success.   Torre's experience on the north side will be
narrated in the next chapter.   His return was on the
29th, on which date all three divisions were back at
the San Lorenzo rancho; and next day at the old
headquarters at Santa Clara.   A council of war determined that the old plan of operations must be
abandoned, and that a new one must include the
coöperation of Pico and his southern forces.   Manuel
Castro was chosen as the man most likely to bring
Don Pio to his senses and to effect a reconciliation;
and a few days later with a small escort he started on
his mission, meeting the governor at Santa Inés.
Meanwhile the general moved with his army southward to San Juan, where he was on July 8th, when
news came that Monterey was in the hands of the
Americans—news that sent Don José in some haste
still farther southward.

Besides the not very brilliant achievements of Castro's army, and the correspondence of which I have
given a résumé, there is but little to be noted during
the revolutionary period of what happened in the
central districts.   On July 1st and 2d, San Francisco
was twice visited by insurgent parties from across the
bay, one of which spiked the guns in the abandoned
fort, and another took Robert Ridley from his house
at Yerba Buena, carrying him as a prisoner to the Sacramento.   This was doubtless done at the instigation of
Leidesdorff, whose sympathy for the revolutionists was
unconcealed, and who was very bitter against Ridley
and Hinckley, who, being Mexican officials, did not
agree with the vice-consul's views.   Hinckley escaped
arrest by having died a day or two before.   Another
arrest of these times was that of Charles M. Weber
with two others, Washburn and Burt, at San José, by
Castro.   Little is known of this affair beyond the fact
that Weber was arrested and carried south as a pris-

oner. According to a current account, supposed to emanate from himself, Weber, having heard of the Sonoma revolt on June 19th by a letter from Lieutenant Bartlett, went to Yerba Buena, and thence across to San Rafael, where he had an interview with Frémont, and by that officer's advice returned to the vicinity of San José to raise a force secretly for the protection of American families in that region, at the same time inviting Fallon of Santa Cruz to raise a force and join him. It was while thus employed that he was arrested, his life being spared only because of Castro's personal friendship. Weber had previously declined a commission as captain of auxiliaries in the Californian army.[19] There is no reason to doubt that Weber and others may have attempted an organization for self-protection; holding themselves in readiness for the results likely to spring from the revolt, which, however, many of them did not approve. It was a current idea among the Californians that Montgomery was permitting his officers with the *Ports-*

[19] *S. José Pioneer*, March 6, 1880; *Tinkham's Hist. Stockton*, 101. June 23d, Weber to alcalde of S. José, declining appointment of captain on account of his business relations with foreigners. In *Halleck's Mex. Land Laws*, MS. June 17th, sub-prefect Guerrero to S. José alcalde. By loud talk of foreigners he has learned that 40 of them are ready to capture S. José, while others do the same thing here at Yerba Buena. Great precautions should be taken. Is not pleased that the son of Ide goes about as he pleases at the pueblo. *S. José, Arch., Loose Pap.*, MS., 37. June 27th, no place or writer's name. The 25 armed foreigners at Sta Cruz intended to start this A. M. It is not known whether they will pass this way, or, as would be more prudent, go to the Sacramento. *Id.*, 39. According to the *Pioneer*, Fallon arrived the day after Weber's arrest. Flores, *Recuerdos*, MS., 10–26, claims to have learned from Mrs Buelna of Weber's hostile plans and concealed weapons, and to have given Castro the information which led to his arrest. Ide, *Biog. Sketch*, 154, says that over 100 had secretly organized under Weber, Bird, and others on the south side of the bay.

Accounts of Castro's preparations by men who took part in them are given in *Pinto, Apunt.*, MS., 101–2; *Ezquer, Mem.*, MS., 23–5; *German, Sucesos*, MS., 24; *Torre, Remin.*, MS., 145–52; *Buelna, Notas*, MS., 22–3; *Castro, Rel.*, MS., 184–95; *Arce, Mem.*, 55, etc.; *Alvarado, Hist. Cal.*, MS., v. 188–202, 229–30, etc.; but these writers add little or nothing to what is revealed in contemporary corresp. Several state that men were forced into the ranks; that they suffered much from hunger; and that Castro made many enemies by his selfishness. It appears that Ex-gov. Alvarado took a prominent part in a private capacity in the warlike preparations. Pablo de la Guerra, *Doc. Hist. Cal.*, MS., iv. 1304, gives some personal items on the subject. C. P. Briggs, in *Napa Reporter*, Aug. 24, 1872, narrates the services of the schooner *Mermaid* at Yerba Buena in conveying volunteers to Sonoma.

mouth's boats to aid the insurgents; but though the sympathies of the naval officers were clearly shown in their correspondence, there is no proof that they were remiss in duty.[20]

Governor Pico was at Santa Bárbara, engaged in making ready for a march against Castro, when on June 23d, by a *violento extraordinario* from Monterey, he received the prefect's communication of the 19th making known the taking of Sonoma. He immediately issued a proclamation, which I append in a note.[21]

[20] Osio, *Hist. Cal.*, MS., 466-7, states that the *Portmouth's* boats were engaged in preventing the crossing of the Californians. Torre, *Remin.*, MS., 145-6, says that Torre on his retreat was pursued by Montgomery's boats. In several communications between Californian officials, their belief in Montgomery's coöperation is manifest. Lancey, *Cruise*, 72-3, quotes from James W. Marshall an account more amusing than probable, to the effect that when the rebels applied on the *Portsmouth* for ammunition, they were met with an indignant refusal; but were told where a large quantity of powder would be put on shore to dry. By a pretended surprise, they overcame the guard and took the powder, whereupon the ship went through the form of firing four guns in their direction!

[21] 'The constitutional governor of the dept of Californias addresses to its inhabitants the following proclamation: Fellow-citizens: The national honor being gravely wounded and compromised in the highest degree at the present time, I have the glory of raising my voice to you, in the firm persuasion that you are Mexicans, that there burns in your veins the blood of those venerable martyrs of the country, and that you will not fail to shed it in defence of her liberty and independence. At this moment your dept. govt has received the unfortunate news, officially communicated by the political authorities of Monterey, and dated four days ago, that a gang of North American adventurers, with the blackest treason that the spirit of evil could invent, have invaded the town of Sonoma, raising their flag, and carrying off as prisoners four Mexican citizens. Yes, fellow-citizens; and who of you on hearing of such fatal perfidy will not quit the domestic hearth, and fly, gun in hand, to the field of honor to avenge the country's honor? Will you be insensible to the oppression in which masters so vile wish to put us? Will the grievous groans of the country not move you? Will you, with serene brow, see destroyed the fundamental pact of our sacred and dear institutions? No! No! Far from me every such suspicion! I do not believe from your patriotism, your blind love of country, that you will permit the beneficent and fruitful tree of sacred liberty to be profaned. The North American nation can never be our friend. She has laws, religion, language, and customs totally opposed to ours. False to the most loyal friendship which Mexico has lavished upon her, to international law, and to the soundest policy, putting in execution her piratical schemes, she has stolen the dept of Texas, and wishes to do the same with that of Cal.—thus to iniquitously dismember the Mexican territory, to tarnish the flag of the *tres garantías* and raise her own, increasing the number of its fatal stars. Fly, Mexicans, in all haste in pursuit of the treacherous foe; follow him to the farthest wilderness; punish his audacity; and in case we fail, let us form a cemetery where posterity may remember to the glory of Mexican history the heroism of her sons, as is remembered the glory won by the death of that little band of citizens posted at the Pass of Thermopylæ under Gen-

The document was much more violent and bombastic in style than that of Castro in the north. The writer evidently had other objects in view than the ordinary one of 'saving his responsibility' with his subjects and superiors, among which extraordinary objects the defeat of insurgents held but a subordinate place. He did not entirely believe in the Sonoma revolt, being disposed to regard it as in some way a device of his rival to justify his own military preparations and assumption of special powers. He was glad, however, by the fervor and ultra Mexicanism of his proclamation to show his zeal at the national capital as an offset to Castro's probable accusations there. He also hoped, by his violent denunciations of the United States and of Americans, to advance his own scheme of an appeal to England. But above all, he desired to create a popular excitement which should largely increase the force with which he was about to march north, thus enabling him to defeat the general and control the future of the country so far as any Californian could control it. This view of the matter is clearly expressed in a subsequent letter written by Don Pio to prominent citizens of Los Angeles in defence of his proclamation.[22] As to the general's ap-

eral Leonidas. Hear their motto: "Stranger, say to Lacedemonia that we have died here obeying her laws." Shall we not imitate this noble example? Shall we consent that the northern republic bring to our soil of liberty the horrible slavery permitted in its States? Shall we suffer human blood sold at a price for vile gain? And finally, must we see profaned the august image of the crucified and the dogmas of our sacred religion? Foreign citizens who tread this soil, the dept. govt considers you under the protection of the laws and treaties. Your property will be respected; nobody will molest you; and as you also are interested in preserving peace and security, the govt invites you to the punishment of the bandits who have invaded the north of this dept. Compatriots, run swiftly with me to crown your brows with the fresh laurels of unfading glory; in the fields of the north they are scattered, ready to spring to your noble foreheads. Respond gladly, Mexicans, to the desires of your fellow-citizen and friend, Pio Pico. Sta Bárbara, June 23, 1846.' Copy from Secretary Moreno's original blotter, in *Moreno, Doc.*, MS., 30-2; copy from original, presented to the society by A. B. Thompson in 1865, in *Cal. Pioneers, Arch.*, MS., 149-56; translation by Lieut Bartlett in *Bear Flag Papers*, MS., 22-4; translation in *Sawyer's Doc.*, MS., 62-5.

[22] June 27th, Pico to Requena, Figueroa, et al., in *Moreno, Doc.*, MS., 33-40. 'Both Mexicans and resident foreigners know the extreme egotism that generally rules hearts; and while they know the imminent danger which threatens us, rather from within than from without, they know also who is the au-

peals of these days to forget past resentments and unite for the country's defence, it does not appear that the governor made any reply to them.   On the 23d and following days he wrote several communications, in which he appealed to the patriotism of citizens, summoned the members of the assembly to Santa Bárbara, and above all urged the sending-forward of men and munitions for his expedition to the north.[23]

The response to Pico's appeals in the south was not more satisfactory than that to Castro's in the north. Not more than a dozen or fifteen men were sent from Los Angeles, after much correspondence.   There was difficulty even in finding guards to preserve order in the city.   On Pico's departure from the capital the foreign residents had taken upon themselves that duty, and had rendered most effectual service; but now, having no wish to serve under Pico in the north, especially when it might become necessary to fight against their countrymen, they chose to be offended at the governor's denunciation of Americans, and threatened to leave the city to the protection of native citizens. Alarmed by the disaffection of the foreigners, prominent men sent to Pico their protests against the tone

thor of so many evils, and are aware of the many appeals which the govt has made to end them.   And what has the govt obtained but insult and outrage upon outrage?   Is is not true that he found great aid in the proceedings of the foreigners to carry his point with the natives? and that for this reason 50 Barbareños were eager to march north under the gov., while before not one would enlist?   The govt is by no means ignorant that it is impossible for us to repel the invasion of foreigners should they attempt one; but with the force now volunteering, we can march without fear to the north and punish the audacity of the com. gen., the cause of all our misfortunes.   Can you doubt that had it not been for the affair of the foreigners the general might already have triumphed over the govt. in these parts?   At the head of 70 men well supplied with all resources he was marching toward these towns, aided by men to be feared for their devotedness to vengeance.   The news about the Americans made him change his route, and here we have the old saying applicable, "No hay mal que por bien no venga."

[23] June 23, 1846, Pico to sub-prefect of Angeles.   He is to march at once with the alcaldes and 50 men.   The northern adventurers must be taught a lesson. *Dept. St. Pap.*, MS., vii. 29–30.   June 23d–24th, Pico appoints several officers to serve among the defensores.   J. P. Ayala, Luis Arenas, and José Fernandez, captains. *Id.*, vii. 33, 35, 36–7.   June 23d, Pico to Figueroa. Trusts that he and the other diputados will come immediately. *Id.*, vii. 28. June 23d, Pico to Bandini.   A patriotic effusion, announcing the news and the duty of all Californians. *Bandini, Doc.*, MS., 79.

of his proclamation, going so far as to advance the theory that the revolutionists of Sonoma were really acting in the governor's interest and against Castro. This theory Don Pio could not accept, claiming that Manuel Castro could not have been thus deceived; but after defending his proclamation at some length, both on general principles and on the special plea that I have cited, he offered to withdraw the document if it had not already been published—as it had.[24] To what extent the Americans allowed themselves to be conciliated by the excuses of the Angelinos and Pico's assurances that he had intended no menace or disrespect to them, is not exactly known; but it is certain that neither they nor any great number of the natives could be induced to engage in any other military service than such as was necessary for the protection of their town and ranchos.

Nor did the members of the assembly obey Pico's summons to Santa Bárbara, even when he on June 29th sent a very earnest appeal, launching the "anath-

[24] June 26th, Coronel to Moreno. Doubts have been thrown on the genuineness of the proclamation in order not to lose the services of the foreigners. *Moreno, Doc.*, MS., 22. June 27th, Pico to Requena, Figueroa, Stearns, Botello, and Gallardo, in reply to their communication of June 25th. *Id.*, 33–40. June 29th, Bandini to P. A long protest against his inconsiderate declaration of the 23d, which had created no enthusiasm, had offended over 100 of the most influential men in Cal., and might precipitate Mexico into a war for which she is not ready. The act of a few men at Sonoma does not justify the term 'bandits' applied to all Americans. *Bandini, Doc.*, MS., 80. June 25th, Botello to Moreno. The proclamation has shattered all our hopes by offending the foreigners. We do not believe in any foreign invasion at the north. *Moreno, Doc.*, MS., 18–20. June 28th, Coronel to Moreno. The foreigners have now learned that the proclamation is genuine—it had been disputed at first—and have retired to their homes much offended. *Id.*, 29. June 30th, Wilson to Bandini, denouncing the proclamation, and claiming that the Sonoma insurgents were acting in Pico's interests. *Bandini, Doc.*, MS., 81. July 1st, Bandini wishes Pico to send trusty men to the north to learn the motives of the insurgents and the general state of affairs. *Id.*, 82. July 8th, Botello to Moreno. Has no faith in a successful resistance. The popular sentiment is against the tone of the proclamation as too severe. *Moreno, Doc.*, MS., 15–17 Botello, *Anales*, MS., 135–7, gives a good account of Los Angeles affairs at this period.

June 24th–9th, miscellaneous corresp. between Sub-prefect Stearns, Alcalde Cota, and others, concerning the measures necessary for the country's defence. Most of the items seem to refer to the preservation of order at the capital rather than to the sending of reënforcements to Pico. *Dept. St. Pap.*, MS., vii. 9–10, 86, 89, 121, 124; *Id., Angeles*, viii. 68; *Moreno, Doc.*, MS., 21; *Coronel, Doc.*, MS., 135–7.

ema of the country against those who do not come
to its defence," and "holding you responsible before
God and the nation if under trivial pretences you do
not set out at once." There are some indications that
the governor still had hopes of securing a meeting of
the consejo general, before which body he had a secret
project to urge. The assembly was convened to consider Pico's request, backed up by eight documents
on the Sonoma revolt; and by Francisco de la Guerra
and Joaquin Carrillo, who had come as comisionados;
but the decision reached was that their presence was
not necessary at Santa Bárbara, especially as Pico
would be absent on his expedition; that more complete information was needed respecting affairs in the
north; and that under the circumstances a weekly
mail should be established![25]

Meanwhile Don Pio went on with his warlike preparations in spite of the Angelinos' lukewarmness in
the cause. He also wrote a letter to Consul Larkin
on June 29th, complaining in bitter terms of what
Americans had done at Sonoma; announcing his suspicion that the government of the United States was
concerned in the acts, which "have the appearance of
downright robbery;" blaming the consul for not having interfered in some way to prevent such scandalous
proceedings; and hoping that for the honor of his nation he would promptly make a satisfactory explanation. Larkin in reply denied that he as consul had
any influence over the Americans who had broken the
laws at Sonoma; and that his government was in any
way concerned. In fulfilment of his duty, he had proffered his aid to the general and prefect, by whom it
had been refused.[26] Not much is recorded of the gov-

[25] June 29th–July 14th, miscellaneous records on the convoking and acts
of the assembly. Some fault was found by Bandini and others with the tone
adopted by Pico toward the assembly. *Dept. St. Pap.*, MS., viii. 112–13,
117–18, 122; vii. 12–13, 90–1; *Id., Pref. y Juzg.*, ii. 162; *Leg. Rec.*, MS., iv.
358–62; *Bandini, Doc.*, MS., 83. Even Guerra, a member residing at Sta B.,
declined to attend the session on pretext of illness. *Dept. St. Pap.*, MS., vii.
121.

[26] June 29, 1846, P. to L. English translation in *Larkin's Off. Corresp.*,

ernor's last days at Santa Bárbara; but it appears
that by the beginning of July he had about 100 men
ready for the march, most of whom were despatched
immediately under Captain Andrés Pico.   Don Pio
followed on or about July 6th, and two days later was
at Santa Inés.   Here Manuel Castro met him, having been sent by the general to effect a reconciliation,
as already stated, and having passed Don Andrés with
his advance force at Los Álamos.   The prefect, as
chief civil authority in the north, as a partisan of Pico
in most of the past controversies, and as a near relation of both chiefs, was by far the most effective me-
diator that could have been employed.   Don Manuel
worked hard to make the governor understand the
true position of affairs, to show that reported dangers
were real and not mere pretences on the general's part,
to explain the absolute necessity of united action, and,
most potent argument of all, to make clear to Don Pio
the unenviable position he must occupy in the eyes of
all Californians and Mexicans should he allow his resentment to outweigh his patriotism at such a time.
Pico was convinced against his will, not that Castro

MS., ii. 167; *Sawyer's Doc.*, MS., 65–8; *Soulé's Annals of S. F.*, 93–5; *Dunbar's Romance*, 34–6; *Lancey's Cruise*, 71.   July 5th, L. to P. *Larkin's Off.
Corresp.*, MS., ii. 132; *Sawyer's Doc.*, MS., 68–70.   Larkin seems disposed to
fan Pico's feeling against Castro, not only by claiming that he had refused his
aid, but by implying that the gen. might easily have retaken Sonoma, and
also that if he would have furnished men Larkin would have captured an
equal number of Americans to hold as hostages for the good treatment of Vallejo and the others.

   June 27th, Pico's bando, requiring great precautions and a strict enforcement of the passport regulations. *S. Luis Ob., Arch.*, MS., 9–10.   June 28th,
gov. to sub-prefect, urging that the 50 men under Gallardo be sent at once.
He has only 68 men, mostly raw recruits—not enough for his expedition.
Dept. St. Pap., MS., vii. 30.   June 30th, Sta Bárbara, the Spanish consul
will advise all of his nation to place their lives and property in security in
view of foreign invasion. *Id.*, vii. 37.   July 2d, Moreno to Andrés Pico.   A
most bombastic letter.   Bloody battle-fields, dying for the country, etc.   Gallardo is on his march with 13 'columns' (one man in a column?) from Angeles.
Pico and the writer will start Monday. *Pico, Doc.*, MS., ii. 89.   July 3d, J.
M. Flores to Pico.   Has no doubt that Cal. is to share the fate of Texas.   Refers to Ide's proclamation.   There is no doubt that supplies are furnished by
the U. S. men-of-war.   The consul has publicly declared that the U. S. will
get Cal. *Dept. St. Pap.*, MS., vii. 68–9.   July 3d, Pico to Capt. Ayala.   Orders to march to join Andrés Pico. *Id.*, viii. 136.   July 8th, Pico at Sta Inés
to Sub-prefect Stearns.   Declares traitors all who do not enlist for the country's
defence. *Id.*, vii. 34.

was acting in good faith, but that his officers and men could not be depended on to fight the general; and at last he reluctantly promised to forget past dissensions, and to unite with Castro against the foreigners.[27] Then they marched northward until the two armies met on or about July 12th at the Santa Margarita rancho, near San Luis Obispo. Castro brought news that Monterey had been taken by naval officers of the United States; the governor and general gave each other a public but not very cordial embrace of reconciliation; and all turned mournfully toward the capital to devise new plans of resistance to *los extrangeros.* I shall follow them later.

[27] *Castro, Servicios Pub.*, MS.; *Id., Relacion*, MS., 201--6.

CHAPTER VII.

BEAR FLAG REVOLT—AFFAIRS AT SONOMA.

June–July, 1846.

Ide in Command—Banner for the New Republic—Star and Grizzly—
Raising of the Bear Flag—The Flags as Relics—Ide's Proclamation—Falsehood and Bombast—Further Organization—Minor Happenings—Ide's Version—Treaty with Alcalde—Todd's Mission to
Montgomery—Misroon at Sonoma—Mormonism—A New Proclamation—Killing of Cowie and Fowler by the Californians—Padilla
and Carrillo—Sortie by Ide—Other Captives—Gibson's Expedition
to Santa Rosa—Insurgents Reënforced—Land Laws—Grigsby's
Return—Ford's Campaign—Padilla Joined by Torre—A Surprise
—Fight at Olompali—Torre Defeated by the 'Bears.'

WE left William B. Ide with twenty-four men in
possession of Sonoma. The alcalde and many citizens
were under arrest. Three Mexican officials had been
sent as prisoners to the Sacramento. This was just
before noon on the 14th of June. For four or five
days it does not appear that there was any increase
in the insurgent garrison; but during that time several
weighty matters of state were disposed of by these
soi-disant founders of a republic. A flag was devised,
manufactured, and raised; a proclamation was written,
embodying the principles, plans, and motives of the
insurgents; the imprisoned Californians were perhaps
released under certain stipulations; and diplomatic
messengers were despatched and received by the commander. Many details respecting each of these matters are involved in more or less uncertainty, as might
be expected from the very nature of the records, chiefly
the memory of individuals concerned; but I proceed

to throw on the whole subject such light as existing evidence can be made to furnish, hoping to reduce prevalent doubts and discrepancies of testimony to a minimum.

The need of a banner was naturally one of the first suggested. The insurgents had no right to unfurl the stars and stripes, as many of them would doubtless have preferred to do; yet any flag devised by Americans must needs have at least a star and a stripe; and the appropriateness of a lone star could not fail to suggest itself to men familiar with the history of Texas, and the similarity of condition between that country and what they hoped to make of California. A simple copy would not, however, suffice, and an additional emblem was required. Somebody proposed the grizzly bear, an animal then common in those regions, and whose reputation for "strength and unyielding resistance" could be attested by every one of those resolute hunters from personal experience. For materials they took what they could find; that is, a piece of common unbleached cotton cloth, the *manta* of the Mexicans, somewhat less than a yard in width and five feet long, and some strips of red flannel about four inches wide. The flannel, the stripe of the flag, made of the requisite length by piecing, was sewn to the bottom of the cotton. In the upper left-hand corner of the white field was outlined in ink, and filled in with red paint, an irregular five-pointed star, fifteen inches in its greatest diameter. Just to the right of the star, and facing it, was painted in like manner what was intended for a bear, statant, though it has been pronounced more like a hog by experts who cared little for the feelings of the last-named animal. Under the two emblems was rudely lettered in black ink CALIFORNIA REPUBLIC. Such was the famous Bear Flag, which has given a name to the revolution, and which caused the insurgents to be known to the natives as Osos. I think there can be no doubt that William L. Todd was the artist who painted it; but respecting the accuracy of

many other current details grave doubts arise from
conflicting testimony. Who first suggested the component emblems of the banner; who furnished the cotton, and who the flannel; whence came the red paint;
was the cloth new or old; had the flannel graced the
undergarment of a fair and patriotic lady, or had it
filled an humbler station as part of a man's red shirt;
who manipulated the needle and thread; who merely
'stood around' in the artist's way; whose knife was borrowed to cut the stuff; and was that knife ever returned
to its owner—these are questions that I cannot answer
so definitely as might be desired; but on some of them
the reader may find light in the appended note.[1]

[1] Wm L. Todd in a letter of June 16, 1872, to Wm Baldridge says: 'At a
company meeting it was determined that we should raise a flag; and it should
be a bear *en passant*, with one star.   One of the ladies at the garrison gave us
a piece of brown domestic, and Mrs Capt. John Sears gave us some strips of
red flannel about four inches wide.   The domestic was new, but the flannel
was said to have been part of a petticoat worn by Mrs Sears across the mountains.   For a corroboration of these facts, I refer to G. P. Swift and Pat Mc-
Christian.   I took a pen, and with ink drew the outline of the bear and star
upon the white cotton cloth.   Linseed oil and Venetian red were found in
the garrison, and I painted the bear and star.   To the best of my recollection, Peter Storm was asked to paint it, but he declined; and as no other person would undertake to do it, I did.   But Mr Storm with several others
assisted in getting the materials, and I believed Storm mixed the paint.
Underneath the bear and star were printed with a pen the words "California
Republic," in Roman letters.   In painting the words I first lined out the
letters with a pen, leaving out the letter "i" and putting "c" where "i"
should have been, and afterwards the "i" over the "c."   It was made with
ink, and as we had nothing to remove the marks of the false letter, it now
remains so on the flag.'   In *Napa Register*, July 6, 1872.   In a letter of Jan.
11, 1878, to the *Los Angeles Express*, reprinted in many other papers, Todd
tells the same story in words but slightly different, saying: 'The following
persons performed the work—Granville P. Swift, Peter Storm, Henry L.
Ford, and myself.'   He also confirms the same version in a letter of March
6, 1878, to the secretary of the Territorial Pioneers.   Copy in *Bear Flag
Pap.*, MS., 41.   Ford, *Bear Flag Revol.*, MS., 12–13, gives an account
which agrees so far as it goes with that in my text; and he claims for himself
the honor of having suggested the grizzly bear.   Ide, *Biog. Sketch*, 130–1;
and also in a quotation from the MS. before publication furnished to the
sec. of the territorial pioneers in a letter of April 16, 1878, from Jas G.
Bleak of St George, Utah—a letter that has been often reprinted—credits
Todd with having done the work; says the flannel was from the red
shirt of one of the men; and erroneously states that the lettering was in
red paint.   In the *Hist. Bear Flag*, we read: 'A national flag was agreed
upon—its base a brown stripe, next above a wide stripe of green cut so as to
represent growing *Tula;* the upper part white to represent the clear horizon,
on the end of the flag-staff a rising star, and in the brown stripe the words
in capitals "California Republic."'   Baldridge, *Days of '46*, MS., i.–vii. 8,
and in *Napa Register*, April 27, 1872, who did not reach Sonoma until some
days after the flag was raised, heard an account on arrival confirming Todd's

The Bear Flag has been preserved for many years in the hall of the California Pioneers in San Francisco; that is, I have found no reason to question the

very nearly, except that he understood the flannel to have been furnished by a native Californian, Chepa Matthews, wife of Wm Matthews. Baldridge complains that some of his statements of former years, correcting popular errors, were not so generally credited as they should have been. McChristian, *Narrative*, MS., 1–5, tells us that Capt. Scott proposed to make a flag if Mrs Hudson would give the stuff, though Mrs Sears gave the white domestic. Phelps, *Fore and Aft*, 284–6, says the flag was a grizzly rampant done on a white cotton sheet with lamp-black. In the *West Shore Gazette*, 13, we are told that Mrs Kelsey furnished the worn-out cotton. Thompson, *Hist. Sonoma*, 15, has it that Mrs Elliott supplied new cotton and flannel. In the *Monterey Californian*, Feb. 13, 1847, we read that the painting was done with lamp-black and poke-berries; and that the letters were on the top. According to Gillespie, in *Cal. Pioneers Soc. Arch.*, MS., 137, the white body of the flag was made of the chemise of Mrs Wm Hudson, and the flannel came from Mrs Sears' petticoat. A chewed stick was used for a brush. McGeorge, in *Petaluma Crescent*, Sept. 10, 1872. Tuthill, *Hist. Cal.*, 172–3, speaks of a pot of berry juice. An account from Semple's MSS. in *Hesperian*, iii. 389–90, has it that the red stripe was stained with berry juice, and under it were the words 'The People's Rights.' In an article prepared for the Pioneer Society by its historian, Hittell described the bear as standing nearly upright, confounding the original flag with another. *S. F. Alta*, Jan. 8, 1878, and in many other papers. According to a 'true history of the Bear Flag,' in the *Santa Rosa Sonoma Democrat*, Aug. 8, 1874, copied in *Napa Register*, Aug. 15, 1874, and in other papers, we are told that the project of a flag came up in a 'casual conversation' between Todd, Dewell, and Cowie. Dewell obtained from Mrs W. B. Elliott the flannel, domestic, and needles and thread. Blue drilling was obtained elsewhere. Cowie and Dewell had been saddlers, and the three young men proceeded to make the flag without consulting any one else, by sewing together alternate strips of red, white, and blue (!), Todd painting a star in the upper corner and a bear in the lower. Swasey, *Cal. '45-6*, MS., 26, seems to have adopted the version just given. Peter Storm has often been credited with having painted the Bear Flag. At a celebration in Napa, Sept. 9, 1873, Storm, introduced by Brannan, stood up and was cheered as the artist, at the same time waving a counterpart of the original. *Napa Register*, Sept. 13, 1873. In 1871 also Storm, visiting S. F., was honored as the painter of the flag. *Calistoga Tribune*, Dec. 21, 1871. It would seem that Storm did paint a flag, but somewhat later and at Napa. Baldridge, *Days of '46*, MS., i.–vi. 8, and in *Napa Register*, April 27th, tells us that it was painted on a piece of greenish fabric at Napa in 1848 for the use of a party going to Sonoma for a celebration of July 4th. He thinks it is one of the flags preserved by the pioneers at their hall in S. F. A correspondent, perhaps Baldridge also, gave the same version to the *Napa Reporter*, and claims to have furnished the materials. He says that Todd's flag was made of 'Dirty Matthews' wife's red flannel petticoat.' Fowler, *Bear Flag*, MS., 2–4, says the material came from a sloop at the mouth of Napa Creek, the writer being present, Storm doing the work, and the bear being represented as standing on its hind legs. Fowler, however, says that this flag was made before June 14th, and was the one hoisted at Sonoma. Knight, *Statement*, MS., 9, thinks that Storm was the painter. In a letter of Feb. 20, 1874, Gen. Joseph W. Revere writes to the soc. of Cal. pioneers: 'At the suggestion of Gen. Sherman, I beg leave to send to your society forthwith a guidon, formerly belonging to the Sonoma troop of the Cal. battalion, 1846, for preservation. This guidon I found among the effects of the troop when I hauled down the Bear Flag at Sonoma and substituted the flag of the U.

genuineness of the flag there preserved, though strictly speaking, it is not so fully proven by documentary evidence as would be desirable. Two other bear flags are preserved by the same society. One of them is of the same size as the original, but differs from it in several respects: the white field is of bunting; the star is much smaller, and black instead of red; the bear, also black, is drawn 'rampant' and with outlines much· less inaccurate than in Todd's effort. Beyond the probability that this is the flag painted by Peter Storm, as indicated in my notes, I have found no proofs respecting its origin. The other flag is the guidon presented by Revere. Its dimensions are 42 by 20 inches; and the material, both of field and stripe, is silk. The bear, statant, is under the inscription, faces away from the star, and is much better drawn than the original. Both material and execution indicate that it was made after Frémont's arrival at Sonoma, and probably after communication had been established with the men-of-war; but nothing definite is known of its origin beyond Revere's statement that he found it at Sonoma in July.

The date on which the Bear Flag was raised has been in late years a topic of much discussion. The writers who have engaged in it have devoted their attention almost exclusively to the date of the taking of Sonoma. Obtaining some slight evidence that the town was taken on June 14th—a date respecting the accuracy of which there can be no possible doubt, it being fully established by the many original documents

S. on the 7th (?) of July, 1846, and have preserved it ever since.' Printed in *Sacramento Enterprise* of Oct. 10, 1875, and in many other places. See accounts of the Bear Flag, containing I believe nothing not already noted, in *S. F. Herald*, July 9, 1858; *S. F. Alta*, July 20, 24, 1852; Jan. 20, 1866; Jan. 8, 1878; Oct. 8, 1874; *Sac. Union*, June 21, 1858; *Id. Mercury*, 1858; *S. José Mercury*, 1861 (Hittell); *Antioch Ledger*, Aug. 15, 1874; *Sta Bárbara Press*, Oct. 10, 1874; *Sta Cruz Sentinel*, March 11, 1876; *S. F. Post*, July 21, 1877; *S. F. Bulletin*, Dec. 20, 1877; *S. F. Call*, Jan. 8, 1878; *S. José Pioneer*, March 1, 1879; *Napa Reporter*, Jan. 18, 1878; *Healdsburg Enterprise*, June 27, 1878; *Petaluma Argus*, Feb. 22, 1878; *Napa Register*, April 13, 1872. Also general résumé in *Upham's Notes*, 563-6; *Lancey's Cruise*, 57-61. Also mention in nearly all the county histories of Cal., and, in fact, in most of the authorities quoted in this chapter and the preceding.

I have presented—they have regarded their diligent investigations as rewarded with conclusive proof that the flag was unfurled on the same day. No such conclusive proof, however, exists. The question is whether the flag was raised on the day of the capture, the next day, or later. There is no contemporary record on the subject of earlier date than June 17th, when Misroon found the flag flying; and no witness, testifying from memory, has had his attention called directly to the question at issue. Ide states, though not in a diary as has been claimed, that the flag-raising was on the 14th. Ford also implies that the flag was raised before night on the first day, though he also states that it was hoisted at sunrise next morning. Bidwell's testimony favors the theory that it was probably not raised on the first day. A few in later times tell us that it was several days after the taking of Sonoma; but most say nothing on the subject. The balance of testimony is therefore in a sense in favor of the 14th; but the evidence is very slight indeed; and it must be regarded as doubtful whether the insurgents had time on that Sunday afternoon to devise, manufacture, and hoist their new banner; especially if, as some say, the halyards were broken, so that the flag-staff in the plaza had to be lowered and raised again.[2]

A proclamation was deemed no less essential than a flag. Some wished to wait until their force should be increased, or until a few prominent persons could be induced to join the movement, or until Frémont's views could be ascertained. But the majority felt that what they had done bore on its face too strong a resemblance to a mere filibustering movement for

---

[2] In the course of the discussion alluded to, the sec. of the territorial pioneers published the statement that 'Bancroft, the Pacific coast historian,' had fixed the date as June 15th; and this statement has been repeated by a dozen writers. While duly flattered by the complimentary title thus circulated in connection with my name, I must protest that I had never formed or expressed any such opinion.

plunder; at least, it was sure to be so represented by enemies, and "how were our forces to be augmented, and who would come to the assistance of those who were only represented as robbers and rebels?"[3] Accordingly a pronunciamiento was decided on.   It was written by Commander Ide, and bore the date of June 15th, having been prepared, as the writer states, between the hours of one and four that morning.   Many copies were made during the next few days, in which vast improvements were made in orthography, and some slight verbal changes were introduced.   A supplemental proclamation was issued on the 18th; and possibly that date was also attached to some copies of the original, a circumstance that has led writers on the subject into great confusion.   I reproduce the document, and add some notes upon the successive stages of its development.[4]   This proclamation consisted first

[3] 'So here we were; by our flag proclaimed 'the California Republic'! 24 self-consecrated victims to the god of equal rights, unknown by any mortal being except 10 men who had dissented from our plan and fled to the protection of Frémont's camp [except 30 or 40 Spaniards who had from a brief acquaintance sworn fidelity to our cause], exposed not only to the wrath of 600 armed men (!), whom we were compelled, in order to avoid the just imputation of violence and crime, to defy in open fight, but to the unmingled scorn of all honorable men whether Mexicans or Americans, if we failed to represent our true character, and the circumstances which compelled us to assume such an unusual position.   Was it prudent to delay a just representation to the public ear?' etc. *Ide's Biog. Sketch*, 135-7.

[4] What purports to be an original in Ide's own writing—Louis R. Lull certifying to the handwriting, Manuel Castro affirming that it was the one sent him as prefect and remaining in his possession since 1846, and there being no reason that I know of to doubt its genuineness—is preserved by the pioneer society, *California Pioneers, Arch.*, MS., 71-5; and was printed in the *S. F. Alta*, Jan. 20, 1866.   Except in its outrageously bad spelling and punctuation, it agrees with the one I print below.

One of the early copies, or originals—for they appear to have been copied both by Ide and by others of the garrison—reached Monterey, and was copied by or for Larkin at the time.   This copy is found in *Larkin's Off. Corresp.*, MS., ii. 69-71; and *Sawyer's Doc.*, MS., 49-51.   It was also sent up the coast, and was first printed in the *Oregon Spectator*, July 23, 1846.   This is the version which I reproduce, differing from the original in orthography only.   Whether the corrections were introduced wholly or in part at Monterey, there are no means of knowing.

A third version is the one that has been most widely circulated, and always under date of June 18th.   It is in substance the same as the preceding, but shows several slight verbal differences; and it is to be noted that the last three paragraphs are written in the first person, 'I also solemnly declare,' etc., instead of 'he also,' etc.   This version first appeared in the *Monterey Californian*, Sept. 5, 1846; and later in *Bryant's What I Saw in Cal.*, 290-1; *Soulé's Annals of S. F.*, 92-3; *Lancey's Cruise*, 63; and in several of the recent county

of a statement of the inducements under which the
revolutionists had settled in California—false from
beginning to end; second, charges of deception and

histories. That such a version was circulated is indicated by two Spanish
translations in *Savage, Doc.*, MS., i. 41; and *Bandini, Doc.*, MS., 75. One
is a copy of a translation certified by Dolores Pacheco, and the other a copy
of what was understood to be a translation by Hartnell. They differ from one
another, and are inaccurate; but both bear the date of June 18th, and both
are written partly in the first person.

Finally, we have the version given by Ide in his letter to Wambough, as
printed in his *Biog. Sketch*, 138-40. This contains many variations from the
original, not, however, modifying the general purport, most of which I introduce in brackets. The proclamation was as follows: 'A proclamation to all
persons, citizens of Sonoma [inhabitants of the county (?) of Sonoma and country around—or in version no. 3—and citizens of the district of Sonoma],
requesting them to remain at peace and to follow [pursue] their rightful occupation without fear of molestation. The commander-in-chief of the troops
assembled at the fortress of Sonoma [com. at Sonoma] gives his inviolable
pledge to all persons in California not found under arms [bearing arms or instigating others to take up arms against him] that they shall not be disturbed
in their persons, their property [religion], or social relations one to another
[to each other], by men under his command. He also [hereby most] solemnly
declares his object [the object of his movement] to be, first, to defend himself [our women and children] and [his brave] companions in arms, who were
invited to this country by a promise of lands on which to settle themselves
and families; who were also promised a republican government; who, when
having arrived in California, were denied even the privilege of buying or
renting lands of their friends; who, instead of being allowed to participate in
or being protected by a republican government, were oppressed by a military
despotism; who were even threatened by proclamation from the chief officer
[one of the principal officers] of the aforesaid despotism [oppressive govern-
ment] with extermination if they would not depart out of the country, leaving all their property, their arms, and beasts of burden; and thus deprived
[were thus to be despoiled] of the means of flight or defence, we were to be
[to have been] driven through deserts inhabited by hostile Indians [savages]
to certain death [destruction.] To overthrow a government which has seized
upon the property of [robbed and despoiled] the missions [and appropriated
the property thereof] for its individual aggrandizement [of its favorites];
[which has violated good faith by its treachery in the bestowment of public
lands]; which has ruined and shamefully oppressed the laboring [and produc-
ing inhabitants] people of California by their enormous exactions [of tariff]
on goods imported into the country, is the determined [this is the] purpose
of the brave men who are associated under his command. He also solemnly
declares [I also declare, etc., in version no. 3] his object in the second place to
be, to invite all peaceable and good citizens of California, who are friendly
to the maintenance of good order and equal rights, and I do hereby invite
them to repair to my camp at Sonoma without delay [and he hereby invites
all good and patriotic citizens in California to assist him to establish, etc.],
to assist us in establishing and perpetuating a republican [liberal, just, and
honorable] government, which shall secure to all civil and religious [and per-
sonal] liberty; [which shall insure the security of life and property]; which
shall detect and punish crime [and injustice]; which shall encourage industry, virtue, and literature; which shall leave unshackled by fetters [shall
foster] commerce, manufactures, and mechanism [by guaranteeing freedom to
commerce]. He further declares [proclaims] that he relies upon the rectitude of our intentions [justice of his cause]; the favor of heaven; [upon the
wisdom and good sense of the people of California;] and the bravery of those

oppression by the authorities—equally false, but in one or two particulars really credited by some of the men; third, some general criticisms of the existing government—well founded in certain respects, but involving no wrong to the rebels, and absurd as coming from them; fourth, bombastic promises of reform and of protection to non-combatants—commendable enough, and of the type usually made a feature of such effusions. As a whole, in truthfulness and consistency, as in orthography and literary merit, it was below the plane of Castro's and Pico's proclamations. In respect of bombast and general absurdity, it stood about midway between the two; but it derived some dignity from the fact that it came from men who meant to fight as well as talk. As a product of filibusterism, pure and simple, it deserves praise not to be awarded from any other standpoint.

Ford tells us that after raising their flag the men completed their organization by electing himself first lieutenant; Samuel Kelsey second lieutenant; Granville P. Swift and Samuel Gibson sergeants. Next morning at sunrise, after the flag had been hoisted anew and the guard relieved, Lieutenant Ford addressed his men on the responsibilities of their position and the necessity of strict discipline. All promised implicit obedience to their officers, as did also fifteen new men who came in that evening—according

who are bound to and associated with him by the principle of self-preservation; by the love of truth [their love of liberty], and by the hatred of tyranny —for his hopes of success. He further declares [premises] that he believes that a government, to be prosperous and happifying [Larkin leaves this word out; while Ide substitutes *ameleiorating!*] in its tendency must originate with [among] its people, who are friendly to its existence; that its citizens are its guardians [last 12 words omitted], its officers are [should be] its servants, and its glory their reward [its common reward]. William B. Ide, commander. Headquarters, Sonoma, June 15, 1846.'

In the various comments on Ide's proclamation I find nothing that seems to require notice, unless it may be the remark of Baldridge, that Ide had a mania for writing and for organization of govt, all his proceedings being regarded by the men as an amusing farce. Tuthill pronounces it 'crude in style, and in its allegations quite unsupported by facts, yet commendably explicit and direct;' and several writers have noted its untruthfulness.

to this writer's statement, which is probably an error.[5]
This is all Ford tells us of events down to the coming
of Misroon; and with the exception of a slight résumé
in another narrative, as appended,[6] we have no other
definite authority on the subject than Ide himself.

Following Ide, the general accuracy of whose narrative there is no good reason to doubt, though it is over-
burdened with patriotic eloquence, bombastic egotism,
and special pleading designed to strengthen his cause
against Frémont, we return to the departure of Grigsby and his prisoners for the Sacramento at 11 A. M.
on June 14th.   After Todd and his assistants had been
put to work on the flag, and while the rest, divided
into two companies, the '1st artillery' and the '1st
rifles,' were puting their arms in order, the commander,
after posting guards and sentinels, "directed his leisure
to the establishment of rules of discipline and order,
and of a system of finance whereby all the defenceless
families might be brought within the lines and supported.   Ten thousand pounds of flour were purchased
on the credit of the government; an account was
opened for the supply of beef on terms agreed upon;
whiskey was altogether a contraband article."   He
also found time to harangue such men as could be
spared from other tasks on their duties.   Then with
an interpreter he went before the thirty or forty im-

---

[5] *Ford's Bear Flag Revol.*, MS., 14–15.

[6] 'Capt. Ide was empowered by the troops to provide provisions for their
subsistence, and to draw orders in behalf of the republic, which were to be
hereafter paid.   Berreyesa, the Mexican alcalde, was sent for, dismissed from
that office, and reäppointed to the same by the new govt.   Berreyesa pledged
himself that the Mexican population of the district of Sonoma should not interfere in the revolution.   Some further measures were adopted, limiting duties on foreign importations to one fourth of the existing rates.   Horace Sanders was appointed commissary.   A national flag was agreed upon, etc.   Capt.
Ide was made captain general; measures were taken to secure public and private property; and in case private property was used by the govt, to adopt
measures for compensating the owners therefor...The general in chief, on the
16th, sent Mr Todd on a mission to Capt. Montgomery...for the purpose of
obtaining a quantity of powder...He declined furnishing it...At the same
time measures were adopted by Gen. Ide in relation to the national domain,
making arrangements for establishing a land office, surveying the country,
and reserving to those who served the state ranchos of some leagues in extent.
In the evening Mr Todd returned with Lieut Misroon,' etc.   *Hist. Bear Flag*,
by Ide, Grigsby, and Nash.

prisoned Californians to explain "the common rights of all men," and his own benevolent intention to right all their wrongs. So eloquently did he put his case that "the Spaniard, even, embraced the commander as he pronounced the name of Washington"! and though told they were at liberty to depart, the imprisoned Berreyesa and his companions chose to remain until a treaty could be made. By a unanimous vote the "powers of the four departments of government" were conferred on the commander; and the evening, after the flag had been raised, was spent in discussions respecting a proclamation.

The proclamation, as we have seen, was written before morning; as was also a letter to Commodore Stockton, and the "remainder of the night was spent in drawing up such articles of agreement and treaty stipulations as were most likely to enlist the good-will of all good citizens of California, without respect to the circumstance of any peculiar origin of its inhabitants." The purport of these stipulations— no copy of which is known to exist, and which are mentioned by Ide alone—was, first, no "individual division" of public property, that being used solely as security for payment for public debts; second, free commerce and no imposts whatever; third, no salaries, "enticements to corruption," for officials; fourth, no involuntary taxation, except as a punishment for crime; fifth, no compulsory military service; last, all Spaniards and Californians, "good friends," on taking a solemn oath to support independent principles and the flag, to be excused from bearing arms against their misguided countrymen, agreeing voluntarily to urge the latter not to resist, and also to furnish all supplies needed for the public service. There was much difficulty in making these stipulations fully understood by the Californians; and still more in obtaining the approval of the insurgents themselves, some of whom "who at first enlisted for plunder and flight to the States, and who proposed to tear down and pillage the house of Vallejo, still earnestly contended that a Spaniard had no right to liberty and but very little right to the enjoyment of life." In fact, it was necessary for Ide to conduct the negotiations without the full knowledge of the garrison, he being sustained in the command only for want of any other man who could insure obedience.

Monday morning a messenger was needed to carry the letter to the naval officer in command at the bay. This letter, as Ide insists, was not a request for aid, but a statement of their acts and purposes, being intended chiefly to prevent any unwarrantable interference of the United States officers by the assurance of an intention ultimately to "unite this fair land with that of our birth." In order to obtain a courier, however, it was necessary to create an impression that his mission was to obtain powder. William Todd volunteered, and on his departure was especially charged by the commander not to ask for anything, but simply to bring back what might be given him! No news was heard from the outside world during the first four days. The time was spent in translating and re-translating treaty and proclamation. "The men were divided into four night-guards of six men each, and into eight day-guards of three men each. One half of the men were at all times by day employed in camp duty; the other half guarded and slept." As no one from abroad came within hailing distance from Sonoma, so it appears that no one was permitted to depart, not even Berreyesa and his companions.

At sunset of Tuesday the 16th, not on the 17th as Ide states, Lieutenant Misroon arrived by boat from the *Portsmouth* at anchor at Sauzalito. He was sent by Captain Montgomery, as already recorded, at the request of Vallejo, to prevent, so far as the personal influence of the naval officers could go, any violence to families and non-combatants, being strictly charged to avoid any meddling with the merits of the revolt. It is probable that Todd reached the ship before Misroon's departure, and returned to Sonoma with him; but there is no allusion to him or his mission in the lieutenant's instructions or report. According to that report Misroon first called on Ide, and obtained from him not only a copy of his proclamation, but both a verbal and a written pledge to prevent all violence to the persons or property of peaceful inhabitants. Then he visited the alcalde, to whom he explained in writing his mission, presenting at the same time the pledge obtained from Ide. And finally, he "called upon the family of General Vallejo, and moderated their distress by the assurances of safety for the general which I had received, and informing them that the prisoners were held as hostages." At his request, the Señora de Vallejo was permitted to send an open letter to her husband by her brother Julio Carrillo, who also carried an account of Rosa's interview with Montgomery, and who, notwithstanding his passport, was thrown into prison on his arrival at New Helvetia. Misroon finally left Sonoma at noon on the 17th. His report of the next day contained copies of the proclamation and pledge, a description of the flag, a statement that the garrison consisted of about twenty-five men, and an expression of his opinion that not only was there no danger of outrages being committed, but that the Californians were very well contented with their position.[7]

[7] June 15th, 16th, Montgomery's instructions to Misroon. June 18th, M.'s report. *Bear Flag Papers.*, MS., 46–57. The pledge given by Ide was as follows: 'I pledge myself that I will use my utmost exertion to restrain and prevent the men in arms under my command (all of whom present acknowledge my authority and approve the measure of forbearance and humanity) from perpetrating any violence, or in any manner molesting the peaceable inhabitants, in person or property, of Cal. while we continue in arms for the liberty of Cal. Wm B. Ide, commander. Sonoma, June 17, 1846.' In a letter of June 19th, from Leidesdorff to Larkin, *Larkin's Doc.*, MS., iv. 167, he describes Misroon's visit; says it was partly due to Todd's arrival; that all was found in perfect order at Sonoma; and tells an anecdote of one of the insurgents being promptly fined $30 for shooting a horse that kicked him! According to the *Hist. Bear Flag*, Misroon 'stated that Capt. Montgomery was in expectation of important news from Mexico, and that in the event of war he would place all the resources of his ship and half of his men under Gen. Ide's command'! Ford simply says that Misroon arrived and 'complimented the party for their orderly conduct.' *Bear Flag Revol.*, MS., 15.

Ide, ignoring altogether Vallejo's messenger and the true nature of Misroon's mission, as well as his efforts at mediation and the documents which he obtained and wrote, represents that officer as having come with Todd, and in consequence of his message, to bring and explain a letter from Montgomery, the letter and explanations being to the effect that no aid, not even a charge of powder, could be furnished; though on receipt of news that war had been declared, the captain would gladly put half his men under Ide's command, and coöperate with his ship against the common foe. Todd, greatly to the sorrow of Ide as he claims, had asked for powder, thus doing incalculable harm to the cause in some manner not very intelligibly explained. Indeed, it is impossible to follow Ide in his ravings at this part of his narrative, as at some others. At night, Misroon was enthusiastic enough in the cause, offering to aid in circulating the proclamation. But next morning a change had come over his mind. He had been talking with the garrison; it was thought best not to issue any proclamation; and the lieutenant even spoke of finding some way to relieve the insurgents from their 'disagreeable situation.' Ide was in a state of terrible anxiety. Evidently Misroon had heard something of current charges against the commander. "He had been charged by Captain Frémont with being a Mormon, and his scheme was denounced as an artifice to betray the whole country into the hands of the Mormons. And it was known that most of the garrison believed the foul slander."[8] But the lieutenant was persuaded

[8] Several early Californians speak of Ide as a Mormon, but there is nothing authoritative on the subject. Many confounded him, I think, with Orson Hyde, and possibly this was the only foundation for the charge of Mormonism. In the *Oregon Spectator*, July 23, 1846, in connection with his proclamation, Ide is said to be a Mormon, one of 'Jo Smith's 12 apostles,' and the query is raised whether the promises alluded to had been made to the settlers as Americans or as Mormons. Ide does not make it quite clear whether the 'foul slander' was the charge of being a Mormon, or that of being engaged in a scheme to win Cal. for that sect, or both. It does not matter whether he was a Mormon or a Methodist. The silence of his biographer, and the peculiar manner of his own references to the subject, leave some doubt as to the truth.

to read the proclamation; it conquered him; he read it aloud to the garrison; all approved it; "joy and animation were kindled in every heart;" triumph was assured; "the battle's won; we'll triumph still, in spite of fears of Mormonism!" Of course it is not to be believed that Ide's statement is true, and that Misroon thus openly gave his support to the insurgents. Fanaticism closely verging on insanity is here and there indicated by the commander's writings.

On June 18th a new proclamation was written, though Ide mentions only the copying of the old one, and was sent, together with a document bearing the signature of Alcalde Berreyesa, to be circulated with translations, both of this and of the original proclamation, south of the bay. A man named Booker, Boker, or Brooker, was chosen as messenger; and a week later he posted the documents at Monterey. I give them in a note.[9] This second proclamation was much

[9] 'A proclamation. All persons who will remain peaceable shall in no wise be molested or injured. The commander of the company of soldiers now in possession of Sonoma promises on his word of honor to all the Californians who do not take up arms against him peace and security, and in case any of the commander's people should in any wise injure any person who is not concerned, on application being made to the above mentioned authority, the offender or offenders shall be punished, the party injured not having taken up arms. The commander wishes to establish a good government for the prompt administration of justice, and with strict attention to individual rights and liberties, and not with the intention of molesting or permitting to be molested any person on account of their religious opinions. The new government will toil indefatigably to the end of acquiring everything that may be beneficial to the country. This government will reduce the marine duties three or four parts in a thousand (?). It will defend its rightful intentions, with the favor of God and the valor of its adherents. The government of the country has ordered us to retire the same way we came, and as this is impossible on account of our poverty, we have determined to make this country independent, and to establish a system of government that will be more favorable to us than such a dangerous and long road back. I order that this be published with a translation, likewise that of the 15th of the present month in English and in Spanish. William B. Ide, commander in Sonoma, June 18, 1846.'

'The 14th day of the present month this present commander took possession of the town of Sonoma, and up to this date there has not been the least disorder, there having been nothing taken but arms, ammunition, and horses; and for whatever else they may have required they have solicited it of individuals, under a promise of payment in full value the moment the government is properly installed in the republic of California, which they are determined to do. José S. Berreyesa, 1st alcalde in Sonoma.'

These doc. are found in *Larkin's Off. Corresp.*, MS., ii. 72; *Sawyer's Doc.*, MS., 53-4, 59-60, with a memorandum by Larkin that they were found posted

more moderate in its tone than the first, the writer omitting all the former false statements but one, and confining himself for the most part to promises of reform in the government. The earlier document had been intended mainly for foreign settlers, and for effect in the outside world; while this one was for the Californians. Ide tells us that it "was written and rewritten, and sent as far as San de Angelos," causing more than half of Castro's army at Santa Clara to desert within three days!

Between the departure of Misroon, on Wednesday the 17th, and the arrival of Frémont, on Thursday the 25th, in addition to a few minor events confusedly recorded by Ide and Ford, there were two about which much has been written; though both, so far as details are concerned, are still involved in some obscurity. The first was the killing of Cowie and Fowler, and the second a fight between Ford and Joaquin de la Torre. On the 18th or 19th, Fowler and Thomas Cowie were sent by Ide to obtain a keg of powder from Moses Carson at the Fitch rancho on Russian River. Disregarding the advice of Ide and Ford, they are said to have neglected all precautions, and to have followed the main road. Before reaching their destination they were captured by a party of Californians under Juan N. Padilla and Ramon Carrillo. These men, twenty or thirty in number, had been for some days ranging through the country, awaiting developments at Sonoma, and expecting reënforcements from Castro. Padilla was a Mexican barber of no influence or standing whatever, and Carrillo was a young Cali-

---

on one of his buildings on the morning of the 27th. This had been done by Boker of Me. or N. H., who was one of the original party that took Sonoma, and who had come south to raise a force at Sta Cruz, etc. He said that Ide was living in Leese's house; and that the party intended to insist on Frémont coming forward openly to take command, else they would either organize without him or break up and retire from the contest. Ide in his letter to Wambough mentions the alcalde's letter and the praclamation as having been sent by Brooker, though he implies that it was the original proclamation. Tustin, *Recoll.*, MS., 9, mentions a Henry Booker living on the Sacramento in 1846, and this may have been the messenger in question.

fornian not noted for his good qualities. The company was composed mostly of wild and irresponsible young fellows, and included several desperate characters; but so far as can be known, they had committed no hostilities on the ranchos round about, as they might easily have done. It was near Santa Rosa that the two Americans were captured, under circumstances of which nothing is known. They were killed by their captors, and they are said to have been mutilated in a most horrible manner. Some state, without details or known authority, that their remains were found later. A noted desperado named Bernardino García, or 'four-fingered Jack,' afterward described the details of the murder, representing the prisoners as having been tied to trees, stoned, and cut to pieces, one of them having his broken jaw dragged out with a reata. His version, or so much of it as could decently be put in print, has been the current one ever since. That the Californians, as a body, or their leaders could have committed so horrible a deed it is impossible to conceive. In the absence of positive original evidence to the contrary, I choose to believe that Cowie and Fowler were killed in an altercation, in an attempt to escape, or by an individual desperado. Testimony, as the reader will see, is vague and contradictory. This affair, however, did much to strengthen the insurgent cause, forcing the settlers through fear to take refuge with their families at Sonoma.[10]

[10] The version given by García was printed in the *Monterey Californian*, Sept. 12, 1846; was repeated in *Bryant's What I Saw in Cal.*, 291-2; and has often been reproduced in the papers of later times. Some additional horrors, from an unknown source, were given in the *S. F. Alta*, July 31, 1853; and repeated in *Lancey's Cruise*, 61-2. Vallejo, *Hist. Cal.*, MS., v. 121-3, followed by Alvarado, *Hist. Cal.*, MS., v. 204-5, desirous of course to clear Carrillo, his wife's brother, from the charge, states that the leaders had no idea of putting the men to death; but while all were holding a council as to what should be done with the prisoners, who were left tied to trees outside, García, a blood-thirsty villain, the terror of the whole region, fearing that they would be released, went out and killed them with his dagger, and returned to boast of his act. This version is at least more plausible than the other. On Aug. 26, 1846, Ramon Carrillo made a sworn statement before Judge Santiago E. Argüello at S. Diego about the northern campaign. He stated that before the capture of Cowie and Fowler two other prisoners had been taken; that the Bear party had seized the horses at Padilla's rancho; and also

Ide claims to have made, apparently just after the departure of Cowie and Fowler, a reconnoissance with ten men for the purpose of protecting the families of settlers, and to have discovered a party of twenty-five Californians, who took alarm and fled, notwithstanding the efforts made to approach them unobserved. This expedition may or may not explain the pursuit mentioned by Ramon Carrillo, and the shot fired at the retreating Californians. At any rate, Ide was convinced "that any attempt to get a fight, just for

that the Bear Flag men had pursued Mariano Elizalde and shot a bullet through his hat. Carrillo took the two men and delivered them to Padilla, who, against his advice and that of others, insisted on having them shot. Four men under a corporal were sent to shoot and bury them. Next day Carrillo was sent to report the affair to Castro, who approved what had been done. Original document found by Benj. Hayes in 1856, in *S. Diego, Archives*, MS.; see *S. Diego Index*, MS., 93; *Hayes' Notes*, 268; *Id., Scrap-books, Cal. Notes*, iv. 124–5. But in 1864, during the excitement caused by Ramon Carrillo's death at the hands of vigilantes, Don Julio, his brother, published a card in the *Sta Rosa Democrat*, June 4, 1864, denying that Ramon had anything to do with the murder of 1846, or that he knew anything of the capture until after the men were killed. He claimed to have proofs of this. See also *Sonoma Co. Hist.*, 107–8. In a letter of July 16th to Montgomery, Grigsby says, 'We have found the two men who were lost on the Sta Rosa farm, horribly mangled.' He names, as concerned in the murder, Ramon Mesa, Domingo Mesa, Juan Padilla, Ramon Carrillo, and Bernardino García, all now believed to be south of the bay; and, apparently, Blas Angelino, in prison; Francisco Tibian (?), Ignacio Valenzuela, Juan Peralta, Juan Soleto (?), Inaguen (?) Carrillo, Mariano Miranda, Francisco García, Ignacio Stiggere (?), all in the north. By Montgomery's letters of July 18th, 20th, it appears that 'four-fingered Jack' was in prison at Sonoma. *War with Mex., Repts, etc., Operations of U. S. Naval Forces*, 1846–7, p. 25–9. In the *Sta Rosa Democrat*, Aug. 8, 1874; *Sonoma Co. Hist.*, 107, etc., it is stated that the remains were buried where they fell, about two miles north of Sta Rosa, on the farm belonging in 1874 to John Underhill, and later to Geo. Moore. Ide, *Biog. Sketch*, 167–8, says the men were sent to Dr Bale's place for the powder. 'They were discovered and captured without resistance, having trusted the promise of the enemy that if they would give up their arms they should receive no harm.' He says they started on the 19th. Ford, *Bear Flag*, MS., 16–17, says it was on the 18th; and that the news was brought back by Sergt Gibson, who was sent out on the 20th. Baldridge, *Days of '46*, MS., 57–8, heard of no definite proof that the bodies were mutilated. He says that Padilla, on returning to Sonoma after the war, was nearly killed by one of the Bear Flag men. Coronel, *Cosas de Cal.*, MS., 155–60, gives a long account of the attack on Padilla in a saloon at Sonoma, the writer being present at the occurrence. He says that both Padilla and Carrillo assured him they were not guilty as charged. Knight, *Statement*, MS., 7–11, tells us that Cowie and Fowler left Sonoma against the advice of their friends in a spirit of bravado. Gomez, *Lo Que Sabe*, MS., 80–4, claims that Padilla confessed the mutilation of the victims. Several state that the two men were on their way to Bodega when captured. I do not deem it necessary to give a long list of references to authorities which merely mention this affair. It would include nearly every one touching on the revolution.

a sample of what could be done, so as in the main to
avoid bloodshed, could not be effectual unless the enemy
were allowed an advantage of five to one; and even
then a retreat must be feigned"!   Soon it was learned
that Todd also had been captured through the treachery of a guide employed to conduct him to the
coast.[11]   Ford tells us, being confirmed in this particular by Carrillo's testimony already cited, that two

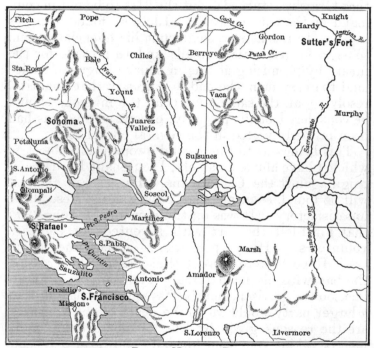

REGION NORTH OF BAY.

others were taken prisoners at about the same time
as Cowie and Fowler.   Suspecting that the four had
been captured, Ford, on the night of the 20th, sent
Sergeant Gibson with four men to Fitch's rancho.
Obtaining the powder, but no news, Gibson started

[11] Ide's letter to Wambough, in *Id.*, *Biog. Sketch*, 164–70. In the *Hist.*
Bear Flag, it is stated that Todd's mission was to carry to the coast a letter
which had arrived from Frémont on the 19th.

back, and near Santa Rosa was attacked by a small
party of Mexicans, one of whom was wounded, and
another brought captive to Sonoma.   It was from him
that information was first obtained about the murder.[12]
It is agreed by all that from about the 19th, the insurgent force rapidly increased, amounting within a
few days to about one hundred men; that many families were brought into Sonoma for protection; and
that Grigsby returned about the 21st to be put in command of the rifle company.   Ide also found time, as
he says, to reconstruct somewhat his financial system
so as to furnish rations to all; and to provide for the
future by promising at least a square league of choice
land to every man who had not already that quantity,
resolving at the same time that the missions should
be considered public properly, except so much as had
been properly vested in the several churches!

This brings us to the second prominent subject to
which I have alluded, namely, Lieutenant Ford's campaign against the Californians.   Particulars about it
will be found, as in all that occurred in these days,
unsatisfactory.   It was on the morning of June 23d[13]
that Ford left the fort with seventeen or eighteen
volunteers.[14]   His purpose was to rescue the prisoners.   Reports were current that Castro was crossing
the bay with his main force.   The danger of an attack on the garrison, and the less apparent danger that
a larger party would cause the death of the prisoners,
are the reasons given by Ide for not sending more
men or taking command himself; and he also repeats
at some length his orders, doubtless for the most part

[12] *Ford's Bear Flag Revol.*, MS., 16–18.

[13] He calls it the 22d himself, but there is some evidence that he is wrong.

[14] Ide says there were 18 besides the leader; Ford, 17; the common version
has it 22; Baldridge thinks there were 10; and the Californians talk of 50 or
60.   Baldridge agrees with Ide that one in every five was chosen, all wishing
to go; and he gives an amusing account of the selection, and of the successful efforts of one Badger Smith to join the party against the wishes of most,
and in spite of the fact that the lucky number of 5 did not fall to his lot.
Ford and Swift made some changes in the men after the first division.   Baldridge was one of those who remained behind; but he gives the best account
extant of the expedition in many of its phases. *Days of '46.* MS., 58–71.

imaginary. Ford was not very friendly to the commander, and generally ignores his authority in his narrative. It does not appear that there was an expectation of meeting any foe but the band of Padilla and Carrillo; and the march was directed toward Santa Rosa, under the guidance, as Ford says, of the prisoner taken by Gibson. It was found on arrival that the Californians had abandoned their camp, though they had left a few muskets in a house near by, which were destroyed. Following the trail at sunset, the 'Bears' reached Padilla's rancho, and learned from an Indian that the enemy would probably camp near the laguna of San Antonio. The pursuers spent the night at a point some half a mile from the laguna; and in the morning 'charged' upon the place, making prisoners of three or four men who were found there. Thence, after obtaining breakfast and changing horses, they directed their course toward San Rafael, and before long came suddenly upon the Californians.

Meanwhile Castro had sent one of his three divisions, fifty or sixty men, under Joaquin de la Torre, across from San Pablo to San Quintin, where they had landed in the evening of the 23d, and proceeded to San Rafael. With part of his men Torre continued his march by night, and having been joined by Padilla's company from Santa Rosa, encamped early in the morning with about fifty men at Olompali, or Camilo's rancho, about midway between San Rafael and Petaluma, where he was found by the 'Bears' in the forenoon of the 24th, and where the fight occurred. The meeting at this point was a surprise to both parties. The Californians were eating a late breakfast at the house, when an alarm was given that the Americanos were attacking the corral. Ford, on coming in sight of the rancho, made a charge upon it, only a few men being in sight, with a view to repeating the affair of San Antonio, and especially of securing a large band of horses that were seen in the cor-

ral. He knew nothing of Torre's force, and even if
the place were garrisoned, expected to meet only Padilla's company, twenty-five at the most. Those in
sight hurriedly retired behind a clump of trees; and
Ford, on reaching the corral and the trees, was surprised to see at the house near by an armed force of
forty-six. The Bears were ordered to dismount and
take refuge behind the trees, where, concealed by the
underbrush, they awaited an attack with their rifles
ready. The Californians made a charge, but at the
first discharge of the rifles Alférez Manuel Cantua
was killed, and Agaton Ruiz was badly wounded.
Torre's men retreated, firing from their saddles in a
random way; and the firing was continued for some
time at long range on both sides, no harm being
done to the Americans, but several of the Californians probably receiving slight wounds.[15] Presently

[15] The earliest account of the affair that I have found is that given in a
letter of the next day, June 25th, from a correspondent, 'Far West,' and
printed in the *Honolulu Friend*, Dec. 1, 1846. 'The first blood shed in battle
in Cal. flowed yesterday on the plains of Sonoma.' Twenty revolutionists attacked and defeated 77 Californians, killing 2, wounding 2, and losing 2.
Capt. Montgomery, in a letter to Larkin of July 2d, tells the story briefly.
Fifteen insurgents attacked by 70 Californians, who surprised them just as
they had put their horses in a corral, but were defeated, losing 4 in killed and
wounded. *Larkin's Doc.*, MS., iv. 192. July 4th, Larkin to U. S. consul at
Honolulu. Torre, driving ahead extra horses, came suddenly upon 15 or 20
men of Ide's party; both fired and parted, the foreigners carrying off the extra
horses, losing a Canadian, named Francis Young, and an American, while
the Californian lost Cantua, Ruiz, and Isidoro. *Id., Off. Corresp.*, MS., i.
125. July 8th, Larkin to Stearns. Represents the two parties as having come
unexpectedly upon each other, fired, and retreated—the Americans into a corral; while Torre—seeing that he had but 60 men against 15—tore off his
shoulder-straps, and did not deem himself safe until half a mile out in the
bay. *Id., Doc.*, MS., iv. 202.

In a deposition made by Ramon Carrillo before Judge Argüello on Aug.
26, 1846, *Hayes' Scrap-books, Cal. Notes*, iv. 125, he said: 'Next day [after
the shooting of Cowie and Fowler] Padilla sent me to Sta Clara to report to
Castro what had happened. Then Castro approved the act. Padilla in his
report urged Castro to send him reënforcements and hasten his march; therefore he sent 50 men under Joaquin de la Torre. We crossed to the other side,
and had a meeting with a party of foreigners at Nonpali. After joining
Padilla I proposed to him to set free his prisoners, and he did so before the
fight. Then the foe fell upon us, all being under the command of Torre, who
ordered us to mount and fire; but seeing that he could gain no advantage,
since most of his men ran away, he ordered the rest to retire. We formed
again in the plain, where we were not attacked; and then we retreated to San
Rafael, with one man killed and two wounded.'

The earliest printed account was that in the *Monterey Californian*, Aug.
15, 1846; and another appeared in the same paper of Sept. 12, 1846. The

Torre's force disappeared in the direction of San Rafael, and the Bears came out from their cover. They attempted no pursuit, but secured such horses as they needed, and returned to Sonoma, where they arrived in the afternoon of the same day, confident that they had killed at least eight or ten of the foe. Though Ford says nothing of the American prisoners, one of

latter was reprinted in the *S. F. Californian*, June 5, 1847; was given in substance in *Bryant's What I Saw in Cal.*, 292–3; and has been often repeated in the newspapers. These accounts represent the forces engaged as 22 or 18 against 85, and the number of killed as 8; the Americans firing 18 or 20 shots, and the Californians 200. Ford is said to have charged on them with several men, 'in such a manner as to draw them to the edge of the wood, where the remainder of the force was stationed.' The prisoners were rescued.

In my text I have followed *Ford's Bear Flag*, MS., 18–22, with some slight modifications derived from *Baldridge's Days of '46*, MS., 58–71, and other sources. Ford says that after leaving guards for his 5 prisoners and 40 horses, he had only 14 effective men; that the Mexicans took his movement to the woods as a retreat, and immediately charged; that his first fire killed 7 and the second volley 3; and that finally, the enemy being out of range, he took his prisoners and 400 horses, and returned to Sonoma. He says nothing of the rescued American prisoners. Baldridge gives a full narrative from the story told by the men on their return. He says they were scattered and careless, not expecting to find any foe at the rancho. Their charge was on the corral, to prevent the horses being turned loose; but fortunately the wood was at hand for their protection. Those that were behind had a narrow escape, and might have been cut off had the Californians acted promptly. The latter renewed their fire from a hill out of musket-range, but the rifles did some slight execution. Burgess, Williams, and Badger Smith were among those behind the main force, the latter distinguishing himself by his desperate courage. Todd escaped from the rancho house and joined his friends while the fight was going on, his companion, an Englishman, refusing to make the attempt. Todd claimed to have saved his life while a captive, solely by threatening the retaliation of his fellows on Vallejo and others at Sonoma. They did not take the horses, or even go over the battle-field, or visit the house. Swift was in reality the leading spirit of the enterprise. Lancey, *Cruise*, 64, follows also Ford and Baldridge through the medium of newspaper articles.

Luis German, *Sucesos*, MS., 18–24, is the only native Californian who gives a tolerably accurate account of the affair, in which he took part. He thinks, however, that there were 40 or 50 Americans, and says they fired from the corral as well as from the wood. The officers deemed it impossible with their escopetas and lances and horses to defeat men fighting from cover with rifles; and therefore ordered a retreat. Such other Californians as mention the matter give no details, contenting themselves with simply stating that Torre was surprised and defeated by the Bears, generally overstating the force of the latter, and several of them severely criticising Torre. Osio, *Hist. Cal.*, MS., 471–3, thinks Ford was thinking of surrender when Torre ordered a retreat! See also *Castro, Rel.*, MS., 195–9; *Id., Servicios*, MS.; *Alvarado, Hist. Cal.*, MS., v. 199–200; *Fernandez, Cosas de Cal.*, MS., 133–5; *Amador, Mem.*, MS., 166–7; *Bernal, Mem.*, MS., 3–4; *Galindo, Apuntes*, MS., 55–6; *Flores, Recuerdos*, MS., 9–10; *Gomez, Lo Que Sabe*, MS., 283–4; *Pinto, Apunt.*, MS., 100. *Vallejo, Hist. Cal.*, MS., v. 129–33, tells us that Ford, finding the Californians taking their siesta, fortified themselves in a corral and opened fire upon the sleeping foe! After a stubborn resistance of an hour and a half, in which

them, Todd, seems to have been rescued, and perhaps the other also. This fight at Olompali reflected no credit on Torre or his men, nor discredit on Ford and his little company; yet the cowardice of the one and the heroic deeds of the other have been greatly exaggerated in current accounts.

two Americans and one Californian fell, the latter retreated. Ruiz was taken captive, ordered shot, and left with five bullets in him, but finally recovered after treatment on the *Portsmouth!* Then the Bears sacked the rancho and beat to death the venerable Dámaso Rodriguez before the face of his daughters and granddaughters! The same Rodriguez, however, on June 28th renders an account of cattle and other property taken from his rancho by Frémont's men, to the value of $1,243. *Vallejo, Doc.*, MS., xii. 227.

Ide, *Biog. Sketch*, 170–4, asserts that Ford rendered a report to him as follows: 'I have done exactly as you ordered. We have whipped them, and that without receiving a scratch. We took their whole band of horses, but owing to the fact that about one half the men (?) retreated with all possible haste, I did not think best to encumber ourselves; so we only picked out each one a good horse.' 'Very well done! I did not order you to bring the horses,' etc., was Ide's reply. In the *Hist. Bear Flag Revol.*, we read: 'Lieut L. H. Ford was despatched in pursuit of a company of Mexicans, and found them; they proved to be 200 in number; gave them a fight, killed 8 and wounded 13; after which they fled. This victory gave a decided character to the revolution, and convinced the Spaniards that it was not prudent to attempt the capture of any more prisoners.' Fowler, *Bear Party*, MS., 4–5, says that the men were with difficulty restrained from plundering the ranchos. In the *S. F. Californian*, May 29, 1847, it is explained that the number of killed was incorrectly estimated from the riderless horses. Later it was learned that only 2 were killed and 2 wounded. Martin, *Narr.*, MS., 27–8, claims to have been one of the party that had the fight, under the command of Gibson. Gillespie, *Frémont's Cal. Claims*, 25–9, mentions the skirmish, in which 24 settlers had defeated 70 Mexicans, killing 1, wounding 4, and rescuing 2 prisoners. Boggs, in *Napa Register*, April 13, 1872, tells us that the wounded Californian (Ruiz) was shot through the lungs by Swift while trying to creep up a gully toward the Bears. He recovered, being treated on board a U. S. vessel; and the writer has often seen him and Swift drink together in later times, the wound being exhibited and the circumstances being narrated. Boggs represents the Californians as using cannon. The sec. of war in his report of Dec. 5th, *29th Cong. 2d Sess., H. Ex. Doc. 4*, p. 51, also says that Torre on his retreat lost 9 pieces of artillery! A writer in the *Napa Reporter*, Oct. 12, 1872, names Grigsby as the commander. See also mention in *Tuthill's Hist. Cal.*, 172; *Sac. Union*, April 27, 1855; and many of the recently published county histories. Tuthill, Smucker, and others, besides speaking of the capture of cannon and of transports, attribute Ford's campaign to Frémont or to men despatched by him. Frémont himself implied as much in his correspondence. Ford accuses a Frenchman—an old mountain man known by most of the party, who lived near the town, apparently Beaulieu, one of Frémont's old party—of having acted as a spy, being allowed to pass in and out of the fort freely. On returning from Olompali, Ford found a wounded horse in Vallejo's corral, left there by the Frenchman, who had reported the fight, but could not give a clear account of his own whereabouts and actions. He was arrested and put in irons.

CHAPTER VIII.

BEAR FLAG REVOLT—FRÉMONT'S CAMPAIGN.

1846.

COMPLAINTS AT SONOMA—FORD'S LETTER—FRÉMONT ON THE SACRAMENTO—
FORCED TO ACT—MARCH TO SONOMA—THE SAN RAFAEL CAMPAIGN—
MURDER OF BERREYESA AND THE HARO BROTHERS—A DASTARDLY ACT
BY FRÉMONT AND HIS MEN—TORRE'S RUSE—THE INSURGENTS SENT TO
SONOMA—A FALSE ALARM—SPIKING THE GUNS OF SAN FRANCISCO—
CAPTURE OF ROBERT RIDLEY—FOURTH OF JULY AT SONOMA—MILITARY
REÖRGANIZATION—CHANGE OF ADMINISTRATION—FRÉMONT ASSUMES
THE CHIEF COMMAND—IDE'S VERSION—THE BATTALION ORGANIZED—
FRÉMONT'S DESIGNS—NEWS FROM MONTEREY—BIBLIOGRAPHY OF THE
BEAR FLAG REVOLT.

SOME days before starting on his expedition against
the Californians, Lieutenant Ford had sent a messenger to the Sacramento, with an announcement that
Castro was said to be crossing the bay with the intention of attacking Sonoma. Ford himself tells us that
his letter was directed to Merritt, requesting him to
raise a force and come to the garrison's relief. Ide
states, however, that the message was addressed to
Frémont, informing that officer "that the men of the
garrison had no confidence in the ability of Mr Ide to
manage matters at the fort at Sonoma, and that they
were in great danger of being betrayed into the hands
of the Spaniards," since the commander had erred in
making conditions of peace with natives of the region.
It is doubtless true that Ide was regarded by many
of the insurgents as too much a man of theories and
dreams for his actual position, a man who regarded
himself as a great leader engaged in founding a re-

public, rather than a filibuster chief.   At any rate, he was deemed eccentric, and was not popular.

Meanwhile Frémont was waiting and watching. Possibly, he thought, it might not be necessary for him to interfere at all; or Castro, by marching directly against him, might give his interference the desired form of self-defence, or bring about a state of war between Mexico and the United States.   But on the same day, June 20th, there arrived Hensley and Reading from Marsh's, and John Neal from Sonoma, with news that the attack was to be directed against the insurgents; and in fulfilment of promises which, as already explained, he had made, Frémont felt himself called upon to act.   On Sunday he came down to Sutter's Fort to make some final arrangements respecting the garrison, and to leave such part of his *impedimenta* as was not needed.   Next day he returned to his camp on American River, and on Tuesday, the 23d, he started with his own company, and a reënforcement of settlers under Hensley, some ninety men in all, for Sonoma, where he arrived early in the morning of the 25th.   This was Frémont's first open coöperation with the insurgents; though a month later, when the insurrection seemed to have been successfully merged in the conquest, he virtually claimed in his letters that all had been done by him or under his orders.[1]

On June 26th, Frémont, reënforced by Ford's men and others from the constantly increasing garrison,

[1] Frémont to Benton, and B. to pres. *Niles' Reg.*, lxxi. 173–4, 191.   I do not give references for Frémont's march from Sac. to Sonoma, as there are neither doubts nor details to be presented.   Ide, letter to Wambough, tells us that Frémont at first criticised and ridiculed the proclamation and all that had been done; but very soon pretended to approve all, except that his own grievances at Castro's hands had not been added to the list named in the proclamation, which he complimented without limit as to style and matter!   But Frémont did not yet propose to take any part in the revolution, desiring simply to visit the bay as an explorer, and to accompany the insurgent army under Ford!   Ide's idea was that Frémont had expected Castro to scatter the insurgents and then attack him, a neutral party; that he came to Sonoma and to San Rafael still intent only on getting himself attacked and thus provoking a war, and that he finally pretended to join the movement when all the work had been done, merely to appropriate to himself the glory; in fact, that he used the Bears as cat's-paws to get his chestnuts from the fire—and there was certainly a color of truth in all this.

which was 75 strong after his departure, marched
with about 130 men to San Rafael. Here Torre and
Padilla were understood to be; and hither Castro
might be expected to come with the rest of his army.
No enemy, however, was found to oppose a peaceable
occupation of the mission buildings, where the insurgent force remained for about a week. The period
was for the most part an uneventful one. Castro did
not deem it best to cross the bay, and the exact
whereabouts of Torre could not be ascertained.

On Sunday, the 28th, the only blood of Frémont's
campaign was spilled, and that under such circumstances as to leave a stain of dishonor upon the commander and some of his men. A boat was seen
crossing from San Pablo. It contained four men,
and was apparently steering for a landing at or near
Point San Pedro, several miles from the mission.
Kit Carson was sent with two or three companions
to intercept them. After starting, Carson turned
back—so testifies Jasper O'Farrell, an eye-witness—
to ask Frémont, "Captain, shall I take those men
prisoners?" The reply, given with a wave of the
hand, was, "I have no room for prisoners." Then
they advanced, alighted from their horses, and from
a distance of about fifty yards deliberately shot three
of the strangers, who had landed and were approaching the mission. The three victims were the twin
brothers Francisco and Ramon de Haro, aged about
twenty, sons of a prominent citizen and former alcalde of San Francisco, and José de los Reyes Berreyesa, an old man who owned a rancho near Santa
Clara. Two divisions of Castro's army being at San
Pablo with the intention of crossing the bay as the
other division had done, one of the Haro boys volunteered to carry a message to Joaquin de la Torre, the
message relating doubtless to details of the plan for
crossing. The other boy wished to accompany his
brother and share his risks; and the old man Berreyesa insisted on being permitted to cross with his

nephews. His son was alcalde of Sonoma, reported to be a prisoner of the Osos; and the anxiety of a father and mother had impelled him to leave his home and seek an opportunity of visiting Sonoma. One of the Castros of San Pablo carried them over in his boat, left them at the landing, and returned; while the others started on foot for San Rafael, knowing nothing of its occupation by the insurgents. Their fate has been told.[2]

[2] Frémont, letter to Benton, *Niles' Reg.*, lxxi. 191, says simply: 'Three of Castro's party, having landed on the Sonoma side in advance, were killed near the beach; and beyond this there was no loss on either side.' Benton, *Id.*, 174, mentions the killing of Cowie and Fowler, 'in return for which three of De la Torre's men being taken were instantly shot.' Gillespie, *Frémont's Cal. Claims*, 28, says that on the afternoon of the 26th 'letters were intercepted which disclosed their plans, and required De la Torre to send horses to the point the next morning to mount 80 men who would be sent over at that time.' These letters, if there be no error, were probably those brought by Haro. Jasper O'Farrell, in the *Los Angeles Star*, Sept. 27, 1856, perhaps taken from another paper, besides narrating the facts of the murder as in my text, states that Carson claimed to have done the act unwillingly by Frémont's order. In the same paper is a letter from J. S. Berreyesa, in which, after narrating the circumstances of the killing, he states that the clothing of his dead father and cousins was stripped from their bodies by their murderers, and that Frémont refused to order the giving-up of his father's sarape, which one of the men was wearing, and which the son finally bought for $25. June 30th, Leidesdorff writes to Larkin of the shooting, which took place 'day before yesterday.' He names Sergt Manuel Castro as one of the killed. This report seems to have been current for a time. *Larkin's Doc.*, MS., iv. 189. Rico, *Mem.*, MS., 19–23, gives the most detailed account of the departure of the messengers, Rico having been the officer immediately concerned in sending the messenger. The first news of what had happened was brought by Torre the next day. Ford is silent on this matter. Ide, in his letter to Wambough, *Biog. Sketch*, 190, says: 'The flying Spaniards drew lots among their number, and three men, prepared with letters (intended to deceive the Bears) in their boots, put themselves in the power of their pursuers, threw away their arms, and fell on their knees begging for quarter; but the orders were to take no prisoners from this band of murderers, and the men were shot, and never rose from the ground...One of the men declared with his dying breath that he expected death, that he came on purpose to die for the benefit of his countrymen'! Bidwell, *Cal. in 1841-8*, MS., 170, and several others name G. P. Swift as one of Carson's companions. Hargrave, *Cal. in '46*, MS., 8, thinks Carson and a Frenchman were alone responsible for the deed. Swasey, Frémont's devout admirer, *Cal. '45-6*, MS., 10, thinks that 'the firing was perfectly justifiable under the circumstances'! Fowler, *Bear Party*, MS., 5, who was present at the time, says that Carson and the Canadian, who were alone responsible, were drunk. Martin, *Narr.*, MS., 29, who claims to have been the sentinel who first saw the boat, and one of the five who captured and shot the men, as well as Chas Brown, *Early Events*, MS., 25-6, who married a sister of the Haros, and several Californians, state that the bodies of the victims were allowed to lie unburied where they fell for several days. Phelps, *Fore and Aft*, 286-90, seems to have originated the absurd story that on one of the men was found an order from Castro to Torre to kill every foreigner he could find, man, woman, and child; and this story has been re-

The killing of Berreyesa and the Haros was a brutal murder, like the killing of Cowie and Fowler, for which it was intended as a retaliation. Its perpetrators put themselves below the level of García and Padilla. The Californians, or probably one desperado of their number, had killed two members of a band of outlaws who had imprisoned their countrymen, had raised an unknown flag, had announced their purpose of overthrowing the government, and had caused great terror among the people—the two men at the time of their capture being actively engaged in their unlawful service. In revenge for this act, the Bears deliberately killed the first Californians that came within their reach, or at least the first after their own strength became irresistible. The three victims were not members of Padilla's party, nor were they suspected of being such, nor charged with any offence. As messengers between Castro and Torre, their mission was a perfectly legitimate one; and so far as was known at the time of the shooting, they were not engaged in any public service whatever. They were in no sense spies, as has been sometimes implied. The statement that they brought orders to kill every man, woman, and child of the foreigners was an absurd fabrication; but had it been true that such papers were found on them, or even had it been proved that they had been the very murderers of Cowie and Fowler, these facts would afford no justification to those who killed them, because such facts could not have been known until after their death. They were given no chance for defence or explanation, but killed in cold blood at long rifle-range. Viewed in its most favorable light, the act was one of cowardly vengeance. Members of the

peated by Lancey, *Cruise*, 68, and copied from him in *Marin Co. Hist.*, 83, and several other works. The newspapers have often mentioned this affair in connection with the famous Haro claim to lands in S. F. The Californians, as a rule, give an accurate account of this occurrence. See *Castro, Rel.*, MS., 190–9; *Alvarado, Hist. Cal.*, MS., v. 207–10; *Vallejo, Hist. Cal.*, MS., v. 138–41; *Berreyesa, Relacion*, MS., 1–7; *Bernal, Mem.*, MS., 1–3; *Galindo, Apuntes*, MS., 56; *Sanchez, Notas*, MS., 15; *Juarez, Narrative*, MS.; *Amador, Mem.*, MS., 167; *Vallejo, Notas*, MS., 115–16.

Bear party, and apologists of their acts, have wisely had but little to say of the matter, always refusing to go beyond vague generalities. Of course John C. Frémont, as commander of the insurgents, is to be held responsible for the murder. That he personally gave the order which led to the result depends on the testimony of one person, a man whose reputation for veracity was good. In justice to Frémont, it is fair to say that the testimony was first publicly given during the political campaign of 1856, at a time when prejudice was generally more potent than love of truth; but justice also requires me to call attention to the fact that Frémont has never, so far as I know, denied the accuracy of O'Farrell's assertion.

Meanwhile scouting parties from the camp at San Rafael were trying to learn of Torre's whereabouts. They were not very successful; but late in the afternoon of the same day the messengers were shot they captured an Indian on whose person was found a letter in which Torre announced his intention of attacking Sonoma early the next morning. This letter, together with the one that had previously been intercepted, having been taken perhaps from Haro's dead body, making known Castro's plan of crossing before the hour of the proposed attack, caused Frémont to fear that Ide's garrison was in danger;[3] and he at once set out with nearly all his force, perhaps against the judgment of Ford and Gillespie, for Sonoma, where he arrived before sunrise on the 29th. There, also, if we may credit Ide's account, a letter had been intercepted, addressed to some of the natives, and disclosing the plan of attack. The citizens were in great terror, and wished to leave the town. This was not permitted; but as night came on they were allowed the jail as a shelter for the men, and Vallejo's house for the women and children. The garrison meanwhile made every preparation for defence; can-

[3] July 30th, Leidesdorff to Larkin also wrote that Torre was to move against Sonoma 'yesterday.' *Larkin's Doc.*, MS., iv. 189.

non, rifle, and musket were loaded and primed, and sentinels were posted. Just before dawn the advanced sentries heard the distant tramp of horses. Clearly, the threatened attack was to be a reality. Without vouching for its accuracy, I quote Ide's melodramatic narrative of what followed. "Thus prepared, in less than one minute from the first alarm, all listened for the sound of the tramping horses—we heard them coming!—then, low down under the darkened cañon we saw them coming! In a moment the truth flashed across my mind; the Spaniards were deceiving us! In a moment orders were given to the captains of the 18-pounders to reserve fire until my rifle should give the word; and, to prevent mistake, I hastened to a position a hundred yards in front of the cannon, and a little to the right-oblique, so as to gain a nearer view. 'Come back; you will lose your life!' said a dozen voices. 'Silence!' roared Captain Grigsby; 'I have seen the old man in a bull-pen before to-day!' The blankets of the advancing host flowed in the breeze. They had advanced to within 200 yards of the place where I stood. The impatience of the men at the guns became intense, lest the enemy came too near, so as to lose the effect of the spreading of the shot. I made a motion to lay down my rifle. The matches were swinging. 'My God! They swing the matches!' cried the well known voice of Kit Carson. 'Hold on, hold on!' we shouted, ''tis Frémont, 'tis Frémont!' in a voice heard by every man of both parties, we cried, while Captain Frémont dashed away to his left to take cover behind an adobe house; and in a moment after he made one of his most gallant charges on our fort; it was a noble exploit; he came in a full gallop, right in the face and teeth of our two long 18's!" [4]

It did not take long for Frémont to convince himself that he had been outwitted; and after a hasty

[4] *Ide's Biog. Sketch,* 187–90.

breakfast he set out again for San Rafael, where he
arrived within twenty-four hours of the time he left it
—to learn that Torre had made good use of his time to
recross the bay and rejoin Castro with all his original
force, and such residents of the northern frontier as
chose to accompany him.   The wily Californian had
written letters expressly intended to fall into the
hands of the Osos, and thus facilitate his own escape.
After retreating before twenty rifles, he had no wish
to face two hundred.   He left San Rafael just before Frémont's first arrival; and, as Castro's force
did not arrive, he soon began to consider his position
a critical one.   Facilities for crossing the bay were
so uncertain that it was not safe to be seen at any
landing while the mission was occupied by the foe;
therefore Don Joaquin feigned an advance into the
interior toward Petaluma, and wrote the letters to be
intercepted.   The ruse was entirely successful; and,
Frémont's force having been sent to Sonoma, the Californians, to the number of 75 or 80, appeared at Sauzalito in the morning of June 29th.   Captain Richardson had an old launch, or lighter, lying at anchor there,
which he declined to lend, but which he permitted
Torre's men to 'take by force;' and all were soon afloat.
Wind and tide were not favorable, and for a long time
they lay near the shore, in great fear lest Frémont
should return, and no less apprehensive of pursuit by
the boats of the *Portsmouth*.   Some were so frightened
that they believe to this day that they were thus pursued.   But long before the Bears had returned to
San Rafael the Californians had landed at San Pablo,
whence, with the other divisions of the 'grand army,'
they marched next day to Santa Clara.[5]

[5] Luis German, *Sucesos*, MS., 18–24, gives the most connected and detailed account of Torre's escape.   Frémont, in his letter to Benton, followed
by the set of authorities that obtained their information from that letter,
claims, in a general way, the credit of having driven Torre away, besides destroying his transports and spiking his cannon south of the bay, as will presently be noticed.   Gillespie, *Frémont's Cal. Claims*, 28, has the assurance to
write: 'Capt. Frémont returned to Sonoma, leaving a force to protect San
Raphael.   This movement, executed with so much promptness, alarmed De

Having thus 'driven' Torre and his men away, Frémont and the Bears had no further opposition to fear north of the bay, and no reason to remain longer at San Rafael; yet before their departure for Sonoma two minor enterprises were undertaken, which, if they served no other purpose, figured somewhat attractively in reports of this grand campaign. On July 1st Frémont and Gillespie visited Phelps on board the *Moscow*, and having removed that gentleman's scruples by the assurance that war had really been declared, and that they were "acting in obedience to orders of the United States government," obtained his coöperation for a movement on San Francisco. Phelps furnished his vessel's launch with a crew, going himself as pilot, to carry Frémont and about twenty of his men across to the old castillo. Wading ashore through the surf, and boldly entering the fort, this band of warriors proceeded to spike the ten guns found there, and to wade back to the boat. In the absence of a garrison, with no powder, it is not surprising that, so far as can be known, not one of the ten cannon offered the slightest resistance. But the energies of the insurgents were not exclusively directed against abandoned guns; for next day ten of their number, under Semple, appeared in the streets of Yerba Buena, at noon,

la Torre to such a degree that he fled with his command in the most cowardly manner to Sausalito, where he stole Mr Richardson's launch, and escaped across the bay'! Phelps, *Fore and Aft*, 286–92, was at Sauzalito at the time, in command of the *Moscow*, and he gives an inaccurate version of what occurred, which has, however, been considerably used by later writers. He says that Frémont sent him, Phelps, word that he would drive Torre to Sauzalito that night, whence he could not escape without the *Moscow's* boats. Phelps proceeded to make all safe, and took the precaution to anchor farther out a launch lying near the beach, putting some provisions on board for Frémont's use! But when Torre arrived in the morning, a boat was mysteriously procured from Yerba Buena, and the launch was reached. Phelps informed the commander of the *Portsmouth*, but he declined to intercept the fugitives. Montgomery, writing to Larkin July 2d, *Larkin's Doc.*, MS., iv. 192, speaks of Torre as having been chased by Frémont, barely escaping by his good luck in finding a large freight boat. Ford, *Bear Flag Revolution*, MS., 22–5, claims that he and Gillespie opposed the march to Sonoma. The *Hist. Bear Flag* agrees for the most part with Ide—naturally, as Ide was its chief author. It speaks of Castro having sent 200 men across the bay. Larkin, *Off. Corresp.*, MS., i. 125, in a letter of July 4th to the U. S. consul at Honolulu, speaks of Torre's defeat, and of the trick by which he escaped.

and captured Robert Ridley, captain of the port, who was taken from his house and sent to New Helvetia. This was doubtless done at the instigation of Vice-consul Leidesdorff, who, as we have seen, had repeatedly denounced Ridley and Hinckley as "more Mexican than the Mexicans themselves," in their opposition to the Bear movement. Hinckley would doubtless have shared Ridley's fate had he not died two days before. Obtaining such supplies as were to be found on the *Moscow*, together with cattle from the ranchos of the region about San Rafael, Frémont returned with the whole insurgent force to Sonoma. Through Benton he ingeniously contrived, without quite committing himself to a falsehood, to create the impression among the people of the United States, not only that he had been in active command of the revolutionists from the first, but that finally, after defeating Torre, he had driven him across the bay, spiking his cannon, destroying his transports, and breaking up all communication between the north and south —thus making the whole campaign a brilliant success![6]

The 4th of July was celebrated at Sonoma by the burning of much gunpowder, reading of the declaration of independence, and a fandango in the evening. Frémont and his men returned from San Rafael that day, or more probably the evening before; at any rate, in time to take part in the festivities.[7] Next day, though some say that also was on the

[6] Frémont to Benton, and B. to pres., in *Niles' Reg.*, lxxi. 173, 191. Montgomery, in two postscripts to a letter of July 2d to Larkin, mentions the spiking of the guns and capture of Ridley. *Larkin's Doc.*, MS., iv. 192. Phelps, *Fore and Aft*, 285–92, gives the fullest account of the first affair—in fact, all we know of it, so far as details are concerned. See also *Bryant's What I Saw in Cal.*, 294–6; *Tuthill's Hist. Cal.*, 173–4; *Lancey's Cruise*, 70, 72; *Upham's Life Frémont*, 233–4; *Yolo Co. Hist.*, 16.

[7] Frémont in his letter to Benton, and Gillespie in his testimony, say that they returned on the evening of the 4th; but the latter speaks of the salutes fired during the day. According to the *Hist. Bear Flag*, the return was on the 3d. Baldridge says that the declaration, a copy which the writer had brought over the mountains, was read by Lieut Woodworth of the navy.

4th, the people were called together to deliberate on matters of public importance. Respecting details of what was accomplished, our evidence is meagre and contradictory to a certain extent; but it is certain that a new military organization was effected, and that Frémont was put in command of the insurgent forces, Ide's authority terminating on that day. Frémont himself says: "In the morning I called the people together and spoke to them in relation to the position of the country, advising a course of operations which was unanimously adopted. California was declared independent, the country put under martial law, the force organized, and officers elected. A pledge, binding themselves to support these measures and to obey the officers, was signed by those present. The whole was placed under my direction. Several officers from the *Portsmouth* were present at this meeting."[8] William Baldridge claims to have been chairman of the meeting, and names John Bidwell as secretary.[9] Bidwell tells us that Frémont—after a speech in which he expressed his willingness to coöperate, criticised some irregularities of the past, and insisted on implicit obedience—named Ide, Reading, and the writer as a committee to report a plan of organization. Unable to agree, each made a report of his own, with the understanding that Gillespie should select one of the three. He chose Bidwell's, perhaps on account of its brevity. As presented by the author from memory, it was a simple agreement to render military service in support of independence.[10]

<hr/>

[8] F. to B. *Niles' Reg.*, lxxi. 191. Benton made some improvements on this as on other parts of the same letter as follows: 'The north side of the bay was now cleared of the enemy, and on July 4th Capt. Frémont called the Americans together at Sonoma, addressed them upon the dangers of their position, and recommended a declaration of independence, and war upon Castro and his troops as the only means of safety. The independence was immediately declared, and war proclaimed.' These statements were repeated in substance by the secretary of war, and by many other writers, some of whom go so far as to say that Frémont was elected governor!

[9] *Baldridge's Days of '46*, MS., 6.

[10] 'To be signed by all willing to prosecute the war already begun, to

The document signed at Sonoma on July 5th, so far as I know, is no longer extant; nor have we any written contemporary record of that day's transactions. Yet it appears clearly to me that no radical changes were effected in the plan of revolt; that nothing like a new declaration of independence was made; that there was no official act ignoring what had been already accomplished. It was simply the formal and public assumption by Frémont of a command which by most of the insurgents he had been expected to assume, or even deemed tacitly to hold from the first. He had virtually thrown off his mask of caution by his San Rafael campaign, and it was hardly possible, even had he desired it, to draw back now. Naturally he required pledges of obedience and discipline; and military reörganization was of course necessary for active operations against Castro.

To one, however, William B. Ide, this day's doings were of no small import, since they put an end to all his greatness. He characterized them as "events and circumstances which changed the character of our enterprise, and presented California to the United States as a trophy of that species of conquest that wallows in the blood of murder, or of that ignoble traffic that makes the price of liberty the price of blood, instead of presenting the same fair land on terms of honorable compact and agreement, such as all the world can participate in without loss or dishonor, by the free, frank expression of voluntary consent and good-will of the parties." Ide regarded himself as the leader of the revolutionists, and as the founder of a republic. He moreover regarded the revolution as a complete success. In his eyes the triumph had already been won; California had been wrested from

wit: the undersigned agree to organize and to remain in service as long as necessary for the purpose of gaining and maintaining the independence of California.' This was signed by all at Sonoma, including Frémont's men, and was signed by others later at the Mokelumne River on the march south; since which time it has not appeared. *Bidwell's Cal. in 1841-8*, MS., 171-4. This author puts Frémont's speech on the 4th, and the fandango on the evening of Sunday the 5th, after the organization.

Mexico. There remained only the trifling formality of taking possession of that part of the country south of San Francisco Bay, and this would already have been wellnigh accomplished had Frémont not prevented the sending of reënforcements to Weber at San José.[11] It was Ide's plan, as he claims, and as there is no good reason to doubt, when once he had fully established a free and independent government, to apply for admission to the American Union on terms to be settled by negotiations, in which of course he personally would play a prominent rôle. This method of annexation in his view would not only give him the fame and profit to which he was entitled, but was more honorable to the United States and just to the Californians than the plan of conquest finally adopted.

Naturally, holding these views, Ide regarded Frémont's 'unwarrantable interference' as a grievous wrong. His theory was that Frémont, finding that his original plan of provoking an attack by Castro had failed, and that the revolutionists had succeeded without his aid, had deliberately plotted with other United States officers to obtain command of the movement. His purpose was believed to be twofold: first, to gain for himself glory as conqueror of California; and second, to give the country to the United States without the troublesome negotiations and treaty stipulations which would be necessary in dealing with an independent government.[12] As to the means by

[11] *Ide's Biog. Sketch*, 191, etc. He says three men had arrived on July 1st, with news of preparations south of the bay. He at once made ready a boat to send arms and other aid; but Frémont managed to prevent the measure on one pretext and another, really to prevent the complete success of the revolution until he could obtain exclusive control. Ide's editor, his brother, says: 'The civil and military authority of Mexico had been thoroughly wiped out; California was not, and had not been, from the 15th of June to the 5th of July under Mexican rule. She was what her rude national flag had from day to day proclaimed, the California Republic. During these 20 days there was no obstruction, by a conflicting party to the exercise by the Bear Flag government of its entire functions and prerogatives of national independence'! p. 207.

[12] Ide's version of the 'second edition revised and corrected' of Frémont's plan is as follows: '1st, secure the command of the independent forces of the Bear Flag republic. 2d, hoist the U. S. flag, and follow up to the entire conquest. 3d, if no war between Mex. and the U. S. ensue,

which the plot was carried out, Ide gives the following explanation: The people were assembled at Salvador Vallejo's house, Frémont's 72 men, with eight or ten 'gentlemen officers' from the ships, under arms in one room; and about 280 of the Bears unarmed in another, with an armed sentry between the two. Then Frémont entered the larger room with Gillespie and others, and made a speech. He still declined to meddle in California politics, but was willing to render aid against Castro, whom he denounced as a usurper, on condition that the insurgents would pledge themselves to "abstain from the violation of the chastity of women," to conduct the war honorably, and to obey their officers implicitly. Ide then made a speech, consenting to the pledge of obedience, to draft which a committee was chosen. The larger assembly named Ide on this committee, whereupon the smaller, 'the council of friends,' named two of their number. In committee meeting the majority, being and representing men who were not connected with the Bear Flag movement at all, favored setting aside all that had been done in the past and starting anew; and this idea was embodied in their report. The reasons urged were: 1st, that July 5th immediately follows the 4th; 2d, that Frémont, as 'advisory leader,' should begin with the beginning; and, 3d, that in changing the 'administration,' a new organization was proper—"or, more definitely, that we who are out of office may have a chance to get in." After an ineffectual attempt to get possession of the chair by the representatives of the smaller body, the majority report was first submitted for approval; and then that of the minority—but here Ide's narrative abruptly terminates. We have no means of

sell out all the military stores of the U. S. to the govt of Cal., and obtain Cal. by treaty with the new govt; but in the event of a war, to seize and acquire the whole by the right of conquest.' The officer who should thus violate national honor would naturally be cashiered by his govt; 'yet as a solace for his dishonor [to use the language of our informant, who was one of said U. S. officers], he will be in town with a pocket full of rocks.' *Biog. Sketch*, 195. Ford's narrative does not include these matters.

knowing this author's version of the final result, or
of the methods by which Frémont succeeded in his
main purpose of obtaining the command, notwithstanding the numerical strength of the Bears as compared with the 'council of friends.' Perhaps Ide
would have represented the adoption of Bidwell's
brief pledge as a victory over those who wished to
blot out all that had been done before July 5th, and
his own withdrawal in favor of Frémont as a compromise intended to prevent dissensions; or perhaps
his claim might be to have resigned in disgust, because his policy could not be fully carried out.

The truth is that Ide greatly overrated his influence
and achievements. He believed himself entitled to the
glory of having organized a great revolution, won a
great victory, and founded a great republic. His companions of the original Bear party looked upon him
as an honest, zealous, but eccentric and somewhat fanatical old man, whose zeal, good sense, and education
rendered him as well fitted for the command as any
of their number after the departure of Semple and
Grigsby, and whose eccentricities and mania for theorizing and writing and making speeches could not be
regarded as a serious fault on the part of a garrison
commander. They cared nothing for his political
theories, and never thought of him as in any sense a
rival of Frémont. It was on the latter's coöperation
that they had founded their hopes of successful revolt
from the first, and they were ready to welcome his
accession to the active command at any time, regarding it as practically an alliance with the United
States. Sympathy is naturally excited in Ide's behalf
by reason of his many good qualities, by his devotion
to what seemed to him a worthy cause, by the earnestness with which he presents his wrongs, and by the
fact that Frémont did unquestionably rob him of a
certain portion of what both parties and the world at
large regarded as fame. But it must be borne in mind
that his cause was in reality a bad one—mere filibus-

terism; that his influence in promoting the revolt had been much less than that of Frémont; and that, far from having conquered California as he believed, he had really accomplished little or nothing toward that conquest. Moreover, it is not easy to comprehend that his plan of giving the country to the United States was in any way more honorable than that by which the annexation was effected, and which he so violently denounces.

Respecting the military organization effected on July 5th at Sonoma, I have found no contemporary records whatever. All that is known of the California battalion as it was at first organized is that it numbered about 250 men of the Bear Flag party and Frémont's explorers; formed into three companies under John Grigsby, Henry L. Ford, and Granville P. Swift respectively as captains; all under the command of Frémont, though it does not appear what was the exact rank and title—perhaps acting major—assumed by that officer; and with Lieutenant Gillespie apparently as adjutant.[13] About the terms of enlistment we have only Bidwell's memory of the paper signed by the volunteers. Ide seems to have joined the force as a private. Something more of detail about the battalion in a later stage of its development will appear in the annals of the conquest. Captain Grigsby with 50 men or more remained at Sonoma. The rest of the

[13] Frémont says nothing of the force; simply mentions that it was organized under his command, that officers were elected, Grigsby and 50 men being left at Sonoma. *Niles' Reg.*, lxxi. 191. Gillespie, *Frémont's Cal. Claims*, 28, says that four companies were organized, one being left at Sonoma, and that the whole force was 224. Hensley, *Id.*, 35, says: 'We organized the "California Battalion," adopting the "grizzly bear" as our emblem, requesting Capt. Frémont to take command of the battalion, and of all the forces and resources of the country, which command he accepted.' In a contribution to the *Alta*, July 3, 1866, Gillespie gave the force as 250, 70 being left at Sonoma; and names himself as adjutant and inspector, with rank of captain. Followed by *Lancey's Cruise*, 73, 102. In the *Bear Flag Hist.*, we read that the volunteers were 'organized into three companies under captains Grigsby, Ford, and Swift, leaving a small artillery company to take charge of the fort.' Ide says nothing of the organization, but states that there were about 350 men at Sonoma. Bidwell mentions the election of captains Ford and Swift only. Baldridge says there was some rivalry for the post of senior captain; but Grigsby was chosen. By different authorities the force of the battalion on arrival at Monterey is given as 160 or 180 men.

force under Fremont started July 6th for the Sacramento, there to make preparations for an advance upon Castro, taking with them such horses, cattle, and other needed supplies as the Bears had accumulated, or as they could find in the adjoining ranchos.

Frémont and his battalion arrived at Sutter's Fort, and moved up to the old camp on the American River on the 9th and 10th of July. It was the avowed intention to march with the least possible delay against Castro in the south; and it is of course impossible to prove that such was not Frémont's real purpose. I suspect, however, that he would have found a plausible pretext for delaying the movement for several weeks, in expectation of news that war had been declared. He was by no means afraid of Castro's forces, nor was he averse to a fight in which old scores might be settled; but his position as an officer of the United States was a delicate one. By postponing hostile action until the news of war should come, he might, thanks to his past caution, set up the plea, if by reason of official censure or other motives it should seem safest, that he had not instigated the revolt or taken any active part in it, but had taken the nominal command at the last for any one of a dozen reasons which his fertile brain would suggest. It is by no means impossible that he might have found it politic under certain circumstances to assume the ground imputed to him by Ide, that he had gained control of the movement solely to remove obstacles, in the shape of an independent government, to the military conquest of the country. The desired tidings arrived, however, on the very day that the battalion camped on the American; so that the movement even from its beginning at Sonoma has been known as a 'pursuit of Castro,' news of whose retreat from Santa Clara reached the Sacramento at about the same time. With the news of Sloat's operations at Monterey, there came a U. S. flag, which was raised next morning, July 11th, over Sutter's Fort; the stars and stripes had already been floating at Sonoma for two days; the Bear Flag revolt was at an end.

In an introductory chapter to the general subject, and in the course of my narrative, I have already said quite enough respecting the causes, effects, and general character of the Bear Flag revolt, and I do not propose to reöpen the subject even en résumé. Neither do I deem it best to notice, except in a passing glance, the actions of the insurgents respecting private persons and property while in possession of Sonoma and the surrounding region. It is not possible to ascertain the exact truth in this matter. Those connected with the movement, almost without exception, both in statements of the time and in later testimony, declare that no outrage or excess was committed; that but little private property except horses was taken, and these always with the consent of the owners, who took receipts to prove their claims against the new government later. It is not necessary to believe that all this was literally true; there can be no doubt that small quantities of plunder were taken by the insurgents from many citizens without any formalities whatever; and it is not likely that the rancheros were eager to part with their horses and cattle, even in exchange for the Bears' promises to pay. Yet it is certain that the leaders did their best to restrain their somewhat unruly followers; and their efforts were, all circumstances considered, successful. Rarely if ever has a filibuster revolt been conducted with so much moderation in respect of private rights. I might introduce here a long list of statements by Californians about outrages committed by the hated Bears; but it would serve no good purpose. Many of these accusations are evidently and absurdly false; others are grossly exaggerated; and I have no means of distinguishing accurately the comparatively few that are well founded. As to the obligations contracted by the insurgents for horses and other supplies from June 14th to July 9th, they were turned over to U. S. officials, together with the so-called public property designed as security for their payment. The matter of 'California claims' in congress is too complicated to be noticed here. These early claims were, however, acknowledged by the United States, in connection with more numerous and important obligations of similar nature incurred during the conquest. The two classes of claims are so blended that it is not easy to determine from existing records the fate of any particular claim of the earlier period. Many of the rancheros lost their receipts; others sold theirs to third parties at nominal prices; and others still presented fictitious claims. Few if any bona fide original claimants ever received payment for the property lost.[14] I append in closing some notes on the bibliography of the Bear Flag revolt.[15]

[14] In *Bear Flag Papers*, MS., 21, is a memorandum of sundries taken from some one on June 21st and July 5th. It is marked 'taken by order of Capt. Frémont.' In *Vallejo, Hist. Cal.*, MS., v. 141-6, and Mrs Leese's *Hist. Bear Party*, there are somewhat vague accounts of troubles between the Bear leaders and Mrs Vallejo and family, the latter being accused of sending arms and ammunition to Padilla and Carrillo.

[15] I name different sources of information—already often referred to in the preceding chapters—approximately in the order of their importance. The *Bear Flag Papers* is a collection of about 80 original documents of 1846 bearing on the capture and occupation of Sonoma, the imprisonment of Vallejo and his companions at Sutter's Fort, and other topics closely connected with the revolt. Almost without exception, these papers contain information not existing elsewhere. Of especial value are the original capitulations and parole papers signed at Sonoma on June 14th, a contemporary narrative by Leese, official reports of Lieut Misroon's visit to Sonoma, and some correspondence of the prisoners. I have no hesitation in putting this collection at the head of the list. For the preservation of such valuable historic records the public is indebted, as I am for their possession, to Gen. M. G. Vallejo. *Leese's Bear Flag; Statement of Jacob P. Leese to Col. J. C. Frémont. Proceedings in Upper California previous to the declaration of the war in this department*, is one of the papers of the collection just mentioned, and merits special notice. It is a narrative of 12 large and closely written pages in Leese's hand; prepared probably in 1847, under circumstances not definitely known; and containing a more detailed account of the taking of Sonoma, in certain respects, and especially of the journey of the captives to Sacramento, than any other. Leese's statements are confirmed by other evidence in some parts; and there is no reason to doubt their accuracy in others.

The manuscripts contained in *Larkin's Doc. Hist. Cal.* and *Larkin's Off. Correspondence*, which bear upon the matter would, if brought together, form a collection much larger, and in some respects more important, than that just mentioned. They consist of more than 200 documents, chiefly correspondence of Larkin, Stearns, Leidesdorff, Frémont, Montgomery, Gillespie, Marsh, and other prominent men, dated in the first half of 1846. They are invaluable in fixing dates; and they throw much light on every phase of what was occurring in all parts of the country. *Buchanan's Instructions to Larkin* is the most important single document, though belonging only indirectly to the Bear Flag revolt. *Sawyer's Documents* consist of copies made from the Larkin papers before they came into my possession; but it includes a few papers that have been lost from the originals. They were given me by the late Charles H. Sawyer.

Other private archives particularly rich in material on the revolt are *Castro, Doc. Hist. Cal.; Documentos para la Hist. de California;* and *Vallejo, Doc. Hist. Cal.* Very many important papers, official and unofficial, are found in these collections and nowhere else, to say nothing of the hundreds of petty communications which, in the aggregate, help so much to perfect the historic record. The smaller collections of *Doc. Hist. Cal.*, bearing the names of Guerra, Pico, Bandini, Olvera, Moreno, Coronel, and Carrillo respectively, also contain each its original and contemporary contributions to current history, with special reference to affairs in the south. The *Cal. Pion. Soc. Archives* and the *Monterey Consulate Archives* furnish each a few items not obtainable elsewhere.

The public archives of the Californian government furnish but meagre information respecting the events of this period. There is hardly anything of value relating to events on the northern frontier in June and July. The archives—notably the *Legislative Records; Depart. St. Papers,* tom. vi.–viii.; *Los Angeles, Arch.;* and *San José, Arch.*—are richer in matters about events preceding the outbreak; though even in this respect they are much less complete than the private archives.

Among personal narratives—that of Leese having been noticed, and after a passing glance at four *Letters from California,* signed 'The Farthest West,' written in June 1846 from Yerba Buena, intended for a New York paper, but originally published in the *Honolulu Friend,* Oct. 15–Dec. 1, 1846, and containing much interesting information on current events—that of William B. Ide merits our first attention. It is found in *A Biographical Sketch of the Life of William B. Ide; with a minute and interesting account of one of the largest emigrating companies (3,000 miles over land) from the East to the Pacific coast. And what is claimed as the most authentic and reliable account of 'the virtual conquest of California in June 1846, by the Bear Flag Party,' as given by its leader, the late Hon. William Brown Ide. Published for the subscribers.* n.p., n.d. (probably Claremont, N. H., 1880), 16mo, 240 p. This little work was edited and printed by Simeon Ide, a brother of William B., and may be noticed in three distinct parts. 1st, biographical matter contributed by different members of the family, and including original letters; a most praiseworthy sketch of the life of a prominent pioneer, containing interesting reminiscences of the overland trip by Ide's daughter, Mrs Healey. 2d, an account of the revolution compiled by the editor from various sources, and of no value whatever; since the aged brother in his New Hampshire home had no facilities for acquiring accurate information; and the men in California to whom the proofs were submitted for revision—or at least those of them whose ideas were followed—were not well qualified for the task. And, 3d, *Ide's Letter to Senator Wambough,* a narrative of the revolt supposed to have been written before 1848, and devoted mainly to a vindication of the author's reputation as the real 'Conqueror of California' against the rival claims of Capt. Frémont. This is by far the most important part of the work. In many respects it is a more complete record than any other narrative. It is most eloquently though quaintly written. There is every reason to believe, from the narrative in question and from other sources, that Ide was an honest and well meaning man. This letter, however, is a piece of special pleading, everywhere colored by a violent prejudice, sometimes amounting to a mania, against Frémont, whom Ide honestly believed to have robbed him of his fame as a conqueror and founder of a republic. The merits of the case have been discussed elsewhere; but the author's grievance and bitter prejudice doubtless lead him at several points away from strict accuracy in the presentation of minor facts, and thus detract from the merit of the narrative. The Wambough letter, with some editorial comments, containing nothing not in the *Biog. Sketch*, was issued separately under the title, *Who Conquered California, etc.* Claremont, N. H. (1880), 12mo, 137 p. Mr Ide quotes once or twice a diary kept by him at Sonoma. It is not very unlikely that this manuscript may some day be brought to light. I have also a MS. copy of *Ide's Biog. Sketch* made before the work was published.

A manuscript report signed by John H. Nash, John Grigsby, and Wm B. Ide as a 'committee' of citizens, and dated Sonoma, May 13, 1847, was furnished to the *Sangamon (Ill.) Journal*, which paper published a 'brief résumé' of its contents reprinted in *Niles' Register*, lxxiii. 110–11, 157. It is not known what has become of the original. I have quoted the summary as *history of the Bear Flag Revolt*. The original had an appendix containing 'matters and things which ought not to be published at the present time,' say the editors. From the closing paragraph, it appears that the report was written to favor the payment of the 'California claims,' and to obtain a 'land premium' and other remuneration for revolutionary services. It was probably written chiefly by Ide, and in general purport does not differ materially from the Wambough letter. Henry L. Ford's *Bear Flag Revolution in Cal.* is a MS. narrative written by the author in 1851, for Rev. S. H. Willey, who published a summary of its contents in the *S. F. Bulletin* and *Sta Cruz Sentinel*. My copy was made from the original in 1877. Ford was a prominent man in the revolt from the beginning, and may be regarded as a trustworthy witness. As he wrote from memory, his dates are inaccurate; and there are some indications that in his recollections he sometimes confounded what he saw and what he read in the early papers; still his statement must be regarded as one of the most important extant.

Among the statements written by Bear Flag men from memory expressly for my use, William Baldridge's *Days of '46* is by far the most valuable and complete; though some useful items are given by Knight, Hargrave, Fowler, McChristian, Marshall, Gregson, and others. Bidwell, *California 1841–8*, gives testimony that has been of great service to me, being somewhat disappointing, however, in comparison with his testimony on other matters, and with what might naturally be expected from a gentleman of Bidwell's intelligence and opportunities. John A. Sutter's *Personal Reminiscences* are not very valuable in this connection, except as showing the author's views on certain points. John C. Frémont has repeatedly promised and as often failed to give me his testimony on the subject. Thomas S. Martin's *Narrative*, by one of Frémont's men, is quite extensive and interesting; but is unfortunately so inaccurate on many matters susceptible of proof as to destroy its value on other affairs.

Original statements by native Californians, of which I have many besides the elaborate histories of Vallejo, Osio, Alvarado, Pico, and Bandini, and the briefer recollections of Manuel Castro, Francisco Arce, Francisco Rico, Estévan de la Torre, and Luis German, with contributions of Antonio F. Coronel and Narciso Botello in the south, are on this subject as on most others very uneven in quality. Side by side in the same narrative are found the most absurd and evident inaccuracies on one point and valuable testimony on another. The Bear Flag revolt is on an average more fairly presented by these gentlemen than are many other topics of California history. Their statements in the aggregate are very valuable when used in connection with and tested by contemporary records; without such accompaniment they would lead the historian far astray on many points. Of course I have no space here to particularize the merits and weaknesses of so many narratives; and no one of them is, on this special subject, notably superior or inferior to the rest.

The *New Helvetia Diary*, MS., is a record of the time which fixes several dates, and is otherwise of considerable value. *Sutter's Diary* is substantially in most respects a résumé of the same record. *Clyman's Diary*, MS., contains some items bearing indirectly on the general topic. In *Niles' Register* of 1846–7, vol. lxx. p. 161, lxxxi. p. 173–4, 187–91, is a valuable collection of correspondence on Frémont's movements, some of it not elsewhere found. It was on Frémont's letter to Benton, and on that of the latter to the president, that were founded brief mentions of the subject in various govt reports of the time, as well as the current popular ideas for several years. *Frémont's Geog. Memoir* and *Kern's Journal* contain some matters pertaining more or less directly to the subject; and *Peters' Life of Kit Carson* may be regarded as containing some original matter in the shape of Carson's testimony, though of little value. *Frémont's Cal. Claims* (30th cong. 1st sess., Sen. Rept no. 75) is a collection of important testimony taken in 1848 from Frémont, Gillespie, Hensley, and many other prominent men, on a subject growing directly out of the revolt.

Phelps' Fore and Aft and *Revere's Tour of Duty* are books written by men who were in California in 1846, and to some extent actors in the scenes described. Both authors fall into some errors, doubtless without any intentional misrepresentation. The *Monterey Californian*, 1846, and the *S. F. Californian*, 1847, contained a good deal of valuable matter on the subject, much of it emanating from Dr Semple, editor of the former paper and a prominent Bear Flag man, a narrative from whose pen appears in the *Hesperian*, vol. iii. Much information, in a certain sense original, being in many instances the personal recollections of pioneers, and in a few cases taking a documentary form, has appeared in California newspapers of later date, of which it is not necessary to give a list here, the *S. F. Alta* and *San José Pioneer* being prominent in this respect. It is well to mention in this connection Thomas C. Lancey's *Cruise of the Dale*, published in the paper last named. It contains more matter on all topics connected with the conquest than any other publication extant, being compiled from newspaper and other sources by a gentleman who came to California in 1846, and who was well fitted in many respects for the task. This work merits more praise than it will ever obtain in its present form, marred by many typographical blunders, and lacking systematic arrangement. Of a similar nature to Lancey's work, though as a rule inferior, except where they have reproduced it literally, are the local county histories of California published during the past few years; the editors having occasionally, however, obtained items that were new and of some value. John S. Hittell's *History of San Francisco* should be noticed here as the only popular work of late years in which a correct understanding of the character of the revolt is shown.

Such are the sources of original information on the Bear Flag revolt; and I may add that most of the authorities cited treat also of later annals, or the conquest. Miscellaneous printed works treating more or less fully of both the Revolt and the Conquest—some of them trustworthy, and others trash, pure and simple; none of them containing original matter; and none of them cited in my pages except occasionally, to show the author's peculiar views, to correct an error, or for some other special purpose—may be found in great numbers in my general list of authorities.

CHAPTER IX.

PRELIMINARIES OF THE CONQUEST.

1846.

THE WAR WITH MEXICO—BEGINNING OF HOSTILITIES—FEELING IN THE UNITED STATES RESPECTING CALIFORNIA—POLICY OF PRESIDENT POLK'S ADMINISTRATION—INSTRUCTIONS TO COMMODORE SLOAT IN 1845 AND 1846 — PLANS FOR PERMANENT OCCUPATION—THE PACIFIC SQUADRON AT MAZATLAN—RUMORS OF WAR—SERVICES OF DR WOOD AND JOHN PARROTT—THE 'PORTSMOUTH' AND 'CYANE' SENT TO MONTEREY—NEWS FROM THE RIO GRANDE—SLOAT'S PLANS—HIS 'UNWARRANTED INACTIVITY'—CHANGES HIS MIND—STARTS FOR CALIFORNIA IN THE 'SAVANNAH' —ENGLISH DESIGNS—THE RIVAL FLEETS—A RACE, IN AMERICAN IMAGINATION—A PROTECTORATE—AN UNFOUNDED CONJECTURE—THE MCNAMARA COLONIZATION PROJECT—TEN THOUSAND IRISHMEN FOR SAN JOAQUIN.

THE conquest of California was a part of the war of 1846–8, between Mexico and the United States. Not only was California a portion, and the richest portion, of the territory transferred from one nation to the other as a result of the war; but it was also the prize chiefly coveted in advance by that element in the northern republic which promoted the conflict. It was the region whose loss Mexico most dreaded, and whose prospective annexation to the United States was looked upon with most disfavor in Europe. Therefore I might appropriately—and in fact, were I writing a detached history of California, should be obliged to—present at considerable length the general annals of the war, and particularly the causes which led to it. I am relieved, however, from this necessity by the fact that the Mexican war is in its general features fully treated in another volume of my work; and I shall therefore confine myself to a brief statement respecting the outbreak of hostilities, and then proceed to consider those phases only of the subject which directly concerned the territory to which these volumes are devoted.

The independence of Texas, effected in 1836 by Americans colonists, while fully recognized by the leading powers of the world, was never so recognized by Mexico, which nation persisted in regarding the lonestar republic as its own territory, and believed that the so-called independence was but a pretext from the first for ultimate annexation to the United States. When the question of such annexation began to be agitated, the Mexicans of course were confirmed in their belief, and the popular feeling became very bitter. Over and over again the government of Mexico declared officially that annexation would be forcibly resisted, and would be made a cause of war. In the United States it was not generally believed that this warlike threat would be carried out. There was, however, a strong opposition to the proposed measure, founded in part on the justice of Mexican claims, but mainly on the danger of extending southern political power. The project was defeated in congress; but, after a presidential election in which its friends were victorious, it was again brought up, and ratified at Washington in March 1845, receiving the final approval of Texas in July of the same year. Before the end of 1845 a military force was stationed, not only on the Texan frontier, but over the line in disputed territory, which Mexico with much reason claimed as her own, whether Texan independence were recognized or not. In Mexico, meanwhile, there was practically no difference of opinion on the merits of the case; but the administration in power, that of Herrera, was inclined to avoid a declaration of war, and to favor delay and diplomatic negotiations, prudently foreseeing the danger of losing, not only Texas, but other parts of the national domain. The popular feeling, however, was irresistibly opposed to every policy of concession; the administration was forced to refuse negotiation with Slidell, the American minister, whose mission it had to a certain extent encouraged; and finally it was overthrown by Paredes, who took advantage of the public sentiment in favor of war to raise himself into power. Another effort to prevent the war was that which aimed at a treaty by which Mexico should recognize the independence of Texas, in return for a pledge against annexation. This plan was instigated by the European powers clearly foreseeing the result of a conflict, but it was rejected by Texas. Early in March 1846 the American army advanced toward the Rio Grande, impeded by protests and proclamations and threats, but no forcible resistance. Early in April the Mexican army was ordered to advance, and General Ampudia, commanding at Matamoros, assumed a hostile attitude, ordering Taylor to retire at once beyond the Nueces until the question of boundaries could be settled. The order was not obeyed. Before the end of April blood had been shed in several minor encounters of small detached parties, and a considerable part of the Mexican force had crossed the Rio Grande. On May 3d an artillery duel was begun between the fortifications on opposite sides of the river, and on May 8th was fought the first pitched battle at Palo Alto. I need not follow the record of military operations further. It was on May 13th that congress voted, and President Polk proclaimed, that "by the act of the republic of Mexico a state of war exists between that government and the United States."

As to the popular sentiment in the United States respecting the acquisition of California, there is little or nothing to be added to what I have said on the same subject for 1845.[1] The threatened war had little bearing on the subject, for it was not generally be-

[1] See *Hist. Cal.*, vol. iv., chap. xxv.

lieved that there would be any war.   It was felt that
California was a most desirable province; that it was
not destined to remain much longer under Mexican
control; that it ought for many reasons to belong to
the United States; and that the rapid increase of
American immigration would inevitably bring about
the desired result, unless it were prevented by European interference.   Those who were opposed to the acquisition founded their opposition mainly on political
and sectional grounds; but many of those who favored
it hoped to see it accomplished by purchase rather than
by methods bearing a dishonorable taint of filibusterism.   On two points there was wellnigh unanimous
agreement—that England was no less eager than the
United States to obtain California, and that no interference by that or any European power must in any
case be tolerated.   Of course, the war once begun,
there was but little disposition on the part of any to
oppose the temporary occupation of California as a
military measure; indeed, during the continuance of
the conflict public attention was but very slightly
directed to the ultimate fate of that country, though
details of military achievements, there as in Mexico,
were closely watched.[2]

Respecting the policy of the administration at
Washington with regard to California, we are left
in no doubt whatever.   From developments in the
Commodore Jones affair of 1842,[3] and from the subsequent naval operations on the coast, I might reasonably infer, as other writers have repeatedly done
before me, that naval commanders had standing instructions during all this period to occupy California
in case of war with Mexico, and to prevent in any

[2] The feeling in the U. S. is well shown in an article on 'California,' published in the *American Review* of Jan. 1846, vol. iii., p. 82–99, in which particular attention is paid to English designs.   I might quote extensively
from newspapers of the time; but I find no such material which throws further light on the subject than has already been obtained from citations of
former years.   Most articles on the Mexican war mention California, but
only incidentally.
[3] See chap. xii. of vol. iv.

event such occupation by England or France. But
we have no need for inference or conjecture on the
subject, since clearly written instructions are extant.
On June 24, 1845, after congress had ratified the
measure which Mexico had declared would be a
casus belli, Bancroft, secretary of the navy, wrote in
'secret and confidential instructions' to Commodore
Sloat, commanding the Pacific squadron, as follows:
"The Mexican ports on the Pacific are said to be
open and defenceless.   If you ascertain with certainty
that Mexico has declared war against the United
States, you will at once possess yourself of the port
of San Francisco, and blockade or occupy such other
ports as your force may permit.   Yet...you will be
careful to preserve if possible the most friendly relations with the inhabitants, and...will encourage them
to adopt a course of neutrality."[4]   In later communications of August 5 and October 17, 1845, Bancroft called Sloat's attention anew to the importance
of carrying out the previous instructions promptly,
substituting in the first the words "in the event of
war," and in the second "in the event of actual
hostilities," for the phrase "if you ascertain with certainty that Mexico has declared war."   The receipt
of these documents was acknowledged by Sloat on
January 28th and March 17th respectively.

In October of the same year Buchanan, secretary
of state, in his instructions to Confidential Agent
Larkin, so often cited in previous chapters, implied
clearly that California would be occupied in the event
of war, stating openly at the same time that European interference would not be permitted.   Accordingly Larkin was instructed, and orders to Frémont
and Gillespie were of like import, to gain the good-
will of the authorities and people, that they might
quietly and voluntarily submit to the proposed occu-

[4] *29th Cong., 2d Sess., H. Ex. Doc. No. 19; Cutts' Conq.*, appen.   These
instructions are often referred to in later correspondence.   See especially
document in *Clarke's Speech on Cal. Claims*, p. 8-9; *Frémont's Cal. Claims*, 71.

pation; or, if there should be no war, as now seemed most likely, that they might be induced to declare their independence and ask for annexation.[5]   Thus the policy of the United States respecting two distinct methods of acquiring California was clearly though not publicly announced in advance.   What may have been the secret intention, in case both plans should prove unsuccessful, we may only conjecture; but as we have seen, though many have believed the contrary, no steps were taken to promote the acquisition by means of a settlers' revolt or other form of direct filibusterism.   Indeed, it was fully believed by the government, as by its agents in California, that the proposed methods of acquisition would prove amply adequate to the purpose.

On May 13, 1846, Bancroft wrote to Sloat: "The state of things alluded to in my letter of June 24, 1845, has occurred.   You will therefore now be governed by the instructions therein contained, and carry into effect the orders then communicated with energy and promptitude."   Next day Buchanan sent to Larkin an official notification that war had begun, and that the Pacific ports would be at once blockaded. On May 15th Bancroft instructed Sloat more definitely, but to the same effect.   "You will consider the most important public object to be to take and to hold possession of San Francisco, and this you will do without fail.   You will also take possession of Mazatlan and of Monterey, one or both, as your force will permit.   If information received here is correct, you can establish friendly relations between your squadron and the inhabitants of each of these three places. . . You will, as opportunity offers, conciliate the confidence of the people in California, and also in Sonora, toward the government of the United States; and you will endeavor to render their relations with the United States as intimate and friendly as possible.   It is important that you should hold possession, at least

[5] *Buchanan's Instructions to Larkin, Oct. 17, 1845*, MS.

of San Francisco, even while you encourage the people to neutrality, self-government, and friendship." In a similar communication of June 8th occur the following passages: "It is rumored that the province of California is well disposed to accede to friendly relations. You will if possible endeavor to establish the supremacy of the American flag without any strife with the people of California. If California separates herself from our enemy, the central Mexican government, and establishes a government of its own under the auspices of the American flag, you will take such measures as will best promote the attachment of the people of California to the United States. You will bear in mind generally that this country desires to find in California a friend, and not an enemy; to be connected with it by near ties; to hold possession of it, at least during the war; and to hold that possession, if possible, with the consent of its inhabitants." Still earlier, on June 3d, Secretary of War Marcy ordered General Kearny to press on overland from New Mexico to California; and in his instructions he was directed to establish temporary civil governments in the regions occupied, to continue in office such authorities as are friendly to the United States and will take the oath of allegiance; and to "assure the people of those provinces that it is the wish and design of the United States to provide for them a free government, with the least possible delay, similar to that which exists in our territories. They will be called upon to exercise the rights of freemen in electing their own representatives to the territorial legislature." Later instructions to Shubrick and Stevenson and Stockton were of the same tenor.[6]

The preceding communications might be cited more fully, and others of similar purport might be mentioned. Some of them will be noticed in other con-

---

[6] The communications cited are found in *Larkin's Doc.*, MS., iv. 121; *U. S. Govt Doc.*, 29th cong. 2d sess., H. Ex. Doc. 19; 31st cong. 1st sess., H. Ex. Doc. 17; *Cutts' Conq.*, append.; *Stockton's Life*, append., etc.

nections; but the citations given suffice for my present
purpose, fully explaining the policy of the United
States, before indicated with sufficient clearness in the
instructions of 1845.   Those of 1846 have no practical importance in connection with naval and military
operations on the Pacific coast in that year, because
they did not reach their destination until later than
July.   In spirit, however, and in some instances with
remarkable fidelity to detail, they were all obeyed
long before they were received.   This shows, what is
otherwise clear enough, that the policy to be observed was well understood in advance—somewhat
better, in fact, than could naturally be accounted for
by the written orders extant—by officers and agents
in the west.   Naval commanders had been kept acquainted with that policy for several years; and there
is no reason to doubt that Gillespie brought to California, and communicated to leading men, exact information about the orders to Sloat.   It is to be noted
that the orders of 1846 go somewhat further than to
prove an intention to maintain a purely military occupation during the war; and indicate a purpose to retain, by one means or another, permanent possession
of California   The selection for the regiment of volunteers of men deemed likely to remain in the country, like other circumstances that might be mentioned,
illustrates the same purpose; and, indeed, as early as
January 1847 the secretary of the navy, in a communication to Commodore Stockton, "foresees no
contingency in which the United States will ever
surrender or relinquish possession of the Californias."
    Thus we see that the administration at Washington
had determined in case of a war with Mexico to occupy California, and as a result of the war to hold
that country as a permanent possession.   If peace
should continue, a scheme had been devised and operations actually begun to promote a revolution of the
natives, and a subsequent appeal for annexation.   In
any event, California was to fulfil its 'manifest des-

tiny,' and become a part of the United States.   Had both plans failed, it may be plausibly conjectured that a revolt of American settlers would have been encouraged; but no such failure was anticipated; and so far as can be known, no steps were taken in that direction.[7]

The Pacific squadron of the U. S. navy, under the command of Commodore John D. Sloat, included in the spring of 1846 the following vessels: the ship *Savannah*, flag-ship, 54 guns; the ship *Congress*, 60 guns; the sloops *Warren, Portsmouth, Cyane*, and *Levant*, each 24 guns; the schooner *Shark*, 12 guns; and the transport *Erie*.   Five of these vessels had visited the California coast during the preceding year, as we have seen.   The English squadron in Pacific waters, under Admiral Sir George F. Seymour, was considerably stronger in vessels, guns, and men.   The two squadrons had been for some time closely watching each other's movements because of possible difficulties

[7] Most writers on California have something to say on the matter of U. S. policy; but I find it necessary to make but few references.   The prevalent opinion, deemed by me an error, that the government did promote the settlers' revolt as a part of the conquest, has been fully noticed elsewhere.   Jay, *Mexican War*, 154–7, and Mansfield, *Mexican War*, 96–7, argue that the war was made for the sole purpose of seizing California, presenting the prompt obedience of orders in advance, as proofs that permanent occupation was intended from the first, and that plans were perfected and orders given long before hostilities began.   See also Thompson's speech of Jan. 27, 1848, in *Cong. Globe*, 1847–8, p. 260; *Dwinelle's Address before Pioneers*, 1866, p. 9–20; *Thompson's Recollections*, 232–5.   Dwinelle says: 'There are gentlemen of the highest respectability residing in Cal. who came here upon the personal assurance of President Polk, in 1846, that the war should not be concluded until Upper Cal. was secured by treaty to the U. S.'   Wood, *Wandering Sketches*, 215, says: 'For many years before Cal. was annexed, the impression seemed to exist in the U. S. Pacific squadron that its most important purpose was to occupy Cal., and its vigilance was directed to the accomplishment of such a duty. The British squadron seemed to have an equally strong idea that its business was to prevent any such act upon the part of ours, and consequently these squadrons went about watching each other.'   In Mexico it was the universal belief that the United States govt was determined to obtain Cal. by filibustering encroachments; and most regarded war as the only means of resisting such encroachment; but a few opposed the war, because they believed it would only hasten the calamity.   Hardly a newspaper published in Mexico that did not frequently contain the most bitter articles in opposition to the American policy respecting Cal.; and the subject was continually alluded to in official writings and discourses.   Quotations would be bulky, and would serve no good purpose.

to arise from the Oregon question, if for no other reason: but more of this hereafter. The movements of Sloat's fleet have no special importance for our present purpose until March, when all the vessels— except the *Congress,* which with Commodore Stockton on board was at Callao en route from the States, and the *Cyane,* which had lately sailed for Honolulu—were cruising on the Mexican coast, being practically all together at Mazatlan.

Sloat, with the Washington orders down to October 1845 in his possession, was awaiting tidings of war which should enable him to carry out those orders. Lieutenant Gillespie had arrived at Mazatlan overland in February, and had sailed February 22d on the *Cyane,* William Mervine commander, for Honolulu and Monterey, arriving at the latter port in April;[8] but it does not clearly appear that he brought instructions to or had any official relations with Sloat. Late in March the military authorities at Mazatlan received news by express from the interior that war had broken out, and that the Mexican Atlantic ports had been blockaded. This report caused much excitement, during which the archives were removed to Rosario, whither the comandante went with his garrison, after warning the people in a bando that the Americans were about to blockade the port. Sloat had no news of an eastern blockade, neither had the English commanders, whose means of communication were better than those of the Americans, and who had before given the latter despatches not otherwise received; but during the excitement news came from California of Frémont's trouble with Castro, and on April 1st the *Portsmouth,* Captain John B. Montgomery, was despatched in haste to Monterey, where she arrived

[8] Details about the exact movement of most of the vessels are but meagrely recorded. The Honolulu papers, the *Polynesian* and *Friend,* afford some information. The *Cyane* arrived at Honolulu March 13th and sailed 19th 'for Mazatlan;' but as Gillespie says he came via the Sandwich Islands, and as there was no record of, or indeed time for, another trip by that route before April 17th, I suppose she touched at Monterey on the way to Mazatlan, for which place she sailed April 19th.

on April 22d, remaining there, and later at San Francisco.[9] The alarming or reässuring news was not confirmed by later despatches from Mexico. The local excitement passed away, and the naval officers resumed their watchful waiting for warlike rumors. Meanwhile the *Shark*, Lieutenant Neil M. Howison, had been sent on April 2d to await the *Congress* at Honolulu; and about the end of the month the *Cyane* returned from Monterey with news that the Castro-Frémont war-cloud in California had passed away.

At the beginning of May William M. Wood, late fleet surgeon, being permitted to return home overland through Mexico, was intrusted with despatches to the government, and was instructed to send back to Sloat any information of importance that might be gathered on the way. Accompanied by John Parrott, U. S. consul at Mazatlan, Wood went up to San Blas by sea, started inland on May 4th, and on the 10th arrived at Guadalajara. "Startling news here reached us," writes Wood, "placing us, and particularly myself, in most unpleasant circumstances. In triumphant and boastful language we were informed of the successful attack upon our forces on the Rio Grande, and the capture of some of our dragoons. The intelligence reached the city about the same time with ourselves; and soon after newsboys were selling extras in the streets, and crying, at the highest pitch of their voices, 'Triumph over the North Americans.' In every respect this was bad news, mortifying to our national pride...Our own position was a cause of much anxiety. Here was war, and we in the centre of the country; I with a hostile uniform in my trunk, and despatches in my cap, which unfortunately stated that one object of my journey was to collect information in relation to expected hostilities. What was to be done, was a

[9] *Larkin's Doc.*, MS., iv. 107, 115, 126–7, containing corresp. on the trip of the *Portsmouth* and the news brought by her of the state of affairs at Mazatlan. See also *Wood's Wandering Sketches*, 346–8, the author of which was at Mazatlan at the time and gives some particulars.

serious question. I had no disposition to be placed
in the position of a spy in an enemy's country; and
yet, to avoid being in such a position, I should at
once surrender myself to the authorities. By pursuing this course, I would be compelled to surrender
or destroy the despatches, and, what was worse, would
lose an opportunity of communicating the state of affairs to the commander-in-chief in the Pacific. The
condition of things left by us on the western coast
seemed to demand that such an opportunity should
not be lost. Whether correctly or not, it was believed that in case of war the British squadron would
attempt to take California under its protection...
After due deliberation, it was determined that we
should continue our journey through the country,
and, if possible, send an express to the commander-
in-chief of our squadron in the Pacific. The latter
was a matter of some difficulty, as all expresses must
be sent through and under authority of the government post-office. However, Mr Parrott was enabled to manage the matter with much skill. The
express went through safely, making ten days' ordinary travel in five days, and delivering, on the 17th
of May, the first news of the war to our forces on the
Pacific." [10]

Having received on May 17th from James R. Bol-
ton, acting consul, the despatch sent by Wood and
Parrott, Sloat at once sent the *Cyane* under Captain
Mervine to California. She sailed on or about May

[10] *Wood's Wandering Sketches,* 348–69. In *McWhorter's Incidents of the
War with Mexico,* a small pamphlet of 10 pages, without date of publication, and devoted to a record of Wood's services, we find Sloat's letter
of April 30th, to the sec. of the navy, explaining Wood's mission; and
also a letter from Sloat to Wood, dated March 20, 1855, in which the doctor's great services are acknowledged, with a statement that the news received from him was what determined the writer to take Cal. Wood was
also complimented for his valuable services by the chairman of the senate
naval committee. Lancey, *Cruise,* 74–8, quotes Wood, and gives full particulars. The services of Parrott, Wood, and James R. Bolton, the latter acting consul in Parrott's absence, are also recorded in the *S. F. Alta,* Feb. 25,
1880; and by A. Williams, in *Pioneer Soc. Arch.,* MS., 120–2. The praise
due Parrott and the others for their service has been somewhat exaggerated,
under the mistaken idea that their acts saved Cal. from being taken by England.

18th, and reached Monterey on or about June 20th.
She brought a letter from Sloat to Larkin, dated May
18th and marked 'strictly confidential.' The original
is in my possession, and, as the best means of making
known the commodore's intentions, I quote as follows:
"From information I have received from Metamoras,
it appears certain that hostilities have commenced on
the north bank of the Rio Grande. It is said the
Mexicans crossed the river with 1,200 cavalry and 400
infantry, and fell in with a reconnoitring party of our
troops of 50 men, which they attacked, killed, and
captured the whole. It was expected in Metamoras
that General Taylor would bombard the town next
day. It is my intention to visit your place immediately, and from the instructions I have received from
my government, I am led to hope that you will be prepared to put me in possession of the necessary information, and to consult and advise with me on the
course of operations I may be disposed to make on the
coast of California. When my force arrives there, I
shall have the *Savannah, Congress, Portsmouth, Cyane,
Warren, Levant,* and *Shark.* Of course you will keep
all this a profound secret until my arrival, as no officer of my squadron has any knowledge of my intended
movements. They are, however, aware that a collision has taken place on the north side of the Rio
Grande between the American and Mexican troops;
and should this subject get into circulation, you will
make as light of it as possible, saying that it has been
only a mere skirmish between the reconnoitring parties. I shall call off Monterey first, and hope to be
there as soon as this, which goes by the *Cyane.* Her
commander has instructions to advise with you whether
it is best for him to remain there or proceed to San
Francisco. I do not think it necessary to write more
particulars, as I am confident you will understand my
object."[11] Sloat's allusion to information which he ex-

[11] May 18, 1846, Sloat to Larkin, in duplicate. *Larkin's Doc.,* MS., iv. 122–
3; *Sawyer's Doc.,* MS., 57–9.

pected to get from Larkin doubtless signified that he knew the nature of the latter's efforts and instructions as confidential agent, and hoped to be told by him how to raise the flag without opposition from the Californians. Larkin, however, thought the allusion might be to despatches sent him from Washington but not received; and he therefore notified Leidesdorff and others to be on the lookout for missing documents by an overland courier.[12]

But Sloat, though he knew that hostilities had begun, and had once made up his mind to act promptly in obedience to his orders, changed his mind, and did not start for Monterey. It is not known that he received contradictory reports from the east, or that he had any reasons for delay, save his natural indecision of character. On May 31st he heard of General Taylor's battles of the 8th and 9th on the Rio Grande;[13] and this news so restored his wavering determination, that on the same day he wrote to the secretary of the navy: "I have received such intelligence as I think will justify my acting upon your order of the 24th of June, and shall sail immediately to see what can be done."[14] His renewed enthusiasm did not last long; though about this time he despatched the *Levant* under Captain Hugh N. Page to Monterey;[15] and we are also told, on authority not the best, of a short cruise off the coast and return to Mazatlan, all with intent to deceive the English admiral.[16]

[12] June 22d, Larkin to Leidesdorff, Montgomery, et al. *Larkin's Doc.*, MS., iv. 119-20; *Sawyer's Doc.*, MS., 62. June 20th, L. had notified Montgomery that Sloat was to come at once. *Larkin's Off. Corresp.*, MS., i. 115.

[13] An extract from the *Savannah's* log, furnished by L. W. Sloat to *Dunbar's Romance*, 38-9, and also printed in *Lancey's Cruise*, 78-9, contains this entry: 'May 31, 1846, received report of Gen. Taylor's victory over the Mexicans on the 8th and 9th of May.' The news of May 31st, according to Williams, in *Cal. Pioneer Soc. Arch.*, MS., 120-5, was received by Bolton from a German correspondent, Fageman, at Durango.

[14] May 31, 1846, Sloat to sec. navy, in *Frémont's Cal. Claims*, 70. Sloat had asked on May 6th to be relieved from his command on account of failing health. *Id.*, 72.

[15] I have found no definite record of the *Levant's* trip, except that she arrived at Monterey on June 30th. *Larkin's Off. Corresp.*, MS., i. 96.

[16] Testimony of Lieut Geo. Minor, in *Frémont's Cal. Claims*, 44. He says

According to the log of the flag-ship, on June 5th the news of Taylor's battles was confirmed, and the capture of Matamoros was announced. This, however, was by no means enough for the irresolute commodore; and he wrote next day to Secretary Bancroft: "I have, upon more mature reflection, come to the conclusion that your instructions of the 24th of June last, and every subsequent order, will not justify my taking possession of any part of California, or any hostile measures against Mexico (notwithstanding their attack upon our troops), as neither party have declared war. I shall therefore, in conformity with those instructions, be careful to avoid any act of aggression until I am certain one or the other party have done so, or until I find that our squadron in the gulf have commenced offensive operations," announcing, however, his intention of proceeding to California to await further intelligence.[17] This extraordinary determination was of course not approved at Washington, and brought out a severe reprimand for the dilatory commander of the squadron. "The department willingly believes in the purity of your intentions; but your anxiety not to do wrong has led you into a most unfortunate and unwarranted inactivity," wrote Bancroft, after dwelling on the previous orders and hints to act promptly; and on the same day, by reason of failing health, in accord-

that when the *Savannah* sailed an English vessel at once started for San Blas, apparently to notify the admiral; and on Sloat's return the same manœuvre was repeated. Lancey, *Cruise*, 78, gives a 'sailor's story,' to the effect that Sloat, suspecting that Seymour was closely watching his movements, resolved to verify his suspicion, and put the Englishman off his guard by a Yankee trick. So a sham trial was got up, and a man condemned to death, a fact much talked about whenever English hearers were present. The *Savannah* put out to sea to hang a 'dummy' at the yard-arm, closely followed and watched by a vessel of the rival fleet. Soon after, a similar affair was planned and talked about; but when the ship sailed to execute the sentence, the Englishman thought it not worth while to watch the operation, and the *Savannah* started unobserved for Cal. !

[17] June 6, 1846, Sloat to Bancroft, in *Frémont's Cal. Claims*, 70. Sloat continues: 'The want of communication with and information from the department and our consul render my situation anything but pleasant; indeed, it is humiliating and mortifying in the extreme, as by my order I cannot act, while it appears to the world that we are actually at war on the other coast.'

ance with his own earlier request, "and for other reasons," Sloat was relieved of his command.[18]

Yet again Sloat changed his mind, in time practically to nullify the censure of the government, and to escape the dishonor in which his removal must otherwise have involved him; for long before the communications cited above had reached him he had done the things which he had been reprimanded for not doing, and thus saved his reputation. The *Savannah's* log, according to the extract published, has this entry: "June 7th, news received of the blockade of Vera Cruz by the American squadron. At 2 P. M. got under way for Monterey." In a later report the commodore writes: "On the 7th of June I received at Mazatlan information that the Mexican troops, six or seven thousand strong, had by order of the Mexican government invaded the territory of the United States north of the Rio Grande, and had attacked the forces under General Taylor; and that the squadron of the United States were blockading the coast of Mexico on the gulf. These hostilities I considered would justify my commencing offensive operations on the west coast. I therefore sailed on the 8th in the *Savannah* for the coast of California, to carry out the orders of the department of the 24th June, 1845, leaving the *Warren* at Mazatlan to bring me any despatches or information that might reach there."[19] It was probably the report of an eastern blockade that determined Sloat's action, since in his letter of the 6th he had declared his intention of awaiting such news. How this news of June 7th was received I am not quite certain. Perhaps it was through another letter from Parrott and Wood, written at the city of Mexico, as several persons state; but there is some confusion in the testimony.[20] I shall

[18] Aug. 13, 1846, Bancroft to Sloat. *Frémont's Cal. Claims*, 71–2.

[19] July 31, 1846, Sloat to Bancroft, in *War with Mexico, Repts Operations of U. S. Naval Forces*, 30th cong. 2d sess., H. Ex. Dec. no. 1, pt. ii. p. 2. Repeated substantially in report of sec. navy, Dec. 5, 1846, 29th cong. 2d sess., H. Ex. Doc. 4, p. 378; and often elsewhere.

[20] Wood in his narrative says nothing of any despatches from the city of Mexico, but implies that those from Guadalajara were the only ones sent to

notice later the possibility that no such determining news was received at all, and that Sloat did not make up his mind until after his arrival at Monterey. At any rate, the commodore sailed on June 8th for California, whither I shall follow him in the next chapter.

One phase of Sloat's experience at Mazatlan, and his voyage to California, yet remains to be noticed; it is that arising from his relations with Admiral Seymour, and brings up anew the old subject of English designs on California. It was believed at the time that England intended to take possession, in the event of war, or at least to assume a protectorate, and thus keep the territory from the United States. It has been the opinion of most Americans ever since, and has been stated directly or indirectly by writers on the conquest almost without exception, that the rival squadrons were closely watching each other's movements at Mazatlan and San Blas in the spring of 1846; that there was a contest between the respective commanders as to which should first obtain definite information that war had been declared, and with it reach California; that had Seymour in the *Collingwood* reached Monterey before Sloat in the *Savannah*, the English flag would have been raised instead of the stars and strips; but that the commodore, either by getting the first news overland, or by sending the admiral off on a false scent, or by a trick which enabled him to sail without the knowledge of his rival, or by the superior speed of his flag-ship, won the race, and

Sloat. Parrott, in an interview printed in the *S. F. Alta*, Feb. 25, 1880, mentions only one despatch. Sloat in his letter of 1845 to Wood speaks of the news from Guadalajara as having determined his action, alluding to no other communication. This letter is also quoted in *Willey's Thirty Years in Cal.*, 14–15. Williams and Lancey, however, on authority not stated, mention a communication sent from Mexico by Parrott May 23d to Bolton, who received it June 7th. Parrott's letter was founded on one received from a friend at S. Luis Potosí, and closed with these words: 'You can tell the commodore if he is with you that I did not write to him, because there is too much risk; that he has a field open to signalize himself, and I wish him a crown of laurels.' This literal citation indicates that the writers saw the original letter, which may have been furnished by Parrott or Bolton. (In a later conversation I understood Mr Williams to confirm this.)

saved California for his government. The tangible
facts in the case are the belief of Americans that England intended to occupy the country; the presence at
Mazatlan of the rival fleets closely watchful one of the
other; a trip of the *Collingwood* to Monterey, arriving
about a week after the U. S. flag had been raised; and
finally, that an Irish subject of Great Britain was attempting in 1845–6 to obtain Californian lands for
colonization. The question for consideration is whether these facts are a sufficient foundation for the current version of former writers, or whether that version
may be deemed to rest on mere conjecture and patriotic prejudice.

In other chapters this subject of English schemes
has been fully treated for earlier years; and our investigation has shown simply that several travellers had
praised California highly, had predicted that it could
not long remain a Mexican possession, had shown the
ease with which it might be occupied by a foreign
power, and had dwelt on the advantages to its people
and to England of its becoming an English province
rather than a territory of the United States; that
some popular writers had echoed the desires of the
travellers, and had ridiculed the claims of the United
States to any exclusive rights in that direction; and
that a part of the English holders of Mexican bonds
had favored an arrangement by which Californian
lands for colonization could be taken in payment, or
as security for the payment, of the debt, though it has
never clearly appeared that even a majority of the
bond-holders decided in favor of such an arrangement.
In 1846 the bond-holders' scheme, so far as outward
manifestations were concerned, was a thing of the
past, unless the McNamara project, of which I shall
speak presently, might be in some way connected with
it. The only new developments of the year in this
connection were the undoubted existence of a party
among the Californians in favor of a British protectorate, and the well known fears, leading to some diplo-

matic efforts, of the English government with regard to the prospective annexation of Mexican territory to the United States in consequence of the war. The former subject has been fully presented already; the latter requires no further remark, as England made no secret of her perfectly natural and legitimate disfavor to the extension of American territory southward and westward at the expense of Mexico.[21]

I find nowhere a single word of official utterance to indicate that England had the slightest intention or desire of obtaining California by conquest or purchase, or that she ever gave any encouragement to the colonization plans of her bond-holding subjects. In the total absence of any such definite indication, and in view of the fact that the testimony in favor of the English scheme, though bulky, is composed wholly of mere statements of belief from men who like myself have had no special facilities for penetrating court secrets in London, I have no hesitation in expressing my conviction that England did not deem California a desirable acquisition at the price of serious complications with another nation; and that she knew perfectly well that trouble with the United States was sure to result from any attempt in that direction. There was never any definite plan on the part of the government to make California an English possession.[22]

[21] I refer only to remarks of Bentinck, Palmerston, Disraeli, and others in parliament. Aug. 1846, *Hansard's Parl. Debates*, lxxxviii. 978–93, when free reference was made to the harm to English interests likely to result from the war. See remarks on the policy of England on this matter in my *Hist. Mex.*

[22] For testimony in favor of the English schemes, all of the nature indicated in my text, see *American Review*, iii. 87–99; *Frémont's Cal. Claims;* Debates in *Congressional Globe*, 1847–8; some of the same speeches printed in pamphlet or book form, as *Dix's Speeches*, i. 281–2; *S. F. Californian*, Oct. 28, Nov. 4, 1848; *Overland Monthly*, iii. 156; *Tuthill's Hist. Cal.*, 178–80; *Ripley's War with Mex.*, i. 294; *Lancey's Cruise;* and indeed almost every authority cited in this and the following chapters, including manuscript statements of pioneers, and very many newspaper narratives. Writers and speakers in 1846 and earlier founded their opinions on prevalent national prejudices, on the Oregon troubles, on the narratives of English navigators on what was known of the bond-holders' affair, and on the suspicions of Larkin and his friends in Cal. In 1847–8, during the 'claims' agitation, opinions of many men were brought out and exaggerated as testimony to magnify the services of Frémont and his Bear Flag battalion. In later times, writers have simply cited the

In its phase of a proposed protectorate, the matter of English intervention assumes, it must be admitted, a somewhat different and more plausible aspect. England made no secret of her opposition to any further extension of American .territory on the Pacific if it could be prevented by diplomacy or other means than war. There could be little doubt that the United States would seize California as soon as war began. There was a party of some strength among the Californians, including the governor, in favor of English interference; they would likely have asked for protection had a British man-of-war arrived opportunely— perhaps did petition for it through an agent sent to Mexico.[23] The question is, Had the British government through any authorized agent encouraged or approved the scheme? Had Admiral Seymour instructions to raise his flag at Monterey? or was he likely to assume the responsibility of such an act? If he intended to do it, the design was by assuming a protectorate, not necessarily to secure permanent possession, but to set on foot a long train of diplomatic correspondence, to prevent the United States being in possession at the close of the war, and thus indefinitely delay if not prevent the dreaded annexation. The aim and the methods would have been legitimate enough; but was any such purpose entertained or any such means devised? As I have remarked, the theory that such was the case is a more plausible one than that favoring conquest or purchase; but that is about all that can be said in its favor. There is the same absence of all positive or documentary evidence, and the same exclusive reliance by its advocates on mere

testimony of the earlier witnesses of both classes, or more frequently have in a spirit of boasting alluded to England's ambition and defeat as matters of historic record requiring no support.

[23] José M. Covarrubias was sent to Mexico, as we have seen, chap. ii., in Feb., and he returned at the beginning of July. *Bandini, Doc.*, MS., 85. Pio Pico, *Hist. Cal.* MS., states that Covarrubias was instructed, if not successful in Mexico, to call on the English admiral and promise a revolt of California on condition of an English protectorate; also that Covarrubias on his return reported that Admiral Seymour had spoken favorably of the scheme.

opinion and conjecture. I proceed to note some items of circumstantial evidence bearing on the subject.

First: the presence of an unusually strong British fleet in the Pacific at this time, and the close and constant watch kept on the movements of the American squadron, are amply accounted for by the pending complications of the Oregon question, which it was thought might at any time result in war between England and the United States. Consequently naval operations of a general nature prove nothing respecting designs on California. Second: the statements of different writers respecting the suspicious actions of the English naval officers, the methods by which Sloat outwitted Seymour, and the race between the *Savannah* and *Collingwood*, are so contradictory in the matter of details, and so inaccurate in respect of minor facts, as to more than suggest their lack of solid foundation.[24] Third: some of the theories advanced sug-

---

[24] Lieut Minor, as we have seen, *Frémont's Cal. Claims*, 43–5, testified that Sloat so manœuvred as to get away from Mazatlan without Seymour's knowledge; and 'a sailor,' *Lancey's Cruise*, 78, explains the method by which the trick was played. According to Minor and others, the *Collingwood* was at San Blas. Benton, *Thirty Years' View*, ii. 692, says: 'Sloat saw that he was watched and pursued by Admiral Seymour, who lay alongside of him, and he determined to deceive him. He stood out to sea and was followed by the British admiral. During the day he bore west across the ocean, as if going to the S. I.; Adm. Seymour followed. In the night the American commodore tacked and ran up the coast toward Cal.; the British admiral, not seeing the tack, continued on his course and went entirely to the S. I. before he was undeceived.' Arriving in Cal. from Honolulu, 'to his astonishment he beheld the American flag flying over Monterey, the American squadron in its harbor, etc. His mission was at an end. The prize had escaped him.' Randolph, *Oration*, says: 'The flag of the U. S. was no sooner flying than the *Collingwood* entered the bay of Monterey. There had been a race.' Wm H. Davis, *Glimpses*, MS., 343–6, learned from Capt. Mervine at the time ∧t Monterey that the rivals had closely watched each other; and that the *Savannah* and *Cyane* left Mazatlan secretly by night, fearing that the *Collingwood* might have pursued them and arrived before them at Monterey. But we know that the *Cyane* had come long before. There are other slight inaccuracies, showing that Davis gives the common report rather than Mervine's direct testimony. W. S. Green published in the *Colusa Sun* a statement—which I find in the *Bakersfield Courier*, Sept. 21, 1870, and which was published in several other newspapers—purporting to have been derived from Sloat's own lips, containing the following: A courier arrived from Mexico, bringing despatches to Seymour but none to Sloat. Seymour after the arrival of the courier was 'all in all' with the leading Mexicans, while they looked daggers at Sloat. The commodore watched the movements of the admiral. The line-of-battle ship hove short on her anchors and made ready for a voyage. The two little American vessels did the same. The *Collingwood* weighed anchor, and with clouds of canvas, etc.

gest troublesome questions. For instance: Minor and others state that Sloat left Mazatlan for a short cruise and then returned, his departure being promptly made known to Seymour. What means could he have adopted more likely to start the admiral for California, and to insure his arrival there in advance? Or if, as Benton says, Sloat sailed as if for Honolulu, but took a tack in the night, what necessity was there for Seymour to follow exactly the same route as his rival? Moreover, why should Seymour have been so anxious to follow every movement of the *Savannah?* If he intended to raise his flag at Monterey, was it absolutely essential that Sloat should be present at the ceremony? Fourth: Admiral Seymour seems to have paid not the slightest attention to the departure of the *Cyane* and *Shark* and *Portsmouth*, and *Cyane* again, and the *Levant*, any one of which for all he knew might have orders to raise the stars and stripes at Monterey, and all but one of which were actually bound for California waters. Fifth: for a naval commander to devote all his energies to watching a single ship, and to leave unwatched for six months a coast of which he intended to take possession, and which was likely to fall into a rival's hands, was, to say the least, a peculiar proceeding. To the ordinary mind California would seem a convenient station for at least part of a fleet whose chief mission was to protect or conquer that country; and there is no indication that the commander of the *Juno* was instructed to forestall, or even to closely watch, the action of the three American ships. Sixth: Sloat, as we have seen, delayed decisive action long after he knew that hostilities had

Within half an hour the *Savannah* and *Preble* (?) were ploughing the bosom of the deep, while the mind of the gallant commodore was made up, etc. Seymour on reaching Monterey told Sloat that only himself and a few leading Mexicans knew of the existence of hostilities when he left Mazatlan! See also *Powers' Afoot*, 316–18. Walpole, *Four Years*, passim, tells us that the *Collingwood* was becalmed off the coast, thus delaying her arrival. Cronise, *Nat. Wealth of Cal.*, 69, says the English vessel arrived within 24 hours after the *Savannah*. Others simply say the *Savannah* outsailed her rival, or that Sloat won on account of getting the news of war first through Parrott. Thus it is seen that the evidence is meagre as well as contradictory.

begun, unable to make up his mind, and disregarding his instructions. Are we to suppose that Seymour, who, as there is no reason to doubt, knew practically as much of events on the Rio Grande as did Sloat, was equally timid and irresolute? Or that he deemed it his duty to copy his rival's stupid blunders as well as to watch his ship? Truly, his delay was inexcusable if his mission was as alleged; and there was no later success, as in Sloat's case, to relieve him of the blame. Seventh: what, indeed, was the need for the admiral to wait for definite news of war at all? Why might he not, if he had such a design as is imputed to him, have raised the flag in June as well as in July? The rapid increase of American immigration, or certainly the acts of the Bears, afforded a plausible pretext for acceding to the request of Governor Pico and his friends. Sloat of course required positive evidence of hostilities, because his proposed action in California was one of war, and by acting hastily, he might compromise his government; but Seymour had no warlike project in view; he was merely to assume protection of a people at the request of its authorities. It is difficult to understand in what respect his act would have been more compromising to his government, or more offensive to the United States, just before than just after the declaration of war. Eighth and finally: there was nothing in the circumstances attending Seymour's visit to Monterey, July 16th–23d, to sustain the theory that he had meditated interference. He and Sloat exchanged the customary courtesies without the slightest disturbance of amicable relations; and having obtained from the Americans a set of spars for his vessel, he sailed away for the Sandwich Islands without meddling in politics, or commenting, so far as may be known, on the change of flag.[25]

[25] In reality, little is known of the *Collingwood's* trip, except the date of her arrival at Monterey. Lieut Fred. Walpole of that vessel wrote *Four Years in the Pacific*, Lond. 1849, 8vo, 2 vol.; but he pays little or no attention to politics or to details of the vessel's movements. That part of his book relating to Cal. is found in vol. ii. p. 204–19. He gives a little sketch of the

I would not flippantly assert that previous writers
have fallen into error on a matter like this, where
from the nature of the case no positive proof against
them can be adduced; but in the absence of like proof
in their favor, it has seemed well to consider the attendant circumstances; and these, as I think the
reader will agree, point almost irresistibly to the conclusion that the danger of English intervention in any
form was a mere bugbear; that the race between the
Savannah and *Collingwood* was purely imaginary.
The contrary belief has been a fascinating one for
Americans; it is agreeable to dwell on a contest in
which we have been the winners.   But the satisfaction
in this case is not well founded, and there is no reason
to believe that there was any intention of raising the
English flag in California.   The reason why the project of a protectorate, if considered, was not approved,
was probably, as in the matter of conquest or purchase,
that 'the game was not worth the candle,' especially
as the candle was likely enough to assume the propor-

Bear Flag revolt and other current events, noting particularly the appearance
and character of Frémont's trappers.   On the subject now under consideration
he says: 'On the morning of the 16th of July, 1846, after a long voyage, we
were becalmed off the coast of Cal. in the bay of Monterey, and, toward the
afternoon, anchored amidst a crowd of American vessels of war.   To our astonishment we found that they had only a few days before taken possession
of the place, hoisted the American colors, and planted a garrison in the town.'
There is no indication that the vessel came by way of Honolulu, as some
writers state.   Green, in the newspaper article already cited as purporting to
come from Sloat, relates a conversation between him and Seymour, which is
to be regarded as purely imaginary.   In his report of July 31st, Sloat mentions Seymour's arrival on the 16th, and departure on the 23d, and the inter-
change of friendly courtesies.   Sloat thought his coming strengthened the
American cause by convincing the natives that he would not interfere. *Niles'*
Reg., lxxi. 133.   July 23d, Sloat notifies Montgomery of Seymour's presence
and his friendly conduct. *War with Mex., Repts Oper. Navy*, 29.   Phelps,
Fore and Aft, 295, and Dunbar, *Romance*, 40, state that Seymour frankly told
Sloat that he had intended to raise the English flag.   Colton, *Three Years*, p.
13-14, notes the holding of a meeting after the flag was raised to discuss the
question of asking English protection; and he quotes the facetious argument
of one Don Rafael (Gonzalez?) against it.   The same writer, however, *Deck
and Port*, 393, says: 'It has often been stated by American writers that the
admiral intended to raise the English flag in Cal., and would have done it had
we not stolen the march on him.   I believe nothing of the kind; the allega-
tion is a mere assumption, unwarranted by a single fact.'   Nidever, *Life and
Adven.*, MS., 130, and Swasey, *Cal. '45-6*, MS., 13-14, mention an exhibition
of marksmanship by Frémont's men which delighted the officers of the *Collingwood*, and reduced their store of silver dollars.

tions of a foreign war. It is well to note finally that
the conclusion reached deprives the Bear Flag cause
of the only merit that could ever with any plausibility
be attributed to it, that of having saved California
from English rule through the influence of Frémont's
action in hastening Sloat's movements.

The McNamara colonization scheme, though it car-
ries me back to 1845, and forward some days past the
raising of the stars and stripes, is treated here because
it has commonly been considered a part of the general scheme of English interference. Of Eugene Mc-
Namara, except in connection with the affair in question, we know only that he was "a native of Ireland,
catholic priest, and apostolic missionary." Before
August 1845, and probably in the spring of that year,
he asked the president of Mexico for a grant of land
in California, to be occupied by an Irish colony. His
avowed object was threefold. "I wish in the first
place," he said, "to advance the cause of catholicism.
In the second, to contribute to the happiness of my
countrymen. Thirdly, I desire to put an obstacle in
the way of further usurpations on the part of an irre-
ligious and anti-catholic nation." He eulogized the
Irish as the best of colonists, "devout catholics, moral, industrious, sober, and brave." He proposed to
bring over one thousand families as a beginning, each
to have a square league of land, and this first colony
to be located on the bay of San Francisco; a second
would be established later near Monterey; and a third
at Santa Bárbara. He desired for a time exemption
from taxes; and claimed to have the approval of the
archbishop of Mexico. There being some hesitation
on the part of the government, McNamara again
urged the advantages of his project and the necessity
of prompt action. "If the means which I propose be
not speedily adopted, your Excellency may be assured
that before another year the Californias will form a
part of the American nation. Their catholic institu-

tions will become the prey of the methodist wolves; and the whole country will be inundated with these cruel invaders;" but ten thousand Irishmen "will be sufficient to repel at the same time the secret intrigues and the open attacks of the American usurpers." In this communication the petitioner asked for land to be hypothecated in payment of the colonists' travelling expenses; and also for the customs duties at San Francisco for a term of years.[26]

The government was disposed to look with favor upon the scheme; though of course there was no thought of granting coast lands, or least of all, at the ports mentioned by the priest;[27] and though there were not wanting those in Mexico who believed Irish settlers more likely to side with the Yankees than the Mexicans.[28] We know very little of the negotiations in Mexico, but on August 11th, Minister Cuevas, in a communication to José M. Híjar, announced that McNamara, highly recommended by the archbishop and others, would come to California with Iniestra's expedition. Híjar was instructed to treat him well, to examine his project, and to consult with the governor with a view to advise the government what was best to be done.[29] There is no evidence, however, that Híjar ever received this communication.

In January 1846, under a new administration, McNamara was informed by Minister Castillo Lanzas that his memorial and plan, in accordance with the

[26] McNamara's petitions to the president. In Spanish with translations, in *Frémont's Cal. Claims*, 19–21, 77–9. The documents have no date, and it is not stated where they were found; but there is no reason to doubt their authenticity. Most of the matter on the subject is given, from the above source, in the *Honolulu Polynesian*, v. 105; and *S. F. Californian*, Oct. 28, Nov. 4, 1848.

[27] Dix, in his speech of March 29, 1848, *Dix's Speeches*, i. 262–81; *Cong. Globe*, 1847–8, p. 560–1, reviews the subject, and conveys the impression that the final grant did include, besides the bay of S. F., some of the best lands and most important military and commercial positions in Cal. ! Mayer, *Mexico Aztec*, i. 343–5, says 'the govt of Mexico granted 3,000 sq. leagues in the rich valley of S. Joaquin, embracing S. Francisco, Monterey, and Sta Bárbara'!

[28] In the *Amigo del Pueblo*, Oct. 25, 1845, we read : '¿Todavia no se conoce que todo él que hable el idioma inglés ha de tener mas simpatías hácia los rapaces Yankees que hácia nosotros?'

[29] Aug. 11, 1845, Cuevas to Hijar. *Frémont's Cal. Claims*, 23.

opinion of the council, would be submitted to congress.[30] The documentary result is not extant; but whether congress acted on the subject or not, the empresario doubtless obtained some encouragement but no positive promises from the government with a recommendation to go to California, select lands suitable for his purpose, and submit his project in regular form to the departmental authorities.[31] The Iniestra expedition not being likely to start soon, if ever, the padre took passage on H. B. M. ship *Juno* for Monterey, where he arrived before the middle of June, or possibly at the end of May. There is no information extant about the *Juno's* visit, except that she left Monterey on June 17th, was at Santa Bárbara on July 1st, and returning, arrived on July 11th at San Francisco.[32] Making known his project to Larkin and probably to others, McNamara sailed still on the *Juno* for the south to see the bishop and negotiate with the governor. On July 1st at Santa Bárbara he submitted his proposition in writing to Pico, having perhaps first broached the subject to him a week earlier.[33] His plan, which had "received the benign coöperation of the venerable and illustrious archbishop of Mexico, and the cordial recognition of the supreme government," was now to bring as soon as possible 2,000 Irish families, or 10,000 souls; and he

[30] Jan. 19, 1846, Castillo Lanzas to McNamara. *30th Cong. 1st Sess., Sen. Rept*, 75, p. 22.

[31] To Larkin on his arrival McNamara said that Pres. Herrera had approved the scheme; but that the new president made objections, on the ground that the Irish would join the Americans, and that he wanted no English-speaking colonists. *Larkin's Off. Corresp.*, MS., ii. 65.

[32] She arrived before June 11th. *Larkin's Off. Corresp.*, MS., i. 90. In a later letter Larkin states incidently that she arrived in May. *Id.*, ii. 81. In *Id.*, ii. 65, he writes, June 18th, that she arrived, and left for Sta Bárbara 'yesterday.' July 11th, Montgomery to Sloat. The *Juno* arrived to-day and anchored at 'Sausolita' (Sauzalito). *30th Cong. 2d Sess., H. Ex. Doc.*, i. pt ii. p. 16.

[33] In the record of the assembly action of July 6th, *Leg. Rec.*, MS., iv. 363–4, the governor's communication to that body is said to have been dated June 24th; and the same date is mentioned in another record of July 7th. *Frémont's Cal. Claims*, 25. Still another says it was written June 24th and submitted on July 2d. *Bandini, Doc.*, MS., 87. There may therefore be some error in the printed date of July 1st, or there may have been more than one communication.

asked for a grant of the land selected between the
San Joaquin River and the Sierra Nevada, from the
Cosumnes southward to the extremity of the Tulares,
near San Gabriel.   This petition was sent by Pico to
the assembly, with documents relating to the project
and with his approval.[34]   Lataillade, the Spanish vice-
consul, also wrote a letter describing and advocating
the colonization scheme.[35]   On July 6th the matter
was brought up in a session of the assembly at Los
Angeles, and was referred to a committee consisting
of Argüello and Bandini.   Their report, rendered
next day in an extra session and approved, was favorable to McNamara's petition, and recommended that
the grant be made under certain conditions; the most
important of which were that land should be granted
only in proportion to the number of colonists presenting themselves; that the title should not be susceptible of hypothecation or transfer to any foreign government or other ownership; and that sections of
good land should be reserved in the region granted.[36]
The committee further recommended that the departmental government should petition congress to allow
the colonists exemption from taxes for a number of
years; and also for the introduction free of duties of
$100,000 worth of merchandise for each 1,000 colo-
nists.

[34] July 1, 1846, McNamara to Pico, and Pico to assembly. *Frémont's Cal.
Claims*, 23.   See also references in note 33.

[35] July 2d, L. to Bandini. *Bandini, Doc.*, MS., 84.   The writer says there
were difficulties in Mexico on account of prospective expenses; but now
he understands that the English crown will bear the expense.   He favors
the plan, because it will create a barrier both against the Indians and the
Americans.   He foresees the raising of the stars and stripes in case of war;
but thinks a period of anarchy will ensue until a regular government is established, during which the country will be overrun by hordes of lawless
strangers; and that while the Irish colonists could not be expected for several years, the title to lands being acquired, England would protect it and
keep the lands from the possession of adventurers.

[36] July 7, 1846, report of special com. on McNamara grant.   Original blotter
in *Bandini, Doc.*, MS., 87.   Also in *Leg. Rec.*, MS., iv. 364–8.   The tract specified within which the colony lands were to be selected—without prejudice to
former grants and with the reservation of alternate sections—was 'on the
river San Joaquin and towards the Tulares, on the southern extremity of the
lagoons or said tulares, between the latter and the Sierra Nevada, and on the
river of Las Ánimas and its region as far as the Cajon de Muscupiabe, near
San Bernardino.'

This favorable action of the assembly was forwarded to Pico on the same day.[37]   It reached Santa Bárbara probably on the 8th; but the governor, it will be remembered, had started a day or two earlier for the north, and did not reach that town on his return until the 12th or 13th.   Then he doubtless made out and signed in due form a grant to McNamara, subject to the approval of the national government. The terms and conditions of the grant were substantially as fixed by the assembly, it being specified, however, that the tract was to be wholly in the interior, twenty leagues from the coast; that each of the 3,000 families—instead of 2,000 as before— should have one league, or less if the tract should not suffice; and that any excess should be reserved by the government.[38]   Thus far all had been apparently regular and in accordance with legal formalities.   But it is to be noted that the final grant, as extant in print—I have not seen the original manuscript—is dated at Santa Bárbara on July 4th.   If the document was really signed on that date, it was in advance of legislative action and invalid; otherwise it was signed after the 12th, and fraudulently dated back, in consequence of Pico's having learned on his northern trip that the United States flag had been raised on the 7th.

With his grant McNamara went up to Monterey. There he explained to Larkin the nature of his scheme somewhat more fully; informed him that he was acting for a private company in London; showed him the title—bearing date of July 4th, which shows that date to be not merely a misprint—and asked his opinion whether the United States would recognize its

[37] July 7th, Figueroa, president, and Botello, sec., to Pico. *Frémont's Cal. Claims*, 25.   July 8th, Bandini to Lataillade, in reply to letter of 2d, already cited.   Has done what he could for McNamara, who appears to be satisfied. *Bandini, Doc.*, MS., 88.   July 8th, Botello to Moreno.   Has been busy with the McNamara affair, which he warmly approves. *Moreno, Doc. Hist. Cal.*, 17–18.

[38] July 4, 1846, Pico's grant to McNamara. Translation from original, in *Frémont's Cal. Claims*, 23–5.

validity. Larkin told him the governor could not grant more than eleven leagues in a single deed; and the reverend empresario sailed on the *Collingwood* for Honolulu en route to Mexico.[39] No attempt was ever made to secure recognition of the title in California. It is said, however, that the grant was in Mexico referred to the 'direccion de colonizacion ó industria,' which body reported adversely on several grounds—chiefly that the price fixed by law for the territory in question, but which McNamara had not even promised to pay, was about $71,000,000! In spite of this report, it appears that the colonization committee of congress approved the project; and that is the last we hear of it.[40]

Such is the history of the famous McNamara colonization project. It appears that a company of speculators in London, taking the hint perhaps from the efforts of the Mexican bond-holders in past years, if not composed in part of the same men—though there is no evidence on that point—and foreseeing that in American or other hands Californian lands were likely to increase very rapidly in value, resolved to become the possessors of as large a tract as possible. To avoid opposition from the authorities in a catholic country, a priest was employed to negotiate in the name of an Irish colony. There was probably no expectation of

[39] Aug. 22, 1846, Larkin to sec. state. *Larkin's Off. Corresp.*, MS., ii. 81.

[40] I have not found any original record of these actions, which are, however, unimportant on account of their date after the American occupation of Cal. I find the information given above with some details in the *Honolulu Polynesian*, iv. 50, Aug. 11, 1847; quoted also in *S. F. Californian*, Sept. 29, 1847. It is to be noted that in this account the legislative action is dated July 3d, and the grant July 4th. On Sept. 27th McNamara wrote from Honolulu to J. A. Forbes a letter quoted in *Hartmann's Brief in Mission Cases*, 65. After raving about the 'asinine stupidity of old Aberdeen' in settling the Oregon question, and referring to his scheme for working the quicksilver mines, he says: 'I am also very desirous of doing something about that grant of land. I will give the Yankees as much annoyance as I possibly can in the matter.' Velasco, *Sonora*, 310, says the grant was confirmed by Santa Anna, and that McNamara went to Europe to make arrangements; but that litigation is expected. Besides the works I have cited, see on the McNamara scheme, *Bidwell's Cal. 1841-8*, MS., 151-2, 176; *Coronel, Cosas de Cal.*, MS., 69; *First Steamship Pioneers*, 170-1; *Hesperian*, iii. 387; *Upham's Life Frémont*, 240-1; *Cronise's Nat. Wea'th Cal.*, 69; *Lancey's Cruise*, 54-5; *Tinkham's Hist. Stockton*, 92; *Yolo Co. Hist.*, 25; and many newspaper accounts.

ever sending to California any such number of families as was talked about; but it was thought that a title might be acquired to lands of great value. In order to get as much as possible on the most favorable conditions, and with the least possible delay, advantage was shrewdly taken of the bitter feeling against all that was American. The scheme met with as much favor as could have been shown to any measure that had to be submitted to two opposing administrations; but evoked little enthusiasm even in Mexico. And when the speculating *presbítero* arrived in California, where colonization on a large scale had always been a popular idea, with all his special inducements of opposition to the Yankee invaders and *lobos metodistas*, he found the authorities by no means in a hurry to disregard the laws and put him in possession of the whole department. He obtained little more than any presumably responsible man might have obtained in ordinary circumstances—the concession of an immense tract of land, valueless then and nearly so for many years later, away from the coast, inhabited by gentile tribes, of extent in proportion to the actual number of colonists sent to occupy it, with title not transferable —hampered, in fact, by all the legal conditions. The chance for speculation on a grand scale was not very apparent. It may be doubted that the London company would have cared for the grant even had their clerical agent not been obliged to tell them that it was fraudulently antedated. At any rate it would have been sold at a low figure to some Yankee speculator during the subsequent years of litigation.

Respecting the international or political aspects of the McNamara project, there is not much to be said; though it is to that phase of the matter that writers have chiefly devoted their attention. Most of them state it as an unquestioned fact that the colony was simply a part of the general plan of the English government to get possession of California; and failed, just as the main plan failed, because the British agents were

too late.   Had there been any such plan—and I have
proved to my own satisfaction there was not—it would
still be necessary to pronounce its relation to the colony
scheme purely conjectural.   It is not unlikely that the
promoters of the colony, like the bond-holders of earlier
years, hoped to acquire a title which should eventually
attract the attention and secure the protection of
the British government.   It is also probable that in
Mexico, and tolerably certain that in California, Mc-
Namara, to advance his interests, sought to give the
impression that to grant his petition would be to secure
English favor; but that the government secretly favored the scheme in any way, I find no evidence.   Indeed, the establishment of 10,000 Irish colonists in a
country as a means of acquiring peaceful possession
of the same was hardly a method that would at any
time have commended itself to the favor of her
Britannic Majesty.

After the conquest it was claimed that McNamara's
intrigues for an immense land grant had been one of
the chief motives of the Bear Flag revolt; and in the
investigation of 'California claims' in 1848, a leading
point made by Frémont and his friends was that the
revolt alone had prevented the success of that scheme,
and had thus saved for American settlers an immense
tract of valuable land.   A dozen witnesses or more
testified positively that such was undoubtedly the fact.
I do not believe that anything whatever was known
of McNamara or his scheme north of the bay before
June 14th, if indeed it was known before July 7th;
but this of course cannot be proved, especially if, as
Larkin states in one letter, the *Juno* arrived in May;[41]
and it must be admitted that such a knowledge would
have been an argument of some force with the set-

[41] June 18th, as we have seen, was the earliest date on which anything
appears on the subject in contemporary documents at Monterey; and June
24th in the south.   That Larkin knew of it a week or more and informed the
settlers in the north, before he wrote on the subject to the sec. state, is not
very probable.   I suppose, moreover, that his statement in *Off. Corresp.*, MS.,
ii. 81, that McNamara arrived in May may have been a slip of the pen on the
part of his clerk.

tlers.   However this may have been, the second proposition that the revolt put a stop to this and other
grants by Pico to Englishmen is a manifest absurdity;
since not only is it certain that it had no such effect,
but obviously its tendency must have been to cause
the governor to make haste in disposing of the public
domain.   Moreover, it is by no means certain that
the success of the colony and a recognition by the
United States of the grant as valid would have been
an unmixed evil.

CHAPTER X.

COMMODORE SLOAT, in his flag-ship, the *Savannah*,
coming from Mazatlan, arrived at Monterey, where
he found the *Cyane*, Captain Mervine, and the *Levant*, Captain Page—the *Portsmouth*, Captain Montgomery, being at San Francisco—on the 1st or 2d of
July. I find no means of determining accurately
which is the correct date, though perhaps the preference should be given to the second.[1]   A midship-

---

[1] Sloat, in his report of July 31st, *U. S. Govt Doc.*, 31st cong. 1st sess., H.
Ex. Doc., i. pt ii., p. 2, says he arrived on July 2d; and this date has been
taken by most writers from his statement.   The fragment of the log published by Lancey and Dunbar reads: 'July 1st, stood into the harbor of Monterey and came to anchor at 4 P. M., in front of the town...The captain of the
port, accompanied by Mr Hartwell [Hartnell], attached to the custom-house
called.   *Cyane* and *Levant* in port.'   The difference between sea and land
time may be made to account for this entry in the log; but Larkin, in several
communications of the period, dates the arrival on the 1st; while in another he says it was the 2d.   Lieut Minor speaks of a 'passage of 23 days,'
leaving Mazatlan on June 8th, which would make the arrival not later than
July 1st.   Midshipman Wilson, in his testimony, says it was July 2d.

man on the frigate states that the commodore sent
an officer ashore to tender the usual civilities, by offering to salute the Mexican flag, which honor was declined for want of powder for a return salute.[2] I
have two original letters before me, bearing date of
July 2d, one of them in Sloat's handwriting, asking
if there is any objection to his men landing for
twenty-four hours in squads of 100; the other, written by his son and secretary, proposing to land and
take a ride with the consul next morning.[3] According to the log, it was also on the 2d that Larkin made
a long call on the commodore, and on his departure
was saluted with nine guns. Next day Sloat landed
to call on the authorities. Of festivities on the
4th, we know only that the ship was dressed and
salutes were fired. Religious service was performed
on Sunday, the 5th, by Lieutenant Trapin; and on
the same day the *Portsmouth's* launch arrived from
Yerba Buena with despatches from Montgomery.
The 6th was passed by Sloat and Larkin on board
the frigate, in preparing proclamations and correspondence, of which I shall speak presently. Nothing more is known of actual events at Monterey
from the 1st to the 6th of July.

We have seen that Sloat, with a sufficiently definite
knowledge of hostilities on the Rio Grande, had long
hesitated to obey his orders from Washington. After
several changes of mind on the subject, he had on
June 6th announced his intention to proceed to California, but not to take possession until he should hear
of a formal declaration of war or of offensive operations by the gulf squadron. Next day he received
additional despatches, supposed to have included a
report that the gulf ports had been blockaded; and on

[2] Wilson's testimony in *Frémont's Cal. Claims*, 40–1. He says the officers
wondered that Sloat should have made this offer, knowing of the Mexican
hostilities.

[3] July 2d, Com. Sloat and L. W. Sloat to Larkin. *Larkin's Doc.*, MS.,
iv. 193–4. The consul is also thanked for books and quicksilver ore, and is
informed that the men, if they make some noise, will also spend $1,000 or
$1,500 in doing it.

the 8th he sailed for Monterey. According to his own official report, he had resolved at the time of sailing to raise the flag in California in consequence of the latest news.[4] His delay of six days after arrival before acting, however, in itself seems to indicate that his vacillation did not end with the departure from Mazatlan. Frémont and his friends point to Sloat's letter of June 6th as showing his purpose when he left Mazatlan; to his delay at Monterey and friendly relations with Mexican authorities there; to the general impression on board the ships that Sloat's final action was determined by the receipt on July 5th of Montgomery's despatches announcing the acts of the revolutionists. And in addition to this, Frémont and Gillespie testify positively that Sloat in his first interview with them gave them distinctly to understand that he had acted upon the faith of their operations in the north, and was greatly troubled on learning that they had acted without authority.[5]

Thus was founded a claim that it was Frémont's acts that caused Sloat to take possession of California for the United States. The claim was to a certain extent well founded. Frémont's operations did unquestionably have an influence in removing Sloat's doubts and strengthening his purpose; though it was by no means the only influence in that direction; and though, had it been so, the chief merit claimed for it, that of having saved the country from England, cannot be accorded to the rebels. I find no reason to doubt that Sloat, as he claimed, left Mazatlan and arrived at Monterey with a determination—as strong as such a man in such circumstances could entertain—to obey his orders and seize the country. His hesitation, very much less inexcusable here than before on the Mexican coast, began at his first interview with

---

[4] *War with Mex.*, *Report Naval Operations*, p. 2. Sloat to sec. navy, July 31st.

[5] Testimony of Frémont, Gillespie, Wilson, and Minor, in *Frémont's Cal. Claims*, 13, 32, 41, 44–5; see also *Benton's Speech* of April 10, 1848; *Cong Globe*, 1847–8, p. 604–6; G. H., in *S. F. Cal. Star and Calif.*, Dec. 9, 1848.

Larkin, and was largely due to the consul's influence. He learned, it is true, that the American settlers were in revolt, and that the Californian authorities were popularly believed to be in favor of English interference, both circumstances calculated in themselves to strengthen his purpose; but at the same time he learned that the coöperation of Frémont and Gillespie with the insurgents was not positively known, and that Larkin did not now apprehend any trouble from the McNamara scheme, or from Pico's favor to an English protectorate. He had not expected definite news or orders from the Rio Grande, or from Washington; but he had hoped to find something to support his resolve in the secret instructions of Larkin and Gillespie. He now learned that those documents contained nothing in addition to his own instructions, and that they were devoted chiefly to a plan of acquiring the country by voluntary separation from Mexico, to be followed by annexation—a plan under which Larkin had been and still was at work with much hope of success. Larkin was not in sympathy with the Bear Flag movement. He was embarrassed in his efforts by it, and puzzled by the reported connection of United States officers with it; and he did not favor, or later wholly approve, the forcible occupation of the country, where he confidently expected to see the stars and stripes raised voluntarily by the Californians. That the views of so prominent a citizen, at the same time U. S. consul and confidential agent of the administration, should have had great influence with the commodore is not to be wondered at. A much more resolute man might have wavered under such circumstances. Both, however, were wrong. Larkin, well founded as were his hopes, had no right to suppose that his government intended to put off the military occupation in case of war, or that such occupation could under the circumstances be effected in the immediate future with the entire approval of the

inhabitants and authorities.   And Sloat should have
obeyed his instructions literally and without delay.[6]

Both Sloat and Larkin being much perplexed as to
what should be done—the former inclining to action
and the latter to delay—on the afternoon of Sunday
the 5th the *Portsmouth's* launch, under Passed Midshipman N. B. Harrison, arrived with despatches
from Montgomery.   The boat had been delayed by

[6] Larkin's position in this matter is by no means a theory, though as
such it might be consistently and successfully presented, the consul's general
views being clearly enough recorded.   I have a statement by Larkin himself
bearing directly on the subject.   He says: 'It was known to the commodore
and the U. S. consul that a severe battle had taken place at or near Matamoros, . . . yet there was no certainty in California that war was declared.   On
the first or second day after the commodore's arrival in this port, he informed
this consulate that he thought it of the greatest importance that he should
land his marine force and take possession of Monterey.   Without official information, either by the commodore or myself, I hesitated to take possession
of California by force of arms, and preferred that the civil governor and military commandant should place their country under the protection of our government.   This subject had been canvassed repeatedly by myself and certain
persons in command on shore, and partially agreed upon should emergencies
create the necessity.   Some of the town authorities and a few principal citizens
of Mexico in Monterey, while the *Savannah* lay at anchor, favored the plan
and proposed to send expresses to Gen. Castro and Gov. Pico. . .There was
during this period a rising of foreigners, most of them unknown in the settlements, at the Sacramento River and jurisdiction of Sonoma.   These circumstances urged many Californians in July 1846 to view with high favor the
plan of coming under a peaceable protection of a foreign government.   There
was a fair prospect of the commandant general and some or all the authorities
of Monterey coming into the arrangement; but it required at least ten days
to come to a conclusion.   On the 4th or 5th of the month a proposition was
thought of in Monterey by some of the citizens to seize on the American consul and carry him off, in order to make further motives to the ship's forces to
land.   Com. Sloat became more and more anxious to land and hoist our flag.
Early on Sunday [it should be Monday] morning of the 6th of July, he sent a
boat on shore for the U. S. consul, who was received in the commodore's cabin
with the exclamation, "We must take the place!   I shall be blamed for doing
too little or too much—I prefer the latter."'   Copy in *Sawyer's Doc.*, MS., 84-
7, of what seems to be a memorandum left by Larkin among his papers.   It
was apparently written considerably later than 1846.   He gets into confusion
in the dates, making the 6th and 7th Sunday and Monday, instead of Monday
and Tuesday.   He also makes the *Portsmouth's* launch arrive in the afternoon
of the same day that he spent with Sloat, who had made up his mind in the
morning; but that is evidently an error.   He adds: 'It is not improbable but
the possession of the country would have been postponed a few days longer
had not Com. Sloat been apprehensive that Admiral Seymour on H. M. ship
of the line *Collingwood* would soon be in port and might wish to hoist the
English flag there.'   In a letter of July 4th to the consul in Honolulu, Larkin
says: 'I closed my Oahu mail last night, supposing that some 15 soldiers sent
in from Castro last night might have carried me off.   I suppose, however,
they did not think of it; although two days back they had it in contempla-
tion.   In the mean time I am dreaming of trying to persuade the Californians
to call on the commodore for protection, hoist his flag, and be his countrymen, or the Bear may destroy them.' *Larkin's Off. Corresp.*, MS., i. 99.

contrary winds, having perhaps left San Francisco on the morning of July 3d. The despatches to Sloat, if there were any such,[7] are not extant, but I have before me a communication from Montgomery to Larkin, dated July 2d, with two postscripts, in which were announced Torre's retreat with Frémont's latest achievements, the spiking of the guns at San Francisco, and the capture of Ridley.[8] This document was probably brought by the launch, and was perhaps the decisive one. At any rate, there can be little doubt that the latest news from the northern frontier, and especially the definite announcement that Frémont was acting with the insurgents,[9] was the last straw which—strengthened the camel's back to bear the burden of responsibility. With clear orders from his superiors at Washington, with positive knowledge of hostilities on the Rio Grande, with the ever present fear of being anticipated by the English admiral, and with importunities, as is very likely, on the part of his commanders,[10] Commodore Sloat dared no longer hesitate, especially as he now foresaw the opportunity, in case the seizure should prove to have been premature, like that of Jones in 1842, of throwing part of the responsibility upon Frémont.

[7] Wilson testified that the arrival was on the 5th. Larkin says it was Sunday. Lancey, *Cruise*, 79, says the passage was 56 hours, on authority not stated. In any case, it is not probable that Montgomery knew of Sloat's arrival; yet, as he expected him, he may have addressed despatches to him, all the same.

[8] July 2d, M. to L. *Larkin's Doc.*, MS., iv. 192. He writes: 'I feel very desirous to learn something more definite concerning the mysteries referred to in them (your letters). Were I enlightened respecting the future designs of our gov't, or concerning the actual condition of affairs with Mex., I could probably do much in the present crisis toward accomplishing objects in view. My neutral position, while all is stirring and exciting about me, renders us quiet spectators of passing events. I am looking for the arrival at this port of both commodores; as this must be the point of all important operations.'

[9] Larkin, in the document cited in note 6, says that definite news was now received of what had before been mere confused rumors; but this is exaggeration, for he already knew tolerably well what was being done at Sonoma.

[10] Davis, *Glimpses*, MS., 345–6, learned from Capt. Mervine that there was a council of war on the night of the 6th (5th), at which Sloat showed himself still irresolute until prevailed upon to decide on action by Mervine, who used very strong language, telling him 'it is more than your commission is worth to hesitate in this matter.'

Accordingly Larkin was summoned on board the flag-ship. The day was spent in preparing correspondence, orders, and proclamations; and before night of July 6th, the launch was started back for San Francisco with copies of papers to be published on the morrow, and a despatch for Montgomery, in which Sloat writes: "I have determined to hoist the flag of the United States at this place to-morrow, as I would prefer being sacrificed for doing too much than too little. If you consider you have sufficient force, or if Frémont will join you, you will hoist the flag at Yerba Buena, or at any other proper place, and take possession of the fort and that portion of the country "[11]

Every preparation having been completed the night before, at 7 in the morning of Tuesday, July 7th, Sloat sent Mervine ashore with two or three officers, bearing a formal demand for the surrender of the post of Monterey, with all troops, arms, and other public property. The summons was addressed to the military commandant, and was delivered to the old artillery captain, Mariano Silva. His reply, written at 8 A. M., was that as he had no authority to surrender the post, and as there were no troops, arms, or other public property, the commodore might settle the matter with General Castro, to whom the summons had been sent. On receipt of this reply at half-past nine, Sloat issued to the crews of all the ships a general order forbidding in the usual terms all plunder and other excesses on shore, and beginning with these words: "We are about to land on the territory of Mexico,

[11] July 6, 1846, S. to M. *U. S. Govt Doc.*, 29th cong. 2d sess., H. Ex. Doc. no. 4, p. 648–9. A writer signing himself 'Vindex,' and claiming to have been at Monterey in 1846, in a semi-official position, writes to the *Alta* of Sept. 11, 1870, to state positively, but erroneously, that Larkin with other prominent Americans called repeatedly on Sloat to beseech him to raise the flag. Mrs Ord, *Ocurrencias*, MS., 142, narrates that the people of Monterey had an idea that the place was to be taken on July 4th; and one man was injured by the crowd rushing out of evening prayers on a false alarm that the Americans were landing.

with whom the United States are at war.   To strike
her flag, and to hoist our own in the place of it, is our
duty.   It is not only our duty to take California, but
to preserve it afterward as a part of the United
States at all hazards.   To accomplish this, it is of the
first importance to cultivate the good opinion of the
inhabitants, whom we must reconcile."

At 10 o'clock 250 men, marines and seamen, were
landed from the squadron, under Captain Mervine,
with Commander Page as second.   This force marched
directly to the custom-house, where Sloat's proclamation was read, the flag of the United States was
raised—there had been no Mexican flag flying for two
months—three cheers were given by troops and spectators; and at the same time a salute of 21 guns was
fired from each of the three men-of-war.   The proclamation in English and Spanish was posted in public
places; two justices of the peace, Purser Price and
Surgeon Gilchrist, were appointed to preserve order
in the place of the alcaldes, who declined to serve; a
summons to surrender, with an invitation to present
himself for a personal interview, was sent to Castro
at Santa Clara; duplicate orders were sent to Montgomery at San Francisco; and letters of information
were forwarded by Larkin to Frémont, Ide, and others in different directions.   Thus Monterey became
permanently an American town.

Next day more correspondence was sent out, including communications from Larkin to Castro, Alvarado, and Stearns; police regulations were perfected; permanent quarters for a large part of the
garrison were fitted up at the custom-house, where
Commandant Mervine also had his headquarters,
while Page lived at the old government house; and a
band of music paraded the town for the entertainment of the new and old American citizens.   On the
9th arrived communications from Castro, at San Juan,
in one of which he manifested his purpose to spare no
sacrifice for the defence of his country, though he pro-

posed to consult the governor and assembly respecting
the means and methods of defence; and in the other
he complained bitterly of Frémont and his 'gang of
adventurers,' demanding an explanation of the relations between the insurgents and the forces commanded by Sloat. This may have indicated a disposition to treat if Sloat would disown in the name of
his government all Frémont's acts; but it was more
likely intended as an excuse, and it was really a sufficient one, for not considering himself bound by past
pledges to Larkin. The commodore also wrote to
Pico: "I beg your Excellency to feel assured that although I come in arms with a powerful force, I come
as the best friend of California; and I invite your Excellency to meet me at Monterey, that I may satisfy
you and the people of that fact."

On the 10th, Narvaez, Silva, and several other officers left Castro and returned to their families; and it
was reported that many of the general's men had deserted him, while others were about to do so. By the
12th there were 300 men on shore; two 18-pound
carronades were mounted as field-pieces; a stockade
and blockhouse were in process of erection; and a
cavalry force of from 35 to 50 men had been partially
organized. Orders for this company of patrolmen had
been issued as early as the 8th, Purser Daingerfield
Fauntleroy and Passed Midshipman Louis McLane
being put in command as captain and lieutenant respectively. It was on the 14th that Sloat announced the
receipt of intelligence that the flag was flying at Yerba
Buena, Sutter's Fort, Sauzalito, and Bodega; Commodore Stockton arrived with the *Congress* on the 15th;
next day came Admiral Seymour in the *Collingwood;*
on the 17th, Fauntleroy with his company was despatched to San Juan; and finally, on the 19th, Frémont and his battalion appeared at Monterey.

Thus without opposition, without much excitement,[12] without noteworthy incidents, Monterey had

[12] The French consul, Gasquet, seems to have objected to the posting of

fallen a second time into the hands of the United States, and was garrisoned by a naval force. I append some bibliographical matter bearing on the topic, including an abstract of the documentary record.[13]

a sentinel near his house. *Larkin's Off. Corresp.*, MS., i. 138; and on this circumstance, as I suppose, Vallejo and Alvarado build up a serious quarrel, in consequence of which Gasquet was arrested and exiled to S. Juan.

[13] Sloat's official report of July 31st, to the sec. of the navy, *War with Mexico, Repts Operations of the Navy*, 2–4, is a condensed narrative of the events noted in my text, to which little or nothing has been added by later writers. The same report, slightly disguised as a 'letter from an officer,' appears in *Niles' Reg.*, lxxi. 133. The report of the sec. of the navy on Dec. 5th, *U. S. Govt Doc.*, 29th cong. 2d sess., H. Ex. Doc. 4, p. 378–9, contains a still briefer account. Each successive point is still more clearly brought out by the documents of the period cited below. Swan, in *Monterey Republican*, Jan. 6, 1870; *S. José Pioneer*, May 4, 1878, tells a story of a frightened sentry at the custom-house, who one afternoon gave an alarm of an enemy coming on seeing the approach of a party of marines who had landed at a point out of sight. There is a notable absence of incidents, real and fictitious, in narratives relating to this period. Ezquer, *Memorias*, MS., 26, was one of the displaced justices. He says he was put under arrest, and that the doors of his office were broken down. Most Californians and others who were at Monterey at the time confine their statements to a brief mention of the occupation. It is not necessary to name them. *Cutts' Conq. of Cal.*, 111., etc., having been published in 1847, deserves mention, though it contains nothing except what was obtained from Sloat's report and the accompanying documents. For an account of the affair as reported in Mexico in August, including a translation of Sloat's procl., with amusingly bitter comments by the editor, see *Bustamante, Mem. Hist. Mex.*, v. 84–90; *Id., Nuevo Bernal Diaz*, ii. 58, 76–81. Other Mexican versions, showing no notable peculiarity, in *Rivera, Hist. Jalapa*, iii. 779; *Guerra, Apuntes*, 354–5; *Dicc. Univ.*, viii. 157; *Restaurador*, Aug. 18, 1846.

The official documents are found, as *Sloat's Despatches*, in *U. S. Govt Doc.*, 29th cong. 2d sess., H. Ex. Doc. 4, p. 640, etc.; and 31st cong. 1st sess., H. Ex. Doc. 1, pt ii. p. 1, etc. Most of them are copied in *Lancey's Cruise*, 79, etc.; and many have been often reprinted elsewhere. I do not deem it necessary to make any further reference to the page where each of these well known routine documents is to be found; nor to give more than a mere mention of their purport. Somewhat more attention is given to documents not before published, chiefly found among Larkin's papers.

1. July 7, 1846, Sloat to com. at Monterey, demanding surrender. 2. Silva to Sloat in reply, referring him to Gen. Castro. Spanish and translation. A correct copy of the original, the printed one being inaccurate, in *Larkin's Doc.*, MS., iv. 199. 3. Sloat's general order to his men before landing, forbidding plunder and disorder. *Dept. St. Pap.*, MS., vii. 70–1. 4. Sloat's proclamation to the inhabitants of Cal. (see my text a little later). Autograph original in the hall of the Cal. Pioneers. Original copies as circulated in English and Spanish, in *Vallejo, Doc.*, MS., xxxiv. 217; *Bandini, Doc.*, MS., 90; *Savage, Doc.*, MS., iii. 15, etc.; with printed copies in many works. 5. Sloat to Castro, in same terms as to Silva, demanding surrender; and adding: 'I hereby invite you to meet me immediately in Monterey to enter into articles of capitulation, that yourself, officers, and soldiers, with the inhabitants of Cal., may receive assurances of perfect safety to themselves and property.' 6. Com. Mervine to citizens, ordering that all stores and shops be closed for two days, and strictly forbidding retail of liquors. *Mont. Arch.*, MS., viii. 58–9. 7. Sloat to Montgomery: 'Your launch left yesterday. I enclose two documents. I hoisted the American flag here to-day at 9 A. M. (?)

Sloat's proclamation was as follows: "To the inhabitants of California: The central government of Mexico having commenced hostilities against the

You will immediately take possession of Y. B., and hoist the flag within reach of your guns; post up the proclamation in both languages; notify Capt. F. and others; put the guns and fort in order. I wish very much to see and hear from Capt. F., that we may understand each other and coöperate together.' 8. Larkin to Frémont. Desires him to send message overland on a subject of which he will soon be informed. 'The commodore wishes you at once to coöperate with him under the new state of affairs, and inform him immediately, calling on Capt. Montgomery for a launch if you need it, to bring him information of your willingness to do so. By land immediately you can send me a courier with a letter in your handwriting, without signature, merely saying you will fall into the plan offered. Show this to Mr Gillespie.' *Larkin's Off. Corresp.*, MS., i. 105. 9. Larkin to Montgomery, enclosing an open letter for Frémont, to be read, shown to Gillespie—who is desired to come down in the launch—and forwarded. Letters in writer's hand to be deemed authentic if not signed. *Id.*, i. 102. 10. Larkin to Ide. Com. Sloat 'has this hour (10 A. M.) raised the flag of the U. S.' 'I presume you will be inclined to desist from any contemplated movements against the natives, and remain passive for the present.' 'I would recommend you to communicate immediately with the commodore.' *Id.*, i. 100. 11. Larkin to Weber and Stokes at S. José, enclosing letter for Ide. To be carried or sent at once. Dr Marsh also to be notified. 'The news will come unexpected to you; but I hope you will be ready to coöperate in calming the minds of those around you.' *Id.*, i. 101. 12. Passport or certificate of Manuel Diaz, that the bearer has a communication for Ide recommending him to suspend hostilities. *Id., Doc.*, MS., iv. 200. 13. Sloat to Larkin. Suggests the posting of reliable persons on each road a few miles from town. *Id.*, iv. 201.

14. July 8th, Larkin to Stearns; with an account of what has occurred, also latest news from the north. *Id.*, iv. 202. 15. Larkin to Sloat, recommending the appointment of a school-master at $1,000 salary. He will contribute one tenth. Thinks it will induce the natives to accept office under the U. S. Called on Castro's wife, and found her very uneasy. Will soon know all Castro's plans. The gen. will probably be at S. Juan to-night. Will come on board to-morrow with David Spence and Dr McKee. Manuel Diaz invited, but prefers to wait a few days. *Id., Off. Corresp.*, MS., i. 100–1. 16. Larkin to Castro. The commodore is anxious for an interview. Assures him of good treatment. *Id.*, i. 108–9. 17. Larkin to Alvarado. Is still friendly to him and Don José. Hopes the latter will enter into a convention with Sloat, as he may honorably do. *Id.*, i. 100. 18. Larkin's circular to Americans, with a full account of the Bear Flag revolt, including the latest news. 19. July 9th, Sloat to Frémont, telling him what had been done, and urging him to make haste with at least 100 men. *Frémont's Cal. Claims*, 73–4. Castro to Sloat (in reply to no. 5). Spanish and translation. 20. Same to same, asking an explanation about Frémont's operations. (One of these two doc. appears in one of the official editions, and the other in the other, each as appendix F.) 21. Sloat to Pico, enclosing copies of summons to Castro; asking an interview and assuring him of good treatment, also dated 12th. 22. Castro to Larkin. His letter to Sloat contains his 'ultimate determination.' *Sawyer's Doc.*, MS., 77–8. 23. Alvarado to Larkin. Thanks for kind attentions. Cannot disregard his obligations to his general. Refers to the efforts of the 'immortal Washington.' *Id.*, 78–9. 24. July 10th, Larkin to Sloat, informing him of the return of Silva and Narvaez, and reported desertion of Castro's men; and suggesting a proclamation of encouragement for such men. *Larkin's Off. Corresp.*, MS., i. 105. 25. July 12th, Sloat to Montgomery, with an account of the situation of

United States of America by invading its territory
and attacking the troops...on the north side of the
Rio Grande, and with a force of 7,000 men under...
Gen. Arista, which army was totally destroyed...on
the 8th and 9th of May last by a force of 2,300 men
under...Gen. Taylor, and the city of Matamoras
taken...and the two nations being actually at war by
this transaction, I shall hoist the standard of the
United States at Monterey immediately, and shall
carry it throughout California. I declare to the inhabitants of California that, although I come in arms
with a powerful force, I do not come among them as an
enemy to California; on the contrary, I come as their
best friend, as henceforward California will be a portion of the United States, and its peaceful inhabitants
will enjoy the same rights and privileges as the citi-

affairs; also another despatch approving his course at San Francisco. 26.
Larkin to Frémont. Urges him to come on to Monterey. The commodore
is anxious for his coöperation. Wishes to organize a body of paid men.
Frémont may promise $15 or $20 per month, and to a great extent choice
of their own officers. *Larkin's Off. Corresp.*, MS. 27. Wm Matthews,
carrying despatches to San Francisco, was stopped at Tucho rancho by
'Chanate' Castro and José Higuera. He was tied to another prisoner and
carried off on horseback; but escaped while the captors were drinking.
Mont. Arch., MS., viii. 45–9.
    28. Muster-roll of Fauntleroy's dragoons from July 12th to Sept. 17th.
49 names. *Cal. Pion. Soc., Arch.*, MS., 239–40. Sloat's communication of
July 8th to Fauntleroy, authorizing him to organize the company, 35 strong,
from the squadron and volunteers, to protect peaceable inhabitants and keep
a watch over the enemy. *Id.*, 231. Also Sloat's proclamation to 'good citizens of Cal. and others,' inviting them to enroll themselves in the company
for 3 months at $15 per month. Doc. not dated, but a Spanish translation
is dated July 13th.
    29. July 13th, five custom-house officers meet and resolve that they
are bound to support the Mexican cause, exhorting all subordinates to join
Castro's force. Hartnell declined to do so, though he signed and approved
the resolution, because of his large family. Guerra was the leading spirit.
Unb. Doc., MS., 211–13. Pablo de la Guerra, *Guerra, Doc.*, MS., iv. 1300–1,
claims that he refused to give up the custom-house flags and boats, commanded his employés to join Castro, and himself left town in all haste to
avoid giving his parole.
    30. July 14th, Sloat's general order announcing the raising of the flag in
the north, and congratulating all who had participated in the change. *Sawyer's Doc.*, MS., 83. 31. Thomas Cole paid $165 for carrying despatches to
S. José and Yerba Buena. Horses and pistols taken from him by Castro's
men also paid for. *Monterey, Consulate Arch.*, MS., ii. 16–17.
    32. July 16th, Larkin to Montgomery. Reports arrival of the *Congress*,
and says all is quiet. About 100 people have asked for passports to pass in
and out of town, though they are not required. *Larkin's Off. Corresp.*, MS.,
i. 107.

zens of any other portion of that territory, with all
the rights and privileges they now enjoy, together
with the privilege of choosing their own magistrates
and other officers for the administration of justice
among themselves; and the same protection will be
extended to them as to any other state in the Union.
They will also enjoy a permanent government, under
which life, property, and the constitutional right and
lawful security to worship the creator in the way
most congenial to each one's sense of duty, will be
secured, which unfortunately the central government
of Mexico cannot afford them, destroyed as her resources are by internal factions and corrupt officers,
who create constant revolutions to promote their own
interests and oppress the people.   Under the flag of
the United States California will be free from all
such troubles and expense; consequently the country
will rapidly advance and improve, both in agriculture
and commerce, as, of course, the revenue laws will be
the same in California as in all other parts of the
United States, affording them all manufactures and
produce of the United States free of any duty, and
all foreign goods at one quarter of the duty they
now pay.   A great increase in the value of real estate
and the products of California may also be anticipated.   With the great interest and kind feelings I
know the government and people of the United States
possess toward the citizens of California, the country cannot but improve more rapidly than any other
on the continent of America.   Such of the inhabitants of California, whether native or foreigners, as
may not be disposed to accept the high privileges of
citizenship and to live peaceably under the government of the United States, will be allowed time to
dispose of their property and to remove out of the
country, if they choose, without any restriction; or
remain in it, observing strict neutrality.   With full
confidence in the honor and integrity of the inhabitants of the country, I invite the judges, alcaldes,

and other civil officers to retain their offices, and to execute their functions as heretofore, that the public tranquillity may not be disturbed; at least, until the government of the territory can be more definitely arranged. All persons holding titles to real estate, or in quiet possession of lands under a color of right, shall have those titles and rights guaranteed to them. All churches and the property they contain, in possession of the clergy of California, shall continue in the same rights and possessions they now enjoy. All provisions and supplies of every kind furnished by the inhabitants for the use of the United States ships and soldiers will be paid for at fair rates; and no private property will be taken for public use without just compensation at the moment. John D. Sloat, commander-in-chief of the United States naval force in the Pacific Ocean."

This proclamation was by no means a model in respect of literary style, though superior to many of the commodore's productions. The preliminary statement that American soil had been invaded by Mexico might be criticised, even from a standpoint not purely Mexican; though Sloat was not responsible for it, and such criticism does not belong here. The position assumed that California was to be permanently a territory of the United States was certainly a novel and very peculiar one, considering the fact that the United States ostensibly fought to resist invasion in Texas; but it was more or less in accord with the spirit of the instructions that Sloat had received, and entirely so with those then on their way to him. In other respects, however, the document was most wisely framed to accomplish its purpose. Moderate and friendly in tone, it touched skilfully upon the people's past grievances—neglect by Mexico, high prices of imported goods, official corruption, and insecurity of life and property; and contained no allusions likely to arouse patriotic, religious, or race prejudices. No proclamation involving a change of nationality could have been more favorably received by Californians of all classes. Many, not before friends to annexation, welcomed the change as a relief from prospective Bear Flag rule; though nearly all would have been better pleased had the lack of all connection between the revolt and the hoisting of the stars and stripes been somewhat more apparent.

The capture of San Francisco by the United States naval forces was an event quite as devoid of incident or romance as the occupation of Monterey just related.[14] The *Portsmouth's* launch, leaving Monterey on July 6th with despatches from Sloat to Montgomery, had a stormy passage of five days; but other despatches, already noticed as sent on the 7th, reached their destination sooner. One copy sent by Henry Pitts by way of San José was delivered at 7 P. M. of the 8th;[15] while the duplicate, which Job Dye took by a coast route, arrived at 1 P. M. of the next day. Before dawn on Thursday the 9th, Montgomery despatched Lieutenant Revere in the ship's boat with a flag to be raised at Sonoma; and at 8 A. M., having landed with 70 men at Yerba Buena, he hoisted the stars and strips "in front of the custom-house, in the public square, with a salute of 21 guns from the ship, followed by three hearty cheers on shore and on board, in which the people, principally foreign residents, seemed cordially to join. I then addressed a few words to the assembled people," writes the cap-

[14] Perhaps I should here credit one man with a laudable ambition to make the preliminaries at least interesting. A soldier's yarn—whether invented by the soldier or by the writer who claimed to take it from his lips I know not—published in the *N. Y. Commercial Advertiser*, June 14, 1867, and reprinted in half a dozen California papers, informs us that the hero was at Tepic when news came that papers had been signed giving Cal. to the U. S., but that England was also after it. He was therefore sent off on horseback with despatches for Capt. Montgomery at S. F., whom he reached, after a series of thrilling adventures, just in time to have the flag raised and the country saved!

[15] Lancey, *Cruise*, 82, says that Pitts was stopped on the way by the Californians; but this occurred I think on his return. Lancey's statement is founded on that of Milton Little. *Monterey Herald*, July 13, 1874; *Sta Cruz Sentinel*, July 25, 1874.

tain to his superior officer,[16] "after which your excellent proclamation was read in both languages and posted upon the flag-staff."[17] Not only was there no opposition, but there was not in town a single Mexican official from whom to demand a surrender. Sub-prefect Guerrero and Comandante Sanchez had absented themselves; Port-captain Ridley was a prisoner at Sutter's Fort; and Receptor Pinto had more than a week before gone to join Castro, first disposing of the custom-house flag, which in 1870 he presented to the California Pioneers, and the archives of his office, which now, thanks to Don Rafael, form an interesting part of my own collection.[18]

After the ceremony a part of the force landed, including all the marines; and the rest, taking up their quarters at the custom-house, remained as a permanent garrison, under the command of Lieutenant H. B. Watson. In a meeting held at Vice-consul Liedesdorff's house, steps were taken, in accordance with a proclamation of Montgomery, to organize a company of 'volunteer guards,' to protect the town and perform duties similar to those assumed by Fauntleroy at Monterey. Purser Watmough was sent with a

---

[16] Montgomery's report to Sloat of occupation of S. F., July 9, 1846. *U. S. Govt Doc.*, 29th cong. 2d sess., H. Ex. Doc. 4, p. 649–50. The story also told briefly in Sloat's report. *Id.*, 641. Bryant, Tuthill, and others have given the date of the occupation incorrectly as July 8th.

[17] The old custom-house, or *receptoría*, stood on what is now Brenham place, on the west side of the plaza, or Portsmouth Square, near Washington street.

[18] Pinto informs me—and the same version appears in the *Sta Cruz Sentinel*, Aug. 13, 1870, the presentation of the flag being recorded in the *S. F. Bulletin*, July 6, 1870; *Suisun Republican*, Aug. 4, 1870, and other papers— that on his departure he committed the trunk containing the flag and documents to the care of Leidesdorff as private property. Rather strangely, Montgomery and Leidesdorff failed to examine the contents, which were subsequently restored to the owner. The papers were presented to me in 1878 by Don Rafael, whose *Apuntaciones* I have often cited as a valuable contribution to Californian history, and now—650 in number, very important as records of the country's commerce, and including many of great interest on other matters—they are preserved in my Library in two large folio volumes, with the following title: *Documentos para la Historia de California. Coleccion del Sr Don Rafael Pinto, Oficial que fué del ejército Mejicano en California, y Receptor de la Aduana de San Francisco en los últimos meses de la dominacion Mejicana. Regalada por el conducto de Tomás Savage á la 'Bancroft Library,' 1878.*

letter to intercept Frémont, erroneously supposed to
be at Santa Clara in pursuit of Castro.   Lieutenant
Misroon with a small party made a tour to the presidio and fort, finding the cannon at the latter place
just as Frémont had left them on July 1st, spiked,
and requiring much labor to render them of any service.   No other public property was found; and no
human beings were seen except a few Indians.   The
U. S. flag was displayed over the fort.   Two days
later Misroon visited the mission and secured a collection of public documents.   The residents had at
first fled on hearing of what had happened at Yerba
Buena; but now they were returning to their homes
and becoming reconciled to the change.   It was also
on the 11th that Revere returned from Sonoma,
bringing news that all was well in the north.   Comandante Sanchez came in on Montgomery's invitation, and pointed out the spots where two guns were
buried, the sub-prefect coming in later and giving up
the papers of his office; and the *Juno* anchored in
the bay, causing some warlike preparations on the
Portsmouth, but showing no disposition to interfere
in any way.   During this period, and until the end
of the month, there were no incidents worthy of notice.[19]   There were no arrests, except of half a dozen
of Montgomery's own men for disorderly conduct.
Some cannon were transferred from Sonoma and
mounted on the side of what is now Telegraph Hill,
to protect the town.   Correspondence of the time
made known at Yerba Buena much of what was occurring at Monterey and at other places.   It was
understood that couriers were sometimes stopped by

[19] Wm H. Davis, *Glimpses of the Past*, MS., 267–8, 346–7, arrived at Yerba
Buena during this period, and chats pleasantly, as is his wont, of what occurred.
He and W. D. M. Howard were arrested late one night while crossing the
plaza, having forgotten the countersign, and were taken to the guard-house;
but Lieut Watson administered no more severe penalty than to force them
to drink a bottle of champagne with him before going home.   Davis says
the guns were got out and all made ready for a fight on board the *Portsmouth*
several times on the arrival of a vessel, once while he was taking breakfast
with Montgomery, there being great fear of trouble with England.   Phelps,
Fore and Aft, 293–4, also has something to say of the events of these days.

Californians on the way to San José; but otherwise no rumor came to indicate that all north of Monterey was not as completely and quietly American as was the little village on San Francisco Bay. Not much is known of the events narrated, beyond what is contained in the documentary record which I append.[20]

[20] The documents relating to the occupation of San Francisco are found annexed to Sloat's report in *29th Cong. 2d Sess., H. Ex. Doc. 4*, p. 648–68, and in *31st Cong. 1st Sess., H. Ex. Doc. no. 1*, pt ii. p. 10–30. They are as follows: 1. July 6th, Sloat to Montgomery, sent by the launch, and already noted. 2. July 7th, same to same, 'telegraphic,' already noted. 3. July 9th, Montgomery to Sloat, in reply to no. 2, narrating events of the occupation as in my text, and enclosing documents of the day. Advises the bringing of two 18-pounders from Sonoma. Has supplied Frémont with stores to the amount of $2,199. 4. Montgomery to his 'fellow-citizens,' an address after raising the flag. Thinks the new standard will 'this day be substituted for the revolutionary flag recently hoisted at Sonoma.' Commends Sloat's proclamation. Invites citizens willing to join a local militia to call at Leidesdorff's house immediately. 5. Montgomery's proclamation, calling upon all to enroll themselves into a military company, choosing their own officers. In case of an attack, all necessary force will be landed from the *Portsmouth*. Announces Watson's appointment as military commandant pro tem. 6. Montgomery to Frémont, announcing what has been done, and requesting his presence at Monterey. 7. Montgomery to Purser James H. Watmough. He is to intercept Frémont at Sta Clara or S. José, and deliver no. 6 to him. 8. Montgomery to H. B. Watson, making him commander of marines and local militia. Encloses list of militia force. Arranges signals for aid in case of attack. 9. Lieut J. S. Misroon to Montgomery. Report of a visit to the presidio and fort with Watmough, Leidesdorff, and several volunteers. At the fort he found 3 brass cannon and 7 of iron. Recommends some repairs at the fort. No cannon at the presidio. 10. July 11th, Misroon to Montgomery. Report of a visit to the Mission with Leidesdorff and a party of marines. 11. Lieut Revere, having returned, reports the success of his mission to Sonoma. 12. Lieut Watson's report of the day. All quiet. Patrol vigilant and obedient. 13. Lieut Misroon for Montgomery (who is confined to his bed) to Sloat. Sends additional documents and details. Reports raising of the flag in the north. Arrival of the *Juno*. Hopes to recover two cannon buried at the presidio and mission. Comandante Sanchez had come in on invitation; had no public property to deliver, but knew where some guns were buried. A stand of colors and a boat taken from the custom-house. This was sent to Monterey by Pitts. Received next day. 14. July 13th, Montgomery to Fallon, about affairs at S. José. 15. July 15th, Montgomery to Sloat. Has received Sloat's of 12th, sent from S. José by Stokes. Is 'wholly at a loss as to the whereabouts of Capt. Frémont,' but thinks he may be at Monterey. Notes arrival of the *Vandalia* from S. Diego. Suggests transfer of arms from Sonoma. Sends correspondence with Fallon. 16. July 17th, Montgomery to Sloat, in answer to telegraphic despatch of 12th, which was delayed 36 hours at S. José. Is fortifying the anchorage. The entrance to the bay can be so fortified as to repel the whole navy of Great Britain. 17. Same to same, on the prisoners at Sutter's Fort. 18. July 18th, Montgomery to Grigsby, on Sonoma affairs. 19. July 20th, Montgomery to Sloat, forwarding correspondence with Grigsby. Suggests a guard on the road to S. José infested by mischievous men. Has 6 men under arrest for disorderly conduct. Good progress on the new fort. The late sub-prefect Francisco Guerrero came in from his rancho on summons, and gave up the papers of his

At Sonoma, where nothing that we know of had occurred since Frémont's departure three days before, Revere arrived before noon of July 9th, having left San Francisco in the *Portsmouth's* boat at two o'clock in the morning. Of what followed there is no other record than that of Revere himself, as follows: "Having caused the troops of the garrison and the inhabitants of the place to be summoned to the public square, I then read the proclamation of Commodore Sloat to them, and then hoisted the United States flag upon the staff in front of the barracks, under a salute from the artillery of the garrison. I also caused the proclamation to be translated into Spanish and posted up in the plaza. A notice to the people of California was also sent the next day, to be forwarded to the country around, requesting the people to assemble at Sonoma on Saturday next, the 11th, to hear the news confirmed of the country having been taken possession of by the United States. An express, with a copy of the proclamation and a United States flag, was also sent to the commander of the garrison at Sutter's Fort on the Sacramento, with a request to do the same there that had been done at Sonoma. The same was also done to the principal American citizen—Mr Stephen Smith—at Bodega, with a demand for two pieces of field artillery...I am happy to report that great satisfaction appeared to prevail in the community of Sonoma, of all classes, and among both foreigners and natives, at the country having been taken possession of by the United States and their flag hoisted; more particularly after the general feeling of insecurity of life and property caused by the recent events of the revolution in this part of California."[21] It will be remembered that Grigsby and about fifty men had been left as a garrison, the main force of the in-

department. He was allowed to depart on parole. *Juno* sailed. No visits during her stay except by boarding officers.

[21] July 11, 1846, Revere to Montgomery. *29th Cong. 2d Sess., H. Ex. Doc. 4*, p. 657. In his *Tour of Duty*, Revere says nothing of this visit, though he speaks of his return to Sonoma as commandant a little later.

surgents having gone to the Sacramento. This fact, perhaps, accounts in part for the commonplace, matter-of-course way in which the Bear flag gave place to the stars and stripes. But while under the former régime, with Ide in command, such an event might have been attended with more diplomacy, speech-making, and general excitement, there is no reason to believe that there would have been the slightest opposition by the revolutionists. Doubtless some of the leading spirits would have preferred that the change should come a little later, accompanied by negotiations which might give themselves personally more prominence; and many adventurers saw with regret their chances for plunder in the near future cut off; but there were very slight, if any, manifestations of displeasure, and no thoughts of resistance. The natives were naturally delighted at the change; and as is usual in such cases, they were disposed to exaggerate the chagrin experienced by the hated Osos.[22]

About the raising of the flag on the Sacramento, we know still less than of the like event at Sonoma, having no official contemporary record whatever. The courier despatched by Revere from Sonoma on the 9th

[22] Vallejo, *Hist. Cal.*, MS., v. 158–61, tells us that the Bears murmured, and even threatened to raise the old flag as soon as Frémont should return. He quotes a letter from his wife, in which she says: 'For two nights the servants have not slept in my room; the danger is past, for a captain from Sauzalito, sent by Capt. Montgomery, who in a letter recommended him highly to me, put the American flag on the staff where before was the Bear; and since then there are no robberies that I know of, although sister Rosa (Mrs Leese) says it is all just the same. In those days were great fiestas, all of us shouting with pleasure and waving our handkerchiefs; but the Osos were very sad. I heard the wife of Capt. Sears say that her husband said, "The American flag had come too soon, and all his work was lost." I and sister Rosa are not afraid any more for your life and that of Salvador and Don Luis' (Leese). On July 16th Capt. Grigsby wrote to Capt. Montgomery: 'The Spaniards appear well satisfied with the change. The most of them, 38, have come forward and signed articles of peace. Should they take up arms, etc., they forfeit their lives and property. All things are going on very well here at present. We have about 50 men capable of bearing arms. There are some foreigners on this side that have never taken any part with us. I wish to know the proper plan to pursue with them, whether their property shall be used for the garrison or not. There are some poor men here that are getting very short of clothing. I wish to know in what way it might be procured for them.' *31st Cong. 1st Sess., H. Ex. Doc. 1*, pt ii. p. 28.

was William Scott.[23] He carried a flag and a copy
of Sloat's proclamation, with orders, or a request, to
the commandant at Sutter's Fort to hoist the former
and publish the latter.   The courier arrived just before night on the 10th; and Lieutenant Kern sent
him on to the American River to the camp of Frémont, whom Montgomery and Revere had supposed
to be far away in the south.   Frémont writes: "We
were electrified by the arrival of an express from
Captain Montgomery, with information that Commodore Sloat had hoisted the flag of the United States.
. . .Independence and the flag of the United States
are synonymous terms to the foreigners here, the
northern which is the stronger part particularly, and
accordingly I directed the flag to be hoisted with a
salute the next morning.   The event produced great
rejoicing among our people;"[24] and, as he might have
added, among the imprisoned Californians in the fort,
who were foolish enough to believe that the change of
flag would effect their immediate deliverance, as it
certainly should have done.   It does not clearly appear whether Frémont went down in person to raise
the flag at the fort on the morning of July 11th, or
simply directed Kern to attend to that duty.   Sutter,
who never admits that he was not in command all this
time, says of the flag: "Lieutenant Revere sent me
one.   It was brought by a courier, who arrived in the
night.   At sunrise next morning, I hoisted it over my
fort and began firing guns.   The firing continued until nearly all the glass in the fort was broken."[25]

[23] *Monterey Californian*, March 20, 1847; *Lancey's Cruise*, 102; and many
newspaper accounts.
[24] Frémont's letter of July 25th, in *Niles' Reg.*, lxxi. 191. Gillespie, *Frémont's Cal. Claims*, 29, says, 'About sunset an express arrived from below,'
impliedly at the fort, 'bearing an American flag to be hoisted at the fort,
and a proclamation from Sloat, announcing the commencement of hostilities
with Mexico and the taking of Monterey. The bear flag had been hauled
down at Sonoma, and the American flag run up in its place immediately
upon the arrival of the news. The flag brought by the express was hoisted
at Sutter's fort at sunrise upon the 11th July under a salute of 21 guns;
and the settlers throughout the country received the news with rejoicings of
great joy and gladness.'
[25] *Sutter's Pers. Remin.*, MS., 151. The *N. Helvetia Diary*, MS., notes

In the Santa Clara Valley, Weber and Fallon had made an effort to raise a force among the settlers, with the view of coöperating with the Bear Flag insurgents. This region being Castro's headquarters, it was necessary to act cautiously; but while an open movement against the Californians was impracticable, some kind of an organization was effected, and a considerable force was in readiness to join Ide and Frémont whenever they should advance from the north. Fallon, with nineteen men from the region of Santa Cruz, was encamped in the hills, awaiting the time for action. Weber's efforts were revealed to the Californians, and with two companions he was arrested and taken to San Juan[26] at or about the same time that Castro transferred his force to that place. On July 7th Pitts arrived from Monterey en route for San Francisco, with communications for Weber and Stokes, and others for Ide and Frémont.[27] He may also have been the bearer of Sloat's despatch to Castro.[28] Next day the general withdrew his troops and started for San Juan. There are indications that Stokes and his friends soon hoisted an American flag; but if so, it was lowered and carried away by some foe to the cause.[29] On the 11th, however, Fallon and his party entered the town from their mountain camp, and the leader notified Montgomery that they were at his command,

the arrival of Frémont on the 10th at the fort and the American River; and also the departure of some men for the camp on the 11th; but says nothing of the flag, and then closes abruptly for several months.

[26] See chap. v., this vol.

[27] July 7th, Larkin to Weber and Stokes, enclosing one for Ide. *Larkin's Off. Corresp.*, MS., i. 101. A communication for Frémont was also doubtless sent by this route as well as through Montgomery. Marsh was to be notified. Larkin suggested that Stokes or Weber should go to Sonoma if possible, otherwise that Cook or Bellamy should be sent. Lancey says that Pitts arrived on the 8th, and this may be correct; but as he left Monterey early on the 7th and reached S. F. at 7 P. M. on the 8th, it seems most likely, in the absence of positive proof to the contrary, that he passed the night at S. José.

[28] John Daubenbiss, who carried the despatch for Frémont, says, *S. José Pioneer*, Aug. 23, 1879, that Castro was parading his troops in town when he started. Lancey, *Cruise*, 73, says, however, that Daubenbiss carried the news that Castro had gone to S. Juan with Weber as prisoner.

[29] Fallon, in his letter to Montgomery, mentioned later, says: 'The flag that was put up here was cut down before we came here, but I hope it shall never happen again.'

and ready to raise the flag.   Montgomery replied on
the 13th with thanks, and instructions to hoist the flag
if the force should be deemed sufficient to defend it.[30]
But though the force increased rapidly to the number
of about forty, no flag could be found at the pueblo.
Hearing of this want, Sloat forwarded the required
bunting on the 13th, and on the 16th it was raised
over the juzgado by Fallon and his patriotic followers.[31]   On the same day, Alcalde Pacheco having declined to serve under the new régime, James Stokes
was appointed by Sloat to hold the office temporarily.[32]   In a few days Fallon and his men went down
to San Juan to join Frémont.

We left Frémont and his Bear Flag battalion encamped on the American River near Sutter's Fort.
At San Francisco and Sonoma it was believed that
Frémont was in hot pursuit of Castro, and in that
belief despatches were sent to intercept him at Santa
Clara, the general's headquarters.   But as a matter
of fact, before the insurgents had completed their
preparations for the pursuit, if indeed the captain
really intended to undertake it, news came that Castro had retreated southward, in consequence of Sloat's
occupation of Monterey.   This news, together with
Sloat's proclamation and his request that Frémont
should join him without delay, seems to have been
brought up the valley by Robert Livermore, and arrived on the 11th, the same day that the flag was

[30] July 12th, Fallon to Montgomery, and the latter's reply of the 13th. *U. S. Govt Doc.*, 29th cong. 2d sess., H. Ex. Doc. 4, p. 660–1.   Fallon says Castro started south 'last Wednesday' (8th); and he asks for some arms as a loan, which the captain is willing to furnish but has no way to send them.   Lancey, *Cruise*, 89, cites two other unimportant letters from Montgomery to Fallon, dated July 15th, 16th, though the former date must be an error.   Win-
ston Bennett, *S. José Pioneer*, May 26, June 2, 1877, claims to have been the one to notify Fallon of Pitts' arrival.   He is inaccurate in some of his details.

[31] Sloat's report of July 31st, and his letter to Montgomery of July 12th. See also *Hall's Hist. S. José*, 146–7, 150–3; *S. José Pioneer*, Sept. 15, 1877; *Sta Clara Co. Hist. Atlas*, 10; *S. José Patriot*, July 23, 1875.

[32] July 16th, Sloat to people of S. José. *S. José, Arch., Loose Pap.*, MS., 33.   They are urged to choose their own local authorities.

raised over Sutter's Fort.[33] It was probably the next
day that Frémont's battalion started down the valley,
about 160 strong, with one or two field-pieces.[34] On
the Mokelumne River, as we are informed by Bidwell,
the Sonoma agreement, or enlistment paper, was
brought out to receive the signatures of all who had
not yet signed; and the document is not known to
have been seen since.[35] Continuing his march rather
slowly down the Sacramento and up the San Joaquin,
Frémont crossed the latter river near what is now
called Hill's Ferry, and crossing the hills, probably by
the Pacheco Pass, arrived on July 17th at San Juan,
which place Castro had abandoned a week before. A
few hours later, Fauntleroy arrived with a squad of
his dragoons from Monterey, having been sent by
Sloat to reconnoitre the country, hoist the flag at San
Juan, and recover some cannon said to be buried there.
The stars and stripes soon floated over the ex-mission
pueblo, probably with salute and cheers and reading
of the proclamation as elsewhere. Thus the last place
in northern California, or at least the last making any
pretensions to the rank of 'town,' came, without the
slightest resistance, under the power of the United
States.[36]

[33] Frémont's letter to Benton. *Niles' Reg.*, lxxi. 191. Livermore is named
as the courier in the *Monterey Californian*, March 20, 1847. John Daubenbiss, in *S. José Pioneer*, Aug. 23, 1879, says, accurately I think: 'Dr Stokes
received the despatch from Pitts, who had brought it from Com. Sloat at
Monterey, and he asked me to carry it to Capt. Frémont, who was at Sutter's
Fort. I rode to the San Joaquin River, and being unable to swim my horse
across the river, I returned to Livermore (rancho), and got Mr Livermore to
carry the proclamation to Frémont, which he did with the aid of his Indians.
I remained at Livermore's until Lieut Gillespie arrived from Frémont's camp,
and then piloted him to S. José, where we found that Capt. Tom Fallon had
hoisted the American flag. We arrived at S. José at midnight, and next
morning I took Lieut Gillespie to Monterey.' In the same paper of Jan. 20,
1877, Harry Bee tells how he himself carried the despatches to Frémont at
Sloat's request; and adds many details of Frémont's words and actions, as of
his own adventures. The story has some foundation in fact. See ii. 714.

[34] Gillespie, in the *S. F. Alta*, July 3, 1866, mentions 2 guns, the 'Sutter,'
that had been mounted on the fort, and the 'Frémont,' a 16-pounder iron gun
mounted upon the running-gear of a Pennsylvania wagon, bought from Sutter
for $600. The 'Sutter' was a brass piece of Russian origin. It was after the
war returned to Sutter, and by him presented to the Cal. Pioneers. Frémont
mentions but one gun on his arrival at Monterey.

[35] *Bidwell's Cal. in 1841–8*, MS., 174; *Willey's Thirty Years in Cal.*, 13.

[36] On Frémont's occupation of S. Juan, see Sloat's report, and report of sec-

The current version is that now or a little later
Frémont and Fauntleroy found and took possession
of a considerable quantity of arms and ammunition
that had been abandoned by Castro at San Juan.
Some writers specify nine cannon, 200 muskets,
twenty kegs of powder, and 60,000 pounds of copper
cannon-balls.[37]   That Castro left most of his cannon
buried, or even that some of the guns had not been
dug up or mounted since the time of Micheltorena,
may well be credited; but that he left at San Juan
any serviceable muskets or powder, in the absence of
more positive proof, I must decline to believe.   Fallon with his men soon came in from San José to join
the battalion; and leaving a small garrison behind,[38]
to relieve which Fauntleroy was soon sent back with
some forty men, the dragoons and the battalion of
Bears marched on Sunday, July 19th, to Monterey,
where Gillespie had arrived two days earlier.   Frémont's men, whose appearance is described in print
by Walpole and Colton, seem to have created a decided sensation in the town.[39]

retary of war, for a brief statement.   Martin, *Narrative*, MS., 31-2, describes
the march slightly.   All the authorities mention Fauntleroy's expedition.
German, *Sucesos*, MS., 25-6, mentions the curious circumstance that while
Frémont and Fauntleroy were at S. Juan a mad coyote came in and bit many
persons.   No one died; but all the dogs in town were immediately shot.

[37] *Monterey Californian*, March 20, 1847; *Tuthill's Hist. Cal.*, 181-2.
Vallejo, *Hist. Cal.*, MS., 170-1, and Alvarado, *Hist. Cal.*, MS., v. 232-3,
267, state that all the arms and ammunition had been removed before Frémont's arrival.

[38] Lancey, *Cruise*, 103, names Daubenbiss and James W. Marshall, and
says there were 7 or 8 others.

[39] 'During our stay Capt. Frémont and his party arrived, preceded by
another troop of American horse.   It was a party of seamen mounted.
Their efficiency as sailors, they being nearly all English, we will not question.   As cavalry, they would probably have been singularly destructive to
each other.   Their leader, however, was a fine fellow, and one of the best
rifle-shots in the States (Fauntleroy?).   Frémont's party naturally excited
curiosity.   Here were true trappers.   These men had passed years in the
wilds, living on their own resources.   They were a curious set.   A vast
cloud of dust appeared first, and thence in long file emerged this wildest wild
party.   Frémont rode ahead, a spare, active-looking man, with such an eye!
He was dressed in a blouse and leggings, and wore a felt hat.   After him
came five Delaware Indians, who were his body-guard; they had charge of
two baggage-horses.   The rest, many of them blacker than the Indians, rode
two and two, the rifle held by one hand across the pommel of the saddle.
39 of them are his regular men, the rest are loafers picked up lately.   His
original men are principally backwoodsmen from Tennessee...The dress of

Naturally an early interview took place between Sloat and Frémont; and for obvious reasons it was not satisfactory to either. The commodore, whose hesitation at Mazatlan and Monterey has already been noted, if he had not exactly been induced to act by the news of Frémont's operations, had at least been greatly comforted thereby. His natural timidity increased by ill health, he had again begun to fear that, like Jones in earlier years, he had acted prematurely; and he had looked forward with anxiety to the opportunity of learning from the captain's own lips the nature of the instructions or information under which he had begun hostilities. His anxiety in this respect is clearly reflected in the letters of himself and Larkin already cited; and it had been greatly augmented by Larkin's opinion that Frémont and Gillespie had acted on their own responsibility. Therefore, when he learned in response to his questions that those officers had pro-

these men was principally a long loose coat of deer-skin, tied with thongs in front; trousers of the same, of their manufacture, which, when wet through they take off, scrape well inside with a knife, and put on as soon as dry. The saddles were of various fashions, though these and a large drove of horses, and a brass field-gun, were things they had picked up in California. The rest of the gang were a rough set; and perhaps their private, public, and moral characters had better not be too closely examined. They are allowed no liquor,...and the discipline is very strict. They were marched up to an open space on the hills near the town, under some large firs, and there took up their quarters in messes of six or seven, in the open air. The Indians lay beside their leader. One man, a doctor [Semple], six feet six high, was an odd-looking fellow. May I never come under his hands! The party, after settling themselves, strolled into the town, and in less than two days, passed in drunkenness and debauchery, three or four were missing. They were accordingly marched away...One of the gang was very uncivil to us, and threw on us the withering imputation of being Britishers...On inquiry, he was found to be a deserter from the marines. In fact, the most violently Yankee were discovered to be English fellows, of high principles, of course.' *Walpole's Four Years in the Pacific*, ii. 215–16. Colton, *Deck and Port*, 390–1, says: 'Monday, July 20th, Capt. Frémont and his armed band, with Lieut Gillespie of the marine corps, arrived last night from their pursuit of Gen. Castro (!). They are 200 strong, all well mounted, and have some 300 extra horses in their train. They defiled, two abreast, through the principal street of the town. The ground seemed to tremble under their heavy tramp. The citizens glanced at them through their grated windows. Their rifles, revolving pistols, and long knives glittered over the dusky buckskin which enveloped their sinewy limbs, while their untrimmed locks, flowing out from under their foraging caps, and their black beards, with white teeth glittering through, gave them a wild, savage aspect. They encamped in the skirts of the woods which overhang the town.' July 22d, Frémont and his men visited the *Congress*.

ceeded without authority from Washington, if not in direct disobedience to instructions, and that they knew nothing whatever about the breaking-out of war, he was grievously disappointed. Instead of comforting assurance, he received matter for increased uneasiness. But he seems greatly to have exaggerated his disappointment and anger, going so far as to state that he had based his own acts entirely on those of Frémont, which, as we know, was by no means true. He did this with a view to save his responsibility in possible future contingencies; the only practical effect was to give Frémont material on which plausibly to found a claim to more credit than he deserved for the conquest of California.[40]

The interview was not satisfactory to Frémont, on the other hand, because Sloat declined to adopt his plans for a prosecution of the conquest, or even to accept the services of the Bear Flag battalion as a part of the United States forces. The filibuster captain felt that, could he get his men once regularly mustered into the service, he was likely to escape from all possibly embarrassing results of his past irregular conduct. He wished, moreover, to have his own wrongs and those of the settlers embodied in the avowed motives of the war, thus identifying the revolt and the conquest; and he counted on making in person a brilliant campaign against Castro. But Sloat was not disposed to show the slightest favor to his schemes, and even declined to do what he had intended, and partially promised directly and through

[40] Testimony of Frémont and Gillespie in 1848. *Frémont's Cal. Claims*, 13, 32. It seems that Gillespie, in his first interview with Sloat before Frémont's arrival, had declined to state on what authority they had acted. Many writers, whom I need not specify, have repeated the purport of this testimony. Baldridge, *Days of '46*, MS., 29–30, met Frémont as he left the ship, and saw by his manner that there was some trouble. A little later he met Sloat's son, who described the interview much as it was described by the officers in their testimony, adding that the commodore was very violent in his denunciations of Frémont's conduct. Tuthill, *Hist. Cal.*, 182–4, suggests that Sloat was also jealous that Gillespie, a naval officer, had been sent past him at Mazatlan to Frémont, a lieutenant of topographical engineers. Benton, *Thirty Years*, ii. 692, states that Frémont's confession left Sloat without orders for taking Monterey, since the commencement of war was not known!

Larkin by letter, that is, to utilize the battalion for service similar to that being performed by Fauntleroy's dragoons. He had raised the flag as ordered by his superiors, on hearing of national hostilities; and he sensibly refused to meddle in the quarrels of Frémont and Castro, or in the fictitious wrongs of the settlers. There was nothing in the letter of his orders, even of those en route which he had not received, that required him to go beyond the occupation of the ports; and now, until by receipt of additional instructions, or at least by news that war had been formally declared, it should be proved that he had made no mistake, the commodore proposed to content himself with what he had done in literal obedience to his superiors. Doubtless Larkin sustained Sloat in his determination.[41]

The misunderstanding between Sloat and Frémont was not destined, however, to have any serious effect on subsequent events—such was the result of Commodore Stockton's intervention. Stockton had arrived in the *Congress*, Captain Dupont, from Honolulu on July 15th, and reported for duty to Sloat. He had sailed in October from Norfolk, and the route was round Cape Horn to Valparaiso, Callao, and the Sandwich Islands.[42] The contents of his 'sealed orders' have never been made public, and indeed, I find no trace of instructions to him of earlier date than November 1846. Doubtless he was fully informed respecting the probability of war, and the policy of his

[41] July 17th, Larkin writes to Stockton that Gillespie, who is about to call on him, seems to have imbibed ' local views' of affairs. Hopes Stockton will cause him to abandon those views, since the writer believes ' we should continue what has been begun without having our minds and views prescribed by the Pacific Ocean and Rocky Mountains; the world at large and posterity will look only for national and extended views for the good of our country in common.' *Larkin's Off. Corresp.*, MS., i. 143. July 24th, Larkin to Frémont, saying that as Sloat has decided not to keep up any interior force, all instructions, etc., in former letters are to be deemed countermanded to this date. *Id.*, i. 144.

[42] *Colton's Deck and Port, or incidents of a cruise in the U. S. frigate Congress to California*, N. Y., 1850, 12mo, 408 p., is a journal of the voyage by Rev. Walter Colton, chaplain of the vessel. It is an interesting and deservedly popular work. Its continuation under another title more nearly concerns California.

government in the case of war or peace, being directed
to join the Pacific squadron and await developments.
It is noticeable that Stockton's original orders were
dated October 17, 1845, the date of the instructions
to Larkin and Gillespie, a fact suggestive of their
probable contents.[43] Frémont and Gillespie had an
interview with Stockton, as well as with Sloat, and
found him to be a man after their own heart. He had
none of Sloat's timidity about assuming responsibility.
He believed that Sloat's orders and information from
the Rio Grande abundantly justified, not only what he
had done, but would justify much more. He was in
favor of accepting the services of the battalion, and of
prosecuting the conquest to a successful issue by a
land campaign. Not only this, but he was willing to
virtually adopt the Bear Flag revolt in all its phases
as part of the conquest, thus imbibing the 'local views'
against which Larkin had warned him.[44]

But what pleased Frémont and Gillespie most of
all was Stockton's assurance that he would soon be
in a position to carry his and their plans into execution. For at their first interview, on July 15th, Sloat
had announced his intention to retire at an early date,
leaving the other commodore in command of the squad-

---

[43] Stockton's letter of Oct. 24, 1845, acknowledging receipt of orders of the
17th, and mentioning the sealed orders, etc. p. 95 of *A Sketch of the Life of
Com. Robert F. Stockton; with an appendix, comprising his correspondence with
the navy department respecting his conquest of California; and extracts from
the defence of Col. J. C. Frémont in relation to the same subject; together with his
speeches in the senate of the U. S., and his political letters.* New York, 1856,
8vo, 210, 131 p. This work is sufficiently described by its title. The tone
is of course warmly eulogistic of the hero, who deserved something of eulogy.
So far as Cal. is concerned, the documentary part of the work is the most valuable, though but few documents are given which are not elsewhere extant;
and the editor for the most part simply echoes the views of Stockton himself,
as expressed in his various reports. Colton, *Deck and Port*, 379, says: ' Mexican papers were received there [at Honolulu] the day before our departure,
stating that hostilities had commenced between that country and the U. S.
on the Texan line. We doubted the correctness of the information, but put
to sea at once, that we might be off Monterey in season for any service which
the possible exigency might require.' The correspondence of the time shows
clearly that Stockton was expected with the *Congress* to join the squadron by
Sloat, Larkin, and Montgomery long before his arrival even at Honolulu.

[44] Stockton's ideas on the subject are clearly expressed in his various reports, and reflected in his acts. as we shall see presently.

ron.[45] Sloat perhaps intended at first to await the arrival of an order for relief from Washington, such an order—in reply to his request of May, and "for other reasons"—being then on the way, coupled with a reprimand, of which he knew nothing; but if so, his disagreement with Stockton respecting the policy to be pursued in California, and the latter's willingness to assume the responsibility of coöperating with Frémont, as well as his own failing health, soon determined him to hasten his departure. Accordingly, on July 23d, as a preliminary step, he made Stockton commander-in-chief of all forces and operations on land. Having already an understanding with Frémont, the new commander on the same day perfected an arrangement by which the 160 'ex-osos' were received as a battalion of volunteers, Frémont being made major and Gillespie captain, to serve under Stockton as long as their services might be required. Other officers remained presumably as on the departure from Sonoma; at least, there is no information extant respecting the reorganization of the battalion until a later period and for another campaign.[46]

Captain Dupont was now transferred to the *Cyane*, Captain Mervine to the *Savannah*, and Lieutenant Livingstone took command of the *Congress*. On Sunday, July 26th, or perhaps next day,[47] the *Cyane*

[45] *Stockton's Report of Operations on the Coast of the Pacific*, Feb. 18, 1848. This detailed report and defence, which I shall have frequent occasion to cite, is found in *31st Cong. 1st Sess.*, *H. Ex. Doc. 1*, pt ii., p. 33–50; and also in *Stockton's Life*, append A, p. 17–30; *Bigelow's Mem. Frémont*, 164, etc.

[46] *Stockton's Report;* Stockton's letter of Aug. 28th to Sec. Bancroft, in *Cutts' Conq.*, 119. Frémont, in his letter of July 25th to Benton, sent home by Sloat, says: 'I received this morning from Com. Stockton a commission of major in the U. S. army, retaining command of my battalion, to which a force of 80 marines will be attached. We are under orders to embark to-morrow morning on the *Cyane*, and disembark at S. Diego.' *Niles' Reg.*, lxxi. 191. Hensley, *Fremont's Cal. Claims*, 36–7, says the men refused to serve at $11 per month, and no rate was specified until August. July 24th, Larkin to Stockton, advising him that a force of men accustomed to rifle and saddle will be necessary, in addition to sailors and marines. Recommends also that he proceed to S. Pedro to act there as the position of Pico and Castro may demand. *Larkin's Off. Corresp.*, MS., i. 110.

[47] The order was to sail on the 26th, and Sloat in his report gives that as the date of departure; but Colton in his journal, *Three Years in Cal.*, 16, states that it was on Monday, July 27th. The other dates are clearly stated

sailed for San Diego with the battalion on board.
On Wednesday the 29th Sloat transferred his broad
pennant to the *Levant* and sailed for home;[48] while
Stockton assumed command of the squadron; issued
a proclamation, which, with the acts accompanying its
enforcement, I shall notice in the next chapter; and
on Saturday, August 1st, sailed in the *Congress* for
San Pedro, having before his departure appointed
Walter Colton as alcalde in place of Price and. Gilchrist, and also sent Revere and Fauntleroy to command the garrisons of Sonoma and San Juan respectively.   The *Portsmouth* was left at San Francisco,
and the *Savannah* at Monterey, the *Erie* being at .
the Hawaiian Islands, and the *Warren* not having
yet arrived from Mazatlan.

in the original reports and by Colton; but have been confused by several
writers, who seem to have followed the *Monterey Californian*, Aug. 15, 1846.
    [48] On the voyage he wrote his report of July 31st, which has been so often
cited in preceding pages. *Sloat's Despatches on Conquest of Cal.*, with accompanying documents, in *U. S. Govt Doc.*, 29th cong. 2d sess., H. Ex. Doc. 4, p.
640 et seq.; and 30th cong. 1st sess., H. Ex. Doc. 1, pt ii., p. 2–50.   Montgomery, on July 25th, one of the documents cited, wrote to Sloat a very kind
and flattering letter of congratulation and good wishes.   Sloat reached
Washington early in November.
    John Drake Sloat was a native of New York, born in 1780.   He joined
the navy in 1800; became sailing-master and lieutenant in 1812; commanded
the U. S. schooner *Grampus* in 1824–5, cruising for pirates in the West In-
dies squadron; served two years in the *St Louis* of the Pacific squadron; was
made commander in 1826; and subsequently commanded at the recruiting
station in New York City and the Portsmouth navy-yard, becoming post-
captain in 1837.   In 1845 Capt. Sloat was appointed to succeed Com. Dallas
in command of the Pacific squadron.   After his return from Cal. he was in
command of the Norfolk navy-yard in 1848–50; revisited California as president of a drydock commission in 1852; was placed on the retired list in
1856; promoted to be commodore when that rank was created in 1862, and
to be rear-admiral in 1866.   He held several other official positions, and died
at his home on Staten Island on Nov. 28, 1867.   He was senior honorary
member of the Society of California Pioneers; and it is chiefly from the resolutions published at his death that I take the preceding notes of his life.
Cal. Pioneer Arch., MS., 53–60; also in many newspapers.

CHAPTER XI.

THE CONQUEST—STOCKTON'S RULE—OCCUPATION OF THE SOUTH.

August, 1846.

Stockton's Proclamation—A Pronunciamiento Filibustero—Castro Retreats Southward—Pico's Proclamation—Action of the Assembly—Vain Efforts of Governor and General for Defence—No Enthusiasm or Resources—Castro at the Mesa—Frémont at San Diego—Stockton at San Pedro—The Commodore Refuses to Negotiate for Fear his Terms may be Accepted—His Weak Excuses—Larkin's Efforts—Castro and Pico Resolve to Quit California—Flight and Farewell Addresses—Pico's Land Grants—Stockton Enters Angeles—Submission of the People—Proclamations and Orders—News from Washington—Election Ordered—Plans for a Civil Government—Garrisons at the Southern Towns—Stockton and Frémont Return to the North.

THE proclamation, or address, issued by Commodore Robert F. Stockton on July 29th, the date of his assuming the command and of his predecessor's departure, is given entire in the accompanying note.[1]

[1] Address to the people of California. 'The Mexican government and their military leaders have, without cause, for a year past been threatening the U. S. with hostilities. They have recently, in pursuance of these threats, commenced hostilities by attacking, with 7,000 men, a small detachment of 2,000 U. S. troops, by whom they were signally defeated and routed. Gen. Castro, the commander-in-chief of the military forces of Cal., has violated every principle of international law and national hospitality, by hunting and pursuing, with several hundred soldiers, and with wicked intent, Capt. Frémont of the U. S. army, who came here to refresh his men, about forty in number, after a perilous journey across the mountains, on a scientific survey. For these repeated hostilities and outrages, military possession was ordered to be taken of Monterey and S. F. until redress could be obtained from the govt of Mexico. No let or hindrance was given or intended to be given to the civil authority of the territory, or to the exercise of its accustomed functions. The officers were invited to remain, and promised protection in the performance of their duties as magistrates. They refused to do so, and departed, leaving the people in a state of anarchy and confusion. On assuming the command ...I find myself in possession of the ports of Monterey and S. F., with daily

The reader will find it a most extraordinary document; and the more closely it is studied, the less commendable it will appear. Stockton's policy of completing the military occupation of California by taking posses-

reports from the interior of scenes of rapine, blood, and murder. Three inoffensive American residents of the country have, within a few days, been murdered in the most brutal manner; and there are no Californian officers who will arrest and bring the murderers to justice, although it is well known who they are and where they are. I must therefore, and will as soon as I can, adopt such measures as may seem best calculated to bring these criminals to justice, and to bestow peace and good order on the country. In the first place, however, I am constrained by every principle of national honor, as well as a due regard for the safety and best interests of the people of Cal., to put an end at once and by force to the lawless depredations daily committed by Gen. Castro's men upon the persons and property of peaceful and unoffending inhabitants. I cannot, therefore, confine my operations to the quiet and undisturbed possession of the defenceless ports of Monterey and San Francisco, whilst the people elsewhere are suffering from lawless violence; but will immediately march against these boasting and abusive chiefs, who have not only violated every principle of national hospitality and good faith toward Capt. Frémont and his surveying party, but who, unless driven out, will, with the aid of the hostile Indians, keep this beautiful country in a constant state of revolution and blood, as well as against all others who may be found in arms, or aiding or abetting Gen. Castro. The present general of the forces of Cal. is a usurper; has been guilty of great offences; has impoverished and drained the country of almost its last dollar; and has deserted his post now when most needed. He has deluded and deceived the inhabitants of Cal., and they wish his expulsion from the country. He came into power by rebellion and force, and by force he must be expelled. Mexico appears to have been compelled from time to time to abandon Cal. to the mercies of any wicked man who could muster 100 men in arms. The distances from the capital are so great that she cannot, even in times of great distress, send timely aid to the inhabitants; and the lawless depredations upon their persons and property go invariably unpunished. She cannot or will not punish or control the chieftains who, one after the other, have defied her power, and kept Cal. in a constant scene of revolt and misery. The inhabitants are tired and disgusted with this constant succession of military usurpers, and this insecurity of life and property. They invoke my protection. Therefore upon them I will not make war. I require, however, all officers, civil and military, and all other persons to remain quiet at their respective homes and stations, and to obey the orders they may receive from me or by my authority; and if they do no injury or violence to my authority, none will be done to them.

But notice is hereby given, that if any of the inhabitants of the country either abandon their dwellings, or do any injury to the arms of the U. S., or to any person within this territory, they will be treated as enemies, and suffer accordingly. No person whatever is to be troubled in consequence of any part he may heretofore have taken in the politics of the country, or for having been a subject of Gen. Castro. And all persons who may have belonged to the govt of Mexico, but who from this day acknowledge the authority of the existing laws, are to be treated in the same manner as other citizens of the U. S., provided they are obedient to the law and to the orders they shall receive from me or by my authority. The commander-in-chief does not desire to possess himself of one foot of Cal. for any other reason than as the only means to save from destruction the lives and property of the foreign residents, and citizens of the territory who have invoked his protection. As soon, therefore, as the officers of the civil law return to their proper duties, under a regularly organized govt, and give security for life, liberty, and property alike to all,

sion of the southern towns, as compared with Sloat's policy, in the last days, of holding Monterey and San Francisco, and awaiting new orders and information, was probably a wise one. Though some thought differently, there is reason to doubt that progress could have been made toward voluntary submission by inaction at this stage of affairs. Instructions from Washington in letter required an occupation of the ports only; but in spirit—and still more so the orders then en route—they involved the raising of the flag at interior towns, if it could be done with safety. I think there can be no doubt that Stockton was fully justified, not only in taking possession of the southern ports, but in extending the occupation to the inland towns, and in utilizing the services of Frémont's battalion for that purpose. That being the case, the only proclamation called for by the circumstances was a simple announcement of his accession to the command, and of his purpose to complete and maintain the military occupation, with a repetition of Sloat's promises and appeals for a peaceful submission.

Nothing of the kind, however, is found in the commodore's address, in which all the motives that had actuated Sloat were ignored, and an entirely new theory was evolved respecting what had been done and what was to be done. The paper was made up of falsehood, of irrelevant issues, and of bombastic ranting in about equal parts, the tone being offensive and impolitic even in those inconsiderable portions which were true and legitimate. Sloat wrote to Secretary Bancroft, after reading the proclamation at sea: "It does not contain my reasons for taking possession of, or my

the forces under my command will be withdrawn, and the people left to manage their own affairs in their own way.'

The document bears no date, and some writers have dated it on the 23d, when Stockton took command on land; others on the 28th, when a copy of it was addressed to Com. Sloat; but there is no doubt that the true date should be the 29th. The proclamation is found in *31st Cong. 1st Sess., H. Ex. Doc. 1*, p. 31–3; also in *Stockton's Life*, 116–18; *Soulé's Annals*, 103–4; *Lancey's Cruise*, 105–6; *Cal. Pioneers, Arch.*, MS., 237–8. Spanish translations, original copies, *Vallejo, Doc.*, MS., xii. 231; *Janssens, Doc.*, MS., 8–14.

views or intentions toward that country; consequently it does not meet my approbation." The third paragraph, describing Castro's outrageous treatment of Frémont, is false from beginning to end; but had it been truth, the following statement that it was on account of these outrages, and to obtain redress for them, that Monterey had been seized, was not only without foundation in truth, but was well known to be so by Stockton, who may charitably be presumed to have been deceived in the first respect. And in all that follows there is hardly a hint at the simple truth that California was to be held—the people being urged and encouraged meanwhile to voluntarily change their allegiance—in military possession until the United States and Mexico should determine its fate by treaty at the end of the war; but there are constant allusions to the punishment of criminals, to boastful and abusive chiefs, to usurpers, and to oppressed inhabitants who had invoked his protection. Unlike his government at Washington, Stockton did not care to make California a territory of the United States, nor did he want a foot of that country for any other reason than to save the lives and property of citizens; his mission was rather to avenge the wrongs of Frémont and of the people, to bring about reforms in local government, to punish the wicked rulers and the equally wicked and misguided Californians who should hesitate to abandon those rulers and should dare to defend their country! Why the wrongs of the poor American settlers and the resulting Bear Flag revolt were ignored by the commodore is a mystery. In the fifth and sixth paragraphs we read of prevalent "rapine, blood, and murder." There is but slight evidence, beyond the limits of the writer's imagination, that there were at this time any unusual disorders; but had there been such disorders, it was certainly an extraordinary idea of Stockton's to throw the responsibility upon the local Mexican authorities who had declined to throw off at a moment's notice their na-

tional allegiance, and accept office under the invaders
of their country!   Castro was not a usurper in any
sense that concerned Stockton as an officer of the
United States, nor was the latter at all concerned in
the faults of departmental rulers or in Mexican neglect of California, except that he might legitimately
refer to them as a means of encouraging the people
to submit with good grace to the inevitable.   The proclamation was in all its phases offensive, impolitic, uncalled for, inaccurate, and most undignified.[2]

W e have not far to go in search of the motives which
prompted Stockton to publish an address so unworthy
of him.   It should have borne the signatures of Frémont and Gillespie, who managed to gain for the time
being complete control over the commodore, and who
dictated the proclamation with the sole view to advance their own interests.   They were shrewd and
lucky adventurers.   Stockton was the more ready to
adopt their views, because by so doing he magnified
the difficulties before him, and his glory in the event
of success; because the address would make a good
impression in the States, where little was likely to be
known about the facts; and because it seemed prudent,
in view of the opinions entertained by Sloat and Larkin, to lay the foundations for a defence of himself
and his government, in case the news of war should
prove unfounded.   In his later formal report to the
government, which I quote at some length below,
Stockton explained the considerations which "seemed
to make prompt and decisive action an imperative
duty"—considerations which, though involving exaggerations of difficulties encountered, in the aggregate
were amply sufficient to justify his action; but which

---

[2] Tuthill, *Hist. Cal.*, 186–7, wittily says that Stockton's proclamation had
a 'Mexican flavor,' but was carried out, 'a very un-Mexican procedure.' The
Californians generally condemn and ridicule the address, though Stockton
himself later became very popular with them. The commodore was never
censured for his absurd utterances, nor does it clearly appear that he ever
admitted their folly.

by no means justified the tone of his pronunciamiento
filibustero of July 29th.[3]

[3] *Stockton's Report*, 34–5. He says: 'The result of my inquiries and investigations showed me that the position I was about to occupy was an important and critical one. The intelligence of the commencement of hostilities between the two nations, although it had passed through Mexico, had reached Com. Sloat in advance of the Mexican authorities.' See *Bandini, Doc.*, MS., 85, for proof that before July 3d Covarrubias had brought news of hostilities on the Rio Grande. 'When he made his first hostile demonstrations, therefore, the enemy, ignorant of the existence of the war, had regarded his acts as an unwarrantable exercise of power by the U. S., and the most lively indignation and bitter resentment pervaded the country.' No such general bitterness existed; what feeling did exist was due to the acts of the insurgents, not those of Sloat; and if all had been as Stockton states, how admirably well calculated was the address to assuage the popular indignation and explain the true motives of the U. S.! 'The public functionaries of the territory were not slow in availing themselves of this feeling, and endeavored to stimulate it to the highest possible degree. A proclamation was put forth, denouncing in the most unmeasured terms all foreigners, but it was unquestionably aimed principally at the citizens of the U. S. and such others as sympathized with them.' He must refer not to Pico's proclamation of July 16th, which was not at all violent in tone; but to the earlier one, not called out by Sloat's acts, but by those of the Bear Flag insurgents! 'Two or three were in fact murdered, and all were led to apprehend extermination from the sanguinary feeling of resentment which was everywhere breathed. The local legislature was in session. Gov. Pio Pico had assembled a force of about 700 or 1,000 (!) men, supplied with seven pieces of artillery, breathing vengeance against the perpetrators of the insult and injury which they supposed had been inflicted. These hostile demonstrations were daily increasing, and by the time that the command devolved on me...the situation had assumed a critical and alarming appearance. Every citizen and friend of the U. S. throughout the territory was in imminent jeopardy; he could count upon no security for either property or life. It was well known that numerous emigrants from the U. S. were on their way to Upper California. These marching in small and detached parties, encumbered with their wives and children and baggage, uninformed of the war and consequently unprepared for attack, would have been exposed to certain destruction'—a mode of theorizing likely to be very forcible in the States, but pure 'clap-trap' all the same. 'It was also ascertained that in anticipation of the eventual conquest of the country by the U. S., many of those in the actual possession of authority were preparing for this change by disposing of the public property, so that it might be found in private hands when the Americans should acquire possession, believing that private rights would be protected and individual property secure. Negotiations were in actual progress thus to acquire 3,000 leagues of land, and to dispose of all the most valuable portions of the territory appertaining to the missions at nominal prices, so that the conquerors should find the entire country appropriated to individuals, and in hands which could effectually prevent sales to American citizens, and thus check the tide of immigration, while little or no benefit would result to the nation from the acquisition of this valuable territory.' More of this later. There was certainly enough of truth in it to make the seizure of the capital at an early date desirable. 'All these considerations, together with others of inferior moment, seemed to make prompt and decisive action an imperative duty. To retain possession merely of a few sea-ports, while cut off from all intercourse with the interior, exposed to constant attack by the concentrated forces of an exasperated enemy, appeared wholly useless. Yet to abandon ground which we had occupied, to withdraw our forces from these points, to yield places where our flag had been floating in triumph, was an alternative not to be thought

Castro's movements in the first half of July, few details being known, have already been described, as have those of Pico in the south.[4] From his northern campaign Castro had returned, after Torre's defeat, to Santa Clara, the 30th of June. From this point he sent Manuel Castro southward, to effect a reconciliation with Pico, and secure his coöperation in defensive measures. The general probably remained at Santa Clara until he received Sloat's despatch of July 7th, departing on the evening of that day, and arriving at San Juan on the 8th. Here he passed one night, and on the 9th, after replying to the commodore's communications, started with his little army for the south.[5] Juan B. Alvarado accompanied him, though holding no command. The position taken by both officers in their communications to Sloat and Larkin is worthy of the highest commendation. To plot a declaration of independence in the interest of the United States had not perhaps been quite a creditable proceeding for Castro or Larkin, or the gov-

---

of, except as a last resource. Not only would all the advantages which had been obtained be thus abandoned, and perhaps never be regained without great expenditure of blood and treasure, but the pride and confidence of the enemy would be increased to a dangerous extent by such indications of our weakness and inability to maintain what we had won.'

[4] See chap. vi. of this vol.

[5] There are no means of proving definitely the date on which Castro left Sta Clara. John Daubenbiss, in a communication already cited, says Castro was at S. José when he started with despatches for Frémont, which must have been on the evening of the 7th or morning of the 8th. Several Californians mention the fact that they encamped one night between Sta Clara and S. Juan, and spent one night at S. Juan. Larkin wrote on the 10th that Castro had arrived at S. Juan on the 8th, had that same day received Sloat's despatch, and had started on the 9th. *Larkin's Off. Corresp.*, MS., ii. 73. Castro in his letter to Sloat, dated S. Juan July 9th, says: 'I received your note last night at Sta Clara.' *Sloat's Despatches*, 646. But this may be an error, for it would seem that he must have got Silva's despatch if not Sloat's on the 7th. Larkin, *Doc.*, MS., iv. 201, writing to Stearns on the 8th, says that Alvarado went to S. Juan a week ago and Castro went 'yesterday, before he heard from the commodore.' In another of same date, *Off. Corresp.*, MS., i. 100–1, he says Castro will probably be at S. Juan tonight. Sloat, in a letter of the 9th, *Frémont's Cal. Claims*, 73, says: 'I have this moment learned by an Englishman, just arrived from Gen. Castro at the Pueblo (S. José), that Castro was probably at St Johns last evening... The Englishman says that when the general read my proclamation to his troops he expressed his approbation of it.' Padre Real, writing from Sta Clara on the 12th, says that his *compadre* Castro left S. Juan 4 days ago. *Vallejo, Doc.*, MS., xxxiv. 221.

ernment at Washington; but for the commanding
general to have betrayed his national allegiance in
time of war by complying with Sloat's demands
would have been in the highest degree dishonorable
—even had Don José had the slightest wish to so
comply after the acts of the insurgents. The force
that Castro led to the south was possibly 150 men,
but probably not over 100. He had about 160 in
his San Pablo campaign, including Torre's men; and
perhaps increased the number at Santa Clara to over
200, though twice that number were talked about.
Many of the militia served, however, against their
will, and left their leader when he started for the
south, some because they were unwilling to leave
their families, and others because they deemed all defensive measures useless, or even favored the success
of the Americans.[6]

On July 11th Castro was at Los Ojitos, near San
Antonio; and from this point he sent a communication to Pico, announcing Sloat's invasion. There was
yet time, he wrote, to save the country; and he was
on the march to join his forces to those of the governor for that purpose. Pico received the news at
San Luis Obispo the same day, and at once sent orders to Los Angeles, countermanding previous orders
to send troops northward to reënforce his army, and
directing that every effort be made to protect the capital.[7] Both chiefs advancing met at Santa Margarita,
perhaps on the same day, but more probably on the
12th, to reconcile their past differences, as elsewhere
recorded. Then they proceeded toward the capital,
but not together, as it is stated, there being still much
jealousy and distrust between the northern and south-

[6] In the letters to be cited in the next note Castro states his force to be
160, but under the circumstances he was sure to overstate it; and Pico says
the number was 200, his motives for exaggeration being stronger still.

[7] July 11th, C. to P., P. from S. Luis to comandante of Angeles, and
Sec. Moreno to sub-prefect. *Dept. St. Pap.*, MS., iii. 73–4, 34. P. to Ban-
dini on July 16th, speaking of his meeting Castro and his 200-men. *Bandini,
Doc.*, MS., 89.

ern officers and men.   Nothing is known in detail of
the march of either division.[8]

Back at Santa Bárbara, on his way to the capital,
Governor Pico issued, on July 16th, the proclamation deemed necessary in such cases.[9]   It was an appeal to the people to defend their country against
foreign invaders, with no peculiar features that require notice.   At the same time Don Pio convoked
the assembly, and going in person some days later
to Los Angeles, brought the subject of the invasion
before the assembled legislators on July 24th, when
he and others made patriotic speeches.   The decision
in this emergency was, as might have been expected,
that the people must be called upon to do their duty,
and that a reglamento must be formed for the organi-

[8] Moreno, *Vida Militar*, MS., 9–11, states that a definite agreement was
made that the two armies should march and encamp 24 hours apart.   The
reconciliation and the subsequent march to Angeles are mentioned in the following narratives, none of which present any details that seem worth repro-
ducing: *Gomez, Lo Que Sabe*, MS., 284–300; *Bernal, Mem.*, MS., 4–11; *Galindo, Apuntes*, MS., 57–8; *Amador, Mem.*, MS., 188–9, 169–70; *Pinto, Apunt.*,
101–2; *Pico, Hist. Cal.*, MS., 146–50; *Osio, Hist. Cal.*, MS., 477–8; *Buelna,
Notas*, MS., 23–5; *Torre, Remin.*, MS., 152-3; *Lugo, Vida*, MS., 30–1; *Ord,
Ocurrencias*, MS., 137–8; *Julio César, Cosas*, MS., 7; *Arnaz, Recuerdos*, MS.,
83–5; *Coronel, Cosas de Cal.*, MS., 72–3; *Pico, Acont.*, MS., 64–5.

[9] Official copy certified by Stearns at Angeles on July 19th, in *Coronel,
Doc.*, MS., 143.   It is as follows: 'Pio Pico, constitutional governor of the
dept of Cal., to its inhabitants, know: that, the country being threatened
by the sea and land forces of the U. S. of America, which occupy the posts
of Monterey, Sonoma, S. F., and others on the northern frontier of this dept,
where already waves the banner of the stars, with threats of occupying the
other ports and settlements in order to subject them to their laws; and the
governor being firmly resolved to make every possible effort to repel this the
most unjust aggression of late centuries, undertaken by a nation which is
ruled by the most unheard-of ambition, and has formed the project of authorizing the robbery without disguising it with the slightest mark of shame,
and only consulting the power held over us because of our political weakness—in the exercise of my constitutional powers, and by virtue of repeated
superior orders by which I find myself authorized, I have determined to decree for strict observance the following articles: 1. All Mexican citizens,
native and naturalized, residing in this dept are required by duty to defend
the country when as now the national independence is in danger.   Therefore
every man without exception, from the age of 15 to 60, will present himself
armed to the departmental govt to defend the just cause.'   2. Sub-prefects
through alcaldes, etc., will at once cause to be formed lists of men, ages, etc.,
in each municipality.   3. But without waiting for the formation of these
lists, citizens will present themselves at once.   4. Any Mexican refusing or
excusing himself on any pretext will be treated as a traitor.   5. Those who
are physically unable to serve in person must aid with their property—all to
be indemnified by the national govt in due time.   6. Sub-prefects to be held
responsible for a strict observance of this decree.

zation of the militia.   Meanwhile Castro and his men
had arrived, and the two chiefs had their work before
them.   There are left but slight fragments of contemporary correspondence to show what was taking place
among the Angelinos in those days; but eked out with
the personal recollections of many men who were actors
or spectators in these last scenes of Californian allegiance to Mexico, they are amply sufficient to indicate
in a general way if not in detail the existing state of
affairs.[10]

[10] July 16th, Pico to Bandiñi, urging him to join the assembly.   Don
Juan in reply pleads ill health as a reason for not serving, though he protests
his patriotism as a true Mexican. *Bandini, Doc.*, MS., 89, 92.   July 16th,
Sub-prefect Stearns to the rancheros.   Threatens fines if they do not fly to the
defence of their country. *Dept. St. Pap.*, MS., vii. 94.   July 17th, Stearns
to Receptor Coronel at S. Pedro, urging him to take steps to learn the exact
truth about the reports from Monterey, whether any proofs existed, etc.
Coronel, Doc., MS., 195.   July 17th, Pico orders sub-prefect to deliver artillery to Capt. Andrés Pico. *Dept. St. Pap.*, MS., vii. 35.   July 18th, ayunt.
is called upon by the gov. for aid; refers the matter to the assembly, but is
duly patriotic. *Los Ángeles, Arch.*, MS., v. 326-7.   July 20th, juez of S.
Vicente.   Indians very treacherous and hostile; but in case of need half the
troops and vecinos may go to fight for the country. *Dept. St. Pap., Ben. Pref.
y Juzg.*, MS., ii. 41-3.   July 23d, B. D. Wilson to Stearns.   Yutes stealing
horses.   Eight Americans have come from Angeles to his rancho, fearing to remain under present circumstances. *Id.*, ii. 45.   July 24th, session of the assembly. *Leg. Rec.*, MS., iv. 370-1.   July 24th, Wilson to Stearns.   Must resign his
office; people refuse to obey, either because they are opposed to the govt or
because they regard him as one of the enemy.   He keeps three armed foreigners to protect his place from Indians; Mexicans will not aid him. *Dept.
St. Pap., Ben. Pref. y Juzg.*, MS., ii. 43-5.   July 24th, Castro complains of
the 'infamous holding-back' of property by certain persons, either from fear
or from having been won over by the foe. *Dept. St. Pap.*, MS., vii. 76.   July
25th, Lugo at S. Bernardino.   Complains of adventurers drifting about, and of
Wilson's efforts to make trouble. *Id., Ben. Pref. y Juzg.*, MS., ii. 43.   July
27th, Figueroa and Botello as an assembly committee propose that—it is a
sacred duty, etc., and the general must ask the gov. for aid, etc. *Dept. St.
Pap.*, MS., vii. 77.   July 28th, Pico to alcalde.   Everybody must be sent to
defend the capital. *Id., Ang.*, xi. 178.   July 29th, reglamento militar in 13
articles, formed by Olvera and Guerra as a committee. *Dept. St. Pap.*, MS.,
vii. 78-80.   July 30th, Pico and Castro resolve to send a com. to collect
arms of private persons, missions, etc., as far as the frontier of Lower Cal.
Id., vii. 36.

For personal reminiscences on this subject—affairs at Angeles July 16th–
Aug. 10th—see the references of note 8, with the pages following those there
named; and also *Temple's Recoll.*, MS., 9-10; *Valle, Lo Pasado*, MS., 44-5;
Arce, Mem., MS., 55-8; *Sanchez, Notas*, MS., 13-14; Pico, in *Hayes' Mission Book*, i. 342, and *Los Angeles Express*, Feb. 4, 1873; *Alvarado, Hist.
Cal.*, MS., v. 245-50; *Juarez, Narrative*, MS.; *Osio, Hist. Cal.*, MS., 478-9;
Wilson's Observ., MS., 61-2; *Castro, Servicios*, MS.; *Botello, Anales*, MS.,
138-9; *Los Angeles Hist.* 41-5.   From all these sources we get in the aggregate much general information, but few details.   Botello tells us that it was
evident to all in the south from the first that Castro did not intend to fight
the Americans.   Jas R. Barton, *Hayes' Miss. Book*, i. 365, says that he with 8

All went wrong from the standpoint of Pico and Castro; that is, if we suppose them to have been in earnest, as to a certain extent they probably were not; or at least, they had no real expectation of success. There were no signs of popular enthusiasm for the cause. Subordinate local authorities issued their routine orders in a spirit of apathy. Few inhabitants rendered more implicit obedience than they were obliged to by fear or pride. Many of influence, natives as well as foreigners, were secretly in sympathy with the invaders; others more or less indifferent took the advice of American friends to hold themselves aloof as far as possible from actively engaging in a useless struggle. Many, especially of the lower classes, were very bitter against the Yankees; but of these some realized that their cause was hopeless, and but few had any confidence in the good faith or ability of the leaders. Personally, Pico and Castro succeeded in keeping up at least an appearance of friendly feeling; but among their subordinates there was constant jealousy and quarrelling. The militiamen of the south refused to obey any but civic officers, while Castro's men of the north regarded themselves as constituting the 'regular army,' and assumed pretensions accordingly. The inhabitants of the city had organized themselves during Pico's absence into a kind of military body for the defence of the town against Castro, but though they did not openly revolt now against the authority of the chiefs, it was well understood that they would not fight against foreigners. Recruits for the regular force came in slowly. From

or 10 others named, left Pico's force when Castro came and went to B. D. Wilson's rancho, where they were persuaded to stay and defend themselves; but they later went back, on Pico's assurance that they would not be harmed. (See Lugo's commun. of July 25th, in this note.) Torre notes that the troops were fed on 'the bull that founded S. Gabriel.' Both he and Gomez note the carelessness and inefficiency of Castro's preparations at the Campo de la Mesa; and speak of the scare and confusion on one occasion when Andrés Pico arrived with a party. Moreno tells how the Angeles troops refused to give up to Castro certain cannon, even at Pico's command. Coronel speaks of a conference lasting all day before the civic troops would consent to obey Castro. Pico mentions the same trouble and his own efforts to overcome it.

outside districts came patriotic sentiments, with regrets that the Indians were troublesome, and no men could be sent. Rancheros and others contributed horses, arms, and other property with evident reluctance and in small quantities. The government had lost its prestige, resources, and credit. In fact, Pico had exhausted all his popularity and power in preparing for the northern campaign against Castro, and had raised less than a hundred men. These were all that he had now in reality under his command, and more than he could properly feed with the public funds at his disposal; but double this number had to be supported, for Castro had brought another hundred, and no funds. All agree that the soldiers had a hard time, being in every respect inadequately provided for. Each party, abajeños and arribeños, thought that partiality was shown to the others; each shifted upon the other the responsibility for the country's critical position; and naturally each constantly diminished in numbers. It has been common for American writers —and even Californians who wish to account for Stockton's easy success by charging the governor and general with cowardice—to speak of Castro's force as 800 or 1,000 well armed and equipped men. There was no time in the last half of July when he could have led out of the city over 200 men to make even the pretence of a fight; and before the enemy actually came, the number was reduced to 100.

In the early days of August Castro established himself with part of his force at the Campo de la Mesa, a short distance out of the city, leaving Manuel Castro and Andrés Pico in command of the forces left, most of which soon joined the general at the Mesa.[11] At about the time of this movement came news that Fré-

[11] Aug. 4th, Castro to A. Pico, announcing his departure, and putting him in command of the auxiliaries. The necessity of complete harmony with D. Manuel and his men is urged. *Pico, Doc.*, MS., ii. 93. Aug. 3d, Castro to Antonio Coronel, urging him to assemble his company, etc. *Coronel, Doc.*, MS., 245.

mont had landed at San Diego, followed soon by the announcement of Stockton's landing at San Pedro. Of Frémont's operations at this time, no official report or other contemporary account is extant. He had sailed with his battalion in the *Cyane* July 26th from Monterey; and had reached San Diego on the 29th, taking possession and raising the flag without opposition or incident, so far as may be known.[12] A week was spent in obtaining horses, which were by no means plentiful, and on August 8th the battalion, about 120 strong, started northward, leaving a garrison at San Diego.   Several Californians vaguely relate that on hearing of Frémont's arrival Castro despatched a party under Villavicencio, with Alvarado as counsellor, to meet the riflemen; but they returned without having seen the foe.

Meanwhile Stockton, with 360 marines and seamen available for an enterprise on land, had sailed from Monterey August 1st on the *Congress*.   On the way down the coast he touched at Santa Bárbara, perhaps on the 4th or 5th, and raised the stars and stripes there, leaving a small garrison.   Strangely, I find no definite record of the date, or of any circumstances connected with this event.[13]   Stockton arrived at San Pedro on the 6th.   Here the flag was raised, and the

[12] July 29th is the date usually given, though I can trace it back only to *Cutts' Conq.*, 154–5, in 1847; and Gillespie, in the *Alta*, July 3, 1866, says it was on the 30th.   Lancey, *Cruise*, 110–13, tells us, on authority not given, that Andrés Pico was found at S. Diego, and would have been put to death by the settlers had not Capt. Fitch answered for his honor, etc.   As it was, Don Andrés was allowed to carry the news to Angeles.   I deem it very improbable that anything of the kind occurred.   Lancey also tells us that the *Cyane* returned immediately to S. Pedro to meet Stockton, arriving on the 5th; and that Frémont started north on Aug. 3d, leaving a garrison of 40 men.   On Aug. 8th, Capt. Dupont, in reply to a petition of Pedro Carrillo and others to leave a guard to protect the citizens, says he has no power to do so, but that Gillespie will remain with a force until orders from the commander come. *Carrillo (Pedro), Doc.*, MS., 4. Martin, *Narr.*, MS., 32–3, says that Merritt with 13 men was left at S. Diego.   Forster, *Pioneer Data*, MS., 30–1, had just arrived at S. Luis Rey when Frémont came there, and had some trouble with that officer about the mission property.   Bidwell, *Cal. 1841–8*, MS., 176–80, gives some general recollections of the expedition, which he accompanied.

[13] *Stockton's Report*, 36.   Phelps, *Fore and Aft*, 309, followed by Lancey, *Cruise*, 110, says the garrison was composed of Midshipman Wm Mitchell and 10 men.

force was immediately landed, to be drilled and otherwise prepared for a march inland.[14]   Next day two
commissioners from Castro arrived.   They were Pablo
de la Guerra and José M. Flores, who after asking
and receiving in writing an assurance that they would
be well received, visited the camp and presented a
letter from the general, which with Stockton's account of the visit is given in a note.[15]   The latter is
not quite intelligible in all respects; but the former
was a simple demand for an explanation of the commodore's purposes, coupled with a clearly implied expression of willingness to enter into negotiations, on
the condition usual in such cases of a suspension of all
hostilities pending the conference.   The letter was an

[14] Here Lancey gives some information, the source of which has escaped my
research.   He says that the *Cyane* was found at S. Pedro, which I question;
and that Lieut James F. Schenck was sent in the launch with 20 men to take
the town.   The 5 men of the garrison escaped, but the officer in command
staying to light his cigarito was made a prisoner and detained on the frigate.
He also quotes from Capt. Paty, of the *Don Quixote*, an account of how he
refused to sell, but allowed Stockton to take by night secretly, three cannon
from his vessel.

[15] Translation in *Stockton's Mil. and Naval Oper.*, 4, preceded by the note
of Guerra and Flores and Stockton's reply, about the reception of the commission.   The translation is evidently slipshod, but I have not found the
original.   'The undersigned, commandant general and chief of the division of
operations in this department, has the honor to direct himself to the commander-in-chief of the U. S. naval forces anchored in the road of S. Pedro,
asking explanations on the conduct that he proposes to follow.   Since knowing that he wishes to enter into conferences on what is most convenient to the
interests of both countries, the undersigned cannot see with serenity one pretend, with flattering expressions of peace, and without the formality that
war between polished nations permits, to make an invasion in the terms that
your lordship has verified it.   Wishing, then [de acuerdo], with the governor,
to avoid all the disasters that follow a war like that which your lordship prepares, it has appeared convenient to the undersigned to send to your lordship
a commission...to know the wishes of your lordship, under the conception
[with the understanding] that whatever conference may take place, it must
be on the base that all hostile movements must be suspended by both forces,
since on the contrary, there will not be negotiations.'   Yours truly, etc.
Stockton, *Report*, 36–7, says : 'Two persons arrived, representing themselves
to be commisioners sent from Gen. Castro, authorized to enter into negotiations with me, and bearing a letter from the general...Before, however, they
would communicate the extent of their power or the nature of their instructions '—it does not appear in the letter that they had any powers or instructions except to learn Stockton's wishes and his willingness for negotiations—
'they made a preliminary demand that the further march of the troops must
be arrested, and that I must not advance beyond the position which I then
occupied.   This proposition was peremptorily declined.   I announced my determination to advance; and the commissioners returned to their camp without imparting further the object of the proposed negotiations.'

indication that Castro was disposed to accede to the well known wishes of the United States; the condition imposed was in every respect a moderate and reasonable one; and there was no good reason why Stockton should not welcome such a proposition, if he really wished to carry out the avowed policy of his government. He wished, however, nothing of the kind. He did not desire Castro's assent to the terms which he was obliged in a certain sense to offer, that is, a voluntary raising of the American flag by the departmental authorities. On the contrary, he wished to avoid the embarrassment of continuing those authorities in power on any basis, preferring, even in case the stars and stripes had to be lowered on account of the non-existence of war, to leave a clear field to the Bear Flag insurgents. Accordingly the commodore rejected "the Mexican proffers of negotiation," by putting his terms in the form of an insulting threat.[16]

In his report of 1848, Stockton gives at some length what he chooses to have regarded as his motives. His first point is that as no act of the local authorities would have been valid without approval of the Mexican government, and as no such ratification could be expected, the Californians would be at liberty to break any compact that might be made. But the only compact thought of was one that from its very nature could not be broken, and one respect-

[16] Aug. 7, 1846, Stockton to Castro, from San Pedro. 'General: I have the honor to acknowledge the receipt of your letter, and with you deplore the war...I do not desire to do more than my duty calls upon me to do. I do not wish to war against California or her people; but as she is a department of Mexico, I must war against her until she ceases to be a part of the Mexican territory. This is my plain duty.' True enough, but this is not the ground taken in the proclamation of July 29th. 'I cannot, therefore, check my operations to negotiate on any other principle'—no other had been proposed or hinted at—'than that California will declare her independence, under the protection of the flag of the U. S. If, therefore, you will agree to hoist the American flag in California, I will stop my forces and negotiate the treaty. Your very obedient,' etc. A Spanish translation was printed in the *Los Angeles California Meridional*, July 18, 1855; in *Coronel, Doc.*, MS., 174. In *Doc. Hist. Cal.*, MS., iv. 1301, Pablo de la Guerra says that after a discussion of two hours he refused to accede to Stockton's demand that the Californians should raise the U. S. flag.

ing which the approval or disapproval of Mexico was
not of the slightest consequence.   Secondly, he claims
that recognition of the Californian authorities, by
negotiating with them, would have involved recognition of them in other matters, notably in that of
granting lands.   To question the right of a governor,
in his capital, under his national flag, and in accordance with Mexican law, to grant lands, because a foreign power had seized some parts of the department,
was certainly a remarkable position to assume; but
still Stockton's point had weight to this extent, that
it was his duty to destroy Pico's authority as a Mexican governor as soon as possible by raising the flag
over Los Angeles.   Could the flag be raised voluntarily by Pico, so much the better for the end in
view.   To gain time, therefore, the commodore declined a conference, for which twenty-four hours
would have been ample time, and then put off his advance from San Pedro four days!   In the third place,
a truce, argues Stockton, would have enabled the
Californians to exterminate the settlers, attack the
immigrants, increase and organize their forces, and
in fact, do all the things that the present movement
was intended to prevent.   Even had the danger of
such acts been originally less absurd and imaginary,
it is not quite apparent that a short delay with a
view to a voluntary submission of the foe could have
been much more disastrous than a longer delay for
hostile preparations.   Finally, the writer says: "Our
march would necessarily have been suspended at the
outset; the sailors and marines must have reëmbarked; the California battalion, so prompt and energetic in volunteering to aid us, must have been abandoned to its own resources, and thus insulated and
unsupported, must either have dispersed or fallen a
sacrifice to an exasperated and powerful enemy"—
thus implying, what there is not the slightest evidence
to support, that Castro proposed a truce to continue
until questions in dispute could be referred to Mex-

ico. With all his lack of brilliancy, it is not likely
that Don José ever conceived so stupid a proposition.
Had he suggested such a plan at the proposed conference, it could have been rejected without great expenditure of time.[17]

It must be evident to the reader, I think, that
Stockton was bound as a representative of the United
States, in view of past negotiations and promises of
his government's confidential agents, to accede to
Castro's request for a conference. The presumption
was that the general was disposed to make the required concessions; and if fruitless, the conference
would involve no delay whatever. Stockton feared
that Castro would yield; hence his refusal. His explanation was special pleading designed to cover up
his real motives. Lest it appear, however, to any one
that the view here presented is exaggerated, I introduce a hitherto missing link in this historic chain,
matter which strengthens my criticism at every point,
exhibits the American commander's conduct in a light
by no means creditable to his honor, and shows that
he has suppressed an essential part of the record. It
has been noticed that Castro alluded to Stockton's
desire for a conference. Larkin came down from
Monterey on the *Congress*, still bent on acquiring
California without the use of force. Immediately, on
arrival at San Pedro, he addressed long communications—the original blotters of which are in my possession—to Abel Stearns, his associate confidential agent,
though also Mexican sub-prefect. This gentleman
was urged without loss of time to consult with Pico,
Castro, the assembly, and leading citizens; and to
place before them in the strongest possible manner
the importance of at once declaring their independence
of Mexico and putting California under the American

[17] Lancey, *Cruise*, 111, states definitely that Castro proposed a truce, 'by
the terms of which each party should maintain its present position, unmolested by the others, until intelligence of a more definite character could be
obtained from Mexico or the U. S., or until the conclusion of peace'! Other
writers have evidently fallen into a similar misunderstanding.

flag.   Stockton's irresistible force was presented, and even exaggerated, to show the folly of resistance. Larkin expressed his belief that the conjecture of war with Mexico would prove unfounded, in which case the flag would probably have to be lowered, and the country would be exposed to the hostile movements of the Sonoma insurgents, reënforced by 2,000 expected immigrants.   There was but one way to avoid this calamity, to prevent the shedding of blood in a useless resistance to Stockton, and to secure future happiness and prosperity.   The leaders were to be assured that the commodore had no desire to wage war; but that he was anxious to have them voluntarily organize a new government, retaining their offices, and that he would gladly enter into negotiations with them.   They were to be urged to come for a conference, accompanied if possible by Stearns and other prominent men, without delay, as the force would probably advance in twenty-four hours.   "Could this proposal be acted on in the pueblo at once, war within the department is at an end.   As the subject has for months been canvassed in California, it does not require long to come to a conclusion."[18]   There can be but little doubt, then, that it was in response to this invitation, virtually sent by Stockton himself, that Castro made overtures for a treaty, insultingly rejected by the commodore, who feared that his terms might be accepted.   If Castro had had half the men accredited to him, half as desperate and hostile as they were represented in Stockton's proclamation; and had they made an attack as they did later on Mervine, in this very region, or on Kearny at San Pascual, the disaster might justly have plunged the proud leader into life-long disgrace.

On August 9th Castro, after holding a council of war with his officers at the Mesa, resolved to leave California, and notified Pico to that affect in writing.

18 Aug. 6, 1846, Larkin to Stearns.   Blotter copies of two letters in *Larkin's Doc.*, MS., iv. 261, 268.

"After having done all in my power," he states, "to prepare for the defence of the department, and to oppose the invasion of the United States forces by sea and land, I am obliged to-day to make known to you with regret that it is not possible to accomplish either object, because, notwithstanding your efforts to afford me all the aid in your power, I can count on only 100 men, badly armed, worse supplied, and discontented by reason of the misery they suffer; so that I have reason to fear that not even these few men will fight when the necessity arises." He announced his intention to leave the country, for the purpose of reporting to the supreme government; invited the governor to go with him; and enclosed two documents which he had written to 'save his responsibility.'[19] One of these was a farewell address to the people, issued a few days later by the general *en camino para Sonora.* "With my heart full of the most cruel grief, I take leave of you. I leave the country of my birth, but with the hope of returning to destroy the slavery in which I leave you; for the day will come when our unfortunate fatherland can punish this usurpation, as rapacious as unjust, and in the face of the world exact satisfaction for its grievances. Friends, I confide in your loyalty and patriotism," etc.[20]

The third document was a copy of Castro's reply to Stockton's communication of the 7th; and it was just such an answer as the commodore had desired and expected. If the general had at one time meditated a dishonorable submission to the enemy with a view of retaining his office, he had now abandoned the idea. His pride and that of his counsellors forbade the acceptance of terms offered in a manner so peremptory and humiliating. His reply was an indignant rejection of the proposal to raise the American

---

[19] Aug. 9, 1846, Castro to Pico, written at the Campo en la Mesa. *Moreno, Doc.*, MS., 12–13.

[20] Aug. (9th), Castro to the people of Cal. *Castro, Doc.*, MS., ii. 134; *Doc. Hist. Cal.*, MS., iii. 263. Possibly this is not the address enclosed to Pico on the 9th, but a later one; but if so, the other is not extant.

flag; and his indignation was not altogether assumed for effect in Mexico, though such was the main purpose of the letter, and though at the time of writing he had resolved to attempt no defence. Stockton wrote a reply to this communication, though he afterward denied having done so; but its purport is not known.[21]

On receipt of Castro's communication and accompanying documents, Pico submitted them to the assem-

[21] Aug. 9, 1846, Castro to Stockton, in *Olvera, Doc.*, MS., 29–32; translation in *Stockton's Mil. and Naval Oper.*, 5–6. In his report of Sept. 18th Stockton says: 'I did not answer his last letter but by a verbal message, which does not properly belong to history.' *Id.*, 2. But I have before me an original autograph letter in which Stockton on August 11th says to Larkin: 'You will proceed with a flag of truce and deliver the accompanying letter to Gen. Castro, which is a reply to one sent by him to me yesterday. You will say nothing more than that you are ready to receive any explanations he may see fit to make of his letters. You will be especially careful not to commit me in anything for the future, or to say anything of our movements or Frémont's.' *Larkin's Doc.*, MS., iv. 250.

Castro's letter to Stockton was as follows: 'With unspeakable surprise I have received your reply to my official note asking explanations of your proposed conduct in the invasion which the naval and land forces of the U. S. under your command have perpetrated in this department in my charge. The insidious contents of that note, and the humiliating propositions which it involves, oblige me, for the honor of the national arms committed to me, to reproduce to you the last of my communications, and to make clear to you to what degree I will sacrifice myself to preserve stainless the post which I hold. Since war exists between the U. S. and Mexico, and as you from duty wage it against this department, a part of Mexican territory, so I, as a Mexican chief of the forces under my orders, am resolved to defend its integrity at all hazards, and to repel an aggression like yours, without example in the civilized world, and all the more so when it is considered that there is as yet no express declaration of war between the two nations. You say that you cannot suspend your operations to negotiate on any basis other than that California declare her independence under the protection of the U. S. Never will I consent that she commit so base an act; but even supposing she should attempt it, she would never carry it out under the degrading conditions that you propose. And what would be her liberty with that protection offered her at the cannon's mouth? I understand it not; but be assured that while it exists I will take care that this part of the Mexican republic, in which I first saw the light, seal not its disgrace and slavery. Still more, believing doubtless that no drop of Mexican blood flows in my veins, and that I know not the scope of my duties, you offer me the most shameful of your propositions, which is to hoist the American flag in this department. Never, never, never! Much might I say to you on this subject; but I only ask you what would you do if the proposition were vice versa. Finally, Mr Commodore, I repeat that I will spare no sacrifice to oppose your intentions; and if by misfortune the flag of the U. S. waves in Cal., it will not be by my consent, or by that of the last of my compatriots, but solely by force; with the understanding that I protest solemnly before the whole world against the means used, or which may be used, to separate this department from the Mexican republic, to whose flag it desires to belong, making you responsible for all the evils and misfortunes that may result from a war so unjust as that which has been declared against this peaceful department. I have the honor,' etc.

bly on August 10th. In a speech he admitted the impossibility of a successful defence; said he saw no other way to preserve the honor of the government than to depart with the general and report to the national authorities; and proposed that the assembly should dissolve, in order that the enemy might find none of the departmental authorities acting. The members, after each had given expression to the proper sentiments of patriotism, voted to approve Pico's resolve, and to adjourn sine die.[22] Then Don Pio issued his parting address to the people. In this document he announced that 'between ignominy and emigration,' he chose the latter. He denounced the ambitious efforts of the United States to secure the fairest portions of Mexican territory, and especially the shameful promises by which the foe had attempted to seduce Californians from their allegiance; and warned them to prove to the world that it was their desperate situation and want of resources, not their consent, that brought them under the usurper's yoke. "My friends, farewell! I take leave of you. I abandon the country of my birth, my family, property, and whatever else is most grateful to man, all to save the national honor. But I go with the sweet satisfaction that you will not second the deceitful views of the astute enemy; that your loyalty and firmness will prove an inexpugnable barrier to the machinations of the invader. In any event, guard your honor, and observe that the eyes of the entire universe are fixed upon you"![23]

It was on the night of the 10th that Pico and Castro left the capital, the latter having disbanded his military force. Their departure and parting addresses have been ridiculed and denounced as a cowardly

[22] Aug. 10, 1846, record of assembly proceedings, in *Olvera, Doc.*, MS., 32–6. Some of Pico's friends have said that he wished to continue the defence, but was not permitted by the assembly.

[23] *Pico, Proclama de Despedida, 10 de Agosto, 1846*, MS. Original in *Pico, Doc.*, MS., ii. 175-6; translation in *Savage, Doc.*, MS., iii. 68-70; *Hayes' Emig. Notes*, 340-1.

flight before the enemy, and an absurd exhibition of
Mexican bombast.   By their selfish incompetence and
foolish strife in past years, these men had done much
to reduce California to her present unhappy condition,
so that she could no longer make even an honorable
show of resistance to the invader.   I have not much
to say in praise of either as man or ruler.   Yet as
they had to choose between flight and surrender, and
as they were Mexican officers, and as it was a firmly
rooted Mexican idea that flight and patriotic protests
saved the national honor in such cases, I think their
final acts deserve some commendation.   They chose
flight attended with some hardship, rather than the
continuance of power that had been promised them
under the American flag, coupled with dishonor in
the eyes of their countrymen.   This shows that they
still retained a praiseworthy pride.

 And here I must notice briefly one phase of this
matter, which is more fully treated in other chapters
relating to the missions and to the subject of land
grants.   It has been a current statement among writers on California that Pico in the last months of his
rule exerted himself to distribute among his friends
—and especially among Englishmen, with a view to
keep them out of the hands of Americans—the largest possible amount of public lands; that he made
haste to sell the mission property, for the most part
to Englishmen also, for whatever prices he could get;
and that he carried away with him some $20,000 of
funds resulting from these sales, or which had been
contributed by the people for the country's defence.
With respect to the last charge, I hasten to say, that
beyond the statements of Don Pio's personal enemies,
and the current rumors growing out of those statements, I find no evidence that he carried out of the
country a dollar of the public funds; and it is very
certain that he could not have obtained any such sum
as that named.   Again, it may be said that the political aspect of Pico's land grants and mission sales, as

part of a scheme to give California to England, is almost purely imaginary. Many men, foreseeing a great increase in the value of lands, were anxious in these last months to secure grants; and the governor, so far as his quarrels with Castro left him free to attend to such matters, was disposed to grant their request. It was by no means discreditable to him, that before his power was gone he was disposed to distribute the public lands among his friends, so long as he acted legally. As to the sales of the missions, they were effected in pursuance of a policy formed in earlier years, with the approval of the assembly. The price was as large as could be obtained, and I find no reason to doubt that the proceeds were patriotically squandered in support of the government, and preparations against Castro. The only question is the legal one of Pico's power to sell the missions at all under existing circumstances, a matter that is not to be discussed here. So far nothing appears against the governor in this respect, taking the various grants as they appear on their face. It would be well for his reputation could we stop here; but there is no room to doubt that some of the titles were written by the governor just before his departure, or even after his return, and fraudulently antedated. Comment is unnecessary.

Pico and Castro, though they both left Los Angeles on August 10th, did not flee together. Castro, accompanied by his secretary, Francisco Arce, and a small party [24]—others having turned back from San Bernardino, and Weber being carried along as a prisoner but soon released—took the Colorado River route to Sonora, and reached Altar the 7th of September. Here he communicated with Governor Cuesta, and sent despatches to Mexico describing the condition of affairs in California and urging measures to recover the country and avenge her wrongs. [25] Of

[24] Arce, *Mem.*, MS., 58–9, says there were 19 men. Jesus Pico, *Acont.*, MS., 66–7, names Salomon Pico, Rudecindo Castro, and three Soberanes.

[25] Sept. 9, 1846, Castro at Altar to Cuesta, and Cuesta's reply of the 13th, in

course no practical attention was paid to the general's
suggestions.   After some military service in Sinaloa,
Castro returned to California in 1848, and departed
again in 1853 to become a Mexican official in Lower
California.   Pico, leaving Los Angeles in the night
of August 10th—after issuing the proclamation already noted, and also notifying the foreign consuls
that California was to be left without a government—
spent the night at Yorba's rancho, and went next day
to San Juan Capistrano, where, and in the vicinity of
his rancho of Santa Margarita, he was concealed by
his brother-in-law, John Forster, for about a month.
He states that he had many narrow escapes from falling into the hands of Frémont's men, and of a party
under Santiago E. Argüello.   This is confirmed by
Forster, and to some extent by others.   It is probable
that the efforts to effect his capture, rather vaguely
mentioned by many writers, have been considerably
exaggerated.   At any rate, Frémont, at Bandini's
intercession, assured Don Pio that he should not be
molested.[26]   It was hoped perhaps that if he could be
induced to remain, he might consent to convoke the

El Sonorense, Sept. 25, 1846. A list of Castro's companions was enclosed, but
unfortunately not printed. Sept. 9th, Castro to min. of war. Explains the circumstances that forced him to leave his post. Awaits orders at Altar, as he
has no means of pursuing his journey. Thinks that with a great effort triumph
would still not be very difficult. The foe has but 3,000 men, most of them
not available except on the coast. In the interior, only the settlers and 400
or 500 hunters were to be feared. Castro thinks no very large number of
immigrants can be expected until next year. Col. Alvarado, Prefect Manuel
Castro, and Capt. Torre, with citizens, are hidden in the mountains, ready to
sally forth and defeat the 'infernal intrigues of our oppressors.' Original
blotter in *Castro, Doc.*, MS., ii. 136. Oct. 15th, reply of min. of war.
Expresses sympathy and indignation. The govt with a view of vengeance is
expediting the march of Gen. Bustamante. *Id.*, ii. 144. In Nov. Escudero,
diputado from Chihuahua, proposed in congress a scheme and loan to recover
New Mexico and Cal., which he thought would be easy. *Escudero, Mem.
Chih.*, 46–9. In his report of Dec. 14, 1846, Min. Lafragua speaks of a new
organization of the Californias into two territories; but the appointment
of gefes políticos had no effect because of the invasion. *Mexico, Mem. Relaciones*, 1847, p. 163.

[26] Sept. 15, 1846, Pico from S. Vicente to Bandini, with thanks for his
efforts. Mentions a letter from Frémont which he has answered. *Bandini,
Doc.*, MS., 97. Capt. Phelps, *Fore and Aft*, 305–6, who was at S. Juan be-
fore Pico's departure, mentions Frémont's letter, and says that he met Don
Pio on the way to S. Diego. He then seemed disposed to give himself up, as
Frémont had urged.

assembly and go through the form of turning over the country to the United States. The fugitive governor, however, was joined by his secretary Moreno,[27] and escaped across the line into Baja California on September 7th. With Macedonio Gonzalez he went on to Mulegé, where he arrived the 22d of October. In November he crossed the gulf to Guaymas, and was subsequently driven to Hermosillo when Guaymas was bombarded by the Americans. Over and over again he wrote to the national government, urging measures for the recovery of California; but no attention was paid to his representations; and he could obtain neither the payment of his salary, thanks for past sacrifices, nor even recognition as still entitled to be called governor. He returned to California in the middle of 1848.[28]

Meanwhile Stockton at San Pedro was engaged in drilling his 360 men, most of them ignorant of the simplest military movements on land, and making other preparations for an advance, from the 7th to the 11th. The commodore's biographer, in a very inaccurate and bombastic narrative of this campaign, which has apparently been the source of most that has since been written on the subject,[29] tells us that when Castro's commissioners arrived, the American commander, regarding them as spies, resolved to deceive them as to his strength. He therefore caused

[27] There is a tradition that they carried away and buried the government archives; but a large part of the documents were retained by Moreno, and their contents now form part of my collection, as *Moreno, Documentos para la Historia de California. Coleccion de D. José Matías Moreno, secretario que fúe del gobierno, año de 1846, la cual existe original en la Baja California, en posesion de la Sra Doña Prudenciana Lopez. Copias y extractos por Thos Savage*, 1878, MS., fol., 138 p.

[28] March 29, 1846, Pico at Hermosillo to min. of rel., describing his movements since leaving Cal., and mentioning the contents and dates of previous reports. *Pico, Doc.*, MS., i. 31–6; *Savage, Doc.*, MS., iii. 76–84; *Hayes' Emig. Notes*, i. 340, 342. See also *Pico, Hist. Cal.*, MS., 161–74; *Forster's Pioneer Data*, MS., 32–5; *Los Angeles Express*, Feb. 4, 1873; *Marion, Recuerdos*, MS., 10–13; *Wilson's Observ.*, MS., 61–2; *Monterey Californian*, Aug. 22, 1846.

[29] *Stockton's Life*, 119–23, followed closely in most respects by Tuthill, Lancey, and others.

his men to march in a circle, one part of which was concealed, until each had come many times into view. He also received Guerra and Flores where his guns were, posting himself by the side of a 32-pounder, while the others, six-pounders, were covered with skins, so as to make it appear that all were of the same large calibre. To what extent the account of these manœuvres is founded on fact, there are no means of knowing; but the additional statements that Stockton, having delivered his message for Castro to the embassadors "in the most fierce and offensive manner, and in a tone of voice significant of the most implacable and hostile determination, waived them from his presence imperiously, with the insulting imperative, 'Vamose';" that another embassy was treated with like insolence, with the successful purpose of intimidating the foe; and that to a third embassy, pompously informing the commander that "if he marched upon the town he would find it the grave of his men," the reply was, "Have the bells ready to toll at eight o'clock, as I shall be there at that time"—may very safely be designated as falsehoods pure and simple.[30]

The march to Los Angeles was begun on August 11th. Larkin had been sent ahead with a message for Castro, but that same afternoon news came of the general's retreat. No enemy was seen, but progress was very slow, as the artillery had to be drawn by oxen or by the sailors themselves. Two nights were spent on the road. Captain Phelps of the *Moscow* arrived at San Pedro the day after Stockton's departure and at once started to overtake him. He gives an excellent account of the expedition and events immediately following, indeed the only one extant, so far as details are concerned. From him we learn that 150 sailors were sent back as soon as Castro's flight was known; that the main force encamped for the night at Temple's rancho, was kept under arms

[30] It is fair to say that the last lie was taken by this writer, as it has been by others, from *Colton's Three Years in Cal.*, 56.

for two hours on account of the alarm created by the
cries of two coyotes; and that Stockton and Larkin
entered the city, where they were joined by the
writer, before the arrival of the troops.[31]   At Castro's
abandoned camp were found ten pieces of artillery,
four of them spiked.[32]   Major Frémont from San
Diego met the marine force just outside the town;
and at about 4 P. M. on the 13th the combined armies
entered the capital, where the flag of the United
States was at once raised with the usual ceremonies,
and, here as elsewhere in California, without the
slightest demonstrations of opposition or disapproval
on the part of the inhabitants.[33]

Some of the Angelinos had fled to their ranchos or
those of their friends as the Americans drew near
the town; others had withdrawn to the hill to see
what the strangers would do with the capital.   The
latter returned to their homes before night, attracted
by assurances that no harm should befall them, and unable to resist the influence of a full brass band.   The
former also returned with few exceptions as the days
passed by.   Frémont and his men made a tour southward in quest of fugitives; but were not able greatly
to advance the cause of reconciliation, on account of

[31] *Phelps' Fore and Aft*, 297, etc.   Of Stockton's army on the march he
says: 'First came the full band of music, followed by Capt. Zeilin and his
marines; then Lieut Schenck and the web-feet; Lieut Tilghman and a battery of four quarter-deck guns mounted on as many bullock carts; the car-
riages of the guns were secured by the breechings, and ready for instant service.   Each cart was drawn by four oxen—the baggage ammunition followed
in similar teams; the purser, doctor, and some other officers—part of them
mounted on rather sorry horses, the others on foot.'   In *Stockton's Life* we
read: 'The enemy were often in sight, threatening their flanks or advance
guard, and hovering on the brows of adjacent hills'!   B. D. Wilson, *Observations*, MS., 62-3, claims that he had gone out to meet the Americans; and
that it was on his invitation that Stockton came with him in advance into
the town.

[32] *Stockton's Mil. and Naval Oper.*, 2.

[33] On Stockton's occupation of Los Angeles, see also *Stockton's Report*, 38–
9; reports of secretaries of war and navy, Dec. 5, 1846, *29th Cong. 2d Sess.*,
H. Ex. Doc. no. 4, p. 52, 379; Stockton's despatches and annexed documents,
in *30th Cong. 1st Sess.*, *H. Ex. Doc. no. 70*, p. 38–42; *Lancey's Cruise*, 111–14;
Tuthill's Hist. Cal., 186–9; *S. F. Bulletin*, Oct. 10, 1866; *Monterey Californian*, Sept. 19, 1846.   The first official act of Stockton at Angeles, as shown
by the records, was the appointment of Larkin as U. S. navy agent. *Larkin's Doc.*, MS., iv. 254.

the bad reputation given him by Castro, though when
better known he became popular in the south.   The
chief influence brought to bear was that of old foreign residents, who counselled submission.   Phelps,
a well known trader, did something in this direction
during a business trip to San Diego and back.   Officials were required to give their parole; others merely
to comply with the necessary police regulations of
military rule.   Castro's men had started in several
parties for their northern homes soon after the general's departure, dispersing as they advanced.   A few
of them were captured and paroled on the way by a
detachment of the California battalion sent in pursuit.[34]   Others were paroled later in the north; while
a few officers of both sections escaped altogether the
humiliation of submission.   The parole records have
not been preserved; but the names of certain officers
who broke their promise will be given later.   Local
authorities as a rule declined to serve; but there were
exceptions; and several prominent abajeños, notably
Bandini and Argüello of San Diego, became openly
partisans of the American cause.[35]   There still smoul-

[34] I find in *Lancey's Cruise*, 117, more particulars of this matter than anywhere else.   He says Lieut Maddox, with the companies of Ford and Swift,
left Angeles Aug. 16th; captured and paroled 15 officers near S. Luis Obispo
after a 'sharp skirmish;' and reached Monterey on Sept. 2d (this date comes
from the *Californian*, Sept. 5, 1846) or 10th.   Alvarado and Jesus Pico
were among those taken; but I do not think Manuel Castro was paroled, as
Lancey states, or that there was any skirmish.   Pico, *Acont.*, MS., 67–8,
mentions the arrest and parole of himself and Alvarado by a party that took
possession of S. Luis.   Alvarado, *Hist. Cal.*, MS., v. 249–50, mentions his
own arrest and parole by Frémont's men; but says that Castro had previously
disbanded his men and taken refuge in the mountains.   Several Californians
describe the march vaguely, but say nothing of any hostile meeting.   I have
before me an original summons sent by Sub-prefect Thompson to Manuel
Castro and his companions to appear before him on complaint of citizens
whose horses they were taking on their retreat.   It is dated Sta Bárbara
Aug. 13th.   *Doc. Hist. Cal.*, MS., iii. 261.   Of course the summons was not
obeyed, though some say that Don Manuel sent back a challenge to Thompson to come out and fight.   On or about Aug. 26th Maddox seized 17 horses
and a mule on Capt. Guerra's S. Julian rancho.   It appears he had an order
for certain animals, but took more than the order called for.   So testifies the
majordomo Gregorio Lopez.   *Guerra*, *Doc.*, MS., vii. 200–1.

[35] In *Bandini*, *Doc.*, MS., 98, I have an address to the people, in which
Bandini and Argüello explain their reasons for accepting the situation, and
urge all Californians to do the same.   It is a long document, but does not re-

dered in the hearts of many Californians a bitter
Mexican prejudice against the invaders, but there
were few if any open manifestations of discontent.
Mounting a few guns on the hill, and organizing a
garrison, Stockton soon retired his naval force to the
Congress. It only remains to notice the commodore's
successive orders, his proposed organization of a civil
government, his placing of garrisons in the southern
towns, and his departure for the north.[36]

On August 17th Stockton published his second
proclamation to the people, signing himself "Commander-in-chief and governor of the territory of California." It merits none of the unfavorable criticism
called forth by the earlier production. In it the commodore simply announced that the country now belonged to the United States, and as soon as possible
would be governed like any other territory of that
nation; but meanwhile by military law, though the
people were invited to choose their local civil officers,
if the incumbents declined to serve. Liberty of conscience and full protection of life and property were
promised to all who should adhere to the new government; none others were permitted to remain. Thieves
were to be punished by hard labor on the public works;
and the California battalion was to be kept in the
service to preserve the peace.[37] It was also on the

quire quotation. The arguments presented rest on Mexico's past neglect
and California's consequent misfortunes; on the inevitable separation from
Mexico sooner or later; on the impossibility of resisting the American forces;
on the necessity of self-preservation; and on the prospective prosperity of the
country under so liberal, fraternal, and strong a govt as that of the U. S.
In *Id.*, 93, 96, I have letters from Frémont and David Alexander to Bandini,
Aug. 22d, 24th, in which both dwell on the glories of American rule, address-
ing Don Juan as a friend of the cause, and Frémont also announcing the definite news of the Mexican war.

[36] In the *Monterey, Consulate Arch.*, MS., ii. 18, Larkin charges up his
expenses on the southern trip $376. Sept. 2d, Olvera informs Moreno that
Luis Vignes had to give up the archives. *Moreno, Doc.*, MS., 23. Hargrave,
Cal. in '46, MS., 8-9, notes the accidental discharge of his gun while he was
doing duty as sentry, and Frémont was in the room above, the bullet narrowly missing him. Tuthill, *Hist. Cal.*, 189-90, and several others represent
Frémont as not having arrived until after the occupation of Angeles.

[37] Aug. 17, 1846, Stockton's proclamation. *29th Cong. 2d sess., H. Ex.
Doc. no. 4*, p. 669-70; *S. Diego, Arch.*, MS., 316-17 (an original); *Monterey Californian*, Sept. 5, 1846; *S. F. Cal. Star*, Jan. 9, 1847; *Bryant's*

17th that Frémont's men started in search of Pico and other Californian fugitives; and on the same day the *Warren*, Commander Hull, anchored at San Pedro from Mazatlan and Monterey, bringing definite news of a declaration of war.[38] On the 15th Stockton had fixed the duties on foreign goods at fifteen per cent ad valorem, and tonnage duties at fifty cents per ton; on the 19th, he proclaimed all the Mexican coast south of San Diego "to be in a state of vigorous blockade," except against armed vessels of neutral nations; and on the 20th he issued orders to commanders Hull and Dupont to blockade the ports of Mazatlan and San Blas with the *Warren* and *Cyane*.[39]

On the 22d of August Governor Stockton ordered an election of alcaldes and other municipal officers to be held in the several towns and districts of California, September 15th.[40] This order, identical in purport with a paragraph of the proclamation of the 17th, was the only step taken by the new governor—except the act of calling himself governor—toward the organization of a civil government. All else took the form of plans for the future. He determined, and announced his intention both to Frémont and to the secretary of the navy, to form a civil territorial government, and to appoint a governor in the person of Frémont, with other territorial authorities to rule after his own departure. He even prepared a plan, or constitution, which he submitted to his government, but did not publish or attempt to put it in op-

What I Saw in Cal., 298–9, etc. All persons during the continuance of military law were required to be within their houses from 10 o'clock to sunrise; and persons found with arms outside their own houses were to be treated as enemies. It will be noticed that this document differs in no important respect from Sloat's proclamation of July 7th.

[38] *Phelps' Fore and Aft*, 303. The arrival of the *Warren* at Monterey on Aug. 12th, and departure on the 13th, are noted in *Colton's Three Years*, 28–9. The vessel brought not only Mexican papers announcing the war, but also Sec. Bancroft's despatch of May 13th.

[39] *Stockton's Despatches, 1846*, in *29th Cong. 2d Sess., H. Ex. Doc. no. 4*, p. 668–75.

[40] *Id.*, 671; *Dept. St. Pap., S. José*, MS., vi. 59–60. The former alcaldes, whether elected or appointed, were to hold the election.

eration.[41] In his later report, the commodore gave somewhat elaborately the motives that impelled him to substitute a civil for a military government, but did not allude to any definite acts beyond the issuance of commercial regulations and the order for local elections; though he tried to create the impression, as he always maintained, that the change from military to civil rule was practically effected at the time.[42] His motives as alleged were good and sufficient; his right as a naval commander ordered to occupy Mexican ports to establish a civil government need not be questioned here; but the fact that he did not organize such a government, while intending to do so, has some importance in view of later complications.

Deeming the conquest complete, Stockton resolved

[41] Aug. 24th, Stockton to Frémont; Aug. 28th, Stockton to Bancroft; no date, form of constitution; in *Stockton's Despatches, 1846*, p. 668–75. To Frémont he says: 'I propose before I leave the territory to appoint you to be governor, and Capt. Gillespie the secretary thereof; and to appoint also the council of state, and all the necessary officers.' To Bancroft he says the same in substance; and adds: 'I enclose to you several despatches marked 1 to 14,' of which no. 6 is the constitution, 'by which you will see what sort of a government I have established, and how I am proceeding.' The document no. 6, without title or date, is as follows, with many verbal omissions for the purpose of condensation: I, Robert F. Stockton, commander and governor, having taken Cal. by right of conquest, declare it to be a territory of the U. S.; and I order that the form of govt, until altered by the U. S., shall be as follows: A governor to hold office 4 years, unless removed by the pres. of the U. S., to be commander-in-chief, and supt of Ind. affairs, to approve laws, grant pardons and reprieves, commission officers, and see to the execution of the laws. A secretary to record and preserve all proceedings and laws, to forward copies each year to the pres. and to congress, and to perform the duties of gov. temporarily, in case of that officer's absence, etc. A legislative council of 7 appointed by gov. for two years, but subsequently elected each year; the council's power to extend to all rightful subjects of legislation; but no law to interfere with primary disposal of land, no tax on U. S. property, and no discrimination in taxes between residents and non-residents. Laws must be approved by the gov. Municipal officers to continue as before, under the laws of Mexico, until otherwise provided for by gov. and council. Council to hold its first session when and where the gov. shall direct; but as soon as possible gov. and council to establish the capital.

[42] *Stockton's Report*, 40. 'Actuated by such considerations, I gave my immediate attention to the establishment, upon a permanent basis, of a civil govt throughout the country, as much in conformity with the former usages of the country as could be done in the absence of any written code.' 'Having achieved the conquest of the country, and finding my military strength ample to retain it, the establishment of a civil govt naturally and necessarily resulted.' Aug. 27th, Thos Frazer writes to Larkin: 'I hear some rumors that Frémont is going to compel Stockton to nominate him as governor. The pretensions of the major run high, because old Benton will stick to him through thick and thin.' *Larkin's Doc.*, MS., iv. 263.

to withdraw his marine force from California, "to leave the desk and camp and take to the ship and sea," and to devote his personal attention to naval operations on the Mexican coast. With this object in view, he ordered Major Frémont to increase his battalion to 300 men, to garrison the different towns, and to meet him at San Francisco on October 25th to perfect final arrangements.[43] All that had been done so far was reported on August 28th to the government at Washington, the report with accompanying documents being sent overland by Kit Carson at that time.[44] On the last day of August Stockton commissioned Gillespie as commandant of the southern department, instructing him to maintain martial law, and enforce the observation of the proclamation of the 17th, but authorizing him also to grant written permits to persons known to be friendly, to be out before sunrise and carry weapons.[45] And finally, on September 2d, the last day of his stay at Los Angeles, he issued a general order creating the office of military commandant of the territory, which was divided into three departments. Frémont was appointed on the same day to fill the new command.[46]

Gillespie was left with a garrison of 50 men at Los Angeles. It would seem that no garrison was left at San Diego, though a few men were sent there a little later. The position of Bandini and Argüello has been already noted; and several citizens accepted office under the new régime. John Bidwell was put in charge of San Luis Rey and the mission property.[47] Stock-

[43] Aug. 24th, S. to F. *Stockton's Despatches*, 675. The garrisons, before and after the increase of force by enlistment, were to be for S. F., 50, 50; for Monterey, 50, 50; Sta Bárbara, 25, 25; Angeles, 50, 50; and S. Diego, —, 25—so that the increase was not chiefly for garrison duty, but 'to watch Indians and other enemies.'

[44] These documents form the collection which I have quoted as *Stockton's Despatches, 1846*, in *29th Cong. 2d Sess., H. Ex. Doc. 4*, p. 668–75.

[45] Aug. 31st, Stockton to Gillespie. *Stockton's Mil. and Naval Oper.*, 7–8. Gillespie might also appoint local civil officers where none were elected.

[46] *Id.*, p. 8. Frémont's appointment as military commandant of the territory is given in *Frémont's Court-martial*, 110.

[47] *Bidwell's Cal. 1841–8*, MS., 180–1. Aug. 18th, Miguel de Pedrorena accepts the office of justice of the peace temporarily. *Hayes' Doc.*, MS., 187.

ton left Los Angeles September 2d; and three days later sailed northward on the *Congress*. At Santa Bárbara on the 7th he took on board Mitchell and his men, formerly left here as a garrison. Here he also met Midshipman McRae, who after crossing Mexico had arrived in a Mexican brig, and who brought despatches dated Washington, May 15th, two days later than those received by the *Warren*.[48] He arrived at Monterey the 15th, where the *Erie* from Honolulu had arrived before him. Meanwhile Major Frémont, with the remnant of his battalion, left Los Angeles and marched northward to the Sacramento Valley. Nothing is known of the march, except that Lieutenant Talbot and nine men were left as a garrison at Santa Bárbara to replace the men taken away on the *Congress*.[49]

Aug. 18th–25th, Pedro C. Carrillo accepts Stockton's appointment as collector of customs. *Carrillo* (*P.*), *Doc.*, MS., 5–7.

[48] Stockton acknowledges the receipt, and mentions his meeting with McRae in his report to the sec. of navy of Sept. 18th, *Stockton's Mil. and Naval Oper.*, 1–2, at the same time stating that he had carried out the orders of May 15th, even to the sending of an overland courier, and so he had, and somewhat more, as the order did not literally require more than the occupation of Californian port towns. The order is found in *29th Cong. 2d Sess.*, *H. Ex. Doc.*, 19; *Cutts' Conq.*, append., 254–5. Phelps, *Fore and Aft*, 309–10, who was at Sta Bárbara, notes McRae's arrival. The brig on which he came was seized by Mitchell. The passenger pretended—it does not clearly appear why—to be an English officer, with despatches for the admiral. Phelps suspected this was not true; and while quizzing him at dinner the *Congress* appeared, and the officer threw off his disguise. He said he had crossed to Acapulco in the disguise of an English officer. Stockton wished to charter Phelps' vessel as a privateer, but the offer was declined for business reasons. In a speech at a banquet of the *Cal. Assoc. Pioneers*, N. Y., 1875, p. 20, Ex-governor Rodman M. Price, formerly purser of the *Cyane*, said: 'This I know, the official news of the existence of war came by Lieut McRae of the navy, a special messenger from Washington to Monterey, and I carried it from there to Los Angeles and delivered it to Com. Stockton.'

[49] In his *Geog. Memoir*, 39–40, Frémont gives an account of the physical features of the country as observed on this march; but the only dates are 'about the middle of Sept. we encamped near the summit of the Cuesta de Sta Inés,' and at the end of Sept. were in the region of Soledad. Lancey, *Cruise*, 120, says that Frémont left Angeles Sept. 8th with 40 men; and Sta Bárbara Sept. 13th with 30 men.

CHAPTER XII.

THE CONQUEST—AFFAIRS IN THE NORTH—REVOLT OF
FLORES IN THE SOUTH.

AUGUST–OCTOBER, 1846.

AT MONTEREY—COLTON'S DIARIES—THE FIRST NEWSPAPER—FAUNTLEROY
AND SNYDER AT SAN JUAN—SAN JOSÉ UNDER HYDE, WATMOUGH, AND
WEBER—SAN FRANCISCO AFFAIRS—RECEPTION TO STOCKTON—REVERE
AT SONOMA—MEETING OF BEAR FLAG MEN—RELEASE OF PRISONERS—
THE WALLA WALLA INVASION—STOCKTON'S GRAND PLANS—JUAN FLACO'S
RIDE—PREPARATIONS TO QUELL THE REVOLT—GILLESPIE AT ANGELES—
VARÉLA'S ATTACK—JOSÉ MARÍA FLORES—PRONUNCIAMIENTO—FIGHT AT
CHINO RANCHO—GILLESPIE'S CAPITULATION—TALBOT DRIVEN FROM
SANTA BÁRBARA—MERRITT FROM SAN DIEGO—MERVINE'S DEFEAT—
MEETING OF THE ASSEMBLY—STOCKTON AT SAN PEDRO—SAN DIEGO
REOCCUPIED.

AFFAIRS at the north from August to the end of
October, during the absence of Stockton and after his
return, may be best and briefly presented in the form
of local annals. Let us glance at each of the northern
settlements, Monterey, San Juan, San José, San Francisco, and Sutter's Fort.

Walter Colton, sometime chaplain in the navy, performed occasional religious service in these times, both
on land and on shipboard. He served as alcalde, at
first by military appointment with Rodman M. Price,
and later by popular election; kept a diary, subsequently
published; and in company with Semple edited and
published a newspaper. From the book and paper,
with some slight aid from other sources, I form a
chronologic summary of local happenings, which is

appended in a note.[1]   Colton's diary is largely devoted
to petty though interesting details of incidents connected with the author's administration of justice, with

[1] Aug. 1st, Stockton sailed on the *Congress* to undertake the conquest of
the south.   Aug. 7th, news that the *Brooklyn* with its Mormon colony had
arrived at S. Francisco.   Aug. 11th, a deserter reports Castro as on his last.
legs, anxious to fly to Mex.   H. B. M. brig-of-war *Spy* arrived from S. Blas.
'She has undoubtedly news of moment, but will not reveal it.'   Aug. 12th,
the *Warren*, Com. Hull, arrived from Mazatlan, bringing the official news of
war.   'The mysterious silence of the officers of the *Spy* is now explained.'   'The
war news produced a profound sensation here.   The whole population were
instantly thrown into groups in the corridors and at the corners of streets.
The hum of voices continued late into the night.   It was an extinguisher on
the hopes of those who had looked to Mexico for aid, or who had clung to the
expectation that the American govt would repudiate our possession of Cal.
They now relinquish all idea of a return to their old political connection, and
appear resigned to their fate.'   Aug. 13th, the *Warren* sailed for S. Pedro.
Alcaldes Colton and Price issued an order strictly prohibiting the sale of liquors
or wines, under penalty of forfeiture, fine, and imprisonment.   Colton relates
several instances of efforts on the part of dealers to evade this law.   Aug. 14th,
20 Indians arrested for stealing horses brought to town.   They were turned
over to Capt. Mevrine, who drew up his troops in a hollow square, with the
Indians in the centre expecting to be shot; but they were set free, and then
taken on board the *Savannah* to inspire them with awe, being furnished with
blankets and handkerchiefs, and dismissed to the air of Hail Columbia, vow-
ing eternal allegiance to the Americans!   Aug. 15th, first number of the *Californian* published.   A man from Castro's camp reported that the general was
disposed to treat with Stockton, having only about 130 soldiers left.   Aug.
18th–19th, some of Castro's officers, including Joaq. de la Torre, arrived and
were paroled, announcing the flight of the general and governor.   Aug. 21st,
Lieut McLane returned from an exped. against marauding Ind.   Aug. 22d,
29th, no. 2 and 3 of the *Californian* appeared.
    Sept. 2d, Lieut Maddox, with captains Ford and Swift and a portion of
their companies, arrived from Los Angeles.   Sept. 3d, despatches from Stockton included his procl. of Aug. 17th; also stated that Gov. Pico had not escaped, but surrendered.   Sept. 4th, first jury impanelled in Cal. to try the
case of Isaac Graham vs Charles Roussillon, 'involving property on one side
and integrity of character on the other.'   The verdict acquitted the Frenchman of fraudulent intent, and found a balance due plaintiff of $65.   Graham
was satisfied, and retracted in writing his charges.   The jury was composed
of Juan Malarin, W. E. P. Hartnell, Manuel Diaz, José Ábrego, Rafael
Sanchez, Pedro Narvaez, Charles Chase, Geo. Minor, Milton Little, Robert
H. Thomes, Florencio Serrano, and Talbot H. Green.   Sept. 4th, Com. Mervine issued an order requiring all of Castro's officers to present themselves
and sign paroles; also those already paroled were to give additional pledges.
Sept. 5th, no. 4 of the *Californian*.   Sept. 11th, an express announced the
arrival of 1,000 Walla Walla Ind. on the Sac., bent on vengeance.   (See
later in this chapter.)   Sept. 12th, no. 5 of the *Californian*.   Ex-gov. Alvarado arrived about this time and was well received by Capt. Mervine and
by the citizens of Monterey.   Sept. 14th, news that 2,000 immigrants had
arrived at the Sacramento.   Sept. 15th, municipal election held, with following results: Alcalde, Walter Colton; alcalde pro tem., Milton Little;
alcalde's councillors, Spence, Hartnell, Malarin, and Diaz; treasurer of municipal funds, Salvador Munras.   Sept. 15th, Stockton arrived in the *Congress*.   Sept. 17th, Larkin recommends the confirmation of T. H. Green as
collector of the port, and the appointment of Hartnell as surveyor and ap-
praiser of the custom-house.   This was done.   Sept. 19th, the *Erie*, the

frequent remarks on the manners and customs of the
people—the whole being an excellent picture of the
times, whose reproduction en résumé is of course impossible.   The *Savannah* remained at anchor in the
bay during Stockton's absence in the south; and Captain Mervine was military commandant of the post.
On the commodore's return Lieutenant Maddox was
made commandant of the central district on Sept. 18th,
and a company of dragoons was organized.   On the hill
in a position commanding both town and harbor were
built by Cecil a block-house and battery, where three
42-pounders were mounted.   The structure, sur-

date of whose arrival from Honolulu is not recorded, sailed for Panamá
with despatches.   No. 6 of the *Californian*.   Sept. 20th (or 22d), the *Savannah* sailed for S. Francisco.   Sept. 25th (or 24th), the *Congress* with Stockton sailed for S. F.   Additional orders on the sale of liquors.   Sept. 26th,
no. 7 of the *Californian*.   Sept. 29th, order forbidding gambling.   A courier from Los Angeles brought news of a revolt of the Californians in the
south.
    Oct. 1st, arrived the French corvette *Brillante*, bringing M. Moerenhaut,
French consul at Monterey.   Oct. 3d, no. 8 of the *Californian*.   Oct. 5th,
news that the *Savannah* had sailed for the south, 'to bring the insurgents if
possible to an engagement; but the probability is that they will instantly disband and fly to the forests.'   Oct. 10th, no. 9 of the *Californian*.   Lieut Maddox's company mustered into the service; 2 officers and 15 men.   30 men
joined later.   Mustered out April 1847.   *31st Cong. 1st Sess., H. Ex. Doc. 24*,
22 h. vol. vii.   Oct. 14th, streets barricaded and other preparations made for
defence.   'Bands have been gathering in the vicinity to make a night assault
on Monterey.   Their plan is to capture or drive out the small American force
here and plunder the town.'   Oct. 15th, alarm still continued.   A company
of Californians seen in the distance.   A despatch sent by the *Barnstable* to
Stockton for aid.   Oct. 16th, Stockton arrived in the *Congress*, having been
met outside by the messenger while en route for the south.   He landed a force
sufficient to protect the town, 50 men and 3 guns under Baldwin and Johnson.   Oct. 17th, no. 10 of the *Californian*.   Oct. 19th, a party of 20 Californians left the town and vicinity to join the insurgents.   The *Congress* sailed
for S. Pedro.   Oct. 23d, the *Vandalia* arrived from the south with news of
Gillespie's capitulation at Angeles and Mervine's defeat at S. Pedro.   Oct. 24th
news of the *Sterling* with Frémont and his men, who had turned back while
en route for the south.   No. 11 of the *Californian*.   Oct. 27th, Lieut W. B.
Renshaw arrived in the *Malek Adhel*, a prize brig taken at Mazatlan.   Oct.
28th, Frémont and his men arrived in a famished condition.   Scouts reported
a large band of Californians in the hills; and it was thought that they intended
to attack the town that night, Maddox being absent with 30 men at S. Juan,
but that their plan was frustrated by Frémont's arrival.   Oct. 29th, Maddox
returned with a field-piece and many horses.   Oct. 30th, a man in charge of
the horses near the town was shot by two of the Californians, but not killed.
Oct. 31st, no. 12 of the *Californian*.   See *Colton's Three Years in California*,
20–84.   In the *S. J. Pioneer*, Oct. 13, 1877, is a narrative of the excitement
caused by the discharge of a cannon when strapped on the back of a mule
that had brought it from S. Juan; also in *Id.*, Jan. 19, 1878, of Mariano Soberanes' tussle with a sentinel, while surreptitiously visiting his family in
town.

rounded by a ditch, was at first called Fort Stockton, but the name was soon changed to Fort Mervine. At first all was quiet; but at the news of southern revolt, the arribeños also began to show disaffection. Bands of Californians, more or less fully organized, ranged the hills and drove off horses, even threatening the town; so that before the end of October much fear was experienced, not only by Americans, but especially by the many native families who had been somewhat prominent in espousing the American cause. Respecting the acts of the rebels in later months I shall have something to say hereafter.

The appearance of the first newspaper is an event which merits notice here. Not only had there never been a paper published in the country, but there had been no subscribers to any paper, except a few in the last two or three years to the Honolulu *Polynesian.* The Mexican official paper was sent with some show of regularity to the Californian government; small packages of different Mexican and Spanish papers were forwarded occasionally by friends to officers, padres, or citizens; while trading vessels sometimes brought to resident foreigners old numbers of journals from the United States, from the Sandwich Islands, or even from Oregon. It was probably Robert Semple who conceived the idea of a Californian newspaper in 1846, as Figueroa had done without any practical results in earlier times. Semple knew something of setting type. Colton favored the scheme, and had had some editorial experience in Philadelphia on the *North American.* The two agreed to edit and publish a paper in partnership. Colton describes his partner as "an emigrant from Kentucky, in a buckskin dress, a fox-skin cap; true with the rifle, ready with his pen, and quick at the type-case." At the government house were found the old press and type, whose products in 1834–42 I have had frequent occasion to cite in past chapters. The apparatus had not been used for several years, having been pronounced

useless, perhaps as a mere excuse, when Pico wished
to transfer it to Angeles in 1845. It had not, as one
of the editors stated, and as many have repeated, been
" picked up in a cloister," or " used by a Roman Catholic monk in printing a few sectarian tracts;" nor had
it ever been used by the padres at all; but had been
the property of Agustin V. Zamorano, who sold it
to the government, which made some slight use of it
in publishing official orders, both at Monterey and Sonoma. Colton says: " The press was old enough to be
preserved as a curiosity; the mice had burrowed in
the balls; there were no rules, no leads; and the types
were rusty and all in pi. It was only by scouring
that the letters could be made to show their faces. A
sheet or two of tin were procured, and these with a
jack-knife were cut into rules and leads. Luckily we
found with the press the greater part of a keg of ink;
and now came the main scratch for paper. None
could be found, except what is used to envelope the
tobacco of the cigar smoked here by the natives. A
coaster had a small supply of this on board, which we
procured. It is in sheets a little larger than the com-
mon-sized foolscap." It was the ordinary Spanish
foolscap on which most of the archives of California
and other Spanish American provinces are written,
the thicker the better for writing, the thinner grades
being preferred for cigarettes, but there being rarely
any opportunity of choice for either purpose. The
font of type being intended for the Spanish language, vv had to serve for w. " The upper room in
the north end of the upper barracks was furnished by
Lieutenant Minor as an office," writes Semple; and the
first number of the *Californian* appeared on August
15th. "A crowd was waiting when the first sheet
was thrown from the press. It produced quite a little sensation. Never was a bank run upon harder;
not, however, by people with paper to get specie, but
exactly the reverse." The paper appeared every Saturday during the rest of the year and later, being

transferred to San Francisco in May 1847. It contained official orders, current news chiefly local, editorials and correspondence on the condition and prospects of the country, contributions from native Californians who favored the new order of things, and several historical articles on the Bear Flag revolt and other past events. By the aid of Hartnell, a portion of the contents was printed in Spanish. The management of the paper reflected much credit on the publishers. Semple, though he had obtained his discharge from Fauntleroy's company in order that he might devote his whole attention to the new enterprise, was absent much of the time in the region of San Francisco Bay, engaged—according to the statement of his partner, who with a type-setting sailor had most of the work to do—in land speculations and in vain search for a wife.[2]

Just before Stockton's departure for the south, Captain Fauntleroy and 'Major' Jacob Snyder with fifty men were sent to occupy San Juan in the place of the small garrison left there by Frémont. Of their experience there all that is recorded is an expedition dur-

[2] The set of *The Californian*, Aug. 15, 1846, to May 6, 1847, nos 1–38, so far as published at Monterey, which I have consulted, and a MS. résumé of which forms a volume in my Library, is that of the heirs of Ramon Argüello, in possession of Juan Malarin of Sta Clara, originally preserved by David Spence. I have also a few specimen numbers of the original. There is a set in the Cal. State Library at Sac.; also one nearly complete in the library of the Cal. Pioneers in S. F. It appears that the first page of no. 1 was printed as a prospectus, bearing the name of Semple alone as publisher. A copy is in *Taylor's Specimens of the Press*, in the Mercantile Library of S. F. In the 'extra' of Jan. 28, 1847, Colton gives an account of the enterprise. A letter of Semple to Fauntleroy explaining the plan and asking his own discharge, is found in *Cal. Pioneers, Arch.*, MS., 225–7. The paper is noticed in the *Oregon Spectator* of Nov. 12, 1846; also in the Honolulu papers. See full particulars in *Colton's Three Years in Cal.*, 32, etc. Francis D. Clark, in a letter of Feb. 22, 1878, in *S. José Pioneer*, March 9, 1878, gives a statement of John R. Gould of Maryland, that he fitted up the office, restored the type, and printed the first numbers of the *Californian*. Gould may be the sailor alluded to by Colton; but as he also says that Semple did not become a partner for several months, the accuracy of his whole statement may be questioned. Gould's claim is also noticed in *Upham's Notes*, 387. The *S. Jose Pioneer*, Dec. 15, 1877, prints a bill for $20, the subscription to the paper for 5 years to John H. Watmough, signed by Semple on Aug. 28, 1846. See also *Hist. Or.*, i. 467, this series, for claim of M. G. Foisy that he worked as printer on the *Monterey Californian*.

ing the first week in August against a party of Indians who had driven off two hundred horses from San José, and who were forced to give up their booty after a fight in which several of their number were killed. It would appear that Fauntleroy's men were subsequently withdrawn; for late in October, after the revolt at Los Angeles had begun to trouble the northerners, Maddox marched with thirty men to San Juan, spiked the iron cannon, took the locks from the muskets, and carried the brass pieces with all horses obtainable to Monterey.[3]

Respecting events at San José from August to October, our information is hardly less meagre. James Stokes was succeeded as alcalde by George Hyde, who was appointed "civil magistrate for the district of Santa Clara, with headquarters at San José," by Montgomery on August 26th. Purser James H. Watmough, being appointed commandant of Santa Clara on the same date, with a company of forty men, was sent down from San Francisco; but of his exploits we know only that on September 14th he is said to have returned to San José from an Indian expedition of two weeks, in which he recovered one hundred horses and killed several gentiles; and that he probably went back to San Francisco before the end of September. Early in October, Charles M. Weber returned from his captivity in the south, and was made military commandant of San José district by Montgomery, who also desired him to accept the position of alcalde. Weber was authorized to organize a military force and defend the town and vicinity if possible, but to retreat to Yerba Buena rather than to run too great risks. No hostilities were committed, however, beyond the occasional cutting of the flag-staff halyards at night; and Captain Weber was able to collect a considerable body of horses, with which he

[3] See Colton's Three Years in Cal., 25, 82; Monterey Californian, Oct. 31, 1846; and Maddox's letter of Oct. 28th to Weber, in S. José Pioneer, March 6, 1880.

is said to have arrived at San Juan just after the departure of Maddox.[4]

At San Francisco, where Montgomery remained in the *Portsmouth* as military commandant of the northern district, while Watson commanded the little garrison on shore, all was peace and quiet, with no ripple of excitement, except on the arrival of vessels or couriers with news from abroad, or on the occasion of a grand social festivity on shore or on shipboard. Lieutenant Washington A. Bartlett was on August 26th appointed alcalde of the San Francisco district, with headquarters at Yerba Buena. September 15th a municipal election was held, at which nearly a hundred votes were cast. The officers elected were Washington Bartlett, alcalde; José de Jesus Noé, second alcalde; John Rose, treasurer; and Peter T. Sherrebeck, collector.[5] In the last days of September the *Savannah* and *Congress* arrived from Monterey, and Stockton was given a public reception the 5th of October. As the commodore landed from his barge, at a point corresponding to what is now Clay street between Montgomery and Sansome, William H. Russell delivered a flowery address of welcome; after which the people marched in procession round the

[4] *Monterey Californian*, Sept. 5, 26, 1846; original letters of Bartlett and Montgomery to Weber, in *Halleck's Mex. Land Laws*, MS.; account from Weber's own statements and papers, in *S. José Pioneer*, March 6, 1880. In one of his letters, Montgomery orders Weber to throw a 'kurral' round his camp to prevent surprise. Sends him three recruits, also powder and clothing. Militiamen can draw no pay except when in actual service. $15 per month for subsistence is too much. Sept. 15th, Alcalde Hyde takes the parole of Capt. José Fernandez. *Vallejo, Doc.*, MS., xii. 241.

[5] *Monterey Californian*, Sept. 5, 26, Oct. 3, 1846; *Hyde's Statement*, MS., 8; *S. José Pioneer*, Jan. 4, 1879. The vote at the election was as follows: alcalde, Bartlett 66, Ridley 29, Spear 1; 2d alcalde, Noé 63, Haro 24, scattering 9; treasurer, Rose 67, Francis Hoen 20, scattering 9; collector, Sherreback 86, J. Cooper 2. The inspectors were Wm H. Davis, Frank Ward, Francisco Guerrero, and Francisco Haro. Aug. 29th, Bartlett enclosed to the alcalde of Sonoma 'rules and regulations for trade in the bay.' *Santa Rosa Sonoma Democrat*, Dec. 30, 1871. On Sept. 15th Montgomery issued an order that Indians should not be held in service except under a voluntary contract, acknowledged before a magistrate, and equally binding upon employer and employé. *Californian*, Oct. 3. Among the festivities are notably a ball at the residence of Leidesdorff on Sept. 8th, at which over 100 ladies, Californian and American, were present; and another on board the *Magnolia* on the 18th.

plaza and back to Montgomery street, where they
listened to a speech from Stockton. The discourse,
in which he narrated the conquest of Los Angeles,
and made known his plans of vengeance on the "cowardly assassins" who had dared to revolt against his
authority, was decidedly of the bombastic and 'spread-
eagle' variety, marked by the same disregard of truth
that had been shown in his first proclamation; but
the speaker was eloquent and the audience pleased.
Then there was more marching; and finally, the governor with prominent citizens made a tour on horseback to the presidio and mission, returning in time
for a collation given by the committee of arrangements at Leidesdorff's residence.[6] The rumor of an
impending Indian invasion had hastened Stockton's
visit to the north. This rumor proved unfounded;
but news of a revolt in the south had reached him
just after his arrival at San Francisco. October 4th,
the day before the reception, Mervine had sailed in
the *Savannah* for San Pedro; on the 13th the *Congress* and the chartered merchant vessel *Sterling*,
Captain Vincent, left the bay for the southern coast,
the former with Stockton on board, and the latter
bearing Major Frémont and his battalion. There is
nothing to be noted at San Francisco after their departure.

Revere had been sent by Montgomery to command
the garrison at Sonoma, consisting of Company B of
the battalion, under Captain Grigsby. Revere tells
us that a few disaffected Californians were still prowl-
ing about the district, in pursuit of whom on one
occasion he made an expedition with sixteen men to

[6] *Monterey Californian*, Oct. 24, 1846, with Stockton's speech in full; *Oregon Spectator*, April 1, 1847; *Davis' Glimpses of the Past*, MS., 349–51, the
author having been present at the reception; *Stockton's Report;* and Lancey,
Cruise, 131–2, who gives additional particulars. He names Frank Ward as
marshal; describes the composition of the procession formed at 10 A. M.; says
that in addition to his reply to Russell made at the wharf, Stockton made a
long speech in reply to a toast at the collation, declaring that if one hair of
the brave men left to garrison the south should be injured, he 'would wade
knee-deep in his own blood (!) to avenge it;' and mentions a ball which
closed the day's festivities, and lasted until daylight the next morning.

the region of Point Reyes. He did not find the
party sought, but he was able to join in a very en-
joyable elk-hunt. The only other feature of his stay
at Sonoma—and a very interesting one, as described
by him, though not very important from an historical
point of view—was an expedition by way of Napa
Valley to the Laguna, now Clear Lake, and back by
the Russian River Valley, in September. With the
exception of a few military and hunting expeditions,
meagrely recorded, this was the first visit to the lake
by a traveler who included in the record a description
of the country.[7] On his return, the lieutenant heard
of the threatened Walla Walla invasion, and hastened
with a force to the Sacramento; while the Vallejos
were commissioned to protect the Sonoma frontier
with a force of Christian Indians, and Misroon before September 11th assumed command of the garrison. Manuel E. McIntosh was now alcalde of Sonoma; and the victims of the capture of June 14th

[7] *Revere's Tour of Duty*, 77–95, 112–18, 130–47. The author's description
of the regions visited is quite extensive. He and his few companions passed
the first night at Yount's; arrived by noon at the place of J. B. Chiles, who was
one of the party, ranking as sergeant; and spent the second night at the rancho
of Greenock (Guenoc?), the frontier settler. Next morning, crossing the last
mountain pass, and riding all day through timbered uplands, broad savannahs,
and shady glades, at sunset they reached the lake near its narrowest part, at
the base of the high sierra—now Uncle Sam Mountain—opposite a pretty
islet. After some hesitation, caused by memories of the servant-hunting
raids of the Californians, the Indians ferried the visitors over on tule balzas
to their island town of 200 or 300 inhabitants. Next day they journeyed
over the sterile obsidian-covered plain, to go round the mountain, into the
beautiful country on the upper lake—now Big Valley—and at sunset reached
Hopitsewah, or Sacred Town, the largest of the rancherías, where the lands
were enclosed and cultivated. Here, on the third day after arrival, a grand
council of native chieftains was assembled to listen to and make the speeches
of such occasions, and transfer their allegiance to the great and good govt of
the U. S. After which a grand dance. Next day Revere's party travelled
over the plain parallel to the lake until noon, and then turning to the left,
climbed the range. They were attacked by Indians, who mistook them for
foes, and one of whom was badly wounded. A difficult trail led them to
the summit at sunset, and they looked foward into another broad valley and
back upon the lake. 'Few white men have visited this magnificent Laguna.
In the course of time it will become famous, and perhaps the "tired den-
zens" of the Atlantic cities may yet make summer excursions to its glorious
shores.' Down into the Russian River Valley they went to the rancho of Fernando Félix, where they spent the day. On the way to Piña's rancho they
killed a huge grizzly; and at Fitch's rancho of Sotoyome they found the annual *matanzas* in progress.

had returned from their imprisonment in August.
On September 25th a meeting of the old Bears was
held, at which, J. B. Chiles being president and John
H. Nash secretary, a resolution was adopted "that
three persons be appointed to act as a committee to
investigate and gather all the information in their
reach in relation to the action of the Bear Flag
party, and report at a subsequent meeting." Semple, Grigsby, and Nash were appointed on the committee, though Semple's place was afterward taken
by Ide; and the resulting report of May 13, 1847,
has already been noticed in this work.[8]

At Sutter's Fort Kern remained in command; being confirmed in his authority by Montgomery on
August 26th, at which date E. J. Sutter, son of the
captain, was made Kern's lieutenant at the fort.[9] In
August also the Sonoma prisoners were released, as
they ought to have been long before. They had appealed to Frémont when Sloat's proclamation and the
United States flag arrived; but not the slightest attention was paid to their appeal. In July a letter of
inquiry about them came from Larkin; and Montgomery interested himself in their behalf.[10] In reply,
Vallejo wrote to both Larkin and Stockton; but before the letters were received, on July 27th, the commodore despatched an order for the release of Vallejo
and his brother-in-law; followed in a few days by a
similar order in behalf of the other captives. All
were required to sign a parole. Vallejo and Carrillo
were discharged on or about the 1st of August, the
former in very feeble health. The others, Salvador
Vallejo, Victor Prudon, and Jacob Leese had to re-

---

[8] Record of the meeting in *Monterey Californian*, Oct. 3, 1846. See chap.
viii. of this volume; also *Hist. Bear Flag Revol.*

[9] *Monterey Californian*, Sept. 5, 1846.

[10] July 16th, Larkin to Vallejo, describing his efforts to learn his fate.
Had sent messengers to Sonoma, and John Murphy had been sent to the Sac.
—for which service he was to be paid by V. $100. *Bear Flag Papers*, MS.,
62. July 17th, Montgomery to Sloat, forwarding Forbes' petition for the release of Vicente Peralta, and also mentioning Vallejo, in whose case he was
personally interested. *Sloat's Despatches*, 24–5, or 661–8.

main in prison a week longer, Don Salvador—and probably the rest, though Leese claims that his captivity lasted until the 13th—being liberated on August 8th by Misroon, the officer sent up by Montgomery for that purpose. Returning to their homes, they found that cattle, horses, and other personal property had for the most part disappeared; but the change of government might enrich those of the number who were the owners of real estate.[11] Montgomery sent

[11] July 29th, Stockton to Vallejo. One of his first acts was to order his release; and he has now sent a courier to Montgomery to have the others freed, whose names he did not know before. *Bear Flag Papers*, MS., 67. No date, copy of Montgomery's order to release Vallejo and Carrillo. *Id.*, 72. Leese, *Bear Flag*, MS., 16–17, thinks the first order named Vallejo's brother-in-law, meaning himself, but applied to Carrillo. July 29th, Larkin to Vallejo. Letters of 23d received this morning. Orders for release sent two days ago to Montgomery. Now repeated, and the courier will tell the conversation he had with Stockton. *Savage, Doc.*, MS., iii. 19; *Larkin's Doc.*, MS., iv. 234. Aug. 3d, Montgomery to V., announcing the pleasure it has given him to order his release, and introducing Lieut Revere, who has instructions to 'mitigate' his parole by accepting simply a promise of friendship to the U. S., or of neutrality. English and Spanish. *Bear Flag Papers*, MS., 70, 73. Aug. 7th, Salv. Vallejo to M. G. Vallejo, in answer to letter of Aug. 4th, which announced that a boat was on the way with the order of release. The boat has not arrived, and even if it does come there is but little hope of freedom; for Kern has said he will not obey any order if the name of each prisoner be not specified, and has even hinted that he is not bound to obey any orders but those of Frémont. *Id.*, 76. Aug. 7th, S. Vallejo, Prudon, and Leese, to Vallejo, expressing their opinion that Kern did not intend to free them, and asking the colonel to write to Montgomery in their behalf. *Id.*, 68. Aug. 6th, Lieut Bartlett to Vallejo, in answer to letter of July 30th. With many expressions of friendly feeling, he says: 'I at once laid your note before Capt. Montgomery, who at once expressed his deep regret that you were yet a prisoner [on the 30th]. He has constantly regretted that you were not liberated on the day the American flag first waved over New Helvetia, which certainly would have been the case had his command extended to that post. He has directed me to assure you that among his first communications to Com. Sloat he stated the names of all persons that had been arrested, ... and requested instructions as to the course he should now pursue with regard to them, at the same time making particular mention of your case.' *Id.*, 74–5. Aug. 8th, V. to Montgomery, in reply to letter of Aug. 3d. Thanks for his efforts; bad state of the writer's health; appeals for the release of his companions. *Id.*, 78–80. Aug. 8th, Lieut Misroon takes the parole of Salvador Vallejo at 'Fort New Helvetia.' *Vallejo, Doc.*, MS., xii. 232. Aug. 12th, V. to Montgomery. 'Muy enfermo salí del Sacramento y peor llegué á mi casa.' Thanks for opportune sending of Dr Henderson. *Bear Flag Papers*, MS., 81. Aug. 17th, Montgomery to V. Sends him documents relating to Misroon's visit to Sonoma in June. Has just returned himself from Sonoma. *Id.*, 58. Aug. 24th, Larkin to V. from Los Angeles. Speaks of having sent a second courier to New Helvetia before leaving Monterey. Sept. 15th, V. to L. Returned from his prison 'half dead,' but is now better. Has lost over 1,000 cattle, 600 tame horses, all his crops, and many other things of value; but will go to work again. *Larkin's Doc.*, MS., iv. 280–1. Sept. 25th, Montgomery to V. Thanks for his services to the U. S.

Dr Henderson to Sonoma to treat Vallejo's illness, and soon visited the colonel in person. Vallejo also came down to San Francisco to be present at Stockton's reception.

The alarm of an Indian invasion from the north, to which I have alluded, had its origin in an affair of the winter of 1844–5. A party of Oregon Indians had come down to trade for cattle, being well received by Sutter, who had known some of the chiefs in Oregon, and permitted to hunt for wild horses, to be exchanged for cattle. Among the party were the Walla Walla chief Yellow Serpent and his son Elijah. The latter, who had been educated by the missionaries, was a turbulent and insolent fellow, who killed one of his companions near the fort, and was prevented by an American from killing another. Among the animals taken by the Indians were some claimed as private property; but which they refused to give up. Grove Cook on going to demand a mule that bore his brand was met by Elijah, who levelled his rifle at him, and told him to take the animal if he dared. Sutter then summoned the chiefs to his office, and insisted that branded animals must be given up to their owners, though the Indians were entitled to a reward for restoring them. They declared that by their customs such animals belonged to those who found them. While the discussion was going on, Sutter left the office; and during his absence, Elijah was shot and killed by Cook in a quarrel, in which, according to the white witnesses present, the Indian was the aggressor; though it would be more reasonable to suppose, in the absence of Indian witnesses, and the safety with which

<hr />

Vallejo, Doc., MS., xii. 242. Sept. 29th, Id. to Id. Invites him to Yerba Buena to meet Stockton. *Id.*, xii. 236. Oct. 19th, Id. to Id. Cannot accede to Vallejo's request that Revere be removed from the command, though he would do so for the cogent reasons urged had the request come a little sooner. *Id.*, xii. 244. Nov. 16th, Id. to Id. A very friendly letter. Regrets that he cannot visit Sonoma before his departure. *Id.*, xii. 249. March 28, 1847, V. to Bandini on his imprisonment and losses thereby. *Bandini, Doc.*, MS., 104. June 14, 1847, V. to Ex-president Bustamante on the same topic. *Vallejo, Doc.*, MS., xii. 304.

an Indian might be killed under the circumstances,
that Elijah was deliberately murdered by Cook. The
whole party of about forty then hurried back to
Oregon with their horses, not waiting to receive the
cattle due them, and eluding the pursuers despatched
by Sutter. Their story was told to the missionaries
and to the Indian agent, White; and these gentlemen
were ready to credit the version given them without
investigation. White wrote on the subject to the
government, to Sutter, and to Larkin.[12]

Yellow Serpent came back to California at the beginning of September, 1846, with some forty of his
people, to trade and to demand justice for the killing
of his son. Reports had come from Oregon, from the
missionaries and by the immigrants, that the Walla
Wallas were bent on vengeance; and great was the
alarm when a frontier settler came to New Helvetia
with the news that a thousand warriors were approaching. The chief and his party had arrived at the cabin
of the settler, Daniel Sill; and the explanation that
nine men had been left ill on the way was interpreted
to mean that 900 warriors were close behind! The
alarm was sent in all haste to Sonoma and Monterey;
and while Stockton came up to San Francisco, every
possible preparation was made for defence along the
northern frontier. Revere, leaving the Vallejos with
a force of Californians and friendly Indians to scour
the country and protect exposed points, hastened to
the Sacramento. Soon after his arrival Revere learned
the true state of affairs, and that there was no danger;
in fact, the Walla Walla chief came in person to have
a 'talk,' announcing that he had come to trade and
not to fight, and urging upon the 'Boston men' who
now owned the country his claim for justice. Both

[12] See *Hist Or.*, i. 285–9, this series. July 21, 1845, Sutter to Larkin, giving full particulars of the affair. *Larkin's Doc.*, MS., iii. 227.   May 16th,
White to Larkin. *Id.*, iii. 155.   White to sec. of war. *Monterey Californian*,
Sept. 19, 1846. See also *White's Concise View*, 49; *Parrish's Oregon Anec.*,
MS., 90; *Gray's Hist. Ogn*, 507–11; *Mission Life Sketches*, 205–7.   Pewpew-
moxmox, the old chief was called in Oregon; Sutter calls him Piopiopio; and
the Californians ' El Cojo Macai.'

soldiers and settlers were anxious for a fight; certain persons tried to keep up the excitement; and many were not disposed to believe in the Indians' peaceful intentions, but rather to make a raid upon all the savages in the valley; but better counsel soon prevailed, and the cheering news was sent southward that the fear of a Walla Walla invasion was groundless.[13]

Some enthusiastic biographers have accorded to Major Frémont the glory of having persuaded the Walla Wallas to forego their plans of vengeance, and thus prevented a disastrous Indian war; but as a matter of fact, Frémont did not arrive until the excitement had passed away. He did, however, obtain some of the savages as recruits for his California battalion. Of the major's operations in the Sacramento during this visit, at the end of September and beginning of October, nothing definite is recorded, except that he succeeded in getting many recruits, whose military operations of the next few months, with what is known of their organization, will be presented in due time. The large influx of immigrants by the overland route, to be noticed elsewhere, made it easy to find soldiers for the battalion at this time.

Stockton's plans on quitting Los Angeles were, as we have seen, to appoint Frémont governor, leave detachments of the battalion as garrisons for the different posts, and to depart with the strength of his fleet to engage. in naval operations on the Mexican coast. He regarded the conquest of California as complete. He had no doubt that the people would soon become devoted subjects of the United States,

[13] *Stockton's Mil. and Naval Oper.*, 9; *Stockton's Report*, 41; *Revere's Tour*, 154, etc.; Sept. 10th–15th, corresp. between Misroon, M. G. Vallejo, and Salv. Vallejo, on the military preparations. *Vallejo, Doc.*, MS., xii. 234–40. See also *Vallejo, Hist. Cal.*, MS., v. 203–8; *Torres, Peripecias*, MS., 77–8; *Juarez, Narracion*, MS.; *Tustin's Recoll.*, MS., 9; *Honolulu Friend*, iv. 158; *Monterey Californian*, passim; *Upham's Life Frémont*, 242–3; *Bigelow's Mem. Frémont*, 172–3. The Californians have an idea, not very well founded I think, that Salvador Vallejo was the originator of the scare, hoping to run up a large bill for horses and other aid, and thus get paid for a part of his past losses.

and believed that his proposed system of civil rule would soon be in successful operation. Arriving at Monterey, his plans were somewhat interrupted by the Walla Walla alarm, which called him to San Francisco; but when he learned that no danger was to be apprehended from the Indians, his prospects again assumed a roseate hue, and his schemes were not only revived, but had been greatly amplified. His project was nothing less than to raise a thousand men in California, to land them at Mazatlan or Acapulco, and with them march overland to "shake hands with General Taylor at the gates of Mexico"![14]   Major Frémont—from this time addressed as military commandant of California, the date of his appointment to that position being September 2d—was sent to the Sacramento to recruit the army which was to conquer Mexico.   It is not necessary to characterize the commodore's project as a "master-stroke of military sagacity" with Lancey, or as the mad freak of an enthusiast seeking notoriety. Much would have depended on the result; and before much progress could be made news came that caused the scheme to be abandoned. At the end of September, John Brown arrived in all haste from Los Angeles with the report that the southern Californians had revolted, and that Gillespie's garrison was hard pressed by the foe. The courier, known as Juan Flaco, or Lean John, had made the distance from Angeles to San Francisco, about 500 miles, in six days, a feat which, variously

[14] *Stockton's Report*, 40.   Sept. 19th, Stockton to Mervine—'confidential'— announcing his plan, and that Frémont had been sent to the north for recruits. Sept. 28th, S. to Frémont, 'military commandant of the territory of Cal.' Anxious to know what his prospects are for 'recruiting my thousand men '— 'private '—in *Stockton's Mil. and Nav. Oper.*, 14–15. Sept. 30th, S. to Mervine.   Instructions for the movements of the *Savannah*, which was to sail at once. *Id.*, 12–13.   Oct. 1st, S. to Sec. Bancroft.   'I will send the *Savannah* on her cruise to-morrow, and the *Portsmouth* in a few days; and will follow myself in the *Congress* as soon as I can, to carry out my views in regard to Mexico, with which I have not thought it necessary or expedient to acquaint the department.   Our new govt goes on well...If any chance is given, I have no doubt an effort will be made by the Mexicans to recover the territory; troops are ready to come from Mexico, but if they are not seen on the way I'll make them fight their first battle at Acapulco, or between that and the city of Mexico.' *Id.*, 13–14.

exaggerated and misrepresented, has made the rider more or less famous.[15] Though Stockton did not attach great importance to the reported revolt, it was sufficient to distract his attention temporarily from his grand schemes of conquest; and he at once ordered Mervine to sail for San Pedro, to Gillespie's relief, which he did on the *Savannah* the 8th of October.[16] Frémont was summoned from the Sacramento, and arrived at San Francisco on the 12th with 160 men, who were embarked on the *Sterling*. This vessel with the *Congress* sailed next day for the south. Stockton, meeting the *Barnstable* with despatches from Maddox, touched at Monterey on the 16th, landing a

---

[15] Brown's own story, as quoted in *Lancey's Cruise*, 126–8, from the *Stockton S. Joaquin Republican*, 1850, is in substance as follows: With a package of cigarettes, the paper of each bearing the inscription, 'Believe the bearer,' and Gillespie's seal, he started at 8 P. M., Sept 24th, hotly pursued by 15 Mexicans. His horse, incited by a bullet through his body, cleared a ravine 13 feet wide, and fell after running 2 miles! Then he started on foot, carrying his spurs for 27 miles to Las Vírgenes. Here he was joined by Tom Lewis, and they reached Sta Bárbara at 11 P. M. of the 25th. At the same hour of the 26th, having been furnished horses successively by Lieut Talbot, Thos Robbins, and Lewis Burton on showing the magic cigarettes, they camped between S. Miguel and S. Luis Obispo, where Lewis gave out; but Brown started again next morning, and late at night reached Monterey. He was offered $200 to go on to S. F.; and started at sunrise on a race-horse belonging to Job Dye. Larkin aided him at S. José, where he was detained 4 hours; and he reached Yerba Buena at 8 P. M. of the 28th—630 miles in 4 days! He slept on the beach, and next morning when the commodore's boat landed gave Stockton the rest of his cigarettes. Gillespie, in the *Sac. Statesman*, May 6, 1858, gives a brief account, agreeing well enough with Brown's, except that the horse leaped into instead of across the ravine, breaking a leg, whereupon the courier had to carry his saddle 4 miles to a rancho; and that he reached Monterey at night of the 28th, slept two hours, and arrived at S. F. at sunrise of the 29th! Phelps, *Fore and Aft*, 311–15, tells us that Stockton got the news on Oct. 1st, when the courier was picked up drunk and carried to the flag-ship, where the cigarettes were found on him. Colton, *Three Years*, 64–5, notes Brown's arrival on the night of Sept. 29th, and his start before sunrise on the 30th. He had 'a few words over the signature of the alcalde rolled in a cigar, which was fastened in his hair...He rode the whole distance (to Monterey), 460 miles, in 52 hours, during which time he had not slept'! Stockton in his reports says the news was received on or about Sept. 30th. Taking the authority of Gillespie and Brown for the date of the start, and that of Colton and Stockton for that of the arrival, we have, as stated in my text, 6 days for the ride. But Bryant, *What I Saw in Cal.*, 327, says the courier arrived Oct. 1st; and it is to be noticed that Stockton in his order of Oct. 1st to Mervine says nothing to indicate that he had received the news. The *Californian* of Oct. 3d says he must have received the news on the morning of the 1st.

[16] Gillespie, in *Sac. Statesman*, May 6, 1858, claims that Mervine, having set sail on or about Oct. 1st, with a fine breeze, stopped at Sauzalito for some frivolous thing, and his departure was delayed for three days by a fog.

force for the protection of the town, and proceeded on his way. Frémont meanwhile met the *Vandalia*, learned that no horses could be obtained at Santa Bárbara, and turned back to Montcrey, where he arrived on the 28th, to prepare for a march southward. He found awaiting him a commission as lieutenant-colonel in the army of the United States.[17] His preparations and his expedition will be noticed later; it is now time to describe the revolt of the abajeños against the authority of their new masters.[18]

Gillespie had been left by Stockton as military commandant of the south, with a garrison of fifty men at Los Angeles. His instructions were to maintain military rule in accordance with the commodore's proclamation; but he was authorized to grant exemption from the more burdensome restrictions to quiet and well disposed citizens at his discretion; and a lenient policy in this respect was recommended. From a purely political point of view, Gillespie's task was not a difficult one; that is, there was no disposition on the part of the Angelinos to revolt against the new régime. In other respects, the prospect was less encouraging. My readers, familiar with Los Angeles annals, know that there was an element in the population of the town that was turbulent, lawless, and hitherto uncontrollable. That the new commandant could convert

---

[17] *Monterey Californian*, Oct. 31, 1846; *Colton's Three Years*, 79–82; *Lancey's Cruise*, 132–3. The commission was signed by the president May 29, 1846.

[18] The following extract from the *Californian* of Oct. 3d will show how the revolt was regarded in the north: 'We learn by the last courier that there has been quite a disturbance at the pueblo below. The more sober portion of the community, it seems, had no participation in the frantic affair. The principal actors in it are a class of hare-brained fellows who wanted a row, cost what it might...As for any prolonged resistance to the existing laws, there is not the slightest probability of such a result. Had there been any serious determination to resist and maintain an attitude of hostility, it would have showed itself when Gen. Castro was there...We do not suppose that any one engaged in this affair expects an ultimate triumph; nor do we suppose that he has looked seriously into the consequences to himself...The ringleaders will be apprehended and tried under martial law, and may suffer death; so much for an affair that can be of no benefit to any one, and must entail sorrow on many. The people of Monterey are wiser.'

these fellows into quiet citizens without a struggle was
not to be expected.   Had he been the wisest of rulers, a
conflict was inevitable; but the character and extent
and results of the conflict depended largely upon his
skill and prudence.   Gillespie had no special qualifications for his new position; and his subordinates were
still less fitted for their duties.   They were disposed
to look down upon Californians and Mexicans as an
inferior race, as a cowardly foe that had submitted
without resistance, as Indians or children to be kept
in subjection by arbitrary rules.   They were moreover
suspicious, and inclined to interfere needlessly with
the people's amusements, and with the actions of individuals.   Little account was taken of national habits
and peculiarities.   In a few weeks many good citizens,
though not perhaps of the best, who, though content
with the change of government, had no desire to be
at once fully Americanized in their methods of life
by process of law, were prejudiced against Gillespie,
characterizing his treatment of themselves or of their
friends in the enforcement of police regulations as oppressive tyranny.   Then came some open manifestations
of lawlessness, to which the commandant was too ready
to impute a political significance.   Arrests were freely
made; and the people found themselves branded as
rebels before they had really thought of rebellion.   A
few ambitious Mexican officers gladly took advantage
of the opportunity to foment the excitement; a degree
of success at first turned the heads of the ignorant
populace; many were led to believe that their country might yet be recovered; and others were either
blinded by their dislike of the men placed over them,
or had not the courage to resist the popular current.
The result was an actual revolt; and there can be little doubt that Gillespie and his men were largely
responsible for this result.[19]

[19] Coronel, *Cosas de Cal.*, MS., 78–80, tells us that Gillespie from the first
dictated needlessly oppressive measures; that two persons should not go about
the streets together; that under no pretext must the people have reunions at
their homes; that provision-shops must be closed at sundown; that liquor

Sérbulo Varela, a wild and unmanageable young fellow, though not a bad man at heart, whom the reader
already knows as a leader in several popular tumults
at Angeles under Mexican rule, soon became involved
in difficulties with Gillespie, doubtless because he was
unwilling to submit to police regulations—though
no details are known. Varela thereupon became a
kind of outlaw, ranging about the vicinity of the
town, keeping out of the reach of Gillespie's men,
but annoying them in every possible way. A dozen
kindred spirits joined him, irresponsible fellows, but
each controlling a few followers of the lower class;

should not be sold without his permission; also deciding petty cases instead
of leaving them to the jueces de paz, searching houses for weapons, and imprisoning Rico and others on mere suspicion. In short, he so oppressed the
people that he came to be regarded as a tryant; and after the first troubles
with Varela, redoubled his persecutions and drove many to join the rebels.
Francisco Rico, *Memorias*, MS., 25-6, says that he was imprisoned for 30 days
because he could tell nothing of the whereabouts and intentions of Ramon
Carrillo. B. D. Wilson, *Observations*, MS., 66-7, was told by the foreigners
who came to his rancho 'that Gillespie's conduct had been so despotic and
unjustifiable that the people had risen...He had established very obnoxious
regulations, and upon frivolous pretexts had the most respectable men in the
community arrested and brought before him for no other purpose than to hu-
miliate them, as they thought. Of the truth of this I had no doubt then and
I have none now. The people had given no just cause for the conduct he
pursued, which seemed to be altogether the effect of vanity and want of
judgment.' Temple, *Recollections*, MS., 10-11, takes the same view of the
matter. John Forster, *Pioneer Data*, MS., 35-7, thinks there would have
been no difficulty if Gillespie had been less exacting and despotic. Ávila,
Notas, MS., 29, attributes the revolt to the same cause. Larkin, during his
later imprisonment, was told by the officers that Gillespie's rigid discipline
and ignorance of Spanish customs and character had forced the people to take
up arms. *Larkin's Off. Corresp.*, MS., ii. 89. 'The discontent was caused by
the ill-advised acts of some of the American officers left in charge of the little
garrisons...Gillespie, with an insignificant and undisciplined military force,
attempted by a coercive system to effect a moral and social change in the
habits, diversions, and pastimes of the people, and reduce them to his standard of propriety. The result of this injudicious effort was the rebellion.' *Los
Angeles Hist.*, 17. Lieut Wise, *Los Gringos*, 44-5, attributes the revolt to
the fact that 'the natives had been confounded and bewildered by speeches
and proclamations,' etc.; and 'the banding together of a few mongrel bodies
of volunteers, who enhanced the pleasure of their otherwise agreeable society
by pillaging the natives of horses, cattle, etc., in quite a marauding, bucca-
neering, independent way; all of course under the apparent legal sanction of
the U. S.' See also *Dicc. Univ.*, MS., viii. 157-8; *Guerra, Apuntes*, 355; *Foster's Los Angeles in 1847*, etc., 42-3. Lancey, *Cruise*, 124, tells us that Pio
Pico and José M. Flores, 'these treacherous enemies of the U. S.,...secretly
collected together the remnant of their former army, and resolved upon
another effort to expel the Americans,' took advantage of Stockton's absence,
and suddenly appeared before Los Angeles with 500 men. This, in substance,
may be called the current version, except in respect to Pico's name.

and these men soon began to dream of raising a force
to attack the garrison, and repeat some of their exploits of earlier years.[20]   It is even said that one of
the number, Manuel Cantua, was for a time jocosely
termed by his companions, governor of California!
Several of the ringleaders were Sonorans, and others
Mexicans.   Gillespie, choosing to regard the operations of these marauders as a treacherous rebellion of
the Californians, greatly aided their cause by his oppressive and arbitrary measures.   Many citizens fled
to the ranchos to await further developments, having
no sympathy for the comandante, even if they had
not much for Varela.

About the middle of September a detachment of
the garrison had been sent to San Diego under Ezekiel Merritt; and before daylight on the 23d Varela,
with perhaps twenty companions, made a sudden attack on the adobe building in which the rest were
posted.   The Californians had no intention of fighting,
but by the suddenness of the assault, by discharging
a few muskets, and by shouts and beating of drums,
they hoped perhaps to surprise and capture the post,
as they had been wont to do in earlier days, or at
least to impress both the garrison and the citizens
with the idea that their movement was a formidable
one.   But Gillespie's men, whatever their faults, were
not to be defeated by noise, and a volley of rifle-balls
followed the fleeing assailants, one of whom was

[20] The earliest definite record of these operations is on Sept. 6th, when
Bonifacio Olivares wrote to Salvador Vallejo: 'Your friend Cantua and I
have thought of giving *rentazos* to the sailors who took Los Angeles. Capt.
Noriega and Flores are coming; if you also come, we will all vote for you to
command and punish the sailors. We have lances and reatas here.' 'P. S. All
that my compadre says is true, and I, who command more than he, also say
it, at the request of M. Cantua, Dionisio Reyes.' Original in *Larkin's Doc.*,
MS., iv. 274. Sept. 15th, Gillespie writes Fitch: 'Election for alcalde going
on, but only 20 voters have appeared. The party of Sonoreños who are disposed to disturb the peace proves to be quite small. I know the names of
the ringleaders, who will not long be at liberty.' *Fitch, Doc.*, MS., 402. The
original rebels included Sérbulo Varela, Hilario Varela, Manuel Cantua, Pedro
Romero, J. B. Moreno, Ramon Carrillo, Pablo Véjar, Nicolás Hermosillo,
Leonardo Higuera, Gregorio Atensio, Bonifacio Olivares, Dionisio Reyes,
Urita Valdés, etc.

wounded in the foot.[21]   After daylight Lieutenant
Hensley was sent out to make a raid about the suburbs
of the town.   The assailants of the night kept out of
his way, as did most residents, though a few were arrested at their homes; but this raid, together with
Varela's demonstration, had the effect contemplated
by the latter, to transform his movement into a general revolt.   The Californians with few exceptions
were persuaded that war had broken out anew, and
that patriotism required them to take sides against
the foreign invaders.   Varela's force was speedily increased to nearly 300 men, divided in bands of which
his original associates styled themselves captains.   But
the chief places were now assumed by Castro's old
officers.   It is not impossible that some of them may
have had an understanding with Varela and the others
from the first; but there is no proof that such was the
case.   Most of these officers were under parole not
to serve against the Americans; and by their act, according to military law, they disgraced themselves
and forfeited their lives; yet they justified their conduct on the plea that Gillespie by his persecution had
virtually renewed hostilities and released them from
their parole.   Captain José María Flores, one of the
paroled officers, and one who had narrowly escaped
arrest, was chosen to act as comandante general; José
Antonio Carrillo was made second in command, resuming his old rank of *mayor general;* while Captain Andrés Pico, as *comandante de escuadron,* took the third

[21] Gillespie says: 'On the 22d at 3 o'clock in the morning a party of 65
Californians and Sonoreños made an attack upon my small command quartered
in the government house.   We were not wholly unprepared; and with 21
rifles we beat them back without loss to ourselves, killing and wounding three
of their number.   When daylight came Lieut Hensley with a few men took
several prisoners, and drove the Californians from the town.   This party was
merely the nucleus of a revolution commenced and known to Col. Frémont
before he left Los Angeles.   In 24 hours 600 well mounted horsemen, and
(armed?) with escopetas, lances, and one fine brass piece of light artillery, surrounded Los Angeles and summoned me to surrender.   There were three old
honey-combed iron guns (spiked) in the corral of my quarters, which we at
once cleared and mounted upon the axles of carts,' etc. *Sac. Statesman,* May
6, 1858.   It is very improbable, to say the least, that no gun in working order
had been left for Gillespie by Stockton.

place.   It is not to be supposed that the leaders had
any confidence in their ability to defeat the Americans; but they thought the fate of California would
be decided by national treaty, and if it remained a
Mexican territory, their efforts would give them glory,
and influence in the future.   In any event, temporary
prominence and power could be secured, and if the
worst came, they could retreat to Sonora.

The main camp of the rebels, where the final organization was effected, was at the place called Paredon
Blanco, just outside the town.   On September 24th
was issued a proclamation, or plan, which I give below.[22]   It was a document of the stereotyped order,

[22] *Pronunciamiento de Varela y otros Californios contra los Americanos, 24
de Set. 1846*, MS.; English translation in *Soulé's Annals*, 113–14; *Stockton's
Mil. and Naval Operations*, 15–16—the latter, followed by other authorities,
dating it Oct. 1st, from a certified copy issued by Flores on that date.

'Citizens: For a month and a half, by a lamentable fatality resulting from
the cowardice and incompetence of the department's chief authorities, we see
ourselves subjugated and oppressed by an insignificant force of adventurers
from the U. S. of N. America, who, putting us in a condition worse than that
of slaves, are dictating to us despotic and arbitrary laws, by which, loading
us with contributions and onerous taxes, they wish to destroy our industries
and agriculture, and to compel us to abandon our property, to be taken and
divided among themselves.   And shall we be capable of permitting ourselves
to be subjugated, and to accept in silence the heavy chain of slavery?   Shall
we lose the soil inherited from our fathers, which cost them so much blood?
Shall we leave our families victims of the most barbarous servitude?   Shall
we wait to see our wives violated, our innocent children beaten by the American whip, our property sacked, our temples profaned, to drag out a life full
of shame and disgrace?   No!   A thousand times no!   Compatriots, death
rather than that!   Who of you does not feel his heart beat and his blood
boil on contemplating our situation?   Who will be the Mexican that will not
be indignant, and rise in arms to destroy our oppressors?   We believe there
will be not one so vile and cowardly.   Therefore, the majority of the inhabitants of this district, justly indignant at our tyrants, we raise the cry of war,
and with arms in our hands, we swear with one accord to support the following articles: 1. We, all the inhabitants of the department of Cal., as members
of the great Mexican nation, declare that it is and has been our wish to belong to her alone, free and independent.   2. Therefore the intrusive authorities appointed by the invading forces of the U. S. are held as null and void.
3. All North Americans being foes of Mexico, we swear not to lay down our
arms until we see them ejected from Mexican soil.   4. Every Mexican citizen from 15 to 60 years of age who does not take up arms to carry out this
plan is declared a traitor, under penalty of death.   5. Every Mexican or
foreigner who may directly or indirectly aid the foes of Mexico will be punished in the same manner.   6. All property of resident North Americans
who may have directly or indirectly taken part with or aided the enemies of
Mexico will be confiscated and used for the expenses of the war, and their
persons will be sent to the interior of the republic.   7. All who may oppose
the present plan will be punished with arms [put to death].   8. All inhabitants of Sta Bárbara and the northern district will be immediately invited

containing a recital of wrongs in which a meagre substratum of fact was eked out with much that was imaginary; a florid appeal to Mexican patriotism; a threat of vengeance on the oppressors and punishment to all who might either give aid to the foe or fail to support the cause of freedom. It was signed by Varela and more than 300 others; possibly not receiving the signature of General Flores until a day or two later. Meanwhile the garrison was summoned to surrender, and the town was surrounded, and in a sense besieged by the Californians. It does not clearly appear that there was any fighting, though some say that Gillespie's men made several sorties, the well mounted natives keeping beyond the reach of rifle-bullets, and confining their efforts to stampeding the horses, cutting off supplies, completing their own preparations, and annoying the Americans as much as possible.[23] On the 24th, as we have seen, Juan Flaco started with the news of Gillespie's position for Monterey and San Francisco.

The first 'battle' of this rebellion—or the second if we count Varela's demonstration against Gillespie—

to accede to this plan. Camp near Los Angeles, Sept. 24, 1846. Sérbulo Varela [written Barelas], Leonardo Cota [and over 300 others].'

[23] On the events of these and the following days much information is derived from the following works: Coronel, Cosas de Cal., MS., 80–107; Lugo, Vida, MS., 32–67; Rico, Mem., MS., 25–35; Botello, Anales, MS., 142–54; Wilson's Observ., MS., 66–91; Forster's Pioneer Data, MS., 35–43; Vejar, Recuerdos, MS., 44–64; Moreno, Vida, MS., 13–23, 35; White's Cal., MS., 27–35; García, Episodios, MS., 8–18; Castro, Servicios, MS.; Palomares, Mem., MS., 58–76; Janssens, Vida, MS., 189–93; Streeter's Recoll., MS., 63–75. Manuel Castro to Pio Pico, in Doc. Hist. Cal., MS., iii. 292; Foster's Angeles in '47, MS., 21–45; Arnaz, Recuerdos, MS., 55–7, 94–5; Ord, Ocurrencias, MS., 184–5; Vega, Vida, MS., 50–7; Los Angeles Crónica, May 23–6, 1877; Hayes' Scraps, Cal. Notes, iii. 35; Davis' Glimpses, MS., 351–4; Osio, Hist. Cal., MS., 480–5. Most of the writers cited were actors in the events described. Their testimony shows no important discrepancies, except in minute personal details, which cannot be presented in the space at my command. See Mexican accounts in Diccionario Universal, viii. 157–9; Guerra, Apuntes, 355–61; and especially Bustamante, Mem. Hist. Mex., MS., v. 218, 242–3; vi. 41–4. At first Don Cárlos María took great comfort from the news that the Anglo-American garrison of 250 men had been killed á palos in a revolt of the town! 'Leccion terrible para los opresores, y que les bajará un tanto su orgullo'! But his later news, though always exaggerated, was much more accurate. Printed accounts by American writers, as a rule, barely mention the revolt, reserving details so long as reverses continued.

was fought at the Chino rancho of Isaac Williams, about twenty-five miles east of Los Angeles, on September 26th–27th. Benito Wilson had been put by Stockton in command of some twenty foreigners to protect the San Bernardino frontier, both against the Indians and against hostile parties that Castro might send from Sonora, if he had crossed the Colorado at all, which was at first doubted. Wilson went to his own rancho of Jurupa, whence he visited the different rancherías of Indians, satisfied himself that Castro had really departed, and made a hunting tour. On his return to Jurupa he was met by David Alexander and John Rowland, who brought news of the rising in town, and also an invitation for the company to go to Chino. This invitation was accepted the more readily because they had used up nearly all their ammunition in hunting; but on reaching Chino, contrary to their expectations, they found that Williams had no powder. By some it was thought best to leave the rancho for the mountains, whence an attempt might be made to join the garrison in town; but most declared that their ammunition was sufficient for the few shots needed to defeat a Californian foe, and it was decided to withstand a siege. That same afternoon the Californians approached; and Isaac Callaghan, who was sent out to reconnoitre, came back with a bullet in his arm.[24]

Sérbulo Varela, Diego Sepúlveda, and Ramon Carrillo had been despatched from the Paredon Blanco with fifty men or more against Wilson. José del Cármen Lugo, already in command of fifteen or twenty men on the San Bernardino frontier, with instruc-

[24] *Wilson's Observations*, MS., is the most detailed and complete narration of the whole affair, supported in most respects by other authorities. Such support is, however, for the most part wanting to Wilson's charge that Williams was a traitor; that he enticed them to Chino by the statement that he had plenty of ammunition; that, while pretending to send a message from Wilson to Gillespie, he directed the courier, Félix Gallardo, to deliver it to Flores; and in fact, that all his efforts were directed to gaining Flores' good-will by the sacrifice of his countrymen. Michael White, *Cal.*, MS., 27, etc., gives a similar version. Some others state that Williams took no part in the fight, acting in a cowardly manner.

tions to watch the foreigners, also marched to Chino.
Lugo claims to have arrived first, and to have been
joined by Varela late in the night, which was probably true.[25]   The Americans were summoned to surrender, and perhaps a few shots were exchanged that
evening, the 26th, though witnesses do not agree on
that point.   There was but little ammunition on
either side; and the Californians lacked weapons also.
The rancho house was of adobe, surrounding a large
interior court-yard, having but few windows or other
openings in the thick walls, and roofed with asphal-
tum.   The whole was nearly enclosed with a ditch
and adobe fence.   About dawn on the 27th, the Californians, many of them on horseback, made a rush for
the house, the movement being accompanied and followed by a discharge of fire-arms on both sides.   Several horses fell in leaping the ditch or fence, throwing
their riders, two or three of whom were wounded, and
one, Cárlos Ballesteros, killed by a rifle-ball.   Inside
the house three were wounded, Perdue, Skene, and
Harbin, the two first-named somewhat seriously.[26]
There was time but for few shots, for the assailants
reached a position close under the walls of the building, where they could not be seen.   Their next step
was to fire the roof.   The owner of the rancho presented himself with his small children, whose uncles,
the Lugos, were among the assailants, and begged
that their lives might be spared.   Varela appeared at
the main entrance, and called upon the Americans to
surrender, promising them protection as prisoners of
war.   The terms were accepted; Wilson's men gave

[25] *Lugo, Vida de un Ranchero*, MS., 34, etc.   Wilson and Coronel confirm
Lugo's statement to a certain extent.   Francisco Palomares, *Memorias*, MS.,
58, etc., claims to have been second in command.   Rico states, and some
others imply, that Ramon Carrillo was the leader.
[26] Stephen C. Foster, *Angeles '47-9*, MS., 25, etc., gives many particulars
of the fight, and the actions of particular individuals, obtained from men who
took part in the affair, six months later.   He describes the firing to have been
done chiefly after the Californians had reached the house, they creeping along
the walls, and exchanging shots at close range through the port-holes.
Skene was wounded by a young Lugo, whose father later cared for the
wounded man.

themselves up;[27] Varela's force set to work to extinguish the fire and secure the plunder; and soon all were on the road to Los Angeles. Sepúlveda and his men in the advance party, and in charge of most of the prisoners, proposed to shoot the latter in revenge for the death of Ballesteros; but Varela interposed his authority, and by the utmost efforts saved their lives. They were turned over to Flores, and eight or ten of the most prominent at least were kept in captivity until January 1847. The rest were probably exchanged for those whom Gillespie had arrested, though there is no agreement in the testimony on this point.[28]

Gillespie and his men were now posted on Fort Hill, where some guns were mounted. Whether he also still held possession of the old barracks is not clear. His position was becoming critical. The Californians, though poorly provided with arms and ammunition, had plenty of food and horses, were flushed with their

[27] The members of this party so far as known were B. D. Wilson, Isaac Williams, David W. Alexander, John Rowland, Louis Robidoux, Joseph Perdue, Wm Skene, Isaac Callaghan, Evan Callaghan, Michael White, Matt. Harbin, George Walters. Also named on doubtful authority, Dotson, Godey, Warner.

[28] Michael White is positive that it was Carrillo and not Varela who prevented their being killed. Lugo claims to have been chief in command throughout the affair, and to have had charge later of those prisoners who had not been exchanged. Véjar names Gerónimo Ibarra as one of the wounded. He also claims to have had much to do himself with saving the prisoners' lives. Several state that the prisoners were exchanged. Coronel thinks that some of them were released on parole. Foster says much of A. M. Lugo's attentions to the wounded, and of his offer to go bail for all. According to Wilson, they were kept at the camp, at Boyle's Height, in a small adobe house, until Gillespie's departure; then taken into town, where the wounded were treated by Dr Den; and all received much aid and attention from Eulogio Célis, while Stearns and other Americans did not make their appearance. Flores offered to release them on a solemn promise not to bear arms or use their influence in favor of the U. S., which they declined. Then a plan was formed to send them to Mexico, which was prevented by a revolt, of which more anon. They were sent to S. Gabriel for a few days, being practically free, but were brought back to prison. Later they were sent for a time to Temple's rancho of Los Cerritos. This was while Stockton was at S. Pedro. Then they returned to their town prison, but were kindly treated, until Stockton's second entry into Angeles. Willard Buzzell, in a newspaper account found in *Hayes' Scraps, Cal. Notes*, iii. 35, says that 13 of Gillespie's prisoners were exchanged for a like number of the Chino men. Buzzell was with Gillespie, but his narrative is in some respects very inaccurate.

victory at Chino, were bitter against Gillespie on old
scores, besides having the death of Ballesteros—a
young man who was liked and respected by all—to
avenge, and outnumbered the Americans ten to one.
Even if Juan Flaco had succeeded in his mission,
which could not be known, it would be long before relief could be expected.   Meanwhile Flores renewed
his demands for a surrender; and finally offered to
permit the garrison to march unmolested to San Pedro, if they would abandon their post in the city.
Wilson, at Flores' request, made known the proposal
to Gillespie, and with it sent his own advice in favor
of its being accepted, on the ground that the post
could not be held, that there was great danger of all
losing their lives in the impending attack, and that
by holding out, no good, but rather harm, would result
to American residents of the south.   Gillespie accepted the offer; marched out with all the honors of war,
his colors flying and drums beating; arrived at San
Pedro without molestation; and four or five days later
embarked on the merchant ship *Vandalia*, which,
however, did not at once leave the port.   He was accompanied by a few American citizens, and also probably by a dozen of the Chino prisoners, for whom he
had exchanged a like number of Californians under
arrest.   The capitulation was in the last days of September, and the embarkation the 4th of October.[29]
There is a general agreement that Gillespie promised
to deliver his field-pieces at San Pedro, but broke his
promise by leaving them on shore spiked and useless.
The terms of the capitulation, however, if they were
put in writing at all, are not extant.[30]

[29] Gillespie says he marched to S. Pedro on Sept. 29th; Wilson thinks it
was on the 28th; and several Californians make it the 30th.   I find no document to settle it.

[30] In addition to the Californians, Bidwell, Buzzell, and other Americans
confirm the spiking of the guns.   Gillespie himself implies that by the treaty
he was to remain on shore at S. Pedro; but says that, 'Flores having broken
the treaty by stopping my supply of water, I safely embarked my party on
board the *Vandalia*, which I had detained to cover my retreat.'   It is unlikely that Flores permitted the Americans to remain at S. Pedro.   Possibly

The garrison of Los Angeles being thus disposed of, there remained the posts of Santa Bárbara and San Diego to be reoccupied by the Californians. Manuel Garfias was despatched to Santa Bárbara with a small force, to be increased by enlistments in that region. It was not doubted that Talbot and his nine men[31] would be willing to depart on the same terms as Gillespie; but Garfias carried a demand for surrender on parole. He sent the demand on arrival, the messenger being accompanied by a small guard, and two hours were allowed for decision. The date is not exactly known, perhaps the 1st or 2d of October,[32] and it was nearly dark. Residents of the place had warned the garrison in advance, and now advised a surrender; but Talbot and his men decided to run away, and thus avoid the necessity of a parole. They started at once, met with no opposition from the guard,[33] and gained the mountains. They were experienced mountaineers, though few were over twenty years of age. They remained a week in sight of the town, thinking that a man-of-war might appear to retake the post. Their presence was revealed to

Gillespie had agreed to embark at once, but delaying on one pretext or another, had his water supply cut off to hasten his movements, seizing upon this act as an excuse for spiking the guns. Rico claims to have been sent to S. Pedro with a message to Gillespie that if he did not embark at once as he had promised he would be attacked.

[31] They were Theodore Talbot, Thomas E. Breckenridge, Eugene Russell, Charles Scriver, John Stevens, Joseph Moulton, Francis Briggs, Durand, William, a Chinook Indian, and Manuel, a New Mexican. Testimony of Russell and Breckenridge in *Frémont's Cal. Claims*, 52-4.

[32] Russell and Breckenridge speak of having been 34 days on the journey from Sta Bárbara to Monterey. This would make the date of starting Sept. 27th or Oct. 4th, according as we include or not the 8 days spent at the mountain camp in sight of Sta Bárbara.

[33] Phelps, *Fore and Aft*, 313-14, tells how they marched out, one of their number sick. They formed in line, their backs against the wall, and told the foe they were ready, daring them to advance, calling them cowards, 'laughing them to scorn,' etc. Finding they would not fight, Talbot marched off in a hollow square, followed by the 'cabaleros,' who reviled the brave squad but dared not attack them! All this is purely imaginary. A letter of Nov. 15th to the *Boston Traveller*, reprinted in *Niles' Reg.*, lxxii. 81, gives an account similar to that of Phelps. Evidently some of Talbot's men on arrival at Monterey indulged in the trappers' propensity for story-telling. Streeter, *Recoll.*, MS., 55-63, says that all the men but one, Russell, favored surrender at first; but as he declared his purpose to escape, the rest concluded to go with him.

Californians by their attempts to obtain cattle and sheep at night; and then some efforts were made to hasten their movements. A party sent out for this purpose once came so near the American camp that a horse was killed by a rifle-ball; American residents, apparently Robbins and Hill, were sent with new demands for surrender; and finally, just after Talbot's men had left their camp, fire was set to the mountain chaparral, with a view to drive them out. They crossed the mountains, receiving aid and guidance from a Spanish ranchero, reached the Tulares, and proceeded to Monterey, where they arrived November 8th, having suffered many hardships on the long journey.[34] After Talbot's flight, American residents of the Santa Bárbara region were arrested, most being paroled, and a few apparently sent to Los Angeles as prisoners. A small garrison was left at the town, and another at San Buenaventura; all under the command of Lieutenant-colonel Gumesindo Flores; while 40 or 50 men were recruited for Flores' army.[35]

At San Diego, as we have seen, no garrison had been left at first; but about September 15th, at the request of Fitch, who reported symptoms of disorder, Ezekiel Merritt was sent with a dozen men by Gillespie to protect the place.[36] Immediately after Gillespie's retreat, and at the same time that Garfias was sent to Santa Bárbara, Francisco Rico marched for San Diego with fifty men. At his approach Bidwell

[34] Arrival at Monterey noted in *Monterey Californian*, Nov. 14th. Lancey, *Cruise*, 130-1, quotes Talbot, source not mentioned: 'I suffered more from downright starvation, cold, nakedness, and every sort of privation, than in any other trip I have yet made, and I have had some rough ones.' Most of the authorities I have cited on the Flores revolt also mention briefly Talbot's retreat.

[35] Nidever, *Life and Adven.*, MS., 116-27, and Dittmann, *Narrative*, MS., 37-9, arrived at Sta Bárbara with Wm Fife from a hunting tour just after Talbot's departure. They were arrested, but Fife and Dittmann, not being Americans, were released. Nidever was sent to Angeles, but ran away and kept hid until Frémont came south. He gives many details of his personal adventures in the mean time, all strictly true, as it is to be hoped.

[36] Sept. 13th, Gillespie to Fitch, who was to furnish provisions. *Fitch, Doc.*, MS., 400. Sept. 15th, Id. to Id., and Bidwell to Fitch. *Id.*, 401-2. Merritt's party was expected on the 16th.

left San Luis Rey and joined Merritt's party. They
were also joined by a few native citizens, and all went
on board the *Stonington*, a whaler lying at anchor in
the bay, taking with them some cannon dug up at
the old fort. Rico, however, did not reach San Diego, being recalled in great haste from Santa Margarita; but it appears that a few mounted Californians
of the district appeared on the hills from time to time,
with sufficient demonstrations of hostility to keep the
Americans on board their vessel for about twenty
days.[37]

Nearly all the male inhabitants of southern California were now, in a certain sense, engaged as soldiers in the revolt; but less than 200 were kept
actually in service, the rest being warned to hold
themselves in readiness for the time of need. In fact,
200 men, or half that number, were more than could
be armed and equipped. The country was ransacked
for old muskets, pistols, and lances, with indifferent
success. An old four-pounder, that had formerly
served on festive occasions for the firing of salutes,
was dug up from the garden of Inocencia Reyes,
where it had been buried on Stockton's first approach; and this was mounted on a pair of wagon-
wheels by an English carpenter. Powder was still
more scarce than weapons; only enough for a few
charges of the *pedrero* could be procured; and to supply the want a quantity of very inferior quality was
manufactured at San Gabriel. News soon came that
the Americans had landed at San Pedro; and José
Antonio Carrillo was despatched in haste with fifty
horsemen to reconnoitre and harass the foe; while
Flores was to follow with the gun. Captain Mervine, having left San Francisco on the *Savannah* October 4th, reached San Pedro on the 6th, and immediately landed about 350 men, who were joined by

Gillespie's men from the *Vandalia*.   On the 7th they
began their march to Los Angeles.   They took no
cannon from the ship; and they could find no horses;
but they remembered Stockton's former march, and
had no doubt the Californians would run at their approach.   In the afternoon they began to see mounted
men of Carrillo's advance guard, with whom a few
shots were exchanged, one of the Californians being
slightly wounded.   At night the Americans occupied
the buildings of the Dominguez rancho; and before
midnight Flores joined Carrillo with sixty men, bringing also the field-piece.   There was more or less firing
during the night, with no other effect than that of
keeping Mervine's party on the alert.   Early the next
morning, October 8th, Flores retired with twenty men,
leaving orders to risk no general engagement, but to
harass and delay the foe as much as possible.   Soon
the Americans advanced, the marines and seamen
forming a solid square in the centre, while Gillespie's
party acted as skirmishers on the right and left.   Carrillo also divided his force into three bodies, about
forty on each flank, and ten with the gun in the centre.   When Mervine came near, the gun was fired by
Ignacio Aguilar, and was immediately dragged away
by reatas attached to the horsemen's saddles, to be reloaded at a safe distance.   This operation was repeated some half a dozen times in less than an hour.
The first discharges did no harm, since the home-made
powder was used; but at last the gun was properly
loaded, and the solid column affording an excellent
target, each shot was effective.   Six were killed and
as many wounded, if indeed the loss of the Americans was not still greater.[38]   No one was hurt on the

[38] 'Four killed and several wounded,' or 'several men killed and wounded,'
is all that Stockton says.   *Report*, 42; *Mil. and Nav. Op.*, 10.   No official
report by Mervine is extant, so far as I know.   Six killed and 6 wounded
is the statement in *Cutts' Conq.*, 127–8, and most often repeated.   Gillespie,
Sacramento Statesman, May 6, 1858, says that Mervine lost 13.   Several Californians state that 12 or 13 were killed, basing their statement on the account of the man employed to move the remains.   Carrillo, in his official report, gave 7 as the number of slain.   Flores, in his report, says they were 12.
Phelps says 7 or 8.

Californian side. The sailors advanced bravely, but in this peculiar warfare bravery was of no avail. Mervine soon perceived that the pursuit of flying artillery and cavalry by marines on foot could only result in useless slaughter; he had no means of knowing, what was indeed true, that the enemy had burned all their effective powder, and could no longer oppose his advance; and he accordingly retreated to San Pedro and reëmbarked. The dead and wounded were carried by their companions; and the former were buried on the little island before and since known as Isla de los Muertos. The Californians claim that Mervine left behind him a quantity of useful articles, including a flag.[39]

During the rest of October a large part of the Californian army, or about one hundred men, was kept between Angeles and San Pedro, the chief encampment being at Temple's rancho of Los Cerritos, and a small detachment being stationed at Sepúlveda's rancho of Palos Verdes, near the anchorage. The men had nothing to do but to watch the *Savannah;* and the leaders were able to devote their attention to perfecting the machinery of their new government, and to the more difficult task of obtaining resources for future warfare. Archives of the Flores régime have for the most part disappeared; but enough remain in my collection from private sources to show the purport of the general's measures.[40] The plan

[39] *Carrillo, Accion de San Pedro contra los Americanos, 8 de Oct. 1846,* MS. The original official report, dated at S. Pedro Oct. 8th; also printed in *El Sonorense,* Jan. 8, 1847. Flores' congratulatory proclamation announcing the victory is in *Janssens, Doc.*, MS., 19–20. There is a general agreement among the different authorities on the general features of this battle, though there is naturally much exaggeration of the forces engaged on the opposite side, especially by American writers. A newspaper item relates that Mervine, before starting on his march, made a speech to his men, alluding, among other things, to the grapes they would find at Los Angeles. This remark was afterward connected by the men with the 'grape' fired from the cannon; and 'Capt. Mervine's grapes, vintage of 1846,' became a current joke.

[40] Agustin Janssens was justice of the peace at Sta Inés, and was made a kind of military commandant in that region; and among his papers are found many of Flores' orders not elsewhere extant. Oct. 9th, Flores' general instructions for Sta Inés district. Keep the largest possible force in arms, with spies on the Monterey road to look out for Frémont, and also toward Sta

was to wage a guerrilla warfare, and thus prevent the naval forces from penetrating again into the interior, leaving the ownership of California to be settled between the national governments. Manuel Castro was sent as commander-in-chief of operations in the north, with Rico as his second in command, and San Luis Obispo as his headquarters. His achievements will be noticed later.

The departmental assembly was reorganized October 26th, being summoned by Flores to resume the functions interrupted by the temporary occupation of the capital by the forces of the United States. The members present were Figueroa, Botello, Guerra, and Olvera; Joaquin Carrillo, a vocal suplente, was sworn in and took his seat. Figueroa acted as president, and Olvera was made secretary. The president in an introductory discourse congratulated the country on the success that was attending the Cali-

Bárbara in case of a landing there. Keep up communication with Sta Bárbara and San Luis Obispo; aid them, and cut off supplies from the foe in case of attack. If the enemy advances on Angeles, harass them with guerrillas in the rear. Scrutinize the passes of all travellers, and arrest all suspicious persons, sending foreigners to headquarters. If attacked by superior forces, fall back on Angeles. *Janssens, Doc.*, MS., 17-19. Oct. 12th, Gumesindo Flores' comandante from S. Luis to S. Buenaventura, the 8th company, is glad Janssens is serving with such zeal. The people are immortalizing themselves. The foreigners here (Sta Bárbara) are rendering good service. Johnson has offered his guns, which go to the pueblo to-day. Make a list of persons who will not aid. Keep a copy of the instructions, and send the original to Monterey. *Id.*, 21-3. Oct. 17th, Flores' general order. One of the best methods of harming the foe being to deprive him of supplies; any one aiding the enemy in any way will be punished as an enemy; rancheros must at once remove their live-stock from the coast beyond the reach of the naval forces; whoever refuses is a traitor. *Id.*, 23-5. Oct. 18th, Capt. J. J. Pico at San Luis Obispo orders Miguel Ávila to deliver certain property, left with him by Dana and Howard, to José García and his men. *Ávila, Doc.*, MS., 21-2. Oct. 20th, Gumesindo Flores to Janssens. A private letter, with miscellaneous gossip about public affairs. All quiet at S. Pedro; a force gone to S. Diego; Frémont's men leaving him because they are not paid; 'Vallejo said to be a general of the Americanos'! *Janssens, Doc.*, MS., 26-7. Oct. 23d, Gen. Flores appoints Manuel Castro comandante of brigade for operations in the north, with Francisco Rico as second in command. *Castro, Doc.*, MS., ii. 147. Oct. 25th, Janssens' circular calling for contributions for defence, since 10 Americans are said to be seducing the Indians in the Tulares to attack the rancheros. Eleven names of contributors, including Wm G. Dana. *Id.*, 28-9. Oct. 26th, Flores decrees any person deserting or leaving military service, or found one league from camp without permit, to be court-martialled and put to death; every traveller without a passport to be arrested. *Id.*, 30-1; *Doc. Hist. Cal.*, MS., iii. 265.

fornian cause, and recommended the choice of a governor and general to fill the places made vacant by the flight of Pico and Castro. It was decided to unite the two commands in one person; and José María Flores, already acting as commander-in-chief, was elected to hold both offices ad interim, until successors should be appointed by the supreme government, or assume the offices by due form of law after the restoration of peace. In the decree announcing this action the country was declared in a state of siege, and martial law in full force. Botello and Guerra were named as a committee to report on ways and means for prosecuting the war. Their report, presented next day, approved in the session of the 30th, and issued as a decree by Flores on the 31st, was in favor of annulling Pico's sales of mission estates, and of hypothecating one or more of those estates as security for a loan of such sums as public necessity might require. Before the assembly Flores took the oath of office, listening and replying on that occasion to a speech of President Figueroa. Neither discourse contained any feature calling for special comment, one being merely an expression of the country's confidence in the new ruler, and the other the usual protestation of unworthiness, coupled with patriotic zeal. The date of the oath is not very clear. In his communications to foreign consuls, Flores makes the date November 1st, but he had already issued, October 31st, the decree mentioned above, and another making Narcisco Botello his secretary.[41]

Meanwhile Stockton, having left Monterey October 19th, arrived at San Pedro with the *Congress* on

[41] Oct. 26th–30th, record of assembly proceedings, in *Olvera, Doc.*, MS., 49. Oct. 26th, decree of assembly electing Flores. *Castro, Doc.*, MS., ii. 150. Oct. 30th, Flores to Carrillo, ordering the publication of the decree of Oct. 26th. *Carrillo (D.), Doc.*, MS., 94. Oct. 31st, Flores' decree naming Botello as secretario del despacho. *Doc. Hist. Cal.*, MS., iii. 267–8. Nov. 1st, Flores to Forbes and Lataillade, announcing that 'to-day' he has taken the oath. *Id.*, 269, 271. Oct. 30th, decree of assembly on missions. *Unb. Doc.*, MS., 360–1. *Janssens, Doc*, MS., 33–5. Oct. 31st, Flores' decree promulgating the preceding. *Soberanes, Doc.*, MS., 326; *Castro, Doc.*, MS., ii. 153.

the 23d, and learned from Mervine the facts of his late disaster. "Elated by this transient success, which the enemy with his usual want of veracity magnified into a great victory, they collected in large bodies on all the adjacent hills, and would not permit a hoof except their own horses to be within fifty miles of San Pedro. I had, however, agreed to land here, to be in readiness to coöperate with the forces under Major Frémont, expected from Santa Bárbara; and therefore determined to do so in the face of their boasting insolence, and there again to hoist the glorious stars in the presence of their horse-covered hills. On our approach to the shore the enemy fired a few muskets without harm, and fled; we took possession, and once more hoisted our flag at San Pedro. The troops remained encamped at that place for several days before the insurgents who covered the adjacent hills, and until both officers and men had become almost worn out by chasing and skirmishing with and watching them, and until I had given up all hope of the coöperation of Major Frémont. Besides, the enemy had driven off every animal, man, and beast, from that section of the country; and it was not possible by any means in our power to carry provisions for our march to the city...The insurgent force in the vicinity was supposed to number about 800 men. The roadstead of San Pedro was also a dangerous position for men-of-war;"[42] and therefore the commodore de-

[42] *Stockton's Report*, 42; *Id., Mil. and Naval Operations*, 11, 16-17, with orders of Oct. 26th for landing, and of the 28th thanking the men for their gallantry. Gillespie with 50 men was to land first, but failed to do so, 'in consequence of a fancied force of the enemy. Not so with the sailors and marines,' who landed in a most gallant manner. Several Californians relate that a letter containing scurrilous nonsense was sent to Stockton's camp by being tied to a dog. All seem to regard this a very funny occurrence; therefore I note it. On Nov. 9th Larkin writes to his wife: 'There is a report here among the natives that two or three miles from S. Pedro the commodore formed his men thus , with the cannon behind them; then sending ahead 100 men, who on meeting the Californians retreated on the main body, losing a few seamen, when the main body opened and gave fire, which killed and wounded about 100 people, many being also taken prisoners. The report appears consistent, and is believed here. If it is true, I hope the Californians are satisfied.' *Larkin's Doc.*, MS., iv. 320.

cided to attack Los Angeles by way of San Diego.
His landing was on October 27th; and his departure
for the south in the first days of November. He had
about 800 men, and with a few light guns might
easily have retaken Los Angeles; but he had evidently
modified his oft-expressed opinions of Californian valor,
and had become somewhat cautious. Of the 800 attributed to the enemy, 700 at least existed only in
the American imagination; for Carrillo had adopted,
as all the native writers agree, the tactics which some
have accredited to Stockton on a former occasion at the
same place—that of displaying his men on the march
among the hills in such a way that each man was several times counted. He also caused large droves of
riderless horses to raise clouds of dust in the distance.
His success in frightening Stockton away was beyond
his expectations, and possibly his hopes; for there is
some reason to suppose that Flores had founded on
the present display and past successes a hope that the
American commander might be induced to consent to
a truce, by the terms of which he would hold the
ports and leave the Californians in possession of the
interior until the national quarrel should be settled.[43]

At San Diego we left the American garrison on
board the *Stonington.* Bidwell went in a boat with
four men up to San Pedro to obtain supplies. He arrived apparently during Mervine's absence on October
7th–8th, and started back at once; but a gale arose,
and the trip was a long and perilous one. As soon as
Mervine returned to his ship and heard the news, he
seems to have sent Lieutenant Minor with a small
party down to reënforce Merritt; and on his arrival

---

[43] B. D. Wilson, *Observations,* MS., 85–8, states that such a plan was made
known to him by J. A. Carrillo; and that as a prisoner he was sent with a
sergeant to an elevated spot near the S. Pedro landing, with instructions on
a given signal to raise a white flag and to communicate to Stockton the proposition for a truce, He saw Carrillo's parade of horses, etc.; and he also saw
the ship's boats full of men approach the shore; but he says they did not land.
He is very positive that Stockton landed no men; but either his memory is
at fault, or the period of his watch was when Gillespie's men failed to land,
as already recorded.

the united forces—or possibly Merritt's men and the whalers before his arrival—landed and again occupied San Diego. The exact date is not known, and our information respecting these events is extremely meagre. Meanwhile, Sérbulo Varela had been sent down from Angeles with a force to operate on the southern frontier. It does not clearly appear whether or not he was in command when the place was retaken, or that any hostilities occurred; but many of his men were unmanageable, and the force gradually dissolved; and on October 26th, after the Americans were again in possession, Captain Leonardo Cota and Ramon Carrillo were sent to replace Varela, and to press the siege. Their tactics here as elsewhere consisted in driving off live-stock and harassing the foe. They were instructed to make no attack, but to keep a close watch on the Americans, report their strength and movements, and cut off their supplies. At the same time they were to see to it that no San Diegan shirked his part of the country's defence, acting to that end in accord with Alcalde Marron.[44]

[44] *Bidwell's Cal. in 1841-8*, MS., 188–98; *Lancey's Cruise*, 135; Stockton's reports, naming Minor as in command at S. Diego. Oct. 26th, Flores' order recalling Varela, and his instructions to Cota and Carrillo. *Olvera, Doc.*, MS., 52–4. Bidwell says he fired at by the natives at S. Juan Capistrano on his way up the coast; that on his return he had thrown overboard, among other things, a keg with a bottle and message, which he had prepared to leave at S. Pedro if no vessels had been found, the Indian finder of which was shot by Flores as a spy; and that immediately on his return Merritt's men and the whalers landed their cannon and retook the town, not without resistance by the foe, at whom the two cannon were fired alternately every 100 yards. Soon Pedrorena went up to S. Pedro for aid, and brought back Gillespie (Minor?) with a part of his force in the *Magnolia*. About this time the Californians attacked the post with a cannon from the hill; but the garrison made a sally, captured the gun, and with it killed one of the enemy's horses. It is possible that Bidwell's version is correct, and that the town was retaken by the original garrison before Minor's arrival.

CHAPTER XIII.

THE CONQUEST—THE FLORES REVOLUTION—FIGHT AT
SAN FASCUAL.

NOVEMBER–DECEMBER, 1846.

STOCKTON AT SAN DIEGO—PETTY HOSTILITIES—PREPARATIONS INTERRUPTED
—U. S. TROOPS COMING FROM THE EAST—AFFAIRS AT ANGELES—ORDERS
AND CORRESPONDENCE—REVOLT AGAINST THE GOVERNOR—CORONEL'S AD-
VENTURES—THE DALTON FINANCIAL SCHEME—THE CHINO PRISONERS—
FLORES IMPRISONED AND RELEASED—ALARMING NEWS—KEARNY'S IN-
STRUCTIONS—HIS MARCH FROM NEW MEXICO—MEETING KIT CARSON—
CAPTURE OF HORSES AND A COURIER ON THE COLORADO—ACROSS THE
DESERT TO WARNER'S AND SANTA MARÍA—REËNFORCED BY GILLESPIE—
FIGHT AT SAN PASCUAL—DEFEAT OF KEARNY BY THE CALIFORNIANS UN-
DER PICO—THIRTY-SEVEN MEN KILLED AND WOUNDED—IN CAMP AT
SAN BERNARDO—REËNFORCEMENTS UNDER GRAY—MARCH TO SAN DI-
EGO—STOCKTON AND KEARNY MARCH ON ANGELES.

EARLY in November 1846 Commodore Stockton,
leaving the *Savannah* at San Pedro, went down to San
Diego with the *Congress*. His plan was to obtain
horses and supplies, and to advance on Los Angeles.
Immediately after his arrival he received by the *Malek
Adhel* despatches from Frémont, explaining that officer's turning-back, and his project of making an overland expedition to the south. Of events at San Diego
for a month after the commodore's arrival, we have
but little information beyond what is contained in his
brief reports—in substance as follows: He found the
town in a state of siege, Lieutenant Minor being in
great need of reënforcements and supplies. The frigate struck in attempting to cross the bar, and was
forced to return to the anchorage outside. Arrangements were made to send a party under Captain Gib-

son of the battalion in the *Stonington* down the coast
to Ensenada after horses and cattle; Mervine was
sent with the *Savannah* to Monterey to aid Frémont
in his preparations; and Stockton, having made a trip
to San Pedro for that purpose, returned to San Diego.
The ship being becalmed on the way, Lieutenant
Tilghman was sent in a boat to urge Minor to hasten
his preparations for the march northward. This time
the *Congress* was brought successfully into the bay
though not without having once dangerously grounded.
"The situation of the place was found to be most miserable and deplorable. The male inhabitants had
abandoned the town, leaving their women and children dependent upon us for protection and food. No
horses could be obtained to assist in the transportation of the guns and ammunition, and not a beef could
be had to supply the necessary food," though, as the
writer somewhat contradictorily adds, Gibson had returned, "driving about 90 horses and 200 head of
beef cattle into the garrison." Meanwhile the Californians held the region roundabout the town. Stockton says: "On the afternoon of our arrival the enemy,
irritated I suppose by the loss of his animals, came
down in considerable force and made an attack; they
were, however, soon driven back with the loss of two
men and horses killed, and four wounded. These skir-
mishes, or running fights, are of almost daily occurrence; since we have been here, we have lost as yet
but one man killed and one wounded." Thus reported
the commodore on November 23d, the only definite
date we have for these events.[1] That there were,
however, any hostilities involving loss of life, I think
there is room for doubt.

More horses were required; and those already obtained needed rest. "During the time required for
resting the horses," writes the commodore, "we were

[1] Nov. 23, 1846, Stockton to Sec. Bancroft, in *Stockton's Mil. and Naval
Oper.*, 11–12. Also to same purport, except as to the killing of three men, in
Id., Report of Feb. 18, 1847, p. 43–4, which is the chief authority for the events
immediately following.

actively employed in the construction of a fort for the more complete protection of the town, mounting guns, and in making the necessary harness, saddles, and bridles.   While the work of preparation necessary for our march was thus going on, we sent an Indian to ascertain where the principal force of the insurgents was encamped.   He returned with information that a body of them, about 50 strong, was encamped at San Bernardo, about 30 miles from San Diego.   Captain Gillespie [2] was immediately ordered to have as many men as he could mount, with a piece of artillery, ready to march for the purpose of surprising the insurgents in their camp.   Another expedition, under command of Captain Hensley[3] of the battalion, was sent to the southward for animals, who, after performing the most arduous service, returned with 500 head of cattle and 140 horses and mules.   About December 3d two deserters, whose families lived in San Diego, came into the place and reported themselves to Lieutenant Minor, the commander of the troops. On receiving information of the fact I repaired to his quarters with my aide-de-camp, Lieut Gray, for the purpose of examining one of these men.   While engaged in this examination, a messenger arrived with a letter from Gen. Kearny of the U. S. army, apprising me of his approach, and expressing a wish that I

[2] Nov. 29th, Gillespie writes to Larkin: 'In consequence of the great want of animals, every horse being driven away, Com. Stockton has landed here with all his force, and intends to maintain this position until we catch horses, and then proceed upon the march to the pueblo.   We hear nothing from Maj. Frémont, but suppose that he must be near the pueblo.   Some few of the enemy show themselves now and then upon the hills opposite to us, beyond the reach of our guns.   We muster now on shore 450 men, and altogether have a fine camp.   The *Congress* is safely moored within pistol-shot of the hide-houses, where she will no doubt lie until the winter is passed.' *Larkin's Doc.*, MS., iv. 334.

[3] 'In November 1846 I was directed by Com. Stockton to go into lower California and get horses, mules, cattle, saddles, and saddle-rigging.   I was directed to proceed by sea, and accordingly went on board the *Stonington*, and disembarked at San Domingo.   In landing we swamped two boats, with the loss of seven or eight rifles, several pistols, blankets, and many articles of clothing.   We succeeded in getting 140 head of horses and mules, and about 300 head of cattle, some saddles and saddle-rigging.   The cattle belonged to Juan Bandini, who was in S. Diego at the time.' Hensley's testimony in *Frémont's Cal. Claims*, 35.   Hensley did not return until about Dec. 20th.

would open a communication with him and inform
him of the state of affairs in California. Capt. Gillespie was immediately ordered to proceed to Gen.
Kearny's camp with the force which he had been directed to have in readiness. He left San Diego at
about half-past seven o'clock the same evening, taking
with him one of the deserters to act as a guide in
conducting Gen. Kearny to the camp of the insurgents."[4]

At Angeles Flores continued to issue as before his
routine orders to subordinates, few of which require
any special notice. It is to be noted, however, that
many of them relate to affairs in the direction of San
Diego, and naturally, since there was the camp of the
enemy. From these documents it appears that a
party of Americans from San Diego may have undertaken an expedition into the interior not mentioned
in Stockton's reports. At any rate, on November 22d

---

[4] *Stockton's Report*, 44–5. Judge Hayes, *Emig. Notes.*, 364–6; *Miscel.*, 41–
2, gives some details of these times gleaned from conversations with the old
Californians, as follows: Bandini, Argüello, Pedrorena, and others were very
friendly to the Americans. J. A. Estudillo was neutral, like Abel Stearns,
who went at first across the frontier, and later to the Cajon rancho. Bandini
entertained sumptuously. Some of the force were quartered at the house of
Doña María Ibañez and part at the Argüello house. Women and children
were gathered within the strong walls of the Estudillo house. The Californians held the fortified Stockton hill (?) so near that Juan Rocha could be
heard shouting to his aunt for *ropa* and *chocolate*. J. M. Orozco amused himself by firing at A. B. Smith when he climbed the flag-staff to fix the flag;
and also at Pedrorena, who was escorting a young lady—merely to scare him.
One day a party came down and drove off some cattle from the flat near the
Argüello house. Then on the 8th day of the siege, Capt. Argüello with a
company ascended the hill, and though wounded in the leg, drove the Californians, under Hermosillo, from their position. They made a new stand behind the ruins of the old presidio walls, but soon retreated toward the mission.
Capt. Pedrorena went in pursuit, and about a mile up the valley met and
exchanged some shots with the advanced guard under Leandro Osuna.
Farther on, an American going to water his mule in a cañada was killed.
Pedrorena was again successful in a charge on the foe at the old mission,
where Ramon Carrillo (?) and others were taken prisoners. From this time
many, disgusted with Hermosillo's conduct in these affairs, began to come in
and give themselves up. Dances and festivities followed. The grand music
of Stockton's naval band is still spoken of by the natives. At one of the
jollifications came the news of Kearny's approach. Marron, *Papeles*, MS.,
14–19, gives some similar reminiscences. Her husband had been forced into
the Californian ranks, escaped, and was retaken and lost nearly all his property.

Andrés Pico was ordered in all haste to proceed with a hundred men to San Luis to cut off the retreat of a body of the enemy which Flores understood to have started for Santa Isabel.   Captain Cota at the same time was instructed to coöperate with Pico; and the hope was expressed that the Americans might be caught between the two forces and destroyed.   Two days later it was learned that the enemy had gone back to San Diego; but still Don Andrés was ordered to make a reconnoissance in the region of the San José Valley; and he seems to have remained in the south, where we shall presently hear from him.   Flores himself a little earlier had announced his intention to march with 200 men to San Diego as soon as a quantity of powder could be manufactured.   He also made an effort to win back the support of Juan Bandini for the Californian cause, but without success.[5]

[5] Nov. 5th, Flores' procl. The country having been declared in a state of siege, all citizens from 15 to 60 years of age must appear to take up arms at the first alarm.   The signal, a cannon-shot, general alarm, and ringing of bells. Those who fail to respond will be put to death as traitors. *Janssens, Doc.*, MS., 35–7; *Olvera, Doc.*, 54–6. Nov. 6th, Flores to com. at Sta Inés.   Robbins, A. B. Thompson, Daniel Hill, and Robert Cruell to remain at Sta Inés till further orders; but may go to Sta Bárbara on business. *Janssens, Doc.*, MS., 37–8. Nov. 6th, Capt. G. Flores to Janssens.   Thinks the latter unfortunate in being appointed military commandant.   'A Mexican is *mal visto*, even if he perform miracles.' *Id.*, 54.   No powder, and not a dollar to buy any. *Id.*, 55.   Nov. 8th, Flores to —— (Antonio Rodriguez?), ordering him to raise and command a 9th company at Sta Bárbara. *Id.*, 38–40. Nov. 12th, 13th, Flores to Cota.   Will soon march to S. Diego.   Understands the difficulty of approaching that place; but you can cut off the enemy's supplies and communications, and shoot every Indian found in his service.   Must report if the enemy had been reënforced by a ship that passed S. Pedro on the 8th. *Olvera, Doc.*, MS., 57–9. Nov. 12th, Flores to Bandini, urging him to support the Californian cause, and assuring him that he shall not be molested in any way for the past.   He calls Don Juan 'Uncle.' *Bandini, Doc.*, MS., 99. Same date, Flores to Cota.   Official letter enclosing one for Bandini; and private letter, in which he says: 'I flatter him a little to see if we cannot turn an enemy into a friend, for our circumstances do not allow us to commit imprudent acts at present.   This man is the one most to be feared now, and it is necessary not to vex him.   You may write to him and try to raise his spirit and fill him with confidence, and see what may be got out of him, especially arms and ammunition.' *Olvera, Doc.*, MS., 58–60.   Nov. 19th, Flores to Janssens.   You may impose a contribution of cattle and grain to support your detachment, not to exceed 15 men. *Janssens, Doc.*, MS., 40–1.   Nov. 22d, Flores to Andrés Pico and to Cota.   Instructions for campaign, as in my text. *Pico, Doc.*, MS., ii. 101–3; *Olvera, Doc.*, MS., 63–7.   Nov. 24th, Flores to Pico. *Pico, Doc.*, MS., ii. 105.   Nov. 30th, Raimundo Carrillo, comandante at Sta Bárbara, orders Janssens to go to S. Luis Obispo and learn what force was there, if proper precautions were taken, and if there was any news of Frémont's movements. *Janssens, Doc.*, MS., 56–7.

Flores was an intelligent and well educated man, who, as far as can be known, had not intrigued for his position, and under difficult circumstances had performed its duties with entire good faith toward the Californians and with fair ability and success. He was, however, a Mexican *de la otra banda;* there were many who thought a native Californian should be at the head of affairs; and the success of the new government was sufficient to inspire jealousies. It is believed, though evidence on this point is not very plentiful or definite, that José Antonio Carrillo, next to Flores in military command, was the officer who chiefly but secretly instigated opposition to the governor. During the San Pedro campaign there are related a few instances of insubordination on the part of Ramon Carrillo and others; about San Diego there had been bickerings between Californian and Mexican officials, resulting in much demoralization of the troops; Joaquin de la Torre was accredited with having used his influence against Flores among northern officers and men; and Manuel Cantua had been put in prison for disobedience of orders and wholesale plundering of ranchos. But the general, declaring that he had not sought the command, that he was willing to resign it, and that success was difficult enough even if all would unite their efforts, declined to engage in any quarrel.[6]

At last for a brief period there was open revolt against Flores' authority. The immediate cause or pretext was his proposed action in the matter of obtaining resources for the war, and disposition of the Chino prisoners. Naturally, as there were no public funds whatever, the task of clothing and supporting the soldiers in actual service was a difficult one. Antonio F. Coronel was despatched to Mexico via Sonora as a commissioner to solicit aid from the national government, taking with him the American

[6] Flores' views are indicated in several communications, especially in those of Nov. 1st, 2d, to Manuel Castro, in *Doc. Hist. Cal.*, MS., iii. 270, 272-3.

flag captured at San Pedro, and also a band of horses and mules. Before he started a party of Sonorans had set out with a much larger band of animals that had perhaps been stolen. At Warner's rancho Don Antonio heard of a party of Americans who had left San Diego to capture his horses; and it was probably his report that caused Andrés Pico to be sent to that region, as already related. On approaching the Colorado crossing, Coronel heard of an American force coming from the east, and also of the horse-thieves encamped in that region; which caused him to turn back, after sending Felipe Castillo to Sonora with his despatches; and he returned to Aguanga, near Temécula, to await further developments. Here he was surprised on December 3d, escaping capture, but losing his animals.[7] Meanwhile Flores devised another scheme for obtaining supplies. Henry Dalton, an English merchant of Los Angeles, who had married a sister of Flores' wife, had a quantity of needed articles in stock, which he was willing to deliver in exchange for drafts on Mexico—of course at a good round price, as is customary in such contracts the world over, and as was justifiable enough in this instance, since Dalton assumed a great risk of losing the whole amount of the investment. In order to promote the payment of the drafts by exaggerating the achievements of the Californians, and at the same time to enhance the general's personal glory, it was proposed to send the Chino prisoners to Mexico. These prisoners were, however, men of considerable influence, several of them being married to natives. Through their friends, prominent among whom were William Workman and Ignacio Palomares, they made every effort to save themselves. Of course they took

[7] *Coronel, Cosas de Cal.*, MS., 104, etc. At the time of his surprise he had come down from his hiding-place in the sierra to meet couriers who failed to appear, and was drying his clothing in a house where he had eaten supper. Barefoot, and clad only in shirt and drawers, he escaped by climbing a tree; and wandered for a long time in the mountains before he could obtain a horse. Popular tradition has given another explanation of his *déshabillé*, much more romantic, but probably less accurate than that given by himself.

advantage of the current prejudice of the Californian officers against Flores. Francisco Rico, lately returned from the north, became the nominal leader of the malecontents; and the most absurd charges were made against the governor, notably that he was preparing to run away to Sonora with the public funds! How he was to pay the balance of his travelling expenses after exhausting the said funds does not appear.

During the night of December 3d Rico and his companions took possession of the *cuartel*, apparently without opposition; and placed Flores under arrest. His imprisonment lasted until the 5th. On that day the assembly in an extra session investigated the matter. Flores admitted his previous plan of sending the prisoners to Mexico, which plan, however, he was willing to abandon. Not the slightest foundation could be adduced for the other charges; and accordingly the assembly denounced the movement as unjustifiable, and especially so at the present critical juncture. Alarming news from the south had arrived the night before; Carrillo and his fellow-conspirators deemed it best under the circumstances not to urge their cause; Palomares and Workman had effected their purpose, since Wilson and his men were to remain; and therefore Flores was restored to power; the opposition to him was silenced temporarily though not eradicated; and Rico in his turn was made a prisoner.[8]

[8] Dec. 5th, 7th, Flores to Cota and to Janssens, relating his arrest. *Olvera, Doc.*, MS., 68–9, 71; *Janssens, Doc.*, MS., 45–6. He thinks that the affair of the prisoners was only a pretext, and that Carrillo and the rest had been influenced not only by the former's ambition, but had been bought with *oro Americano* to ruin their country, which he believes has had a very narrow escape. Dec. 5th, action of the assembly. *Olvera, Doc.*, MS., 49–51; *Pico, Doc.*, MS., ii. 109–10. Dec. 4th, Olvera wrote to Coronel, describing the affair. *Coronel, Cosas de Cal.*, MS., 115. Narratives also in *Wilson's Observ.*, MS., 82–5; *Rico, Mem.*, MS., 30–5, whose version is that the assembly, composed mainly of Mexicans, would not listen to his well founded charges. *Botello, Anales*, MS., 152–3; *Dicc. Univ.*, viii. 159–60. Dec. 5th, Flores to Cota, mentioning Coronel's letter, in which he announced hostile operations of the Americans. Cota is ordered to do his best to recapture the horses and punish the foe. If this be impossible, he is to reoccupy his former position. *Olvera, Doc.*, MS., 69–70. Dec. 7th, Flores to Janssens. Cannot send a man, for the enemy is upon us. Consult with Jesus Pico, collect the greatest possible force and keep it ready. *Janssens, Doc.*, MS., 45.

The alarming news to which I have referred was
Coronel's report that a party of Americans had captured his animals near Ahuanga.   Flores was greatly
puzzled to account for the presence of the enemy in
that quarter, since he could not understand how they
had left San Diego and penetrated into the interior
without being seen by the forces of either Pico or Cota.
As a matter of fact, they had come not from San Diego, but from the opposite direction.   They were the
men from whom Stockton had received a letter on or
about December 3d; and it is now time to explain
their presence in California and to follow their movements.

Colonel Stephen W. Kearny, leaving Fort Leavenworth at the end of June, 1846, occupied Santa Fé
and accomplished the conquest of New Mexico in August, as related in another part of this work.   Before
he started on this expedition he received orders, dated
at Washington, June 3d, to march across the continent from Santa Fé and take possession of California.
He was to coöperate with the naval forces, which
would be found probably in possession of the ports;
and having secured the country, he was to organize
a temporary civil government.   I append some extracts from the instructions forwarded to Kearny at
different dates.[9]   They will prove of some importance

[9] June 3, 1846, instructions of Sec. of War Marcy to Col. Kearny. 'It
has been decided by the pres. to be of the greatest importance in the pending war with Mex. to take the earliest possession of Upper Cal. An expedition with that view is hereby ordered, and you are designated to command it.
To enable you to be in sufficient force to conduct it successfully, this additional force of 1,000 mounted men has been provided to follow you in the
direction of Sta Fé...When you arrive at Sta Fé with the force already
called, and shall have taken possession of it, you may find yourself in a condition to garrison it with a small part of your command, as the additional
force will soon be at that place, and with the remainder press forward to Cal....
It is understood that a considerable number of American citizens are now settled on the Sacramento River, near Sutter's establishment, called New Helvetia, who are well disposed toward the U. S. Should you on your arrival
find this to be the true state of things, you are authorized to organize and receive into the service of the U. S. such portions of these citizens as you may
think useful to aid you to hold possession of the country. You will in that
case allow them, so far as you shall judge proper, to select their own officers.
A large discretionary power is invested in you in regard to these matters, as

in connection with later complications, besides showing the ideas of the government at Washington respecting the future status of California.   At about

well as to all others...The choice of routes by which you will enter Cal. will
be left to your better knowledge, etc....Though it is very desirable that the
expedition should reach Cal. this season,...yet you are left unembarrassed
by any specific directions in this matter.   It is expected that the naval forces
of the U. S., which are now or soon will be in the Pacific, will be in possession of all the towns on the sea-coast, and will coöperate with you in the conquest of Cal....Should you conquer and take possession of N. Mex. and Cal.,
or considerable places in either, you will establish temporary civil governments therein, abolishing all arbitrary restrictions that may exist, so far as
it may be done with safety.   In performing this duty, it would be wise and
prudent to continue in their employment all such of the existing officers as
are known to be friendly to the U, S. and will take the oath of allegiance to
them...You may assure the people of those provinces that it is the wish and
design of the U. S. to provide for them a free govt, with the least possible
delay, similar to that which exists in our territories...It is foreseen that
what relates to civil govt will be a difficult and unpleasant part of your duties, and which must necessarily be left to your discretion...The rank of
brevet brigadier-general will be conferred on you as soon as you commence
your movement toward Cal.'   *Cal. and N. Mex., Mess. and Doc.*, 236–9.
June 18th, 'Since my last letter it has been determined to send a small force
round Cape Horn to Cal...Arrangements are now on foot to send a regiment
of volunteers by sea.   These troops, and such as may be organized in Cal.,
will be under your command.'   June 5th, the proclamation sent you, intended for Gen. Taylor, to issue to the Mexicans, will not answer our purpose for Cal.   *Id.*, 239–40.   Sept. 12th, volunteer regiment about to sail.
'This force is to be a part of your command; but as it may reach its destination before you, the colonel, J. D. Stevenson, has been furnished with instructions for his conduct in the mean time.   I send you a copy; also a copy of
instructions to the commander of naval squadron, a copy of a letter to Gen.
Taylor, etc., and a copy of general regulations relative to the respective
rank of naval and army officers.   These, so far as applicable, will be looked
upon in the light of instructions to yourself.'   *Id.*, 241–2.   Dec. 10th, 'It is
presumed that you will not find a state of things in Cal. requiring you to
remain in that country, but that you will deem it proper to leave affairs there
in charge of Col. Mason, recently sent out, and return to Sta Fé.'   Jan. 11,
1847, 'It is proper to remark that the provisions of the law established for
New Mexico go in some respects beyond the line designated by the president, and propose to confer upon the people of the territory rights under
the constitution of the U. S.; such rights can only be acquired by the action of congress...Under the law of nations the power conquering a territory or country has a right to establish a civil govt within the same as a
means of securing the conquest, and with a view of protecting the persons
and property of the people, and it is not intended to limit you in the full
exercise of this authority.   Indeed, it is desired that you should exercise it
in such a manner as to inspire confidence in the people that our power is to
be firmly sustained in that country.   The territory in our military occupation
acquired from the enemy by our arms cannot be regarded, the war still continuing, as permanently annexed to the U. S., though our authority to exercise civil government over it is not by that circumstance the least restricted.'
Id., 244–5.   Jan. 11th, extract of letter to Stockton, forwarded to Kearny.
On Nov. 5th you were informed that the pres. 'has deemed it best for the
public interests to invest the military officer commanding with the direction
of the operations on land, and with the administrative functions of govt over
the people and territory occupied by us.'   This was before the receipt of

the time of Kearny's expedition, arrangements were made for the sending of several different bodies of troops to California; but as none of these accompanied Kearny or reached their destination in 1846, it will be more convenient to defer an account of military preparations until I come to treat of results in the annals of 1847.

It was on September 25th that General Kearny—for his commission as general had already reached him—left Santa Fé with 300 of the 1st dragoons for California.   The line of march was down the valley of the Rio Grande.   Nothing of interest occurred until the army on October 6th reached a point some thirteen miles below Socorro.   Here was met Kit Carson, with fifteen men, including six Delaware Indians, en route from Los Angeles to Washington with despatches from Stockton.   Carson brought the news that the conquest of California had, at his departure in August, been already fully effected by Stockton and Frémont; that there was no longer the slightest opposition to the American rule; that Stockton was engaged in organizing a civil government; and that Frémont was to be made governor.

This news caused the general to modify his plans, and to send back 200 of his 300 dragoons under Major Sumner to Santa Fé.   He retained companies C and K, or 100 dragoons, under Captain Benjamin D. Moore, Lieutenant Thomas C. Hammond, and Lieutenant John W. Davidson.   His staff consisted of Captain Henry S. Turner, acting assistant adjutant-general; Captain Abraham R. Johnston, aide-de-camp; Major Thomas Swords, quartermaster; Lieutenants William H. Emory and William H. Warner of

Stockton's despatches of Sept. 18th, 19th, which were received Dec. 26th. Then follows a general disquisition on the nature of military occupation. 'This right of possession, however, is temporary, unless made absolute by subsequent events,' coupled with a general approval of Stockton's acts, though 'at present it is needless, and might be injurious to the public interests to agitate the question in Cal. as to how long those persons who have been elected for a prescribed period of time will have official authority.' The number of appointments should be made as small as possible. *Id.*, 246-7.

the topographical engineers, with a dozen assistants
and servants;[10] and Assistant Surgeon John S. Griffin.
Antonio Robidoux was the guide, and Carson became
his associate. The latter was unwilling to turn back,
desiring to deliver his despatches in person, and also
to visit his family; but Kearny insisted and became
responsible for the safe and speedy delivery of the
papers. The whole force of officers and men was
therefore 121. Two mountain howitzers were taken
under the charge of Lieutenant Davidson. The men
were mounted chiefly on mules; the luggage was carried at first in wagons, which were, however, soon
abandoned in favor of pack-mules.

The 15th of October, in the region of Fra Cristóbal,
they left the valley of the Rio Grande, and turned to
the westward into the mountains, passing the old copper mines, and striking the upper Gila five days later,
without adventures requiring mention.[11] On November 9th they emerged from the mountains into the
valley of the lower Gila; and on the 22d reached the
vicinity of the Colorado junction. The march had
been a hard one; many animals had been lost, some
eaten, and the rest were in bad condition; but there

---

[10] Those named were J. M. Stanley, draughtsman; Norman Bestor, assistant;
Jas Early, W. H. Peterson, Baptiste Perrot, Maurice Longdeau, François Von
Cœur, François Ménard, Jas Riley, Dabney Eustice, and Williams.

[11] There are two diaries of the whole trip extant. The most complete is
Emory's *Notes of a Military Reconnoissance from Fort Leavenworth in Missouri to San Diego in California.* Washington, 1848. Being *30th Cong. 1st Sess.,
H. Ex. Doc. 41,* p. 55-126; the diary being from Sept. 25, 1846, to Jan. 20,
1847. The other is Dr Griffin's *Journal of a trip with the First U. S. Dragoons from New Mexico to California in 1846,* MS. copy in the handwriting
of Judge Hayes from the original. A part has been printed in the *Los
Angeles History.* A third diary is Capt. Johnston's *Journal* printed with that
of Emory, p. 567-614. It terminates on Dec. 4th, the author having been
killed in battle by the Californians on the 6th. Lieut Cooke also gives a diary of the march down the Rio Grande; but he turned back to Sta Fé, and
the rest of the journey is described from the journals of other officers. *Cooke's
Conquest of Cal.,* 68-86, 228-56. The expedition is briefly described in letters
of Gen. Kearny of Dec. 12th, 13th. *30th Cong. 1st Sess., Sen. Ex. Doc. 1,* 513-
16; still more briefly in Major Swords' report of Oct. 8, 1847. *30th Cong.
2d Sess., H. Ex. Doc.,* i. 226-8; and mentioned from the above sources in several govt documents. I have also a MS. *Statement on San Pascual,* by Asa
M. Bowen, who was with this expedition; and *Notes on S. Pascual,* MS., by
Wm H. Dunne. I might give a long list of accounts made up from the preceding.

had been no serious mishap or suffering.   Here they found a small party with a band of 500 horses coming from California and bound for Sonora.   These men gave alarming but contradictory reports of the revolution at Los Angeles; and a bearer of despatches was also captured, whose papers confirmed the news that a large portion of the country was in possession of the Californians, including the region through which they were to pass.   The Americans obtained all the horses they desired; and though most in the band were unbroken, many of the dragoons succeeded in getting a fresh mount.   There is a degree of mystery about the men who had the horses.   They told all kinds of stories about themselves.   Coronel says they were horse-thieves proceeding to Sonora with stolen animals; possibly some of the rancheros had sent the horses to Sonora on speculation, thinking that if not sent out of the country they were sure to fall into the hands of either the native or American armies, or certain Mexican officers may have been interested in the venture; but I think there was no foundation for the statement made by some of the men that the horses belonged to Flores or Castro.[12]

[12] Emory says: 'Each gave a different account of the ownership and destination of the horses.   The chief of the party, a tall, venerable-looking man, represented himself to be a poor employé of several rich men engaged in supplying the Sonora market with horses.   We subsequently learned that he was no less a personage than José María Leguna [Segura?], a colonel in the Mexican service.'   Emory inplies that the Mexicans were kept in arrest for a while, and released, the animals being taken as contraband.   He mentions a woman of the party to whom a child was born in camp.   Johnston says: 'They lied so much that we could get but very little out of them,' though it appears their reports about affairs in Cal. were very nearly accurate.   'The letters being opened were resealed by Capt. Turner, and all returned to the man, who was discharged.   These fellows tell various stories about the horses; they all acknowledge that a part of them belong to Gen. Castro...Nov. 24th, completed our trading with the Mexicans; Capt. Moore's men being in part remounted on wild horses, on which never man sat, they got of course many tumbles; but they stuck to the furious animals until they succeeded.'   Dr Griffin says the horses, 20 in number, were bought at $12 each, or for $2 and a broken-down animal; and the Mexicans were surprised at being paid at all. Lugo, *Vida de un Ranchero*, MS., 50-1, says that Capt. Segura ran away to Sonora with a band of horses and other property; and that he and Diego Sepúlveda started in pursuit and went nearly to the Colorado.   He says it was suspected that Segura acted in secret accord with Flores, who sent the funds in advance, intending to flee to Sonora himself soon.   It is not unlikely that the

Kearny's men forded the Colorado November 25th; and next day, provided with bunches of grass and mezquite-beans for the animals, they set out to cross the Californian desert. The worst of the desert had been passed at noon on the 28th, when they reached the Carrizo Creek; but the march had been attended with greater hardships than any before experienced. Both men and animals were completely exhausted; and many of the latter, of which there were 250 at the Colorado, had been lost on the way. Pressing on, they reached Warner's rancho of Agua Caliente the 2d of December; and here their troubles, so far as lack of water and food was concerned, were at an end. The route had been for the most part farther south and a more difficult one than that usually followed from the Colorado to San Gabriel.[13] Warner was absent, but every attention was shown to the Americans by Marshall. The Indians of the region were also friendly. Here they were visited by Stokes, an English ranchero of the region, who volunteered to carry a letter to Stockton, and who delivered it at San Diego, as we have seen, the 3d of December.[14] Here also they learned that not far

mail-carrier taken by Kearny was the Felipe Castillo despatched by Coronel, though it is said that his despatches bore date of Oct. 15th.

[13] The route was as follows: Nov. 26th, 22 or 24 m. to Álamo; Nov. 27th, 31 or 32 m. to salt Laguna; Nov. 28th, 27 or 22 m. to Carrizo Creek; Nov. 29th, 20 m. to Bayo Cita, or Bayeau Chitoes (Vallecito?); Dec. 1st, 18 m. to S. Felipe, deserted Indian village; Dec. 2d, to Warner's rancho. The hardships of the march are described in detail by Emory, Johnston, and Griffin. The fresh horses obtained at the Colorado suffered more than the mules. On the way a Mexican family was met on their way to Sonora.

[14] The letter, in *Stockton's Mil. and Nav. Op.*, 26-7, is as follows: 'Headquarters, army of the west, camp at Warner's, Dec. 2, 1846. Sir: I this afternoon reached here, escorted by a party of the 1st regiment of dragoons. I came by order of the pres. of the U. S. We left Santa Fé on the 25th Sept., having taken possession of N. Mex., annexed it to the U. S., established a civil govt in that territory, and secured order, peace, and quietness there. If you can send a party to open communication with us on the route to this place, and to inform me of the state of affairs in Cal., I wish you would do so, and as quickly as possible. The fear of this letter falling into Mexican hands prevents me from writing more. Your express by Mr Carson was met on the Del Norte, and your mail must have reached Washington 10 days since. You might use the bearer, Mr Stokes, as a guide to conduct your party to this place. Very respectfully, etc.' Stockton's reply was as follows: 'Headquarters, S. Diégo, Dec. 3d, 6:30 P. M. Sir: I have this moment received your note of yesterday by Mr Stokes, and have ordered Capt.

away was a band of horses and mules said to belong to the government; and Davidson with twenty-five men was sent to capture them, in which enterprise he was successful. These animals were those of Coronel's party at Ahuanga; but the horses were most of them unbroken, and therefore of no great use for the coming emergency.[15] On the 4th Kearny marched down the valley to Santa Isabel, where his men were as hospitably entertained by Stokes' majordomo 'Señor Bill,' as they had been by Marshall at Agua Caliente. Next day they marched on to the rancho of Santa María. On the way they met Gillespie, Lieutenant Edward F. Beale, and Midshipman James M. Duncan with thirty-five men and a four-pounder, the 'Sutter gun,' sent by Stockton from San Diego.[16] At different points in the past few days they had heard reports, tolerably accurate, though not fully credited, respecting the state of affairs in California. They had learned that they were likely enough to meet the enemy upon their route; and even that a party escorting prisoners to Mexico was soon expected to arrive. Now these reports, except the last, were fully confirmed by the new-comers. Stockton announced that a hostile force was posted not many miles away, and suggested a surprise. The soldiers,

Gillespie with a detachment of mounted riflemen and a field-piece to proceed to your camp without delay. Capt. G. is well informed in relation to the present state of things in Cal., and will give you all needful information. I need not, therefore, detain him by saying anything on the subject. I will merely state that I have this evening received information by two deserters from the rebel camp of the arrival of an additional force of 100 men, which, in addition to the force previously here, makes their number about 150. I send with Capt. G., as a guide, one of the deserters, that you may make inquiries of him, and, if you see fit, endeavor to surprise them. Faithfully, your obedient servant, Robt F. Stockton, commander-in-chief and governor of the territory of Cal., etc.'

[15] Capt. Johnston says: 'After them came a party of French, English, and a Chilian, claiming their riding animals, as they were going out of the country, which the general gave them. Many of the animals from the herd were put into service, and arrangements made to secure the balance by driving them into some safe place in the mountains.'

[16] 'The force which accompanied Capt. Gillespie consisted of a company of volunteers, composed of Acting Lieut Beale, Passed Midshipman Duncan, 10 carbineers from the *Congress*, Capt. Gibson, and 25 of the California battalion.' *Stockton's Report*, 45. The whole number was 39.

after their unresisted occupation of New Mexico, and their tedious march across the continent, made no secret of their desire to be brought face to face with the foe. Kit Carson had affirmed along the march that the Californians were cowards and would not fight. The battalion men from San Diego doubtless confirmed this view more or less fully. An attack was therefore decided upon; and in the evening Lieutenant Hammond was sent out to reconnoitre.[17]

Captain Andrés Pico, as we have seen, had been sent southward by Flores on November 22d, to cut off the retreat of a party of Americans understood to have left San Diego for the region of Santa Isabel. The alarm proved to be a false one—or at least, the Americans returned before Pico arrived; but Don Andrés remained in the south, making his headquarters at San Luis Rey and Santa Margarita, coöperat-

[17] Emory says: 'We heard that the enemy was in force 9 miles distant.' After Hammond had been seen by the foe, 'we were now on the main road to S. Diego, all the by-ways being in our rear, and it was therefore deemed necessary to attack the enemy and force a passage.' Johnston—the last entry of his journal—says, on Dec. 4th: 'We heard of a party of Californians, of 80 men, encamped at a distance from this [Sta Isabel]; but the informant varied from 16 to 30 miles in his accounts, rendering it too uncertain to make a dash upon them in the dark; so we slept till morning.' Dr Griffin tells us that Gillespie's men camped soon after the meeting, while the rest went on some 10 miles to a point two miles beyond Sta María. 'A party of the enemy being reported in our vicinity, it was first determined that Capt. Moore should take 60 men and make a night attack; but for some reason the general altered his mind, and sent Lieut Hammond with the men to reconnoitre.' Kearny, in his report of Dec. 13th, says: 'Having learned from Capt. Gillespie of the volunteers that there was an armed party of Californians, with a number of extra horses at S. Pascual, three leagues distant on a road leading to this place, I sent Lieut Hammond, 1st dragoons, to make a reconnoissance.' Geo. Pearce, one of the dragoons, still living in 1880, says in the *Son. Co. Hist.*, 581–2, that he, Pearce, was sent by Kearny to summon Capt. Moore to an interview; that Moore opposed a reconnoissance, favoring an immediate attack; but his objections were overruled, and Hammond, Sergt Williams, and 10 men were sent to reconnoitre. Pearce heard their report, 'that as they neared some Indian huts at...S. Pascual, the guide stopped them and called attention to a dim light in one of the huts, and told them that Pico and his men were occupying those huts; that Sergt Willams and the guide [the same native Californian who had reported at Warner's rancho] absolutely went to the door of the hut and saw a number of men sleeping, and a lone Indian sitting by the fire. They beckoned the Indian without the hut, and while conversing with him, a sentinel hailed the main party, and the whole detachment instantly retreated...As they retreated they distinctly heard the shouts of the enemy "Biva California"!'

ing with Captain Cota in watching and keeping supplies from the enemy, awaiting Flores' approach with
the main force to assist Stockton's expected advance.
He had perhaps taken 100 men, as ordered, from
Angeles, but had lost many who absented themselves
on one pretext or another, and had also picked up a
few recruits, until his force, as nearly as can be ascertained, numbered about 80, most Californians making
it considerably less.   Of his movements, like those of
Cota, nothing is known in detail until December 5th,
when he was encamped at the Indian pueblo of San
Pascual, where he had arrived that day, or possibly
the day before.   His purpose was to cut off the retreat of Gillespie, whose departure from San Diego on
the 3d was known, and whose mission was supposed
to be to obtain cattle and horses.   Pico had no expectation when he went to San Pascual of meeting
any but Gillespie's men; and Cota, or some of his
subordinates, had been sent to cut off the Americans'
retreat if by chance they should take another return
route.   Before night on the 5th the Indians brought
in reports that a large force was approaching, and not
far distant; but as these reports were somewhat contradictory, and did not agree with what was known of
Gillespie's party, the only enemy whose presence was
suspected, but little attention was paid to them, or
even to messages from Coronel, describing the taking
of his horses by a party coming from the east.   So
far as any reliance can be placed in the statements of
his companions, Pico was inexcusably careless; and
even sent away most of his horses to feed at a distance
of several miles.   It was a cold and rainy night.
Between 11 o'clock and midnight the sentry was
alarmed by the barking of a dog.   To his 'Quien
vive?' no reply was given, but he thought he could
see retreating forms; and a party sent out to reconnoitre found a blanket marked 'U. S.' and the trail
of the enemy's scouts.   Now the horses were sent for
in all haste, and preparations for defence were made,

though even then it could hardly be comprehended that thirty-five men on a raid for live-stock would venture on an attack by night. At early dawn, however, on the 6th, the near approach of the Americans was announced; and hardly could the Californians mount their horses, lance in hand, before the advance guard of the foe was seen riding at full speed down the hill upon them.[18]

Kearny had 160 men under his command at Santa María. The force of the enemy at San Pascual, ten miles distant, had been correctly reported, as is shown by Johnston's journal, at 80; but no certainty could be felt on this point. Hammond returned about 2 A. M. from his reconnoissance, reporting that he had seen the camp of the enemy, and had been seen but not pursued by them. The call to horse was sounded without delay, and the army was soon on the march. The San Diego force had encamped at some distance from the general's camp, but all were reunited soon after the start. The order of march was as follows: Captain Johnston commanded an advanced guard of twelve dragoons mounted on the best horses; close behind was General Kearny with lieutenants Emory and Warner of the engineers, and four or five of their men; next came Captain Moore and Lieutenant Hammond with about fifty dragoons, mounted, many of them on mules, followed by captains Gillespie and Gibson with twenty volunteers of the California battalion; Lieutenant Davidson was next in the line, in charge of the two howitzers, with a few dragoons to manage the guns, which were drawn by mules; and finally, the rest of the force, between fifty and sixty men, brought up the rear under Major Swords, protecting the baggage, and protected by Gillespie's field-

---

[18] On these preparations, as on the following conflict, much information is derived from *Hayes' Miscellany*, 38–40; *Id., Emig. Notes*, 400–2, being reminiscences of old Californians collected by Judge Hayes during an acquaintance of many years; *Coronel, Cosas de Cal.*, MS., 115–19; *Forster's Pioneer Data*, MS., 37–42; *Botello, Anales*, MS., 154–6; *Véjar, Recuerdos*, MS., 66–80; *Moreno, Vida Militar*, MS., 25–31; *Palomares, Mem.*, MS., 88–95; *Osio, Hist. Cal.*, MS., 492–500.

piece.   It required more than the ardor of anticipated
victory to make the march a tolerably comfortable
one.   The animals were either stiff and worn out by
their long journey, or partially unbroken and unmanageable; while the men's clothing was soaked by the
night's drizzling rain, and the cold was now intense.
In the gray dawn of morning they drew near San
Pascual; and as they came in sight of the Indian village and the enemy's camp, a charge was ordered by
the general, and down the hill dashed Captain Johnston and his men at a gallop.

It was no part of Californian cavalry tactics to
stand still and receive a charge.   Had Gillespie's forty
men come down upon them in a compact body, Pico's
company would have retired at least far enough to
find favorable ground for a countercharge; and had
Kearny's force appeared in like manner—of whose
presence Don Andrés had as yet no knowledge—they
would have retreated promptly to the hills to await
an opportunity for a sudden dash or to content themselves with harassing the foe and driving off his animals.   But seeing less than twenty horsemen coming
down the hill, the Californians made a stand, discharged the few muskets and pistols they had, and
with lances ready received the shock of the advancing
dragoons.   Captain Johnston received a musket-ball
in the head and fell dead; a dragoon also fell, badly
wounded.   Of the very brief hand-to-hand conflict
that ensued at the Indian village, naturally no participant has been able to give a clear account; and it
is not known if there were any casualties beyond
those mentioned.   Overpowered by numbers and confused by the fall of their leader, the Americans perhaps
fell back a very short distance after the first shock;
but at that moment Kearny's main force appeared
on the scene; and Pico's men fled.

Filled with enthusiasm at the sight of the retreating foe, the gallant Captain Moore called on his men
to charge in pursuit, and was followed by all that had

come up. Not all of Moore's and Gillespie's force
had been able to do so; but it seems hardly probable
that enough of them had been kept back by their
animals' lack of speed to justify Dr Griffin's opinion
and that of Dunne that not more than fifty men saw
the enemy. No order was observed in the pursuit;
all rushed onward pell-mell, each urging his animal at
full speed. Between the fleetest and freshest horses,
however, and the slowest and most worn-out mules,
there were many gradations of speed; and the effect
on the relative position of the different pursuers may be
readily imagined. What were Pico's plans, if he had
any, it is impossible to know; his movement has been
called on the one hand a cowardly retreat, and on the
other a deliberate trap for the Americans; I am inclined to think it was neither, but rather the instinct-
ive tactics of Californian warriors in favor of sudden
dashes and short decisive conflict. However this may
have been, after running half a mile, more or less, to
ground more favorable for cavalry evolutions, and noting the line of pursuers extending with frequent and
irregular intervals far to the rear, Don Andrés suddenly wheeled his column and rushed back to meet
the Americanos. The conflict, though brief, was terrible. Kearny's men derived but slight benefit from
their fire-arms, either because the rain had rendered
them useless, or because most of them had been discharged at long range upon the flying foe. It was
sabre against lance—sabres and clubbed guns in the
hands of dragoons and volunteers mounted on stupid
mules or half-broken horses against lances, the enemy's
favorite weapons, in the hands of the world's most
skilful horsemen. The Americans fought with desperate valor against heavy odds and with fearful loss
of life; and they stood their ground. For ten minutes, perhaps less, the hand-to-hand conflict raged;
and then, when the force of the assault had somewhat
spent itself, and when the two howitzers had been
brought up, the Californians again fled. This time

the Americans were in no condition to pursue. The
mules attached to one of the howitzers took fright,
however, and dashed wildly after the enemy, who
captured the gun and killed the man in charge of it.

The battle of San Pascual, the most famous and
deadly in Californian history, was at an end. The
Americans camped on the battle-field. Lieutenant
Emory was sent back to bring up Major Swords'
party, who were a mile in the rear, and had not been
attacked; and he also recovered the body of Johnston
at the village where the first fight occurred. Eighteen men had been killed in the fight; nineteen were
wounded, three of them fatally; and one was missing.[19]
Only one death and one wound were caused by fire-
arms; but all the other dead and wounded had three
lance-thrusts on an average in each body, some having ten. The dead were buried in the night under a
willow-tree east of the camp; but the remains were
subsequently removed to Old San Diego, where I saw
rude boards in honor of their memory in 1874. Johnston was the first victim, as we have seen, being shot
in the first charge. Moore fell early in the second
charge, with a lance through the body, after a desperate resistance. Hammond is said to have received
the thrust that caused his death in a few hours while

[19] There are some slight variations in different reports. Kearny says there
were 18 killed and 16 wounded; Emory makes it 18 killed and 13 wounded.
In tables contained in *31st Cong. 1st Sess.*, *H. Ex. Doc. 24*, p. 10, 28, the number is given as 17 killed and 16 wounded. The best authority, however, is
Griffin's quarterly report of Dec. 31st, of which I have the original blotter in
Griffin's Doc., MS., 4–5. In a letter of Feb. 14, 1847, the doctor puts the loss
at 17 killed and 18 wounded. *Id.*, 22. In his *Journal*, p. 28, he makes it 18
killed and 18 wounded, or 35 in all (?). The killed were: dragoons, Capt. Abraham R. Johnston, Capt. Benj. D. Moore. Co. C, Wm C. West, corporal;
privates Geo. Ashmead, Jos T. Campbell, John Dunlop, Wm Dalton, Wm
C. Lucky, and Samuel F. Repoll. Co. K, Otis L. Moor, 1st sergeant; Wm
Whitness, sergeant; Geo. Ramsdale, corporal; David W. Johnson, farrier;
and privates Wm C. Gholston, Wm H. Fiel, and Robert S. Gregory. Henry
Booker, or Baker (?), private Cal. battalion. François Menard, private top.
engineers. Missing, and supposed to have been killed, Hugh McKaffray, Co.
K, 1st dragoons. The wounded were: Lieut Thos C. Hammond, 1st drag.,
died Dec. 6th; Sergt John Cox, died Dec. 10th, at S. Bernardo; Jos B.
Kennedy, priv. Co. C, died Dec. 21st, at S. Diego; Gen. S. W. Kearny, Capt.
Arch. Gillespie, Capt. Gibson, Lieut Wm H. Warner, Jos. Antonio Robi-
doux, David Streeter; and 10 others slightly.

trying to save Moore. Gillespie, a skilful swordsman, fought bravely, but was unhorsed and left for dead on the field with three lance-wounds in his body. Warner also received three wounds; while Kearny escaped with two. Gibson of the battalion was slightly wounded, and Robidoux, the guide, more seriously. Respecting the losses of the Californians at San Pascual there is no agreement of testimony. One man, Pablo Véjar, whose horse fell in the action, was made a prisoner, and there was perhaps another. About a dozen men were wounded, one or two perhaps seriously; but I think that none were killed.[20]

Captain Turner assumed command in consequence of Kearny's wounds. The day was consumed in dressing wounds, and in making rude ambulances for the moving of the disabled. Alexis Godey, a man named Burgess, and one or two others were sent to San Diego with a letter to Stockton, asking for reenforcements, for supplies, and for carts in which to carry the wounded. Stokes seems to have preceded Godey, starting before he knew the exact results of the battle. "When night closed in," writes Emory,

[20] Capt. Pico's report of Dec. 6th, received by Flores at 4 A. M. on Dec. 7th, and by him communicated to subordinates, *Janssens, Doc.*, MS., 45-6, says that the victory was gained 'without other casualty on our side than 11 wounded, none seriously, since the action was decided *á pura arma blanca.*' Gen. Kearny says in his report: 'The number of their dead and wounded must have been considerable, though I have no means of ascertaining how many, as just previous to their final retreat they carried off all excepting six.' It is hard to resist the conclusion that the general deliberately misrepresents; for it is certain that no dead Californians were left on the field; and that no wounded fell into the hands of the Americans is proved by the fact that a little later, when Pico proposed an exchange of prisoners, Kearny had but one, Véjar, to exchange. Sergt Falls tells me that he and his party sent to search the field found one Californian with a broken leg. Dr Griffin speaks of seeing one man fall after a shot by Lieut Beale; he speaks of two prisoners; and says, 'I think the enemy must have suffered as much as we did.' He says that a little later he sent to Pico an offer to care for his wounded, but the capt. replied that he had none. Pablo Véjar says that one man, Francisco Lara, was killed and 12 were wounded, one of them, Casimiro Rubio, fatally. Several Californians speak of Lara's death; but in the *Los Angeles Hist.*, 24-8, Lara is said to have been wounded, captured, and to have had his leg amputated at S. Diego, living for a long time at Angeles. Botello tells us that a Sonoran was wounded and died a little later of fright. Osio says a boy became frightened, was unable to run, and was killed. Judge Hayes, personally acquainted with the participants in the battle and their friends for many years, could never find evidence that any of Pico's men were killed.

"the bodies of the dead were buried under a willow to the east of the camp, with no other accompaniment than the howling of myriads of wolves. Thus were put to rest together and forever a band of brave and heroic men. The long march of 2,000 miles had brought our little command, both officers and men, to know each other well. Community of hardships, dangers, and privations had produced relations of mutual regard which caused their loss to sink deep in our memory...Our position was defensible, but the ground covered with rocks and cacti made it difficult to get a smooth place to rest, even for the wounded. The night was cold and damp; and sleep was impossible." The Californians were not far away, and keeping a close watch. Pico had reported to Flores that the defeated Americans were encamped and besieged on a little height near the battle-field without water; that he was waiting only for the arrival of the division under Cota and Hermosillo to attack them; and that not one could escape. And Flores replied, thanking Don Andrés for his brilliant service to the country, and promising a reënforcement of 80 men, horses, and a field-piece.[21]

Early on the 7th, Kearny having resumed command, his army, described by Emory as "the most tattered and ill-fed detachment of men that ever the United States mustered under her colors," set out on its march down the valley, taking a route to the right, along the hills; while the Californians, whose pickets were part of the time in sight, retired in the same direction, keeping to the left, nearer the dry bed of the stream. Late in the afternoon they reached the ran-

[21] Capt. Turner's letter of Dec. 6th is given in *Stockton's Mil. and Nav. Op.*, 27–8. Dec. 7th, Flores to Janssens, with Pico's report. *Janssens, Doc.*, MS., 45–6. Dec. 7th, Flores to Pico, in *Pico, Doc.*, MS., ii. 111–12. Pico claimed to have defeated 200 Americans, killed over 30, including Gillespie, and taken one of the enemy's two cannon, with a loss of only 11 slightly wounded. This showed considerably less exaggeration than Kearny's report written a week later, that he had defeated 160 Californians—the maximum force on paper of Pico's and Cota's men united—of whom 6 had been left on the field, the rest of the killed and wounded being carried away.

cho of San Bernardo, deserted by all but a few Indians, where they found, however, some chickens and cattle.   Here they turned to the left, crossing the enemy's trail, and approached the river-bed in search of better feed for their animals; but when they had advanced a mile and reached the foot of a detached hill, the enemy came upon them from the rear.   We have no intelligible account of this skirmish of San Bernardo; but it would appear that after an exchange of shots at long range, the Americans, leaving their cattle, marched up the hill; that Pico's men started by a longer course to prevent the success of that movement; that a small party reached the summit on one side before the Americans who were ascending from the other side; but that they promptly retired before the rifle-balls of Gibson's volunteers. At any rate, Kearny formed his camp on the hill; while Pico withdrew his force to a position across the creek.[22]

It was apparent that an attempt to advance would almost certainly result in a loss of the wounded, and of the baggage, if not in further disaster; and it was resolved to remain for a time on the defensive. A small supply of water was obtained by digging, and some of the least emaciated mules were killed for food. Early on the 8th a man arrived from Pico's camp with a flag of truce, bringing sugar and tea, and a change of clothing sent by a friend for Gillespie, and a proposition to exchange four prisoners just captured.

[22] Kearny says: 'Reaching S. Bernardo, a party of them took possession of a hill near to it and maintained their position until attacked by our advance, who quickly drove them from it, killing and wounding five of their number (!), with no loss on our part.' Emory says: 'A cloud of cavalry debouched from the hills in our rear, and a portion of them dashed at full speed to occupy a hill by which we must pass, while the remainder threatened our rear. Thirty or 40 of them got possession of the hill, and it was necessary to drive them from it. This was accomplished by a small party of 6 or 8, upon whom the Californians discharged their fire; and strange to say, not one of our men fell. The capture of the hill was then but the work of a moment, and when we reached the crest, the Californians had mounted their horses and were in full flight...They had several badly wounded.' Griffin remarks: 'The enemy again appeared and made another rush to occupy a hill where they could annoy us. They got to the top about the time we got halfway up, when the fight commenced; but after two or three minutes the rascals ran, leaving 3 of their spears on the field.'

There was but one Californian to be exchanged, and with him Emory proceeded to an interview with Pico. It was Godey's party that had been captured near San Bernardo on the return from San Diego, which place they had reached in safety. Burgess was the man exchanged; the others were sent to Los Angeles. At night Beale, Carson, and an Indian volunteered to go to San Diego, a mission which they performed successfully.[23] On the 9th Sergeant Cox died from the effects of his wounds, and was buried. On the 10th, as the horses and mules were feeding at the foot of the hill, the Californians made a characteristic attempt to stampede the animals by driving upon them a band of wild horses, some of them with dry sheep-skins tied to their tails. By good luck and active exertion the success of this trick was prevented; and it even proved an advantage, for one or two fat animals were shot for food.

The wounded having improved in condition so that most of them could ride, and there being but little hope that Beale and Carson could reach San Diego and return with reënforcements, Kearny decided to make a new start next day. An order had already been issued to destroy all property that could not be transported.[24] Before dawn on the 11th, however, reënforcements made their appearance in the shape of about 200 marines and sailors under Lieutenant Gray, Stockton's aide-de-camp, who had left San Diego on the evening of the 9th on or before the arrival of Beale and Carson.[25] When the sun rose the enemy

[23] In Peters' *Life of Kit Carson*, 290–6, is an account of their adventures on the way, adopted by Lancey, *Cruise*, 143. Carson's account of the whole S. Pascual campaign as given in Peters' work, p. 278–96, is grossly inaccurate. It is said by this authority and others that Lieut Beale from his excitement and exposure became mentally deranged for a time.

[24] Dec. 9th, order signed by Capt. Turner, a. a. a. general, in *Griffin's Doc.*, MS., 3.

[25] Stockton, *Report*, 45, tells us that he first heard of Kearny's defeat, with no particulars, from Stokes in the evening of Dec. 6th. Next morning, Dec. 7th, Godey and his companions arrived with a letter from Capt. Turner (given in *Lancey's Cruise*, 142). Preparations were made to march with all the force that could be spared; and the advance under Lieut Guest was ordered to march to the mission. Preparations seem to have proceeded somewhat slowly; for

had disappeared, leaving the cattle at San Bernardo. This sudden disappearance, and the fact that they were seen no more, cannot be entirely accounted for by the aid of any records extant; not even by the supposition of Emory that "our night attack had filled them with the unnecessary fear of being surprised" by the marines and sailors! Pico's force had been increased to about 150 by the arrival of Cota's company; and Ramon Carrillo with 50 men, leaving Angeles at 4 P. M. on the 10th, had perhaps arrived before Kearny's departure.[26] That no attack was made on Kearny's camp is easily understood; the Californians had a pardonable aversion to charging on horseback up a hill to meet cannon-balls and rifle-bullets. They had hoped that Kearny might be kept cut off from communication with Stockton until forced to surrender or to expose himself to renewed attack by resuming his march. The arrival of Gray's company removed all chance of successful attack upon the Americans, if they were prudent enough to march in compact order. But Pico's policy naturally, and in accordance with general orders, would have been to hover about the enemy, seeking opportunities to annoy him, driving off his animals, and otherwise impeding his march. Yet, upon learning Gray's approach, he simply withdrew, reporting to Flores that Kearny had received reënforcements and marched for San Diego, he being unable to prevent it for want of horses! And Flores thereupon ordered him to leave his own and Carrillo's men to act as scouts in the south, and with Cota's

before the advance started an Indian arrived (night of the 8th or morning of the 9th) with reports indicating that Kearny's need of assistance was more urgent than had been supposed. Therefore it was decided to send only a part of the force for rapid movement. At 10 P. M. (of the 9th) Beale arrived and confirmed the worst reports; and Lieut Gray with 215 men was sent to Kearny's relief. Emory makes Gray's force '100 tars and 80 marines.' Griffin says there were 120 marines and 80 sailors.

[26] Dec. 10th, Flores to Pico, in reply to letter of the 8th. Has been delayed for want of horses; but sends Carrillo, and will follow himself to-morrow. Pico must not relax the siege. Nothing is to be feared from S. Diego; for the captured despatch of Stockton, a translation of which is enclosed, says it is impossible to send aid. *Pico, Doc.*, MS., ii. 115.

company to march to Los Angeles—an order which Don Andrés obeyed before it was received, and more than obeyed, since he retired with two companies, leaving but one. This was not a brilliant ending for the campaign; and it is not unlikely that the disaffection accompanying the late revolt against the governor had much to do with it.[27]

At 10 A. M., December 11th, Kearny's army marched from the hill camp of San Bernardo, and proceeded unmolested down the valley. The camp for the night was Alvarado's rancho of Peñasquitos, where, and at other points along the way, they found considerable quantities of cattle, sheep, and poultry, all confiscated as belonging to enemies. At about 4 P. M. on the 12th, they marched into San Diego, where they were hospitably received by Stockton and by the inhabitants.[28]

[27] Dec. 15th, Flores to Pico, on receipt of his report of the 11th. The want of horses has been a serious drawback all along. Owners keep them hidden, but it is noticeable that they are readily enough found for the enemy. It is reported that more U. S. troops are coming from New Mexico, and scouts have been sent to the Colorado. Pico is to recruit his horses in the Sta Ana region. Cota and Hermosillo with their men and the captured gun will come to the city. *Pico, Doc.*, MS., ii. 119–23. It seems that Pico left San Luis Rey and went to Sta Ana with his force before receiving Flores' order, leaving Cota's company in the south. Cota on the 14th asked to be relieved; and Flores on the 17th, in reply, complained bitterly of Pico's disobedience, and of the general indifference and insubordination of officers and men. The order to Pico has been repeated, and if disobeyed Cota may abandon the south. If the Californians do not care to defend their country, he will not be responsible. *Id.*, 127–9; *Olvera, Doc.*, MS., 60–3.

[28] I have described the S. Pascual campaign from information derived from all existing sources, the original authorities having been cited on previous pages, notably in notes 11 and 18. I add the following items, which could not conveniently be introduced in my text. Emory says: 'We subsequently received authentic accounts that Pico's number was 180 men engaged in the fight, and that 100 additional men were sent him from the pueblo, who reached his camp on the 7th'! Griffin affirms that Burgess reported Stockton to have refused to send reënforcements, and on this account Kearny wished to move at once; but the navy officers pledged themselves very strongly that the commodore would send relief. It should be noted that Kearny's report and Emory's notes are accompanied by a plan of the battle, which has been several times reprinted in other works. Items from *Hayes' Miscellany*, and *Id.*, *Emig. Notes;* some of them also published in *Los Angeles Hist.:* Capt. Moore was killed by Leandro Osuna. Gillespie was lanced and unhorsed by Francisco Higuera, or 'El Güero.' Gabriel García killed the man in charge of the howitzer. Juan Lobo and J. B. Moreno were conspicuous in the fight. Philip Crossthwaite saved the life of Véjar, the prisoner whom one of the Delaware Indians (?) was about to kill. José Ant. Serrano claims to have left the field while the fight was raging, and to have found Pico, Cota, and Tomito Sanchez safely out of danger on Soto Hill! Foster, *Angeles in 1847,*

It is difficult to regard the affair of San Pascual otherwise than as a stupid blunder on the part of Kearny, or to resist the conclusion that the official report of the so-called 'victory' was a deliberate misrepresentation of facts. True, the Americans remained in possession of the battle-field; but this fact by no

MS., 8–10, relates what others confirm, that Higuera would have killed Gillespie if he had not been in so much of a hurry to get away with his fine saddle and bridle. He later offered to return the articles, but Gillespie declined to receive them, as their loss had saved his life. Wm H. Dunne, *Notes on S. Pascual*, MS., remarks that Stokes was in the fight and died soon after from fright and exposure on the way to S. Diego; the officers were full of wine during the fight; the men regarded the fight as a stupid and criminal affair on the officers' part; Emory showed great gallantry on the taking of Mule Hill; Kit Carson was thrown from his horse and had his rifle broken. In the *Alta*, Nov. 14, 1868, Gillespie refutes with much indignation the statement of 'C. E. P.' (Chas E. Pickett), in the same paper, that the Americans were under the influence of wine. Emory in a letter of March 15, 1847, to the *N. Y. Courier and Enquirer*, tries to refute the insinuation in the *Monterey Californian*, Jan. 28, 1847, that discredit was thrown on the American arms by the action of S. Pascual. *Niles' Reg.*, lxxiii. 205. Jan. 22, 1847, Larkin briefly describes the battle in a letter to Vallejo. *Vallejo, Doc.*, MS., i. 22.

The campaign of S. Pascual has been frequently described at secondhand in books and newspapers. Brackett, *Hist. U. S. Cavalry*, 71–6, gives a very good general account. Phelps, *Fore and Aft*, 314–15, talked with Pico a few weeks after the battle, and was told that he had not intended to risk a fight; but that on seeing the disorder of Kearny's men he could not resist the temptation. Pico also told Botello, *Anales del Sur*, MS., 154–6, that his charge was a pure accident. Bowen, *Statement on S. Pascual*, MS., says: 'They proved to be about 400, and they killed all of us but 32 or 33. We were all wounded more or less.' Streeter, *Recoll.*, MS., 95–9, gives a narrative derived from the statement of David Streeter, his cousin and one of the wounded dragoons. John A. Swan, in *S. José Pioneer*, April 27, 1878, names Henry Booker as the man in charge of the howitzer. He was perhaps the man who had brought news of the Bear Flag revolt to Monterey, in June. Bidwell, *Cal. in 1841–8*, MS., 199–204, who was at S. Diego at the time, adds nothing to the general accounts. In the life of Stockton, p. 135, it is declared that the disaster was much more serious than represented in Kearny's report. An account credited to A. A. Hecox, in the *Sta Cruz Times*, Aug. 27, 1876, is perhaps as inaccurate as any extant; unless indeed it be excelled in that respect by that of Wm H. Davis, *Glimpses of the Past*, MS., 361–5, a writer who on many points is one of the most careful and accurate of all who have recorded their recollections. Lancey, *Cruise*, 138–47, gives a complete account from the official reports and journals, but he intersperses fragments from unreliable sources. He speaks of Juan Andado (?), who lost a leg carried away by a 6-lb. ball. Lieut Rhuson (Rheusaw?) and Sergt Jones, of the battalion, distinguished themselves at S. Bernardo. Gillespie in the *Alta*, July 3, 1866, followed by Lancey, says the 'Sutter' gun was kept back with the baggage, against his protest; that a howitzer was fired by him, holding the foe in check until the field-piece was brought up and drove them back; and that at S. Bernardo the gun killed several of the enemy. It is, however, pretty certain that no cannon was fired at S. Pascual; and there is no evidence beyond this statement of Gillespie that any was fired at San Bernardo. An account in the *Chihuahua Farol*, Aug. 10, 1846, and the *Sonorense* of Aug. 20th, has it that Kearny was killed and that his men shamefully capitulated!

means sufficed to make of defeat a victory, since the
enemy uninjured was free to occupy any one of a dozen
equally defensible positions on the way to San Diego.
There was no reason for the attack on Pico's forces;
and even a bloodless triumph could have done the
enemy's cause but slight harm.   Entering California
with but a small part of his original force, after a long
and tedious march, men and animals exhausted, Kearny
finds the country in revolt.   Instead of joining Stockton, which he might have done without risk or opposition, and proceeding as commander-in-chief to devise
means for completing the conquest, he attempts a night
attack upon an unknown force of mounted Californians,
knowing that the alarm had been given, and that surprise was impossible.   Coming in sight of the enemy,
he orders a charge, and permits a part of his men, be-
numbed with cold, their fire-arms wet and useless, their
sabres rusted fast in the scabbards, mounted on stupid
worn-out mules and half-broken horses, to rush in
confusion upon the Californian lances, presenting a
temptation to slaughter which the enemy—even if they
are as cowardly as their assailants believe—cannot resist.   Individually, the Americans fight most bravely:
nothing more can be said in praise.   Many lives are
recklessly and uselessly sacrificed.   An irresponsible
guerrillero chief would be disgraced by such an attack
on Indians armed with bows and arrows; but Kearny
was a brigadier-general commanding regular troops
of the United States.   Success would have brought
him no glory; defeat should have brought him disgrace.   It does not appear that any of his officers opposed the general's plans.   It has been said that all
were under the influence of wine; fortunately—for the
reputation of California wine, fiery liquid though it
may have been in its primitive stages of development
—this theory is but slightly supported by the evidence.
Stockton suggested the attack; but we may charitably
suppose that he did not realize the condition of Kearny's force; and he certainly is to no extent responsible

for the criminally blundering manner in which his suggestion was followed.   It is noticeable that Stockton was slow to respond to Kearny's appeal for aid after the disaster; even refusing at first to send reën-forcements, if we may credit the statement of Burgess, and the letter which fell into Pico's hands.   Too little is known, however, on this point to make it the ground of unfavorable criticism.

Of Governor Flores' operations, and those of his subordinates in and about the capital, after the San Pascual campaign and until the end of December, there is nothing to be said, except that those operations consisted of rather feeble preparations to resist the invader, not without certain petty bickerings and jealousies among the officers.   The Californian cause had decidedly lost strength during the past few weeks. The effect of military success at Angeles, Chino, San Pedro, Natividad, and San Pascual had been more than neutralized by internal feuds and jealousies showing the weakness of the new government.   It was wellnigh impossible to obtain supplies.   The rancheros concealed their horses to prevent their seizure.   There was no powder except the poor stuff made at San Gabriel.   The Americans were reported to be advancing from the north and east, as well as preparing for an attack from the south.   Men of the better class were convinced by reflection that there was no hope of successful resistance; and not a few were already devising schemes for securing pardon and protection from the foe when the collapse should come.   At the end of the year it was the general opinion, sustained by the acts of the military chiefs, that the first conflict was to be with Frémont rather than with Stockton.

At San Diego Kearny's arrival with his wounded dragoons and worn-out animals did not hasten but rather retarded preparations for beginning the campaign.   The wounds healed favorably, except those of Streeter, sixteen in number, and of Kennedy, who had five in the brain, and died.   Captain Hensley returned from his raid across the frontier and brought a large number of cattle and horses, the latter in poor condition.   Vegetables and bread were scarce; and the men were reduced to short rations of everything but fresh meat.   Major Swords was sent to Honolulu on a trading vessel chartered for the trip in quest of supplies.   The *Portsmouth* and *Cyane* arrived to join the *Congress*.   The men were constantly drilled for land evolutions; and the marines and sailors are said to have executed on their broncos several movements not laid down in any authority on cavalry tactics. Relations between the general and commodore were ostensibly amicable.   Meanwhile small parties of Californians came in from day to day, including some even of those who had been at San Pascual, to give themselves up, and receive assurances of protection. They brought all kinds of rumors about the whereabouts and plans of Flores and of Frémont.   The only news at the same time exciting and true was that of the killing of ten *gente de razon* at the Pauma rancho by Indians.   On December 29th all was at last ready, and the Americans, 600 strong, with Kearny in command of the troops under Stockton as commander-in-chief, started on the march to Los Angeles.   More will be said of this army in the next chapter, when I come to speak of its achievements.   Progress was slow and uneventful.   The first camp was at Soledad; the second at Peñasquitos; and on the last day of 1846 they encamped near San Bernardo, where Kearny's men had been besieged so recently.[29]

[29] *Griffin's Journal*, MS., 33–44; and *Id.*, in *Hayes' Emig. Notes*, 379, is the chief source of information on the last days of the stay at S. Diego.   See also *Emory's Notes*, 113–16; *Stockton's Report*, 45–6; Swords' report in *30th Cong. 2d Sess.*, *H. Ex. Doc. 1*, p. 226–7; *Hayes' Miscel.*, 27–9; *Davis' Glimpses*, MS., 368–70; *Bidwell's Cal. 1841–8*, MS., 204.   Some matters connected with the relations between Stockton and Kearny may be noticed more conveniently elsewhere.   In the *Los Angeles Hist.*, 33, it is related that Juan Bandini and his family came up from Baja California with Hensley; and that on the way his daughters made an elegant U. S. flag for the troops—the first ever made in California— for which the young ladies were serenaded, and thanked by the commodore in person.

CHAPTER XIV.

AFFAIRS IN THE NORTH—NATIVIDAD AND SANTA CLARA.

November, 1846—January, 1847.

Frémont's California Battalion—Official Plunder of the Rancheros —Successful Recruiting—Indian Allies—Organization and List of Officers—Manuel Castro and Other Officers Break Paroles and Join Flores—From San Luis to the Salinas—Burroughs and Thompson at San Juan—Capture of Larkin—Americans at Los Verjeles—Approach of the Californians—Fight at Encinalito— Foster Killed—Battle of Natividad—Death of Burroughs— Losses—Castro's Retreat—March of Frémont's Battalion from San Juan to Santa Bárbara—Condemnation and Pardon of Jesus Pico—Disastrous Crossing of the Cuesta de Santa Inés—More Forced Contributions—Sanchez's Revolt—Alarm at the Pueblo— Marston's Expedition—Campaign of Santa Clara—End of War in North—Loss of the 'Warren's' Launch—Wreck or Murder.

It has been recorded that Frémont, with about 160 men of the battalion, sailed for the south in the *Sterling* to coöperate with Stockton against the southern Californians, but having met the *Vandalia,* and learned not only of Mervine's disaster, but that no horses could be obtained at Santa Bárbara or San Pedro, he resolved to return for reënforcements and animals, and to advance on Los Angeles from the north by land. The vessel was becalmed on approaching Monterey; but a few officers were sent ashore October 24th, and on the 28th Frémont and his men landed from the *Sterling.* I append a few items of chronologic happenings at Monterey in these days, as an aid to the reader in following the subsequent record.[1]

[1] From *Colton's Three Years; Monterey Californian;* and *Bryant's What I Saw;* repeated by Lancey and many other writers. Oct. 24th, boat from the *Sterling.* Oct. 27th, *Malek Adhel,* a prize brig taken by the *Warren* at Maza-

Officers were at once despatched in all directions by
Lieutenant-colonel Frémont, for he found this new commission awaiting him at Monterey, with orders to enlist recruits for the battalion, and above all to obtain
the largest possible number of horses in the shortest
possible time.   How they were obtained did not much
matter, for the necessity was urgent.   Receipts were
given, to be settled by the government after the end
of the war; friends of the cause were treated with
some courteous formalities, if they turned over their
animals without delay; while the lukewarm or hostile
were plundered without ceremony of all their property
that could be utilized.   The commander cannot be
blamed for the proceeding; but doubtless much bitter
feeling was provoked, and justly, by the arbitrary
methods employed by most of his agents.[2]   The United

tlan, arrived under Lieut W. B. Renshaw.   Oct. 28th, the *Sterling* arrived
with Frémont.   Capt. Maddox had gone to S. Juan with 30 men.   Oct. 29th,
Maddox returned with a brass field-piece.   Large number of Californians
reported in the hills, perhaps intending to attack Monterey.   Oct. 30th, a
man guarding Frémont's horses shot by two Californians.   Oct. 31st, enlistments actively going on among newly arrived immigrants, by efforts of Montgomery in the north.   Nov. 5th, second rain of season.   Nov. 9th, Talbot
and his men from Sta Bárbara arrived.   Nov. 12th, Grigsby arrived from Sonoma with 30 men and 60 horses.   Hastings expected from S. José with 60
men and 120 horses.   Nov. 14th, the *Savannah* arrived with news from S.
Diego.   Nov. 16th, Delaware scout arrived with news of a fight between
Americans and Californians; also capture of Larkin.   Nov. 17th, Frémont
with his 300 men left Monterey for S. Juan.   Nov. 27th, prize brig *Julia*,
Lieut Selden, arrived from S. Francisco with news that a force had been sent
to protect S. José.   Dec. 1st, seven prisoners escaped from jail.   Dec. 2d–8th,
etc., county deemed unsafe out of town.   Dec. 17th, the *Julia* sailed for south.
Dec. 22d, news of Bartlett's capture at S. F.; forces sent to S. José.   Dec.
30th, the *Dale* arrived with a large mail.
    [2] Nov. 1st, all efficient horses but 3 taken from Fitch's rancho, 29 in num-
ber, worth $730. *Fitch, Doc.*, MS., 406, 422.   Many mistakes, with harsh and
arbitrary measures, provoking much angry feeling. *Hyde's Statement*, MS., 3.
'Every one who can raise among the emigrants 30 or 40 men becomes a captain and starts off to fight pretty much on his own hook.   Nor is he very
scrupulous as to the mode in which he obtains his horses, saddles, etc.   He
takes them wherever he can find them, and very often without leaving behind
the slightest evidence by which the owner can recover the value of his property.   He plunders the Californian to procure the means of fighting him.
Public exigency is the plea which is made to cover all the culpable features in
the transaction.   This may justify, perhaps, taking the property, but it can
never excuse the refusal or neglect to give receipts.   It is due to Stockton and
Frémont to say that this has been done without their sanction.   Still it reflects reproach on our cause, and is a source of vast irritation in the community.   No man who has any possible means of redress left will tamely submit
to such outrages; and yet we expect the Californians to hug this chain of deg-
radation, and help to rivet its links.' *Colton's Three Years*, 158.   All Amesti's

States finally assumed the obligation, as we shall see, to pay these 'California claims;' and while many rancheros received no compensation, others were paid for property that they had never lost. Such are the fortunes of war. It is not possible to form a connected narrative of the operations by which supplies and recruits were gained, for no official report was ever made on the subject; but Frémont's efforts were very successful, and within a month over 200 recruits were obtained for the battalion. Many immigrants had lately arrived at New Helvetia, and were ready to enlist for the war at twenty-five dollars per month. Bryant, Jacob, Grayson, and Lippincott were active in enlisting the new-comers; and they also raised a company of Walla Walla and native Californian Indians for the service, known as the spies, or more commonly as the 'forty thieves.' A company of Indians was also formed to serve at New Helvetia under Kern and Sutter, thus releasing the old garrison for service in the south. Captain Hastings had come back to California, and entered with much zeal into the congenial work, raising a company of 60 or 80 men in the central region. Captain Grigsby came down to Monterey with his Sonoma garrison of Bear Flag men. Louis McLane exerted himself with much success to organize an effective artillery company, for which several field-pieces were found.[3]

horses, saddles, and blankets taken without receipts. He then started with his family for another rancho in an ox-cart; but was met by Capt. Sears' men, who took the oxen and left the family in the road. *Vallejo, Hist. Cal.*, MS., v. 182-3; *Pinto, Apunt.*, MS., 104-5. Alcalde Chabolla of San Juan was beaten for refusing to give up his saddle. *Weeks' Remin.*, MS., 117. All German's horses were taken, 100 in number; but he went to Monterey to see Frémont, who gave him back a horse and mule, and also some money. G. had tried to save 11 fine horses by concealing them, but a neighbor pointed them out. *German, Sucesos*, MS., 13-15; Amador, *Mem.*, MS., 172-3, gives some details of the process of plundering. Most of the rancheros were left without horses for their work. See also *Cooke's Conq.*, 218-20. Weber's raids for horses are described in *S. José Pioneer*, March 6, 1880; *Lanccy's Cruise*, 191-2; *Tinkham's Hist. Stockton*, 103-4; with some correspondence found also in *Halleck's Mex. Land Laws*, MS. Howard and Mellus on complaint to Montgomery got a permit to retain such horses as were necessary for their business. In the *Eureka West Coast Signal*, Dec. 20, 1876, I find a burlesque narrative of Frémont's coming in person to Sonoma to get Vallejo's horses.

[3] *Bryant's What I Saw* and *Colton's Three Years* contain much information

It was a motley army in respect of race, language, weapons, and especially uniform; but it would have proved a most formidable and effective one against any foe existing in California. It contained many lawless, ignorant, and unprincipled men; but there was also a strong element of intelligent and brave Americans, thoroughly in earnest, and skilled riflemen; while the leaders were well fitted by character and experience to discipline and control such a force. The different parts of the battalion were reunited at San Juan, after some stirring events to be noticed presently, late in November. The whole force at that time, according to Bryant, who was an officer present at the time, was 428 men. No muster-rolls were sent to Washington; and none have been preserved so far as I know, though I have some partial lists mentioned in a note, and utilized in my biographical sketches. According to the official report, when the force was mustered out in April 1847 the total number of men enlisted had been 475 mounted riflemen and 41 artillerymen, in ten companies.[4] I append in a note the organization of the battalion into companies, with a full list of officers.[5]

which has been widely copied. See also *Frémont's Cal. Claims; Honolulu Friend*, iv. 190; *Tuthill's Hist. Cal.*, 200–3; and *Lancey's Cruise.* Sutter, *Person. Remin.*, MS., 153–4, says that he, at Frémont's request through Russell, organized the Walla Walla company under a Canadian named Gendreau; also a company of reformed horse-thieves from the Mokelumne and Stanislaus under José Jesus. Nov. 9th, Larkin writes to his wife of Frémont's rapid progress. He will have 400 to 450 men. Some fear that after his force departs Monterey may be attacked. *Larkin's Doc.*, MS., iv. 320. Sutter says F. had officers who could not sign their names. Many 'que ni conocian la o por lo redondo.' *Alvarado, Hist. Cal.*, MS., v. 234.

[4] *31st Cong. 1st Sess., H. Ex. Doc. 24*, p. 22 h.

[5] Official list in *Frémont's Cal. Claims*, 61–3; with corrections from *Brackett's List*, MS.; *Bryant's What I Saw*, 365–8; *Swasey's Cal.*, MS., 19; and other sources. John C. Frémont, lieut-col. commanding battalion (lieut-col. in U. S. A.) Archibald H. Gillespie, major (1st lieut U. S. marines). Pearson B. Reading, paymaster. Henry King, commissary (capt.) Jacob R. Snyder, quartermaster (called maj.) Wm H. Russell, ordnance officer (maj.) Theodore Talbot, adjutant (lieut). John J. Myers, sergeant-maj. and later lieut. Detached officers serving in south and elsewhere: captains, Samuel J. Hensley, Samuel Gibson, Santiago E. Argüello, Miguel Pedrorena, Charles Burroughs (killed before the battalion went south), Bell, and Wm A. T. Maddox (2d lieut U. S. N.) First lieutenants, Hiram Rheusaw, James H. Barton, Edward M. Kern (at Sutter's Fort), Luis Argüello, Benj. D. Wilson, Felipe Butron (?), Montgomery Martin, and Alexis Godey. Second lieut,

On hearing of Flores' revolution, Manuel Castro
and several other officers left Monterey, breaking
their paroles, and made haste to offer their services
to the new general, who on October 23d appointed
Castro commandant of military operations in the

Andrew J. Grayson. Quartermaster, John Bidwell (capt.) Among officers signing a receipt for pay are Ed Gilchrist, surgeon, and Geo. Waldo,
rank not mentioned.

Company A, composed chiefly of Frémont's original explorers. Richard
Owens, capt.; Wm N. Loker, 1st lieut (adjutant later); Benj. M. Hudspeth,
2d lieut (capt. later); Wm Findlay, 2d lieut (capt. later). Co. B, Henry L.
Ford, capt.; Andrew Copeland, 1st lieut. Co. C, Granville P. Swift, capt.;
Wm Baldridge, 1st lieut; Wm Hargrave, 2d lieut. Co. D, John Sears,
capt.; Wm Bradshaw, 1st lieut. Co. E, originally Co. C, or 3d co. of the
organization at Sonoma in July. List of members extant, see below. John
Grigsby, capt.; Archer (or Archibald) C. Jesse, 1st lieut; David T. Bird, 2d
lieut. Co. F, Lansford W. Hastings, capt.; M. M. Wambough, 1st lieut;
James M. Hudspeth, 2d lieut. List of members probably extant. Co. G,
Bluford K. Thompson, capt.; D. A. Davis, 1st lieut; James Rock, 2d lieut.
Partial list of members, see below. Co. H, composed mainly of Walla
Walla and Cal. Indians. Richard T. Jacob, capt.; Edwin Bryant, 1st lieut;
Benj. S. (also called Geo. M.) Lippincott, 2d lieut, acting asst quarter-
master in Jan. Artill. Co. A, Louis McLane, capt., major later (lieut U. S.
N.); John K. Wilson, 1st lieut, later capt. (midshipman U. S. N.); Wm
Blackburn, 2d lieut. Artill. Co. B, apparently organized after the battalion
went south. First lieut A. Girard in command. Muster-roll of 28 names
extant.

In *Grigsby's Papers*, MS., 6-7, 11, 13-14, I find a compact of 33 men of
Co. E, dated Oct. 29th at Sonoma, to serve under Frémont; also list of 33
names (4 new ones being substituted for 4 of the old), with dates of enlistment
from Oct. 4th to Nov. 14th, chiefly at Sonoma. Horace Sanders, orderly
sergeant. In *Cal. Pioneer Soc., Arch.*, MS., 35, I find a list of 57 privates
and 12 officers, without reference to companies, who acknowledge receipt of
pay. In Id., 45, is a muster-roll of Girard's company of artillery, 28 names,
enlistments July to Nov., dated March 25, 1847. In Id., 101-3, is a contract
between Frémont and 71 men, dated at San Juan, Nov. 20th, enlistments
from different dates of Oct. and Nov. This would seem to be Hastings' Co. F,
since Hudspeth and Wambough appear among the names. In Id., 209-10, is
a similar contract with 31 men of the San José company (Thompson's Co. G).
Enlistments for 3 months from Nov. 20th. In Id., 211-12, is similar contract,
dated Monterey, Nov. 10th and 28th, enlistments from different dates of
Sept.-Nov., with 20 men of Co. B (Ford's), 4 of Co. A, and 3, company not
specified. C. P. Briggs, in *Napa Reporter*, Sept. 7, 1872, says that Frémont
wished to break up Thompson's company to fill up the ranks of the others;
but Thompson protested, and after much trouble his men were organized into
a separate company. T. had been Weber's lieutenant at S. José; and there
are indications that W. declined to join the battalion with his men, from dislike of Frémont. In *McKinstry's Papers*, MS., 20-3, is a pay-roll of 50 Indian
soldiers of the New Helvetia garrison, Lieut J. A. Sutter, certified by Lieut.
Kern. Nov. 9th to Feb. 26th, pay of troopers $12.50 per month; infantry,
$6; lieut, $50. Thus we have approximately complete lists for companies B,
E, F, G, and Girard's artillery, about 190 names. For most members of Co.
A, see list of Frémont's explorers in vol. iv., p. 583, of this work. The names
of the Indians in company H, are of no special importance. For companies
C and D, and McLane's artillery, we have no lists; but many additional
names will be found, as well as all those referred to in this note, in my biographical sketches of pioneers.

north, with headquarters at San Luis Obispo. His
instructions were to enlist with or without their consent all capable of bearing arms, and to seize all munitions of war wherever they could be found. Horses
and other supplies were also to be taken as found and
needed, though preferably from foreigners who had
favored the invaders. Powder and horses would be
sent from the south if possible. Francisco Rico was
named as second in command; and Jesus Pico, comandante at San Luis, was ordered to put himself and
men at the orders of the northern chief. The policy
to be followed as in the south was that of harassing
the foe by a guerrilla warfare, cutting off supplies,
preventing communication, stampeding horses, and
watching for opportunities to attack advantageously.
Arriving at San Luis early in November, Don Manuel set himself to work, and with the coöperation of
Rico, Pico, the brothers Joaquin and Gabriel de la
Torre, José Antonio Chavez, and others, he soon raised
a force of about 100 men, many of whom became
soldiers unwillingly. Castro's quest for supplies was
similar in methods to that of Frémont in the north,
but was less successful, since the prospect of payment
was deemed less favorable; though a stirring appeal
from the prefect-commander was issued to Californian
patriots the 7th of November. The same day he reported to Flores what had been accomplished. The
horses were in bad condition; the men had few and
poor weapons; and there was no powder to speak of;
yet he hoped to take some powder from the foe, and
he intended to march for the north two days later.
He probably did start on the 9th or 10th, and two or
three days later, his force being increased to 125 or
130 on the way, he reached the Salinas River in the
region of Soledad. Pilarcitos, Tucho, and half a
dozen other places are named in different narratives
as the sites of military camps in these days, all in the
Salinas Valley below Soledad. The plan of the Californians was to capture as many as possible of Fré-

mont's horses, and thus keeep the battalion from aiding Stockton in the south.[6]

Meanwhile all was quiet at Monterey, but for the bustle of Frémont's preparations. Several of the paroled officers, like Juan B. Alvarado and the Estradas, were keeping their pledges; while Pablo de la Guerra and perhaps a few others were put under arrest in consequence of news from the south.[7] On November 4th it was reported that one of the Torres had recently gone south with 30 men and 200 horses, causing much loss to farmers between Monterey and San Luis.[8] We are told also that several men of the Monterey district, with a knowledge of Castro's movements, were secretly active in collecting arms and ammunition, with a view to coöperate with the approaching force;[9] but if this was true, their operations were not suspected. There were some fears of possible hostilities at the end of October; but it was believed that the return of the battalion had removed all grounds of anxiety. Meanwhile the work of military reorganization was going on actively, and recruits were coming from all directions to swell the force.

On Sunday, the 15th of November, Captain Charles Burroughs, a newly arrived immigrant who had taken

[6] Oct. 23d, Flores to Castro. Appointment and instructions. *Castro, Doc.*, MS., ii. 147. Oct. 30th, J. J. Pico to Castro from S. Luis. *Doc. Hist. Cal.*, MS., iii. 266. Nov. 7th, Castro's report to Flores. *Fernandez, Doc.*, MS., 15. Nov. 7th, Castro's procl. and appeal to Californians. *Doc. Hist. Cal.*, MS., iii. 274. In *Castro's Servicios*, MS., a report of 1847, we have a general account of the prefect's plans and operations during this campaign. The author attempts no explanation of his parole, but admits that he was a prisoner at Monterey. He seems not to have been captured with the rest on the way north, but to have submitted voluntarily, with an idea that the war was over. Alvarado, *Hist. Cal.*, MS., v. 256–8, says the army was organized in three divisions or companies of over 30 men each: 1st, veterans under Gabriel de la Torre; 2d, militia under Jesus Pico; 3d, Mexicans and New Mexicans under Herrera and Quintana. See also *Ord, Ocur.*, MS., 145–6.

[7] Guerra states that he was kept in close confinement until Feb. '47, on account of his great influence on the Californians. *Doc. Hist. Cal.*, MS., iv. 1301. There are other contemporary references to his captivity.

[8] *Mont. Californian*, Nov. 7, 1846.

[9] Torre, *Remin.*, MS., 160–74, gives some details, and names Cárlos and José Antonio Espinosa, Estévan and Pablo de la Torre, and Antonio Ruiz de la Mota as the leaders. They raised a force of some 30 men, and were somewhat successful in getting supplies; but they do not appear to have joined Castro either before or after the fight.

an active part in recruiting, arrived at San Juan Bautista from the Sacramento with about 34 men and a
drove of several hundred horses. The same day there
arrived Captain Thompson with about the same number of men from San José, and all camped for the
night at San Juan.   Knowledge of their presence,
and especially that of the horses, was promptly forwarded to Castro's camp on the Salinas.   It was also
on the 15th that Thomas O. Larkin set out with one
attendant, William Matthews, from Monterey for
Yerba Buena. He had previously sent his family
there for safety, and had just received from his wife a
letter making known the illness of his child, together
with a message from Captain Montgomery, who desired an interview.   Larkin had no suspicion of danger, and stopped for the night at Los Verjeles, the
rancho of Joaquin Gomez, sending Matthews on to
San Juan, and intending to follow him next morning.
But news of his trip reached Castro's camp,[10] and
Chavez conceived the project of capturing the consul.
The other officers, while admitting the advantage of
such a capture, seem to have opposed the act as likely
to make known their presence prematurely and prevent the success of their main purpose; but Chavez
either overcame their fears, or, as some say, undertook
the enterprise without their consent; and at any rate,
he appeared about midnight at Gomez's rancho with
a dozen men.   Larkin was roused from sleep, obliged
to dress in haste, and carried on horseback as a prisoner to the Salinas camp; but he was treated with
the greatest kindness by all the Californian officers
from the beginning to the end of his captivity.   The
plan was to utilize the possession of so important a
man in later negotiations for a truce, exchange of
prisoners, surrender, or escape from consequences of
broken paroles, as circumstances might require.   They

[10] Alvarado, *Hist. Cal.*. MS., v. 259-64, and several other Californians
state that the Fench consul, Gasquet, sent the information of Larkin's departure to Castro; but perhaps this is an error.

also tried at first to induce the prisoner to aid their attempt on San Juan by writing letters to put the garrison on a false scent; but Larkin refused to write; and they in turn refused his proposition to be exchanged for Pablo de la Guerra and others under arrest at Monterey. On the 16th the whole force started northward in four divisions, Larkin being taken along closely guarded. The plan, as he understood it, was for a small party to attack San Juan in the night, and by a retreat to draw out the garrison in pursuit, to be cut off by the main body.[11]

As had been feared, Larkin's capture resulted in making Castro's presence known to the Americans. So far as can be determined from the complicated and contradictory testimony, Captain Thompson started from San Juan early on the 16th for Monterey, to consult with Frémont, accompanied by a small guard and leaving the rest of his men in camp. He seems to have taken a short cut; while Captain Burroughs,

[11] Larkin's captivity is fully described in his original letters in my possession. Nov. 25th, L. to his wife, from Sta Bárbara. *Larkin's Doc.*, MS., iv. 333. Dec. 4th, Id. to Id., from Angeles. *Id.*, iv. 347. Jan. 11th, Id. to Id., from Angeles after release. *Id.*, v. 5. Jan. 14th, Id. to sec. state, from Angeles. *Id.*, *Off. Corresp.*, MS., ii. 90–1. Jan. 22d, Id. to Vallejo, from Angeles. *Vallejo, Doc.*, MS., i. 22. The writer gives many petty details, and often repeats that from Castro and his officers, as well as from Flores and others in the south, he received always the best of treatment; though on a few occasions he was threatened by irresponsible soldiers. In the *Californian* of Feb. 13, 1847, he published a card of thanks in Spanish, to Nic. A. Den, J. A. Carrillo, J. M. Flores and wife, Eulogio Célis and wife, Doña Luisa Argüello de Zamorano, R. S. Den, and Luis Vignes. The news of his capture was published in Id., Nov. 21, 1846; and in Id., Feb. 27, 1847, a kind of journal of his captivity, which has often been reprinted wholly or in part, as in *Bryant's What I Saw*, 361–3; *Frémont's Cal. Claims*, 75–6; *Lancey's Cruise*, 147–8, 180–1; and various county histories. See also, on Larkin's captivity, *Rico, Mem.*, MS., 41–5; *Gomez, Lo Que Sabe*, MS., 49–50; *Botello, Anales*, MS., 170–1; *Soulé's Annals*, 763–4; *Tuthill's Hist Cal*, 200; *Davis' Glimpses*, MS., 355–6; *Ord, Ocur.*, MS., 146; *Savage, Doc.*, MS., 23; and indeed, nearly all the references for the Natividad affair in the following notes. After the fight Larkin was hurried south, by a party under Rico and Noriega. Rico absurdly talks of a plot to kill him and N. and release the prisoner, who was to pay $1,000. Larkin was carried to Sta Bárbara and finally delivered to Flores, at Angeles, by whose order he was shown every kindness, though closely guarded. It was proposed at one time to send him to Mexico with some of the Chino prisoners, as already related; but he was finally released on Jan. 9th, the day before Stockton's occupation of Angeles, and returned to Monterey on the *Cyane* early in February.

with all his men and horses, set out a little later by the main road. At Gomez's rancho Thompson not only learned what had happened there in the night, but saw and pursued ineffectually two scouts who had been sent by Castro to make observations. Failing to capture these, Thompson sent a warning to Burroughs and hastened back to San Juan to bring up his men. Meanwhile Burroughs reached the rancho, learned what had occurred, and sent out a party of six or eight scouts southward into the plain to learn the enemy's whereabouts and numbers.[12]

The Californians advanced northward, Joaquin de la Torre with a dozen horsemen as scouts in advance. Then came the vanguard under Castro, followed by Chavez's company, with Larkin in charge, while Rico commanded the rear guard, including a party in

[12] It is impossible to be entirely certain about the details of these events. One of the best accounts extant is that by 'E. C. K.' (Kemble, I think), in the *S. F. Californian*, Aug. 21, 1847. His version is in substance that of my text, except that he seems to represent Thompson as having accompanied Burroughs in the morning, and as first sending and then coming back to S. Juan for his men; but he also speaks of T. having sent a man to warn B., which is inconsistent with the theory that T. had accompanied B. Again 'K.' (perhaps also Kemble) wrote an account for the *Sac. Union*, 1869, which I take from the *Los Angeles Star*, Dec. 25, 1869, in which he represents Burroughs, after his scouts had met the foe, to have sent Lieut Rock (of Thompson's co., but who had accompanied B.) back to S. Juan to bring up Thompson and his men. 'K.' was one of T.'s men. Again, Winston Bennett, *Pioneer of '43*, says that when Burroughs sent back for aid, being attacked, a messenger was sent to overtake T., who had started with 3 men for Mont. across the hills. T. was overtaken, returned, and marched to aid B. Lancey, *Cruise*, 148-9, following 'Kemble and others,' has it that B. and T. both started for Mont. with a small guard, leaving their companies at S. Juan; that B. sent back to his lieut to bring up the force as soon as he learned the presence of the foe on reaching Gomez's rancho; and that T. came back about the same time to lead his men, having also learned the presence of the foe, and sent a warning to B. Swasey, *Cal. in '45-6*, MS., 15 et seq., ignores all this preliminary matter, and implies that the entire forces under B. and T. (and erroneously Grigsby), advanced to Gomez's rancho, heard of the foe, and finally determined on an attack. Francisco Rico, *Mem.*, MS., 35 et seq., and several other Californians mention the meeting between Castro's scouts and a party of 8 Amer., some of them naming Thompson. Vicente P. Gomez, *Lo Que Sabe*, MS., 316 et seq. (other versions by G., p. 35, 49), says that he and his brother, sons of Joaquin G., owner of Los Verjeles, were the scouts, and gives particulars of the pursuit by Thompson's men. Most of the Californians think that Matthews, Larkin's companion, camped near the rancho, escaped capture, and carried the news to S. Juan; but none of the American witnesses say anything of Matthews. I have no doubt, from a careful study of the testimony, that the version of my text is in substance correct.

charge of horses and munitions under Sergeant Lázaro Soto. It was perhaps 3 o'clock P. M., or even later, when the advance arrived at the Natividad rancho and met the American scouts. These were the men, six to ten in number, who had been sent out by Burroughs before Thompson's arrival. They included George Foster, often called captain, John (or James) Hayes, the two Delaware Indians, Tom Hill, and James Salmon, and several Walla Wallas. I think they had been in the vicinity several hours. On seeing the foe, two or three of the Indians fled to the rancho to give the alarm, while the rest posted themselves in the *encinalito*, or little grove of oaks, close at hand, where they were presently attacked by Torre, and completely surrounded as soon as Castro and Chavez came up. The fight at the grove lasted an hour, according to the estimate of Larkin, who was a spectator. The consul was desired to go to the Americans and induce them to surrender; but refused to do so unless he could offer a safe retreat to San Juan or Monterey, to which Castro would not consent. The riflemen behind trees had an advantage notwithstanding the disparity of numbers against the horsemen with their few ineffective muskets. Lieutenant Chavez and Alférez Juan Ignacio Cantua were badly wounded,[13] and probably two or three Californians were killed, to be scalped by the Indian warriors. But Foster, riddled with musket-balls, at last fell dead at the foot of the tree that had protected him; and Hayes was disabled by serious wounds in the thighs. Then the main body of the Americans appeared in sight; 25 or 30 men were left

[13] Larkin saw an officer who crept up to get a view shot, and carried off by one of his companions. This was probably Cantua, the standard-bearer, and Alvarado names Mariano Soberanes as the man who distinguished himself by carrying off the wounded man on his horse, thus saving him from the tomahawks and scalping-knives of the Indians. Alvarado's informant, Juan de Mata Boronda—whose version is also given in *Vallejo, Hist. Cal.*, MS., v. 166–70—and some other natives state that the Americans drew the Californians into an ambush at the grove; but this seems unfounded, except by the fact that the Californians were surprised at finding the grove occupied by a foe.

to besiege the few remaining scouts; Rico's rear guard was moved up; and the Californian army, about 65 strong, was drawn up on the plain to the right or east of the grove, to meet the enemy.[14]

When Thompson arrived with reënforcements from San Juan, after the scouts had been sent out but before the encinalito fight began,[15] there arose a discussion as to what should be done. Thompson and many of the men in both companies favored an advance to attack the Californians; but Burroughs with much reason hesitated to incur the needless risk of engaging in a conflict which might result in a loss of his horses and the failure of all Frémont's plans. The controversy became heated as time passed on, and taunts of cowardice were flung at the captain by the irresponsible volunteers, Thompson, a reckless fire-eater, becoming extremely violent in his remarks.[16] If any further incentive was needed, it came presently in reports from the Walla Walla scouts of what was going on at Natividad.[17] Detaching fourteen men to guard the horses in Gomez's corrals, and committing

[14] Swasey makes the grove fight a part of the general engagement, stating that the scouts entered the woods to the right as the Americans advanced, both fights going on together; but this seems to have no support. A writer in the *Sta Cruz Times*, Aug. 27, 1870, tells us that the grove siege lasted 4 hours before the main body appeared; but this is doubtless an error, unless we include all the time spent by the scouts at the grove before the enemy appeared.

[15] Some imply the contrary, and some even state that the fight began before a demand for aid was sent to S. Juan at all; but this seems very unlikely. 'K.' says Thompson arrived at 9 A. M., and before noon the line was drawn up on the edge of the plain, though the advance did not begin till 3 P. M. This may be accurate, and it is possible that the scouts were posted in the grove; but that the fight had begun or was known to be raging at the time of his arrival I cannot believe. 'E. C. K.' has it that the message reached S. Juan at 10 A. M., and the force arrived at the rancho an hour later, which is more probable. Lancey says it was 5 P. M. when the scouts left the main body for Natividad, but this may be a misprint.

[16] Red-haired, sorrel-top, hell-roaring Thompson are some of the names by which he was known.

[17] Bennett says that Foster's Walla Wallas broke through the Californian lines and brought the news of Foster's death and Hayes' wounds, B. being the interpreter of the message for Thompson. All this seems to me extremely improbable, especially as Bennett is clearly wrong in several other particulars. These Walla Wallas were probably those who left Foster before the fight began, but possibly men who had been sent out to see what had become of Foster's company, and saw the fight from a distance. This theory agrees with the *Sta Cruz Times* account.

to their care a field-piece found at the last moment to be unserviceable for the fight, Burroughs gave the order to advance, and the little army of about fifty men began their march, perhaps half an hour or more after the encinalito fight had begun.

The Californians were superior in numbers and were skilful horsemen; but their weapons were a miscellaneous collection of improvised lances, reatas, ineffective escopetas, and pistols, with powder for only a few discharges of the fire-arms. The Americans were, most of them, but indifferent riders; but they were well armed with rifles and had plenty of ammunition. Coming in sight of the enemy, Burroughs' men advanced rapidly over the plain. Castro's men fired their muskets at long range, doing no harm. The Americans, halting, discharged their rifles, and at once charged upon the foe at full speed, with wild shouts, in a manner more creditable to their valor than to their discipline, each man for himself, with Captain Burroughs in advance on his gray charger 'Sacramento.' The charge was a blunder like that committed at San Pascual a little later, and with similar results. The Californians feigned flight, in accordance with their usual tactics;[18] but presently turned to attack their pursuers, as they came at full speed over the plain in disorder and armed with empty rifles. At the same time apparently the 20 or 30 men at the grove rushed up to attack the Americans on the rear or flank.[19] Some writers describe what followed as a desperate hand-to-hand fight, lasting from ten to twenty minutes; but this is shown by the results to be an exaggeration. In such a conflict a large number of Americans must have fallen. But

[18] Indeed, 30 or 40 of them ran away in good earnest, according to Larkin, who was still a spectator. These were probably men who were serving against their will. During the fight, Lorenzo Soto, in his wrath at seeing a relative fall, rushed upon Larkin to kill (or scare?) him, but L. saved himself by backing his horse behind others! L. was, however, compelled to change animals successively until he was reduced to a '$1 horse and $2 saddle.'

[19] Henry Marshall, Statement, MS., 2–3, was wounded by a lance in this part of the fight, which he describes more fully than any other, being followed by Lancey. 'E. C. K.' also mentions this movement, stating that 2 Americans were killed and one wounded.

I suppose that only the foremost pursuers, and a few of Castro's men, came actually to close quarters for a very brief period. The brave Burroughs, however, leading the charge, fell dead, pierced by a pistol-bullet;[20] two or three others were killed; and several were wounded. Very soon, however, the Americans fell back into a more compact body; some of those in the rear, who had either reserved their fire at first or had time to reload, fired upon the advancing foe, killing and wounding several; and Castro's men again fled.[21] The Californians remained in sight until nightfall, and may have indulged in some charges and evolutions at a safe distance; but there was no more fighting, and at last the enemy disappeared in the distance. Larkin describes the fight as having lasted some twenty or thirty minutes, and says the Californians disappeared in successive detachments. The Californians say that the Americans finally dismounted and took refuge among the trees, which is not unlikely; and that they retreated because they had no possible chance of success against the rifles, especially as they had no more powder. Captain Thompson withdrew his force to Gomez's rancho to bury his dead, care for the wounded, and make preparations for defence, since a renewal of the attack

[20] 'E. C. K.' says: 'He fell headlong from his horse, his unloaded rifle in hand, shot down by a swarthy New Mexican, in the act of turning upon him.' 'K.' says the dashing 'hidalgo rode up abreast, with the other sent his bullet through our leader's body.' Christian Chauncey, an eye-witness, tells us that Burroughs was shot by 'Three-fingered Jack,' who wished to get his horse and saddle, though the horse escaped. *S. F. Alta*, Aug. 8, 1853. Lancey identifies the 'swarthy New Mexican' with 'Three-fingered Jack,' as Bernardino García, the murderer of Cowie and Fowler at Sta Rosa in July. According to *Sta Cruz Times*, Torre was the man who killed Burroughs; Alvarado says it was Juan de Mata Boronda; and Swasey, who gives one of the best accounts of the battle, is positive that it was Manuel Castro himself. Clearly it is not known who fired the shot. Swasey notes that B. had in his pocket a packet of letters for men at Monterey, the corner of each being cut off and blood-marked by the ball.

[21] It is said that Burroughs had at first ordered every alternate man to fire; but in the excitement little attention was paid to the order. Thompson, however, induced some of his men to reserve their fire, and was thus able at last to repulse the enemy. Wm M. Boggs, in *Napa Register*, May 4, 1872, following Gregson—see also *Gregson's Statement*, MS., 4–5—says that the arrival of Weber with reënforcements put an end to the fight; but this is only a confused reference to Thompson's arrival at an earlier hour.

was feared. Tom Hill, with perhaps another Indian
named McIntosh, was sent to Monterey with a message for Frémont, and is said to have had a fight on
the way, in which he was wounded.[22]

The Americans lost at Natividad four or five
men killed, including Burroughs, Foster, Ames, and
Thorne;[23] and five or six wounded, including Hayes,
Hill, Marshall, William McGlone, and James Cash.
At least, these are the losses reported; but it is possible that they were more numerous, though the Californians doubtless exaggerate in their narratives.[24]
Foster was buried at the foot of the tree where he
fell; the others were interred at Gomez's rancho, and
a salute fired over their graves. The Californian
loss was perhaps about the same as that of the Americans, though really little is known about it beyond the
wounding of Chavez and Cantua at the grove. That
so few were killed on the American side is accounted
for by the short duration of the fight at close quarters;
but that the rifles did so little execution, especially at

[22] The Delaware's arrival is noted (incorrectly as on the morning of the
16th) in *Colton's Three Years*, 96-7; also his fight on the way, in which he
met 3 Californians, killing one with his rifle, another with his tomahawk,
while the third fled. Swasey implies that Hill's wound was received in the
fight before he started for Monterey, from the fragments of a bullet. Lancey
has it that he got a lance through the hand from the Indian he tomahawked
on the way. 'E. C. K.' says Charles McIntosh and an Indian were sent to
Monterey. See also *Californian*, Nov. 21, 1846, for adventures of the Walla
Walla messengers.

[23] 'Billy the Cooper' is mentioned by several authorities as having been
killed. His real name was not known; but he was possibly the man called
Thorne by 'E. C. K.' and others.

[24] 'Pioneer' (John A. Swan), in reminiscences called out by 'K.'s' article,
Savage, Doc., MS., iii. 20 et seq., was personally acquainted with the killed
and wounded, and many others who took part in the fight, and he thinks the
loss was heavier than reported. 4 killed and 5 wounded is 'E. C. K.'s' statement. Larkin says 4 killed and 2 or 3 wounded, perhaps not including the
grove fight; and again he says there were 10 or 12 killed and wounded on
each side. Gomez states that 4 dead and 9 wounded were brought to the
rancho, 6 more dead found and buried at the grove, and 3 bodies found later
by the people of Natividad. José Ant. Alviso, *Campaña de Natividad*, MS.,
son of the owner of the rancho, who claims to have first informed Castro of
the presence of the Americans at S. Juan, says 4 Amer. were killed and 4
wounded. Rico says that in the main fight he saw 8 or 9 Amer. killed, and
heard of more, besides those killed at the grove. In a report of the time,
Castro claimed to have killed 21 of the enemy. *Fernandez, Doc.*, MS., 53.
Pico says the Amer. lost 2 officers and several soldiers killed. Flores in Dec.
reported that 11 Amer. had been killed.

the grove, where the enemy came near enough to riddle Foster's body with musket-balls, is remarkable; and, indeed, it is not unlikely that the loss may have been greater than represented. From a dozen to twenty was the estimate of the Americans, who of course had no means of knowing the truth.[25] The dead were probably buried at Alisal rancho. Lieutenant Chavez was cared for secretly at some of the ranchos, and finally came to Monterey in January, where for a long time he eluded the vigilance of officials, largely by the aid of prominent ladies.[26] The Californians after leaving Natividad dispersed for the most part as they advanced southward. Rico with a small party hastened with Larkin to the capital, where Castro also made his appearance later with 25 or 30 of his army. Though the Americans were the attacking party, and were content to remain on the defensive after the fight, yet the result was practically a victory for them, since the Californians were forced to abandon their projects of seizing the horses and harassing the battalion by a guerrilla warfare.[27]

Frémont and his men left Monterey November 17th as soon as the news arrived from Los Verjeles. He

[25] Alviso says the Cal. lost 4 wounded. Rico says he lost 4 killed and 4 wounded, besides several killed before at the grove. Loss about same as the Amer. according to Alvarado. Vallejo gives the loss as 3 killed and 4 wounded; including Vicente Soto and Bautista García. 3 killed and 5 wounded according to Castro's report. Mrs Ord says 2 killed. Inocente García, *Hechos*, MS., 97-8, says his son Bautista was wounded; also heard from a fugitive at S. Luis that a cholo and a cook from S. Luis and several from Monterey had been killed. Piço says several of his own men were killed and wounded. Nidever, *Life*, MS., 129-30, says an Italian cutthroat named Antonio was killed on the Cal. side. Larkin says 3 Californians were killed, besides José García from S. America; and 7 wounded. Gomez says the Walla Wallas scalped 4 Californians.

[26] Many stories are told of Chavez's adventures in trying to avoid arrest. Once he was concealed in bed between two women, which prompts Rev. Walter Colton, *Three Years*, 145, to wickedly quote a verse from *Don Juan*. See also Ord, *Ocurrencias*, MS., 152-4; Gomez, *Lo Que Sabe*, MS., 95-6. Lancey, *Cruise*, 151, tells us Chavez was taken on board the guard-ship at Monterey and had his wounds dressed.

[27] Besides the references already given on the Natividad affair, see *Honolulu Friend*, iv. 190; *Martin's Narr.*, MS., 35; *Osio, Hist. Cal.*, MS., 479-80; *Larios, Vida*, MS., 23-4; *Amador, Mem.*, MS., 170-2; *Upham's Life Frémont*, 242-5; *Taylor's Eldorado*, i. 194; and many of the county histories.

made some expeditions in different directions in search
of such parties of the enemy as might still be lurking
in the district; but found no Californians, and in four
or five days united his forces at San Juan, where he
remained till the end of November. Some parties of
recruits joined the force there, and one from the Sacramento did not arrive until the army had started
southward. At San Juan the organization of the battalion, as already described, was completed; and on
the 29th the army started on its march to coöperate
with Stockton against Flores. The march was for
the most part uneventful, and requires no extended
description. Bryant's diary is in print, and is supplemented by many other narratives more or less complete.[28] The rains of an extremely wet season had
begun, and progress was consequently slow and difficult along the muddy way. The old grass was spoiled
by the rain, and the new was not sufficient to keep the
horses in strength. Many of the animals had to be
abandoned on the way, and still more could barely
carry their saddles without the riders, so that a large
part of the march was performed by the men on foot.
Luggage was carried by pack-mules. Beef was almost
the only article of food, cattle being driven along with
the army and killed at each halt as required. Many
of the men were ill, but only one death occurred. The
route was up the San Benito, over the hills to the
Salinas, up that valley and past San Miguel to San
Luis, where they arrived the 14th of December.

There is no reason to doubt that Frémont and his
officers exerted themselves to prevent disorders and
outrages on the march, and with a high degree of

[28] *Bryant's What I Saw*, 365–91; itinerary of dates and distances in *Grigsby's Papers*, MS., 9–12; weather record in *Frémont's Geog. Mem.*, 41–2. Other
narratives will be mentioned in later notes on special points; but the following may be named as not requiring further mention, though some of them are
accurate enough: *S. F. Star*, Jan. 9, 1847, copied in other papers; *S. F. Alta*,
Dec. 18, 1852; *Martin's Narr.*, MS., 36–8; *Lancey's Cruise*, 156–65; *Tuthill's
Hist. Cal.*, 200–3; *Upham's Life Frémont*, 242–9; *Dicc. Univ.*, viii. 160; *Cutts'
Conq.*, 160–2; *Honolulu Friend*, iv. 190; *Yolo Co. Hist.*, 20; and several other
local histories.

success, considering the unfavorable circumstances. There was some complaint and insubordination among the men and subaltern officers, requiring a court-martial for the trial of certain offenders on December 7th.[29] The trail of Castro's retreating force was crossed; and on the 8th two Californians were arrested, as were several later. An Indian servant of Jesus Pico was taken on the 12th, and next day shot as a spy after trial. The evidence against him has never been made public, but the act was doubtless an unjustifiable compliance with a bitter popular feeling in the army. On the same day the rancho of Ojitos was plundered, its buildings being burned by a scouting party.[30] At San Luis Obispo it was thought there might be an armed force, and the place was accordingly surrounded and taken by a sudden assault on the 14th in the rainy darkness of night; but only women, children, and non-combatants were found.[31]

The house of Pico, the former commandant, was

[29] *Bryant*, 371. Swasey, *Cal. 1845-6*, MS., 21, mentions James Savage as one of the worst malecontents, and says that several officers were reduced to the ranks, there being also several desertions. Swasey, p. 24-5, notes that on one occasion shots were heard in advance, and the men were found engaged in a battle with grizzly bears, of which 26 were killed. Boggs, in *Napa Register*, May 4, 1872, notes a mirage by which a madroño tree was made to appear a large force of the enemy. Also in Id., June 1, 1872, is described a practical joke in which the bugler, Butler, was made to blow his morning blast and rouse the camp, mistaking the moon for the sun.

[30] Pico, *Acont.*, MS., 70, says the Indian, named Santa María, had been sent out by him to watch the Americans. It is generally stated that papers were found on his person, perhaps communications to the enemy. *S. José Pioneer*, Jan. 27, 1877. Paso Robles is mentioned by several as the place where he was arrested. Swasey says the shooting of the Indian was opposed by many of the officers, but it was deemed unsafe to disregard the feelings of the undisciplined men. Janssens, *Vida*, MS., 197, says that Frémont farther south mentioned the different outrages as the acts of detached parties, whom he could not control. Serrano says Los Ojitos was burned because the owner had two sons in the Californian army; also that the bell-ringer of San Luis was threatened with death for having rung the vesper bells, and soon died of fright. Gonzalez, *Mem.*, MS., 42-3, denounces these acts as cowardly, and notes that an American tried to mount a wild colt and was killed, probably an error.

[31] Swasey, *Cal. '45-6*, MS., 21-2, graphically describes the amusing scenes of this night assault, including Capt. Sears' valiant charge over adobe walls into a sheep corral. He also notes that many were made ill by eating ravenously of the pumpkins and frijoles found at San Luis. There have been reports that the inhabitants were surprised at a ball, but this seems to have no foundation in fact. See *Bryant*, 374; *Janssens, Vida*, MS., 193; *Pico, Acont.*, MS., 71; *Lancey's Cruise*, 160.

searched with special zeal, but was found to be occupied by Henry J. Dally, from whom it was learned that the owner was probably at Wilson's rancho; and a party was despatched at once to arrest him, under Dally's guidance. They returned next day with their prisoner, and on the 16th he was tried by court-martial. Pico had not only broken his parole in taking up arms for Flores, but he had been prominent in the movement, had forced many Californians into the ranks, and had taken part with them in the campaign of Natividad. These facts were made known to Frémont through certain communications that had been delivered to him by Petronilo Rios a few days before, and which were produced at the trial. The sentence was that Don Jesus, familiarly known as Totoi Pico, must be shot, a fate that he technically deserved. But his wife, accompanied by her fourteen children and many women of San Luis, came to throw herself at the American leader's feet, begging for her husband's life. Frémont could not resist her tearful pleadings, to which were joined the solicitations of his officers and of some of his men whom Pico had befriended in former years. He granted a pardon, and though it provoked much temporary dissatisfaction among his rude followers, the act gained for him the life-long gratitude and devotion of Don Jesus, who accompanied the battalion to the south, rendering every assistance in his power. Several others were arrested, but released in the region of San Luis, including Joaquin Estrada, Inocente García, and Mariano Bonilla, the latter being left as alcalde to preserve order at the ex-mission.[32]

[32] *Pico, Acontecimientos*, MS., 67–73. He says the documents had been intrusted by him to Reed, owner of S. Miguel rancho, who had sent them to Capt. Villavicencio by Rios, who was taken by Frémont. Dally, *Narrative*, MS., 27–41, gives complete details of the affair. Both Dally and Breck had been arrested by the Californians during the military preparations, but released on parole. It appears from his statements and from other evidence that some of the Californians on returning from Natividad were very bitter, and swore they would kill all foreigners, who were advised by the officers to keep in close retirement until the danger was past. Some were arrested for protection. Streeter, *Recoll.*, MS., 67–75, also gives many details of the

Leaving San Luis on the 17th, the battalion continued its march southward without incidents requiring notice,[33] and on the 24th climbed the lofty Cuesta de Santa Inés by a difficult pass not far from that of the modern stage route. The afternoon of Christmas was spent in descending the southern slope of the mountain, an operation rendered difficult and even perilous by the rain which fell in torrents all the afternoon and night with a continuous gale of wind. Horses to the number of a hundred or more fell over the precipices or were drowned in the mountain torrents; the cannon and other luggage were left scattered along the way; the men slid rather than marched down the slippery rocks, waded the gullies, and at dark, storm-drenched and half-frozen, lay down to rest near the foot of the mountain without protection from the pouring rain, some not arriving till late at night. Next day the guns and some other effects were brought down to camp; and on the 27th the battalion went on to Santa Bárbara. No enemy appeared to resist their advance; a few foreigners came out to meet them; but the town was wellnigh deserted. Here Frémont remained a week in camp before proceeding southward, whither we shall accompany him later.[34]

troubles of foreigners in those days. Inocente García went to Sta Bárbara with Pico and Frémont. In his *Hechos*, MS., 92–100, he gives many particulars. Martin, *Narr.*, MS., 36–7, one of Dally's and Pico's captors, has also something to say on the subject. Swasey, *Cal. '45–6*, gives an eloquent account of the pardon scene; as also does Talbot in *Cutts' Conq.*, 160–1. See also *Bigelow's Mem.*, 145–7; *Davis' Glimpses*, MS., 378–9; *Lancey's Cruise*, 117, 161. Dec. 16th, Bonilla's appointment as alcalde of S. Luis. *Bonilla, Doc.*, MS., 20. It is hard to say what Frémont, *Court-martial*, 378, means by the statement that he captured Pico 'with 35 others, among them the wounded captain who had commanded at La Natividad'!

[33] Janssens, *Vida*, MS., 193–5, who was living near Sta Inés at the time, gives some unimportant details of the passage of Frémont's army.

[34] Davis, *Glimpses*, MS., 357–60, 374–6; Dittmann, *Narrative*, MS., 39–41; Streeter, *Recoll.*, MS., 75–81; and Nidever, *Life*, MS., 127–9, give some details about Frémont's arrival and stay at Sta Bárbara. The last-named takes particular pleasure in recounting his services in aiding in the search of houses belonging to prominent citizens like Guerra. See also, on the march of the battalion and passage of the mountains, *Gregson's Statement*, MS., 5–6; *McChristian's Narr.*, MS., 5–8; *Bennett's Pioneer of '43*; *Bidwell's Cal.*, MS., 201–4; *Sta Cruz Sentinel*, March 21, 1868.

With their vivid descriptions of hardships experienced in crossing the Cuesta de Santa Inés many writers mingle sarcasm, ridicule, and blame, directed against Frémont for his choice of a route over the summit, instead of by the comparatively easy Gaviota pass. They accuse him not only of bad judgment and excessive timidity in his fear of hostilities along the way, but of having deliberately prolonged his march from the beginning to the end, with a view to avoid an encounter with the foe at Los Angeles. The charge of cowardice or lack of energy is an unjust one, though it may be clear to us, knowing the exact condition of affairs, that the trip over the mountains involved needless risks and hardships. But at the time, the strength of the Californians in men, horses, and weapons was grossly exaggerated; rumors of impending attack were current at every point; and there were probably definite warnings of danger at the pass from persons whom the leader deemed trustworthy, making it seem important to take an unusual route, which but for the violent storm would have involved no very serious hardships. Unfavorable comment on Frémont's action in this matter, as on his achievements as an explorer in earlier years, has sprung largely from the political prejudices of 1856. The average American cannot be trusted to testify fairly in the case of a political foe, being in that respect strikingly similar to the citizen of any other nation.

A final northern campaign of the war remains to be put on record before we return to the operations of Stockton, Kearny, and Frémont in the south. Could we credit all that has been written of this campaign, a long and somewhat interesting story might be told. Reduced to approximate limits of truth, the record is much less bulky and loses something of its fascination. While the organization and outfit of the battalion were in progress, Captain Weber took an active part in procuring horses for that force, and most of his volunteer company joined Frémont under Thompson; but Weber raised another company for the protection of San José and the adjoining region, since there was no lack of rumors respecting impending hostilities by bands of roving Californians. Lieutenant Pinkney, of the *Savannah*, with midshipmen Watmough and Griffin, and a company of 50 men or more, was also sent by Captain Mervine from Yerba Buena to garrison the pueblo, while Weber was busy in obtaining horses for the battalion. Many immigrants came down from the Sacramento to Santa Clara, fortifying the ex-mission, and organizing a company of about 30 men, under Joseph Aram as captain, for the protection of their families and those of their companions who were absent with Frémont. Thus the garrisons at Monterey, San Francisco, San José, and Santa Clara were amply sufficient for protection. There was much difficulty in obtaining supplies of food; and Frémont's methods of plundering every rancho where cattle or other stores could be found were to a great extent those still employed.[35]

Throughout the preceding troubles many Californians of the better class had remained quietly on their farms, submitting not cheerfully but without resistance to the exchange of their animals and other property for Frémont's receipts. Their patience, however, had been sorely tried during the process by the outrageous acts of different irresponsible Americans, who carried on the work of plunder under a show of military authority but beyond the control of the battalion officers;[36] and it was completely exhausted when

[35] On the organization of Weber's, Pinkney's, and Aram's companies, see *Hall's Hist. S. José*, 155-7; *Hecox*, in *Sta Cruz Times*, July-Aug. 1870; *Lancey's Cruise*, 192. Nov. 26th, J. A. Forbes at Sta Clara certifies that in consequence of immigrants' fears of attack a wall is to be made in front of mission with only one entrance. Doña Silveria Pacheco rents her house for this purpose at $12 per month. *S. José, Arch., Loose Pap.*, 57.

[36] 'They are a class of persons who have drifted over the mountains into the country from the borders of some of our western states. It is a prime feature in their policy to keep in advance of law and order, and to migrate as often as these trench on their irresponsible privileges. Their connection with our military operations here is a calamity that can only find a relief in

it became evident that the depredations were to be continued after the departure of both armies. They were ready to resist if an opportunity should present itself. About the 8th of December as is generally stated, but later I think, since the news did not reach Monterey till the 22d, Alcalde Bartlett with five men started down the peninsula from Yerba Buena on one of the usual raids for cattle—that is he went to 'purchase' supplies. Francisco Sanchez, who had a rancho in the San Mateo region, and who had lost his own horses and those of Howard and Mellus under his care at the hands of Weber, could not resist the temptation to retaliate. So with a small party he waylaid Bartlett and his companions, making them prisoners and carrying them to a camp in the hills. It is not probable that there had been any formal organization or plan before, but now reënforcements came in from different quarters until Sanchez had perhaps 100 men. Some were impelled by exasperation at past losses; others by fear of vicarious punishment for Sanchez's act; and there was probably a party of some 20 men who had been recruited by Torre, Espinosa, and Mota for Castro's army but had not joined that force, and had been ranging about the country secretly since the fight at Natividad, joined perhaps by a few members of the dispersed army.[37] The plan, so far as any plan was formed, was to utilize the prisoners, with such other advantages as they might gain, to exact from the Americans a treaty to protect their property and put an end to depredations.[38] No acts of hostility were committed.

the exigencies of war...The principal sufferers are men who have remained quietly on their farms, and whom we are bound in honor as well as sound policy to protect. To permit such men to be plundered under the filched authority of our flag is a national reproach.' *Colton's Three Years*, 155.

[37] Estévan de la Torre, *Remin.*, MS., gives some details, but he does not state that the men of his party joined Sanchez, or indeed give any information about this affair.

[38] Colton describes them as with few exceptions 'men of the better stamp, men who had a permanent interest in the soil, and had refused to join the rash spirits of the south.' They stated 'that they had taken up arms not to make war on the American flag, but to protect themselves from the depredations

In the eyes of the Americans this act of Sanchez
was the outbreak of a new rebellion, in which the Californians took advantage of Frémont's departure to
rise, 200 strong, for the purpose of committing outrages on the unprotected immigrants.[39] As soon as
proper steps for defence could be taken, but somewhat
tardily it would appear if Bartlett was captured on
the 8th, Captain Weber marched from San José with
33 men on the 25th to attack the foe; but changed
his mind and went to San Francisco for orders and reenforcements. Sanchez is said to have taken advantage of Weber's absence to approach San José the next
day, hoping to find the pueblo unprotected, but to
have retired on finding Pinkney and his garrison prepared to fight.[40] Meanwhile, a force was fitted out
and despatched on the 29th by Commandant Hull,
who had succeeded Montgomery at San Francisco.
This force of about 100, including Weber's company,
was commanded by Captain Ward Marston of the marines.[41] The march was down the peninsula, delayed

of those who under color of that flag were plundering them, . . . and that on
assurance being given that these acts of lawless violence should cease, they
were ready to return quietly to their homes.' *Three Years*, 152.

[39] For instance, Hecox, *Sta Cruz Times*, July 23, 1870, talks of Sanchez's
men as raiding through the county, capturing Bartlett, and then turning their
attention to Sta Clara in hopes to make short work of the men and 'appropriate the women to their own use'!

[40] Hall, *Hist. S* *José*, 157 et seq., followed by others, speaks of a warning
sent to Pinkney by Sanchez, but I doubt that there was any correspondence
at all. The same writers say that Forbes went to the Californian camp to
negotiate for a release of the prisoners. Sanchez put Bartlett in Forbes'
keeping for several days, and offered to give up all the captives in exchange
for Weber; but the authorities at S. F. being consulted refused to consent to
any such arrangement. I do not believe that any such proposition was made,
and I think it most likely that Forbes' visit and the partial release of Bartlett
were later occurrences. See note 45. In *S. José Pioneer*, March 6th, it is
stated that Pinkney was sent down to take Weber's place at this time, and it
may be true that P. had previously retired and now returned; as this would
explain the approach of Sanchez. Hall represents Bartlett as having cried
like a child when sent back to the Californians, expecting to be killed!

[41] According to list in *Monterey Californian*, Feb. 6, 1847, followed by Bry-
ant, Hall, Lancey, and also in *S. F. Pacific News*, Dec. 12, 1850, from *Civil,
Lit. and Naval Gazette*, the force was made up as follows: Capt. Ward Mars-
ton, with Asst Surgeon J. (or Marius) Duval as aid; 34 marines under Lieut
Robert Tansill; 10 seamen with a field-piece under Master Wm F. Delong
(D. Gough or de Longh or De Iongh) assisted by Midshipman John Kell;
John Pray as interpreter; 33 mounted San José volunteers under Captain Chas
M. Weber, with lieutenants John Murphy and John Reed; and 12 mounted

somewhat as it appears by the quality and quantity of aguardiente found at one of the halting-places; and on January 2d the enemy was seen on the Santa Clara plain. As the Americans advanced along the road, the Californians on horseback hovered about them on front and flanks at a safe distance, Marston firing grape from his field-piece and Sanchez replying apparently with a few musket-shots.[42] Thus the two forces slowly approached Santa Clara, being in sight of each other for several hours. Either at the beginning or at some later point of the advance the gun and part of Marston's force seem to have become mired in crossing a marshy spot, and Sanchez made a 'charge;' that is, his men came for a few minutes within gunshot, and slightly wounded two of the Americans,[43] but retired as soon as the cannon was again in condition to be used. As they drew near to the mission, perhaps Captain Aram came out to aid Marston; at any rate, the Californians disappeared from sight, going toward the Santa Cruz mountains. The Americans, making no attempt to pursue the foe, repaired to the mission, and the 'battle of Santa Clara' was at an end. It has generally been described, though with many curious complications of detail, as a sharp engagement of several hours, in which Marston's gallant band attacked the enemy in a strong position, broke their line, drove them back inch by inch under a constant shower of bullets, and finally caused them to flee with four or five men killed and as many wounded, so demoralized that there was nothing left for them but unconditional surrender! No Californian was hurt; and evidently Sanchez had no intention of risking a fight, unless by

Yerba Buena volunteers under Capt. W. M. Smith and Lieut John Rose, including a few men under Captain Julius Martin—or 101 men in all. Jan. 9th, Richardson to Fitch. Mentions Bartlett's capture and the departure of Marston's force. *Fitch, Doc.*, MS., 411.

[42] The Californians are said to have had a field-piece given up later; but it is not stated that it was used.

[43] One of Weber's men and a marine from the *Dale*. Lancey names them as Jackson Bennett and Robert Heeney. I. M. Baker assures me that he saw the men wounded.

good fortune the marines might be tempted into a
pursuit resulting in a hand-to-hand conflict on horseback.[44]

In the evening a messenger came in from Sanchez
with a flag of truce, doubtless to explain the grievances which had driven his countrymen to arms, and
to offer submission on condition that the United States
officers would guarantee protection of property; and
an armistice was agreed upon until a reply could be
obtained from San Francisco.[45] Next day, the 3d,

[44] The earliest account in the *Monterey Californian*, Jan. 16, 1847, mentioned no fight, but says that Weber was driven into Sta Clara by the Californians, the leaders met under a flag of truce, and the Californians agreed
to disperse under proper guaranties. In the next accounts, Id., Feb. 6,
1847; *Bryant*, 415-16, there had been an hour's fight, 2 Amer. wounded, Cal.
losing a horse, and 'probably' some men killed and wounded; but the Cal.
were able to escape, having superior horses. In the *S. F. Cal. Star*, Jan.
9, 1847, is a report that Marston had captured the whole party of Cal. and
ended the war. In Id., Jan. 23d, the version is that the enemy had retired
from their 'fortifications' near S. F., on Marston's approach, and retreated to
near Sta Clara, where they made a stand; but the cannon in a few hours
brought out a flag of truce, leading to a satisfactory settlement and full pardon of all. In Id., Feb. 6th, the battle is described as in *Californian* and a
list of officers is given; but after this was put in type it was learned that 4
Cal. had been killed and 5 badly wounded! In the *Annapolis Civil, Lit. and
Naval Gazette* of 1850, or earlier, appeared an elaborate account of the battle,
and especially of the evolutions of Marston's forces, from the journal of an
officer. I have no doubt this account is correct enough, except in the impli-
cation that the enemy were within gunshot and defeated by the said evolutions. This writer also says the Cal. had 5 killed and 'a considerable
number' wounded. Hall and Lancey are guided by the accounts mentioned,
but are somewhat careful not to commit themselves as to the bloodshed. It
must be admitted that only the long distance between the combatants prevented an exciting affair. The *S. José Pioneer* of Mar. 6, 1880, on Weber's
authority, represents W. as having been the prominent man of the affair, and
as having by his generalship saved the army from defeat when involved in
the mustard growth at the creek crossing and charged by Sanchez at full
gallop. The battle 'was of short duration, about 2 hours, for experience has
shown that Mexican valor is unequal to American pluck, and Sanchez, the
last revolutionist of the period, was obliged to capitulate to Capt. Weber,
the man of all men whom he most desired as a prisoner.' Hecox, *Sta Cruz
Times*, notes that the immigrants crept out through the mustard to attack the Californians in the rear, putting them to flight. Eight Cal. were
killed! Miguel Flores, *Recuerdos*, MS., 16-21, gives a confused account of
the fight. Secundino Robles, *Relacion*, MS., 15-25, gives a detailed narrative, which is pure fiction from beginning to end. Henry Marshall, *Statement*,
MS., 3-4, narrates the affair briefly but with tolerable accuracy. See also
Ryan's Judges and Criminals, chap. xvi.; *Hyde's Statement*, MS., 9; *Cooke's
Conq.*, 276; *Davis' Glimpses*, MS., 356; *Tinkham's Hist. Stockton*, 105; and
the different county histories.

[45] Lancey speaks of an offer by Sanchez to surrender on certain conditions,
a reply that it must be unconditional, an assurance from S. that he would die
first, etc. It was during the term of this truce, I think, that Forbes took a
prominent part in negotiations; and then, if at all, that Bartlett was intrusted
temporarily to his care, and not earlier, as Hall has it. See note 40.

Captain Maddox arrived with his company of 50 men or more. News of his approach came through Sanchez, and an officer was sent to meet him, make known the truce, and prevent an attack by his men, who were eager for the fray—so eager that they had only taken ten days to come from Monterey![46] Two days later a reply came from the commandant at San Francisco, probably to the effect that the surrender must be nominally unconditional, but with unofficial assurances, confirmed by prominent citizens, that property should be no longer seized without the proper formalities and receipts.[47] On the 7th arrived Lieutenant Grayson with 15 men from the north to join Maddox;[48] and on the 8th the treaty was concluded, Sanchez giving up his prisoners and arms, and his men retiring quietly to their farms. Marston and his men returned to Yerba Buena to receive congratulations from Captain Mervine for their valor and success. The war in the north was at an end.[49]

[46] Maddox left Monterey Dec. 22d or 23d. *Colton's Three Years*, 128; *Mont. Californian*, Dec. 26, 1847. I do not mean to imply that M. and his men were timid and did not come as fast as was necessary; but simply to expose the absurdity of current accounts about the difficulty of restraining the force from attacking Sanchez.

[47] According to Colton and the *Californian*, Sanchez and his companions protested that they had no intention of fighting against the U. S., but only desired to protect themselves from lawless depredations; and their terms were acceded to.

[48] Boggs, in *Napa Register*, Mar. 30, Apr. 20, 1872, was one of these men, recruited by himself, Grayson, and Martin in the Sonoma region. After exciting adventures in crossing the bay they reached S. F. after Marston's departure, and even after the fight of the 2d. They were sent down by water to the Sta Clara landing, stole round the hostile camp, joined Maddox, and charged into the midst of the Californians! Then they learned that there was a truce to terminate at 9 o'clock next morning. At that hour they charged again (!), but were met by Bartlett with news of his release. Maddox sent him back with an order to surrender in 10 minutes, and Sanchez obeyed. B. took from Sanchez' men as many horses as were needed, and then marched with Maddox for San José, and soon to Monterey via Sta Cruz. B. gives many details, the value of which may be estimated from the fact that one of their exploits on this march was the arrest of Gen. Castro at Sta Cruz!

[49] Jan. 12th, Mervine to the army. 'It is a novel instance in the history of Cal. that her unrivalled cavalry were obliged to surrender and lay down their arms in consequence of being so effectually entrapped as to deprive them of their usual alternative, and render escape impossible'! Special thanks to the volunteers and Capt. Smith, who on 13th replies: 'Our watchword is inscribed upon our banner, and we trust that you will find us semper paratus.' *Mont. Calif.*, Feb. 6, 1847. Lancey says that Sanchez was detained for a while on the *Savannah*.

A sad event in northern annals of 1846, which may as well be recorded here as elsewhere, was the loss of the *Warren's* launch and twelve men, including two sons of Captain Montgomery—William H., acting master of the *Warren*, and John E., his father's secretary—with Midshipman Daniel C. Hugenin.[50] The boat was despatched late in November or early in December from Yerba Buena to New Helvetia, the officers having some business to transact with Captain Kern, and perhaps carrying $900 with which to pay off the garrison. They never arrived at Sutter's, and after several weeks Robert Ridley was sent in another launch up the Sacramento and San Joaquin, finding no traces of boat or crew. Ridley's opinion was that they had been lost in a gale shortly after setting out; and this became the prevalent theory among men acquainted with the circumstances, though there were those who thought the officers had been murdered by the crew, or that possibly all had been killed by the Indians. The question whether young Montgomery was alive or dead figured in later litigation respecting certain lands in San Francisco.[51] In later years a report became current in the newspapers that one of the missing men, apparently Ladd, had been seen in New York, and confessed that his companions murdered the officers, destroyed the boat, and fled with the money, some of them perhaps joining the Indians.[52]

[50] The sailors of the crew were: Geo. Rodman, Anthony Sylvester, Alex. McDonald, Sam. Turner, Sam. Lane, Milton Ladd, John W. Dawd, Gilman Hilton, and Lawton Lee.

[51] *Mont. Californian*, Jan. 23, 1847; *S. F. Cal. Star*, Jan. 23, 1847; *Davis' Glimpses*, MS., 352; *Honolulu Polynesian*, iv. 51; and inaccurate mention in *Sherman's Mem.*, i. 35. See also *Cal. Repts*, 1 Sawyer, 668–9.

[52] A correspondent of the *S. F. Bulletin*, June 17, 1869, claims to have met an early Californian who met one of the party in New York and heard his story. A 'Pioneer,' in *Id.*, June 22d, says that in 1857 or 1858 he met a miner—still living in 1869—who pointed out a man as one of the murderers, and gave details of his having with a companion worked at various ranchos, one of the two being hanged after the gold discovery at Hangtown. This story is repeated in other papers. Wm T. Wheeler, *Loss of the 'Warren,'* MS., a boy on the *Warren* in 1846, and well acquainted with Ladd and Turner, is strong in the belief that the officers were murdered. He cites some mysterious acts and words of his chum Turner at parting; and he thinks in case of wreck some part of the boat or the water-cask would surely have come to light.

CHAPTER XV.

THE CONQUEST COMPLETED BY STOCKTON AND FRÉMONT.

JANUARY, 1847.

STOCKTON'S ARMY—THE ADVANCE FROM SAN BERNARDO TO LOS COYOTES—
PROPOSITIONS FROM FLORES—A PROCLAMATION—SAND-STORM—FORS-
TER'S SERVICES—CHANGE OF ROUTE TO AVOID AMBUSH—PREPARATIONS
OF THE CALIFORNIANS—FROM LA JABONERÍA TO PASO DE BARTOLO—THE
BATTLE OF THE SAN GABRIEL—STOCKTON'S REPORT—DEFEAT OF THE
CALIFORNIANS—FIGHT OF THE MESA—ENTRY INTO LOS ANGELES—FRÉ-
MONT'S MARCH FROM SANTA BÁRBARA TO SAN FERNANDO—THE CALIFOR-
NIANS AT LOS VERDUGOS—EFFORTS OF JESUS PICO—FLORES TRANSFERS
COMMAND TO ANDRÉS PICO—ARMISTICE—TREATY OF CAHUENGA—THE
WAR AT AN END—FRÉMONT AT ANGELES—FLIGHT OF FLORES AND MA-
NUEL CASTRO TO SONORA.

WE left Stockton and his army of about 600 men
encamped at San Bernardo on December 31, 1846.
They had left San Diego two days before for an advance on Los Angeles. The composition of the force
is given in the appended note.[1] Only Gillespie's vol-

[1] Commodore Robert F. Stockton, U. S. N., commander-in-chief. Gen.
Stephen W. Kearny, in command of the division. Lieut Stephen C. Rowan, U.
S. N., of *Cyane,* major. Capt. Wm H. Emory, U. S. top. engineers, acting ad-
jutant general. Lieut Geo. Minor, U. S. N., of *Savannah,* quartermaster, assisted by Daniel Fisher. Purser Wm Speiden, of *Congress,* commissary, as-
sisted by John Bidwell (capt. of volunteers). John Southwick, carpenter of
Congress, chief engineer in com. of sappers and miners. Doctors John S.
Griffin, U. S. A., Andrew A. Henderson, of *Portsmouth,* and Chas Eversfield,
of *Congress,* surgeons. Capt. Miguel Pedrorena, of Cal. battalion, and Lieut
Andrew F. V. Gray, U. S. N., aides-de-camp of commander-in-chief.
 1st division, or battalion, commanded by Capt. J. Zielin: Zielin's marines,
Co. C, musketeers of *Portsmouth,* Capt. Benj. F. B. Hunter, acting lieut U.
S. N.; Lieut Ed. C. Grafton, midshipman U. S. N. Co. F, carbineers, Capt.
James M. Duncan, passed mid.; Lieut Joseph Parrish, mid. Co. E, car-
bineers of *Cyane,* Capt. J. Fenwick Stenson, passed mid.; Lieut Edmund
Shepherd, mid. Co. G, carbineers of *Congress,* Capt. John Reed (Peet or
Peco), sailmaker.
 2d battalion, commanded by Capt. Henry S. Turner: Companies C and

unteer riflemen were mounted; and the luggage was carried in ten ox-carts. Horses and oxen in small numbers, as well as small food supplies, were obtained at several points along the route. Says Stockton: "Our men were badly clothed, and their shoes generally made by themselves out of canvas. It was very cold and the roads heavy. Our animals were all poor and weak, some of them giving out daily, which gave much hard work to the men in dragging the heavy carts, loaded with ammunition and provisions, through deep sands and up steep ascents, and the prospect before us was far from being that which we might have desired; but nothing could break down the fine spirits of those under my command, or cool their readiness and ardor to perform their duty; and they went through the whole march of one hundred and forty-five miles with alacrity and cheerfulness."[2] Leaving San Bernardo the 1st of January, 1847, they encamped successively at Buenavista, San Luis Rey, and Las Flores, in their uneventful progress.[3] Reports came in that Frémont was

K, U. S. 1st dragoons, united and dismounted, 55 men; Lieut John W. Davidson. Co. D, musketeers of *Cyane*, Capt. Edward Higgins, acting lieut U. S. N.; Lieut John Van Ness Philip and Albert Allmand, acting lieutenants, also Wm Simmons, commodore's clerk. Artillery co. of sailors, 6 guns, 45 men. Capt. Richard L. Tilghman, lieut U. S. N.; Lieut Wm H. Thompson, passed mid.

3d battalion, commanded by Capt. Wm B. Renshaw, lieut U. S. N.: Co. B, musketeers of *Savannah*, Capt. Renshaw; Lieut Geo. E. Morgan; Philip H. Haywood and Robert C. Duvall, mid. Co. A, musketeers of *Congress*, Capt. John Guest, passed mid.; Lieut Theodore Lee and Benj. F. Wells, mid. There were 379 sailors and marines in all the divisions.

4th battalion: squadron of mounted volunteers, including 30 Californians, acting as guards or skirmishers on front, rear, and flanks; under command of Capt. Arch. H. Gillespie, also captains Samuel Gibson, Sam. B. Hensley, and Santiago E. Argüello; lieutenants Luis Argüello, Hiram Rheusaw, and ——. 84 men, besides 3 employés of the topographical engineers. The total force was 607 men, of whom 44 were officers.

The authorities for this list are Stockton's official report in *Stockton's Mil. and Nav. Op.*, 31 et seq.; *Emory's Notes*, 115; and a MS. list by Brackett, in *Miscel. Hist. Pap.*, 31. The company lettering is from Brackett; according to Stockton's account of later events, companies E, F, and G were respectively Co. A, carbineers of the *Cyane*, Co. C, carb., and Co. A, carb. of the *Congress*. Lieut H. B. Watson is also named.

[2] Report of Feb. 5th, in *Stockton's Mil. and Nav. Op.*, 31.

[3] *Griffin's Diary*, MS., 44 et seq., and *Emory's Notes*, 116 et seq., are the best original authorities for the march, the former being much the more complete. Jan. 1st, J. A. Pico sent word that he had horses for the army, but

approaching Los Angeles from the north, and that the Californians had gone to meet him 600 strong under Andrés Pico. Soon after they left Las Flores on the 4th, three men appeared—William Workman, Charles Flügge, and Domingo Olivas—under a flag of truce, bringing a letter from Flores, dated on the 1st. In this communication the general suggested, rather than asked for, a truce to await confirmation of a current report that peace had been made between Mexico and the United States, and thus avoid a useless spilling of blood.[4] But Stockton peremptorily refused to enter into negotiations with Flores, declaring him to be a man without honor, who had broken his parole, and would be shot as a rebel if caught.[5] The envoys made a plea in behalf of the people; but the commodore would listen to nothing but propositions of unconditional surrender. Workman, however, accompanied the army to San Juan Capistrano, where on the 5th he induced Stockton to issue a proclamation offering a general amnesty to all Californians except Flores, on condition that he should be given up as a prisoner.[6] It was noted that at the pass be-

was distrusted. Jan. 2d, at S. Luis some sailors broke into the church and committed petty thefts. Forster came in with reports. Hensley went to Pico's rancho of Sta Margarita and brought in some horses and 45 oxen next day.

[4] Jan. 1st, Flores to Stockton, in *Stockton's Mil. and Nav. Op.*, 19–20, evidently a not very accurate translation. F. says he had been urged by foreign residents to communicate with S. through them as mediators for an honorable adjustment, but has not felt at liberty to do so until now, when such action is required by the rumors of peace. He denounces S. for the unjust war he is waging, and expresses the determination of himself and men to defend their country to the last if S. declines the truce. In *Olvera, Doc.*, MS., 71–3, is a blotter of a somewhat similar letter, written by Flores on Dec. 31st; but he must have made great changes in it if the translation may be trusted at all. In this copy F. expresses his joy on the news of probable peace, and his surprise that S. should have started from S. Diego under such circumstances; and he writes simply to save his responsibility in case blood shall be shed after a treaty has been made. Nothing is said of the unjust war or resolution to resist, etc. Forster, *Pioneer Data*, MS., 45 et seq., is the only one who names Olivas; and he also notes the fact that each of the three ambassadors finally met a tragic death.

[5] Griffin, Forster, and others represent Stockton as having shown much anger, especially at the idea of Flores' claiming to be governor of Cal.

[6] Spanish translation in *Olvera, Doc.*, MS., 75. Stockton says nothing of this document, but it is mentioned by Griffin, who feared a pretended acceptance by the people.

tween Las Flores and San Juan a small force of the
enemy might easily have defeated the army.

Stockton's camp of the 5th was at Los Alisos; next
day he marched to Santa Ana; and on the 7th to Los
Coyotes. John Forster accompanied the army and
rendered valuable aid in obtaining supplies and information. A violent wind, raising clouds of dust, continued through the night and morning of the 6th–7th,
of which, as Emory says, the enemy should have taken
advantage for an attack. Conflicting rumors had
been received about Flores' movements, the general
impression being that his first meeting would be with
Frémont rather than Stockton; but in the region of
Los Coyotes reliable information was obtained that
the Californians would make a stand at the San
Gabriel River; and indeed, the enemy's scouts were
seen, making some hostile demonstrations.[7] Next
morning, the 8th of January, anniversary of the battle
of New Orleans, as the soldiers did not need to be
reminded, the advance was resumed. Though the
official reports make no allusion to any change of plan
or route, I have no doubt that the original intention
was to proceed by the most direct way, crossing the
San Gabriel at the lower ford, but was changed in
consequence of information received through Forster
that the Californians occupied a most advantageous
position on the lower route.[8] At any rate, Stockton

---

[7] Griffin, *Diary*, MS., 52, says they even captured two vaqueros, and also
Forster, whom they released, for he soon came back to camp.

[8] Forster, *Pioneer Data*, MS., 49 et seq., as in conversation, states positively that such was the case. He learned that Flores, though supposed by
the Americans and non-combatant Californians to be at S. Fernando awaiting
Frémont, had really passed Angeles in the night and had posted his men in
ambush in the willows and mustard at a point near the modern Gallatin, where
Stockton's men could be attacked at a fearful disadvantage. This is confirmed,
as we shall see, by Coronel and other Californians. In his narrative, Forster
says he got the information from an Indian. He also mentions interviews
with Ramon Carrillo, who was willing to abandon the cause of Flores, but
feared punishment for breaking his parole and for his supposed part in the
killing of the Bear Flag men at Sonoma. Forster promised to intercede with
Stockton, from whom he got a written guaranty, but could not find Carrillo
again. He claims that Carrillo knew nothing of Flores' real movements—not
a very plausible claim. Dr Griffin also noted in his diary Carrillo's reported
presence and desire for pardon. In 1874 Forster stated that having fallen

soon swerved to the right after leaving Los Coyotes, and directed his course toward the upper ford, the Paso de Bartolo. He approached the river between 2 and 3 o'clock in the afternoon, and found the enemy in possession of the opposite, or north-western, bank, the Californian scouts having been seen before in the distance.

What has been said of Flores' operations during the last half of December,[9] may be literally applied to the first week in January. There exists no documentary record of what was being done by the Californians in these days, but there is nothing of mystery connected with the subject. Dissensions continued between the leaders, Flores being less to blame than the others for this state of things, but still much discouraged. His original intention had been to so harass the foe by a guerrilla warfare as to limit the American occupation to a few points until either aid or news of a treaty should come from Mexico. With the hearty coöperation of all, even with his limited resources, he might have accomplished much in this direction. But there was no longer any popular enthusiasm whatever. Such patriotic zeal as had at first existed, and had been fanned into flame by early successes, had now disappeared in consequence of official disputes and mismanagement, calm reflection, and the personal hardships resulting from war. There was left no hope of success. The only remaining stimulants to action were a degree of stubborn national pride, and a fear of punishment for past offences, fomented by the officers who had broken their paroles. The Californians were not in earnest,

into the stream he went back to a house to dry his clothing. Here he met a party of Californians, among whom was a friend anxious to secure Stockton's protection, but fearful because of his Sonoma record; and from him, for a promise of protection, the information was received. Thus it appears clear enough that Carrillo was the informant, though Forster thought it desirable, on second thoughts, to conceal the fact. The Californians, however, generally attributed the revelation of the plan to Lorenzo Soto.

[9] See p. 355 of this volume.

and they accomplished nothing.   Their scouts retired
before the advance of Stockton and Frémont, not
even driving off the cattle and horses along the route.
The letter of January 1st was sent by Flores merely
in the hope of gaining time.   What reasons if any he
had for expecting news of a treaty I do not know;
but Stockton's verbal reply was not encouraging, and
still less so his later written offer of armistice to the
people if they would give up their general.   As the
enemy approached from south and north the situation
became more critical, and no new resources were developed.   It was thought that Frémont would arrive
first, or at least that the first conflict should be with
his forces, and the Californian army was accordingly
stationed for several days at San Fernando; but
Stockton's advance was perhaps more rapid than had
been expected; and at the last the plans were changed.
On the 6th or 7th the army was moved rapidly and
secretly, without entering the town, to the vicinity
of the San Gabriel River, and posted at La Jabonería in the willows and mustard at a spot commanding the route by which Stockton was expected to
pass.   But early on the 8th the scouts brought news
that the plan had been revealed and the Americans
were marching for the upper ford.   The disappointment was great at losing an expected advantage; but
Flores at once set out up the river, and reached the
Paso de Bartolo shortly before the Americans made
their appearance.[10]

---

[10] *Coronel, Cosas de Cal.*, MS., 120, etc.   Andrés Pico seems to have been
in command at S. Fernando, while Flores and Carrillo remained in the south,
ordering Pico to join them after Stockton had reached Sta Ana.   Pico's
route was by Los Verdugos and Arroyo Seco.   The lower ford is called
Los Nietos.   This writer names the Sonoran, Lorenzo Soto, as the man who
revealed the ambush.   Most of the Sta Bárbara company deserted in the
night of the 7th.   Larkin's journal, in *Mont. Californian*, Feb. 27, 1847, mentions the encampment for 2 or 3 days at S. Fernando.   Rico, *Mem.*, MS., 48
et seq., mentions the ambush and change of route, but thinks the warning
was given by one Dominguez.   Each narrator is inclined to attribute this act to
some personal enemy; but I have already noted the probability that Ramon
Carrillo was the man.   Manuel Castro, *Servicios*, MS., in presenting the
troubles of the Californians, throws the blame chiefly on Flores, as cowardly
and incompetent, inspiring no faith, keeping his place by intrigue, and thus

Flores posted his men, nearly 500 in number, on a bluff, or bank, forty or fifty feet high, skirting the river bottom at a distance of from 400 to 600 yards from the water. The two cannon, nine-pounders apparently, were placed opposite to and commanding the ford. Two squadrons of horsemen under Andrés Pico and Manuel Garfias were stationed on the right a few hundred yards southward, and another squadron under José Antonio Carrillo on the left at a greater distance up the stream. A party of skirmishers seems to have been sent across the river, and to have retired as the Americans advanced. Stockton's order of march was as follows: Centre, Turner's 2d division, with Hensley's riflemen as advance guard, and two guns on each flank; right, 1st division under Zielin; left, 3d division under Renshaw; rear, 4th division under Gillespie, with two guns under Thompson, and guard of 49 men under Haywood, the cattle and wagons being in the centre, in what the sailors termed a 'Yankee corral.' The army halted about a quarter of a mile from the river to make final preparations, and then moved forward again to attack the Californians. I append in a note Stockton's official report of the engagement that followed, interspersed with items from other sources.[11]

robbing real patriots of their due glory! Osio, *Hist. Cal.*, MS., 487 et seq., tells us the Californians had no advantages but their courage. To the ambush he adds Flores' plan to fire the mustard on the enemy's approach, and charge under cover of the smoke! He does not name the 'spurious Californian' who betrayed his country. Botello, *Anales del Sur*, MS., 156, etc., gives a good account of the preparations, agreeing for the most part with that of Coronel. He says Ramon Carrillo commanded a party of scouts in the south, and José Carrillo (son of Don Cárlos) a similar party in the north to watch Frémont, while the rest of the force was concentrated at S. Fernando. It was on the 7th that the army countermarched secretly to La Jabonería. But Stockton turned off at Los Nietos and spoiled the plan. Palomares, *Mem.*, MS., 76 et seq., gives some particulars of the retreat of the scouts before Stockton's advance, as well as of Flores' general movements. Avila, *Notas*, MS., 32 et seq., calls the upper ford Corunga, implying that it was distinct from Bartolo. In *Los Angeles Hist.*, 23, it is called Curunga, or Pico Crossing.

[11] Report of Feb. 5, 1847, to Sec. Bancroft, in *Stockton's Mil. and Nav. Oper.*, 32 et seq. Stockton also briefly describes the battle in his reports of Jan. 11th, *Id.*, 17–19, and Feb. 18th, *Stockton's Report*, 47–8; but gives no additional information. There are mentions also in several other official reports of different officers, but no details. These documents have been often

From the testimony thus cited, the official report somewhat ridiculously magnifying the battle of San Gabriel for effect at Washington, it appears that Stockton's force forded the river under a constant fire

reprinted wholly or in part, especially by Cutts, Bryant, *Stockton's Life*, Lancey, etc. A brief but clear account is given in *Emory's Notes*, 119–20. See also Californian narratives as cited in note 10.

'A detachment of marines, under Lieut Watson, was sent to strengthen the left flank. A party of the enemy, 150 strong, had now crossed the river and made several ineffectual efforts to drive a band of wild mares upon the advance party.' There is no other authority for this attempt, though Castro, *Servicios*, MS., and others speak vaguely of having captured some horses and saddles at some time during the fight; and Griffin says 21 horses were lost, having been tied by the volunteers before the fight, and forgotten until it was too late. 'We now moved forward to the ford in broken files; Capt. Hensley's command was ordered to dismount, and, acting as skirmishers, it deployed to the front and crossed the stream, which is about 50 yards in width' (Emory says: 'The river was about 100 yards wide, knee-deep, and flowing over quicksand. Either side was fringed with a thick undergrowth. The approach on our side was level; that on the enemy's was favorable to him '), 'driving before him a party of the enemy which had attempted to annoy us.' García, *Hechos*, MS., 102–3, is the only Californian who says anything of this party, which he says was of 200 men under Joaquin and Gabriel de la Torre. Emory says that on approaching the thicket they received the scattering fire of the enemy's sharpshooters. 'The enemy had now taken their position upon the heights, distant 600 yards from the river and 50 feet above its level; their centre or main body, about 200 strong, was stationed immediately in front of the ford, upon which they opened a fire from two pieces of artillery, throwing round and grape shot without effect.' (Emory says: 'As the line —of skirmishers—was about the middle of the river, the enemy opened his battery, and made the water fly with grape and round shot.') 'Their right and left wings were separated from the main body about 300 yards.' The Californians say that Carrillo's division was 1,000 or 1,500 yards away; and several add that he was stationed there on pretext of guarding a pass to the hills, but really because Flores distrusted him. 'Our column halted upon the edge of the stream; at this time the guns were unlimbered to return the enemy's fire, but were ordered again to be limbered and not a gun to be fired until the opposite bank of the river was gained.' It is stated in *Stockton's Life*, 144 et seq., and confirmed by other witnesses, that Kearny ordered the guns unlimbered before crossing, as was doubtless the most prudent course, but Stockton countermanded the order. Half-way across, K. sent a message that it would be impossible to cross, as there was a quicksand; but S. dismounted, seized the ropes, and declared, 'Quicksand or no quicksand, the guns shall pass over.' The phrase as heard by Forster, who was present, was 'Quicksands be damned,' etc. See also *Bidwell's Cal.*, MS., 207 et seq. He says Kearny showed much suppressed anger at this and before at Stockton's reply to Flores' letter; but I fancy this is an exaggeration. 'The two 9-pounders, dragged by officers as well as men and mules, soon reached the opposite bank, when they were immediately placed in battery. The column now followed in order under a most galling fire from the enemy, and became warmly engaged on the opposite bank, their round shot and grape falling thickly amongst us as we approached the stream, without doing any injury, our men marching steadily forward. The dragoons and *Cyane's* musketeers, occupying the centre, soon crossed and formed upon a bank about 4 feet above the stream. The left, advancing at the same time, soon occupied its position across the river. The rear was longer in getting across the water; the sand being deep, its passage was delayed by the baggage carts; however, in a few

from the enemy's guns, which under ordinary circumstances would have caused great loss of life, but had practically no effect because of the bad powder used, planted his artillery on the right bank, and soon si-

moments the passage of the whole force was effected, with only one man killed and one wounded, notwithstanding the enemy kept up an incessant fire from the heights.' (Emory says: 'On the right bank of the river there was a natural banquette, breast-high. Under this the line was deployed. To this accident of the ground is to be attributed the little loss we sustained from the enemy's artillery, which showered grape and round shot over our heads.') Neither gives the chief reason for the slight loss of life, which was the worthlessness of the powder made at San Gabriel. Emory's further statement, 'Whilst this was going on, our rear was attacked by a very bold charge, and repulsed,' is unintelligible, to say nothing of the 'bull.'

'On taking a position upon the low bank, the right flank, under Capt. Zielin, was ordered to deploy to the right; two guns from the rear were immediately brought to the right; the 4-pounder under Thompson, supported by the riflemen under Renshaw. The left flank deployed into line in open order. During this time our artillery began to tell upon the enemy, who continued their fire without interruption. The 9-pounders standing in plain view upon the bank were discharged with such precision'—most witnesses state, as was doubtless true, that Stockton himself aimed one of the guns—'that it soon became too warm for the enemy to remain upon the brow of their heights; eventually a shot told upon their 9-pounder, knocked the gun from its trail, astounding the enemy so much that they left it for four or five minutes. Some 20 of them now advanced, and hastily fastening ropes to it, dragged the gun to the rear.' Coronel says that the brow of the hill protected the Californians, but at the same time prevented their own guns being fired effectively except as they were advanced to the brow, discharged, and dragged back; and soon both were dismounted by the Americans' fire. Rico claims that the guns were at first of no service; but that after they were put by Flores in his charge they were dragged forward by reatas and fired with much effect. Osio says Flores' best gun was dismounted at the first shot. Forster says the second shot, aimed by Stockton, destroyed one of the wheels of the enemy's gun, but still they continued to fire it 7 or 8 times, the balls only reaching half-way. Both Coronel and Botello represent the artillery conflict as much less hot than does Stockton. Emory says that it required one hour and 20 minutes to cross the river and silence the enemy's guns.

'Capt. Hensley's skirmishers now advanced and took the hill upon the right, the left wing of the enemy retreating before them. The 6-pounder from the rear had now come up; Capt. Hensley was ordered to support it, and returned from the hill.' Neither Emory nor any one else mentions this movement. 'This movement being observed, the enemy's left made an attempt to charge the two guns, but the right flank of the marines under Zielin, being quickly thrown back, showed too steady a front for the courage of the Californians to engage, who wheeled to the left and dashed to the rear across the river. At this time the enemy were observed collecting on our left and making preparations to charge our left flank. Gen. Kearny was now ordered to form a square with the troops on the right flank, upon which the left flank, in case of being worsted, might rally. The right wing of the enemy now made an unsuccessful attempt to charge our left, but finding so warm a reception...they changed their purpose and retired, when a discharge of artillery told upon their ranks. The dispositions for charging the heights were now made. The troops having been brought into line, the command "Forward" being given, on they went (the artillery in battery) charging the heights, which the enemy's centre contested for a few moments, then broke in retreat; their right wing charging upon the rear under Gillespie, encumbered with packs, etc,... but re-

lenced the Californian battery. Then his men were formed in squares and advanced toward the bluff. Flores ordered a charge by his horsemen; but the movement was clumsily executed, as by men whose heart was not in the work; some of the companies failed to coöperate promptly; an order to halt from an aid increased the confusion; and the few who came within reach of the Americans were quickly repulsed. Then the Californians retired, and Stockton took possession of their post on the bluff without further opposition. The engagement had lasted probably a little less than two hours from the time when the first shots were fired. The American leader distinguished himself by his valor and skill, though his policy at the ford could not have been justified in case of disaster.

ceiving a well directed fire from the guard, which hurled some of them from their saddles, they fled at full speed across the river we had just left. The other portion of their forces retreated behind their artillery, which had taken position in a ravine, and again opened fire upon our centre; our artillery was immediately thrown forward—the troops being ordered to lay (sic) down to avoid the enemy's cannon-balls, which passed directly over their heads. The fire from our artillery was incessant, and so accurate that the enemy were from time to time driven from their guns until they finally retreated. We were now in possession, where, a short time before, the insurgents had so vauntingly taken strong position; and the band playing Hail Columbia,' etc. Emory describes this last part of the battle, doubtless much more accurately, as follows: 'Half-way between the hill and the river, the enemy made a furious charge on our left flank. At the same moment our right was threatened. The 1st and 2d battalions were thrown into squares, and after firing one or two rounds, drove off the enemy. The right wing was ordered to form a square, but seeing the enemy hesitate, the order was countermanded; the 1st battalion, which formed the right, was directed to rush for the hill, supposing that would be the contested point, but great was our surprise to find it abandoned. The enemy pitched his camp on the hills in view, but when morning came he was gone. We had no means of pursuit.' Emory also gives a plan of the battle. Griffin's account agrees well with Emory's. He says the plain was about 250 yards wide, though Southwick by pacing made it 900 paces. Wilson, Observ., MS., 92, etc., who was a spectator at a distance, says a part of the Californians charged and seemed for a time to have broken the American line. Ávila, Notas, MS., 34 et seq., was also a looker-on, and gives a similar account. The Californian authorities already cited, though their accounts are confused in detail, all agree that a charge was ordered and partly executed; but state that the failure of Carrillo to promptly obey orders, or at least to arrive in time, and an order to halt given by Diego Sepúlveda, one of Flores' aids, caused a failure of what at first seemed likely to be a successful movement. No witnesses support Stockton's account of the final scenes of the fight, reopening of artillery fire, etc.; and I have no doubt they are purely imaginary. Juan Bautista Moreno, Vida, MS., 31–3, was in command of one of the charging companies, and was seriously wounded. The battle is described on authority of Agustin Olvera in Los Angeles Hist., 23–4. For additional authorities on this fight and that of the next day, see note 13.

The sailors and marines, like the dragoons and volunteers, behaved admirably, and displayed all the bravery required by circumstances, losing two men killed and eight wounded. The Californian loss was probably the same in killed, but the exact number wounded is not known. Each party as usual greatly overrated the enemy's loss.

The Americans encamped near the original position of Flores' right wing, and are said to have been aroused by firing on the pickets at midnight; but no further hostilities were committed. The Californians at nightfall were in sight on the hills, but in the morning had disappeared. Many of them dispersed, and the rest repaired to the Cañada de los Alisos, not far from the main road to town. Here, ashamed to run away and give up the struggle, they posted themselves in a favorable position and awaited the enemy's approach. At about 9 o'clock in the morning of January 9th Stockton resumed his march for Los Angeles; but instead of following the road he turned to the left into the open plain as soon as he became aware of Flores' position, apparently just before noon. The Californians, however, approached and fired their cannon and the Americans replied. This artillery duel at long range continued for several hours as the army advanced at oxen's pace in a compact square over the plain, with some slight loss, chiefly of animals, on both sides. On one or two occasions the cavalry charged upon the square, coming within a hundred yards or less, but did not succeed in breaking it, and were repulsed by the musketry. Flores lost one man killed, and an unknown number wounded; Stockton, five wounded.[12]

[12] The Americans killed on the 8th were: Fred Stearns (or Strauss), seaman of *Portsmouth*, Thos Smith, seaman of *Cyane* (accidental), and Jacob Haight (or Hait), volunteer (died 9th); Stockton in his report says one was killed on the 9th, but perhaps refers to Haight, who died on that day. Wounded on the 8th, Wm Cope (or Coxe), seaman of *Savannah* (severely), Geo. Bantam, of *Cyane* (accidental), Pat. Campbell, of *Cyane*, Wm Scott, marine of *Portsmouth*, Joseph Wilson, of *Congress*, Ivory Coffin, of *Savannah*, and James Hendy, of *Congress;* on the 9th, Mark A. Child, Co. C dragoons (severe), James Campbell, seaman *Congress* (accidental and severe), Geo. Crawford, boatswain's mate *Cyane* (severe), Lieut Rowan and Capt. Gillespie, slightly contused by

About 4 o'clock the Californians retired, and the 'battle of the Mesa' was at an end.   Respecting particulars there is no agreement, and I do not deem it necessary to reproduce all the versions or to notice the various inaccuracies and exaggerations of each witness. Stockton crossed the Los Angeles River and encamped on the right bank about three miles below the town.[13]

Next morning, the 10th of January, a flag of truce was brought to Stockton's camp by Célis, Ávila, and Workman, who came to intercede in behalf of the Angelinos.   They said that no resistance would be made to the Americans, and were promised kind treat-

spent balls.   Dr Eversfield's report in *Griffin's Papers*, MS., 18–19; reports of Griffin and Emory in *Stockton's Mil. and Nav. Op.*, 36–7; *Id.*, *Life*, appen., 16–17.   Thus the total was three killed and 12 wounded, though generally stated as 1 killed and 14 wounded.   This is the statement in *31st Cong. 1st Sess.*, *H. Ex. Doc. 24*, p. 18, where it is said that the man killed was an officer. Stockton himself says 3 killed and 14 wounded.

The Californians lost 3 killed in both fights: Ignacio Sepúlveda, Francisco Rubio, and a Yaqui Indian known as 'El Guaymeño.'   The only wounded men named are Capt. Juan B. Moreno and Alférez Ramirez; but there may have been a dozen more slightly wounded.   Ávila says only 2 were wounded at the Mesa.   In his report Stockton says the loss was between 70 and 80, besides many horses.   In *Stockton's Life*, 147, it is stated that over 70 were killed and 150 wounded!

[13] See Stockton, Griffin, Emory, Coronel, Botello, Ávila, and other authorities as cited in preceding notes.   Coronel notes the exploits of a boy of 12 years, named Pollorena, who captured a horse and saddle from the Americans, being uninjured by the many shots sent after him.   A scrap in handwriting of José Castro, in *Doc. Hist. Cal.*, i. 523, says: 'Mr Flores on this occasion hid himself in a little thicket of alders, and this was the only occasion when he saw the enemy.'   Griffin tells us that in the morning of Jan. 9th Soto arrived with a flag of truce, reporting Frémont's arrival at S. Fernando, and two U. S. vessels at Sta Bárbara.   Gen. Kearny gives a brief account of the campaign in his report of Jan. 12th. *30th Cong. 1st Sess.*, *Sen. Ex. 1*, p. 516–17.   Emory gives a sketch also of the Mesa battle-field; and I have also the 2 plans on a larger scale from other govt documents.   Gillespie, in the *S. F. Alta*, July 3, 1866, has something to say of what was accomplished by his 'Sutter' gun, which at La Mesa, at one discharge, took 9 of the enemy from their saddles!   The earliest printed account of the campaign, and a very good one, was that in the *Mont. Californian*, Jan. 28, 1847; often reprinted in other newspapers.   See also *S. F. Cal. Star*, Jan. 16, Feb. 13, 1847; *Valdés, Mem.*, MS., 32–4; *Alvarado, Hist. Cal.*, MS., v. 268–70; *Davis' Glimpses*, MS., 321, 360–78; *Fernandez, Doc.*, MS., 60–1; *Vallejo, Doc.*, MS., xxxiv. 254; i. 22; *Julio César, Cosas*, MS., 10; *Bowen's San Pascual*, MS., 33; *Cutts' Conq.*, 129–31, 201–6; *Bryant's What I Saw*, 398–400; *Cooke's Conq.*, 263–9; *Phelps' Fore and Aft*, 311–19; *Tuthill's Hist. Cal.*, 197–200; *Ripley's War*, i. 482–5; *Quigley's Irish Race*, 227–9; *Frignet, Cal.*, 77; *Brooks' Hist.*, 257–9; *Capron's Hist.*, 41–2; *Dicc. Univ.*, viii. 160; *Lancey's Cruise*, 170–89; *Yolo Co. Hist.*, 21; *Hayes' Scraps, Cal. Notes*, iii. 33, 36; *Ind.*, v. 236; *Sacramento Union*, Apr. 27, 1855; *S. F. Alta*, Jan. 9, 1853.

ment and protection for the citizens.[14] At 10 A. M., or
a little later, the army broke camp and advanced
slowly up the river. Notwithstanding the assurances
just received, it was deemed wise to neglect no precaution, and the advance was in military order as if to
meet a foe. About noon the troops entered the city
by the principal street, directing their march to the
plaza with flying colors and band playing. Many
families had retired to the ranchos or San Gabriel;
small parties of Flores' horsemen, perhaps, disappeared from view as the Americans entered; but the
hill was covered with curious spectators of the pag-
eant. A few reckless and drunken fellows indulged
in threatening and insulting acts, and were fired on by
some of the sailors; but otherwise there was no opposition to the entry.[15] A strong detachment with artillery was posted on the hill; Gillespie raised over his
old quarters the flag he had been obliged to lower four
months ago; and the Californian capital was once more
in possession of the invaders. On the 11th Stockton,
as governor and commander-in-chief, issued an order

[14] *Ávila, Notas*, MS., 30-1, 35-6; also mentioned by others. Ávila says
they were sent by Flores, which may or may not be accurate. Their visit
was about 9 o'clock.

[15] Griffin tells us that one of these fellows struck down another and attempted to lance him, which act brought out a cry of 'Shoot the damned
rascal,' and a volley from the sailors which did no harm. Kearny swore at
the men first for firing without orders, and then for not shooting better.
Stockton merely says their progress was 'slightly molested by a few drunken
fellows who remained about the town.' But Emory makes a much more serious matter of it. He says: 'The streets were full of desperate and drunken
fellows, who brandished their arms and saluted us with every term of reproach.
The crest overlooking the town in rifle-range was covered with horsemen engaged in the same hospitable manner. One of them had on a dragoon's coat
stolen from the dead body of one of our soldiers after we had buried him at
San Pasqual. (Griffin also mentions this.) Our men marched steadily on
until crossing the ravine leading into the public square, when a fight took
place among the Californians on the hill: one became disarmed, and to avoid
death rolled down the hill toward us, his adversary pursuing and lancing
him in the most cold-blooded manner. The man tumbling down the hill was
supposed to be one of our vaqueros, and the cry of "Rescue him" was raised.
The crew of the *Cyane*, nearest the scene, at once and without orders halted
and gave the man lancing him a volley. Strange to say, he did not fall.
Almost at the same instant, but a little before it, the Californians from the
hill did fire on the vaqueros. The rifles were then ordered to clear the hill,
which a single fire effected, killing two of the enemy.' I have no doubt this
is fiction.

of congratulation to the "officers and men of the southern division of U. S. forces in California, on the brilliant victories obtained by them over the enemy, and on once more taking possession of the ciudad de Los Angeles."[16]

There was no further disturbance in town, except such as was naturally caused by the effects of California wine on the sailor-soldiers. Families gradually returned to their homes on assurance of protection from the new authorities, and for several days the chief excitement arose from speculations and rumors respecting the whereabouts of Flores and Frémont. It was reported that the latter had run away to Sonora; but also at first that he had gone to attack the battalion; and later that it was pardon not battle that the remnants of the force sought at San Fernando. From San Luis on the 3d Stockton had despatched a messenger to Frémont by way of San Diego and Santa Bárbara; and on the 9th, before the fight, a courier had come into camp with news that Frémont was at or near San Fernando. In the afternoon of the 10th General Kearny sent a letter to the colonel, announcing the occupation of Angeles and asking for information respecting his position and needs. It rained in torrents all day the 11th, but Lieutenant Emory made some progress in planning fortifications, also obtaining from Griffin an official statement of casualties which he reported to Stockton, while the latter, in addition to his congratulatory order already cited, found time to write a brief report to Secretary Bancroft on recent happenings, in which he said: "We have rescued the country from the

---

[16] *Stockton's Mil. and Nav. Op.*, 20; *Id.*, *Life*, appen., 9. 'The steady courage of the troops in forcing their passage across the Rio San Gabriel, where officers and men were alike employed in dragging the guns through the water, against the galling fire of the enemy, without exchanging a shot, and their gallant charge up the banks against the enemy's cavalry, has perhaps never been surpassed; and the cool determination with which in the battle of the 9th they repulsed the charge of cavalry, made by the enemy at the same time on their front and rear, has extorted the admiration of the enemy, and deserves the best thanks of their countrymen.'

hands of the insurgents, but I fear that the absence
of Colonel Frémont's battalion will enable most of the
Mexican officers who have broken their parole to escape to Sonora." Emory broke ground for his fortifications on the 12th; while Kearny sent another note
to Frémont, and also wrote a brief report of the campaign addressed to the adjutant general. In the
morning of the 13th an armistice, signed the day before and perhaps received by Stockton the preceding
evening, was given by the latter to Kearny, who
wrote two more notes at noon and 2 P. M. to Frémont;
and also wrote to Stockton, expressing his fear that
the riflemen, in ignorance of what had occurred at
Angeles, might be embarrassed in their movements,
or that Frémont might capitulate and retire to the
north. He offered to take half the force and march
to effect a junction. The commodore's reply is not
known, but, perhaps before a decision could be made,
Russell arrived with definite news from Frémont in a
letter for Kearny. On the 14th Frémont himself
appeared with his battalion; and the same day both
Kearny and Stockton reported his arrival to the government at Washington.[17]

Frémont and his battalion, after a week of rest,
marched from Santa Bárbara the 3d of January, probably informed, though I find no definite record on the
subject, of Stockton's proposed advance. An additional cannon was obtained from the prize schooner
Julia, which vessel also went to render aid in case an

[17] All the communications referred to may be found in *Frémont's Court-
martial*, 6–7, 73–4, 85, 88, 108–9, 162, 243–4, 272, 400, 403–4; *Stockton's Life*,
appen., 8–9, 16–17, 35, 46; *Id.*, *Mil. and Nav. Op.*, 20, 36–7; *30th Cong. 1st
Sess.*, *Sen. Ex. Doc. 1*, p. 516–17; *Griffin's Diary*, MS.; and *Emory's Notes*,
122. Most of the correspondence has been often repeated in other publications which it is not necessary to name. I have in *Olvera, Doc.*, MS., 77, one
of the documents issued by Stockton to the people. It permits Agustin
Olvera and Narciso Botello to come to Angeles without molestation, dated
Jan. 12th. This was doubtless an attempt to bring into his presence the members of the old assembly, who might make some kind of a surrender by virtue
of their legal authority. It appears from Botello's narrative and from *Los
Angeles Hist.*, 16–17, that none of the ex-legislators were induced to present
themselves.

attack should be made at the Rincon pass; but no foe was seen until they arrived at San Buenaventura on the 5th. Here a small party of Californians appeared at a distance, but ran away at the approach of the riflemen and the discharge of two cannon. As a precaution, a detachment was sent to occupy a hill about a mile from the mission during the night. As they advanced next day up the valley of the Santa Clara, in the face of a dust-laden gale, the enemy again appeared, 60 or 70 strong, and remained in sight for some time, entertaining the Americans with a variety of equestrian antics, but always at a safe distance. The Indian scouts under Tom Hill rode towards the Californians and exchanged a few harmless shots with them; and once an attempt was made by the battalion to cross a spur of the hills with a view of attacking an imaginary foe on the flank; but the route was found to be impracticable, and the army wisely returned to their plodding way up the valley. Each day small parties of Californian scouts were seen on the hills, but there were no hostilities. The 8th brought a renewal of the sand-storm. Supplies for man and beast were plentiful at the ranchos, and the horses were daily gaining in strength. I follow Bryant's journal, additional details from other sources being either hopelessly contradictory or obviously erroneous. The Californians give some unimportant particulars of their movements in the hills.[18]

[18] *Bryant's What I Saw*, 386 et seq.; *Frémont's Geog. Mem.*, 42; *Nidever's Life*, MS., 132–5; *Lancey's Cruise*, 181–8; *Tuthill's Hist. Cal.*, 203–5; *Martin's Narr.*, MS., 38–40; *S. F. Alta*, Dec. 18, 1852. Frémont, *Court-martial*, 379, says: 'A corps of observation, of some 50 or 100 horsemen, galloped about us, without doing or receiving harm, for it did not come within my policy to have any of them killed'! Arnaz, *Recuerdos*, MS., 89–91, says he was arrested by Frémont at S. Buenaventura, and threatened with death if he did not reveal the whereabouts of the priest, José M. Rosales. José E. García, *Episodios*, MS., 18–23, was one of the scouts under José Carrillo's command, and gives a description of events. He says his party was joined at Sanchez's rancho by a force from S. Buenaventura under Raimundo Carrillo and Demesio Dominguez; and he speaks of a plan to surprise the Americans at Carrillo's rancho, which failed by the accidental discharge of a musket. Foster wrote for the *Los Angeles Express* an account of a blunderbuss and cutlass which were among the trophies of Frémont's campaign, copied in *S. José Pioneer*, Feb. 16, 1878.

Frémont has been criticised unfavorably and without much justice for the slowness of his march by the same men who have found fault with his crossing of the Cuesta de Santa Inés. His delay is ascribed to a desire to keep out of danger until others should have defeated the foe. If, however, he knew from the first, as he certainly did at the last, what were Stockton's plans, his movements were well timed, since he arrived at San Fernando the day after Stockton entered Los Angeles. If he was ignorant of those plans, there was no possible motive for haste, and every reason to advance slowly and cautiously in compact order. His horses were weak; his troops as horsemen were without skill or discipline; he had Natividad in mind; and he had heard of San Pascual. Had he rushed forward, as his opponents of later years pretend to think he should have done, he would have given the enemy their only possible chance of success; and had the Californians been half as numerous and well prepared as they were believed to be, the result would have been most disastrous to the battalion. In the morning of the 9th a messenger came into camp with a letter from Stockton, dated at San Luis Rey on the 3d—an explanation of the commodore's movements and plans, and a warning to proceed with great caution.[19] As they entered the San

[19] 'My dear colonel: We arrived here last night from S. Diego, and leave to-day on our march for the City of the Angels, where I hope to be in 5 or 6 days. I learn this morning that you are at Sta Bárbara, and send this despatch by way of S. Diego, in the hope that it may reach you in time. If there is one single chance for you, you had better not fight the rebels until I get up to aid you, or you can join me on the road to the pueblo. These fellows are well prepared, and Mervine's and Kearny's defeat have given them a deal more confidence and courage. If you do fight before I see you, keep your forces in compact order; do not allow them to be separated, or even unnecessarily extended. They will probably try to deceive you by a sudden retreat or pretend to run away, and then unexpectedly return to the charge after your men get in disorder in the chase. My advice to you is to allow them to do all the charging and running, and let your rifles do the rest. In the art of horsemanship, of dodging, and running, it is in vain to attempt to compete with them.' *Frémont's Court-martial*, 272–3, with mention in *Id.*, 85, 229, 379; *Stockton's Life*, 143–4; *Bryant*, 389.

The messenger's name was George W. Hamley, Hanly, Hawley, Hamlin, Hamblin, or Hamlyn—being written in all these ways—master of the *Stonington*. He sailed from S. Diego on the *Malek Adhel;* landed at S. Buenaventura

Fernando plain on the 11th, two Californians met
them with the news that Stockton had defeated the
Californians, and had occupied Angeles the day before; a little farther on was met a Frenchman with
Kearny's note for Frémont.[20]   Then the battalion
advanced and occupied the mission buildings of San
Fernando about 1 P. M. of the same day.   Before
night Jesus Pico was despatched to the camp of the
Californians.

It is not possible, nor very important, to follow the
Californian forces in all their movements after the
fight of January 9th.   Many simply dispersed and
went home, as others had done before.   The rest in
small detachments visited the different ranchos, some
going to San Fernando, but retiring with Carrillo's
party before Frémont's arrival.   The chief points of
reunion were the ranchos of San Pascual and Los
Verdugos, about 100 men being assembled at the
latter place on the 11th.   One of Flores' last acts on
the 9th, before quitting the city, was to release Larkin and the other prisoners.[21]   There was much dis-

on the 8th; and was guided by Pedro Carrillo to Frémont's camp at the Willows, passing round a camp of the enemy.   Forster thinks Lieut Beale was
the man sent from S. Luis; and Wilson, *Observ.*, MS., 102–3, states that Daniel
Sexton carried this message or an earlier one.   As to the courier who reached
Stockton's camp on the morning of the 9th, according to Griffin, there is no
record of his having been sent by Frémont.   He was probably sent by Americans in Angeles, who had heard of F.'s approach.

[20] 'Pueblo de Los Angeles, Sunday, Jan. 10, 1846 (7), 4 P. M.   Dear Frémont: We are in possession of this place with a force of marines and sailors,
having marched into it this morning.   Join us as soon as you can, or let me
know, if you want us to march to your assistance; avoid charging the enemy;
their force does not exceed 400, perhaps not more than 300.   Please acknowledge the receipt of this, and despatch the bearer at once.   Yours, S. W.
Kearny, Brigadier-General U. S. A.'   *Frémont's Court-martial*, 73, 403.
Frémont did not send an immediate answer as requested; and he received
three more notes of similar purport from Kearny during the next two days,
before he sent an answer.   *Id.*, 73–4, 403–4.   It does not seem necessary to
copy them.   They were familiar in tone, and more and more urgent in the
request for news.

[21] Larkin's letters describing his captivity as already cited.   Larkin was
taken out to the battle-field in the afternoon, and it was then decided to release him; but at his request Flores and other officers escorted him back to
town.   On movements of the Californians in these days, most of the references also covering the subsequent capitulation, see *Coronel, Cosas*, MS.,
129–30; *Rico, Mem.*, MS., 52–3; *Botello, Anales*, MS., 167–9; *García, Episodios*, MS., 23–5; *Lugo, Vida*, MS., 63–7; *Janssens, Vida*, MS., 196; *Osio,
Hist. Cal.*, MS., 502–4; *Fernandez, Cosas*, MS., 148–9; *Julio César, Cosas*,

cussion among officers and men about the best course to be taken in the immediate future. None thought of further resistance; and it does not appear that any thought of complying with Stockton's conditions by giving up their leader, though Flores, having enemies in the camp, was very cautious in his movements. Such being the state of affairs, Jesus Pico made his appearance late on the 11th,[22] being apparently arrested and brought into camp at Los Verdugos. He came to urge not only submission, but submission to his new master and friend, Frémont. He was a man of some influence, came to men who had no fixed plans, dwelt with enthusiasm on the treatment he had received, and without much difficulty persuaded his countrymen that they had nothing to lose and perhaps much to gain by negotiating with Frémont instead of Stockton. A message was sent to the party at San Pascual, and by the latter to Flores and Manuel Castro, at some other point not far away.[23] Flores came in response to this invitation, and all went to Los Verdugos to hold a final council, in which an appeal to Frémont was decided on. The general had resolved, however, to quit California, and started the same night for Sonora; but before his departure he formally transferred the command to Andrés Pico.[24]

MS., 10; *Wilson's Obs.*, MS., 98–100; *Palomares, Mem.*, MS., 88–9; *Los Angeles, Hist.*, 16–17. None of the particulars or errors seem to require special notice.

[22] At midnight, according to the *Los Angeles Hist.*, 16, but I have no doubt it was earlier.

[23] 'SS. Dⁿ Manuel Castro and D. José Mª Flores. At this moment there has arrived a messenger from the Verdugos rancho with the enclosed note' (not extant), 'and a junta of friends has resolved on communicating this news to you; since they have Don Jesus Pico secured at that point where are also assembled 100 men, so that we only wait for your opinion to march and see what guaranties can be obtained. We advise all the friends to come and take advantage of this opportunity, if they deem it best. San Pascual, Jan. 11, 1847. Francisco de la Guerra, José Antonio Carrillo.' Translation from original in my possession. *Castro, Doc.*, MS., ii. 159.

[24] 'Comandancia General. No pudiendo continuar con el mando que interinamente he obtenido, y habiendo variedad de opiniones respecto á los movimientos que deben emprenderse; se entregará Vd del mando de esta Division, por corresponderle por su graduacion. Dios y Libertad. Campo

Then Francisco de la Guerra and Francisco Rico were chosen as representatives and went with Don Jesus to San Fernando. They were well received by Frémont, who promised all the Californians could desire, named commissioners to negotiate a treaty, and signed an armistice suspending hostilities.[25] On the return of Guerra and Rico, José Antonio Carrillo and Agustin Olvera were appointed by Pico as treaty commissioners for the Californians and the camp was moved to the region of Cahuenga. Frémont's commissioners were Major P. B. Reading, Major William H. Russell, and Captain Louis McLane; and the battalion moved its camp to the rancho of Cahuenga. Here the negotiations were completed and a treaty drawn up in English and Spanish before night; and next morning, January 13th, it received the signatures of the respective commandants, Frémont and Pico, the document with a letter to General Kearny being presently carried by Russell to Los Angeles.[26]

en los Verdugos. Enero 11, 1847. José Mª Flores. Sr Mᵒʳ Gʳᵃˡ D. Andˢ Pico.' From the pencil original, in *Olvera, Doc.*, MS., 78.

[25] 'To all, etc. In consequence of propositions of peace...being submitted to me as commandant of the Cal. battalion of U. S. forces, which has (sic) so far been acceded to by me as to cause me to appoint a board of commissioners to consult with a similar board appointed by the Californians; and it requiring a little time to close the negotiations, it is agreed upon and ordered by me that an entire cessation of hostilities shall take place until tomorrow afternoon (Jan. 13th), and that the said Californians be permitted to bring in their wounded to the mission of San Fernandez, where also, if they choose, they can remove their camp, to facilitate said negotiations. Given, etc., Jan. 12, 1847. J. C. Frémont, Lieut-colonel U. S. A. and Mil. Com. Cal.' In *Stockton's Mil. and Nav. Op.*, 21. This armistice was sent to the city and was received by Kearny from Stockton in the morning of the 13th. How it was sent to Stockton does not appear. See also on these and the following negotiations, *Pico, Acont.*, MS., 73–5; *Los Angeles Hist.*, 16–17.

[26] 'Articles of capitulation made and entered into at the ranch of Cowenga this 13th day of Jan., A. D. 1847, between, etc. Art. 1. The commissioners on the part of the Californians agree that their entire force shall, on presentation of themselves to Lieut-Col. Frémont, deliver up their artillery and public arms, and they shall return peaceably to their homes, conforming to the laws and regulations of the U. S., and not again take up arms during the war between the U. S. and Mexico, but will assist and aid in placing the country in a state of peace and tranquillity. Art. 2. The com. on the part of Lieut-col. Frémont agree and bind themselves, on the fulfilment of the 1st art. by the Californians, that they shall be guaranteed protection of life and property whether on parole or otherwise Art. 3. That until a treaty of peace be made and signed between the U. S. of N. America and the republic of Mexico, no Californian or other Mexican citizen shall be bound to take the oath of allegiance. Art. 4. That any Cal. or other citizen of

Frémont also marched for the city, which, as we have seen, he entered with his battalion on the 14th, having been rejoined by Russell on the way.

By the terms of this capitulation, the original of which is in my possession, and the somewhat clumsy translation of which has been given in a note, the Californians were pardoned for all past hostilities, and were free to go to their homes on giving up their public arms—two cannon and six muskets as it proved—and promising not to take up arms during the war. They were guaranteed protection, with all the privileges of American citizens, without being required to take an oath of allegiance; and they were free to depart if they so desired. There were no exceptions, and even

Mex. desiring, is permitted by this capitulation to leave the country without let or hindrance. Art. 5. That in virtue of the aforesaid articles, equal rights and privileges are vouchsafed to every citizen of Cal. as are enjoyed by the citizens of the U. S. of N. America. Art. 6. All officers, citizens, foreigners, or others shall receive the protection guaranteed by the 2d art. Art. 7. This capitulation is intended to be no bar on effecting such arrangements as may in future be in justice required by both parties. P. B. Reading, major Cal. Battalion; Wm H. Russell, ordnance officer Cal. Bat.; Louis McLane, Jr., com. artill. Cal. Bat.; José Antonio Carrillo, com. de esquadron; Agustin Olvera, diputado. Approved, J. C. Frémont, lt-col. U. S. army, and mil. com. of Cal.; Andrés Pico, com. de esquadron y en gefe de las fuerzas nacionales en Cal. Additional article: That the paroles of all officers, citizens, and others of the U. S., and of naturalized citizens of Mexico, are by this foregoing capitulation cancelled, and every condition of said paroles from and after this date are of no further force and effect, and all prisoners of both parties are hereby released. (Same signatures as above.) Ciudad de Los Angeles, Jan. 16, 1847.' Official printed copies in *Stockton's Mil. and Nav. Op.*, 22–3; *War with Mex.*, 63–5, printed in Spanish and English in *Monterey Californian*, Feb. 13, 1847. Often reprinted in English. Original 7 articles of the 13th, with autograph signature, in *Carrillo (D.), Doc.*, MS., 113–16. This is in the handwriting of J. A. Carrillo, and the signatures to the additional article are copied by him. In *Olvera, Doc.*, MS., 76, I have a copy from the original, including all the articles. There are copies in various collections.

Jan. 14th, Padre Ordaz, at S. Fernando, certifies that F. and party lived on the mission sheep and cattle, and carried off what horses they could find. This certificate to protect the lessee. *Pico, Pap. Mis.*, MS., 157. Jan. 16th, Russell acknowledges receipt from Andrés Pico of 2 pieces artillery with 6 charges of grape, and 6 muskets, according to the treaty. *Olvera, Doc.*, MS., 76–7. Jan. 18th, Angeles blotter of 6 articles suggested by Carrillo and Olvera in accordance with art. 7 of the treaty, and said to be approved by Stockton; but without signatures, in *Id.*, 79–81. This document provided for the continuance of incumbents in office at their desire; popular elections; a recognition of the govt debt by the U. S.; payment of back salaries(!); protection of priests; and payment of damages for property destroyed by Americans! It is possible that these measures may have been favorably considered with a view to a subsequent treaty with Mexico.

Flores might have claimed protection. The wisdom of granting such liberal terms cannot be questioned; since a rigorous enforcement of military laws by inflicting due punishment on officers who had broken their paroles would have done great harm by transforming a large part of the native population into guerrilla bandits. That the Californians should have preferred to treat with Frémont rather than with Stockton, under the urging of Jesus Pico, is easily understood. That Frémont should have made a treaty at all, when the commander-in-chief was so near and there were no urgent reasons for haste, is more remarkable. Under ordinary circumstances, it might be plausibly suspected that he acted under secret instructions from Stockton, who desired an excuse for not carrying out his former threats; but such was probably not the fact. Frémont's motive was simply a desire to make himself prominent and to acquire popularity among the Californians, over whom he expected to rule as governor. It was better to adopt conciliatory methods late than never. True, his treaty might not be approved; but even then he would appear as the natives' advocate; and it is not unlikely that he already foresaw certain strong reasons why his acts were sure to be approved by one commander or another. Stockton was perhaps slightly offended at Frémont's assumption of responsibility, and he even pretended to disapprove the conditions of the treaty, though I have no doubt he would have granted the same conditions, especially now that Flores had escaped. At any rate, the reasons at which I have just hinted, and of which I shall have much to say in the next chapter, were amply sufficient to prevent any controversy between the commodore and lieutenant-colonel. An additional article was annexed to the treaty by the commissioners and the original commandants on the 16th; and it was virtually approved by Stockton, though I find no evidence that he appended his signature to any copy of the document. In his report of the 15th to his government he wrote: "Not being able to negotiate with me, and having lost the battles of the 8th and 9th, the Californians met Colonel Frémont on the 12th instant on his way here, who, not knowing what had occurred, entered into the capitulation with them, which I now send to you; and although I refused to do it myself, still I have thought it best to approve it."[27] The conquest of California was completed. It only remained for the new rulers to preserve order, to regulate details of civil and military administration, to quarrel among themselves, and to await the completion of a national treaty.

As we have seen, General Flores started for Sonora in the night of January 11th, after turning over the command to Andrés Pico. Both Flores and Castro believed that in view of their part in the late campaign their absence would aid the Californians in obtaining favorable terms from the Americans; they had besides a degree of pride as Mexican officers that made surrender seem disagreeably humiliating; and it is doubtful if the former would have remained if he had been sure of unconditional pardon. The two leaders met and were joined by about 80 men in the San Bernardino region on the 12th or 13th; but after reflection on the hardships of the journey, for which they were but ill prepared, and on the not cheerful prospect of enforced military service in Mexico, more than half the fugitives, including Coronel and his party, wisely decided to stifle their Mexican pride and return to their homes. Some half a dozen officers and 30 privates resolved to accompany Flores and Castro, the former including Garfias, Juan and Tomás Soberanes, Francisco Limon, and perhaps Diego Sepúl-

[27] Stockton to Bancroft, Jan. 15, 1847, in Stockton's *Mil. and Nav. Op.*, 21. Kearny in his report of the 14th, *Frémont's Court-martial*, 80, says: 'The enemy capitulated with him yesterday near San Fernando, agreeing to lay down their arms, and we have now the prospect of having peace and quietness in this country.'

veda and Segura.[28] Most of the men were Sonorans or Mexicans, who followed their natural inclinations in quitting California; and it may be doubted that any besides the two leaders were influenced by either fear or pride.

The journey of the refugees over the desert was a tedious one, involving much suffering; and it is said that Alférez Limon died on the way. On the Gila, when for some time there had been no other food than the flesh of their horses, Flores with three officers and a small guard took the best animals and pressed on in advance of the company.[29] The route was through Papaguería by way of Sonoita; and from Zoñi, where he arrived on February 2d, Flores sent back some provisions and horses for his companions.[30] From Altar on the 5th Flores addressed to Governor Cuesta and Vice-governor Redondo brief reports of past occurrences in connection with the invasion by "los pérfidos Norte Americanos," and an appeal for aid. The reply from the governor at Ures contained expressions of sympathy for the exiles, and of indignation against "our implacable enemies," but gave no hope of material aid, though within a month or two the munificent sum of $15 was paid out of the treasury on this account.[31] Castro soon arrived at Altar, and the two went on to Hermosillo, whence Don Manuel wrote on May 16th to Pio Pico a brief account of the ills that had befallen California; and at

[28] Statements of Coronel, Botello, and Larkin. Botello, the governor's secretary, says he wished to go, but was advised by Flores not to do so. He says he gave $500 to Limon, presumably government funds. Lugo, *Vida*, MS., 66-7, says he dissolved his party at Cucamonga, and was urged by F. to go with him, but declined. He also states that he was sent by Frémont in March to follow Flores' trail, picking up 60 abandoned horses.

[29] Alvarado, *Hist. Cal.*, MS., 268-72, gives some details, apparently obtained from Castro, who in his *Relacion*, MS., does not include a narrative of these events. Alvarado claims that Flores treacherously abandoned Castro and the company to save himself, but I have no doubt that this is erroneous.

[30] Feb. 3d, Flores to Castro from Zoñi. *Castro, Doc.*, MS., ii. 174. 'Paciencia, amigos, y constancia, porque la república está perdida.'

[31] Feb. 5th, Flores to Cuesta and Redondo; Feb. 12th, reply from Cuesta. *Castro, Doc.*, MS., ii. 178, 181, 183; *Sonorense*, March 5, June 11, 1847; *Fernandez, Doc.*, MS., 18-21; *Bustamante, Nuevo Bernal Diaz*, ii. 108-10; *Id., Mem. Hist. Mex.*, MS., vi. 167-9.

Álamos in June he issued a written appeal for contributions to enable him and his two companions to reach Mazatlan. The total contribution in sums from two reals to ten dollars was $59.[32] It is not necessary here to follow the subsequent career of the two officers. Both were somewhat prominent in annals of the Mexican north-west during the next few years, and Castro returned later to California, where he still resides as I write in 1884.[33]

In January General Bustamante, commanding the western department at Guadalajara, had received from Flores in California a report of his revolt and successes at Angeles, Chino, and San Pedro, with an appeal for aid to continue his victories over the invaders. Later Flores had sent a courier with reports of the triumphs at Natividad and San Pascual; but this man failed to reach his destination, and was found by the general on his way to Sonora. Bustamante promptly applied to the minister of war for troops to be sent to California; ordered the governor and comandante general of Sonora to sent immediate reënforcements to Flores to secure his triumph pending the arrival of the troops from Mexico; and congratulated Don José María and his patriotic associates for their brave and successful movement against the foreign invaders. It is tolerably certain that all this would have resulted in nothing under any circumstances; but the governor's letter from Ures, congratulating the Californian hero, and regretting his inability to obey Bustamante's order,[34]

[32] May 16th, Castro to Pico. *Doc. Hist. Cal.*, MS., iii. 292. June 7th, Castro's original subscription paper, with 17 signers. *Id.*, i. 504.
[33] See biographical sketches of ·Castro and Flores. In June 1849, Flores, then sub-inspector de Colonias Militares de Occidente, proposed to go to Cal. for his family, but was not at that time permitted to do so. *Doc. Hist. Cal.*, MS., iii. 300.
[34] Jan. 18th–19th, Bustamante to Flores and others; Feb. 4th, gov. to Flores. *Castro, Doc.*, MS., ii. 164, 167–8, 173, 175, 182.
I make no attempt to name all the accounts of the conquest in 1846–7 that have been printed; but I have before me the following references, mostly additional to those given in other notes, some of them accurate enough, but none adding anything of value to the record that is before the reader: *Arco, Iris*, Aug. 1847–Jan. 1848, passim; *Biglow's Mem. Frémont*, 147 et seq.; *Brackett's U. S. Cav.*, 64–77; *Bustamante, Invasion*, 65–6; county histories, see

was dated February 4th, the very day that Flores, no longer triumphant, made his appearance at Altar!

names of counties; *Farnham's Life Cal.*, 419–26; *Ferry, Cal.*, 17–43; *Frost's Hist. Cal.*, 27–34; *Id., Hist. Mex.*, 435–56; *Furber's 12 Vol.*, 267–71; *Goodrich's Hist. Amer.*, 859–61; *Guerra entre Mex.*, 353–61; *Hittell's Hist. S. F.; Id.*, editorials in *Alta* (cited by me on special points); *Honolulu Friend*, 1846–7; *Hughes' Doniphan's Exped.*, 23–42; *Jay's Mex. War*, 144–50; *Jenkins' Hist. Mex. War*, 125–35; *Lancey's Cruise*, passim; *Los Angeles Star*, Mar. 16, 1872, and other dates; *McKune*, in *Terr. Pion.*, 1st An., 40–2; *McClellan's Golden State*, 89–109; *Mansfield's Mex. War*; *Mayer's Mex. Aztec*, i. 345–6; *Mex. War Heroes*, ii. 204–7; *Niles' Register*, 1846–7.   See index; *Oswald, Cal.*, 9–21; *Oregon Spectator*, 1846–7; *Ripley's War Mex.*, i. 295–8; *Robinson's Cal.*, 73–85; *Ryan's Judges and Crim.*, chap. xi.–xii.; *S. F. Alta*, Sept. 24, 1866; July 7th of dif. years, and many other dates; *S. F. Bulletin*, July 20, 1867, and many dates; *S. F. Cal. Star*, 1847–8; *S. F. Post*, July 21, 1877, etc.; *S. F. Sun*, Sept. 5, 1856; *S. José Pioneer*, passim; *Sta Cruz Sentinel*, Apr. 22, 1876; *Soulé's Annals S. F.*, 90–124; *Sutter's Diary*; *Upham's Life Frémont*, 235–51, *Williams' Lecture*, June 11, 1878, in S. F. papers.

CHAPTER XVI.

STOCKTON'S CONTROVERSY WITH KEARNY.

JANUARY–FEBRUARY, 1847.

POLICY OF SLOAT AND STOCKTON—A RÉSUMÉ OF THE CONQUEST—KEARNY'S
INSTRUCTIONS FROM WASHINGTON—LATER ORDERS—STATE OF AFFAIRS
ON THE GENERAL'S ARRIVAL—DISCUSSION AT SAN DIEGO—THE CAM-
PAIGN—THE COMMODORE AS COMMANDER-IN-CHIEF—AT LOS ANGELES
—KEARNY AND FRÉMONT—THE CONTROVERSY BEGUN—THE GENERAL'S
AUTHORITY NOT RECOGNIZED—HE GOES TO SAN DIEGO AND MONTEREY—
ARRIVAL OF COMMODORE SHUBRICK—A POLICY OF PEACE—STOCKTON'S
LAST ACTS AS GOVERNOR—GENERAL CONCLUSIONS—KEARNY IN THE
RIGHT—STOCKTON IN THE WRONG—FRÉMONT'S ACTION JUSTIFIED—
RULE OF FRÉMONT AS GOVERNOR—LEGISLATIVE COUNCIL—PROCLAMA-
TION—FINANCIAL TROUBLES.

THE war in California was at an end, and the forces
of the United States were in full possession. Who
was to rule the country until an international treaty
should fix its destiny? So accustomed had become
the inhabitants to controversies between their civil
and military chiefs that they would perhaps have
questioned the legitimacy of an harmonious administration. Be this as it may, the old ways were not to
be abruptly and radically broken up in this respect at
least under the new régime. Under existing conditions, there were abundant opportunities, if few
reasons, for a quarrel at Los Angeles.

In July 1846 Commodore Sloat, acting under instructions from Washington to "at once possess yourself of the port of San Francisco, and blockade or
occupy such other ports as your force may permit,"
had not only occupied Monterey and San Francisco,

but, relying on presumed instructions to Frémont, had also raised the flag at different points of the northern interior, proclaiming a conciliatory policy, for his instructions also required him "to preserve if possible the most friendly relations with the inhabitants," and "encourage them to adopt a course of neutrality." His policy, when he learned that Frémont had no additional orders, was to hold the ports and await further news and instructions, having some doubts whether war had really been declared. He was not in sympathy with the American revolutionists, and was not disposed to utilize their battalion for an aggressive warfare on the Californians. But he soon retired, and was succeeded in command of the naval squadron by Stockton. The latter had no orders of later date than Sloat's, but he decided promptly to extend the occupation to the southern ports and to Los Angeles, the capital. In this respect he acted wisely, but no more can be said in his favor. In utter disregard of his government's policy, as made known to a confidential agent, and without any good reason, he adopted the aggressive policy of the Bear Flag men and filibusters, issued an offensive and warlike proclamation, and on going south practically refused to receive the voluntary submission of the Californian leaders, thus disobeying the spirit of his instructions. Yet he was in a sense successful; the south was occupied without resistance. Then the commodore, deeming the conquest complete, resolved to organize a temporary civil government and to leave Frémont in charge as governor, reporting his intention at the end of August, and making Frémont military commander early in September.[1]

Certain dishonorable and imprudent phases of these proceedings not being fully understood, there was no reason why they should not be approved at Washington. Notwithstanding the blunders and braggadocio

[1] For details of what is briefly referred to here see chap. x.-xi. of this volume.

and filibusterism of Frémont and Stockton, really the
greatest obstacles to the conquest, these officers might
plausibly claim to be the conquerors. The purpose
to organize a civil government, if not altogether regular and commendable, was in accordance with orders
then on the way to the naval commander.[2] Had the
conquest proved permanent and complete as reported,
had Stockton organized his government as intended,
making Frémont governor, and had reports of such
action reached Washington before other measures had
been adopted, doubtless all would have been approved
and the governor's appointment confirmed. But a
serious revolt occurred, which involved both in the
south and north all the fighting and bloodshed that
attended the war in California; and the commodore
and colonel were forced to postpone all thought of
civil organization and give all their energies to the
military task of putting down a revolt that was
largely due to their own errors. Stockton with his
naval force proceeded to San Diego to renew operations against Los Angeles; Frémont as military commandant hastily ransacked the country for recruits
and supplies for his battalion, and marched south to
coöperate with the commodore, after some of his men
had engaged in a fight at Natividad; and garrisons of
marines and volunteers were left to protect the northern posts, and, as it proved, to engage in some slight
warlike service. Details and results have been recorded in preceding chapters. But before the conquest was really accomplished, and the leaders were
ready to think again of civil affairs, several things
had happened to affect their plans.[3]

[2] July 12th, Sec. Bancroft to Sloat. The sending of an artillery company,
and of the N. Y. volunteers soon to start, is announced; and Sloat is instructed to extend his possession to S. Diego, and if possible to Los Angeles.
'This will bring with it the necessity of a civil administration. Such a government should be established under your protection; and in selecting persons to hold office, due respect should be had to the wishes of the people of
Cal.' News of Kearny's appointment and a copy of his instructions are
enclosed. 'The govt relies on the land and naval forces to coöperate with
each other in the most friendly and effective manner.' Doc. in *Frémont's
Court-martial*, 59–60; *Stockton's Life*, 30.

[3] The later theory of Stockton and Frémont, that the revolt was a mere

The administration at Washington on the outbreak of the Mexican war, taking it for granted that the naval forces would occupy the ports, but not anticipating that they would be able to do much more, resolved to send a military force by land and sea to coöperate in the conquest or occupation. General Kearny was selected to take command, and in June was ordered—as soon as he should have completed the conquest of New Mexico—to march across the continent. His instructions were to take possession of California, to assume command not only of the troops that accompanied him, but of those to be sent after him by sea and land, and of such volunteers as might be organized among the settlers, and to establish a temporary civil government.[4] It was hoped, but not confidently believed, that Kearny might reach California in the winter of 1846-7.

There were as yet no definite instructions on the course to be followed if the things the general was sent to do should be done before his arrival by others, for no such emergency was foreseen; but there were later orders throwing light on the government's intention. In July the artillery company was despatched by sea, with orders dated in June,[5] and the instruc-

local and insignificant matter, not interfering at all with the conquest previously effected or the civil govt already organized, merits no consideration whatever; but it is fair to notice that the revolt was put down mainly by their efforts, their energy deserving some commendation.

[4] See chap. xiii. of this volume for details of Kearny's instructions and operations. The essential points of the former were as follows: June 3, 1846. 'It has been decided by the president to be of the greatest importance in the pending war to take the earliest possession of Upper California. An expedition with that view is hereby ordered, and you are designated to command it... You are authorized to organize and receive into the service of the U. S. such portion of these citizens as you may think useful to aid you to hold the possession of the country... It is expected that the naval forces of the U. S... will be in possession of all the towns on the sea-coast, and will coöperate with you in the conquest of Cal... Should you conquer and take possession of N. Mex. and Upper Cal., or considerable places in either, you will establish temporary civil governments therein... It is foreseen that what relates to the civil govt will be a difficult and unpleasant part of your duty, and much must necessarily be left to your own discretion.' June 18. Announcement of the proposed sending of troops by sea, artillery and N. Y. volunteers; 'these troops and such as may be organized in Cal. will be under your command.' Cal. and N. Mex., Mess. and Doc., 1850, p. 236, 240.

[5] June 20th, Scott to Capt. Tompkins. He is not to be 'under the orders

tions already cited were sent to the naval commander, alluding to the possibility of having to establish a civil government before Kearny's arrival, but not implying that this was to affect the general's authority.[6] And in September instructions to Colonel Stevenson, given after the reception of unofficial reports that Monterey had been occupied, were based on the idea that the New York volunteers would arrive before Kearny, that the latter would come later to take command, and that probably before his arrival not much would be accomplished in the interior.[7]

strictly speaking of any naval officer,' but is to coöperate with the naval forces in the occupation of Cal. ports. 'You may find on the north-west coast an army officer with higher rank than your own, when of course you will report to him, and if ashore, come under his command. *Cutts' Conq.*, 251.

[6] See p. 413 for instructions of July 12th. If Kearny's instructions, enclosed with these, were to be disregarded, surely an order to that effect would have been given in clear language. In the instructions of Aug. 13th, 17th, to the naval commander, Sec. Bancroft says: 'A military force has been directed to proceed to Cal. for the purpose of coöperation with the navy' in taking and holding S. F., Monterey, S. Diego, and if possible 'San Pueblo de los Angeles.' 'A detachment...has sailed in the *Lexington.* A regiment ...will soon sail from N. Y., and a body of troops under Brig.-gen. Kearny may reach the coast over Sta Fé. Copies of so much of the instructions to Tompkins and Kearny as relates to objects requiring coöperation are herewith enclosed. The president expects and requires the most cordial and effectual coöperation between the officers of the two services,...and will hold any commander of either branch to a strict responsibility for any failure to preserve harmony and secure the objects proposed.' *Cutts' Conq.*, 107, 256.

[7] Sept. 11th, sec. war to Stevenson. 'Instructions have been given to the naval commander,...and you are directed to coöperate with him in carrying out his plans. The regiment under your command, as well as the company of Capt. Tompkins, is a part of Gen. Kearny's command; but it may be that he will not be in a situation to reach you, by his orders, immediately on your debarkation. Until that is the case, yours will be an independent command, except when engaged in joint operations with the naval force. It is not expected that you will be able to advance far into the country...In the event of hostile resistance, your operations must be governed by circumstances, and you must use the means at your command to accomplish the object in view—the military occupation of the country. It is not, however, expected that much can be done, if preparations shall have been made to resist, until the forces under Gen. Kearny shall have entered the country.... Where a place is taken by the joint action of the naval and land force, the naval officer in command, if superior in rank to yourself, will be entitled to make arrangements for the civil govt of it while it is held by the coöperation of both branches. All your powers in this respect will of course be devolved on Gen. Kearny, whenever he shall arrive.' *Cutts' Conq.*, 249–50. Sept. 12th, sec. war to Kearny, enclosing the instructions to Stevenson. 'This force is to be part of your command; but as it may reach the place of its destination before you are in a condition to subject it to your orders, the colonel...has been furnished with instructions for his conduct in the mean time.' *Cal. and N. Mex., Mess. and Doc.*, 1850, p. 241.

The next orders, in November—issued after news had come of Sloat's operations, of Stockton's accession to the naval command, and of his acceptance of Frémont's battalion of volunteers, but before the reception of the commodore's plans for civil government —were positive to the effect that Kearny on his arrival, and the ranking military officer before, was to be recognized as civil governor; and these orders were sent by Colonel Mason, who was to command after Kearny's departure.[8]

Thus we see that Kearny by the original orders of June 1846 was required to conquer California in co-operation with the naval forces, to command all troops and to direct all land operations in the province, and to establish a temporary civil government, being governor by virtue of his military command. The later orders cited, though not received till after the controversy began, confirm the apparent meaning of the first, and show that Kearny did not misinterpret them. They show that the administration anticipated the possibility—though not a probability—of the conquest being extended to the capital, and of a civil government being organized by the naval forces under Stockton, the regulars under Tompkins, and volunteers under Frémont and Stevenson, before Kearny's arrival and assumption of the command. They do not show that the general's authority was to be af-

---

[8] Nov. 3, 1846, Gen. Scott to Kearny. 'It is desirable that the volunteers' (Frémont's men), 'if not originally mustered, should be caused by you to be regularly mustered into service retrospectively under the volunteer act of May 13th.' The appointment of collectors, etc., 'appertains to the civil governor of the province, who will be, for the time, senior officer of the land forces in the country.' 'As a guide to the civil governor of Cal., in our hands, see the letter of June 3d last.' 'After occupying with our forces all necessary points in Upper Cal., and establishing a temporary civil govt therein, as well as assuring yourself of its internal tranquillity, ...you may charge Col Mason, ...or the land officer next in rank to your own, with your several duties, and return yourself' to St Louis. *Frémont's Court-martial*, 48–50. Nov. 5th, sec. navy to Stockton. 'The president has deemed it best for the public interests to invest the military officer commanding with the direction of the operations on land, and with the administrative functions of govt over the people and territory occupied by us. You will relinquish to Col Mason or to Gen. Kearny, if the latter shall arrive before you have done so, the entire control over these matters.' *Id.*, 51–2.

fected by such events; nor do they indicate that under any circumstances the position of civil governor could be held by any other than the ranking military officer.   Kearny, as we have seen,[9] started from Santa Fé in September, earlier than had been expected, with three hundred dragoons.   Presently he met Carson, Stockton's messenger, with despatches for Washington, and news that California had been conquered and a civil government organized by Stockton and Frémont.   Nothing indicates that he questioned the accuracy of the report; neither did he find in it anything to modify his instructions or duties.   He sent back two thirds of his dragoons, believing that the other troops provided for would suffice for holding the country, and continued his march across the continent.   Had he on arrival found Carson's report strictly true, all being tranquil, and civil affairs being quietly administered by the commodore or lieutenant-colonel, he would have been entitled, beyond question I think, to assume the military command, and with it the governorship.

But, as the reader knows, he found no such state of things.   He learned that Stockton had not organized but only planned a civil government, and that the conquest was yet to be effected before the plans could be carried out.   The necessity for military service, instead of having disappeared, was much more urgent than had ever been anticipated at Washington.   But Kearny, after the disaster of San Pascual— which reflected no credit on his ability as an officer —entered San Diego under peculiar circumstances, wounded like many of his men, deprived of his best officers who had been killed, his whole command perhaps saved from destruction by the commodore's aid. The delicacy of his position, courtesy due to the naval commander, and the fact that Stockton was actively engaged in organizing an expedition against the enemy prompted the general not only to abstain from de-

[9] See chap. xiii. of this volume.

manding the chief command, but to decline it when proffered by Stockton.[10]

The two officers, however, had some correspondence, conversation, and even argument respecting their claims to the ultimate command. Kearny showed his instructions, expressed his opinion that under them he was entitled to the governorship, and probably announced his intention to assume that position later. Stockton, on the other hand, showed copies of his earlier reports explaining his plans for a civil government, and made an argument in support of his theory that the general's contingent instructions had been superseded by events, since he and Frémont had already done the things that Kearny was ordered to do.[11]

[10] So Stockton states, offering a certificate of two of his aids who were present as witnesses. The point was not touched in Kearny's testimony in the court-martial, but there is no contradictory evidence. Stockton says: 'After Gen. Kearny arrived, and in my quarters and in presence of two of my military family, I offered to make him commander-in-chief over all of us, and I offered to go as his aid-de-camp. He said no; that the force was mine, and that he would go as my aid-de-camp, or accompany me. A few days after this, and when Gen. K. had removed to other quarters, I made a formal call upon him;...during that interview I made the same offer to him, pretty much in the same language, and received pretty much the same answer. My motives for making this offer were two: the first was his high character as a soldier; the second was, I desired he should know that I was disposed, on his first arrival, to give all power into his hands, without making a question of rank at all.' *Frémont's Court-martial*, 189; and to same effect in *Stockton's Report*, Feb. 18, 1847, with more explanations that the offer was made, 'although it was my decided opinion...that I was entitled to retain the position in which I was placed of commander-in-chief.'

[11] Kearny's testimony: 'In that conversation'—that of Dec. 28th, and the only one held on the subject as he states—'I told Com. S. that he had seen... the instructions of the president to me relating to Cal.; that I had come to Cal. with but a small military force; that deference and respect for his situation, he being then in command of the Pacific squadron and having a large force of sailors and marines, prevented me, at that time, from relieving him and taking charge of the civil govt; that as soon as my command was increased I would take charge of affairs in Cal. agreeably to my instructions. Com. S. said in reply that he had in Aug. reported the state of affairs in Cal. to Washington, and that he could not permit himself to be interfered with until he received an answer to that report.' *Frémont's Court-martial*, 79, 81–3. Stockton's testimony: 'About the time when Gen. K. was leaving my quarters, he handed me his instructions, and when I read them, I was simple enough to believe that he had handed them to me that I might be gratified by seeing how fully and thoroughly I had anticipated the wishes of the govt. (!) When I returned the papers with a note of thanks...I sent him copies of some of my own despatches to the govt, that he as a friend might participate in the pleasure I felt...After this at S. Diego the general in a conversation with me introduced the subject of the governorship, and intimated that he thought

Doubtless the commodore regarded Kearny's non-acceptance of the immediate command as indicating a probable yielding at the last. There would be time enough, however, to settle these matters after the taking of Los Angeles; and at San Diego there was no interruption of friendly relations. It would seem, however, that the general took at least one slight step to strengthen himself in a foreseen controversy;[12] thus indicating, as also by certain later acts, that he did not fully appreciate the strength of his position. It had been understood that Kearny after declining the chief command would serve in the campaign as Stockton's aid; but just before marching from San Diego a new arrangement was made at the general's request. All agree that Kearny accepted and exercised throughout the expedition the immediate command of the troops, and that Stockton reserved for himself, as publicly announced to the officers, the position of commander-in-chief and acting governor of California, his temporary authority as such being fully recognized by the general. Yet a little later there was much dispute about the relative positions of the two offi-

he ought to be governor under his instructions. This of course amazed me, because I had more than once voluntarily offered to place him at the head of affairs in Cal., which offer he had as often refused. We argued the matter, however, he relying upon his instructions.' Stockton in *Id.*, 190, and to same effect elsewhere. Dec. 16th. Stockton to Kearny, returning with thanks despatches and sending copies of his own letters, etc., 'that you may see how far the wishes of the govt have been anticipated.' *Stockton's Mil. and Nav. Op.*, 28.

[12] It is difficult to attach any other meaning to K.'s letter of Dec. 22d, advising S. to march as soon as possible on Los Angeles to form a junction with Frémont's force, and adding, 'I shall be happy, in such an expedition, to accompany and to give you any aid either of head or hand of which I may be capable.' *Frémont's Court-martial*, 47. Next day Stockton replied in a note explaining that his purpose to march on Angeles at the earliest possible moment had been made known to K. in conversation the morning before, and implying some surprise that K.'s advice had been deemed necessary. *Id.*, 111. K. in his reply of the same date, alluding to the conversation, says, 'If I had so understood you, I certainly would not have written my letter to you of last evening.' *Id.*, 112. It is possible that K. really misunderstood S.'s plans, but it seems unlikely; especially as in his report of Jan. 17, 1847, he says, 'The march of the troops from S. Diego to this place was reluctantly consented to by Com. Stockton on my urgent advice,' *Id.*, 95; and in his later testimony that the expedition to Angeles 'was organized in consequence, as I believe, of a paper which I addressed to Com. S.'—the one cited above. *Id.*, 47.

cers, Kearny denying that he had been in any sense
under the commodore's orders. The evidence leaves
no possible doubt, I think, that in this dispute Stockton was right and Kearny wrong, that the former did
act as commander-in-chief of the forces, issuing in that
capacity many routine orders, which were obeyed,
some of them against the general's commands. So
clearly is this established that I do not deem it necessary to present in detail the bulky testimony, especially as the matter had no such importance in the
general controversy as was imputed to it then and
later.[13]   Kearny had a right by his instructions and

[13] Kearny admits that he recognized S. as acting governor, and even as
commander-in-chief 'of California,' that is, of all forces except those at S.
Diego, but claims that he retained no authority over K. or the troops over
which K. was put in immediate command, and that his so-called 'orders'
were regarded as mere 'suggestions.' In other words, K. claims to have assumed the military command in accordance with his rank and instructions as
far as was possible at S. Diego before absent portions of the forces should report to him, or should be formally turned over by Stockton. The distinction
is, however, a very fine one, hardly satisfactory to the mind not imbued with
military technicalities; and as I have said, the testimony that Stockton acted
practically as commander-in-chief is overwhelming.

Stockton's testimony in *Frémont's Court-martial*, 191–4, 199, 201, and to
same effect in other reports. 'I did not send my aid to Gen. K. to say to
him that I ordered him to do this and that; but I sent all my messages to
him in the most respectful and considerate manner...Most of the execution
of details was confided to Gen. K. as second in command.' Testimony of
Lieut Gray, as S.'s aid, in *Id.*, 210–11; Lieut Minor, *Id.*, 241–2. Certificate
of Mosely and Speiden of the navy to K.'s original offer to go as S.'s aid. *Id.*,
430. Russell's testimony on K.'s later admission that he had served under
K. *Id.*, 262. Kearny's testimony in *Id.*, 47, 61, 70, 116–17, 322–5. He re-
represents S. as saying at S. Diego, 'Gentlemen, Gen. K. has kindly consented to take com. of the troops on this exped. You will therefore look
upon him as your commander. I shall go along as gov. and com.-in-chief in
Cal.' 'I exercised no com. over Com. S., nor did he exercise any over me.'
'He was considered by me as com.-in-chief in Cal. until he had on Dec. 29th
turned over a portion of that com. to me.' 'During the march many messages were brought to me from Com. S.; these I looked upon as suggestions
and as expressions of his orders.' Lieut Emory, *Id.*, 161–3, 171–2, testifies
that K. was in command, but that 'my information is confined very much to
the immediate com. of the troops.' 'Com. S. claimed to be gov. and com.-
in-chief...On the march Com. S., I understood, did several acts in that capacity.' He mentions also an instance where he obeyed S.'s order on the
location of a camp. In *Id.*, 70, is Emory's report of casualties, dated Jan. 11th,
and addressed to 'His Excell. R. F. Sockton, Gov. of Cal., etc.;' and in *Id.*,
108–9, K.'s advice and offer to march with part of the troops, addressed to
'Com. R. F. Stockton, Gov. of Cal., com'd'g U. S. forces.' John Bidwell,
Cal. 1841–8, MS., 204–7, says: 'I as quartermaster received orders from both,
and obeyed both so far as I could. S. was determined to command. A conflict was growing between the two. Sometimes I thought I could see K. bite
his lips with rage.' Testimony of John Forster, *Pioneer Data*, MS., 45, and
of B. D. Wilson, *Observ.*, MS., 105–9, that S. was in command. See also

by his rank of brigadier-general—Stockton's assimilated rank being that of colonel—to assume whenever he thought best the military command, involving the civil governorship. He deferred the act, as he had also a right to do. His subsequent efforts to ignore Stockton's real position in the campaign must be attributed to a wish to strengthen himself for a coming controversy, and later to the spirit aroused by that controversy.

During the campaign, as at San Diego, there was no interruption of friendly relations, apparently at least; and the same state of things continued for about a week at Los Angeles, though Bidwell and a few others thought that the general was angry at Stockton's attitude on the march, and Emory testified that Kearny forbade the reading of the commodore's congratulatory order to the troops. Meanwhile, however, it is not unlikely that divers petty occurrences, not recorded, furnished fuel for the coming fire; at any rate, it became more and more evident to Kearny that Stockton did not intend voluntarily to surrender the command. He also began to foresee that the attitude of Frémont and his battalion of volunteers would be a factor in the problem. He had determined to assert his authority as soon as his force should be increased, and the nearest source of such increase was the battalion. He did not yet claim au-

narrative of the campaign in chap. xv. of this volume. In the *Monterey Californian*, Jan. 28, Feb. 13, 1847; *S. F. Californian*, June 26, July 17, 1847; reprinted as an appendix to Benton's speech of July 1848 in the *Cong. Globe*; and also as appen. D of *Stockton's Life*, 43–8—is a mass of correspondence on this subject. It contains not only Stockton's statement, but certificates from some 15 naval officers affirming most positively that S. held the chief command, and that K., commanding the troops by S.'s appointment, was considered by all the officers as second in command. I have no space for the bulky details.

In his report to the govt of Jan. 12th, Kearny wrote: 'At the request of Com. S., who in Sept. last assumed the title of Gov. of Cal., I consented to take com. of an exped. to this place...Com. S. accompanied us,' etc. Then follows an account of the battle, etc. *U. S. Govt Doc.*, 30th cong. 1st sess., Sen. Ex. Doc., 1, p. 516–17. Stockton, in his report of Jan. 11th, represented himself as having been 'aided by Gen. Kearny.' *Stockton's Life*, appen. 8. In his four notes to Frémont, dated Jan. 10th, 12th, 13th, *Court-martial*, 73–4, Kearny did not name Stockton at all, and in one of them he said, 'I am here in possession of this place.'

thority over the volunteers; to assume it by a general
order, and require compliance from Stockton and Frémont, would be to precipitate the controversy; and
he chose rather to gain his end by more indirect
methods.   His notes to Frémont, and his proposition
to join him, on January 10th–13th, were due in part
to the motive alleged, anxiety for the safety of his
force; but also, and chiefly, to a desire for friendly
relations with Frémont, and to the hope of obtaining
from that officer at least a technical 'report' to himself as commander.   In this last respect his crafty
plan was successful, for on the evening of the 13th,
Major Russell arrived from the battalion's camp with
the required report.[14]

Russell had been sent by Frémont to deliver the
letter, to learn who was in actual command, and to
report to that officer the capitulation of Cahuenga.
Having called on Kearny and learned that he recognized Stockton as commander-in-chief, the major proceeded to report the treaty to the commodore.   That
evening he had at least two interviews with each of
the chiefs, and finally passed the night with Kearny
and Turner at their quarters, engaging in long conversations on current events.   As to the general purport of results, there is no essential discrepancy in
testimony.   Russell learned that Kearny, while yet
recognizing Stockton as commander-in-chief, claimed

[14] 'On the march, Jan. 13, 1847.   Dear Sir: I have the honor to report to
you my arrival at this place, with 400 mounted riflemen and six pieces of artillery, including among the latter two pieces lately in the possession of the
Californians.   Their entire force, under the command of D. Andrés Pico, have
this day laid down their arms and surrendered to my command.   Very respectfully, your obedient servant, J. C. Frémont, Lt-col. U. S. A., and military commandant of the territory of Cal.   Brig.-gen. S. W. Kearny, commanding U. S. forces, Puebla de los Angeles.'   In *Frémont's Court-martial*,
37, and elsewhere.   It was later claimed by Frémont and his friends that
this letter—drawn out by friendly notes addressed to 'Dear F.,' etc., and
asking for information as to his whereabouts—did not constitute a 'report' of
his command to Gen. K. in a military sense; but a military court decided
otherwise.   Another point made by the same party with some force was, that
in the immediate controversy at Los Angeles, K. did not urge this report as
the foundation for his authority over the battalion, but reserved it as the
foundation of later charges.   This document was really the basis of the verdict in one of the two principal phases of the court-martial.

the right, under his instructions, to assume the command and organize the civil government; that he was friendly to Frémont and disposed to encourage his hopes for the governorship; and that he fully approved the treaty of Cahuenga. He also learned that Stockton still maintained his authority to hold the civil and military command as unimpaired by Kearny's arrival and instructions; that he disapproved the capitulation; but that he changed his mind in this latter respect after listening to arguments.[15] There is no doubt that both the general's and commodore's approval of Frémont's recent acts was founded mainly on their own immediate interests, as the making of the treaty had been an irregular proceeding.

Russell left town in the morning of the 14th, met Frémont five or six miles out, and reported the state of affairs at the capital. This report was to the effect that the lieutenant-colonel would have to choose between the general and commodore, since each claimed a right to organize a civil government, either would probably make Frémont governor, and both approved the treaty of Cahuenga. A controversy was clearly foreseen; Russell believed that Kearny was more friendly than Stockton; and Frémont apparently agreed with him. There was, however, as yet

---

[15] Testimony of Russell and Kearny in *Frémont's Court-martial*, 87–8, 243–5, 251–2, 262–5, 268, 321–4, 392. They agree on the points mentioned in my text. Russell states, however, that K. relied exclusively on his instructions and admitted—against R.'s opinion—that Stockton outranked him. This is denied by K., and is very improbable. R. also says that Stockton claimed to be acting under written instructions not shown, which is not supported by any other evidence. And finally, Russell makes K.'s encouragement of F.'s hopes for the governorship amount almost to a promise, at least to a statement that he intended soon to leave Cal., and proposed, if his authority was recognized, to make F. governor; but Kearny denies that he made any promise, announced any intention, or offered any other encouragement to F. than to speak of him in favorable terms. It is to be noted that in their testimony R. would naturally—and probably did—exaggerate and K. underrate the encouragement to F.'s hopes; that F. was at the time the ranking army officer in Cal. next to K., and would naturally be left in command on the latter's departure, though Lieut-col Cooke was expected soon to arrive; and that Frémont in his defence, p. 392, notes, as a very strong indication against K.'s testimony and in support of R., the fact that Capt. Turner, a witness for the prosecution, was not questioned about the conversation between R. and K., most of which was in his presence.

no call for a decision; the battalion marched into the city early on the 14th; and Frémont called on both chiefs, first on the commodore, no particulars being known about either interview. Indeed, so far as the controversy is concerned, no developments of this day or the next are recorded. Kearny reported to the government Frémont's arrival and capitulation, and alluding to the troops en route by land and sea, said: "On their arrival I will, agreeably to the instructions of the president, have the management of things in this country,"[16] thus perhaps implying a doubt whether he would be able to obtain control before the coming of reënforcements. And Stockton, reporting the same matters, said: "The civil government formed by me is again in operation in the places where it was interrupted by the insurgents...I will immediately withdraw my sailors and marines, and sail for the coast of Mexico;"[17] thus taking it for granted that there was to be no opposition to his authority. Yet while there is no definite record of what was being said and done in the matter, it was well known to Kearny and to many others at Los Angeles that Stockton intended to ignore the general's authority. Indeed, he had on the 14th tendered to Frémont and Russell their commissions as governor and secretary of state.

On the 16th, therefore, Kearny ordered Stockton either to show his authority from the government or to take no further action in relation to a civil organization.[18] The commodore in his reply of the same

---

[16] Jan. 14, 1847, K. to adj.-gen., in *Frémont's Court-martial*, 80.

[17] Jan. 15th, S. to Sec. Bancroft, in *Stockton's Life*, appen. 9–10. This was sent by Lieut Gray, who left Los Angeles for the east on the 16th. *Griffin's Diary*, MS.

[18] Jan. 16, 1847, Kearny to Stockton. 'Sir: I am informed that you are now engaged in organizing a civil govt, and appointing officers for it in this territory. As this duty has been specially assigned to myself by orders of the president,...in letters to me from the sec. war, of June 3 and 18, 1846, the originals of which I gave you on the 12th, and which you returned to me on the 13th'—there seems to be no other record of this corresp.—'and copies of which I furnished you with the 26th of Dec., I have to ask if you have any authority from the president, from the sec. navy, or from any other channel of the president's, to form such a govt and make such appointments? If you have such authority and will show it to me, or will furnish me with

day declined to obey the general's order, on the ground that the conquest had been completed and the civil government put in operation before his arrival. He also suspended Kearny from the command of the troops conferred on him at San Diego, as he had a right to do so far as the sailors and marines were concerned.[19]

Thus in clear terms the general asserted his authority, which Stockton refused to recognize, and to enforce which the former's force was less than a hundred dragoons. The only source of possible increase at the time was the battalion; therefore Kearny sent to Frémont, through Emory, a test order to make no changes in the organization of the battalion.[20] This order was delivered in the evening, and later Frémont called upon Stockton at the latter's request to receive his commission as governor, seeing at that

certified copies of it, I will cheerfully acquiesce in what you are doing. If you have not such authority, I then demand that you cease all further proceedings relating to the formation of a civil govt for this territory, as I cannot recognize in you any right in assuming to perform duties confided to me by the president. Yours resp., S. W. Kearny, Brig.-gen. U. S. A. Com. R. F. Stockton, U. S. N., acting gov.' In *Frémont's Court-martial*, 90, and often repeated elsewhere.

[19] Jan. 16, 1847, Stockton to Kearny, in *Id.*, 118. 'Sir: in answer to your note received this afternoon, I need say but little more than that which I communicated to you in a conversation at S. Diego: that Cal. was conquered and a govt put into successful operation; that a copy of the laws made for me for the govt of the territory, and the names of the officers selected to see them faithfully executed, were transmitted to the pres. of the U. S. before your arrival in the territory. I will only add that I cannot do anything, nor desist from doing anything, or alter anything on your demand; which I will submit to the president and ask for your recall. In the mean time you will consider yourself suspended from the command of the U. S. forces in this place. Faithfully, your obed. serv., R. F. Stockton, com.-in-chief. To Brevet Brig.-gen. S. W. Kearny.'

[20] 'Headquarters army of the west, ciudad de Los Angeles, Jan. 16, 1847. By direction of Brig.-gen. Kearny I send you a copy of a communication to him from the sec. of war, dated June 18, 1846, in which is the following: "These troops and such as may be organized in Cal. will be under your command." The general directs that no change will be made in the organization of your battalion, or officers appointed in it, without his sanction or approval being first obtained. Very resp., W. H. Emory, Lieut and A. A. A. Gen. To Lieut-col J. C. Frémont, mounted riflemen, commanding battalion Cal. volunteers.' *Court-martial*, 5. See also *Id.*, 78, 118, 163, 194, 395, 399, 401. The particular change anticipated was the appointment of Gillespie to command the battalion in Frémont's place. Kearny says the order to F. was written— but perhaps not delivered—before he received S.'s letter, and even before he wrote to S.

interview the communications that had passed between the general and commodore, and showing the
latter Kearny's order to himself.[21] Next morning,
the 17th, Frémont wrote a reply, in which he declined
to obey the general's order, on the ground that he had
received his appointment from Stockton, and on arrival at Los Angeles had found that officer still recognized as commander. "I feel myself, therefore,
with great deference to your professional and personal
character, constrained to say that until you and Commodore Stockton adjust between yourselves the question of rank, where I respectfully think the difficulty
belongs, I shall have to report and receive orders as
heretofore from the commodore."[22]

Leaving this reply to be copied by the clerk, Frémont, in response to a note—"Dear Colonel: I wish
to see you on business"—called at Kearny's quarters.
During the interview the reply was brought in, and
after being signed was given to the general, who
earnestly advised the lieutenant-colonel, as a friend
and senior officer, to take back and destroy the paper,
offering to forget its contents. But Frémont declined
to reconsider his refusal to obey, even when Kearny
implied a willingness a. make him governor in four or
six weeks, on his own departure. There is some con-
tradiction, more apparent than real, and resulting from
the exaggerations of controversial prejudice, respect-

[21] Stockton's testimony. *Frémont's Court-martial*, 196–7. F.'s com. as
governor. *Id.*, 175–6. Other commissions by S. bore the same date.

[22] Jan. 17, 1847, Frémont to Kearny. 'Sir: I have the honor to be in receipt of your favor of last night, in which I am directed to suspend the execution of orders which, in my capacity of mil. com. of this territory, I had
received from Com. Stockton, gov. and com.-in-chief in Cal. I avail myself
of an early hour this morning to make such a reply as the brief time allowed
for reflection will enable me. I found Com. S. in possession of the country,
exercising the functions of mil. com. and civil gov., as early as July of last
year; and shortly thereafter I received from him the commission of mil. com.,
the duties of which I immediately entered upon, and have continued to exercise to the present moment. I found, also, on my arrival at this place some
three or four days since, Com. S. still exercising the functions of civil and
military gov., with the same apparent deference to his rank on the part of all
officers (including yourself) as he maintained and required when he assumed
in July last. I feel myself, etc. (as in text), with considerations, etc. J. C.
Frémont, Lt-col. U. S. A. and mil. com. of the ter. of Cal. To Brig.-gen. S. W.
Kearny, U. S. A.' *Id.*, 6, 231.

ing this interview,[23] but I have no doubt that, without definite promises on either side, each believed the date of appointment to be the essential point at issue. Frémont certainly understood that by yielding he could have the governorship later; and Kearny probably believed that by offering an immediate appointment he could secure obedience.

Finding his authority and his instructions from the government thus ignored by Stockton and Frémont, and having no troops with which to enforce his orders, Kearny wrote to the commodore: "I must for the

[23] See testimony in *Id.*, 38–9, 76, 78–81, 87, 91–2, 101, 164, 252–3, 380–96. Kearny says: 'Having finished the reading, I told F. that I was a much older man than himself, that I was a much older soldier than himself, that I had great regard for his wife and great friendship for...Col. Benton;...that these considerations induced me to volunteer advice to him, and the advice was that he should take back that letter and destroy it, that I was willing to forget it. Lt-col. F. declined taking it back, and told me that Com. S. would support him in the position he had taken. I told him that Com. S. could not support him in disobeying the orders of his senior officer, and that if he persisted in it he would unquestionably ruin himself. He told me that Com. S. was about organizing a civil govt, and intended to appoint him as gov. I told him Com. S. had no such authority, that authority having been conferred on me by the president. He asked me if I would appoint him governor. I told him I expected shortly to leave Cal.,...that as soon as the country was quieted I should most probably organize a civil govt, and that I at that time knew of no objections to my appointing him as the gov. He then stated to me that he would see Com. S., and that unless he appointed him gov. at once, he would not obey his orders, and left me.' It would seem unlikely that F. should make this last statement, since both he and K. knew that S. would make him gov. at once; and F. in his defence makes several strong points against parts of K.'s testimony. This 'bargaining for the governorship' is what he deems most seriously to affect his honor, and he accuses K. of testifying falsely on the interview. It is to be noted, however, that K. does not state positively that F. offered obedience in return for an immediate appointment; that F., with all his righteous indignation on the charge of 'bargaining,' omits all details of the interview; and that the extract of a letter to Benton—'Both offered me the post of gov.; Com. S. to redeem his pledge immediately, and Gen. K. offering to give the commission in four or six weeks'—introduced by F. as his own testimony, seems to support K.'s testimony and the theory that 'time' was made the test. The matter, however, is one that affects the personal veracity of the two officers more than it does the general controversy. It appears, also, that at this interview F. expressed sorrow for the dissensions between S. and K., and perhaps tried to bring about an interview, which K. desired but would not ask for.

This reply of Frémont refusing obedience was made the foundation of the principal accusation against him before a military court. In defence, he made the point that K., at the interview, by offering to permit the paper to be destroyed, to forget its contents, and to consider the matter of making F. governor, condoned the act of disobedience, or 'mutiny.' This is true to the extent that K. was technically at fault; but the dishonor in such cases always pertains not to the officer who shows such leniency, but to the recipient who uses it against him.

purpose of preventing collision between us, and possibly a civil war in consequence of it, remain silent for the present, leaving with you the great responsibility of doing that for which you have no authority, and preventing me from complying with the president's orders." He also announced in writing his intention to withdraw with his dragoons; and reported the state of affairs to the adjutant-general at Washington.[24]

On the 18th about 10 A. M. General Kearny marched from Los Angeles with his dragoons, having no further communication with Stockton or Frémont, and reaching San Diego on the 23d. He told Lieutenant Emory, sent east with despatches a few days later, that he would assume control as soon as his force should be sufficiently increased; but the arrival of the battalion of Mormon volunteers, over three hundred strong, under Lieutenant-colonel Cooke,[25] who reported to the general at San Diego on the 29th, was not deemed to justify such a step. Cooke was ordered to station his men at San Luis Rey and await further developments; and Kearny embarked on the *Cyane* January 31st, reaching Monterey on February 8th. Here he found Commodore W. Branford Shubrick, who had arrived the 22d of January in the *Independence*, to succeed Stockton in command of the Pacific squadron. On the 25th Shubrick had written a friendly letter to Frémont as the senior military officer in the

[24] Jan. 17, 1847, Kearny to Stockton. The quotation in my text is preceded by a reference to preceding corresp. of the 16th, and a statement that by the battles of the 8th and 9th, and capitulation of the 13th, Cal. 'might now for the first time be considered as conquered.' *Court-martial*, 79–80. Jan. 17th, K. to S. 'I have to inform you that I intend to withdraw to-morrow from this place with the small party which escorted me to this country,' addressed to S. as 'acting governor of Cal.' *Id.*, 195. Jan. 17th, K. to adj.-gen., enclosing copies of corresp. with S. and F. 'It will be seen by the pres. and sec. war that I am not recognized in my official capacity, either by Com. S. or Lieut-col F., both of whom refuse to obey my orders or the instructions of the pres.; and as I have no troops in the country under my authority except a few dragoons, I have no power of enforcing them.' *Id.*, 94–5.

[25] On the Mormon battalion, see chap. xviii., this volume. Record of K.'s departure from Los Angeles, also Emory's departure, in *Frémont's Court-martial*, 87, 92–3, 165, 383. *Griffin's Diary*, MS., is authority for the arrival at S. Diego.

country, not knowing that Kearny had arrived, but
three days later had written a similar letter to the
general. On the 28th the *Lexington* had arrived with
Captain Tompkins and an artillery company, as fully
recorded in another chapter; and next day Shubrick
had sent the *Dale* southward with the letter to
Kearny and another to Stockton, requesting his presence at Monterey. Kearny found the new commodore disposed to recognize his authority as military
commander-in-chief, and to disapprove Stockton's act
in organizing a civil government in opposition to the
general's instructions, but also to favor a peaceful
settlement of the dispute. He had, moreover, the
instructions addressed to Sloat on July 12, 1846, as
already cited, which authorized the naval officers to
organize a civil government. The general agreed
with Shubrick that it was best not to reopen the controversy, but to wait for more explicit instructions
from Washington. Therefore he started for San
Francisco, February 11th, on the *Cyane;* while the
commodore reported the decision to Frémont and to
the government.[26]

[26] *Shubrick's Rept*, Feb. 15th, is a narrative of events since his arrival. In
it the only remark bearing on the controversy is, 'I have recognized in Gen.
K. the senior officer of the army in Cal.; have consulted and shall coöperate
with him as such; and I feel that I am particularly fortunate in having so
gallant a soldier,' etc. Shubrick's letters of Jan. 25th and 28th to Frémont
and Kearny are not extant, but are mentioned in *Id.*, and *Frémont's Court-
martial*, 9. The general's account of his arrival and consultation with Shubrick is in *Kearny's Rept*, March 15, 1847. He says: 'On my showing to
Com. Sh. my instruc. of June 3, 18, 1846, he was at once prepared to pay all
proper respect to them; and being at that time com.-in-chief of the naval forces,
he acknowledged me as the head and com. of the troops in Cal...He then showed
me the instruc. to com. Sl. of July 12th,...and as they contained directions
for Com. Sl. to take charge of civil affairs, I immediately told Com. Sh. that
I cheerfully acquiesced and was ready to afford him any assistance in my
power. We agreed on our separate duties, and I then went to S. F.,' etc.
Frémont's idea of this agreement, in *Court-martial*, 419–20, is that it was
virtually an acknowledgment of the legitimacy of the position assumed by
himself and Stockton. Shubrick's letter of Feb. 13th to F., *Id.*, 417, in reply to F.'s of Feb. 7th, to be noticed later, was non-committal and friendly.
'While the gen. was here, we consulted fully as enjoined on me by my
instruc., and on him by his, on the measures necessary to be taken by us for
the security of Cal. I am looking daily for the arrival of Com. St., when I
shall of course receive from him a full account, etc. It is to be hoped that
the pleasure of the president on civil govt, etc., will soon be known.' Has
no funds to spare for F. In his report of same date to the govt, *Id.*, 296, Sh.

Meanwhile Commodore Stockton, still holding the position of governor down to the date of his departure, left Los Angeles the 19th of January and marched with his marines and sailors to San Pedro, where all embarked on a man-of-war for San Diego. Here on the 22d he reported the civil government to be in successful operation. On February 4th he sent a longer report on the troubles with Kearny, demanding that officer's recall, "to prevent the evil consequences that may grow out of such a temper and such a head"! and next day he wrote a full report of the recent campaign, from which I have quoted extensively in the preceding chapter.[27] Also in February and March the commodore and his naval officers took some pains to enlighten the public respecting his position as commander in the final campaign, as already recorded.[28] As to his correspondence or conversation with Shubrick, if he had any, nothing is known. From Frémont during January, February, and the first ten days of March, we have, so far as the controversy is

alludes to the 'unfortunate difference' between St., K., and F. 'I have exchanged opinions with Gen. K., and shall continue to concert with him such measures as may seem best...With regard to the civil govt,...measures have been, in my opinion, prematurely taken by Com. St., and an appointment of gov. made of a gentleman who I am led to believe is not acceptable to the people of Cal.'; but Sh. intends to await further instructions and confine his efforts to keeping quiet possession of the territory. The despatch of the 13th was sent east by Lieut Talbot, reaching Washington June 3d.

[27] A letter of Jan. 19th signed by 12 citizens of Los Angeles, and presumably recognizing the legitimacy of S.'s proceedings, was offered as evidence, but not allowed to be read. *Frémont's Court-martial*, 195. Jan. 22d, St. to Bancroft. A brief report, sent by Lieut Gray, containing an allusion to K.'s 'perilous condition after his defeat at S. Pascual.' S. was somewhat too fond of these sly hits. *Stockton's Life*, appen. 10. Feb. 4th, Id. to Id. 'As the guardian of the honor and services of the navy, I take leave to send you the following narrative. This case requires no argument; nor will I make a single remark in relation to the extraordinary conduct of Gen. K. or the indefensible language of his notes: "demands," "personal collision," "civil war," and the bold assertion that the country was not conquered until the 8th and 9th of Jan. by the troops under his command, speak for themselves.' *Id.*, 10–12. Stockton's rept of Feb. 5th, in *Id.*, 12–16; *Id.*, *Mil. and Nav. Oper.*, 30. This was sent by Lieut Beale, and reached Washington May 31st. *Frémont's Court-martial*, 366.

[28] See note 13 of this chapter. Feb. 5th, certificate of Spieden and Mosely at S. Diego, in *Frémont's Court-martial*, 430. March 9th, Capt Zielin to captains Pedrorena and Argüello, asking for their reports of the battles, and particularly for their testimony as to who was in command. *Savage, Doc.*, MS., iii. 72.

concerned, only three letters, addressed to Benton, to Shubrick, and to W. P. Hall, all written to defend his position and that of the commodore who had appointed him.[29]

Thus the annals of the controversy have been brought down in a sense to the end so far as Stockton was concerned, and to the end of its first phase in Frémont's case. And here I may say, as has been implied in what precedes and as the facts fully justify me in saying, that on the merits of the dispute, Kearny was in the right and Stockton in the wrong. General Kearny, in obedience to instructions from Washington, had marched to California, had coöperated with the naval officers in conquering the country, and was entitled to the chief command. Stockton's claim to have effected the conquest and organized a civil government before the general's arrival was unfounded; but had it been supported by facts, it would by no means have justified his disobedience. His position was untenable, and popular sympathy for him as a conqueror unfairly deprived of the glory of his achievement has been misplaced through a misconception of the facts. He had shown a creditable degree of energy and skill in overcoming obstacles for the most part of his own creation, in putting down a revolt

[29] Feb. 3, 1847, F. to Benton, only a brief fragment on K.'s offer of the governorship, quoted in note 23. A longer extract of perhaps the same letter is found in *Bigelow's Mem.*, 197–8. Feb. 7th, F. to Shubrick, in reply to note of Jan. 25th, explaining his reasons for having refused to recognize K.'s authority—that is, that K.'s contingent instructions had been superseded by events. 'I trust the foregoing explanation will fully satisfy you that the position I take is an incident of the extraordinary circumstances surrounding me, and is borne out by a rigid adherence to the line of duty.' He also explains that he is financially hard pressed, and hopes Sh. can advance money for govt expenses. *Frémont's Court-martial*, 9–10. Feb. 11th, F. to Hon. Willard P. Hall. 'I learn with surprise and mortification that Gen. K., in obedience to what I cannot but regard as obsolete instructions, means to question my right, and...I cannot...yield or permit myself to be interfered with by any other until directed to do so by the proper authorities.' 'Intimations... have reached me that you were using your talents and high character as a member of the American congress, in your intercourse with citizens of this place and the troops under my command, to raise doubts, if not questioning altogether the legitimacy or validity, of my tenure of office;' therefore wants to know if the intimations are founded in fact. *Id.*, 10–11; Hall's testim. *Id.*, 208–9.

that but for his own folly would have had no existence.   No more can be honestly said in praise of the
commodore's acts and policy in California.   Against
Kearny's position in the dispute nothing can be urged,
and against his conduct—his blunder at San Pascual
affecting only himself and his men—nothing more
serious than a savor of sharp practice in certain minor
proceedings indicating a lack of confidence in the
real strength of his position, or perhaps an excess of
personal bitterness against his rival.

As far as Frémont is concerned, his action in disobeying Kearny's order, or rather in leaving the two
chiefs to settle their own quarrel, must I think be
approved; that is, as compared with the only alternative.   Like Stockton, he merits no praise for earlier
proceedings.   He had perhaps done even more than
the commodore to retard the conquest.   His mishaps
as a political adventurer call for no sympathy.   But
his cause was identified with that of Stockton, who
had adopted his views, had saved him from a position
that might have been dangerous, had given him his
command, had approved his irregular acts at Cahuenga, and depended upon his support in his own
assumption of authority.   There is, or should be,
honor even among filibusters.   For Frémont to have
deserted his patron at the last, particularly when
Kearny's offer of the governorship was sure to make
the transaction appear a bargain, would have been
dishonorable and treacherous.   True, the colonel's act
was declared later by a military court to be technically mutinous disobedience of a superior's orders.
This amounts to little, and is all that can be said
against Frémont.   Had there been no further developments in the controversy, the verdict would possibly
have been different; or rather it is probable that no
charges would have been preferred.

Commissions to Frémont as governor and Russell
as secretary of state were issued by Stockton on Jan-

uary 16th, but their respective terms of office began on the 19th, when the commodore turned over the command on his departure from Los Angeles. It had been intended to make Gillespie secretary, but he preferred to be major of the battalion, and his commission was dated the 18th.[30] Besides a governor to succeed himself, Stockton also appointed on the 16th a legislative council of seven members, as follows: M. G. Vallejo, David Spence, J. B. Alvarado, Thomas O. Larkin, Eliab Grimes, Santiago Argüello, and Juan Bandini. The council was summoned, by Stockton's proclamation of the 18th, to convene at Los Angeles the 1st of March; but no meeting was ever held. Some members declined to serve; there was apparently a degree of sectional dissatisfaction; and finally no council was deemed necessary by a new administration.[31] After the commodore's departure the battalion was paraded, the commissions were read by Secretary Russell, and the new government went into operation. On the 22d Governor Frémont issued

[30] On these commissions, already recorded indirectly, see *Frémont's Court-martial*, 175–6, 194, 203, 252, 257–8, 384, 410.

[31] Jan. 16, 1847, Vallejo's original commission signed by Stockton. *Vallejo, Doc.*, MS., i. 20. I find no other appointments, and no official list of the members. Jan. 18th, Stockton's proclamation convening the council for March 1st. *Id.*, xii. 260. Jan. 22d, Frémont to Vallejo, enclosing commission, with much flattery. *Id.*, i. 21. Jan. 22d, Larkin to V., enclosing F.'s letter. L. himself will not serve; will send a vessel for V. and Grimes. *Id.*, i. 22. Jan. 29th, Bandini to V., urging him to accept and work for the good of his country, as he intends to do. *Id.*, xii. 264. Jan. 29th, Lieut Revere to V., urging him not to accept, since the peace will not be permanent, and Frémont's course can not be approved. *Id.*, xii. 265. Jan. 31st, Semple, Colton, and Talbot H. Green urge V. to accept. *Id.*, xii. 266–8. Feb. 15th, V. to F. Accepts the position. *Id.*, xii. 277. Jan. 26th, Bandini to Stockton, declining on account of ill health. *Bandini, Doc.*, MS., 103. Feb. 26th, at a public meeting at Sonoma it was resolved that the district north of the bay was entitled to one third of the council, and Gen. Kearny was asked to increase the number of members to 15, giving the district 5; and Vallejo, Boggs, Grigsby, Stephen Cooper, and W. A. Richardson were recommended. *Unb. Doc.*, MS., 138–9. According to *S. F. Cal. Star*, March 6th, the citizens of Sonoma selected Vallejo, Boggs, and Cooper. Feb. 26th, a meeting also held at Sta Clara, and Elam Brown selected. *Id.* March 4th, Kearny to alcalde of S. F. 'I have not called any such council, nor do I at present contemplate doing so.' *Cal. and N. Mex., Mess. and Doc., 1850*, p. 289–91. April 13th, Larkin writes to Stockton that many blame him (L.) that the council did not meet. 'You kindly sent us the *Cyane*, but Com. Sh. prevented her departure. The members could not go by land and get there in time.' *Larkin's Off. Corresp.*, MS., i. 137.

a proclamation or circular announcing the establishment of civil rule. "I do hereby proclaim order and
peace restored to the country, and require the immediate release of all prisoners, the return of the civil
officers to their appropriate duties, and as strict an
obedience of the military to the civil authority as is
consistent with the security of peace and the maintenance of good order where troops are garrisoned."[32]

For a period of about fifty days Frémont was
recognized in a sense throughout California as governor, though it does not appear that he had occasion
to exercise his authority directly beyond the Los
Angeles district.[33] Nor were his duties as ruler
onerous even at the capital. Part of the volunteers
were discharged, and the rest were stationed at San
Gabriel. Locally all was quiet, the Angelinos devoting themselves as in earlier times to social pleasures,
and the governor, as all agree, winning many friends
among the natives by joining in their festivities and
adopting to some extent their ways of dress and life.
The happenings of those days, however, are but
meagrely recorded. Official orders were for the most
part of a petty routine nature; and indeed, the only
ones known are such as were subsequently included
in charges against Frémont as supplementary acts of
disobedience.[34]

[32] Jan. 22, 1847. Frémont's circular. *Monterey Californian*, Feb. 6th;
Bryant's What I Saw, 414; *Cutts' Conq.*, 164.
[33] Lieut-col Cooke, *Conq. Cal.*, 283, under date of March 12th, writes:
'Gen. Kearny is supreme—somewhere up the coast; Col Frémont supreme at
Pueblo de los Angeles, Com. Stockton is "commander-in-chief" at S. Diego;
Com. Shubrick, the same at Monterey; and I, at San Luis Rey; and we are
all supremely poor; the government having no money and no credit; and
we hold the territory because Mexico is poorest of all.' Cooke, however,
was a foe to Frémont. Feb. 20th, J. B. Hull, commandant of the northern
district, proclaims that civil authority has taken place of the military; and
revokes all past orders bearing on civil rights. But he says nothing of any
governor. *S. F. Cal. Star*, Feb. 20, 1847.
[34] Jan. 24th–27th, orders in connection with courts-martial, by which Lieut
Rock was cashiered for drunkenness and fighting with Private Geo. Smith.
Jan. 25th, order to Capt. J. K. Wilson to recruit men for a 2d artillery co.
at $25 a month for three months. Feb. 5th, order to Major Louis McLane to
proceed northward for the purpose of obtaining recruits; also to examine the
defences of Yerba Buena, and erect a fort on White Island. Feb. 13th,
Accepts the resignation of captains Ford, Gibson, Finlay; and lieuts Bald-

The chief difficulty experienced was to obtain funds and supplies for the battalion. Holders of claims for property taken in the past complained that payment was too long delayed, and these complaints, with a prevalent doubt that Frémont's authority to contract debts would be recognized by his successors, increased present financial troubles. Yet men were found willing in consideration of high prices to risk delays and losses. I shall have more to say of these 'California claims' a little later; only two need be mentioned here. From Antonio J. Cot in February the governor obtained a loan of $3,000 at three and two per cent per month; and from Eulogio Célis in March another of $2,500 at two per cent after eight months. With Célis he also made a contract to furnish 600 head of beef-cattle for $6,000, payable in eight months; but the battalion was discharged, and Frémont's authority was gone, before any of the beef was eaten.[35]

ridge, Rheusaw, Blackburn, J. Scott, J. R. Barton, and J. M. Hudspeth. They are blamed for resigning at such a time by Adj. Loker in his order. March 2d, F. binds himself in name of U. S. to pay $5,000 to John Temple for White (or Bird) Island in S. F. Bay. *Frémont's Court-martial*, 7, 8, 12, 16, 17, 62, 63, 408.

[35] *Cal. and N. Mex., Mess. and Doc., 1850*, p. 328–9, 363–73; *Frémont's Cal. Claims* (no. 75), p. 35–6; *Id.* (no. 817). These claims were presented for payment after F.'s departure, and without his having left any record of the transactions. The cattle contract was perhaps somewhat 'crooked.' On April 26th F. certified that Célis had delivered the cattle, and gave to C. a certificate that $6,975 (including the hides which C. was originally to have retained) was due him from the U. S. govt.; but in fact the cattle were not delivered by C. until May 1st and July 7th, and then to Abel Stearns to breed for three years on F.'s account for half the increase! F.'s defence was that he put the cattle in private hands to secure himself if the govt should not acknowledge the debt; and this is plausible if not regular, but it does not explain his certificate of delivery. Hensley testified that he received the cattle for the battalion; but this does not agree with Stearns' receipts.

CHAPTER XVII.

FRÉMONT'S CONTROVERSY WITH KEARNY.

MARCH–MAY, 1847.

NEW INSTRUCTIONS—CIRCULAR OF SHUBRICK AND KEARNY—THE LATTER
ASSUMES THE GOVERNORSHIP—PROCLAMATION AND REPORT—COMMO-
DORE BIDDLE—ORDERS TO FRÉMONT, GILLESPIE, AND COOKE—TURNER
IN THE SOUTH—FRÉMONT'S DISOBEDIENCE, EXCUSES, AND HIS FAMOUS
RIDE TO MONTEREY—QUARREL WITH KEARNY—COOKE AT LOS AN-
GELES—MASON AND FRÉMONT—A CHALLENGE—RUMORS OF MEXICAN
INVASION—KEARNY IN THE SOUTH—STEVENSON SUCCEEDS COOKE—
JOURNEY OF KEARNY, FRÉMONT, AND COOKE OVERLAND TO THE STATES—
STOCKTON GOES EAST—PETITION ON THE GOVERNORSHIP—FRÉMONT'S
TRIAL BY COURT-MARTIAL—FOUND GUILTY AND PARDONED—THE POP-
ULAR VERDICT—BENTON'S TIRADE IN THE SENATE—THE CALIFORNIA
CLAIMS—EXPENSES OF THE CONQUEST.

AT San Francisco Kearny found Colonel Richard
B. Mason of the 1st dragoons and Lieutenant Watson
of the navy, who had arrived the 12th of February, and
with whom the general returned to Monterey by the
Savannah on the 23d.[1] Mason and Watson brought
instructions, dated Washington November 3d and 5th,
for both general and commodore, which were positive
to the effect that the senior officer of the land forces
was to be civil governor. They also required that
the volunteers of the battalion should be mustered
into the service regularly if it had not already been
done, that Frémont should not be detained in California longer than the necessities of the service might
require, and that the military and naval chiefs should

---

[1] *Kearny's Rept*, Mar. 15th; *S. F. Cal. Star*, Feb. 27, 1847. About the 25th
Lieut Beale left Cal. for the east. *Frémont's Court-martial*, 271.

hold frequent conferences, acting always in harmony. Colonel Mason was to be recognized as commander and governor in the absence of Kearny, who was permitted to retire as soon as tranquil possession should be insured and a temporary civil government organized.[2]

Had Stockton been still in command of the squadron, he would probably have refused compliance with these orders, on the ground that they were issued before his report of August had been received; but Shubrick was impelled by inclination as well as duty to obey. Accordingly on the 1st of March the general and commodore issued a joint circular, in which the former assumed the governorship, and Monterey was named as the capital.[3] Kearny issued on the same day general orders and instructions to Cooke, Frémont, and Gillespie, which will be noticed presently, and bearing which Captain Turner started for the south next day. Also on the 2d there arrived Com-

[2] Nov. 3, 1846, Scott to Kearny. Nov. 5th, Sec. of Navy Mason to Stockton, in *Frémont's Court-martial*, 48–53. See quotations from these instructions in note 8, chap. xvi. of this volume. They were written after Sloat's arrival at Washington with Monterey news of July 28, 1846. It was supposed that Mason might arrive and take command before Kearny.

[3] March 1, 1847. 'To all whom it may concern, be it known: That the president of the U. S., desirous to give and secure to the people of Cal. a share of the good government and happy civil organization enjoyed by the people of the U. S., and to protect them at the same time from the attacks of foreign foes and from internal commotions, has invested the undersigned with separate and distinct powers, civil and military; a cordial coöperation in the exercise of which, it is hoped and believed, will have the happy results desired. To the commander-in-chief of the naval forces the president has assigned the regulation of the import trade, the conditions on which vessels of all nations, our own as well as foreign, may be admitted into the ports of the territory, and the establishment of all port regulations. To the commanding military officer the president has assigned the direction of the operations on land, and has invested him with administrative functions of government over the people and territory occupied by the forces of the U. S. Done at Monterey, capital of Cal., this 1st day of March, A. D. 1847. W. Branford Shubrick, Commander-in-chief of the naval forces. S. W. Kearny, Brig.-gen. U. S. Army, and Gov. of Cal.' The original, printed in English and Spanish, of which I have several copies; also in *Cal. and N. Mex., Mess. and Doc.*, *1850*, p. 288; *S. F. Cal. Star*, March 6, 1847; and often reprinted elsewhere. It is to be noted that in *Frémont's Court-martial*, 12, is cited a letter of Feb. 23d, from Shubrick to Frémont, in which the former says: 'Gen. K., I am instructed, is the commanding mil. officer in Cal., and invested by the president with the administrative functions of govt over the people and territory.' I find no other mention of this document.

modore James Biddle on the *Columbus.*   He did not, however, disturb Shubrick in his command of the northern Pacific squadron;[4] and he fully approved the position assumed by Kearny, who on the 4th, but antedating it to the 1st, issued to the people in English and Spanish a proclamation in which he offered protection to all interests, and encouraged the natives to hope for all the rights and privileges pertaining to citizens of a United States territory.   There was no allusion to the controversy except indirectly, in a kind of apology for irregularities in the past.   While the distinct civil government set up by Stockton was ignored, there was practically no radical change in proposed measures or policy.   California was to be held as a conquered province, and ruled by the military commander, through the old officials as nearly as possible in accordance with the old laws until the United States should provide a territorial government; for as before the permanence of possession was taken for granted.   I append the proclamation in a note.[5]

[4] Arrival of Biddle, March 2d. *Kearny's Rept.; Monterey Calif.*, March 6, 1847.   Biddle's decree of March 4th, raising the blockade on the west coast except at Mazatlan and Guaymas. *Id.*, March 13th.   March 6th, B. to Larkin on same subject. *Larkin's Doc.*, MS., v. 34.   March 15th, Larkin to Stockton on Biddle's arrival, with much flattery for St.   Thinks B. and Sh. will work against St., though the latter has done more for the country than both combined are likely to do. *Off. Corresp.*, MS., i. 120–1.

[5] March 1, 1847, 'Proclamation to the people of California.   The president of the U. S. having instructed the undersigned to take charge of the civil government of Cal., he enters upon his duties with an ardent desire to promote, as far as he is able, the interests of the country and the welfare of its inhabitants.   The undersigned has instructions from the president to respect and protect the religious institutions of Cal., and to see that the religious rights of the people are in the amplest manner preserved to them, the constitution of the U. S. allowing every man to worship his creator in such a manner as his own conscience may dictate to him.   The undersigned is also instructed to protect the persons and property of the quiet and peaceable inhabitants of the country against all or any of their enemies, whether from abroad or at home; and when he now assures the Californians that it will be his duty and his pleasure to comply with those instructions, he calls upon them all to exert themselves in preserving order and tranquillity, in promoting harmony and concord, and in maintaining the authority and efficacy of the laws.   It is the wish and design of the U. S. to provide for Cal., with the least possible delay, a free government similar to those in her other territories; and the people will soon be called upon to exercise their rights as freemen, in electing their own representatives to make such laws as may be deemed best for their interests and welfare.   But until this can be done, the laws now in existence, and not in conflict with the constitution of the U. S., will be con-

About this time the first detachment of Colonel Stevenson's New York volunteers arrived at San Francisco, as is fully recorded in another chapter; and after issuing a few minor orders respecting these troops and local affairs in the north, General Kearny wrote a general report of his proceedings since leaving Los Angeles, which was dated the 15th of March and sent east by the *Savannah*. In this report he says: "The Californians are now quiet, and I shall endeavor to keep them so by mild and gentle treatment. Had they received such treatment from the time our flag was hoisted here in July last"—that is, if the policy of Sloat and Larkin had been continued instead of the filibusterism of Frémont and Stockton—"I believe there would have been but little or no resistance on their part. They have been most cruelly and shamefully abused by our own people—by the volunteers

tinued until changed by competent authority; and those persons who hold office will continue in the same for the present, provided they swear to support that constitution, and to faithfully perform their duty. The undersigned hereby absolves all the inhabitants of Cal. from any further allegiance to the republic of Mexico, and will consider them as citizens of the U. S. Those who remain quiet and peaceable will be respected in their rights, and protected in them. Should any take up arms against or oppose the government of this territory, or instigate others to do so, they will be considered as enemies, and treated accordingly. When Mexico forced a war upon the U. S., time did not permit the latter to invite the Californians as friends to join her standard, but compelled her to take possession of the country to prevent any European power from seizing upon it; and in doing so, some excesses and unauthorized acts were no doubt committed by persons employed in the service of the U. S., by which a few of the inhabitants have met with a loss of property. Such losses will be duly investigated, and those entitled to remuneration will receive it. California has for many years suffered greatly from domestic troubles; civil wars have been the poisoned fountains which have sent forth trouble and pestilence over her beautiful land. Now those fountains are dried up; the star-spangled banner floats over Cal.; and as long as the sun continues to shine upon her, so long will it float there over the natives of the land, as well as others who have found a home in her bosom; and under it agriculture must improve and the arts and sciences flourish, as seed in a rich and fertile soil. The Americans and Californians are now but one people; let us cherish one wish, one hope, and let that be for the peace and quiet of our country. Let us as a band of brothers unite and emulate each other in our exertions to benefit and improve this our beautiful, and which soon must be our happy and prosperous, home. Done at Monterey, capital of Cal., this first day of March, A. D. 1847, and in the 71st year of the independence of the U. S. S. W. Kearny, Brig.-gen. U. S. A., and governor of California.' An original in MS., with K.'s autograph, in *Vallejo, Doc.*, MS., xxxiv. 260; print, English and Span., in *Bear Flag Pap.*, 30; also in *S. F. Cal. Star*, March 20, 1847; *Cal. and N. Mex., Mess. and Doc., 1850*, p. 205; and often reprinted.

[American emigrants] raised in this part of the country and on the Sacramento   Had they not resisted, they would have been unworthy the name of men.   If the people remain quiet and California continues under our flag, it will erelong be a bright star in our union."[6]

Kearny's orders of March 1st, carried south by Captain Turner, required the California battalion to be mustered into the service at once by Lieutenant-colonel Frémont, who was to bring to Yerba Buena by way of Monterey and there discharge all volunteers declining to continue in the service.   Frémont was also directed to deliver in person at Monterey, with as little delay as possible, all public documents under his control pertaining to the government of California. Lieutenant Gillespie of the marines was relieved from his duties as an officer of the battalion, and ordered to report to the commander of his corps at Washington. Lieutenant-colonel Cooke was made military commandant of the southern district, with instructions to post his command—consisting of the dragoon company, the Mormon battalion, and the volunteers—at such places as he might deem most eligible for the preservation of peace.   Los Angeles was suggested as headquarters, and a conciliatory policy toward the inhabitants.[7]

---

[6] *Kearny's Report*, March 15, 1847.
[7] March 1, 1847, 'Headquarters 10th mil. department.' 'Orders no. 2.' i. Mustering in the volunteers. ii. Relieving Gillespie. iii. Putting Cooke in command. iv. Cooke to name an officer to receive public property at S. Diego.   v. Maj. Swords and Paymaster Cloud to report at Monterey. 'By order of Brig.-gen. S. W. Kearny, H. S. Turner, captain, a. a. a. general.' In *Frémont's Court-martial*, 13, 33, 221.   Same date, K. to F., referring to the general order, directing him to bring archives, and adding: 'I have directions from the general-in-chief not to retain you in this country against your wishes a moment longer than the necessities of the service may require; and you will be at liberty to leave here after you have complied with these instructions and those in the order referred to.' F. is addressed as 'Com'g bat. of Cal. volunteers.' *Id.*, 32–3, 102, 424. Same date, K. to Cooke, general instructions, leaving details to his judgment. 'It is highly important that a very discreet officer should be in com. of the troops you may station at the city of the Angels, which has been for so long a time the capital, and the headquarters of the Mexicans and Californians when in arms against us. Great discontent and animosity, on the part of the people there, toward the Americans have existed, and in consequence of complaints made by them of the

Turner reached Los Angeles on March 11th, delivering his orders and the joint circular to Frémont, who next day promised obedience, while the captain continued his journey to San Luis Rey, where he made known the orders to Cooke. Frémont's obedience consisted in submitting the order for mustering to the volunteers, all of whom declined to be mustered, though the officers had no serious objections, as the change would not materially affect their pay; and this result was communicated to Cooke on the 16th in reply to that officer's note of the 14th inquiring how many of the volunteers had been mustered. In this letter, written by Russell as 'secretary of state,' Cooke is informed that "the governor considers it unsafe at this time, when rumor is rife with a threatened insurrection, to discharge the battalion, and will decline doing so; and whilst they remain in service, he regards his force as quite sufficient for the protection of the artillery and ordnance stores at San Gabriel." Meanwhile, on the 15th, in view of a prospective absence in the north—though he did not start for a week—Frémont issued to Captain Owens, acting commandant of the battalion, instructions not to leave San Gabriel, not to obey the orders of any other officer, and not to turn over to any one the public arms and munitions. On the 18th he drew bills of exchange against the government in favor of one F. Hüttmann for $19,500; and on the 21st, as governor, he authorized Collector Alexander at San Pedro to receive government orders in payment of duties.[8]

volunteers engaged in our cause. It is not necessary to inquire if these complaints are well founded or not. The fact that the people have been unfriendly and opposed to us is sufficient to make it our duty to reconcile and make friends of them, and this most desirable object may be effected by a mild, courteous, and just treatment of them in future.' *Id.*, 140–1.

[8] Testimony and documents in *Frémont's Court-martial*, 13–16, 148–9, 420 et seq.; *Cooke's Conquest*, 284–6. Frémont claimed that the order to Alexander was merely a repetition in writing of one given earlier verbally, and was given to protect A. The traders who bought up the claims at a large discount and paid them as duties at par evidently made a good speculation. *Rept Court Claims*, 229, p. 20. On the Hüttmann bills, see *U. S. Govt Doc.*, 36th cong. 1st sess.

There were rumors in these days of impending
revolt among the Californians, though there is no evidence that these rumors had the slightest foundation
beyond the imagination, or rather the pretensions, of
Frémont and his partisans. Says the former, after
dwelling on the tranquillity of his past rule: "Suddenly, and in the beginning of March, all this was
changed. Men armed to the teeth were galloping
about the country. Groups of armed men were constantly seen. The whole population was in commotion, and everything verged toward violence and
bloodshed. For what cause? The approach of the
Mormons, the proclamations incompatible with the
capitulation of Cowenga, the prospect that I was to
be deposed by violence, the anticipated non-payment
of government liabilities, and the general insecurity
which such events inspired. Such was the cause;"
and the effect was that Frémont went to Monterey
to lay the alarming state of things before General
Kearny. Or rather these alarms were invented later
as an excuse for disobeying Kearny's orders.[9] It is
true, however, that the Missouri volunteers had succeeded in arousing some feeling against the Mormons;
and that there was a degree of uneasiness among
both Americans and Californians about the recognition of Frémont's debts by the U. S. government.

Frémont's real motive for visiting the north at this
time was probably a wish to learn whether the late
orders were founded on new instructions from Washington or were but a reopening of the old controversy,
and also to ascertain if the general was disposed as
governor to assume the debts of the past administra-

[9] Frémont's defence, in *Court-martial*, 422. Hensley in his testimony,
Id., 232-3, slightly confirms the rumors of impending troubles, but he alludes
chiefly to the end of March and to April, when there were reports of an approaching Mexican force. Indeed, in order to furnish any foundation whatever for Frémont's statements, it would be necessary to group all alarming
symptoms of the entire year, apply them to the month of March, and then
greatly to magnify the sum total. Murray, *Narr.*, MS., 76-7, mentions the
rumors of revolt as heard at Sta Bárbara. Similar reports at S. José in the
north in March. *Unb. Doc.*, MS., 169-70.

tion.[10]   He started from Los Angeles early on March
22d, with Jesus Pico and Jacob Dodson, on his
'famous ride,' reaching Monterey at nightfall of the
fourth day, or the 25th.[11]   The same evening, with
Larkin, he called on Kearny as a matter of etiquette;
and next morning, by a request through Larkin, he
obtained an interview with the general.   According
to the latter's statement—and there is no other definite information about the interview—Frémont made
known his desire for a conversation, but objected to
the presence of Colonel Mason, and when Kearny
insisted that the colonel, as the officer who would succeed to the command, might properly listen to any
conversation on public affairs, Frémont made an
offensive reply, to the effect that Mason was perhaps
there intentionally to take advantage of some un-
guarded expression of his.   Then the general, deeming
the last remark an insult, referred to his orders of
March 1st, and asked Frémont to state distinctly,
before the conversation could proceed, whether he intended to obey those orders or not.   The lieutenant-colonel hesitated, was given an hour or a day for consider-

[10] Cooke, *Conquest*, 287, says that Turner had returned to Los Angeles and
started for Monterey, being convinced that F. did not intend to obey Kearny's orders; whereupon F., as soon as he knew T.'s sudden departure, started
to overtake him, but failed, reaching Monterey several hours after T.'s arrival.   Gen. Sherman, *Mem.*, i. 25, gives the same version.   This may be true,
though unsupported by other evidence.

[11] On his ride F. and Pico rode Cal. mustangs, driving six unsaddled to be
caught with the lasso for frequent changes by Dodson, Frémont's servant and
a skilful vaquero.   They slept the first night at Capt. Robbins' rancho near
Sta Bárbara, and the second at S. Luis Obispo, where the 9 horses were
changed for 8 fresh ones from Pico's caballada.   The third camp was in the
upper Salinas valley, where they were threatened and kept from sleep by
grizzly bears.   Starting on the return in the afternoon of the 26th, Frémont
rode one horse—a gift from Pico—to within 30 miles of S. Luis, as a test of
his endurance.   At San Luis they took the original horses, and having slept
again at Sta Bárbara, they arrived at the city early in the afternoon of the
29th.   They had been absent $8\frac{1}{2}$ days, had ridden over 800 miles, and had
been actually in the saddle probably about 100 hours.   Accounts of this ride
were published in the *Washington National Intelligencer*, *N. Y. Herald*, and
N. Y. Times; from which they were reproduced in *Bigelow's Mem.*, 152–6;
N. Y. Herald, May 29, 1876; *Sta B. Press*, June 3, 1876; *Watsonville Paja-
ronian*, May 15, 1879; *S. F. Belletin*, May 31, 1876; *S. F. Call*, Jan. 21, 1879;
and many other newspapers.   Pico, in his *Acontecimientos*, MS., 76–7, gives
a brief account of the ride.   He says Dodson gave out on the last day of the
return.

ation, and left the room.   He had meanwhile tendered his resignation from the army, which offer was declined.   He came back about an hour later and promised obedience.   Kearny expressed great satisfaction at this conclusion, and repeated verbally the substance of past orders, requiring him to report at Monterey at the earliest possible date, but permitting him to come by land after embarking the volunteers at San Pedro.[12]

I think it probable that the manner and words of Frémont at this interview were the turning-point of the controversy, and determined the general's later course and accusations; but it is also likely that the tone assumed by Kearny was most annoying to the younger officer's pride.   Frémont left Monterey the same day, and two days later Colonel Mason was sent to the south as inspector of troops, " clothed with full authority to give such orders and instructions in that country upon all matters whatever, both civil and

[12] *Frémont's Court-martial*, 17, 34, 104–7, 423, 427. Frémont gives no particulars of the interview; but ridicules the idea that he should have come so far merely to insult the general and offer to resign his commission; and he implies that he asked K. about the claims, and was told that they would not be recognized, also that he disclaimed any intention to insult the general. Doubtless his final promise to obey was founded on information from Larkin as to the nature of the late instructions from Washington. Lieut Sherman, *Memoirs*, i. 25, says: 'All the troops and the navy (?) regarded Gen. K. as the rightful commander, though Frémont still remained at Los Angeles, styling himself as governor, issuing orders, and holding his battalion of Cal. volunteers in apparent defiance of Gen. K. Col. Mason and Maj. Turner were sent down by sea with a paymaster, with muster-rolls and orders to muster this battalion into the service of the U. S., to pay, and then to muster them out; but on their reaching Los Angeles F. would not consent to it, and the controversy became so angry that a challenge was believed to have passed between M. and F....Turner rode up by land in 4 or 5 days, and F. becoming alarmed, followed him, as we supposed, to overtake him, but he did not succeed. On F.'s arrival at Monterey he camped in a tent about a mile out of town and called on Gen. K., and it was reported that the latter threatened him very severely, and ordered him back to Los Angeles, immediately to disband his volunteers, and to cease the exercise of authority of any kind in the country. Feeling a natural curiosity to see F....I rode out to his camp and found him in a conical tent with one Capt. Owens...I spent an hour or so with F. in his tent, took some tea with him, and left without being much impressed with him.' Sherman has evidently confounded two different visits of F. to Monterey. In *Id.*, p. 23, he represents F. as claiming his position 'by virtue of a letter he had received from Col. Benton'! and on p. 27, 'all agreed that if any one else than Frémont had put on such airs, K. would have shown him no mercy, for he was regarded as the strictest kind of a disciplinarian.'

military, as you may think conducive to the public interest,"[13] and bearing an order requiring Frémont to obey Mason, to authenticate and complete any unsettled accounts against the government, and to report at Monterey in twelve days after embarking the volunteers, bringing with him the members of his original exploring party.[14]

On March 23d, the day after Frémont's departure from Los Angeles, Secretary Russell started east with despatches understood to include a petition from Californians for Frémont's appointment as governor.[15] On the same day, after Russell's departure, Cooke arrived from San Luis with the dragoon company and four companies of the Mormon battalion, which troops were posted in and near the town. Gillespie rode out to receive Cooke in a friendly manner, but exercised no authority, having obeyed Kearny's order relieving him of his command. Captain Owens was in command of the battalion at San Gabriel, and when Cooke called on him the 24th he professed to have no knowledge of the orders issued by Kearny and Shubrick, nor would he obey the commandant's order to turn over a part of the artillery to the dragoons. He based his refusal on Frémont's written order already cited, and he urged Cooke to await Frémont's return. There was no quarrel or unfriendly feeling. In his report of the 25th the commandant, while professing amazement at the prevailing ignorance of military law, and denouncing " this treason or mutiny which jeopardizes the safety of the country, and defies me in my legal command and duties," yet deemed it best to " sacrifice all feeling or pride to duty, which I think plainly forbids any attempt to crush this resistance of

[13] March 29, 1847, Kearny to Mason. *Cal. and N. Mex., Mess. and Doc.*, *1850*, p. 307. Mason doubtless had verbal instructions respecting his prospective dealings with Frémont.

[14] March 28, 1847, Kearny to Frémont. *Court-martial*, 17–18, 34, 424. March 31st, Biddle orders Gillespie to report for duty. *Id.*, 221.

[15] Testimony of Cooke and Russell, in *Frémont's Court-martial*, 125, 266, 268. Russell seems to have gone overland, but there is no information about his party or journey. He reached Washington in July.

misguided men. It would be a signal of revolt. The general's orders are not obeyed!"[16] Doubtless he acted wisely in preventing a rupture between the Mormons and the Missourians.

Frémont arrived at Los Angeles on the 29th; but nothing is known of what occurred during the following days. With Cooke he had no intercourse whatever. Mason arrived on the 7th of April or earlier.[17] He had some interviews with Frémont, Cooke being present at Mason's request, but nothing is known of details, except that their relations were not friendly, and that Frémont deemed himself insulted by Cooke's presence as a witness.[18] On the 12th the colonel called for a list of Frémont's civil appointments, and for all records, civil and military. The list and a few papers were furnished next day, with an explanation that the main record had been sent to Washington,[19]

[16] Testimony of Cooke, Gillespie, and Loker, in *Frémont's Court-martial*, 14, 122–7, 134–7, 201–3, 273, including: March 25th, Capt. J. K. Wilson's note to Cooke declining to turn over artillery; Owens' order to Wilson to same effect; and Cooke's report to Capt. Turner; Cooke says Wilson was at first inclined to obey. He was shown, but not permitted to copy, Frémont's order to Owens. Dr Sanderson and Lieut Davidson accompanied Cooke to S. Gabriel. C. expresses doubt that the proposition for being mustered had ever been properly presented to the volunteers. One of the howitzers which Owens was ordered to give up had been captured from Kearny at S. Pascual, and given up to Frémont at Cahuenga. There were frequent attempts to introduce this gun in the court-martial, apparently for no other purpose than to ventilate Kearny's misfortune at S. Pascual. An extract from Cooke's original diary on these happenings at Los Angeles is given in his *Conquest of Cal.*, 288, etc. Cooke's report to Turner was sent by express to Monterey, but could not have arrived in time to affect the instructions to Mason.

[17] April 7, 1847, Gillespie to Larkin, mentioning the arrival of M. 'at this moment' as very fortunate. Speaks highly of M., though his measures are harsh according to orders. *Savage, Doc.*, MS., ii. 76. At this time Frémont hoped to start 'next week.'

[18] Cooke, in *Frémont's Court-martial*, 142 et seq. C. and F. were introduced by M., but F.'s manner did not indicate a desire for further acquaintance, and they did not speak to each other later at Angeles or on the march east. A report of M. to Turner dated April 10th and narrating his official acts down to date, I have not found.

[19] April 12, 1847, Mason to Frémont. April 13th, F. to M. *Cal. and N. Mex., Mess. and Doc.*, *1850*, p. 308. 'My position here having been denounced as usurpation by Gen. K., I could not anticipate from him any call for these papers; and in requiring, myself, from the general govt, means and authority to comply with my engagement, it became necessary that these and other objects should be thoroughly made known.' The only civil appointments had been Santiago Argüello and Pedro Carrillo as collectors of the ports of S. Diego and S. Pedro.

doubtless carried by Russell.   Frémont was annoyed by the matter and manner of an order to bring in a band of horses that had been sent to graze in the country in preparation for later use by the explorers. On the 14th Mason had to send two messengers before Frémont would come to his quarters to answer questions about the horses; and when he did come, he used language which caused the colonel to reply, "None of your insolence, or I will put you in irons." On being informed that Mason would hold himself personally responsible for these words, the ex-governor returned to his quarters, and at once sent Major Reading with a demand for an apology, followed on refusal by a challenge.   This was accepted the same evening by a verbal arrangement with Reading, double-barrelled shot-guns being chosen as the weapons; but in a note of the 15th the colonel announced the necessity of postponing the duel until the parties should meet at Monterey, for which place Mason started a few days later.[20]

The affair, however, became known to General Kearny, whose positive orders prevented a hostile meeting.   There is no reason to doubt that both officers were willing enough to butcher each other; but perhaps neither much regretted that superior orders and circumstances prevented a duel.   In several respects Frémont shows to better advantage in this affair than his rival.[21]

[20] I find no record of the exact date; but his general report to Kearny is dated at Monterey, April 26th.   It is a general statement of the condition of affairs in the south, containing nothing to be noted. *Cal. and N. Mex., Mess. and Doc., 1850*, p. 309.

[21] The best account of the whole matter is that in *Bigelow's Memoir*, 203–13, probably from *Benton's Speech*, including the following correspondence: April 14th, Frémont to Mason, demand for an apology; M. to F., declining to apologize; F. to M., challenge; May 27th, Reading to F., testifying to M.'s verbal acceptance and choice of weapons; April 15th, M. to F., postponing the meeting; F. to M., consenting to a meeting at Monterey; May 4th, Kearny to F., order to proceed no further in the matter; May 19th, M. to F., thinks that K.'s orders make a postponement proper; May 4th, Biddle to M., urging a postponement; May 22d, F. to M., consents to postponement, but wishes to be apprised of the earliest moment when the meeting can take place 'consistently with your convenience and sense of propriety;' May 24th, M. to F., will inform him when 'peculiar official obligations' are 'so far removed as to

For three weeks after the rupture between Mason and Frémont the latter showed no haste to obey orders and depart, though it appears that the last of the volunteers were discharged on April 19th.[22] The ex-governor was doubtless somewhat occupied with financial matters pertaining to his late administration, and on April 26th he tried to put one of these matters on a better footing by certifying the receipt of cattle from Célis.[23] His later excuses for delaying his departure were the danger of travelling in those days, and the fact that the orders did not seem to him urgent!

enable me to meet you.' On his arrival at Monterey, F. is said to have visited M.'s quarters without accepting an invitation to sit, for the purpose of making his presence known. Finally, in 1850, Senator Frémont, at Washington, received a letter from Mason, informing him that he could have satisfaction by coming to St Louis. F. paid no attention to this, and M.'s death occurred a little later. An unsuccessful attempt was made to bring up this matter in testimony at the court-martial. Foster, *Los Angeles in 1847*, MS., 19–21, gives a brief account of the affair, claiming to have been present at Pryor's house when the quarrel took place. He says, and others imply, that there was a 'woman in the case,' an appointment with whom prevented F. coming at M.'s first and second summonses. The affair is mentioned by Hargrave, *Cal. in 1846*, MS., 9–10, who was with Frémont. Boggs, in *Napa Register*, May 18, 1872, besides other blunders, says the challenge was sent to Kearny. Möllhausen, *Tagebuch*, 289–92, says the duel was fought.

While I cannot accept Bigelow's theory that Mason deliberately by repeated insults drew out a challenge from F. with a view of killing him, yet the choice of an unusual weapon, for his skill in the use of which M. was famous, reflects in my opinion no credit on the colonel; and it would appear that there was nothing to prevent M. fighting at Los Angeles if he had wished to fight. Without adopting the opinion of Benton and others that the letters of Kearny, Mason, and Biddle were collusive and designed to extricate M. from the affair, it may be noted that K.'s duty by the rules of war was to arrest both parties, and his act of postponing the duel in a written order was a strange proceeding; though his failure to arrest and bring to trial was in one sense as favorable to F. as to M., and in another sense not so, since F. was to be arrested on another charge.

[22] Official statement. *U. S. Govt Doc.*, 31st cong. 1st sess., H. Ex. Doc., 24, p. 22 *h*, by which it appears that the men were discharged April 1–19. There are no details, but most of the men soon found their way northward.

[23] See note 34 of chap. xvi. In a letter to Snyder of Dec. 11, 1849, F. explains this transaction. He says that when Kearny's order came (March 11th) Andrés Pico had gone to S. Luis Obispo (?) to bring the cattle. On F.'s return from Monterey, where K. had refused to accept the contract, Pico had arrived at S. Fernando with 400 or 500 of the cattle, and it was resolved to put them in the keeping of Stearns on the usual terms, to await the action of the govt. Accordingly F. gave Célis a receipt for all the cattle, only part of which had been delivered. C. was trusted to deliver the rest, and F. signed the receipt, as he claims a right to do, to bind the govt, as he had to leave the country immediately. *Bigelow's Mem.*, 394–6. Stearns received 481 head (those at S. Fernando probably) on May 1st from Célis. Perhaps there had been some kind of a theoretical transfer to Hensley, and back to Célis for safe keeping. It was in February that F. through Larkin had purchased the Mariposas estate from Alvarado for $3,000.

Meanwhile, in addition to increasing Indian depredations, there came alarming rumors that a Mexican army under General Bustamante was coming to reconquer California. Captain Moreno and other refugees returning from Sonora were supposed to have brought the reports; and it was also said that Limantour had landed artillery on the frontier, and brought commissions for leading Californians. A message was sent in haste to the general, Captain Stockton sent a vessel down the coast, scouts were despatched to watch the Colorado route, fortifications were strengthened at Los Angeles, and a close watch was kept on the crowd assembled at a horse-race at Santa Ana; but it was a false alarm, wholly without foundation so far as can be known.[24]

The rest of the New York volunteers having arrived, and a company of volunteer cavalrymen under Lieutenant Burton having been mustered in on April 22d, Kearny left Monterey for the south on the *Lexington*. Accompanied by Colonel Stevenson and two companies of his regiment, he landed at San Pedro and arrived on May 9th at Los Angeles, to "find the people of this part of California quiet, notwithstanding some rumors to the contrary, circulated, and I fear originated, by some of our own officers to further their own wicked purposes." One of the general's motives in visiting the south was doubtless to hasten Frémont's motions. Of their interviews at this time we know only that Frémont asked permission to go with his exploring party to join his regiment in Mexico, or to go directly east from Los

[24] The reports began on April 20th. A good account of the whole affair is given in *Cooke's Conquest*, 299–303. The writer thinks the active preparations and arrival of reënforcements caused Bustamante's expedition to miscarry. In his report of April 28th, *Cal. and N. Mex., Mess. and Doc., 1850*, p. 286, Kearny says: 'I do not place much credit in the latter part of the above (Bustamante's approach), but it has much excited these excitable Californians; and it becomes necessary to reënforce the command at Los Angeles.' May 1st he sent to Wash. copies of all papers relating to his civil administration. *Id.*, 287; and May 3d he announced his intention of going south. *Id.*, 303. *Stockton's Report* contains a mention of his trip down the coast.

Angeles, both requests being denied,[25] and that he was finally induced to obey orders and start by land for Monterey on May 12th. Lieutenant Sherman, who was serving as Kearny's aid, had started a day or two earlier with a detachment of Mormons. On the 13th the general, in reporting Frémont's departure, said: "His conduct in California has been such that I shall be compelled on arriving in Missouri to arrest him and send him under charges to report to you;"[26] though this intention was not made known to the offending officer. Cooke's resignation was accepted both as commandant of the southern district and of the Mormon battalion, Colonel Stevenson assuming the former command. Kearny left town on the 14th, embarked at San Pedro, and arrived at Monterey on the 27th, Frémont and his explorers making their appearance two days later. Gillespie had in the mean time reported to Commodore Biddle. The topographical party being paraded before the general's quarters, those who wished to remain in the country separated themselves from the main party, and Frémont was ordered to discharge them. He was required to remain in town instead of camping with his men outside, was not permitted to send for Kern and King who were absent, or to visit Yerba Buena as he desired, and was ordered to turn over his surveying instruments to Lieutenant Halleck.[27]

I have expressed my opinion that Frémont's technical disobedience in January was justified by his duty to Stockton. His continued disobedience in March, before the visit to Monterey, may, I think, to a certain extent, be regarded as a part or continuation of the same acts, covered more or less fully by

[25] *Frémont's Court-martial*, 103–4, being Kearny's testimony. Sherman, *Mem.*, i. 27, was sent to F. with a notice that K. desired to see him, and F. came back with S. to the general's quarters. This was probably on the 10th.
[26] May 13th, Kearny to Adj.-gen. Jones. *Cal. and N. Mex., Mess. and Doc., 1850*, p. 303. K. also wrote to Benton about F.'s conduct. *Court-martial*, 41.
[27] Testimony of Kearny and Turner. *Frémont's Court-martial*, 113–14, 149–50.

the same justification, the only difference being that Shubrick, succeeding Stockton, now joined his authority to that of the general.   For it must be noted that Frémont, so far as the evidence goes, knew nothing of new orders from Washington, and supposed Kearny to be attempting merely an enforcement of the old instructions, relying on an increase of troops and the commodore's support.   But this palliation of his offence ceases with his knowledge, acquired, at least unofficially, on March 25th, that the general and commodore had new authority for their measures. Most of Frémont's alleged reasons for disobedience were mere excuses, though he certainly had a plausible ground of complaint against Kearny for not making known his new instructions, and for disregarding all formalities and courtesies of transferring the command after having in a sense acknowledged the lieutenant-colonel as acting governor.   Yet the manner and tone of Frémont as well as Kearny were doubtless much more annoying than is shown by the records; and a quarrel once in progress, if the parties keep within the bounds of their legal rights, that is quite as much as can be expected.   The path of the adventurer is not altogether an easy and pleasant one; and in the popular sympathy as for a martyr which his brilliant father-in-law succeeded in working up for him, Frémont got much more than his desert.[28]

Leaving the military and civil command to Colonel Mason, Kearny left Monterey on May 31st with his escort.[29]   Frémont and his topographical party started

[28] That the instructions of Nov. 5, 1846, were not made known to F. seems, however, to have been the fault of Stockton, who received them in March from Biddle.   F. claims that these instructions were 'mandatory to the naval commander to *relinquish* the control of the civil administration, and to "turn over" the papers connected with it.   The only way in which they could be *obeyed* was for that commander to inform me of the order he had received, and take from my hands the office and the archives, that he might, as directed, "relinquish" and "turn them over" to Gen. Kearny.   For some purpose yet unexplained—unless its object is seen in this prosecution—they were not obeyed.' *Court-martial*, 421.   The *S. F. Cal. Star* of June 5, 1847, has a good editorial on Frémont and Kearny, with praise and blame for both.

[29] May 30th, 31st, K. to Adj.-gen. Jones.   In each he announces his intention to start 'to-morrow,' but the start was on the 31st. *Cal. and N. Mex.*,

the same day under orders to accompany the general, the two parties camping each night not far apart. The route was by San Juan and the San Joaquin and Sacramento valleys,[30] and they arrived on the 13th in the region of Sutter's Fort, where preparations for the overland trip occupied several days.[31] Here Frémont asked in writing to be permitted, at his own expense and with a few companions, to proceed in advance to the states; but the permission was refused; and similar requests later were denied, in one case the proposition being to take a short route for exploring purposes.   It is claimed by Frémont that from the start, though not under arrest or having any intimation that he was to be arrested, he was forced to submit to many indignities at the general's hands.[32] The start from the vicinity of New Helvetia was on June 16th and from Johnson's rancho on the 18th. Kearny's party consisted of himself, Major Swords, captains Cooke and Turner, Dr Sanderson of the Mormon battalion, who had resigned, Lieutenant Radford of the navy, a brother-in-law of Kearny, Willard P. Hall, Edwin Bryant, William Fallon as guide, a Mormon escort of thirteen men, perhaps a few of Emory's engineer assistants who had come to Cali-

Mess. and Doc., 1850, p. 303–6.   Maj. Swords started June 1st and overtook the party at S. Juan.
[30] Major Swords in his report of Oct. 8, 1847, to Quartermaster-general Jesup, U. S. Gov. Doc., 30th cong. 2d sess., H. Ex. Doc., i. p. 229 et seq., gives the most complete account of the uneventful journey.   See also Tyler's Hist. Morm. Bat., 299–304.
[31] In the N. Helv. Diary, MS., 63 et seq., it is recorded that on the 12th Loker arrived at the fort, reporting that K. had camped at Daylor's and F. at Murphy's.   On the 13th, 14th, and 15th Sutter received visits of pleasure and business from the general and his associates; and on the 16th visited K.'s camp to witness the departure.
[32] Testimony of Loker and statements of F., in Frémont's Court-martial, 273–86, including F. to K., June 14th, and K. to F. in reply, of same date. One of the chief indignities complained of—besides the refusals to grant his requests, which were in accord with instructions to K. from Washington, and for which refusals no reasons were given—was the being required to camp near and in the rear of the Mormon escort.   There was also some difficulty about a band of horses which had been left on the Cosumnes since Bear Flag times, and of which Swords by Kearny's orders took the best.   It appears by the N. Helv. Diary, MS., that some of the horses were used to pay off the Walla Walla volunteers.

fornia with Kearny, and an unknown number of servants.[33]

Frémont's party consisted of William N. Loker and nineteen of the original exploring party, whose names in most cases are not definitely known,[34] with an unknown number of servants and other attachés. The journey was a rapid and uneventful one by the usual emigrant route. On the 22d Kearny was at Mountain Lake, finding and burying the remains of many who had perished there the preceding winter, members of the Donner party. He passed Fort Hall in the middle of July, and subsequently met the stream of immigrants bound for California and Oregon. He arrived at Fort Leavenworth the 22d of August; and on the same day ordered Frémont, after having arranged the accounts of his men, to consider himself under arrest and report himself to the adjutant-general at Washington.

About a month after Kearny's departure Stockton left San Francisco, and proceeded by way of Sonoma to the Sacramento Valley to prepare for the overland journey.[35] Lieutenant Gillespie was intrusted with prepa-

[33] Kearny's report of May 13th, *Cal. and N. Mex., Mess. and Doc., 1850*, p. 303; *Bryant's What I Saw*, 453, the author not giving any diary or narrative of the return journey; *Cutts' Conq.*, 213–15; *Niles' Reg.*, lxxiii. 5, where the total number is given as 50 or 55; *Cooke's Conquest*, 306. He says there were about 40 men, exclusive of Frémont's party. No names are known except those given in the text, and those of Quigley, John Binley, and N. V. Jones of the Mormons.

[34] The number is given as 19 by Loker in his testimony and in a letter from Kearny. It seems as if there should have been more, and Martin—who in his *Narrative*, MS., 40 et seq., gives a good account of the trip—implies that there were about 40. Martin is the only name positively given; but Breckenridge, Godey, Moore, Owens, and Wise were at Wash. ready to testify at the court-martial, and were probably of the returning party; and there may be added the following, who started again with Frémont in 1848: Creutzfeldt, Preuss, Praule, Haler (?), Morin, Hubbard (?), Scott (?), Steppenfeldt, and Duketel (?); also probably some of the Delawares.

King and Kern were not of the party; and it was attempted to show later that they were left behind by Kearny intentionally by his hasty departure, they being at Monterey and Yerba Buena occupied in closing up affairs. But this charge was probably not well founded, since the names of both men appear in the *N. Helv. Diary*, MS., during the days when both parties were near Sutter's Fort.

[35] Departure of Stockton June 28th, with a salute from the guns of the men-of-war. *S. F. Cal. Star*, July 3, 1847. In *N. Helv. Diary*, MS., 78 et seq. Stockton's presence is mentioned. He seems to have crossed at Hardy's and gone to Johnson's on the 15th.

rations, but was not permitted by Commodore Biddle,
at Kearny's suggestion, to visit the northern districts
before the general's departure.   Thus, as it was claimed,
the start was delayed.[36]   The party is said to have
numbered forty-nine, "a heterogeneous collection of
all nations almost, and professions and pursuits," but
Stockton, Gillespie, Hensley, and Louis Lafleur are
the only members whose names are definitely known.[37]

The start from Johnson's rancho was on the 19th
or 20th of July, and the arrival at St Joseph, Missouri, early in November.   Our only narrative of the
journey is that given by Stockton's biographer, which
is filled almost exclusively with praises of the commodore's bravery in resisting the attacks of the Indians, who sent an arrow through both his thighs; of
his diplomatic skill, shown in avoiding other Indian
fights; of his achievements as a hunter among the
buffalo; and of his remarkable wisdom in conducting
the whole enterprise.   There was nothing, if we may
credit this eulogist, which the 'conqueror of California' could not do more brilliantly than other men.[38]

It was the general understanding that Major Russell, leaving California in March, had carried to Washington a petition signed by many southern Californians for the appointment of Frémont as governor.
In May another similar petition was signed by many

----

[36] It was charged that K. delayed G. intentionally so as to deprive Fré-
mont of his testimony.   K. admitted that he had favored Mason's idea that
G.'s presence on the Sacramento might make trouble, and had suggested
Biddle's order; but denied that he knew of G.'s plan to go east at this time.
Frémont's Court-martial, 308.

[37] J. B. Chiles was probably one of the number; and of the other witnesses
at Washington in Nov., Wm Findlay, J. Ferguson, Wm and James Brown,
R. Jacob, and L. C. Vincenthaler may have come with Stockton or with Frémont a little earlier.   Three Rocky Mountain trappers were engaged as guides
and interpreters.   One of them, described as having a Crow wife, was perhaps Greenwood.   Kern and King of Frémont's party started with Stockton,
but after four days were left sick in the mountains.   See testimony of Gillespie and Hensley in *Frémont's Court-martial*, 218–28, 233–4.

[38] *Stockton's Life*, 159–66.   'Tears coursed down the weather-worn cheeks
of the bold and hardy mountaineers when they took the last friendly grip
of the commodore's hand.   They implored him if he ever made another
overland journey to send for them.   Lawless, reckless, desperate, wicked,
and callous, as many of them were, Stockton had found the tender spot in
each man's heart.'   He reached Washington about Dec. 1st.

in the south, and received some signatures in the
north, where, when the affair became known, a strong
opposition was excited. This was based on three
leading motives, all more or less analogous and intertwined. First was Frémont's unpopularity among
the natives and others, fomented by the ex-members
of the battalion clamorous for their pay, and by other
holders of unpaid claims; second, the influence of Governor Mason and his friends, naturally opposing a
change of rulers; and third, a sectional spirit against the
natural theory that Frémont would unduly favor the
south, where his friends for the most part resided, or
where his past irregularities had least affected the
property of the people. Possibly the real merits of
the case had also an influence; for it would certainly
have been the worst of policy to reopen old controversies by a return of the ex-governor, whatever may
have been the merits of his cause. His friends in
the north tried to create an impression that his return
would promote the payment of the claims, the non-
payment of which was due to his foes; but without
success. A public meeting was held at San Francisco to remonstrate against him, a committee being
appointed to seek evidence against his fitness, and a
counter-petition being circulated. Larkin also wrote
to the secretary of state in opposition to Frémont.
But the administration probably never thought of
making the appointment.[39]

It was on September 17th that Frémont reported
at Washington, calling for the charges against him,

[39] Record of the S. F. meeting of June 14th in *S. F. Cal. Star*, June 19th;
S. F. Californian, June 19th. The prominent men named were Nathan
Spear, R. M. Sherman, H. Petitt, Frank Ward, T. J. Farnham, Jasper
O'Farrell, Robt Semple, Dr Wiersbicki, Thompson, Leese, Leidesdorff, Murphy, and Guerrero. An editorial in the *Star* also opposes Frémont in a moderate spirit. In *Taylor's Spec. Press*, 630, is a blank form of the petition
against F. for signatures. His Bear Flag exploits, partiality for the south,
and unpaid accounts are the points urged against him. June 30th, Larkin to
sec. state. *Larkin's Off. Corresp.*, MS., ii. 117–18. He says Abrego, after
signing the petition for F., gave a courier $20 to overtake the memorial and
erase his name. Alvarado also regretted having signed the paper. See also
mention of the matter in *Tuthill's Hist. Cal.*, 222–3; *Soulé's Annals of S. F.*,
195.

and demanding an early trial.[40]   The order convening
a court-martial bore date of September 27th, the court
assembled at Washington the 2d of November, and
the trial lasted till January 11, 1848.   Captain John
F. Lee was judge-advocate of the court, and Frémont
was defended by Senator Benton and William Carey
Jones.   Respecting the court, the charges, and the
published record of proceedings, I append some particulars in a note.[41]   The testimony, oral and documentary, has already been presented in spirit, and
largely in literal quotations as a record of the controversy in California; and it is not my purpose

[40] Sept. 17th, F. to adj.-general, in *Bigelow's Mem.*, 217–20. This work
also contains Frémont's final defence, and the most complete account of all
connected with the trial extant, except the original record.

[41] *Message of the President of the U. S. communicating the Proceedings of
the Court-martial in the trial of Lieut-colonel Frémont, April 7, 1848* (cited by
me as *Frémont's Court-martial*), in *U. S. Govt Doc.*, 30th cong. 1st sess., Sen.
Ex. Doc., 33. (Wash. 1848.) 8vo, 447 p. The court was composed of the
following officers: Brev. Brig.-gen. G. M. Brooke, Col S. Churchill, Col J. B.
Crane, Brev. Col M. M. Payne, Brev. Lieut-col S. H. Long, Lieut-col R. E.
Derussey, Lieut-col J. P. Taylor, Brev. Lieut-col H. K. Craig, Maj. R. L.
Baker, Maj. J. D. Graham, Maj. R. Delafield, Brev. Maj. G. A. McCall (replaced by Col T. F. Hunt), and Maj. E. W. Morgan. The witnesses examined were, for the prosecution, Kearny, Cooke, Turner, Bryant, and Emory;
for the defence, Stockton, Gillespie, Hall, Gray, Talbot, Hensley, Minor,
Russell, Beale, Loker, and Swords.
The charges were as follows: i. Mutiny. 1st specification, that Frémont,
having reported to Kearny, his superior officer, on Jan. 13, 1847, and having
received K.'s order of the 16th to make no changes in the battalion, with a
copy of K.'s instructions from Washington, did by his letter of the 17th refuse to obey; 2d spec., that he disobeyed the same order further and assumed
to act as commander, by directing Capt. Wilson on the 25th to raise a co. of
artillery; 3d spec., same, by authorizing McLane on Feb. 5th to recruit men;
4th spec., that he reasserted his resistance, etc., by his letter of Feb. 7th to
Shubrick; 5th spec., that he avowed and justified his mutiny, etc., by his letter of Feb. 11th to Hall; 6th spec., that he assumed to act as gov., in contempt
of lawful authority, by his deed of an island to Temple on March 2d; 7th spec.,
that on March 15th, having received the joint circular of K. and Shubrick and
general orders no. 2 of March 1st, and having promised obedience, he further
disobeyed by his orders to Capt. Owens not to give up arms, etc., causing O.
to disobey Cooke; 8th spec., that on March 16th he made known to Cooke in
writing his refusal to obey orders and discharge the volunteers, still assuming
to act as gov.; 9th spec., that on March 21st he continued his assumption,
disobedience, contempt, etc., by his order to Alexander to accept govt payment for duties; 10th spec., same, by divers orders from Jan. 24th to Feb.
13th on court-martial and resignation of officers; 11th spec., that F., after receiving K.'s verbal orders of March 26th, and written orders of the 28th, disobeyed those orders by remaining at Los Angeles until after May 9th. ii.
Disobedience of the lawful command of his superior officer; spec. 1–7 corresponding to spec. 1, 2, 3, 7, 8, 10, 11, of the first 1st charge. iii. Conduct to
the prejudice of good order and military discipline; spec. 1–5 corresponding
nearly to spec. 4, 5, 6, 7, 10, of the 1st charge.

to attempt any minute analysis here. The matter filling the bulky record of over four hundred pages may for convenience of comprehension be divided into four parts, of which the first, consisting of the routine verbiage and repetitions deemed essential in such documents, needs no further notice.

The second portion is composed of matter intended mainly for the people of the United States rather than the military court. It was the evident, and indeed avowed, aim of Frémont and his friends to make the trial cover the entire field of Californian annals in 1846–7, so far as those annals were favorable to themselves. They wished to magnify the opposition of the natives and other obstacles to success in order to exhibit Stockton and Frémont as conquerors and heroes. They were disposed to make much of the errors and belittle the efforts of other officers. They would dwell on San Pascual, and say little of Chino, Gillespie at Los Angeles, Mervine at San Pedro, Burroughs at Natividad. In all this they had a decided advantage. They were permitted to go in this direction far beyond the real questions at issue, though not so far as they wished, or as the historian might desire. Moreover, for the jury they had in view, their questions not permitted to be answered, unsupported implications, and arguments on what was to be proved by testimony not admitted, were quite as effective as the legitimate evidence introduced. And it cannot be denied that they won a victory; that the verdict of popular sympathy was in Frémont's favor. In this phase of the trial the prosecution could do nothing but limit the extent of irrelevant testimony. Could they have known, however, and proved the facts revealed in this volume respecting the true character of Frémont's and Stockton's part in the conquest from the beginning, they would have had an easy road to victory over the pretending conquerors.

The third class of material consisted of a long series of counter-charges, expressed or implied, against

Kearny, including also attempts to refute certain similar accusations against Frémont introduced by Kearny and his friends in their testimony, but not included in the formal charges. These petty complaints on the part of the defence were intended mainly for the public, though some of them properly supported, as they were not in most instances, might have had an influence on the court.[42] Many of these matters have been noticed in the preceding pages. In the aggregate they seem to show on the part of General Kearny an animus against his opponents prompting him to conduct in certain minor transactions not creditable to his high position; yet not too much importance should be attached to this phase of the affair, since only one side of the case was presented. A wide latitude was given to Frémont's brilliant defenders, while Kearny, not being on trial, was deemed to require no defence and no counter-attack on his foe. The popular verdict in this as in the former branch of the case was in Frémont's favor; for resulting admiration of the path-finder and conqueror was hardly

[42] Kearny's statement that F. tried to 'bargain' with him for the governorship is the one against which, as most affecting his honor, F. protested most earnestly. During the trial K. is accused of remembering only what was favorable to himself until hard pressed in cross-examination or confronted with written proofs of the things he had forgotten; also of false or contradictory testimony on a few details; and of unduly multiplying, complicating, and exaggerating his charges. The attempt was made to show that he tried to keep away important witnesses for the accused; and had not only sent secret accusations to the government, but had indirectly worked up public sentiment against his foe through the newspapers. Besides various indignities on the march east and in the manner of the arrest, his keeping his contemplated charges a secret from Frémont was regarded as irregular, as was his refusal to permit F.'s departure for Mex. or the U. S. without giving any reasons. Various insults were mentioned or hinted at, as the insisting on Mason's or Cooke's presence at interviews, sending Mason south with authority, parading the explorers offensively at Monterey, forcing F. to sleep in town, sending the Mormons to 'crush' him, etc. And, of earlier date, attention was called to his denial of Stockton's position as commander on the march to Los Angeles; his claim that the expedition was undertaken at his own urging; his crafty efforts to draw out from F. at San Fernando a 'report;' and his failure to mention this pretended report during the first controversy, or to attempt any suppression of F.'s mutiny—even encouraging his hope for the governorship after the mutiny was committed. Much stress was also put upon his neglect to make known his instructions of Nov. 5th, or to call for a formal transfer of the command.

less marked than disapproval of a general who had unworthily persecuted an officer of lower rank.

Fourth and last, we find matter pertaining legitimately to the charges of mutiny, disobedience, and conduct to the prejudice of good order and military discipline. The evidence was clear and conclusive. Whatever name might be given to the offence, Frémont had disobeyed in January and March three distinct orders, or sets of orders, given by his superior officer. His defence from a strictly legal point of view had no force whatever. The prosecution might have rested their case on the documentary evidence alone; they made no argument, while permitting Benton almost without limit to manufacture public opinion in behalf of his protégé. The reading of the argument for defence occupied three sessions of the court; and after three days of deliberation a verdict of guilty on all the twenty-three specifications of the three charges was brought in on January 31st, the sentence being dismissal from the service.[43] Seven members of the court signed a recommendation of clemency, on account of previous professional services and of the peculiar circumstances in which the accused was placed between two officers of superior rank each claiming the command. President Polk on February 16th accepted the verdict, except on the charge of mutiny, and approved the sentence, but remitted the penalty, ordering Frémont to resume his sword and report for duty. But the lieutenant-colonel declined to accept the president's clemency, and sent in his resignation, which was accepted on March 14th.[44] The court-martial had been an excellent ad-

[43] Remarks by the court: ' With all the latitude of evidence and the broader latitude of defence, the court has found nothing conflicting in the orders and instructions of the govt; nothing impeaching the testimony on the part of the prosecution; nothing in fine to qualify, in a legal sense, the resistance to authority of which the accused is convicted. The attempt to assail the leading witness for the prosecution (Kearny) has involved points not in issue, and to which the prosecution has brought no evidence. In the judgment of the court his honor and character are unimpeached.'
[44] Bigelow's Mem., 317–18.

vertisement for the young adventurer, and he had no further use for his commission. He would return to California to seek political honors and wealth from his Mariposas estates. He started before the end of the year with a private exploring party, which was broken up with a loss of ten men frozen to death before reaching New Mexico. But in 1849 Frémont arrived in California, where we shall hear of him again.

Commodore Stockton's course in the Californian controversy was never made the subject of official investigation; but not having been allowed to testify as fully as he desired at the trial, on February 18th he addressed to the secretary of the navy a complete narrative defence of his conduct, a document which I have often had occasion to cite. Inheriting a large fortune, the commodore resigned his commission in 1849. In 1851–2 he represented his state, New Jersey, in the senate of the United States; and was subsequently an aspirant for the presidency. It was in support of this ambition that a eulogistic biography was published in 1856, a work largely devoted to Californian matters and fully utilized in these chapters.[45] It would add materially to the dramatic interest of this comedy of errors could I say that the 'conquerors' were opposing candidates in the presidential contest of 1856; but only one could secure the nomination. Stockton died at his New Jersey home in 1866.

General Kearny did not aspire to the presidency or even to the senatorship; but he was nominated in July 1848 for the brevet of major-general for "gallant conduct at San Pascual, and for meritorious conduct in California and New Mexico." This roused

[45] The full title of this anonymous work is: *A Sketch of the Life of Com. Robt F. Stockton; with an appendix, comprising his correspondence with the naval department respecting his conquest of California; and extracts from the defence of Col. J. C. Frémont in relation to the same subject; together with his speeches in the senate of the United States, and his political letters.* N. Y. 1856, 8vo, 210, 131 p., portrait.

afresh the wrath of Thomas H. Benton, who made in
the senate a speech of thirteen days, the 'substance'
of which filled over sixty quarto pages of fine type!
In this most extraordinary discourse the senator took
up, besides the details of the San Pascual campaign,
every point brought out or hinted at in the late trial,
repeating all that had been claimed in defence of Frémont and Stockton, and supplementing each step with
a torrent of ingenious misrepresentation and bitter
invective. In respect to San Pascual his general
position that Kearny merited nothing but censure is
fully supported by the facts; yet even here the speaker's partisan spirit and unfairness are manifest. As
to other phases of the subject, Benton aimed to prove
not only that the general had been wrong in all the
controversy, but that, with his rascally confederates
Emory, Cooke, Mason, and Biddle, he had engaged
in a deliberate and villanous plot, first to rob Stockton of the governorship, and then to crush the saintly
Frémont for having dared to refuse coöperation. He
avowed his purpose to hold up Kearny, and in hardly
less degree his associates, as criminals meriting nothing but contempt. Space does not permit me to cite
Benton's opinions and arguments, or to refute them,
except as I have done so in presenting the general
record. I have presented the controversy in a spirit
of fairness, finding something to praise and blame in
the conduct of the different parties, but little of saintly
innocence or diabolic villany on either side. It is
hard to account for Benton's vindictive bitterness
after what had been virtually a victory for his son-in-
law. I think that any reader of the speech familiar
with the events and men involved, even if favoring
the senator's general views, would at this day regard
the tirade as a ludicrous overshooting of the mark.
In temporary conclusion the senator said: "I must
break off. The senate has no time to hear me further. The first division of the subject is not through;
two other divisions remain to be taken up (!); but I

must break off.   A time will come in open session to
finish what is only begun.... After the conspiracy of
Catiline, Cicero had a theme for his life; since this
conspiracy against Frémont, and these rewards and
honors lavished upon all that plotted against his life
and character, I have also a theme for my life."[46]
But it does not appear that Benton ever found an
opportunity to resume this part of his life-work; indeed, General Kearny died before the end of the year.

This seems to be the proper place for a connected
view of the 'California claims,' often alluded to in this
volume, though in most phases the subject is too complicated for detailed notice within the space at my
command.   The claims were debts incurred for government expenses during the rule of Frémont and
Stockton in 1846–8.   So far as there were naval
funds available, these current expenses to the extent
of about $30,000 were paid; but for the rest property
had to be taken from natives and foreigners in California, with or without their consent.   At first the
Bear Flag men seized the property of Californians
north of the bay to supply their own needs and to
weaken a so-called foe; and when the cause was nominally merged in that of the United States, certain
remnants of the property were transferred with the
battalion.   Thus was founded the smallest and least
definite portion of the claims.   Next, after the raising of the stars and stripes, and chiefly for the needs
of the battalion in the autumn of 1846, both native
and foreign residents were plundered indiscriminately
in the north and central districts; though receipts for
supplies taken, mainly horses and cattle, were generally given to the victims, many of whom willingly
parted with their property and all looked to the United
States for payment.   Then there were the debts incurred in the spring of 1847 during Frémont's rule,

[46] *Benton's Speech in the U. S. Senate, July 1848, on the promotion of General Kearny*, in *Cong. Globe*, 1847–8, appen. 977–1040.

and mainly in the south, all duly certified, and a large portion consisting of money loaned on Frémont's drafts on the government cashed by the merchants. These advances were obtainable only at very high rates of interest; and the matter was complicated by the fact that part of the liabilities were incurred when government funds would have been available but for the political controversy; and finally, pay due the volunteers formed also a considerable element of the indebtedness.

That the government was morally bound to pay these claims of all four classes has never been seriously questioned, though trouble was sure to arise in settling particular demands. Nor can Frémont and Stockton be blamed for their general policy in creating the debts, though wrongs were done and errors committed in individual cases. Payment was expected as soon as peace should be restored; and but for the quarrel between rulers, many of the claims would have been promptly settled with naval funds by Stockton. He made an effort in that direction, the success of which was prevented by Shubrick and Biddle; and he is said to have paid before his departure certain claims for which he felt a peculiar personal responsibility.[47] In the last days of Frémont's rule the fear that the debts of his administration would be repudiated, or that at the least long delays must be expected, caused much excitement, and not a little unfavorable feeling towards the ex-governor; but this was for the most part undeserved. He showed commendable zeal in doing the little in his power to protect the creditors and himself. Kearny and Biddle cannot be blamed, I think, for refusing, in view of technical irregularities of the past, to pay the claims. The financial muddle was the result of circumstances, for which Stockton more than any other man was responsible.

Yet the existence of these unpaid claims remained

[47] *Stockton's Life*, 159. It is said that his drafts were all duly honored; but I find no official record of amounts or details.

as the most serious obstacle to tranquillity in California. Soon after the departure of Kearny and the rest, Governor Mason called the attention of the government to the bad feeling excited by the claimants, expressing his opinion that "a speedy payment will do more toward reconciling the Californians to the change of flags, and be worth more to the United States, than ten times the money it will take to pay the debt;"[48] and urging that a discreet and disinterested citizen be sent to investigate and settle the claims. Larkin also wrote to explain the matter and urge prompt payment.[49] The secretary of war recommended immediate action, Frémont having presented a memorial on the subject, and in February 1848 the matter was referred by the senate to the military committee, whose report was dated the 23d, containing testimony on the value of the services rendered by Stockton and Frémont, with something respecting the necessity, nature, and amount of the indebtedness incurred.[50] On the 3d of March Mr Cass introduced a bill appropriating $700,000, and providing for a board of commissioners to consist of Frémont and two other officers of the battalion, whose adjudication was to be final. Many speeches were made, but the only difference of opinion was respecting the constitutionality

[48] June 18, 1847, Mason to adj.-gen. *Cal. and N. Mex., Mess. and Doc., 1850*, p. 312. Another object to be gained was to enable disbursing officers to sell their drafts at par, instead of at 20 per cent discount. Yet on the 21st, *Id.*, 328–30, Mason sends a warning about the claim of Cot for money lent to Frémont; and also the govt claims received for customs dues by his order. Meanwhile, he advised individual claimants to collect evidence to substantiate their claims, which would doubtless be settled at an early date. *Id.*, 327, 361. It was on Oct. 9th that he sent a warning and the documents respecting the Célis claim. *Id.*, 363–73. Mar. 13th, M. Soberanes to Mason, complaining of the burning and plundering of Los Ojitos by Frémont, and enclosing certificates. *Unb. Doc.*, MS., 202–3.

[49] June 30th, Aug. 23d, Larkin to sec. state. *Larkin's Off. Corresp.*, MS., ii. 118–20. March 15th, L. to Stockton, urging him to do something. Says Capt. Hall has accepted and approved many of the claims, so as to strengthen confidence of the holders in Stockton's govt. *Id.*, i. 120–1. See also article in *S. F. Calif.*, June 12, 1847.

[50] *U. S. Govt Doc.*, 30th cong. 1st sess., Sen. Rept, 75, being the important document I have so often cited as *Frémont's Cal. Claims*. F.'s estimate of the amount needed was about $500,000, but he suggested an appropriation of $600,000. More attention was given, however, to the salvation of Cal. from falling into British possession than to the subject proper of the investigation.

and personnel of the board, the obligation to pay the debt being admitted. The bill passed the senate on April 28th; but the house brought up Mason's recent charges against Frémont, amended the bill, and so delayed it that it was left as unfinished business on adjournment in August. Nothing more was heard of the subject for four years.[51]

In 1852 the matter came up again in congress, the legislature of California having also taken some action in favor of a settlement.[52] Without serious opposition or extended debate, by act of August 31st the secretary of war was directed to appoint a board of three commissioners to investigate, at Washington, all claims connected with the service of the California battalion, an appropriation of $168,000 being made for the purpose.[53] The board, appointed on September 6th, consisted of Brevet-colonel Charles F. Smith, Lieutenant-colonel Charles Thomas, and Major Richard B. Lee. They made three reports, in accordance with which many of the claims were paid, in 1853–4; but these require no special notice, because included in a later final report.[54]

Meanwhile one of the claims presented itself in peculiar shape. On March 18, 1847, Frémont had by allowing a premium of $4,500 obtained $15,000 from F. Hüttmann for drafts on the government. These drafts, not being accepted by Secretary Buchanan,

[51] *Cong. Globe*, 1847–8, p. 261, 284, 423, 558–71, 604–8, 627–31, 676–8, 685, 696–708, 1049, 1069; also *Houston's Sen. Repts*, 30th cong. 1st sess., passim. The matter being referred to a house committee, a substitute bill was reported on Aug. 18th, reducing the appropriation to $500,000, and appointing disinterested members for the board. *U. S. Govt Doc.*, 30th cong. 1st sess., H. Rept., 817. Frémont explains in this report the irregularities of the Célis claim.

[52] *Cal. Sen. Jour.*, 1852, p. 554–9, being a report of a committee made on Feb. 5th. Maj. Snyder was chairman, and devoted the report mainly to an inaccurate explanation of the causes that led to the acts of Frémont in June 1846.

[53] Sec. 6 of army appropriation bill, *U. S. Stat. at Large*, x. 108. The section is repeated in many of the reports to be mentioned in the following notes.

[54] *Frémont's Cal. Claims, Reports of Board of Commissioners*, 1853–5. The report of Dec. 29, 1853, is not given, but alluded to in the next; Report of March 13, 1854, in *U. S. Govt. Doc.*, 33d cong. 1st sess., Sen. Ex. Doc., 49; Report of Dec. 5, 1854, in *Id.*, Sen. Ex. Doc., 8, H. Ex. Doc., 13, 33d cong. 2d sess.; Report of April 18, 1855, in *Id.*, 34th cong. 1st sess., Sen. Ex. Doc., 63.

were protested; suit was brought in London, where Frémont was arrested and put in jail, though soon released on bail; and judgment was obtained for the original $19,500, with interest and costs, all amounting to $48,814. A bill was accordingly introduced in congress for Frémont's relief, resulting in a long discussion, in which the story of the conquest and the claims was once more gone over. Finally, by act of March 3, 1854, it was decided to pay the $48,814, but to charge the original $15,000 to Frémont until he should prove that the money had been spent for the public service. This he had not proved in August of the same year, when the amount was deducted from the larger sum due him on accounts of later date than 1848; nor had the proof been furnished as late as 1856. I know nothing of the final settlement, or of the use originally made of the money obtained from Huttman. There was another similar draft of $1,000 in favor of William Wolfskill, about which nothing appears in later times; nor is anything known respecting the final disposition of the Célis claim for money and cattle. I suppose that Frémont settled these matters privately with the claimants, and probably very much to his own profit so far as the cattle were concerned.[55]

In the same congress there was much discussion respecting an item of the appropriation bill, devoting $31,000 to the claims, and $10,000 to the expense of sending a commissioner to California for additional information, but nothing seems to have been accomplished in this direction.[56] The reports of the com-

[55] Discussion in congress on the bill for Frémont's relief, in *Cong. Globe*, 1852–3, p. 231, 254–5, 593–603, 649, 1010, 1012, 1019, 1033, 1036–7, appen. 370. Act of March 3d, in *U. S. Stat. at Large*, x. 759. Also a very full account of the Hüttmann affair, including a curious itemized bill of the London attorneys, filling 30 p. of print, in *Frémont's Accounts*, 1842–56, in *U. S. Govt Doc.*, 34th cong. 1st sess., Sen. Ex Doc., 109, p. 40, 88–140. It appears that additional costs to the amount of $2,150 were passed to F.'s credit. The failure of F. down to 1856 to prove that the money had been devoted to public uses suggests that it had not been so used, with curious complications respecting the interest and costs paid by the govt; but the details of these accounts are not entirely clear to me.

[56] *Cong. Globe*, 1852–3, p. 795–6, 1034, 1056. Aug. 5, 1854; it was ordered

mission in 1854 showed progress in settling the claims; on April 3, 1855, the secretary of war issued an order dissolving the board; and its final report was made on April 19th. By this report it appears that 363 claims had been presented, amounting to $989,185. Of this the amount allowed and recommended for payment—provision being made by congress for all but $8,129 before the date of the report—was $157,365; disallowed, chiefly reductions in the amount of claims allowed, $157,317; suspended for lack of sufficient evidence, $307,927; ruled out as not within the jurisdiction of the board, including $3,695 payable without its action, and some claims for destruction of property by American or Mexican troops recommended for consideration, $186,509; withdrawn, and in some cases resubmitted at lower rates, $147,800; registered too late for investigation before April 19th, $28,570. Of the whole number only four claims were entirely disallowed, while 180 were allowed without reduction. The largest allowance was $48,700 to General Vallejo, and the smallest $2.50 to Nathan Barbour for a pair of shoes. A notable reduction was that in the case of Captain Phelps, who claimed $10,000 for the use of his boat by Frémont in crossing the bay to spike the guns at San Francisco in 1846, but was obliged to be content with $50![57] The commissioners seem to have accepted the certificates and testimony of Frémont and his officers as sufficient to establish the claims; but they reduced the amounts by fixing a schedule of prices for horses, cattle, grain, arms, saddles, and other supplies much lower than the rates charged by the claimants.

The pay of the volunteers seems not to have been

that the battalion muster-rolls be put on file and made to correspond to Reading's pay-rolls. *U. S. Stat.*, x. 582.

[57] M. G. Vallejo received $48,700 out of a claim for $117,875; S. Vallejo, $11,700 of $53,100; Sutter, $9,832, his entire claim; Argüello, $6,800 of $21,688; T. H. Green, $6,425 of $11,205; C. A. Carrillo, $4,035 of $14,010; Leese, $3,934 of $6,189; A. J. Cot, $3,435, his full claim; Julio Carrillo, $2,670 of $17,500; John Temple, $2,144 of $15,766. Part of the reductions were, however, among the suspended claims. The records of the commission were not published; but sample cases are given in *Frémont's Accounts*.

included in the claims thus disposed of; and I am not able to say when or how these men got their arrears of wages, if at all. Nor can I find any record of further investigation or final settlement of the suspended or unconsidered claims left by the board to the amount of about $335,500. In August 1856 the senate called for and obtained a statement of Frémont's accounts running back to 1842, and including many transactions of later date than 1848; but this report throws no light on our present subject, except as already noted.[58] The court of claims succeeded to the functions of the board, but so far as I can learn never considered any of the suspended claims. Two other claims were, however, taken up, that of Blas P. Alviso for the horses taken at the beginning of the Bear Flag revolt, and that of Vallejo for the use of his buildings at Sonoma for seven years. The court decided against Alviso's claim for $2,050, and mainly on the ground that the government was not responsible for property taken before the U. S. flag was raised, thus reversing the position impliedly taken before; and in favor of Vallejo's claim of $20,600, reduced to $12,600.[59] In April 1860 a senate committee reported against taking further action on a number of claims, with few exceptions new, on the grounds that one—that of Alviso—had been rejected by the court, and that no reasons were given why the claims had not been submitted at the proper time to the board of commissioners.[60] It is probable that most of the suspended claims were spurious, having been sent before the board as experiments, and others rested on so slight a basis that not even the battalion officers had the assurance to certify them. That many were never repaid for property actually taken by Frémont's men is certain; and there is no reason to doubt that others were paid for articles never lost.

[58] *Frémont's Accounts*, 1842–56, 8vo, 144 p. Report of sec. treas. Aug. 16, 1856, in *U. S. Govt Doc.*, 36th cong. 1st sess., Sen. Ex. Doc., 109.
[59] *Id.*, Rept Court Claims, 204, 229; *Id.*, H. Rept. 7.
[60] *Id.*, Sen. Rept, 198.

CHAPTER XVIII.

THE MORMON BATTALION.

1846–1848.

Westward Migration of the Mormons by Sea and Land—The Plan to Occupy California—Elder Little Applies to the Government for Aid—Timely War—Polk's Promises—Kearny's Instructions—Colonel Allen's Call—Theory of the Saints—A Test of Loyalty and a Sacrifice—Recruiting the Battalion—List of Officers—Tyler's History and Bigler's Diary—March to Santa Fé—Death of Colonel Allen—Smith in Command—Doctor Sanderson—Calomel and Arsenic—Cooke in Command—His Journal—March across the Continent—Fight with Wild Cattle—Arrival at San Diego—In Garrison at San Luis Rey and Los Angeles—Mustered Out—Re-enlistment of One Company—Homeward March to Salt Lake in Several Detachments and by Different Routes—A Festival of 1855—A Ram in the Thicket.

It was in the spring of 1846 that the Mormons began their westward migration from Nauvoo, Illinois, and at the same time a ship-load of them went from New York to California. By midsummer the advance of the overland line had been extended to Council Bluffs on the Missouri River, and the *Brooklyn* had landed over two hundred of the saints at San Francisco. The annals of this people, including all the circumstances leading to their exodus, pertain to the *History of Utah*, as presented in another work of this series. In a later chapter of this volume Brannan's immigrant company will be noticed with others of the year. Here only a few brief remarks are called for. The Mormons had not definitely determined where in the far west they would choose their new home. Wherever beyond the Rocky Moun-

tains natural advantages of soil and climate might
appear best supplemented by isolation and prospective
non-interference, there should be established the new
Zion.   Apparently it was deemed likely that experi-
mental settlements in several different regions might
be maintained for some years before the final choice
could be made.   Yet there can be no doubt that California was the spot on which Brigham Young and
his followers had fixed their chief attention as probably best adapted to their purpose.   But there is
nothing whatever to support the theory, more or less
current among their enemies, that they intended to
occupy the land in opposition to the United States,
joining hands with Mexico or England if their own
strength should not suffice.   Existing and prospective
international complications might for years be expected to aid them in establishing themselves on the
Pacific; later their policy would be dictated by their
interests as limited by the possibilities; but the Mormons were always loyal to the republic, to the extent
at least of preferring it to any other government than
their own theocratic system.   The settlers' revolt at
Sonoma, the early occupation of the coast province
by the United States, the rapid influx of gentile immigrants, favorable prospects in the Salt Lake region,
and the peculiar conditions resulting from the discovery of gold were the leading factors that fixed the
Mormon realm in Utah rather than in California.

The Latter-day Saints believed they had just cause
of complaint that the national government had refused
to protect them against the oppressions which forced
them to quit their homes in Missouri and Illinois,
and they did not hesitate to apply at Washington for
aid in their enforced exodus.   There were roads to be
opened, forts to be built along the transcontinental
highway to Oregon, military and naval stores to be
transported to the interior and to the western coast;
in fact, there was work to be done for the government
which the exiles could do as cheaply as anybody, and

the compensation would be of the greatest assistance
to the migrating families.   Application was also made
for more direct aid.   Elder Samuel Brannan's device
seems to have been to share the profits with certain
influential men at the national capital in return for
aid, or at least for non-interference; though his contract was not approved by the church council.   But
more on this matter elsewhere.   Elder Jesse C. Little
represented Mormon interests in the east, and in the
letter of appointment and instructions to him, dated
January 26, 1846, was the following suggestion: "If
our government should offer facilities for emigrating
to the western coast, embrace those facilities if possible.   As a wise and faithful man, take every honorable advantage of the times you can."   Armed with
letters of introduction to prominent men, Little went
to Washington, where with the aid of Amos Kendall, Thomas L. Kane, and others, he soon secured
the attention of President Polk, with whose plans
respecting California the reader is familiar.

No secret was made of the intention to settle in
California.   It was mentioned in some of the introductory letters to which I have alluded; and in a petition addressed by Little to the president he wrote:
"From twelve to fifteen thousand Mormons have already left Nauvoo for California, and many others
are making ready to go; some have gone around Cape
Horn, and I trust before this time have landed at the
bay of San Francisco.   We have about forty thousand in the British Isles, all determined to gather to
this land, and thousands will sail this fall.   There are
also many thousands scattered through the states,
besides the great number in and around Nauvoo, who
will go to California as soon as possible, but many of
them are destitute of money to pay their passage
either by sea or land.   We are true-hearted Americans, true to our native country, true to its laws, true
to its glorious institutions... We would disdain to receive assistance from a foreign power, although it

should be proffered, unless our government shall turn
us off in this great crisis and compel us to be foreigners.   If you will assist us in this crisis I hereby pledge
my honor as the representative of this people, that
the whole body will stand ready at your call, and act
as one man in the land to which we are going; and
should our territory be invaded, we will hold ourselves
ready to enter the field of battle, and then, like our
patriotic fathers, make the battle-field our grave, or
gain our liberty."[1]

While negotiations were in progress, news came that
hostilities with Mexico had begun; and most opportunely in certain respects for the Mormon designs,
though defeating their purposes in other directions.
Little's memorial quoted above was drawn out by
Kendall's announcement that the administration had
resolved to occupy California, and was disposed to
accomplish that object through the Mormons, by aiding them to hasten their journey across the continent.
The project promptly arranged by Polk and his advisers, if we may credit Little's version, was for a thousand picked men to press on overland, and 'make a dash'
into California, while another thousand were to be sent
out by sea on a U. S. transport.   Possibly the elder
in his enthusiasm was disposed to exaggerate the
president's promises; while on the other hand we may
readily imagine that Polk, on further consideration,
either with or without the promptings of enemies to
the church, or of promoters of other military and colonization schemes, concluded that he had promised too
much, that it was not altogether desirable or necessary to allow the Mormons too much power in California; that it would be as well to use rather than be
used by them; and that there would be no difficulty

---

[1] *Life of Brigham Young; or Utah and her Founders. By Edward W.
Tullidge*, N. Y. 1876, 8vo, iv. 458, 81 p.   Little's instructions and petition
are quoted from this work, which contains a more complete account of the
transactions at Washington than I have found elsewhere; though the leading
facts are given in other works.   It was in a conversation with Kendall about
the Mormons that Stevenson claims to have first suggested the idea of sending a volunteer regiment to Cal.

in obtaining other volunteer colonist soldiers. Churchmen believe that Thomas H. Benton did more than than any other to turn the president against them, which is not at all unlikely.

Whatever may have been the original proposition, and it is well to remember that details of preceding negotiations rest almost exclusively on Mormon authority, the final decision was to raise a battalion of five hundred men, to be mustered into the U. S. service for twelve months, and to march by Santa Fé to California, where they were to be discharged at the expiration of their term, retaining their arms and accoutrements. Little and Kane went to Fort Leavenworth with despatches for Colonel Kearny, who on June 19th issued to Captain James Allen of the 1st dragoons the order appended in a note.[2] Allen started at once for the north, and on June 26th, at Mount

[2] June 19, 1846, Kearny to Allen. 'It is understood that there is a large body of Mormons who are desirous of emigrating to California, for the purpose of settling in that country, and I have therefore to direct that you will proceed to their camps and endeavor to raise from amongst them 4 or 5 companies of volunteers, to join me in my expedition to that country, each company to consist of any number between 73 and 109; the officers of each company will be a captain, 1st lieut, and 2d lieut, who will be elected by the privates and subject to your approval, and the captains then to appoint the non-commissioned officers, also subject to your approval. The companies, upon being thus organized, will be mustered by you into the service of the U. S., and from that day will commence to receive the pay, rations, and other allowances given to the other infantry volunteers, each according to his rank. You will, upon mustering into service the 4th company, be considered as having the rank, pay, and emoluments of a lieut-colonel of infantry, and are authorized to appoint an adjutant, sergeant-major, and quartermaster-sergeant for the battalion. The companies, after being organized, will be marched to this post, where they will be armed and prepared for the field, after which they will, under your command, follow on my trail in the direction of Santa Fé, where you will receive further orders from me...You will have the Mormons distinctly to understand that I wish to have them as volunteers for 12 months; that they will be marched to California, receiving pay and allowances during the above time, and at its expiration they will be discharged and allowed to retain, as their private property, the guns and accoutrements furnished to them at this post. Each company will be allowed 4 women as laundresses, who will travel with the company, receiving rations and other allowances given to the laundresses of our army. With the foregoing conditions, which are hereby pledged to the Mormons, and which will be faithfully kept by me and other officers in behalf of the govt of the U. S., I cannot doubt but that you will in a few days be able to raise 500 young and efficient men for this expedition.' The subject is included in Sec. Marcy's instructions of June 3d to Kearny, who was to enlist a number of Mormons not to exceed one third of his entire force. *Cal. and N. Mex., Mess. and Doc., 1850*, p. 236.

Pisgah, Iowa, one of the principal camps of the Mormons, issued a circular announcing his mission. In this document he repeated the substance of Kearny's instructions, and added: "This gives an opportunity of sending a portion of their young and intelligent men to the ultimate destination of their whole people, and entirely at the expense of the United States, and this advanced party can thus pave the way and look out the land for their brethren to come after them. Those of the Mormons who are desirous of serving their country, on the conditions here enumerated, are requested to meet me without delay at their principal camp at Council Bluffs, whither I am now going to consult with their principal men, and to receive and organize the force contemplated to be raised. I will receive all healthy, able-bodied men of from eighteen to forty-five years of age. I hope to complete the organization within nine days from this time."[3] By the high council of Mount Pisgah, Captain Allen was sent westward with a letter to President Young at Council Bluffs, the main and frontier encampment. Here a council was held the 1st of July, at which it was determined by Young and his advisers that the battalion as called for must be raised; and corresponding orders were issued at once.

Thus is explained the origin of the Mormon Battalion, involving, it would seem, nothing mysterious or underhanded in any of its phases. The Mormons had asked for aid in moving part of their people to California; the government needed a volunteer force which in no other way could be raised so promptly; the favor was mutual. The Mormons, however, not receiving aid to the extent or of the kind they had hoped for, regarded the action taken as a mere requisition for troops, and in numbers out of all proportion to the population that was to furnish them.[4] In its

[3] June 26, 1846, Allen's circular to the Mormons, in *Tyler's Hist.*, 114; *Tullidge's Life Young*, 42.

[4] 'It may well be imagined that many of the saints hesitated. It was not from lack of courage either. The danger would never have caused them to

best aspect, the call for troops was a test of Mormon
loyalty; some have claimed to regard it as a device
to weaken the saints and hasten their destruction;
and it has even been given out as the secret history of
the transaction, "as President Young was afterward
informed on the best of authority," writes George
Q. Cannon, "that Thomas H. Benton got a pledge
from President Polk that if the Mormons did not
raise the battalion he might have the privilege of
raising volunteers in the upper counties of Missouri
to fall upon them and use them up."[5]   Some think

shrink; but they had been deceived so many times by those who held authority in the nation that they looked upon this new requisition with distrust...
Assistance in emigrating with their families westward would have been hailed
with joy.   Work of any kind and at any price on the route of their proposed
journey, by which they could earn a subsistence, would have been considered
a godsend.   But joining the army and leaving their families in such a condition was repugnant to their feelings.   Such a thing had never been thought
of, much less asked for, by the saints.   The assertion which has been made
by their enemies, that they desired and solicited the privilege of joining the
army to go against Mexico, leaving their wives and children homeless and
destitute wanderers on the banks of the Missouri, is a base libel on the character of the saints.   They were loyal citizens, but they never expected such
a sacrifice would be required of them to prove their loyalty to the government.   Though Captain Allen represented the call as an act of benevolence
on the part of the govt, and assured the saints that here were hundreds of
thousands of volunteers in the states ready to enlist, it is doubtful whether
he would have got one of the saints to join him if it had been left to his own influence.' *Tyler's Hist.*, 115–16.   'One view is that the govt, prompted by
such men as Benton, sought to destroy, or at least to cripple, the Mormons,
by taking from them 500 of their best men in an Indian country and in their
exodus; while the other view is that the govt designed their good and honor.
The truth is, that a few honorable gentlemen did so design; but it is equally
true that the great majority heartily wished for their utter extinction; while
Sen. Douglas and many other politicians, seeing in this vast migration of Mormons the ready and most efficient means to wrest California from Mexico,
favored the calling of the battalion for national conquest without caring what
afterward became of these heroic men who left their families in the wilderness, or whether those families perished by the way or not...The reader has
noted Mr Brannan's letter, received by the leaders before starting; they
looked upon this "call" for 500 or 1,000 of the flower of their camps as the
fulfilment of the threat.   The excuse to annihilate them they believed was
sought; even the govt dared not disperse and disarm them without an excuse.   At the best, an extraordinary test of their loyalty was asked of them,
under circumstances that would have required the thrice hardening of a
Pharaoh's heart to have exacted.'   *Tullidge's Life Brig. Young*, 44–5.

   [5] All the speakers at a reunion of the battalion in 1855 regarded the raising of the troops in the light of a sacrifice which had saved their people.   Father Pettegrew addressed the women as 'wives and daughters of those men
who were offered a sacrifice for the church of Jesus Christ of Latter-day
Saints,' men ordered 'to go and fight for the rights of the people before
whom they were fleeing.'   Said President Kimball: 'I know that resulted in
the salvation of this people, and had you not done this, we should not have

that the leaders looked upon the raising of the battalion as an advantage to their cause.

Whatever their views, the Mormon chiefs set themselves to work most zealously as recruiting officers. Young, Kimball, and Richards rode back to Mount Pisgah, sending letters to encampments farther east. Doubtless there was a little hesitation among the people, since the enlistment of married men involved many hardships for their families;[6] but promises of protection for women and children, with predictions of exemption from disaster to the men, joined to eloquent and authoritative teachings on duty to the nation and the church, rapidly overcame all opposition. The battalion, about five hundred strong, was recruited in about two weeks; and four companies and part of the fifth were mustered in at Council Bluffs the 16th of July, the fifth company being filled a little later. I append a list of officers. The name of each member of the battalion who reached California will be found in the Pioneer Register at the end of these volumes.[7]

been here. President J. M. Grant had visited Washington and testified to Benton's bloody project; and if we could not have raised the complement of men, what would have been the fate of this people? Israel must have been put in the tomb, unless by the interference of high heaven a ram had been found in the thicket...Yes, brethren, had it not been for this battalion, a horrible massacre would have taken place upon the banks of the Missouri.' President Young took the same view of Benton's project. 'Without doubt, this was decreed in Washington, and I was moved upon to forestall it. As quick as this idea entered my mind it came to me, I will beat them at their own game. Did we not do it?'

[6] Thomas L. Kane, in *The Mormons: A discourse delivered before the Historical Society of Pennsylvania, March 26, 1850*, says: 'The call could hardly have been more inconveniently timed. The young, and those who could best have been spared, were then away from the main body, either with pioneer companies in the van, or, their faith unannounced, seeking work and food about the south-western settlements to support them till the return of the season for commencing emigration. The force was therefore to be recruited from among the fathers of families, and others whose presence it was most desirable to retain. There were some, too, who could not view the invitation without jealousy...But the feeling of country triumphed. The union had never wronged them. "You shall have your battalion at once if it has to be a class of elders," said one, himself a ruling elder. A central mass meeting for council, some harangues at the more remotely scattered camps, an American flag brought out from the storehouse of things rescued and hoisted to a tree mast—and in three days the force was reported mustered, organized, and ready to march.'

[7] An official report, *U. S. Govt Doc.*, 31st cong. 1st sess., H. Ex. Doc., 24 p. 22 g, gives the number mustered in as 15 officers and 481 men, joined

It should here be stated that the experiences of the Mormon battalion have been written by Sergeant Tyler in a manner that leaves little or nothing to be desired.[8] I have followed his work as my chief authority. The troops started on their journey the 20th of July. "There was no sentimental affectation at their leave-taking. The afternoon before their march was devoted to a farewell ball; and a more

later 7, resigned and discharged 3, deaths 7, desertion 1, and mustered out in Cal. 17 officers and 468 men. There is apparently some error here, to say nothing of the fact that about 150 men did not reach California. Tyler gives the names of 506 men, including officers and the men left behind. Kane says there were 520 men. Other authorities speak of the number as about 500.

List of officers in the Mormon battalion: Commander, Lieut-col. *James Allen; later Lieut A. J. Smith; and finally Lieut-col. Philip St George Cooke, all of the 1st U. S. dragoons. Adjutant, Lieut Geo. P. Dykes, and later Lieut P. C. Merrill; quartermaster, Lieut *Sam. L. Gully, and later Lieut Geo. Stoneman; sergeant-major, James H. Glines, and later James Ferguson; quartermaster-sergeant, Sebert C. Shelton, Redick N. Allred; surgeon, Dr Geo. B. Sanderson; assistant-surgeon, Dr Wm L. McIntyre; spiritual directors, David Pettegrew and Levi W. Hancock.

Co. A, Capt. Jefferson Hunt; lieut, Geo. W. Oman, Lorenzo Clark, *Wm W. Willis; sergeants, James Ferguson, Phinehas R. Wright, Reddick N. Aldred, Alex. McCord, Wm S. Muir.

Co. B, Capt. Jesse D. Hunter; lieut, *Elam Luddington, Ruel Barrus, Philemon C. Merrill; sergeants, Wm Coray, Wm Hyde, Albert Smith.

Co. C, Capt. James Brown; lieut, Geo. W. Rosecrans, Sam. Thompson, Robert Clift; sergeants, Orson B. Adams, Elijah Elmer, Joel J. Terrill, David Wilkin, Edward Martin, Daniel Tyler.

Co. D, Capt. *Nelson Higgins; lieut, Geo. P. Dykes, Sylvester Hulett, Cyrus C. Canfield; sergeants, Nathaniel V. Jones, Thomas Williams, Luther T. Tuttle, Alpheus P. Haws.

Co. E, Capt. Daniel C. Davis; lieut, James Pace, Andrew Lytle, *Sam. L. Gully; sergeants, Sam. L. Brown, Richard Brazier, Ebenezer Hanks, Daniel Browett.

Those whose names are marked with a * did not reach Cal. There were seven or eight young men who went as servants to the officers, whose relatives they were in most cases. For biographical notices of each officer and private, see my Pioneer Register and Index.

[8] *A Concise History of the Mormon Battalion in the Mexican War, 1846–1847*. By Sergeant Daniel Tyler, no place (Salt Lake City), 1881, 8vo, 376 p. 'Neither labor, pains, nor expense has been spared in the effort to make this a just and authentic history. The author has not aimed at sensational effect, nor made any attempt at literary embellishment, but rather endeavored to offer a plain statement of facts and give due credit to all concerned,' says Tyler in his preface, and the result shows that no better man could have undertaken the task. Naturally his narrative is marked by that display of faith which is a characteristic of all religious writers; but this, while adding a charm, detracts in no respect from the value of the record. His authorities are chiefly diaries written by his comrades at the time, and letters written by them in later years. The 'introductory' includes a sketch of *The Martyrdom of Joseph Smith*, by President John Taylor, and Col Kane's discourse of 1850 on *The Mormons*, as already cited; also a poem on the Mormon battalion by Mrs Eliza R. Snow. There is appended an account of the battalion festival at Salt Lake City in 1855.

merry dancing rout I have never seen, though the
company went without refreshments, and their ball
was of the most primitive," writes Colonel Kane.
One of the soldiers' last acts before departure was to
subscribe a large part of their pay for their families
and the Mormon poor. The elders made parting
addresses of encouragement, and Brigham Young
formally predicted, as he had done before, that "not
one of those who might enlist would fall by the
hands of the nation's foe; that their only fighting
would be with wild beasts." That their subsequent
safety resulted from this prediction the Mormons had
no doubt; and that they were under divine protection soon became evident to them when a tornado
threw down the trees of a forest in which they were
encamped without harming a man. The captains and
some of the men were accompanied by their families,
and there were in all about eighty women and children who started on the journey. Much of their
way was through a country inhabited by their old
foes, the Missouri 'mobocrats,' but there were no
hostilities and few hardships. The arrival at Fort
Leavenworth was on August 1st, and here the battalion remained two weeks, drawing their arms and
accoutrements, with forty dollars in money for each
man, most of which was sent back to the church by
elders Hyde, Taylor, and Little, who here took final
leave of their soldier disciples. Here Lieutenant-
colonel Allen fell sick and died before the end of
August. He was very popular with his men, none
of whom have anything but words of praise for him.

On the 12th and 14th of August the troops started
on their long march to Santa Fé; and now their
troubles began. It is not necessary to chronicle here
the hardships and petty adventures incident to such
a journey, though as given in the Mormon diaries[9]

[9] Besides the diaries quoted by Tyler, I have Henry W. Bigler's *Diary of
a Mormon in California*, MS., which contains a most valuable and interesting record, not only of the march to Sta Fé and thence across the continent,
but of the later discovery of gold in California.

the narrative is not without a charm. Sufferings resulted mainly from heat and bad water, and there was much sickness, with several deaths; but there were also miraculous cures attributed to faith, prayer, and baptism. One phase of the battalion's troubles, however, merits somewhat more extended notice—that resulting from complaints against the officers. On the death of Allen, Lieutenant A. J. Smith of the regular army was sent from Fort Leavenworth to take command temporarily. The Mormon privates and part of their officers claimed that the command belonged to the senior captain, Hunt, and that Colonel Allen had promised such an arrangement in the event of his own removal from the position. The fact that such a promise had been made was comfirmed by Brigham Young. On the other hand, it was claimed that Allen had no right to make the promise; nevertheless a council of the Mormon officers with only three dissenting votes decided in favor of Smith. From that time the lieutenant was naturally an object of dislike to the soldiers, who looked on him as unfriendly to the Mormons, cruel in his treatment of the sick, and perhaps disposed to destroy the battalion by overwork and privations. Only divine protection enabled the saints to survive, and only the patriotic devotion that had prompted the original sacrifice of their enlistment kept them from mutiny. Such was their view of the matter;[10] yet their wrongs must be

[10] 'And on the brave battalion went
    With Colonel Allen, who was sent
    As officer of government.
    The noble Colonel Allen knew
    His " Mormon boys " were brave and true,
    And he was proud of his command
    As he led forth his " Mormon band."
    He sickened, died, and they were left
    Of a loved leader soon bereft !
    And his successors proved to be
    The embod.ment of cruelty.
    Lieutenant Smith, the tyrant, led
    The cohort on in Allen's stead
    To Santa Fé, where Colonel Cooke
    The charge of the battalion took.'
                    Mrs Snow's poetical version.

'It would have been difficult to select the same number of American citizens from any other community who would have submitted to the tyranny and abuse that the battalion did from Smith and Sanderson. Nor would we have done so on any consideration other than as servants to our God and patriots to our

regarded as in some measure imaginary. Raw recruits chafe under the discipline imposed by an officer
of the regular army, and often attribute to him the
hardships of their march. It was hard for the Mormons to realize their position as volunteers in the U.
S. service, and they were prone to include in their
list of grievances all that did not please them.

It was not, however, against their leader that the
bitterest feelings were excited, but against Sanderson,
the surgeon of the battalion. The Mormons have
their own views on medical science, and do not entertain the highest respect for the methods of the schools.
They rely for the cure of ordinary ailments on herbs;
while for more serious illness prayer, anointing with
oil, laying-on of hands, and baptism are prescribed.
And now, a 'mineral quack' had against their will
been made superior to Dr McIntyre, 'a good bo-
tanic physician,' and insisted on dosing them with
his 'calomel and arsenic.' The Mormons claimed
that their religion discountenanced the taking of mineral medicines. Adjutant Dykes, however, affirmed
that they had no such religious scruples, and that the
church authorities themselves took such medicines, and
Captain Hunt would say no more than that it "was
rather against our religious faith." Therefore Smith
supported the surgeon and insisted that his instructions must be followed, though subsequently a letter

country.' *Tyler's Hist.*, 147. All were delighted when the acting colonel
was arrested by a sentinel for not giving the right password. 'The appointment of Smith, even before his character was known, caused a greater gloom
throughout the command than the death of Colonel Allen had.' *Id.*, 144.
Young's letter affirming Allen's promise to leave the command to Hunt. *Id.*,
155-6. 'Whether Col Smith had had no experience in travelling with teams,
or whether he desired to use up the teams and leave the battalion on the
plains helpless, does not appear.' *Id.*, 159. 'It appears that the colonel and
surgeon are determined to kill us, first by forced marches to make us sick,
then by compelling us to take calomel or to walk and do duty.' Rogers' journal in *Id.*, 160. 'While privates were punished by him for the merest trifles,
officers could go where and do what they pleased.' *Id.*, 177. 'And now commenced a series of the most trying cruelties. Our commander was not of
himself cruel and wicked, but he was weak, and became to a great extent
the creature of Dr Sanderson, a rotten-hearted quack that was imposed upon
us as our surgeon.' Ferguson in *Id.*, 365. Bigler and all the rest confirm the
lieutenant's cruelty, weakness, and want of skill.

from President Young was received, saying: "If you are sick, live by faith, and let surgeons' medicine alone if you want to live." For a time the doctor dealt out his drugs, which the patients put anywhere but down their throats; but presently Sanderson learned how his prescriptions were being treated, and thereafter in some cases obliged the sick to take the potions from an old iron spoon in his presence. The wrath of the soldiers and the troubles of the doctor may be imagined; the controversy was kept up till the end; and the Mormons were satisfied that all deaths in the battalion were due to the surgeon's quackery.[11] Indeed, the chief cause of complaint against Smith was his

[11] 'The surgeon was from Mo., did not belong to our people, and had been heard to say he did not care a damn whether he killed or cured; and for this our sick refused to go at sick-call and take his medicine, and Smith was told, straight up and down, there and then, before we would take Dr Sanderson's medicines we would leave our bones to bleach on the prairie.' *Bigler's Diary of a Mormon*, MS., 9. Sept. 2d, 'Smith began to show his sympathy for the sick by ordering them out of the wagons, and swore if they did not walk he would tie them to the wagons and drag them.' *Id.* But Tyler relates that Sergt Williams defended the sick and threatened to knock the colonel down. *Tyler's Hist.*, 144. Young's letter of August 19th on medicine. *Id.*, 146. 'It was customary every morning for the sick to be marched to the tune of "Jim along Joe" to the doctor's quarters, and take their portion from that same old iron spoon,' and the doctor 'threatened with an oath to cut the throat of any man who would administer any medicine without his orders.' *Id.* The author having a fever begged to be left on the road and reported dead rather than take the drugs. *Id.*, 148. He had to take them, but to neutralize their effect he drank a large quantity of water against the doctor's orders. *Id.*, 150. Alva Phelps was suffering severely. 'The doctor prepared his dose and ordered him to take it, which he declined doing, whereupon the doctor with horrid oaths forced it down him with the old rusty spoon. A few hours later he died, and the general feeling was that the doctor had killed him. Many boldly expressed the opinion that it was a case of premeditated murder. When we consider the many murderous threats previously made, the conclusion is by no means far-fetched.' That evening a dancing star was noted in the east. *Id.*, 158. All were glad when the doctor left with the advance party of the well, leaving the sick behind. *Id.*, 163.

'A doctor which the government
Has furnished proves a punishment.
At his rude call of "Jim along Joe"
The sick and halt to him must go.
    Both night and morn this call is heard,
    Our indignation then is stirred.
    And we sincerely wish in hell
    His arsenic and calomel.'
            Hancock's song on the *Desert Route. Id.*, 183.

To Boyle the doctor 'gave the usual dose—calomel—which he did not swallow, but consigned it to the flames. The writer and another elder or two were called upon to anoint him with oil and lay hands upon him, and before night he was well.' *Id.*, 209. Calomel gave out and arsenic was substituted long before Cal. was reached. *Id.*, 215. David Smith killed by the doctor's medicines. *Id.*, 274.

support of Sanderson; and another, Adjutant Dykes, though a Mormon and a preacher, was regarded as an apostate because he had favored Smith and only mildly opposed the doctor.   Says Elder Hyde: "It was plainly manifest that Lieutenant Dykes sought to gain favor of and please the wicked rather than favor his brethren."   And Tyler, that "Dykes became so notorious for his officious and captious manner, that the battalion accorded to him the title of 'accuser of the brethren.'"   And another saint: "There are a few like G. P. Dykes that go into error, and who will not do right.   Brother Dykes has gone into errors and is damned; he has the curse of his brethren upon him for his follies and misdoings."

The route proposed had included Bent's Fort, where supplies were expected and where perhaps the winter might be passed; but to gain time the commander decided on a shorter way, much to the displeasure of his men.   On the Arkansas River, about the middle of September, many of the families were detached and sent to pass the winter at Pueblo under Captain Higgins with a guard of ten men.   This division of the battalion was also opposed, as was a later one of October 3d, when the stronger half of each company was sent on in advance, leaving the feeble to follow more slowly.   The two divisions arrived at Santa Fé the 9th and 12th of October, and were saluted with a hundred guns by order of General Doniphan, an old friend of the Mormons, who were delighted to know that no such honor had been paid to Colonel Sterling Price, their enemy, on his arrival a few days before. From Santa Fé 88 men deemed unfit for prospective hardships were sent back to Pueblo for the winter under Captain Brown and Lieutenant Luddington, and with them went also the laundresses of the battalion.   Again, on November 10th, after the start from Santa Fé, 55 sick under Lieutenant Willis were detached for Pueblo.   Of the 150, more or less, thus left en route, it is only necessary to state that they never came to California, but most of them found their way to Salt Lake the next year.

General Kearny had already left Santa Fé for California with his dragoons, as the reader will remember;[12] but he had left Lieutenant-colonel Philip St George Cooke, of the 1st dragoons, with orders to take command of the battalion and open a wagon route to the Pacific by the Gila route. Cooke assumed the command the 13th of October. Lieutenant Smith became acting commissary of subsistence; Lieutenant George Stoneman, of the 1st dragoons, acting quartermaster instead of Gully, who soon left the service; Lieutenant Merrill, adjutant instead of Dykes, who resumed his place in the company; and James Ferguson was appointed sergeant-major. Major J. H. Cloud, paymaster U. S. A., accompanied Cooke. Stephen C. Foster, called "doctor" in the narratives, was employed as interpreter. The guides were Weaver, Charbonneau, and Leroux, and a Mr Hall seems to have served in a similar capacity. Dr Sanderson continued his services as surgeon.

For the march from New Mexico to California we have, in addition to Tyler's work and Bigler's diary, the official journals and reports of the commander.[13] Of this officer the Mormons speak in favorable terms, describing him as a stern man of forbidding manner, a strict disciplinarian, but impartial in his orders, and

[12] See chap. xiii. of this volume.

[13] *Journal of the march of the Mormon battalion of infantry volunteers, under the command of Lieutenant-colonel P. St George Cooke (also captain of dragoons), from Santa Fé, New Mexico, to San Diego, California, kept by himself by direction of the commanding general of the army of the west,* in *U. S. Govt Doc.*, special sess. (30th cong.), Sen. Doc. no. 2, Washington, 1849, 8vo, 85 p. This journal extends to Jan. 30, 1847.

Report of Lieut-col P. St George Cooke, of his march from Santa Fé, New Mexico, to San Diego, Upper California (1846–7), in *U. S. Govt Doc.*, 30th cong. 1st sess., H. Ex. Doc. 41, p. 549–63, with a map of the route. This is a report to Gen. Kearny, dated at San Luis Rey Feb. 5, 1847.

The Conquest of New Mexico and California; an historical and personal narrative. By P. St Geo. Cooke, brigadier, brevet major-general, U. S. A. Author of *Scenes and Adventures in the Army; or, Romance of Military Life,* etc. N. Y. 1878. 12mo. This contains a condensed narrative of the march, with much additional matter, though hardly enough to justify the author in presenting the book as he does in a preface as the 'first historical narrative of the conquest,' and 'a connected and permanent record.'

a man of great energy and perseverance. They were delighted that a captain was the first to be put under arrest for failure to comply with the regulations; and they were pleased with some flattering things he said of them in later years. In his journal the colonel says: "The battalion were never drilled, and though obedient, have little discipline; they exhibit great heedlessness and ignorance, and some obstinacy." And in his later work: "Everything conspired to discourage the extraordinary undertaking of marching this battalion 1,100 miles, for the much greater part through an unknown wilderness without road or trail, and with a wagon train. It was enlisted too much by families; some were too old, some feeble, and some too young; it was embarrassed by many women; it was undisciplined; it was much worn by travelling on foot and marching from Nauvoo;[14] their clothing was very scant; there was no money to pay them or clothing to issue; their mules were utterly broken down; the quartermaster department was without funds, and its credit bad; and mules were scarce. Those procured were very inferior, and were deteriorating every hour for lack of forage or grazing. So every preparation must be pushed—hurried."

They started October 19th down the valley, obtained such supplies and fresh animals on the way as the inhabitants could be induced to part with for exorbitant prices, sent back 58 of the feeblest, as already noted, and the 13th of November left the Rio Grande for the south-west, 340 strong, accompanied by only five women, who were wives of officers and transported at their husbands' expense. The guides declared it impossible to follow the Gila route proper, or that taken by Kearny, who had left his wagons behind; and a circuit to the south through Sonora was determined on. The country proved to be almost unknown to the guides, who presently recommended a

[14] And by Lieut Smith's tyranny and blunders, and most of all by Dr Sanderson's calomel and arsenic, as the Mormon writers assert.

route by Janos and Fronteras; but on learning that
Janos lay toward the south-east, Cooke determined
to turn to the right, and did so the 21st of November, moved thereto, the Mormons believed, by divine
interposition; for at the suggestion of Father Pettegrew and Brother Hancock, their spiritual advisers,
they sent up fervent prayers the night before "that
the Lord might change the colonel's mind," and accordingly that officer ordered a turn to the west, saying "he would be damned if he would go round the
world to reach California." The way followed was
from a point on the Rio Grande in latitude 32° 40',
south-westward to San Bernardino on the later boundary of the two republics at the corner of four states,
westward to the Rio San Pedro, down that stream
northward, and thence west to Tucson, and to Kearny's
trail on the Gila.

For infantry with wagons for which they must find
or make a road, with worn-out animals and short
rations, the journey was much more difficulty than
that of Kearny's company, or any that had previously
crossed the continent in these latitudes.

> "How hard, to starve and wear us out
> Upon this sandy desert route,"

was the chorus of a song by which the saints relieved
their minds along the way. Nothing short of long
extracts from the diaries, for which I have no space,
would adequately picture their toils, which I do not
attempt to catalogue. Their sufferings were, however, less severe than between Fort Leavenworth and
Santa Fé, because the families and the feeble had
been left behind. On December 11th on the San
Pedro there was an exciting battle with a band of
wild bulls, described by Levi Hancock in a song, in
which affray several men were wounded, including
Lieutenant Stoneman, who as I write is governor of
California. They were at Tucson in the middle of
December, but the town had been abandoned by the
garrison and most of the people, though Cooke had

some correspondence with the comandante. The Mexicans began to plan on paper an organization for defence,[15] but the Americans did not stay to be annihilated. The day after Christmas they were on the Gila, having three days before received a letter from Kearny; on January 8th the junction of the Gila and Colorado was reached; on the 15th news came back of the disaster at San Pascual; and on the 21st the battalion encamped at Warner's rancho, where the Mormons were not inhospitably received.[16] News respecting the state of affairs in California, though of vital interest to the new-comers, need not be recalled to the memory of my readers, who are familiar with the situation. Cooke proposed at first to go to Los Angeles, where he thought his aid might be needed; but presently came an order to march to San Diego, where the battalion finally arrived the 29th of January, and where the commander issued next day a congratulatory order, with well merited compliments to the Mormons for the manner in which they had performed their difficult task.[17]

[15] Some correspondence on the subject in *El Sonorense*, Jan. 1, 8, 1847; as there had been in *Id.*, Oct. 23, 1846, a warning of Kearny's approach.

[16] Notwithstanding that, 'unlike the hospitable Pimas, he hid his bread and drove his cattle into the mountains,' as Ferguson remarks. Cooke, Tyler, and the rest speak not unfavorably of Warner.

[17] 'Headquarters Mormon Battalion, Mission of San Diego, Jan. 30, 1847. (Orders no 1.) The lieut-colonel commanding congratulates the battalion on their safe arrival on the shore of the Pacific Ocean, and the conclusion of their march of over 2,000 miles. History may be searched in vain for an equal march of infantry. Half of it has been through a wilderness where nothing but savages and wild beasts are found, or deserts where, for want of water, there is no living creature. There, with almost hopeless labor, we have dug deep wells, which the future traveller will enjoy. Without a guide who had traversed them, we have ventured into trackless table-lands where water was not found for several marches. With crowbar and pick and axe in hand, we have worked our way over mountains, which seemed to defy aught save the wild goat, and hewed a passage through a chasm of living rock more narrow than our wagons. To bring these first wagons to the Pacific we have preserved the strength of our mules by herding them over large tracts, which you have laboriously guarded without loss. The garrison of four presidios of Sonora concentrated within the walls of Tucson gave us no pause. We drove them out with their artillery, but our intercourse with the citizens was unmarked by a single act of injustice. Thus, marching half naked and half fed, and living upon wild animals, we have discovered and made a road of great value to our country. Arrived at the first settlement of California, after a single day's rest, you cheerfully turned off from the route to this point of promised repose, to enter upon a campaign, and meet, as we supposed, the

The war in California was at an end when the battalion arrived, and in the garrison life of some six months there is but little that demands notice. The Mormons have always been disposed to overestimate the value of their services during this period, attaching undue importance to the current rumors of impending revolt on the part of the Californians and of the approach of Mexican troops to reconquer the province. They also claim the credit of having enabled Kearny to sustain his authority against the revolutionary pretensions of Frémont. The merit of this claim will be apparent to the reader of preceding chapters. But during the interregnum of military occupation a garrison force was essential, and in this respect, as in their march across the continent, the Mormons did faithful service, giving no cause for unfavorable criticism. Devoting themselves zealously to military drill under the instructions of Cooke and Stoneman, they became so proficient in the manual of arms as to elicit high compliments from Colonel Mason and other regular-army officers. At first the men suffered from want of proper clothing, and for want of other food than fresh beef; but gradually their needs were supplied. They made some complaints of petty wrongs, else had they not been volunteers. Many were sorrowful that inexorable discipline would not allow them to retain their flowing beards to be shown at Salt Lake. Dr Sanderson still prescribed, but only one man was thought by them to have been killed by his drugs. A sentinel was found asleep at his post, but the sentence of a court-martial was very mild, and was remitted by the colonel—"a specific and direct answer

approach of an enemy; and this, too, without even salt to season your sole subsistence of fresh meat. Lieutenants A. J. Smith and George Stoneman, of the 1st dragoons, have shared and given valuable aid in all these labors. Thus, volunteers, you have exhibited some high and essential qualities of veterans. But much remains undone. Soon you will turn your attention to the drill, to system and order, to forms also, which are all essential to the soldier.'

Tyler, p. 255, says: ' The foregoing order, one of those simple acts of justice so rarely done to Mormons, which was not read until Feb. 4th, six days after it was written, was cheered heartily by the battalion.'

to prayer." The dragoons were stanch friends of the
Mormons, but the men of Frémont's battalion were
regarded as foes. Doubtless many of the latter, immigrants from the western states, were hostile, and
circulated among the Californians damaging reports
on Mormon character; but it is probable that this
enmity, especially that of Frémont himself, and the
rumored threats to attack the camp and "wipe the
saints out of existence," were seen through the glasses
of prejudice. It is true that the Californians had
formed in advance a very unfavorable opinion of the
Mormons, but equally true that the latter by their
conduct succeeded in almost entirely removing this
feeling. In morals and general deportment they were
far superior to other troops in the province, being
largely under the control of their religious teachers.
Church meetings were held often, and sermons were
preached by Captain Hunt, the spiritual guardians
Pettegrew and Hancock, or by elders Hyde, Tyler,
and others. With a view to the future necessities of
themselves and families, they were allowed to hire
themselves out as farmers and artisans, and did so to
a considerable extent, especially at San Diego, where
they burned bricks, dug wells, and made log pumps,
to the great advantage of themselves and of the citizens.[18]

The battalion left San Diego on February 1st, and
on the 3d took possession of San Luis Rey, where
part of the force was stationed for two months. On
the 15th Company B under Captain Hunter was sent
to garrison San Diego. At the end of the month
Lieutenant Thompson was despatched to the Colorado

---

[18] On the popular feeling against the saints, see *Frémont's Court-martial*,
233, 242–3, 259–63. In *Foster's Angeles in '47*, MS., 6–7, 35–41, is found some
slight information on the battalion, including a long yarn about some trouble
between J. A. Carrillo and the Mormon officers. See also, for mention of the
arrival, etc., *Ripley's War with Mex.*, i. 489; *Griffin's Pap.*, MS., 23; *Cutts'
Conq.*, 69, 209; *Julio César, Cosas de Ind.*, MS., 10–11; *Los Angeles Express*,
Nov. 17, 1871; *S. F. Cal. Star*, Feb. 6, 1847; *Bryant's What I Saw*, 416–17;
Warren's Mem., 54–5; *Hughes' Doniphan's Exped.*, 244–8; *Millennial Star*, x.
23–4; xi. 47–8; *Tullidge's Women of Mormondom*, passim.

to bring wagons left there.   From the 2d of March
Stoneman with his dragoons took the place of Company B at San Diego for two weeks, after which the
Mormons resumed the post.   News of the assumption of the command by Shubrick and Kearny came
on the 14th, with Cooke's appointment to the military
command in the south; and four days later the main
body of the battalion marched to Los Angeles, Lieutenant Oman being left at San Luis with thirty-two
men until April 6th, when the post was abandoned,
and all of the four companies were reunited at the
pueblo.   At the same time the men petitioned for
discharge, but the petition was suppressed by the
officers.   On the 11th Company C was sent to hold
a position already occupied by the dragoons in Cajon
pass, and eleven days later Lieutenant Pace was sent
with another detachment to relieve the first company;
but this force was recalled in haste on the 24th, and
the Mormons were set at work building a fort on the
hill at Los Angeles in consequence of reports that a
Mexican force was approaching.   The saints declined
on May 4th an offer of discharge on condition of enlisting for five years as dragoons.   On the 8th came
the first letters from absent families at Council Bluffs
and Nauvoo; and the same day Lieutenant Thompson was sent with twenty men of Company C against
some hostile Indians in the mountains, six of whom
were killed, and two of the Mormons wounded with
arrows.   Next day General Kearny arrived with the
New York volunteers and Colonel Stevenson, who
succeeded Cooke in command of the southern district.
After some efforts to promote a reënlistment of the
Mormon volunteers, Kearny departed on the 13th
with Cooke, whose resignation had been accepted,
and who took with him twelve of the men as a body-
guard, three from each company.   A small detachment was sent to San Pedro on the 10th of June;
and next day John Allen, an apostate Mormon, was
court-martialled and soon drummed out of camp, as

he had previously been expelled from the church.
During the rest of June and the first half of July
there is nothing requiring special notice, though there
were continued efforts to secure a promise of reënlistment. Company B arrived from San Diego on July
15th; next day all were mustered out by Lieutenant
Smith in the unceremonial way that might have been
expected from the battalion's bête noir of earlier times;
a few days sufficed for paying off the men; and on
the 20th one company of Mormon volunteers under
Captain Daniel C. Davis was mustered into the service for an additional term of six months.[19]

There was an earnest effort by the authorities to
secure a reënlistment of the battalion for another
term of garrison duty. Favorable conditions were
offered, and the command was to be given to Captain
Hunt. Kearny made a speech on the subject before
his departure, and Stevenson was active in the matter under Governor Mason's instructions, visiting the
San Diego company in June, and making a speech at
Los Angeles on his return. He presented as a strong
attraction the privilege of choosing their own officers,
with the fact that the Mormon commander would be
the third in rank among officers in California, and
might become first. The company officers favored
the proposition, and urged the men to reënlist as the
best means of aiding the cause and their absent families. The men as a rule had no serious objections;
but the religious advisers, the parties really in control,
decided adversely. Father Pettegrew thought that
duty to the families demanded a return, which would
be sanctioned by the church leaders. Elder Hyde

---

[19] Tyler's Hist., passim; Bigler's Diary, MS., contains many details of the
experience of Co. B at S. Diego from March 17th to July 9th. Sergt Hyde and
18 men were posted in the fort on the hill. Religious services were held
regularly, Hyde being the preacher; and there was also a 'young men's club'
for debate, etc. Capt. Hunter's wife died April 27th. On May 4th six months'
pay was received, and chiefly devoted to the purchase of an outfit for return
to Salt Lake. Sam. Miles acted as assistant to the alcalde; and on June
24th Lieut Clift was appointed alcalde of the post. The Mormons entirely
conquered the original prejudice of the Dieguinos against them, and effected
a kind of industrial revolution in the town.

believed that their sacrifice of the past was enough,
being satisfactory to God and probably to the government. Elder Tyler could see, in the light of past de-
ceptions, no ground for confidence that promises respecting the command would be kept. "Were not
our noses put upon the grindstone? and were they not
still there?" It is said that Stevenson's closing remarks gave offence. They were: "Your patriotism
and obedience to your officers have done much towards removing the prejudice of the government and
the community at large, and I am satisfied that another
year's service would place you on a level with other
communities." This Tyler compares to the action of
a cow that gave a good bucketful of milk and then
kicked it over. "It was looked upon as an insult
added to the injuries we had received without cause.
We could challenge comparison with the world for
patriotism and every other virtue, and did not care to
give further sacrifice to please pampering demagogues."
Doubtless Pettegrew's opinion was regarded as an
order not to be disobeyed; the government officers, as
is frequently the case under such circumstances, looked
about for some ulterior motive. Stevenson's theory,
as reported to Mason, was that it was designed to
make room for other Mormon soldiers. "They desire to get the military control of the country, and
from time to time will supply from 100 to 1,000 men
for the service, until their whole community shall
have had some experience as soldiers, and become furnished with arms; which by the time the civil government shall be organized will give them control as well
of the ballot-box...This I know to be their calcula-
tion, for Hunt and his officers have so expressed themselves to me." And in the same report it is stated
that Captain Hunt was about to start for Monterey
to proffer his services to raise a new battalion of Mormons from those on their way to the country. But
Father Pettegrew finally permitted the formation of
one company to remain as a garrison at San Diego,

and seventy-eight volunteers were obtained from the different companies. They were promised disbandment in March of the next year, and transportation to Bear River or San Francisco on discharge. Captain Hunter also remained, to be made Indian agent at San Luis Rey.[20]

I have already stated that about 150 of the battalion never came to California, but found their way from New Mexico to Salt Lake, where they were discharged from the service. The first of the saints to return eastward were twelve men who were detached to accompany Kearny and Cooke on the overland route. Their names are not known, except John Binley and N. V. Jones, who kept a diary. Three of them went with the general by sea, leaving the pueblo on May 13th, while the rest accompanied Lieut Sherman by land to Monterey,[21] arriving the 25th and starting again the 31st. Something is said elsewhere of Kearny's march, but nothing occurred of importance in this connection. Two parties of Mormons westward bound were met on the plains in July and August. They reached Fort Leavenworth in September, where the saints were discharged with $8.60 each for overtime, and soon found their way to Council Bluffs to rejoin their families.[22]

[20] June 5, 1847, Gov. Mason to Stevenson, enclosing a letter to Hunt on efforts to be made for reënlistment. *Cal. and N. Mex., Mess. and Doc., 1850*, p. 326–7. June 7th, Id. to Lieut Smith, on muster in and out. *Id.* July 23d, Stevenson to Mason, the letter quoted in my text. *Id.*, 347–8. July 27th, Id. to Id., announcing reënlistment and conditions. *Id.*, 345–6. In his report to the adjutant-general of Sept. 18th, Mason says: 'Of the services of this battalion, of their patience, subordination, and general good conduct, you have already heard; and I take great pleasure in adding that as a body of men they have religiously respected the rights and feelings of these conquered people, and not a syllable of complaint has reached my ears of a single insult offered or outrage done by a Mormon volunteer. So high an opinion did I entertain of the battalion and of their special fitness for the duties now performed by the garrisons in this country, that I made strenuous efforts to engage their services for another year.' *Id.*, 336. In the *S. F. Alta*, Jan. 3, 1854, is mentioned a rejected claim on the treasury for $85,000 for mileage for the battalion, being the difference between commutation by the overland and isthmus routes.

[21] Sherman, *Mem.*, i. 28, says there were about 40 men, and that they were under his command on the march to Monterey. Tyler says there were 12 under Stoneman, and is confirmed by Kearny as to the number.

[22] *Tyler's Hist.*, 299–304, following Jones' diary.

The members of the battalion mustered out on July 16th, and who did not reënlist, were ready for departure in a few days, numbering about 240 men. Paying no attention to the late military organization, they formed themselves after the manner of the Israelites into companies of hundreds, under Andrew Lytle and James Pace; William Hyde, Daniel Tyler, and Reddick N. Allred being captains of fifties, and other chiefs being named as captains of tens. Elisha Averett was put in command of ten pioneers, one of whom was Henry W. Bigler, whose diary is the principal authority for the journey.[23] The pioneers started on July 21st, Allred and his fifty on the 23d, the rest a little later, and on the 27th all were reunited at the San Francisco rancho near the Santa Clara River. Here they purchased a supply of cattle for meat, starting again on the 28th, and reaching what was perhaps Kern River the 1st of August. It is not easy or necessary to trace their exact route. There were no serious hardships, though at first they were troubled by men who claimed some of the horses they had bought as stolen property; and later there was some difficulty in obtaining Indian guides. An unsuccessful effort was made to find Walker's pass, and then they directed their course for Sutter's Fort, where they arrived August 26th, encamping on the American River, two miles from the fort. Here they met Captain Hunt, who had come by the way of Monterey and San Francisco.[24] A few wished to remain over winter, to take advantage of Californian wages, and they were permitted to do so, Hancock

[23] *Bigler's Diary of a Mormon*, MS., 43 et seq. Closely followed by Tyler, 305 et seq. Elder Tyler a little earlier had a dream, or vision, in which 'the eyes of my understanding were then opened, and I was filled with the glory of God throughout my whole system. I saw that we travelled northward and eastward instead of south and east as anticipated;' and in which he foresaw many things and places connected with their journey and future destiny.

[24] Hunt is not named by the Mormon writers, but his arrival on the 25th is noted in *N. Helv. Diary*, and also that of other Mormons a day or two later and earlier. Some men of the battalion had been sent in advance of the main body to make arrangements with Sutter for supplies. Bigler gives many details, for which I have no space.

and Pettegrew deciding that it would be no sin, and all offering their prayers for success.

Part of the men left New Helvetia on the 27th, the rest following a day or two later to follow Kearny's trail over the Sierra. On September 5th the Mormons were at the scene of the Donner disaster, where many fragments of human bodies were lying unburied. Next day they met Samuel Brannan returning from a visit to the eastern saints. He announced the arrival of the advance party of immigrants in Salt Lake Valley, but gave a gloomy picture of prospects there, and advised all, except those whose families had reached Salt Lake, to turn back and work till spring, when very likely the church would be tired of the dreary desert and come to California. Presently, after Brannan's departure, Captain James Brown, originally of the battalion,[25] was met with letters for many, and an epistle from the twelve apostles, advising those of small means to remain in California through the winter. About half of the men followed this counsel, returning at once to New Helvetia, where they were

[25] Bigler says he had a detachment of the battalion, which had been left at Pueblo, and which was bound to Monterey to get their discharge papers. Neither the numbers nor names are given, unfortunately, because they should be included in my Pioneer Register. Probably there was but a small escort. In his report of Oct. 7th, Gov. Mason, *Cal. and N. Mex.*, *Mess. and Doc.*, *1850*, p. 355, writes: 'When on my way up to San Francisco, I was overtaken by Captain Brown of the Mormon battalion, who had arrived from Fort Hall, where he had left his detachment of the battalion to come to California to report to me in person. He brought a muster-roll of his detachment, with a power of attorney from all its members to draw their pay; and as the battalion itself had been discharged on the 16th of July, Paymaster Rich paid to Captain Brown the money due the detachment up to that date, according to the rank they bore upon the muster-rolls upon which the battalion had been mustered out of service. Captain Brown started immediately for Fort Hall, at which place and in the valley of Bear River he said the whole Mormon emigration intended to pass the winter. He reported that he had met Captain Hunt, late of the Mormon battalion, who was on his way to meet the emigrants and bring into the country this winter, if possible, a battalion, according to the terms offered in my letter to him of the 16th of August, a copy of which you will find among the military correspondence of the department. In my letter I offered Captain Hunt the command of the battalion, with the rank of lieutenant-colonel, with an adjutant; but I find, by the orders lately received, that a battalion of four companies is only entitled to a major and acting adjutant. I will notify Captain Hunt of this change at as early a moment as I can communicate with him. I am pleased to find by the despatches that in this matter I have anticipated the wish of the department.'

hired by Sutter to work on his mill-race. Bigler was of this party, and Tyler of those who continued their journey. The latter arrived at the Salt Lake settlement on October 16th.[26] Many remained here, but thirty-two kept on after a stay of only two days, and after a journey of two months without adventure calling for special notice joined their people at winter quarters on the Missouri River the 18th of December, 1847.

The company of reënlisted Mormon volunteers[27] started the 25th of July from Los Angeles for San Diego, where they arrived August 2d. Lieutenant Barrus with a detachment of twenty-seven men was sent a few days later to occupy San Luis Rey. Two of the company died during this second term of service. As before, the work of the Mormons was rather that of mechanics than of soldiers, since there were no disorders requiring military interference. Says the writer of one diary: "I think I whitewashed all San Diego. We did their blacksmithing, put up a bakery, made and repaired carts, and in fine, did all we could to benefit ourselves as well as the citizens. We never had any trouble with Californians or Indians, nor they with us. The citizens became so attached to us, that before our term of service expired they got up a petition to the governor to use his influence to keep us in the service. The petition was signed by every citizen in the town."[23] The term expired in January, but the men were not mustered out and paid off until the middle of March 1848. More than half remained for a time, some permanently, in California, scattering northward to the

[26] Tyler notes that they brought from Cal. various kinds of seeds, which were found very useful in the valley, especially the club-head wheat and a prolific variety of pea.

[27] The officers of this company were: Captain Daniel C. Davis; lieutenants, Cyrus C. Canfield, Ruel Barrus, and Robert Clift; sergeants, Edmund L. Brown, Samuel Myers, Benj. F. Mayfield, and Henry Packard. There were four corporals, two musicians, and 68 privates, whose names appear in my Pioneer Register.

[28] Henry G. Boyle's diary, in Tyler's Hist., 330.

mines, towns, and farms; but a party of twenty-five, under Boyle as captain, went to Williams' rancho to make ready for an overland journey. They started on April 12th with one wagon and 135 mules, followed the southern route by Mojave and the Santa Fé trail, and reached Salt Lake the 5th of June.

The experience of the detachment that returned to work through the winter at Sutter's Fort is clearly recorded in Bigler's diary, but belongs to the annals of the gold discovery, as recorded elsewhere.[29] In May 1848 preparations for a migration were begun, and Daniel Browett with a small party made a preliminary exploration for a new wagon route over the Sierra. By the end of June arrangements had been completed, about forty-five men[30] were gathered at Pleasant Valley, near Placerville, and Brouett with Allen and Cox had started in advance to make new explorations. The main company started on July 2d. Jonathan Holmes was leader, or president, and Lieutenant Thompson captain. On the 19th they found the bodies of Brouett, Allen, and Cox, who had been murdered by the Indians at a place that still bears the name of Tragedy Spring. The route was south of the lake and into Carson Valley, where they encamped the 5th of August. Thus with much toil but without serious disaster the Mormons opened a new wagon road over the mountains. Soon they struck the old Humboldt trail, on which they met several parties of emigrants, announcing to the latter the news that gold had been discovered. The arrival at Salt Lake was on September 25th. It should be added that a large part of the saints left behind by the different detachments of the battalion found their way, with many of Brannan's men, to the Salt Lake

[29] See vol. vi. of this work. Tyler in one place gives the number of this detachment as 40, but elsewhere says that more than half of the party turned back. The two statements seem contradictory, though the exact number of the eastward-bound company is not known.

[30] So says Bigler. Tyler says 37. There was one woman, the wife of Sergt Coray. There were 17 wagons, 150 horses and mules, and about the same number of cattle.

settlement in 1848–9, though a few spent the rest of
their lives in California.

Respecting Captain Hunt's project of raising a new
battalion of Mormons, we are told that Colonel Stevenson, by Governor Mason's instruction, wrote a letter to President Young on the subject, alluding to the
old prejudices against the saints, which in California
had been so completely dispelled by intercourse with
the volunteers until there had come to exist a strong
feeling of respect for them, and a general desire that
they should remain in the service and become permanent residents. But Young persisted in his view that
the original enlistment had been a necessary sacrifice,
which there was no call to repeat. According to Cannon, "he said he did not want the battalion to reënlist
for another six months. He regretted that he did not
have clothing for them; but he would rather wear
skins, he said, than go back to the United States for
clothes."[13] The probability would seem to be that
Young would gladly have furnished another battalion
had it still been the intention to establish his people
in California; but the determination to find their
promised land in Utah rendered it undesirable to part
with the bone and sinew of the saints.

Tyler appends to his admirable history of the battalion the record of a festival held by survivors and
their friends at Salt Lake City in February 1855, including speeches and reminiscences by comrades and
church dignitaries, including President Young. There
is a strong vein of religious faith running through all
that was said, making the record all the more fascinating. The old idea of the enlistment as a sacrifice that
saved the whole Mormon people from massacre was
brought out in an intensified form; indeed, the motto
of the festival was, "The Mormon battalion—a ram
in the thicket." The many hardships of the march,
the promised and fulfilled immunity from bloodshed,
the frequent miraculous cures of the sick, the wagon-

<hr>

[31] Geo. Q. Cannon's *History of the Church*, quoted in *Tyler's Hist.*, 343–5.

roads opened and other achievements, the prayers and piety of the men, the vain threats of Frémont and his wicked followers, the finding of gold, and the return to join the brethren in their new home—-all were pictured anew to eager listeners. Praise from president and others high in power was lavishly bestowed, with something of blame and no end of good counsel. Song and dancing supplemented the speech-making. It is pleasing to fill one chapter of a volume with saintly doings, even if they do not seem to differ very radically, but for certain peculiarities in the telling, from the deeds of those not of the faith as recounted in other chapters.

CHAPTER XIX.

NEW YORK VOLUNTEERS AND ARTILLERY COMPANY.

1846-1848.

CONGRESS CALLS FOR VOLUNTEERS—LETTER TO STEVENSON—POLICY OF THE
GOVERNMENT REVEALED—RECRUITING IN NEW YORK—IN CAMP AT
GOVERNOR'S ISLAND—CLARK'S HISTORY AND MURRAY'S NARRATIVE—
FIRST OR SEVENTH—LIST OF OFFICERS—CHARACTER OF THE MEN—CAMP
LIFE AND DRILL—POPULAR RIDICULE—DISCONTENT AND DESERTION—
HABEAS CORPUS—INSTRUCTIONS—STEVENSON'S TROUBLES—RESISTING
ARREST—A BAFFLED SHERIFF—NEWSPAPER COMMENT—VOYAGE OF THE
'PERKINS,' 'LOO CHOO,' AND 'DREW'—LATER VESSELS AND RECRUITS—
THE COLONEL'S VALOR—AT RIO—ARRIVAL AT SAN FRANCISCO—DISTRI-
BUTION OF THE COMPANIES—GARRISON LIFE—DISBANDMENT—COMPANY
F, 3D U. S. ARTILLERY—IN GARRISON AT MONTEREY—DESERTING FOR
THE MINES—SHERMAN'S MEMOIRS—BURTON'S COMPANY—THE DRAGOONS.

AN act of congress dated May 13, 1846, authorized
the president of the United States to call for and
accept the services of volunteers for the Mexican war,
and on June 26th the following communication was
addressed by William L. Marcy, secretary of war,
to Colonel Jonathan D. Stevenson of New York
City: "The president having determined to send a
regiment of volunteers around Cape Horn to the
Pacific, to be employed in prosecuting hostilities in
some province of Mexico, probably in Upper California, has authorized me to say that if you will organize
one on the conditions hereinafter specified, and tender
its services, it will be accepted. It is proper it should
be done with the approbation of the governor of New
York. The president expects, and indeed requires,
that great care should be taken to have it composed
of suitable persons—I mean persons of good habits—

as far as practicable of various pursuits, and such as would be likely to desire to remain, at the end of the war, either in Oregon or any territory in that region of the globe which may be then a part of the United States. The act of the 13th May last authorizes the acceptance of volunteers for twelve months, or during the war with Mexico. The condition of the acceptance in this case must be a tender of services during the war, and it must be explicitly understood that they may be discharged without a claim for returning home wherever they may be serving at the termination of the war, provided it is in the then territory of the United States, or may be taken to the nearest or most convenient territory belonging to the United States, and then discharged. The men must be apprised expressly that their term of service is for the war—that they are to be discharged as above specified, and that they are to be employed on a distant service. It is, however, very desirable that it should not be publicly known or proclaimed that they are to go to any particular province in Mexico. On this point great caution is enjoined. The communications to the officers and men must go so far as to remove all just ground of complaint that they have been deceived in the nature and place of the service. It is expected that the regiment will be in readiness to embark as early as the 1st of August next, if practicable. Steps will be immediately taken to provide for transportation."[1]

Stevenson was a colonel of militia, a ward politician, and ex-member of the legislature. Just what wires were pulled by him and his friends to secure this new position it is neither possible nor important to know; but he had done some service for the administration that seemed to call for reward, and he was reputed to be a man of some energy and executive ability.[2] The policy of the administration re-

[1] Report of sec. war, July 17, 1846. *Niles' Reg.*, lxx. 344.
[2] Thos C. Lancey, in his *New York Volunteers*, an article founded presum-

specting California is so well known to readers of this and the preceding volumes of my work as to require no further remark; but it must be noted that the letter to Stevenson which I have quoted, made public in July at the request of congress, was one of the earliest documents in which the administration clearly revealed its purpose to make the Mexican war one of permanent conquest, since the destination of the volunteers as settlers for California was but slightly veiled with a view to possible diplomatic contingencies. It was deemed but remotely possible that the men would arrive in time to aid in the conquest, but they might probably be utilized in garrison duty during the military occupation, and they would certainly serve as a nucleus for the Americanizing of the new province, either by remaining at the close of the war as settlers or—in case of unlooked-for happenings—by being disbanded in Oregon, to return as immigrants, and await or hasten the operations of manifest destiny. This newly revealed phase of the project naturally made the Stevenson letter a text for much comment in congress and elsewhere, but without important results.[3]

ably on an unpublished narrative by Col Stevenson, and printed as part of *Clark's First Regiment*, 52–68, gives some particulars, to the effect that Stevenson in the legislature had made a speech in support of the administration's policy in declaring war. Soon visiting Washington and hearing of the proposed Mormon battalion, he mentioned his desire to go to Cal. Postmaster-general Kendall, his friend, reported the remark to President Polk, who at once conceived the idea of sending a regiment of volunteers, an idea which, with the choice of a commander, was approved by John A. Dix, Daniel S. Dickinson, W. L. Marcy, and other prominent men consulted. At a subsequent interview the president questioned the colonel closely as to his previous pursuits and experience. The appointment was approved by the cabinet and by Gen. Scott. Stevenson returned home, received his instructions of June 26th, applied to the governor for permission to raise a regiment on June 30th, and on July 4th made the project public at a meeting of militia officers, the matter being published in the next morning's papers, and the work of recruiting being begun on the 7th. Frisbie, *Remin.*, MS., says that Stevenson owed his place to the friendship of Marcy.

[3] See speech of Ashmun of Mass., July 27, 1846, in H. of R. *Cong. Globe*, 1845–6, appen. 809. Mr A. caused to be read the Stevenson letter, and extracts from the administration organ in Washington. 'From these papers it will be seen, 1st, that the administration now openly proclaims that congress has declared war upon Mexico—that our government has made war openly in the face of the world! It is no longer half reluctantly asserted that the war exists by the act of Mexico; but boldly and unhesitatingly,

Recruiting offices were at once opened at different
points in New York City, and also at Albany, Bath,
and Norwich, three companies being raised outside of
the city, and seven mainly within its limits. The
recruiting officers were for the most part those who
became commissioned officers of the respective companies. No secret was made of the regiment's destination and prospective service, though in consequence
of the precautionary instructions already cited, there
was perhaps no formal publication of the colonizing
scheme. No volunteer dreamed of conflict with any
foe; all regarded themselves as immigrant adventurers
bound for a distant land of many charms, under the
protection of government. There was but slight pretence of patriotism, and no fear of danger; neither did
there present themselves at first any obstacles more
serious than the declamations of politicians who disapproved the Mexican war. By the end of July the
ranks of all the companies were filled, and they were
sent to Governor's Island, where on the 1st of August
the regiment—except apparently one or two companies from the interior—was mustered into the
United States service by Colonel Bankhead, commandant of the post.[4] The regiment was mustered
as the 7th N. Y. Volunteers, because arrangements

that we have made the war!' And after an analysis of the Stevenson letter,
he continues: ' It is no longer pretended that our purpose is to repel invasion
—to strike and defeat the military organizations which Mexico may set on
foot to contend for the boundaries of Texas. The mask is off; the veil is
lifted; and we see in the clearest characters invasion, conquest, and colonization emblazoned on our banners. We are no longer engaged in a defensive war; but we behold an expedition about to sail from New York to a distant region of the globe, which it cannot possibly reach in less time than
from four to six months, commanded by a mere political fortune-hunter of
not the highest character, and destined to accomplish the conquest and dis-
memberment of a sister republic, whose weakness seems to make her a ready
prey to men whose pursuits are those of plunder.'

[4] According to the official reports, there were 767 men at this time, and
Lancey makes the number 800 a little later. It had been the idea to raise
1,000 men. Clark's recapitulation of the muster-rolls shows a total of 844,
not perhaps including recruits who enlisted after the regiment sailed for Cal.
The official report, *House Ex. Doc.*, 24, 31st cong. 1st sess., p. 22ª, makes the
total number, including 188 recruits, 955 officers and men. If the whole regiment was mustered Aug. 1st, there must be errors in Clark's dates of arrival
of companies from the interior; but Murray also says the country companies
arrived later.

had been previously made for the organization of six other regiments from New York; but as the latter were never raised, or rather were consolidated into one, mustered into the service later, Stevenson's regiment became the 1st N. Y. Volunteers, and the name was formally changed by orders from the war department. But the other regiment had also been mustered in as the first, its colonel declined to comply with the order requiring a change, and Burnett's regiment is still known as the first in New York.[5] I append a list of regimental and company officers as taken from the muster-rolls by Francis D. Clark, and published in his latest monograph on the subject.[6]

[5] *Clark's First Regt*, 76, 91.
[6] *The First Regiment of New York Volunteers commanded by Col. Jonathan D. Stevenson, in the Mexican War. Names of the members of the regiment during its term of service in upper and lower California, 1847-8, with a record of all known survivors to the 15th day of April, 1882, and those known to have deceased, with other matters of interest pertaining to the organization and service of the regiment. Compiled by their comrade, Francis D. Clark.* New York, 1882, 8vo, 94 p., with an appendix of 16 p., bringing the record down to Aug. 1, 1883. Portraits of author and of Col. Stevenson. The author, a member of Co. D, and later resident of N. Y. City, began in 1870 to collect information respecting his surviving and dead comrades; and besides taking a prominent part in all anniversary reunions, serving as secretary, replying to toasts, and writing newspaper items on his chosen subject, published a *Roll of Survivors*, New York, 1871, single sheet, and again a *Roll of Survivors*, N. Y. 1874, 8vo, 20 p. He was secretary of the associated pioneers of the territorial days of Cal., and mainly the author of the pamphlet report of that organization. *Cal. Assoc. Pion.*, N. Y. 1875, 8vo, 58 p.; also contributing a narrative of his regiment's experience to the *Cal. Territorial Pioneers, First Annual*. He deserves much credit for his intelligent efforts, and his book calls for no unfavorable criticism so far as the author is concerned. As a monograph, however, the book might well have been made much larger by the addition of interesting personal and local reminiscences; and it does not speak well for the survivors of the regiment, many of whom are rich, that they did not give more encouraging support to the enterprise. Perhaps they reserved their best efforts for the time when the colonel's long-promised narrative shall appear.

Official list of 1st N. Y. Volunteers: Colonel Jonathan D. Stevenson, Lieut-col. Henry S. Burton, Major James A. Hardie, Surgeon Alex. Perry; Ass't surgeons, Robert Murray and Wm C. Parker; commissary, Capt. Wm G. Marcy; adjutant, Lieut J. C. Bonnycastle; ass't quartermaster, Capt. Joseph L. Folsom; sergeant-major, Alex. C. McDonald; quartermaster-sergeants, successively, Stephen Harris, Geo. G. Belt, and James C. Low; drum-major, Geo. Batchelor; chief musicians, Joseph Vevis and Frederic Grambis; sutler, Sam. W. Haight; clerk, James C. L. Wadsworth.

Co. A. Capt. Seymour G. Steele; lieutenants, Geo. F. Penrose, Charles B. Young, and Geo. F. Lemon; sergeants, S. O. Houghton, Walter Chipman, and Edward Irwin.

Co. B. Capt. James M. Turner (did not go to Cal.); lieutenants, Thomas

For names of all members of the regiment, officers
and privates, with biographical notices of many, I refer the reader to the Pioneer Register at the end of
this and the preceding volumes.   Five or six of the
officers were of the regular army and graduates of
West Point.   The regiment was almost exclusively
made up of young unmarried men, many of whom
were minors.   The leading motive for enlistment was
the immigrant's hope to better his condition in a new
country; many were attracted solely by a love of adventure, and but for the ice would as readily have
gone to the north pole; while others had records, as-
sociations, and debts, from which they were willing to
run away.   Captain Steele's company, if we may
credit the *Herald* of the time, was composed of tem-
perance men.   Mechanics were most numerous, including thirteen printers; and there were also clerks and
farmers.   Many were men of good education, family,
and prospects.   Says Walter Murray: "There were

E. Ketchum, Henry C. Matsell, and E. Gould Buffum; sergeants, Charles
Richardson, James G. Denniston, and *John Wilt.

Co. C.   Capt. John E. Brackett; lieutenants, Theron R. Per Lee, Thomas
J. Roach, Chas C. Anderson, Wm R. Tremmels (not in Cal.), and *Geo. D.
Brewerton; sergeants, Edmund P. Crosby, Wm Johnson, and *Geo. Robinson.

Co. D—many of its members from Philadelphia.   Capt. Henry M. Naglee; lieutenants, Geo. A. Pendleton, Hiram W. Theall, and Joseph C. Morehead; sergeants, Henry J. Wilson, Aaron Lyons, and Wm Roach.

Co. E.   Capt. Nelson Taylor; lieutenants, Edward Williams, Wm E.
Cutrell, and Thomas L. Vermeule; sergeants, John M. O'Neill, Henry S. Mor-
ton, and Abraham van Riper.

Co. F.   Capt. Francis J. Lippitt; lieutenants, Henry S. Carnes, Wm. H.
Weirick, John M. Huddart, and *Jeremiah Sherwood; sergeants, James
Mulvey, James Queen, John C. Pulis, and *Thomas Hipwood; chaplain, T.
M. Leavenworth.

Co. G.   Capt. Matthew R. Stevenson (son of the colonel); lieutenants,
John McH. Hollingsworth, Jeremiah Sherwood, *Wm W. Weirick, and
*Wm H. Smith; sergeants, John Connell, Geo. Jackson, Geo. Robinson,
Walter Taylor, and Wm B. Travers.

Co. H—raised at Albany, N. Y.   Capt. John B. Frisbie; lieutenants,
Edward Gilbert and John S. Day; sergeants, Eleazar Frisbie, Wm Grow,
Henry A. Schoolcraft, and James Winne.

Co. I—raised at Bath, N. Y.   Capt. Wm E. Shannon; lieutenants, Palmer B. Hewlett, Henry Magee, Wm H. Smith, and *John McH. Hollingsworth; sergeants, Joshua S. Vincent, Joseph Evans, and Joseph B. Logan.

Co. K—raised at Norwich, N. Y.   Capt. Kimball H. Dimmick; lieutenants, John S. Norris, Geo. C. Hubbard, Roderick M. Morrison, *Theron R.
Per Lee, and *Geo. D. Brewerton; sergeant, Jackson Sellers.

The names marked with a * are those of officers transferred to other companies, on the rolls of which they also appear.

men of pretty much every class except the most opulent; a large proportion of steady mechanics of all trades, with a smart sprinkling of the b'hoys of New York City, and not a few intemperates and ne'er-do-wells."[7] This rough element was strong enough to give the regiment a bad name in some respects, as we shall see. Some of the volunteers achieved later notoriety as criminals, ending their career in prison or on the gallows; while others could never so far forget their early training as to devote themselves to any other industry than the vicious one of machine politics in its different branches. Yet there can be no doubt that the standard of character and ability was much higher than in most volunteer regiments of this or any other period. An extraordinary number, both of officers and men, reached in their western home and elsewhere enviable positions in military and political life: as lawyers, judges, and merchants; as men of wealth and local influence. And a majority of the rest may point with pride to their humbler record as respectable law-abiding citizens. Without indorsing current declarations to the effect that "patriotism was the ruling motive of these brave men," we may suppose that under circumstances demanding such qualities they would have been as brave and patriotic as other men.

With military drill and discipline at the island camp, where the regiment remained nearly two months,

[7] *Narrative of a California Volunteer, by Hon. Walter Murray*, MS., 212 p. The author was a private of Co. A, detailed as cook during the encampment at Governor's Island, and in later years a prominent citizen of California. His narrative is by far the most complete extant on the enlistment, encampment in N. Y., voyage of the *Loo Choo*, and experience of his own and the other companies that served at Sta Bárbara and in Lower California. Unfortunately—though this does not much impair its value so far as regimental annals are concerned—the MS. terminates abruptly before the return of the writer to Alta California. John B. Frisbie's *Reminiscences*, MS., written in Mexico, 1884, contains some details about the history of the regiment.

Another original MS. in my possession is Capt. Albert G. Brackett's *Sketch of 1st Regiment New York Volunteers*. It is a carefully prepared account en résumé of the organization and achievements of the regiment, none the less creditable to the author from the fact that it is less complete than Clark's work published several years after this MS. was furnished for my use. The author is, I think, a son of Capt. Brackett of Co. C.

reality began to take the place of romance in the minds of many volunteers. Many ran away, and more escaped the service, more or less reluctantly, by the aid of their parents, armed with writs of habeas corpus, designated at the time as writs of 'non-Californium' by newspaper writers and others who were wont to refer flippantly to the 'baby regiment.' There were the usual ludicrous happenings in connection with the work of transforming raw recruits into soldiers; as when a sentinel, after repeated instructions that no one must be allowed to pass without the countersign, hailed the next comer with the conventional "Who goes there?" "A friend," was the reply. "Then say 'Newport,' or I'll shoot;" or when another guard started to chase a man who had eluded his vigilance, all the volunteers in sight following the two at full speed in their eagerness to bet on the result of the race. Murray also notes the disastrous effects of the coffee and other rations concocted by himself and other cooks of like inexperience. Because of political opposition to the project of sending out this body of warrior-colonists, and for lack of the excitement and solemnity sometimes arising on such occasions from prospective danger and bloodshed, Stevenson's regiment had to endure somewhat more than its due share of ridicule; but this did no harm, and the places of those that left the ranks were filled without much difficulty.[8]

Among those remaining as well as those who retired there were causes of dissatisfaction more or less serious. Recruiting officers had talked of land grants in California, and the men, when their first enthusiasm had cooled, realized that the government, to say nothing of lands, had not even bound itself to carry them to California at all. Then they were

[8] Besides the narratives already cited, the best authorities on the experience at Governor's Island are articles in various newspapers of the time, many of which I find reproduced or quoted in *Niles' Register*, vol. lxx.-i., passim. The *N. Y. Herald* of Aug. 10 and Sept. 6, 1846, gave to its readers pictures of the encampment.

legally entitled, under the laws of New York, to choose their own company officers; but in few cases, if any, were they really permitted to do so. Again, the prices charged for articles of clothing were deemed excessive, so much so that several companies refused to receive these articles on their pay account, being confined in consequence for insubordination. Somewhat serious disturbances were reported in the newspapers, and on one occasion at least the regular troops were called out to quell disorders.[9]

Late in August three stanch ships were chartered for $65,000—a reasonable rate, as even the newspapers admitted, though they did not fail to note a willingness on the part of certain friends of the administration to furnish inferior vessels at double the price—to carry the regiment round the Horn to the Pacific coast; and on board was placed a large and well chosen assortment of arms, munitions, and implements for war or peace. Instructions from the war department to Colonel Stevenson were dated September 11th. The regiment was to be a part of the force under General Kearny; but as the latter might not arrive so soon as the volunteers, the colonel might for a time find himself in chief command of the

[9] 'On the 18th the regiment was marched to the guard-house to receive their bounty money previous to embarking. The men of Co. C—the first company marched up—refusing to pay the prices charged for their clothing, viz.: $5 for jackets, $3 for pants, and $1.50 for caps. They were willing to pay a fair price, but were confined for insubordination. Co. A then came up, and refused. They were marched back to their quarters and confined to their tents. Col Bankhead, finding the refusal general, told them they would be compelled to embark without their pay—which they preferred to taking the clothing at the prices charged.' *Niles' Reg.*, lxxi. 57. 'The uniform of the regiment, which will soon be completed, designed by Major Hardie, is very neat and serviceable; pantaloons of dark mixed gray with scarlet strip or cord up the seam of the leg, blue coats with scarlet trimmings, a new style of French cap, very becoming; the first dress parade will take place next Sunday.' *N. Y. Herald*, Aug. 3, 1846. See also extracts from the *Union*, *U. S. Gazette*, and *Tribune*, in *Niles' Reg.*, lxxi. 386, 402. 'It is likely that some of the young men who expected to enjoy the "largest liberty" under the rule of such a colonel, and the most lawless license in the El Dorado they seek, will find themselves under restraints which they neither anticipated nor desired.' *N. Y. Com. Advocate*, in *Id.*, 20. 'We hear that a sort of court-martial was held on Governor's Island yesterday, and the ringleader in the recent kick-up there among Col Stevenson's volunteers was convicted of mutiny and ordered to be shot!' *Tribune*, in *Id.*, lxx. 402.

land forces. "It is not expected that you will be able to advance far into the country; nor is it advisable for you to undertake any hazardous enterprises. Until you shall fall under the command of General Kearny, your force will be mostly if not wholly employed in seizing and holding important possessions on the sea-coast;" but "where a place is taken by the joint action of the naval and land force, the naval officer in command, if superior in rank to yourself, will be entitled to make arrangements for the civil government of it while it is held by the coöperation of both branches;" so that Stevenson's chance to be for a brief time military governor of California was very slight. Instructions to Kearny and the naval commanders were enclosed to him, as were his to the others; but as the military occupation was completed and Kearny was on the ground long before the volunteers arrived, the policy as well as the facts of military occupation being moreover well known to the reader, there is no need of entering more fully into the details of this document.[10]

But while ships were ready and instructions signed there were yet vexatious delays of departure resulting from complications between the colonel and his enemies. It is not easy or very important to determine the merits or even the exact nature of the complications referred to, which are but vaguely recorded in papers of the time. The colonel's own version, as presented by Lancey, is in substance as follows: Thomas J. Sutherland, a military adventurer, being refused a position on the staff, used insolent and threatening language, and was ordered out of the tent and off the campground. In his anger he devoted himself to plots of vengeance, and some fifteen days before the time set for sailing Stevenson received a warning through the war department of prospective attempts to prevent his departure, and to make a certain captain, Shannon or Naglee, I suppose, colonel in his place. Presently,

[10] Sept. 11, 1848, Sec. Marcy to Stevenson. *Cutts' Conquest*, 248–50.

through a friend in the sheriff's office, there came more information, to the effect that seventy or eighty men who had joined the regiment, but had been unable at the last to pass the medical examination, had been induced to bring suit for false imprisonment, claiming damages to the amount of $80,000. Writs of attachment were made out and were to be served on the day of sailing; but thanks to the warning, Stevenson was able to baffle the efforts of his foes and to escape the sheriff's posse.[11] There is no good reason to question the general accuracy of this testimony, though there is room for suspicion that it does not include quite the whole truth, that the suits for false imprisonment were not the only ones pending, and that all opposition to the gallant colonel did not proceed from the plots of the disappointed Sutherland. The evidence extant is for the most part vague, and it may involve nothing more discreditable to Stevenson's reputation than the fact that the class of metropolitan politicians which he represented was not—in 1846—regarded as meriting unqualified praise. I append some extracts which will illustrate the spirit of the time, showing what

[11] Lancey, in *Clark's First Reg.*, 55, etc. Embarking the troops in great haste, Col S. gave orders that no one should be permitted to board or leave the vessel without his written permission; and men were stationed at different points with 32-pound shot to sink any boat that might persist in making fast. Several attempts were made by officers of the law to reach the colonel by sending false messages or false names, and by other devices; and once the heavy shot was dropped alarmingly near a boat belonging to the foe. At midnight the colonel with an escort armed to the teeth found his way with muffled oars to hold a parting interview with his three motherless daughters in Brooklyn. For two days after the forces embarked a strict guard was kept up. The guns were manned, loaded with grape and canister, and kept ready for instant service. S. explained to a few trusty friends 'that he intended to resist arrest at all hazards, even if the sheriff's boat had to be blown out of the water'! The pilot of an approaching steamer was given five seconds to back off, or be a dead man, and he chose to save his life. And finally, as the flag-ship was towed out to sea, another steamer bearing the sheriff's posse left the wharf in pursuit, but was distanced in the race. About five miles out the colonel made a parting visit to the other two ships; and on the *Susan Drew*, 'did not notice the extended hand' of the captain who had plotted against him and who was to have been make colonel. 'When, however, this gentleman placed his hand in his, Col S. looked him steadily in the eye. The officer at that glance flushed guiltily, and knew then that the colonel was aware of his perfidy toward him. Slowly the checkmated villain withdrew his hand and slunk away '!

was thought and said of the volunteers and their commander.[12]

The departure from New York was on the 26th of

[12] In his speech of July 27th in congress, Ashmun says of the Stevenson letter: 'It is addressed—not to an officer of the army whose habits and education fit him for mere military service of the ordinary kind—not to a man who has been distinguished by any public service in the field—but a mere political adventurer, who is only known to the world as a partisan from the neighborhood of the Five Points, and the region where the Empire Club holds sway, and where the doctrine that "to the victors belong the spoils" is acknowledged and practised.' *Cong. Globe*, 1845-6, app. 809. There was some jealousy on the part of other volunteer organizations for favors shown to this regiment, especially as a son of Sec. Marcy was to go as paymaster. *Mechanics' Journal*, in *Niles' Reg.*, lxx. 344. 'For ourselves, we have never believed that this expedition would sail under the command of J. D. Stevenson; and warrant for such an opinion may be found in the well known Glentworth affair. A man who has ever found it necessary to be an *alias* should never be intrusted with a military command, or made the associate and companion of gentlemen. How Gov. Marcy can justify it to his conscience and to the country for having recommended Stevenson for this highly important command we cannot conjecture.' *N. Y. Courier and Enquirer*, in *Id.*, 416. The same paper prints some of Sutherland's charges, in substance as follows: 1st, forcing the men to purchase unsuitable clothing at excessive prices, his son-in-law being the pretended contractor. 2d, falsely reporting company rolls as complete, in order to obtain commissions for incompetent favorites. 3d, using his influence to exclude men of capacity and experience (that is, Sutherland himself!), and accepting only men who would become his 'suppliant underlings.' 4th, declaring his intention to run away from his government convoy, and not to obey the president's orders in Cal.! And 5th, duplicity practised on president, governor, and others, 'unbecoming an officer and a soldier.' In the *S. F. Californian*, Oct. 6, 1847, is an extract from the *N. Y. Express* on statements in the legislature on the clothing swindles. 'The difficulties are not yet ended. The colonel has chartered four vessels, but as things look now, one will be amply sufficient, unless he sails very soon. The circuit court is crowded this morning with the parties and witnesses to a case of *habeas corpus*, which is to test the legality and validity of Col Stevenson's commission. Gen. Sutherland continues to be the active instrument of opposition, and will perhaps succeed in breaking up the enterprise. If he does not, it will fall to pieces of itself, most likely. In either case, a partisan of the govt has been liberally rewarded, and it is "all right."' *North American*, in *Niles' Reg.*, lxxi. 39. 'Col Jonathan D. Stevenson—a motion was yesterday made for the appointment of a receiver of the property and effects of this gentleman, upon a creditor's bill filed against him, in which N. Dane Ellingwood was complainant. The motion was granted. Will not this stop his supplies from the government? He is also under bail, which was put in upon his arrest under a writ of *ne exeat* to stay within the jurisdiction of the court.' *N. Y. Tribune*, in *Id.*, 57. 'The Cal. expedition is off at last, shorn somewhat of its numeric force, as it has long been almost wholly of its moral. Its departure has been signalized by a prolongation of that unhappy compound, made up almost equally of misfortune and misconduct, which has attended it from the beginning; and it requires no very abiding or superstitious faith in omens to believe that the issue will be useless and inglorious in strict conformity with the inception and progress.' 'We put on record at this time our unhesitating confidence that as a specimen of utter hopeless failure this Cal. expedition will stand without a superior, perhaps without an equal, in the annals of any nation'! *Com. Advertiser*, Sept. 28, 1846, in *Id.*, 68. More of the Ellingwood suit in Nov. *Gazette and Times*, in *Id.*, 146.

September. Each of the three transports carried three complete companies and part of another, Company E being the one that was divided. The *Thomas H. Perkins*, 697 tons, under Captain James P. Arther, well known in California, bearing the commander's penant, carried companies B, F, and G, with Colonel Stevenson, Surgeon Perry, and Quartermaster Folsom. The *Loo Choo*, 639 tons, James B. Hatch master, and also familiar with the western coast, carried companies A, C, and K, under the command of Major Hardie, having also on board Assistant-surgeon Parker and Chaplain Leavenworth. The *Susan Drew*, 701 tons, Putman master, carried companies D, I, and H, under the command of Lieutenant-colonel Burton, with Commisary Marcy and Assistant-surgeon Murray. All the fleet was under the convoy of the U. S. sloop-of-war *Preble*. So sudden was the departure, for reasons that have been given, that over forty men and officers, including Captain Taylor and lieutenants Vermeule and Penrose, were left behind. These men were despatched on November 13th on the *Brutus*, Adams master, under Captain Taylor. Subsequently two hundred recruits were raised by the efforts of Captain Turner, who had returned from Rio Janeiro. Half of this force sailed on the *Isabella*, Briggs master, from Philadelphia, under Lieutenant Thomas J. Roach; and the other half on the *Sweden*, Knott master, from New York, under Lieutenant Thomas E. Ketchum— all in August 1847.

The voyage of all the transports was a most uneventful one. On the *Perkins* it is related that Captain Arthur had laid in a store of poultry as a consideration of being permitted to join the officers' mess, but subsequently changed his mind with a view to sell his chickens. The officers refused to purchase, but the men were not averse to stealing, and the captain's speculation was not a profitable one. Not many of the volunteers were able to resist sea-sickness, which kept the colonel for several days in his state-room, and left him "but the ghost of his former self," and so weak that for a long time he had to be supported by two soldiers; but the weakness was of the body and not of the spirit, if we are to judge by Stevenson's own account of his methods in enforcing discipline and quelling incipient mutiny.[13] During the last week of November all the ships were together at Rio Janeiro, where certain complications between the United States minister and the Brazilian government afforded the warlike colonel and his men an opportunity to show their patriotic enthusiasm. They even had the honor of adding something to the diplomatic difficulties. To the quartermaster-sergeant's wife had been born on the *Perkins* a daughter, and at her christening as Alta California Harris, Minister Wise indulged in some comparisons between the event and the recent christening of a "royal bantling of the Brazilian nation." For this patriotic pleasantry the government was thought to be contemplating an order that every American vessel must quit the port. No such order, however, was issued, and consequently the New York volunteers did not appear with fixed bayonets in the streets of Rio. All sailed again at the end of November, and proceeded on their uneventful way round Cape Horn. Murray describes the

[13] A sergeant in transmitting orders to his detachment said: 'I have given you the order, and I don't care a damn whether you obey it or not.' For this the colonel reduced him to the ranks, and set him to cleaning the ship. For refusing to perform this duty he was triced up by the thumbs and wrists. This caused discontent, 'until at length, seeking to frighten Col S. into relaxing his severity, Capt. Folsom, who had before presumed on his superior's friendship, entered his cabin, and in rather an insolent manner said to him: "Col S., do you know that there will be a mutiny on this vessel this afternoon?" "No, sir," replied Col S., "but I do know that there will not be a mutiny. And further, Capt. F., you know that I sleep over 900 tons of gunpowder, but you do not know, sir, that I have a train laid from that powder to my berth." "What?" stammered the captain. "Col S., you surely do not mean to say—" "Yes, sir, I do; and you can rest assured that before I will suffer the command of this vessel to pass from me there will not be a plank left for a soul on board to cling to; and now, sir, let the mutiny proceed"! Pale as a spectre, and with eyes fairly emerging from their sockets, the thoroughly alarmed officer hastily excused himself and hurried forward, where he no doubt imparted the fearful threat.' What slight traces of mutiny still remained disappeared after the colonel had promptly knocked down a soldier who spoke disrespectfully of his authority. *Lancey*, 63–4.

voyage of the *Loo Choo,* but his narrative contains nothing calling for notice, unless it be the drowning of a sailor near the cape, the death of Lieutenant Tremmels in a fit of apoplexy, caused by the excitement of the accident, and a narrow escape from grounding in entering Valparaiso, where this craft and the *Drew* arrived in January 1847, the other transport not entering any port between Rio and San Francisco.

The *Perkins* was first to reach San Francisco, where she landed the first detachment of volunteers the 6th of March, 1847. Next to arrive was the *Drew,* on the 19th; while the *Loo Choo,* which had been first at Rio and at Valparaiso, was delayed by a calm in the tropics, and did not anchor at Yerba Buena till March 26th. The *Brutus,* bringing the men who had been left behind, without having touched at any port after leaving New York, arrived on April 18th; and the next day the convoy *Preble* came into port, having touched at Callao.[14] As offensive military operations were at an end, and General Kearny was at Monterey, it only remained to put the regiment at his disposal for garrison duty. Companies H and K were stationed at the San Francisco presidio, under Major Hardie as commandant of the post, with Captain Folsom and Dr Parker; and here these companies remained to the end of their service, except that Company H exchanged posts with the Sonoma company for a short time in August 1848. Companies A, B, and F were assigned to Santa Bárbara, under the command of Lieutenant-colonel Burton, with Surgeon Perry; and

[14] The dates of arrival are given in the *S. F. Cal. Star,* March 13, 27, April 24, 1847. In *Larkin's Doc.,* MS., iv. 33, I have a letter of Capt. Arther of the *Perkins,* dated March 6th, the date of arrival. Stevenson desired Arther to carry his troops to Monterey, but the captain refused, demanding $5,000 for the trip, or later $3,000. He published a defence of his action in the *Star,* where some unfavorable criticism had appeared. Murray, *Narr.,* 55–6, says the first comers told those who arrived later a dismal story of the country, the climate, and the prospective dog's-life before the volunteers. Alfred A. Green's *Life and Adventures of a '47er,* MS., may be noticed here as containing a brief narrative of the voyage, which is alluded to in few words by several members of the regiment who have given me their reminiscences. The *Isabella* and *Sweden,* with two hundred recruits, arrived at Monterey in February of the next year.

they sailed on March 31st in the *Moscow*, landing the 8th of April. Company F remained at Santa Bárbara during the whole term of its service; but A and B sailed for La Paz the 4th of July, leaving Captain Lippitt in command of the post. Companies D, E, G, and I left San Francisco in the *Lexington* April 3d for Monterey. Company D engaged in some expeditions in pursuit of Indian horse-thieves, and the 5th of March, 1848, sailed for La Paz in the *Isabella*, with the recruits that had come on that vessel. Companies E and G left Monterey in the *Lexington* May 5th, and served as a garrison at Los Angeles from the 9th to the time of their discharge, Colonel Stevenson being commandant of the post and of the southern district. Company I remained at the capital till December 28th, then going to garrison San Diego in place of the Mormons, the post being from that time under the command of Captain Shannon. Finally Company C left San Francisco in April, and was stationed at Sonoma under Captain Brackett. A detachment of twenty-five men were sent to garrison Sutter's Fort from June to September, under Lieutenant Anderson. In May 1848 the company was ordered to Lower California, but was sent back to Sonoma from Monterey; and on August 5th it went to San Francisco, being replaced on the northern frontier by Frisbie's men of Company H.[15]

After the arrival of the volunteers and their distribution to the different garrisons, there is but little to be added to regimental annals but the record of disbandment. The men performed their military duties well enough, though at several points there were complaints of disorderly conduct on the part of the rougher element; but their real achievements, as wisely in-

---

[15] The distribution is given in *Clark's First Regiment;* in *Brackett's Sketch*, MS.; in the *S. F. Californian* of April 10, 1847; and scattered items are found in many different accounts, which there is no need to specify, since Clark's work is entirely satisfactory. The services of Naglee's company, as mounted men, against the Indians, are mentioned in Mason's reports of June 18th and Oct. 7th. *Cal. and N. Mex., Mess. and Doc., 1850*, p. 312, 355.

tended by the government from the first, were not as
soldiers, but as settlers and citizens of a new country,
under circumstances in some respects more wonder-
fully favorable than had been dreamed by the youth-
ful adventurers in New York. Petty happenings of
garrison life—though fully related by Murray for
Santa Bárbara, and less completely elsewhere by
other writers—do not belong to the history of the
regiment, but to local annals of the garrison towns,
not very exciting even when eked out with occurrences not military in their nature. An accidental
explosion at Los Angeles on the 9th of December,
1847, by which several men were killed and others injured, was perhaps the most notable event in this connection. The companies that were sent south saw
some actual service in the peninsula, losing two men
in battle, but their experience belongs to another part
of my work.[16]

The volunteers had enlisted 'for the war,' and
accordingly, on receipt of news that the war had been
ended by the treaty of May 30th, orders were issued
by Governor Mason for the mustering-out of the
regiment. This was on August 7, 1848. On the
15th Lieutenant Hardie of the 3d artillery—major of
the regiment, who now resumed his position in the
regular army, but retaining command of the post—
mustered out companies C and K at San Francisco,
and Company H on the 25th as soon as it arrived from
Sonoma. Captain A. J. Smith of the 1st dragoons
mustered out Company F at Santa Bárbara the 8th of
September, the staff companies E and G at Los
Angeles on the 18th, and Company I at San Diego on
the 25th. The remaining companies, A, B, and D,
on their arrival from Lower California, were mustered
out by Captain Burton of the 3d artillery, late lieutenant-colonel of the volunteers, at Monterey on October
23d and 24th. The field-officers were mustered out

---

[16] See *Hist. North Mex. States*, ii., this series. These companies returned
in the *Ohio*, arriving at Monterey Oct. 14, 1848.

by Captain Burton at Monterey the 26th of October.
In his report of December 27th to the war department, giving details of the disbandment, Governor
Mason wrote in complimentary terms of Stevenson,
Burton, and Hardie, and of the faithful and efficient
service each had rendered in his district, extending
the praise also to subaltern officers and soldiers. I
append in a note some items of interest on the disbandment, gleaned from the official documents.[17]

[17] *Cal. and N. Mex., Mess. and Doc., 1850*, containing all the correspondence. Sept. 18, 1847, bad conduct of Lippitt's men at Sta Bárbara, Mason's
report. p. 335.   Nov. 11th, 'Lieut Burton reports much insubordination, and
that the company officers have little or no control over their men.   A similar
state of things exists among some of the companies in Upper Cal.' p. 422.
June 17, 1848, Brackett's company at Sonoma reduced from 60 to 23 men
by desertions for the gold-fields. p. 621-3. Aug. 7th, Lieut W. T. Sherman
(a. a. a. general) to Maj. Hardie.   Order to discharge the volunteers at S. F.
Maj. Rich, the U. S. paymaster, is expected on the *Olga* to pay off the
men, but they must be discharged and wait for pay if he does not arrive. p.
633. Aug. 7th, Id. to comandante at S. José, to proceed with detachment to
S. F. for discharge.   This is the only record I find of such a detachment. p.
633.   Aug. 11th, Sherman to Capt. A. J. Smith, who is to go south on the
Anita to discharge the southern companies.   Unserviceable property was to
be sold at auction.   'As many citizens may feel insecure in consequence of the
withdrawal of all military force, you are authorized to leave with the alcalde
or other trusty citizen a few arms and some ammunition, taking his receipt
for the same.   The arms will be delivered out of those which were taken from
the citizens of Cal. during the past war, and may be distributed to persons
who can be trusted, who stand in need of such protection.' p. 637-8.   Aug.
16th, Sherman to Quartermaster Folsom at S. F.   Volunteers to be paid according to laws of congress and instructions of the war dept.   Gov. M. 'is
not aware of any law that entitles officers of this regiment to mileage, or any
other allowance, to the place of enrolment.' p. 638. Aug. 21st, Id. to Paymaster Rich at S. F.   He is to go south on the *Anita*, after turning over to
Maj. Hardie money to pay the S. F. volunteers lately mustered out. p. 639.
Aug. 20th, Stevenson to Mason.   An appeal that the volunteers in the south
be permitted to retain their arms, and to have 15 days' rations.   Otherwise
they will be left in a bad condition, with scanty means to reach the mines.
The Mormons were allowed to retain their arms, and were furnished transportation to Salt Lake, for less service than that of the N. Y. volunteers; and
Gen. Kearny had assured S. that like favors should be shown to Stevenson's
men. p. 644-5. Aug. 26th, Sherman in reply for Mason declines to permit
the retention of arms.   The Mormons kept theirs by a special agreement at
the time of enlistment; Gen. Kearny left no instructions on the subject, or
record of his promise; and moreover, it would be unwise to leave U. S. guns
of late patterns in the hands of private individuals, because in such case it
would be impossible to distinguish these arms from those improperly acquired.
But as to rations, if Maj. Rich decides against allowing any travelling expenses, provisions will be given for the journey to Monterey or S. F.; and
women, sick men, etc., will be transported on the *Anita*. p. 642. Aug. 21st,
Sherman to Capt. Lippitt.   The auction sale of provisions will give the Sta
Bárbara men a chance to get supplies for their journey to the mines. S. to
Hardie, permitting the issue of a certificate of honorable discharge. Id. to
Id., about paying off the men, Rich not having arrived. p. 640. Aug. 25th,

Official statistics of the regiment as published in the government documents are as follows: Mustered in at New York in August 1846, 38 officers and 729 men; joined later, 188 men; officers resigned, six; men discharged, 136; died, 33; killed in action, two; killed by accident, seven; wounded by accident, two; deserted, 323; mustered out in California 1848, 39 officers and 658 men. According to Clark's researches, nothing is known respecting the death or whereabouts if living of about four hundred and fifty of the men. Of the rest about one hundred and thirty were living in California as late as 1883, and about the same number had died in California before that date. On their discharge nearly all found their way as soon as possible to the gold mines, whence year by year such as did not die there scattered with and without gold over the Pacific territories. Their fate was far from being the disastrous one predicted by hostile newspapers at the start. The volunteers performed well enough the duties assigned them as soldiers and settlers; and the result fairly justified the views of the administration that promoted the organization. The colonel, the oldest man in the regiment at starting, was still a resident and federal office-holder of San Francisco in 1885; while not a few other members of

Anita at Mont., awaiting Rich. Aug. 28th, Rich had arrived, and had paid off S. F. volunteers. p. 603–4, 643–4. Oct. 9th, sec. of war to Col Mason. Volunteers insisting on returning to the U. S. might be retained in the service until an opportunity for return occurred. If discharged in Cal., they will be entitled to 3 months' extra pay. p. 258. I find no other record about this extra pay. Dec. 27th, Mason's report to sec. of war. 'About the time of the disbanding of the three companies from L. Cal. at this place (Monterey), some of the individuals of these companies committed gross acts of pillage upon public and private property, took forcible possession of a public building belonging to the town authorities, which they occupied for some days, and wantonly injured to a considerable extent.' p. 649–53. March 3d, Mason writes that many of the volunteers had brought with them to Cal. arms and ammunition, which they sold to Californians. All that could be found were seized, to be returned after the war was over. p. 488. In the *S. J. Pioneer* of Nov. 21, 1877, is an account of the circumstances attending the mustering-out of the last companies at Monterey, and the men's departure for the mines. The facts and dates of the disbandment are also given in *Clark's First Regiment*. It appears that Lieut Sherwood, being absent on detached service at the mustering-out of his company, was not formally discharged until 1873.

the regiment held positions of honor in California and elsewhere.[18]

The first United States troops sent to California after the declaration of war against Mexico were companies C and K, first dragoons, marching from Santa Fé under General Kearny, and arriving in December 1846. Next came the Mormon volunteer battalion, which, crossing the continent, forded the Colorado and entered California on January 10, 1847. The third detachment was an artillery company of the regular army, which came by sea later in January. Fourth was the regiment of New York volunteers, arriving by sea in March of the same year; and finally, at the end of 1848, there came overland from Chihuahua four additional companies of dragoons under Major Graham. Three of the five bodies of troops have been noticed in this and earlier chapters; the other two, the artillery company and dragoon battalion, require attention here.

Company F third artillery was composed mainly of new recruits enlisted for a term of five years in Pennsylvania and Maryland during the spring of 1846. About half the company were foreigners, chiefly Irish and German. It was organized and drilled at Fort McHenry, and thence transferred to Governor's Island, its captain, Henry S. Burton, accepting a command in the New York volunteers, and his place being taken by Captain Christopher Q. Tompkins. The first lieutenants were Edward O. C. Ord and William T. Sherman; the second lieutenants, Lucien Loeser and Colville J. Minor. Dr James L. Ord, not of the army, served by contract as assistant surgeon; and Lieutenant Henry W. Halleck of the engineers ac-

---

[18] Statistics in *U. S. Govt Doc.*, 31st cong. 1st sess., H. Ex. Doc. 24, p. 22ª. In addition to authorities on Stevenson's regiment already mentioned, I might cite a long list of newspaper articles, chiefly in the form of anniversary reunions, speeches, and lists of survivors; but these furnish nothing in addition to what has been presented, except biographical material utilized elsewhere.

companied the detachment. The rank and file numbered 113 men.[19] General Scott's instructions to Tompkins were dated June 20, 1846;[20] and on the 14th of July the company embarked on the U. S. ship *Lexington*, commanded by Theodorus Bailey, the vessel carrying also a large supply of guns and military stores. The voyage was an uneventful one, without a single death or other casualty; and is well described, like the company's later experience, by General Sherman in his memoirs.[21] Touching at Rio Janeiro, doubling Cape Horn in October, and calling at Valparaiso in November, the *Lexington* anchored at Monterey on January 28, 1847, after being driven up to the latitude of San Francisco.[22]

The artillerymen of Company F on landing at Monterey relieved the naval garrison under Maddox and Baldwin, took possession of the block-house on the hill and of the custom-house, soon building an additional fort, and some of the officers being quartered at private houses in the town. Captain Tompkins resigned his place and went east on a sailing vessel in

[19] See all the names in my Pioneer Register at the end of these volumes. A copy of the muster-roll has been furnished me from Washington by Adj.-gen. L. C. Duncan. The roll contains 131 names; but as other authorities give the number at starting as 112 or 113 men and 5 officers, it is probable that the others were later recruits. The names are given also by Kooser and Lancey. The non-commissioned officers were as follows: sergeants, Charles Layton, John E. Noble, James H. Carson, Harvey Maxim, Lewis Curman, and Patrick Hand; corporals, Richard H. Bell, Patrick Reid, Henry A. Hoffman, and Owen Leavy.

[20] In *Cutts' Conq. Cal.*, 251–2. Similar in purport to instructions to other officers already given. He was to coöperate with the naval officers, to take charge of ordnance and army stores, to erect and defend forts, etc. The artillerymen were to be merely passengers on the U. S. ship, except in case of action, when they were to render aid.

[21] *Memoirs of General William T. Sherman. By himself.* New York, 1875, 8vo, 2 vols. Chap. i. p. 1–60, is devoted to 'early recollections of California,' 1847–8. The narrative is interesting and valuable, though in minor details the author is not always an accurate witness.

[22] Kooser makes the date of arrival Jan. 23d, and Sherman Jan 26th; but Lancey, *Cruise of the Dale*, 211 et seq., seems to be the best authority, being an entry from his original diary. Lancey gives a good account of the company's history, including the substance of the accounts by Sherman and Kooser. Dr Ord, *Remin.*, MS., makes the date of arrival Jan. 27th. In the *Monterey Californian*, Jan. 28, 1847, it is stated that the *Lexington* 'has just arrived.' See also *S. F. Calif.*, Feb. 6, 1847; *S. F. Cal. Star*, Feb. 6, 1847. In *Niles' Reg.*, lxxi. 146, is a letter from a member of the company at Rio, Sept. 11th.

May.   Lieutenant Sherman acted at first as quartermaster and commissary, and later as assistant adjutant-
general under Colonel Mason, serving only for a very
brief period as company officer.   Lieutenant Minor
died in August of a malignant disease brought from
Manila on the *Columbus*, which also killed nine of the
soldiers.   Thus Ord and Loeser were chiefly in charge
of the company, until the latter in the summer of
1848 was sent east with despatches, and a little later,
on the disbandment of Stevenson's regiment, Captain
Burton resumed his original place in command of the
company.   Garrison life at Monterey, though a feature
in local annals of the town and in the personal reminiscences of the company's members, had no salient
points which can be brought out in the space at my
command.   Private Benjamin Kooser, who spent the
rest of his life in California, being well known as editor of several newspapers, wrote several interesting
articles on the annals of the company.[23] Sergeant
Carson was another who gained some reputation as a
writer in later years.[24]   Sherman, Ord, and Halleck
acquired a great national reputation as military commanders after having taken somewhat prominent
parts in Californian affairs; and information about the
more humble career of other officers and soldiers of
Company F may be found in other parts of this work.

The discovery of gold furnished an attraction more irresistible to the regulars than to the volunteers, because
they could not like the latter look forward to an early
discharge.   Accordingly they took advantage of every
favorable opportunity to desert for the mines.   By the
end of August there had been thirty-three desertions,

[23] *Kooser's Pioneer Soldiers of California*, published in the *S. F. Alta*, 1864,
being then partly reproduced from the *San Andreas Independent* of an earlier
date, and all reproduced in the *S. José Pioneer*, Jan. 19, 1878.   See also *Twenty
Years Ago in Cal.*, in *S. F. Bulletin*, Jan. 31, 1867, from the *Sta Cruz Sentinel*.
These articles contain names and reminiscences of the writer's comrades, 46
of whom were known to have died before 1864, and 16 were known to be
living.
[24] *Carson's Early Recollections of the Mines*, Stockton, 1852, being the first
book printed at Stockton.

and only about fifty men were on duty.[25] The movement continued, though we have no further statistics, and in September Governor Mason began to grant furloughs for a few months to trustworthy soldiers who desired a few months of mining life. A few remained faithful to the end of their term in 1851, and some even reënlisted. After an absence in the Tulares and at San Diego, the company, renewed for the most part, served again at Monterey from 1852 to 1857, being then sent to Fort Yuma, where in 1864 one of the original members, William Rafter, still answered to the roll-call.[26]

A small company of volunteer cavalry was mustered into service at Monterey in April 1847, under the command of Lieutenant B. Burton, and rendered some service against the Indians with Naglee's men during the rest of the year, being mustered out in December.[27] The *Huntress* brought a detachment of recruits from New York in September 1848, of whom nothing is known, except that, according to Mason's report of November 24th, "just so fast as they recovered sufficiently from the scurvy to leave the hospital, they went off" for the mines; and in December only twelve of the number remained on duty.[28] The dragoons of Company C, under Captain Smith and Lieutenant Stoneman, including the members of the original Company K, numbered eighty-three men in August 1848, having lost none by desertion as long as they were kept on garrison duty in the south; but on being transferred to San Franciso and other northern points about this time, desertions began, as had been predicted.[29]

[25] *Cal. and N. Mex., Mess. and Doc., 1850*, p. 603, 643.

[26] *Kooser's Pion. Sold.* He gives a blank form of the first furlough granted by Mason.

[27] *U. S. Govt Doc.*, 31st cong. 1st sess., H. Ex. Doc., 24, p. 22 *h; Cal. and N. Mex., Mess. and Doc., 1850*, p. 355–8.

[28] *Id.*, 648–9; *S. José Pioneer*, Nov. 21, 1877.

[29] *Cal. and N. Mex., Mess. and Doc., 1850*, p. 603, 633, 638, 642–3, 648. Nineteen men under Stoneman sent to S. F. in Aug. Twelve desertions before Nov. 24th.

After the war was ended in Mexico a battalion of dragoons marched from Coahuila in August 1848, by way of Chihuahua and Tucson, to California. It consisted of companies A and E first dragoons, under Lieutenant Cave J. Coutts and Captain Daniel H. Rucker, and companies D and E second dragoons, under lieutenants Reuben P. Campbell and Elias K. Kane, acting as captains. It was under the command of Brevet Major Lawrence P. Graham of the second dragoons, and numbered 275 men, besides 205 teamsters and other workmen enlisted for a year from July 1st, or nearly 500 men in all. They left Chihuahua at the beginning of September, were at Tucson late in October, crossed the Colorado into California late in November, and arrived at Warner's rancho on December 29th. The journey is well described by Coutts in his diary, a copy of which is in my possession. It was attended by much toil and hardship, most of which, according to the writer, was due to the incompetence and drunkenness of the commander. Between him and the company officers, and among the latter, there was much dissension on the march and later. I have no space for the quarrels or for details of the march; and the Californian experience of this battalion does not come within the limits of this volume. So late did the dragoons arrive that they had no opportunity even to desert for the mines before the end of the year; and I have not thought it best to include their names in my Pioneer Register. Major Graham was commandant in the south, and several of the officers were somewhat prominent in 1849; but, with the exception of Colonel Coutts,[30] who became a leading citi-

[30] *Coutts' Diary of a March to California in 1848*, MS. Copied in 1874 from the original furnished by the author. It includes some experiences of 1849, among others the service of Coutts' company as escort to the boundary commission. Sherman, *Memoirs*, i. 61, mentions the arrival of Graham's battalion, as does Gov. Mason in his report of Dec. 27th. *Cal. and N. Mex., Mess. and Doc., 1850*, p. 649; also items relating to the dragoons in 1849, in *Id.*, 690–915, passim. In the report cited Mason says: 'I was in hopes that the news of the discovery of the gold mines in this country, together with its effects on the troops stationed here, would have reached the department before any more were ordered out, for every day adds to my conviction that no sol-

zen of southern California, little is heard of officers or men in the country's later annals.

dier should be sent to California for some years to come, unless congress provide them pay bearing some proportion to the amount they can make in the country, and, at the same time, devise some laws by which deserters, and those who entice them away, employ them, and purchase from them their arms, accoutrements, clothing, and other public property, which they steal and carry off, can be more summarily and severely punished; the present laws being entirely inadequate, as long experience has proved. Troops are needed here, and greatly needed; but of what use is it to send them, with the positive certainty of their running off to the gold mines as soon as they arrive, taking with them whatever public property they can lay their hands on ? To arrest them is impossible, as they receive every encouragement to desert and every facility to elude pursuit. I cannot but apprehend that Major Graham's men will desert nearly as fast as the horses recover strength to travel, for the wages in the country continue as extravagant as when I last wrote, and the gold mines hold out fully as tempting a prospect as ever.'

CHAPTER XX.

PIONEERS—DONNER PARTY—THE MORMONS.

1846-1848.

THE foreign male population not of Spanish blood has been given as 150 in 1830, 300 in 1835, 380 in 1840, and 680 in 1845. This population—no longer foreign under the treaty of Guadalupe Hidalgo—may be put at 4,200 in 1848, counting only persons whose names are known. New-comers of the last three years numbered 3,900. Of these 2,020 came as soldiers in the volunteer or regular army; 120 in the navy, not including the muster-rolls of men-of-war, which would amount to several thousands; 360 were overland immigrants; 320 came by sea, about half of them immigrants proper; and of 1,080 it is not known how they came. Meanwhile departures and deaths as recorded numbered about 280, though there are at least twice as many of whose later presence there is no definite record. I suppose that the total population, including half-breed children, was less than 7,000. I do not present separate lists of the pioneers for 1846–8, as I have done for earlier years, because they would be very long, and at the same time an unnecessary repetition of my Pioneer Register and Index, which is completed in this volume, and contains in alphabetical arrangement all the names for these and other years. As pioneer records are somewhat less complete for this than for earlier periods, and as I am obliged to put this chapter in type before the completion of the register, the figures given here must be taken as approximations only, though not misleading.

My register of pioneers for the year 1846 contains in round numbers, not including mere visitors or the naval muster-rolls, as already explained, about 1,000 names. They may be roughly classified as follows: overland immigrants, not including females, 250; officers, dragoons, and servants in General Kearny's escort from New Mexico, 120; or a total of 370 who came by land, 50 of which number entered California only to die in the snows of the Sierra or at the fight of San Pascual. Then there were about 230 men who came by sea, 100 or more of these belonging to the navy, and a like number being the Mormon colony from New York. Finally, we have about 400 men whose presence is known but not the manner of their coming. These include 160 members of the California battalion, many of whose names should doubtless be added to the list of immigrants; 40 of Fauntleroy's dragoon volunteers, many of whom were sailors; 130 men shown by the records to have been at some place in California; and 70 later residents whose arrival is somewhat definitely ascribed to this year.

Early in the spring many foreigners, chiefly immigrants of 1845, left California, some of them dissatisfied with the country or its political condition, others not having come with an intention of remaining. One party of thirty or more went to Oregon, some names being known, but nothing respecting the organization or journey.[1] There were also several small parties that came southward from Oregon, leaving but slight trace in the records beyond the names of a few members.[2] The other departing company was that of Clyman, Hastings, and Hudspeth, consisting of nineteen men, three women, and three children, starting over the mountains eastward late in April at about the same time as the others for Oregon. Hastings and Hudspeth were bent on exploration in behalf of new immigrations, as we shall presently see.[3] The coming of Kearny and his dragoons from New Mexico has been sufficiently described elsewhere in this volume; and I find no trace this year of other immigrants by this route, or by any other land route than that of the Humboldt and Truckee.

I have the names of about 200 male immigrants who came over the Sierra by the Truckee route, besides perhaps another hundred of those who probably came that way. I do not suppose the total immigration numbered much more than 500 men, women, and children; though the estimate has generally been higher. The general subject of overland immigration for the year may be briefly disposed of, the ex-

---

[1] The party included James Barrett, Jarvis Bonney, Truman Bonney, Julian Bradshaw, Elijah Bristow, John Chamberlain, Wm Dodson, Jones, R. C. Keyes, Abner Frazer, Wm Frazer, McDonald, H. O'Brien, James Owens, John Owens, R. K. Payne, W. R. Roulette, Allen Sanders, Charles Savage, Felix Scott, and E. F. Skinner; and also probably many of the following: Martin Brown, M. Coleman, W. C. Cooper, C. Dornte, Duncan, Hayes. Geo. Hibler, Huet, A. Kinney, Lenoir, Thos Owens, and Sipp; though some of these may have gone east instead of north.

[2] June 26, 1846, a party of seven, including Wambough and Wood. *N. Helv. Diary*, MS., 54. Chas E. Pickett was probably one of these men. It appears that the party was attacked by the Rogue River Indians. A large party, including many Canadians, left Or. together, but was soon divided into many smaller ones. The smallest was that of Rich. C. Kirby and perhaps Alfred Baldwin, which followed that of Wambough. *Sta Cruz Co. Hist.*, 25.

[3] *Clyman's Diary*, MS., 5–6, 148, unfortunately ending with the departure from Cal. See also *Doc. Hist. Cal.*, MS., iii. 122; *Sutter-Suñol Corresp.*, MS., 34; *N. Helv. Diary*, MS., 44. Boggs, *Across the Plains in '46*, met Clyman's party at Laramie, but gives no particulars. Wm Sublette, Owen Sumner and family, Henry Owens, Clemens and family, Wilson and family, and Reddick; also perhaps G. M. Smith, Ed Owens, Isaac A. Flint, A. H. Crosby, M. R. Childers, and Benj. Carpenter.

periences of one company only requiring extended notice. Several times in earlier years the same journey had been made under similar circumstances, by the same route, with like motives, hardships, and adventures, as recorded in earlier volumes of this history. Names of immigrants with brief biographic notices are given elsewhere in my Pioneer Register. Personal reminiscences of the long, dreary, and toilsome journey, admitting no profitable condensation, though fascinating in their details, are much too bulky for reproduction here. No two parties had exactly the same experiences, but the variations lose their life and interest when presented en résumé. Bryant and Thornton of the California and Oregon trains respectively have presented particulars in published diaries that leave but little to be desired.[4]

From May to July some two thousand emigrants, with about 500 teams of oxen, mules, and horses, plodded their way over the plains between Independence, Laramie, and Bridger. From each of many towns or regions of the western states a small party under its own captain had found its way to the rendezvous on the Missouri. Here or out on the plains these parties met and travelled together in various combinations, forming at different times one, two, or three great companies under regularly chosen chiefs, with minor detachments extending far to the rear or front. The principal families of each little party generally but not always remained together to the end; but there were frequent transfers of miscellaneous

---

[4] *What I Saw in California: Being the journal of a tour, by the immigrant route and South Pass of the Rocky Mountains, across the continent of North America, the great desert basin, and through California, in the years 1846, 1847...By Edwin Bryant, late alcalde of St Francisco.* N. Y., 1848, 12mo, 455 p., 2d ed. There were six American editions, an English, and two French in 1848-9. This work has been often cited in the preceding pages, and is an excellent authority, not only on the overland journey, but on events in Cal. The author went back with Gen. Kearny in the summer of 1847.

Oregon and California in 1848. By J. Quinn Thornton. N. Y., 1849, 12mo, 2 vols. See *Hist. Oregon,* this series, for details respecting the author and his work. He gives, like Bryant, a diary of the overland journey from day to day.

members, and the party groupings were always changing. Some of the parties, as distinguished by the
names of their leaders, were those of Russell, West,
Reed and Donner, Boggs, Gordon, Cooper, Dickenson, Young, Craig and Stanly, Aram, Brown, Ritchie,
Bryant and Jacob, Lippincott, Grayson, Graves, Harlan, Breen and Murphy, and Dunleavy. I make no
attempt to trace the complicated company changes,
to condense the diaries, or to name the members of
the different parties; but append some general notes
on the subject.[5] Except in a few instances, there is

[5] In *Niles' Reg.*, lxx. 128, 208, 211; lxxi. 146, 151, are items on the emigrants. Those bound for Cal. are estimated at 500 persons; 350 were under
Russell's command at one time. In the Fort Bridger region great discontent
was reported in July. In *Id.*, 32, is mentioned a project to colonize S. Diego
with 500 or 1,000 emigrants to start from Ft Smith in April. For many details respecting the immigration of this year, see *Hist. Oregon*, i. 552 et seq.,
this series. Many biographic sketches in newspapers and county histories
afford items of information about the companies.

Bryant and Jacob from Kentucky were accompanied in the last stages of
the journey by Wm H. Russell, Hiram Miller, John C. Buchanan, Wm H.
Nuttall, James McClary, Brookey, and Brown. With mules and no wagons
they left Bridger July 20th, took the route by the south of Salt Lake,
reached the Humboldt Aug. 7th, its sink the 19th, Truckee Lake 25th, and
Johnson's rancho 30th, being the first party to arrive. Full details in *Bryant's What I Saw.*

Col Russell seems to have started with Thomas West, who like Russell
was at one time captain of the united emigrants. West's party from Missouri included his four sons, and his son-in-law Thomas Campbell and family. B. S. Lippincott and party with 6 wagons seem also to have been with
West during much of the journey. They had a fight with Indians on the
Humboldt, one Sallee being killed, and several wounded, including L. himself.
West and Lippincott were perhaps the third party to cross the Sierra, the
second being Craig and Stanly, who left Fort Hall July 23d, and were overtaken by Bryant near the sink of the Humboldt Aug. 18th, being 12 or 15
days in advance of the other emigrants.

Ex-gov. L. W. Boggs from Missouri and party came by Fort Hall and the
Humboldt, being in company with Thornton and the Oregon train much of
the way. Wm M. Boggs was at one time captain of the company. He has
published a narrative, entitled *Across the Plains in '46*, in *Calistoga Tribune*,
Oct. 14–Dec. 21, 1871; but the names of only three families are known, those
of A. J. Grayson, James Savage, and Wm Bryant. It appears that Grayson at first had been at the head of a small party, the members of which had
quarrelled with and left him. Apparently in company with Boggs over the
mountains was the party of Elam Brown, also from Missouri, consisting of 14
families and 16 wagons. Adams, Allen, Stilwell, and Crowley are the names
known, besides some who went to Oregon. They are said to have reached
Johnson's on Oct. 10th. *Contra Costa Co. Hist.*, 519–22; *Sta Cruz Co. Hist.*,
27; *S. J. Pion.*, Jan. 26, 1878. Thornton, i. 181, represents the Brown and
Allen party as having tried the Applegate cut-off to Or. Stephen Cooper's
party, including the Carriger and Wardlow families, were also apparently in
company with Boggs and Brown. They are said to have reached the mountains Sept. 21st and the lake on the 24th. *Sonoma Co. Hist.*, 674. And with

but meagre information respecting dates or other details of progress west of the Salt Lake region; and unfortunately the New Helvetia diary does not cover the period of overland arrivals this year.

A portion of both the California and Oregon immigration were induced to attempt a shorter way, or cut-off, to their respective destinations. Applegate met the Oregonians at Fort Hall and persuaded part of them to follow him down the Humboldt with the Californians for several hundred miles and thence to the Willamette. The result, as elsewhere recorded in my *History of Oregon*, was not disastrous; but a controversy respecting the merits of the two routes has been kept alive, chiefly through the bitterness of Thornton, down to the present day. The Californians were met in the region of Fort Bridger by Hastings and Hudspeth, and several parties were induced to save several hundred miles and to avoid many hardships by taking the cut-off south of the lake, partly explored by Frémont in earlier years. Hastings, in his partisan zeal, supported by the proprietors of the fort for their own interests, exaggerated the advantages and underrated the difficulties of the new route; but though not a very wise counsellor in such matters, he doubtless acted according to his

them—or possibly a little in advance, as Oct. 1st is given as the date of arrival at Johnson's—was Joseph Aram's party of 12 wagons and over 50 person's, including the Imus, Isbel, White, Berry, and Hecox families. *S. J. Pion.*, July 8, 1882; *Cal. Christ. Advoc.*, July 2, 1863.

The parties of Gordon, Dickenson, and Young seem to have been connected; though Dickenson and Gordon seem to have taken the Fort Hall route; while Young took the cut-off. *Bryant*, 27, 50, 99; *Thornton*, i. 38, 134, 164; *S. F. Bull.*, Aug. 11, 1876; *S. J. Pion.*, March 20, 1880; *Lancey*, 151. Gordon's party is said to have included John Williams. Sam. C. Young, in *S. J. Pion.*, Nov. 9, 1878, describes the trip, and names, besides himself and family, his son-in-law Arthur Caldwell and family, John McCutchen, Buchalas, Jos. Gordon, Jacob Gordon, Duncan Dickenson, W. Hoover and fam., Jacob Russ, Simpson, and McMonigle. Some of these names are probably erroneous, as is certainly the date of Oct. 16th for crossing the summit. It was perhaps on the 5th or earlier. Geo. Harlan's party was another that took the cut-off and probably crossed the mountains about the same time as Young under the guidance of Hastings. These were the last parties to cross, except those of the Donner company. No dates or other particulars are known about the Dunleavy party, or that of M. D. Ritchie, which included John Stark, and perhaps also Cyrus, Tucker, and Jesse.

judgment honestly, and he made no serious error. Bryant decided to follow the new route, but left letters advising others with families and wagons not to attempt it—letters which are said not to have been delivered. His party with pack-mules, being guided by Hudspeth for a part of the way, was the first of the season to reach California. Two other parties, those of Harlan and Young, were guided by Hastings in person, had much difficulty in finding a way for their wagons, lost much of their live-stock in the Salt Lake desert, but at last reached the old trail, and were the last to cross the Sierra. I have now to write of those who were left behind.

On the 20th of July, at Little Sandy stream, several of the parties formed a new combination, chose George Donner for their captain, and thus formed the "Donner party" of 87 persons, 36 being men, 21 women, and 30 children—five of the latter infants, 49 of the whole number belonging to four families, those of Donner, Graves, Breen, and Murphy. The names are given in a note.[6] There was nothing remarkable

[6] Those whose names are marked with a '*' died in the Sierra; those marked '†' died before reaching Cal. Of the survivors those marked '1' were still living in 1880; those marked '2' died before that date; it is not known what became of the rest. McGlashan is the chief authority for this note. See all the names in my Pioneer Register and Index, in this and the preceding volumes.

*George Donner, wife *Tamsen, daughters [1]Elitha C., [1]Leanna C., [1]Frances E. (child), [1]Georgia A. (ch.), [1]Eliza P. (5 yrs). *Jacob Donner (brother of Geo.), wife *Elizabeth, daughter [2]Mary M., sons [2]Geo. Jr, *Isaac (ch.), *Lewis (ch.), *Samuel (ch.); sons of Mrs D. by a former husband, Solomon Hook (ch.), *William Hook (ch.). [2]James F. Reed, wife [2]Mary W., sons [1]James F. (5 yrs), [1]Thomas K. (3 yrs), daughters [1]Virginia E. (12 yrs), [1]Martha F. (8 yrs). *Baylis Williams and half-sister Eliza Williams. *John Denton, *Milton Elliott, *James Smith, Walter Herron, [1]Noah James. These 29 were from Springfield, Ill., and constituted what had been originally the Reed-Donner party; Reed being the most prominent member.

*Franklin W. Graves, wife *Elizabeth, sons [1]Wm C., [2]Jonathan B. (7 yrs), *Franklin W. Jr (5 yrs), daughters [1]Mary A., [1]Eleanor, [1]Lovina, [1]Nancy (9 yrs), [2]Elizabeth Jr (infant); son-in-law *Jay Fosdick, wife [2]Sarah Graves, †John Snyder. These 13 came from Marshall co., Ill., and had originally formed a separate party. What others the party had included, if any, does not appear.

[2]Patrick Breen, wife [2]Mary, sons [1]John, [1]Edward J., [1]Patrick Jr (ch.), [1]Simon P., [1]James F. (ch.), [2]Peter (ch.), daughter [1]Isabella M. (infant). *Patrick Dolan. These 10 were Irish, and came from Keokuk, Iowa. They joined

in the composition of the company, which included rich and poor; American, Irish, and German; Protestant, Catholic, and Mormon. Most members were well enough provided with the necessary outfit. George Donner was a man of some wealth, and was carrying a stock of merchandise to California for sale. On July 22d they parted from the Oregon train, reached Fort Bridger on the 25th, and finally resolved to take the cut-off.

They started on the 28th, only a few days behind Hastings, from whom they soon received a letter advising a new change of route to avoid obstacles encountered by the other company in the Weber Cañon. Reed and two companions were sent to overtake the advance company, obtain additional information, and explore the route—an operation which consumed a week or more; and then the whole party started by the new cut-off. It proved a most difficult way, so much so that all of August passed before they reached open country on the lake shore. From the southern extremity of the lake, where Halloran died of consumption on September 3d, they directed their course to the north-west, crossing the desert from the 9th to

the train at Independence, but it does not appear whether any others were of the same party.

Mrs *Lavinia Murphy, a widow, sons *John L., *Lemuel B. (13 yrs), [1]Wm G. (11 yrs), [2]Simon P. (ch.), daughter [2]Mary M.; sons-in-law, †Wm M. Pike and wife [2]Harriet F. (Murphy) and child.   [1]Naomi L. Pike (2 yrs), and *Catherine Pike (infant), [2]Wm M. Foster and wife [1]Sarah A. C. (Murphy) and son *George (infant).   These 13 are said by McGlashan to have come from Tennessee; but according to Tyler, *Hist. Morm. Bat.*, 312, who got his information from Mary Murphy (Mrs Johnson), Mrs Murphy had lived at Nauvoo and later at Warsaw, accepting an engagement to cook and wash for the emigrants with a view to reach with her children the ultimate destination of the saints.

[2]Wm H. Eddy, wife *Eleanor, son *James P. (ch.), daughter *Mary (infant), from Belleville, Ill.   [1]Wm McCutchen, wife [2]Amanda M., daughter *Harriet (infant), from Jackson co., Mo.   [1]Louis Keseberg, wife [2]Philipine, son *Louis, Jr (ch.), daughter *Ada (infant), a German family that had come to America two years before.   Other Germans were †Wolfinger and Mrs W., *Joseph Rhinehart, *August Spitzer, and *Charles Burger.   †Hardcoop was a Belgian.   *Samuel Shoemaker came from Ohio; *Charles T. Stanton from Chicago; †Luke Halloran from Missouri.   *Antonio and [1]Juan Bautista were of Spanish race from N. Mexico.   The party affiliations of these 22 before reaching Ft Bridger are not known.   There were also two Cal. Indians, *Luis and *Salvador, who joined the company later.

the 15th with great suffering and loss of cattle. One family lost all their oxen; much property had to be abandoned; new hardships and losses followed before they reached the head waters of streams flowing into the Humboldt. The remaining supply of food was believed to be insufficient for the journey. McCutchen and Stanton volunteered to bring relief from California, and started, each with a horse, before the 20th. It was about the end of September when the company struck the old emigrant trail on the main Humboldt, long after the last parties had passed. Belated and destitute, they began to realize their danger.

The second stage of this disastrous journey covers in time the month of October, including the march down the river and into the mountains. At Gravelly Ford, on October 5th, in an unfortunate quarrel over their teams, Snyder was killed by Reed, and the latter was banished from the party. Accompanied by Herron, he passed on in advance, hoping to bring back relief for his family. Hungry and foot-sore, the rest plodded their way onward. At the sink of the Humboldt on the 12th twenty-one head of cattle were stolen by Indians. Several families had no oxen or horses left. The old Belgian Hardcoop, unable to walk, was left to die, as was also the German Wolfinger, the latter under circumstances suggesting foul play on the part of his countrymen. On the 19th, in the region of the modern Wadsworth, Stanton was met, returning from Sutter's Fort with succor. He had seven mules, five of them loaded with flour and beef, and was accompanied by two Californian Indians, Luis and Salvador.[7] An unfortunate delay of several days for rest in the region of Reno was marked

[7] Not much is known of the journey to Cal. and back. Stanton and McCutchen had left the company about Sept. 20th, had overtaken the hindmost party of emigrants—that of Young—and had crossed the Sierra with them. Sutter was prompt to furnish food, animals, and the Indians; McC. was too ill to return; but S. hastened back over the mountains. His generous zeal—destined to prove fatal to himself—was the more noticeable that he had no relatives in the company.

also by the death of Pike, accidentally shot by Foster. On the 23d, alarmed by indications of an impending storm, they resumed their journey, but when they reached the region of Truckee and the lake, at the end of October, the snow was falling, and was already several feet deep on the summits.

The worst of later calamities might perhaps have been avoided at this time, either by an earnest and well directed effort to cross the range, or by careful preparations for a winter in camp; but there was no acknowledged and capable leader, no agreement in opinion, no unity of plan or action, only a wild desire for escape on the part of some, a yielding to despair by others. For three weeks or more the frightened emigrants in small detached parties wasted their strength, in frequent, frantic, and vain efforts to break through the snowy barrier; and when they had so far regained their senses as to realize the necessity of concerted action, there came a week of storm, ten feet or more of snow, which required all energies to be directed for a time to the preservation of life. Most of the cattle, their main reliance for food, had strayed and perished, being buried in the snow, where only a few were ever found. Remaining animals were slaughtered and carefully preserved. A cabin built by the Stevens party in 1844 was still standing near the lake shore; and others were hastily constructed. There were a few unsuccessful efforts to take fish from the lake. Eddy killed a bear and some ducks. Some six miles eastward, on Alder Creek, the Donner families with five or six others were encamped in tents and brushwood huts, worse off in some respects than those at the lake, George Donner being disabled by an accident, and Jacob Donner, a feeble man unfitted for such hardships, the first to die. Shoemaker, Rhinehart, and Smith died here before the 21st of December, and Williams at the lake on the 15th. On the 16th a volunteer party of fifteen, known as the 'forlorn hope,' started on improvised snow-shoes over the mountains. I will follow them later.[8]

There were sixty-one persons left in the mountain camps, most of them ill and weak, with nothing to eat but hides. Snow-storms still continued. The stump of a tree cut when the snow was deepest was found by later measurement to be twenty-two feet high. Patrick Breen's diary, as written from day to day through this terrible winter, is in my collection, the most precious and fascinating record and relic of these events. I make no attempt to portray in words the horrors of the situation. It was more than two months before any message came from the outside world. Burger died December 30th, young Keseberg January 24th, John L. Murphy on the 31st, Eddy's child and McCutchen's February 2d and 3d, Spitzer and Mrs Eddy on the 7th, Elliott on the 9th, and Pike's child on the 20th. At last, when it had been resolved by most to eat the bodies of the dead, as a few had probably done already, the first relief party of seven men arrived on February 19th with a slight supply of food, and the charitably false report that all of the forlorn hope were safe. Three days later they started on their return with twenty-one of the survivors,[9] leaving thirty-one too weak for the journey or unwilling to abandon others needing their care. A week later, on the 1st of March, the second relief of ten men—including Reed and McCutchen—arrived, to leave one of their number and to start back on the 3d with seventeen of the sufferers,[10] leaving fourteen.

---

[8] The members of this party were Eddy, *Stanton, *Graves, *Dolan, *Fosdick and wife, Foster and wife, *Lemuel Murphy, Mrs Pike, Mary Graves, Mrs McCutchen, *Antonio, *Luis, and *Salvador. Those marked with a * died on the way.

[9] These were Elitha, Leanna, and George Donner Jr; Mrs Reed with her children Virginia and James; Mrs Keseberg and *child; Wm G. and Mary Murphy; Wm C., Eleanor, and Lovina Graves; Edward and Simon Breen; *Wm Hook, Noah James, Mrs Wolfinger, Naomi Pike, Eliza Williams, and *John Denton.

[10] These were the seven Breens, Martha and Thomas Reed, *Isaac and Mary Donner, *Mrs Graves with her four children Nancy, Jonathan, *Franklin Jr, and Elizabeth Jr, and Solomon Hook.

Five of these—Mrs Elizabeth Donner, Lewis and Samuel Donner at Alder Creek, the children of Foster and Eddy at the Lake—died in the short period that elapsed before the coming of the third relief at a date not exactly known. This party of four, including Eddy and Foster, carried away five of the survivors.[11] Keseberg and Mrs Murphy at the lake camp were unable to travel; George Donner at Alder Creek was dying, and his wife, though in good health, nobly refused to leave him. These four were left for another month to suffer torments that proved fatal to all but one.

Before proceeding with the annals of the different relief parties, I introduce some remarks on authorities for the whole subject. Patrick Breen's original diary must be regarded as the best record of events at the lake cabins, and in substance it has been several times published.[12] The early papers of California published information about the immigrants' disasters and efforts made to relieve them.[13] Bryant and Thornton, com-

[11] Frances, Georgia, and Eliza Donner, Simon Murphy, and Juan Bautista. Eddy, in *Thornton*, ii. 228, says that 'Clarke carried his booty, and left a child of one of the Donners to perish.' It is possibly true that Lewis Donner was left, as there is no record of the date of his death.

[12] *Diary of Patrick Breen, one of the Donner Party, 1846-7. Presented by Dr George McKinstry to the Bancroft Library.* MS., 16mo, 15 leaves. It was printed in the *S. F. California Star*, May 22, 1847; *Nashville (Tenn.) Whig*, Sept. 1847; *Bryant's What I Saw*, 256; *Thornton's Or. and Cal.*, 201; *McGlashan's Hist.*, 93, and elsewhere. Thornton's extracts are more garbled than the others; but none are literally accurate, there being changes and omissions in nearly every entry. The variations are not, however, historically of any special importance. The diary extends from Nov. 20th to March 1st. I reproduce literally the first and last entries, to show the general nature of alterations in the printed versions. 'Friday Nov. 20th 1846 came to this place on the 31st of last month that it snowed we went on to the pass the snow so deep we were unable to find the road, when within 3 miles of the summit then turned back to this shanty on the Lake, Stanton came one day after we arrived here we again took our teams & waggons & made another unsuccessful attempt to cross in company with Stanton we returned to the shanty it continuing to snow all the time we were here. we now have killed most part of our cattle having to stay here untill next spring & live on poor beef without bread or salt it snowed during the space of eight days with little intermission, after our arrival here, the remainder of time up to this day was clear and pleasant frezing at night the snow nearly gone from the valleys... Mond. March the 1st to fine & pleasant froze hard last night there has 10 men arrived this morning from bear valley with provisions we are to start in two or three days & cash our goods here there is amongst them some old they say the snow will be here untill June.'

[13] See *Monterey Calif.*, Feb. 13, March 27, 1847; *S. F. Cal. Star*, Jan. 16,

panions of the sufferers in the early part of their journey, devoted a portion of their published diaries to
the subject, the former confining himself chiefly to correspondence of the time, and the latter taking testimony from survivors, especially from Eddy.[14]   In 1856
Mrs Eliza W. Farnham published a narrative drawn
mainly from the testimony of Mrs Breen.[15]   In 1871
an article by F. H. McDougal, based on the statements
of Mrs Curtis, called out narrative statements from
Reed and McCutchen;[16] and in 1877 William C.
Graves published his version in a series of newspaper
articles.[17]   Meanwhile there was printed in books and
newspapers a great mass of material on the subject,
which I do not deem it necessary to catalogue, though
most of it is before me, because it is made up, so far
as it has any foundation except imagination, from the
authorities I have cited, and oftener than otherwise
hastily and at second-hand.   Finally, C. F. McGlashan
published a volume on the subject in 1879, treating it
in a manner that has left little or nothing to be desired.   All the facts that I am able to utilize, and
many more, may be found in his work.   Consulting
all the earlier versions cited above, the author supplemented results by correspondence and personal interviews with surviving members of the party, thus
acquiring a mass of personal items of which he made
excellent use.   On no other topic of early Californian
history would any single work so fully suffice for my
purpose.[18]   I have a few original manuscripts which

Feb. 13, March 6, 13, April 10, May 22, June 5, 1847; *Oregon Spectator*, April
1, June 24, 1847.

[14] *Bryant's What I Saw in Cal.*, 249–65, letters from Sinclair and McKinstry. *Thornton's Or. and Cal.*, ii. 96–246.   This is the most complete narrative published in early times.   Both Bryant and Thornton, as we have seen,
give Breen's diary.

[15] *Farnham's Cal. In-doors and Out*, 380–453.   Reprinted also in *Hollister
Central Calif.*, March 22–April 19, 1871.

[16] These three articles were written for the *Pacific Rural Press*.   I find
McDougal's article in the *Hollister Central Calif.*, Feb. 1, 1871; and those of
Reed and McCutchen in the *S. J. Pioneer*, April 28, May 5, 1877.

[17] *Graves' Crossing the Plains in '46*, in *Healdsburg Russ. River Flag*, April
26 to May 17, 1877, and *Id.*, Dec. 30, 1875.   This account also reproduces
Breen's diary.

[18] *History of the Donner Party.   A Tragedy of the Sierra.   By C. F. Mc-*

throw light on certain phases of the matter, notably the narratives of John Breen and of Daniel Rhoads, the latter a member of one of the relief parties.[19]

The 'forlorn hope' of fifteen persons already named started from the lake camp to cross the Sierra on December 16th, taking rations for six days. This journey lasted thirty-two days, and was in some respects the most horrible episode of the winter's events. Stanton, who had perhaps saved the lives of all, was himself left to die on the 23d. When they had been four days without food, on Christmas they reached the 'camp of death,' where a snow-storm confined them for a week. Antonio, Graves, Dolan, and Lemuel Murphy died and were eaten. Again they pressed on; the strings of their snow-shoes furnished a new-year's dinner; Fosdick died on the 4th of January; and on the same day Eddy killed a deer. No food on the 7th; the two Indians had refused to eat human flesh, and ran away to save their lives, but they were soon overtaken, and were shot by Foster. About the 11th the survivors reached a ranchería and were fed with acorn bread—all the Indians had to give. Eddy, more dead than alive, was led to Johnson's rancho, whence a party returned and brought in the other six survivors, probably on the 17th.[20]

We have seen that Stanton and McCutchen had reached Sutter's Fort in October, and that the former had recrossed the mountains with two Indians, all three to perish, but bearing relief that saved the lives of many. Next Reed and Herron left the company,

Glashan. S. F., 1880, 8vo, 261 p., portraits and illustrations. The first edition was issued at Truckee in 1879.

[19] Breen's Pioneer Memoir, MS., p. 1-45; Rhoads' Relief of the Donner Party, MS. See also Burnett's Recoll., MS., i. 377-94, the author having taken testimony of Eddy, Foster, and other members; Thornton's Or. Hist., MS., 26-30; Rabbison's Growth of Towns, MS., 6-8.

[20] The rescuers are named by Eddy, in Thornton, ii. 154-5, as John Howell, John Rhodes, Segur (?), and Tucker, who started first on foot; and Ritchie, Johnson, Joseph Varro (Verrot), and Kiser (Seb. Keyser), who followed next day on horseback. This is confirmed, except in names and numbers, by Sinclair's letter, in Bryant, 255, written at the time, before the 'first relief' had started.

and after a most perilous journey succeeded in reaching a small party of belated emigrants in Bear Valley, met Stanton on his return, and finally arrived at the fort, probably at the end of October. Here they hastily collected supplies and horses, were joined by McCutchen, obtained the services of two Indians, and started to return. They found it impossible to push their way through the mass of snow that had fallen, and were obliged to turn back, rescuing Jotham Curtis and wife of the late immigrants, who from some strange freak had encamped in the upper Bear Valley. It was believed by experienced men at the fort that the Donner party by killing their animals and preserving the meat might live at their mountain camp till relief could reach them; and Reed went south in quest of aid. Before anything could be effected, however, the survivors of the forlorn hope had arrived at Johnson's with reports necessitating immediate action.[21]

The news was sent to the fort as soon as possible by an Indian runner; volunteers were called for, and a relief party was fitted out, largely through the efforts of Sinclair, Sutter, Kern, and McKinstry, who became responsible for the payment of wages by the government.[22] A company of thirteen, known as the 'first relief,' left Johnson's rancho on the 5th of February; but only seven went beyond Bear Valley, whence they started on the 15th. These were Reasin P. Tucker, Aquila Glover, Riley S. Moultry, John Rhoads, Daniel Rhoads, Edward Coffeemire, and Joseph Sells.[23] They reached the lake on the 19th,

[21] Statements of Reed and McCutchen in *Rural Press*. In these statements, and still more in *Thornton*, ii. 182–94, many details are given of dealings with Curtis, who seems to have been a peculiar character. Mrs Curtis was authority for the account that drew out replies from R. and McC. It is not clear that Herron accompanied them in this attempt at relief.

[22] In Nov.–Dec. 1847, Ritchie made a claim for $171 for services in rescuing the immigrants. Gov. Mason hopes soon to get instructions enabling him to pay such claims. *Cal. and N. Mex., Mess. and Doc., 1850*, p. 448.

[23] Sells, or Sel, is named by Eddy and McKinstry; but he is called Joseph Foster by Tucker, and Geo. Foster by Rhoads. Coffeemire is said to have been a sailor, and is called Coffeymier and Copymier, also by Rhoads 'Mike.'

and started back three days later with twenty-one of the immigrants, three of whom died on the way.[24] All were on the point of starvation from failing to find a cache of supplies, when on the 27th they met another relief party, and being thus succored they reached Johnson's the 2d of March, and Sutter's two days later.

The party thus met was the 'second relief' of ten men under Reed and McCutchen. They had not been able to accomplish anything in the south until the excitement of the Sanchez, or Santa Clara, campaign was over, but then at Yerba Buena and north of the bay great interest was aroused. A public meeting was held; Captain Hull, General Vallejo, and other prominent men exerted themselves; a subscription of some $1,500 was raised; twenty volunteers or more were enlisted; Brittan Greenwood was engaged as guide; supplies were furnished from the naval stores; business men furnished schooners for transportation to Sonoma and New Helvetia; and Lieutenant Selim Woodworth volunteered to command the expedition. All this before the receipt of Sinclair's letter announcing the arrival of Eddy and others of the forlorn hope.[25] Reed and McCutchen, with Greenwood, went by way of Sonoma, arrived at New Helvetia in advance of Woodworth's party in the schooner, and pressed on to Johnson's rancho. From this point, with seven companions—Charles Cady, Charles

Wm Eddy started but returned with the horses on the 11th, perhaps with Verrot. On the same day Wm Coon and George Tucker were left in camp to guard provisions. On the 15th, at Bear Valley, M. D. Ritchie, Adolf Brüheim, and Jotham Curtis declined to go any farther. McGlashan quotes from diaries by R. P. Tucker and Ritchie and a narrative by Geo. Tucker. He makes Tucker the captain. McKinstry, in *Bryant*, 255, makes Glover the captain, and quotes his diary. Eddy, also, in *Thornton*, ii. 167, names Glover as the chief.

[24] See note 9 for names of those rescued by the 1st relief.

[25] See *S. F. Cal. Star*, Feb. 6, 13, 1847. McGlashan, p. 126, gives a memorial addressed to Gov. Stockton by citizens of S. José. Reed describes his efforts in the *Rural Press*. An account of the meeting at S. F. is given in *Thornton*, ii. 158–61, including an eloquent appeal by Dunleavy. Alcalde Bartlett, Capt. Mervine, Lieut Maury, W. A. Richardson, Wm Pettet, John Fuller, Ward & Smith, Howard & Mellus, are also named as active in these preparations.

Stone, Nicholas Clark, Joseph Gendreau, John Turner, Hiram Miller, and Matthew Dofar [26]—constituting the second relief, started on February 23d, met on the 27th the other party, as already noted—including Reed's wife and children—and on March 1st, in two parties, reached the lake camps. Two days later, leaving Clark, Cady, and Stone, and taking seventeen of the immigrants,[27] they started on the return. From the 5th to the 7th, while Gendreau, Turner, and Dofar were far in advance, and Cady and Stone were in the rear, having left the camps to overtake their companions, the rest of the party were in Summit Valley, at what was known as 'starved camp,' where three of the immigrants died. A heavy snowstorm prevented progress, and the caches of food had been destroyed by wild beasts. At last the five of the relief took three of the others and started on, and the number of parties was increased from three to four. But the advance reached Bear Valley, where Woodworth was encamped; returned with two companions, John Stark and Howard Oakley, to meet Reed; Cady and Stone came up; and all the fifteen soon reached Woodworth's camp. There were, however, eleven of the immigrants left in the snow at 'starved camp.'

Then was organized the 'third relief.' Woodworth and his men had moved slowly and accomplished nothing. Probably they had done their best, but they had little skill or experience in this kind of work. Meanwhile Eddy and Foster had partially regained their strength, and after some additional efforts at Yerba Buena, had overtaken the naval division in Bear Valley. Five volunteers were obtained, and the party set out at once, the exact date not being known. Stark, Oakley, and Stone volunteered to rescue the eleven at 'starved camp,' and were left

[26] Of Dofar nothing more is known. He may have been Dupas. Gendreau is generally called Jondro.
[27] See note 10 for names.

there by their companions, succeeding in their purpose only after the most extraordinary efforts, since nine of the number had to be carried. Eddy, Foster, Miller, and William Thompson pressed on over the mountains; met Clark and Juan Bautista trying to escape; and reached the lake about the middle of March. Leaving four adults, as already mentioned, they brought out four children and Juan Bautista. Little is known of their return; but they seem to have overtaken Stark and the Breens; and on their arrival at the camp in Bear Valley all seem to have proceeded to Johnson's rancho, and perhaps all to New Helvetia, Woodworth declining or pronouncing it impracticable to attempt a rescue of the four left in the mountains.

Again, by the efforts of Alcalde Sinclair and others at the fort, and by an offer of half of any property that might be saved, nine men, constituting the 'fourth relief,' were induced to start in April.[28] These were William Fallon, William Foster, John Rhoads, R. P. Tucker, J. Foster, Sebastian Keyser, and Edward Coffeemire. Starting from Johnson's on the 13th, they reached Donner Lake on the 17th. Of the four who had been left by the last relief, George Donner and his wife and Mrs Murphy had died, and only Keseberg survived, having preserved his life by eating the bodies of his dead companions. Keseberg had been an unpopular member of the company. Fallon and his men were disappointed at not finding a large amount of money which Donner was believed to have possessed, and which they had hoped to share; they suspected Keseberg of having killed Mrs Donner and concealed the money; and their suspicions were confirmed when, on threats of being hanged, he gave up a small amount which he said Mrs Donner had intrusted to him for her children.[29]

[28] Thornton mentions also another expedition in March, consisting of J. Rhoads, Stark, Coffeemire, Sells, Tucker, Wm Foster, and Graves, which was not able to penetrate beyond Bear Valley on account of melting snows. *Or. and Cal.*, ii. 231.

[29] Fallon's diary is quoted in *Thornton's Or. and Cal.*, ii. 232 et seq.; and

In view of the utter impossibility of knowing the exact truth in this matter, the lack of definite testimony even of most of the accusers, the doubtful character of Fallon, the hope of gain actuating the party, the bitter feeling shown in their version, the evident exaggeration and falsehood of many details respecting the state of things at the camp, the straightforward statement of the accused to McGlashan in 1879, and the fact that, in the face of popular prejudice and testimony stronger than could ever again be obtained, he obtained a nominal verdict against Coffeemire in a suit for slander at Sutter's Fort in May 1847 [30]—in view of all this, I believe that Louis Keseberg is entitled to a verdict of not guilty.   He has been merely the unfortunate object about which has crystallized all the pop-

his version is also given by Bryant, who went east with him.   The version has often been repeated with all its sickening details of mangled corpses found at the camps, 'a large pan full of fresh liver and lights,' 'two kettles of human blood,' with plenty of beef untouched, and Keseberg as a fiendish ghoul boasting of his fondness for human flesh.   He is also accused of having murdered Wolfinger, been responsible for the death of Hardcoop, of having feigned disability to depart with the relief parties, and of having murdered and eaten Foster's child.   K.'s own version, as related in 1879, is given by McGlashan, who also represents Tucker's testimony as being much more favorable to the accused than the current version.

[30] I have two original papers connected with this case, the general result of which—a verdict of $1 damages—is remembered by several witnesses.   May 2d, Alcalde Sinclair to Sheriff Geo. McKinstry, sending summons for witnesses, and asking McK. also to be on hand as a witness; also orders the selection of a jury of 6 or 12 men.   Wood and Rhoads to be added to the jury list.   'The nature of the trial you are acquainted with.   The plaintiff wanted the moderate charge of $1,000 to be put down for damages!!!'   May 4th, Sinclair to McK., summons to Mrs Wolfinger as a witness for the next day. *McKinstry's Pap.*, MS. 30, 34.

The popular story circulated by such prominent men as Dr Bushnell and Bishop Kip and Bret Harte, that Geo. Yount, the Napa pioneer hunter, had a dream which revealed the danger of the Donner party, and led to their being saved, deserves brief mention.   Its only foundation was probably in Yount's statement that he had such a dream.   It is not likely that the dream lost anything in the telling, either by the old trapper or by those who repeated the story.   At any rate, Yount did not go to the relief of the sufferers, and his dream did not lead in any way to their rescue.

On June 2, 1847, the remnants of the Donner property were sold for the benefit of the children. *N. Helv. Diary*, MS., 59.   According to the *Alta*, June 22, 1868, the first railroad train from the east had among its passengers a woman who, as a little girl, had been one of the Donner party.   Many relics of the party were dug up in 1879; and a cabinet with some 200 of these articles was kept at Truckee for a time. *S. J. Pioneer*, Nov. 15, 1879. According to newspapers of the same year, there was a plan to erect a monument at Donner Lake to the memory of the party.

ular horror excited by the cannibalism of the Donner party.

Of the 36 men, 21 women, and 30 children making up the original party of 87, there perished 22, 5, and 12 respectively, or a total of 39, while the survivors numbered 48. For biographic mention of each, as of members of the different relief parties, I refer the reader to my Pioneer Register and Index in these volumes. About 30 were still living in 1880. In June 1847 General Kearny and his party, including Fallon and Bryant, on their way to the east, gave burial to the remains of such victims as they could find; and this work was completed in September by the returning Mormons of the battalion.

In thus recording the experiences of this ill-fated company, I have designedly made no attempt to paint in words the horrors of their journey. The plain facts are sufficiently horrible. I have also omitted for the most part all allusions to individual acts seeming to justify censure or eulogy. Such acts of both classes have been attributed to nearly every adult in the party, and to some of the rescuers. Soon after leaving Fort Bridger dissensions arose between parties, cliques, and families; serious quarrels ensued before the time of their greatest trials; and the prejudices thus developed colored all later testimony. There is not an original narrative which does not show traces of the writer's personal likes and dislikes, or which does not contain directly or indirectly accusations or complaints. It is neither possible nor desirable to investigate the details. Doubtless most committed errors of judgment, were moved by their troubles to say and do foolish things, or were driven in the insanity of starvation to petty acts of apparent cruelty and selfishness; but on the other hand, there were few, if any, who did not on one occasion or another show traits of heroic self-sacrifice. Most of them ate human flesh, and they did right; it was the necessity, not the act, that was deplorable; and the few who at the prompting of stomach or conscience refused the revolting food deserve no special commendation. These immigrants acted as others would have done under like circumstances, though under a competent leader and with unity of purpose and action they might have escaped the worst of their misfortunes. I think McGlashan has done wisely in suppressing disagreeable details and dwelling on the noble deeds of each member; but his kindly exaggeration of praise, no less than the disgusting accusations of other writers, is unsuited to my work. Yet it is well to note the self-sacrifice of Stanton and Mrs Donner, the manly efforts of Reed and Eddy, and the bravery of the rescuers from California; also to point out that the killing of Snyder, so far as we may know, was an act of self-defence; and that the most serious charges against Keseberg had but slight foundation in fact.

One phase of the Mormon migration to California has already been noticed in a chapter devoted to the battalion of volunteer soldiers.[31] This battalion marched from the far west, but the migratory movement was intended to include the whole church, and there were many of the faith living in the eastern states. In a farewell message to saints in the east, dated at New York, November 8, 1845, Orson Pratt explained the general plan to migrate en masse beyond the limits of "this wicked nation," and called upon the brethren to sell their property, purchase teams, and go to Nauvoo for a start with the rest in the early spring. Such as might not be able to provide a proper outfit for the overland journey—and it was clearly set forth that poverty-stricken saints would not just now be welcome at Nauvoo—were counselled to take the cheaper route by sea; and it was announced that Elder Samuel Brannan would be left in

[31] See chapter xviii. of this volume. See also *Hist. Utah*, this series, for a general account of the Mormon movement westward.

charge of this emigration to charter a vessel, or half a dozen vessels if necessary, and start in January for the Pacific coast.[32] Brannan was a native of Maine, who after a residence in the west—during which he had imbibed the true faith, but had been wellnigh killed by fever and ague—returned to New York to publish the *Prophet* and preach to the saints of the metropolis. He was a man of more ability and zeal than high principle; still few better could have been selected to lead this people around Cape Horn to the land of promise.

Very soon the ship *Brooklyn* of 450 tons, Richardson master, was chartered at $1,200 per month; and the rate of passage for adults was fixed at $50, though an additional sum of $25 was required for subsistence. It was hoped, however, that more favorable terms could be secured for later companies, since a New York merchant proposed to carry Mormons at $16 per ton, if he could secure the carrying of certain government stores. There were over 300 applicants for passage on the *Brooklyn,* but most of them were too poor to pay the sum required, and had to remain behind, though some were aided by contributions from richer brethren. A large supply of implements for farmers and mechanics—enough for 800 men, as was estimated, with a view to later accessions to the colony—was put on the ship, which carried also three flouring mills and a printing-press, with all the material pertaining to the *Prophet* newspaper. Books, especially those for school use, were not forgotten; and 179 volumes from a benevolent lawyer of Brooklyn were added to the library at the last moment.[33]

[32] Nov. 8, 1845, Pratt's message, in *Nauvoo Times and Seasons,* v. 1043.

[33] *Nauvoo Times and Seasons,* vi. 1094, 1112–14, 1126–8, including Brannan's announcements, explanations, and instructions to the faithful about preparations for the voyage, and prompt assembling at New York. Also a series of rules and regulations for conduct on the trip in 21 articles. I. M. Vancott was the man who gave 179 volumes of Harper's Family Library. A negro cook and steward were employed at $16 and $18 per month. Exact dates in the preparations of Nov. to Jan. are not clear, from the fact that most of the items in the *Times and Seasons* are taken from the *N. Y. Messenger* without naming dates of the latter.

The whole number of emigrants finally leaving New York was 238,[34] including 70 men, 68 women, and 100 children. They were chiefly American farmers and mechanics from the eastern and middle states, and included a few—just how many it is impossible to state—who were not Mormons. I append a list of names.[35]

[34] According to my list in next note, though as will be seen there are a few uncertain items in the matter of children. Kemble, *Twenty Years Ago*, says there were 238 souls, about a dozen not being Mormons. Eagar says there were 236, all Mormons but Frank Ward. The *Times and Seasons*, vi. 1126, makes the number 230, with 3 or 4 not Mormons.

[35] I have three lists of the Mormon immigrants, the most complete of which is that published in the *Honolulu Friend*, July 1, 1846, as a passenger list on the arrival of the *Brooklyn* at that port. Another was made before the vessel left N. Y., and is found in the *Nauvoo Times and Seasons*, vi. 1113; but many changes were made apparently before departure. The third list is one made out by Wm Glover, *Mormons in Cal.*, MS., in 1884, with notes as to what became of the different members. There were probably a few non-Mormon passengers not named in the following list. See a biographic notice of each member in my *Pioneer Register and Index*.

Brannan's company of Mormon immigrants, 1846: Isaac Addison, wife, and daughter; Silas Aldrich (died at sea), wife Prudence, son Jasper, and daughter; Wm Atherton and wife; Julius C. Austin, wife, and 3 children; Samuel Brannan, wife, and child; Alondus L. D. Buckland, and mother Hannah D. Buckland; Newell Bullen, wife, and 3 children; Charles C. Burr, wife, and child; Nathan Burr and wife; John Cade (possibly Kincaid) and wife; Sophia P. Clark; Abram Combs, wife, and 3 children; Mrs Fanny M. Corwin; John Eagar, Lucy Eagar, and daughter (perhaps 2) Mary Eagar, Thomas Eagar; Elias Ensign (died at sea), Miss Eliza Ensign (died at sea), Jerusha Ensign and son; Wm Evans, wife, and 4 children; Joseph R. Fisher, Mary Ann Fisher; Jerusha Fowler, and 4 children (a child of John (?) Fowler died at sea); Wm Glover, wife, and 3 children; Isaac Goodwin, wife (died at sea), and 6 children; Jonathan Griffith, wife, and 2 children; Mrs Mary Hamilton (and perhaps children); A. G. Haskell; Jacob Hayes; Joseph Hicks; John M. Horner and wife; Elisha Hyatt, wife, and son; Cyrus Ira (or Irea); John Joyce, wife, and child (perhaps 2); Mrs Isabella Jones; Ed. C. Kemble; George Kittleman, John Kittleman, Sarah Kittleman, Thomas Kittleman, Wm Kittleman, wife, and 6 children; Richard Knowles, and wife; Samuel Ladd (or Johnson); Emmeline A. Lane; Isaac Leigh (or Lee), and wife; James Light, wife, and child; Angeline M. Lovett; Patrick McCue, wife, and 4 children; Earl Marshall and family; Moses A. Meder, wife Sarah D., and child; Barton Mowry, wife, and 2 sons; Origin Mowry and family (?); Rinaldo Mowry; Ambrose T. Moses, wife, and 4 children; Miss Mary Murray; Edwin Narrimore, Mercy M. Narrimore (apparently remained at Honolulu for a time), and child; Joseph Nichols, wife Jerusha, and child (a child also died at sea); Lucy Nutting; Howard Oakley; E. Ward Pell, wife, and 2 daughters; Robert Petch, wife, and 2 children; John Philips; Peter Pool, Mary Pool, Elizabeth Pool; Christiana Read, Hannah T. Read (Jimison?), and child, John Reed, Rachael Reed; Isaac R. Robbins, wife, and 2 children; John R. Robbins, wife, and 2 children (2 children died at sea); Henry Rowland (Roulan, or Rollins) and daughter (?), Isaac Rowland; Eliza Savage; James Scott; George W. Sirrine, John J. Sirrine, wife, and child; Horace A. Skinner, wife, and child; Amelia Smith; Orrin Smith, wife, and 6 children; Robert Smith, wife, and 2 children; Zelnora S. Snow; Mary Sparks and family; Quartus S. Sparks, wife, and child;

Besides superintending preparations for the departure of this particular company, Elder Brannan devoted much attention to the general welfare of the whole Mormon people in their new western home, and this not altogether to the neglect perhaps of his own interests and those of certain friends. He discovered, or pretended to have discovered, that the government would probably take steps to prevent the Mormon migration, on the ground that they intended to take sides with either Mexico or England against the United States. But the shrewd Samuel also discovered a remedy for all prospective misfortune. He learned that Amos Kendall and certain influential associates, acting through one Benson as agent, and claiming President Polk as a 'silent party' to the project, would undertake to prevent all interference if the Mormon leaders would sign an agreement "to transfer to A. G. Benson & Co. the odd numbers of all the lands and town lots they may acquire in the country where they may settle." Accordingly such a contract was drawn up by Kendall, signed by Brannan and Benson, witnessed by Elder Appleby, and sent to President Young for approval. In relation to this matter, I am unable to say whether Brannan was made to believe by certain men for their own interests that the saints were in danger and that they had influence with the government, being thus induced to sign the contract for protection, or whether

---

Daniel Stark, wife, and 2 children; George Still, wife, and 3 children; Simeon Stivers; Wm Stout, wife, and child; Jesse A. Stringfellow; Thomas Tompkins, wife, and 2 children; Frank Ward (not a Mormon); Caroline Warner and 3 children; George K. Winner, wife, and 6 children (a child died at sea).

The list in *Times and Seasons* contains the following names, not in the Honolulu list, of persons who probably could not finally raise the passage money: Dan. S. Baldwin, Manena Cannon, Jonas Cook, James Embly, J. M. Farnsworth, Wm Flint, Joseph France, John Hairbaird, Wm Mack, Stephen H. Pierce, Wm C. Reamer, Dan. Richardson, Charles Russell, Susan A. Searls, James Smith, Sam. Smith, and Simeon Stanley. One Ferguson, an Irishman from Waterford, is named by Maguire. *Irish in Amer.*, 269. Lincoln is named by Findla, *Statement*, MS., 3–4, as a Mormon preacher. Clark, of 'Clark's Point,' S. F., is called a Mormon by Sherman. *Mem.*, i. 52. Marshall and Oakley are not named in the Honolulu list, though there is no doubt about their coming. Ladd was known as Johnson in Cal.

the scheme was one devised by the crafty elder himself as a means of becoming a partner in the proposed
speculations of Benson & Co. in California. Brigham
Young and his council declined to approve the contract, and no very serious results to the Mormons
ensued; but the war with Mexico may have interfered with the plans of the speculators, of which nothing more is known. It is noticeable that Lansford
W. Hastings was a Californian agent in this affair,
and that he also represented it as a project secretly
supported by the government.[36]

It was on February 4th that the *Brooklyn* sailed
from New York with her load of emigrants. She was
not a fast sailer, but excellent preparations had been
made for the comfort of the passengers. Elaborate
regulations had been drawn up for all the details of

[36] *Tullidge's Life of Brigham Young*, 18–24, contains the best account of
this matter, with quotations from original documents. In his letter of Jan.
26th to Young, Brannan says: 'I had an interview with Amos Kendall, in
company with Mr Benson, which resulted in a compromise'—a previous letter of the 12th had made known the impending danger to the saints—'the
conditions of which you will learn by reading the contract between them and
us...K. is now our friend, and will use his influence in our behalf in connection with 25 of the most prominent demagogues in the country. You will
be permitted to pass out of the states unmolested...I shall select the most
suitable spot on the bay of S. F. for the location of a commercial city. When
I sail, which will be next Saturday at one o'clock, I shall hoist a flag with
"Oregon" on it...I am aware that it (the contract) is a covenant with death,
but we know that God is able to break it and will do it. The children of Israel
in their escape from Egypt had to make covenants for their safety and leave it
for God to break them; and the prophet has said, "As it was then so shall it be
in the last days."...Mr Benson's address is No. 39 South St., and the sooner you
can give him answer the better. He will spend one month in Washington to
sustain you, and he will do it, no mistake. But everything must be kept
silent as death on our part, names of parties in particular. I now commit this
sheet to the post, praying that Israel's God may prevent it from falling into the
hands of wicked men.' In a postscript to a copy of the contract he says: 'It
is no gammon, but will be carried through if you say "amen." It was drawn
up by Kendall's own hand; but no person must be known but Mr Benson.'
In his journal Brigham Young writes: 'The council considered the subject,
and concluded that as our trust was in God, and that as we looked to him
for protection, we would not sign any such unjust and oppressive agreement.
This was a plan of political demagogues to rob the Latter-day Saints of
millions, and compel them to submit to it by threats of Federal bayonets.'
March 3d, Hastings to Larkin, predicts great things for Cal. from the vast
tide of immigration. Benson & Co. are about to establish a great commercial
house in Cal. and will send two ships a year, bringing immigrants free of
charge. This is a confidential govt arrangement, B. & Co. not really bearing
the expense. The motive of the govt will be clear to L. *Larkin's Doc.*, MS.,
iv. 55.

routine conduct, and there were days when several of
the rules were not broken. Strict attention was paid
to the duties of religion; yet before the end of the
voyage four leading members had to be excommunicated for improper views and conduct, or what seemed
such to the immaculate Samuel.[37] Besides these spiritual backsliding there were ten deaths, and two
births, the infants being named Atlantic and Pacific.
In each ocean a storm put all in danger. Once Captain Richardson gave up the vessel as lost; but the
Mormons paid no heed to such terrors, for were they
not in the keeping of the Lord, and bound for a land
of promise? It is even claimed that faith somewhat
strengthened them to bear the pangs of sea-sickness.
The last storm struck the ship when she was near the
latitude of Valparaíso, and trying to make that port,
driving her back nearly to the cape. The first anchorage was at the island of Juan Fernandez on May
4th. But here they got for nothing the supplies that
would have cost dear at Valparaiso.[38] After five days
they continued their voyage, arriving at Honolulu on
June 20th, and remaining there ten days, being hospitably welcomed, and honored by Mr Damon with a
kindly notice in the *Friend*.[39] Here they met Commodore Stockton, about to sail for Monterey, and
learned something of the prospect that California
would soon be occupied by the United States. Much
of the time during the remainder of the voyage was

[37] Brannan's letter in *Liverpool Millen. Star*, ix. 307. Elder Pell, B.'s
counsellor, was one of the culprits. 'Wicked and licentious conduct' was
shown by 'evidence of the most disgusting character,' if we may credit B.
The trial was after leaving Honolulu.

[38] I have a copy of a letter from one of the passengers, written at Juan
Fernandez on the 5th, and describing the voyage to that point as pleasant and
uneventful.

[39] *Honolulu Friend*, July 1, 1846, including, as we have seen, a list of the
Mormons. Quoted also in the *Millennial Star*, ix. 39-40. John P. Gregson,
then on the *Erie*, in a letter of 1875, says one of the Mormon elders and family remained at Honolulu on account of ill health, and conversed freely with
the writer about the plans of the saints. Glover says that Orrin Smith's family was the one left at the islands. Mrs Narrimore and son arrived at S. F.
in 1847 on the *Don Quixote*, and may therefore have remained at Honolulu.

spent in military drill, with a view to possible hostility on the part of the Mexicans.[40]

The arrival at San Francisco was on July 31st, and of course there was not the slightest opposition to the landing from United States officials, as there would probably have been none had the Californians been still in power, though it is true that immigrants from the western states had not given the Mormons a good name.[41]   Brannan and his associates were doubtless somewhat surprised to find the stars and stripes floating over their land of promise, and it is even possible that the pious elder's first remark, as reported, was, "There is that damned flag again"!   But it has been the fashion greatly to exaggerate their disappointment.   Could the Mormons have established themselves, fifty or a hundred thousand strong, in the country while it was yet a Mexican possession, it might have better suited their plans, since it would have given them a vantage-ground for negotiations with the United States.   Possibly in certain contingencies they would have acted against that government had their interests seemed to require it; but that they expected or desired such a state of things may

[40] Glover names Ladd and Robt Smith as teachers of tactics; and says the drill continued until Capt. R., fearing a mutiny, stopped it.   Kemble says the teacher was a deserter from the U. S. army.   Eagar represents the arms as having been bought at Honolulu on the advice of Stockton.

Wm Glover's *Mormons in California* is a MS. record of the voyage and all connected with the immigrant company, written from memory in 1884, at the request of Franklin D. Richards, and furnished for my use by the latter.   It is of especial value in its information on what became of the different members, and is supplemented by a letter of July 31, 1884.   *Twenty Years Ago.   The 'Brooklyn' Mormons in California*, is a very complete narrative of the whole matter, probably the best extant, published in the *Sacramento Union*, Sept. 11, 1866, and written by one of the company, whom I suppose to have been E. C. Kemble.   John Eagar's brief narrative is a MS. furnished by Mr Richards, with *Glover's Mormons*.   It is not of great value, containing several erroneous statements.   In the *Times and Seasons*, vi. 1126–7, is a full account of circumstances attending the departure from N. Y.   Brief account by the 'wife of Col Jackson,' in *Tullidge's Women*, 445–8.   Californian songs of the Mormons, in *Young's Wife No. 19*, p. 111, 116–17; *Marshall's Through America*, 179–80.   Mention of Brannan's company may be found in most works on early California.

[41] March 2d, Gov. Pico to assembly, on rumors of an intended Mormon immigration. *Olvera, Doc.*, MS., 14–15; *Dept. St. Pap.*, MS., ix. 16–17. March 4th, Larkin to U. S. sec. state, on the same reports, which he represents as having caused much fear. *Larkin's Off. Corresp.*, MS., ii. 42.

well be doubted. There had been nothing secret or mysterious about their purpose to occupy California, but they had hoped to be first in the field, and masters of the situation, the grantors not recipients of favors in their dealings with a government that had not protected them against the mobs in Missouri and Illinois. Yet, though they had not expected the war to break out so soon, they must have known what was likely to happen before they left the states; news at Honolulu had left but slight doubt as to the result; and now, if not entirely pleased, they were prepared to make the best of the situation, taking comfort from the thought that they had at least escaped complications with the Mexicans, and had saved a considerable sum in duties that would have had to be paid on their cargo.

Thus San Francisco became for a time very largely a Mormon town. All bear witness to the orderly and moral conduct of the saints both on land and sea. They were honest and industrious citizens, even if clannish and peculiar. There was no practice of polygamy to excite animosities. They had a few months' provisions left on disembarking, but they owed something on their passage money. After camping for a time on a vacant lot, some went to Marin county to work as lumbermen and thus pay their debts; others were put in possession of the old mission buildings; all sought work at whatever tasks presented themselves, making themselves generally useful; while a party of twenty was sent into the San Joaquin valley to prepare for the coming of the Nauvoo saints by the overland route. Many of them appear in the town records of 1846–7 as the grantees of building lots. Yet all was not tranquil in the community. Four had been expelled from the church on the voyage, as before remarked, and three more soon after landing. Some of the company made complaints against Brannan, whose misdeeds are not clearly specified, but who was apparently exonerated after a legal investigation.   Before the end of 1846 twenty "went astray after strange gods, serving their bellies and lusts," as the elder expressed it; that is, they declined to follow his instructions.   In January 1847 Brannan began the publication of the *Yerba Buena California Star*, using the material of the old *Prophet* office; and it was continued through this year and the next.   It was not issued as an organ of Mormonism but as a newspaper, though I think some special 'extras' were devoted to church affairs, not being generally circulated.[42]

Brannan wrote from Yerba Buena on the 1st of January: "We have commenced a settlement on the River San Joaquin, a large and beautiful stream emptying into the bay of San Francisco; but the families of the company are wintering in this place, where they find plenty of employment, and houses to live in; and about twenty of our number are up at the new settlement, which we call New Hope, ploughing and putting in wheat and other crops, and making preparations to move their families up in the spring, where they hope to meet the main body by land some time during the coming season." [43]   The site of New

---

[42] Jan. 1, 1847, Brannan to the brethren from the *Star* extra in *Millen. Star*, ix. 306–7.   He expects another shipload of immigrants, 2 vessels being reported as having sailed, one from N. Y. and the other from Boston.   (The *Xylon* to leave in N. Y. in April with Mormons. *Or. Spectator*, Aug. 20, 1846.)   'A few of the passengers on our arrival endeavored to make mischief and trouble by complaints of the bad treatment they had received during the passage, which induced Capt. Montgomery to institute a court of inquiry, before which the larger portion of the company were cited to appear for private examination.   But the truth was mighty and prevailed!' Tuthill, *Hist. Cal.*, 214–15, says the first jury trial in Cal. was won by Brannan on this occasion.   In *Ryan's Judges and Criminals*, 59–60, is a burlesque account of the controversy, implying that the quarrel was about funds.   The *Monterey Calif.*, Oct. 10, 1846, contains a brief notice of a split in the Mormon ranks, which by scattering them will be good for the country.   The Mormons are spoken of as a plain, laborious, frugal people, not meriting the opprobrium cast upon them.   Aug. 19th, justice of the peace at S. Diego uses the 'Mormon invasion' as an incentive to patriots to furnish 100 horses for the troops. *Hayes' Doc.*, MS., 188.   Glover states that only two of the Mormons enlisted in the California battalion, and this mainly through his own opposition, many of them having been willing to enlist at first.

[43] *Millen. Star*, ix. 306.   According to *Solano Co. Hist.*, 312, a site was selected by L. W. Hastings at Montezuma, where H. resided for several years; but the place did not suit the brethren, and they went elsewhere.

Hope was on the north bank of the Stanislaus, about a mile and a half from the San Joaquin. William Stout was in charge of the party that went in a launch from Yerba Buena to found the first settlement in San Joaquin county. A log-house was built and a saw-mill, eighty acres were seeded and fenced, and in April the crops promised well, but not much more is known of the enterprise, except that it was abandoned in the autumn. The company is said to have had trouble with Stout, who soon left the place, as did others.[44] The reason for abandoning the enterprise was not, however, these dissensions, but the receipt of news that the church had decided to settle at Salt Lake. Brannan went east to meet President Young and the main body, leaving New Helvetia late in April, reaching Fort Hall on June 9th,[45] and meeting the saints at Green River about July 4th, to come on with them to Salt Lake Valley. He was not pleased with the decision to remain there and found a city, and soon started back sorrowful with the news. In the Sierra he met the returning members of the battalion on September 6th, giving them a dreary picture of the chosen valley, and predicting that Young would change his mind and bring his people to California the next year.[46]

The members of the *Brooklyn* company were like-

[44] In *S. Joaq. Co. Hist.*, 100–1, the settlement is called Stanislaus City. It is said that after the planting and fencing was done Stout claimed the farm, and advised the others to select farms for themselves! This made trouble, Brannan was summoned, and it was decided that the house and farm must be reserved for the twelve apostles, whereupon Stout soon departed. A meagre crop of potatoes and a flood are mentioned. Buckland, the last to quit the place, went to Stockton in Nov., the rest of the company having gone to the south. The land was abandoned until 1851. See also *S. J. Pioneer*, June 23, 1877. Glover, *Mormons in Cal.*, MS., says 'the company was broken up and every one went to work to make a fit-out to go to the valley as best we could. The land, the oxen, the crop, the houses, tools, and launch, all went into Brannan's hands, and the company that did the work never got anything.'

[45] June 19th, Brannan writes to a friend in N. Y. from Fort Hall. Will start next day with 2 men and part of the horses. *Mill. Star*, ix. 305. Glover says B. was accompanied by Charles Smith. Meeting with Young. *Tullidge's Life Young*, 166.

[46] *Tyler's Hist. Morm. Bat.*, 315. Brannan's return is announced in the *S. F. Cal. Star*, Sept. 18, 1847.

wise disappointed to learn that the new home of their people was to be in the far interior.   Some declined to leave the coast region; the rest, giving up their dreams of a great city at New Hope, devoted themselves half regretfully to preparations for a migration eastward.   The discovery of gold in the spring of 1848 reunited most of them at the mines of Mormon Island; but their experience as miners belongs to a later volume.   Nearly one hundred adults, with some forty children, found their way in different parties, chiefly in 1848–50, to Utah, where many of them are still living as I write.[47]   The rest, forty-five adults and sixty-five children, according to my lists, remained behind.   Most of them, like the leader, apostatized from the true faith; a few in later years joined Mormon communities at San Bernardino or in Arizona, while a few either died in the faith, or living, retain something of their former theories.   Probably about a dozen of all who came on the *Brooklyn* are still residents of California.

Pioneers of 1847, according to my register, were 1,900, or about twice as many as those of the preceding year,[48]   They may be classified in round number as follows: Overland immigrants, not including females, and in reality only a small part of the whole number, 50; volunteers of the Mormon battalion, 350; a total of 400 known by name to have come by land routes. The regiment of New York volunteers, or soldier immigrants, 950; officers and men of the artillery company, U. S. regulars, 120; other known arrivals by sea, 70, including 20 in the navy; making a total of 1,140 who came by water.   Men whose coming is ascribed to 1847 in records of later years, 60; those whose presence at some point in California is shown by records of the year, 300; or a total of 360 to be

[47] Glover, *Mormons in Cal.*, MS., describes the journey of himself and a few others across the Sierra in the spring of 1849, and names most of those still living.

[48] See beginning of this chapter.

divided in unknown proportions between arrivals by sea and land.

My register for 1848 contains 520 names. Classified as above, they included 35 overland immigrants, 25 from Oregon, 140 known to have come by sea, 100 whose arrival merely is ascribed to this year, 50 mentioned for the first time as being in the mines, and 170 found at other places without any definite record respecting the manner of their coming. To this number of 520 there should be added, however, 480 men—dragoons, teamsters, mechanics, and servants—who came under Graham from Mexico, arrived in southern California late in December, and with few exceptions are not named in my lists. Thus the total number of registered new-comers for the year was 1,000, though necessarily the record is less accurate than for earlier times. For later years even an approximately correct register is an impossibility.

The overland immigration to Oregon in 1847 was very large; that to California much smaller than had been expected, though it was understood in advance that prevalent uncertainty in the east respecting the political situation, together with reports of the Donner disasters of the past year, would have an unfavorable effect. Oregon agents at forts Hall and Laramie also did much to discourage those who had California in view, not adhering more strictly to the truth in their statements than had Californian agents at the same points a few years earlier. Yet a party of about fifty came down from Oregon, arriving in June or earlier.[49] The regular immigration by the Humboldt and Truckee route may have numbered two hundred

[49] *S. F. Calif.*, July 10, 1847; *Or. Spectator*, June 10, 1847. Charles Bennett and Stephen Staats, who later returned to Or., are named as members of this party. The *S. F. Cal. Star*, Feb. 13, 1847, predicts a large immigration in the autumn and an immense one the next. In the *Monterey Calif.*, Aug. 29, 1846, is an extract from the *Little Rock Gazette*, announcing the coming of an Arkansas company in 1847. See letters in praise of Cal., though mingled with doubts on the actual state of affairs, in *Niles' Reg.*, lxxiii. 111; *Cutts' Conq.*, 263-4; *S. F. Bulletin*, June 16, 1877; *Belfast (Me.) Repub. Jour.*, in *Eureka West Coast Signal*, May 24, 1871; *Newark (N. J.) Advertiser* (letter of June 17th from Monterey).

souls, though, as we have seen, only about fifty names are known.   The parties were met by Kearny and later by Stockton, and were passed by Brannan on his return from Salt Lake, news from these sources being published in the papers.   They had no remarkable experience on the way, and arrived with seventy wagons at New Helvetia in the first half of October. Charles Hopper, a pioneer of 1841, now returning with his family, was in charge of the main company as guide or captain.   There was another small party that attempted a northern cut-off to the upper Sacramento, but was obliged to take the Appleton route to Oregon.[50]   As far west as Salt Lake Valley the Mormon trains formed a prominent element in the year's immigration.

Of the overland parties of 1848 still less is known, but the immigration was perhaps not less numerous than in 1847, though there are only about thirty-five names on the records.   The only narrative of the trip extant is that written from memory by J. P. C. Allsopp, who came with a small party from New Orleans by way of St Louis and Independence.   Several of the number stopped at Salt Lake to become Mormons, and seven, crossing the Sierra by the Carson Valley route, arrived at San Francisco in December.[51] James T. Walker with a party of eight started in 1847, but, being belated, was obliged to spend the winter in the Green River country, and came on to

[50] Aug. 23, 1847, Hunsacker and Smith arrive at the fort with news of the immigration. *N. Helv. Diary*, MS., 100.   Sept. 4th, news from Ft Hall in extracts from a diary kept perhaps by Brannan's companions.   1,500 wagons turned aside to Or. *S. F. Cal. Star.*   Sept. 18th, Brannan's report.   25 wagons probably at Truckee; others farther back. *Id.*   Oct. 3d–9th, arrival of immigrants at Sutter's.   Gerke, Fairchild, Fourgeaud, and Beston named. *N. Helv. Diary*, MS., 118–20.   See also *Sutter's Diary*, 9.   Oct. 16th, Capt. Hopper's company of 60 wagons crossing the S. Joaquin on the way to S. José.   Also mention of the party (Wiggins) which took the northern route. *S. F. Cal. Star;* also *Hist. Or.*, i. 623, this series.   Oct. 21st, Sutter to Vallejo.   Immigration very small, only 70 wagons. *Vallejo, Doc.*, MS., xii. 315. See also *Honolulu Polynesian*, iv. 51, 137, 146.   James Findla, *Statement*, MS., was a member of Hopper's company, and gives a brief account of the journey.   In Dec. a caravan of about 212 New Mexicans arrived at Los Angeles to trade. *S. F. Californian*, Dec. 29, 1847.
[51] *Allsopp's Leaves from my Log*, MS., 34–45.

California this year.[52] Bigler of the returning Mormons gives some information of parties met by the way.   On August 15th at the sink of the Humboldt they met eighteen emigrant wagons from Fort Hall. Ten more were met on the 26th; and next day Captain Hensley came up with a party of ten men on mules, who, after failing to follow the Hastings cutoff, had discovered a new and better route.   Three days later appeared Captain Chiles with forty-eight wagons, claiming to have found a better way than Hensley's, but the latter's was taken by the Mormons, since Chiles' trail could not be found.[53]

[52] *Contra Costa Co. Hist.*, 686.
[53] *Bigler's Diary of a Mormon*, MS., 89–95.   In the *Oregon Spectator*, Sept. 7th, is a report from advance immigrants that there were 600 wagons on the way, 300 of which would probably go to Cal.

CHAPTER XXI.

MISSIONS—INDIAN AFFAIRS—COMMERCE.

1346-1848.

Sale of Mission Estates—Act of the Assembly in April—The Montesdeoca Order—Pico's Sales from May to July—Purchasers and Terms—The Tornel Order—Evidences of Fraud—Action of Flores' Government—Decision of the Courts—Policy of Kearny and Mason, 1847-8—Ecclesiastical Affairs—Bishop and Friars—Vicars—Indian Affairs—Sutter, Vallejo, and Hunter as Sub-Indian Agents—Local Items—Commerce and Maritime Affairs—Meagre Data for 1846—Statistics—Mason's Communications—Collectors—Removal of Burdens—Free-trade—New Tariff from Washington—War Contributions—Modifications by Mason and Shubrick—Gold-dust for Duties—U. S. Revenue Laws Introduced with the Treaty—The First Steamer in California Waters—List of Vessels, 1846-8.

In accordance with Governor Pico's regulations of October 28, 1845, authorized by the territorial junta in its resolution of May 28th, three missions were sold and four rented to private individuals before the end of the year, as has been recorded in the preceding volume.[1] Six other establishments were to be sold in January, but a purchaser was found for only one, that of Soledad, bought by Feliciano Soberanes for $800 on the 4th. The sale of San Francisco was in later years ascribed to February 10th, but Santillan's title was doubtless fraudulently antedated. There

---

[1] See vol. iv. p. 546-53. The establishments sold were S. Juan Capistrano to Forster and McKinley for $710, Purísima to Temple for $1,110 (but the title was made out on Dec. 6th to J. R. Malo), and S. Luis Obispo to Scott, Wilson, and McKinley for $510. Those rented were Sta Bárbara to N. A. Den and Dan. Hill at $1,200, S. Buenventura to Arnaz and Botello at $1,630, Sta Inés to Covarrubias and Carrillo at $580, and S. Fernando to Pico and Manso at $1,120.

were also six missions remaining to be rented under the regulations, as soon as obstacles arising from their debts could be removed, but these obstacles proved insuperable. Respecting the governor's legal right with the junta's approval to sell the mission estates at this time, doubts were expressed by able men in the litigation of later years; but the wisdom of the policy and the good faith of the sales cannot be questioned. The titles acquired by the purchasers of the four missions named were finally confirmed.[2]

In his address to the assembly on March 2d, Governor Pico explained the condition of affairs, and called upon that body to devise some means of saving the missions from total ruin. The debts were large, creditors clamorous, and products limited. If leased, the amount of rent that could legally be applied to the payment of debts would be insignificant; if not rented, the expenses of administration would eat up all the revenue.[3] The result was a resolution introduced by Juan Bandini[4] on March 23d, approved by the assembly on the 30th, signed by the president and secretary on the 3d, and published in a bando by Pico on the 4th of April. It authorized the government to "carry into effect the object of the decree of May 28, 1845," and if necessary for that purpose, to sell the mission estates at auction, distributing among the Indians any surplus of funds that might exist, and in any case providing for the maintenance of the padre and the expenses of public worship. It was to have no effect on what had already been done under the earlier decree. I append a translation.[5]

[2] Land commission, no. 224, 410, 476, 526, in *Hoffman's Repts.*
[3] March 2, 1846, Pico to assembly. *Olvera, Doc.,* MS., 17–18. See also *St. Pap. Miss.*, MS., xi. 64.
[4] In *Bandini, Doc.,* MS., 66, are blotter copies, with erasures, interlineations, etc., showing the development of the measure. Also in *Dept. St. Pap.,* MS., viii. 89–95, as presented on March 23d, with a preamble explaining the necessity of such action. March 28th, Figueroa writes to Pico on the project. He was probably one of the committee.
[5] March 30, 1846, decree of assembly on missions, published by the governor on April 4th:
Article 1. The government is authorized to carry into effect the object

Before anything had been done to carry this decree into effect, there arrived from Mexico, dated November 14th and submitted to the assembly on April 15th, an order of the national government suspending all proceedings for the sale of mission property.   This, without recorded comments, was referred on May 13th to the committee on missions, and nothing more is heard of it for several years.[6]   In original

of the decree of 28th May last, published by this honorable assembly, respecting missions; to which end, seeing the impracticability of renting, mentioned in article 3 of said decree, the departmental government will act in the manner which may appear most conducive to obviate the total ruin of the missions of San Gabriel, San Luis Rey, San Diego, and the remainder, which are in similar circumstances.

Art. 2. As most of these establishments are owing large amounts, if the property on hand should not be sufficient to satisfy their acknowledged debts, attention shall be had to what the laws determine respecting bankruptcies, and steps shall be taken accordingly.

Art. 3. Should government, by virtue of this authority, find that, in order to prevent the total ruin which threatens said missions, it will be necessary to sell them to private persons, this shall be done at public auction, the customary notice being previously given.

Art. 4. In case of sale, if, after the debts be paid, any surplus should remain, this shall be divided among the Indians of the premises sold, government taking care to make the most just distribution possible.

Art. 5. In any case, care must be taken to secure a sufficient amount for the maintenance of the padres and the expenses of public worship, the government being at liberty to separate a part of the whole establishments, whether in lands for cultivation, landed or other property, at its discretion, which will be sufficient to secure both objects, the respective priests being previously heard and attended to.

Art. 6. The premises set apart according to the foregoing article shall be delivered as a sale at a perpetual interest of four per cent; and the proceeds shall be applied precisely to the objects mentioned in said article 5.

Art. 7. What has been done agreeably to what was ordained in the decree of the honorable assembly of the 28th May, before cited, remains in full force; and these presents shall in no manner alter the contracts made and measures taken by government, in accordance with said decree of May 1845; nor shall they in future put any obstacle in the way of what may be done in accordance thereto.

Art. 8. The government will remove any obstacles not foreseen in this decree; and within six months at furthest will notify this honorable assembly of the result of its fulfilment.

Halleck's Rept., 166–7; *Leg. Rec.*, MS., iv. 325–8; *Dept. St. Pap. Angeles*, MS., x. 88–9. The original bando is also in my possession. *Doc. Hist. Cal.*, MS., iii. 155; and it has often been reprinted in Spanish and English.   In later litigation, the lawyers attempted to show that Pico's reference to the date of this document as April 3d was an evidence of fraud, but there is no foundation for such a theory.

[6] Nov. 14, 1845, Minister Montesdeoca to gov. of Cal.   'It has come to the knowledge of the president that the departmental govt has made arrangements to sell at public auction all the property belonging to the missions, which your predecessor had ordered to be returned to the respective missionaries for the management and administration of their temporalities; therefore, he has seen fit to notify me that that govt must report on those particu-

archive records of later months of 1846, there is found
but little to indicate that the Montesdeoca order was
not obeyed, at least to the extent of suspending the
sales.[7] Yet in later years there were produced title
deeds signed by Pico, showing the sale at different
dates between May 4th and July 4th of twelve missions, including the four which had been rented in
1845. I append a list, referring the reader to local
annals for more particulars.[8] These titles vary considerably in form. In none is there any allusion to a
sale by auction, and it has never been claimed that
the sale was of that character as required by the decree. The consideration, even where a definite sum is
named, was in most cases an amount already due from
the government for past advances, and in the other
cases there is no evidence respecting the payment or
use made of the money.[9] Most of the titles require

lars, suspending at once every proceeding connected with the alienation of
the property in question pending the resolution of the supreme govt.' *St. Pap.,
Mis. and Col.*, MS., ii. 404-5; *Hartman's Brief*, 49-50; *Leg. Rec.*, MS., iii.
329-30, 341, and often reproduced. This order had no bearing on the governor's power to grant in regular form ranchos that had formerly been used by
the missions, but referred only to buildings, cattle, lands in use, etc. *Hoffman's
Opinions*, passim. It was also claimed that the order referred only to the 13
missions restored to the padres in 1843, and not to S. Juan Bautista. *Holli-
day's Brief*, in *Panaud* v. *U. S.*, *Hayes' Miss. B.*, 366, p. 14.

[7] May 13th, Pico calls upon all creditors of the missions to present their
claims and proofs. *Castro, Doc.*, MS., 84; *S. Luis Ob.*, *Arch.*, MS., 8; *Dept.
St. Pap.*, *Pref. y Juzg.*, MS., ii. 117. There are also, in *St. Pap. Mis.*, MS.,
xi. 61-6, and *Unb. Doc.*, MS., some records on the sale of S. Diego, S. Fernando,
S. Buenaventura, and Soledad.

[8] Missions sold by Pico in 1846: May 4th, S. Juan Bautista to O. Deleissèques for a debt; May 5th, S. José to Andrés Pico and J. B. Alvarado for
$12,000; May 18th, S. Luis Rey to Cot and José Ant. Pico for $2,437; June
8th, S. Rafael to Ant. Suñol and A. M. Pico for $8,000, S. Buenaventura to
José Arnaz for $12,000, S. Diego to Santiago Argüello for past services to govt,
and S. Gabriel to Reid and Workman for debt; June 10th, Sta Bárbara to
Rich. Den for $7,500; June 15th, Sta Inés to Covarrubias and Joaquin Car-
rillo for $7,000; June 17th, S. Fernando to Célis for $14,000; June 30th,
orchard of Sta Clara to Castañeda, Arenas, and Diaz for $1,200; July 4th,
S. Miguel to P. Rios and Wm Reed; June 4th, Soledad to Soberanes for $800.
The three sold in 1845, as already recorded, were Purísima, S. Luis
Obispo, and S. Juan Capistrano. A fraudulent title to S. Francisco was
dated Feb. 10th. Respecting the disposition of S. Cárlos, Sta Cruz, S. Antonio, and Solano nothing appears, except that at the latter a house was
granted by Castro to Prudon on June 3d.

[9] Pico has been accused of carrying away large sums to Mex., but there is
nothing to support the charge. In his *Hist. Cal.*, MS., 133-4, 171-2, he speaks
of the mission sales, without throwing much light on the subject. He says he
sold in 1846 only five missions; that the sales of S. Gabriel and S. Luis Rey

the purchaser to pay the mission debts, and to provide for the padre's support and the expenses of public worship, also reserving from the sale the church and priest's residence. Some of them make provision for remnants of the community Indians. Nearly all refer to the assembly's act as the grantor's authority,[10] and also to a general authorization from the supreme government, without naming any definite order or date, or alluding in any way to the Montesdeoca order. In later years a Mexican order of March 10th, declaring the governor and general 'facultados ampliamente' to defend the country, was produced as legalizing the sales.[11] I regard the document in itself as sufficient, although the courts did not take this view of it.[12] But the date of receiving this order is not known; it is improbable that it arrived before May 4th, when the sales began, or before the middle of June, when most of them had been effected; had it been in his possession, Pico would almost certainly have cited it; and during the period between the reception of the Montesdeoca order on April 15th and the unknown date when the Tornel order came to hand the governor had no right to sell the mission estates.[13]

In the case of several missions, it was proved clearly enough that the titles and corroborative papers in pri-

did not go into effect; that the sale of S. Fernando was virtually a mortgage to secure sums contributed to the govt (it is true the deed contained a provision that the property might be redeemed within 8 months); S. Diego was given to Argüello for past services; and the consideration for S. Buenaventura was merely nominal. Not a dollar ever came into Pico's hands.

[10] Copies of most of the titles are printed in Spanish and English in *Hartman's Brief, in Miss. Cases*, appendix. A noticeable peculiarity is that the date of this act is generally given as April 13th, instead of 3d (*trece* for *tres*).

[11] March 10, 1846, Tornel to Castro and Pico. The original in my possession. *Pico, Doc.*, MS., ii. 171.

[12] *Hoffman's Opinions*, 12, 38; *U. S. Sup. Court Repts*, 1 Wallace, 745, 766. The 'ample powers,' it seems to me, must have included the power to raise funds by selling the only national property in the province.

[13] A point not noticed, so far as I know, by the land lawyers was this: the Tornel order authorized Pico and Castro to adopt measures for the defence of Cal. against the Americans, but for nearly the whole period of the alleged mission sales Pico was straining every nerve—not to resist the Americans, for he did not believe an invasion imminent—but to defend himself against Gen. Castro! The absence of the Tornel order from the archives may be explained either by the late date of its reception, or, if it came in June, by Pico's unwillingness to admit to the sureños that Castro had also the 'ample faculties.'

vate hands had been written after Pico's return to
California in 1848, or at least after the raising of the
United States flag in July 1846, and fraudulently
antedated. That the same was true of others is
strongly indicated by various circumstances: notably
the absence of original archive evidence, the error in
date of the assembly's decree, with other irregularities
in the documents,[14] the mystery enshrouding the alleged
payment of large sums of money, the delay of purchasers in making known their claims, and the failure
to call certain witnesses in the resulting litigation.   I
suppose, however, that several of the establishments
were deeded more or less in good faith before July 7,
1846, to creditors of the government who were willing
to take the risks of obtaining confirmation of their
titles; but I do not venture to name the missions so
disposed of.

The only subsequent action of Californian authorities in this connection was a decree of the assembly
on October 30th, promulgated by Governor Flores
on the 31st, which annulled Pico's sales, and authorized the new ruler to mortgage some of the missions,
and thus raise funds for a continued resistance to
American invasion.[15]   Of course under the United
States régime this act had no validity except as an
argument respecting the view taken by Californians
of the sales and their legality.   As to the ultimate
fate of these mission titles, the supreme court decided

[14] On the other hand, if Pico had written the titles after his return in 1848,
he would naturally have cited the Tornel order in his possession.   The suspicious circumstances are catalogued and exaggerated by Hartman and others.
The Mex. treaty commissioners in 1848 assured the U. S. representative that
there had been no land grants since May 13, 1846.

[15] Oct. 27, 1846, measure introduced by com. on ways and means. *Olvera*,
Doc., MS., 46–8.   Oct. 30th, 31st, decree approved by assembly and published
by Flores.   Original in *Soberanes*, *Doc.*, MS., 326; also in *Halleck's Rept.*,
167; *Castro*, *Doc.*, MS., ii. 153; *Janssens*, *Doc.*, MS., 33–5; *Unb. Doc.*, MS.,
360–1.   Unfortunately this decree does not name the missions that have been
sold, and it may possibly refer to the sales of 1845.   It also provides that the
missions shall continue in the possession of the lessees.   This might indicate
ignorance that the leased missions had been sold; but it must be noted that
by some of the deeds the purchasers were to have possession only on the
expiration of the lease.

in 1863, in the cases of San Gabriel and San Luis Rey, that Pico had no right to make the sales; but before that decision was rendered, the titles of San Diego, San Buenaventura, San Fernando, Soledad, and San Juan Bautista had been finally confirmed by the land commission and district courts, while the other six had been rejected by the same tribunals. The 'church property' proper, including the church buildings, priest's house, and lands to the extent of six to one hundred and ninety acres at each of the twenty-one establishments, was finally confirmed to the archbishop, representing the catholic church.

It soon became evident to the new rulers of California that there was room for much doubt respecting the true ownership of the mission estates, and during 1847–8 they wisely adhered to the policy of maintaining the matter in statu quo. On March 22, 1847, Kearny ordered that four establishments in the north should remain in charge of the priests, without prejudice to the rights of claimants, until proper judicial tribunals should be established.[16] This caused some trouble at Santa Clara, where American immigrants had taken possession. Governor Mason announced that "the government fully recognizes and will sustain the rights of the priests at the missions and to all mission property, against all who cannot in due course of law show a just and sound legal title;" and he once ordered a military force under Captain Naglee to eject the immigrants; but Padre Real finally permitted them to remain till after harvest, and longer by paying a small sum for the support of the church.[17] In the south the occupants, whether priests, lessees,

[16] March 22, 1847, Kearny's order that S. José, Sta Clara, Sta Cruz, and S. Juan remain in charge of the priests. *Halleck's Rept*, 168; *Arch. Arzob.*, MS., v. pt ii. p. 73–4, etc.

[17] *Cal. and N. Mex., Mess. and Doc., 1850*, p. 343–4. P. Real had sold some mission lands, under orders from Gen. Castro of May 25 and June 16, 1846; but Mason on Jan. 3, 1848, declared all such sales void. Neither did he permit claimants under the alleged Pico sale to take possession of the orchard. At Sta Cruz, on complaint of the padre, forbade the sale of lots by the alcalde. *Id.*, 433. Prudon's occupancy of a building at Sonoma was sustained against the padre's claim and alcalde's decision.

or purchasers, were allowed to remain in possession; nor was interference permitted with the Indians who were living on certain tracts of disputed lands. Even a claimant under a grant from Governor Flores was temporarily sustained at Santa Inés. In the case of certain occupants who claimed a double title, that of lessee was preferred, and an effort was made to obtain documentary evidence for future use as well as to prevent a waste of property by a strict investigation of accounts. For alleged abuses, the lessee of San Buenaventura was ejected after investigation by Colonel Stevenson; and San Diego was also leased by the American authorities. In current correspondence there is little but local items.

"Of general mission and ecclesiastical matters outside of those connected with the disposal of estates, a bare mention will suffice." This remark on the subject for 1845 will apply equally well to the period of 1846–8. At the beginning there were thirteen surviving friars, six Fernandinos, and seven Zacatecanos; at the end only one of the former, Padre Ordaz, was left, with six of the latter. The year of the American conquest brought death to five of the missionaries. The old organization was kept up to a certain extent, Padre Duran retaining the prefecture in the south until his death in June 1846, and Ánzar being succeeded by Gonzalez as chief of the Zacatacan friars. Even the formality of assigning stipends for each of the missions was kept up in Mexico, though of course no money was forwarded.[18] Bishop García Diego, being seriously ill in April 1846, appointed fathers Duran and Gonzalez as his vicars, who after the bishop's death in May took charge of the ecclesiastical government; and after Duran's early death, Gonzalez retained the position for the rest of the period.[19]

[18] *Mex., Mem. Hacienda*, 1846–8.
[19] April 19, 1846, bishop to PP. Duran and Gonzalez, with appointment. April 20th, pastoral letter of D. and G., asking for prayers, etc. April 22d, bishop announces the appt accepted by D. and G. April 28th, gov. announces the matter. May 1st, 3d, death and burial of the bishop. May 6th, circular

Church matters led to few complications during the military occupation, though American ideas of marriage as a civil contract troubled the priests considerably, and their complaints caused Governor Mason to issue, in August 1847, an order forbidding alcaldes to perform the marriage ceremony when either of the parties was a member of the catholic church. Entire freedom was guaranteed in matters pertaining to religious belief and worship; but beyond the preaching of the Mormon elders at San Francisco, and some slight beginnings of protestant service there and at San José and Santa Cruz, there was little to interrupt the current of old-time religious customs.

Indian affairs, the doings of gentiles and apostates, will afford a few items for local annals of 1846–8; but the general subject requires but brief treatment. Naturally, the quarrels of Californian rulers, followed by the war of American occupation, tended to promote rather than check the ravages of horse-thief tribes roaming through the broad interior. During the first half of 1846 complaints of depredations were of constant occurrence, especially in the Los Angeles region, where propositions to effect a loan, to send out an armed force, or to station a garrison at the Cajon pass were always pending; and where parties of volunteers under Lugo, Salazar, Palomares, Wilson, and others made several effective raids. Many Indians were killed, recovered property was distributed among the captors, and captive women and children were brought to the ranchos to work and be educated. In April the assembly went so far as to resolve in seven articles to devote surplus revenues to active efforts against

of the vicars. May 19th, sub-prefect orders their recognition. *Sta Clara, Parroquia*, MS., 29; *Doc. Hist. Cal.*, MS., iii. 187; *Dept. St. Pap.*, MS., vii. 118; *Id.*, *Pref. y Juzg.*, ii. 62, 65, 118, iv. 65; *Id.*, *Angeles*, xi. 172; *Sta Bárbara, Lib. Mis.*, MS., 39; *S. Luis Ob.*, *Arch.*, MS., 25; *Arch. Arzob.*, MS., v. pt ii. 66. Oct. 7, 1847, the chapter of the metropolitan of Mex. approves Gonzalez's title as vicario capitular y gobernador de la mitra de Californias. *Arch. Obisp.*, MS., 26. In *Corresp. Mis.*, MS., 13–37, is an undated appeal of P. Gonzalez to the pope in behalf of Cal., asking for the power to administer confirmation.

the savages![20]   At the same time, in reply to urgent
petitions from the people of San José for protection,
Governor Pico authorized the prefect to organize a
vigorous campaign, and to pay expenses with $6,000—
from Castro's part of the revenues![21]   Of Indian affairs
in the Sacramento Valley at this time something has
been said in connection with Frémont's operations.

During the war in the last half of 1846 prominent
phases of the general subject, and almost the only
ones of which anything is recorded, are the fears of
Walla Walla invasion, the enlisting of Kern's Indian
garrison at New Helvetia, and the formation of an
Indian company to serve in the California battalion,
all of which have been noticed elsewhere.   Here I
may mention a kind of census, by which the native
population of the region about the fort, the district
including the ranchos and settlements of the valley,
was made 2,665, a number increased to about 22,-
000 by Bidwell's estimate of the next year for the
region above the Buttes.[22]   In the San José district
a somewhat extended campaign of Purser Watmough
with San Francisco volunteers is recorded in September.[23]   In the south the only noticeable event was
the massacre of eleven men at Pauma rancho in
December by Garra's band of Cahuillas and fugitive
ex-neophytes of San Luis Rey.   These men had retired to Pauma to avoid military service either for or
against Flores.   There was an unfounded theory that
they were really killed in the fight at San Pascual.
The Indians were instigated by William Marshall,
who doubtless led them to suppose their acts would
be approved by the Americans.   Marshall was afterwards hanged for this offence; and in January Garra's

[20] Leg. Rec., MS., iv. 332-3; Doc. Hist. Cal., MS., iii., 192; Dept. St. Pap.,
MS., viii. 97-9; Id., Pref. y Juzg., ii. 123.   If the surplus did not suffice,
civil employés were to be called upon for part of their salaries.
[21] Dept. St. Pap., MS., vii. 45-8; Doc. Hist. Cal., MS., iii. 191; S. José
Arch., MS., Loose Pap., 31.
[22] Originals in McKinstry's Pap., MS.
[23] Mont. Calif., September 26, 1846.   Long account by C. P. Briggs in
Napa Reporter, Aug. 31, 1872.

band was drawn into an ambush, and most of the offenders slain by a force of friendly Indians and Californians under Lugo.[24]

In 1847–8 under American rule depredations of hostile Indians still continued, and the records show but slight change in methods or results of warfare against them. None of the local happenings are of sufficient importance to call for notice here. In April General Kearny appointed Sutter as sub-Indian agent for the district of the Sacramento and San Joaquin, and Vallejo for the Sonoma district extending to Cache Creek and Clear Lake. Their salary was to be $750. They were to have no power to spend public money, but were to deal chiefly in good advice, explanation of recent changes in government, and promises of reward or threats of punishment from the president of the United States as the 'great father' of the Indians, mainly bent on taking care of his good children. Both Vallejo and Sutter had large experience in dealing with the Indians of their respective districts, and no better men could have been selected for the position. In August Captain J. D. Hunter was appointed agent for the southern district, with headquarters at San Luis Rey, and additional instructions were issued by Governor Mason, in which he enjoined upon the agents the care and protection of Indian servants and ex-neophytes, as well as the keeping in check of gentile bands. Statistics and information on manners and customs were also called for, and a new supply of promises furnished, though there were as yet no funds available for the purchase of gifts.[25] In the Sacramento Valley

[24] See local annals of S. Diego, chap. xxiii. of this volume.

[25] April 7, 1847, Sutter's appointment. April 14th, Vallejo's. Aug. 1st, Hunter's. Aug. 16th, Mason's instructions. *Cal. and N. Mex., Mess. and Doc., 1850*, 294–7, 344–5, 358–9; *Vallejo, Doc.*, MS., i. 23–4; xii. 311; *S. F. Californian*, April 10, 17, 1847. Oct. 30th, Vallejo's recommendations on regulations for Indian matters. *Vallejo, Doc.*, MS., xii. 317; *Unb. Doc.*, MS., 94–7. Nov. 29th, Mason's order forbidding sale of liquor to Indians. Original print in English and Spanish. *Vallejo, Doc.*, xii. 319; *S. F. Californian*, Dec. 8, 1847. In April 1848 Vallejo offered his resignation, which was not accepted. April 15th, May 25th. *Vallejo, Doc.*, MS., xii. 342, 346.

there were complaints of outrages by settlers, notably in July, when Armijo, Smith, and Egger killed a dozen Indians in capturing some forty for laborers, an act that resulted in a trial of the offenders by a special court. San José residents also abused the Indians, and took horses from them on the Cosumnes; and the records contain frequent mention of depredations and of expeditions in preparation. Also in the districts of Los Angeles and San Diego complaints and raids continued, the dragoons being defeated on one or two occasions by the Indians. The same state of things continued in the early part of 1848, but the items are vaguely recorded or unimportant. In May there were alarming rumors in the Sonoma district, but they were believed to have no other foundation than a desire to prevent the removal of troops and the recall of citizens from their search for gold. Better founded were the fears at Los Angeles in August on the disbanding of the volunteers at the end of the war; but arms were furnished the citizens, and no serious disasters resulted.

At the end of this chapter I give a list of vessels shown by different records to have visited the coast in 1846–8, though it is doubtless not so complete as the similar lists for earlier years. Of commercial and maritime annals during this period of transition from Mexican to United States methods, beyond what has been included in the narrative of political events, there is naturally little to be presented. Particularly is this true during the period of military operations from June 1846 to January 1847. Statistical and other records are meagre; but slight attention was paid to the observance of any system; there were no notable controversies or other happenings; and the series of petty detached items that might he put in print would be uninteresting as well as valueless. From January to July 1846 commercial affairs were in the same condition as in the preceding year, the only change being an order of Governor Pico in March abolishing the tax of $600 per year on each foreign vessel.[26] The Monterey custom-house remained in charge of Guerra, and finally of Hartnell,[27] while Ábrego retained control of the treasury.[28] A few petty regulations on trade and the collection of duties were issued by Governor Stockton or his subordinates.[29] Exports of the year were estimated by Larkin at 80,000 hides, 60,000 arrobas of tallow, 10,000 fanegas of wheat, soap to the value of $10,000, and furs $20,000, 1,000 barrels of brandy and wine, 200 ounces of gold, and 1,000,000 feet of lumber.[30]

Of trade statistics for 1847–8 we have still but fragmentary items, San Francisco having become now the chief port of entry, doing more business probably than all the others combined, and attracting some attention as a Pacific metropolis threatening the supremacy of Honolulu.[31] Exports and imports at San Francisco for the last quarter of 1847 were $49,598 and $53,590 respectively, the former including $30,354 of Californian products, and $31,741 of

[26] Mar. 28, 1846, Pico abolishes the tax on foreign vessels. *Dept. St. Pap., Ben. Cust.-H.*, MS., viii. 14; against protest of administrator at Mont. *Dept. St. Pap., Ben.*, MS., iii. 86.

[27] In May Hartnell was admin., José Rafael Gonzalez, com. de celadores, and the celadores, Benito Diaz, Ant. Chavez, Jacinto Rodriguez, and Wm A. Hartnell. *Doc. Hist. Cal.*, iii. 204. Hartnell was inspector in Sept., and Talbot H. Green collector in Nov.

[28] There are no complete accounts extant. In April receipts from customs were $26,826; the outlay was $32,566, including $11,552 for extraordinary expenses; and the balance in the treasury May 1st was $10,835. *Dept. St. Pap.*, MS., xiii. 16–17.

[29] Aug. 15th, Stockton fixed a tariff of 15 per cent on imported goods, and a tonnage duty of 50 cents. *Cutts' Conq.*, 125. Sept. 4th, S. orders collector of S. Diego to collect $10 anchorage on whalers instead of the tonnage. *Miscel. Hist. Pap.*, MS., no. 3. Aug. 29th, elaborate regulations for inspectors of hides and tallow for the region round S. F. Bay, approved by the comandante, and signed by Alcalde Bartlett. Sauzalito, Corte Madera, S. Rafael, Petaluma, Sonoma, Napa, Sutter's Landing, and Dr Marsh's Landing were the places where produce might be shipped for Yerba Buena, besides others apparently on the Contra Costa. *Sonoma Sta Rosa Dem.*, Dec. 30, 1871. Sept. 6th, trade regulations of Capt Montgomery. *S. F. Munic. Repts*, 1866–7, p. 519.

[30] *Larkin's Descrip. Cal.*, MS., 94. July 24th, L. writes to his cousin in Boston very enthusiastically on commercial prospects. *Doc.*, MS., iv. 227.

[31] See *Hon. Polynesian*, iv. 78, 135, v. 17. It need not be added that the Hawaiians did not altogether admit the danger, or fear the annihilation of their trade.

the latter coming from the Sandwich Islands. An estimate of the time was \$250,000 for the year's imports from Honolulu at all the ports.[32] Arrivals of merchant vessels at San Francisco for the year ending April 1848 were eighty-five.[33] Exports from Santa Bárbara from March to September 1847 amounted to \$27,780.[34] At Monterey sixty-seven vessels arrived in thirteen months ending October 9, 1848, of which fifty-five were traders with a tonnage of 11,504 tons. The amount of duties collected at Monterey in the same period was \$25,000, and in all California \$120,000, according to a record kept by a naval officer.[35] In August 1847 Larkin wrote to the government, "the commerce of California has trebled within a year. The regular traders of many years' standing from Boston appear to have retired from the trade, which is now carried on by transient vessels from the Sandwich Islands, South America, and the United States."[36]

From the beginning of 1847 we have a series of communications that passed between Governor Mason, the collectors of ports, and military commandants of the several districts, on commercial affairs and the collection of revenues. Most relate to the appointment of collectors and their duties in various matters of official routine.[37] These collectors received a salary of \$1,000, except at San Francisco, where it was \$1,200; and they made quarterly returns to the military commandants of their respective districts, the

[32] *S. F. Calif.*, Mar. 29, 1848. Of the exports \$33,890 went to Honolulu, \$7,286 to Sitka, \$5,000 to Mazatlan, \$2,000 to U. S.; imports from U. S., \$6,791, Oregon, \$7,702, Chili, \$3,676, S. I., \$31,741, Sitka, \$2,471, Bremen, \$493, Mex., \$712. Copied in *Annals of S. F.*, 198; *Cronise's Nat. Wealth*, 63; *Hunt's Merch. Mag.*, xix. 52, etc.

[33] *S. F. Alta*, Apr. 17, 1852.

[34] *Carrillo, Doc.*, MS., 15. Duties for quarter ending June 30th were \$307. *Id.*, 11, 16.

[35] *Niles' Reg.*, lxxv. 208. For 6 months ending Feb. 1847, the number of trading vessels entering Monterey was 23. *Larkin's Off. Corresp.*, MS., ii. 112.

[36] *Larkin's Off. Corresp.*, MS., ii. 120. In June L. had written, 'Goods are falling off in price; produce from the ranchos is rising.' *Id.*, i. 159.

[37] *Cal. and N. Mex., Mess. and Doc., 1850*, passim; also the same or similar letters in MS. collections, and in the *S. F. Star* and *Californian*.

resulting funds being subject to the governor's orders for expenses of the civil government.[38]   As to system, the ports were still regarded as Mexican, and in theory the old regulations were followed, except as modified by circumstances, according to the views of the new authorities.   Practically, and in accordance with promises by different commanders during the war, the old burdens were largely removed, much to the satisfaction of both the people and traders.   In February it was ordered that certain staple articles of food should be admitted free for six months; and by the regulations of March and April the cargoes of American vessels were to be admitted free, those of foreign vessels to pay fifteen per cent on the value at the port of entry, with five cents per ton anchorage, and fees amounting to four dollars.[39]   Even under these regulations there was much smuggling, but of several confiscations recorded none seem to require notice.

In October, however, there came from Washington new orders, including tariff regulations formed in March for all Mexican ports in possession of the United States.   It was decided to open all these ports to trade, to collect heavy specific duties as war contributions, and thus to force the Mexican government by the loss of revenue and by popular complaints of high prices to treat for peace.   As a war measure directed against a hostile people, this was perhaps good policy; but the regulations were absurdly inapplicable to the condition of California, where the natives were not only submissive, but without national influence, and where American residents were the

[38] The collectors were: at San Diego, Pedro C. Carrillo, Santiago Argüello, and from June Miguel Pedrorena; at S. Pedro, Dav. W. Alexander; at Sta Bárbara, Pedro C. Carrillo; at Monterey, Talbot H. Green; at S. F., Wm A. Richardson.

[39] Feb. 11, 1847, Shubrick's order for free admission of beef, pork, bread, flour, butter, cheese, sugar, and rice for six months. *S. F. Cal. Star*, Feb. 20, 1847.   March 29th, Biddle's orders to collectors. *Carrillo, Doc.*, MS., 7–8; and other orders of like import in April.   No vessel could clear for Mex. ports not held by the U. S.   Nothing but specie, treasury notes, or drafts to be received for duties.

chief purchasers of imported goods.[40]   Mason and
Shubrick recognized at once the injustice and impolicy
of such a measure in California, and decided not to
enforce its most onerous requirements.   Explaining
their reasons to the government and announcing in
proclamations that the continuance of their lenient
policy would depend on the good behavior of the
people, they issued in October a new series of regulations radically different in many respects from those
of the national authorities.[41]

[40] *U. S. Govt Doc.*, 30th cong. 1st sess., H. Ex. Doc. 1, p. 552–89; with
correspondence at Washington preceding and following the new regulations,
which bore date of March 30th, and was sent to Cal. on May 10th.   The
essential features were as follows: Ports open to all but Mex. vessels; $1 per
ton for all port charges; a high specific duty—too long for reproduction here
—on all imported goods; all goods to be unloaded at the first port entered;
goods shipped from port to port to pay the same duties as if coming from
abroad, and this coasting trade to be open only to American vessels;
military stores contraband; mining machinery free, and also all U. S.
stores; exports free; all Mex. monopolies and prohibitions annulled; strin-
gent regulations for all details of collection, confiscation, etc.; and the collection of revenue to be in the hands of military officers.

[41] Oct. 20, 1847, Mason's commercial regulations in *Honolulu Polynesian*,
iv. 114, in 26 articles.   Oct. 9th, Shubrick and Mason to people of Cal.,
threatening to enforce the orders on military contributions in case of any disturbance of the peace. *S. F. Californian*, Oct. 20, 27, 1847.   Some regulations by Shubrick on Sept. 15th are referred to, but I have not found them.
Oct. 14th, 20th, various instructions from Mason, in accordance with the new
regulations. *Cal. and N. Mex., Mess. and Doc., 1850*, p. 404–10.   Sept. 23d,
'all vessels, not American, engaged in the coast trade pay the same duties as
when coming from a foreign port.' *Id.*, 397.   Editorial on the tariff regulations, in *S. F. Calif.*, Nov. 24, 1847.   Call for a meeting at S. F. to prepare
a memorial to congress on the subject. *Id.*, Dec. 1, 1847.   Objections to the
new system. *Niles' Reg.*, lxxii. 209–10, 219.   The tariff is also given in *Amer.
Almanac*, 1848, p. 178.   Nov. 10th, Larkin to sec. state, in defence of Mason's
course in substituting a modified tariff. *Larkin's Off. Corresp.*, MS., ii. 12.
Nov. 11th, Mason to adjutant-general, defending the liberties he has taken,
and explaining some of his innovations. *Mess. and Doc., 1850*, p. 422–5.
'Promises and assurances founded upon these instructions (those to Kearny of
June 3, 1846) have gone forth to the people of Cal. as a solemn pledge on the
part of our govt.   It was believed and received by the people generally as a
pledge; but some of our enemies have asserted that these promises were made
by us to delude them into subordination, after which the same high duties and
restrictions on commerce would be restored.   Now, these persons pass for
prophets, because after nearly a year of quiet, high duties are again ordered
to be laid, with restrictions on the coast trade, that will in a great measure
prevent the expected competition and reduction of prices; this, too, with the
avowed declaration to treat the Californians as open enemies, subject to military contributions...I would most earnestly recommend that these duties and
restrictions be withdrawn.'   May 10th, sec. war to Kearny, forwarding the
new regulations.   Whalers not subject to duties or tonnage unless engaging
in trade.   Vessels which left the U. S. before the new orders need pay duties
at each port only on the goods landed there. *U. S. Govt Doc.*, 30th cong. 1st
sess., H. Ex. Doc. 1, p. 566–7.   Oct. 13th, the last-named privilege extended

For the specific duties was substituted an ad valorem rate of twenty per cent; tonnage was reduced from one dollar to fifteen cents; the rule requiring all the cargo to be landed at the first port was ignored; the privilege of the coasting trade was extended to all vessels owned in California; products of the country might be freely shipped from one port to another; and no duty was to be collected on lumber. The collection of revenue was now imposed on the military commandants, and the collectors, except at San Pedro where there was no military post, lost their places.

I find no evidence that the government at Washington ever disapproved the military governor's innovations, or that more than a tacit approval was given. Some slight modifications were adopted before Mason's protest was received; and in November others more important, changing the specific to ad valorem duties of twenty and thirty per cent on two classes, or lists, of imports—but all apparently without the slightest reference either to California's needs or the governor's acts. The revised regulations arrived in April 1848.[42] Except that the coasting trade was now declared open to all vessels, I find no indication in commercial correspondence of the time that any essential changes were made. At the end of July, however, Mason instructed his officers to receive for duties gold-dust at very low rates on deposit, redeemable for coin in three and six months.[43]

In August 1848, on receipt of news that the war

to all vessels, Amer. and foreign. *Id.*, 586. A vessel may proceed from port to port to make up a cargo of exports free of all duties. *Id.* Nov. 10th, the former Mex. export duty on precious metals to be collected. Approved by pres. Nov. 16th. *Id.*, 587.

[42] April 28, 1848, Mason to Folsom, forwarding the modifications of Nov. 5, 1847, not given. *Cal. and N. Mex., Mess. and Doc., 1850*, p. 544–5. July 26th, custom-house and port regulations by Mason, with no reference to rates of duties. *Id.*, 583–5. Miscellaneous corresp. of 1848, in *Id.*, passim. The substance of the modifications of Nov. 5th is given in *S. F. Cal. Star*, May 20, 1848.

[43] *Mess. and Doc., 1850*, p. 664, Mason to Howard, Gillespie, and Ward. Also other orders to same purport. M. had at first consented to take gold if melted into some convenient form, but finally decided that he had no right to do so. In Sept. it was decided to issue sea letters to vessels owned by Americans, which should serve as registry papers temporarily. *Id.*, 671.

had been ended and a treaty signed, the authorities decided, without special instructions from Washington, that as California was now a part of the United States, the national revenue laws must be enforced. Accordingly the collectors were reappointed and furnished with copies of the regular custom-house regulations for their guidance, though they were still, in the absence of orders to the contrary, under the supervision of the military chiefs.[44] There was no subsequent change in 1848, American vessels entering free and foreign imports paying duties as at any American port. In the early part of 1849, however, and before the revenue laws were formally extended to California by act of congress, a new view of the matter was taken by Governor Mason; namely, that foreign cargoes could not be legally admitted in California, where there was no regular port of entry; yet, to prevent inconvenience and expense, the authorities would take the liberty of admitting such cargoes on payment of duties and fees.[45] Of the amount of military contributions and irregularly collected revenues collected in 1847–8, I find no definite record; but before the convention of 1849 the amount yet unexpended was nearly a million, and, as we shall see, the disposition to be made of this 'civil fund' became a subject of discussion later.

In maritime annals of this period the appearance of the first steamer in Californian waters merits a passing notice,[46] among the vessels of 1846–8, with a list

[44] Id., 592, 655–60. Pedrorena was appointed at S. Diego, Aug. 7th; Alexander continued at S. Pedro; Lieut Carnes apparently continued at Sta Bárbara; and Edward H. Harrison appointed at S. F. after Edward Gilbert had declined.

[45] Feb. 24, 1849, Mason to Harrison. Id., 694–5. Oct. 9, 1848, sec. war decides that no duties can be collected on Amer. goods or such as have paid duties in U. S. ports; but he gives no instructions on foreign imports. Id., 258. In March Gen. Smith introduced still another variation in theory not affecting the practice; namely, that foreign vessels might land their goods by 'depositing' the amount of duties and fees, 'subject to such disposition as congress may make of them.' Id., 713.

[46] The best authority on this subject is Geo. McKinstry in original letters found in McKinstry's Pap., MS., 40–4, the author having made the trip to

of which I conclude this chapter.[47]   The steamer had no name, but has since been called the *Sitka*.   Her dimensions were: length 37 feet, breadth of beam 9 feet, depth of hold $3\frac{1}{2}$ feet, drawing 18 inches of

Sacramento on the steamer.   A notice of the arrival from Sitka is found in the *S. F. Cal. Star*, Oct. 23, 1847.   Notice of the steamer at Sonoma Nov. 25th, when there was a celebration, with toasts to the 'rival towns of Sonoma and S. F.' *Californian*, Dec. 1, 1847.   See also *Annals of S. F.*, 197; *S. F. Directory*, 1852; *Hutchings' Mag.*, iv. 4; *Sac. Directory*, 1871, p. 103; *Sacramento Illust.*, 8; *Hon. S. I. News*, ii. 50; *S. F. Alta*, May 4, 1858; Nov. 12, 1872; *Sac. Union*, May 19, 1858; *S. F. Bulletin*, Feb. 26, 1868; and many other newspaper articles.   Some accounts describe the boat as a stern-wheeler; and some say she was 60 ft long and 17 ft wide.

[47] Vessels on the coast of California, 1846–8:

Abigail, Amer. whaler; Barnard, master; at S. F. July–Aug. 1846.

Admittance, prize ship; at Mont. June, Sept. 1847; under command of Lieut Revere.

Alford, Hamburg brig; at S. F. March 1846.

Alice, Hinckley, master; at S. F. Sept. 1847.

America, whaler; Nash, master; at S. F. Sept. 1846.

Anäis, French schr; Limantour; at Sta B. and S. Pedro July–Aug. 1847. Also at Mont. and S. F. in May.

Angola, Amer. bark; 311 tons; Sam. Varney; at Mont. from Salem and Honolulu for Sitka in June 1846, consigned to Larkin.   Again at Mont. and S. F. in Nov. 1847, from Honolulu.

Anita, Amer. bark; Woodworth and Shoive; on the coast 1847–8.   Cargo cost $25,000; $\frac{1}{3}$ sold for $20,000; duties, $12,000.

Antonita, schr, built in Cal. 1847; Rousillon & Sainsevain, owners; E. Gray, master; 34 tons, 40 ft long, 6 ft 8 in. deep, 12 ft 4 in. wide.   Permit to trade Nov. 23d.

Ariel, Haw. schr; Griffin; from Honolulu; wrecked 200 miles from S. F. in Oct. 1848.   Passengers and crew saved.

Armata, Amer. ship; Fitch; at S. F. from New London Sept. 1847.

Baikal, Russ. brig; Lieut Rudierkof; at Mont. in Sept. 1846.

Barnstable, Amer ship.   Arr. S. Diego in March 1846; Hall, master; at Sta B. and S. Pedro in Aug.   Aids Com. Stockton in Oct. at Mont. and S. F. On the coast throughout 1847, and in spring of 1848.

Belfast, brig from N. Y.; at S. F. Oct. 1848.   Said to have been the first vessel to discharge cargo without lighters.

Benj. Rush, Amer. ship; L. H. Smith; at S. F. Sept. 1846.

Bowditch, Amer. ship; Borden; from Rhode Island; at S. F. Sept. 1847.

Brillante, French corvette; E. de Bouzet.   Arr. S. F. from Callao Sept. 24th, Mont. Oct. 1st–7th, 1846, with the consul Moerenhaut on board.

Brooklyn, Amer. ship; 450 tons; Richardson.   Arr. S. F. from N. Y. with Mormon colony July 31, 1846.   Visited other ports, and sailed in Sept. for Panamá via Honolulu.   (See chap. xx.)

Brutus, Amer. ship; Adams.   Arr. S. F. April 17, 1847, from N. Y. with part of the N. Y. volunteers.   (See chap. xviii.)

Cabinet, Amer. whaler; Bottene; at S. F. Aug.–Sept. 1846.

Cadboro, H. B. Co.'s brig; at S. F. Jan. 1846, with crew of the U. S. schr *Shark;* wrecked in the north.

California, Amer. ship; Fisher; at S. F. Sept. 1847, from N. Bedford.

Callao, Engl. bark; Hüttmann; at Mont. in Sept. 1848.

Caroline, bark; Halsey; at S. F. Sept. 1846.

Charles, Amer. ship; Thomas Andrews; brought naval stores and a private cargo to Mort. 1847.   Sold $\frac{1}{4}$ of the cargo at immense profit at S. F. after the

water, and having side wheels moved by a miniature engine. She was built at Sitka by an American as a pleasure-boat for the officers of the Russian company, and was purchased by Leidesdorff, being brought

discovery of gold in 1848. The supercargo took gold-dust and carried it home overland across Mexico, but the anxieties of the trip killed him.

Charles and Edward, schr; at Sonoma and S. F. Sept. 1848.

Citizen, ship; Lansing; at S. F. Aug. 1847, from N. W. coast.

Clementine, whale ship; Hashagen; at S. F. Oct.–Nov. 1847.

Collingwood, Brit. man-of-war; Admiral Seymour; at Mont. in July 1846, from Mazatlan, thence to Honolulu. (See chap. ix.)

Columbia, H. B. Co.'s bark; Duncan; at S. F. April 1847, from Columbia River. At Honolulu in May.

Columbus, U. S. ship; Commodore Biddle, Capt. T. W. Wyman; at Mont. and S. F. March–July 1847. (Chap. xvii.)

Columbus, Amer. whaler; Hutchins; at S. F. Aug.–Sept. 1846.

Commodore Shubrick, Hawaiian schr; 60 tons; Von Pfister; at S. F., Mont., and Sta Cruz in April–June 1847. She came back from Honolulu in Sept., Mohran (or Morgan), and was sold to Ruckel & Cooke, Elliot Libbey becoming master. Licensed to trade by Gov. Mason Nov. 11th.

Commodore Stockton, schr; Young, and later Kinch; running between Mont., S. F., Bodega, and Oregon Jan.–Dec. 1847.

Concepcion, Cent. Amer. brig; Beristain; at S. Pedro and Sta B. in Sept. 1847. She reloaded her cargo after paying duties, and departed before Feb. 1848.

Confederacion, Chil. ship; Jones, master; Rich. Carson, sup.; at the ports June–Oct. 1847.

Congress, U. S. frigate; Com. Stockton, Capt. Dupont, Lieut Livingstone. Arr. Mont. from Honolulu July 15, 1846. On the coast through 1846–7–8.

Constantine, Russ. brig; at S. F. from Sitka Jan. 1847.

Copia, Amer. whaler; Taber; at S. F. Aug. 1847.

Corea, Amer. ship; Hempstead; at S. F. from New London Nov. 1847.

Covington, Amer. ship; Duval; at S. F. from Warren, R. I., Sept. 1847.

Currency Lass, schr; Geo. McLean; at S. F. and other ports from Honolulu April–May 1847, and again from Nov. 1847 to Jan. 1848. Perhaps had made a trip in 1846 also.

Cyane, U. S. man-of-war; Mervine and Dupont; on the Californian and Mexican coast during the conquest in 1846–7. Some details of movements have been given in my chapters. She arrived at Norfolk, Va., in Oct. 1848.

Dale, U. S. man-of-war; W. W. McKean; on the coast Dec.–Jan. 1846–7; again in Cal. ports May–Sept. under Selfridge; and in Oct.–Nov. 1848 under Rudd.

Don Quixote, Hawaiian bark; Paty; on the coast March–April, 1846, from Honolulu. Carried Castillero as commissioner to Mex. Again on the coast Aug.–Nov. and in Feb. 1847.

Eagle, brig; Levett; at S. F. Feb. 1848 from China.

Edward, Amer. ship; John S. Barker; at S. F. Sept. 1846.

Elizabeth, Amer. whaler; Hall; at S. F. Aug.–Sept. 1846.

Elizabeth, Amer. brig; King; on the coast from Honolulu Jan.–Dec. 1847, and wrecked near Sta B. Feb. 1848.

El Placer, brigantine, 60 tons; Charles Wolters, master and owner; a prize of the *Cyane*, formerly the *Manuel Adolfo*. Amer. sea-letter granted by Gov. Mason Nov. 15, 1848.

Emily Morgan, Amer. ship; Ewer; at S. F. from New Bedford, Aug. 1847.

Erie, U. S. store-ship; Turner; at S. F. and Mont. Aug.–Sept. 1846, and

down to San Francisco in October 1847 on the *Nas-lednik*. Having made a trial trip on November 15th, she ventured later to Santa Clara and then to Sonoma. Finally, on the 28th of November, she started on the

again Feb.–Oct. 1847, bringing Col Mason, and Lieut Watson, who took command of the ship.

Euphemia, Hawaiian brig; 150 tons; Thos Russum; at Mont. March–Aug. 1846 from Honolulu. Wm H. Davis, sup. and part owner, gives many details in his *Glimpses*, MS., 335 et seq., 353–4. She came back in Nov.–March 1846–7; also in July–Sept. 1847; and in 1848 with Vioget as master.

Euphrates, Amer. ship; Edwards; at S. F. Sept. 1847 from New Bedford.

Europa, Bremen whaler; Curns; at S. F. Aug. 1846.

Eveline, Amer. brig; Goodwin; at S. F. Aug. 1847 from Honolulu.

Fama, Amer. ship; Nye; came from Honolulu in 1845, and was wrecked near Sta B. on Feb. 26, 1846.

Ferdinand, French whaler; at S. F. Sept. 1846.

Flecha, schr; Mont. May 1848.

Francisca, Amer. brig; Lemoine; on the coast from Honolulu Feb. 1847; and again in June, being wrecked at Sta B. in Nov.

General Kearny, schr; Shelly, and later Menzies; at S. F. and other ports April–May 1847. Had some trouble about entering as an American vessel.

Georgiana, Amer. bark; Kelly; at S. F. Aug. from Valparaiso for Honolulu.

Golden Gate, pilot-boat from Boston; at S. F. Dec. 1846.

Haalilio, Haw. schr; Smith; left Honolulu Oct. 1848 for S. F.

Hannah, Amer. brig; Chever; on the coast Jan.–March 1846. Carried despatches from Larkin to Mazatlan.

Henry, Amer. brig; Bray, and later Wm R. Kilborn; at S. F. from Columbia Riv. Aug. 1847, and again in Nov.–Dec., landing goods at Sta Cruz. In May 1848 she was at Mont. bound to Mazatlan with naval stores.

Herald, Engl. frigate; Capt. Kellett; at S. F. on surveying service Sept. 1846.

Hindoo, probably fictitious name of a ship attacked by pirates; the novel *Amelia Sherwood* being founded on the voyage.

Honolulu, Amer. schr; Newell; left Honolulu for S. F. in June 1847. Made two trips to Cal. in 1848.

Hope, Haw. schr; King; wrecked in Dec., perhaps on coast of Lower Cal.

Huntress, Amer. ship; Spring; brought recruits to S. F. from N. Y. in Oct. 1848.

Independence, U. S. man-of-war; Com. Shubrick, Capt. Page; on the coast Jan.–Oct. 1847.

Iris, Amer. bark; Hewes; at S. F. Sept. 1847 from New Bedford.

Isaac Howland, Amer. whaler; Corey; at S. F. Aug. 1846.

Isaac Walton, Amer. ship; Allyn; 800 tons; brought naval stores from N. Y. in Aug. 1848.

Janet, Engl. bark; Dring; at S. F. from Columbia River and Calcutta Aug. 1847. Her cargo was seized, and she was deserted by captain and crew in Oct. 1848 (?).

Janus, Amer. whaler; Hammond; at Honolulu from S. F. Dec. 1846.

Jeanette, Amer. whaler; Atkins; at S. F. July–Aug. 1846.

John Young, Haw. brig; at S. Pedro and Sta B. Aug. 1846.

Jóven Guipuzcoana, Peru. bark, 200 tons; Barker (or Vaca); on the coast from Callao Aug.–Dec. 1846. Back from Honolulu April–Aug. 1847. Handford also named as master.

Juanita, Mex. schr; Scott; carried Covarrubias to Mex. in Feb. 1846. In July in trouble with the revenue officers at Sta B. At Mont. in Nov.

Julia, U. S. prize schr; Lieut Selden; on the coast Nov. 1846–Sept. 1847;

great voyage of her career to Sacramento, carrying
ten or a dozen souls, including the owner, George
McKinstry, L. W. Hastings as far as Montezuma,
and Mrs Gregson and baby—the latter serving a use-

then sold in Oct., and in Nov. arrived at Honolulu under Moran.   Came back
as *Julian* under Hawaiian flag in Oct. 1848.

Juno, Brit. man-of-war; Blake; on the coast June–July 1846.   McNamara
passenger.

Kekauonohi, Haw. schr; Treadway; left Hon. for S. F. Aug. 1848.

Keone Ana, Haw. brig; Jeupas; on the coast from Lima Sept.-Oct. 1847.
Duties at S. Diego, $1,676.   Duties at Sta B., $104, refunded.

Lady Adams, brig; Hanna; at S. F. from Callao Jan. 1848.

Lambayacana, schr; left S. F. for Valparaiso in Aug. 1848.

Laura Ann, Engl. brig; Thomas; on the coast July–Oct. 1847.   Back
from Hon. Dec.-Jan. 1847–8, and again at S. F. in Oct.

Levant, U. S. man-of-war; Page; at Mont. June 30–July 28, 1846, when
she sailed for the U. S. with Com. Sloat.

Lexington, U. S. transport; Bailey; brought Co. F 3d artill. from U. S.;
on the coast Jan.–June 1847, and again in Oct.–Nov.

Lion, French transport; at S. F. from Hon. Sept. 1846 and probably
earlier.

Louisa, schr; at Mont. and S. Pedro May 1848.

Magnet, Amer. ship; Wilbur; at S. F. Sept. 1846.

Magnolia, Amer. ship; Simmonds; on the coast Sept.–Nov. 1846.

Malek Adhel, Mex. brig; captured by the *Warren* at Mazatlan in Sept.
1846, and sent to Mont. under Lieut Renshaw with dispatches in Oct. and to
S. Diego in Nov.   She was sold to Phelps in Sept. 1847, and was on the
coast until 1848 under Hall and Phelps.

Maria Helena, Chil. bark; Curphey; at S. F. and Mont. July–Oct. 1847.

Maria Teresa, Mex. brig; Hanks; at Mont. and S. F. May and Sept. 1846.

Mary Ann, Haw. schr; Paty; on the coast June–Nov. 1847, thence to
Honolulu under Russum.   A part of her cargo was seized at S. F. by the
revenue officers.

Mathilde, Danish brig; 130 tons; Rabbens; on the coast April–Oct. 1847.

Mermaid, schr; at S. F. June 1846.

Moncoba, Engl. bark; at S. F. March 1846 from Columbia Riv.

Moscow, Amer. bark; Phelps; on the coast from Jan. 1846, engaged in
trade and also aiding Frémont and Stockton in their operations.   She carried
a company of the N. Y. volunteers down the coast in 1847, but was wrecked
before the end of the year.

Mount Vernon, U. S. store-ship; Given; on the coast April–May and
again in Aug. 1847.

Narwal, French whaler; G. Radon; at Mont. Sept. 1846.

Naslednik, Russ. bark; Harnden; at S. F. Oct. 1847 from Sitka.

Natalia, Chil. bark; Luco; at S. F. from Hon. Dec.–March 1847–8.

New Perseverance, French brig; Boyer; at S. F. Sept. 1848.

Obed Mitchell, ship; Wing; at S. F. from N. W. coast Aug. 1847.

Ohio, U. S. man-of-war; Com. Jones, Capt. Hardy; on the coast from
Oct. 1848.

Olga (?); Teschemacher, sup.; 1846.

Pacific, ship; Edwards; at S. F. from N. W. coast Aug. 1847.

Paladian, Amer. whaler; McLane; at S. F. July–Aug. 1846.

Pandora, Brit. brig; Wood; at S. F. Sept. 1846 on surveying service.

Parachute, Amer. ship; Duval; at S. F. Sept. 1846.

Patriot, Bremen whaler; Mensing; at S. F. Aug. 1846.

ful purpose in 'trimming' the little craft. The trip
was made in six days and seven hours, one of the
passengers saving the odd hours by leaving the
steamer and walking. Returning to Yerba Buena,

Portsmouth, U. S. man-of-war; Montgomery; on the coast from April
1846 to late in 1847.
Preble, U. S. man-of-war; W. F. Shields, and later James Glynn; on the
coast in April–May, also Oct. 1847, and in April–May 1848.
Prescott, Amer. whaler; Mallory; at S. F. Aug.–Sept. 1846.
Primavera, Mex. brig; W. Stenner; on the coast from April 1847. Sold
in June by creditors at Los Angeles to E. Célis for $1,000, and resold to Ed.
A. King. Wm S. McKinney became master; and his license to trade was
issued by Gov. Mason Nov. 13th.
Providence, French schr; Mitchell; left Hon. for S. F. Aug. 1847. Per-
haps *Prudence*, Louis.
Providence, brig; Hinckley; at S. F. from Hon. March 1848.
Rhone, Amer. ship; Hill; at S. F. from Baltimore and Hon. Aug. Oct.
1848.
Roman, Amer. ship; Shockley; at S. F. Sept. 1846.
Sabine, Amer. brig; Vincent; at S. F. from Boston March 1848. Back
from Honolulu in Aug.–Sept. under Chaffield.
Sagadahoc, Amer. schr; Barmore; left Hon. for S. F. Oct. 1848.
Santa Cruz, Cal. schr; Lowe; on coast 1846–7.
Sarah Parker, Amer. whaler; Russell; Mont. Sept.–Oct. 1846.
Savannah, U. S. man-of-war; Com. Sloat, and later Capt. Mervine; on the
coast from July 1846 to March 1847.
Seis de Junio, Chil. brig; at S. F. from Hon. June–July 1848. In trouble
about duties.
South Boston, Amer. whaler; Hoxie; at Hon. from S. F. Feb. 1847.
Southampton, U. S. store-ship; R. D. Thorburn; on coast from Sept. 1847
to end of 1848.
Spy, Brit. man-of-war; Wooldridge; at Mont. Aug. 1846.
S. S., Haw. schr; Molteno; left Hon. for S. F. Jan. 1848.
Starling, Haw. schr; Hinckley; left Hon. for S. F. Feb. 1848.
Sterling, Amer. ship; G. W. Vincent; on the coast in 1846, being used as
a transport for the Cal. battalion.
Stonington, Amer. whaler; Geo. W. Hamley; on the coast Aug. 1846 to Feb.
1847, aiding Stockton in his operations at S. Diego.
Susanita, launch, schooner-rigged; bought of Vioget by Brannan, and sent
up to Sacramento in 1848 under Grimshaw.
Sweden, ship; Nott; at S. F. from N. Y. Feb. 1848.
Tasso, Amer. bark; Libbey; on the coast from 1846 to Oct. 1848.
Tepic, Engl. brig; Luce; at S. F. July 1848, and again from Hon. in Sept.–
Oct.
Thomas H. Perkins, Amer. brig; Arther; at S. F. from N. Y. in March
1847, bringing part of the N. Y. volunteers.
Thomas H. Benton, U. S. brig; at Sta B. Aug. 1847.
Toulon, bark; Crosby; at S. F. from Columbia Riv. Jan.–April 1847.
Triad, ship; Horton; at S. F. from N. W. coast Aug. 1847.
United States, Amer. whaler; Stevens; at S. F. Sept. 1846.
Valiant, French whaler; Des Prairies; at Mont. April 1846.
Vancouver, H. B. Co.'s bark; at Mont. and S. F. April 1846, from Colum-
bia River.
Vandalia, Amer. ship; Everett; on coast from 1846 to May 1847. Cargo
cost $37,000; sold for $134,000; duties, $27,000.
Vesper, Amer. ship; Clark; at S. F. Sept. 1847.

she was wrecked at her anchorage in a gale; but was raised, hauled inland by oxen, and transformed into a launch or schooner. As the *Rainbow* she ran on the Sacramento River after the discovery of gold.

Warren, U. S. man-of-war; Hull, and later Lanman; on the coast from Aug. 1846 to the end of 1848.

Wave, Haw. sloop; Quimby; left Hon. for S. F. Oct. 1848.

Whiton, Amer. bark; R. Gelston; at S. F. from N. Y. in April 1847; again in July and Nov. from Columbia River.

William, U. S. prize schr; at Mont. from S. Blas March 1847. Under English colors. Case tried before admiralty court at Mont. Sold at auction in April. At S. F. in Aug.

William Neilson; Weston, master; at Hon. from Cal. July 1846.

Xylon, Amer. ship; Millington; on the coast from N. Y. and Hon. in March–April 1847.

Zack Taylor, schr; built at Sta Cruz in 1848 (?) by Blackburn.

CHAPTER XXII.

THE RULE OF GOVERNOR MASON.

1847–1848.

Mason's Proclamation and Reports—Fears of Revolt—Visits to the South and North—Return of José Castro—The Cañon Perdido at Santa Bárbara—Return of Pio Pico—His Claims for the Governorship—Imprisonment and Release—Treaty of Guadalupe Hidalgo—Mason's Proclamation—California in Congress, 1846–9—Causes and Effects of the War—Slavery in the Territories—Opposition to the Acquisition of California—Debates on Territorial Government—Final Unsuccessful Efforts—Military Rule—Rights of Conquerors—Views of Congress and Administration—Policy of Sloat, Stockton, Frémont, and Kearny—Mason's Theory and Practice—Items—Alcalde Nash at Sonoma—Trial of Armijo—Barrus and Foxen—De Facto Government after the Treaty.

THE war in California had ended in January 1847, and the ensuing controversies between rival chieftains in May. The departure of Frémont and Kearny and Stockton removed for the most part all cause for dissension, and left the country tranquil. It also wellnigh removed all elements of interest in territorial annals, so far as the sequence of events is concerned. Since dropping the chronologic thread at the end of Kearny's rule as governor, I have devoted four chapters to subjects pertaining wholly or in part to Mason's rule in 1847–8; namely, the Mormon battalion, New York volunteers and artillery company, immigration, missions, Indian affairs, and trade. Most items in the records and correspondence of the period, outside of local and personal affairs, have been disposed of in connection with the subjects mentioned; but there are a few other matters that require notice in this final chapter of the regular series; notably matters pertaining to the civil and municipal government, and to congressional discussion on the destines of California, besides a brief glance at minor events in the order of their happening.

On May 31st Colonel Richard B. Mason, on the departure of General Kearny, proclaimed his assumption of the position of governor and commander-in-chief of United States forces in California by order of the president.[1] During the month of June, as indeed all other months of his rule, Mason's attention was chiefly occupied with routine details of military, revenue, and municipal affairs, his correspondence taking the form almost exclusively of replies and instructions to local subordinates on various minor matters, which, as already explained, I make no effort here to trace. On June 18th he reported to the government, expressing his need of mounted troops for Indian service, giving attention to the 'California claims,' and stating in general: "The country continues to be quiet, and I think will remain so, though the people dislike the change of flags, whatever may be said or written to the contrary, and in the southern part would rise immediately if it were possible for Mexico to send even a small force into the country; nothing keeps them quiet but the want of a proper leader and a rallying point"—a view that was much exaggerated.[2]

In July Lieutenant-colonel Burton was sent on the *Lexington* with two companies of the New York volunteers to take possession of Lower California, which was accomplished without serious difficulty.[3] Apprehensions of revolt continued, though almost entirely unfounded. Colonel Stevenson had complained in

[1] May 31, 1847, Gov. Mason's proclamation. *Los Angeles Arch.*, MS., iii. 65; *S. F. Californian*, June 12, 19, 26, 1847.

[2] June 18th, Mason to adj.-general. *Cal. and N. Mex.*, *Mess. and Doc.*, *1850*, p. 312.

[3] Kearny's order of May 30th, founded on that of sec. war of Jan. 11th; Mason's order to Burton June 1st; and M.'s report to govt of B.'s departure July 21st. *Id.*, 310, 323, 331. For the occupation of L. Cal., see *Hist. North Mex. States*, ii., this series.

June that "prominent Californians" had threatened
to cut down his flag-staff, and was authorized to say
that "such an act will be considered an act of war,
and punished accordingly."[4]   Captain Lippitt, left in
command at Santa Bárbara, soon learned that the
Californians were about to attack his post, and sent
Mr Sparks to Monterey to explain the danger.   The
governor went on the *Dale* to Santa Bárbara, where
he remained a week, and "became fully satisfied that
there were no just grounds to apprehend a popular
outbreak; and that if threats had been made, they
were nothing more than the expression of natural feelings resulting from the bad conduct of some of the
men composing the garrison."   Stevenson also came to
assure him of prevailing quiet at Los Angeles; and
Mason, back at Monterey, explained the state of
affairs in his report of September 18th, devoted mainly
to the military condition and needs of the country.[5]
Then he went to San Francisco, where he was entertained at a grand ball, found all in a satisfactory
condition, but was called back by the arrival of Toler

[4] *Cal. and N. Mex.*, etc., 341. Mason to Stevenson, July 14th. July 7th,
Fitch in a private letter says: 'The inhabitants are almost unanimously
opposed to the U. S. govt, and detest us from the bottom of their hearts, in
particular the new-comers'! *Fitch, Doc.*, MS., 447. July 27th, 'Z.' writes
to *S. F. Californian*, Oct. 6, 1847, on the danger of a revolt at Los Angeles
if the military force should be reduced. He says the southern people differ
from those of the north; 'they drink harder, gamble more, and have a more
obscene code of ethics, by far, and have consequently less sympathy with us.
They are Mexicans.'

[5] July 16th, Lippitt to Sherman; July 21st, Mason to adj.-gen.; Sept. 18th,
Id. to Id. *Cal. and N. Mex.*, etc., 330–1, 335–9. In this report he says:
'When you remember the extent of the coast and frontier; the great numbers
of Indians upon the immediate border, who know that a change of government has been effected in this country, and are watching its effects upon the
character of the people, as to whether it is better for them to live on as
thieves and robbers or as friendly tribes; and also the immense amount of
property on deposit, you can readily appreciate my anxiety in contemplating that event. There are other dangers in this country I must point out.
The number of natives and foreigners in the country are nearly balanced,
and of course a strong jealousy exists between them, not only on the score
of which government shall prevail, but as to ideas of personal liberty, property, and all the every-day dealings of life. There are subordinate jealousies,
too, between the foreigners of different nations, the old settlers and the new;
and indeed, when you remember that a great part of these foreigners are
deserters from ships, and men who have been accustomed to lead a lawless
life, you can see what confusion would result from the sudden withdrawal
of strong authority, well backed by force.'

with despatches before he could extend his tour, as had been intended, to Sonoma and New Helvetia. His report was dated October 7th; and in the next, of November 11th, devoted mainly to commercial topics, he reported a continuance of tranquil prosperity, with good news from the peninsula.[6] In December there was a renewal of alarming rumors, with which the presence of Sonorans was in some way connected, and which brought out on the 27th a proclamation requiring all Sonoreños in the territory to appear within ten days before the military authorities to explain their business, under penalty of arrest and treatment as enemies and spies.[7] Meanwhile an overzealous sentinel at Los Angeles having fired his gun at the approach of a horse or cow failing to give the countersign, the garrison was called to arms, the guns were made ready, and finally a lighted fuse was dropped into the ammunition-chest, causing an explosion that partially destroyed the guard-house and killed several dragoons and volunteers.[8]

In 1848 fears and rumors of revolt continued. Some were inclined to connect the return of José Castro with revolutionary plots, while others took the view that his return without an army indicated the end of all plottings. Three of the men suspected, Antonio Chavez, Francisco Rico, and Gabriel de la Torre, were obliged to give bonds of $5,000 each that

[6] Arrival at S. F. and ball. *S. F. Cal. Star*, Sept. 25, Oct. 2, 1847; *S. F. Californian*, Sept. 29, Oct. 6, 1847. Oct. 7th, Mason to govt. *Cal. and N. Mex.*, etc., 355-8. 'It affords me much pleasure to assure the department that the most perfect harmony subsists between the members of the naval and land forces on this coast, and that the most friendly intercourse is kept up between the officers. I have had frequent occasion myself to ask assistance of commodores Biddle and Shubrick, and my requests have been granted with promptness and politeness; and in return I have afforded them all the assistance in my power. Our consultations have been frequent and perfectly harmonious, resulting, I hope, in the advancement of the common cause of our country.' Nov. 11th, rept on commerce. Much insubordination among the volunteers.

[7] Sonorans at S. José, rumors of hostilities. *S. F. Californian*, Dec. 15, 1847. Dec. 27th, Mason's proclamation. *Bonilla, Doc.*, MS., 28; *Cal. and N. Mex.*, etc., 450.

[8] The accident was on Dec. 7th. *Los Angeles Hist.*, 30; *Clark's First Regiment*, 76-7.

they would commit no act of hostility. This was in February, and at the same time Castro was travelling very slowly from Los Angeles northward, having come back to California under a passport signed by Mason in the preceding June. He was notified by the governor of the prevalent rumors respecting impending revolt, and thereupon came to Monterey and gave a solemn promise to abstain from all political interference.[9]

Still other revolutionary developments are to be noticed at Santa Bárbara. In April, when forces were being organized to fight the Indians, a plot was revealed to use these forces against the Americans with a view to the taking of both Santa Bárbara and Los Angeles; but an investigation by Colonel Stevenson showed no definite foundation for charges that had been made against certain leading citizens.[10] Meanwhile, however, the affair of the *cañon perdido* tended to increase popular excitement and official fears. A six-pound gun belonging to the *Elizabeth*, that had been carried from the barracks to the beach for shipment, disappeared in the night of April 5th. All efforts to find it were unsuccessful; some said it had been carried in a cart toward Los Angeles, others that it had been put on board a vessel; the authorities

[9] Feb. 5, 1848, bonds given by Chavez and the rest. *Unb. Doc.*, MS., 131; *Vallejo, Doc.*, MS., xii. 331. March 14th, Chavez allowed to go to S. Blas. *Cal. and N. Mex.*, etc., 492. July 17, 1847, Mason's passport to Castro. *Id.*, 323. Feb. 7, 9, 1848, Mason to Castro. *Id.*, 472, 474. April 12th, Mason's report of both affairs. *U. S. Govt Doc.*, H. Ex. Doc. 1, pt ii. 103–4. March 4th, trouble thought to be brewing near S. José by a party in the redwoods under one Beverley. *Unb. Doc.*, MS., 8–9. Nov. 14th, Manuel Castro urged by his mother and brother-in-law to return to Cal. *Doc. Hist. Cal.*, i. 505.

[10] Testimony at the investigation of April 18th–20th, in *Guerra, Doc.*, MS., i. 219–28. Capt. Lippitt had been told by Pedro Carrillo, who got his information from his brother José, and he from the mother of Juan Rodriguez, that the latter, lying behind the counter at Camarrillo's store, had overhead a consultation on the proposed revolt between Francisco and Pablo de la Guerra, Antonio Rodriguez, Juan P. Ayala, José Lugo, and perhaps Cesario Lataillade. Rodriguez and his mother as witnesses knew nothing of the matter. José Carrillo had heard some remarks on the ease with which the barracks might be taken. Pedro Carrillo had represented the matter to Lippitt as an idle rumor, with the understanding that nothing should be done. March 10th, Alcalde Pedro Carrillo testifies to good feeling between troops and citizens, as shown particularly on Washington's birthday. *Carrillo, Doc.*, MS., 10.

were inclined to connect the disappearance with current rumors of revolt, and to believe that the Barbareños, if as patriotic as they claimed to be, might clear up the mystery. Local officials and prominent citizens were offended at the suspicions cast upon them, but they could not learn who had taken the gun. Accordingly, at the end of May, Governor Mason imposed a military contribution of $500 on the town, to be paid pro rata by all inhabitants, but to be repaid to the town on discovery of the guilty individuals, or proof that they were not residents of Santa Bárbara. This act caused much excitement and indignation, especially among American residents; the alcaldes offered their resignation, which was not accepted; and some individuals made trouble about paying their assessment; but the amount was collected, and in August was turned over to the alcalde to be used as a municipal fund. Ten years later the cannon was found. Five men—probably without the knowledge of others, and possibly with a vague idea that the gun might be useful in some rising of the Mexicans—had dragged it away in the surf by the aid of a yoke of oxen, and buried it in the sand of the beach. It is not of record that the municipal fund was ever devoted to public uses, the tradition being that it disappeared in an effort to double it at monte; but the affair gave names to two streets of the town still called Cañon Perdido and Quinientos Pesos.[11]

[11] April 12th, Mason, by Sherman, to José de la Guerra; April 20th, Guerra's reply; Apr. 27th, Mason's reply; May 19th, G.'s reply; threats of penalty, protests, explanation of details, etc. *Guerra, Doc.*, MS., i. 83–94; *Doc. Hist. Cal.*, MS., iv. 1184–6. May 31st, July 21st, Mason's order for a military contribution, and later explanation. Addressed to Stevenson. *Cal. and N. Mex.*, etc., 572, 615. July 11th, Stevenson to Mason. Has collected $385; thinks the Barbareños not guilty. Two Americans were exempt for past services. *Unb. Doc.*, MS., 151–6. It appears that at first the tax was $2 per head, but later changed to a percentage on property. José Ant. Aguirre was not allowed to leave the port on the *Guipuzcoana* till he had paid his quota of $45. *Guerra, Doc.*, MS., vii. 202–4. Corresp. of July–Aug. on resignation of the alcaldes Pedro C. Carrillo and E. Ardisson. Both refused to pay the tax, and some of their property was seized. *Unb. Doc.*, MS., 195–6; *Miscel. Hist. Pap.*, MS., 9; *Cal. and N. Mex.*, etc., 589. Aug. 7th, Mason's order to Lippitt to turn over the $500 as a municipal fund. *Id.*, 591. José E. García, *Episodios*, MS., 1–7, was one of the 5 who buried the cannon, and he gives a

Last in the series of alarming circumstances, and last development in Mexican rule over California, was the return of Pio Pico, with claim to be recognized as governor. His pretensions were characterized by Mason as absurd, and so they were so far as any chance of success was concerned; yet they were plausible enough from certain points of view. The armistice of February 29th suspended all hostilities pending the ratification of a treaty, and left Mexican civil officials free to exercise their functions. Pico, being in Sonora, understood this to restore him temporarily to authority, and he applied to the naval officer in command for permission to return in his official capacity, which was denied, with the assurance that there was no objection to his coming as a private citizen.[12] Don Pio crossed to the peninsula in May, and arrived at San Diego on the 6th of July, reaching Santa Margarita three or four days later, and going to Workman's La Puente rancho on the 15th, and to San Gabriel on the 17th. Meanwhile Colonel Stevenson became alarmed at Pico's return without a passport, at his failure to report to the military commandant at San Diego, and especially at current rumors of his having said he came with full powers as governor; and issued an order requiring him to present himself at once on penalty of being treated as a spy. Two detachments of troops sent to bring in Don Pio did not find him; but having heard of the order and sent Hugo Reid to explain matters, he came in voluntarily, with the assurance that he had no hostile intentions,

full account of the affair. His companions were José Ant. de la Guerra, José Lugo, José Dolores García, and Pacífico Cota. Streeter, in his *Recollections*, MS., 83–9, gives many details; as also does Stephen C. Foster, *Los Angeles in 1847–9*, MS., 31–4.

[12] May 10th, Com. Rudd to Pico, on the *Dale* at Guaymas, in reply to request of April 22d. Regrets his inability to carry P. across to Mulegé. Original in *Pico (Pio) Doc.*, MS., ii. 181. That other Mex. officers took the same view as Pico is shown by an order of April 22d, from Gen. Anaya at Mazatlan to the 'Mexican comandante general of Cal.,' to proceed under art. 1 of the armistice to elect authorities to rule Cal. as part of the Mex. republic. *Unb. Doc.*, MS., 392–3. Also by a letter of Gov. Parás of N. Leon, announcing on April 4th his own restoration, and sent to Pico as gov. of Cal. *Pico, Doc.*, MS., ii. 177.

and was permitted to go on to San Fernando.[13]   Here
he summoned Covarrubias, his former secretary, and
on the 22d addressed official letters to both Stevenson and Mason to inform them that he came in consequence of the armistice as Mexican governor of
California "to establish in the towns of this territory
the benefits of said armistice," and to ask for the issuing of the corresponding orders to give his mission
due effect![14]   The colonel after receiving another letter of inquiry replied that although Pico's position
was not tenable, that matter would be left for the
decision of Mason, but meanwhile he must take no
steps and abstain from conversation tending to foment
discontent on penalty of imprisonment.   Don Pio in

[13] July 17th, Stevenson's order to Pico. Original in *Pico, Doc.*, MS., ii. 183.
July 20th, Stevenson's report to Mason. *Cal. and N. Mex., Mess. and Doc.,
1850*, p. 599.   July 21st, Mason to Stevenson, in reply to a letter not extant,
on Pico's arrival.   P. must be required to give a written parole, treated with
the respect due his rank, but watched carefully. *Id.*, 572.   Pico gives a clear
account of the whole matter in his *Hist. Cal.*, MS., 174–8.   Stevenson represents Pico as denying 'ever having said that he came back with powers to
resume his gubernatorial powers,' but Pico says he simply disavowed any
hostile intentions, and was allowed to go to S. Fernando and open an 'official
correspondence.'
[14] July 22d, Pico to Stevenson and to Mason, blotter originals in *Pico,
Doc.*, MS., ii. 185–8.   The following English translation of the letter to
Mason is in *Cal. and N. Mex.*, etc., 602: 'Most Excellent Sir: As Mexican
Governor of California, I have come to this country with the object that the
armistice agreed upon in the city of Mexico, on the 29th of last February,
by the generals in chief of the forces of the United Mexican States and
those of the United States of the North, he observed herein.   In making
this declaration to your excellency, the just principle on which it is founded
fills me with confidence; and from the favorable information which I possess
respecting the qualifications which adorn your excellency, I trust that my
mission to California will produce its due effect.
'For which reason, and in due observance of the before-mentioned armistice, I have the honor to address myself to your excellency, requesting that
you will be pleased to expedite your orders to the end that, in the places
in California occupied by the forces of the United States of America, no im-
pediment be placed in my way toward the establishment of constitutional
order in a political, administrative, and judicial manner.
'It is my desire that the Mexicans and Americans look upon and consider
themselves with the most sincere fraternity; and in accordance with this
principle, I feel disposed to co-operate with your excellency in surmounting
any difficulties which may arise in the business which occupies us.
'This opportunity offers me means of protesting to your excellency the
assurances of my distinguished consideration and high respect.   God and
Liberty! San Fernando, July 22, 1848. Pio Pico. His Excellency R.
B. Mason, Governor and Commander-in-chief of the forces of the United
States in California, Monterey.'   July 25th, Pico to Stevenson; July 28th,
Stevenson's reply; July 29th, P.'s reply; July 30th, S.'s reply. *Pico, Doc.*,
MS., ii. 193, 197–8, 201–6.

reply came to the city, complained in writing of the threat as uncalled for, since he would be the last to encourage disturbances in his country, and was permitted to go to his rancho of Santa Margarita to await Mason's response.[15] Governor Mason, who on July 26th had sent a warning in relation to Pico's possible action in antedating records of land grants, received his letter on the 3d of August, and his answer was an order to Stevenson to arrest Don Pio, confine him at Los Angeles, prevent his conferring with any of his countrymen, and send him north by sea at the earliest opportunity. There is no definite record of the date or duration of his confinement, but Pico and others agree that he was kept under arrest for a week or more at Stevenson's quarters. Mason's order for his release, on receipt of news that a treaty had been signed, was dated August 8th, and was accompanied by some bluster in very questionable taste about the ex-governor's pretensions.[16]

The treaty of Guadalupe Hidalgo, concluded on February 2d, ratified at Washington March 10th and at Querétaro May 30th, put an end to the war, and gave California permanently and formally to the United States.[17] The news reached California on the

[15] Aug. 5th, Stevenson's pass to Pico. *Pico, Doc.*, MS., ii. 211–13. This and the preceding 7 documents of the correspondence were printed in Spanish in the *Los Angeles Cal. Meridional*, July 18, 1855. See *Coronel, Doc.*, 174.

[16] July 26th, Mason to Stevenson on land titles. By prompt and discreet action it was hoped to get on the right side of Don Pio before the holders of fraudulent grants could reach him. *Cal. and N. Mex.*, etc., 668–9. Aug. 3d, Mason's order of arrest. *Id.*, 631–2. Aug. 8th, countermand. 'Had it not been for this, you may inform Pico, he would have been sent to Oregon or some other foreign country. The manner in which he entered California might have subjected him to the treatment of a spy; and his subsequent conduct, after his conversation with you, together with his absurd pretensions to the government of the country, made him merit harsher treatment than he now receives. You will please inform him that Upper California is now American territory, and that he is at liberty to leave it or not, as he pleases; but so long as he continues in Upper California he must be cautious how he acts toward our authorities, civil or military. I have the honor to be your obedient servant, W. T. Sherman.' *Id.*, 635. Aug. 23d, Mason's report to govt. *Id.*, 601. *Pico, Hist. Cal.*, MS., 174–8, says he refused to accompany the officer sent to arrest him, and was left to present himself voluntarily the next day. He was treated with courtesy and allowed many favors.

[17] See *Hist. Mex.*, v., this series, for full account of the negotiations and

6th of August, and was announced next day in a proclamation by Governor Mason. Making known the cession of Upper California, the boundary, and the choice of citizenship offered, the governor continues: In the mean time the Mexicans " will be protected in the free enjoyment of their liberty and property, and secured in the free exercise of their religion. They, however, are reminded that, as war no longer exists, and as Upper California now belongs to the United States, they owe a strict obedience to the American authorities, and any attempt on their part to disturb the peace and tranquillity of the country will subject them to the severest penalties. From this new order of things there will result to California a new destiny. Instead of revolutions and insurrections, there will be internal tranquillity; instead of a fickle and vacillating policy, there will be a firm and stable government, administering justice with impartiality, and punishing crime with the strong arm of power. The arts and sciences will flourish, and the labor of the agriculturist, guided by the lamp of learning, will stimulate the earth to the most bountiful production. Commerce, freed from the absurd restrictions formerly imposed, will be greatly extended; the choked-up channels of trade will be opened, and the poisoned fountains of domestic faction forever dried up. Americans and Californians will now be one and the same people, subject to the same laws, and enjoying the same rights and privileges; they should therefore become a

resulting treaty. Also *Tratado de Paz*, Mex. 1848, 8vo, 55 p., in Engl. and Spanish. The territory corresponding to Texas, N. Mex., Arizona, and Cal. was ceded to the U. S. for $15,000,000, and the amount of all decided and pending claims against Mexico. The boundary was the middle of the Gila and a straight line from the Colorado junction to the Pacific, at a point one league below the southernmost point of the port of S. Diego. Free navigation of the Gila and of the Colorado and gulf below the junction was assured. Mexican residents of the ceded territory were free to remain or depart as citizens of Mexico or the U. S., but must choose within a year, a failure to do so being equivalent to a decision to become citizens of the U. S. All property rights were to be inviolably respected, including those of the church and of all ecclesiastical or religious corporations or communities. Mexican grants of land were to be recognized; and legitimate titles in Cal. were to be such as were legitimate under Mex. law before May 13, 1846.

band of brothers, emulating each other in their exertions to develop the wealth and resources, and to secure the peace, happiness, and permanent prosperity, of their common country."[18]

Reporting his action to the government on August 19th, Mason was later occupied with the disbandment of the volunteers, with consequent fears of Indian hostilities, with details of an anomalous system of government, and with various routine matters, besides affairs connected with the gold excitement. He says: "I do not anticipate any rebellion or revolution on the part of the Californians, although the southern district must be entirely abandoned by the military force now there; and in fact, the minds of all men are so intently engaged upon getting gold, that for the present they have not time to think of mischief;" yet he did not cease to urge upon the government the necessity of providing additional means of security.[19]

Congressional action on the territory acquired from Mexico is a subject that can neither be disregarded nor satisfactorily treated in connection with Californian annals of 1846–8. Not only does its treatment involve much repetition in the history of New Mexico, Texas, and of the Mexican war as presented in

[18] Aug. 7th, Mason's proclamation of peace. *Cal. and N. Mex.*, *Mess. and Doc.*, *1850*, p. 590–1. Original print in English and Spanish. *Pico (Pio)*, *Doc.*, MS., ii. 215.

[19] Aug. 19th, Mason to govt. The letter announcing the treaty was dated Querétaro May 30th, and was sent up from La Paz overland by Col Burton. *Cal. and N. Mex.*, etc., 597. June 23d, Buchanan to Larkin, with the news. *Larkin's Doc.*, MS., vi. 134. Aug. 23d, Mason to govt. Ammunition sent to Oregon for Ind. war; also furnished to Cal. rancheros for protection, Pico's return, fortifications urgently needed at S. F., no laborers can be hired for less than $10 or $20 per day. *Cal. and N. Mex.*, etc., 601. Aug. 25th, Id. to Id. Paying off of troops, continued desertions, crews of merchant vessels mutinous, but no power to arrest them, no equipments. *Id.*, 603. Aug. 28th, desertions, troops must be better paid or it is of no use to send them; those faithful now deserve reward. 'Should any rebellion take place, no future promise of pay, however great, would call 100 men from the mines.' Not an ounce of ammunition can be bought. *Id.*, 643. Nov. 24th, Mason wishes to be relieved, 'the war being over, and the soldiers nearly all deserted.' Many people of L. Cal. have been brought here, orders given to feed and quarter them for two months. *Id.*, 648–9. Dec. 27th, compliments to officers for past services. Reports of several horrible murders and robberies, including that of Reed and family at S. Miguel. *Id.*, 649–53.

other volumes of this series, but it belongs inseparably to the grandest and most complicated topics of United States history, national development, territorial extension, the struggle between slavery and freedom, nullification, abolition, secession, and all the successive steps that led to the greatest war of modern times. How futile the attempt to present en résumé even an outline view of these matters; yet a résumé, and that of the briefest, is obviously all that can be offered here.

Texas in 1844–5 was regarded in the United States as including a strip of territory extending from the gulf to latitude 42°, along the Louisiana boundary of 1819, and westward rather indefinitely into Mexican possessions. The people at this time strongly favored its annexation, because of a general desire for enlarging the republic in accordance with manifest destiny, of a theory that the country had been needlessly yielded to Spain in 1819, and of popular sympathy for the supposed wrongs of Texan settlers. With additional strength as a popular measure in support of certain presidential aspirations, and as a field for profitable land speculations, a treaty of annexation was signed in 1844; yet it was rejected in the senate by a vote of two to one. This result was due to the fact that by the treaty the United States would have assumed the existing war with Mexico, that by its terms Texan boundaries were arbitrarily extended to the Rio Grande, and that annexation by treaty was not deemed the best method of procedure. To the majority the idea of an aggressive war on Mexico was not a pleasing one; a minority favored the measure at any cost, either desiring war or believing it might be avoided.

Early in 1845 the project was presented in a modified and more acceptable form, that of a joint resolution to admit territory "rightfully belonging" to Texas, under a constitution to be submitted to congress, and with the condition that four new states might be formed under the provisions of the Missouri

compromise, prohibiting slavery north of latitude 36°
30′. This passed the house by a vote of 120 to 97.
In the senate it could be passed only by the addition of a peculiar amendment or alternative substitute
providing for preliminary negotiations at the president's discretion, and then by a vote of 27 to 25, with
the understanding that negotiations with Mexico
should be opened by Polk, the president-elect, before
submitting the resolution of congress to Texas. But
President Tyler in the last days of his term, having
approved the bill, at once despatched it to Texas by a
special envoy. Thus the measure was carried in
March by a trick. If President Polk was to any extent a victim, he proved a very willing one, since he
made no effort to recall the envoy, and the administration became fully committed to the measure, which
was accepted by Texas in July. Accordingly, in
December the state was admitted by the new congress
by a vote of 141 to 56 in the house, and 31 to 14 in
the senate. There was a strong opposition from the
north to the extension of slavery, but many who opposed annexation on account of Mexican complications
deemed themselves bound by the action of the last
congress.

Mexico had repeatedly announced that the annexation of Texas would be taken as a declaration of war,
and as such it was intended by the administration;
but for fear that Mexican threats might not be carried out, the declaration was renewed by the advance
of United States forces to the Rio Grande. Hostilities began in April 1846, and in May the president
called upon congress for means to prosecute the war
and repel invasion. The war bill was passed by both
houses almost unanimously, and signed by President
Polk on May 13th. There were protests against the
preamble, which falsely declared the war to exist by
act of Mexico, but the actual beginning of hostilities
created a military spirit which few cared to resist,
especially as there were some real grounds of com-

plaint against Mexico. And as yet the war had no other avowed purpose than that of repelling invasion, obtaining indemnity for past grievances, and effecting a settlement of Texan boundaries.

Not only were immediate steps taken to enlist volunteers for active service and to occupy frontier provinces of Mexico, but the purpose of the war party to permanently hold California and New Mexico began to be revealed, notably by proceedings in connection with organizing the New York volunteers and Mormon battalion. In August, at the end of the session, the president called upon congress for funds to be used in making peace, that is, as an advance payment to Mexico for concessions in fixing boundaries. A bill to grant $2,000,000 for 'extraordinary expenses' not specified, caused a warm discussion and strong opposition. Whigs denounced the war and the proposed acquisition of territory, which were defended by democrats. At last a substitute bill, giving $30,000 for negotiations, and $2,000,000 for expenditure if needed on ratification of a treaty, with the 'Wilmot proviso,' prohibiting slavery in any territory that might be acquired, was passed in the house by a vote of 87 to 64. In the senate the rejection of the Wilmot proviso probably, and certainly any action on the bill, was prevented by a Massachusetts senator who spoke 'against time' until final adjournment.

Before the matter came up again at the second session of the twenty-ninth congress several victories had been won on the field of battle, California and New Mexico had been occupied, and the intention to wage a war of conquest, and force Mexico to pay its cost, had become more clearly apparent. In his December message the president alluded to the establishment of a civil government in the provinces named. In the senate a resolution to refer this part of the message to the committee on territories was defeated on the ground that it would be absurd to take any action respecting territory not yet belonging

to the United States. In the house, however, such
a resolution was adopted, as was another calling on
the president for information on the civil government,
with copies of all instructions on the subject to
Kearny, Stockton, and others. Discussion took a
wide range, and gave congressmen an opportunity to
repeat their opinions on the war and its probable results, as well as on the rights of the government
under international law in conquered provinces.

But the chief topic of debate at this session was
the 'three million bill,' of like purport, save in amount,
to that defeated before. The whole subject of the
Mexican war was now much more fully considered
than ever before, and on the main issues at least there
was no longer any concealment. Whigs, with few
exceptions, denounced the war as unjust and aggressive from the first, and still more earnestly in its
newer aspects as a war of conquest. They favored a
treaty adjusting Texan boundaries and providing for
a payment of the old claims. They opposed the dis-
memberment of Mexico, the enforced collection of
indemnity for expenses of the war, and the use of
money to purchase a peace. Some of them declared
their belief that the three millions were to be used as
a bribe for Mexican officials, and pointed to the return of Santa Anna under a United States passport.
They opposed the acquisition of California and New
Mexico, because the republic was large enough, because the population of those provinces was undesirable, because of the irregular methods proposed, and
especially because of difficulties in connection with
the slavery question. Southern whigs were particularly anxious and earnest in urging this phase of the
matter, declaring that the acquisition of new territory
would result in endless controversy and perhaps in
breaking up the union. Webster and other conservatives in the north held the same view. Democrats,
on the other hand, justified the war as provoked by
Mexico, freely admitting the intention to force the

enemy to pay its cost, advocating the acquisition of
California and New Mexico as both justifiable and
desirable, and defending the purchase of a peace.
Most urged a vigorous prosecution of the war for the
purposes indicated, though Calhoun with a small following favored a defensive policy, a mere holding of
the occupied provinces till Mexico should yield. The
danger to be feared from the slavery agitation was
represented as purely imaginary, though some speakers admitted that disunion would result from northern attempts to interfere with southern rights in
newly acquired territory—attempts which as they
trusted would never be made. Opponents of the bill
were plausibly denounced as willing to prolong the
war by insisting on irrelevant issues.

Slavery in new territory was, of course, the real
point of contention. Abolitionists in the north were
now openly, and disunionists in the south secretly,
in favor of forcing the issue. Conservatives in both
sections wished to avoid it. The Wilmot proviso or
its equivalent introduced in both houses at this session
was made the text of the controversy. Southerners
opposed it, claiming that congress had no right to pro-
hibit slavery in the territories, and generally expressing acquiescence in the Missouri compromise. Northerners, including many anti-slavery men, opposed it as
premature, since it was absurd for congress to legis-
late on territories not yet belonging to the United
States; as needless, since slavery was already prohibited by Mexican law in California and New Mexico,
where it could, moreover, never exist for natural reasons; and as tending both to prolong the war and
to excite sectional controversy. Its advocates included abolitionists, men opposed to the extension of
slavery, those doubting the possibility of extending
free soil, and a few conservatives who regarded the
proviso as the best means of defeating the bill.
Doubtless there was a southern radical element secretly approving the proviso as a means of agitation.

In the house the three-million bill was passed in February 1847, with the Wilmot proviso, by a vote of 115 to 105, but this house bill went no farther. In the senate the proviso was defeated by a vote of 31 to 21, and the bill was passed on March 1st by 29 to 24. It passed the house two days later by 115 to 81, the proviso as an amendment being defeated by 102 to 97.

Though funds were thus placed at the president's disposal, there was much hard fighting to be done before Mexico could be forced to yield. Santa Anna, whether or not he had made and broken any agreement respecting a treaty, served a useful purpose to the United States, exhausting Mexican resources by a compact resistance. At last, in March 1848, the treaty of peace, ceding California and New Mexico for $15,000,000, was referred to the senate and ratified by the requisite two-thirds vote. In July it was communicated to the senate as having been finally ratified by Mexico in May. Meanwhile, at the first session of the 30th congress discussions on the president's message, on the Oregon question, and on various resolutions for and against the right of congress to legislate on slavery in the territories had afforded opportunity for keeping the old questions alive, without leading to any practical result, or even to the evolution of any new theories. In his message of July 6th the president announced that California and New Mexico now belonged to the United States, that the temporary military government in those provinces had ceased to exist, and that a territorial civil government was an urgent necessity, at the same time recommending a spirit of mutual concession in establishing the new order of things. On July 22d, in compliance with resolutions of congress, adopted not without debate, he communicated additional information on boundaries and on the past military rule.

So fully had earlier debate made known the views of congress on the questions at issue, that it was deemed useless to attempt the passage of any territorial bill either prohibiting or permitting slavery. Neither the north nor south would yield, and each party of course held the other responsible for the failure to provide a government for California. In the senate a select committee reported on July 19th a bill to make territories of Oregon, California, and New Mexico, with the compromise feature of leaving the matter of slavery to be settled by the courts, facilities being provided for easy and prompt appeal to the United States supreme court. In the discussion it was advocated by southern whigs and by democrats generally; but its opponents declared it to be an evasion rather than a compromise, that it was a southern measure, that the supreme court as constituted would support slavery, that congress should not relinquish control over the matter, and that the bill in its details was faulty. It was passed on July 26th, after a continuous session of twenty-one hours, by a vote of 33 to 22; but in the house, after brief discussion, it was laid on the table by a vote of 112 to 97. Congress adjourned in August, and California had no government. But the Oregon bill, excluding slavery, was finally passed by both houses, though the senate favored making the Missouri compromise the basis of its action, and the president announced that he would not have approved the bill but for the fact that Oregon was north of latitude 36° 30′.

Before congress met again in December 1848, the gold excitement had added a new element of interest and importance to the pending controversy. Again the president urged the necessity of a government. In the discussions of this session more attention was given than before to the people, conditions, and needs of California, though these were still but secondary topics. Slavery in the territories was the real question and the subject of voluminous speeches. I cannot present even en résumé the complicated network of bills, substitutes, amendments, and points of order by which each party strove to gain an advantage. The north was resolved to restrict slavery, and would entertain no proposition for compromise. Once the house in committee of the whole passed a resolution to cede back to Mexico the new territory, retaining San Francisco for the $3,000,000 already paid. An offer of private speculators to take California and pay the cost of the war was mentioned. The house also passed a bill for Upper California similar to the Oregon bill, prohibiting slavery, by adopting the ordinance of 1787; but the senate did not act on this proposition. Considerable importance was attached in debate to the danger of losing California if a government was not speedily provided for her rapidly growing and adventurous population.

The impossibility of obtaining territorial governments being apparent from the first, Senator Douglas introduced and most zealously advocated a bill to admit California and all the new territory at once as a state of the union, the people having, of course, the right to decide the slavery question for themselves. This was cutting the gordian knot indeed; but besides being a solution that would be practically a defeat for the south, though certain prominent southerners favored a similar measure in the house, it had several objectionable features. The judiciary committee reported adversely, on the grounds that congress had no power to create but only to admit a state, that the population was scanty and unfit, that the right to divide the state later as was proposed could not be reserved, and that boundary troubles with Texas were inevitable. Failing in this, Douglas offered a substitute bill admitting California, and providing for the admission of New Mexico as soon as her population should be sufficient; but the measure was not favorably considered.

The final effort was to attach the matter to appropriation bills. An amendment of the army bill, giving to the inhabitants the rights of habeas corpus, trial by jury, and freedom from martial law, was rejected, perhaps because the 'inhabitants' included negroes. But an amendment to the civil and diplomatic bill, extending the revenue, Indian, and land laws over California and New Mexico, was adopted in the senate by 25 votes to 18, the south expecting some advantage from the implied extension of the constitution to the provinces. The house substituted an amendment authorizing the president to hold the new provinces by using the army and navy to maintain existing laws, and also extending the United States revenue laws; but this was not accepted by the senate, chiefly because the Mexican laws prohibited slavery. Finally, on March 4th, after an all-night session and complicated debate, the senate receded from its original amendment, and thus passed the appropriation bill, leaving California as before without a government. Then at the last moment before adjourning, and not without protests from southern senators against the protection of any property rights where their own were ignored, a bill was passed extending the revenue laws over California, and establishing a collection district there.[20]

The matters thus presented extend chronologically somewhat beyond the limits of this chapter and volume, but belong to what precedes rather than to what follows. Later developments connected with the admission of California as a state, after the people had formed a constitution, will be treated in a later volume. We have seen that the subject of California in congress, down to the middle of 1849, includes really but very little of California and a good deal of congress, or congressional action on matters that were national rather than provincial in their scope.

As we have seen, not only did congress after the treaty of 1848 consider the government that should

[20] For the voluminous debates of which I have attempted to present an outline, see *Cong. Globe*, 1845-9, 29th and 30th congresses. Also *Benton's Debates* and *Houston's Debates* for the same period.

be provided for California, but earlier, in December 1846, the system that had actually been put in operation there. A resolution calling upon the president for information and explanation on the subject was passed after long debate, which was, however, merely a part of the general controversy, with but slight bearing on the state of affairs in the far west. Certain peculiarities in the proclamations of Sloat, Kearny, and Stockton afforded a favorable opportunity to attack the administration, to denounce the war, and particularly the apparent purpose to make it a war of permanent conquest. After the discussion had served its partisan purpose the matter was dropped, as the president's explanation was unassailable on the point nominally at issue, and his plans of conquest were otherwise clearly enough announced. The debate, however, brought out the views of congressmen respecting the civil government of conquered provinces as regulated by international law. Mr Douglas took the ground, more or less fully supported by others, that by the act of occupation California and New Mexico became United States territory, and as such immediately subject to the control of congress. On the other hand, Mr Rhett and a few followers expressed very radical opinions in favor of the arbitrary and unlimited powers possessed by the president as commander-in-chief. Neither of these extreme views, however, was generally supported.[21]

The position assumed by the president from the beginning to the end of the war, both in messages to congress and instructions to subordinates, supported in the debates by conservative members with citations from writers on international law, and carried out

[21] Debates in 2d sess. 29th congress, in *Cong. Globe*, 1846–7, p. 13, 20, 33, 37–9, 43–4, 46, 67, 75–6, 85, 87, 345. The president's explanatory message is also found with accompanying documents as *U. S. Govt Doc.*, 29th cong. 2d sess., H. Ex. Doc. 19. See also, on civil government, *Cong. Globe*, 1847–8, p. 910–16, 989–92, including the message of July 22, 1848. Also *Globe*, 1848–9, p. 191. The most complete treatment of the subject, in all its phases, is found in the speech of Mr Seddon of Va., Dec. 10, 1846, in *Globe*, p. 23–6.

more or less uniformly by the successive commanders in California, was in substance as follows: War having been regularly declared, the executive, as commander-in-chief, could use his forces to conquer and hold any part of the Mexican territory as an act of war. The first object was to obtain possession, to overcome all armed resistance, and to secure submission on the part of the people. This accomplished, it became a right and duty to protect citizens in their individual rights, and thus prevent anarchy. To this end the conquerors acquired the powers of sovereignty temporarily lost by Mexico. Methods would depend largely on the judgment of commanders, and might vary with circumstances; but a conciliatory rather than an oppressive policy was required. Strict martial law might be enforced if deemed necessary; otherwise, the people being submissive and friendly, a temporary civil government might be established as a legitimate feature of military rule. The nature of the system to be introduced was not to be determined by the people; Mexico was entitled to no voice in the matter; the power of the conqueror was absolute, except as limited by the requirements of humanity and justice, constituting what is called international law and usage. Other things being equal, it was natural and right to continue the old Mexican methods; but the conqueror might legitimately conciliate popular favor for his government and nation, as well as promote the cause of justice, by annulling oppressive acts of Mexico; and in introducing modifications deemed convenient or essential to safety, he might properly take the institutions of his own nation as a model. By the conquest California did not become United States territory; the president had no power to make or declare her such; she did not come under the protection of the constitution or of legislation by congress. What powers of permanent annexation or government congress and the executive might legitimately have assumed over California before the treaty is a question that need not be considered, since there was no attempt to exercise such powers. The government set up was a temporary one, and a part of the military rule by conquerors. Commanders in California were responsible to the president, under whose orders they acted; and he was responsible to congress in this matter of civil government to no greater extent than in any other matter connected with the prosecution of the war.

Instructions from Washington, with consequent proclamations and acts of Sloat, Stockton, Frémont, and Kearny down to the middle of 1847, have been fully presented in the narrative of events.[22] In the instructions no irregularity is to be found, unless it may be in that requiring an oath of allegiance to the United States from officials. No more than an oath of obedience to the new authorities could be properly demanded.[23] In New Mexico General Kearny went so far in his proclamations as to elicit from the president a statement that certain parts were not "approved or recognized," but for the rest, including the acts of Sloat and Stockton, he said in his message of December 1846: "If any excess of power has been exercised, the departure has been the offspring of a patriotic desire to give the inhabitants the privileges and immunities so cherished by the people of our own country. Any such excess has resulted in no practical injury, but can and will be early corrected in a manner to alienate as little as possible the good feelings of the

[22] See instructions to Sloat et al., p. 195–9, this vol.; Sloat's procl. of July 7, 1846, p. 234; Stockton's procl. of July 29th, p. 255; Stockton's procl. of Aug. 17th, p. 283; Stockton's proposed government, p. 284; instructions to Kearny, p. 334; treaty of Cahuenga, Jan. 13, 1847, p. 404; Jan. 22d, Frémont's procl. and govt, p. 432; Kearny's procl. of March 1st, p. 437–8.

[23] It is in the instructions of July 12, 1846, that we read: 'The object of the U. S. has reference to ultimate peace with Mex.; and if, at that peace, the basis of the *uti possidetis* shall be established, the govt expects through your forces to be found in actual possession of Upper Cal. This will bring with it the necessity of a civil administration. Such a govt shall be established under your protection; and in selecting persons to hold office, due respect should be had to the wishes of the people of Cal., as well as to the actual possessors of authority in that province. It may be proper to require an oath of allegiance to the U. S. from those who are intrusted with authority.

inhabitants." Of proceedings in California no special disapproval was ever deemed necessary.

Sloat, in his conciliatory proclamation of July 7th, went far beyond his instructions or the authority of his chief, in promising that California should be permanently a territory of the United States; yet he practically attempted nothing but the military occupation of certain points; and Stockton, while in his warlike and impolitic tirade of the 29th he went still further astray by declaring that his only purpose was to protect oppressed citizens and foreigners, and that he would withdraw his forces as soon as that purpose should be effected, simply proceeded to extend the military occupation, and take the paroles of submissive Mexican officers. In his proclamation of August 7th he continued military law, while promising some changes in the near future;[24] and in his elaborate system of territorial government soon devised, local rule under Mexican law was provided for, and the features of his scheme to which exception might be taken on legal grounds were never approved or carried into effect. Then after the revolt and reconquest came the treaty of Cahuenga, January 13, 1847, the terms of which were entirely unobjectionable, requiring from the Californians only present submission to the American authorities, but no oath of allegiance, and not treating them as in any sense citizens of the United States. Stockton's system of civil government was then partially established; Frémont was appointed governor, and in his proclamation of January 22d he simply required " the return of civil officers to their appropriate duties, and as strict an

[24] 'The territory of Cal. now belongs to the U. S., and will be governed as soon as circumstances may permit by officers and laws similar to those by which the other territories of the U. S. are regulated and protected. But until the gov., sec., and council are appointed, and the various civil departments of the govt are arranged, military laws will prevail, and the commander-in-chief will be gov. and protector of the territory. In the mean time the people will be permitted' to elect civil officers to administer the laws according to former usages. The system of govt devised by Stockton about this time, and sent to Washington for approval, may be found in *Cutts' Conq.*, 123.

obedience of the military to the civil authority as is consistent with the security of peace." The controversies of those days referred to the governorship, and not to the system of government.

Thus far Sloat, Stockton, and Frémont had acted without instructions, yet, while by their unfortunate differences in act and promise and theory they had done much to retard Californian peace and prosperity, they had not gone far astray in the matter of civil government and its administration by conquerors. Kearny, acting under definite instructions of June, July, and November 1846, and in the light of experience, in his acts of March 1847 had no occasion to make radical changes in the methods before observed. His requiring from officials an oath to support the constitution was illegal, besides not being in accord with the capitulation of Cahuenga, but it was in his instructions. He dispensed with the legislative council, being under no obligation to follow Stockton's ideas, but the council had not acted. His promise of a regular territorial government may be understood as referring to the formation of a treaty; his absolution of the inhabitants from all allegiance to Mexico was but a farce; his prediction that the stars and stripes would float over California as long as the sun should shine upon her was as harmless an expression of his opinion and that of his superiors as had been the earlier one of Sloat.

Governor Mason succeeded Kearny at the end of May, and made no innovations in system followed by his predecessors. All the successive commanders among themselves and with the national authorities practically agreed respecting essential features of the temporary military and civil rule; and the president's excuses for irregularities in 1846, as previously quoted, will apply with equal force to later informalities. Instructions of January now received were much more definite than earlier ones, approving in a general way what had been done, but explaining the rights of con-

querors, and containing a warning that the existing
government was but temporary, and that California
could not yet be considered a territory of the United
States.[25] Thus, pending a treaty of peace, there was
but little opportunity for subsequent misunderstanding or theorizing on the general system, though perplexing details of application were likely to present
themselves. Alcaldes who had been elected or appointed continued to administer justice according to
their ideas of Mexican law and the old usages, appealing in difficult or complicated cases to the governor,
whose policy was to interfere as little as possible,
particularly in questions affecting property rights.
Naturally, in places where both the alcalde and the
people were foreigners, some very peculiar versions of
Mexican law and of old customs obtained; but petty
local affairs were well enough managed as a rule,
though there was no lack of complaint that the country was without law. Local annals given in later
chapters will furnish some illustrative items, especially
on the municipal troubles of San Francisco, San José,
and the larger towns. I append some brief notes;[26]

[25] See p. 334–5 of this vol. for instructions to Kearny. I quote here more
fully those to the naval commander: 'The course of our govt in regard to
Cal....depends on those on whom the constitution imposes the duty of making and carrying treaties into effect. Pending the war, our possession gives
only such rights as the laws of nations recognize, and the govt is military,
performing such civil duties as are necessary to the full enjoyment of the
advantages resulting from the conquest, and to the due protection of the
rights of persons and of property of the inhabitants. No political right can
be conferred on the inhabitants thus situated, emanating from the constitution
of the U. S....Unless incorporated, with the assent of congress by ratified
treaty or by legislative act, our rights over enemies' territory in our possession are only such as the laws of war confer, and theirs no more than are
derived from the same authority....In the discharge of the duty of govt...
it has not been deemed improper or unwise that the inhabitants should be
permitted to participate in the selection of agents to make or execute the
laws to be enforced....I have regarded your measures...as founded on this
principle, and so far as they carry out the right of temporary govt under existing rights of possession they are approved. But no officers created, or
laws or regulations made to protect the rights or perform the duties resulting from our conquests, can lawfully continue beyond the duration of the
state of things which now exists, without authority of future treaty or act
of congress....The president foresees no contingency in which the U. S. will
ever surrender or relinquish possession of the Californias.'

[26] June 2, 1847, Mason to Alcalde Boggs, explaining the system of govt as
per instructions of Jan. 11th. Cal. and N. Mex., Mess. and Doc., 1850, p. 317.
See S. F. Cal. Star and Californian, 1847–8, for much comment by editors

and there are a few cases that may be somewhat more fully noticed in this connection.

The case of Alcalde Nash at Sonoma was the only one in which the military authority in civil matters

and correspondents on matters of govt. In March a man came to Mont. with a paper from an alcalde which stated that he had been convicted of horse-stealing, and desired a new hearing. *Mont. Calif.*, Mar. 20, 1847. Mar. 26th, Kearny orders the dismissal of an old suit for winnings at a race. *Cal. and N. Mex.*, etc., 291. Mar. 24th, Colton appointed judge of the admiralty court of Cal. *Id.* April 10th, Kearny orders that liquor shops be closed on Sunday, drunken and disorderly persons to be arrested and punished. *Los Ang. Arch.*, MS., iii. 46–7. If a man is not content with the alcalde's decision, let him wait for the establishment of other courts. *S. José Arch.*, *Loose Pap.*, MS., 5. April 24th, Kearny to Bellamy, in answer to complaint. 'During the existence of the war there must of necessity arise many cases of great hardship and injustice, which for the time being are without remedy.' *Cal. and N. Mex.*, 299. May 1st, alcalde remonstrates with K. for setting aside his proceedings. *Unb. Doc.*, MS., 117. May 5th, K. recommends arbitrators in a divorce case. *Cal. and N. Mex.*, 305. June 1st, Larkin to *N. Y. Herald*, writes: 'We must live on in lawless blessedness. We have, however, a fair supply of lawyers, and each can produce the laws of his native state and urge on the alcalde their adoption as most applicable to the case in hand.' *Off. Corresp.*, MS., i. 158. June 5th, alcaldes decline to take the oath of allegiance, which would make them traitors to Mex. *Unb. Doc.*, MS., 204. June 16th, Mason orders an alcalde to come to Mont. and bring with him a prisoner and witnesses. *Cal. and N. Mex.*, 323. June 14th, Mason writes: 'The alcaldes are not "authorities of the U. S.," nor are they Mex. authorities. They are the civil magistrates of Cal., and therefore the "authorities of Cal.," subject to removal from office by the gov.' *Id.*, 321. Only one change of venue can be granted. *Id.*, 333, 376. July 3d, alcalde may call for military aid to enforce his decrees. *Id.*, 339. He must apply in writing. The slightest possible force to be used. There are many other communications on this matter. July 24th, order of Gen. Scott, making the martial law a supplemental code for punishment of serious crimes by or against military men, circulated and to be enforced in Cal. *Id.*, 353. Aug. 4th, troops cannot take charge of prisoners except in grave cases. *Los Ang. Arch.*, MS., iii. 99. A murderer at Sta Cruz shot by alcalde's order. *Unb. Doc.*, MS., 108. Aug. 23d, 'The civil officers would be most willing to shift upon mil. the disagreeable task of arresting and guarding their criminals, but this must not be permitted. Officers in command are only expected to aid civil officers when the latter are unable to enforce their decrees; and even then a sound discretion should be exercised.' *Cal. and N. Mex.*, 349. Aug. 25th, 'Your auth. as alcalde in all cases between citizen and citizen is the same as it was under the Mex. law. But when a soldier is concerned, then mil. law must have precedence.' *Id.*, 354. Oct. 25th, alcaldes may have jurisdiction over crimes committed on board ships, as there are no other courts. *Id.*, 404. Oct. 26th, alcalde may sentence a man for manslaughter to 7 years' hard labor on public works, and may send him to Mont. *Id.*, 410. Alcalde can not be required to retry old cases. *Id.*, 412. Nov. 1st, instructions on formalities in a trial for murder. *Id.*, 413. Nov. 29th, Mason's order of fine of $50 to $100, and imprisonment of 3 to 6 months for selling liquor to an Ind. *Id.*, 437, and elsewhere. Dec. 3d, there are no courts other than alcaldes'; and Mason declines to appoint a special court, though he has done so in some cases. *Id.*, 439. Dec. 20th, Mason suggests an additional penalty of 50 lashes for stealing horses. *Id.*, 445. Dec. 22d, if a jury cannot agree in a reasonable time, a new one may be empanelled. *Id.*, 446. Dec. 29th, in cases involving over $100 a jury of six men shall decide. *Id.*, 452, and elsewhere. March 2d,

was disputed. John H. Nash was an old man who
had come overland from Missouri in 1845, and had
been elected alcalde in 1846. In consequence of reported irregularities in his management of the office,
General Kearny appointed L. W. Boggs, an abler but
not a better man, to succeed him in April 1847. Nash
denied Kearny's right to remove an alcalde elected
under the system established by Sloat and Stockton,
refusing to turn over the records of his office, and being supported by the citizens, who, to the number of
seventy, headed by Ide and Grigsby, held a public
meeting to petition for his reinstatement. He was
egotistic and eccentric, much like Ide in some respects,
and even proposed to make an effort at Washington for
Kearny's removal. For a time in May Sonoma had
practically no alcalde, each declining to act; but Mason
declined to revoke his predecessor's order as being presumably well founded, and early in June ordered Captain Brackett to use force for the transfer of records,
at the same time sending Nash a peremptory order.
The latter still declined to obey, and Brackett excused
himself from the performance of an act that would
make him unpopular. Meanwhile in June Boggs was
performing the duties of his office. In July Lieutenant Sherman was sent by Mason to arrest Nash

1848, grave cases must be tried by jury, which must award a sentence if
they convict; but the verdict and testimony must be sent to gov. for approval. *Id.*, 488. Men cannot be punished for crimes they will probably commit when they have a chance. *Id.* Mar. 9th, Mason writes: An attempt on
the jail 'would afford me an excellant opportunity of making an example on
the spot of some of the lawless characters with which this country is infested,
and I shall always have a halter ready.' *S. José Arch., Loose Pap.*, MS., 43.
April 17th, alcalde has convicted a man of selling liquor, without jury, because Californian jurymen have on two occasions refused to find a country-
man guilty. *Unb. Doc.*, MS., 122. Apr. 12th, Mason will not take any action in disputes about horse-races. *Cal. and N. Mex.*, 508. April 29th,
M. will not disturb the decision of arbitrators. *Id.*, 546. May 8th, debts
contracted in U. S. cannot be collected here during the war. *S. José Arch.,
Loose Pap.*, MS., 29. May 21st, Hartnell sent to S. F. to attend to printing
a Spanish translation of laws to be pub. by Mason. *Cal. and N. Mex.*, 555.
May 31st, M. proposes to build prisons, appropriating $1,000 for each, and
citizens to pay the rest. *Id.*, 558. Aug. 23d, Hartnell to get $2,000 salary
as govt interpreter and translator. *Id.*, 659. The support of civil prisoners
must be paid from municipal funds. *Id.*, 569. A mil. commandant reprimanded for too hasty action in civil matters. *Id.*, 575.

and bring him to Monterey.   Argument and sea-sickness on the way brought the old gentleman to terms, and Mason at once sent him home at public expense, " fully sensible of his error," and promising an immediate surrender of all the papers of his office, with full accounts of his administration.[27]

Antonio M. Armijo, Robert Smith, and John Egger, of the Sonoma district, were arrested in August 1847, and charged with the murder and kidnapping of Indians in the Sacramento Valley.   The affair gave rise to much correspondence and excitement.   Vallejo and Sutter were appointed as special judges to try the case with a jury of twelve, and Boggs was added to the number later.   For want of an impartial jury and for other reasons, the case was transferred from Sacramento to Sonoma, where it was tried in October, Captain Brackett acting as prosecutor, and Sutter being absent.   The accused were acquitted; and Governor Mason declined to approve an exorbitant bill of about $2,000 for costs of the trial.[28]   A similar special court, consisting of Stephen C. Foster and Abel Stearns, was appointed in April 1848 for the trial of several members of the Mormon battalion at Los Angeles on a charge of passing counterfeit gold coin.   Each had a separate trial before a jury, and Lieutenant Ruel Barrus was found guilty, confessing that he had played at monte with counterfeit money, and was sentenced to five years' imprisonment at hard labor, but the governor, in consideration of his youth and other palliating circumstances, reduced the term to one year.   The

[27] Documentary record very complete in *Unb. Doc.*, MS., 82–3, 107–13, 116, 143, 145, 316; *Cal. and N. Mex., Mess. and Doc., 1850*, p. 289, 295, 317–20, 325, 343, 377; *S. F. Cal. Star*, May 22d; *S. F. Californian*, July 24th, Sept. 4th.   Also a very good and interesting account in *Sherman's Mem.*, i. 30–8.   Green, a lawyer, with whom Nash lived, seems to have incited him to resist, and to have attempted some bluster at the time of his arrest.   Pickett and Scott with Boggs himself were Nash's enemies.   Boggs claimed in Aug. that N. had not rendered his accounts, accusing him of making fraudulent deeds of town lots, and of changing the original map.   J. R. Snyder and Tim. Murphy were appointed commissioners to investigate.

[28] *Cal. and N. Mex., Mess. and Doc., 1850*, p. 343–4, 348–9, 384, 394–5, 419–22; *Unb. Doc.*, MS., 89–90, 124–6, 292–3, 297–8, 313.   One of the items not allowed was lawyer Green's bill for $200.

others were acquitted.[29] Yet another special court was that appointed to try Benjamin Foxen in May at Santa Bárbara. He had killed Agustin Dávila near Santa Inés for stealing his chickens. Estévan Ardisson and Pedro C. Carrillo were the judges; the jury included six Americans and six Californians; and the verdict was manslaughter, for which Foxen was sentenced to four years' imprisonment.[30]

News of the treaty putting an end to the war brought some perplexing questions respecting the government of California. How they were settled is best explained in Mason's own words. In his proclamation of August 7, 1848, he said: "The congress of the United States, to whom alone this power belongs, will soon confer upon the people of this country the constitutional rights of citizens of the United States; and no doubt in a few short months we shall have a regularly organized territorial government; indeed, there is every reason to believe that congress has already passed the act, and that a civil government is now on its way to this country, to replace that which has been organized under the rights of conquest. Such territorial government will establish all local claims and regulations which, within the scope of its legitimate powers, it may deem necessary for the public welfare. In the mean time the present civil officers of the country will continue in the exercise of their functions as heretofore, and when vacancies exist or may occur, they will be filled by regular elections held by the people of the several towns and districts, due notice of such elections being previously given. The existing laws of the country will necessarily continue in force till others are made to supply their place." And his position was further explained in his report to the adjutant-general.[31] A similar

[29] *Unb. Doc.*, MS., 17, 37–9; *Cal. and N. Mex., 1850*, 39–41, 562, 570–1. C. C. Canfield and Sam. Myers were the others accused.

[30] *Cal. and N. Mex.*, etc., 505–7, 570; *Unb. Doc.*, MS., 63, 365–70.

[31] Aug. 7th, Mason to people of Cal. *Cal. and N. Mex., Mess. and Doc., 1850*, p. 590–1. Aug. 19th, Mason to adj.-gen. *Id.*, 597–8. In the latter doc-

view of the situation was taken by the national authorities. In his message of July 6th, the president wrote: "The war with Mexico having terminated, the power of the executive to establish or to continue temporary civil governments over these territories, which existed under the laws of nations whilst they were regarded as conquered provinces in our military occupation, has ceased. By their cession to the United States, Mexico has no longer any power over them; and until congress shall act, the inhabitants will be without any organized government. Should they be left in this condition, confusion and anarchy will be likely to prevail."[32] And later, when congress had

ument he says: 'The above are the only instructions I have received from the department to guide me in the course to be pursued, now that war has ceased, and that the country forms an integral part of the United States. For the past two years no civil government has existed here, save that controlled by the senior military or naval officer; and no civil officers exist in the country save the alcaldes appointed or confirmed by myself. To throw off upon them or the people at large the civil management and control of the country would most probably lead to endless confusions, if not to absolute anarchy; and yet what right or authority have I to exercise civil control in time of peace in a territory of the United States? or, if sedition and rebellion should arise, where is my force to meet it? Two companies of regulars, every day diminishing by desertions that cannot be prevented, will soon be the only military force in California; and they will be of necessity compelled to remain at San Francisco and Monterey, to guard the large depots of powder and munitions of war, which cannot be removed. Yet, unsustained by military force, or by any positive instructions, I feel compelled to exercise control over the alcaldes appointed, and to maintain order, if possible, in the country, until a civil governor arrive, armed with instructions and laws to guide his footsteps.

'In like manner, if all customs were withdrawn, and the ports thrown open free to the world, San Francisco would be made the depot of all the foreign goods in the north Pacific, to the injury of our revenue and the interests of our own merchants. To prevent this great influx of foreign goods into the country duty-free, I feel it my duty to attempt the collection of duties, according to the United States tariff of 1846. This will render it necessary for me to appoint temporary collectors, etc., in the several ports of entry, for the military force is too much reduced to attend to those duties.

'I am fully aware that in taking these steps I have no further authority than that the existing government must necessarily continue until some other is organized to take its place; for I have been left without any definite instructions in reference to the existing state of affairs. But the calamities and disorders which would surely follow the absolute withdrawal of even a show of authority impose on me, in my opinion, the imperative duty to pursue the course I have indicated, until the arrival of despatches from Washington (which I hope are already on their way) relative to the organization of a regular civil government. In the mean time, however, should the people refuse to obey the existing authorities, or the merchants refuse to pay any duties, my force is inadequate to compel obedience.'

[32] *Congress. Globe*, 1847–8, p. 901. Similar views in the message of July 24th. *Amer. Quart. Rev.*, i. 560–4.

adjourned without providing for the government of
the new provinces, the president, through Secretary
Buchanan, in a letter of flattery, congratulation,
promise, and advice, announced the existence of a *de
facto* government, to be continued in accordance with
the governor's views until another should be legally
substituted.[33]

And thus the country was governed as before dur-

[33] Oct. 7, 1848, Buchanan to Wm V. Voorhies, agent of the post-office department. *U. S. Govt Doc.*, 30th cong. 2d sess., H. Ex. Doc. 1, p. 47–50;
Cal. and N. Mex., etc., 6–9. The purport is also given in Sec. Marcy's letter
to Gov. Mason, dated Oct. 9th. *Id.*, 258–9. Buchanan writes: 'In the mean
time the condition of the people of California is anomalous, and will require,
on their part, the exercise of great prudence and discretion. By the conclusion of the treaty of peace, the military government which was established
over them under the laws of war, as recognized by the practice of all civilized
nations, has ceased to derive its authority from this source of power. But is
there, for this reason, no government in California? Are life, liberty, and property under the protection of no existing authorities? This would be a singu-
lar phenomenon in the face of the world, and especially among American citizens, distinguished as they are above all other people for their law-abiding
character. Fortunately, they are not reduced to this sad condition. The termination of the war left an existing government, a government *de facto*, in full
operation; and this will continue, with the presumed consent of the people,
until congress shall provide for them a territorial government. The great law
of necessity justifies this conclusion. The consent of the people is irresistibly
inferred from the fact that no civilized community could possibly desire to
abrogate an existing government, when the alternative presented would be to
place themselves in a state of anarchy, beyond the protection of all laws, and
reduce them to the unhappy necessity of submitting to the dominion of the
strongest.

'This government *de facto* will, of course, exercise no power inconsistent
with the provisions of the constitution of the United States, which is the
supreme law of the land. For this reason, no import duties can be levied in
California on articles the growth, product, or manufacture of the United States,
as no such duties can be imposed in any other part of our union on the productions of California. Nor can new duties be charged in California upon
such foreign productions as have already paid duties in any of our ports of entry, for the obvious reason that California is within the territory of the
United States. I shall not enlarge upon this subject, however, as the secretary of the treasury will perform that duty.

'The president urgently advises the people of California to live peaceably
and quietly under the existing government. He believes that this will promote their lasting and best interests. If it be not what they could desire and
had a right to expect, they can console themselves with the reflection that it
will endure but for a few months. Should they attempt to change or amend
it during this brief period, they most probably could not accomplish their
object before the government established by congress would go into operation. In the mean time the country would be agitated, the citizens would be
withdrawn from their usual employments, and domestic strife might divide
and exasperate the people against each other; and this all to establish a government which in no conceivable contingency could endure for a single year.
During this brief period it is better to bear the ills they have than fly to
others they know not of.'

ing the rest of 1848 and later; as well governed as it is likely to have been under any system that congress could have devised. It was probably well for California that no regular territorial government was put in operation. The people doubtless had the right from August to organize a provisional government for themselves. The president advised them not to do it, while Senator Benton took it upon himself to give contrary advice.[34]   Governor Mason, before receiving the letters of Buchanan and Marcy, favored such a movement in case congress should be known to have adjourned without action.[35]   And some local efforts in the same direction were made before the end of the year; but these matters belong properly to the annals of 1849–50—the constitutional convention, and the admission of California into the union as a state.

Here as well as anywhere may be added a few items respecting the foreign consulates in California in 1846–8.   Thomas O. Larkin's functions as U. S. consul ceased of course with the treaty.   He was notified to this effect by Secretary Buchanan in a letter of June 23, 1848, with approval of his past performance of duties.   Meanwhile he had been appointed U. S. naval agent by Stockton in August 1846, receiving in October 1847 the president's appointment of March.   There are no circumstances connected with his official career in these years that call for further notice than is given elsewhere.[36]   James A. Forbes retained the position of British vice-consul.[37] J. S. Moerenhaut was French consul from October 1846, and appointed Etienne Jourdain as vice-consul

    [34] Benton's letter was dated Aug. 27th.   See *S. F. Alta*, Jan. 11, 1849; *Burnett's Recol.*, MS., ii. 18–20.
    [35] Nov. 25th, Mason to Kemble, referring to a conversation on the subject. *Unb. Doc.*, MS., 140–1.
    [36] Aug. 13, 1846, appointment as naval agent. *Larkin's Doc.*, MS., iv. 254.   June 23, 1848, Buchanan to L. *Id.*, vi. 134.   See also *Mont. Consulate Arch.*, MS., ii., and *Mont. Navy Agent Accts*, MS., i. ii.
    [37] His claim to exemption from paying duties on goods imported by himself was not allowed by Mason in Dec. 1847. *Cal. and N. Mex.*, *Mess. and Doc.*, *1850*, p. 446–7.

at Yerba Buena in December 1848. Moerenhaut had occasion to present for settlement the grievances of Pierre Atillan, Clement Panaud, and of Richards and Maube, who had suffered in property at the hands of Frémont's men.[38] Cesareo Lataillade received his exequatur as Spanish vice-consul in April 1846, and took possession of his office in June. In 1847 he was allowed to reside at Santa Bárbara. His chief effort was to obtain redress for the imprisonment of José Noriega at Sutter's Fort by the Bear Flag men.[39] Late in 1848 George Trail Allen was appointed Hawaiian consul in California.[40]

[38] *Cal. and N. Mex.*, etc., 254, 320, 322, 379, 566; *Unb. Doc.*, MS., 99–103, 285–6. Mason could grant no relief; but in the case of R. and M. orders came from Washington to appoint an investigating board.

[39] *Doc. Hist. Cal.*, MS., ii. 30; iii. 167, 236; *Dept. St. Pap.*, MS., vi. 37, 40; *Larkin's Doc.*, MS., iv. 145; *Id.*, *Off. Corresp.*, i. 110; *Unb. Doc.*, MS., 16, 391–2; *Los Ang. Arch.*, MS., iii. 173–4; *Cal. and N. Mex.*, 297, 427, 430; *S. F. Calif.*, Aug. 7, 1847.

[40] *Unb. Doc.*, MS., 132; *Cal. and N. Mex.*, 687.

CHAPTER XXIII.

LOCAL ANNALS—SAN DIEGO TO MONTEREY.

1846–1848.

San Diego Events—Frémont, Stockton, and Kearny—Massacre at Pauma—Mormons and New York Volunteers—Municipal Affairs —Ranchos—Revenue—San Diego Mission—San Luis Rey—Padre Zalvidea—San Juan Capistrano—Los Angeles District—Index of Occurrences—Sub-prefect and Alcaldes—Mormons, Dragoons, and Volunteers—Ranchos—San Gabriel—Padre Esténega—San Fernando Mission — Santa Bárbara — Pueblo Government — Land Grants—Mission—Bishop García Diego—President Duran—San Buenaventura—Santa Inés—Purísima—Monterey District—Summary—Town Affairs—San Cárlos—San Luis Obispo—San Miguel —Murder of Reed Family—San Antonio—San Juan Bautista— Soledad—Santa Cruz and Branciforte.

CHAPTER XXIV.

Local annals of 1846–8, a period of transition from the old to the new, must be compressed within narrow limits; and this may be done without omission of essential matter or serious inconvenience, except at one or two points, where, however, matters pertaining to the effects of the gold discovery are reserved for another volume. The time of military and mission statistics was past, and I shall attempt no estimates of local gains or losses in population, the gain for the whole territory, but for the foreign immigration and the final influx of gold-seekers, being very small. There are lists of municipal officers which are worth being placed on record, with here and there a local occurrence to be added to the index of events recorded in other parts of this work, all to be presented mainly in fine-print notes.

Nothing happened at San Diego, though much interest was felt, and a few prominent citizens went to the capital to participate, in the political controversies of the time, until the Americans came under Frémont in July 1846, to be driven out in August, but to return in November under Stockton, who here made his final preparations for the reconquest of the south.[1] The coming of Kearny, his disaster at San

[1] San Diego events. 1846. Feb.–May, minor Ind. troubles, chiefly in the form of rumors. *Dept. St. Pap., Ben. P. & J.*, MS., ii. 124–9. Election for the consejo general in May; Bandini summoned to the capital. This vol., p. 45–51. Warner in corresp. with Larkin. *Id.*, 63. Occupation by Frémont for the U. S. at the end of July. *Id.*, 266–7. July 21st, padron showing 73 men fit for military duty. *Dept. St. Pap., Ben. P. & J.*, MS., ii. 159. Aug., Phelps' efforts at reconciliation; Bandini and Argüello favor the U. S.; probably no garrison left at first. *Id.*, 282, 286–7. Sept., Merritt and a few men sent to garrison S. D. from Los Angeles. *Id.*, 308. Reoccupation by the Californians. *Id.*, 316–18. Oct., reoccupation by Americans. *Id.*, 324–5. Stockton's arrival in Nov., and his preparations to march on Los Angeles. *Id.*, 326–9 et seq. Kearny's arrival in Dec. from N. Mex.; battle of S. Pascual; relations of Stockton and Kearny; they start for Los Angeles. *Id.*, 339–56, 385, 417, et seq. Dec., massacre by Ind. at Pauma. *Id.*, 567–8. The victims were Sergt Francisco Basualdo, José M. Alvarado, Manuel Serrano, Ramon Aguilar, Dominguez (known as Dominguito), an old man, Santiago Osuna, José Lopez, Santos Alipás, Eustaquio Ruiz, Juan de la Cruz, and a New Mexican not named. There is much mystery about this affair. There were theories that the Ind. were incited by the Americans; that they were incited by Flores indirectly—that is, instructed to attack all attempting to quit Cal. or join the Americans; that there was no massacre, the victims having been killed in the fight at S. Pascual; and that they were first captured by the S. Luis fugitives in connection with an effort to bring back the latter to the mission, and were treacherously killed by the Cahuilla allies. Estudillo, *Datos*, MS., 45–9, says the S. Pascual Ind. tried to save the victims but were too late. About the Ind. chiefs engaged on both sides there is great confusion of testimony. See *Machado, Tiempos Pasados*, MS., 37–42; *Julio César, Cosas de Ind.*, MS., 11–13; *Hayes' Em. N.*, 595–6; *Id., Memorab.*, 139–41; *Id., Scraps, Ind.*, i. 100, 141.

1847. Jan., campaign against the Ind. in consequence of the Pauma affair noted above. *Lugo, Vida*, MS., 51–63; *Hayes' Em. Notes*, 577–8; *Julio César, Cosas*, MS., 13–14. The evidence is still conflicting; but the S. Luiseños under the chiefs Manuelito Cota and Pablo Apis seem to have been the victims of an ambush and bloody fight near Ahuanga, the Cahuillas under Juan Antonio aiding the Californians under José del Cármen Lugo and Ramon Carrillo. More complaints of Ind. depredations in April. *S. D. Arch.*, MS., 319; *Hayes, Doc.*, MS., 200–2; *Unb. Doc.*, MS., 303. Jan.–Feb., return of Kearny and Stockton from Los Angeles; arrival of the Mormon battalion; Co. B, Capt. Hunter, as a garrison. This vol., pp. 428–30, 486–9. March, garrisoned for two weeks by Lieut Stoneman and the dragoons. *Id.*, 489. July, departure of the Mormons to be mustered out, and petitions of citizens on the need of a garrison. *Id.*, 490; *S. D. Arch.*, MS., 322; *Fitch, Doc.*, MS., 446. Return of the reënlisted Mormons, Capt. Davis, in Aug. *Id.*, 451; this vol., p. 495.

1848. Arrival of Co. I, N. Y. Volunteers, to take the place of the Mormons, who were mustered out in March; Capt. Shannon becomes commandant of the post. *Id.*, 514. Feb., complaints against Shannon's men for engaging

Pascual, and the massacre of a dozen Californians by the Indians in December were also more startling events than had occurred in this region for years. Leading citizens cheerfully embraced the cause of the United States from the first; and others who fled to serve under Flores for a few months soon returned after their defeat, and the course of events in 1847–8 was as tranquil as ever, the garrisons of Mormon and New York volunteers being received as welcome additions to the population, giving new life to the little town and to the social festivities that alone interrupted the chronic monotony of existence there. José Ramon Argüello succeeded his father as sub-prefect and held

in mercantile speculations, introducing military clothing free of duties. *Cal. and N. Mex., Mess. and Doc.*, 482–3. Jan.–April, more trouble with the Ind., several chiefs being imprisoned; Charbonneau implicated. *Bandini, Doc.*, MS., 108; *S. D. Arch.*, MS., 328, 331. July, return of Pio Pico. This vol., p. 588. Sept., Shannon's company mustered out. *Id.*, 515. Dec., Graham's battalion of U. S. dragoons arrives at Warner's rancho. *Id.*, 522–3.

Municipal affairs. 1846. José Ramon Argüello appointed sub-prefect Apr. 3d, sworn in Apr. 12th. He held the office till the Americans came. *Dept. St. Pap.*, MS., vii. 16; *Id., Ben. P. & J.*, ii. 11, 50, 85, 128. Jueces de paz, José Antonio Estudillo and Juan M. Osuna. The latter at first declined the office and possibly did not act. Aug. 18th, Miguel Pedrorena took Estudillo's place in the latter's absence. Sept. 15th, Joaquin Ortega and Henry D. Fitch elected. 1847. Jueces de paz, or alcaldes as they were usually termed, Henry D. Fitch and perhaps Philip Crosthwaite elected. *Hayes' Em. Notes*, 486–91; but Thomas Ridington soon took C.'s place, and was acting at times as 1st juez in June–July, also as sheriff. June 23d, Fitch declining to serve longer, Lieut Robert Clift of the Mormon co. was appointed by Col Stevenson, and confirmed by Gov. Mason Dec. 10th. Feb. 5th, Alcalde Fitch's bando of police regul. *S. D. Arch.*, MS., 319. Additional regul. May 15th. *Id.*, 320. April, alcalde has trouble with Warner, who refuses to obey his orders, and Thos Russell accused of an attempted murder; gets instruc. from Kearny. *Fitch, Doc.*, MS., 431; *Cal. and N. Mex.*, 301–3. June, Johnson fined $50, with 2 months' work, for stabbing with intent to kill. *S. D. Index*, MS., 96. July, court-house and school in course of construction. *S. D. Arch.*, MS., 319. 1848. The resignation of Robert Clift as juez or alcalde was accepted Feb. 19th; Juan Bandini and E. L. Brown were appointed as 1st and 2d alcaldes by Stevenson March 29th, and by Gov. Mason April 15th. Bandini resigned Sept. 27th on account of illness, and Juan María Marron was elected Oct. 3d, being approved by the gov. Dec. 2d.

Custom-house affairs. 1846. Henry D. Fitch as receptor resigned and was succeeded by Pedro C. Carrillo in April. *Dept. St. Pap., Ben. Cust.-H.*, MS., vi. 7–8; *Id., P. & J.*, ii. 127. Aug. 18th, Carrillo was reappointed by Com. Stockton, and took the oath on the 24th. *Carrillo, Doc.*, MS., 5. In March the assembly proposed the opening of the port to foreign trade. *Dept. St. Pap.*, MS., viii. 134. Sept., purchase of a boat for $60 and furniture and stationery $77 for acct of U. S. *Carrillo, Doc.*, MS., 14. 1847. Carrillo after Feb. was apparently succeeded by Santiago Argüello; and June 24th, Miguel Pedrorena was appointed. This vol., p. 446, 572; *Fitch, Doc.*, MS., 421;

the place till the Americans came. Municipal affairs were but very slightly interrupted under the new régime; and the successive justices of the peace, or alcaldes as they were generally termed, were José Antonio Estudillo, Miguel Pedrorena, Joaquin Ortega, Henry D. Fitch, Thomas Ridington, Robert Clift, Juan Bandini, and Juan M. Marron. The revenues of the port were managed successively by Fitch, Carrillo, Argüello, Pedrorena, Shannon, and Pedrorena again, acting as receptores, or collectors. About a dozen ranchos within the district were granted by Governor Pico to private owners in 1846; and during 1847–8 an effort was made to keep the matter of titles for these and earlier grants in statu quo for presentation to later tribunals. San Diego mission had no resident padre after the departure of Padre Oliva in August 1846. The remaining property was ceded in

Hayes, Doc., MS., 203. From Oct. under the new orders the mil. commandant was required to act as collector. This vol., p. 574. 1848. C. C. Canfield acting as collector in Feb.; Capt. Shannon in July. *Fitch, Doc.*, MS., 486, 522; but Aug. 7th, Pedrorena was reappointed, with a salary of $1,000, if the collections should amount to that sum over expenses. *Cal. & N. Mex.*, 654.

Private ranchos in S. Diego district 1846–8. *Camajal y El Palomar, 4 l., granted in 1846 to J. J. Warner, who was cl. Cañada, see S. Vicente. Guadalupe, mission, in B. Cal., 5 l., 1846, Juan Bandini. *Leg. Rec.*, MS., iv. 321. Island, 1846, Pedro C. Carrillo; Billings cl. Mission, 1846, Sant. Argüello, who was cl. Monserrate, 3 l., 1846, Isidro M. Alvarado, who was cl. Otay, 2 l., 1846, Magdalena Estudillo, who was cl. Pala, see S. Luis Rey. Palomar, see Camajal. Potrero, see S. Jacinto. S. Felipe, see Valle. S. Jacinto Nuevo y Potrero, 1846, Miguel Pedrorena, whose heirs were cl. S. Jacinto Viejo y Nuevo, sobrante, 5 l., 1846, María del Rosario Estudillo de Aguirre, whose husband was cl. *S. Luis Rey & Pala, 12 l., 1846, Scott & Pico; Wm C. Jones cl. Sta Rosa, 3 l., 1846, Juan Moreno, who was cl. S. Vicente, cañada, 3 l., 1846, Juan Lopez; Domingo Yorba cl. Sobrante, see S. Jacinto. Valle de S. Felipe, 3 l., 1846, Felipe Castillo; John Forster cl. *Valle de las Viejas, 4 l., 1846, Ramon Osuna et al.; Wm Williams cl.

S. Diego Mission. 1846. Jan. 6th, inventory made by Pico and Manso, signed also by P. Oliva. Engl. translation in *U. S.* v. *Argüello, cl. brief on Excep. before Surveyor-gen.*, 120–2; *Hayes' Legal Hist. S. D.*, 45. Total value, $1,654, of which $1,000 is for main building; live-stock 110 cattle, 65 horses, 4 mules; credits $19,588, of which $18,816 is due for supplies to troops; debt $1,474, of which $500 due to Miguel Pedrorena has been paid with the Sta Mónica rancho. June 8th, Gov. Pico's deed of sale to Santiago Argüello, who gets all the lands and other property excepting the church and padre's dwelling, but is bound to support the padre and worship, and to pay the mission debts. The consideration is money due to A. from the govt. for past services. *Hartman's Brief in Miss. Cases*, app. 80–3. July 24th, gov. orders P. Oliva to surrender the estate by inventory to Argüello. *Unb. Doc.*, MS., 390. A ground plan of the mission buildings, no date. *St. Pap., Miss.*, MS., vii. 3. P. Oliva left the mission when the Americans came. *S. Diego, Lib.*

June to Santiago Argüello in payment for past services. Though Argüello's title was confirmed in later years, the American authorities did not permit him to hold the property in 1847–8, putting it in charge of E. L. Brown, and later of Philip Crosthwaite, who was given a lease for two or three years. Naturally the buildings gradually went to ruin, but there were a few aged Indians left whose claim to support was recognized in theory at least. At San Luis Rey, Father Zalvidea, the senior of the little remaining band of Fernandinos, died early in 1846, and the mis-

Mis., MS., 57. 1847. Oliva at S. Juan in Oct. complains that the commandant had removed the roofs of mission buildings at S. Diego. *Unb. Doc.*, MS., 97, 389. Oct. 17th, Captain Davis to Stevenson, P. Oliva on his departure left a man in charge. J. A. Estudillo shows a power of attorney from Oliva; and Sant. Argüello has a bill of sale from the gov., probably antedated. *Id.*, 97–8. Sergt E. L. Brown seems to have been put in charge of the mission, no exact date. *Hayes' Em. Notes*, 150. 1848. April 26th, P. Prefect Jimeno permits the alcalde to take material from the ruined buildings —not pertaining to the church edifice!—to build a new church in town. In May there were some efforts to obtain a padre from Lower Cal., and P. Mancilla agreed to come. *S. D. Index*, MS., 141; *Hayes' Miss. B.*, i. 407. Aug. 6th, Crosthwaite receives the property from Brown. There were 53 cattle, 43 horses, 13 asses, 33 sheep, and 44 goats. In June there had been only 107 animals instead of 186. *Unb. Doc.*, MS., 173. Aug. 9th, Stevenson to gov., if left in present state the property will soon disappear. It should be sold. Some old Ind. still remain, and they might receive rations from the post. *Id.*, 159. At this time or in Oct. Crosthwaite leased the mission for 3 years (or 2 years). He went to the mines, leaving his father-in-law, Bonifacio Lopez, in charge, and when he came back in 1849 found the U. S. troops quartered here. *Crosthwaite*, in *Hayes' Em. Notes*, 154. Aug. 18th, Gov. Mason having received from Stevenson an inventory ordered the property put at the disposition of Padre Gonzalez of Sta Bárbara—perhaps only the church property. *Cal. & N. Mex.*, 596. Sept. 8th, P. Gonzalez to Stevenson, has received the governor's orders; but the property is already rented for 2 years. He has sent the inventory to the padre prefecto Jimeno. *Unb. Doc.*, MS., 214–15.

San Luis Rey. 1846. May 18th, deed of sale to José A. Cot and José A. Pico for $2,437. *Hartman's Brief*, app. 83–5; *Unb. Doc.*, MS., 277–9. July 24th, gov. orders the admin., Marron, to deliver the property to Cot and Pico. *St. Pap., Miss.*, MS., xi. 53. John Forster, *Pioneer Data*, MS., 22–3, 30, says that he took possession for the purchasers, and then left Marron in charge for C. and P. See also *Marron, Pap.*, MS., 9. In Aug., Frémont put John Bidwell in charge, removing Marron and having some trouble with Forster. *Bidwell's Cal.*, MS., 181; *Forster's Pion. Data*, MS., 30–1; *Lorenzana, Mem.*, MS., 17–18. The latter thinks Godey was put in charge. She also says, p. 22, 27, that on Aug. 25th P. Oliva came up from S. Diego and stayed two months before going to S. Juan. P. Zalvidea had died earlier in the year. Aug. 22d, Cot complains to Stockton of forcible dispossession at the hands of Frémont, and asks for reinstatement, though willing to leave the question of title to the courts. Stockton left the matter to Gillespie and nothing was done, as appears in a later complaint of Cot in Oct. of the next year. *Unb. Doc.*, MS., 277–9. Bidwell had to retire in Oct. at the time of the Flores revolt. This vol., p. 267, 286, 318; and José Alipás seems to have

sion had no later resident minister, except perhaps
Padre Oliva for a short time in the same year. The
San Luis estate was sold in May to Cot and Pico for
$2,437; but their agent was dispossessed by Frémont,
and they failed to regain possession. Some doubts
were expressed then and later about the genuineness
of the sale; but the title was finally rejected on the
ground that the governor had no power to sell the
missions. Juan M. Marron was in charge until Au-

commanded a small military force here until Stockton took the place the
next Jan. *Estudillo, Datos*, MS., 47. The S. Luis neophytes were concerned
in the Pauma massacre of Dec., as related in another paragraph of this note.
1847. Jan.–April, Stockton's arrival, and Mormon garrisons. This vol., p.
386–7, 428, 441, 488–9. June–Aug., complaints of Ind. depredations. They
broke into the church, stole the crucifix, and threatened another raid. *S. D.
Arch.*, MS., 320; *S. F. Californian*, Sept. 15, 1847. Aug. 1st, Capt. J. D.
Hunter of the Mormon battalion appointed sub-Indian agent with headquarters at S. Luis. This vol., p. 568. Mormon garrison under Lieut Barrus. *Id.*,
495. Aug. 2d, Gov. Mason to Hunter, he is put in charge of the mission
property only to protect it; if any priests come they are to be treated with
kindness and given rooms and supplies and anything they want, even the
entire management of the Ind. *Cal. & N. Mex.*, 348. Sept. 1st, Stevenson
to gov., the Ind. are pleased at Hunter's appointment; but complain that live-
stock has been removed, which should be recovered. S. says the Ind. have
raised grain enough for their wants, and their settlement shows more evidence of comfort than most of the ranchos of rich Californians. *Unb. Doc.*,
MS., 92–3. Nov. 24th, gov. to J. A. Pico, request to turn over any mission
property in his possession to Hunter, and to furnish an inventory of all such
property that may have been at any time in his possession. *Pico, Doc.*, MS.,
ii. 131. Nov. 24th, gov. sends a blank appointment for alcalde, to be filled
out by Stevenson with name of John Shannon (Charbonneau?) or any other.
Cal. & N. Mex., 434. Dec. 1st, gov. to Hunter on conciliatory measures
with J. J. Warner and the Ind. whose land W. claims, so as to keep the Ind.
quiet, and leave question of title for the courts. *Id.*, 438. 1848. Jean B.
Charbonneau alcalde until Aug., when his resignation, offered because as a
half-breed he was thought to favor the Ind. too much, was accepted by the
gov. *S. D. Arch.*, MS., 333; *Unb. Doc.*, MS., 364–5; *Cal. & N. Mex.*, 587–8.
Jan. 31st, Hunter reports that he has raised a small wheat crop on the mission farm at Pala, and has induced the Ind. to do the same. *Unb. Doc.*, MS.,
62–3. In Sept., Hunter intended to resign, *Id.*, 174; and Dec. 17th, he was
granted a leave of absence for 6 months, Wm Williams to take charge of the
mission in his place. *Cal. & N. Mex.*, 681.

José María de Zalvidea was born at Bilbao, Vizcaya, Spain, on March 2,
1780, taking the Franciscan habit Dec. 13, 1798, and coming to the Mex. college of S. Fernando in Sept. 1804. He arrived in Cal. in Aug. 1805, and his
missionary service was at S. Fernando in 1805–6, at S. Gabriel in 1806–26, at
S. Juan Capistrano in 1826–42, and at S. Luis Rey in 1842–6. From the first
he was rated by his superiors as one of the best and most zealous of the friars,
as priest, teacher, and manager of temporalities. *Autobiog. Autog. de los
Padres*, MS.; *Sarría, Inf. de 1817*, MS., 45–6; *Payeras, Inf. de 1820*, MS.,
125. Zalvidea's great field of labor was at San Gabriel, where he toiled in-
cessantly for 20 years, and with the greatest success, to build up the temporal
interests of his mission, but never neglecting spiritual affairs or sacrificing the
love of his neophytes or the esteem of all who came in contact with him. He

gust 1846, and John Bidwell from that time till October. A garrison of the Mormon battalion held the place during the greater part of 1847; and from August Captain Hunter as sub-Indian agent for the south took charge of the mission, being succeeded temporarily by William Williams at the end of 1848. Hunter found a considerable number of Indians, who under his protection tilled the soil with much industry

was doubtless in those days a model missionary, and then and later was regarded by the common people as a saint. He gave much attention to viticulture at S. Gabriel, being the first to introduce this industry on a large scale, and taking the greatest pride in his immense vineyard. In my list of authorities a diary of exploration in 1806, and a petition of 1827 in behalf of the Indians, bear his name. In political controversies he took no part; in 1829 he was willing to swear allegiance to the republic so far as was consistent with his profession; and in 1838 he declined a passport to retire, on the ground that there was none to take his place. His transfer in 1826, against his wishes, was doubtless mainly because his services were needed at S. Juan in the place of Padre Boscana; but also because some of his idiosyncrasies—notably that connected with his vineyard, which he proposed to protect by an iron fence—had assumed the form of insubordination to his superiors, or perhaps suggested that a change might be mentally beneficial. All this has, however, been much exaggerated in current accounts of later years, as has also Zalvidea's brooding over the change and its effect on his mind. Somewhat eccentric at first, he became more so in his old age, and finally during his stay of four years at San Luis he became probably in some respects insane. Among those who write from personal acquaintance with the padre are Estudillo, *Datos*, MS., 35–40; Marron, *Recuerdos*, MS., 3–9; Alvarado, *Hist. Cal.*, MS., iii. 113–14; Coronel, *Cosas de Cal.*, MS., 217–19; Janssens, *Vida*, MS., 167; Davis, *Glimpses*, MS., 134–6, Julio César, *Cosas de Ind.*, MS., 6–7; White, *Cal.*, MS., 64–5; Serrano, *Apuntes*, MS., 183–6; Perez, *Recuerdos*, MS., 5–6; and Lorenzana, *Mem.*, MS., 14–16. There was also in 1874 a newspaper discussion between Ex-gov. Downey and Gen. Vallejo about the padre's character and his acts at S. Gabriel. Nearly all agree as to his many eccentricities in the last years, most of them, as is understood, having been noticed in less degree from the first. When addressed he invariably replied, 'Vamos, sí señor,' and turned his eyes partly away. His method of eating was to mix all that was put before him, solid and liquid, sweet and sour, in one dish, and then devour the mass; or if this was prevented, he would take the dishes in succession, butter, wine, meat, etc., without regard to the order, always swallowing the entire contents of one dish before beginning another, and never leaving anything on the table. On rising he cleaned his horn spoon and fork, while a servant cleaned his earthen basin, and carried all three to his room, putting his napkin in his girdle. Most of his time he spent in reading devotional books, walking meanwhile about the mission, and occasionally stopping to make strange gestures and exclaim, 'Va-te Satanás,' as if engaged in a conflict with the evil one, or driving away evil thoughts. While thus engaged he paid no heed to warnings of danger, and on several occasions wild cattle charged upon him without harming him or evoking anything but a slight reproof for throwing dirt upon his book. He made frequent use of the scourge, and wore belts with iron points penetrating the flesh. In his last months he would have no watchers at night, and was always found covered with blood from self-inflicted wounds in the morning. Yet even in the midst of all this madness in devotional matters, he showed himself to have a clear head and the most practical and liberal ideas on all

and success.   Jean B. Charbonneau acted as alcalde for a time.   Padre Vicente Pascual Oliva came to San Juan Capistrano in the autumn of 1846, and died there in January 1848.   There seems to have been no other resident minister during the period; and nothing is known of progress at the pueblo, which, however, had a population of 113 souls, according to a padron of 1846.   John Forster, who had purchased the mission

other subjects.   He was a tall man, of fine presence and fair complexion; always courteous in his manners, with a smile and kind word for all, and never annoyed by the presence of others even in his maddest moments.   He was skilled in the native tongue, in which he used to preach on Sunday at S. Gabriel, according to Hugo Reid.   There is no evidence that he ever had an enemy or said an unkind word of any man.   He refused to quit S. Luis, where he believed his services to be needed; but finally it was thought best to remove him to S. Juan.   A cart was prepared with all possible conveniences, by advice of Padre Oliva and Apolinaria Lorenzana, who had nursed him for some days.   The night before the journey was to be made Zalvidea died. He was buried in the mission church, at the left of the altar.   The date is not known, but it was apparently early in 1846.

San Juan Capistrano.   1846.   John Forster juez de paz, Juan Ávila suplente. *Dept. St. Pap.*, MS., vii. 86; viii. 141–5; *Id., Ang.*, xi. 170; *Id., Ben. P. & J.*, iv. 63.   March, padron of S. Juan showing a pop. de razon of 113. *Dept. St. Pap.*, MS., viii. 141–5.   P. Oliva came here to live in the autumn. *S. Diego, Lib. Mis.*, MS., 57; *Lorenzana, Mem.*, MS., 22, 27.   Gov. Pico concealed for a time in this vicinity after his flight from Angeles in Aug.   This vol., p. 278.   1847.   Forster reappointed alcalde by Gov. Mason July 14th. *Cal. & N. Mex.*, 374.   Resigns Dec. 3d because the Ind. agent, Hunter, interferes and the troops decline to aid him.   *Unb. Doc.*, MS., 129–30.   1848. Blas Aguilar alcalde.   In Aug. he objects to being deemed subordinate to the alcalde of Los Angeles. *Los Ang. Arch.*, MS., iii. 221–2.   The S. Juan mission registers show that P. Tomás Esténega officiated occasionally in 1843 –6; P. Ign. Ramirez de Arrellano in 1844; and P. Blas Ordaz in 1847–8.

Vicente Pascual was born July 3, 1780, at Martin del Rio, Aragon, and became a Franciscan at the convent of Nra Sra de Jesus in Zaragoza, Feb. 1, 1799.   He came to Mexico in 1810 and started for Cal. in 1811, but was delayed by the revolution and by a serious illness at Acapulco, and did not arrive until Aug. 1813.   He served at S. Cárlos, as supernumerary, in 1813–14, at S. Fernando in 1814–15, at S. Francisco in 1815–19, at S. Miguel in 1819–20, at S. Diego in 1820–46, and at S. Juan Capistrano in 1846–8.   Ordinary merit, good application, and a certain ability as preacher were the qualities accredited to him by his superiors. *Autobiog., Autog. de los Padres*, MS.; *Sarría, Inf. de 1817*, MS., 71–2; *Payeras, Inf. de 1820*, MS., 123.   Not much is known of this padre, who seems to have been a very commonplace man, with few notable merits or defects.   Duhaut-Cilly, *Viaggio*, ii. 19–21, mentions the poor quality of food and the uncleanly service at the padre's table, and his expressions of surprise that no one seemed to care to eat with him. Oliva's moral character was not in all respects above suspicion, though there is no definite evidence against him.   He declined to take the oath of republican allegiance in 1826 and later.   When the Americans came he left S. Diego, where he had lived for 26 years, and after a short stay at S. Luis, came to S. Juan probably in Oct.   He died here Jan. 2, 1848, without receiving the sacraments, as the rains prevented Padre Ordaz from arriving in time; but Ordaz buried him on the 29th in the presbytery of the mission church. *S. Juan Cap., Lib. Mis.*, MS., 11–12.

property in 1845, and to whom it was confirmed in later times, was not disturbed in his possession. He served as alcalde in 1846–7, and Blas Aguilar was his successor.

Los Angeles had an unusually interesting history in 1846–7 as the capital, and as the centre of the Californians' last or only resistance to foreign invasion; but this was also the history of California in those years, and has been narrated with all desirable detail in the earlier chapters of this volume. Therefore here, even more than elsewhere, does an index suffice.[2] Leading events of 1846 were Pico's controversy with Castro and the north, involving fears of local invasion; Stockton's occupation of the city in August; and Flores' revolt, including the fights at Chino and San Pedro. At the beginning of 1847 came the reoccupation by United States forces, the final submission of the Californians, and the controversies of Stockton, Frémont, and Kearny, ending in the triumph of the

[2] Los Angeles events. 1846. Jan.–July, political affairs in the controversy of Pico vs Castro, sessions of the assembly, etc. This vol., p. 30–53. Lists of inhab. in the region, including one of 427 men capable of bearing arms in July. *Dept. St. Pap.*, MS., vii. 64–5; *Id.*, *Ben. P. & J.*, ii. 159–60. April 18th, Pio Pico sworn in as constitutional gov. by Mex. appointment. This vol., p. 40. March–Aug., Indian affairs, showing frequent alarms at rumors of invasion from the Colorado River bands, with several expeditions from the S. Bernardino region. On one occasion 18 Ind. were killed at S. Francisco rancho, having revolted after being captured. It was at one time resolved to station a guard at the Cajon. Six Yuta families came to Jurupa to settle. *Bandini, Doc.*, 67; *Dept. St. Pap.*, vi. 11, 80, 86–7, 92–3; viii. 104–10; *Id.*, *Ang.*, viii. 64, 71; *Id.*, *Ben.*, iv. 36–9; *Id.*, *P. & J.*, ii. 48; iv. 62; *Leg. Rec.*, iv. 346–8. June, news of the Bear Flag, cool response of the Angelinos to Pico's calls. This vol., p. 140. Action of the assembly on the McNamara scheme. *Id.*, 218–19. July, action of the gov., assemb., and general on news of Sloat's invasion. *Id.*, 263–6. Aug., the American forces at S. Pedro 6th, negotiations, flight of Pico and Castro 10th, Stockton takes the city 13th, Gillespie left in command 31st. *Id.*, 266–87. Sept.–Oct., Gillespie's acts and policy, Varela tumult 23d, Flores' revolt, fight at Chino rancho 26–7th, Gillespie driven out, Mervine's defeat at S. Pedro Oct. 8th, sessions of the assembly, Stockton at S. Pedro 23d. *Id.*, 305–25. Nov.–Dec., Flores' operations, Rico's sub-revolt, Dec. 3d. *Id.*, 329–34, 355. Larkin at Angeles as a prisoner. *Id.*, 365. Return of Manuel Castro's army from the northern campaign. *Id.*, 372.

1847. Jan., defence by Flores and capture by Kearny and Stockton, battle of the S. Gabriel 8th, battle of la Mesa 9th, city occupied by U. S. forces 10th, arrival of Frémont and his battalion 14th, flight of Flores and Castro 11th, treaty of Cahuenga 13th. *Id.*, 385–407. Jan.–Feb., controversy between

latter and the removal of the capital from Los Angeles to Monterey in March. Subsequent annals of 1847–8—a period of semi-military rule under Colonel Stevenson as commandant of the south with garrisons from the Mormon battalion, New York volunteers, and U. S. dragoons—offer but little of general importance, though including items of local interest as appended in my note. Abel Stearns served as sub-prefect for a time before the Ameri-

Stockton, Kearny, and Frémont, departure of K. and S., Frémont as gov. *Id.*, 422–35. March–May, Frémont's controversy with Kearny, Capt. Turner arrives 11th, Frémont's ride 22d, Col Cooke in command 24th, F.'s return 29th, Col Mason's arrival April 7th, Frémont vs Mason 14th, arrival of Kearny May 9th, F.'s departure 12th, Stevenson succeeds Cooke. *Id.*, 440–50. March–May, slight details of troubles with Ind., by whom on one occasion the dragoons were repulsed with three men wounded. *Los Ang. Arch.*, MS., iii. 48–50, 54–5; v. 434–5, 445–6; *Savage, Doc.*, MS., ii. 76; *Unb. Doc.*, MS., 87–8, 115–16, 330; *Lugo, Vida*, MS., 67–8; *Moreno, Vida*, MS., 33–5. March–July, the Mormons at Angeles. This vol., p. 489 et seq. May, etc., Co. E and G, N. Y. volunteers, at Angeles as a garrison. *Id.*, 514–15. May, efforts to obtain the services of a parish priest in place of the sickly presbyter Jimenez del Recio. The president would not permit P. Ordaz to serve. *Los Ang. Arch.*, MS., iii. 59–62. June, artillery sent from Monterey for the Angeles fortifications. *Cal. & N. Mex.*, 328. July, etc., rumors of troubles with the Californians. This vol., p. 583 et seq. Dec. 7th, explosion. *Id.*, 515, 585. The killed were Sergt Travers and Private Legare of the N. Y. vol., and Private Stokely of the dragoons; 10 others were wounded. *Griffin's Pap.*, MS., 124–7. At an election for ayunt. in Dec. there were 96 voters, 22 of whom could write. *Los Ang. Ayunt. Rec.*, MS., 80.

1848. Jan. 4th, a slight temblor, according to a newspaper. Feb. 6th, a force to be posted at the Cajon to keep Ind. raiders in check. *Unb. Doc.*, MS., 43–4. April 15th, a N. Mex. caravan under F. E. Vigil and Juan I. Morsine to start on return. *Dept. St. Pap., Ang.*, MS., viii. 77. April, trial of Barrus and other Mormons for passing counterfeit money. This vol., p. 610–11. July, return of Gov. Pico. *Id.*, 588. Aug. 8th, orders to Stevenson on breaking up the military post, and removing the guns and war-stores. *Cal. & N. Mex. 1850*, p. 635–6. Aug. 20th, Stevenson to gov., an earnest appeal against leaving the people exposed to Ind. raids without troops or arms. *Id.*, 645–6. List of over 100 land-owners with their water rates. *Hayes, Doc.*, MS., 209. There were 259 voters for the ayunt. *Los Ang. Arch.*, MS., v. 469.

Municipal goverment and list of officials. 1846. Abel Stearns sub-prefect in June–July, appointed June 17th, sworn in 20th, Narciso Botello secretary. It will be remembered that Stearns was also sub-confidential agent of the U. S.! Members of the ayuntamiento: alcaldes Juan Gallardo and José L. Sepúlveda; regidores Leonardo Cota, Luis Jordan, Miguel Pryor, and Julian Chavez; síndico Alexander Bell, secretary Ignacio Coronel. Cota, Jordan, and Chavez acted as jueces at different times. Chavez is also named as juez de aguas, and Casildo Aguilar as celador. In Feb. the ranchos of S. Bernardino, Yucaipa, Napolitan, Jurupa, Huapa, and Cucamonga were formed into a separate district, with B. D. Wilson as juez de paz and José del Cármen Lugo as suplente. Aug. 20th, Louis Robidoux succeeded Wilson by Stockton's appointment. Francisco García was juez of S. Feliciano, with José Salazar as suplente. Ignacio Coronel was receptor at S. Pedro in

can occupation; and municipal affairs, except as interrupted by the military rule of Gillespie in August and September 1846, and of Frémont in January 1847, were managed by an ayuntamiento with Juan Gallardo and José Salazar as successive alcaldes; but for 1848, though an ayuntamiento was elected, it was

July. Jan. 21st, gov. orders payment of $4,656, the balance of the $5,000 paid for A. M. Lugo's house bought for use of the govt. *Unb. Doc.*, MS., 388. Other accounts say that he bought the house of Isaac Williams, paid $600 on account, and in June mortgaged the building to Célis for $2,000. *Hayes' Crim. Trials*, 1 et seq.; *Botello, Anales*, MS., 127. June, the ayunt. has its feelings wounded by an order to submit all its acts to the govt for approval. *Los Ang. Arch.*, MS., v. 348–51; *Dept. St. Pap., Ben. P. & J.*, MS., ii. 81.° July, sub-prefect tells alcalde that he has no right to leave town without his (Stearns') permission. *Dept. St. Pap.*, MS., vii. 94.

1847. The city was under military rule in Jan., as it had been since the preceding July, but on Feb. 10th the following ayunt. was elected: Alcaldes José Salazar and Enrique Ávila; regidores Miguel N. Pryor, Julian Chavez, Rafael Gallardo, and José Ant. Yorba; síndico José Vicente Guerrero; sec. Ignacio Coronel. Primary election on the 7th. There were frequent absences and consequent temporary promotions. Juez de policía Pedro Cabrera from Oct.; juez auxiliar at Sta Ana Teodosio Yorba; zanjeros Basilio Lusiano and Mariano R. Roldau. Alcalde at S. Bernardino Louis Robidoux, reappointed by Gov. Mason June 1st. Receptor at S. Pedro, Pedro Carrillo, succeeded by D. W. Alexander. Municipal receipts for the year $1,219. *Los Ang. Arch.*, MS., v. 432. In June a regidor was fined $10 for impoliteness. In Aug. Alcalde Ávila tendered his resignation on account of disagreements with the mil. com. *Id.*, 415–18. Dec. 18th, an election of alcaldes for the next year was held, no other members of ayunt. named. On the 19th Col Stevenson complained to Gov. Mason that the alcaldes-elect were of the worst class, one of them noted for his hatred of Americans, and the other an ignorant and vicious fellow; many citizens ask that Foster be appointed juez de 1ª instancia to supervise the alcalde's acts. *Unb. Doc.*, MS., 128–9. Meanwhile the gov. on Dec. 10th (perhaps antedated) had appointed Foster, and ordered the alcalde to surrender the records on Jan. 1st; and on the 29th he directs Stevenson to declare the election void, as having been held without the governor's authority. *Cal. & N. Mex. 1850*, p. 443, 451.

1848. Alcaldes elected as above but not acting, Ignacio Palomares and José Sepúlveda; alcalde and juez de 1ª instancia from Jan. 1st by governor's appointment as above, Stephen C. Foster; 2d alcalde from May Vicente Guerrero; Abel Stearns síndico from Jan.; jueces de campo from Feb. 12th Antonio Ign. Ávila, Agustin Machado, Tomás Serrano, Juan Ramirez, Antonio Salazar, Francisco Lopez; Henry Cardwell alguacil mayor, or sheriff, appointed May 30th; auxiliary alcalde for S. Antonio, S. Rafael, etc., Hilario Morillo; collector at S. Pedro Dav. W. Alexander. On Jan. 1st Stevenson met the old and new ayunt., introducing Foster as the appointed alcalde. Salazar preferred, and seems to have been permitted, to deliver the office to Palomares, his elected successor, leaving P. to surrender to Foster. P. and his associates wished to retain their offices, and that Foster should be juez de 1ª inst., or prefect, to supervise their acts; they were permitted to petition to that effect, but did not do so in the time allowed, and Foster was installed. Stevenson then appointed Stearns síndico and Aguilar collector, those elected declining to serve. At first citizens refused to do the regular guard duty, but yielded gradually to a system of fines. Letter of Stevenson Jan. 11th. *Unb. Doc.*, MS., 159–67. Jan. 13th, Stevenson's procl., annulling the election. *Los Ang. Arch.*, MS., iii. 155·6. Feb. 8th, S. has appointed subordi-

not permitted to be installed, and Stephen C. Foster
served as alcalde by the military governor's appointment, not without considerable dissatisfaction on the
part of the citizens at not being allowed to choose
their own officers as had been promised them; yet
Foster seems to have ruled for the most part wisely,

nate officials; Foster is gaining respect; all is going smoothly. *Id.*, 156–7. May
16th, Foster to gov., explaining his difficulties owing to the unfriendly feeling
of the people, and suggesting the town's financial and other needs. *Id.*, 72–3.
Aug. 20th, Foster offers his resignation, which on Stevenson's advice is not
accepted, and F. is promised all possible aid and is urged to retain the place.
On Sept. 6th, F. withdrew his resignation and thanked the gov. for his confidence. F. was at the same time govt interpreter and translator for the
southern mil. district. *Id.*, 28–9, 33; *Cal. & N. Mex. 1850*, p. 639–60.

Additional municipal matters. Items of police regulations on prisoners,
vagrants, use of liquors, lighting shops, carrying arms, etc., are omitted. In
the administration of justice there are no cases that require notice. In April
1846 the citizens petitioned for the removal of the Ind. rancheria; and in June
the gov. sold its site to Juan Domingo for $200 to raise funds for a mil. expe-
dition. *Los Ang. Arch.*, MS., iii. 28–30; v. 336, 338, 399; *Id.*, *Ayunt. Rec.*,
16; *Dept. St. Pap.*, *Ben. P. & J.*, MS., iv. 54. The Ind., however, were still
at this rancheria in 1847, or had formed another. In Nov. its removal was
ordered, it being a resort of vice; and again in Feb. 1848 a similar order was
issued. *Los Ang. Arch.*, MS., iii. 133–5, 165; v. 429–30. May 29, 1846, the
ayunt. chooses two experts in company with the 2d alcalde to survey the
town ejidos, measuring 2 leagues from the church to each point of the com-
pass (which would give 16 sq. leagues !) and erect boundary monuments. *Id.*,
v. 344. April 1847, lot 10 x 30 v. sold for $20. *Id.*, 487. July, owing to
abuses and scarcity of salt, the authorities take charge of the only salina. *Id.*,
409. Murder of a Frenchman, not named, July 4th–5th. *Id.*, iii. 87–90. A
man asks to be relieved from payment of fee on his lot, because he has built
a house on it; but is obliged to pay on the unoccupied part. *Id.*, v. 412.
July 22d, a committee on streets reports that the cemetery street is too narrow
and that the síndico's instructions on the subject are illegal; wants more
light; and the ayunt. decides in substance that the matter must be regulated
as well as possible under the circumstances without being too particular about
trifles. *Id.*, *Ayunt. Rec.*, MS., 98–100. Aug., complaints that land-owners
object to paying the water rates. *Id.*, *Arch.*, iii. 103–4. Oct., Valle asked
for a lot 200 v. front by 75 v. deep, having contracted to supply the town
with meat and needing plenty of room; but only 100 v. front were granted.
Id., *Ayunt. Rec.*, 92–3. Dec., Sant. Argüello got a title to lot 44 x 96 v.,
saying that he had bought the land when the formalities were different,
and like many others had no proper title. *Id.*, 96. Aug. 1, 1848, Alcalde
Foster's decree on regulations for use of the water for irrigation. *Coronel,
Doc.*, MS., 249–51.

Private ranchos in Los Angeles district. Los Álamos y Agua Caliente,
6 l., granted in 1846 to Francisco Lopez et al.; Agustin Olvera cl. Ánimas,
see Rio. Boca de la Playa, 1½ l., 1846, Emigdio Véjar, who was cl. *Cahuenga, 4 l., 1846, Luis Arenas; Nic. Morchon cl. *Cajon de los Negros, 3 l.,
1846, Ignacio Coronel; Wm Workman cl. *Cienega, 20 l., 1846, Agustin
Olvera, who was cl. Tomás de Santiago, 4 l., 1846, Teodosio Yorba, who
was cl. Palos Colorados, 1846, José L. Sepúlveda, who was cl. Negros, see
Cajon. Playa, see Boca. *Rio de las Ánimas, 6 l., 1846, Leonardo Cota and
Julian Chavez; J. F. Jones et al. cl. San Fernando mission lands, 14 l.,
1846. Eulogio de Célis, who was cl. *San Gabriel mission, 1846, Workman
and Reid, who were cl. Mission lot 500 x 200 v., 1846, Simeon, who was

and there was but slight ground for complaint of
Stevenson's policy and acts. But for the constant
depredations of Indian horse-thieves, which the new
like the old authorities were unable to prevent, quiet
and good order prevailed for the most part throughout the district. About twenty new ranchos were
granted to private ownership by Governor Pico in
1846; and all matters of title and possession were as
a rule left in statu quo after the change of flag. At
San Gabriel Padre Esténega died early in 1847, and

cl. *Id., 25 x 40 v., 1846, Andrés Duarte et al., who were cl. Id., 400 x
200 v., 1846, José Ledesma, who was cl. Sta Anita, sold by H. Reid to Henry
Dalton for $2,000 in May 1847. (It sold for $200,000 in 1874.) Los Ang.
Arch., MS., v. 488. Sta Catalina Island, 1846, Thomas M. Robbins; J. M.
Covarrubias cl. Santiago, see Tomás. Sierra, 4 l., 1846, Bernardo Yorba,
who was cl. Id., 4 l., 1846, Vicente Sepúlveda, who was cl. *Sierra de los
Verdugos, 1846, Antonio F. Coronel, who was cl.

San Gabriel. 1846. Jan.–May, Mariano R. Roldan and Henry Dalton
are named as encargados, or perhaps majordomos. Pedro Romero juez de
campo. Los Ang., Ayunt. Rec., MS., 46; Dept. St. Pap., Ang., MS., viii. 63–4,
71; Id., Ben. P. & J., iv. 65; St. Pap., Miss., MS., xi. 60–1. Feb. 20th,
the vecinos, 40 whites and 100 Ind., ask that the ex-mission be declared a
pueblo, complaining of mismanagement on the part of the padre and majordomo. But the govt decided in March that the thing could not be done, as
the mission had a heavy debt. Dept. St. Pap., MS., vii. 14–16; Leg. Rec.,
MS., iv. 319, 325. In May the alcalde reported that the farmers had to
leave their ranchos and gather at the mission for protection against Indians.
In June Hugo Reid was auxiliary administrator and juez de paz. Dept. St.
Pap., MS., vii. 83, 89. June 8th, the mission estate was granted to Hugo
Reid and Wm Workman, in payment for past services to the govt, they binding themselves to pay all debts, support the padre, and pay the expenses of
worship. Deed in Hartman's Brief, 85–7; Hayes' Miss. B., 368. Reid was
probably put in possession, but dispossessed by Stockton and Frémont,
though I find no definite records on the subject. Powder for the Cal. army
made here in Oct. This vol., p. 318. 1847. Bernardino Lopez, encargado
de justicia, though Roldan's name is also mentioned in May; Joaquin Valenzuela juez de campo; Francisco Villa zanjero. Manuel Olivera seems to have
been put in charge of the mission property by the American authorities.
Part of Cal. battalion stationed here; trouble between Owens and Cooke.
This vol., p. 434, 441, 445. May 24th, Col Stevenson requires that all not
legally entitled to live at S. Gabriel must quit the houses and lands at once;
and no taverns must be established. Olivera must be protected in the discharge of his duties. Los Ang. Arch., MS., iii. 63. P. Ordaz' signature
appears on the register from May 14th. S. Gab., Lib. Mis., MS., 60. June
8th, Pres. Jimenez to Stevenson, at his request has ordered Ordaz to take
charge of the mission, but not of the secular administration. Unb. Doc.,
MS., 266–7; yet later the padre seems to claim to be in charge also of temporal
matters. Los Ang. Arch., MS., iii. 84–6, 102, 309. He remained here till
1850. May and July, Lopez and the Ind. protest against Olivera's arbitrary
acts and insist on his removal. Id., 54–6, 84–5, 92, 95–7. It seems that P.
Esténega had allowed the Ind. to retire from the community to their ranchos
or those of others; Olivera required them to return, which they were unwilling to do unless O. was removed. The result is not recorded. Aug. 4th, P.
Ordaz asks the alcalde of Los Angeles to order the ex-neophytes to repair the

Padre Ordaz took charge as curate a few months later. In June 1846 the mission estate was sold to Reid and Workman in payment of past aid to the government; but they were apparently dispossessed by the United States officers in August, and the next year Manuel Olivera was put by them in charge as administrator of the property. The purchasers' title was finally declared invalid on the ground that the governor had no right to sell the missions. A few Indians still lived in the vicinity under the care of the padre, and an auxiliary juez de paz with a few other petty officials managed local affairs in subordination to the alcalde of the city. At San Fernando Father Ordaz remained until May 1847, and he was the last resident minister. The mission had been

church and curate's house. He is told that they are at his orders, but not at the administrator's. On the 20th the padre protests against the granting of a lot without his consent. *Id.*, 102, 105, 109–10. 1848. Feb., Gov. Mason to Stevenson, says the man in charge has lately sold a still worth $800 or $1,000 for $200. *Cal. & N. Mex. 1850*, p. 479. Stevenson begs Ordaz to oblige his protégé Guillermo Novarro to quit the place, because the settlers complain of his selling liquor and buying stolen goods. *Los Ang. Arch.*, MS., iii. 168–9. March, creditors claim $3,014 and they should be secured. *Unb. Doc.*, MS., 266. Evidently Reid and Workman had not paid the mission debt; but on the other hand they had not been kept in possession of the estate.

Tomás Eleuterio Esténega (or Estenaga) was born in the province of Vizcaya about 1790, became a Franciscan at Cantabria, came to the Mex. college in 1810, and to Cal. in 1820. After remaining for a few months as supernumerary he served at S. Miguel in 1820–1, at S. Francisco in 1821–33, and at S. Gabriel in 1833–47. Prefect Payeras described him soon after his arrival as a pious and worthy missionary, but in bad health. *Payeras, Inf. de 1820*, MS., 131–2. Esténega was tall, slender, and of fair complexion; and bad health always impaired his usefulness, though there was an improvement after his transfer to the south. He was generally well liked by his neophytes, and not unpopular with others. Though declining to take the oath to republicanism he promised obedience to the govt; in 1832–3 he served temporarily for several months at S. Rafael; in 1834 he was held as a prisoner for a time by the Ind., and was also involved in the famous 'conspiracy' of Duran and Guerra; in 1841 he was accused of neglecting the morals of his neophytes, and the same year declined to officiate at the fiesta of Sept. 16th; and in 1843 he took the oath to the 'bases constitucionales.' I find no trace of him in the mission registers of S. Gabriel after 1845, and, rather strangely, no record of his death. But it appears that he died there early in 1847, since the juez on May 8th writes of what the 'late' Padre Esténega did 'over two months ago.' *Los Ang. Arch.*, MS., iii. 54–6.

San Fernando. 1846. Jan. 1st, inventory signed by P. Ordaz and the lessees; live-stock 710 head wild animals, 92 cattle, 16 horses, 375 sheep, $2,048; furniture, tools, etc., $122; total $2,170. *Pico, Pap. Mis.*, MS., 156. June 17th, sale of mission estate for $14,000 to Eulogio de Célis. Deed in *Hartman's Brief*, 89–92; *St. Pap., Miss.*, MS., xi. 65. Célis was bound to support the padre and worship, also to give the Ind. the use of the lands they rented in 1845 to Pico and Manso, who apparently held possession in 1846–8, though the property was sold in June 1846—subject to the lease, I suppose— to Eulogio Célis for $14,000, the title of Célis being in later years confirmed.   There were no occurrences at this ex-mission to be noted except the occupation by Frémont's battalion in January 1847, and the signing of the treaty of Cahuenga which put an end to the war in California.

Santa Bárbara took but slight part in the stirring events of the conquest of 1846–7, though it was here that Governor Pico, hearing of invasion in the north, issued his patriotic but not very effective proclamations.   From August to October 1846, a small garrison of Frémont's battalion was posted here; and from April 1847 a detachment of the New York volunteers, at first under Lieut-colonel Burton and later of Captain Lippitt, garrisoned the place; but excepting the episode of the cañon perdido, there was nothing exciting, even from a local standpoint.[3]   When we add to the peaceful sequence of Santa Bárbara events the absence of the municipal records, it is not surprising

occupied during their life-time.   Presumably he bought subject to the lease, though nothing is said on the subject.   The purchaser was not to take possession for 8 months, during which time the govt might redeem the property. On the date of sale, June 17th, I have an original order from Gov. Pico to the 'lessee' to pay the rent as it becomes due to Andrés Pico and Juan Manso on account of a debt of $3,000 due them from the govt. *Pico (Pio), Doc.*, MS., ii. 85.   Andrés Pico named as lessee in Sept. 1847. *Dept. St. Pap., Ang.*, MS., viii. 76.   1847.   Jan., Cal. army and Frémont's battalion in possession; treaty of Cahuenga. This vol., p. 401 et seq.   1848.   Gov. Pico's return. *Id.*, 589.

[3] Sta Bárbara events, etc.   1846.   Lieut-col Gumesindo Flores comandante, except as interrupted by the U. S. occupation.   Jan., several officers of the company resign. This vol., p. 35.   Feb., wreck of the *Fama. Id.*, 578.   May, plan for a 'consejo general' never assembled. *Id.*, 37, 44–7.   June, Gov. Pico here; news of the Bear Flag revolt at Sonoma; Pico's proclamation and appeals. *Id.*, 138–42.   July, assembly refuses to meet at Sta B. *Id.*, 37.   McNamara's proposed colony and his visit. *Id.*, 215–19.   Another proclam. on receipt of news of U. S. occupation of Monterey. *Id.*, 263.   Aug., Stockton touches here on his way south, leaving a garrison and raising the U. S. flag. *Id.*, 267.   Sept., Mitchell and his men replaced by Talbot and volunteers of the battalion as a garrison. *Id.*, 286–7.   Oct., reoccupation by the Californians under Garfias; Talbot driven out. *Id.*, 316–17.   Nov., Raimundo Carrillo comandante, under Flores. *Id.*, 330.   Dec., Frémont arrives with the battalion. *Id.*, 376.

1847.   April, arrival of Co. A, B, and F, N. Y. vol., under Lieut-col

that local annals of the district are for the most part
a blank. Anastasio Carrillo served as sub-prefect
until the United States flag was raised; and town affairs were managed by the following justices of the
peace: Antonio M. Ortega in 1846, Pablo de la
Guerra in 1847, and Pedro C. Carrillo in 1848. Colo-

Burton; July, Co. F remains as a garrison under Capt. Lippitt as comandante
of the post. *Id.*, 513–16. Many details of camp life at Sta B. in *Murray's
Narr.*, MS.; *Green's Life*, MS. July, rumors of trouble with the Californians. This vol., p. 584. Custom-house receipts; Pedro C. Carrillo collector.
Id., 571–2.
　　1848. Feb., Gov. Mason has heard very unfavorable reports about the
conduct of Co. F, and complains of the soldiers having clubbed together to
purchase large quantities of supplies free of duties for purposes of trade.
Cal. & N. Mex. 1850, p. 481–2. March, citizens authorized by juez to make
expeditions to the tulares in quest of wild live-stock, on which a certain
amount must be paid into the town treasury. *Sta B. Arch.*, MS., 65–7.
April, affair of the *cañon perdido*. This vol., p. 586–7. Sept., mustering-out
of the N. Y. vol. *Id.*, 515; records, etc., turned over on Sept. 8th by Capt.
Lippitt to Capt. Smith. *Unb. Doc.*, MS., 21–2.
　　Municipal affairs. 1846. Anastasio Carrillo sub-prefect Jan.–June, though
often desiring to be relieved. Jueces de paz Antonio M. Ortega and Juan P.
Ayala, Juan Camarrillo having been appointed juez 2° but excused at his own
request. Estévan Ortega collector of munic. taxes. 1847. No records until
May since June 1846. On May 9th Pablo de la Guerra and Luis Carrillo
were elected 1st and 2d alcaldes. They declined the governor's appointment
and refused to take the oath of allegiance to the U. S.; yet in some way they
seem to have retained the positions throughout the year. *Unb. Doc.*, 15,
123–4, 204–5. Aug., gov. to Alcalde Carrillo, has ordered Capt. Lippitt to
discontinue military proceedings against two men for insulting women and
theft. Is willing to yield the jurisdiction in such cases to the alcaldes when
as now he has reason to believe them influenced by proper motives. *Cal. & N.
Mex. 1850*, p. 354. Dec. 11th, alcalde to gov., criticising the decree forbidding the sale of liquors to Ind., which he has not enforced. Moderate drinking is good for working men, and the Ind. will not work for anything else.
Abuse of liquor is what should be punished; and the whites behave worse in
this respect than the Ind. *Unb. Doc.*, MS., 197–201. 1848. There had been
an election, if not two, in Jan.–Dec., but one set of alcaldes declined to serve,
against another apparently the citizens protested, and Pablo de la Guerra
went on serving until on Feb. 8th Gov. Mason appointed Pedro C. Carrillo
and Estévan Ardisson as alcaldes. *Unb. Doc.*, MS., 25, 372–3; *Cal. & N.
Mex. 1850*, p. 473–4. It seems that another Don Pedro (Don Pablo?) would
have been appointed, but he declined to accept the offices from a mil. gov.
May, Stevenson threatens Carrillo with removal if he refuses to obey. More
trouble in Aug. *Unb. Doc.*, MS., 335, 194. July, Capt. Lippitt reports that
there are no civil magistrates. *Id.*, 10. Trial of Benj. Foxen for the murder
of Agustin Dávila by the two alcaldes appointed as a special court by the
gov. This vol., p. 611. Gervasio Ayala, Estévan Ortega, and Inocente Lorenzana jueces de policía. *Sta B. Arch.*, MS., 67. Gerónimo Ruiz zanjero at
Carpinteria. *Id.*, 71. March, munic. regulations by the 1st alcalde. *Unb.
Doc.*, MS., 25–7. Trouble with Ind. thieves: Ticó authorized to make a raid.
Sta B. Arch., MS., 69–71. April, gov. declines to interfere with the decision of an umpire in a horse-race. *Cal. & N. Mex. 1850*, p. 508–9. June,
the military must aid the civil authorities in guarding prisoners; much fault
found with Lippitt's comp. *Id.*, 565. July, Stevenson has visited Sta B.,
and has arranged munic. matters there, though he had to remonstrate with

nel Stevenson, in command of the southern military district, had generally some fault to find with the jueces, but the difficulties never assumed any serious form. Only seven or eight ranchos were granted by the governor in this district. The mission, which had been rented in 1845, was sold in June 1846 to Rich-

the alcalde. *Unb. Doc.*, MS., 23–4. The town must raise funds for expenses of admin. of justice; gov. finds fault with both Lippitt and Carrillo for their acts in several minor cases. *Cal. & N. Mex. 1850*, p. 569–76. Sept., the mil. com. releases a prisoner for want of civil authorities and a jail. *Unb. Doc.*, MS., 22. Dec. 13th, Ramon Rodriguez buried; he was shot at Ortega's rancho while trying to arrest evil-doers. Dec. 20th, a boy 7 years old found dead from stabs near town. Dec. 28th, Lynch, Remer (or Raymond), and Quin shot, for murder at S. Miguel. *Sta B., Lib. Mis.*, MS., 41-2.

Private ranchos. Cañada de S. Miguel and Cañada del Diablo, 2 l., granted in 1846 to Ramon Rodriguez, whose heirs were cl. *Cuyama, 11 l., 1846, Cesareo Lataillade; whose widow was cl. Diablo, see Cañada. Goleta, 1 l., 1846, Daniel Hill, who was cl. Liebre, 11 l., 1846, José M. Flores, who was cl. S. Buenaventura mission, 12 l., 1846, José Arnaz; M. A. Rodriguez de Poli, cl. S. Marcos, 8 l., 1846, Nicholas A. Den, who was cl. (Stevenson annuls the grant to R. S. Den, in Oct. 1848. *Arch. Sta B.*, MS., xi. 51.) S. Miguel, see Cañada. Sta Bárbara mission, 1846, Richard S. Den, who was cl. *Sta Inés mission, 1846, José M. Covarrubias, who was cl. Sta Inés, land near, granted by Gov. Flores in 1846 to Joaquin Ayala, who in '47 was allowed by the govt to retain possession, though his title could not be good. *Savage, Doc.*, MS., ii. 78. The grant of a house at the presidio by Gen. Castro to Nicolás Lopez was in Feb. 1848 declared null. *Cal. & N. Mex. 1850*, p. 479.

Sta Bárbara mission. 1846. Jan., several letters of P. Duran to gov. on the delivery of the rented mission property, and about lots assigned to the Ind. and for support of the padres. *Arch. Arzob.*, MS., v. pt ii. 69–72. March 24th, inventory of the property valued at $6,387. *Hayes' Miss. B.*, i. 373–6. June 8th, bond of Den and Hill, who pledge their ranchos of Dos Pueblos and S. Pedro to return all the property in good condition after the term of nine years. *Id.*, 372; *Unb. Doc.*, MS., 279. June 10th, deed of sale to Richard S. Den for $7,500. *Hartman's Brief*, app. 96–9; *Hayes' Miss. B.*, i. 377. July 1848, the govt orders the investigation of the lease by Col Stevenson. *Cal. & N. Mex. 1850*, p. 573–4. Aug. 18th, govt annuls the act of Alcalde Carrillo in putting R. S. Den in possession of S. Márcos, one of the mission ranchos, though not on the ground that the mission sale was illegal. *Id.*, 596. I find nothing about the final disposition of R. S. Den's title, except that it was confirmed by the land commission, but that in his later suit against Den and Hill to get the property he was defeated in the U. S. circuit court on the ground that Pico had no power to sell the mission estate. Death of García Diego, succession of Duran and Gonzalez, and death of Duran. This vol., p. 565-6. Late in 1848 Presbyter José M. Rosales was for doctrinal irregularities sent away from Cal. by the gov. of the diocese, Gonzalez, notwithstanding the petition of 50 citizens that he be retained for Los Angeles, the original of which is in *Carrillo (D.), Doc.*, MS., 121-4.

Francisco García Diego was a native of Mexico, and had been 'lector de artes y de sagrada teología' at the Franciscan college of Guadalupe de Zacatecas, when sent to California in 1833 as comisario prefecto in charge of the Zacatecan band of missionaries. He became minister of Sta Clara, where he remained until 1835, discontented with the general condition of affairs, but performing acceptably the routine duties of his position, and showing himself to be a well meaning and intelligent man. Then he went to Mexico, to come

ard S. Den for $7,500, but the lessees seem to have kept possession throughout 1846–8.   Den's title was confirmed by the land commission, though there are indications that it was practically annulled in later litigation.   Padre Duran, the venerable president of the Fernandinos, died at his post early in 1846, one

back in 1841 as the first bishop of California.   The country needed no bishop, and García Diego was in no way fitted to overcome obstacles that would have discouraged a younger and more energetic man.   Without priests or money he could accomplish nothing, and only at Sta Bárbara did he receive hearty popular support.   Advanced in years, somewhat overweighted by the dignities of his office, grievously disappointed at the failure of his subjects to support his grand schemes for their good, he became peevish, and even childish, rarely leaving his home at Sta Bárbara, though he made an episcopal tour to the north in 1844.   The kind-hearted and inoffensive old man, having left the governorship of the diocese to PP. Duran and Gonzalez, died at midnight of April 30, 1846, at the age of 60 years, 5 months, and 24 days.   He was buried May 3d by P. Gonzalez in a new tomb made for the purpose in the mission church. *Sta B.*, *Lib. Mis.*, MS., 39; *Arch. Arzob.*, MS., v. pt ii. 67; *Doc. Hist. Cal.*, MS., iii. 197; *Arch. Obisp.*, MS., 25.

Narciso Duran was born Dec. 16, 1776, at Castellon de Ampurias, Catalonia, and became a Franciscan at Gerona May 3, 1792.   He came to Mexico in 1803 and to Cal. in 1806, serving at S. José in 1806–33, and Sta Bárbara in 1833–46.   In 1817–20 he was praised by his superiors as a most zealous and efficient missionary, fit for the prelacy. *Autobiog. Autog. de los Padres*, MS., *Sarría, Inf. de 1817*, MS., 69–70; *Payeras, Inf. de 1820*, MS., 139.   Duran was president of the Fernandinos in 1825–7, 1831–8, and 1844–6, being comisario prefecto in 1837–43, and governor of the diocese after the bishop's death in 1846.   In all the mission chapters of the last three volumes of this work, the reader has found Padre Narciso's name more prominent than that of any other friar, and several of his writings appear in my list of authorities.   He was a most earnest and successful missionary, the only fault ever found with him in this respect being an excess of zeal in the forcible conversion of gentiles for his mission of San José; while as prelate he was a worthy successor of Sarría, Señan, and Payeras.   Throughout the troublous times of secularization he managed the mission affairs with marked ability.   To a greater extent than most of his comrades he was a politic and practical man, contenting himself with a part when all could not be won.   Though an able and bitter foe to secularization, yet as a choice of evils when he realized that secularization could not be prevented he gave honest and valuable advice respecting the practical working of the successive schemes.   Though he often became impatient and despondent, these moods never lasted long; and though he engaged in many controversies and wrote many bitter and sarcastic things, he yet retained the esteem of most adversaries, and was always beloved by the people of all classes, being especially popular and influential at Sta Bárbara in the later years.   Rather strangely I find no direct trace of his presence at S. José before 1811.   An immense music book, written in colors on home-made parchment and bound in heavy boards and leather, has an explanatory preface signed ' Fr. N.' in 1813.   In 1817 he was present at the founding of S. Rafael.   He refused the oath to republicanism in 1826; refused to aid the revolutionist Solis in 1829; and in 1831, suffering from the gout, obtained a promise of his passport for Habana.   In 1832, discouraged at the mortality among his Ind., he writes ' la paciencia no me alcanza, y no veo las horas de tirar esta carga.' Figueroa recommended his exile in 1833, and Duran never had friendly feelings for this governor, believing him to be a much overrated man.   In 1836 he had a controversy with Chico, and became an earnest and most valuable

month after the death of Bishop García Diego of the
Zacatecanos; but Padre Gonzalez still remained
throughout this period and for nearly thirty years
longer, to become the last survivor of all the Californian missionaries. The mission of San Buenaventura
had also been rented, but was sold for $12,000 in June
1846 to José Arnaz, one of the lessees. His title as
purchaser, though confirmed by the courts in later
years, was not recognized by the government in 1846–
8, and he was even ousted as lessee in 1848, Isaac
Callaghan obtaining a lease from Colonel Stevenson,
and being also juez auxiliar, as José Moraga and

supporter of Alvarado even against Carrillo, his personal friend. In 1839 he
again thought of departure and obtained a new passport, having already one
from Figueroa. In 1845 he ordered the balance due him to be paid to the
neophytes. In 1845-6 his advice was sought and in many respects followed
by Gov. Pico in the matter of renting and selling the missions. In physique
Duran was of medium stature, somewhat stout, of fair complexion, and blue
eyes. Mofras, *Explor.*, i. 199, gives a portrait, only a tolerable likeness according to P. Gonzalez, says Taylor. His death occurred on June 1, 1846, at
5 P. M., and he was buried June 3d, by Padre Gonzalez, in the church vault.
Sta B., Lib. Mis., MS., 40; *Arch. Arzob.*, MS., v. pt ii. 72. Only two of the
Spanish Fernandinos, Oliva and Ordaz, survived him.

San Buenaventura. 1846. José Moraga appointed juez de paz in Jan.
May 20th, the Ind. authorize the gov. to dispose of the mission for govt
needs. *Miscel. Doc.*, MS., 14–24. June 8th, deed of sale to José Arnaz for
$12,000 due him. *St. Pap., Miss.*, MS., xi. 61–3; *Hartman's Brief*, app. 92–
6. June 10th, assembly approves grant of 400 varas to Fernando Ticó. *Leg.
Rec.*, MS., iv. 354. June 19th, inventory of various effects delivered to the
lessees, including 1,273 head of cattle. *Pico, Pap. Mis.*, MS., 77–9. Arnaz,
Rec., MS., 83, says he paid Botello $1,000 for his interest in the lease. Gov.
Pico here with his army in June. This vol., p. 48. Occupied by the Calif. in
Oct. *Id.*, 317. 1847. Frémont and his battalion arrive Jan. *Id.*, 400.
1848. Francisco Ortega juez de paz until May 26th, when he was removed
by Col Stevenson and Isaac Callaghan appointed in his place; and Gov.
Mason, though criticising Stevenson's act, confirmed the appointment on
June 11th. Jan. 7th, gov. authorizes 6 Ind. to continue their occupation of
mission lands unless José Moraga can show a legal right to dispossess them.
Cal. & N. Mex. 1850, p. 454. Feb.–June, imperfect details of Stevenson's investigation of Arnaz's acts in disposing of mission property. The corresp.
seems to indicate that Arnaz was regarded merely as lessee, and that his bill
of sale was not presented. At any rate, he was ousted and his vineyard and
other property were seized as security. *Id.*, 479, 504, 549, 563–4; *Los Ang.
Arch.*, MS., iii. 175–84, 191–2; *Unb. Doc.*, MS., 331–4. It was in connection with this change that Callaghan was appointed to succeed Ortega; and
apparently in Aug. Callaghan became lessee. *Cal. & N. Mex. 1850*, p. 588.
Streeter, *Recoll.*, MS., 91–5, claims to have been a partner of C., his brother-
in-law, and says nothing was heard of Arnaz's ownership till 1850. Arnaz,
Recuerdos, MS., 91–3, however, says that his title as owner was presented to
Stevenson and by him declared a forgery. The Arnaz title was finally confirmed by land commission and U. S. courts, though litigation lasted many
years, and many men in that region still regard the title as fraudulent. I

Francisco Ortega had been before him. Presbyter José M. Rosales remained in charge of spiritual interests until expelled by his prelate late in 1848, and Alejandro M. Branchi was the next curate from 1849. Santa Inés was sold to the lessees, Covarrubias and Carrillo, for $7,000 in June 1846; but though they kept possession until after 1848 under their lease, their title by purchase was finally declared invalid. Joaquin Carrillo, Agustin Janssens, Francisco Cota, and José M. Covarrubias are named as successive jueces de paz; and Padre Joaquin Jimeno continued as curate, being also rector of the ecclesiastical seminary, an institution which, with Padre Francisco de Jesus Sanchez as vice-rector, still maintained a precarious existence. Purísima was entirely abandoned, and nothing about the establishment appears in the records.

Though no longer the capital, Monterey had still the custom-house, the prefectura, and the military comandancia, being still as in former years the centre

have found no satisfactory reasons to doubt that the sale was made in good faith.

Santa Inés. 1846. Joaquin Carrillo juez de paz in Jan.; Octaviano Gutierrez juez 2° in June; Agustin Janssens juez and military comandante in Oct. Jan., corresp. between P. Jimeno, Juez Carrillo, and the gov. about support of the padre, who complained, and proposed that the rent of $580 should be equally divided between the Ind. and padre. *Dept. St. Pap.*, MS., vii. 100. June 15th, deed of sale to Covarrubias and Joaquin Carrillo for $7,000. *Hartman's Brief*, app. 99–102; *Unb. Doc.*, MS., 280–1. Interview between Gov. Pico and Pref. Castro in June. This vol., p. 143. Some unimportant troubles with the Ind. are described by Janssens. *Vida*, MS., 188–91. 1847. Sept. 6th, Gov. Mason calls upon the lessees for copies of their contract, also accounts of rents, etc. *Cal. & N. Mex. 1850*, p. 392. Nov. 29th, gov. declines to recognize the sale to Covarrubias and Carrillo, because the sale had not been at auction as required, and because their acts in continuing to pay rent in 1846–7 was against the theory of a purchase. They must be regarded as renters, and must settle up and show receipts on that basis. *Id.*, 436. 1848. Francisco Cota juez auxiliar, succeeded in March by José M. Covarrubias; though Janssens claims to have been juez in Jan. Dec. 31st, financial condition of the ecclesiastical seminary, Fr José Joaquin Jimeno rector, Fr Francisco de Jesus Sanchez vice-rector; receipts for 1848 ($58 from parents of pupils, $667 from sales of live-stock, $250 from bishop, $239 from rector, $300 from vice-rector, from Americans $25, and alms $96), $1,635; expend. $1,846, deficit $211; deficit of 1847, $337. Crops 226 fanegas of grain. Cattle at end of 1848, 1,706 head. *Savage, Doc.*, MS., ii. 83; *Sta Inés, Lib. Mis.*, MS., 35.

of all political developments in the north, as fully
indexed in my note.[4] During the first half of 1846
the controversy between Castro and Pico was the
chief topic of consideration, though sectional feeling
was less intense here than at Los Angeles; and the
popular attention was also much directed to foreign

[4] Monterey events. 1846. Jan.–June, Monterey and Castro versus Los
Angeles and Pico. This vol., p. 30–53. Larkin's efforts in behalf of the U.
S. *Id.*, 54 et seq. Jan., Frémont's visit. *Id.*, 4. Quarrel of Man. Castro and
Cambuston. *Id.*, 34. March, Frémont's operations at Gavilan. *Id.*, 9–21.
March–April, junta of military men to save the country. *Id.*, 41–2, 59 et seq.
April, arrival of Gillespie on the *Cyane.* *Id.*, 27–8, 200. May, delegates for
the Sta Bárbara consejo. *Id.*, 45 et seq. June, arrival of the *Juno* and Mc-
Namara. *Id.*, 217. Castro's efforts against Pico and the U. S. *Id.*, 51–3.
Ide's Bear Flag proclamation posted here. *Id.*, 159. July, arrival of Com.
Sloat and raising of the U. S. flag. *Id.*, 224–38. Arrival of Frémont and
Gillespie; Sloat succeeded by Stockton; radical change of policy. *Id.*, 248–60.
Aug.–Sept., chronological summary of local happenings, including movements
of war vessels, publication of the 1st newspaper, 1st trial by jury, etc. *Id.*,
288–93. Nov.–Dec., a like summary; also organization of the Cal. battalion,
imprisonment of Larkin, and campaign of Natividad. *Id.*, 357–77.
1847. Jan., arrival of Co. F, third artillery. *Id.*, 519. Arrival of Com.
Shubrick. *Id.*, 428–9. Return of Capt. Maddox and company from the Sta
Clara campaign. Feb., Kearny arrives from the south. *Ib.* March, arrival
of Com. Biddle; Kearny assumes the governorship; Frémont's visit and quarrel with Kearny. *Id.*, 436–8, 443–4. April, arrival of four companies of the
N. Y. vol., Co. I remaining as a garrison until Dec. *Id.*, 514. Grand ball
given by the naval officers on April 9th. *S. F. Californian*, Apr. 17, 1847.
About this time two barrels of liquor were smashed on the wharf by Lieut
Sherman, an event that John A. Swan never forgets to mention. Volunteer
cavalry co. under Lieut B. Burton. This vol., 521. May, arrival of Kearny
and Frémont from the south, and departure for the east; Gov. Mason in command. *Id.*, 450–1. July 4th celebrated at the capital. *S. F. Calif.*, Sept. 8,
1847. In the same paper the progress of the town is noted; 27 houses being
erected; the 1st brick house in Cal. lately completed by Dickenson; great improvements at the fort on the hill under direction of Lieut Ord; Miss Eager's
school very popular. Nov., Larkin writes that town lots have risen from $100
to $2,000. *Larkin's Off. Corresp.*, MS., ii. 124. Dec. 30th, a fire in José
Abrego's house, extinguished by the aid of citizens, soldiers, and sailors.
Calif., Jan. 19, 1848. Disgraceful conduct of some of the volunteers at a ball
given at the barracks. *Id.*, Oct. 20, 1847. 1848. Feb. 26th, subscription for a
ball on Washington's birthday $355. *Larkin's Doc.*, MS., vi. 38. May 29th,
news of the discovery of gold. *Colton's Three Years*, 242. Sept., a board of
trustees appointed by the alcalde to manage a stone building erected for public uses. *Ashley, Doc.*, MS., 264. Oct., mustering-out of last comp. and staff
of N. Y. volunteers. This vol., 515–16.
Municipal affairs. 1846. Prefect Manuel Castro, with Florencio Serrano
as secretary. Jan., Castro complains that the ayunt. has been installed without notice to him; insists on his rights. *Castro, Doc.*, MS., i. 255. French
consul complains that Castro is not legally prefect, being under 30 years of
age. *Dept. St. Pap., Ben. P. & J.*, MS., ii. 4. May, Castro offers his resignation, *Id.*, 58, which was not accepted. The prefect's part in political and
military affairs of Jan.–July has been fully recorded in other chapters. Alcaldes—elected in Dec., taking possession Jan. 1st, approved by gov. Jan. 22d,
—Manuel Diaz and Joaquin Escamilla; regidores Ignacio Ezquer, Francisco
Arias, Rafael Estrada, Job F. Dye; síndico Florencio Serrano, secretary Am-

intervention as a source of relief from prevalent evils. Meanwhile the Montereyans were willing to wait in patience for whatever fate might have in store for them, listening to Larkin's appeals in behalf of the United States, and startled only by Frémont's absurd performance at Gavilan and the American settlers' filibusterism on the northern frontier. In July the stars and stripes were raised without the slightest opposition, and the old capital became a garrison town, whose uneventful progress was duly recorded in a weekly newspaper and in Alcalde Colton's diary. The coming of Company F, third artillery, and the restoration of the capital were the events of 1847; while the next year can hardly be said to have had any dis-

brosio Gomez. Diaz wished to be excused in Jan., but was required to serve. Ezquer often served as juez 1° in Diaz's illness. Auxiliares de policía, Teodoro Gonzalez, Juan Antonio Vallejo, Francisco Granados, Adalberto Thoms, Guillermo Gomez, and Jesus Soto. Jueces de campo Agustin Escobar, Estévan de la Torre; id. of the valley (Salinas) ranchos, José Antonio Alviso, Agustin Martinez, Andrés Juarez, Francisco García, and Felipe García; id. S. Cárlos, Juan de Mata Boronda. Jueces auxiliares, of the valley ranchos, Santiago Estrada and Joaquin Buelna, with Andrés Soto and Prudencio Espinosa as suplentes; id. S. Cárlos Juan Rosales. Tithe-collector Francisco Pacheco. In July, by U. S. military appointment, Edward Gilchrist and Rodman M. Price were made alcaldes; but Gilchrist was succeeded by Walter Colton on July 20th; and on Sept. 15th, at a popular election with 68 votes out of 338, Colton was chosen alcalde with Milton Little as substitute; councillors David Spence, W. E. P. Hartnell, Juan Malarin, and Manuel Diaz; treasurer Salvador Munrás. *Mont. Calif.*, Sept. 19, 1846. Jan., police regulations in 17 articles. *Doc. Hist. Cal.*, MS., iii. 83. April, instructions to jueces auxiliares. *Mont. Arch.*, MS., viii. 28–9. Aug., etc., regulations on sale of liquors, etc. *Mont. Californian.* Aug. 15, Sept. 26, Oct. 3, Oct. 31, Dec. 19, 1846. 1847. Alcalde Walter Colton; councillors, etc., not named; Wm R. Garner sheriff. The municipal record is very slight, showing only a few minor regulations of different dates, though Colton in his published diary gives occasional amusing incidents in the administration of justice. In Oct. two Ind. were shot for murder. *S. F. Calif.*, Oct. 20th. 1848. Colton still serving as alcalde until Oct., when Florencio Serrano took his place. Wm R. Longley was appointed 2d alcalde on Jan. 13th, Wm R. Garner still served as clerk.

Ranchos. Laguna de Tache, 11 l., 1846, Manuel Castro; id. and J. Clark cl. S. Juan Bautista, orchard, 400 v., 1846, Ollivier Deleissèques; C. Panaud et al. cl. *S. Juan Capistrano del Camote, 10 l., 1846, T. Herrera and G. Quintana. S. Lorenzo, 11 l., 1846, Rafael Sanchez, who was cl. *S. Miguel, 1846, Wm Reed, Petronilo Rios, and M. García; Rios cl. S. Miguelito, 500 v., 1846, Miguel Ávila, who was cl.; *2 l., id. grantee and cl. Soledad, mission, 2 l., 1846, Feliciano Soberanes, who was cl. Ranchos without names; 6 l. to José Castro, Robt B. Neligh cl.; to *T. H. Green, who was cl.; 1,500 v. to José Castro, Patrick Breen cl.; Carmelo (perhaps not in Monterey district), 10 l., Wm Knight; J. G. Morehead cl. Tucho, 1 l., 1846, Joaquin Arroyo. *Doc. Hist. Cal.*, MS., i. 502. In 1847-8, Alcalde Colton was called upon to furnish copies of grants of town lands with details as to the titles; particularly with reference to the lots within Halleck's survey of lands in the

tinguishing local feature before the news of gold came to depopulate the town. Manuel Castro ruled as prefect down to the American occupation; and Manuel Diaz as alcalde presided over the ayuntamiento that managed municipal affairs. After the change of flag, Edward Gilchrist was made alcalde, but was soon succeeded by Walter Colton, who ruled till late in 1848 and was followed by Florencio Serrano. As Monterey was the residence of the military governor, the municipal authorities had but little to do, though the reverend alcalde has woven into his published narrative a series of amusing experiences in the administration of justice. Ranchos granted in 1846 were only about a dozen, including several of the ex-mission estates. For San Cárlos mission there is no record whatever; and it is not even clear who was the resident priest at Monterey, though the names of Real, Ánzar, and Ambris appear on the registers. At San Luis Obispo, Padre José Nicolás Gomez served as

vicinity of the fort—or those of Shubrick, Bailey, Doyle, Spence, Green, and Deleissèques; also a map of Fort Hill is given. *Halleck's Report*, 169–75.

S. Cárlos, no record of ex-mission affairs, or rather no affairs of which to make a record. The names of PP. Real, Ánzar, and Ambris appear on the registers, though neither resided at the mission.

S. Luis Obispo. José Ortega juez succeeding Estrada, Jan.–March, with Victor Linares as juez 2°; Jesus Pico juez Feb.–Sept. García, *Hechos*, MS., 95, says that Pico as mil. com. took the baton by force from O., being unwilling to be ruled by a man who had an Ind. wife. In Sept. Mariano Bonilla was appointed juez, and served through the year. Jan. 4th, juez to gov., the buyers of the mission have not yet appeared. Describes the buildings, which are in bad condition, except the church. *Dept. St. Pap., Ben. P. & J.*, MS., ii. 62–3. Feb. 9th, some Ind. have run away and carried off the alcalde's wife. *S. José Arch.*, MS., loose pap., 30. Feb. 20th, P. Gomez to gov., can not understand why after all his labors there comes an order to turn over the property to others. *Dept. St. Pap.*, MS., vii. 105–6. Feb. 26th, jueces de campo appointed, not named. Pico, *Acont.*, MS., 79–80. March 7th, Linares orders P. Gomez to turn over property to Pico for Scott and Wilson; Gomez appeals to bishop, who asks gov. to reserve certain storerooms and the mills. Gov. promises to investigate. *Arch. Arzob.*, MS., v. pt ii. 65–6. March 10th, Gomez to gov., complaining of lack of means of support, also of his mortifications and insults. *Dept. St. Pap.*, MS., vii. 42–3. March 29th (?), possession given to Pico. *Id., Ben. P. & J.*, ii. 63. April 18th, Linares, juez 2°, reprimanded by sub-prefect for insubordination. *S. Luis Ob., Arch.*, MS., 2. Apr. 28th, order of juez about use of water for irrigation. *Id.*, 3. June 1st, Pico reports an Ind. fight in which 6 were killed. *Dept. St. Pap., Ben. P. & J.*, MS., ii. 46. June 12th. Gov. Pico orders enlistment of men for his mil. exped. to the north. *S. Luis Ob., Arch.*, MS., 12. June 22d, 25th, doc. connected with the putting of John Wilson in formal possession of the ex-mission estate, with measurements, etc. *Hartman's Brief*, app. 71–4. Janssens, *Vida,*

curate; and pueblo affairs were directed successively by José Ortega, Jesus Pico, Mariano Bonilla, and John M. Price as justices, or alcaldes. The purchasers of 1845 seem not to have been disturbed in their possession of the ex-mission estate, their title to which was in later years declared to be valid. San Miguel was subject spiritually and municipally to the curate and justice of San Luis. The estate was sold in July to Rios and Reed, and their possession was not disturbed by the new authorities, though the purchase was declared invalid by the courts later. The murder of Reed and his family in December 1848 was the most notable event of San Miguel annals during this period. At San Antonio, Padre Doroteo Ambris

MS., 190, mentions the arrest of Williams, an American, by a party of drunken Californians, who were finally induced by J. to release him, when made to understand the danger to Mex. prisoners in Amer. hands. This was just before Frémont's arrival. July–Dec. Gov. Pico and Gen. Castro meet; news of capture of Mont.; Skirmish between Lieut. Maddox and Calif.; Man. Castro has his headquarters at S. Luis; capture of the place by Frémont, trial of Jesus Pico, etc. This vol., p. 144, 262, 282, 321, 362, 374–5. 1847, Mariano Bonilla alcalde until Oct., when he resigned, as he had tried to do in April; Gov. Mason offered to appoint any one the people could agree on, but there is no record of a new appointment. May 30th, alcalde's regul. on sale of liquors, etc. *Mont. Arch.*, MS., xiii. 14–15. June 6th, Wm G. Dana at Nipomo complains of S. Luis as a sink of debauchery, where the alcalde's authority has no weight; Ind. are raiding, horrid murders are reported, and farmers will have to quit their ranchos if no military aid is sent. *Unb. Doc.*, MS., 168. Bonilla had made like complaints, and on June 16th was ordered by Gov. Mason to come to Mont., bringing three criminals and three witnesses with him. *Cal. & N. Mex. 1850*, p. 323. Aug. 24th, juez ordered by gov. to turn over to the priest all the property held by the padres at the raising of the U. S. flag. *S. Luis Ob., Arch.*, MS., 5; *Bonilla, Doc.*, MS., 24–5. 1848, Alcalde John M. Price, appointed by Gov. Mason Jan. 25th. He was first elected, but the gov. disapproved the election, at the same time sending the appointment. *S. Luis Ob., Arch.*, MS., 24; *Cal. & Mex. 1850*, 462–3. Price was accused by Miguel Ávila of having stolen his cow, and when P. was made alcalde A. thought his case not improved, and he petitioned the ayunt. of Mont. for a trial without the alcalde's intervention. *Ávila, Doc.*, MS., 17–18. Feb., police regulations. *S. Luis Ob., Arch.*, MS., 15–18. March 21st, gov. orders Price to organize an exped. against the Ind., ammunition to be supplied by the govt. *Id.*, 23–4; *Cal. & N. Mex. 1850*, 495–7

S. Miguel. 1846, mission in charge of the juez and padre at S. Luis Obispo. July 4th, estate sold, as was claimed, to Petronilo Rios and Wm Reed; but very little is known of the transaction. Reed lived here since 1845 or earlier. 1847. Sept., gov. orders that Reed be left in possession, a satisfactory provision for the priest being made, and the title being left for later settlement. *Bonilla, Doc.*, MS., 24, 26; *Cal. & N. Mex. 1850*, p. 396, 436–8. Nov. 30th, gov. orders that the S. Miguel Ind. be put in possession of lands granted them in 1844. *Ib.* 1848. Dec., murder of Reed and family by a party of tramps, formerly soldiers. Reed entertained these fellows for several days with his usual hospitality, but unfortunately revealed the fact

had charge as curate; but there is no record of events, or of the mission estate, which apparently was never sold. At San Juan Bautista the curate was Padre José Antonio Ánzar in 1848, and there was probably no other resident priest during the period. Quintin Ortega and José María Sanchez were the municipal

that he had quite a large sum of gold in his possession, having recently returned from a trip to the mines where he had sold a flock of sheep. Leaving S. Miguel the villains went only to Sta Margarita, and after dark returned and murdered all the occupants of the ex-mission, making a heap of the corpses in one of the rooms, and carrying off the gold and other valuables. The victims were Reed, his son aged 2 or 3 years, his wife María Antonia Vallejo, her unborn child, her brother José Ramon, Josefa Olivera a midwife who had come to attend Mrs Reed, her daughter aged 15 and nephew aged 4, an Indian servant aged over 60 and his nephew of 5 years, and a negro cook. The murderers were apparently five in number, were pursued by a force of men from Sta Bárbara under Lataillade, and were finally overtaken on the coast near the Ortega rancho. One of the number after being fatally wounded shot and killed Ramon Rodriguez, who rashly rushed upon the party; another jumped into the sea and was drowned; and the other three, Joseph Lynch, Peter Remer (or Raymond), and Peter Quin, were executed at Sta Bárbara on Dec. 28th. Samuel Brenard is given as the name of one of the party not taken alive. Details are given by Catarina Ávila de Rios, *Recuerdos*, MS., widow of Petronilo Rios, Reed's partner, then living at Paso de Robles, and who buried the victims. *Streeter's Recoll.*, MS., 195–9; *Janssens, Vida*, MS., 207–9; *Sta B., Lib. Mis.*, MS., 42.

S. Antonio. No record of any disposition of the estate in 1846. This vol., 561; and no claim before the land commission in later times, except that for the church property as elsewhere. Doroteo Ambris in charge as curate, but perhaps not living here continuously, from Feb. 1846. *S. Antonio, Lib. Mis.*, MS., 26. Vicente P. Gomez, *Lo Que Sabe*, MS., 204–16, says that he at the request of P. Ambris and with Gov. Mason's approval took charge during 1847–8, gathered about 35 Ind. fam., raised good crops, but became tired of living alone exposed to the attacks of passing miners, and gave up the place.

S. Juan Bautista. 1846. Jueces de paz, Quintin Ortega and Angel M. Castro, with Joaquin Soto and Antonio Castro as suplentes. After the Amer. occupation Matthew Fellom was appointed alcalde. *Cutts' Conq. Cal.*, 125. Chabolla is also named in Nov. March 15th, juez Angel Castro asks for leave of absence. *Doc. Hist. Cal.*, MS., iii. 135. March, affairs connected with Frémont's fiasco at Gavilan. This vol., p. 9–20. May 4th, sale of the orchard of S. Juan to Ollivier Deleissèques on account of govt indebtedness. *Hartman's Brief*, 102–6. June–July, events connected with the U. S. occupation; Castro's headquarters; Frémont and Fauntleroy. This vol., p. 51, 231, 233, 245, 247–8, 254, 261. Oct., occupied by Maddox. *Id.*, 290–4. Nov., Cal. battalion organized; fight at Natividad. *Id.*, 360–72. Estolano Larios, *Vida*, MS., 24, says that his rancho, Palos de Lanza, was so named from the lanceshafts here obtained for the fight at Natividad. 1847. Alcalde José María Sanchez. In Nov. Julian Ursúa was elected, and Gov. Mason, though declaring the election null and void, appointed Ursúa; but U. seems not to have been willing to act, and Sanchez retained the place. March, order that the mission property remain in charge of the priest. This vol., p. 564. May, Deleissèques asks the French consul to reclaim for him the orchard granted him by Pico, but of which the U. S. govt has dispossessed him. *Unb. Doc.*, MS., 287. 1848. Alcalde José M. Sanchez. March, José Castro buys Deleissèques' title, and asks to be put in possession, which Mason declines to

chiefs. The ex-mission orchard was sold in May 1846 to Ollivier Deleissèques, and though he did not obtain possession in 1846–8, his title was finally confirmed. Soledad was sold in June 1846 to Feliciano Soberanes, who retained possession, and whose title was confirmed. The ex-mission has no other annals. I

permit unless the priest consents, as he probably will. *Unb. Doc.*, MS., 263, 268, 271; *Cal. & N. Mex. 1850*, p. 490.

Soledad. 1846. Sold June 4th to Feliciano Soberanes for $800. *Hartman's Brief*, app. 110–13; *St. Pap. Miss.*, MS., xi. 66. There is no record for 1847–8, but apparently Soberanes was not disturbed in his possession. Gomez, *Lo Que Sabe*, MS., 217–18, says the buildings were in ruins, and it was a desolate looking place, having, moreover, a bad reputation as a place where travellers had to pay heavily for hospitalities, and where their horses were apt to be put astray, involving a compensation for their recovery.

Sta Cruz and Branciforte. 1846. Jueces de paz José Bolcof and Macedonio Lorenzana, suplentes Guadalupe Castro and Roman Rodriguez. Juez de campo Isidro Salazar. On the American occupation Bolcof was desired to continue in office, either alone or with John Hames, *Larkin's Off. Corresp.*, MS., i. 140–1; but apparently declined; and Joseph L. Majors was appointed in Aug. with Wm Thompson as 2d, and Lawrence Carmichael as secretary. Jan. 21st, juez has given the Castros possession of S. Andrés lands, *Castro, Doc.*, MS., i. 281, at which the juez of Mont. complains. *Id.*, 283. March, lumbermen refuse to pay taxes. This vol., p. 57. According to a resolution of the ayunt. the town lands extend one league in each direction from the mission. *Sta Cruz Arch.*, MS., 109. All claimants must present their titles for inspection. *Id.*, 108. April, killing of Henry Naile by James Williams at the house of Wm Buckle. The two men had a quarrel about their property rights in the Sayante saw-mill, N. being struck and challenging W. to fight a duel, perhaps threatening to kill him next day or on sight. Next day W., concealed at Buckle's house, shot N. as the latter passed, and then gave himself up with the claim of having acted in self-defence. Witnesses examined were Wm Buckle, Joseph L. Majors, John Hames, Wm Blackburn, Jacob R. Snyder, Joseph R. Foster, and Williams, the testimony being favorable to W. The result is not given, but I think W. was acquitted. *Mont. Arch.*, MS., v. 2–9. Graham claimed Naile's arms, but the juez refused to give them up. *Doc. Hist. Cal.*, MS., iii. 171. April 15th, John Marsh and others inform Larkin of the affair, asking him to take steps to bring the murderer to justice. *Larkin's Doc.*, MS., iv. 90. Jas W. Weeks, *Remin.*, MS., 107–8, was coroner in this case. Jan., building and launch of the schooner *Sta Cruz*, built by Charles Roussillon for Pierre Sainsevain. *S. José Pioneer*, Aug. 2, 1875. Oct. 15th, María en Gracía Rodriguez complains to Alcalde Majors that her sister-in-law has slandered her and her daughters; desires that she be made to give satisfaction, or be punished according to American laws. *Sta Cruz Arch.*, MS., 33. Rancho of S. Vicente granted to Blas A. Escamilla, to whom it was later confirmed. *Land. Com.*, no. 608. 1847. Alcaldes Majors and Thompson till June; later Wm Blackburn and Wm Anderson. Beginning of protestant worship, by Hecox, Anthony, and Dunleavy. *Cal. Christ. Advoc.*, July 2, 1863; This vol., p. 566. March, order that the mission remain in charge of the priest. *Id.*, 564. June 21st, gov. sends to Blackburn his appointment, and directs him not to permit encroachments on Sainsevain's land. *Cal. & N. Mex.*, 1850, p. 332–3. Aug., Pedro Gomez, who murdered his wife on the 14th, was convicted before Alcalde Blackburn and a jury, and was shot by B.'s sentence on the 16th. *Sta Cruz Arch.*, MS., 100; *S. F. Calif.*, Sept. 8th; *S. F. Cal. Star*, Sept. 11th. Nov., a man for cutting the mane of A. Rodriguez's horse was condemned to have

find no definite record of any resident curate at Santa
Cruz and Branciforte, where the successive jueces
and alcaldes were José Bolcof, Joseph L. Majors, and
William Blackburn, with the aid of four councillors
in 1848. The murder of Henry Naile in 1846, the
execution of a wife-murderer by Alcalde Blackburn's
order in 1847, with a municipal controversy and vain
attempt to oust the famous alcalde in 1848, were
prominent among local happenings.

his own hair cut close in front of the alcalde's office. *Willey's Centen. Sk.*,
25. Nov. 24th, the priest of Sta Cruz (not named) complained to gov. that
the alcalde had been granting lots belonging to the mission; therefore the
gov. calls on the alcalde for his authority to do so, and for documents and
map to show that a town has been organized; otherwise he has no right to
dispose of lands. *Cal. & N. Mex. 1850*, p. 433–4. In later years there were
also charges that the priest (Anzar of S. Juan?) had improperly disposed of
some mission property. *Unb. Doc.*, MS., 273–4. 1848. Blackburn and
Anderson alcaldes. A. A. Hecox acting alcalde in Nov. March 18th, a
town-council elected, consisting of Jos L. Majors, Manuel Rodriguez, John
Hames, and Geo. W. Sirrine; approved by gov. on 24th on petition of citizens. They were to act as advisers to Blackburn. *Sta Cruz Arch.*, MS., 108;
Unb. Doc., MS., 340. April 28th, petition of J. W. Powell and 26 others
for the removal of Blackburn and appointment of James G. T. Dunleavy in
his place; also counter-petition of 134 citizens in Blackburn's favor. *Unb.
Doc.*, MS., 7–9, 23. March 20th, council decides that the beach is the best
and only suitable site for the town. *Sta Cruz Arch.*, MS., 108. Oct., alcalde
of Mont. complains that Alcalde Anderson refuses to obey his summons to
appear in a suit; and is instructed by the gov. that A. is subject to him and
must obey. *Cal. & N. Mex.*, 1850, p. 675.

CHAPTER XXIV.

LOCAL ANNALS OF THE NORTH.

1846–1848.

IN local annals of 1846–8, as already explained, no estimates of population have been given, since no reliable foundation for such estimates exists in contemporary records for most of the settlements. In the aggregate there was a small gain in the Hispano-Californian population, which was slightly less in 1845 and slightly more in 1848 than 7,000 souls. The number of foreigners has been given elsewhere as approximately a little less than 7,000. Probably a total of 14,000, or 7,500 and 6,500 for the two classes, would be as accurate an estimate as it is possible to make of the population in the middle of 1848. There were still from 3,000 to 4,000 ex-neophyte Indians leading a somewhat civilized life at or near the towns and ranchos, with perhaps nearly twice as many scattered among the gentiles. Estimates of the period have but slight value, but agree well enough with these figures in a general way.

San Francisco in 1846–8 was in some respects the most thriving town in California, its future greatness as commercial metropolis of the coast being clearly foreseen even before the discovery of gold—an event destined to give the bay settlement an immediate development not dreamed of by the most enthusiastic citizen. In view of this latter growth, even the most petty local affairs assume an additional interest and importance; and fortunately, besides the ordinary sources of information, we have two local newspapers from which to draw material. Thus the aggregate of items is much more bulky here than elsewhere; but they are best presented, as in chapters devoted to other towns, in the form of a classified note. It is well to add here that in the *Annals* and the work of John S. Hittell we have two very satisfactory records already before the public, much more complete for this than for earlier periods of San Francisco history. I refer the reader also to the end of this chapter, where by means of a plan and accompanying notes I have attempted to give a clear idea of the town's development before the discovery of gold.[1]

[1] Summary of S. F. events, 1846. Jan., Frémont's visit on the way from N. Helvetia to Monterey. This vol., p. 3. Feb. 7th, Vice-consul Forbes thanks the receptor for having attended the funeral of the 'British subjects interred yesterday.' *Pinto, Doc.*, MS., ii. 221–2. March 16th, Sub-prefect Guerrero to receptor, asking the loan of a Mex. flag, as he has to enter town with an armed force to publish a commun. from the prefect. *Id.*, 229. End of March, Lieut Talbot at Y. B. to obtain supplies for Frémont. This vol., p. 22. April, visit of Gillespie on his way from Mont. to overtake Frémont. *Id.*, 28. May, Benito Diaz chosen delegate for the consejo general at Sta B. *Id.*, 45. June 7th, Gillespie's 2d visit to get supplies for Frémont. *Id.*, 102, 126. June 15th, news of the capture of Sonoma by the Bears; steps taken by Capt. Montgomery of the *Portsmouth*. *Id.*, 129–32. July 1st, 2d, visit of Frémont, Semple, and the Bears; spiking the guns at the presidio; capture of Ridley. *Id.*, 136, 177–8. July 9th, Montgomery takes possession for the U. S. *Id.*, 238–41. July 11th, arrival of the British *Juno*. *Id.*, 240. July 31st, arrival of the *Brooklyn* with Brannan's Mormon colony. *Id.*, 550–1. Aug.–Oct., local happenings, including a grand ball on Sept. 8th, an election on the 18th, a grand reception to Com. Stockton on Oct. 5th, and the commodore's departure on the 13th. *Id.*, 295–6. Nov., loss of the *Warren's* launch. *Id.*, 384. Dec., capture of Alcalde Bartlett by Sanchez, and the resulting Sta Clara campaign in Jan. *Id.*, 379 et seq. A Christmas celebration mentioned in the *Sac. Union*, Jan. 1, 1873.

Events of 1847. Jan. 9th, publication of the 1st newspaper, the *California Star*. Jan. 16th, first news of the Donner party's peril. More definite news came in Feb.–March, and much space was given to the subject in the

In the first half of 1846 San Francisco took locally
but slight part in the political and military movements that were agitating the territory; yet it was
here that Frémont, having already captured the unoccupied San Rafael and shot three inoffensive Californians, accomplished the crowning achievement of
his campaign by spiking the presidio guns and capturing that valiant Mexican chief Robert Ridley. Then
the United States flag was raised in July, and in the
same month the Mormons came to double the town's
population. In December Alcalde Bartlett was captured while engaged in a raid on the Californians'
live-stock; and in January 1847 the first newspaper
appeared. At this time steps were taken officially to
prevent the permanent substitution of Yerba Buena
for the town's original name. A chief motive was

columns of the *Star* until June. See also this vol., p. 539. Jan. 23d, Alcalde
Bartlett issued the following order: 'Whereas the local name of Yerba Buena,
as applied to the settlement or town of San Francisco, is unknown beyond
the immediate district, and has been applied from the local name of the cove
on which the town is built—therefore, to prevent confusion and mistakes in
public documents, and that the town may have the advantage of the name
given on the published maps, it is hereby ordered that the name of San Francisco shall hereafter be used in all official communications and public documents or records appertaining to the town.' Published in the *Star*, Jan. 30th.
Both the order and the reasons given for it were proper and timely. Yet, as
has been often pointed out, one phase of the leading motive was not mentioned
in the order; namely, that Francisca, the rival town on the Strait of Carquines,
was likely to gain a decided advantage in the outer world by the resemblance
of its name to San Francisco. Gen. Sherman, *Mem.*, i. 55–6, and in an oft-
repeated newspaper interview, has something to say on the subject. There
was and has been ever since much opposition to the so-called change on the
part of the numerous class who date the history of the state and city back
only to the coming of American immigrants. The publishers of the *Star*,
though bitterly hostile to Semple and Benicia, kept the name Yerba Buena
at the head of its columns for a time, submitting to the inevitable under protest in the issue of March 20th. From Jan.–Feb., three lawyers, Jones, Pickett, and Hastings, advertise in the *Star*, and in Feb. the first auction sale of
goods is advertised by Dickson and Hay. Feb., visit of Gen. Kearny, who
meets Mason and Watson. This vol., p. 436. March, meeting to protest
against the lack of representation for the immigrant element in the proposed
governor's council; Dunleavy nominated. *Star*. March 6th, arrival of the
Perkins with part of N. Y. volunteers; arrival of the rest of the regiment
March 19th and 26th on the *Drew* and *Loo Choo*. This vol., p. 513. April
17th, arrival of the *Brutus;* semi-monthly mail for S. Diego. *Star*. May
22d, the *Californian* first appears at S. F., being transferred from Monterey. May 29th, a grand illumination in honor of Gen. Taylor's victory in
Mexico. *Star*. June 8th, fire in the bush back of town, causing some alarm.
Star of 12th. June 14th, public meeting to protest against Frémont as gov.
This vol., p. 455. July 4th, grand celebration, decoration of men-of-war,

doubtless fear of rivalry on the part of Francisca at the strait of Carquines; but the action was most opportune. It has been generally but inaccurately regarded and deplored as a change of name; but Yerba Buena was but a comparatively modern designation for a part of San Francisco; and to have taken from the great founder of the Franciscan order the honor of naming California's great city would have been a most unfortunate piece of barbarism. So far as events are concerned, there is nothing in the later annals of 1847–8 that requires further notice than is given in the note. Descriptive and statistical statements by visitors and residents appearing from time to time in books, manuscript reminiscences, and especially in the *Star* and *Californian*, have considerable interest, a prominent element being that of enthusi-

salutes from guns on ship and shore, meeting at Brown's Hotel, oration by Dr Semple. The Y. B. M. R. C., Scherrebach, orderly sergt, had called a meeting in advance to make arrangements. *Star* and *Californian* of the 10th. July, anniversary of raising U. S. flag in Cal. celebrated in a supper given by Alcalde Hyde at Sherreback's house. *Californian*, July 10th. Aug. 14th, the *Star* notes a ball at Brown's a few days before. Sept., visit of Gov. Mason, with Maj. Rich and Lieut Sherman, entertained by a ball. This vol., p. 584. Sept., breaking up of the Mormon establishment, or dissolution of the firm of Brannan & Co.; commissioners appointed to settle the business; and from this time advertisements appear of property for sale at S. F. and elsewhere, including the set of Harper's Family Library presented to the colony on leaving N. Y. *Star*, Oct. et seq. Oct., arrival of the 1st steamer for Leidesdorff. This vol., p. 575–81. Oct. 20th, a fierce norther, beaching several craft. *Star*. Nov., murder of Dörnte by Beverley at Denike's bakery. *Star*, 20th. Rainy season set in before the 3d. *Californian*. Nov. 18th, first thanksgiving dinner of New Englanders at Brown's Hotel, presided by Admiral C. W. Wooster, ending with a ball. Besides the records in the two newspapers, E. C. Kemble wrote his recollections of the affair 20 years later. *S. F. Bulletin*, Dec. 23, 1868. Dec. 4th, call for first meeting of Odd Fellows at the Portsmouth House; regular meetings later. *Star*. Jan. 1, 1848, the sloop *Stockton*, Briggs, was advertised for regular tri-weekly trips to Sonoma. March, discovery of gold first announced. May, capsizing of Capt. Richardson's boat, drowning 5 persons; the gold fever raging in town.

Descriptions, statistics, etc. (See plan and notes at end of this chapter.) Yerba Buena is mentioned naturally by many visitors, both in print and MS., but the descriptions and figures given are, as a rule, vague, inaccurate, and of no real value. The general purport is that in 1846 the place had from 25 to 50 buildings, mostly shanties, and a population of from 100 to 200; but that in 1847–8 it had greatly increased in size and in activity. Most mentions are not worth analysis here, though the reproduction of them all en masse, did space permit, would have some interest. Wm H. Davis furnished the *S. F. Call* of March 11, 1877, a list of about 50 persons residing at Yerba Buena in July 1846, representing a population of 150, with 23 buildings. The *Star* of Jan. 30, 1847, gives a slight description of the town and its surround-

astic predictions respecting the town's future greatness. A careful statement by Gilbert in August
1847 makes the population 459; number of buildings
157, of which half had been erected in the last four
months; places of business 41. Before the gold-fever
began to rage in May 1848, the number of inhabitants had probably increased to about 900 and that
of buildings to 200. Many of these are shown on a

ings, giving Y. B. a pop. of about 500, a gain of 300 in two years; it 'is rapidly improving, and bids fair to rival in rapidity of progress the most thriving
town or city on the American continent. It is no doubt destined to be the
Liverpool or New York of the Pacific.' Again, in the issue of March 13th,
the *Star* indulges in enthusiastic prophecies. If labor and lumber can be obtained, from 300 to 500 houses will go up within a year. There are many
similar articles in both papers. Lieut Wise in March, *Los Gringos*, 70-1,
found the population 'composed of Mormons, backwoodsmen, and a few very
respectable traders from the U. S. Very rare it was to see a native.' Frisbie, *Remin.*, MS., 30, Murray, *Narr.*, MS., 56-9, and others of the N. Y. vol.
have something to say of the town as they found it in March. Fifty houses
built in the last month, according to the *Star* of April 17th. James C. Ward's
Diary contains many items on local affairs from April. Hyde, *Hist. Facts*,
MS., 14-15, thinks that by June there were 600 inhab. The *Star* of Aug.
28th and Sept. 4th contains some comparatively careful statistics, which have
often been republished, as follows: pop. in June, of whites, exclusive of the
N. Y. volunteers, 375, or 247 males and 128 females, Ind. 34, Sandwich Isl.
40, negroes 10, total 459. Of the whites, 228 were born in the U. S., 38 in
Cal., 27 in Germany, 22 in England, 14 in Ireland, 14 in Scotland, 6 in Switzerland, 5 in Canada, and 21 in various countries. Increase during the past
year about 100 per cent. Over four fifths under 40 years of age; 273 can
read and write. The white males include 10 professional men, farmers 12,
traders 16, clerks 13, navigators 7, laborers 20, hotel-keepers 3, 26 carpenters,
and 62 other mechanics. Places of business number 1 apothecary shop, 3
bakeries, 2 blacksmith shops, 3 butcher shops, 1 cabinet-maker shop, 2 carpenter shops, 1 cigar-maker's shop, 2 cooper shops, 7 grocery stores, 1 gunsmith's shop, 2 hotels, 2 mills (horse and wind), 2 printing-offices, 1 shoe shop,
8 stores, 2 tailor shops, 1 watchmaker's shop, total 41. On April 1st there
were 31 frame buildings, 26 adobes, and 22 shanties, or 79 buildings; at the
end of August there had been added 47 frames, 11 adobes, and 20 shanties,
total 79; grand total, 157 buildings. (See end of this chapter.) The writer,
'E. G.' (Edward Gilbert), 'cannot suppress a desire to say that S. F. is destined
to become the great commercial emporium of the north Pacific coast,' notwithstanding the claims of Monterey and Benicia. Sherman, *Mem.*, i. 32–4,
whose visit was in Sept., has much to say of the town, its lots, and its prospects. In the *Californian* of Dec. 3d appeared a dream on the future greatness of S. F., signed 'Niña,' and said to have been written by Mrs Larkin.
It was reproduced in the *Alta* of Sept. 14, 1851, and in other papers. About
the end of 1847, the pop., according to a school census, was 473 men, 177 women, and 60 school children, or 710 in all, with enough more to raise the total
to over 800. In the *Alta* of Feb. 17, 1867, A. D. Piper gives many interesting items about S. F. in 1847, as utilized elsewhere. See also *Parker's S. F.
Directory*, 1852-3; *Colville's S. F. Directory*, 1856; *Ryan's Judges and Criminals;* besides the *Annals of S. F.;* and *Hittell's Hist. S. F.* The *Star* of
March 18th gives the pop. by school census as 812, besides children too young
for school. According to *Ward's Diary*, in March 1848 the town was 3 times
as large as in March 1847, having about 600 pop. The pop. at this time, at

plan at the end of this chapter.   Until the coming of
the Americans in July 1846, Francisco Guerrero continued to serve as sub-prefect, and Jesus Noé was the
juez de paz.   Under the military rule of the United
States, Washington A. Bartlett was alcalde from
August to February 1847; Edwin Bryant from that
time till May; George Hyde from June, aided—or
embarrassed, as he viewed it—by a council of six—
Glover, Howard, Leidesdorff, Jones, Parker, and

the news of the gold discovery, according to the *Annals*, 200, was about 850,
with 200 buildings.   The *Californian* of April 26th gives 192 buildings and
1,000 inhabitants.
     List of municipal officers.   1846.   Sub-prefect, Francisco Guerrero until
July; Francisco de Haro sometimes acting temporarily.   A secretary asked
for in Jan., but no appointment given.   Jueces de paz, appointed in Dec.
1845 for this year by prefect at nomination of the sub-prefect, Jesus Noé and
José de la Cruz Sanchez, suplentes Vicente Miramontes and Robert Ridley.
Ridley was suspended early in April by the sub-prefect, on complaint of Noé,
and also on account of R.'s quarrels with Leidesdorff, the two having a fight
in Guerrero's presence. *Castro, Doc.*, MS., ii. 60.   The others held office till
July.   John C. Davis treasurer, Francisco Ramirez collector; jueces de campo,
Candelario Valencia, José M. Flores, Rodolfo Miramontes, and Leandro Galindo, all appointed Jan. 4th by a junta of the jueces and suplentes. *Castro,
Doc.*, MS., i. 246.   From the occupation by the U. S. on July 9th, there
were no civil authorities until Aug. 26th, when Lieut Washington A. Bartlett was appointed alcalde of the district.   On Sept. 15th the following were
elected: alcaldes Bartlett and Jesus Noé, treasurer John Rose, collector Peter
T. Sherreback.   See this vol., p. 295.   Noé seems not to have accepted the
office, for from the date of Bartlett's capture by Sanchez in Dec., probably
by appointment of Capt. Hull on Dec. 10th, George Hyde acted as alcalde.
     1847.   Alcalde Washington A. Bartlett (Geo. Hyde acting until B.'s re-
turn about Jan. 10th), with J. G. T. Dunleavy as municipal clerk.   Feb. 22d,
Edwin Bryant was appointed alcalde by Gen. Kearny, and took possession
the same day, Bartlett returning to his naval duties.   John C. Buchanan was
Bryant's clerk.   There is no mention of a 2d alcalde.   Sherreback still continued to serve as collector, and presumably Rose as treasurer, though I find
no record.   E. Ward Pell acted as sheriff, in March–April at least..   May 2d,
Bryant offered his resignation, and May 28th Gov. Kearny appointed George
Hyde to succeed him.   Hyde assumed the office on June 1st.   Frank Ward
was acting alcalde during Hyde's absence in June, by temporary appointment
of Major Hardie.   Jasper O'Farrell was appointed surveyor by the gov. on
July 6th at request of Leidesdorff and others, dated June 28th.   Council, or
ayuntamiento, appointed by Hyde on July 28th; W. A. Leidesdorff, R. A.
Parker, J. P. Thompson, P. T. Sherreback, J. Rose, and B. R. Buckelew.
Council elected on Sept. 13th, Wm Glover, W. D. M. Howard, Wm A.
Leidesdorff, E. P. Jones, Robert A. Parker, and Wm S. Clark.   Wm Pettet
was secretary of the council, having been the alcalde's sec. before, until Sept.
27th, when E. P. Jones succeeded him, being succeeded by W. F. Swasey on
Oct. 4th.   Leidesdorff was made treasurer.   Oct. 2d, gov. appointed T. M.
Leavenworth 2d alcalde.   Oct. 11th the council appointed Henry Smith and
W. S. Thorp constables, Smith being also jail-keeper; but on Dec. 17th Thomas
Kittleman was appointed constable in place of the above.
     1848.   Alcaldes Hyde and Leavenworth to the end of March.   By gov-
ernor's appointment of March 27th, John Townsend became 1st alcalde from

Clark—from September until March 1848; John Townsend from April to August; and T. M. Leavenworth from September to the end of the year and later. The administration of municipal affairs in 1847–8 was attended by continuous and bitter controversy, a prominent element of which was connected with charges against Alcalde Hyde preferred by citizens and members of the council. The merits of the quarrel are somewhat obscure, and the whole matter is too complicated for discussion here, even if I were

April 1st, Leavenworth still holding his place. Council as before, with E. C. Kemble as secretary from April 10th. From June, Leavenworth, in Townsend's absence, was acting 1st alcalde. Chas V. Gillespie notary public from July 29th. Aug. 29th, T. M. Leavenworth chosen 1st alcalde; the election was declared null, but at a new election on Oct. 3d Leavenworth was reëlected. At the same time B. R. Buckelew and Barton Mowry were chosen members of the council in place of Glover and Leidesdorff.

Municipal government and controversies. 1846. Jan. 4th, sub-prefect to prefect, complains of lack of an office and a secretary; of the quarrels between Forbes, Leidesdorff, Ridley, and Hinckley, whom he has tried in vain to reconcile; with troubles with deserting sailors, whom the U. S. vice-consul will not permit to be confined. *Castro, Doc.*, MS., i. 251. Feb. 16th, same to same, has many prisoners from all parts of the partido, and the juez moves slowly; wants a lot to build a house on the water side of the plaza, to be used perhaps as a casa municipal. *Id.*, ii. 14. March 12th, is unable to borrow from the merchants the little money needed to buy ammunition for the force about to march against a foreign foe. *Pinto, Doc.*, MS., ii. 227. C. E. Pickett, *Paris Expos.*, 13, claims to have declined the alcaldeship. Ryan, *Judges and Crim.*, 61, relates that at the 1st election a reckless fellow, Joe Downey, clerk of election, managed by fraudulent tampering with the ballots to get himself elected alcalde, but was arrested and carried drunk on board the *Portsmouth*.

1847. Jan., C. E. Pickett, or ‘Yerba Buena,’ in the *Star* accused Alcalde Bartlett, the ‘vaquero general,’ of misappropriating town funds, failing to have a survey made, etc., besides criticising the acting alcalde, Hyde, for such offences as smoking in court. Thereupon Bartlett called on Capt. Hull for an investigation, which was made by Howard, Leidesdorff, and Guerrero as a committee, who completely exonerated the alcalde from having mismanaged any part of the municipal receipts, amounting to $747. *Star*, Jan. 9–30, 1847. Jan. 30th, discharge of fire-arms prohibited in town. Feb. 17th, Com. Hull announces the restoration of civil authority. March, complaint of no post-office. April, gov. decides that the munic. auth. should provide an office for the alcalde outside the building occupied by the military. May, Hyde's appointment provoked much opposition. A public meeting was called, by a notice reading: ‘The people's voice stifled by intrigue. People of S. F., rally for your rights! A majority has petitioned the gov. to appoint John Townsend...Geo. Hyde is appointed! Will you submit to this? The proclam. of Stockton gives you the right of electing alcaldes...Assemble at Brown's Hotel this evening (May 30th), and assert your rights.’ In Feb. there had been an altercation at a public meeting between Hyde and Dunleavy on one side and Jones and Brannan on the other. Leidesdorff informed the gov. that the opposition to Hyde came from the friends of Cal. independence from the U. S., supported by the Mormons. Maj. Hardie attended the meeting of the 30th, and refused to permit an election. *Unb. Doc.*, MS., 68,

disposed to take sides with either party. It is clear enough that personal enmities, business cliques, and newspaper rivalries were leading factors in the controversies; that the Mormon influence played no other part than that of bugbear among the foes of that sect; and that there was a strong feeling in favor of election and against military appointment that would have rendered almost any appointed alcalde unpopular. Yet so much smoke is generally indica-

109-10. In June Hyde left town for Monterey, and his absence was pronounced 'culpable negligence,' etc., by the *Star* of the 26th. Major Hardie reported that on account of the prevalent disorders he had appointed Ward to act as alcalde. *Unb. Doc.*, MS., 119. Hyde, however, declared to the gov. that the Mormons abused him because he sought to check their influence. *Id.*, 105. On July 15th the gov., just after H.'s visit, had written an order for the election of a council, but was called away and completed the letter on Aug. 15th, after the appointment of the 1st council. He authorized the alcalde to hold an election, or not, as he deemed best. *Cal. & N. Mex. 1850*, p. 378-9. The appointment of July 28th is recorded in the *Californian* of the 31st. J. P. Thompson was sec. The alcalde at a meeting said he had proposed the council to the gov., who had not objected. At the election of Sept. 13th 200 votes were cast; the judges were Vioget, Leavenworth, and Robert Gordon; the clerks W. F. Swasey and W. Hood. The unsuccessful candidates for councilmen were Everhart, J. S. Lincoln, C. L. Ross, Stephen Harris, B. S. Lippincott, Wm Pettet, John Sirrine, E. H. Harrison. *Id.*, Sept. 15th. A notice of the election had been published in the papers, both of which approved the measure, and later the men chosen. At the first meeting, on Sept. 16th, Howard, Jones, and Clark were appointed a committee to frame a code of laws. At the next meeting, on the 21st, the code was reported and adopted; then came trouble. Dr Jones moved to appoint a com. of 5 citizens to investigate the affairs of the alcalde's office, an alteration of the records, 'an enormous outrage,' having been charged in the *Star* of Aug. 21st, and there being other charges; but Hyde protested warmly, and after a wordy altercation the meeting was adjourned without the appointment of the committee. An incorrect report was furnished the papers, both of which disapproved Hyde's action, though the *Californian* of Sept. 29th published a defensive letter, in which H. denied having prevented a full investigation. At the meeting of the 24th the matter was taken up, and the council made itself a com. of investigation against the vote of Jones and Glover. The citizens also, through Ward, Brannan, and Ross, sent charges to the gov., with a petition for H.'s removal; and Mason on Oct. 1st ordered the council to make an investigation. *Cal. & N. Mex. 1850*, p. 361-2. There is no record of progress in the investigation during the rest of the year; but the *Star* continued to make charges, and the *Californian*, while disposed to criticise the council for inaction, to publish Hyde's letters, which finally brought out in the *Star* of Oct. 30th a collection of letters from Brannan, Folsom, Pickett, and Ross. Clearly there was a bitter quarrel, but as to its merits we are left for the most part in darkness.

1848. In Jan.-Feb. there are but slight indications of the continuance of the controversy, and none at all of the investigation supposed to be in progress. The two papers continued to snarl at each other, the *Californian* criticising the council, which was mildly defended by the *Star*. Hyde found it necessary to deny his alleged ownership in the former paper. Charges were made against Leidesdorff, the treasurer, provoking several letters and edito-

tive of more or less fire, and in view of the character
of some of the accusers and the earnestness of their
doubtless exaggerated statements of prevalent lawlessness, it is perhaps necessary to conclude that
Hyde was not altogether a model alcalde. Much
opposition was also developed against Leavenworth,
though it did not produce definite results until after
the end of the period now under consideration.

rials, and a resolution for investigation in the council. Early in March, 4 of
the 6 councilmen sent an undated request to the gov. to remove Hyde, implying that the charges against him had been substantiated; but the gov. required something more definite. March 9th, Hyde to gov., declaring the
charges slanderous and fully refuted; but the council are not gentlemen
enough to retract the accusations. There is a bitter feeling against him on
the part of certain men; Leidesdorff, formerly his friend, has turned against
him; he is disgusted with his thankless position, and wishes to come to Monterey and resign. Similar request on the 11th. *Unb. Doc.*, MS., 41–2, 27–8.
March 10th, prominent citizens, including Fourgeaud, Jones, J. C. Ward,
Brannan, Howard, W. H. Davis, E. H. Harrison, Leidesdorff, C. L. Ross, G.
W. Whittock, Henry Mellus, etc., petition the gov. for the removal of Hyde
and Leavenworth, and the appointment of Townsend and Buchanan. They
represent the town as in a disgraceful state of disorder; bloody street-fights
of almost daily occurrence; the alcalde defied, publicly insulted on the bench,
not daring to endanger his personal safety, and moreover, the open associate
of the worst characters. Another petition of the same date supports Townsend's claims. Same date, Leidesdorff, in a private letter to the gov., explains
that the accumulation of testimony has changed his opinion of Hyde, who is
responsible for all the lawlessness, prevents the council from effecting reforms,
is suspected of being the author of scurrilous articles in the *Californian*, and,
like the professional gamblers McDougall and Lippincott, is the writer's personal foe on account of his efforts to suppress gambling. *Unb. Doc.*, MS., 29–
32. March 18th, Jones and Leidesdorff of the council to gov., declaring that
Hyde prevented the progress of the investigation by legal quibbles and long
cross-examination of witnesses on matters foreign to the case, continued for
2 months, until the patience of the investigators was exhausted, the accusers
withdrew from the prosecution in disgust, and the witnesses went home; yet
2 of the charges were fully sustained by the evidence and were admitted by
the accused, viz.: 1st, changing numbers on the town map; 2d, granting lots
to later applicants, ignoring the rights of earlier ones. Of the council, Glover
and Howard, through sickness and absence, have not been present at meetings; Parker thinks he has said enough in the earlier report, and Clark declines to unite with J. and L.; therefore, only these two sign, and they ask
the gov. to treat the report as a 'private communication'! *Id.*, 39–40; *Calif.*,
Apr. 5th. March 19th, 20th, Hyde to gov., complaining that, despite his
efforts to have the investigation completed, nothing has been done for months;
the council has acted most unjustly by waiting so long before recommending
his removal; they are influenced solely by personal enmity; but he tenders
his resignation as he has done before, and recommends that the alcalde in
future have nothing to do with the council, which should choose its own president. March 20th, Clark to gov., dissenting from the views of the 4 councilmen against Hyde, as not supported by evidence. *Unb. Doc.*, MS., 171–3,
80–1. The *Star* of the 25th has an editorial against Hyde, who had gone to
Monterey to influence the gov. in his own behalf. The *Calif.* of the 22d had
an editorial against the proceedings of the council, also noting H.'s departure
to consult the gov. Also on the 25th, the gov. replied to Leidesdorff and

Town lots to the number of about 1,200 were granted or sold for the benefit of the municipal treasury during the three years; at first for purposes of actual settlement, under condition of fencing and building; later without conditions, though still at nominal prices of $12 and $25 each for lots of 50 and 100 varas; and finally at auction, the purchasers, especially of beach and water lots, being for the most part speculators who paid in some instances as high

Jones, declining to treat their commun. as 'private,' or to remove Hyde, as no proper investigation had been held and no details of testimony had been furnished. This corresp. was published in the *Californian* of April 5th, with an editorial favorable to Hyde. But as we have seen, on March 27th Hyde's resignation was accepted and Townsend was appointed. In his *Hist. Facts*, MS., 16–26, Hyde, in reply to the statements of Jones and Leidesdorff, and to that of the *Annals of S. F.*, 201, that 'some 9 or 10 charges of a criminal nature were made, only two of which were established by proof,' denies positively that these two charges were substantiated, or that they were ever admitted by himself; and he gives copies of letters from W. D. M. Howard, R. A. Parker, and W. S. Clark of the council, written in 1855 in reply to his own letters, and confirming his statement that he was completely exonerated from the 2d charge, while the 1st one was not 'established by proof.' In June–Aug., Alcalde Townsend went to the mines, and the citizens sent petitions to have Ed. Gilbert, and later J. D. Hoppe, appointed 1st alcalde. The gov. declined to make an appointment, but on Aug. 7th directed the 2d alcalde to hold an election, at which on Aug. 29th Leavenworth was elected by 99 votes against 76 for Hoppe. K. H. Dimmick, Wm Evans, and John S. Norris were the judges. On the same day Howard, W. H. Davis, Jones, and 40 others protested to gov. against the election as illegal, and the gov. on Sept. 4th sustained their view, on the grounds that sufficient notice had not been given; that the franchise had been limited to the town, whereas it extended to the district; and that Mexicans and other classes of residents had been denied the right to vote. He ordered a new election, with at least 3 weeks' notice, and named Howard, Gillespie, Dimmick, Clark, and J. C. Ward as judges. *Unb. Doc.*, MS., 73–4, 19, 78–80; *Cal. & N. Mex. 1850*, p. 568, 593, 661–2. Sept. 8th, 29 citizens ask for an election for 2 councilmen. *Unb. Doc.*, MS., 158. Sept. 16th, gov. orders the election of councilmen to take place on the same day as that for alcalde, Oct. 3d. *Cal. & N. Mex. 1850*, p. 667. Sept. 22d, Leavenworth to gov., has advised his friends to give Hyde, Ross, etc., 'ample rope to hang themselves with.' Their assertions will be proved false. *Unb. Doc.*, 36. Of the 2d election, at which Leavenworth was reëlected, I have no other record than that in the *Annals of S. F.*, 206, where it is stated that 158 votes only were cast. There seems to have been no further serious controversy before the end of the year, though trouble was brewing for 1849.

Pueblo lands. Beyond the fact that the alcaldes continued to grant lots, there was nothing in developments of 1846–8 which had any special bearing on the town's claim to 4 leagues of land, or the great question of later litigation. *Wheeler's Land Titles in S. F.* contains, besides an excellent résumé of land annals down to the date of publication in 1852, lists of about 1,200 lots granted to private owners in 1846–8, dates, lots, grantees, and grantors being specified. 1846. There had been 61 lots granted previously at Yerba Buena, and 18 were granted before July 9th, making 79 at the end of Mex. rule; while in July–Dec. there were 39, or a total of 116 at the end of 1846. These grants were made according to the Vioget survey of 1839, and with the con-as $600. During the earliest phases of the 'flush times' before the end of 1848 some of the lots on favorite corners changed hands for $10,000; and 40 years later many then not deemed desirable are worth more than a million each; while four miles beyond the limits of O'Farrell's survey lots sell from $6,000

dition of fencing and building on the lots within a year. Oct. 8th, Larkin, Grimes, and Wm H. Davis petition Com. Stockton for land on the water side of Montgomery St. for a wharf. *Larkin's Doc.*, MS., iv. 303.

1847. Total no. of lots granted 762, of which 248 were water-lots obtained like many others for speculative purposes, being beyond the limits of actual improvements. Total no. at end of the year 878. Jan. 16th, the *Star* in an editorial advised the people that no title to beach and water lots could in any way be obtained; but argued that the lots ought to be sold for the benefit of the town, and hoped this would be rendered legally possible. At a public meeting in the plaza on Feb. 15th, enlivened by harsh words between Parson Dunleavy and Editor Jones, resolutions to the above effect were adopted. *Star*, Feb. 20th. Accordingly, Gov. Kearny, who probably had no authority to do anything of the kind, on March 10th proceeded to 'grant, convey, and release' to the town all the title of the U. S. in the beach and water lots between Fort Montgomery and the Rincon, except lots to be selected by army and navy officers for government use, the lots to be sold at auction for the benefit of the town. *Cal. & N. Mex. 1850*, p. 291, often repeated elsewhere. Halleck, *Report*, 123–4, regarded this as an order for the selection of lands needed by the govt, and a release of U. S. title to the rest, if the lots were within the limits of the town—not as a land grant by a territorial governor. March 16th, Alcalde Bryant announced the sale for June 29th, and Jasper O'Farrell was employed to make a survey for the purpose; terms one fourth cash, and one fourth in 6, 12, and 18 months, with interest at 10 per cent. *Vallejo, Doc.*, MS., xii. 282; *S. F. Cal. Star*, March 20th and following nos. Feb. 1st, W. S. Clark applied to the gov. for a confirmation of his title to the lot on Broadway and Battery, where he was to build a wharf; but the gov. said he had given up all authority in the matter, though recommending the grant to the local authorities. *Cal. & N. Mex. 1850*, p. 297–8. Similar reply to Wm Pettet. *Id.*, 301–2. Advertisement of sale in *Californian* from May 23d. June 21st, Gov. Mason decides, in the case of Buckelew, that any loss sustained by an owner by changes in the streets should be paid by the town, but that other (beach) land cannot be granted in compensation except by public auction. *Cal. & N. Mex. 1850*, p. 333. June 23d, gov. orders Maj. Hardie to select the lots needed by the govt for custom-house, wharves, etc., before the sale. *Id.*, 339–40. The Rincon site of the later marine hospital was also reserved under this order. By advertisement of July 10th the sale of beach-lots was postponed to July 20th. In the newspapers of July also holders of Mex. titles to lots, who had not complied with the conditions, were ordered to present their titles at the alcalde's office. The sale took place July 20th–23d, when nearly 250 lots, each 45 x 137½ feet, were sold. The beach-lots brought as high as $600, while water-lots sold from $50 to $400. The results announced in the *Calif.* and *Star* of July 25th. Hittell, *Hist. S. F.*, 114, says that all those between Clay and Sacramento streets were reserved for possible public uses, and sold 6 years later at an average of $12,000 each. Aug. 23d, Larkin says house-lots in S. F. have increased 500 per cent. *Off. Corresp.*, MS., ii. 120–1. Sept. 22d, charge from citizens that the records had been tampered with, some 20 grants having been erased for some informality. *Californian.* Something has been already said on this subject. Hyde, in his *Hist. Facts*, MS., admits that some errors of his predecessors were corrected on the map, though not by him; and Wheeler's lists show opposite many num-

to $10,000. In 1846, but for buildings and fences
vaguely outlining unnamed streets on a small area,
there were no public improvements; but in 1847 the
region extending some half a mile in different directions from the plaza was surveyed and mapped by
Jasper O'Farrell, street names being permanently
fixed. Gradually, as needed, a few streets were graded

bers such notes as 'erased, deed void, not taken out as required by law.   Geo.
Hyde.'   Meanwhile, O'Farrell's survey extending over land as well as water,
and far beyond the limits of Vioget's survey, lots were granted, about 500 in
number, at $12 each for 50-vara lots, and $28.62 for 100-vara lots, of which
few were granted.   Sept. 27th, council decides that hereafter lots shall not
be forfeited for failure to fence and build, all conditions being removed. *Star*,
Oct. 2d.   Sept 30th, gov. to alcalde, orders not to grant any more lots south
of Rincon Point and east of a certain line. *Cal. & N. Mex. 1850*, p. 361.
Oct. 11th, council ratifies the action of the alcalde in having granted more
than one lot to one person. *Star*, Oct. 16th; *Calif.*, Oct. 13th.   Oct. 28th,
council orders that hereafter all lots on land or water must be sold at auction.
Star, Oct. 23d.   Nov. 22d, C. E. Pickett, two citizens, and a soldier, petitioned the gov. to appoint a special court to settle land titles in S. F., a
scheme which Gov. Mason on Dec. 14th declared impracticable. *Cal. & N.
Mex. 1850*, p. 470.   1848.   Total no. of lots granted this year, 388, making
1,266 in all; 36 were of the beach and water lots, 300 of the 50-vara survey,
10 of the 100-vara survey (below Market St), 17 100-vara lots in the region of
the lagoon, 6 at North Beach, and 10 at Clark's Point.   Jan. 5th, advertisement of sale of the rest of the water-lots at auction on Feb. 1st; postponed to
1st Monday in March. *Star*, Jan 8th, Feb. 3d.   I find no record of the sale,
and the 36 lots appear on Wheeler's list as having been 'granted on petition'
to W. S. Clark and W. C. Parker on Sept. 9th and 25th.   In connection with
the plan at the end of this chapter, some additional items on the location of
the earlier grants may be found.
    Streets and public improvements.   See plan and notes at end of this chap-
ter.   The survey made by Vioget in 1839 has already been mentioned.   By
it lots were granted throughout 1846, but it gave no name to streets.   In Jan.
1846 Jacob R. Snyder obtained authority from the sub-prefect to survey
lands—chiefly outside of the town, perhaps—for the owners. *Doc. Hist. Cal.*,
MS., iii. 48.   But of the results in town, if there were any, nothing is known.
I have found no definite record of the naming of streets at first, but evidently
Montgomery, Kearny, Clay, Washington, Jackson, and some other leading
streets were named in 1846, after the raising of the U. S. flag in July.   In Oct.
Larkin and others petitioned the gov. for land on Montgomery St for a wharf,
but nothing was accomplished.   Except a general outlining of streets by fences
and buildings on a part of the lots, and the wooden bridge over the neck of
the lagoon, there were no street improvements before the end of 1846.   At
the end of the year or beginning of 1847 the necessity of a new survey was
agitated at a public meeting and in the *Star*, but there was a general disagreement about what to do and how to pay for it.   In Feb., however, a Yerba
Buena corresp. of the *Honolulu Friend*, v. 84, writes that a man was then engaged in surveying the place and laying out streets; also that there was a hope
of having a wharf in a few months.   This may have been O'Farrell, who was
perhaps already at work making a semi-official extension of the Vioget survey.
The result was probably a map signed by Alcalde Bartlett Feb. 22d, and preserved in the Sacramento State Library and S. F. hall of records, a photographic
copy of which is described in the *Alta* of Feb. 27, 1875.   It covers the tract
included between Vallejo, Powell, and Sutter streets.   Powell St has no

through sand hills to the water front. On one occasion it was resolved to open California Street from Kearny to the bay, at a cost of $150. The only other improvements were the filling-up of the lagoon at the corner of Jackson and Montgomery streets, and the construction of two wooden wharves at the foot of Clay and Broadway streets, respectively, representing at that period rival sections of the town.

name; Battery is Battery Place; Sansome is called Sloat; Pacific is Bartlett; Sacramento is Howard; there is no Pine St between Bush and California; and Dupont and Stockton are reversed, Dupont being farthest west. The lots and grantees seem not to agree in all cases with those indicated on the later survey. The lot at the s. E. cor. of Vallejo and Sansome is marked as the graveyard. The *Californian* of July 24th mentions this burial-place on Sansome and Broadway, calling attention to the necessity of selecting a new place. And according to the *Alta* of Feb. 4, 1851, Anderson of the N. Y. vol., who died in Sept., was buried far out of town in the North Beach region, this being the beginning of a new cemetery, which already in 1851 was in process of destruction. O'Farrell's regular survey of the town was begun probably in March, though perhaps virtually a continuation of earlier work as above, and completed in Aug., in connection with the sale of water-lots. It included three divisions, the beach and water lots between Clark's Point and the Rincon, the 100-vara survey south of Market St, and the 50-vara survey adjoining the original Yerba Buena. Says Hittell, O'Farrell's survey covered 'an area of about 800 acres. His map included the district bounded by the lines of Post, Leavenworth, and Francisco streets and the water front, and south of Market St it showed four full blocks fronting on Fourth St, and 11 full blocks fronting on Second St. There were besides a few fractional blocks. O'F. disliked many things in Vioget's little survey, but some he could not change. Kearny and Dupont streets were too narrow, but these could not be widened without an expense of several thousand dollars, which nobody wanted to incur. It was considered indispensable, however, that the acute and obtuse angles of V.'s lots should be corrected, and to do this a change of 2½ degrees was necessary in the direction of some of the streets. This transferred the situation of all the lots, and was subsequently called "O'Farrell's swing" of the city. For years, on account of the swing, buildings were to be seen at various places projecting a little beyond the general line of the street. The corner of Kearny and Washington streets was the pivot of the swing, and the main monument or starting-point was established there. The new map gave to the streets the names which they now have.' *Hist. S. F.*, 114–16. Lots granted before the end of 1846 were chiefly in the tract bounded by California, Stockton, and Broadway streets and the water front, 27 lots within this space remaining unsold; south of California only 7 lots had been sold, west of Powell 17, and north of Vallejo 13. In Sept. 1847 the council appointed a committee to consider the subject of building a wharf; and in Oct. the construction of two wharves was ordered, $10,000 being appropriated to that at the foot of Clay St, and $2,000 to that on Broadway, which was to be 10 x 150 feet. The Clay-St result was ridiculed in the *Californian* of Nov. 10th as a 'monument to the folly of the town,' fortunately not strong enough to last through the winter; but it was decided to extend the wharf to 49 x 547 feet, at a cost of $11,000, for which $1,000 was appropriated Nov. 27th. The Broadway structure 'took a start seaward' in Dec., but $2,000 more was appropriated, and the work went on slowly till suspended in Jan. 1848 for lack of funds; and in Feb. all wharf work was ordered to be stopped, except so far as material was on hand for the Clay-St structure. The last we hear of

A private school was opened by J. D. Marston in April 1847; after much agitation of educational projects by citizens and press a school-house on the plaza was completed in December; and finally a public school under Thomas Douglas as teacher was open

the wharves before the gold excitement is a record of various 'reports of progress,' not unmixed with protests, in April; for besides the usual 'jobs,' there was much rivalry between property owners of the 'old town' and those at Clark's Point. Meanwhile, the project of filling up the lagoon had been agitated since October, and work had been actually begun near the corner of Montgomery and Jackson in Jan., the widening of Montgomery St at that point being favorably considered. In Oct. O'Farrell was paid $300 on account for his labors as surveyor; and negotiations with him were opened to run the town boundary after the completion of the survey. In Nov. the council decided to open Broadway from Sansome to the bay, and California from Kearny to the bay, the appropriation being $150. The sum of $2,000, soon increased by $500, was appropriated in Jan. 1848 for general street improvements. In April Gerke took a contract to grade Pacific Street, and it was resolved in March to complete the work, citizens being allowed to work out their indebtedness to the town. In March there were also petitions for moving fences to correspond with the survey, and for opening Jackson St to Sansome; but only reports of progress in April appear as results.

Education. I find no record of any school in operation or even proposed in 1846, under either the Mexican or American rule. But the *Star* of Jan. 16, 1847, urged the importance of attending to educational interests, having counted 40 children in the streets who ought to be in school. A lot and $50 in money were editorially offered. In the next number, Jan. 23d, a subscription and a public meeting were proposed. A meeting was held and a committee of 5 appointed; but nothing more was accomplished, as appears from editorials in the same paper of Feb. 6th and March 6th. According to the *Annals*, 677, a private school was opened in April by Marston, a Mormon, as Fitzgerald, *Educ. in Cal.*, MS., 2, states, though there was no such Mormon in the *Brooklyn* colony; but I find no definite information about this school. In July and Aug. both *Star* and *Californian* continued to agitate the matter, and it was complained that the lot selected had been granted by the alcalde to private ownership. In June, however, Lieut Ed. Gilbert had taken a census showing 129 persons under 20 years, and 56 between 5 and 15 years. *Star*, Aug. 28th. At a council meeting of Sept. 24th, Leidesdorff, Glover, and Clark were appointed a com. on the building of a school-house. They reported progress on Oct. 4th, and were empowered to receive sealed bids, which were opened on the 11th, and that of Mr Stark accepted. Its completion was announced in the *Star* of Dec. 4th, though with a complaint of the council's lack of energy as likely to defer the opening of a school, and another that 'the nut-brown of red-wood lumber is not sufficiently fanciful for San Francisco,' and the appearance of the exterior should be improved. Also mention in the *Californian* of Dec. 29th. The *Annals*, 675, has a view of the structure. On Feb. 1, 1848, at a public meeting presided by E. H. Harrison, with E. C. Kemble as sec., Brannan, Ross, and Harrison were chosen as a committee to canvass the town for scholars, select a teacher, and suggest to the council the propriety of ordering an election of 5 school commissioners. *Star*, Jan. 29th, Feb. 5th. On Feb. 14th the council ordered an election for the 21st, when Fourgeaud, Ross, Townsend, John Sirrine, and Wm H. Davis were chosen as trustees. *Id.*, Feb. 19th, 26th. They advertised for a teacher on March 1st. *Id.*, March 4th. The council on the 17th appropriated $400 for the payment of a teacher; and on April 1st the school was announced to begin on the 3d, under Thomas Douglas, a graduate of Yale; tuition $5 to $12

in April and May 1848. Besides the weekly meetings of the Mormons there was no regular religious
service at San Francisco until November 1848, when
Rev. T. D. Hunt, presbyterian, was employed as
town chaplain; but there had been occasional preaching by naval chaplains and others; and in May 1847
a sabbath school was organized through the agency
of Oregon methodists, with J. H. Merrill as superintendent. The *California Star*, San Francisco's
first newspaper, was published by Samuel Brannan,
with E. P. Jones and E. C. Kemble as successive

per quarter. The opening was as announced. *Id.*, March 18th, Apr. 1st, 8th.
On May 2d the council declared the trustees illegally chosen, and ordered a
new election on the 13th, when L. W. Hastings, Ross, Davis, Brannan, and
Fourgeaud were chosen. *Id.*, May 6th, 13th, 20th. Meanwhile the school
continued prosperously enough under the care of Douglas, until perhaps the
early part of June, when the gold excitement seems to have carried patrons,
trustees, and finally the teacher to the mines, and educational matters were
neglected until 1849, though in Nov. an advertisement for a teacher appeared
in the *Star and Californian*.

Church and religious affairs. In 1846, the priest at the mission remained
on duty until the raising of the U. S. flag; and subsequently priests from
abroad occasionally visited Dolores; but there was never any catholic service
at Yerba Buena. Brannan and other Mormon elders held religious services
at private houses every Sunday from the time of their arrival in July. There
is no record of any protestant service in 1846, though it is not impossible that
such service may have been performed on some occasion by a chaplain of the
naval force. On May 8, 1847, at a public meeting, Rev. T. M. Leavenworth
(episcopalian) urged the importance of a church, presenting a document for
the signatures of those interested; and a committee was named to carry the
matter further. *Star*, May 8th. It does not appear that anything was accomplished as a result of this effort. But on the 16th Rev. James H. Wilber
of the Oregon methodist mission, a passenger on the *Whiton*, organized a sabbath school, which was addressed by Leavenworth, included a promising
class of kanakas, was put in charge of J. H. Merrill as superintendent and
J. D. Marston as secretary, and was to meet every Sunday forenoon at the
alcalde's office. Rev. Wm Roberts, superintendent of the Oregon missions,
promised a library as soon as the books could be found in the hold of the
vessel. *Id.*, May 22d. In the same paper of July 24th preaching by Newell,
chaplain of the *Independence*, was announced for the next Sunday. Ward in
his *Diary*, in 1848, notes that 'Capt. L. H. Thomas, a most estimable Welsh
gentlemen, reads prayers every Sunday in the school-house, and Mrs C. V.
Gillespie has organized a Sunday-school, the first on the Pacific Coast.' In
October 1848 Rev. T. D. Hunt, presbyterian, arrived from the Sandwich Islands, and from Nov. 1st officiated at the school-house as chaplain of the
town, at a salary of $2,500. *Annals*, 688.

Newspapers. On the *Brooklyn*, in July, arrived the press, type, and general outfit of the *Prophet*, a Mormon paper that had been published in N. Y.
by Samuel Brannan, who doubtless intended to continue its publication as a
church organ in Cal. This became undesirable as soon as it was revealed
that Cal. was not to be the promised land of the Mormons; but the plan of
publishing a newspaper was not abandoned. It is said by Hittell, *Hist. S.
F.*, 109, that a sheet of printed matter describing Taylor's victory in Texas

editors from January 9, 1847, to June 10, 1848. The *Californian*, transferred from Monterey, was published and edited successively by Robert Semple, B. R. Buckelew, Robert Gordon, H. L. Sheldon, and other associates from May 22, 1847, with some gaps in May–August 1848, to November 11th. Then it was swallowed up by its former rival, and the *California Star and Californian* appeared from November 18th, to be known at the beginning of 1849 as the *Alta*

was issued in Oct. 1846, but I have not seen it. The first number of the *California Star* was issued on Jan. 9, 1847, Elbert P. Jones taking the position of editor, temporarily, as he announced, in the absence of the man who was to be permanent editor—presumably Kemble. The paper was of 4 pages, 8¼ x 12 inches of print, subscriptions $6 per year. A prospectus of the usual style was signed by Brannan as publisher. The *Star* was a very good local newspaper, its editorial and other departments showing no special ability or lack of it on the part of the managers, who as usual in such cases sometimes indulged in expressions more coarse and violent than good taste would justify. The paper was complimented for its neat appearance by its Monterey contemporary in Jan., but the compliment was not returned. On April 17th Jones withdrew from the editorship on account of 'circumstances' not explained, which prevented any connection between himself and the publisher; and Edward C. Kemble and John Eagar took charge until Brannan's return from the east, when Kemble became the regular editor. On Jan. 22, 1848, vol. ii. no. 3, the paper was enlarged to 10½ x 16¾ inches of print, taking—as an advertisement—three columns of Brandreth's pills. The issue of April 1st with a supplement was sent overland to the states to the number of 2,000. It was published regularly each week until June 10th, or vol. ii. no. 23; and its suspension on account of the gold excitement was announced in an extra sheet of June 14th. *The Californian*, as has been related elsewhere, was established at Monterey by Colton and Semple in 1846, with the material that had been used by the Californians since 1834. Its San Francisco existence began with no. 1 of vol. ii., on May 22, 1847, Robert Semple being publisher and editor, the size being 4 pages of 3 columns each about 16 inches long—subsequently increased to 4 columns on a page, or the same size of the enlarged *Star*—and the price of subscription being $5. From the issue of July 17th, vol. ii. no. 9, B. R. Buckelew succeeded Semple as proprietor and editor; from Aug. 28th, no. 15, the 'The' was dropped from the title, which became simply *Californian;* and from the issue of Sept. 8th, no. 17, the day of publication being changed from Saturday to Wednesday, Robert Gordon was named as editor. In Dec., Gordon seems to have been publisher as well, but early in 1848 Buckelew's name reappears. In April the editors were Buckelew and J. D. Hoppe; and in May Buckelew sold out to Hoppe, H. L. Sheldon, and perhaps Jos. Dockrill, Sheldon being the editor. On May 17th the 3d volume was begun, but on the 24th a fly-sheet had to be issued announcing temporary suspension on account of the impossibility of retaining workmen. This is the way the *Star* of June 3d puts it, 'Gone too —. The *Californian* ceased issue with an annunciatory "slip" on Tuesday last. Verdict of inquest—fever.' I have another slip of June 2d, containing two columns of news on treaty with Mexico, Frémont's trial, etc., two advertisements, and the following editorial: 'For the purpose of convincing what there is left of the "public" that the *Californian* is not extinct, nor yet altogether used up, we, in our triple character of editor, printer, and devil, have compiled, set up, worked off, and circulated this extra, which we hope will do our readers

California. Military and revenue affairs require no further mention than is given in my note and in other chapters of this volume. The same may be said of the few ranchos granted or pretended to have been granted in 1846, only one of them subsequently confirmed; and of the mission at Dolores, where there was no regular curate except for a time in 1846, and where no definite or formal disposition is known to have been made of the remnants of the ex-mission estate.

much good; for it would probably very much perplex his Satanic Majesty to tell at what precise period they will hear from us again.' A number was issued on July 15th, and another in Aug.; and the publication was regular from Sept. 2d, vol. iii. no. 5, to Nov. 11th, no. 15, Sheldon still being editor. Then Kemble returned from the mines, bought out the *Californian,* and from Nov. 18th published *The California Star and Californian,* which was in reality a continuation of the *Star,* beginning with vol. ii. no. 24, where that paper had stopped. Early in Jan. 1849, Ed. Gilbert having become associated with Kemble, the name was changed to *The Alta California,* which still appears regularly in 1886; and through all its changes the typographic peculiarities of the original *Star* heading have been preserved.

Military matters. Francisco Sanchez was nominally comandante at S. F. until the end of Mexican rule, though practically no military duties were performed by him or any other. After the U. S. flag was raised in July, Capt. John B. Montgomery of the navy, succeeded before the end of the year by Capt. Hull, was in command of the district; but Lieut H. B. Watson was put in command of the garrison, being succeeded late in the year by Capt. Ward Marston, and the latter in Feb. 1847 by Lieut Robert Tansill. The old custom-house was occupied by the military, and a battery of guns from the presidio had been established near the foot of Vallejo Street, called Fort Montgomery, and giving a name to Battery St. On Feb. 17th Hull and Tansill announced the end of military rule and the resumption of their functions by the civil authorities, and Tansill departed in April. Meanwhile, from the arrival of the N. Y. volunteers in March, companies H and K were stationed at the presidio as a garrison, and Major James A. Hardie was commandant of the post, Capt. J. L. Folsom being assistant quartermaster down to Aug. 1848, when the volunteers were mustered out, and apparently later as lieut of artillery, a small garrison of dragoons being stationed here. There are many communications of Hardie and Folsom to the gov., in which they complain of prevalent disorders at S. F.

Custom-house affairs. Rafael Pinto continued as receptor to the end of Mexican rule, Robert Ridley being captain of the port; Lieut W. A. Bartlett was put in charge of the revenues by Montgomery after the raising of the U. S. flag; and Wm A. Richardson was appointed by Stockton collector and captain of the port, to succeed Bartlett in Oct. A year later, in Oct. 1847, the collection of revenues devolved on the military officers by orders from Washington, and Capt. Folsom was put in charge from the 1st, holding the position until, on the news of peace with Mexico, Lieut Edward Gilbert having declined the place, Edward H. Harrison was appointed on Sept. 3d, at a salary of $2,000. See p. 567 et seq. of this vol. for revenue and commercial affairs.

Ranchos. *Mission estate granted in 1846 to Prudencio Santillan, title rejected by the U. S. courts as having been fraudulently antedated. J. R. Bolton was the chief claimant; also preëmption claim of *Francisco Rufino to a mission lot rejected. *Presidio lands, ½ league, 1846, granted to H. D.

A very good outline of local affairs in the San José region is given in Hall's history, which with supplemental items from the usual archive and other sources is represented and indexed in the appended note.[2]

Fitch, whose widow was claimant. His petition of May 13th for the land where he proposed to build a mill is given in *Dwinelle's Colon. Hist.*, add. 95–6. *Punta de Lobos, 2 l., 1846, Benito Diaz; J. C. Palmer et al., cl. This land extended from Pt Lobos to the laguna de Loma Alta. Larkin owned the claim which was submitted to the American authorities in Oct. 1846–June 1847, and was pronounced invalid in a report by Capt. Folsom. Documents in *Halleck's Report*, 173–9. San Mateo, 2 l., 1846, Cayetano Arenas; W. D. M. Howard, claimant.

Mission. Prudencio Santillan served as curate until July 1846, leaving his post on the coming of the Americans, and not returning to reside permanently until after 1848. Nothing whatever seems to have been done in consequence of the order of sale issued in 1845. Jan. 4, 1845, the sub-prefect forwarded to the prefect for the gov. a petition of residents that they be permitted to continue their residence in the ex-mission buildings in order that the majordomo might not remove the roofs, as he had done in the case of other abandoned dwellings. They also recalled an earlier order of Gov. Alvarado to establish a pueblo at Dolores; and as there are no Indians, and as there is no room for live-stock at Yerba Buena, they desire to form at Dolores 'a frontier (!) to the town at Y. B.,' which is being formed entirely of foreigners.' *Castro, Doc.*, MS., i. 248. This shows that there was still a majordomo—perhaps Vazquez, still?—as there was also in April, at $20 per month. April 20th, sub-prefect to prefect, says that P. Santillan wants two rooms for schools, and the majordomo should be ordered to give them up. His salary is a useless expense; he lives in the house and sells brandy, has no duties to perform, and his cattle are always about the church. There is an old order for granting lots, etc., but nothing can be done, for the majordomo pays no heed to the civil authorities. *Id.*, ii. 64. The grant of the mission estate to Padre Santillan in Feb. has no special interest in connection with the annals of this period, because his claim was not known until after 1848, and was, besides, shown to be fraudulent. Nor are there any events that call for mention. Sept. 18, 1847, Capt. Folsom was ordered to obtain the records existing at the mission and send them to the governor's office for safe-keeping. *Cal. & N. Mex. 1850*, p. 397. Feb. 5, 1848, gov. orders that P. Santillan be consulted about lands that may be put in his charge for the use of the Ind.; also about such movable property as may exist. *Id.*, 472. On Jan. 22d, Robert Ridley was made subaltern alcalde at the mission by Hyde, with authority from the gov. *Id.*, 452; *Star*, Jan. 15th.

[2] San José events. 1846. Visit of Frémont in Jan. This vol., p. 3. Feb., Frémont again at S. José and Fisher's rancho. *Id.*, 6–8. March, 78 citizens sign a petition for an Ind. expedition. *Dept. St. Pap.*, MS., vii. 47–8. April, local authorities indorse the declaration in favor of Paredes. This vol., p. 41. Delegates chosen for the Sta Bárbara consejo. *Id.*, 45. In March–May there was considerable popular excitement about Pierre Sainsevain's grist-mill, which he had established the year before by permission of the govt. Over 20 citizens—two of whom could write their names—petitioned for the removal of the dam represented as very prejudicial to the welfare of the town. There was a sharp correspondence, Sainsevain claiming that the movement was a device of some pícaros whom he had refused to trust, his mill being a public convenience. The prefect finally ordered the removal of all obstructions in the stream so far as demanded by public convenience and health, leaving the owner at liberty to sue for damages. Original corresp. in *Doc. Hist. Cal.*, MS., iii. 136–7, 207–8, 210, 214, 228, 498–9. June–July, operations of Gen. Castro at Sta Clara, in his efforts against Pico, the Bears, and the U. S. This

This was the centre of General Castro's military operations in the first half of 1846; but the change of flag was effected here as elsewhere without hostilities. The native element was more prominent than in other sections of the north, and as the valley was also a favorite rendezvous of the immigrants who looked down with contempt upon the whole Spanish race, it is not strange that there was some clashing and disorder, which, however, never assumed serious proportions. The Santa Clara campaign between Sanchez and Marston was the end of the war in the north. Indian horse-thieves were continuously troublesome to the rancheros, as they had ever been. Raids by and against them were of frequent occurrence; but the new authorities, like the old, seem to

vol., p. 51, 53, 105, 108–9, 132–3, 185, 261. Arrest of Weber and others. *Id.*, 136. July, raising the U. S. flag. *Id.*, 245–6. Local happenings Aug.– Oct., Watmough in command. *Id.*, 294–5. Bryant, whose visit was in Sept., describes S. José as a village of 600 or 800 inhab., in a fine valley, of adobe buildings and very irregular streets, with thousands of ground-squirrels burrowing in the plaza, and men and women of all classes engaged in gambling. *What I Saw*, 315–17. Dec.–Jan., 1847, Lieut Pinkney's garrison, Weber's efforts, the Sta Clara campaign, final hostilities of the war in the north. This vol., p. 377–83. Feb., meeting to elect a member of the council. *Id.*, 433. Feb. 16th, Hull orders Weber to disband all volunteers. *S. José Pioneer*, March 6, 1880. Action of citizens in behalf of the Donner party. This vol., p. 539. First visit of a steamer to the embarcadero. *Id.*, 578. Beginning of protestant worship. *Id.*, 566. In *Hall's Hist. S. José*, 188–9, *S. José Pioneer*, March 3, 1877, are some items about early buildings. In *Ward's Diary* is what purports to be a view of the town, which would serve equally well for an adobe house or two on a plain anywhere else. Dec., a military guard desired; Gov. Mason orders an investigation of quarters, supplies, etc. *Cal. & N. Mex. 1850*, p. 447–8. Aug. 7, 1848. Order to send detachment of N. Y. volunteers to S. F. to be mustered out. *Id.*, 633. Hall, 196, notes a snowfall of two or three inches about Christmas.

Indian affairs. March 15, 1846, petition of 78 citizens for a force of 100 men to fight Indians, whose raids are becoming unbearable; bitter complaints that the custom-house receipts are wasted by the employees living in great style and working 2 or 3 hours a month, while the workers of the country have to pay double price for their goods, and defend themselves against the Ind., who might be annihilated at a small expense by continued and systematic effort. *Dept. St. Pap.*, MS., vii. 45–8. Apr. 30th, Gov. Pico orders a campaign, appropriating $6,000 for the purpose—from Castro's part of the revenue! *Doc. Hist. Cal.*, MS., iii. 191. July, etc., renewed depredations after the U. S. took possession; complaints of the failure of citizens to provide for defence; campaign of Purser Watmough, killing several Ind. and recovering 100 horses. *S. José Arch.*, MS., loose pap., 32; this vol., p. 567. From Feb. 1847, after the removal of the garrison, complaints were renewed. The gov. decided that troops at S. José would accomplish nothing, since the Ind. came in small parties, having an understanding with other Ind. on the ranchos; but it was thought best to send a company to the S. Joaquin Valley to watch

have had only moderate success in checking the depredations of these robbers, who often had confederates
among the rancho Indians.   Before the change of
flag, San José was subject to the sub-prefect of San
Francisco.   The jueces de paz, later called alcaldes,
were successively Dolores Pacheco, James Stokes, and
John Burton in 1846; Burton and James W. Weeks
in 1847; Weeks and Charles White in 1848.   Each
of the alcaldes was involved in more or less contro-

the passes, with a force of 35 Cal. volunteers on horseback. Felipe Butron
was appointed a lieut to raise and command these men. They seem to have
started late in April, but we have no account of their achievements. The
citizens in May urged the appointment of B. K. Thompson as Ind. agent on
the S. Joaquin. *S. José Arch.*, MS., loose pap., 17, 41, 49; *Unb. Doc.*, MS.,
146-7, 311; *Vallejo Doc.*, MS., xii. 288; *S. F. Californian*, June 19, 1847.
Sept. 6, 1847, preparations for a grand campaign; Ind. on ranchos to be furnished with papers, which they must show or be treated as horse-thieves.
Ind. caught stealing should be shot; if merely loitering about, they should be
sent to the alcalde. *Cal. & N. Mex. 1850*, p. 355.   July 1848, José de Jesus,
a S. Joaquin chief, acting in behalf of the whites against the horse-thieves.
Unb. Doc., MS., 74-5. Bernal, *Mem.*, MS., 11-23, gives many details of an
exped. in April 1848, in which 8 Ind. of a party of 9 were killed and many
horses recovered; and Larios, *Vida*, MS., 7-16, 25-7, describes an attack by
Ind. on his father's rancho of Sta Ana near Hollister in Sept.
   Municipal officers. 1846. During the first half of the year S. José was
subject to the sub-prefect of S. Francisco. Jueces de paz Dolores Pacheco
and Pedro Chabolla, suplentes Valentin Higuera and José Fernandez. These
were appointed in Dec. 1845 by the prefect, though the sub-prefect's recommendation was for José Noriega and Pacheco, with Chabolla and Higuera as
suplentes. *Castro, Doc.*, MS., i. 235. Jueces de campo appointed by Alcalde
Pacheco Jan. 25th, Joaquin Higuera, José Félix, José M. Alviso, and Agustin Bernal, juez de policía Francisco Palomares; síndico Salvio Pacheco.
Juez de paz of the contra costa Joaquin Estudillo of S. Leandro, suplente
Antonio M. Peralta appointed Dec. 15, 1845, approved Jan. 22, 1846. Al-
calde from July 16th, by Sloat's appointment, James Stokes. According to
the *Californian* of Sept. 5th, Geo. Hyde was appointed civil magistrate of the
Sta Clara district on Aug. 26th, but I find no evidence that he served. John
Burton was appointed by Montgomery temporary alcalde on Oct. 19th, *S. J.
Arch.*, MS., ii. 35, and served throughout the year. I find no support for
Hall's statement that Burton was alcalde and Stokes juez de paz from July.
1847. John Burton alcalde until Sept. Wm Fisher was appointed Aug. 30th,
but declined; and on Sept. 14th James W. Weeks was appointed. Ignacio
Alviso auxiliary justice in March. L. C. Anthony sheriff in Nov. Estudillo
was still juez of the contra costa, though in April the citizens petitioned for
the appointment of Elam Brown. 1848. Alcalde James W. Weeks, who had
sent in his resignation in Dec., until Feb. 9th, when Charles White was appointed 1st alcalde and Dolores Pacheco 2d alcalde. White resigned on July
16th on account of opposition among the Mexican population and the lack of
a military guard; and Wm Byrne was appointed on July 26th; but Bryne declined to accept the office and White continued to act. H. K. Dimmick was
elected alcalde on Dec. 12th for the next year. In the contra costa, Elam
Brown was appointed March 30th to succeed Estudillo as alcalde.
   Pueblo affairs and administration of justice. 1846. Jan., complaints of
vagabonds killing cattle, encouraged by traders who buy the hides. *Doc.*

versy, arising chiefly from class and race prejudices. They had but little skill in the administration of municipal affairs, but for the most part did their best under unfavorable circumstances to maintain order, though the town did not achieve a flattering reputation in this respect. The inability of the government to furnish a military guard for interior posts did much to increase the difficulties, the force of Indian horse-thieves and Mexican vagrants being gradually sup-

Hist. Cal., MS., ii. 28, 33. Jan.–May, instructions to jueces de campo, and police regulations. *Estudillo, Doc.*, MS., ii. 94; *S. José Arch.*, MS., loose pap. 31-2; *Castro, Doc.*, MS., i. 261. Alcalde Pacheco tried to avoid accepting the office on account of legal irregularities and because of opposition from a part of the people; and vague complaints were made against him after he did accept, by A. M. Pico and others. *Doc. Hist. Cal.*, MS., iii. 13, 184; *Castro, Doc.*, MS., i. 274, 277-9. Before Stokes' appointment an election was talked of, but not held. *Larkin's Off. Corresp.*, MS., i. 139. 1847. Jan., the juez of the contra costa claims equal authority with him of S. José, complaining of Burton's summons to him to appear before him. *Estudillo, Doc.*, MS., ii. 98. Feb., Com. Hull gives instructions in the matter of complaints against Weber. *S. José Arch.*, MS., loose pap., 7. March, alcalde ordered by Kearny to dismiss the old suit of Gabriel Castro against Antonio Hernano for winnings at a horse-race. *Cal. & N. Mex. 1850*, p. 291-2, 301-2. April, if Stokes is not satisfied with the decision of the alcalde's court, he must wait for higher tribunals to be established that he may appeal. *Id.*, 295. May 1st, alcalde and junta protest against Kearny's setting aside legal proceedings; the alcalde wants to resign, as his rights are invaded. *Unb. Doc.*, MS., 117-18. June 5th, 8 citizens ask the gov. to appoint an alcalde in Burton's place, and also to station a guard. *Id.*, 114. Oct. 18th, murder of an Ind. by another. *S. F. Calif.*, Oct. 20th. Oct., a man named Chute convicted by a jury of manslaughter. Gov. recommends a sentence of 7 years of hard work. *Cal. & N. Mex. 1850*, p. 410-11. Dec. 2d, P. Real complains of men who stand at the church door to look at the women as they came from mass, a practice that should be stopped in the interests of religion, morality, and public tranquillity. *Soberanes, Doc.*, MS., 328. Dec. 28th, J. S. Ruckel to gov., reporting increasing lawlessness; states that the late alcaldes Burton and Weeks, though upright men, commanded no respect; recommends White and a guard of 6 temperate men under a sergeant. *Unb. Doc.*, MS., 132-3. 1848. Jan., complaints of horse-thieving, which is not all the work of Ind., since the Bernals were attacked by 6 foreigners. *Id.*, 46. March, three men, Hands, Higgins, and Williams, arrested and sent to Monterey for the intention to commit robberies, etc. Gov. Mason objected to this, but did not send the men back. Hands enlisted; Higgins was a deserter sent to S. F.; and the other was shipped to Mazatlan. *Cal. & N. Mex. 1850*, p. 487-8. Reported organization of a party of marauders in the red-woods under one Beverley. *Unb. Doc.*, MS., 8-9. April, alcalde tried a Mex. for selling liquor, without a jury, because in earlier cases the native element of the juries refused to commit. *Id.*, 122. May, gov. does not know whether Alcalde Brown of the contra costa is subordinate to S. José or not. July, alcalde complains of dangers resulting from the political intrigues of Salvio Pacheco and the violence of his son Juan Ignacio against foreigners. No native will deal justly with foreigners. The writer is accused of favoring the natives, yet fears for his life if Pacheco is punished. *Unb. Doc.*, MS., 76-7; but White was urged to do his best and continued in office. Dec., three men, Matthew Freer, Wm Campbell, and David A. Davis, for highway rob-

plemented by foreign marauders from ship and army,
three of whom were hanged for highway robbery at
the end of 1848.   A junta, or council of twelve members, subsequently reduced to six, there being no end
of controversy respecting their election or appointment, shared the alcalde's tasks in 1847–8.   The attention of the council seems to have been chiefly
directed to the town streets, squares, and lots, several
surveys being made during this period; but their
greatest achievement was perhaps the distribution of
the outside pueblo lands in 500-acre tracts among
resident heads of families, an action that in later

bery and attempted murder, were convicted by a jury, and hanged on Dec.
18th. *Id.*, 340, 34; *S. J. Arch.*, MS., loose pap., 8–9, 55.

Junta or council.   In Dec. 1846 Alcalde Burton appointed a committee,
or council, of 12 citizens to aid in managing the pueblo affairs.   The men selected were Antonio Suñol, Dolores Pacheco, José Fernandez, José Noriega,
Felix Buelna, Salvador Castro, Wm Fisher, Isaac Branham, Grove C. Cook,
Charles White, Julian Hanks, and J. W. Weeks.   *Hall's Hist.*, 174–5.   In
Feb. 1847 this committee was ratified by a meeting of the people, and the
committee was named a junta.   May 1st, ten of the above, all except Castro
and Cook, represent to Kearny that they had been so chosen, complaining
that K. had decided a case on hearsay evidence, ignoring the alcalde and
junta. *Hist. Doc.*, MS., 117–18.   July 3d, Weeks and others object to the
election as illegal, and propose that the gov. appoint 3 Californians and 3
Americans, recommending Pacheco, Noriega, Castro, Fisher, Hanks, and
Thomas Campbell. *Id.*, 130.   It appears that a new election of 6 councilmen
was ordered, and that two elections were held, the gov. in Nov. deciding that
only the 1st was valid, but if any members elect were not actual residents
their places must be supplied by a new election. *Cal. & N. Mex. 1850*, p.
417.   On Nov. 15th Noriega, Castro, Campbell, James F. Reed, Robert B.
Neleigh, and John Murphy were elected.   Next day Charles White and 6
others protested against Reed and Murphy as non-resident gamblers chosen
by a small vote.   Reed is also accused of having killed a man (the Donner-
party affair?).   They also declare Weeks an unfit man for alcalde, and will
present charges if necessary.   The gov. then appointed J. S. Ruckel, Weeks,
and a third to be selected by them, to investigate the election and decide the
matter equitably.   I do not find their definite report; but Ruckel reported
privately in favor of a new alcalde and an appointed council. *Id.*, 431–2; *Unb.
Doc.*, MS., 120–1, 132–3.   Fisher, Castro, White, Noriega, Suñol, and Pacheco are spoken of as 'a majority of the late junta' meeting on Dec. 31st.
Id., 45–6.

Pueblo lands.   Feb. 11, 1847.   Alcalde Bartlett of S. F. advises Burton to
sell lots at the regular prices, 25 cents per front vara.   There are complaints
of his charging $100 for a 100-vara lot. *S. J. Arch.*, MS., ii. 34.   One of the
first acts of the junta, probably in Feb., was to order a survey of the town
into blocks, streets, and squares, 50-vara lots to be sold for $12.50 and fees,
and no person to buy more than 4 lots, or half a block.   In May the survey
was made by Wm and Thomas Campbell.   The alcalde's grants of these town
lots were finally sustained, even against earlier titles claimed by Weber and
Pico.   In June the junta, their action being ratified by the alcalde and people, decided to have the outside pueblo lands surveyed into tracts of 2,000

years was annulled by the courts. Town lots at San José, as at San Francisco, were sold by the alcaldes at 25 cents per front vara. Of the few land grants made in 1846 only one, with a few mission lots, was subsequently confirmed by the land commission. Santa Clara, under the care of Padre José María Real as parish priest, has been included, so far as events are concerned, with the town, having been, indeed, more prominent than the latter in the semi-

varas square, or 500 acres—or less if the land were not enough for all—one of which should be reserved for a school, and the rest should be distributed, one to each, among the actual citizens who were heads of families, the rest being reserved for distribution to later citizens, and each tract paying an annual tax of $3. The survey was made by J. D. Hutton in July–Aug., and the tracts were distributed by drawing lots, the alcalde issuing titles which were in later years not sustained by the courts. *Hall's Hist. S. J.*, 176–82. In 1848 a new survey was made by C. S. Lyman, U. S. surveyor, the streets and squares being much extended. *Id.*, 182–4. See *Alta*, Dec. 15, 1869, for a decision of U. S. Circuit Court in one of the '500-acre' cases. In Jan. 1848 the alcalde complained that Hutton had defrauded the citizens by certifying tracts of 500 to 380 acres to contain 500. He should be prosecuted for obtaining money under false pretences. *Unb. Doc.*, MS., 45–6. March 10th, gov. decides that alcaldes have no right to dispose of pueblo lands. *S. J. Arch.*, MS., loose pap., 14.

Ranchos granted in 1846. *Calaveras, 8 leagues, Francisco Pico, who was claimant. Huecos, 9 l., Luis Arenas and John Roland, R. claimant. *New Almaden mine, Andrés Castillero, who was claimant. *S. José mission estate, Andrés Pico and J. B. Alvarado, who were cl. *Sta Clara, embarcadero, 1,000 varas, Basilia Bernal, who was cl. Mission lands, Juan C. Galindo, *Antonio M. Osio, Francisco Arce, *José Arnaz; *orchard to Castañeda, Arenas, and Diaz—Larkin cl. June 3, 1847, gov. to Gabriel Alviso, declaring his lack of authority to grant lands. *Cal. & N. Mex. 1850*, p. 318–19. Aug. 24th, alcalde directed not to interfere in the land quarrel of Forbes and Cook. *Id.*, 389. Nov. 24th, gov. cannot settle disputes on land boundaries in the contra costa. *Id.*, 435. March–Apr. 1848, the gov. decides that Iñigo has no claim to certain lands as against Castro. *Id.*, 498–9, 542–3.

Sta Clara mission. Padre José M. Real continued in charge as curate and temporal manager of Sta Clara, and also of mission S. José. 1846. May 25th and June 10th, P. Real authorized by govt to sell mission lands to pay debts and support himself and the church. *Unb. Doc.*, MS., 269–70. June 30th, sale of the orchard and buildings pertaining to it for $1,200 to Juan Castañeda, Luis Arenas, and Benito Diaz; deed in *Hartman's Brief*, 116–18. This deed was later proved to have been fraudulently antedated. *Hoffman's Opin.*, 15. 1847. Diaz was negotiating with Larkin for the sale of the Sta Clara orchard, and on Feb. 14th wrote to the padre to say, in Larkin's name, that the only obstacle was the Indian title, and to ask if for a fair compensation to the Ind. he could remove that obstacle. On its face there was nothing dishonorable or irregular in this proposition; but Real chose to consider himself insulted by a request to commit the 'bajeza de vender los intereses de unos inocentes,' and wrote a sharp letter to Larkin on the 19th. Original in *Savage, Doc.*, MS., ii. 57–8; copy in *Larkin's Doc.*, v. 20. The padre also went so far as to publish the two letters in the *Star* of March 20th. In reply, Larkin published his reply to Real of Feb. 24th in the *Star* of April 10th. In this reply he had denied having authorized Diaz to write such a letter, or

military developments connected with the change of
government in 1846–7. The mission orchard was
claimed to have been sold for $1,200 in May 1846,
but the purchasers did not get possession, and their
title was afterwards declared invalid. There was also
much controversy between the priest and the immi-

known its purport, expressed indignation at Real's insulting tone, and reminded him that in 1846 he was very willing to deliver the property to another party, notwithstanding the rights of his innocents. In a letter to
Forbes of Mar. 4th, *Larkin's Off. Corresp.*, MS., i. 114, L. speaks of the same
matter, and of Real's disposition to exceed his powers as a kind of sub-Indian
agent. Kearny's order that the property remain in care of the priest was
dated March 22d. In the *Star* of April 27th, Diaz published an explanation.
May 1st, Alcalde Burton gives notice to all persons to quit the mission, unless
allowed by the padre to remain. *S. J. Arch.*, MS., loose pap., 30. June 14th,
Real to gov., sends a list of effects lost by the forcible occupation of the two
missions by immigrants and troops, amounting to $4,007, besides damages to
buildings, gardens, etc., not less than $15,575. *Unb. Doc.*, MS., 254–7.
June 24th, gov. orders all occupants to vacate the buildings at Sta Clara and
S. José immediately, the alcalde being directed to enforce the order. *Cal. &
N. Mex. 1850*, p. 334. July 10th, gov. to Capt. Naglee, ordering him to go
to the mission with his company and eject the immigrants, using force if they
would not yield to persuasive means. *Id.*, 340–1. But next day, at a personal interview between Real and Gov. Mason, the former consented to permit the immigrants to remain until after harvest, and later, by making a
special arrangement with the priest and paying rent for the benefit of the
church. Therefore, Naglee was ordered simply to take a position in the valley, and hold himself in readiness to sustain the civil authorities. *Id.*, 334–5,
343–5. Oct. 14th, Real to gov., protesting against the fraudulent disposal of
the orchards. Larkin, on Sept. 16th, had furnished an expediente of 16 doc.
showing his title. *Unb. Doc.*, MS., 275, 277. Possession was not given, and,
as I have said, the title was not finally confirmed. In the *Star* of Oct.–Dec.
was advertised for sale a tannery at Sta Clara, as part of the property of the
late Mormon concern of Brannan & Co. Nov., etc., corresp. on the sales of
mission lands by Real, which were annulled by the gov. This vol., p. 564;
Halleck's Rept. 129, 168; *Cal. & N. Mex. 1850*, p. 429–30, 448, 452–3. In
Nov., Real claimed some special privileges as a priest in personal litigation,
not regarding the alcalde a 'competent judge' in his case; but the gov. refused
to take such a view of the matter. *Id.*, 435.

S. José mission. This establishment, with Sta Clara, was under the care
of Padre Real as parish priest; and most of the corresp. given above may be
applied to this mission also. Of local events, nothing whatever appears in
the records. May 5, 1846, the mission estate was sold, as was claimed later,
to Andrés Pico and J. B. Alvarado, for $12,000. Deed in *Hartman's Brief*,
107–10. But the purchasers were not put in possession, and it was later decided, as in the case of Sta Clara, that the deed was fraudulently antedated.
March 20, 1847, Col. Mason reported to Kearny having visited the mission
and found the immigrants in possession, they having broken open the doors
and done much damage. *Unb. Doc.*, MS., 146. Larkin had also acquired a
title to the orchard of this establishment, and on Apr. 4, 1848, complained
that the property was neglected, demanding possession, or that Real be required to give security for its preservation. *Id.*, 276. But his request was
not heeded, and his title was later pronounced invalid. In May 1847 he
seems to have rented the property to James F. Reed, but the bargain probably had no effect. *Larkin's Doc.*, MS., v. 130.

grants who had taken possession of the mission buildings; but the intruders yielded to the governor's
threat of ejecting them by force, and finally came to
terms with the padre.   There was also a pretended
sale of San José mission, which did not go into effect.
Padre Real had charge of this establishment as well
as that of Santa Clara.

The great event of Sonoma annals for the period
was the seizure of the place on June 14, 1846, by the
American filibusters, whose operations under the Bear
flag have been fully narrated.   Other occurrences are
somewhat dwarfed by the glory of this great outburst
of patriotic folly; and from the downfall of Mexican
power on the frontier to the gold fever of 1848, there
was hardly a ripple of excitement in the little town;
Grigsby, Revere, and Brackett were the successive
military commandants; and the savages were for the
most part easily controlled by the efforts of Vallejo as
sub-agent of Indian affairs.   The town had about 260
inhabitants in 1848.[3]   Municipal affairs were directed

[3] Sonoma and northern frontier events.   1846.   Jan., quarrel about the
alcaldeship, to be noted later in this note.   May, Prudon chosen delegate to
the Sta B. consejo. This vol., p. 45.   June, Castro's visit. *Id.*, 51, 105–6.
June 14th, capture of Sonoma by Bear-flag men, and subsequent happenings.
Id., 109–21, 145–68.   June–July, Frémont's campaign. *Id.*, 169–90.   July
9th, raising of U. S. flag. *Id.*, 242–3.   Lieut Revere put in command. *Id.*,
254.   Occurrences from Aug. *Id.*, 296–8.   1847.   Feb., public meeting on the
governor's council; call for a military force. *Id.*, 433; *Unb. Doc.*, MS., 140.
April, three stores, town growing fast. *S. F. Calif.*, May 29th.   Co. C, N.
Y. vol., Capt Brackett, stationed here. This vol., p. 514.   April, et seq., trou-
bles with Alcalde Nash. *Id.*, 608–10.   Aug., trial of Armijo et al. for outrages on Ind. *Id.*, 610.   Nov., visit of the 1st steamer, *Sitka*, at the landing.
Id., 578.   Andrew Hoeppner's medical springs near Sonoma advertised in S.
F. papers from May.   A visit, view of Vallejo's house and the church. *Ward's
Diary.*   Sketch of the town in '47. *Napa Register*, Jan. 4, 6, 1877.   In the
S. José Pioneer of Sept. 15, 1847, is an account of a theatrical performance,
claimed to be the first in Cal., in 1847, by members of the garrison and others.
1848.   Jan., 45 houses and about 260 inhabitants. *Star*, Jan. 8th.   Corre-
spondence of the *Californian* of March 22d, on the notable improvement of the
town.   May, decision to remove garrison, and consequent fears of the people.
Cal. & N. Mex. 1850, p. 556–8.   June, Brackett's co. reduced by desertion.
This vol., p. 516.   Aug., Frisbie's Co. H takes the place of Co. C, and all
mustered out. *Id.*, 515.

Indian affairs.   1846.   During the exciting times of the Bear revolt and
U. S. occupation nothing is heard of the hostile Indians; but in 1847 troubles
recommenced, though not reaching very serious proportions.   April, M. G.

under Mexican rule by José de los Santos Berreyesa
as juez de paz, after a torrent of ink had been shed
in controversy about the office; then after an interregnum of military rule, and· perhaps a short rule
of Manuel McIntosh, the famous John H. Nash
became alcalde, ceding the place, not without a struggle, in 1847 to Lilburn W. Boggs, who was aided by
a council of six citizens, and continued to preside over

Vallejo appointed Ind. agent for the district. This vol., p. 568. May, skirmish between Fernando Félix and party and Ind.; one white man killed; investigation by Vallejo. *Savage, Doc.*, MS., iii. 28–31. May 26th, V. to gov.,
the Yucaya chief sent in a party with articles taken in war, promising to use
his influence for peace, The Ind. armed to resist outrages, which must be
stopped. *Unb. Doc.*, MS., 314–15. July, Brackett to gov. announces that the
Ind. have been stealing Salv. Vallejo's stock. *Id.*, 301–2. Investigation of
the matter. *Savage, Doc.*, MS., iii. 32–5. Aug., gov. to Vallejo, approving
his policy; cannot increase the garrison. *Cal. & N. Mex. 1850*, p. 380–1.
1848. Apr., V. asks to be relieved; white settlers should not be permitted
to settle on lands of the gentiles until some arrangement has been effected.
Vallejo, Doc., MS., xii. 342. May, threatened hostilities in consequence of
removal of Brackett's company. The gov. had not much faith in the danger,
declared it impracticable to retain the garrison; the people must defend
themselves, and V. must use his influence; intruders must be removed. In
an emergency, aid will be sent from S. F., also ammunition. But the garrison was finally retained till Aug. *Id.*, xii. 346; *Cal. & N. Mex. 1850*, p.
556–8, 613–14. New depredations in the Clear Lake region in Dec. *Id.*, 682.
Kelsey and Stone had settled near the lake and were grossly ill-treating the
natives, who took a bloody vengeance in 1849.

Municipal official list. 1846. Jueces de paz, appointed by prefect in
Dec., and approved by gov. Jan. 22d, José de los Santos Berreyesa and Joaquin Carrillo; suplentes, Dámaso A. Rodriguez and Antonio Valle. The preceding juez, José de la Rosa, had a quarrel with Berreyesa, and found in his
actions some pretext for refusing to turn over the office until Jan. 9th, when
he put B. under arrest and swore in Rodriguez the suplente as juez 1°, and
Carrillo next day as juez 2°. There was no end of corresp. and charges, but
the details are not worth presenting. Berreyesa took possession on March
5th, and Rosa was fined $50, trying to avoid payment on the ground that he
was an employee of the com. general. Original corresp. in *Doc. Hist. Cal.*,
MS., iii. 12, 14, 17–18, 20, 25–9, 30–1, 34–6, 41–5, 127, 129, 139–40. By the
Bear-flag men in June there was a pretence of keeping Berreyesa in office for
a short time; but for several months under the insurgents and the U. S. there
was only military rule. It vaguely appears that Manuel McIntosh acted as
alcalde in the autumn for a while; but later, at a date which I have been unable to find, John H. Nash was elected by the citizens. 1847. Nash alcalde
until April. For an account of Nash's refusal to give up the office, see this
vol., p. 608–10. L. W. Boggs was appointed by Kearny to succeed Nash on
April 10th, taking possession of the office in June. June 14th, James F.
Reed was appointed sheriff. Oct. 28th, Andrew Hoeppner appointed 2d alcalde. Dec. 3d, election of a town council, consisting of Quin Fine, John G.
Ray, John Lewis (or Davis), L. P. Leese, Jesse Beasly, and H. A. Green.
Unb. Doc., MS., 122; *S. F. Calif.*, Dec. 15th. May, alcalde asks gov. for
information about the extent of his jurisdiction; whether, as Vallejo says, it
extends to the Sac., Bodega, S. Rafael, and Napa. There is no jail, and the
troops are tired of guarding prisoners. *Unb. Doc.*, 110–11. Trial of Armijo
et al. See this vol., p. 610. Dec., gov. to alcalde, on powers of the council,

local government in 1848.   Only three or four ranchos
were granted on the northern frontier in 1846.   In
the disposal of town lots, Vallejo's past acts as director of colonization were recognized temporarily by the
military authorities; and the sale of lots by the alcaldes
continued here as elsewhere.   The only reference to
ex-mission affairs was in connection with a citizen's
claim under General Castro's grant for one of the
buildings, which was sustained against the alcalde's
decision.   San Rafael in 1846–8 was under the rule
of Ignacio Pacheco as juez de paz, and later of Timothy Murphy as alcalde, the latter being still in charge

referring him to instructions for the council of S. F., as printed in the *Star*
and *Californian* in Oct. *Cal. & N. Mex. 1850*, p. 446. 1848. Boggs continued to serve as alcalde.

Lands. The ranchos granted in 1846 were Chimiles, Napa, 4 l., to José
Ign. Berreyesa, Gordon and Coombs cl.; German, 5 l., to Ernest Rufus, C.
Mayer cl.; Rincon de Musulacon, 2 l., to Francisco Berreyesa, J. Horrel et
al. cl.; and *Yucuy, Lake, 8 l., to J. J. Berreyesa, who was cl. April, Vallejo presents to gov. his authority, under Figueroa's orders of 1835, for having granted lands on the northern frontier and town lots at Sonoma, authority
which he had exercised down to Feb., but which he now surrenders. *Vallejo,
Doc.*, MS., xii. 284–5; *St. Pap., Miss. & Colon.*, MS., ii. 405–6. The gov.
in reply assured V. that he had no doubt that his acts would be recognized
by the U. S. govt. *Cal. & N. Mex. 1850*, p. 292–4. May, the alcalde thinks
the old powers should be restored to Vallejo. *Unb. Doc.*, MS., 113. June
7th, gov. to alcalde, authorizes him to carry out so much of V.'s former instructions as applied to the sale of town lots; and the sales by Nash must be
considered valid. *Cal. & N. Mex. 1850*, p. 321. Lots were sold by the alcaldes here as elsewhere, and the titles were sustained in later years. Some
of the charges against Nash, as against Hyde at S. F., were to the effect that
he had sold lots improperly, and tampered with the map and records. Snyder and Murphy, as we have seen, were commissioned to investigate these
charges. May 17, 1848, gov. to alcalde, denying the right of the council, or
any other authority, to dispute a title given by Vallejo to Juan Castañeda
before the U. S. flag was raised. *Id.*, 551.

Mission. In June 1846 Gen. Castro gave Victor Prudon one of the ex-mission buildings in payment of amounts due him from the govt. In March
1847 Alcalde Nash decided against Prudon in favor of the church, with $420
damages; but Gov. Mason overruled this, and ordered that P. be left in possession. In the litigation of later years, however, the title of the church was
confirmed. In Sept. 1847 the gov. ordered Capt. Brackett to secure all records
pertaining to the mission, and send them to Monterey. *Vallejo, Corresp.*,
MS., 12; *Cal. & N. Mex. 1850*, p. 293–4, 396; *Unb. Doc.*, MS., 258.

San Rafael. 1846. Jueces de paz, Ignacio Pacheco and Gregorio Briones,
appointed by the prefect and approved by gov. From the military occupation in June to the end of 1847 I find no definite record of any civil authorities, though I think that Pacheco and perhaps Murphy may have served as
alcaldes. June 1st, Gen. Castro to Col Vallejo, orders a distribution of all
remaining mission property to the Ind., reserving only a few horses for the
national defence. *Vallejo, Doc.*, MS., xii. 218. A few days later Castro
visited S. Rafael to get the horses, which, being sent under care of Francisco

of the ex-mission property. The estate was perhaps sold in June 1846 to Suñol and Pico for $8,000, but the purchasers failed to secure possession. Two other ranchos in Marin County were granted this year. The only stirring local events were in connection with the Bear revolt, or the operations of Torre, Ford, and Frémont, including the fight at Olompali, the bloodless capture of the mission, and the murder of the Haro brothers. Bodega, though honored by a formal raising of the stars and stripes in July 1846, and the appointment of a civil magistrate, had no history during this period, except as a rancho and the site of a prosperous saw-mill. Napa in 1848 was surveyed as a town site, had one or two buildings, and was honored in the San Francisco press with the title of Napa City. Benicia had also its beginning and a much

Arce, served as a pretext to the Bears for opening hostilities. This vol., p. 105 et seq. It was at the same date, June 8th, that the ex-mission estate, as was claimed, was sold by Gov. Pico to Antonio Suñol and Antonio M. Pico for $8,000. Deed in *Hartman's Brief*, 113-16. The purchasers did not obtain possession, and their title was later decided to be invalid, E. A. Breed et al being the claimants. Other ranchos granted in 1846 were Baulines, 2 leagues, Gregorio Briones, to whom the grant was confirmed; and *Buacocha, 2½ l., M. Teodora Peralta, who was claimant, rejected. June-July, fight at Olompali, Frémont's campaign, Torre's operations, murder of the Haros and Berreyesa. This vol., p. 164-77. 1847. April, Kearny to Murphy, asking for an inventory of mission property in his charge, also information about a debt to Hartnell. *Cal. & N. Mex. 1850*, p. 297-8, 302-3. Sept., Capt. Folsom ordered to obtain the mission records and send them to the governor's office for safekeeping. *Id.*, 397. 1848. Tim. Murphy, alcalde. Feb., inquiries ordered by gov. about mission property that may be taken for use of the Indians. *Id.*, 472.

Bodega. This place had no beginning as a town in 1846-8; but the U. S. flag was raised here in July. This vol., p. 232; and Stephen Smith was appointed civil magistrate for the region. *Monterey Calif.*, Sept. 5th. Subsequently Bodega was subject to the jurisdiction of the Sonoma alcalde in 1847 -8. For nearly a year the operations of Smith's saw-mill were suspended during the war by the flight of Indian laborers and the seizure of horses by the Americans; but in 1847-8, on account of the active demand for lumber at S. F., the industry became very profitable.

Napa. According to the *Napa and Lake Co. Hist.*, 232 et seq., the town site of Napa was surveyed by Nathan Coombs early in 1848, the adobe rancho houses of Juarez and Higuera being the only buildings standing in the vicinity. The first building was a saloon, built by Harrison Pierce—still standing in 1881—in May, completed in time to be deserted for the mines on the outbreak of the gold fever, but occupied by Pierce in the autumn. Yet it is to be noted that Wm F. Swasey and Chas C. Southward advertised in the *Star* of April-June a store at Napa City. In Aug. the election of a subordinate alcalde was ordered. *Cal. & N. Mex. 1850*, p. 595.

Benicia. At the end of 1846 M. G. Vallejo and Robert Semple devised the scheme of building a new city on the Strait of Carquines. For this pur-

more ambitious career, of which full details from original sources are given in my note. General Vallejo gave five miles of land, on which Robert Semple, with Larkin as a partner, undertook to build a city at the Carquines Strait, which should be the Pacific metropolis. Two hundred lots were sold and

pose, on Dec. 22d V. deeded to S. an undivided half of a tract of 5 square miles of the Soscol rancho, the deed being put on record at Sonoma and S. F. The town was to be named Francisca, in honor of Vallejo's wife, Doña Francisca Benicia Carrillo. V.'s chief motive was to increase the value of his remaining lands, by promoting the settlement of the northern frontier; and he was willing to dispose of his interest in the proposed town. The earliest original record that I have found is a letter of May 4, 1847, in which Semple writes of Larkin's desire to buy the general's interest, and expresses his approval if the change suits Vallejo. S. is closing up his business, and will move his newspaper to Francisca by Aug. at latest. *Vallejo, Doc.*, MS., xii. 289. Accordingly, on May 18th at Sonoma, Semple deeded back his half of the property to Vallejo. Original in *Bear Flag Pap.*, MS., 31. Next day, the 19th, Vallejo deeded whole property, reserving the right to some town lots, to Semple and Larkin for a nominal consideration of $100. *Vallejo, Doc. Hist. Cal.*, MS., xii. 291; *San Francisco Californian*, July 3d. Semple transferred his paper in May, not to Francisca but to S. F.; and the issues of May 29th and June 5th contained notices of the proposed town, sale of lots, establishment of a ferry, etc. Meanwhile Semple had gone in person to Francisca to start his ferry and have the town site surveyed by Jasper O'Farrell. Doubtless the city founders had counted on deriving an advantage from the resemblance of the name Francisca to San Francisco, against Yerba Buena, a name little known in the outside world. But the dwellers on the peninsula, as we have seen, had checkmated them by refusing in Jan. to permit Yerba Buena to supplant officially the original name. Accordingly the speculators deemed it wise to yield; Semple writes on June 12th from 'Benicia,' and after a parting wail in the *Californian* of the 12th, the change to Benicia is announced in the issue of the 19th. In his letter of the 12th to Larkin, Semple says the plan is completed and the lots are numbered; several have been selected by men who propose to build; two men are preparing to open stores; S. will have three frames ready for putting up in July; five men are getting out lumber; 50,000 ft could be sold in 3 weeks; S. has bought 1,000 varas opposite (Martinez) for a ferry-house; plenty of coal at the point opposite Mare Island! 'Benicia is making quite a stir in the great city of S. F.' *Larkin's Doc.*, MS., v. 159. On June 29th articles of agreement were signed at S. F. by Semple and Larkin. Lots of even number were to belong to L. and odd numbers to S.; wharves and all privileges equally divided; each to sell or convey his interest without interference by the other; each donates 4 squares for public uses; each gives a lot for ferries, and 4 lots in 100 for town use. *Calif.*, July 25th. S. returned at once to the strait; and in July Larkin contracted with H. A. Green of Sonoma for lumber, and with Samuel Brown to build 2 two-story wooden houses for $600 and 2 miles of land at the Cotate rancho. *Larkin's Doc.*, MS., v. 177, 179, 181, 202, 249. In Aug., as appears from Semple's letters, the doctor contracted for 50,000 feet of lumber at $40, opened a small store, wrote to the gov. to secure an alcaldeship (which the gov. declined, after consultation with Larkin, on Aug. 23d. *Cal. & N. Mex. 1850*, p. 389); Vallejo sent Indians to build him a house, Charles Heath was employed in boat-building, Stephen Smith agreed to establish a lumber-yard if the town continued to prosper, McClurg and Haight agreed for 16 lots to build a store and warehouse in which to keep a good supply of goods and lumber, Maj. Stephen Cooper decided to settle at

fifteen or twenty buildings erected before the gold excitement, which latter event was deemed extremely favorable to the prospects of the town. Francisca was the name at first selected, in the vain hope that the name of San Francisco would be permanently changed to Yerba Buena, but it was the new estab-

Benicia, a ditch was dug, and a brilliant success became a matter of certainty! *Larkin's Doc.*, MS., v. 200, 204–5, 210, 227. Meanwhile, and in Sept., as appears from original corresp., there was a fair demand for lots abroad. V. Bennett, John H. Brown, J. Hudspeth, A. J. Grayson, J. W. Eggleston, David W. Chandler, John Couzens, Samuel R. Palmer, H. Smith, Wm Gordon, Josiah Belden, C. W. Wooster, John W. H. Drummond, and B. R. Buckelew signified their willingness to take the lots assigned them. One of them writes that he has credited the price, as a matter of form, 'merely nominal of course.' *Id.*, 238, 246, 254, 260, 276, 316. Wm I. Tustin, *Recoll.*, MS., 5–8, says that he arrived early in the summer with his wife and child, just as O'Farrell was departing, and while Semple was absent in quest of lumber. He therefore claims to have been the first resident, and to have built the first house. The 2d was built by Henry Crouch for Semple; the 3d by Wm (or Benj.) McDonald, later Pfister's store; and the 4th for Cooper as a hotel. A similiar account is given by S. C. Gray in *Solano Co. Hist.*, 149 et seq. Cooper, in *S. F. Star*, Apr. 1, 1848, tells us that the 1st house was begun on Aug. 27th. The original corresp. shows that Tustin's house and several others were occupied before Sept. 7th. In a letter of Nov. 11th, Semple, *Bear Flag Pap.*, MS., 34–6, writes that there were 15 fine houses under cover, and several more in process of construction. On the 20th he sent a more detailed report, showing, as supplemented by earlier allusions, a total of 16 buildings, as follows: Wm I. Tustin's adobe 40 x 18 ft, Semple's adobe store 40 x 18, occupied by E. H. Von Pfister, Semple's wooden house 30 x 25, in which Stephen Cooper lives, Semple's 2-story wooden house 36 x 18, Cooper's 2-story adobe hotel 36 x 18, Landy Alford's house 18 x 16, Nathan Barbour's house 18 x 16, Briggs & Russell's frame house 28 x 20, Forbagh's (Benj. Forbush?) adobe house 18 x 20, Wm Bryant's frame house 24 x 12, 'elegantly built,' Henry (or Wm) Russell's frame house 24 x 12 (Bryant and Russell were partners), Charles L. Benedict's wooden house and grocery 18 x 16, Vallejo's building 130 x 36, intended to be raised to 2 stories the next year, blacksmith's (Fine, who died in 1848) adobe shop 18 x 17, and 2 houses 23 x 19 and 18 x 16, built by Barbour for owners not named. Some of these were not quite furnished, even when occupied, and there were half a dozen other frames ready for shipment or erection. The foundations for Larkin's two houses were ready, but Green and Brown were very slow about going on with the building. Meanwhile, and before the end of the year, Semple had a canal 13 ft wide between 1st and 2d streets, and had made much progress on road and wharf; he had found plenty of chalk, quicksilver, and coal in the vicinity; and had many applications for lots, the price of which was raised from $20 to $50. John S. Williams had selected lots and prepared to build; Henry Smith was mentioned as engaged in building; and Green made a new contract to put up Larkin's houses. The doctor was full of enthusiasm, was delighted at the success of vessels in reaching his port, and had no doubt that Benicia was to be the Pacific metropolis in spite of the lies told at the villages of S. F. and Sonoma. His great trouble was Larkin's lukewarmness in the cause. It required the most persistent urging to induce L. even to visit the place late in the autumn. That a man in his senses should look out for a few dimes at Monterey and neglect interests worth millions of dollars at Benicia seemed to Semple incomprehensible. *Larkin's Doc.*, MS., v. 250, 258, 304, 315, 344, 351–2, 354. The doctor's marriage about Christmas to Maj. Cooper's daughter did not dampen his

lishment that had to change its name. Semple's faith
and industry, like his disgust at the comparative lukewarmness of others, were unlimited. It is still believed by many that opportune coöperation with a
little good luck in 1848–9 might have made Benicia
in reality a formidable rival to the city on the penin-

zeal. The *Solano Co. Hist.* names as present at the festivities, besides some
that had been named above, David A. Davis, Charles S. Hand, Edward Higgins, F. S. Holland, Henry Matthews, George Stevens, and Wm Watson.
At the end of Dec., 28 citizens petitioned the gov. for a new district to be set
off from Sonoma under an alcalde. *Unb. Doc.*, MS., 127–8; and on Jan. 3,
1848, the gov. granted the petition, appointing Stephen Cooper alcalde, and
on the same day (!) consulting Alcalde Boggs at Sonoma as to the desirability
of the proposed change. *Cal. & N. Mex. 1850*, p. 452–3. The boundaries of
the Benicia district were: from mouth of Napa River up that stream to head
of tide-water, east to top of ridge dividing Napa from Sac. valleys, northwards
along that ridge to northern boundary of Sonoma district, east to Sac. River,
and down that river and Suisun Bay to point of beginning. Early in 1848,
E. H. Von Pfister began to act as Larkin's agent, and I have many of his
original letters, as well as Semple's. There was much corresp. about lumber,
contracts, and projected buildings; Higgins and Hand did some work on Larkin's foundations; Persifor F. Smith applied for lots for a residence and store;
Faust dug a well; Hand did some work on a school; Green was always on
the point of beginning to do something on Larkin's houses; R. L. Kilburn
of Napa wished to settle here and make contracts for buildings; Cooper fenced
Larkin's square and planted it with locust trees, projecting also a vineyard;
Semple predicted that there would be 100 houses before the end of the season,
meanwhile working day and night and economizing to pay his debts, also
building or repairing with the aid of Wood a launch in addition to his old ferry-
scow (Tustin says the scow was built in Napa Creek by Chas Heath, and the
sloop at Benicia, being painted green and called the *Greenhorn*), and meanwhile dreaming of a horse-power ferry-boat; a gale blew down one of the
doctor's frames and part of Pfister's store; Fine, the blacksmith, died; E. L.
Stetson tried to form a partnership with Pfister or start a store of his own;
Russell sold his house and left town; Davis and Fine opened a store at the
ferry-house on the contra costa, which hurt von P.'s business, so that he
thought of taking James Creighton as a partner; and Mr Brunt is named as a
house-owner. *Larkin's Doc.*, MS., vi. 28, 33, 35, 46–9, 61, 68, 72, 93, 97. In
the *Star* of April 1st Maj. Cooper has a letter of March 22d, in which he says:
'There are now 14 houses of adobes and frame, the smallest 18 ft by 16, and
the largest 56 by 20 ft, 2-story. We have here 8 carpenters, one blacksmith,
and one wagon-maker, a tavern, and two stores. There has been upwards of
200 lots sold, averaging about $18 each, 60 or 70 of them sold on condition
that the purchasers shall within the present year build a house to cover 600
sq. feet, many of which are in progress of erection.' He adds that the ferry
has paid $150 a month, which has been donated, with lots, for the benefit of
schools. But in May came the gold fever to interrupt for a time Benicia's
progress toward greatness. On May 19th Semple wrote that in three days
not more than two men would be left; on the same day Von Pfister announced that in two months his trade had been only $50, and that he was
going to the Sacramento, leaving Larkin's business in charge of Cooper; and
now H. A. Green came at last to work on Larkin's long-delayed houses, actually completing one of them! Semple remained, for his ferry and transportation business became immensely profitable. *Id.*, v. 121; vi. 112, 116. The
doctor promptly realized that the discovery of gold, notwithstanding its temporary effects, was to be the making of Benicia and a death-blow to its rival,

sula. Stockton, under the efforts of Charles M. Weber, made a beginning as a town, and achieved a considerable development during the early golden times as a centre of trade for the southern mines. New Hope, on the Stanislaus, was cut off in its infancy as a settlement by the resolution of the Mormon potentate to fix the 'new hope' of his people in the far interior.

S. Francisco. All that was needed was to establish a wholesale house, obtain for ships the privilege of discharging their cargoes, if not of paying duties, at the strait, and induce one or two prominent shippers to make use of the privilege. Scores of traders came to B. from the mines, anxious to buy there and avoid the dangers and delays of a trip to S. F. If Larkin would only see his opportunity! But the Monterey capitalist was apathetic, blind to his opportunities as his partner thought. Exhortations, entreaties, and even threats seem to have had but little effect on him. Semple from July to Dec. tried to make him understand that he was years behind the times, that he was by no means the 'live go-ahead Yankee' for whom S. thought he had exchanged Vallejo, that he must wake up. On July 31st he threatened if L. did not come and go to work by Aug. 20th, to having nothing more to do with him. In Dec. his indignation knew no bounds, when he learned that L. was thinking of erecting a row of buildings in Yerba Buena! This he declared the hardest blow yet aimed at Benicia, worse than all the lies that had been told, since it showed that the chief owner had no confidence in the new town. 'For God's sake, name a price at which you will sell out,' he writes, and offered $15,000 for Larkin's interest. *Id.*, 150, 154, 244. Of actual progress in the last half of 1848 we have no definite information; but Bethuel Phelps finally became a partner with Semple and Larkin; and several years elapsed, as we shall see, before Benicia's dreams of metropolitan greatness came to an end. Many men of good judgment yet believe that could a beginning of wholesale trade have been made in 1847-8, Benicia would have been the great city; while others regard Semple's project as the baseless vision of an enthusiast. It should be added here that Vallejo's original title to the Soscol rancho was finally, and most unjustly, rejected by the U. S. supreme court; which caused the holders under Semple and Larkin much trouble until they were relieved by an act of congress. At Montezuma, J. Laird advertised his ferry from Feb. 1848 as affording the best crossing of the Sacramento for travellers from Sonoma and San José or Sutter's Fort. *Star, Californian.* Halo Chemuck or Chamo was the name of a new town on the river in the same region, projected by Bidwell, Reading, and Hoppe, and several cabins were built before the gold fever began to rage. *Californian,* Aug. 28, 1847. *Star and Calif.,* Dec. 9, 1848.

Stockton. In 1844-5 C. M. Weber, through Wm Gulnac, had obtained the French Camp rancho. The first settlers, living in tule huts, were Thomas Lindsay, killed by the Indians, and David Kelsey, who died of small-pox. In 1846 Weber made efforts to induce immigrants to settle on his grant, but fear of Indians and the outbreak of the war prevented success. In Aug. 1847 Weber himself moved to the place from S. José, and besides attending to his business as a ranchero, laid out a site called Tuleburg as the nucleus of a town of the future. Except the captain's employees, however, the place can hardly be said to have had any inhabitants until the gold fever broke out in March–May. Then Tuleburg became the headquarters of a mining company organized by Weber to operate in different diggings. This company being dissolved, the captain gave his attention from Sept. to the town, resurveyed and renamed Stockton, where he built a store. Thus the town dates in reality from the gold excitement, and this slight mention is all that is called for

At New Helvetia, or Sutter's Fort, from the time of
the settlers' revolt early in 1846 to the discovery of
gold at the beginning of 1848, there was nothing in
the course of events or development that requires

in this volume. See Gilbert's account in *S. Joaquin Co. Hist.;* and *Tinkham's
Hist. Stockton.* The Mormon settlement of New Hope, on the Stanislaus,
where several cabins were erected and other improvements made in 1846-7,
has been mentioned in this vol., p. 552-3. In April 1847 a letter in the *Star*
indicates 10 or 12 settlers, and 3 or 4 houses completed. In the *Star* from
Oct. is advertised, in connection with the dissolution of the firm of Brannan
& Co., the sale of all the improvements at New Hope, Robbins, Stark, and
Glover being agents.

New Helvetia events. 1846. Jan.–April, visits of Frémont and Gillespie.
This vol., p. 3, 22, 24, 29. Jan., Mr Trow preparing stakes to lay out a new
town on the Sacramento. *N. Helv. Diary,* MS., 32. Survey by Hastings and
Bidwell finished Feb. *Id.,* 34. The new town is called Sutterville in *Yolo
Co. Hist.,* 30, and Nueva Helvetia in *Bryant's What I Saw,* 272. June, preliminaries of the settlers' revolt. This vol., p. 77 et seq. First operations:
Taking of Arce's horses, 10th. *Id.,* 105 et seq. June 16th, Vallejo and other
prisoners from Sonoma; E. M. Kern in command at the fort; chronologic
affairs to July 10th. *Id.,* 120-9, 170. July, return of Frémont from Sonoma,
9th; missing U. S. flag, 11th; march of the battalion for Monterey. *Id.,* 184-
6, 243-4, 246-7. Aug.–Oct., Kern and E. J. Sutter in command; release of
Sonoma prisoners; Walla Walla Indian scare. *Id.,* 298-302. Sept., John
Sinclair elected alcalde. *Unb. Doc.,* MS., 296; *McKinstry's Pap.,* MS., 9.
Oct.–Nov., enlistment of immigrants for the battalion, also an Ind. garrison
for the fort. This vol., p. 359. Arrival of immigrants. *Id.,* 524 et seq.
Measures for relief of Donner party, Oct.–Feb. *Id.,* 537 et seq. 1847. Sin-
clair still acting as alcalde for the district; Geo. McKinstry sheriff. June-
July, departure of Kearny, Frémont, and Stockton for the east. *Id.,* 452-4.
June-Sept., 25 N. Y. vol. under Lieut Anderson garrison the fort. *Id.,* 514.
Aug., Mormons here on their return east. *Id.,* 493. Arrival of immigrants.
Id., 554-7. Arrival of the 1st steamer in Dec. *Id.,* 578-9; *N. Helv. Diary,*
MS., 143. Dec., statistics furnished by Sutter to govt: white pop. 289, half-
breed, Hawaiian, and negro 16, tame Ind. or ex-neophytes 479, gentiles
21,873 ! Sixty dwelling-houses at the fort; 6 mills in the district, and a tannery; no schools, but the new town will have one next year; 14,000 fan.
wheat raised this season. *McKinstry's Pap.,* MS., 28; *Unb. Doc.,* MS., 91-2,
296, 307. 1848. Sinclair alcalde and McKinstry sheriff. An election of 4
subordinate alcaldes was ordered in Aug., and in Nov. Sinclair was reappointed by the gov. The discovery of gold was in January. Ind. affairs of
1846-8 are briefly mentioned in this vol., p. 566 et seq., and except numerous
petty details too bulky for reproduction, nothing beyond this brief outline is
obtainable.

Ranchos of the Sacramento and S. Joaquin valleys granted in 1846,
most of the titles being finally pronounced invalid, were as follows: Cañada
de Capay, Yolo co., 9 leagues, Santiago Nemesis and F. Berreyesa, Jasper
O'Farrell claimant; *Moquelamo, Calaveras, 11 l., Andrés Pico, who was cl.;
*Sacramento, Colusa, 11 l., Manuel Diaz, who was cl.; ranchos not named,
in Butte Co., to Dionisio and Máximo Fernandez, who was cl.; 11 l. to *Henry
Cambuston, who was cl.; in S. Joaquin Co., 8 l. to A. B. Thompson, who was
cl.; 11 l. to *José Castro, who was cl.; 11 l. to *José Castro, B. S. Lippincott
cl.; 11 l. at junction of S. Joaquin and Stanislaus rivers to *John Rowland,
who was cl. March 5, 1848, Gov. Mason refuses to recognize a lease of lands
to Sutter and Marshall by the Indians. *Cal. & N. Mex. 1850.* p. 490.

fuller notice than is given in the appended note. John Sinclair acted as alcalde of the district under the American rule, and the population at the end of 1847 was estimated at nearly 300, besides Indians.

I append a plan of San Francisco in 1848, as promised at the beginning of this chapter, with a long explanatory note.[4]

[4] San Francisco and its buildings before the outbreak of the gold fever in May 1848. In these notes and the accompanying plan I have attempted to fix the location of the principal buildings of the town. Including shanties, there were standing about twice as many structures as I have indicated, but many of them were mere out-buildings connected with those located, and respecting the sites of the rest there is no agreement among witnesses. I have also indicated the original owners of the lots in each block. The blocks contained six or four 50-vara lots each, which are referred to by number in this order. The numbers given to the blocks are arbitrary, for my own convenience and that of the reader. Buildings are referred to by letters on the plan. My special authorities, in addition to the many cited elsewhere in this and earlier local chapters on S. Francisco, are the following: official maps of S. F., showing blocks and lots; *Wheeler's Land Titles*, showing the grantees of lots; advertisements and items in the *Star* and *Californian* of 1847–8; original corresp. of Leidesdorff, Ross, Sherman, and others, in *Larkin's Doc.;* Swasey's *View of S. F. in 1846–7*, published in 1884, founded on the recollections of Stevenson, Hyde, and Vallejo, besides those of the author, and a work of considerable merit; A. D. Piper's recollections, in the *Alta* of Feb. 17, 1867; J. C. Ward's *Diary*, in the *Argonaut;* and the testimony of the following men, as given to me in interviews of 1885: Wm H. Davis, Wm S. Clark, Charles V. Gillespie, Richard M. Sherman, and John H. Brown. Except Juana Briones' house, and perhaps one or two more in the North-Beach region, there were probably no buildings beyond the limits of my plan, though the limits of Vallejo, Powell, and Bush streets are arbitrarily chosen, the survey, as elsewhere explained, extending considerably farther. My plan shows also the extent of water subsequently filled in and covered by the growing city. In no respect is more than approximate accuracy claimed. All the buildings not otherwise removed, except two, were destroyed by the fires of 1849–51.

Block 1. Lot-owners, 1 John Travers 1847, 2 Josiah Belden (beach), 3 L. Everhart '48, 4 Henry Huber (beach). Block 2. Lot-owners, all in 1847, 1 Roland Gelston, 2 Wm H. Peterson, 3 J. M. Stanley, 4 Ed Bryant, 5 Ed Burgess, 6 Laz. Everhart.

Block 3. Lot-owners, all in 1847, 1 Jas. F. Reed, 2 Christian Russ, 3 Adolph Russ, 4 Robert Semple, 5 McK. Beverley, 6 Charles Russ. Ward tells us that Semple gave his lot in '48 to J. C. Buchanan, probably to show his faith in Benicia. Buildings: *a*, the Russ brothers put on the corner lot a ship's caboose, building additions as required, and occupying the premises from 1847. Until after the gold fever this was the southern frontier of settlement. It was separated from the next buildings north, and hidden from view, by a high sand bank (not shown in Swasey's view) lying between Pine and Cal. streets. The lots have not changed owners, and are still in 1885 the site of the Russ House, a more pretentious structure than the original.

Block 4. Lot-owners, all in '47, 1 Benj. Kilburn, 2 James Barrett, 3 Philip Brown, 4 E. P. Jones, 5 Geo. McDougall, 6 Charles Docente. The

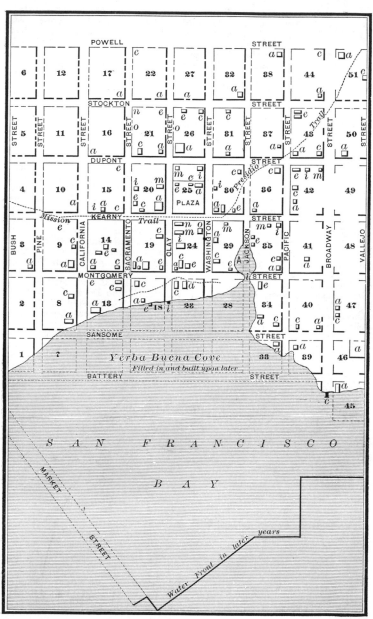

SAN FRANCISCO IN 1848.

mission trail, or road, followed approximately the line of Kearny and Mission streets to the mission, 3 miles south-westward. Block 5. Lot-owners, all in '47, 1, 2, 4, 5 C. L. Ross, 3 J. M. Curtis. 6 Jean Kleinshroth. Block 6. Lot-owners, 1, 4 not sold till '49, 2, 3, 5, 6 E. P. Jones in '48. Block 7. Beach-lots sold to B. S. Lippincott and C. L. Ross.

Block 8. Lot-owners, 1 sold in '49, 2 Wm S. Clark 47, 3 L. W. Hastings '47, 4 Dionisio García '46, 5 John Townsend '47, 6 W. A. Leidesdorff (beach). Buildings: c, Dr Townsend, late in '47, erected a wooden residence on his lot, where he lived with his family and had his physician's office in '48 and later. His alcalde's office was apparently not here. At a, Starkey, Janion & Co., merchants, had their store, with a separate office, on the Leidesdorff lot in '49–50. It was probably built in '48. They had also an office in '48 at the cor. of Clay and Kearny, probably in the City Hotel.

Block 9. Lot-owners in '47, 1 Charles C. Burr, 2 Charles Heath, 3 Jos. Hicks, 4 Basil Hall, 5 Eliab Grimes '46, 6 Robert Ridley '44. Buildings: a, adobe house, or rather a mixed structure of wood and mud, built by Ridley on his lot in '46. E. W. Pell lived here with Ridley for a time. Early in '47 it was bought by Leidesdorff, who spent the rest of his life there. Leidesdorff's cottage is described as the only house in town which had a garden, being the southernmost house until Russ built one over the sand hill far out in the suburbs. Ward gives a view of the cottage, with some other buildings in the distance northward. W. D. M. Howard lived here after L.'s death in '48–50. Above this building, at c, Swasey has an unnamed structure, which is also remembered by others. It was probably a shanty erected by Grimes to hold the lot. Ross mentions a house and lot on cor. of Pine and Kearny, offered to him in '48 for $350.

Block 10. Lot-owners in '47, 1 Howard Oakley, 2 Geo. McKinstry, 3 Geo. Panano, 4 Keari Palani, 5 J. A. Sutter, 6 Jacob Döpken. Block 11, lot 1 E. H. Harrison '48, 2 C. L. Ross '47, 3 C. W. Wooster '47, 4 Rich. Knowles '47, 5 J. B. McClurg '47, 6 John Philips '47. Block 12, lots 1, 2, 3 sold in '49, 4 James Lick '48, 5, 6 Wm S. Clark '48.

Block 13. Lot-owners, '47, 1 John R. Robbins, 2 Leidesdorff (beach), 3 Wm Pettet, 4 blank. Buildings: a, Leidesdorff's warehouse, on the beach, at what was later Leidesdorff and Cal. streets. Built by L. probably in '44 or '45, and used by him till his death in May '48, also apparently as U. S. quartermaster's warehouse. There was a small pier, or wharf, at the landing near the building. S. H. Williams & Co. had a store here in '49, and probably occupied the old warehouse before the end of '48. Wm Pettet had a wooden building on his lot at c, occupied perhaps at first by himself as a painter. In June '47 Gelston & Co. occupied the store with the *Whiton's* cargo in charge of C. L. Ross. They left this place in July or Aug. for the cor. of Washington and Montgomery (block 29), after having occupied for a short time Larkin's store on the beach (block 18 or 23). Wm Foster occupied the building next as a furniture shop, being succeeded in April '48 in the same business by McLean & Osburn, as appears from advertisements in the *Californian*. Before the end of '48 McL. & O., or perhaps Osburn in company with Brannan, built a better wooden building west of the other, near the corner. This was the lot on which Donahue & Kelly's bank stood later. Post and Cooke are named as early owners.

Block 14. Lot-owners, 1, 2, 4, 5 John Fuller 1837 and '47, 3 Francisco Sanchez '45, 6 C. W. Flügge '44. Davis, a later owner of 3, is certain that he bought of Flügge, and not Sanchez, the numbers being transposed on the official map. Near the middle of his 100-vara lot, at e, Fuller in 39 put up three small wooden buildings, in which he lived with his family from that time. One of the three, that on the left, or south, was occupied by Leidesdorff in '45–7, until he moved to the Ridley place (block 9). Dr E. T. Bale's family lived here with Fuller in '44–5. In March '47 Fuller's property was advertised to be sold by the sheriff, but his occupation seems not to have been disturbed. The property is described in the adv. as bounded on the north by Howard St (Sacramento). An alley in this block still bears the name of Fuller

Place. Lot 3, on which stood the granite building so long occupied by Wells, Fargo & Co., was bought in '45 by Wm H. Davis, who built on it a wooden shanty, a, and a red-wood fence. Mrs Montgomery occupied the house for a time in '45-6; and in '49 Davis put up a brick building, leased to govt for a custom-house, and burned in '51. Lot 6 was bought by Wm M. Smith, who at c built in '47 or '48 a house occupied by his partner, Frank Ward, till '49.

Block 15. Lot-owners, 1 J. M. Hudspeth '47, 2 Geo. McDougall '47, 3 Henry D. Fitch '46, 4 James R. Berry '44, 5 E. T. Bale '44, 6 Wm S. Hinckley '44. According to Swasey, Robert Ridley had a house at a in '47, which is confirmed by Brown; but others do not remember such a building, or that Ridley had a house in town after quitting his house in block 9. Block 16. Lot-owners, '47, 1 Geo. K. Winner (?), 2 Christina Read, 3 Asa Stevens, 4 J. Handerick, 5 Keaniu Cuani, 6 Wm Johnson '44. Block 17. Lot-owners, '47, 1 blank, 2 Robert Roberts, 3 Mills L. Callender, 4 L. C. Gray, 5 G. D. Lemoine, 6 Robert Smith.

Block 18, beach-lots, granted in '46 to the wife of James A. Forbes. A portion seems to have been owned by Larkin in '47, though there is some confusion in the matter. Ross, representing Gelston & Co. in Pettet's store (block 13, c), tried in '47 to buy or lease Larkin's lot, 'opposite, on the corner, in a line with Ward.' Larkin's Doc. He did not get the lot, but rented from Larkin his 'house on the beach, on the Forbes' lot,' at $50, occupying it for less than a month as a store. A sick man occupied it in Oct. In Feb. '48 Larkin's ' little white house under the hill'—apparently the same—was vacant, and Ross, as L.'s agent, had a chance, by improving it and moving it to the corner, to lease it for $300 to Mowry and wife for a shoe-shop and coffee-saloon. This was done—or at least the improvements were made. At the same time, Ross desired to obtain a lease of the Forbes' lot on which to build a warehouse on the beach, else he would have to build on his own lot, next to Starkey & Janion (block 8). It does not appear that he succeeded before the end of '48. All this appears from original corresp. in Larkin's Doc.; but nobody remembers anything about the matter, and it is complicated by the fact that L. had another Forbes' lot in block 23, and also lots with some buildings in block 21 on the hill. Wm H. Davis informs us that the Hudson's Bay Co. built a kind of warehouse at c in '42-3, and it was still standing in '47-8; but he remembers no other building in the block except a shed at a, built by himself for Paty & Co. in '44, which was removed before '48. Davis thinks the wharf at e, foot of Commercial St., later known as Long Wharf, was begun in '48, but this seems doubtful. On the Clay-St. wharf at i, as recorded elsewhere in this chapter, considerable work was done before the gold excitement in '48, but nobody remembers that the result was of any practical use at that time. I suppose that the building at c may have been identical with the Larkin building alluded to above. The dotted line crossing this block and the one next north indicates the position of a steep bank rising from the beach. Near Clay St. it was about 10 feet high, but diminished in both directions, and disappeared just above Washington and below Sacramento streets. In '35 et seq. Capt. Richardson's Indians are said to have had a temascal near the foot of Sacramento St.

Block 19. Lot-owners from '40, 1, 2, 4, 5 Jean Vioget, 3, 6 J. P. Leese. At a, about the corner of the later Commercial St., Leese built in '38 a large wooden store, and adjoining it, in '39, a small kitchen. L. lived here till '41, when he sold the buildings and both lots to the H. B. Co. Wm G. Rae, for the company, built an additional structure south of the kitchen in '42, used at first for a stable, and later as a warehouse; advertised as a warehouse at cor. Sac. and Montgom. streets in '47. The main building, used as a dwelling and store, is mentioned by every visitor, and is fully described in the narrative of Mrs Rae. After Rae's death in '45, Forbes occupied the buildings for a time, until in '46 the property was sold to Mellus & Howard, who lived and traded here in '46-8, Howard, however, moving his residence to the Leidesdorff cottage (block 9, a) in May '48. On the northern lot, at e, M. & H. erected late in '48 the first brick building in town. Perhaps John

Fuller had a shanty here in '38, before moving to his house in block 14.　At *c*, on his own land, Vioget in '40-1 erected a wooden structure, in which he lived and kept a drinking and billiard saloon till about '44.　He was succeeded in the same business—still remaining owner—by Juan N. Padilla, Robert Ridley, and (perhaps later) J. H. Brown, down to Aug. '47, when it was refitted and kept as a hotel by E. P. Jones, to the gold excitement, though it had been advertised for sale by Vioget in Oct. '47.　The name had been changed from the Vioget House to Portsmouth House in July '46. Swasey has a separate building below the hotel as Jones' residence, which would seem an error.　Piper describes the hotel as 'a small cluster of one-story buildings.'　Late in '48 a part was occupied as a store by Finley, Johnson & Co.; and another part, the N. W. cor., as a hardware store by C. E. Wetmore.

　　Block 20.　Lot-owners, '43, 1 Trinidad Moya, 2 Vicente Miramontes, 3 José Benavides '46, 4 Juan Castañeda, 5, 6 Leidesdorff.　The City Hotel, at *a*, was a large adobe building erected by Leidesdorff in '46.　It is mentioned as a new building in the *Star* of Feb. '47, and was kept as a hotel by John H. Brown—being often known as Brown's Hotel—until Oct., when Mr and Mrs Skinner took charge.　The rooms fronting on the streets were much used in '47-8 as offices and stores.　Shelly & Norris, Jasper O'Farrell, Alcalde Hyde, A. J. Grayson (book and variety store), McDonald, auctioneer, Wm S. Clark, C. V. Gillespie, McDougall & Parker, brokers, and Starkey, Janion & Co., seem to be among those who thus used the rooms.　In the last half of '48 Brown was again in charge, R. A. Parker being the lessee at $2,000.　The *Annals*, 346, has a view of the building, and quotes an account published in the *Alta* just after its destruction by the fire of '51.　In '48-9 the City Hotel was the headquarters of the gamblers; and was from '49 leased at $16,000, and sublet for stores and rooms at a great profit.　It was a low building with a veranda in front.　The adobe house at *c* was built in '46 by Vioget on the Benavides lot, V.'s wife being a Benavides, and occupied by him in '47-8.　At *e* on the same lot, according to Davis, was a small two-story wooden house where the Grimeses lived in '47-8, and where Capt. G. died. D. thinks this also may have been built by Vioget in '46.　Above Grimes, at *i*, Vicente Miramontes built on his own lot about '44 a wooden house, in which he lived with his family to '48 and later.　Swasey's no. 21, accredited to Noé, may be intended for this house.　At *m*, Wm Pettet advertises, in April '48, a store for the sale of glassware, etc., 'opposite the school-house.'　Swasey has a group of 3 buildings here, one of them being the residence of Padilla. Dr Fourgeaud seems also to have had an office in this vicinity.

　　Block 21.　Lot-owners, 1 Wm Kittleman '47, 2, 3, 5, 6 J. P. Leese '36, 4 Newell Bullen '47.　At *a* Leese built in '36 the first house in town, as elsewhere recorded (vol. iii. p. 709), where the St Francis Hotel stood later.　It is not known that it was occupied after Leese left it, and it was perhaps removed about '40.　Davis is positive that it was not there in '46-8, though Swasey gives a small building not named.　At *c*, or at Sac. and Dupont, according to the *Alta* of Oct. 26, 1852, the U. S. military authorities built a kind of block-house in '46.　Nobody remembers such a structure, though Gillespie locates the jail in this vicinity in '48.　The 100-vara lot, however, became the property of Larkin, and in '47 had on it a shed that had been built by Capt. Hull for a hospital, doubtless the blockhouse as above.　A man named Antonio occupied it for L., but was ejected by order of Shubrick. L. had a cellar dug for a new house, and there are several communications on the subject.　Later in '47 L. had two small houses rented for $3 and $7; also—perhaps the same—two sheds rented to a baker for $9.　*Larkin's Doc.* There may be some confusion between this and L.'s other lots in blocks 18, 23, q. v.　Block 22.　Lot-owners, '47, 1 Matthew J. Haan, 2 Robert Petch, 3 Howard Oakley, 4 Wm Pettet, 5 Daniel Clark, 6 John Sirrine.

　　Block 23.　Lot-owners, southern lot (beach) Nathan Spear '49, northern J. A. Forbes '46, perhaps owned later by Larkin.　See note on block 18, there being some confusion about these Forbes-Larkin lots.　At *a*, on the northern

half of the Spear lot, Ward & Smith had their large wooden store in '47-8.
It was advertised as 'No. 3 Montgomery St.,' this and the building nearly
opposite being the only ones in town that indulged in numbers. Wells &
Ward (J. C.), according to Davis, occupied part of the building in '48; and he
also states that the *Star and Californian* at the end of that year was published here. In April, Ross occupied W. & S.'s 'warehouse,' which may have
been the same building. *Larkin's Doc.* About the same time Mowry was living in W. & S.'s yard, but soon moved to Larkin's house near by. *Id.* At *c*,
Davis states that at the foot of the bank was a spring, where in '38-9 Fuller,
living diagonally opposite, had a kind of wash-house or shed. Late in '47
R. M. Sherman bought the southern half of the lot, and employed W. H.
Merrill to erect a wooden store, which was occupied by Sherman & Ruckel
in '48. In 1885 Sherman still owns the property, and has an office in the
Sherman Building. The dotted line, as before explained, shows the bank rising abruptly from the beach. S. says that he had a bridge from his front
door to the bank, which proves that it was in the street at this point; others
think it was not so far west. C. L. Ross seems to have had a lumber-yard
on the flat either in this block or the one next north.

Block 24. Lot-owners, 1 Geo. Allen '42, 2 Nathan Spear '46, 3 Spear and
Mrs Hinckley '47-6, 4 Peter Sherreback '42, 5 Wm S. Hinckley '39, 6 Juan
A. Vallejo '40. Lot 3 was at first owned by Spear & Hinckley, but the partnership was soon dissolved and the lot divided. At *a*, in '38, Spear put a ship's
house from the *Kent* on the corner of his lot for temporary use till he could
erect another building. Later he used it as a sleeping-room, and Kent Hall
seems to have stood here till after '48. At *c*, next northward, Spear built his
wooden store in '38-9, just north of Kent Hall and farther back from Montgomery St. Here he lived and traded till '46, when he sold out to Wm H.
Davis the building and his half of the lot. Davis lived here for a year, as did
his clerks later, and kept store till '49, when it was removed to make room
for a new building erected by the lessees Bleeker, Van Dyke, and Belden. It
was advertised as 'No. 2 Montgomery St.' The firm was Davis & Carter
in '48. C. E. Pickett made the store his home in '46-8. Davis owned also
lots 2 and 5. At *e*, Capt. Hinckley built an adobe house in '40 on his half of
the lot, where he lived with his family till his death in '46, and his widow
later. Alcalde Bartlett had his office here for a time in '46-7. In April '47
the house was leased to Ward & Smith for 8 years, and was occupied as a
dwelling by Smith, who married Mrs Hinckley. It was removed in '50. The
site corresponds nearly to the corner of the later Merchant St. Davis thinks
that adjoining it on the north a small wooden office was built early in '48, and
used by Ward & Smith. The Vallejo lot next north was purchased by Larkin, and had no building till after '48, though Swasey erroneously puts a
building on it. The lot was for sale in '47-8, and there were many offers for
the whole or part by Ross, Boggs, Hastings, and Holbrook, from $800 to
$4,000. *Larkin's Doc.* In '48, after the gold fever began, it was sold to Bran-
nan for $10,000. At *i*, in '39-40, Spear built a 2-story heavy frame building
for a mill run by mule power. Daniel Sill was the builder and miller. It
stood about 15 ft back from Clay St. Not used as a mill after '45, being
bought by Davis in '46, and used as a storehouse, the machinery being sold.
In '48 Davis sold the building to Cross, Hobson & Co., who occupied it as
store, office, and dwelling. At *m*, Robert A. Parker had a store in '48-9, advertised from April '48 as a 'new store opposite the Portsmouth House,'
Parker moving there from his old 'adobie store.' There was free grog on the
occasion of putting up the sign in April. Swasey and Leighton occupied it
in '48, succeeding Parker. Swasey calls it the Ross building. Brown declares there was no such building between the mill and the adobe. Davis remembers it as a wooden store, and thinks it was built by Gelston. Holbrook
brought out on the *Sabine* a store all ready to put together, and in March '48
was in search of a site. I think this may have been the same building. At
n was Paty's adobe, probably built by Benito Diaz about '46, and sold to Capt.
Paty in '47. Davis thinks this was Parker's adobe store in '47-8, but the

weight of evidence seems to be against him. McDonald & Buchanan, auctioneers, seem to have been here Jan.–May '48, though their place is advertised both at s. e. and n. e. corner of the plaza, and Gillespie thinks he remembers them at the latter. Wm Beere had a cabinet-maker's shop in the rear of this building in '48; and Wm Hendricks a barber-shop in this or that adjoining, being advertised as opposite the Portsmouth House. At o, on his own lot, Peter Sherreback built a wooden house in '43, which he occupied through '48. John Sullivan, S.'s brother-in-law, lived with him in '44–6. The Hinckley lot, east of this, had, like the Vallejo lot, no buildings.

Block 25. Lot-owners, 1 Jesus Noé '43, 4 Stephen Smith '46, 2, 3, 5, 6 town plaza from the time of Vioget's survey in '39. On the plaza, at a, the adobe custom-house with tile roof was built in '44–5, as recorded in vol. iv. p. 669–70. From July '46 it was the U. S. military barracks, and later occupied by the alcalde and revenue officers. It stood till the fire of '51. A view is given in the Annals, 255. Adjoining the custom-house, at c, there was a jail built later. Clark remembers the jail, and it is on Swasey's view. Davis, Gillespie, and others fail to remember any such building. At e, on the plaza, was the small wooden school-house built in '47, as recorded in note 1 of this chapter. At i, on his own lot, Stephen Smith in 45–6 built a wooden house, which he perhaps occupied for a short time. In '46 he leased it to Brannan, who lived there and published the Star, which in Feb. '48 was moved up Washington St. to the next block, Brannan being succeeded in this house by Gillespie. There is a picture of Brannan's house—possibly the one farther up the street—in the Annals, 347. In the other corner, at m, Jesus Noé lived in a wooden house on his own lot in '46–8. Swasey's location of Noé's house is inaccurate.

Block 26. Lot-owners, 1 Wm Glover '47, 4 Sam. Brannan '47, 2, 3, 5, 6 Wm A. Richardson '36 (though in Wheeler's schedule E this 100-vara lot is left blank). At a was the adobe 'casa grande' built by Richardson in '37 on the site of his tent of '35 (see vol. iv. p. 668–9, 709). It was one of the largest buildings in town in '46–8. R. and family lived here till '42, his house being mentioned by all the early visitors. Its site was nearly that of the later Adelphi theatre. James McKinley bought it at the end of '42, and Wm H. Davis occupied it as agent of McK. & Paty in '43–5, Benito Diaz also residing here part of the time. Many of the Mormons wintered here in '46–7. Davis thinks the building was unoccupied from the time he left it except for miscellaneous occasional uses; but Josiah Belden states that he (B.) occupied it as a store for Paty in '46–7 (though this may possibly have been at n in block 24); and it is stated by Wm S. Clark, A. D. Piper, and a writer in the Alta of Sept. 21, 1851, that R. A. Parker had his store here. I think this must have been Parker's store at the 'adobie house' advertised in the Star from July '47 to March '48, when he moved to m in block 24. David Dring was the owner in '49–50. This was the only building of '47 still standing in the region of the plaza in Sept. '51. In May '52 it was taken down, having been undermined by winter rains. This left standing only one building (a in block 51) that dated back before the discovery of gold. Alta, May 3, '52. The office of the Star, as appears from an advertisement of Feb. 3, '48, was moved (from i block 25) about 100 varas up Washington St., 'within a stone's-throw of the old windmill.' I suppose that Brannan moved the office, and perhaps his residence, to his own lot at c, though nobody seems to remember such a change. Swasey has several small unnamed buildings in this vicinity. Wm Glover built a house and lived on his lot at e.

Block 27. Lot-owners, 1 Wm Evans '47, 2 John Eagar '47, 3 Wm H. Montgomery '46 (Ed. Hudson '47), 4 Daniel Stark '47, 5 Wm J. Powell '46, 6 John B. N. Montgomery '46. Block 28, beach-lots granted to Dionisio García in '39. Nobody remembers any buildings on the block. In Oct.–Dec. '48, Edmonson & Anderson's centre market is advertised as on the cor. of Washington and Montgomery St. 'opposite Ross' N. Y. store,' and may have been here.

Block 29. Lot-owners, 1, 2, 4, 5 John C. Davis '39, 3 Francisco Guerrero

'43, 6 Gregorio Briones '45. At *a*, John C. Davis built his wooden house with carpenter and blacksmith shop in the rear about '39. As blacksmith, D. was succeeded in May '47 by E. Walcott, and in Nov. Davis & Co. by Rose & Reynolds, with D. as their agent. John Finch was also connected at some time with this business. Davis probably lived here off and on till his death. R. M. Sherman rented the house from the widow late in '48. On the Guerrero lot at *c*, perhaps a little nearer Montgomery St, C. L. Ross built his 'New York store,' and occupied it from Oct. '47, as per advertisement in the *Star*. All remember this store, still occupied by Ross in '49. In the corner below Ross' store, Swasey and Brown put Wm Reynolds' house, which others do not remember. In July, a new building at the cor. of Washington and Montgomery was used for preaching on one Sunday, and was immediately occupied as a store by Gelston & Co., who moved from their old 'store on the beach,' about the site of which there is some uncertainty (see note for blocks 13, 18). This appears from editorial items in the *Star* of July 24th, 31st, but G. & Co.'s adv. still continued 'Montgomery St on the beach.' Ross' adv. begins Oct. 16th and G. & Co.'s disappears Nov. 6th, R.'s adv. reading both 'Mont. St on the beach' on 'Cor Wash. and Mont.' This is somewhat confusing, but I have no doubt that Ross and G. & Co. occupied the N. Y. store together for a time, R. having been at first G. & Co.'s agent, or perhaps a partner. I think this was the only building near the corner. Ross had a lumber-yard somewhere on the beach, and at one time he occupied Ward & Smith's warehouse (*a*, block 23). From July '47, Lazarus Everhart advertised his tailor-shop at the 'Laagggoonn.' Clark remembers this shop at *e* as a ship's caboose, which he thinks was 'Kent Hall' (moved here from block 24, *a*); but Davis thinks it was a shanty farther N. w. at Jackson St. From April '48, Geo. Eggleston kept the Washington market, apparently at *m*, and later in the year Karl Schlottour had a bakery in the rear of the market. The lagoon at A. is represented on the city map, presumably from O'Farrell's survey, as longest from N. to S., almost reaching Washington St; but all witnesses agree that it was longest from E. to W., and that it did not touch the Guerrero lot. At *i*, Alcalde Hinckley is said to have built a slight wooden bridge in '44. The 'valley of dry bones,' a name which seems to have originated from some experience of the N. Y. volunteers, was at the cor. of Kearny and Jackson, according to the *Star* of Jan. 15, '48.

Block 30. Lot-owners, 1, 2, 4, 5 J. B. R. Cooper, 3 Fran. Haro '43, John Finch '47, 6 Domingo Félix '43. From perhaps as early as '44–5 Finch, known as Tinker, lived and kept a saloon and bowling-alley at *a*. Thompson was his partner in '47–8. The building was quite a large frame. From March '48, Conway & Westcott (though W. ran away presently) advertised the Colonnade Hotel, on Kearny a few doors from the plaza. I think this may have been the Tinker building, but possibly a distinct one. Dörnte, a man who was murdered in '47, is said by Clark and others to have lived on this block at *e*. On the Cooper lot at *c*, John Cooper, a cousin of J. B. R., is said to have built a wooden shanty in '40, where he kept a groggery for a year or two, after which Hiram Teal used it as a store to '43. Its later occupants are not remembered. David Ramsey's store was advertised as 'opposite the custom-house,' perhaps at *i*, from March '48; and the *Star and Californian* office as on Washington St and the plaza in Dec.

Block 31. Lot-owners, 1 Joel P. Dedmond '44, 2, 3, 5, 6 Francisco Sanchez '37, 4 Wm Richardson '44, J. C. Buchanan '47. Capt. Paty in '44–5 bought the Sanchez 100-vara lot, fenced it, and built a shanty at *a*. John Halls, who advertises as a surveyor in '47–8, is located here by Gillespie. At *c* there was another shanty, said to have been occupied by a Lascar named Jacinto in '39–47.

Block 32. Lot-owners, 1 Robert Henry, 2 John S. Misroon, 3 blank, 4 James Early, 5 A. A. Andrews, 6 blank. Andrews built a wooden house at *a*—not apparently on his own lot, since several remember clearly that it was on the corner—where he lived from '45 to Nov. '47. Wm H. Davis bought the property in '46, and lived there from Nov. '47 to '50. On this lot also seems to have stood the windmill noted by several as a prominent landmark in '46–7. Piper says it had been built to grind wheat.

Block 33. 6 beach-lots, owned by Pettet, Jones, Leidesdorff, and Joice. At *a*, seems to have been situated B. R. Buckelew's watchmaker's shop, advertised from April '47, though B.'s lot was in the next block. This region was sometimes known as Buckelew Point. It would seem that in this building must have been the office of the *Californian;* at least, nobody remembers it elsewhere.

Block 34. Lot-owners, 1 Hoen & Dohling '46, 2 beach-lots owned by Ellis, Dixon & Hay, and Hood, 3 blank, 4 Leandro Galindo '46, 5 Máximo Fernandez '46, 6 Geo. Denike '47. At *c*, on his own lot, Denike from '46 had a bakery, saloon, etc. It was here that Dörnte was murdered by Beverly in '47. From May '48 D. advertised his new hotel on the same site. At *a*, Dickson & Hay built the 'Beehive' store in '47, which they advertised from Jan. '48 as adjoining Ellis' and opposite Ross' lumber-yard. They moved at this time from their 'old premises adjoining Leidesdorff's'—possibly a room in the City Hotel. At *e* was an adobe building occupied in '47–9 by A. J. Ellis as a boarding-house and groggery. Everybody remembers how a bad taste in E.'s whiskey led to the discovery of a drowned Russian sailor in the well. It was on Hoen's lot, and Clark thinks H. lived here before he moved to block 43; Davis says the house was built by Benito Diaz in '44, and by him sold to Ellis in '47. In Feb. '48, L. W. Perry, a painter, had a shop at the cor. of Jackson and Montgomery, perhaps at this corner adjoining Ellis.

Block 35. Lot-owners, 1 John Martin '43, 2 B. Diaz and J. B. Mesa '44, 3 J. M. Santa María '46, 4 Gregorio Escalante '43, 5 Bruno Valencia '43, 6 Cárlos Glein '44. From about '45 Cárlos Glein had a blacksmith-shop, and perhaps a residence, on his lot at *a*. Near at hand, perhaps at *c*, John Ellick kept a grog-shop in '47–8, being part of the time in partnership with Denike. Somewhere in this vicinity must have been Prudon's adobe in '39–43, but I cannot locate it, unless perhaps it may have been at *m*, where Davis remembers an adobe shanty, occupied in '45–8 by Escalante and Ramirez; but D. evidently confounds this building in some respects with that of Cáceres (block 36), whom he calls Valle. At *e*, Piper mentions two small adobes, one of them unfinished, in '47. They were evidently on the Diaz-Mesa lot. Davis thinks one was begun in '43–4 by Diaz and never finished; the other was built by John Cooper about '44. At *i*, on the site of the modern Commercial Hotel, Hood & Wilson advertised their carpenter-shop from April '48.

Block 36. Lot-owners, 1, 2, 4, 5 Francisco Cáceres '38, 3 Juan B—— '43, 4 blank. The Bazaar, a market, was advertised from May '48, and is located by Gillespie at *a*. Swasey puts John Sullivan's residence at about the same spot, but others do not remember it. On his own lot at *c*, Francisco Cáceres built an adobe house in '38–9, and lived there with his family till '44, and perhaps later, though part of the family moved to S. Rafael, where they had a land grant. On the map of '47, Prudon is named as the owner of the lot, which he obtained, according to Davis, by marrying Cáceres' daughter. Between the Sullivan and Cáceres houses on Swasey's view are two buildings not named, and which I cannot identify.

Block 37. Lot-owners '46, 1 Wm P. Reynolds, 2 John Duncomb, 3 Juan Yvain, 4 Wm M. Smith, 5 Miguel Pedrorena '45, 6 Wm Fisher '45. From March 48, Henry Hartman advertised a tin-shop on Pacific between Dupont and Stockton, perhaps at *a*. Block 38. Lot-owners, 1 Julius Martin '47, 2 Rafael Guirado '47, 3 Lázaro Peña '45, 4 Lewis Rogers '47, 5 Martin Murphy '47, 6 Wm Pettet '47. Near the S. E. cor. of Pacific and Powell, in a little depression, Davis remembers that José Antonio Ortega had a little shanty house in '38–41, perhaps at *a*. See also block 41.

Block 39, beach-lots not sold till after '48, except no. 3 (cor. Broadway and Sansome), which was bought by B. R. Buckelew in '47. But B.'s house was, as we have seen, not on this lot. The only building on the block was A. B. Thompson's hide-house at *a*, at the head of a little cove, and accessible to boats at high tide. Davis remembers it as early as '38-9, and Clark in '46-8.

Block 40. Lot-owners, 1 S. J. Hensley '46, 2 Manuel E. McIntosh '46, 3 Jacob Harmand '47, 4 Thomas Kittleman '46, 5 Christian Thomas '47, 6 Jasper O'Farrell '47. At *a*, Hood (of H. & Wilson, see block 35) had a shanty house in '46-7, according to Clark's recollection. In Nov. '48, DeWitt & Harrison advertised their removal to their new store 'on Sansome St., opposite the govt reserve,' and their place is located by Clark at *c*. Block 41. Lot-owners, 1 Bernal '44, 2 E. S. Marsh '47, 3 P. B. Reading '46, 4 John Connell '47, 5 Hugo Reid '47, 6 John Allen '47. The house shown by Swasey as that of Ortega would seem to have been in this block, at *a*, but I find nobody who remembers it. See block 38.

Block 42. Lot-owners, 1 Thomas Smith '45, 2 Vardeman Bennett '47, 3 Eusebio Soto '45, 4 John Couzens '47, 5 Geo. Wisner '46, 6 V. Bennett '47. At *a* was perhaps Francis A. Hammond's shoe-shop advertised from April '48 as on Pacific St. near Bennett's. At *c*, Bennett kept a groggery, bowling-alley, and sailor's retreat from '45, sometimes with Thompson as a partner. According to Hittell, B. refused to be 'swung' out of his original lot by the O'Farrel survey, and his title was sustained by the courts in '59. Smith also kept a saloon and bowling-alley at *e* on his own lot in '46-8, with Wm Patterson as a partner part of the time. His adv. appears from Oct. '47. Marston's school of '47, according to the *Annals*, was in a shanty on Dupont bet. Pacific and Broadway, say at *i;* but nobody remembers it. On his own lot at *m*, Couzens probably had a house besides his place in block 47.

Block 43. Lot-owners, '46, 1 Aug. Deck, 2 Elliot Libby, 3 Francis Hoen, 4 J. C. Frémont '47, 5 J. H. Watmough, 6 John Allig (Ellick). At *a* and *c*, on their respective lots, Hoen and Ellick are remembered by Clark and Davis to have had houses in '46-8. At *e*, J. Montgomery & Co. advertised the Shades Tavern and bowling-alley, with a store next door eastward, perhaps all in one building, in the last months of '48. Very likely the buildings were not erected till after the gold excitement in May. Block 44. Lot-owners, 1 James Murphy '47, 2 Thos Kerr '47, 3 Wm Reynolds '44, 4 J. E. Montgomery '46, A. J. Grayson '47, 5 Daniel Murphy, 6 John Rose '44. I think Rose may have had a shanty on his lot at *a*, though nobody mentions it.

Block 45. Lot-owners, '47, 1, 2 Wm S. Clark, 3 Chas Albien, 3 (beach) Clark, Pettet, and Buckelew. At *a*, on the lot which he still owns in '85, Wm S. Clark, who gave the name to Clark's Point, built a warehouse in '47 -8. The 'new warehouse at foot of Broadway at the stone pier' was advertised to let in March '48. In the wharf at *c* the first piles were driven by Clark, and considerable work was done by the city, as recorded in note 1 of this chapter. The battery, or Fort Montgomery, of 1846, which gave a name to Battery St., was in the next block north, between Battery St and the water, at the foot of the hill.

Block 46. Lot-owners, '47, 1 J. H. Ackerman, 2 Peter Wimmer, 3 Alex. Hatler, 4 Ira T. Stebbins. Lot no. 3, or *a*, was designated as a cemetery at the cor. of 'Sloat' and Vallejo streets in the Bartlett map, and several bodies were buried there in '46-7, but none after '47, the burial-place being transferred to North Beach. Block 47. Lot-owners, '47, 1 Pika Paele, 2 Henry Harris '46, 3 J. D. Hoppe, 4 Geo. Pott, 5 John B. Faust, 6 Geo. M. Evans. An advertisement of '47 mentions 'H. Harris' house (*a*) above Couzens' slaughter-house (*c*), where Geo. Evans also lived.' The houses are also remembered by Clark.

Block 48. Lot-owners, '47, 1 Michael Foley, 2 E. P. Jones, 3 Michael Morey (or Murrey), 4 Aug. Tieroff, 5 F. J. Lippitt, 6 Aquila Glover. Block 49. Lot-owners, '47, 1 Stephen A. Wright, 2 Kale Puaani, 3 Robert Whittaker, 4 James McClary (McClurg?) '46, 5 blank, 6 James Greyson (Gregson?).

Block 50. Lot-owners, 1 E. P. Jones '46, 2 John Thompson '47, 3 Enoch P. Jewett '47, 4 Frank Ward '46, 5 Henry Smith '47, 6 John D. Harris '47. W. H. Merrill's American House, a kind of boarding establishment, was built in '47, a two-story wooden building. Merrill kept the place through '48. It is mentioned in the *Star* of Nov. 27, '47, as a new building, where the festivities attending Wm H. Davis' marriage were celebrated. Davis locates it at *a;* some others think it was not in this block. F. J. Lippitt had his law-office at Merrill's in Dec. '48. It seems likely enough that Jones and Ward put some slight improvements on their lots granted in '46, but they are not remembered.

Block 51. Lot-owners, '47, 1 Barton Mowry, 2 Richard Moffatt, 3 Wash. A. Bartlett, 4 Origin Mowry, 5 R. M. Sherman, 6 John Joyce. At *a* was built in '47 an adobe house with wooden roof, for Mowry. The 2d floor was used by the Mormons for their meetings. This was one of the two old buildings that escaped the fires, and it was the only one left after '52. It was still standing in '67, when A. D. Piper, who helped to build it, wrote his recollections for the *Alta* of Feb. 17th. At *c*, Sherman began a house in '48, Merrill being the builder, which was sold to S. A. Wright in '49.

ADDITIONS.—After the preceding pages were in type, Wm Glover of Farmington, Utah, a member of the Brooklyn colony, and a prominent citizen of S. F. in '46–8, furnished me a supplementary statement on the subject, which includes not only his own recollections, but those of eight others of the Mormon colony. The testimony is of value; most of it confirms what I had printed; and the additions by blocks are as follows: Block 8, *a*, Wm Stout. 9, *e*, John Halls. 10, *a*, Dr Parker. 13, *c*, *e*, John and Isaac Robbins. 15, *c*, James Ferguson; *e*, Carrington's carpenter-shop; *i*, Hiram Grimes (?). 16, *a*, Christina Read. 17, *a*, Robert Smith. 21, *e*, Joseph Nichols; *n* and *o*, Thos and Wm Kittleman. 22, *a*, John Sirrine; *e*, Robert Petch. 26, *a*, Parker's store; *c*, Brannan's house, and *Star* office a little farther east; *o*, Beers' cabinet-shop. 27, *a*, Julius Austin. 37, *a*, Daniel Clark. 42, *a*, A. Buckland. 44, *c*, A. J. Grayson. 50, *a*, Merrill's place in next block north. 51, *e*, John Joyce.

R. ('Il Signor'), 1827, sup. of the *Héros*. iii. 129–30.   Raabes (Claudio), at S. Gabriel '46.   Rabbens, or 'Raben,' 1847, mr of the *Mathilde*. v. 579. Rabbettoile (Pierre), 1847, Co. F, 3d U.S. artill.; 'Rabbittaile' on the roll; living in '64.   Radford, 1847, lieut on the U. S. *Warren*, who went east overland with Kearny. v. 452.   Radon (G.), 1846, mr of the *Narwal*. v. 579.

Rae (Wm Glen), 1841, nat. of Scotland, and agent of the H. B. Co., in charge of the Cal. establishment of the co. at S. F. '41–5.   He was an able man of business, and a jolly, popular bon-vivant.   In '45 he was driven by a complication of causes, arising from business, political, and domestic troubles aggravated by dissipation, to commit suicide at the age of 31. iv. 216–19, 593–4, 665–8; v. 679.   Rae's wife was Eloise, daughter of Dr John McLoughlin, and they had a son and 2 daughters.   The widow became Mrs Harvey, and died at Portland, Or., in '84 at the age of 68.   In a MS. *Life of Dr Mc-Loughlin*, she had furnished me a valuable sketch of her experience in S.F. Her property was left to her son, Joseph McL. Harvey, but the will, acc. to the newspapers, is contested by the daughters of Rae, Mrs Wygant and Mrs Myrick.   Raeckman (Israel), 1846, Cal. Bat. (v. 358).   Rafter (Wm), 1847, Co. F, 3d U. S. artill. (v. 518); still in the service '64. v. 521.   Raggio (Luigi), 1847, Ital. from Mex.; justice of the peace S. Luis Ob. '51; S. Benito Co. '67–81 with family.   Ragsdale, 1837, mr of the *True Blue*. iv. 106.

Rainey (Dav. P.), 1847, Co. B, Morm. Bat. (v. 469).   Rainsford (John), 1829, Irish sailor from the Islands, known as 'Kanaka Jack,' and as Joaquin Solis from his personal resemblance to the convict. iii. 179.   He worked as a lumberman; joined the comp. extranjera in '32. iii. 221; appears on Larkin's books from '34; got a Mont. lot in '35; age 30 in '36; sold out in '37; at S.F. in '39–41, acting as interpreter and mr of a launch on the bay. iv. 130. In '42 he lived at Sonoma, getting naturalization papers, and perhaps visiting the Geysers; grantee of a Napa rancho by the Sonoma alcalde in '45. *Land Com.*, no. 804; died in '46.

Ramirez (Agapito), at Los Ang. '45–6, iv. 522, 541.   R. (Angel), **1834,** Mex. ex-friar and ex-revolutionist, in charge of the Mont. custom-house '34– 6; a leading supporter of Alvarado at first and later a conspirator against him; an intriguing, vicious fellow, who died in '40.   His wife, or mistress, in '36 was Francisca Gutierrez, who came with him overland from Tepic. Biog. iii. 587– 8; ment. iii. 357–8, 261, 297, 370–3, 377, 452, 455, 469, 477, 487, 513, 523–5, 569, 573, 670–2, 677, 683, 688; iv. 96, 163.   R. (Angeles), at Los Ang. '46. R. (Aquilino), killed at S. Buen. '38. iii. 554.   R. (Antonio), at Los Ang. '39, age 25.   R. (Francisco), Chileno at S.F. '43–6; age 40 in '45; collector in '46. v. 648.   R. (Ignacio), first man buried at Mont. 1770. i. 175.

Ramirez (José), 1820, Mex. sub-lieut of artill. '20–26, when he returned to Mex. ii. 263, 371, 381, 422, 470, 510, 537, 674; iii. 25. He was an old man of 60, and soon died, leaving a widow, María de Jesus Ortega, of Sta B., who returned to Cal., and in '75 was still living at Sta Clara.   R. (José), resid. of Branciforte '28–30. ii. 627; wife Margarita Lorenzana, child. Riviano (Bibiano?), Vicente, Victor, Andrés, José Arcadio, Luis, Estefana, Bárbara. R. (José Ant.), carpenter-instructor 1792–5; at Los Ang. '21. i. 615; ii. 351. R. (José Guad.), soldier at S. Juan B. before 1800. i. 558.   R. (José María),

1825, Mex. alférez, who came with Gov. Echeandía, and was soon attached
to the S. Diego comp. iii. 13–14, 16, 24, 78. He married Dolores Palomares,
and in '30 was tried and acquitted for bigamy. Took part in the revolt of '31,
and was the slayer of Vicente Gomez. iii. 204, 673; in '33–4 comisionado to
secularize S. Diego mission. iii. 326, 620, 630; in '35–6 admin. of S. Antonio
(possibly another man). iii. 354, 687–8; in '36 at Mont.; also comisionado of
Sta Inés. iii. 426, 463, 663–4; iv. 46. He was involved in the sectional quarrels of '37–8, being more than once arrested in the south. iii. 504, 555, 566;
in '40 was grantee of land at Los Ang. iii. 634; iv. 635; and in '44 is ment.
as lieut, being also instructor and adjutant of the Los Ang. comp. of defensores. iv. 407–8. An Alf. Ramirez was wounded at the S. Gabriel in Jan. '47.
v. 396.   R. (José María), soldier at Mont. '36, age 33, nat. of Oajaca.   R.
(Juan), at Los Ang. in '36, one of the vigilantes. iii. 432; age 32 in '39; juez
de campo '36, '40, '48. iii. 636–7; v. 626; justice of the peace in '50.   R.
(Manuel), 1801, Mex. convict. ii. 170.   R. (María Potenciana), wife of Macario Castro 1777. ii. 141.   R. (Miguel), síndico at Branciforte '36. iii. 697;
in '45, age 50, nat. of Tepic, wife Margarita Lorenzana, son Canuto b. '26 at
B.; prob. same as José above.   R. (Ramon), at S. Gabriel '46.   Ramon
(José), Ind. grantee of Purísima, Sta Clara.   Ramos (José), Mex. convict
settler 1798. i. 606.

Ramsay, mr of the *Good Hope*. ii. 284.   Ramsdale (Geo.), 1846, corp.
Co. K, C, 1st U.S. dragoons. Killed at S. Pascual. v. 346.   Ramsey (Chas),
1848, settler in Solano Co., still in Green Valley '78.   R. (Dav.), 1847, corp.
Co. H, N.Y.Vol. (v. 499); kept a store at S.F. '48. v. 683.   R. (John W.),
1847, Co. E, N.Y.Vol. (v. 499).   Rand, or Ran (Caleb), 1847, settler in Sta
Clara Val. with wife from '46–7; went to Or. '72; d. '79.   R. (Geo.), 1847,
perhaps of N.Y.Vol. (v. 499), under another name.   R. (Joshua), 1847, Co.
C, N.Y.Vol. (v. 499); d. before '82.   Randall (Andrew), 1847, gunner on
the U.S. *Portsmouth;* in '50 called a doctor and scientist; in '53 apparently
the claimant for several ranchos. iii. 677, 712; iv. 655, 670, 672.   R. (Chandler G.), 1847, said to have been orderly sergt in N.Y.Vol., but not on the
rolls; a carpenter at S. José from '49 to his death in '58, age 36.   R. (Charles
G.), 1847, Co. B, N.Y.Vol. (v. 499); d. S. José after '50; doubtless same as
preceding.   R. (Eli), 1847, at Stockton. *Tinkham.*   R. (John), 1826, mid.
on the *Blossom* '26–7.   Randolph (Isaac N.), 1846, Co. C, 1st U.S. dragoons
(v. 336); kept a hotel at Sonoma '48; in Amador Co. from '53 to '63, when he
committed suicide.   R. (J. B.), 1847, lieut on the U.S. *Columbus.*   Raney
(McKee), 1848, nat. of Va, settler of S. Joaq., apparently living in '84; also
called 'Reany.'   Rangel (Juan José), 1829, Mex. convict set at liberty '34.
Ranguel (Manuel), at Los Ang. '46.   Ransch (Joseph A.), 1847, at S.F.
asking for land; perhaps 'Rausch.'

Ratiguende (Wm), 1828, doubtful name; mr of the *Fénix.* iii. 147.
Rausch (Nicholas J.), 1847, Co. K, N.Y.Vol. (v. 499); owner of S.F. lot;
later a prominent German citizen of S.F. where he died in '63.   Rawson
(Dan. B.), 1847, Co. D, Morm. Bat. (v. 469).   Ray (Charles), 1823, mr of
the *Plowboy.* ii. 492.   R. (David), 1848, immig. from Or. with wife and 5
children; died on the Yuba the same year. *Burnett.*   R. (John G.), 1846,
memb. of the Sonoma council '47. v. 668; Cal. claim of $250 (v. 462); in '60
kept a hotel on the Geyser road. The John Ray who came to Rose Bar with
his family in '48, *Yuba Co. Hist.,* 83, may be he or David.   Rayaty (Julian),
at Los Ang. '39, age 26.   Raymond (Almon P.), 1847, Co. D, Morm. Bat.
(v. 469).   R. (Fred.), 1847, nat. of Mass., who died at S.F. May 27th.   R.
(Peter), 1846, Co. E, Cal. Bat. (v. 358); murderer of J. R. von Pfister in the
mines Oct. '48, but escaped from jail. I think he may possibly be the Peter
Remer executed at Sta B. in Dec. for the Reed murder. v. 632.   Raymore
(Thos), 1832, memb. of the comp. extranjera at Mont. iii. 221.   Raynor
(Wm), 1846, Co. C, 1st U.S. dragoons (v. 336).

Read (Christina), 1846, of the Mormon colony. v. 546; owner of a S.F. lot.
v. 679.   R. (Edward), 1844, Amer. from Mazatlan, who went mad on the
voyage, and seems to have died at S. Pedro. iv. 453.   R. (Hannah T.), 1846,

of the Morm. colony with a child. v. 546; perhaps Mrs Jimison later.   R.
(John), 1826 (?), Irish sailor said to have come from Acapulco this year. iii.
176. I find no original record of his presence before '33 except that in '34 several witnesses testified to having known him for 6 years, or since '28. Prevented by Ind. from cultivating the Cotate rancho, and serving for a time as
majordomo of S. Rafael, acc. to current sketches he came to Sauzalito in '32.
Weeks claims to have visited him in the Sauzalito cabin in '31. His boat
running occasionally to Yerba Buena, may be regarded as the 1st ferry. From
'33 his name appears on Larkin's books and in various records. iii. 365; iv.
117. He was naturalized in Sept. '34, and in Oct. was grantee of the Corte de
Madera del Presidio rancho. iii. 711. In '35 he was godfather at the baptism
of Geo. Yount, and in '36 married Hilaria, daughter of José Ant. Sanchez,
being appointed admin. of S. Rafael, and perhaps serving as alcalde the next
year, when he was visited by Edwards. iii. 718; iv. 86. Henry A. Peirce describes a visit to his place in '41, and he died in '43, leaving 4 children. The
widow was still living in '72 with a daughter by a 2d husband. The son, John
J., b. in '37, inherited his father's estate and was still living in '80, with wife
Carlota Suarez and 2 children. Another son was Richard, b. about '39. One
daughter, Inés, Mrs Deffenbach, lived in '80 in the adobe house built by her
father; the other, Hilaria, married J. Boyle of S.F.   R. (Rachel), 1848,
married at S. F. to F. Weaver.   R. (Wm B.), 1847, Co. F, 3d U. S. artill.
(v. 518).

Reading (Pierson B.), 1843, nat. of N.J. and overl. immig. in the Chiles-
Walker party. iv. 393–4, 400. He entered Sutter's service as clerk and chief
of trappers, making wide explorations in '44–5, commanding at the fort during Sutter's absence in the Micheltorena campaign, and getting in '44 a grant of
the S. Buenaventura rancho. iv. 483, 486, 673. In '46 he was active from the
first in promoting the settlers' revolt, and served '46–7 in the Cal. Bat. as
paymaster, with rank of major, owning a lot at S.F., and having a 'Cal. claim.'
v. 127–8, 170, 179, 360, 404–5, 447, 674, 685. After his discharge he settled
on his Shasta Co. rancho, but in '48–9 engaged extensively in mining operations on Trinity River, where Reading Bar bore his name, and in '49 had a
store at Sac. in company with Hensley and Snyder, besides taking part in
political affairs. In '50 he went east to settle his accounts as paymaster, and
to pay a large debt at Vicksburg resulting from a business failure of '37, and
returning was candidate for governor in '51, barely missing election. Subsequently he devoted himself to agriculture in northern Cal.; married Fanny
Washington in '56, and died in '68 at the age of 52, leaving a widow and 5 children. Maj. Reading was a man of well-balanced mind, honorable, energetic,
and courteous; one whose Californian record seems never to have furnished
material for adverse criticism.

Real (Antonio Suarez del), 1833, Mex. friar of the Zacatecas college, who
served at Sta Cruz '33–44, and retired to his college in the latter year, or perhaps in '45. iii. 319, 693–5; iv. 371, 657, 662, 675. Padre Real was a dissolute
man addicted to more than one vice, and even accused of theft, but credited
with having been kind and indulgent to his neophytes. Sir Geo. Simpson,
Laplace the French voyager, and Josiah Belden have something to say of the
friar's character.   R. (José María del Refugio Sagrado Suarez del), 1833,
brother of Antonio, Mex. friar of the Zacatecanos, missionary at S. Cárlos to
'43, and priest at Sta Clara, with charge of S. José and S. Cárlos from '44. iii.
319, 679–80; iv. 5, 427, 549, 638, 651, 657, 682. In '46–7 he was in some difficulty about sales of mission lands and encroachments of immigrants. v.
564, 663, 665–7; and in later years his troubles with the authorities continued
to some extent, until in '51 the guardian called on P. Gonzalez to suspend
Real if he could not be induced to leave Cal. voluntarily. He went in '52; in
'53 writes from S. José del Cabo, L. Cal.; and in '55 he had severed his connection with the college and was serving as parish priest at Mazatlan. Padre
José María somewhat resembled his brother in character, though an abler man,
with more skill in concealing his irregularities. It was most unfortunate for
the general reputation of the Cal. padres—a most excellent body of men, as

is fully shown in these volumes—that the Real brothers, Quijas, Mercado, and a few other black sheep of the fold were the friars whose conduct was best known to the foreign immig., and on whom many pioneers have founded their estimate of the missionaries.   Reamer (Wm C.) of the Mormon col. of '46; did not come to Cal.   Reausseau (Charles), 1847, Co. D, N.Y.Vol. (v. 499); d. in S.F. '68.

Recio (Antonio M. Jimenez del), parish priest at Los Ang. '47. v. 625; prob. came in '45 or earlier.   Rector (Geo. W.), 1847, nat. of Ky; resid. of S. Luis Ob. Co. '68–83.   Reddick, 1845, one of Frémont's men perhaps. iv. 583; went east with Sublette in '46, or perhaps to Or. v. 526.   Redmond (John B.), 1848 (?), Irish settler of Marin Co. '64–80.   Reed (B. F.), 1846, Cal. claim of $300 (v. 462).   R. (Edward), 1831, mr of the *Harriet*.   R. (Geo.), 1828, mr of the *Rascow*. iii. 148.

Reed (James Frazier), 1846, nat. of Ireland and a prominent member of the Donner party from Ill., accomp. by his wife, 4 children, and his wife's mother, Mrs Sarah Keyes. The latter died in May at the age of 90. In Oct., before reaching the mts, Reed, in a quarrel, killed John Snyder and was banished from the company.   With one companion he crossed the Sierra, and after an unsuccessful attempt to recross with relief, served as lieut in the Sanchez campaign, and in Feb. '47 went back to the lake in the 2d relief. All the family saved their lives and settled at S. José, where R. became wealthy and held local offices, dying in '74, and his wife, Margaret W., in '61. James F. Jr was living at S. José in '80, as was Thomas K., also Virginia E., wife of John M. Murphy, with 6 children, and Martha J., widow of Frank Lewis, with 7 children.   Portraits of father, mother, and the daughters in McGlashan's work. v. 508, 530, 532, 534, 664, 666, 668, 676.

Reed (John), see 'Read.'   R. (John), 1837 (?), nat. of N.C., who came from N. Mex.; often accredited to the Workman party, but his name is not in Rowland's list, and Given is positive he was not of the party. iv. 118, 278. Accredited to '37 by the *Los Ang. Co. Hist.*, but perhaps did not come till after '41. Served against Micheltorena in '45. iv. 495; signed the declaration against Castro in June '46, and in Stockton's campaign of 46–7 served as sergt in the Cal. Bat. A visit to Sutter's fort is recorded in '47. He was a son-in-law of John Rowland, and became owner of La Puente rancho, where he died in '74, leaving a widow, but no children.   R. (John), 1846, of the Mormon colony. v. 546; perhaps should be 'Read,' or the others 'Reed.'   R. (John), 1846, lieut in Marston's force Sta Clara campaign. v. 350.   R. (John), 1846, sailmaker on the *Congress*, acting capt. in Stockton's Bat. '46–7. v. 385. R. (Joseph), 1847, accredited to N.Y. Vol., but not on roll; in St Helena '75. R. (Martin), 1830, asked permission to cut timber at S.F.; may be an error for 'John Read.'   R. (P. H.), 1847, on the *Vandalia* at S.F. and Mont.   R. (Rachel), 1846, of the Mormon colony. v. 546; perhaps 'Read.'   R. (Richard), 1845, deserted from the *Hopewell* at S. Diego.   R. (Thos B.), 1845, doubtful name of an overl. immig. iv. 578.   R. (Wm), 1826, claimed to have been with Jed. Smith. iii. 153.   R. (Wm), 1837, Engl. sailor and lumberman in Mont. district '37–8; being also named as pilot and mate of the schr *California* '37–9. iii. 532; iv. 101.   He married a native and settled near S. Miguel before '46, in which year, with Petronilo Rios, he got a grant of the mission rancho. v. 561, 637.   Returning to his home from a successful trip to the mines he was murdered in Dec. '48, with wife, children, and servants—11 persons in all—by 4 robbers, some of them discharged N.Y. Volunteers. One of the assassins was killed in the pursuit, and the others, calling themselves Lynch, Remer, and Quinn, were executed at Sta B. Dec. 28th. v. 592, 639–40.   R. (Wm), 1842, trader at S.F. from N. Orleans, aged 32, with wife and 3 children, John, Maria, and Eliza, the last born or S.F. Padron in *Dwinelle*.

Reer (James), 1846, Cal. Bat. (v. 358).   Reese (Dav.), 1847, Co. F, 3d U.S. artill. (v. 518).   R. (Geo.), 1847, ditto.   R. (James), 1846, Co. E, Cal. Bat. (v. 358).   Reeves (S. C.), 1848, Columbia River pilot who came to Cal. on the news of gold, in a long-boat rigged for the trip; returned to Or. as mr of the *Jóven Guipuzcoana*, but came back to navigate S.F. bay on the

Flora, and was drowned in '49. *Hist. Or.*, i. 589, 808.   Reffe (Winchester),
1847, nat. of Ky and overl. immig.; a farmer near Stockton '49-56; settler in
Lake Co. '65-80; wife Lucy Maxwell.   Regalado (Pedro) inválido corp. of
S. F. comp. '39-40.   R. (Victor), 1848, nat. of Texas who came from Sonora
to the mines; later at Los Ang.   Reichart (John), 1847, Co. F, 3d U.S.
artill. (v. 518); supposed to be living in '67.

Reid (Hugo Perfecto), 1834, nat. of Scotland, who had been 6 years in
Mex., coming to S. Diego in Aug. '34 with a pass from Gefe Pol. Monterde at
La Paz. iii. 412. He settled at Los Ang., aged 23, and in '35 was accused of
complicity in the Apalátegui revolt. iii. 285; iv. 117. He is ment. in various
records from this time, and seems to have been engaged in trade with Leese
and Keith. Becoming naturalized in '39, he settled on the Sta Anita rancho,
granted to him in '41-5. iv. 635. I have several of his letters to Hartnell,
who aided him in getting the land against the efforts of J. A. Carrillo in behalf of the Lopez family. In '39 he had a wife, Victoria, and 3 children, the
wife having a grant of the Cuati rancho in '38. iii. 633. He is named as mr of
the *Esmeralda* in '42-3. iv. 565; in '43, '46, encargado de justicia at S. Gabriel,
iv. 637, of which establishment he was purchaser with Workman in '46. v.
561, 627-9. In '47 he sold Sta Anita to Dalton. v. 628; was owner of a S. F.
lot. v. 685; is named as sec. of a meeting at S.F. on land matters; visited the
mines in '48, being also Pio Pico's agent to explain the motives of his return.
v. 588; and in '49 was a member of the constit. convention. He gave much
attention to Ind. manners and customs, on which subject he wrote a valuable
series of papers, published in the Los Ang. *Star*. i. 180. His death was in '52.
Felipe and José Dolores seem to have been his sons, iv. 119, the former being
at S. Juan B. in '49.   R. (Joseph), 1847, Co. H, N.Y.Vol. (v. 499); at Napa
'71-82.   R. (Patrick), 1847, corp. Co. F, 3d U.S. artill. v. 519; supposed to
be living '64.   R. (Wm), 1835, Amer. physician at Los Ang., accused of
complicity in the revolt. iii. 242-5, 285. The ayunt. passed complimentary
resol. on his medical services; prob. confounded with 'Keith,' q.v.   Rein-
hart (John), 1846, Co. F, Cal. Bat. (v. 358).   Reintrie (Henry), 1842, sec. of
Com. Jones. iv. 310, 321; a nat. of Cuba of French parentage, who was sec.
on the *Independence* in '47; in '68 vice-consul-general at Habana.   Reisch
(Jacob), 1847, Co. G, N.Y.Vol. (v. 499).

Remer (Peter), 1848, one of the murderers of the Reed family at S. Miguel, executed at Sta B. in Dec. v. 632, 640. I think he was Raymond of the
N.V.Vol., '47, who killed Pfister in Oct. '48.   Remington (Darius C.), 1847,
Co. K, N.Y.Vol. (v. 499); in Wash. Ter. '74.   Remon (José Ant.), 1819, at
Los Ang. ii. 354.   Renard (Wm), 1840, mr of the *Francis Henrietta;* letters
of introd.; perhaps did not come.   Rendall (John), 1826, mid. with Beechey.
iii. 121.   Rendon (Guadalupe and Julian), at Los Ang. '46.   R. (Ignacio),
settler at Los Ang. '10-19. ii. 349, 354.   Renom, 1817, boatswain on Roquefeuil's vessel, d. at S.F. ii. 288.   Renshaw (Wm B.), 1846; lieut U.S.N.,
acting capt. in Stockton's bat. '46-7; came from Mazatlan with despatches
on the *Malek Adhel* Oct. '46. v. 290, 357-8, 386, 391-5.   Repeto (James),
1846, Co. C, 1st U.S. dragoons (v. 336).   Repoll (Sam. F.), 1846, killed at S.
Pascual. v. 346; prob. the following.   Repose (Sam. T.), 1846, Co. C, 1st
U.S. dragoons (v. 336).

Requena (Manuel), 1834, nat. of Yucatan, a trader who came by sea from
Guaymas, sold his vessel, and remained in Cal. In '35 he was fiscal at the
Apalátegui trial. iii. 285; alcalde of Los Ang. '36. iii. 418-19, 431, 481, 636;
took a prominent part '36-8 in the southern opposition to Alvarado, and after
the affair at Las Flores retired for a time across the frontier. iii. 491, 504, 518,
548-9, 555, 558, 561, 565. In '39-41 he was a member of the junta. iii. 590,
604; iv. 193; in '44 alcalde. iv. 411, 633; and in '45 ministro of the sup.
tribunal and suplente congressman. iv. 532, 539-40; v. 50. In the troubles of
'46-7 he seems to have taken but slight part; but in '50-67 he was often
member of the city council. He died in '76, at the age of about 72, having
always been a citizen of excellent standing and much local influence. His
wife was Gertrudis Guirado, who died in '74. His daughter married Dav. W.

Alexander, from whom I obtained copies of a small collection of *Requena*, *Doc. Hist. Cal.*   Retar (Henry), 1840, sailor on the *California.*   Revell (Andrew or Joseph), 1848, S.F. letter list.

Revere (Joseph Warren), 1846, nat. of Mass., and lieut on the *Cyane.* He was the officer sent to raise the U.S. flag at Sonoma in July, and remained in com. of the northern district for several months, making a tour to Clear Lake—the 1st ever described in print—and visiting Sutter's fort to repel the threatened Walla Walla invasion. v. 59–60, 128–9, 238, 242–3, 254, 296–7, 301, 433, 667. In '47 com. of the prize *Admittance.* v. 576; later claimant for a Marin Co. rancho. iv. 673. His *Tour of Duty,* published in '49, contained an interesting narrative of his adventures and observations in Cal. He resigned in '50 to become a ranchero in Mex., soon entering the govt service, but in '61 reëntering that of the U.S. as colonel of a N.J. regiment. He rose to the rank of brig.-gen., but was dismissed from the army by court-martial in '63 for alleged misconduct at Chancellorsville. He resided at Morristown, N.J.; published another book, *Keel and Saddle,* in '72; took much interest in pioneer Cal. matters. v. 148–9; and died in '80.   Revilla (Cristóbal), 1775, mate on transports '75–6. i. 241, 287.

Rey (Chas), 1823, mr of the *Plowboy.* ii. 492.   R. (Cristóbal), in trouble 1797. i. 639.   R. (Joseph), 1842, French lumberman in the contra costa. Reyes (Antonio), at Los Ang. i. '19–39; ii. 355; and Ant. María '46–8, perhaps the same.   R. (Dionisio), in Los Ang. revolt '46. v. 308.   R. (Fecundo), at Los Ang. '46.   R. (Francisco), settler at Los Ang. 1787; alcalde '93–5; owner of ranchos; d. before 1816. i. 461, 553,561–2, 612, 661–3; ii. 172, 185, 349. R. (Ignacio), juez de campo at Los Ang. '45. iv. 634.   R. (Inocencia), ment. at Los Ang. '46. v. 318.   R. (Isidro), aux. alcalde at Los Ang. '38. iii. 636; age 26 in '39; cl. for Boca de Sta Mónica '52. iii. 633.   R. (Jacinto), settler at Los Ang. 1804. ii. 349.   R. (José), saddler-instructor 1792–5. i. 615.   R. (José), convict settler of 1798. i. 606.   R. (José), corp. of S.F. comp. '20–8; perhaps same at Los Ang. '46–8; Sta. B. '50.   R. (Manuel), at Los Ang. '46. R. (Martin), settler at Los Ang. 1790. i. 461.   R. (Saturnino and Seferino), at Los Ang. '46–8.

Reynolds, 1810, mr of the *Sultan* '10–14. ii. 282.   R. (Ed. D.), 1847, purser on the U. S. *Southampton.*   R. (Sam.), 1843, visited Cal. from Hon. R. (Stephen), 1833 (?), Mass. trader at Honolulu, often named in Cal. corresp. of '30–44, many of his original letters being in my collection. I think he visited Cal., but find no positive record. He died insane in Mass. about '53, having lost his property in a sugar plantation at the Islands.   R. (Wm), 1847, Co. C, Morm. Bat. (v. 469).   R. (Wm), 1845, named at S. F.; also as alcalde of S. Rafael, and later claimant for part of Nicasio rancho. iv. 587, 593, 672, 677. There may be some confusion between him and the following. R. (Wm John), 1839, Engl. sailor and carpenter on the *Index,* who left the ship and settled at S.F. in '43. iv. 119. In '44, being 25 years old, he became a Mex. citizen, owner of a lot, iv. 669, and corporal in the defensores. He worked as a carpenter with Davis and Rose, spending much of the time, '45–6, in Napa Valley, where he seems to have worked on a mill, and where he built a small vessel, the *Londresa.* His visits at N. Helv. are recorded in the *Diary* of '45–7; and he is said to have been married in '46 (?) by Alcalde Boggs. There is no reliable record of the part he took in the revolt of '46, though some vague and inaccurate reminiscences are recorded in the Napa *Register* of '72.   He was familiarly known as Chino Reynolds, was rarely detected in telling the truth about early events, and died in '76 at Sonoma. R. (Wm P.), 1845, son of Stephen, b. in Manila, mate on the *Fama.* iv. 565; worked for Davis & Grimes; served in Fauntleroy's dragoons (v. 232, 247); owner of S.F. lot. v. 684; in '49–52 was in charge of Lugo's rancho, Los Ang., and later a trader; still at Los Ang. '58.   Rezánof (Nikolai Petrovich), 1806, Russ. chamberlain, who visited S.F. to establish commercial relations bet Alaska and Cal. ii. 38, 67–80, 182, 219.

Rhea (John), 1831, Amer. trapper from N. Mex. in the Wolfskill party, who settled at Los Ang., where he kept a saloon, with a billiard-table, from

'34 to '36, but is thought to have gone east about '37. iii. 387, 405. Rhett, 1845, perhaps one of Frémont's party. iv. 583. Rheusaw (Hiram), 1845, overl. immig. of the Swasey-Todd party. v. 576, 587. He is ment. at Sutter's fort early in '46; and went south with Frémont in Aug., remaining there with Gillespie, and ranking as lieut in the Cal. Bat. during the final campaign. v. 360, 386, 435; Cal. claim of $15 (v. 462). I have no record of him after his discharge from the service in April '47. Rhinehart (Joseph), 1846, German memb. of the Donner party, who perished in the snow. He had no family. v. 531, 533.

Rhoads (Daniel), 1846, son of Thomas, nat. of Ill., and overl. immig. with wife and his father's family. He worked for Sinclair on the Grimes' rancho, and was a member of the 1st Donner relief, v. 538, of which he has furnished for my use a valuable narrative in MS. Working in the mines '48-9, after a visit east he settled in '51 on a rancho near Gilroy, moving in '57 to the Kings River country, and living in '83 at the age of 62 near Lemoore, Kern Co. He had at that date a son and three daughters. Portrait in *Kern Co. Hist.*, 168. R. (Henry C.), 1846, son of Thomas, in Fresno Co. '72. R. (H.), 1847, visited Cal. on the *Gen. Kearny*. R. (John B.), 1846, oldest son of Thomas; member and perhaps capt. of the 1st Donner relief, and also memb. of the 4th; on the jury in the Keseberg trial. v. 538, 541. He settled in the Sac. Valley, was a memb of the legislature '63, and died in '66. R. (Thomas), 1846, nat. of Ky, a Mormon, and overl. immig. with wife and 12 sons and daughters. He settled on the Cosumnes, and the visits of different members of the family are often recorded at Sutter's fort in '47. In that year Mrs R. died on Sutter's launch while being carried to S.F. for medical aid, and was buried at Benicia. R. subsequently went to Utah, where he died in '69 at the age of 77. The sons, Daniel, Henry, John, Thomas, and Wm B., are named in this register. Of the daughters, Elizabeth married Sebastian Keyser in '46, and in '72, as Mrs Pierce, lived at Kingston, Fresno Co.; Sarah married Wm Daylor in '47, in '51 became the wife of Wm R. Grimshaw, and in '72 lived at the Daylor rancho with 7 children. Grimshaw's narrative has been my chief source of information about the Rhoads family. A 3d daughter married Jared Sheldon in '47, and in '72 lived at Daylor rancho with 2 children. The youngest daughter went to Utah and married John Clawson. The wife of T. Elder is also named as a daughter of R. R. (Thomas Jr), 1846, son of Thomas; prob. the T. Rhoads who served in the Cal. Bat. (v. 358); drowned while crossing the plains in '52. R. (Wm B.), 1846, son of Thomas; in Fresno Co. '72. Rhodes (Jonas B.), 1848, at S. F. from Valparaiso. R. (Stephen C.), 1846, sailor on the U.S. *Dale;* came back to Cal. in '49, and died at S.F. '50 at the age of 40.

Rice (Daniel), 1832, Amer. carpenter from S. Blas. iii. 408; at Los Ang. '40, age 30; married a Romero about '35. R. (Geo. Joseph), 1826, nat. of Mass., who came from Hon. on the *Rover*. iii. 176; ii. 558; and settled at Los Ang. In '28 he made a trip to Hon. on the *Héros* for his health, returning by L. Cal. and S. Diego, obtaining naturalization and a license to marry in '29. His wife was a Lopez, and he was for a time associated in business with John Temple, the partnership being dissolved in '32. I have several of his letters of '31-4. In the later years he kept a billiard-saloon, which he sold to Fran. Figueroa about '35; and he is said to have left Cal. for the east about the same time. R. (John), 1830, Amer. shoemaker from N. Mex. iii. 180; at Los Ang. '36, age 25. R. (Joseph M.), 1846(?), Soc. Cal. Pion. R. (Thos), 1825, mate on the *Rover*. R. (Wm H.), 1846, died in Alameda Co. '67; said to have been a sailor in the navy '46. R. (Wm), 1826, mr of the *Warren* '26, '29 (?). iii. 149.

Rich (Wm), 1841, botanist in U.S. ex. ex. iv. 241, 243. R. (Wm), 1847, maj. U.S.A., and paymaster '47-8; came on the *Preble*. v. 517, 646. Richards (Henry), 1842, sentenced at Los Ang. to 10 years of presidio in Jalisco for murder; nothing known of the case. iv. 296, 342, 633. R. (James), 1847, Co. E, N.Y. Vol. (v. 499). R. (Q.), 1847, Co. E, Morm. Bat. (v. 469). R. (Nathaniel), 1833, mr of the *N. America*. iii. 383. R. (Pierre), 1844, Frenchman in Mont. district; fined for buying smuggled goods; had a claim for damages done by Frémont. iv. 453, 566; v. 615.   R. (Peter F.), 1847, Co. B, Morm. Bat. (v. 469); reënl.   R. (Wm), 1829, British subject who got a carta.

Richardson (A.), 1846, mr of the *Brooklyn*, which brought the Mormon colony. v. 545, 576; d. in N.Y. '84 at the age of 86, and his wife the same day aged 77.   R. (Artemas W.), 1847, Co. C, N.Y. Vol. (v. 499); county surveyor in Tuolumne; d at Sonora '54.   R. (Benj.), 1848 (?), a capitalist of S.F. and N.Y. whose arrival is doubtfully accredited to this year in newspaper sketches of '84.   R. (Charles), 1847, sergt Co. B, N.Y. Vol. v. 504; d. at sea '55.   R. (Henry), 1844, clerk on the *Sterling;* d. in Cal. iv. 453.   R. (Henry P.), 1847, trader on the coast '47–8; owner of S.F. lot and of property at Benicia.   R. (Paul), 1840 (?), a noted trapper and mountaineer, who several times crossed the continent to Or., and may have entered Cal. before '48, as he did in '49. iv. 120.

Richardson (Wm Antonio), 1822, Engl. mate on the whaler *Orion* who 'left' his vessel at S.F., was permitted by Gov. Sola to remain on condition of teaching his arts of navigation and carpentry, and in '23 was baptized at the mission by P. Esténega, receiving at that time the name of Antonio, and being 27 years old. ii. 478, 495–6, 591. I have his autograph letter of '23 in Spanish, and many of later date. In '24 he was in trouble about debts. ii. 526; and this was by no means the last occurrence of such difficulties; but in '25 he married María Antonia, daughter of Comandante Ignacio Martinez. ii. 592; iii. 29; and in '27–9 he applied for naturalization—obtained in '30— calling himself a piloto, with some ideas of ship-building, speaking Spanish, and having a capital of about $3,000, besides some live-stock, and producing a certificate from P. Altimira of great usefulness to the mission by carpenter-work, and teaching calking to the Ind. He had a boat that traders could hire, served as pilot on the bay, as in the case of Duhaut-Cilly. ii. 590; was more than suspected of smuggling with the support of his father-in-law, and in '29 was employed to vaccinate Ind. at different missions, iii. 168, whence his later title of doctor. At the end of '29 he moved with his family to S. Gabriel, where he made his home till '35, though making trading trips up and down the coast in different vessels. ii. 558; iii. 143, 285, 382. In '35, returning north, after aiding in founding Sonoma, he erected the 1st structure in S.F., a kind of tent, or shanty, replaced in '36 with a large adobe building; became the owner of town lots; declined the office of alcalde in '37; and from the 1st day of '37 served as capt. of the port by Vallejo's appointment. iii. 295, 512, 700, 705, 709; iv. 97–8, 116, 153, 601–2; v. 682. His private business was the collection of country produce by a launch running on the bay. In '36 he became owner of the Sauzalito rancho, granted to Galindo in '35; and in '41 he went there to live, though still holding his office of capt. of the port of S.F. till Nov. '44, with no little trouble arising from his interested leniency to whalers who insisted on going to Sauzalito 'for wood and water.' iv. 245, 314, 376, 430, 665–6, 669–70, 683. In '46 he afforded some slight aid to the Californians against the Bears. v. 176; but under Stockton's appointment served again as capt. of the port and collector in '46–7. v. 572, 659, 433, 539. Had a Cal. claim of $6,683 (v. 462); was claimant for Sauzalito, where he spent the rest of his life, and his wife for Pinole. iii. 713; iv. 672; was a witness in the Limantour and other land cases; and died in '56, leaving a widow, still living in '80, a son, and 2 daughters. Capt. R. was a skilful sailor and an energetic man of business; and though somewhat too often involved in business difficulties, and severely criticised—as who was not?—in land litigations, is still given a good name by men of all classes who knew him in the early days. A biog. sketch is given in the *Marin Co. Hist.*, 386, the very inaccurate nature of which would not be noticed here but for the statement that it is founded on an original diary.   R. (Wm B.), 1832, Amer. tailor said to have come on the *Espía*, though I find no other record of such a vessel. iii. 408. Named in Larkin's books from '33; and in '40 at Mont., age 30, and married. In '46 he served in Co. B, Cal. Bat. (v. 358), and was still living in Mont. Co. '50. Called also Rocherson and Rickerson. Sometimes a Wm R. appears in the records, at Sonoma and elsewhere, who cannot be identified with Wm A. or Wm B., so that there may have been a third of the name   Richer, see 'Nief.'

Richie (Benj.), 1847, Co. C. Morm. Bat. (v. 469).   Richmond (Wm), 1847, Co. D, ditto.   Richter (Carl), 1832 (?), writes to Hartwell, in Russian, from Sitka, and seems to have spent some time in Cal., being a friend of the padre prefecto.   Rickman (Robert), 1841, overl. immig. of the Bartleson party; visited Mont. in Jan. '42 with letters from Sutter, but went east the same year. iv. 267, 270, 275, 342.   Rico (Francisco), nat. of Mont. b. about '20; in '42-4 clerk and celador of the Mont. custom-house, being also grantee in '42-3 of S. Lorenzo and Ranchería del Rio Estanislao ranchos. iv. 339, 377, 431, 655, 672. In the revolution against Micheltorena '44-5, Rico took a prominent part from beginning to end. iv. 460, 462, 487, 501, 505, 588. In his *Notes* of '45 Larkin describes him as an honorable, straightforward man of good standing but little property. In '46-7 as capt. of defensores he was an active supporter of the Flores movement, being 2d in com. in the Natividad campaign, chief of a sub-revolt against Flores, and finally commissioner sent to treat with Frémont. v. 45, 307, 316-18, 321, 333, 362, 365, 368, 372, 404. As late as Feb. '48 he was required to give bonds to commit no hostilities against the U. S. v. 585-6. In later years he was a ranchero in Mont. Co., being apparently supervisor in '56. In '77 he gave me his *Memorias*, a narrative confined exclusively to the events of '44-7 which fell under his personal observation, the general accuracy of his statements being well attested by original documentary records. In '85 I have not heard of his death.   R. (Martin Gonzalez), appointed in Mex. district judge for Cal. in '29, but never came.   R. (Vicente), sergt at Sta B. '29-30. iii. 78, 114.   Ricord (John), 1847, N. Y. lawyer who had been attorney-gen. of the king of the Sandwich Isl. An unfavorable letter from Com. Biddle to Gov. Mason respecting his record at Hon. and in the U.S. preceded him in Cal., and he was unable with all his arts to secure a high govt position. He opened a law office at Mont., and in '48 was a speculator in quicksilver mines.

Riddell (D. A.), 1834, mr of the *Wm Lye*. iii. 384.   R. (Timothy W.), 1834, mr of the *Martha*. iii. 383.   Ridington (Thomas), 1833, Amer. sailor, who landed from the *Ayacucho* and settled at S. Diego as a shoemaker, age 33. iii. 409. In '35 he applied for naturalization, and in '38 got provisional papers from Cárlos Carrillo as gov. His arrest was ordered in '40, iv. 15, but he was not exiled; and in '44 and '47 he served as justice of the peace. iv. 618-20. I find no record of him after '48. His wife was Juana Machado, widow of Dámaso Alipás, who still lived at S. Diego in '78, with 4 married daughters, giving me a narrative of *Tiempos Pasados*.   Ridley (Robert), 1840, Engl. sailor and clerk, who appears on Larkin's books from Jan., being in com. of Sutter's launch, and for a time in charge of Ross '41, acting also as clerk for Spear and Rae at S.F. iv. 117, 120, 129, 138, 186, 233, 668-9, 678-9. In '44 he was naturalized, owner of a lot, corporal of the militia, and married to Juana Briones of North Beach, all at the age of 25. He was a pronounced cockney, a fine-looking fellow, prone to gossip and big stories, capable of drinking prodigious quantities of brandy, and popular with all classes. In '45 he got a grant of Sonoma rancho. iv. 671; and this year or the next built a house in town—the Leidesdorff cottage, at the corner of Montgomery and California streets. He was capt. of the port in '46, and for a time 2d alcalde; but having a fight with Leidesdorff—whose letters are full of denunciation of this 'greatest blaggard in town'—he was removed from the office. v. 648-9. In July, as a Mexican official, he was arrested by the Bears and cast into prison at Sutter's fort, but released in time to get some votes for alcalde in Sept. v. 126, 129, 136, 178, 239, 295, 644-5, 659. In '47 keeping a saloon at S.F.; he went on a voyage of search for the *Warren's* launch. v. 384, 680; later appears at Mont. for a time; but in '48 was appointed alcalde at S.F. mission, where he spent the rest of his life, dying in '51. His heirs were unsuccessful claimants for the Visitacion rancho. v. 671. His name was prob. Robert T., though the 2d initial is written also J. and F., and he is also called Richard and Joseph.

Riely, 1847, of Lee & R. at Mont.   Rielson (Geo.), 1846, at Bernal's rancho near S. Leandro.   Riffe (Wm), 1846, Cal. Bat. (v. 328); prob. same as 'Reffe.'   Rigby (Geo. F.), 1847, Co. F, N.Y. Vol. (v. 499); at S. José '50. Riley (James), 1846, with Kearny from N. Mex. as asst in the engineer dept. v. 337.   R. (James), 1847, Co. D, N.Y. Vol. (v. 499); owner of S.F. lot '48. Ringgold (J.), 1841, lieut U.S.N., com. of the *Porpoise* in U.S. ex. ex. iv. 232, 235, 568.   Rins (Louis), 1840, refused grant of Sta Catalina Isl. as a foreigner; doubtful name.   Rioboo (Juan Antonio García), 1783, Span. friar who served as supernumerary at S.F. and S. Diego, retiring in '86. Biog. i. 455-7; ment. i. 379, 388, 404, 422, 459.

Rios (A.), land-owner at S. Juan Cap. '43. iv. 621.   R. (Cayetano), soldier of S. F., drowned '17-18. v. 202, 382.   R. (Gregorio), at Los Ang. '46. C. (Joaquin), sub-majordomo at S. Juan B. '35; land-owner at S. Juan Cap. '41. iii. 692; iv. 626.   R. (Petronilo), Mex. sergt of artill. at S.F. '27-40. v. 592; iii. 71, 584, 672, 702; prob. came in '24-5. In '36 named in Mont. padron as 30 years old, wife Catarina Ávila, child. José Camilo b. '34, María Lina '35, José Simon '36.   In '42 grantee of S. Bearnabé rancho, Mont. iv. 655; in '46 grantee with Reed of the S. Miguel estate. v. 375, 561, 637, 639-40; and in '52 claimant for Paso de Robles. iv. 655. He still lived in S. Luis Ob. Co. '60; and in '77 his widow, living at Sta Clara, gave me her *Recuerdos* of the Reed murders at S. Miguel in '48.   R. (Santiago), juez de paz at San Juan Cap. '42-3, where he was also grantee of land. iv. 627.   R. (Severiano), settler at S. Juan Cap. '41. iv. 626.   R. (Silverio), at S. Diego '31. iii. 201; in '39 at Sta Ana rancho, Los Ang.; in '46 at S. Juan Cap., age 45, wife Francisca, child. Salvador b. '39, José Dolores '41, José Santos '45.   R. (Silverio), at S. Juan Cap. '46, age 32, wife Primitiva (?), child Margarita b. '39, Manuel '42.

Riper (Abraham van), 1847, sergt Co. E, N.Y. Vol. v. 504.   Ripley (Francis L.), 1833 (?), nat. of Ga, who in newspaper sketches is said to have visited Mont. this year as mate on a whaler. iii. 409. In '48, being wrecked on the L. Cal. coast he came up to Mont. on the *Ohio*, and, except a short time in the mines, spent the rest of his life in Mont. Co., being city recorder and county surveyor for several terms. He died at Sta Rita '79.   Ripoll (Antonio), 1812, Span. friar who served at Purísima and Sta B., and fled from Cal. in '28; a very enthusiastic missionary. Biog. 578; ment. ii. 235, 264, 354, 364, 366, 394, 416, 423, 530-2, 534-5, 655; iii. 92-4.   Rippstein (Jacob), 1846, overl. immig. with Hoppe and Buckelew; Co. F, Cal. Bat. (v. 358); owner of S.F. lot '47; in Yuba Co. '85, a farmer.   Riser (John J.), 1847, Co. C, Morm. Bat. (v. 469); reënl.; settled in Cal. on discharge, visiting Utah '48-50, and '51-82 in Alameda Co. with wife and 6 children, Catharine, Geo. C., Chas W., May B., Franklin A., and Helen R.

Ritchie (Archibald A.), 1848, a sea-captain who bought land in Solano Co.; later successful cl. for several ranchos. iv. 671, 674; of the S.F. firm R., Osgood, & Co.; d. in '56, leaving a family.   R. (M. D.), 1846, nat. of Pa, known as 'colonel' for services in the Blackfoot war, overl. immig. with family. v. 528-9. Working a while for Sutter and being one of the first Donner relief. v. 538-9; he settled at Napa in '47, working on the ranchos of Boggs and Bale, and renting a mill of Vallejo in '48. He died at Napa in '74, having lost his wife in '73, leaving 6 married daughters—Mrs Stark and Poulson of Lake, Mrs Pond, Cooper, and Hecox of Napa, and Mrs Howard of Solano—with 32 grandchildren.   Riter (Henry), 1847, Co. B, N.Y. Vol. (v. 499). R. (Levi), 1848, Mormon who went to Salt Lake '49. *Glover.*   Rithey (Wm M.), 1846, Co. F, Cal. Bat. (v. 358); at Sutter's fort '47.   Ritschard (John), 1848, resid. of Sac. '48-52; d. in Switzerland '77.   Rittenhouse (J. B.), 1844, purser on the U.S. *Levant.*   Ritter (Henry), 1839, deserter from the schr. *California* at S.F.   R. (John), 1847, Co. A, Morm. Bat. (v. 469); reënl.

Rivas (Juan), at Los Ang. '46-8.   Rivell (Andrew), 1848, in S.F. letter list.   Rivera (Antonio) Mex. sold. in the Hidalgo piquete at Mont. '36, age 27.   R. (Francisco), Alvarado's comisionado to Mex. '42. iv. 283; grantee of

S. Luis Gonzaga, Mariposa, '43. iv. 673.   R. (Joaquin), mason-instructor 1792-5. i. 615.   R. (Pascual) corp. at the Col. Riv. pueblos, killed by Ind. i. 359, 362.   R. (Salvador), mason-instructor, 1792. i. 615, 684.   Rivera y Moncada (Fernando Javier), 1769, capt. in com. of the Loreto garrison from 1756 or earlier, and in '69 in com. of the 1st exped. by land to Cal., accompany-ing Portolá also on the 1st exped. from S. Diego to Mont. and S.F. i. 115-25, 132-6, 140-1, 150-5; returned to L. Cal. '70-1. i. 165, 167, 171-2, 175, 178, 182. In '74, by appointment of Aug. 17, '73, he came back to Cal. to succeed Fages as mil. com. of the province from May 25th. i. 216-18, 220, 225-6, 231, 238, 486, 608. His rule lasted until the arrival of Gov. Neve Feb. 3, '77, and then he went to Loreto to act as lieut-gov. of L. Cal. For events of his rule, including his troubles with Anza and Serra in '76, see i. 230, 232-5, 244-5, 248-9, 255-7, 264-73, 276, 279-80, 286-8, 292, 294-5, 298-309, 683. In '78-9 he was commissioned to raise colonists for Cal., and at the Colorado River on his way was killed by the Indians July 17, '81. i. 319, 339-44, 361-3, 487; ii. 44. On his character and family, see i. 363-4.   Riviere (P.), 1847, doubtful name in *N. Helv. Diary* '47-8.

Roach (Chas T.), 1848, in S.F. letter list.   R. (John), 1830, Amer. from N. Mex. iii. 180; in the comp. extranjera at Mont. '32. iii. 221; also named in a list of '36.   R. (Thomas), 1846, gunner in Stockton's Bat., campaign of '46-7, according to a newspaper sketch.   R. (Thomas J.), 1847, lieut Co. C, N.Y.Vol. v. 504, 511; deputy collector of the port of S.F., where he engaged in trade after a tour in the mines. In '50 he settled at Trinity bay, and in '52, being county judge elect of Klamath, was drowned in trying to cross a moun-tain stream, at the age of 28. His brother, Philip A. Roach, is a well-known citizen and official of S.F.   R. (Wm), 1847, sergt Co. D, N.Y.Vol. (v. 504); county sheriff of Mont. for several terms; in Sept. '66 his body was found in a well near Watsonville.   Roan (Francis), 1847, Co. F, 3d U.S. artill. (v. 518).   Roane (Archibald), 1847, Co. F, N.Y.Vol. (v. 499); d. at George-town, D.C., '79.   R. (John), 1847, musician of N.Y.Vol.

Robb (James B.), 1847, Co. D, N.Y.Vol. (v. 499).   Robbins, 1842, men-tioned as a lieut. with Com. Jones. iv. 308.   R. (Isaac R.), 1846, one of the Mormon colony with wife and 2 children. v. 546; a councillor of the church in Utah '84.   R. (John), 1833, at Mont.   R. (John R.), 1846, one of the Mormon colony, v. 546, with wife and 2 children, 2 children also having died on the voyage; agent to settle affairs of Brannan & Co. 47; owner of a S.F. lot. v. 678; in Utah '84.   R. (Thomas M.), 1823, nat. of Mass. and mate on the *Rover* '23-5. ii. 495; mate of the *Waverly* '26-8. iii. 147, 149, 154. About '30 he settled at Sta B., where he opened a store, commanded the *Sta Bárbara* schooner, and in '34 married Encarnacion, daughter of Cárlos Carrillo. ii. 573; iii. 140, 384; iv. 117. He is named in the padron of '36 as an Amer. trader, age 35, a catholic with wife and child. In '37-9 Capt. R. commanded the govt schr *California* in the service of Alvarado and Vallejo, winning an honorary commission as capt. in the Mex. navy. iii. 531; iv. 101-2, 552, 569, 580; v. 317. His name does not appear except in private commer-cial records in 40-4, though I have a copy of his MS. *Diary* of weather and movements of vessels at Sta B. for the 1st quarter of '43. In '46 he was gran-tee of La Calera rancho and Sta Catalina Isl. iv. 642; v. 628; being also in some slight trouble with the Flores govt. v. 330, 304; Cal. claim of $143 (v. 462). He was claimant for La Calera in '52, and died in '57, his widow living until '76. Capt. Robbins is remembered as a hospitable, good-natured old salt, whose store was a general rendezvous for seafaring men and traders, who were always welcome at his table.

Roberts (Mrs), 1847, first person buried at Benicia, drawn to the grave by an ox-team. *Tustin;* perhaps 'Rhoads,' q.v.   R. (Geo.), 1836, nat. of Ga, at Sonoma and Ross; baptized at S. Rafael '38 as Jorge María. iv. 118.   R. (J.), 1846, Cal. Bat. (v. 358); perhaps same as preceding.   R. (James), 1840, at S. Diego.   R. (L.), 1847, Co. E, Morm. Bat. (v. 469); in '82 a farmer at Kaysville, Utah.   R. (Robert), 1847, owner of a S. F. lot. v. 679.   R. (Sam.), 1847, Co. E, N.Y.Vol. (v. 499); chief of the Hounds at S.F. '50, sentenced to 10 years in the penitentiary. *Pop. Trib.*, i. 90, 99-100.   R. (Wm), 1847, Or. missionary at S. F. v. 657.   R. (Wm), 1848, Amer. sailor at the mines.   Robertson, 1848, kept a gambling and grog shop at Sta B.   R. (John), 1848, Engl. from Chile on the *Confederacion;* kept a bakery and saloon at Mont., going soon to the mines. Settled in Salinas Val., and died there in '70 at the age of 55.   R. (Robert), 1840, at S. Diego '40-8. iv. 15, 120. Robeson (Thomas), 1846, Co. C, 1st U.S. dragoons (v. 326).

Robidoux (Antoine), 1846, nat. of St Louis, Mo., who had lived 15 years in Mexican provinces and married a Mex. wife. He came with Kearny as guide from N. Mex., and was severely wounded at S. Pascual. v. 337, 346-7. Going east in '47 he came back after '49 to remain until '54. From about '56 he lived at St Joseph, Mo.—founded by his brother—where he died in '60 at the age of 66. The name is variously written, but I follow his autograph. R. (Louis), 1844, brother of Antoine, who came from N. Mex. in '44, having possibly visited the country before. iv. 265, 453. He purchased the Jurupa rancho, where he settled with his family, a man of considerable wealth. In the troubles of '46-7, being juez de paz at S. Bernardino, v. 625-6, he favored the Americans, was one of the chino prisoners (v. 311), and served in the Cal. Bat. He was cl. for Jurupa and S. Jacinto. iv. 621, 633; was a prosperous ranchero down to about '62; and died in '68 at the age of 77.   Robinson, 1838, mate of the *Llama*. iv. 91.   Robinson, 1841, storekeeper at S. Diego. iv. 619; perhaps 'Robeson.'   R., 1847, of the firm R. & Townsend at Mont. '47-8.

Robinson (Alfred), 1829, nat. of Mass., who at the age of 23 came on the *Brookline* as clerk, and remained in Cal. as agent of Bryant & Sturgis of Boston. He was baptized as José María Alfredo before '33, travelling up and down the coast from S. Diego to S.F. to bargain for the purchase of hides and the sale of goods, often mentioned in commercial records, and many of his original letters—generally signed 'Alfredo' or 'Robinson'—being in my collection. iii. 137, 146, 179, 258, 374; iv. 116; v. 590-1, 619-20. Early in '36— obtaining in his haste a dispensation of two bans with a hint from Padre Duran to contribute $20 to the church—he married Ana María, daughter of Capt. José de la Guerra y Noriega; and in '37 with his wife sailed for Boston via Honolulu. iv. 101. He came back on the *Alert* in '40 to resume his former agency, remaining till '42, when he again went east via Mazatlan, carrying despatches from Com. Jones to the govt, and also gold to the Phil. mint from the Los Ang. placers. iv. 297, 320, 403, 562, 640. While prevented by a certain personal reserve and dignity from achieving the 'hail fellow well met' popularity of some of his contemporaries, Robinson always inspired respect by his straightforward dealings; and his alliance with the leading family of southern Cal. naturally did much to give him a good standing among Californians. In '46 he published anonymously his *Life in California*, a standard work, followed by most writers on the annals of '30-42, and worthy of much praise, though showing here and there the personal and political prejudices of the author and his father-in-law. For notice of the book, with citations on various topics and a sketch of the author, see iv. 343-5; ii. 176, 563, 620-5; iv. 2-3, 6, 20, 35-6, 332-5; v. 98. In '49 he came back to Cal. as agent of the Pacific Mail Steamship Co., in later years becoming agent for the sale and management of several large estates in the south; and in '85 still lives at S.F. —the oldest surviving pioneer so far as my records show. In '80 he furnished a brief *Statement*, which has been found useful in connection with his book and his original correspondence. His wife, after living in the east I think from '37 to '50 or later, died at Sta B. in '55. There were 8 children, 2 of them b. before '40, James (who died at West Point at the age of 17), Alfredo, Miguel, James 2d, Elena, María, Antonia, and Paulina. One of the sons lives at S.F. '85, his wife being a daughter of Horace Hawes.

Robinson (Christopher F.) 1847, at Mont. from Hon. '47-8.   R. (Edward R.), 1830 (?), Amer. sailor, said to have touched at Mont. iii. 180; then 'coasted off and on' for 10 years, and settled in the Sac. Val. Mentioned 45-8 in the *N. Helv. Diary;* in '47 married Mrs Christina Patterson and lived on Dry Creek,

ROBINSON—ROCHE, 699

S. Joaq. Co.; but went to the mines in '48; testified in a land case '60; near Gilroy '72; and in S. Joaq. Co. '78.   R. (Geo.), 1839, mate on the *California* schr, who seems to have died before '42. iii. 532; iv. 101, 119.   R. (Geo.), 1842, officer of marines on the *United States. Maxwell.*   R. (Geo.), 1846, Co. C, 1st U.S. dragoons (v. 336).   R. (Geo.), 1847, sergt Co. G, N.Y. Vol. v. 504.   R. (James), 1841, nat. of the Bermudas, sailor disch. from the *Julia Ann;* still at Mont. 42.   R. (J. F.), 1848, passp. from Hon.   R. (L.), 1846, Co. F, Cal. Bat. (v. 358).   R. (Robert), 1835, Scotch sailor, in trade at S. Diego to '50. iii. 423.   R. (T.), 1847, gunner on the *Columbus.* R. (Wm), 1847, Co. D, Morm. Bat. (v. 469).   R. (Wm), 1847, Co. D, N.Y. Vol. (v. 499).   R. (Wm), 1848 (?), sup. of a N.Y. vessel wrecked in S. Amer., said to have arrived this year; at Benicia '49; later county judge of Shasta, and finally a filibuster in Peru.   R. (Wm D.), 1847, Co. D, N.Y. Vol.; (v. 499); owner of S.F. lot; watchman at Mont. '48; still at Mont. '72-82.   R. (Wm M.), 1847, nat. of S. Joaq. Pion. Soc.

Robles (Avelino), soldier S.F. comp. '27-30; killed at Branciforte '39. iii. 588.   R. (Antonio), nat. of Zacatecas; at Branciforte '28, wife Rosalía Merlopes, child. José Raimundo, Teodoro, Secundino, Guadalupe, Nicolás, Fulgencio, and Estefana. In the padron of '45 he appears as José Antonio, age 70, wife Gertrudis Merlopes age 50. He had settled at B. in 1797. i. 569; regidor 1805; comisionado '17; secretary '27; and alcalde '33. ii. 156, 390, 605, 627. iii. 696-7. He died in '42 and his widow in '49.   R. (Fulgencio), son of Antonio, a rough character, killed in '42. iv. 663.   R. (Juan José), 1769, soldier of the 1st exped.; from '76 sergt of the S. Diego comp.; killed on the Colorado '81 by Ind. i. 342-3, 362, 452.   R. (Manuel), soldier at S. Diego '71-2.   R. (Miguel), alcalde at S. Luis 1781.   R. (Nicolás), son of Antonio, in trouble at Branciforte '39. iii. 588; named in '43.   R. (Rafael), soldier of the S.F. comp. '19-30.   R. (Ramon), at Mont. '36, age 27; nat. of Branciforte; wife Perfecta Castro, child Felipe b. '33.   R. (Secundino), son of Antonio, b. '13; maj. of Sta Clara mission from '41. He claims to have been one of the discoverers of the N. Almaden quicksilver mine about '28; and respecting affairs of the mine, and on the Sanchez campaign of '46-7; in '77 at his rancho of Sta Rita, Sta Clara Co., he gave me a *Relacion.* He was also one of the claimants of Rincon de S. Francisquito. iv. 672. His wife was Antonia García, and they had 29 children. Still living in '81.   R. (Teodoro), brother of Secundino, and with him cl. for S. Francisquito. iv. 672.   Robredo (José), 1791, lieut in Malaspina's exped. i. 498.

Roca (José), 1796, Mex. sergt of artill., son-in-law of lieut Sal.; mentioned to 1802, and after an absence came back in 1805. i. 540-1, 648, 679; ii. 30-1, 144, 147.   R. (Ramon), appointed capt. of the S. Diego comp. '17, but never came to Cal.   Rocha (Antonio José), 1815, Portuguese who came on the *Columbia.* ii. 273, 393; naturalized '31; in '36 living at Sta B. with his wife, Josefa Alvarado, and 5 children, age 45; perhaps the grantee of La Brea '28. ii. 350, 565, 633. An Antonio R. was assessor at Los Ang. '69-70.   R. (Cornelio), 1798, Mex. convict settler. i. 606.   R. (Juan Estévan), corp. at S. Diego, 1775. i. 250-1.   R. (Juan José), 1825, Mex. brevet alférez who came with Echeandía under sentence of banishment for 2 years. iii. 13-14. He was put in com. of the Mont. detachment of the S. Blas comp., and is often named in the records of later years, being comisionado for the secularization of S. Juan Cap. in '33-4, in charge of S. Gabriel '36-7, and acting com. of the southern force in the sectional war of '37. ii. 549; iii. 13-14, 36, 61-2, 69, 73, 99, 204, 326, 346, 481-2, 488, 491, 495, 504, 520, 626, 644-5, 648. He died at S. Diego, at a date not recorded. His wife was Elena Dominguez; and a son Manuel died at S. Diego in '54.   R. (Ramon), soldier at Sta B. before '37   Roche (Eugene de la), 1845, came from Hon. to S.F. this year or the next acc. to his testimony and that of others in the Santillan case. Rochin (Francisco), soldier of the S.F. comp. '27-37; at S. José '41, age 30, wife María Archuleta, child Francisco b. '40; still at S. José '47.   R. (Ignacio), soldier at Sta B. executed for murder 1795. i. 638, 669. His wife was Ana María Bojorques.   R. (Leandro), regidor at S. José '35. iii. 730; in '41

named in the padron as 32 years old, wife María Fran. Romero, child. José
Ant. b. '30, Petra '27, Concepcion '28, Efigenia '29.   R. (Lúcas), soldier of
Mont. comp. '36, age 15.   R. (Miguel), killed by his wife '33.   B. (Vicente),
drummer in the Hidalgo piquete at Mont. '36, age 11.   Rochon (Z.), 1846,
came to Sta Clara Co., where he still lived in '82.
    Rock (Geo.), 1836, first appears at Sonoma as a witness against a horse-
thief. iv. 118; seems to have had a rancho near Sonoma, and in '37 was nominal grantee of S. Julian, Sta B., iii. 655–6, being in '37 grantee of Guenoc,
Lake Co. iv. 671. According to the *Lake Co. Hist.*, he lived at Guenoc from
about '48, as agent for Jacob P. Leese.   R. (James), 1841, Amer. deserter
from the U.S. ex. ex. iv. 279; though there is a record that seems to show
the banishment of a woman for *trato ilícito* with Santiago Rock in '40. He
settled at S. José, where in '45 he signed the call to foreigners. iv. 599. In
'46 he served as lieut of Co. G, Cal. Bat., but was cashiered by court-martial
in Jan. '47. v. 361, 366, 434; and was killed by Ind. in S. Joaq. Val., according to the *S.F. Star* of July 24, '47.   Rockwell (Orrin P.), 1848, guide to
the Mormons on the journey east. *Tyler.*   'Rocky Mountain Jack,' 1826,
claims to have been one of Jed. Smith's party. iii. 153.
    Roderick (John), 1841, Engl. mate of the schr *California* '41–2; mr of the
Bolivar '44–5. iv. 279, 563.   Rodford (Wm), 1845, lieut on the U.S. *Warren.* iv. 587.   Rodgers, 1838, mr of the *Flibbertygibbet.* iv. 103.   R.(1843), at
Mont., mr of a vessel. *Peterson.*   R. (Geo.), 1845 (?), lumberman before '46.
iv. 587. *Brown.*   R. (James), 1842, nat. of Md, deserter from the U.S.
Cyane, and captured by Salv. Vallejo March '43.   Rodman (Geo.), 1845,
coxswain of the *Warren's* launch, lost in S.F. bay '46. iv. 587; v. 384.   R.
(Robert C.), 1847, sailmaker on the U.S. *Columbus.*   Rodrian (Chas), 1847,
Co. K, N.Y. Vol. (v. 499); owner of S.F. lot.
    Rodriguez, at S.F. '44, age 20.   R., corp. at Sta Cruz '24. ii. 519, 522.
R., sailor sirviente at Sta Cruz 1795. i. 496.   R. (Alejandro), alcalde of Branciforte '35. iii. 696–7; in '36 at the Trinidad rancho, Mont., age 44, wife
Concepcion Martinez, child. Manuel b. '18, José '23, María del Sacramento
'26, and Juan Buenaventura '32; at Branciforte '45, age 50 (?), with the same
family less Manuel; died in '48.   R. (Antonio), 1829, Mex. convict, liberated '33.   R. (Antonio), drummer in the Hidalgo piquete '36, at Mont., age
13.   R. (Antonio), soldier at Sta B. '32; wife Mariana Arellanes; commended for valor '24. ii. 552; juez or alcalde at Sta B. '39–40, '44. iii. 654–5;
iv. 642; arrested in '45, served under Flores '46, suspected of hostile intentions '48. iv. 542; v. 330, 586; justice of the peace '51–2.   R. (Antonio),
mentioned as 103 years old at Los Ang. '73.   R. (Antonio), alcalde of Branciforte '37, and grantee of S. Vicente rancho '39. iii. 678, 695, 697; also of
Bolsa del Pájaro '36. On the Branciforte padron of '45 he is named as 46
years old, nat. of Cal., wife Dolores Galindo, child. Guadalupe b. '22, Magin
'31, Venancio '34, Miguel '37, José María '43, Balvaneda '35, Adelaida '38,
and María Ant. '41.   R. (Antonio), regidor at S. José '37. iii. 729–30.   R.
(Antonio Catarino), 1809, Span. friar, who served chiefly at S. Luis Ob. and
Purísima, dying in '24. Biog. ii. 580; ment. ii. 155, 159–60, 236, 292, 369, 384,
387, 394, 529, 532–3, 581, 618, 655.
    Rodriguez (Dámaso Antonio), corp. of Mont. comp., transf. to Sta B. comp.
in '18; sergt '21–30, ii. 572, being a leader of insurgents in '29, iii. 78, and
alférez from '31. From '33 he was alférez of the S.F. comp., sometimes com.
of the post, iii. 396, 573, 701–2, being an inválido at Sonoma on full pay from
'37. In '44 he was instructor of the Sonoma defensores, grantee of Lac
rancho, and perhaps 2d alcalde of S. Rafael. iv. 407–8, 671, 677. In '46
named as supl. juez, and as in the Olompali fight with the Bears, which took
place on his land. v. 168, 688; had a Cal. claim of $2,675 (v. 462). He died soon
after '46.   R. (Fecundo), at Mont. '36, nat. of Cal., age 22, wife Guadalupe
Robles, child. Rafaela b. '33, Concepcion '36.   R. (Felipe), at Sta B. before
'37, wife Rafaela Soto; soldier of S.F. comp. '44; prob. 2 men.   R. (Francisco), Sta Cruz poet of '18. ii. 245; in '28 at Branciforte, wife Rafaela Castro,
child. Jesus, Escolástica, Benita, and Antonia; alcalde in '30. ii. 627; grantee

of Arroyo del Rodeo '34. iii. 677; still living in '55.   R. (Fran.), at Los Ang. '43-6; justice at Alamitos '56.   R. (Giacundo), at Sta Cruz '43.   R. (Ignacio), grantee of Conejo rancho 1802 et seq. ii. 112, 172, 516, 664.

Rodriguez (Jacinto), nat. of Cal., first mentioned in public records as lieut of militia and employed by Alvarado in '36. iii. 491. From '39 he was alférez of the Mont. comp. aiding in the arrest of the foreigners in '40. iii. 671; iv. 23, 282, 652. Celador of the Mont. and S. F. custom-house '43-46, being grantee of the Jacinto rancho, Colusa, in '44. iv. 377, 431, 463, 557, 570, 671. Named in the Branciforte padron of '45 as 31 years old, wife Guadalupe ——, child. Rafaela b. '32, Concepcion '35, Guadalupe '36, and Josefa '39. Alcalde at Mont. in '49 and member of the constit. convention, the reasons for such a choice by the Montereyans not being very apparent. He still lived in Mont. Co. '74 and later, a man of some property. I obtained from him a brief *Narracion* of his recollections of early events. His oldest son, Porfirio, died at Mont. '77.   R. (José), sirviente at S.F. 1777. i. 297.   R. (José), soldier at Sta B. 1832, wife Bernarda Rosas.   R. (José), prisoner at Mont. '47; alias 'Letra.'   R. (José), síndico at S. F. '38. iii. 705; at S. F. '42, age 35, wife Romana Miramontes, child. María b. '38, María '40, José and Francisco '37; perhaps the same who had a Cal. claim of $46 (v. 462), and was at S. José '50.   R. (José), at Branciforte '45, age 21.   R. (José), soldier, carpenter, and teacher at Mont. 1796-1800. i. 643.   R. (José Antonio), soldier at S. Antonio '93 and earlier; corp. of the escolta at S. Miguel '97. i. 560; invál. at Branciforte from '99, being comisionado of the villa for some years to 1810. His wife was María Vicenta de Leon, and 6 of his sons were soldiers of the Mont. comp. after 1800. i. 571; ii. 156, 171, 390. He died in '37.   R. (José Ant.), at Trinidad rancho, Mont., '36, age 26, wife María Elena Castro; juez at S. Juan B. '44. iv. 661; perhaps was drowned in attempting to save goods from the *Star of the West* in '45.   R. (José Brígido), son of José Ant., b. at S. Antonio 1793; soldier of the Mont. comp. 1811-30; a tailor by trade. From '34 he was a ranchero in Sta Cruz Co., and in '77, at the age of 84, residing near Soquel, he gave me his *Recuerdos Históricos*. He died in '80, leaving only one surviving member of his family, an aged sister.

Rodriguez (José María), at Sta B. before '37 with wife Cármen Dominguez and 5 children; at Los Ang. '46.   R. (Juan), resid. at S. Diego '30. ii. 546. R. (Luis), at Sta B. before '37 with wife María Arrellanes and 3 children. R. (Manuel), Mex. soldier of the Mont. comp. at Soledad 1791-1800. i. 499; in 1819 comisionado of Branciforte. ii. 390; being an invál. corporal; síndico in '39 and alcalde '44. iii. 697; iv, 408, 664; in '45 on the padron as 68 years old, nat. of Sinaloa, with a daughter Josefa b. '11.; memb. of town council '48. v. 642; though this may have been the following.   R. (Manuel), at Branciforte '45, age 28, wife María Gonzalez, child. José b. '42, Santa '44. R. (Manuel), 1795, Mex. cadet and alférez of the S.F. comp. though serving in the S. Diego comp., of which he became lieut and comandante. In 1806 he was made capt. of the S.F. comp. and sent to Mex. as habilitado general, dying in '10. Biog. ii. 98-9; i. 646-7; ment. ii. 11-15, 39, 106, 109, 125, 188-9, 370, 421.   R. (María Engracia), at Sta Cruz '47. v. 641.   R. (Matias), soldier at S. Juan B. before 1800. i. 558.   R. (Nemesio), soldier of S.F. comp. '41-2.   R. (Norberto), soldier at Sta B. before '37.

Rodriguez (Pablo), Ind. settler at Los. Ang. 1781-6. i. 346, 348.   R. (Pedro), at Trinidad rancho, Mont., '36, age 25, wife Gertrudis Espinosa, child. Juan de Parma b. '32, José '35.   R. (Ramon), grantee of Agua Puerca '43 and Cañada de S. Miguel '46. iv. 655; v. 632; killed '48 in attempting to arrest the murderers of Reed in Sta. B. Co. v. 632, 648.   R. (Ramon), in Branciforte '28, wife Teresa Soto, child José de la Cruz. ii. 627; in '45, age 40, wife María Ignacia Alviso.   R. (Sebastian), sergt of the Mont. comp. '28-30, and comisionado of Sta Cruz '31. ii. 609; iii. 307; in 36 at the Trinidad rancho, Mont., nat. of Cal., age 50, wife María Perfecta Pacheco, child. José b. '12, Jacinto '13, Francisco '17, Teresa '22, Desiderio '23, Bernabé '26, María Ant. '28, Cármen '30, Ramona '32. iii. 679. Grantee of Bolsa del Pájaro in '37, iii. 677, for which he was cl.—as also for Rincon de la Ballena,

Marin, iii. 678—and about which there was much litigation between his heirs and those of his brother Alexander. He or another of the name is named as a retired soldier with the rank of alférez in '44–5. iv. 408. He died in '54 or '55. R. (Tomaso A.), grantee of Llajome rancho, Napa. iv. 671.

Roe (Chas), 1832, one of the comp. extranjera at Mont. iii. 221.   Roeder (Louis), 1847, Co. C, N.Y. Vol. (v. 499).   Roether (Chas), 1845, German immig. prob. of Grigsby-Ide party. iv. 579, 587. His name often appears in the *N. Helv. Diary* '45–7; settled at 'Charley's rancho' in Butte Co., moving in '58 to Feather River in Yuba, where he died in '68, leaving a widow and 3 children.   Rogenade (Jacob), 1848, nat. of Poland, who came with the U.S. dragoons (v. 522); murdered at Los Ang. '54.

Rogers, 1847, teamster in Sutter's employ.   R. (James), 1834; Engl. mr of the *Iolani* '35; on Larkin's books '34–43; arrested in '40 but not exiled. iii. 382, 412; iv. 17, 23.   R. (John P.), 1848, from Or. to the mines; brother-in-law of Gov. Burnett.   R. (Lewis), 1847, owner of a S.F. lot. v. 684. R. (M.), 1848, passp. from Hon.   R. (Sam. H.), 1847, Co. B, Morm. Bat. (v. 469); in Ariz. '81.   R. (Seth), 1827, mr of the *Andes* '27–9.   R. (Wm.), 1847, Co. F, 3d U.S. artill. (v. 518).   R. (Wm H.), 1847, Co. A, N.Y. Vol. (v. 499); at Brooklyn, N.Y., '74–84.   R. (Wm J.), 1843, mr of the *John Jay.* iv. 566.   Roget (Dr), 1848, intending to settle at Benicia.

Rohlman (John), 1843, Ger. settler in Sta Clara '76; carta '44, then in Sac. Val.; perhaps the name should be 'Rohlan.' iv. 400.   Rojas, at Los Ang. '37. iii. 504.   R. (Feliciano), at Corralitos rancho, Mont., '36, age 16, nat. of Mex.; in '41 at S. Juan Cap. iv. 626.   R. (Justiniano), Ind. said to have been baptized at Sta Cruz in 1791 at the supposed age of 40; d. Sta Cruz 1875, a famous centenarian.   Rojo (José María), at Sta B. before '37 with wife Altagracia García, juez de paz in '39. iii. 657–5; grantee of Cuyama in '43. iv. 642.

Roland (Fred. C.), 1828, Engl. sailor, age 23, who landed at S. Pedro, went to Los Ang., and sailed from S. Diego '29 on the *María Ester;* yet apparently at Los Ang. '30. ii. 558.   R. (John), 1841, overl. immig. of the Bartleson party, who seems to have returned east in '42. iv. 270, 275.   R. (John), 1846, grantee of Los Huecos, Sta Clara, and of land on the S. Joaq., for which ranchos he was cl. in '52. v. 665. At N. Helv. '48. I do not know if this was the same man as the preceding, Rohlman or Rohlan, John Rowland of the south, or distinct from all.   Roldan (Mariano), aux. alcalde in Los Ang. dist '36. iii. 636; grantee of La Habra '39, iii. 633, when he was 39 years old; juez de campo '40. iii. 637; at S. Gabriel '46–7. v. 626, 628. He seems to have been a Mex. who came about '36 and went back after '47.   Rolfe (Tallman H.), 1847 (?), nat. of Me, who came from Or. '47 or '48, salesman for Brannan & Co. at Sutter's fort '48, and later alcalde in Yuba Co., but was a printer by trade, perhaps working on the *S. F. Star*, and later connected with many papers in Cal. and Nev., being long the editor of the *Austin Reveille* and *Nevada City Gazette*. He died at S. Bern. in '72. Some sketches represent him as having come in '46 and served in the Cal. Bat.   Rollin, 1786, surgeon of La Pérouse's exped. i. 435.   Rollins (Henry), 1846, according to Glover one of the Mormon colony (v. 546), with son Isaac and a daughter; prob. 'Robbins,' q. v.   R. (John), 1843, at Mont.; perhaps 'Robbins.'   R. (John), 1847, Co. D, Morm. Bat. (v. 469); in Springville, Utah, '82.   R. (John), 1847, Co. E, ditto.

Romaldo, neoph. grantee of land, S. Luis Ob. '42.   Roman, tailor of 1798. i. 598.   R., neoph. accused of murder '27–8. iii. 193.   R. (Richard), 1848, doubtful date; at Vallejo '51; state treasurer '49.   Romana (Miguel), 1841, sup. of the *Jóven Carolina.* iv. 566.   Romero, a discov. of silver near Mont. '25. ii. 667.   R., soldier ment. '34, '37. iii. 257, 638.   R. (Abelino), at S. José '41, age 52, nat. of Cal., wife Juana Rubio, child. Matilde b. '24, Pedro Ant. '29, Victoria '31, José Ant. '34, Francisco '37, Rosario '39.   **R.** (Antonio), two sirvientes of the name at Sta Clara 1777. i. 306; one grantee of S. José land 1783. i. 350; regidor '85. i. 478; alcalde '90. i. 478; in '95–7 owner of a rancho near Mont. i. 683, 716.   R. (Antonio), perhaps son of the preceding, regidor at Mont. '33-4; grantee of rancho '40. iii. 673, 679. R. (Antonio), soldier at Sta B. before '37; settler at Los Ang. 1807. ii. 350. R. (Balbino), gunner at the Mont. revolution of '36. ii. 461. R. (Domingo), 2d alcalde at Los Ang. '35; in trouble '40. iii. 635, 639. R. (Felipe), black-smith at S. Diego 1775. i. 250; wife in '78 Rosario Marquez, several children born before '83. R. (Domingo), soldier at Sta B. before '37; at Los Ang. '39, age 47. R. (Florencio), at S. José '41, age 36, wife Encarnacion Miranda, child. José b. '35, Patricio '37, José Ant. '39. R. (Gabriel), soldier at the Colorado pueblos, killed by Ind. 1781. i. 359, 362. R. (Guadalupe), at Los Ang. '46; named in '58 as a centenarian. R. (Ignacio), soldier of the S.F. comp. '28-31. R. (Inocencio), soldier of the S.F. comp. '23-33; in '37 alf. of militia at S. José. iii. 732; in '44 grantee of a Contra Costa rancho. iv. 671. R. (Javier), tanner at S. José '41, age '38, nat. of L. Cal. R. (Joaquin), at Los Ang. '46.

Romero (José), 1823, Mex. capt. who made an exploring exped. from So-nora to Cal. '23-5. ii. 507-9, 542, 568; iii. 14. R. (José), soldier of the S.F. comp. '19-22, '30; in '41 at S. José, nat. of Cal., age 42, wife María García, child. Teodosia b. '30, Estefana '31, García '33, José '32, Lovribano (?) '35, and Poliarno (?) '38. R. (José), at S. Isidro rancho, Mont., '36, age 48, nat. of Cal., wife Paula Cantua, child. José b. '29, Aguilino '32, María '31, Fran-cisco '34, and Juan '35. R. (José), Mex. at Branciforte '45, age 48, child. José b. '37, Dolores '40. R. (José), at Los Ang. '46. R. (José Antonio), settler at the Colorado pueblos, killed by Ind. 1781. i. 359, 362. R. (José Antonio), soldier and settler at S. José 1777. i. 212. R. (José Ant.), teacher at S. José '23. ii. 603; at Mont. '26. ii. 612; maj. and alcalde S. Cárlos '35. iii. 354, 674, 680; being also grantee of Cañada de Laureles. iii. 677. R. (José Ant.), at Sta B. '37, wife Dorotea Alanis, 5 children. R. (José María), soldier of artill. militia 1801-10. ii. 190. He was a son of Juan María, b. about 1788. In '77, living at Los Nietos, he gave me some vague *Memorias* of the olden times. ii. 237-8.

Romero (José Mariano), 1834, Mex. teacher who came with the H. &. P. colony (iii. 259), and established what he called a normal school at Mont., writing also a *Catecismo de Ortología*, printed at Mont. in '36. He opposed the Cal. revolutionists, and left the country with Gutierrez in '36. iii. 463. R. (Juan María), corp. of the Sta B. comp. 1788; his wife was Lugarda Sal-gado. R. (Juan María), 1816, Irish interpreter in the *Lydia* case at Mont. ii. 276. R. (Manuel), at Los Ang. '39-48. R. (María), miner of Carmelo Vol. '25. ii. 667. R. (Mariano), soldier of the S.F. comp. '22-33. R. (Mar-tin), 1818, Paraguayan of Bouchard's insurgents. ii. 237. R. (Miguel Ant.), soldier at the Colorado pueblos 1780-1. i. 359. R. (Pedro), settler at S. José 1791. i. 716; wife Guadalupe García, child María Guad., in '93. R. (Pedro), settler at Los Ang. 1790. i. 461. R. (Pedro), at Los Ang. '45-6. iv. 541; v. 308, 628. R. (Pierre), 1831, Fr. laborer at Los Ang., age 53, from N. Mex. iii. 387, 405. R. (Rafael), Span. locksmith at Mont. '20-8. iii. 51. R. (Teodoro), grantee of Potrero de Felipe Lugo '45. iv. 635. R. (Tomás), soldier at Sta B. '32, wife Felipa Lugo; sergt '35. iii. 650; alférez '39. iii. 583. R. (Vicente), soldier on the southern frontier from '25; in later years at S. Diego. His *Notes of the Past* were dictated to Benj. Hayes.

Romeu (José Antonio), 1791, Span. lieut-col and gov. of Cal. from April 16, '91, to his death on April 9, '92. He was an officer from whom much was expected, especially in financial reforms; but though presumably a competent man, and certainly a conservative and amiable one, he was prevented by ill health from attending to any but routine duties during his brief term. Rule and biog. i. 481-500; ment. i. 370, 389, 393, 441, 471, 474, 479, 501-2, 530. Romeu's body was buried at S. Cárlos, and has been multiplied in current newspaper sketches into the remains of dozens of governors. Romie (Ernest), 1841, doubtful name of a German at Mont. *Toomes;* at S.F. '84. *Swan.* R. (John F.), 1843, tailor at Mont. '43-8; also visiting Sutter's fort; had a son at school '46. iv. 400. Roody (John L.), 1846, farrier Co. C, 1st U.S. dra-goons (v. 336). Rook, 1848, from Hon. on the *Sagadahoc.* Roper (John),

1832, one of the comp. extranjera at Mont. iii. 221. Ropiam, 1816, Hawaiian sailor on the *Albatross*. ii. 275. Roquefeuil (Camille), 1817, mr of the *Bordelais* '17-18, and author of a narrative of-the *Voyage*. ii. 287-91, 222, 251, 331, 373, 419.

Rosa, ment. at Mont. 1798. i. 691. R. (Cárlos), at S. Diego 1803. ii. 13. R. (José de la), 1834, Mex. printer who came with the H. & P. colony. iii. 263, 289; going to Sonoma and becoming a kind of protegé of Gen. Vallejo; had some skill as a musician, and also worked at mending clothes and tinware. In '45 he was alcalde at Sonoma, being also the grantee of Ulpinos. rancho, for which he was the unsuccessful claimant in '54. iv. 674, 678-9. In '46 he was the messenger sent to Capt. Montgomery with news of the Bear revolt, also having a quarrel with Berreyesa. v. 129-30, 668. In 1875 Don Pepe was still living at or near Martinez. Rosales (Bernardo), settler of 1779-83. i. 350, 605. R. (Cornelio), soldier at S. José mission 1797-1800. i. 556. R. (José Ant.), at S. José '30. R. (Juan), at S. Francisquito rancho, Mont., '36, nat. of Mazatlan, age 48, wife Isidora García, child. José b. '33, María '36; in later years juez de paz. iii. 678, 680; iv. 653; v. 637. Rosales Pacheco (José María), 1843, Mex. priest who served as curate at S. Buen. till '48, and in '49 at S. Antonio; also as chaplain of Flores' army '46-7. He was sent away by his superior in '49-50 for some ecclesiastical offence. iv. 371, 422, 644-5; v. 400, 632, 635. Rosalío (Eugenio), owner of Mont. rancho 1795. i. 683. Rosamel (J. de), 1840, com. of the Fr. corvette *Danaïde*. iv. 35-6, 103. Rosas (Alejandro), Ind. settler at Los Ang. 1781-6. i. 345, 348. R. (Basilio), ditto. i. 345-6, 348-9, 460. R. (Feliciano), at Los Ang. '46. R. (José), convict settler of 1798. i. 606. R. (José), maj. at Soledad '36. iii. 691. R. (José Ant.), nat. of Los Ang. and soldier, shot and his body burned at Sta B. 1801 for a *crimen nefando*. i. 639-40; ii. 119. R. (Juan), settler at S. José 1791-1800. i. 716. R. (Manuel), fifer of S.F. comp. '39-42. R. (Ramon), at Los Ang. '46. R. (Sinforóso), at Los Ang. '46.

Rose (John), 1818, Scotchman of Bouchard's insurgents captured at Mont., age 27; in '21 at Purísima, his spiritual welfare being the object of much anxiety to the authorities. ii. 232, 241, 248, 292, 393, 412, 444. Rose (John), 1841, Scotch carpenter and sailor registered at S. Blas since '39, who touched at Cal. ports in '41-2, and landed permanently at Mont. from the *Clarissa* in Nov. '43, settling at S.F. and going into partnership with Davis and Reynolds as carpenters and builders. iv. 279. In '44, being 36 years of age, he obtained a town lot, was naturalized, and served as corporal in the defensores. iv. 669, 593. In '46-7 he was town treasurer. v. 295, 648; served as lieut in the Sanchez campaign. v. 381; was a member of the council. v. 648. In '46 his firm built a schooner in Napa Creek, and in '47-8 a mill for Salv. Vallejo, going to the mines in '48. Rose gave his name to Rose bar on the Yuba, and was the first settler of Nevada Co., where he had a trading post from '49. Still living at Smartsville in '80 and prob. in '85. R. (John M.), 1847, Co. G, N.Y.Vol. (v. 499). R. (Thomas), 1847, employed by Larkin to carry despatches. R. (Wm), 1843, Engl. naturalized; prob. an error. Rosecrans (Geo. W.), 1847, lieut Co. C, Morm. Bat. v. 477. Rosencrantz (Andrew), 1847, Co. F, 3d U. S. artill. (v. 518). *Lancey;* not on the roll. Rosenberg (N.), 1833, mr of the *Polifemia* '33-5. iii. 383. Rosentiel (Anton), 1847, musician N. Y. Vol. (v. 499); d. S.F. '55. Rosete (Marcos), soldier of the Hidalgo piquete. Rosistof, 1838, mr of the *Sitka*. iv. 106.

Ross, 1846, came to Sta Clara Val. *Hall;* went to the mines '48. R. (Chas L.), 1847, nat. of N.J. who came on the *Whiton* with a cargo of goods for sale, member of the firm Gelston & Co., a prominent merchant and landowner of S.F. '47-9, also taking part in public affairs, and serving as school trustee. v. 650-1, 656-7, 678-9, 681, 683. He lived in S.F. for some years after '50; kept a hotel in Calistoga '66; returned to S.F.; and shortly before '85 went to the Sandwich Isl. In '80 he furnished me a statement of *Experiences of '47*. R. (Geo. W.), 1842 (?), in S.F. almshouse '81, said to have come in '42. iv. 341. *Chronicle.* R. (Henry), 1831, sailor on the *Catalina;* at S. Diego again '34 with Hugo Reid. R. (John), see 'Rose.' R. (J.),

1876, Co. F. Cal. Bat.; later Co. B, artill. (v. 358). R. (Sam. H. P.), 1848, nat. of La, who came on the *Major Tompkins*, and went to the mines, age 18. Afterward trader, county surveyor, assoc. judge, and superintendent of schools in Merced Co.; d. at Hopeton '73. R. (Wm), 1828, mr of the *Times*. iii. 149. Rossen (Joseph), 1848, an Or. pioneer of '43 who came to Cal. '48; at Weaverville '73. Rossignon, 1848, Fr. trader in the mines with Ama- ador and Suñol, who ran away to Peru with the profits of all three. Prob. ' Roussillon,' q. v.

Rotchef (Alex.), 1836, Russian manager at Ross '36-41. iv. 117-18, 129, 153, 164, 171-6, 179-86; iv. 233. Roteta (Antonio V.), 1825, naval officer on the *Asia*. iii. 25-6. Roth (John), 1848, German sailor in the navy, disch. in '48; in the mines '48-51; trader at Mont. '52-73; d. at Castroville '79, leav- ing a wife. Roudon (Guadalupe), at S. Bern. '46, age 35. Rouelle (Jean B.), 1841 (?), Canadian trapper from N. Mex. iv. 278-9. Nothing is known of his coming, but he is named as the discoverer of gold in '42 in the S. Fernando region. iv. 631. A few years later he moved with his family to the Sac. Val., and was there during the mining excitement, being named in the *N. Helv. Diary*. Finally settled on Feather River. Romissillon, 1802, Polish count who sailed with Cleveland and Shaler. ii. 11, 22. Roulam (Henry), 1846, of the Mormon colony. See 'Rowland.' Rouleau (François), 1836, Fr. laborer at Los Verjeles rancho, Mont., age 30. Roulette (Wm R.), 1845, overl. immig. of the Grigsby-Ide party; lived in Capay Valley '45-6; prob. went to Or. '46. iv. 579-80; v. 526. Round (Joseph), 1845, mr of the *Pacific*. Rous- seau, 1846, with Gillespie when he met Gen. Kearny. Roussillon (Charles), 1843 (?), Fr. trader who 1st appears at Los Ang. this year, but is said to have come in '37, or even in '33. iv. 400. From '44 he was in the Mont. district, chiefly at Sta Cruz, where he had a mill and dealt in lumber, building a schooner in '46, v. 641, and in '47-8 being a partner of Sainsevain. The 1st jury trial in Cal. was that of Graham vs R. in '46. v. 289. I have some of his business corresp., but no record after '48. Perhaps he went to S. Amer. See 'Rossignon;' age 31 in '45.

Rowan, 1842, doubtful name of a trapper at Los Ang.; came again to Cal. '50. v. 341. R. (H.), 1847, lieut on the U. S. *Cyane*. R. (James), 1799, mr of the *Eliza*. i. 545, 706; and of the *Hazard* 1802-4. ii. 11, 17-18, 24-5, 108, 119, 122, 130. R. (James), 1847, Co. G, N.Y.Vol. (v. 499); in '48 teamster for Brannan & Co. at Sac. R. (Stephen C.), 1846, lieut U. S. N., and acting maj. of Stockton's Bat.; wounded at the Mesa Jan. '47. v. 385, 395; in later years vice-admiral. Rowe, 1848, at Sonoma, called one of the N.Y.Vol. R. 1848, went to Hon. on the *Currency Lass*. R. (James), 1816, sailor on the *Lydia*. ii. 275. Rowland (Henry), 1846, of the Mormon colony with his son Isaac and perhaps a daughter. v. 546. They were generally called 'Rollins' by the Mormons. Henry R. died in the faith before '80. R. (John), 1841, nat. of Pa and leader of the Workman-R. immig. party from N. Mex., where he had lived 18 years, amassing considerable wealth and marrying a native wife. iv. 276-9, 637. He was suspected of complicity in certain revolutionary or filibustering schemes in connection with the Texans, and this was a lead- ing motive of his emigration; indeed, warnings were sent to Cal., but they did not prevent his getting in '42 a grant of La Puente rancho in company with Workman. iv. 331, 635. Then he went to N. Mex. and brought his family, spending the rest of his life on his rancho. iv. 343. In '45 he joined the other southern foreigners in their opposition to Micheltorena. iv. 495, 508; and was one of the Chino prisoners in '46, v. 314, having a Cal. claim of about $1,500 (v. 462); but as a rule took no part in public affairs, being noted for his retir- ing disposition and fondness for home life. He died in '73 at the age of about 80. His son Wm R. was sheriff in '73, and he or another son married a daughter of Bernardo Yorba. Roy (C.), 1822, mr of the whaler *Alert*. ii. 474. R. (Chas), 1823, mr of the *Plowboy*. ii. 492; perhaps Ray. R. (Pierre), 1782, Fr. sirviente at S. Buen. i. 377. Royabe (Claudio), at Los Ang. '46. Royal (B.), 1845, at Sutter's fort '45-6; perhaps one of Sub- lette's men.

Rub (Geo.), 1847, Co. C, N.Y. Vol. (v. 499).   Rubí (Mariano), 1790,
Span. friar whose missionary service was at S. Antonio and Soledad. He
retired in '93, and was prob. expelled from the college for immorality. Biog.
i. 499; ment. i. 388, 492, 576, 597.   Rubio (Casimiro), at Los Ang. '43-5. iv.
541, 633; fatally wounded at S. Pascual '46. v. 347.   R. (Francisco), soldier
of the S.F. comp. '24-31; executed in '31 for crime committed in '28. His was
one of the causas célebres of Cal. ii. 592, 594; iii. 191-3, 699.   R. (Francisco),
at Los Ang. '46; killed at the S. Gabriel fight Jan. '47. v. 396.   R. (José
M. de J. Gonzalez), see 'Gonzalez.' iii. 318, 724.   R. (José), at Los Ang. '46-8.
R. (Manuel), at Los Ang. '46.   R. (Mateo), nat. of Flanders, soldier of the S.
Diego comp. in 1779 and earlier, and a settler at Los Ang. 1794-1819. i. 454;
ii. 349, 354. His wife was Ursula Dominguez, and the birth of 4 children is
noted before 1790, one of them being Francisco Ramon.   R. (Nabor), Mex.
at Mont. '36, age 40.   R. (Rafael), soldier of the S.F. comp. '24-6.   R.
(Santiago), at Los Ang. '19. ii. 355.   R. (Tomás), at San Juan Cap. '46, age
30, child Candelaria; at Los Ang. '48.
    Ruckel (Joseph L.), 1847, a prominent trader at S.F., S. José, and Mont.
'47-8, of the firms Sherman & R. and R. & Cooke. v. 663. About '55 he went
to Or., where he became a steamboatman and pres. of the O. S. N. Co., still
there in '74-5.   Rucker (Dan. H.), 1848, capt. of dragoons in Graham's battalion. v. 522.   R. (R. A.), 1848, at S.F. and Mont.   Rudacof, 1846, Russ.
naval lieut on the *Baikal* at S.F.   Rudd (John), 1848, came from Callao on
the *Lady Adams* and took com. of the U.S. *Dale.* v. 577.   Rudenstein
(John), 1846, asst surgeon on the U.S. *Dale*, d. '69.   Rudierkof, 1846, Russ.
lieut; prob. same as 'Rudacof.' v. 576.
    Rufus (Ernest), 1844, nat. of Germany, about the manner of whose coming,
perhaps earlier, nothing appears. iv. 453. He was naturalized in March '44,
appointed in July a lieut in Sutter's army, fighting for Micheltorena, and in
Dec. got a grant of the Cazadores rancho in Sac. Val. iv. 479, 485, 671, 680.
In '45, in partnership with Wm Benitz, he leased the Ross property from Sutter; and in '46 was grantee of the Rancho de German, north of Ross. iv. 679;
v. 669. He sold the rancho, or parts of it, to Glein and Hägler in '47, but
seems still to have resided in Sonoma Co. as late as '79.   Ruggles (John),
1847, Co. K, N.Y. Vol. (v. 499); at Sac. in '82.
    Ruiz, mentioned in 1798. i. 670.   R. (Agaton), wounded at the Olompali
fight. v. 166-8.   R. (Anselmo), at Los Ang. '39-46, age 25 in '34.   R.
(Cárlos), at Sta B. before '37, wife María Ant. Verdugo, 4 children.   R.
(Catarina), widow of M. Nieto, grantee of Las Bolsas '34.   R. (Efigenio),
settler at Los Ang. 1790. i. 461.   R. (Eustaquio), killed at Pauma '46. v.
617.   R. (Francisco), com. de policía at S. Diego '36, regidor '37. iii. 616.
R. (Francisco), at Los Ang. '39-48.   R. (Francisco María), nat. of L. Cal.
and sergt of the Sta B. comp. from 1795, alférez 1801, lieut 1805, and from
1806 comandante at S. Diego, being promoted to capt. in '20 and retired
from active service in '27. He received a grant of the Peñasquitos rancho, and
died in '39 at the age of about 85. He never married. Biog. ii. 5, 39-41; ment.
i. 636, 665; ii. 50, 85, 99-101, 109, 117, 191, 240, 245, 340-1, 345, 451, 457,
546-8, 551-2, 571, 663; iii. 7-8, 612.   R. (Fructuoso), settler at Los. Ang.
1799; regidor 1802. ii. 110, 349.   R. (Gerónimo), zanjero at Carpentería '48.
v. 631.   R. (Guadalupe), at S. Gabriel '46.   R. (Hilario), soldier at Sta B.
before '37.   R. (Joaquin), grantee of Bolsa Chica, Los Ang., '41, being also
claimant '52; at Los Ang. 13, '39, '46; age 47 in '39. ii. 350; iii. 639.   R.
(José), inválido settler at Los Ang. '15. ii. 349.   R. (José), soldier at Sta B.
'32, wife Isabel Uribe.   R. (José), at Sta B. '32, wife Maria Ign. Lugo, child.
Deogracia, Gerónimo, Baltazar, Hilarion, and Gabriel; in '45 a ranchero.
R. (José Manuel), brother of Francisco M., lieut in L. Cal., appointed to Cal.
in '24 but did not come; he became gov. of L. Cal. ii. 515, 540.   R. (José
Pedro), grantee of Calleguas rancho Sta B. '47, his heirs Gabriel et al. cl. iii.
655.   R. (José María), settler at S. José 1791-1800. i. 716.   R. (Juan), settler at Los Ang. '12. ii. 350; at Sta B. '50.   R. (Juan María), mentioned
in 1801. ii. 171.   R. (Leon), 1842, Mex. sub-lieut of the batallon fijo '42-5.

iv. 289.   R. (Manuel D.), mason-instructor 1792–5. i. 615.   R. (Manuel García), made alférez 1789, but did not come to Cal. i. 340.   R. (Mariano), at Los Ang. '39, age 25.   R. (Martin), settler at Sta B. '32, wife Catalina Lizalde; at Los Ang. '46.   R. (Nicolás), at Sta B. '37, wife Encarnacion Pico, and 5 children.   R. (Santiago), mason-instructor 1792–5. i. 615, 684–5.   R. (Toribio), ditto. i. 615.   Ruiz de la Mota, see 'Mota.'

Rule (John H.), 1847, Scotch teacher at Mont., from Callao on the *Guipuzcoana.*   Ruinville (Geo. W.), 1839, at Mont., as per Larkin's books.   Rumschöttel (Richard), 1847, Co. C, N.Y. Vol. (v. 499); hospital steward at Sac.; at Vallejo '71–4; drowned at Stockton '74.   Runyan (Levi), 1847, Co. D, Morm. Bat. (v. 469).   Rupe (Henry), 1847, Co. F, 3d U.S. artill. (v. 518); supposed to be living in '64.   Ruschenberger (W. S. W.), 1836, surgeon on the U.S. *Peacock*, and author of a *Narrative* of the voyage. iv. 140–2; iii. 680. Rush (Madison), 1847, acting lieut on the U.S. *Columbus.*

Russ (Adolph Gustav), 1847, son of J. C. C., born in Germany '26; of Co. C, N.Y. Vol. (v. 499); owner of a S.F. lot; in the mines '48. He settled in S.F., where he still lived in '82, having been a member of the legislature in '67. His *Biography* and *Remembrances* in my col. of MSS. are brief sketches of the family and of S.F. affairs in early times. He married Frances Simon in '51, and had 5 children surviving in '79.   R. (August), 1847, brother of A. G., b. N.Y., drummer of Co. F, N.Y. Vol.; still living in S.F. '82.   R. (Chas Christian Ed.), 1847, brother of A. G., b. in Germany '28; fifer of N.Y. Vol.; owner of a S.F. lot. v. 676. After his disch. at Sta B. he went to the mines in '48, making many later mining tours down to that of Frazer River in '58. The intervals were filled in with business enterprises at S.F. He married in '52, and was the father of 7 children. Still a rich and prominent citizen of S.F. in '82; life and portrait in *Contemp. Biog.*   R. (Henry B.), 1847, brother of A. G., who came, as a boy, with the family; in later years supervisor of S.F., where he still lives in '85.   R. (Jacob), 1846, overl. immig. of Young's party. v. 529.   R. (J. C. Christian), 1847, German of Co. C, N.Y. Vol. (v. 499). He had made a fortune as a jeweller in N.Y., and lost it by burglarly one night when he closed his shop and went to see a procession in honor of Gen. Jackson. He enlisted with 3 sons, and was accomp. by his wife and other children. Opening a jeweller's shop at S.F., he obtained, as did his sons, building lots, v. 676, and rapidly regained his fortune during the flush times. He became the owner of much real estate, besides the original lot on which he built the hotel still owned by the family and called the Russ House. His house on this lot was in '47–8 the southern limit of settlement, being separated from the town by a sand hill. He also built a residence on Harrison St in the far-off wilderness, and the Russ Garden near by was from '57 a popular place of suburban resort. He died in '57, and his widow, Christina, in '80. The sons are named in this *Register;* a daughter, Mrs Mebius, died in Dresden '85.

Russell, 1846, mr of the *Sarah Parker.* v. 580.   R. (Chas), 1846, of the Mormon colony, but prob. did not come to Cal. v. 547.   R. (Eugene), 1845, one of Frémont's men, and of the Sta B. garrison '46. iv. 583; v. 316; later in Co. A, Cal. Bat. (v. 358). He applied for land in the S. José district '46. R. (Geo. W.), 1847, sailor on the *Independence;* applied to Larkin for a clerkship.   R. (Henry or Wm), 1847, carpenter and builder at Benicia, a partner of Bryant and of Briggs. v. 672.   R. (John), 1845, sailor on the *Benj. Morgan.*   R. (J.), 1848, passp. from Hon.   R. (Robert E.), 1846, of Cal. Bat. (v. 358); Cal. claim $46 (v. 462); witness at Wash. '48; at S. José '50. Perhaps same as Eugene.   R. (Thomas), 1835, Amer. sailor picked up by the *Pilgrim* at Sta B. and landed at S. Diego in '35. iii. 412. He became a permanent resident of S. D., and is named by Dana in his *Two Years.* In '36, with one Weldon, he made an exped. in search of buried treasure at the Colorado River missions, the affair causing more excitement than increase of wealth. iii. 613. The same year he was in trouble through sending a challenge to Lumsden for a duel. iii. 618. In '40 he worked as a carpenter, being married to a native, 37 years old, and a naturalized citizen. Next heard of in '47, when he was in trouble for refusing obedience to the alcalde, or perhaps for an attempt to commit murder. v. 618; and in '48 ment. by Buffum in the mines at Weber Creek. A man of the same name was cl. for land in Sta Cruz Co. '52. R. (Wm), 1845, Amer. at Mont.; perhaps the owner of a S.F. lot '47; or one named in Napa Val. '47-8; or as present at Dr Semple's marriage at Benicia '47. v. 672; or some of these may be the following. R. (Wm), 1847, Co. G, N.Y. Vol. (v. 499).

Russell (Wm H), 1846, nat. of Ky who had been somewhat prominent in local politics, memb. of the legislature, U.S. marshal, etc.; also serving in the Florida war. He came to Cal. overland with Bryant and Jacobs. v. 528; made a flowery oration at the S.F. reception of Com. Stockton in Oct. v. 295-6; served as ordnance officer with rank of major in the Cal. Bat. v. 160, 399; and was one of the commissioners to make the treaty of Cahuenga, v. 404-5, being somewhat active in the Frémont-Kearny controversy, and sec. of state at Los Ang. during Frémont's rule as gov. v. 422-4, 432-3. In March '47 he was sent east with despatches, his chief mission being to secure F.'s appointment as gov. v. 445, 454; and he was one of F.'s principal witnesses at the court-martial. v. 420, 423, 456. He came back to Cal. in '49, and practised law at S. José, Sac., and S.F. to '54 or later; about '61-2 was U.S. consul at Trinidad de Cuba, but resigned and returned to Ky, where he died. A daughter married a grandson of Henry Clay. A second wife was married about '62. Russell was a boastful man of many words, and a hard drinker, but honorable, intelligent, and popular, with much ability. R. (Wm W.), 1847, lieut of marines on the U.S. *Independence.* Russum (Thos), 1846, Engl. mr of the *Euphemia* and *Mary Ann* '46-7. v. 578-9; heard of in England in later years. Ruth (John), 1847, Co. G, N.Y.Vol. (v. 499). Rutledge (John), 1847, acting lieut on the U.S. *Erie.* Rutter (Henry), 1841, employed on Leese's launch at S.F. R. (John), 1829, mr of the *Planet.* iii. 148.

Ryan (Edward), 1847, Co. B, N.Y.Vol. (v. 499); d. S.F. '66. R. (Geo. F.), 1843, Irishman who got a pass in Dec. R. (Geo. P.), 1847, went to Hon. on the *Gen. Kearny.* R. (P. H. W.), 1847, Co. A, N.Y.Vol. (v. 499). R. (Q.), 1847, blacksmith at Mont. R. (Wm), 1845, sailmaker on the U.S. *Savannah.* R. (Wm Redmond), 1847, Co. D, N.Y.Vol. (v. 499). He returned east by Panamá, and wrote his *Personal Adventures in Upper and Lower Cal.,* 1848-9, published in London '50. Died at N. Orleans '52. Ryder (Geo. W.), 1847, arr. Oct., according to Soc. Cal. Pion. roll; died S.F. '68, age 49.

Saavedra (Ramon A.), 1790, Span. com. of transport and exploring vessels on the coast 1790-7. i. 506, 523-4, 542, 706, 728; ii. 184. See also *Hist. N. W. Coast,* through index. Sabici (Matias), 1834, Ital. sailor who came from Mex. with the H. & P. colony, and settled at Mont. after working for a while at the Palo Colorado as a sawyer. iii. 412. He is mentioned at Los Ang. in '47, and seems to have married a daughter of Wm Wolfskill. Sabas, (José), at Los Ang. '48. Saenz (Ignacio), Mex. convict of 1791. i. 606. S. (Juan), soldier of the S.F. comp. '19-30. S. (Luis), ditto '42. S. (Macario), of S.F. militia '37. S. (Manuel), soldier of S.F. comp. '32-3; militia '37; at Sonoma '44, age 30. S. (Pablo Pedro), of S.F. militia '37, exiled in '39. iii. 580; perhaps Pablo and Pedro. S., see also 'Sais,' 'Saez.' S. de Lucio, see 'Lucio.' Saez (José, Justo, and Miguel), settlers at S. José 1797. i. 717. S. (Nasario), settler at S. José 786. i. 477; wife Micaela Sotelo, child. in '93, Miguel, Juan, Benedicta, and Felipa. Sagarra (Eduardo), Peruvian shot for stealing at Mont. '31. iii. 191, 669, 673, 679. S. (Mateo), 1818, of Bouchard's insurgents, captured at Mont. ii. 232. Sahr (Albert), 1847, owner of S.F. lot.

Sainsevain (Pierre), 1839, French carpenter, age 20, who arrived at Sta B. on the *Ayacucho.* iv. 117, 119. His passport was dated Bordeaux, Nov. '38. He was a nephew of Louis Vignes, whom he joined for a time in the manufacture of wine at Los Angeles. In '43 he was grantee of the Cañada del Rincon rancho, iv. 655, and from '44 owned a saw-mill at Sta Cruz, being from '46 in partnership with Roussillon, building a schooner in '46, v. 641, and also from '46 having a flour-mill at S. José, which gave rise to some local troubles. iv. 685; v. 660. He went to the mines in '48, Sainsevain Bar being named for him; and in '49 was a member of the constit. convention. In later years he became one of the most prominent vineyardists and wine-makers in the state. His wife, married in '45, was a daughter of Antonio Suñol. St Clair (Trouett), 1843 (?), trapper who prob. came from N. Mex. about this year. iv. 400; ment. by Schallenberger and in the *N. Helv. Diary* '44–5; still living in Sta Cruz Co. as late as '79.   St Germain (Baptiste), 1831, Fr. from N. Mex.; prob. with Wolfskill. iii. 387.   St John (Augustus A.), 1847, Co. B, N.Y.Vol. (v. 499).   St J. (Henry), 1843 (?), Engl. sailor, and later sugarplanter in the Sandw. Isl., said to have come to Cal. this year. iv. 400. He was later a miner and cattle-dealer, who attempted suicide at S.F. '83.   St J. (J.), 1848, passport from Hon.   St J. (Stephen M.), 1847, Co. E, Morm. Bat. (v. 469).   St Quintin (Joseph), 1847, Co. C, N.Y.Vol. (v. 499).   Sais (Domingo), soldier of the S.F. comp. '26–33; of S.F. militia '37; grantee of Cañada de Herrera, Marin, '39. iii. 711. He had been elector and regidor of S.F. '37–9. iii. 705; and his age was '39 in '44. His name is written also 'Saenz' and 'Saez,' which are perhaps more correct forms; at least, it is impossible to distinguish between them in Cal.   S. (Miguel), settled at Los Ang. 1806. ii. 350.   Saizar de Vitoria, see 'Vitoria.'   Sajat (Lewis T.), 1847, owner of S.F. lots.

Sal (Hermenegildo), 1776, Span. soldier who came with Anza; guardaalmacen at S.F. '78–82; alférez '82; lieut '95. He served at Mont. 1782–1800 (except '91–4 at S.F.); much of the time as habilitado and comandante. In 1800, being retired as capt., he died at Mont. Though a quick-tempered man, he was a faithful officer, strict disciplinarian, and excellent accountant. Biog. and fam. i. 678–80; ment. i. 297, 335, 396–7, 441, 463, 467–8, 490, 493–6, 501, 509–11, 514, 516–18, 526, 537, 547, 551–2, 569, 572–3, 588–94, 634, 680, 692–707, 718; ii. 143, 191; iii. 11.   Salamanca (Secundino), 1791, Span. lieut in Malaspina's exped. i. 490.   Salazar, 1796, com. of the *Concepcion* and *Activo* '96–7. i. 540, 544.   S. (Alonso Isidro), 1791, Span. friar, who was a founder of Sta Cruz, where he served until his retirement in '95, writing in Mex. an important report on the *Condicion Actual de Cal.* Biog. i. 497–9; ment. i. 494, 566, 576, 579–80, 603–4, 618, 626, 661.   S. (Antonio), at Los Ang. '46; juez de campo '48. v. 626.   S. (Canuto), fifer of the S.F. comp. '39–42; in '54–5 at S.F., age 28; witness in the Santillan case.   S. (Dionisio), at Branciforte '45, age 28, wife Perfecta Castro, child. Encarnacion b. '40, and Juan '41.   S. (Fulgencio), soldier of the S.F. comp. '38–42.   S. (Ignacio and Jesus), at S. Bern. '46.   S. (Isidro), teamster at Mont. '47.   S. (Jorge), soldier at Mont. '36, age 25.   S. (José), convict settler 1798. i. 606.   S. (José), soldier of S.F. comp. '38–43. iv. 667; Cal. claim (v. 462).   S. (José Antonio), N. Mexican trader and settler from '39. iv. 81, 278, 387; in '46 supl. juez at S. Feliciano rancho. v. 625; in '47 alcalde at Los Ang. v. 626; still there in '48.   S. (José María), regidor at Branciforte '34. iii. 696, 588; in '45 on the padron as a nat. of Cal., age 60, wife Hermenegilda Rios, child. Isidro b. '15, Jorge '19, Juan '25, Maria Refugio '30, Refugio '33.   S. (Juan), com. of the guard at S. Fern. '23. ii. 570; in '27–30 acting habilitado at Sta B. and S. Diego. ii. 543, 572; iii. 114. In '31–4 he was promoted from sergt to alférez, and was once a prisoner during the sectional wars in '37. He was acting com. of S. Diego, and is ment. as late as '46. iii. 482, 503–4, 541, 608–10; iv. 617; v. 566.   S. (Miguel), soldier at S. José mission 1797. i. 556. S. (Ramon), at Los Ang. '46.

Sales (Alex.), 1833, Amer. hunter from N. Mex., at Los Ang. '36, age 29. Prob. Cyrus 'Alexander,' q.v.; also ment. in the campaign of '45. iv. 495.   S. (Francisco), grantee of land at S. Gabriel '45. iv. 637.   Salgado (Augustin), at Los Ang. '46.   S. (Francisco), ditto; in S. Luis Ob. 50–8.   S. (Tomás), juez aux. Mont. dist '44. iv. 653.   Salines, 1842, Frenchman in Sutter's employ. iv. 341; prob. the Salinas named in *N. Helv. Diary* '45–8.   Sallalla (Faustino), soldier at the Colorado Riv. pueblos 1780–1, killed by Ind. i. 359, 362.   Salleman, 1847, doubtful name of a Frenchman at S. José.   Sallee, 1846, of West's overl. party, killed on the Humboldt. v. 528.   Salmon (Alejo), colegial at Sta Inés '44. iv. 426.   S. (James), 1846, Delaware Ind.

in the fight at Natividad. v. 367; at Sutter's fort '47.   Salvador, Cal. Ind. sent by Sutter to relief of the Donner party '46. He refused to eat human flesh, but was himself shot and eaten. v. 531–2, 534, 537.   Saly, 1845, at Sta B.   Samlyn (Henry), 1847, Co. F. Cal. Bat. (v. 358).   Samop (Jaime), Ind. alcalde at S. Diego 1799. i. 655.   Sam Tetoy, Ind. chief, later called 'Solano,' q.v. ii. 329.   Sampson (Z.), 1848, passp. from Hon.

Sanchez (Antonio), soldier at Sta B. before '37.   S. (Estévan), soldier at Sta B. '32, wife Romana Lopez.   S. (Francisco), son of José Ant.; soldier of the S.F. comp. '24–5; in '27–8 elector and sec. at S.F. and S. José. ii. 592, 605; in '35 sec. iii. 704; in '37 sec., capt. of the militia, elector, and grantee of town lots. iii. 506, 511, 701, 705; v. 683; in '38–9 acting-com. at S.F. and grantee of S. Pedro rancho, S. Mateo co. iii. 563, 701, 713. He served as juez de paz in '43. iv. 665; in '42 is named on the padron as a nat. of S. José, age 35, wife Teodora Higuera, child. Luisa b. '34, Luis '36, Dolores '38, and Pedro; in '44 capt. of defensores. iv. 407, 468, 667; in '45 capt. of the post, and grantee of town lot. iv. 666, 669; v. 678. In '46 was acting com. at S.F., though absent at the capture by the U.S. v. 4, 17, 61, 239–41, 659; and in '46–7, provoked by the depredations of the Americans, he headed a kind of revolt, with a view to obtain guaranties, taking captive Alcalde Bartlett and his guard, who were making a plundering tour. v. 379–83. Don Francisco still lived at S.F. mission in '55. He is remembered as a hospitable man, though somewhat hostile to Amer., and always regarded by them with suspicion.

Sanchez (Francisco de Jesus), 1842 (?), Mex. friar of the Zacatecanos, who was apparently left behind in L. Cal. when the others came in '33. iii. 319. He was minister at S. Buenaventura '42–3 and '52–3; at Sta Inés '44–50, being vice-rector of the seminary. iv. 425–6, 644–5; v. 635. He is named occasionally at S. Gabriel and Sta B. to '58, but I have found no later record of him.   S. (Francisco Miguel), 1774, Span. friar who served at S. Gabriel, and temporarily at other missions, till his death in 1803. Biog. ii. 113–14; ment. i. 299, 388, 451, 459, 495–6, 511, 576, 664, 719.   S. (Gil), regidor at Mont. '36, tithe col. at Branciforte '39, grantee of Arroyo de la Laguna '40, killed Robles '42, agente de pol. '45. iii. 675, 676, 697; iv. 653, 663.   S. (Hilario), grantee of Tamalpais '45. iv. 674.   S. (Isidro), son of José Ant., of S. F. militia '37, age 23 in '42, wife Teodora Alviso, child. Dolores b. '37, Isabel '40, and Narcisa '41; involved in the assault on Capt. Libby '45.   S. (Jacobo), in revolt at Los Ang. '45. iv. 538–9.   S. (Joaquin), sirviente at Sta Clara 1776. i. 306.   S. (Joaquin), 1801, sergt sent from Mex. to superintend cultivation of hemp. i. 620–1; ii. 178, 181.   S. (Joaquin), soldier of the S. F. comp. '23.   S. (José), 1791, piloto in Malaspina's exped. i. 490.

Sanchez (José Antonio), nat. of Sinaloa, soldier of the S.F. comp. from 1791, corp. from 1805, sergt from 1806, brevet alférez from '20, and alférez from '27, or, as some records indicate, from '32. He was for some years corp. of the Sta Cruz escolta. i. 496, 526, 535; was later engaged in over 20 Ind. campaigns and exploring exped., especially in '17–26, being famous for his skill and courage as an Ind. fighter. ii. 91–2, 126, 232, 322, 329, 335, 339, 371, 445, 497–9, 538, 584; iii. 111–12, 123. In '27–35 he was the grantee of Buri-buri rancho, S.F. ii. 591–5, 664; iii. 711; in '29–33 com. at S.F., though involved in the revolt of '29. iii. 75, 96, 223–4, 333, 365, 701; but in '32–4 apparently attached nominally to the Mont. comp. iii. 671. In '36 he was retired from active service, living on his rancho or at the mission; is named on the padron of '42 as 67 years of age; and died in '43, being denied the comforts of religion on his death-bed, and for a time Christian burial, through some quarrel with the friars, to whom he was always hostile. iv. 373. He was a good man, of known honesty and valor, but very ignorant and unfit for promotion. His sons were José de la Cruz, Francisco, Manuel, and Isidro. His daughters married Fran. de Haro, two Valencias, and John Read.   S. (José Ant.), settler at S. José 1791–1800. i. 716.

Sanchez (José Bernardo), 1804, Span. friar who served chiefly at S. Diego and S. Gabriel till his death in '33. A very prominent missionary and president of the Fernandinos in '27–30. Biog. iii. 641–2; ment. ii. 47, 99, 106–7, 110, 159, 344, 366, 394, 442, 487, 560, 564, 567, 569, 580, 655, 657; iii. 87, 91–2, 94, 96, 102, 108, 142–4, 155, 309–10, 315–16, 337–8, 347, 351.   S. (José de la Cruz), son of José Ant., elector at S.F. '35, regidor '36–7. iii. 704–5; grantee of S. Mateo rancho '36–41, and admin. of S. F. mission '36–40. iii. 713, 715; named in the padron of '42 as 40 years old, wife María Josefa Merido (?), child. Soledad b. '23, Concepcion '30, José María '34, Ricardo '37, and Francisco. He was supl. juez de paz '43, sergt of defensores '44, 2d alcalde '45, and 2d juez de paz in '46. iv. 665, 666–7; v. 648. He continued to live at the mission till his death in '78.   S. (José Joaquin), at Los Ang. '25. ii. 559. S. (José María), 1824, Mex. who in '35 was grantee of Llano de Tequesquite rancho. iii. 677; age 30 in '36; juez at S. Juan B. '37. iii. 692; his rancho sacked by Ind. '38. iii. 693; iv. 75; Cal. claim '46–7 (v. 462); alcalde at S. Juan B. '47–8. v. 640. He was cl. for Las Ánimas, Sta Clara, '52

Sanchez (Juan), sirviente at S.F. 1777. i. 297.   S. (Juan), grantee of Sta Clara rancho, Sta B., '37. iii. 656; wife Inés Guevara and 4 children before '37; still in Sta B. Co. '54.   S. (Juana María L.), 2d baptism at S.F. 1776. i. 291.   S. (Macario), at S. José 1800.   S. (Manuel), prob. son of José Ant., elector at S.F. '35 and petitioner for Cañada de Guadalupe rancho. iii. 704, 711; alf. of militia '37. iii. 701; in '42 age 30, wife Francisca Solis, child. Manuel b. '31, Rosario '37, Dolores '38, Juan Francisco '41.   S. (María Josefa), Cal. claim for $9,030 (v. 462).   S. (Miguel), 1829, Mex. convict liberated in '33. S. (Rafael), Ind. executed at Mont. '45. iv. 654.   S. (Rafael), 1842, Mex. sub-lieut of the batallon fijo '42–5, acting also as Micheltorena's sec. He remained in Cal. as custom-house officer in '45; is mentioned in the annals of '46, serving on the 1st jury and getting a grant of S. Lorenzo rancho. iv. 289, 513, 557; v. 35, 41, 45, 61, 289, 637.   S. (Ramon), 1826, Mex. sup. of the Sta Apolonia, and mr of the Magdalena, 27–8. iii. 147–8.   S. (Ramona or Romana), grantee of Butano, Sta Cruz, '44. ii. 591.   S. (Teodoro), juez de campo at Laguna Seca '35. iii. 674.

Sanchez (Tomás), at Los Coyotes rancho, Los Ang., '39, age 37; collector of taxes at Los Ang. '43. iv. 633. After '49 he was somewhat prominent as sheriff; still living in '77.   S. (Tomito), at S. Pascual '46. v. 352; perhaps same as Tomás.   S. (Urbano), owner of the Sta Apolonia '26. iii. 148, 682; prob. not in Cal.   S. (Vicente), settler at Los Ang. '14–19. ii. 349, 354; arrested and sent to Sta B. in irons '22. ii. 559; elector and prob. alcalde '26–7. ii. 560; iii. 33; member of the dip. '28. iii. 41–2. In '29–32 he as diputado, alcalde, and citizen was involved in a complicated series of troubles, being deposed and imprisoned, and in turn imprisoning others. The details cannot be presented, even if anybody ever understood them. He was a vicious, gambling, quarrelsome fellow, though of some intelligence and wealth; and political quarrels between Echeandía and Victoria had something to do with his troubles, about which suits were pending as late as '44. ii. 561; iii. 187–8, 195–6, 200, 205, 212, 230, 630, 634. In '36–9 he had something to do with the vigilance com., and with the sectional quarrel on both sides. iii. 417, 432, 491, 504, 565, 636. In '42–4 his name appears, being the grantee of Ciénega or Paso de la Tijera, and also comis. de zanjas. iv. 295, 629, 633–4; and in '45 he was again alcalde, not free from popular complaints. iv. 497, 523, 633. I have no later record of him.   Sancho (Juan Bautista), 1804, Span. friar who served at S. Antonio till his death in '30. Biog. ii. 621; ment. ii. 152, 385, 388, 655.

Sandeau, 1846, a mountaineer with Kearny from N. Mex. Lancey.   Sandels (G. M. W.), 1842, Swedish scientist who came from Mex. on the schr California, and went to Hon. on the Diamond in '43. He wrote an account of his observations under the name of 'King's Orphan.' iv. 345–6, 363, 565, 640, 650, 665.   Sanders (Allen), 1845, Amer. blacksmith from Or. in the McMahon party, working for Sutter Jul.-Dec. In the spring of '46 he visited Napa and Sonoma, married Miss Bonney, and in March went with the Bonneys to Or., where he is said to have been living in '80. iv. 572; v. 526.   S. (Horace), 1845, overl. immig. of the Grigsby-Ide party. iv. 579, 587. He was perhaps a

Bear Flag man. v. 110; and served as sergt Co. E, Cal. Bat. v. 361; having a Cal. claim of $20 (v. 462). Thos Knight states that in '70-1, S. was living near Carson, Nev.   S. (Richard T.), 1847, Co. E, Morm. Bat. (v. 469).   Sanderson (Geo. B.), 1847, asst surg. U.S.A., surg. of the Morm. Bat., and an object of the most intense dislike on the part of the Mormons. He went east with Gen. Kearny. v. 446, 452, 477, 480-2.   Sandoval (Josefa), 1791, wife of Gov. Romeu. i. 488, 490.   S. (Luciano), 1842, cornet of the batallon fijo '42-5. iv. 289.   S. (Pánfilo), 1828, Mex. convict liberated '34.

San Estévan (Antonio), 1831, chief of a N. Mex. caravan. iii. 396.   Sands (J. R.), 1847, mr of the *Benj. Tucker.*   Sanford, 1843, at Sutter's fort '45, and perhaps an overl. immig. of the Chiles party. iv. 393, 578.   S. (Sam.), 1847, Co. D, N.Y.Vol. (v. 499).   Sanger (John), 1844, mr of the *Newton; d.* at S. Diego. iv. 567; perhaps 'Sawyer.'   Sangrador (Miguel), tanner-instructor 1792-5. i. 615, 725.

Santa Ana, soldier at Sta B. '24. ii. 532.   Santa Cruz (José Antonio), com. de policía at Mont. '33, '36, juez de campo '35. iii. 673-5; age 43 in '36, nat. of Mex., wife Gertrudis Villavicencio, child Juan José.   Santa María, 1815, teacher who came with Gov. Sola. ii. 426.   Sta M., Ind. sirv. at S. Luis Ob., shot by Frémont. v. 374.   Sta M. (José María), clerk of the court at Mont. '42; owner of S.F. lot '46. v. 684.   Sta M. (Vicente), 1776, Span. friar who served chiefly at S. Buen., where he died in 1806. Biog. ii. 121-2; ment. i. 240-1, 246, 287, 300, 302, 376, 382, 385, 388, 399, 466, 522, 553, 576, 674; ii. 159-60, 490.   Santiago (Juan José Norberto), 1786, Span. friar, who served at S. Juan Cap. and retired in 1810. Biog. ii. 110; ment. i. 388, 423, 458-9, 474, 563, 576, 657; ii. 114, 159-60, 197.   Santillan (José Prudencio), 1841, Mex. novice of Ind. parentage who came with the bishop and soon became a priest. iv. 195. He was parish priest at S.F. mission in '46-50, though much of the time absent; and went to Mex. in '50. His chief and only fame rests on his claim of '50 to the misssion lands under a grant of Gov. Pico in '46, a grant which after a long and famous litigation, though approved by the land com. and district court, was finally declared invalid by the U.S. sup. court, being doubtless fraudulently antedated. v. 558, 659-60. Santillan became asst curate at Mazatlan before '56, and my last record of him is that in '59 he was arrested for refusal to celebrate the return of peace at the order of Gov. Pesqueira; yet in '78 the holders of the land claims professed to be able to produce him as a witness.   Santos, sirv. at Soledad 1791-1800. i. 499. S., neoph. grantee of Rincon del Alisal, Sta Clara, '44. iv. 672.   S. (Guadalupe), at Mont. '36, age 26.

Sargent (Constantine), 1846, purser's clerk on the U.S. *Congress*, committed suicide at Mont. Dec.   S. (Henry S.), 1848, nat. of Conn. recently from Or.; d. at S.F. Oct.   S. (James K.), 1847, Co. F, N.Y.Vol. (v. 499).   Sarmiento (José M.), 1842, Mex. lieut of the batallon fijo; died on the voy. to Cal. iv. 289.   Sarría (Vicente Francisco), 1809, Span. friar whose missionary service was at S. Cárlos and Soledad until his death in '35. He was prefect in '13-19, '23-30, and president '23-5; one of the ablest, best, and most prominent of the Fernandinos. Biog. iii. 688-9; ment. i. list of auth.; ii. 88, 148, 159-60, 217-18, 240, 327-30, 364, 383, 386, 394, 396-409, 451-3, 461, 491, 501-5, 512-13, 517-18, 521, 525-6, 535, 622-3, 655, 657, 659, 662; iii. 7, 16-19, 87, 89-91, 128, 191, 336, 338, 350-1.   Satte (Juan José), 1827, Moorish servant from S. Blas on an Engl. ship; at S. José '29, age 42.

Sauerweid (Alex. A.), 1848, Russian, in S. Joaq. Co. '78.   Saunders (John), 1838, Amer. or Irish sailor at Mont. and Sta Cruz '38, '43; at S.F. '44, age 30. iv. 119. He went to sea again in '47-8, but returned in '52-3, soon shipping again.   S. (Theodore R.), 1847, Co. A, N.Y. Vol. (v. 499); in N.Y. city '82.   S. (Wm L.), 1833, trapper named in Mont. lists of '34. In '34 he writes Capt. Jos. Walker a severe letter denying any indebtedness and claiming to hold a receipt from Bonneville. He may therefore have come in '33 with Walker (iii. 389), or in '32 with Dye, who mentions a Saunders in his party.

Savage (Chas), 1845, at Sutter's fort. iv. 578; went to Or. '46. v. 526; and was at Jacksonville '81. S. (Eliza), 1846, of the Mormon colony. v. 546; in Utah '84. S. (James D.), 1846, overl. immig. who served in Co. F, Cal. Bat. v. 374 (358); named in the *N. Helv. Diary*, 47–8. He had been a trapper and mountaineer, having great influence among the Ind., by whose aid he is said to have acquired much wealth in the gold mines. In '48–9 he had trading posts on the Mariposa and Fresno; and in later times rendered great service to govt and to settlers as interpreter, commissioner, and major in com. of a volunteer battalion. He was probably the discoverer of the Yosemite Valley. In '52 he was killed at the Kings River reservation in a quarrel with Maj. Harvey, the county judge. An ignorant man of much natural shrewdness, he made many warm friends and bitter foes. It is related of him that he made it a point to marry a chief's daughter in every tribe; exchanged hardware and whiskey by weight, ounce for ounce, with the Ind., for gold-dust; and bet his weight in gold on the turn of a card in a S.F. gambling-house. S. (Levi), 1847, Co. D, Morm. Bat. (v. 469); at Lorqueville, Utah, '82.

Sawis (Nathaniel), 1816, doubtful name of a deserter from the *Albatross*. ii. 275. Sawyer (John), 1844, mr of the *Newton;* d. at S. Diego '45. iv. 453, 567. S. (Joseph), 1828, Scotchman at S. Diego '28–9. Saxton (Chas), 1847, Co. G, N.Y. Vol. (v. 499). Schaffer (J. R.), 1848, nat. of Va; at Hon. from S.F. on the *Tepic;* dist attorney of S. Joaq. Co.; d. in '75, perhaps in Idaho.

Schallenberger (Moses); 1844, nat. of Ohio, and overl. immig. as a boy in the Stevens party. His remarkable adventures at Donner Lake, where he was left by the party and passed the winter alone, are noted in iv. 445–7, 453–4, as related in his MS., *Overland in '44.* He appears in various records of '46–8 as clerk and trader at Sutter's fort, S. José, Mont., and Sta Cruz; but finally settled at S. José, where he acquired considerable property, and was still living in '85. I have been unable to obtain information about his career in late years or his family. His sister was the wife of Dr Townsend of the Stevens party, and his daughter Maggie in '84–5 was a teacher, who from her father's notes wrote the MS. narrative of the overland trip. Schenck (James F.), 1846, lieut on the U.S. *Congress*, serving in Stockton's Bat. '46–7; nat. of Ohio; rear-admiral '79. v. 268, 281. S. (Woodhull S.), 1845, lieut on the U.S. *Portsmouth.* Schiller (Ed.), 1847, Co. A, N.Y. Vol. (v. 499); d. Texas '81. Schimer (Earnest), 1847, Co. G, ditto. Schlottour (Karl), 1847, Co. F, ditto; baker at S.F. '48. v. 683; at Rough-and-Ready '82.

Schmidt (Geo. W.), 1848, German who died at S. Diego '73; an early steamboat man. S. (Jacob), 1847, cooper at N. Helv. S. (Karl), 1821, Russian manager at Ross, succeeding Kuskof '21–6. ii. 464–5, 506–7, 642, 648. iii. 146. Schmölder (B.), 1846 (?), author of the *Neuer Wegweiser*, who styles himself in June '47 as Capt. 'from Cal.' He sought to organize a German colony. Schneider (Johann), 1846, Co. B, Cal. Bat. (v. 358). Schoa (Juan), at Los Ang. '46. Schoolcraft (Henry A.), 1847, sergt Co. H, N.Y. Vol. v. 504; Sutter's agent, recorder, and alcalde at Sac. '48–9. He went east, and while returning with an appointment as collector of Sac. died at sea near Acapulco '53. Schoonmaker (Jacob J.), 1847, Co. A, N.Y. Vol. (v. 499); at Vineland, N.J., '82. S. (Milton C.), 1847, ditto; d. at Stockton '50. Schreador (Geo.), 1847, Co. D, ditto; d. Napa Co. '82. Schreiber (Chas), 1846, Cal. Bat. v. 358; one of the Sta B. garrison. Schroeder (Martin), 1847, Engl. mr of a vessel, married at Mazatlan, who brought his family in '49 via Hon.; d. at S. José '81, leaving 5 children. Schroth (Chas), 1848, on roll of the Soc. Cal. Pion.; living in S.F. '81.

Schubart (Peter), 1842, Dane naturalized in Feb.; also called 'Serbia.' iv. 341. Schultz (Ernest), 1847, owner of S.F. lot. Schultze (Fred.), 1847, Co. F, N.Y. Vol. (v. 499). Schulz, 1848, cooper at Sutter's fort. Schumacher (John), 1847, Co. G, N.Y. Vol. (v. 499); at Los Ang. '82. Schwartz (John L.), 1841, Dutch immig. of the Bartleson party. 270, 275, 279. In '44–5 he obtained a grant of Nueva Flandria on the Sac. Riv., iv. 672, where he established a fishing station and built a boat. He and his place are described by Bryant in '46 and Buffum in '48; also mentioned in *N. Helv. Diary,* '45–7. He died in '51 or '52, and his brother George was unsuccessful cl. for the rancho in '53. Schweitzer (Philip), 1847, Co. F, 3d U.S. artill. (v. 518).

Scollan (John), 1847, Co. A, N.Y. Vol. (v. 499); at Sta B. '82.   Scott (Andrew), 1847, Co. D, N.Y. Vol. (v. 499).   S. (Antonio J.), 1846, grantee of S. Luis Rey and Pala.   S. (Chas G.), 1847, sergt Co. B, N.Y. Vol. (v. 499); treasurer of S.F.; d. in Nicaragua '56.   S. (Felix), 1845, nat. of Va and prob. overl. immig. iv. 578–9. One of his daughters died at Sutter's fort Jan. '46. In March he went to Or., v. 526, where he became a prominent settler, visiting Cal. again about '51–3, and being killed by Ind. in '58. See *Hist. Or.*, i. 750.   S. (Gabriel), 1846, had a 'Cal. claim' (v. 462).   S. (G. J.), 1848, had a cabin on the Capay rancho, Yolo Co.

Scott (James), 1826, nat. of Scotland, who first visited Cal. as sup. of the *Olive Branch* and *Waverly*, being mr of the *Huascar* in '27–8. iii. 176, 154, 147. From '30 he seems to have considered Sta B. his home, though constantly on the move, as shown by his business corresp. in my collection. ii. 573; iii. 409; iv. 117; sup. and mr of various vessels; also otter-hunter. iv. 144, 209, 566; v. 578. From '39, or earlier, to '47 a partner of Capt. John Wilson; ment. in mission accounts '40. iii. 657, 660; in '45 purchaser of S. Luis Ob. and grantee of Cañada de Chorro rancho. iv. 553, 558, 655, 658–9. Not friendly to Amer. in '46–7, but not much heard of in those years. He died at Sta B. in '51. S. (James), 1833, Engl. sailor on the *Catalina*. iii. 409; in Mont. dist. '34–5; in trouble on the schr *California* '39.   S. (James), 1846, of the Mormon colony, excommunicated at S.F. v. 546; owner of S.F. lots '47.   S. (James R.), 1847, Co. E, Morm. Bat. (v. 469).

Scott (John), 1831, sup. of the *Ayacucho* '31–5. iii. 381; perhaps James. S. (John), 1845, possibly of Frémont's party, but prob. the following. iv. 583, 587, 453.   S. (John), 1845, overl. immig. of the Grigsby-Ide party. iv. 579, 587. Acc. to the *Yolo Co. Hist.* he lived as a hunter in Capay Val. to June '46; he was prob. one of the Bears. v. 110; and served as a lieut in the Cal. Bat. v. 435. Swan remembers a Jack Scott in the mines from Sta Cruz '48. S. (Leonard M.), 1847, Co. E, Morm. Bat. (v. 469).   S. (Sam.), 1847, nat. of Ky and overl. immig.; a trader at Sta Clara, successful miner who built the first house at Placerville, and finally a settler near Snelling, where he died in '81, leaving one son, Moses.   S. (Wm), 1846, marine on the *Portsmouth*, wounded at the San Gabriel in '47. v. 395.   S. (Wm), 1847, Co. C, N.Y. Vol. (v. 499); owner of S.F. lot; county treasurer of S.F.; killed in Nicaragua.

Scott (Wm W.), 1845, brother of John and overl. immig. of the Grigsby-Ide party. iv. 579, 587. He came from St Louis mainly for his health, and took part in the Bear revolt, being also, it is said, the man who in July '46 carried the U.S. flag from Sonoma to Sac. v. 110, 148, 244. In '46–8 he kept a store at Sonoma, being, I suppose, of the firm S. & Boggs often named, and sometimes visiting Sac. with goods for sale. In '47 he married Mary Ann Smith; in Jan. '48 he killed a man named McRice; and I have his autograph letter of Feb., in which he attributes his bad conduct to the use of liquor, and solemnly 'swears off' forever. Later in the year he appears as a carpenter in Sutter's employ, and is said to have been at the Coloma mill when gold was found. A man of the same name settled in Scott Valley, Lake Co., in '48, and was still living in '54. The preceding items may refer to more than one man. Scriver (Chas), see 'Schreiber.' v. 316.   Scullen (John), 1847, Irishman of Sta B., said to have been killed by Ind. in Ariz. '66; prob. 'Scollan,' q.v.

Seagrim (Thos), 1839, sailor on the schr *California*.   Seaman (Stephen), 1846, acting sailmaker on the U.S. *Dale*.   Searles (Geo.), 1847, Co. D, N.Y. Vol. (v. 499).   Searls (Susan A.), 1846, of the Mormon colony, prob. not coming to Cal. v. 547.   Sears (Franklin), 1845, nat. of Mo. who crossed the plains to Or. in '44, and came to Cal. in the McMahon party, 572–4, 587, gaining an unenviable reputation as an Indian-killer. He is named in the *N. Helv. Diary* '45–6, and in March '46 was nearly killed by a fall from his horse at Sutter's fort. Recovering, he joined Frémont and went south, serving at S. Pascual under Gillespie and in Stockton's campaign. An account of S. Pascual by Boggs in the *Napa Registr*, May 11, '72, seems to be founded on his statements. In '48–9 he took out large quantities of gold near Bidwell's Bar; and in '51 settled at Sonoma, where he was living in '80 at the age of 63. His wife was Margaret Swift, and there were 2 children surviving in '80, one of them, Rachel, being the widow of J. R. Snyder. S. (John), 1845, brother of Franklin, and overl. immig. of the Grigsby-Ide party, iv. 579, 587, with his wife. He was a blacksmith and settled at Sonoma, where he was prob. a Bear Flag man—indeed, Mrs S. is credited with having furnished flannel for the famous flag. v. 110, 147-8. He was capt. of Co. D, Cal. Bat. v. 359, 361; had a Cal. claim (v. 462); and was in the Feather River mines '48. He seems either to have left Cal. or died soon after this date.

Sebastian, Ind. who died at Nicasia '80, said to be about 100 years old. S., 1773, Ind. who was the 1st Christian to make the trip by land from Cal. to Sonora. i. 221. S. (Narcisco), 1844, Canadian at Sta Rosa, having left Ridley's service. Secondi, or Sagondyne (James), 1845, Delaware Ind. of Frémont's party. iv. 583; still in F.'s employ '53. Seely, 1845, in N.Y. '84, claiming to have been one of Frémont's party; also declared by a newspaper corresp. to be the original of Bret Harte's 'Yuba Bill.' Segundo (Angel), sirviente at S.F. 1777. i. 297. Segura (José María), 1842, Mex. capt. of the batallon fijo, who remained in Cal. after Micheltorena's departure, acted as com. at Los Ang. for a time in '46, and seems to have departed with Flores in '47. iv. 289, 364, 492, 513; v. 408. Seibert, 1847, in Sutter's employ '47-8. Seider (Geo. F.), 1847, Co. A, N.Y.Vol. (v. 499). 'Seis Cuartillas' (Theodore), 1834, French carpenter at Mont. Sel, see 'Sells.' Selden (Ed. A.), 1846, mid. on the U.S. Columbus, act. lieut in com. of the prize Julia '46-7. v. 358, 378. Selfridge (Thos O.), 1847, capt U.S.N., com. of the Columbus and later of the Dale. Sellers (Jackson), 1847, sergt Co. K, N.Y.Vol. v. 504. Sells (Joseph), 1846, at Sutter's fort '47-8; also called Selly and Sel; member of the Donner relief parties. v. 538, 541.

Semple (Robert), 1845, nat. of Ky and overl. immig. of the Hastings party. iv. 586-7; a printer and dentist by trade. In '45-6 he was engaged in farming with Johnson and Keyser, first becoming prominent in the Bear revolt. v. 79, 106-7, 110, 114-19, 298, 644. Though a pronounced filibuster and conspirator, he doubtless exerted his influence with much success to restrain the lawless vagabonds of his party from the commission of outrages. In July he went to Mont., served for a time in Fauntleroy's dragoons (v. 232, 247), and then with Walter Colton published at Mont. the 1st Cal. newspaper, the Monterey Californian. v. 291-3, 658. Early in '47 the paper was transferred to S.F., and Semple, obtaining from Vallejo a large tract of land on Carquines Strait, devoted his energies, in company with Larkin, to the building of a great city at Benicia, as fully recorded in v. 670-4, at the same time taking an interest in various political matters, delivering a 4th of July oration at S.F., and owning a S.F. lot, which he patriotically gave away to show his faith in Benicia as the metropolis. v. 433, 455, 646, 676. His great speculation of city-building was not very successful, but he made a large amount of money in '48-50 by running a ferry-boat across the strait. In '49 he was a member and president of the constit. convention; but does not appear later in public life. He moved to Colusa Co., where he died in '54 at the age of 48, his death being the result of a fall from his horse. Dr S. was a good-natured, popular, and honorable man, of much intelligence and natural ingenuity, of some education, a good speaker—indeed, there were few things he could not do fairly well, though noted for obstinate faith in his way of doing things as always the best. His height was about 6 ft. 8 in., giving rise to no end of amusing stories, true and false, respecting such achievements as wading the strait of Carquines. In '47, being a widower, he married Frances, daughter of Stephen Cooper, by whom he had a daughter, Mary Benicia. His widow is living in '85 as Mrs Van Winkle. A son, John W., came to Cal. in '49, dying in '50; and also a brother, C. D., who was claimant for the Colus rancho. v. 671. Señan (José Francisco de Paula), 1787, Span. friar who served at S. Cárlos and S. Buenaventura until his death in 1823. A model missionary, who was president in 1812-15, and '20-3, being also prefect in '23. Biog. ii. 490-1; ment. i. 388, 469, 572, 576-7, 598, 604-5, 674, 685; ii. 121-2; 159, 209, 240, 258, 270, 317, 326-7, 333, 351, 394, 396, 398, 405, 410-11, 451-3, 479, 487, 493, 497, 499-502, 569, 571,

578, 580, 655, 657.   Senar (Francisco), 1828, doubtfu ˙name of an Irish sailor at Mont. '28–9.   Septem (Henry), 1816, sailor of the *Albatross*. ii. 275.

Sepúlveda (Diego), one of the grantees of S. Bernardino rancho '42; somewhat prominent in the Flores revolt at Los Ang. '46–7. v. 312, 320, 407–8. S. (Dolores), son of Juan José, b. S. Diego 1793, settler at Los Ang. 1812, still living there '46–8, having been accidentally wounded in '39. ii. 349, 565, 595.   S. (Dolores), killed by Ind. at Purísima '24. ii. 529.   S. (Dolores), soldier of the S.F. comp. '37.   S. (Encarnacion), grantee of Ojo de Agua '40. iv. 633.   S. (Enrique), prisoner at S. Buen. '38; grantee of S. Pascual '40. iii. 554–5, 634.   S. (Fernando), son of Francisco, at Los Ang. '39–'46; ment. in '40–3. iii. 632–3, 639.   S. (Francisco), settler at Los Ang. '15. ii. 349; in '25 regidor and acting alcalde ii. 559; iii. 11; in '31 in the operations against Victoria, by whom he was imprisoned. iii. 196, 208; in '36–7 comisionado of S. Juan Cap. iii. 626–7; 49 years old in '39, when he was grantee of S. Vicente and Sta Mónica. iii. 634; ment. in '40–3; iii. 639; iv. 629. In '52 he was cl. for the rancho.   S. (Ignacio), killed at the S. Gabriel '47. v. 396.

Sepúlveda (Ignacio), son of José, b. before '48, educated in the east as a lawyer. In later years he became a very prominent lawyer of Los Angeles, and one of the foremost of all the native Californians in respect of both ability and character. He was a member of the legislature in '64; served in Mex. under Maximilian; was county judge in '70–3, district judge from '74, and superior judge from '80, resigning his position in '83 to accept a responsible position as representative of Wells, Fargo, & Co. in Mex., where he has since resided to '85. His *Historical Memoranda*, i. 644, is a valuable contribution to my collection of original MS.; and he has otherwise aided me in my work. His wife, who died before '77, was an American, and there was a daughter.   S. (Isabel), at S. Rafael '42. iv. 237.   S. (José), regidor at Los Ang. '33–4. iii. 635; in '36–8, active among the vigilantes, alcalde, grantee of S. Joaquin rancho, and somewhat prominent on both sides in the sectional quarrels between north and south. iii. 432, 485, 495–9, 509–10, 518–19, 565, 633, 636. His age was 37 acc. to the padron of '39, when he was regidor and took part in a tumulto. iii. 589, 636; iv. 633; sub-prefect in '45. iv. 632–3. He was cl. for S. Joaquin in '52, and died in Sonora '75. His wife was a sister of Juan Ávila.   S. (José), two of the name at Los Ang. '39, a shoemaker and farmer.   S. (José), juez de campo at S. José '43. iv. 685; still there in '55. S. (José del Cármen), at Los Ang. '46–8.   S. (José L.), juez de paz at Los Ang. '42. iv. 632; 2d alcalde '46, '48. v. 625–6; grantee of Palos Colorados '46. v. 627; nominated for prefect '45; memb. of the council '50. I am not sure that he was not the same man as José above.   S. (José Manrico and José Miguel), at Los Ang. '46.   S. (Juan), soldier of the S.F. comp. '20–7; at S. José '41, age 41, wife Francisca Pacheco, child. Demesio b. '29, Silveria '31, Lucía '33, María Ant. '35, Sebastian '38, Bartolomé '39.   S. (Juan), juez de campo at Palos Verdes '40. iii. 637; 2d alcalde at Los Ang. '45, taking some part in politics. iv. 497, 539, 633; age 27 in '39; alcalde in '49; supervisor '54; county assessor '57–8.   S. (Juan María), at Los Ang. '46; justice of the peace '56.   S. (Manuel), at Los Ang. '46–8.   S. (Patricio), soldier at Sta B. before '37.   S. (Rafael), settler at Los Ang. 1789. i. 461.   S. (Vicente), grantee of La Sierra, Los Ang., '46. v. 628.

Serbia (Pedro), 1842, Danish resid. of S.F., age 26; same as 'Schubert,' q.v., and probably intended for 'Sherrebeck,' q.v.   Serer (Domingo) corporal at Mont. '36, age 26.   Serna (Manuel), reputed centenarian of S. Diego '79. S. (Patricio), Mex. soldier of the Hidalgo comp. at Mont. '36, age 33.   Serra (Junípero), 1769, Span. friar, 1st president of the missionaries, and founder of many missions, who died at S. Cárlos Aug. 28, 1784. Biog. i. 409–16; ment. i. 116–23, 129, 134–5, 137–8, 164–8, 170, 175–7, 181, 183–4, 187–94, 199–221, 224, 227, 229–31, 238–9, 244, 246, 248–9, 255, 257, 268, 270–1, 280, 287, 297–-304, 309, 320–8, 330–1, 333, 351, 373, 376, 378, 382, 386, 388–400, 414–15, 422, 455, 457, 459, 469, 473–4, 476, 486, 671, 687.   Serrano (Florencio), 1834, Mex. of the Hijar & Padrés colony. iii. 263, 268; who served in '35 as clerk of the admin. at S. Antonio, and as teacher. iii. 687; and from '36 as clerk of different offices at Mont. taking part in the revolt against Alvarado in '37, and being sec. of the ayunt. in '38. iii. 524–5, 675. In '44 he was 2d alcalde. iv. 653, 656, 404, 411; and in '45–6 síndico and sec. of the prefecture, serving on the 1st jury in '46. iv. 652–3; v. 289, 636. In '48–9 he succeeded Colton as alcalde of Mont. v. 637–8; being before and later engaged in trade. His wife was Rita, sister of Joaquin de la Torre, and there were several sons who supported Don Florencio in his old age, poverty, and blindness. He died in '77 at the age of 63. He was of Span. parentage, of fair education and good repute. Shortly before his death he dictated for me his *Apuntes*, a full statement of his life and recollections of Cal. affairs, which throws light on many topics. S. (Francisco), alcalde at Los Ang. 1799. i. 661.   S. (Ignacio), at Los Ang. '46.   S. (José), juez de campo, Los Ang. '35. iii. 635; grantee of Cañada de los Alisos '42–6, iv. 634, being also cl. in '52.   S. (José Antonio), son of Leandro, at S. Juan Cap. '41. iv. 626; grantee of Pauma '44. iv. 621; in the fight at S. Pascual '46. v. 352; still living at S. Diego '75, age 61. His wife was a daughter of Rosario Aguilar.   S. (José S.), at Los Ang. '46.   S. (Leandro), son of a soldier of the 1st exped., b. at S. Diego; for many years majordomo of Pala for the mission S. Luis Reg.; in '28 maj. at S. Juan Cap., and grantee of Temescal, ii. 547, 663; iii. 612, where he spent the rest of his life, dying in '52. His wife was Presentacion Yorba and later Josefa Montalba. S. (Manuel), killed by Ind. at Pauma '46. v. 617.   S. (Rafaela), at S. Diego '21, '41. ii. 546; iv. 619.   S. (Tomás), juez de campo at Los Ang. '48. v. 626. Servin (Ignacio), 1842, Mex. sub-lieut in the batallon fijo '42–5. iv. 289, 513; still in Cal. '46. v. 41.

Sessions (Wm B.), 1847, Co. A, Morm. Bat. (v. 469).   Sessor (Peter), 1847, Co. F, N.Y. Vol. (v. 499); in S.F. '82.   Settle (Josiah), 1840 (?), nat. of Ohio said to have crossed the plains to Cal. this year; prob. an error, though he may have come from N. Mex. iv. 120. Went to Or. '52, to Wash. Ter. '60, and died at Seattle '76.   Sevy (Thomas), see 'Levy.'   Sexton (Daniel), 1841, nat. of La and overl. immig. of the Workman party. iv. 278–9. He worked as a carpenter in the Los Ang. region, and finally settled at S. Bern.; claims to have raised the U.S. flag at his camp '40. iv. 342; served in the campaign against Micheltorena '45. iv. 495; carried a message from Stockton to Frémont '47. v. 402; married an Ind. woman; cl. for land in Los Ang. '52; still living in '84.   S. (Geo. S.), 1847, Co. A, Morm. Bat. (v. 469); Co. reënl.   S. (Lorin), 1847, Co. I, N.Y. Vol. (v. 499).   Seyman (James), 1848, at Sutter's fort.   Seymour (Chas H.), 1848, on roll of Soc. Cal. Pion.; d. S.F. after '81; an employé in the mint.   S. (Sir Geo. F.), 1846, admiral in com. of the British Pac. squadron at Mont. on the *Collingwood*, July. v. 199–214, 232, 577.

Shadden (Thos J.), 1843, Amer. immig. of the Hastings party from Or. accomp. by his family. iv. 390, 400. In '44 he obtained a land grant in Yolo Co. iv. 674; is named in '45–6 as visiting Sutter's fort from S. José, Sta Cruz, and other points; and had a 'Cal. claim' of $837 (v. 462). A son is said to have been born in '47. Shadden settled on the Cosumnes, where he lived in a cabin of tules in '49, having been before that date a miner and trader in mules. He went to Or. about '51.   Shaler (Wm), 1803, mr of the *Lelia Byrd* 1803–4, and author of a *Journal* pub. in 1808, which was prob. the 1st extended account of Cal. published in the U.S. ii. 10–14, 21–4, 102–3, 109, 119, 122, 143–4, 183.   Shannon (John). v. 621; see 'Charbonneau.'   S. (Wm E.), 1847, capt. Co. I, N.Y. Vol., in com. at S. Diego '47–8, being also collector. v. 504, 514, 617, 619. In '49 a trader, of firm S. & Cady, at Coloma, also alcalde, member of the constit. convention, and district judge. From Dec. '49 a lawyer at Sac., where he died in '50 of cholera.   Sharkey (Frank L.), 1847, Co. I, N.Y. Vol. (v. 499); at Norwich, Conn., '82.   Sharnon (John), 1847, alcalde at S. Diego; prob. 'Charbonneau,' q. v.   Sharp (Matthew W. or A.), 1847, Co. I, ditto; at S. Diego '48; died near Coloma '50.   Shattuck, 1842, lieut U.S.N. with Com. Jones at Mont. iv. 308.

Shaw, 1846, overl. immig. who died on the Calaveras in '49.   S. (Charles), 1846, Co. C, 1st U.S. dragoons (v. 336).   S. (James), 1848, guide to returning Mormons.   S. (James B.), 1846, nat. of Australia; resid. of Sonoma Co. '51–77. *Son. Co. Hist.*   S. (Thomas), 1824 (?), nat. of Mass. I have his autograph letter, apparently written at S. Pedro Oct. 28, 1824, but there may be an error. ii. 526. In '26–8 he was clerk and sup. on the *Courier* and *Waverly.* iii. 154; in 30–1 on the *Pocahontas*, making a contract to carry away Gov. Victoria. iii. 148, 210, 383; in '33–5 sup. and sometimes mr of the *Volunteer*, *Harriet Blanchard*, and *Lagoda.* iii. 382, 384, 410. He was in Boston '36, not expecting to revisit Cal.; but in '39–40 he came back as sup. of the *Monsoon*, his name often appearing in commercial corresp. and mission accounts. iii. iv. 105; iii. 623, 727. He is said to have died in Boston about '66.

Shea (Wm), 1840, one of the exiled foreigners not known to have returned. iv. 18.   Shearman, 1844, mr of the *Menkar.* iv. 567.   Shehey, 1847, died at Sutter's fort Oct.   Sheldon (Geo.), 1848, passp. from Hon.   S. (Henry B.), 1848, editor and part owner of the S.F. *Californian.* v. 658; sec. of the guards; owner of a lot at S. José. Went to the Sandw. Isl. about '65.   S. (Jared), 1840, nat. of Vt, who came from N. Mex. or Sonora with a pass dated March 9, '40. iv. 117, 120. Possibly he had visited Cal. before, as his arrival is often credited to '34 or '32. He was naturalized in '43, then describing himself as a carpenter who had arrived in '40, being in '44 grantee of the Omochumne rancho on the Cosumnes. iv. 672; where he was a partner of Wm Daylor, and where he spent the rest of his life but for his service in the Micheltorena campaign, iv. 486, 501, and a brief experience in the mines. In '51 he was killed in a difficulty with miners about a dam. His wife, married in '47, was a daughter of Thomas Rhoads, and survived him with 3 children, Wm b. '48, Sarah '49, and Catherine '51 (drowned in '52).   Shelikof (Paul), 1825, Russian manager of Ross '25–9, succeeding Schmidt. ii. 648, 650–1; iii. 213.   Shelly (Pearson B.), 1847, mr of the *Gen. Kearny.* v. 518; and trader at S.F. '47–8, of firm S. & Norris. v. 680; also owner of S.F. lot.   Shelton, 1842, at S.F.; prob. 'Sheldon,' q.v.   S. (Sebert C.), 1847, Q.M. sergt Morm. Bat., but reduced to ranks Co. D. v. 477.   Shepherd (Edmund), 1846, mid. U.S.N., acting lieut in Stockton's Bat. '46–7. v. 385.   S. (Lafayette), 1847, Co. A, Morm. Bat. (v. 469).   Sherman (Heran V. S.), 1847, Co. H, N.Y. Vol. (v. 499); d. before '82.   S. (J.), 1837, named in Larkin's accounts.

Sherman (Richard M.), 1846, nat. of R.I., who passed his boyhood on a farm, and then went to sea for 5 or 6 years, coming to Cal. from Honolulu as clerk on the *Euphemia*, leaving the vessel at S.F., where he worked as bookkeeper for Paty & Davis, and in '47–8 made a trip to the Isl. as sup. of the *Euphemia.* He became the owner of a town lot, on which he built a store in which the firm of S. & Ruckel did business in '48–50. v. 681, 686. In '51 he went east, but returned on a business visit in '55–6. He resided in Mass. and at Providence, R.I., till '84, when he returned to S.F. to take charge of his real estate interests, including the 'Sherman building,' on the lot purchased by him in '47, in which he has an office in '85, at the age of 72. In an interview, and also in a letter from R.I., he gave me some information about early S.F. and his own life. His 1st wife, married in '54, was Sally S. Mauran, who died in '65; the 2d, of '69–70, was Emma F. Mitchell; and the 3d, '78–85, Kate Field.   Five children survived in '85, Harry M., Elizabeth M., Adeline M., Ethel, and Richard M. Jr.

Sherman (Wm Tecumseh), 1847, nat. of Ohio, graduate of West Point, who came to Cal. as lieut Co. F, 3d U.S. artill., and in '47–50 served most of the time as adj.-gen. under the military governors. v. 444, 450, 492, 518, 520, 609, 636, 646; also of the firm Warner, Sherman, & Bestor at Coloma '48–9. He went east with despatches in '50; but, having resigned his army commission, came back in '53 to conduct as partner the banking business of Lucas, Turner, & Co. until '57. His Californian experience of '47–57 is fully narrated in the early chapters of his *Memoirs*, a most interesting and accurate record, except in a few comparatively unimportant details. Sherman was later superintendent of a La military academy and president of a St Louis street railroad until in '61 he reëntered the military service as colonel. His subsequent career in the war of '61–5 and since is a prominent part of U.S. history, which I make no attempt to summarize. He reached a higher position than any other pioneer named in this register; and in '85 is still living as retired general of the army. His wife, married in '50, is the daughter of Hon. Thomas Ewing. The general has often revisited Cal., taking a deep interest in pioneer matters.

Sherreback (Peter), 1840, nat. of Denmark, who came by sea and settled at S.F. as a trader. iv. 117, 120. He was baptized and naturalized in '41–2; síndico '43. iv. 666; agente de policía '44. iv. 666; being married the same year or the next to Mary, sister of John Sullivan. In '45 he was owner of S. F. lands, and aided Sutter in support of Micheltorena. iv. 486, 669, 673; v. 681–2. He was collector in '46–7. v. 295, 648; and memb. of the council '47. v. 678. He still lived at S.F. in '55 and later, but I find no mention of his death. His widow was still living in '60. The original name was probably 'Scherrebach,' but it is written in a great variety of ways. Sherwood (Jeremiah), 1847, lieut Co. G, N.Y.Vol. v. 504, 517. In '48–9 clerk for Brannan & Co. at Sac.; later member of N.Y. legislature; d. N.Y. City '83. Scheuer (Pierre), 1834, Fr. mason at Mont., age 27, married to María J. García. Perhaps same as 'Cheorette,' q.v.

Shields (H.L.), 1847, lieut Co. F, 3d U.S. artill. on muster-roll; but did not come to Cal. (v. 518). S. (Sam.), 1831, Amer. from N. Mex. in the Wolfskill party. iii. 387, 405; d. at Los Ang. a few years later. S. (W.F.), 1847, capt. in com. of U.S. *Preble.* Shipley (Otto), 1847, Co. F, 3d U.S. artill. (v. 518). Shipp (Wm), 1847, ditto. Shirland (E.D.), 1847, Co. G, N.Y.Vol. (v. 499); nat. of N.Y. and settler in Placer Co. from '50; capt. in war of '61–5; county clerk and recorder of Sac.; at Auburn '82. Shirley (Paul), 1846, on the roll of the Soc. Cal. Pion.; d. in Ohio '76. Shislylind (Gustaff), 1847, musician Co. G, N.Y.Vol. (v. 499).

Shockley, 1846, mr of the *Roman.* Shoemaker (Sam.), 1846, one of the Donner party from Ohio; died in the Sierra. v. 531, 533. Shoetzof, 1803, in charge of a party of Aleut. hunters. ii. 25, 63, perhaps Shvetzof. Shoive, 1847–8, mr of the *Anita.* v. 576. Shooks (Wm), 1841, doubtful name at S. Diego. *Toomes.* Shooter (Chas), 1847, Co. D, N.Y.Vol. (v. 499). Short (J.O.B.), 1846, nat. of Ky, and overl. immig. with his mother—later Mrs Merriner—who settled at S. Rafael, where he still lived in '80 with wife, Mary Miller, and 5 children. S. (Jacob), 1846, brother of J.O.B., and his partner in '80. S. (Patrick), 1832, Irish priest who came in exile from Honolulu with P. Bachelot; in '34–6 an associate of Hartnell in his school near Mont.; left Cal. in '37, and went to Valparaíso, where he still lived in '70. iii. 317–18, 364, 384, 408, 670, 677–8; iv. 102. Shotwell (Geo.), 1841, overl. immig. of the Bartleson party, accidentally killed on the journey. iv. 269. Shreve, 1848, mr of a vessel at S.F. Shrives, 1848, mr of the *Anita.* Shrives (Dan B.), 1847, Co. F, N.Y.Vol. (v. 499). Shroter (Chas), 1847, Co. G, ditto; at S.F. '82. Shubrick (Wm Bransford), 1846, commodore U.S.N., in com. of Pacific squadron '46–7, on the *Independence.* v. 428–9, 437, 636. Shulters (John), 1847, Co. H, N.Y.Vol. (v. 499). Shultz (Ernst), 1847, owner of S. F. lot. Shumway (Aurora), 1847, Co. C, N. Y. Vol. (v. 469); reënl. Shurts (Watson), 1847, Co. F, N.Y.Vol. (v. 499).

Sibrian see 'Cibrian.' Sibs (Sam.), 1836, doubtful name of a witness at Sonoma. Sicard (Pierre Théodore), 1833, Fr. sailor and carpenter who on applying for naturalization in '40 claimed a resid. of 7 years. iii. 409. He was in the Mont. dist '34 and at the S. Pablo rancho '40. In '42–4 he worked for Sutter at Hock Farm; and in '44 got a grant of the Nemshas rancho on Bear River adjoining Johnson's, iv. 672, where he settled in '45. His visits from Bear River to Sutter's fort in '45–8 are often recorded in the *N. Helv. Diary;* in 48–9 a miner and trader on the Yuba, where a flat and bar took his name. Though deemed rich in those days, he became poor; was living with Claude Chana in '71, and died before '79. Sickels (J. F.), 1847, surgeon on the U.S. *Independence.* Siddons (Wm M.), 1848, on the roll of the Soc. Cal. Pion. Sierra (Benito de la), 1775, Span. friar who visited Cal. as chaplain on the *Santiago* and *S. Antonio,* and died at S. Blas '77. He had served in L. Cal. '69–73. i. 240–1, 287, 310. Sigler (Wm), 1845, at Sutter's fort Nov.; prob.

an overl. immig. In the spring of '46 he carried despatches up the valley to Frémont. He was murdered at Moon's rancho Tehama Co. in '49 or '50. iv. 578, 583; v. 24.

Sill (Daniel), 1832, nat. of Conn., trapper and carpenter who came from N. Mex. in the winter of '32-3, settling at Sta B., where he hunted otter under Capt. Dana's license, and was partner in a bakery in '34. iii. 388, 408. In '35 he came to Mont. and got a carta; and from '39 or earlier lived at S.F., building a mill for Spear in '39-40. v. 681; named by Farnham as one of the foreigners arrested in '40. iv. 17. From '44 he spent most of his time in the Sac. Valley, working as a blacksmith for Sutter part of the time. In '46 he bought a rancho of Lassen where he had a cabin. v. 301; and in '49 was joined by his son Daniel and daughter Harriet—later Mrs Mahew. He died in '62, at the age of 66.   Sillen (D. S.), 1846, Cal. Bat. (v. 358).   Siltzer (Henry), 1847, Co. G, N.Y.Vol. (v. 499).   Silva, family at S. Dieguito rancho '31. iii. 612.   S. (Antonio), 1840 (?), Portuguese deserter from a whaler, employed for several years at Petaluma by Gen. Vallejo. iv. 120.   S. (Mariano), 1840, Mex. capt. of artill. at Mont. '40-6; went to Mazatlan '47 or '48. iv. 31, 198, 293, 307-8, 311, 357, 652; v. 41, 230, 232-3.   S. (Mariano), at Los Ang. '39; in '46 at S. Juan Cap., age 37, wife Francisca Perez.   S. (Mariano), nat. of Chile, patron of the custom-house boat at Mont. '45.   Silvas (Antonio M.), at Los Ang. '39, age 37.   S. (Cárlos), owner of land at S. Juan Cap., 41. iv. 626.   S. (Clara), at S. Juan Cap. '46, age 40, child. Gerónimo b. '29, Guadalupe '32, Lugarda '37, and Fernando '38.   S. (Diego), at S. Bern. '46, age 24.   S. (José), settler at Los Ang. 1789. i. 461.   S. (Juan), at Mont. '36. iii. 617.   S. (Mariano), at Los Ang. '46, age 35.   S. (Ramon), owner of land at S. Juan Cap. '41. iv. 626.   S. (Teodoro), at Los Ang. '10-16; ii. 110, 350.   Silverio, neophyte who killed his wife at Mont. 1798. i. 691.

Sime, 1848, in the legislature '55; John L. in S.F. guard '49.   Simental (José C.), 1800, sentenced to 6 years in Cal. as a settler. i. 606.   Simeon, Ind., grantee of lot at S. Gabriel '46. v. 627.   Simmonds (Stephen), 1835 (?), nat. of N.Y., landing at Sta B. from the whaler *Liverpool Packet*, and becoming an otter-hunter with Nidever for several years. Named in '39-40 at Sta B. and Mont. Making voyages in different vessels; he was in '44 sick in care of the consulate, and is said to have died at Branch's rancho about '45. iii. 413.   Simmons, 1848, lieut on the U.S. *Ohio*.   S. (Alex. R.), 1846, mid. on the U.S. *Columbia*. '46-7.   S. (Bezer), 1843, nat of Vt, mr of the *Magnolia* '43-6. iv. 400, 567; v. 579. Later of the S.F. firm S., Hutchinson, & Co.; member of the council '49; d. in '50 at the age of 40. His assignees were cl. for the Novato rancho. iii. 712. His wife was a sister of Frederick Billings, and died in '49.   S. (Charles), 1847 (?), miner and later trader at Reno, Nev., where he died '79; accredited by the newspapers to N.Y. Vol. Left a daughter at Livermore, Cal.   S. (Wm), 1846, clerk in the navy, acting lieut in Stockton's Bat. '46-7. v. 386.   S. (Wm A.), 1847, Co. B, Morm. Bat. (v. 469).   Simon (Lem.), 1828, Amer. sailor of the *Gen. Lucre* left at S. Diego drunk.   S. (Luis), 1828, Engl. arrested for having no pass; prob. same as preceding.   Simons (Maurice), 1846, passed mid. on the U.S. *Congress*.

Simpson, 1827, mr of the *Cadboro*. iii. 146.   S., 1845, doubtful name of an overl. immig. iv. 578.   S., 1846, ditto; may have gone to Or. v. 529. S. (Geo.), 1841, at S.F. on the *Cowlitz*.   S. (Sir Geo.) 1841, chief of the H. B. Co., visiting Cal. on his trip round the world, and author of a *Narrative* which contains much valuable information on the country. ii. 77-8; iv. 191, 209, 218-21, 235-6, 250-3, 259-61, 333, 343, 564, 639-40, 650-1, 665, 678. S. (Henry I.), 1848, author of *Three Weeks in the Gold Mines*, in the form of a letter written at Mont. in Sept. He claims to be of the N.Y.Vol., but perhaps writes under an assumed name; or still more likely the letter is a fraud concocted in N.Y.   S. (Wm), 1844, Engl. who got a passport.   S. (Wm), 1828, witness against Capt. Bradshaw. iii. 133.   Sims (Jack), 1846, aided in building the *Sta Cruz* schr. *S. J. Patriot*.   S. (Joseph), 1847, Co. D, N.Y. Vol. (v. 499); Engl. settler in Sac. Co. '79-80, with wife Mary L. Moor, and 3 children.

Sinard ('Major'), 1847, visitor at Sutter's fort.   Sinclair (Archibald), 1847, Co. D, N.Y.Vol. (v. 499).   S. (John), 1839, Scotchman for some years in employ of the H.B. Co. in Or., later editor of a paper at Honolulu, who in Dec. '39 was at Mont. asking for a carta, and in '40 at Sutter's fort. iv. 117, 119, 139. In '41 he was sent back to the Isl. by Sutter to make arrangement for consignments of goods, going on the *Llama* and returning on the *Julia Ann*. His negotiations for Sutter were not very successful, but he made a bargain with Grimes, by virtue of which on his return in Dec. '41 he obtained naturalization, and in '42 took possession of the El Paso rancho, north of N. Helv., as the representative of Grimes, to whom it was granted in '44. iv. 229, 237, 566. He was visited in '42-3 by Sandels and Yates, who describe him as a very intelligent man fond of grog; also by Frémont in '44, iv. 438, when he was an officer in the N. Helv. militia. iv. 479, 680. He was Sutter's aide in the Micheltorena campaign. iv. 485-6; is often named from '45 in the *N. Helv. Diary;* and in '46-9 he was alcalde of the Sac. district, v. 675, having a Cal. claim of $450 (v. 462), taking part in relief measures for the Donner party, v. 538, 541, and finally dying in '49 on his passage by steamer to the States.   S. (Wm), 1845, clerk for Rae at S.F. iv. 593.   S. (Wm B.), 1828, Amer. carpenter, age 25, who left his vessel at Sta B., escaping with 3 others in a boat to Sta Catalina Isl.   Singleton (A. W.), 1848, passp. from Hon.   Sinova (José F.), settler at Los Ang. 1785-6; 2d alcalde in '89. i. 346, 348, 461.   Sinton (Rich. H.), 1848, a well-known citizen of S. F. down to '85, whose arrival is accredited, erroneously I suppose, in various publications to '47 or '48.

Sipole (Wm), 1847, Co. F, 3d U.S. artill. (v. 518); d. before '64.   Sipp, 1846, Amer. ship-carpenter from Or. in the McMahon party, who prob. went back to Or. in '46. iv. 572; v. 526.   Siptler (J.), 1846, in Cal. Bat. (v. 358).   Siralde (Mariano). at Sonoma '44, age 27; perhaps 'Lizalde.'   Sirey (James), 1847, Co. D, N.Y.Vol. (v. 499); settled at Stockton '48; at S.F. '71-4; Stockton '75; d. before '82.   Sirrine (Geo. W.), 1846, of the Mormon colony. v. 546; of Stout, S., & Meder, lumber dealers at Sta Cruz '47; memb. of the town council '48. v. 642. In Ariz., still in the faith, '85.   S. (John J.), 1846, ditto, with wife and child. v. 546; in '47 candidate for the council and owner of a S. F. lot. v. 650, 680; an elder and school trustee '48. v. 656; presid. of the council '48; in Ariz. '85.   Sisk (Thos J.), 1848(?), survivor of the Texan-Mier massacre; died at Grass Valley '69.   Sisson (Reuben), 1847, Co. K, N.Y.Vol. (v. 499); d. S. Rafael '49.   Sitjar (Antonio, or Buenaventura), 1771, Span. friar who served at S. Antonio—being also founder of S. Miguel—until his death in 1808. Biog. ii. 151-2; ment. i. 173, 176, 196, 298, 388, 411, 469, 498, 552, 560, 576, 587, 688-9; ii. 147, 159-60.   Swarthout (Nathan), 1847, Co. D, Morm. Bat. v. 469.

Skeckett (Job), 1845, Delaware Ind. in Frémont's party '45-7 (iv. 581). Skee (Alex.), 1827, mr of the *Huascar* '27-8. iii. 147.   Skein (Joseph), 1847, Co. E, Morm. Bat. (v. 469).   Skene (Wm), 1846, one of the chino prisoners, wounded. v. 313-14.   Skillington (H.), 1848, at Hon. from Mont.   Skinner (Eugene F.), 1845, overl. immig. from N.Y. in the Grigsby-Ide party, with a family. Working for Sutter and visiting S.F. and S. José, he went in '46 to Or., where he founded and named Eugene City, dying there in '64, and leaving a widow and 3 children. iv. 579-80; v. 526.   S. (A. A.), 1848, Or. pioneer of '45, judge of the Or. sup. court, brother of Eugene, said to have made a trip to the gold mines; d. at Sta Cruz '77.   S. (Horace A.), 1846, of Mormon colony, with wife and child. v. 546; in '47-8 he kept the City Hotel at S.F. v. 680; in Utah '84.   S. (John), 1847, Co. A, N.Y.Vol. (v. 499); at S. José '50; at Campo Seco '71-4.

Slocum (Wm A.), 1837, U.S. commissioner on the *Loriot*, and author of a *Report*. iv. 146-7, 165.   Slade (Philip O.), 1832, nat. of N. H. who came by sea. iii. 408; in Mont. dist. '33-5; naturalized '39, being a sawyer at S. Rafael; last appears at S.F. '40.   S. (Thompson), 1846, Co. F, Cal. Bat. (v. 358.   S. (Wm D.), 1847, Co. H, N.Y. Vol. (v. 497). A printer who was city marshal at Yreka; d. before '82, prob. in '63.   Slague (John), 1836. Fr. sailor on the *Ayacucho*, age 19. Slater (Richard), 1847, Co. E, Morm. Bat. (v. 469); mail-carrier for Brannan '48. Slausum, 1834, Eng. sailor, age 46, at Mont. Sleight (Peter), 1847, Co. K, N.Y. Vol. (v. 499). Slepe (Jerome), 1834, Eng. hatter in a Mont. list, age 27. Sloat (John D.), 1846, nat. of N.Y. in com. of the Pacific squadron, raising the U.S. flag in Cal. July. v. 37, 195–215, 224–54, 411–12, 580. Com. Sloat was a timid, irresolute man; but after he decided to take possession of the Cal. ports his policy was entirely praiseworthy as compared with that of Stockton, his successor. Biog. note v. 254. S. (Lewis W.), 1846, son of John D., and his sec. on the *Savannah*. v. 225. He came back to Cal. about '54 and was a notary public at S.F. for several years. Slobodchikof, 1806, chief hunter on the coast from Alaska. ii. 40; in '13–14 clerk of Kuskof at Ross, visiting S.F. ii. 204, 302, 304, 373. Slocum, 1844, mate of the *Newton*. Slover (Isaac), 1828, Kentuckian trapper of Pattie's party who went back to Sonora with a pass in Nov. iii. 163, 166–7, 178. He came back with a N. Mex. colony about '41–3, settling at S. Bernardino, where he was killed by a bear in '54, at the age of about 80. Slover Mt still bears his name. Slusser (Levi S. B.), 1847, nat. of Pa; in Sonoma Co. '48–77. Sly (James C.), 1847, Co. B, Morm. Bat. (v. 469); a miller in Sutter's employ, also in the mines '48, exploring a new route and Salt Lake Val. S. (John), 1846, Co. F, Cal. Bat. (v. 358).

Smith, naturally many of the name cannot be identified. S., 1831, sailor drowned at Sta B. iii. 405. S., 1831, about to leave Hon. for Cal. S., 1844, officer on the *Modeste*. S., 1845, Engl. who got a pass for Sonora. S., 1846, from Hon. on the *Euphemia*. S., 1847, had a project of establishing a colony on the Moquelumne, transferring his claim to McKinstry in '48. *S. Joaq. Co. Hist.* S., 1847, mid. on the U.S. *Independence*. S., 1847, owner of a saw-mill near S.F. S., 1848, at Sutter's fort from Sta Clara; lately from Or. S., 1848, mr of the *Haalilo*.

Smith (A. B.), 1837(?), committed suicide at S. Diego '67, said to have been a resid. for 30 (20?) years; ment. at S.D. '46. iv. 118; v. 329. S. (Albert), 1847, sergt Co. B, Morm. Bat. v. 477; also Q.M. sergt at Manti, Utah, '81. S. (Alex.), 1846, ment. by Michael White as in the Los Ang. region, known as 'Stuttering Alec.' S. (Andrew J.), 1847, capt. in the 1st U.S. dragoons, who came with the Morm. Bat., of which he was acting com. for a time in the east. v. 477, 479–83. He was the officer who mustered out the Morm. Bat. and part of the N.Y. Vol., subsequently taking com. of the dragoons. v. 490, 515, 631. He went east with Sherman in '50; and in the war of '61–5 became a general. S. (Azariah), 1847, Co. B, Morm. Bat. (v. 469); author of a song for the bat.; at the Coloma mill '38 when gold was discovered. S. (Chas), 1824, named in an archive record as an otter-hunter. ii. 527; perhaps Karl 'Schmidt.' S. (Chas), 1828, Engl. deserter from a Fr. whaler at Todos Santos; at S. Diego '28–9. S. (Chas), 1846, powder-boy on the *Dale*. S. (Chas), 1846, Co. G, Cal. Bat. (v. 358). S. (Chas), 1847, Co. I, N.Y. Vol. (v. 499). S. (Chas), 1847, with Brannan on trip to Salt Lake. v. 553; perhaps C.C. S. (Chas F.), 1847, Co. I, N.Y. Vol. (v. 499); d. before '82. S. (Chas R.), 1825 (?), said to have been at Sta B. in charge of Dana's store. *S. Luis Ob. Co. Hist.*; in '29 writes from Hon., and had visited Cal. before; in '31 came on the *Louisa* as sup.; in '32 joined the comp. extranjera. iii. 221; ment. in Larkin's accts '36. S. (C.C.), 1847, trader at Sutter's fort '47–8, a partner of Brannan; made a trip to Hon. on the *Tepic* '48. S. (C. S.), 1848, passp. from Hon.

Smith (D.), 1847, Co. B, artill. Cal. Bat. (v. 358). S. (D.), 1848, at Hon. from Mont. S. (David), 1847, Co. E, Morm. Bat. (v. 469); d. in April at S. Luis Rey. v. 481. S. (D. W.), 1846, Co. G, Cal. Bat. (v. 358). S. (Edward), 1848, overl. immig. from Mo., with wife, son, and 5 daughters; postmaster at S. Juan B.; died about '57. One of his daughters married John Breen in '52. S. (Elijah M.), 1847, Co. I, N.Y. Vol. (v. 499); at Aurora, Mono Co., '82 S. (Elisha), 1847, Co. E, Morm. Bat. (v. 469). S. (Ezekiah), 1847, at Sutter's fort; prob. Azariah. S. (F.), 1846, Cal. Bat. (v. 358). S. (Frances R.), 1846, married to W. W. Scott at Sonoma, June. S. (Frazer),

1814, mr of the *Isaac Todd*. ii. 271–2.   S. (Fred.), 1848, German farmer at S. José '50–76.   S. (Fred C.), 1845 (?), said by his son, Budd S.—U.S. consul at S. Blas—to have come as mr of the bark *Helvetia*, but I have no other record of such a vessel this year. iv. 587.

Smith (G. M.), 1845, at Sutter's fort, apparently an overl. immig.; also the same or another at Sonoma '45–6; perhaps the father of Frances R. iv. 579–80, 526.   S. (Geo.), 1825, mr of the *Spy* '25–7. iii. 149.   S. (Geo.), 1846, Co. C, 1st U.S. dragoons (v. 336).   S. (Geo.), 1846, Co. F, Cal. Bat. (v. 358); had a fight with Lieut Rock, and was sentenced by court-martial to 22 months of hard labor. v. 434.   S. (Gerard D.), 1847, Co. C, N.Y. Vol. (v. 499).   S. (H.), 1848, passp. from Hon.   S. (Henry), 1846, at Sutter's fort; interested at Benicia. '47–8. v. 672; perhaps Henry C.   S. (Henry), 1846 (?), keeper of a sailor's boarding-house at S.F., owner of lot, constable, and jail-keeper '47. v. 648, 685; perhaps same as the following.   S. (Henry), 1847, Co. I, N.Y. Vol. (v. 499); drowned in Feather River '49.   S. (Henry C.), 1845, nat. of Ohio, and overl. immig. with the Hastings party. iv. 586–7. He served, perhaps, in the Cal. Bat. (v. 358); had a 'Cal. claim' for $25 (v. 462); was a memb. of the legislature from Sta Clara Co. '52; cl. for land. iv. 673; supervisor of Washington, Alameda Co., '55; in Nev. '61–4; in Alameda Co. from '65 to his death at Livermore in '75, at the age of 51. His wife was Mary van Gordon, married in '46, and his surviving children were Julia A. (Mrs Hargrave), Emma L., Franklin P., and Charles.   S. (Henry J.), 1847, Co. F, N.Y. Vol. (v. 499).   S. (Hiram), 1846, Co. F, Cal. Bat. (v. 358).   S. (I.), 1845, at Sutter's fort Apr. '46.   S. (Isaac P.), 1846, Co. F, Cal. Bat. (v. 358); at Sutter's fort '47.   S. (Israel), 1848, present at the discov. of gold acc. to the county histories.   S. (I. T.), 1846 (?), nat. of Ia and overl. immig.; a settler in Sonoma Co. from '51 to his death in '79, leaving a wife and two children; called also I. P.

Smith (J.), 1846, Cal. Bat., Co. B, artill. (v. 358).   S. (J. J.), 1846, Co. F, Cal. Bat. (v. 358).   S. (Jack), 1846, at Sutter's fort from up and down the valley '46–8.   S. (Jacob), 1816, pilot of the *Lydia*. ii. 275.   S. (James), 1827, capt. of a vessel at S.F.   S. (James), 1841, nat. of Engl., naturalized in '44, when he had been 3 years in Cal., being then a farmer in the Sac. Val. iv. 279. Often named in the *N. Helv. Diary* from '45. In Jan. '46 he married the widow Marshall, and died in '48. Bidwell thinks the widow married Gregson, and was living in Sonoma Co. '64, having a son named Marshall; but there may be some confusion here; see 'Gregson.'   S. (James), 1844, mr of the *Hibernia* '44–5, iv. 566, 587, who in later years established a line of packets between S.F. and Honolulu, being well known as Capt. 'Jim' Smith. He died at New London, Conn., in '68, at the age of '65, leaving no family, as I am informed by Capt. H. H. Watson.   S. (James), 1846, of the Donner party from Ill., dying in the mountains. v. 530, 533.   S. (James), 1848, passp. from Hon.   S. (James G.), 1847, Co. F, N.Y.Vol. (v. 499); drowned in Amer. Riv. '49.   S. (James M.), 1847, Co. K, ditto.

Smith (Jedediah), 1826, Amer. trapper chief who came from Salt Lake via Colorado Riv. and Mojave to S. Gabriel. In '27 he went to Salt Lake from the S. Joaquin Val. and returned, being the 1st to cross the Sierra. From Cal. he went to Or., and in '31 was killed by the Ind. in N. Mex. See record of his visit. iii. 152–60; ment. ii. 551, 569, 600; iv. 263.   S. (John), 1834, Engl. carpenter, age 28, in Spear's service at Mont. iii. 412; also a 'tailor' Smith the same year. Named in Larkin's accounts '36–40; arrested in '40 but escaped exile. iv. 17. There may be some confusion between this man and the following.   S. (John), 1837, nat. of Nova Scotia, who came by sea; asked for naturalization in '42, being a carpenter in the Sac. Val. and 5 years a resident. iv. 118. Sutter says S. obtained land from him near Marysville; naturalized in '44, and got a grant of land in Yolo Co. iv. 674; living on his rancho '45–8, ment. in the *N. Helv. Diary*, a partner and neighbor of Michael Nye.   S. (John), 1845, Amer. sailor on the *Morea* in trouble at S.F.   S. (John), 1846, Fauntleroy's dragoons (v. 232, 247).   S. (John), 1846, Co. C, 1st U.S. dragoons (v. 336); sentenced by court-martial to imprisonment at

Los Ang. '47.   S. (John), 1847, Co. E, Morm. Bat. (v. 469); in Utah '82.
S. (John), 1847, Co. F, 3d U.S. artill. (v. 518); living '64.   S. (John), 1848,
passp. from Hon.   S. (John F.), 1833, Fr. carpenter from the Sandw. Isl. at
Sta B. iii. 409; where he built the 1st wooden house, and died in '66. *Huse.*
S. (John G.), 1847, perhaps of N.Y.Vol. (v. 499), under another name.   S.
(John H.), 1848, passp. from Hon.   S. (John M.), 1847, Co. E, N.Y.Vol. (v.
499).   S. (Joseph), 1845, doubtful name of an overl. immig. iv. 578.
    Smith (L. H.), 1846, mr of the *Benj. Rush.* v. 576.   S. (Lewis), 1847,
Co. B, N.Y.Vol. (v. 499).   S. (Lot), 1847, Co. E, Morm. Bat. (v. 469); re-
enl.; in Ariz. '82.   S. (Napoleon B.), 1845, nat. of Ohio, and overl. immig.
in the Hastings party with his brother Henry C. iv. 586-7. He worked a
while for Sutter, and then became a lumberman in the S. Antonio redwoods,
but perhaps took some part in the revolt and war of '46-7. In '48-9 he went to
the mines, and kept a store at Mission S. José, being sub-prefect for a time in '49.
Later he became a trader at Martinez, being county assessor, and memb. of
the legislature in '52. In '57-85 he lived on a rancho in Contra Costa Co. His
wife was Margelina, daughter of Elam Brown, and he has 8 children: Frank
(b. Jan. '48, the 1st in Contra Costa), Lawrence M., Sarah C., Louis N., Ellen
J., Elam, Timothy S., and Warren C. I have a full *Biog. Sketch* of ' Bony '
Smith written in '75.   S. (Oliver), 1848, doubtful name at Benicia.   S.
(Orrin), 1846, of the Mormon colony, with wife and 6 children, excommunicated on the voy., and perhaps left for a time at Hon. His daughter Amelia
was in Utah '84. v. 546, 549.   S. (O. K.), 1848, nat. of N.Y., and overl.
immig.; memb. of the legisl. '61, being a farmer at Visalia, age '39.   S.
(Persifer F.), 1848. Gov. Smith did not arrive till '49, nevertheless by a slip
of his pen he writes at S.F. in March '48, inquiring for Benicia lots. v. 673.
    Smith (R.), 1833, mr of the *Fakeja.* iii. 382.   S. (Robert), 1846, of the
Mormon colony, with wife and 2 children; teacher of tactics on the *Brooklyn;*
owner of S.F. lot '47; died in the faith about '49. v. 546, 550, 679.   S.
(Robert), 1847, at Sonoma and N. Helv.; known as 'Growling' Smith, and
arrested for outrages on Ind. v. 569, 610. He may have been the ' Badger '
Smith of the Bears in '46. v. 167.   S. (Sam.) 1837, named in Larkin's accounts.
S. (Sam.), 1845 (?), at Sonoma and N. Helv. '45-8; iv. 587; seems to have had
a rancho in the Sac. Val. '47, also working for Larkin. Sam. S. of Baltimore is
named in the *El Dorado Co. Hist.* as having come in '43 and kept the 1st
store at Kelsey. At S.F. as a witness '47 and owner of a town lot. Acc. to the
Marin Co. Hist., a Sam. S. lived in the Pt Reyes region in '46.   S. (Simeon
P.), 1847, in S.F. letter-list.
    Smith (Stephen), 1841, nat. of Md., who had spent some time in Peru, and
who visited Cal., prob. on the *Corsair,* in '41. iv. 279. I have his letter of
July written at Callao after his return from Cal. On this 1st visit he made
arrangements with Gov. Alvarado to introduce a steam-mill; and in '43 he
came back from Baltimore with the engine—the 1st in Cal.—and mill machinery on the *George Henry.* iv. 395-6, 565-6. As soon as he could be naturalized he got a grant in '44 of Bodega, where he had set up his mill, and
where he lived for the most part from that time. iv. 186, 392, 670, 679. In '45,
visiting S. Blas, Smith was arrested on a charge of being engaged in filibustering schemes for the U.S., but soon released, as there was no proof. iv. 601.
As he later told Lieut Sherman that he came to Cal. on the assurance of Webster that the U.S. would surely have the country, it is possible that in the
earlier years he talked indiscreetly. In '45-6 he owned lots in S.F., and
built a house at the cor. of Dupont and Washington streets. iv. 669, 673; v.
682. In '46 he raised the U.S. flag at Bodega, and in '46-8 served as civil
magistrate. v. 242, 670. In the flush times his mill was a very valuable
property, and he was cl. for not only Bodega, but the Blucher rancho. iv. 670.
He died at S.F. in '55 at the age of 69. His wife was a Peruvian, a sister
of Manuel Torres; who married Tyler Curtis in '56; and he left three children,
Manuela, Stephen, and James B., all of whom seem to have been living in '75.
The daughter, born at Bodega '46, married John M. English, and lived in Oakland '81.

Smith (Theodore), 1847, Co. F, N.Y.Vol. (v. 499).   S. (Thomas), 1841, at S. José. iv. 279; naturalized '44, when he claimed to have been a resid. since '42; owner of S.F. lot 45, where he kept a saloon '46-50, a stout and stuttering Englishman. iv. 669; v. 682, 685.   S. (Thomas), 1845, overl. immig. of the Swasey-Todd, or possibly the McMahon, party. iv. 576-7, 573; apparently at Sutter's fort '46-7.   S. (Thos), 1846, sailor in Stockton's Bat., fatally wounded at the S. Gabriel, Jan. '47. v. 395.   S. (Thos), on the roll of the Society of California Pioneers as having arr. in Sept.   S. (Thos J.), 1845, ditto, arrived S.F. Dec. iv. 587; perhaps the cl. of S.F. Mission lots in '52; at Gold Hill, Nev., '81.   S. (Thos L.), 1829 (?), Kentuckian trapper and mountaineer, known as 'Peg-leg' Smith from his wooden leg. The chronology of his wild career is confusing; but he may have stolen horses in Cal. in '29 and several times later, as he was fond of boasting in late years. iii. 172, 179. In '41 'El Cojo Smit' was reported to be in com. of a party of vagabonds from N. Mex. iv. 208, 278, 342. After '49 he lived in Cal., and died at S.F. in '66.

Smith (W.), 1846, Cal. Bat., Co. B, artill. (v. 358), enlisting at Mont. Oct.   S. (Willard), 1847, musician Co. D, Morm. Bat. (v. 469); in '82 at Littleton, Utah, stake president and probate judge.   Smith (Wm), 1800, mate of the *Hazard*, perhaps visiting the coast several times before 1808. ii. 17, 24-5, 95-6. In 1810-11, as mate of the *Albatross*, he was engaged in fur-hunting on the coast, especially in taking seals at the Farallones. ii. 93. In '16 he came back from China in com. of the *Albatross*, and was arrested for smuggling at Sta B., though his vessel escaped capture. ii. 275-7, 362, 248, 633. He was a nat. of Va, whose voyages and adventures in all parts of the world would fill a volume. In '36 or earlier he found his way to Cal. again. iv. 103, 141; and now, too old to command, he still made his home on board Boston vessels on the coast or at the Islands, being transferred from one to another according to his whims, and occasionally spending a few months on shore. He died at Sonoma on May 5, '46, at the age of 78.   S. (Wm), 1824, mr of the *Young Tartar*. ii. 519.   S. (Wm), 1827, Amer. carpenter in the Mont. dist. '29, age 22. iii. 176. Ment. as a sawyer working for Cooper in '31; 'Bill the Sawyer' at S. José '33, married to a Sais; in Mont. lists of '34; also near Pt Reyes; at Sonoma and S.F. '37-9; one of the arrested foreigners '40. iv. 17; Engl. carpenter, age 42, at S. José '41; wife María Josefa Sais, child. Daniel b. '33, José '36, Patricio '37, José S. '39, María '38; one of Sutter's men in the Micheltorena campaign '45. iv. 495; at S. José, S.F., and in the Sac. Val. '46; owner of a lot at S.F. and settler at Benicia '47—all these may be one or half a dozen Bill Smiths for all that I know.

Smith (Wm H.), 1847, lieut Co. I, N.Y.Vol. v. 504; owner of S.F. lot. Still at S.F. '52; in Tuolumne Co. '74.   S. (Wm M.), 1845, nat. of Ga, who came with Capt. Paty from S. Blas. iv. 587. A droll fellow, who had been a circus-rider, known as 'Jim Crow' Smith; in '46-8 member of the S.F. firm of Ward & S., owning lots and building a house, besides serving as capt. of volunteers in Marston's Sta Clara campaign. v. 381, 539, 679, 681, 684. In '48 he married the widow of Capt. Hinckley, and in '49 moved to Martinez. After a while he went to the bad altogether, being a violent and dangerous man when intoxicated, and about '54 he killed himself.   S. (Wm Taylor), 1846, lieut on the U.S. *Dale*.   Smyth (Wm), 1826, mate of the *Blossom*. iii. 121; artist from whose drawings Forbes' *California* was illustrated. iv. 151.

Snitter (Lewis), 1847, Co. E, N.Y.Vol. (v. 499).   Snook (Joseph Francisco), 1830, Engl. mr of the *Ayacucho*, who had been on the Mex. coast in Virmond's employ since '24. iii. 146, 180. He was naturalized in '33, and in '33-9 mr of the *Catalina*. iii. 381; iv. 102, 117. In '38 he purchased of Berry a rancho at Pt Reyes or Tomales, confirmed next year by the diputacion. Before this time he had married María Antonia, daughter of J.B.Alvarado of S. Diego, and he talked of quitting the sea and forming a partnership with Fitch; but in '40-2 he commanded the *Jóven Guipuzcoana*. iv. 12, 104, 305, 566; and the *Juanita* in '46. In '42 he was grantee of the S. Bernardo rancho,

S. Diego, iv. 621, where he lived with his family, dying suddenly in April '47 or '48. His widow married Henry Clayton.   Snow (A.), 1847, at Benicia. *B. Tribune.*   S. (B. F.), 1848, passp. from Hon.   S. (R. D.), 1848, ditto.   S. (Ze nora S.), 1846, of the Mormon colony. v. 546; in Utah '84.

Snyder (Elijah), 1847, Co. E, N.Y.Vol. (v. 499); at Trenton, N.J., '75. S. (Jacob R.), 1845, nat. of Pa, and overl. immig. of the Swasey-Todd party. iv. 576, 587. Mentioned at Sta Cruz and various other points in '45–6, employed as a surveyor. v. 654, 641. He served as quartermaster in Fauntleroy's dragoons. v. 293–4; and later in the Cal. Bat., ranking as major. v. 360. In '47 he was appointed surveyor for the middle department of Cal., and also commissioned to investigate charges against Alcalde Nash of Sonoma. v. 610, 465. In '48–9 with Reading and Hensley he had a trading post at Sacramento, and was a member of the constit. convention; from '50 memb. of a S.F. firm; in '52–3 state senator; in '53–60 treasurer of the U.S. mint at S.F. About '62 he retired for the most part from public life to a rancho at Sonoma, where he died in '78 at the age of 65. He was a man of fine personal appearance, of good abilities, of excellent character, and of well-deserved popularity. Portrait in *Colton's Three Years; Sonoma Co. Hist.* His 1st wife, of '50, was Susan H. Brayton; the 2d, of '74, was Rachel J. Sears; and he had no children.   S. (John), 1846, of the Donner party from Ill., killed by Reed on the Humboldt before reaching Cal. v. 530, 532.   S. (John), 1847, Co. E, Morm. Bat. (v. 469).

Soberanes, occupant of Sauzal rancho '23. ii. 616, 664.   S. (Agustin), sirviente at Sta Clara 1776. i. 306; still at S. José 1794.   S. (Ezequiel), son of Mariano, volunteer officer under Castro at the taking of Los Ang. '45. iv. 492.   S. (Feliciano), at Mont. '26, and regidor '29–30. ii. 612; grantee of Alisal '34. iii. 676; named in the padron of '36 as a nat. of Cal., age 47, wife María Ant. Rodriguez, child. Josefa b. '13, Pánfilo '15, Gabriela '18, Francisco '19, José Ant. '21, José María '23, Cármen '25, Mariano '28, Feliciano '29, José Andrés '31, Francisca '32, and José Mateo '33. Alcalde in '38–9. iii. 675, 697; grantee of S. Lorenzo in '41. iv. 655; and in '41–5 the admin. of Soledad mission, of which estate he became the owner. iv. 194, 559, 660–1; v. 558, 637, 641; being in '45 juez 2° at Mont., iv. 653, 656, where he still lived in '51.   S. (Francisco), grantee of Sanjon de Sta Rita, Merced, '41. iv. 673. S. (Guadalupe), alférez of auxiliary cavalry '45–6. v. 41; in Mont. Co. '50. S. (José Ant.), mentioned at Sutter's fort '47.   S. (José María), a soldier of the 1st exped. of 1769–74; at Soledad 1791 et seq.; in 1795 an inválido in possession of the Buenavista rancho, Mont. i. 683, 441, 499. Prob. ancestor of most of the Soberanes here registered.   S. (José M.), son of Feliciano, ment. in '46. v. 41.   S. (Josefa), daughter of Feliciano, grantee of Los Coches '41. iv. 655.   S. (Juan), sub-lieut of militia '46. v. '41; went with Flores to Mex. '47. v. 407.   S. (Mariano), soldier of the S.F. comp. '19–21; in '23 alcalde of Mont., síndico '27, alcalde '29–30. ii. 611–12; iii. 49, 76, 82, 194; in '35 admin. of S. Antonio. iii. 354, 687–8; in '36 living at Alisal, age 40, a widower—his wife had been a daughter of Ignacio Vallejo—7 child. Mariano b. '19, Juan '21, Ezequiel '23, Tomás '25, Guadalupe '28, Victor '29, Ignacio '31. In '42 he was grantee of Los Ojitos rancho. iv. 655; in '45 juez at S. Miguel. iv. 660. In '46 he was arrested with his sons, and his property at Los Ojitos destroyed by Frémont. v. 374, 464, for which Don Mariano had a Cal. claim of $19,930, of which $423 was paid (v. 462). He was cl. for Los Ojitos in '52, and the rancho is still owned by his sons in '85.   S. (Mariano), son of the preceding; grantee of S. Bernardo rancho '41—though this may have been the father. iv. 655. He was somewhat active in the final campaign of Natividad against the Amer. v. 290, 367; and was still in Mont. Co. '78. His son, Clodomiro, was for a short time employed in my Library, and a small collection of *Doc. Hist. Cal.* bears his name.   S. (Pánfilo), son of Feliciano, juez de paz at Mont. '43; custom-house guard at Mont. and S.F. '44–5. iv. 557, 653, 656.   S. (Tomás), clerk in the Mont. custom-house '44. iv. 431; went to Mex. with Flores '47. v. 407.   Sobradelas (Pablo), 1825, Span. marine from the *Aquiles;* ordered to depart in '28–30. iii. 51–2.   Sohns (John), 1847, Co. D, N.Y.Vol. (v. 499).

Sola (Faustino), 1786, Span. friar who served for brief terms at S. Luis
Ob. and S.F., retiring in 1790, and dying at the college of S. Fernando in
Mex. 1820. He was a brother of Gov. Sola. i. 388, 423, 469-70, 474; ii. 471.
S. (Pablo Vicente), Span. lieut-col, who ruled Cal. as gov. from Aug. 15, '15,
to Nov. 22, '22, being promoted to colonel in '19, and leaving Cal. as dip. to
the Mex. congress in '22. Except that he was a member of the junta de Cal.
in Mex. in '25, iii. 3-5, nothing is definitely known of his later life. For his life
and character, see ii. 470-3; on his rule in Cal. ii. 208-470, passim; miscel. mention. i. 662; ii. 78, 188, 479, 485, 514, 562, 565-6, 569, 571, 580, 587, 604, 607,
616, 642, 674, 676; iii. 3, 5, 11, 33, 109.   Solano (Francisco), Ind. chief of the
Suisunes, who from '35 was an ally of Vallejo at Sonoma, doing more than
any other to keep the Ind. of the northern frontier in order. iii. 295, 360, 598;
71-3, 444, 674. He was the grantee of Suisun rancho in '42. His original
name was Numa or Tetoy, and the name Solano, given him at baptism from
that of the mission, passed from him to the county. I have no record showing
the date of his death. His widow, Isidora, was still living at Sonoma in '74,
at an advanced age, and furnished a *Relacion* that is not without interest.
Solar (José María), at Branciforte '30. ii. 627.   Solares (Pedro), soldier at
the Colorado Riv. pueblos 1780-1. i. 359.   Solas (Matias), sirviente at Soledad 1791-1800. i. 499.

Soler (Juan), 1774, guarda-almacen at Mont. i. 224. There was some complaint of his unfitness for the place in '78-9; and he died at Mont. in '81.   S.
(Nicolás), 1781, Span. capt. who held the position of ayudante-inspector of the
Cal. troops in '81-8; a prominent officer and inveterate fault-finder, generally
in trouble because things were going to the dogs. He became comandante at
Tucson, and died in '90. Biog. i. 397-8; ment. i. 334, 370, 383, 385, 392-6,
411, 443, 451, 462-3, 467, 471-2, 479, 484, 676; ii. 571.   S. (Pablo), 1792,
surgeon of the Cal. troops at Mont. to 1800. i. 439, 501, 679-80.   Soleto
(Juan), doubtful, '46. v. 162.   Solis (Joaquin), 1825, Mex. convict who in
'29 headed a revolt of Californian soldiers, and in '30 was sent as a prisoner
to Mex. For full account of the revolt, see iii. 68-85; mention of Solis. ii. 576,
591, 604, 615, 664; iii. 16, 149.   Solórzano (Francisco), settler at Los Ang.
'16. ii. 350.   S. (José Antonio), sergt of the Mont. comp. '32-3. iii. 671, 673.
S. (Ramon), soldier of the S.F. comp. '39-42; at Sonoma '44, age 19.

Somera (José Antonio Fernandez, or Angel), 1771, Span. friar at S. Gabriel,
forced by illness to retire in '72. i. 137, 176, 187-9, 192-3.   Somers (Fred.),
1847, Co. B, N.Y.Vol. (v. 499).   Somoza (Antonio María), 1842, Mex. lieut
in the batallon fijo '42-5, adjutant, instructor, and com. at Los Ang. '44-5;
still in Cal. '46. iv. 289, 354, 407, 538; v. 41.   Soncho (Francisco), juez de paz
at S.F. '42. iv. 665, 667.   Soret (Angelina), 1847, owner of a S.F. lot.   So-
ria (Francisco), alcalde of Mont. (?) '29. ii. 612; in '28 resid. of Branciforte,
wife Rita Pinto, child. José, Cecilia, Cármen, and Gregorio; juez de paz at
B. '32, regidor '38, juez de campo '43, 2d alcalde '45. iii. 588, 696-7; iv. 663-
4; in '45 at B., age '50, wife Guadalupe Juarez, child. José Ant. b. '27, Miguel '33, Cineda (?) '36, José '44, Cecilia '28, Benita '35, Prudencia '37.   S.
(José), at Branciforte '45, wife María de Jesus Robles, child. Refugio '43, Teresa '44.   S. (Juan José), alcalde of Mont. '28. ii. 612; and prob. '29.   Sosa
(Mariano), visiting Dominican friar at S. Gabriel '31-2. iii. 641.

Sotelo (Francisco), settler at Los Ang. 1803. ii. 350.   S. (Gabriel), ditto
'15. ii. 350.   S. (Gabriel), S.F. militiaman '37.   S. (José), at S. Bernardino
'46, age 45.   S. (José María), at Branciforte '45, age 50, wife Encarnacion.
S. (Juan), soldier in S.F. comp. '42, militia S.F. '37.   S. (Mariano), soldier
of S.F. comp. '34-9.   S. (Pedro D.), at Los Ang. '46.   S. (Ramon), settler
at Los Ang. 1805; killed at Purísima '24. ii. 350, 412, 529, 566. In '17 P.
Payeras writes of him as 'el famoso criminal de California.' Miguel Sotelo,
perhaps his descendant, was a famous outlaw killed by the sheriff at Los
Ang. in '78.   S. (Venancio), at Los Ang. '48.   S. (Vicente), at S. Bern. '46,
age 22.

Soto, sailor sirviente at Sta Cruz. i. 496.   S. (Andrés), at Mont. '38; supl.
juez of ranchos '46. v. 637.   S. (Antonio), settler at S. José before 1800,

regidor 1809–10, alcalde '18, dying suddenly in that year. i. 716; ii. 134, 378. S. (Antonio), soldier of S.F. comp. '19–29; in '41 at S. José, age 42, wife María G. Briones, child. Ramon b. '22, Raimunda '27, Angel '28, Nieves '30, Concepcion '32, Francisco '39, Felipa '40.   S. (Antonio 2d), soldier of the S.F. comp. '19–27.   S. (Bernardino), had a Cal. claim '46–7 of $873 (v. 462). S. (Casilda), grantee of La Merced, Los Ang., '44. iv. 635.   S. (Casimiro), at Mont. '36, age 28, wife Eleuteria Castro, child María Trinidad b. '34.   S. (Domingo), at S. José '41, age 22; and living with him Jesus, age 18, Fernando 12, and José Ant. 14.   S. (Eufemio), juez de campo Mont. '37. iii. 675.   S. (Eugenio), body found hanging at Sta Cruz '38. iii. 697.   S. (Eugenio), at Branciforte '45, age 40, wife ——, child. Ramona b. '35, Juana '37, Rosalía '40, and Josefa '44.   S. (Eusebio), militiaman at S.F. '37; owner of a town lot '45. iv. 669; v. 685.   S. (Felipe), at S.F. '37–44.   S. (Fernando), owner of a Russian River rancho '46. *Raven.*   S. (Flores), at Los Ang. '46.

Soto (Francisco), 1st child b. at S.F. 1776, son of Ignacio. He became a soldier in the S.F. comp., was a corp. in 1810, and was promoted to sergt for bravery in an Ind. campaign of that year; also made an exped. in '13, and another in '20. ii. 91, 204, 324, 339. He was possibly the Fran. S. at S. Matías rancho, Mont., '36, age 57, child Lorenzo b. '21.   S. (Francisco), corp. in S.F. comp. '19; sergt '20–9; ment. in '27–8. ii. 584, 592; iii. 66–7, 111, 156. I am unable to distinguish the different men bearing this name.   S. (Francisco), grantee of Bolsa Nueva rancho '29. ii. 615, 664.   S. (Francisco), corp. died of wounds received in an Ind. exped. '29. iii. 111–13.   S. (Francisco), at Mont. '36, age 28, wife María de Los Angeles, child. Ascension b. '32, Trinidad '34, Gertrudis '36.   S. (Francisco), at S. José '41, age 34, wife Bárbara Castro, child. Ana María b. '34, Francisco '36, Vicente '38, Encarnacion '39; in '42–4 grantee of S. Lorenzo, Alameda Co., for which his widow was cl. in '52. iv. 673.   S. (Francisco), at S. José '41, age 24.   S. (Francisco), grantee of S. Vicente, Mont., '35–42. iii. 678.   S. (Francisco), prob. some one of the preceding; sergt of the Mont. comp. '35–6. iii. 671; a supporter of Alvarado and comisario de policía. iii. 461, 675; ment. as lieut in '39. iii. 588; admin. of Sta Cruz '39–40. iii. 695; went to Mex. with Covarrubias in '40. iv. 13, 15, 24; but is ment. again in '42. iv. 308.

Soto (Gervasio), soldier of the S.F. comp. '19–31; resid. of Branciforte '36. iii. 697; at S.F. age 54 in '44; at S. José '45. iv. 686.   S. (Guillermo), soldier of the S. Buen. escolta 1786, when his wife, Nicolasa Ramirez, died; settled at Los Ang. 1789. ii. 349; alcalde in '98 and 1809. i. 661; ii. 110.   S. (Ignacio), soldier of S.F. comp. from 1776; in 1793 at S. José, wife Bárbara Espinosa, child. Antonio b. '76, Francisco María '77, Dámaso '78, Isidoro '80, Josefa (who married José Sanchez) '83, Joaquin '84, José Francisco, Rafaela, Bernarda, Tomás, Juan, Rafael, and Dolores. i. 291, 477.   S. (Ignacio), soldier of the S.F. comp. '24–30.   S. (Ignacio), corp. at Mont. '36, age 22. S. (Ignacio), soldier at Mont. '36, age 26.   S. (Ignacio), at S. José '41, age 33, wife Teresa Martinez.   S. (Isidoro), soldier retired with rank of lieut '44. iv. 408; in '36 at Mont., age '55, wife Marcela Linares; married sons Lázaro and Joaquin.

Soto (Jesus), sergt who went to Mex. with Castro '40; aux. de policía '46 at Mont. iv. 13, 30; v. 637.   S. (Joaquin), son of Isidoro, at Mont. '36, age 33, wife Dolores Cantua, child. Joaquin b. '24, Luisa '26, Bárbara '27, Josefa '32, Laran (?) '34; possibly the grantee of Piojo in '42. iv. 655; juez de paz at S. Juan B. '46. v. 640; and still in Mont. Co. '51.   S. (Joaquin), son of Ignacio; married at S. José 1803 to María de la Luz Berreyesa. ii. 138.   S. (Joaquin), resid. of Branciforte '30. ii. 627.   S. (Joaquin), juez de campo at Los Carneros, Mont., '35. iii. 674.   S. (Joaquin), at S. Matías rancho '36, age 51, wife Juana Butron, child. Bárbara b. '24, Antonia '25, Deogracias '28, María '30, Adelaida '31, María '33, Salvador '34. iii. 678.   S. (Joaquin), at S. Bernardino '46, age 35.   S. (Joaquin), grantee of Cañada de la Carpintería '45. iv. 655.

Soto (José) soldier of the S.F. comp. '21–9.   S. (José María), settler at Los Ang. '15. ii. 349.   S. (Josefa), grantee of Capay rancho '35–44. iii. 711;

iv. 671. S. (Juan) soldier of the S.F. comp. '19–24; in '41 at S. José, age 55, wife Petra Pacheco, child. José b. '19, Francisco '25, José Ignacio '30, Guadalupe '33, Silverio '34, and Juana '35. S. (Lázaro), son of Isidro, at Mont. '36, age 34, wife Solecita Cantera, child. Isidro b. '28, General (?) '31, Ramon '34, and Joaquin '35; grantee of Cañada de la Segunda '39. iii. 677; at Mont. '46. S. (Lorenzo), at the Natividad fight '46. v. 368; in the south '47. v. 389–90; cl. for Los Vallecitos '52. iii. 612. S. (Luis), at S.F. '42, age 23. S. (Manuel), soldier of the S.F. comp. '23–31. S. (Manuel), at Branciforte '28. S. (María Ant. Mesa de), widow at S. José '41, age 39, child. Juan Cap. b. '23, Jesus '25, Dolores '27, Juan Cris. '29, Francisco '31, José Ignacio '33, Patricio '35, José Cruz '37, and Celia '39. S. (Meliton), in the Solis revolt of '29, sent to Mex. iii. 73, 77–8, 82–5. S. (Milano), Mex. soldier at Mont. '36, age 33. S. (Pedro), soldier at S.F. '42. S. (Rejis), settler at Los Ang. 1789. i. 461. S. (Raimundo), worked for Larkin '48 on his rancho. S. (Ramon), at S.F. '44, age 20. S. (Teodora), grantee of Cañada del Hambre and Las Boleus, Contra Costa, in '42. iv. 671. S. (Tiburcio), at Mont. '36, age 30, wife Concepcion Zuñiga, child. José de Jesus b. '29, Raimundo '30, Vicenta '33, Juliana '34, and Miguel '35. Sonervoit (Alex.), 1847, Co. E, N.Y. Vol. (v. 499); at Los Ang. '77. Sout (W.), 1846, Cal. Bat., Co. B, artill. (v. 358). Southward (Chas C.), 1847, clerk for Parker at S.F.; owner of town lots; in '48 trader at Napa in partnership with Swasey. v. 670; at Vallejo after '50; Trinidad '54; Vallejo '77. Southwick (John), 1846, carpenter on the U.S. *Congress;* capt. and chief engineer in Stockton's Bat. '46–7. v. 385. Southworth (Eli), 1838, nat. of Mass., visited Cal. from Hon. on the *D. Quixote,* and possibly earlier, '33–5, on the *Loriot.* iv. 103, 119, 141. In '43–5 he lived at S.F. as a partner in Paty's business, being named in the padron of '44 as 25 years old. After '48 he engaged in the lumber business; and from '53 he lived with William H. Davis at S. Leandro until his death in '57. Souza (Wm), 1847, Portuguese fruit-dealer at Sta Clara '63–76.

Spalding (Josiah), 1840, mr of the *Lausanne,* in trouble with the authorities. iv. 104, 121, 171–4. A Mass. man who died about '70; his daughter at Mont. in '84. S. (J. C.), 1848, passp. from Hon. Sparks (Isaac J.), 1832, nat. of Me, and long a resid. of St Louis, Mo., who came from N. Mex. with Young's party of trappers. iii. 388, 408. He engaged in otter-hunting on the coast, and in '34 seems to have made a trip to N. Mex., or at least got a pass. iii. 395; in '35 aiding in the removal of Ind. from S. Nicolás isl. iii. 361, 652. From '35 he lived at Sta B., keeping a store from '36 in a house bought of Foxen, but devoting himself mainly to otter-hunting, for which he received several licenses. iv. 81, 117; asked for naturalization in '37, estimating his property at $2,000; grantee of a rancho in '39, he having become a catholic before '36. He was not arrested in '40. iv. 24; but in '41 was in some trouble because of a young woman who bore him two children, iv. 280, being threatened with a fine of $19 (!) if he did not put an end to the scandal, and the woman being finally exiled to Los Ang. In '43 he was grantee of Huasna rancho, S. Luis Ob., for which he was later cl. as also for Pismo. iv. 655; iii. 678. He served rather unwillingly under Frémont for a time in '46–7, had a Cal. claim of some $900 (v. 462), and in '47 was sent to Gov. Mason to explain the state of affairs at Sta B. v. 584. He gave up hunting, except as a pastime, after '48; made an unsuccessful trip to the mines; and later led the life of a prosperous ranchero in S. Luis Ob. Co. till his death in '67 at the age of 63. He was regarded as an honest and active man. His portrait was published in the *Hesperian* of '59, with a sketch of his early life. A family is mentioned in the later years, but I find no record to show whom he married. S. (Mary), 1846, of the Mormon colony with children. v. 546; daughter of Mrs Hamilton; not named in the Honolulu list; and possibly wife of Q. S. S. (Quartus S.), 1846, of the Mormon colony, with wife and child. v. 546. Called also Q. L. and Q. C.; nat. of Conn., teacher and preacher, who seems to have left the church; said to have been a lawyer at S.F. in later years, but not in the directories. S. (Stephen), 1846, sailor on the *Dale.* Sparrowhawk, 1846 (?), mr of the *Jóven Guipuzcoana,* who settled at Stockton, and died '61 acc. to newspapers. Spatz (Conrad), 1847, Co. B, N.Y.Vol. (v. 499); killed in L. Cal, '47.

Spear (Nathan), 1823, nat. of Boston, druggist's clerk with his brother Paul in B., who made a trip to the Sandw. Isl. in '19, and another on the *Rover* in '23, touching at Mont. In '29 he came again to the Islands, in '30 married Jane Holmes, and in '32 came to Cal. in time to join the comp. extranjera at Mont., iii. 221, 408, where he opened a store, obtaining a carta, and owning a schooner, the *Nicolás*, which ran to Sta Cruz. iv. 83, 141. His name occurs often in commercial records of each year, and I have many of his letters. In '36 he formed a partnership with Leese and Hinckley to open a store at S.F., whither he moved in '38, leaving his Mont. store in charge of Wm Warren. At this time the partnership was broken up by a quarrel over $13,000 of profits, but Spear continued the business in the store at the cor. of Montgomery and Clay streets; transferred the *Nicolás* to S.F. bay for the collection of produce, adding the *Isabel* to the fleet—Wm H. Davis, his nephew and clerk, being generally in com. of one of the schooners; and built a mule-power grist-mill; being arrested as a matter of form in '40. iii. 705, 709; iv. 17, 82, 116, 130, 245, 250, 668; v. 681. In '45 he was injured by Californians in an assault on Capt. Libby. iv. 569, 665-6; and is named as a witness at the Rae inquest. iv. 593. In '46-7 he is named as owner of lots, candidate for alcalde, and taking some slight part in politics. v. 295, 455, 680-1; but on account of ill-health moved to Napa Val. with his family in '46, denouncing a quicksilver mine on the Bale rancho. He returned to S.F. at the end of '48, and died there Oct. '49 at the age of 47. He was an enterprising man of business, honorable in his dealings, gentlemanly in his manners, and scholarly in his tastes though of limited education. He never became a Mex. citizen, and therefore obtained no land grant. His wife, a half-breed Hawaiian, died in Napa '48; and there was one son, William N., b. at Napa '46, who in '78 gave me a valuable collection of his father's *Papers*. He died before '84.   Spect (Jonas), 1848, nat. of Pa, who came overland to Or. in '47, and to S.F. on the *Henry*, possibly at the end of '47. In '48 he was a very successful miner, being the discoverer of gold on the Yuba. He kept a store at Sacramento; was elected to the 1st state senate; was a founder of Frémont, where he lived till '56; a resid. of Vernon till about '68, when he moved to Colusa, dying there in '83 at the age of 66. Portrait in *Colusa Co. Hist.*, 42; *Yolo Co. Hist.*, 26; see also *Hist. Or.*, this series, p. 629.   Spedding (Matthew), 1848, Engl. farmer in Sta Clara '76.   Speiden (Wm), 1846, purser on the U.S. *Congress;* commissary in Stockton's Bat.; witness at the Frémont court-martial. v. 385, 420.

Spence (David), 1824, nat. of Scotland, who had lived a few years at Lima, and came to Cal. on the *Pizarro* to superintend the meat-packing establishment of Begg & Co. at Mont. ii. 519, 526. In '27 he started in business for himself, iii. 128, and was prosperous from the beginning, being cautious, close, and energetic. His name often appears in the records of each year, and I have many of his business letters. In '28 he was baptized at Sta Cruz as David Estévan; in '29 married Adelaida, daughter of Mariano Estrada, taking an active part in the protection of Mont. during the Solis revolt. iii. 71, 74, 82, 49; ii. 609; and was naturalized in '30. In '34-9 he was grantee of Encinal y Buena Esperanza rancho, of which he was cl. and permanent owner. iii. 677; in '35 alcalde. iii. 673. In '36 he was a member of the diputacion, and in this and the following years was secretly a supporter of Alvarado's govt, choosing not to act openly as a member of the 'congress,' yet exerting quietly much influence in municipal and legislative matters. iii. 426, 454-5, 460, 469, 501, 524; iv. 86, 116, 148. He was elector and juez de paz in '39-40, furnishing information to Laplace, giving Sutter a letter of introduction, and doubtless favoring the exile of Graham and his vagabonds. iii. 675-6; iv. 8-9, 128, 136, 154-5; ment. '41-2. iv. 212, 309-10; in '43-5 member of the junta departamental. iv. 361, 411, 425, 521, 540; in '45 in com. of the foreign guard to protect Mont. during the Micheltorena troubles, being also appointed prefect by Gov. Pico, but apparently declining the office. iv. 515, 522, 653. In '46, though popularly believed to have intrigued for an English protectorate, he was regarded by Larkin as friendly to the U.S., was member of the council after the change of flag, and of the legislative council in '47. v. 28, 61, 68, 234, 289, 433, 637. He subsequently served as prefect in '49–50, and as county supervisor in '58–60. About '48 he gave up his mercantile enterprises, and devoted himself chiefly to the care of his estate and the raising of live-stock. In '73 he furnished me some brief *Historical Notes*, and died in '75 at the age of 77. Don David had an excellent reputation among the pioneers of Cal., few exerting so wide and good an influence. While not exactly popular by reason of his conservatism and closeness in money matters, obstinate as any of his race, and making enemies as well as friends, he yet merited and received the respect of all classes. His wife survived him but a month, and his only son David, born in '30 and educated at Honolulu, iv. 103, died in '68, leaving 3 sons and a daughter, who inherited their grandfather's large estate.

Spence (Geo.), 1846, Co. E, Cal. Bat., enlisting at Sonoma in Oct. (v. 358). S. (Robert), 1846, ditto; in the mines '48.   Spencer, 1839 (?), on board the Boston trader *Sophia*, acc. to the S. Diego *World* of Feb. 15, '73, when S. revisited S.D.   S., 1809–10 (?), hunter reported to have been in Cal. ii. 89, S. (Oscar H.), 1846, Irishman on roll of Soc. Cal. Pion.; d. at Vallejo '76, age 52.   S. (Wm W.), 1847, Co. D, Morm. Bat. (v. 469).   Spidle (John), 1847, Co. S, ditto; badly hurt at Los Angeles.   Spiel (Henry), 1845, overl. immig. of the Swasey-Todd party. iv. 576, 587 (though John H. Brown says that he went to Or. and came to Cal. in '46). He served in Co. B, artill. of the Cal. Bat. (v. 358), and settled at Sta Cruz, where, acc. to Brown, he was accidentally killed about '53.   Spitler (John), 1846, Co. E, Cal. Bat., enlisting at Sonoma in Oct. (v. 358).   Spitten (John D.), 1846, Co. C, 1st U.S. dragoons (v. 336).   Spitzer (August), 1846, German immig. of the Donner party, who died in the mts. v. 531, 534.   Spooner, 1848, from Hon. on the *Sagudahoc;* perhaps Sam. B. at S. José '50.

Sprague (Richard D.), 1847, Co. C, Morm. Bat., musician (v. 469); reënl.; at Brigham City, Utah, '82.   S. (Thomas), 1848, doubtful date in a newspaper sketch.   Spriggs (Thos), 1847, died in Sonoma Co. '51.   Spring, 1848, mr of the *Huntress.* v. 578.   Springer (James Peter), 1841, nat. of Ky, and overl. immig. of the Bartleson party. iv. 270, 255, 279. He returned east in '42. iv. 342; is said to have made the overl. trip several times, being engaged in promoting immigration; and finally came to Cal. with his family in '52, settling at Saratoga, Santa Clara Co., and being a member of the legislature of '59. He died in '61, leaving a widow and daughter. An account of the trip of '41, by him, is given in *Taylor's Discov. and Founders*.   S. (Lewis), 1847, painter at Mont. '47–50.   Sproston, 1847, mid. on the U.S. *Independence.* Squires, 1848, saddler at Sutter's fort.

Stack (Garrett), 1847, Co. E, N.Y. Vol. (v. 499).   Stadmuller (Joseph), 1847, Co. F, 1st U.S. artill. (v. 518).   Stagg (Wm), 1816, sailor on the *Albatross.* ii. 275.   Stall (Alfred B.), 1847, Co. I, N.Y. Vol. (v. 499); d. before '82.   Standage (Henry), 1847, Co. E, Morm. Bat. (v. 469); in Ariz. '82.   Stanley, 1845, in Sutter's employ '45–6. iv. 578.   S. (Fabius), 1846, lieut on the U.S. *Dale;* nat. of N.C.; later rear-admiral; at Washington, D.C., '79.   S. (John M.), 1846, nat. of N.Y. and artist with Kearny from N. Mex. v. 337; owner of S.F. lot '47. v. 676; went by sea to Or. and thence to the islands; in '51–2 connected with the survey of the Northern Pac. R. R.; d. at Detroit '72.   S. (J. R.), 1846, at Sta Cruz '81. *S. J. Pion.* An R. Stanley of '44 is also mentioned in '78. *Id.*   S. (Joseph), 1842, sailor on the *United States;* at Reno, Nev., '83.   S. (Simeon), 1846, of the Mormon colony; did not come to Cal. v. 547.   Stanly, 1846, overl. immig. v. 528, who joined the Cal. Bat. (v. 358), and died on the march south in Dec.   Stanton (Chas Tyler), 1846, nat. of N.Y. and overl. immig. of the Donner party from Chicago. He crossed the Sierra to Sutter's fort and went back to aid the party, though he had no relatives among the number. Again he volunteered to cross the mts for succor, but died in the attempt. v. 531–2, 534, 537. Portrait in *McGlashan's Hist.* I have a long letter from his brother, Philip V. N. Stanton, to Geo. McKinstry in '48, containing much information about the young man's life, character, and family.

Stargenigge (John), 1847, shingle-maker at Mission S. José.   Stark (Benj. F.), 1847, from Hon. on the *Currency Lass*, returning on the *Toulon*. S. (Daniel), 1846, of the Mormon colony, with wife and two children. v. 547; owner of a S. F. lot '47. v. 682; builder of a school-house. v. 656; commissioner to settle the affairs of Brannan & Co.; member of the S. F. council in '49; living in Utah '84.   S. (Henry), 1847, Co. B, N.Y. Vol. (v. 499).   S. (John S.), 1846, nat. of Ky and overl. immig. with M. D. Ritchie, whose daughter, Mary J., was his wife. v. 529. He took part in measures for the relief of the Donner party. v. 540-1; settled in Knights Valley; county judge of Napa '50-1; memb. of the legislature '51, '55-6; lived near Calistoga '51-68; in Lake Co. from '68 to his death at Guenoc in '74, leaving a widow and 8 children.   Starke (Fred.), 1845, German sailor who deserted from a whaler at Sauzalito. iv. 587; a ranchero in different parts of Sonoma Co.; miner in '48-9; in '80 on a farm near Petaluma with his wife Mina Hastler.   Starkey, 1848, Engl. merchant of the S.F. firm of S., Janion, & Co. v. 678, 680; d. at S.F. about '50.   Stayton (James), 1847, Co. B, N.Y. Vol. (v. 499). d. on the Calaveras '52.

Stearns (Abel), 1829, nat. of Mass. who had lived 3 years in Mex., where he was naturalized in '28, and arrived at Monterey in July '29. iii. 179. He came with the intention of obtaining a large tract of land, to be selected in the Sac. or S. Joaq. valleys, which, apparently in payment of some claim, the Mex. govt. had offered him. His associate in this scheme was Geo. W. Ayres, q.v. Being meanwhile for a year or two in the employ of Capt. Cooper, Stearns seems to have selected his land, or at least to have reached a point where the action of the diputacion was required, and in urging a meeting of that body he excited the enmity of Gov. Victoria, by whom he was banished to the frontier to return as one of the leading inciters of the revolution of '31. iii. 49, 179, 193-4, 200-2, 630. Nothing more is heard of the land project; and in '33 S. settled at Los Ang. as a trader. I have much of his business correspondence from year to year. In '34 he obtained a town lot, and also a building at S. Pedro, which he enlarged and used as a warehouse. His dealings were chiefly in hides and liquors; and from '35 he was often in trouble by reason of smuggling operations; and also in '35 severely wounded in a quarrel about a barrel of wine sold to Wm Day. iii. 375, 417, 631-2, 641; iv. 95, 116, 208. Don Abel was, perhaps, not more addicted to contraband trade than Larkin, Fitch, Spence, and others, but he was less cautious and less fortunate in keeping on the right side of the authorities. In '36 he was síndico. iii. 636; and for some reason that is not very clear, but perhaps for his agency in the matter of the vigilantes, was ordered to leave Cal. by Gov. Chico, becoming in this and the next few years a strong supporter, in a quiet way, of Alvarado, even as against Cárlos Carrillo. iii. 197, 424, 428-9, 501, 565. In '39 his name is mentioned in connection with the flag tumult. iii. 589; in '42 entertained Com. Jones. iv. 321; sent gold from the S. Francisquito placers to the Philadelphia mint. iv. 297; and purchased the Alamitos rancho and its live-stock for $6,000 as a foundation for his future landed wealth. He was somewhat active in the movement against Gov. Micheltorena in '45, being also a suplente of the assembly. iv. 495, 497, 508, 540. In '46 he was sub-prefect and also worked earnestly—both as a foe of Mex. and friend of the U.S.—to further the plans of Larkin, by whom he was formally appointed a sub-confidential agent of the U.S. His efforts and those of his chief were defeated at the last by Stockton's perversity, if, indeed, there was any remaining hope of success after the rascally acts of Frémont and his associates. v. 50, 63, 66, 71, 231, 264, 271-2, 625. In the warlike events of '46-7 he remained neutral as a Mex. official, though he had some small Cal. claims (v. 402), and is mentioned in the annals of '47-8, being síndico in the latter year. v. 329, 435. 448, 610, 626. In '49 he was a member of the constit. convention, and later served as assemblyman, supervisor, justice of the peace, and member of town council. He was cl. for the Laguna and Alamitos ranchos. iii. 633; iv. 621; and the owner of many more, becoming the largest owner of land and cattle in southern Cal. His wealth was somewhat affected by the drought of '63–4 and by other reverses, yet he left an immense estate at his death, which occurred at S.F. in '71, when he was 72 years of age. Don Abel was a shrewd man of business; somewhat tricky in the petty transactions of early years, but apparently honorable in the larger operations of later times; a man of quick temper and strong prejudices, but hospitable, not penurious, a good friend, and kind husband. He hated Mexico and the Mexicans, but liked the Californians to such a degree as to cause at times some hostility on the part of Americans. In person he was very ugly, being known sometimes as Cara de Caballo, and having an impediment in speech from the cut inflicted by Day in '35. His wife was Arcadia, daughter of Juan Bandini, as beautiful as her husband was ugly, raising the personal appearance of the family to a high average, who survived him without children, inherited the bulk of his estate, married Robt S. Baker, and still lives in southern Cal. in '85. S. (Fred.), 1847, killed at the S. Gabriel. v. 395; perhaps 'Strauss.'

Stebbins (Ira), 1845, overl. immig. of the Hastings party. iv. 586–7; working for Sutter in '45–6, later at Sonoma, and prob. one of the Bears, since he is recorded as having arrived at N. Helv. from Sonoma on June 17th. v. 110, 128; owner of S.F. lot '47. v. 685; said to have been killed in the south by Murieta's men. His name is written Ira H. and Isaac T.; possibly two men. Steel (Austin), 1845, mr of the *Dromio* (?). S. (James), 1841, an employé of the H. B. Co. S. (Joseph), 1826, Boston trader, and mr of the *Harbinger* '26–8, of the *Planet* '29–30, *Chalcedony* in '32–3, *Sarah and Caroline* and *Kent* '36–8, and *Roger Williams* in '40. His name constantly appears in commercial records of all these years, and he was evidently a humorous and popular trader. iii. 93, 146–8, 176, 381, 384, 461, 563; iv. 104–6, 117. Steele (Geo. E.), 1847, Co. A, Morm. Bat. (v. 469); reënl. S. (H. A.), 1841, lieut on the *St Louis*. S. (Isaiah C.), 1847, Co. A, Morm. Bat. (v. 469); reënl. S. (Seymour G.), 1847, capt. Co. A, N.Y. Vol. v. 503–4; in Humboldt Co. '74; at S. Diego '82. Steers (Andrew J.), 1847, Co. B, Morm. Bat. (v. 469); reënl.

Steingraudt (Louis), 1846, Co. C, 1st U.S. dragoons (v. 336). Stenner (Wm), 1831, nat. of Mass. and mate of the *Ayacucho*. iii. 405; for 2 years in charge of the hide-houses at S. Diego; in '33 obtained a passport; perhaps the same who was mr of the *Primavera* in '47, v. 580, having a Cal. claim of $450 (v. 462). Stenson (J. Fenwick), 1846, passed mid. U.S.N., and acting capt. in Stockton's Bat. '46–7. v. 385. Stephens, 1848, miner at Coloma. S. (Alex.), 1847, Co. D, Morm. Bat. (v. 469); in Sutter's employ '47–8, and at the Coloma mill when gold was found. S. (Alfred), 1837, on Larkin's books. S. (Charles), 1848, at Sutter's fort. S. (John), 1798, Boston sailor at S. Diego. i. 545, 654. S. (Peter), 1847, Co. F, N.Y.Vol. (v. 499); d. at S.F. '49. S. (Thos H.), 1848, owner of S.F. lots. S. (Wm), 1836, Engl., age 35, in a Los Ang. list. Stepp, 1845, one of Frémont's men, separated for a while from the party, but accompanied Gillespie up the valley to rejoin it. His full name was prob. 'Steppenfeldt,' or possibly there may have been another of that name. iv. 583; v. 24, 453.

Sterling, 1840 (?), at Sta Rosa in '77, known as 'Major' S., said to have visited S.F. in very early times on a coasting vessel. iv. 120. S. (Chas B.), 1847, nat. of La, clerk for naval agent Larkin at Mont. '47–8, and later employed by him in the Sac. Val., where he wrote long letters on his adventures in the mines. He prob. came as purser on a man-of-war; was the 3d settler in Colusa Co.; married Lucinda Stewart '49 in Yolo Co.; and died after '50 at a date not recorded. Sterrett (Isaac), 1842, lieut in com. of the U.S. *Relief*. iv. 314, 568. Stetson (Ed. L.), 1841, clerk on the *Don Quixote* '41–2, named in Larkin's accounts and by Davis. iv. 341; mr of the *Warren* at Honolulu and Mazatlan '45–6; in '47–8 clerk for Larkin at Mont. and Benicia, and later for Brannan at Sac.; at S.F. '51. Stetyel (Geo.), 1848, in S.F. letter-list.

Stevens, 1840, mr of the *Leonidas*. iv. 104. S., 1845, mr of the *Wm C. Nye*. iv. 570. S., 1846, mr of the *United States*. v. 580. S., 1847, mid. on the U.S. *Independence*. S. (Mrs), 1845, at Mont., went east on the *Admittance*. S. (Alex.), 1847, Mormon at the Coloma mill when gold was found. S. (Asa), 1847, owner of S.F. lot. v. 679. S. (Charles), 1847 (?), at S.F. '54.

Annals. S. (Elisha), 1844, nat. of Ga and capt. of the overl. immig. party to which I have given his name. iv. 445–8, 453, 679. I find no record of him in the following years; but in '72–83 he was living on Kern River, with an excellent memory of early times as he wrote, which however he proposed to utilize one of these days to make a book which should bring him money and fame. Alleged portrait and biog. in *S. F. Post*, Dec. 26, '83. I have in '85 received neither a copy of his book nor news of his death. S. (Geo.), 1847, at Benicia. v. 673. S. (Geo. A.), 1847, mid. on the U.S. *Dale*. S. (Isaac), 1842, at Sta Cruz '42–3. S. (James), 1840, mr of the *Roger Williams* and *Cervantes.* iv. 12, 104; also on the coast in '45 and perhaps in '48. S. (James), 1845, doubtful name of an overl. immig. iv. 578; also Richard. S. (John), 1837, at Mont. S. (John), 1840, on the *Lausanne* acc. to a letter pub. in the county histories. iv. 121; yet not named as a passenger at Hon. and not known to have remained in Cal., unless he may be the following. S. (John), 1846, Co. A, Cal. Bat. (v. 358), one of the Sta B. garrison. v. 316. S. (John H.), 1847, Co. G, N.Y.Vol. (v. 499); at Stockton '71–4. S. (Joshua T.), 1845, mr of the *United States.* S. (Lyman), 1847, Co. B, Morm. Bat. (v. 469); in '81 at Orderville, Utah. S. (Thos H.), 1848, owner of S.F. lots. S. (Wm), 1846, sailor on the U.S. *Dale.* S. (Wm), 1847, at Sutter's fort. Stevenson, (B. W.), 1847, mid. on the *Independence.*

Stevenson (Jonathan D.), 1847, nat. of N.Y., democratic politician, and militia officer, who came to Cal. as colonel in com. of the regiment of N.Y. volunteers. For a record of the regimental history, see v. 499–518; and for additional mention of Col Stevenson's career in '47–8, v. 415, 439, 449–50, 489–90, 497, 565, 584, 588–9, 625, 631–2. From May '47 to the end of the war and mustering-out of the volunteers in '48 he was military commandant of the southern district, with headquarters at Los Ang. The colonel never had an opportunity of showing his prowess as a warrior, but he was a man of much energy, of strong will, and good executive ability, a strict disciplinarian, who performed the duties of his position in a very creditable manner. After '48 he settled at S.F. as a real estate agent, and was particularly interested for some years in developing the latent greatness of New York of the Pacific, being the claimant for the rancho of Los Médanos, Contra Costa. iii. 712. From '72 he held the position of U.S. shipping commissioner at S.F., where he still lives in '85 at the venerable age of 85 years. Portrait in *Annals of S.F.*, and *Clarke's Hist.* The public has often been led to expect the publication of his recollections of a long and active life, a work that could not fail to be of deep interest. In '47 Col S. was a widower, having 3 daughters in N.Y.; in '51 he married again and has several daughters born in Cal. S. (Matthew R.), 1847, son of the colonel and capt. of Co. G, N.Y.Vol. v. 504; died at Sackett Harbor, N.Y., '63. S. (Wm), 1847, Co. F, 3d U.S. artill. (v. 518); supposed to be living in '64.

Steward (James), 1826, on the *Rover.* S. (S.), 1848, at Mont. Stewart (Alfred V.), 1846, at S.F. '46–7. S. (Chas), 1848, passp. from Hon. S. (Frank S.), 1847 (?), at a reunion of surviving N.Y. Vol. '84. S. (J. B.), 1847; mid. on the U.S. *Columbus.* S. (James), 1847, Co. D, Morm. Bat. (v. 469). S. (John C.), 1835, sailor on the *Pilgrim* who settled at S. Diego in '38; married Rosa Machado, and still lived at S. D. in '77. S. (Robert B.), 1847, Co. D, Morm. Bat. (v. 469). S. (Thomas), 1824, Scotch carpenter on the *Royal George*, arrested at Sta B.; at Mont '29; at S. D. '36. ii. 526. S. (Thos K.), 1848, on Amer. River; at Sac. '61. S. (Wm M.), 1848, sec. of Com. Jones, making a trip with Colton to the mines; owner of S.F. lots, memb. of the council, justice of the peace, and candidate for gov. in '49; still at S.F. '54.

Stickney (John), 1836, mr of the *Keat* and perhaps of the *Sarah and Caroline* '36–7. iv. 104, 106. Stiggere (Ignacio), doubtful name of a Californian at Sonoma. v. 162. Still (Geo.), 1846, of the Morm. colony, with wife and 3 children. v. 547. Sarah Still, who in '48 was married to J. D. Marston, may have been his daughter. He did not go to Utah. Stillman (Dexter), 1847, Co. B, Morm. Bat. (v. 469). Stillwell (Joseph), 1846, overl. immig., who served in Co. E, Cal. Bat., enlisting at S. José in Nov. v. 528 (358); he was a son-in-law of S. C. Young, still at S. Jose in '50.   Stilts (Jesse), 1846, arrived. *Hittell.*   S. (John), 1846, prob. overl. immig., enlisting at Sonoma in Oct. in Co. E. Cal. Bat. (v. 358); settler in Solano Co. '48, and still there in '78.   S. (Marion), 1846, prob. son of John; nat. of Mo.; in Solano Co. '78. Stirling, see 'Sterling.'   Stivers (Simeon), 1846, nat. of N.J. and memb. of the Mormon colony. v. 547. He was a carpenter at S.F., moving in '48 to Mission S. José, where he still lived in '82 with wife, Anna M. Jones, and child. Letitia M. b. '59, Simeon E. '61, Charlotte J. '64, Sam. '66, Champion D. '69, Anna M. '72, Mark '74, and Edward '78.   Stock, 1841, mr of the *Leonidas.* iv. 566.

Stockton (Robert Field), 1846, nat. of N.J. of an old and prominent family, who left Princeton college in 1811 to become a midshipman in the U.S.N.; served with credit in the war of 1812 and later; and in '46 as captain came to Cal. on the *Congress,* succeeding Com. Sloat in command of the Pacific squadron, and holding the position of military gov. of Cal. till Jan. '47. He returned east overland in '47, resigned his commission in '49, was U.S. senator from N.J. in '51–2, was mentioned as a democratic candidate for the presidency several times, and notably in '56, and died '66 at the age of about 70 years. His career in connection with Cal. affairs is fully recorded in v. 232, 251–87, 289–90, 295–6, 302–29, 356, 385–435, 449, 453, 456, 460, 463, 539, 549, 577, 644; iv. 673. It is too complicated and too much the history of the country in '46–7 to be presented en résumé here. Com. Stockton was brave, resolute, energetic, and in many respects an agreeable gentleman, but an insatiable thirst for popularity and fame was his most marked characteristic, and may be supposed to have determined his policy in Cal.—a policy which, however we may admire some of his acts and qualities, merits nothing but condemnation. His adoption, in opposition to the views of Sloat and Larkin, of the filibustero plans of Frémont and his associates may charitably be regarded as a mere error of judgment; yet it is hard to resist the conviction that the true state of affairs was known to him, and that his warlike proclamation to a peaceful people, his blustering tirade against imaginary evils, his willingness to identify a criminal revolt of vagabond settlers with the legitimate military occupation, his practical refusal to accept the voluntary submission of the Cal. authorities, his whole policy of conquest which was to produce such unhappy results—that all this was chiefly due to his personal vanity and ambition rather than to his honest opinion respecting the interests of his nation. To the same motive may be ascribed his later policy—not without plausibility and dignity in certain aspects—in the controversies with Gen. Kearny. Stockton was beyond comparison an abler and more honorable man than Frémont, yet his reputation as 'conqueror' of Cal.—notwithstanding his energetic and praiseworthy surmounting of obstacles that but for his folly would not have existed—is as unmerited, though not so fraudulent, as that of the 'pathfinder.'   S. (Wm B.), 1847, Co. F, N.Y. Vol. (v. 499); d. before '82.   Stoddard (Rufus), 1847, Co. B, Morm. Bat. (v. 469); worked as a brick-maker and builder at S. Diego.   Stokely (John), 1846, Co. C, 1st U.S. dragoons (v. 336); killed by the explosion at Los Ang. Dec. '47. v. 625.

Stokes (Edward), 1840, Engl. sailor who came from Hon. on the *Fly,* having possibly visited Cal. before. iv. 104, 120. He married Refugio, daughter of José Joaquin Ortega, and in '43–4 was grantee of the Pamo and Sta Isabel ranchos. iv. 621. In '46 he rendered aid to Kearny by carrying despatches to Stockton at S. Diego. v. 339. The date of his death after '50 does not appear, but his widow married Agustin Olvera, and was still living in '70. S. (James), 1834 (?), Engl. sailor who in Cal. became a doctor; first appearing on the records of '35, when he served as consulting physician in the case of Gov. Figueroa, but prob. left some vessel a year or two earlier. iii. 412, 296. He is occasionally named as doctor, druggist, and trader at Mont. in '35–43. iv. 117, 342; married María Josefa Soto in '44; appears at Mont., S. F., N. Helv., and S. José in records of '45, being in com. of a detachment of the

Mont. guard, iv. 515, but appears to have considered S. José his home from this year. In '46 Dr S. is vaguely accredited in tradition with having intrigued for an Engl. protectorate, but was the 1st to raise the U.S. flag at S. José, where by Sloat's appointment he served for a time as alcalde after the change of flag, owning also a lot in S.F., and having a Cal. claim. v. 34, 68, 245–6, 294, 662. He became the owner of the Verjeles and Natividad ranchos, Mont. Co., for which he was later claimant. iii. 679; iv. 656; and in '48 made a trading tour to the mines. I find no record of him or his family after '52. Stolze (Adolphus), 1847, Co. F, N.Y.Vol. (v. 499).

Stone, 1833, at Mont. acc. to Larkin's accounts.   S., 1847, settler in Lake Co. with the Kelseys, killed by the Ind. in '49. Nothing more seems to be known about the man. Possibly he was the following.   S. (Chas), 1847, of the 2d Donner relief party. v. 539–40.   S. (Elisha), 1841, of the original Bartleson party; did not come to Cal. iv. 269.   S. (Heber), 1847, Co. B. N.Y. Vol. (v. 499).   S. (Henry), 1847, owner of S.F. lot.   S. (Joseph M.), 1848, passp. from Hon.   S. (Mahlon), 1846, at Los Ang.   S. (Wm W.), 1808 (?), a resid. of Cal. from '48, and at Angels from '57 to his death in '62; said to have visited the coast in 1808 (prob. an error) and at other dates before '48.   Stoneman (Geo.), 1847, nat. of N.Y., graduate of West Point, and lieut of Co. C, 1st U.S. dragoons, coming to Cal with the Mormon Bat. as quartermaster, but soon rejoining the dragoons. v. 477, 483, 485, 489, 521, 617. Down to '55 or a little later he was engaged in garrison, exploring, or Ind. service on this coast. At the beginning of the war of '61–5 he was a major in the regular army, reaching the rank of brevet major-general of volunteers, and gaining an enviable reputation as a cavalry officer. After the war he returned to Cal. and settled near Los Angeles, holding later the position of railroad commissioner, and being as I write in '85 governor of California. In these official capacities he will require some notice in a later volume; and in the case of so prominent a pioneer, it is to me a matter of regret that I have no data for a more complete sketch of his earlier Cal. experience. Stope (Gerard), 1836, Engl. at Mont.   Stoppard (Moses), 1847, Co. K, N.Y. Vol. (v. 499).   Storer (Geo.), 1847, nat. of N.Y., from Hon. on the *Francesca;* settled in Sonoma; in Mendocino township '77; there is perhaps confusion between this man and Geo. 'Story.'

Storm (Peter), 1833 (?), Norwegian sailor, whose coming is credited in current sketches to this date with doubtful accuracy. iii. 409. Farnham names him as one of the foreigners arrested in '40. iv. 17. The 1st definite record is that he lived at S.F. in '44, age 40. He settled in Napa Co. in '44–5, and probably took part in the Bear revolt of '46. v. 110, 147–9. He spent the rest of his life mainly in Napa, and died at Calistoga in '77.   Story (Edward), 1848, Amer. lawyer with Brooks in the mines; said to have been alcalde at Mont. earlier (?).   S. (Geo.), 1847, Co. C, N.Y.Vol. (v. 499); near Healdsburg in '80.   Stothers (John E.), 1847, Co. F, ditto; d. at Oakland after '70.   Stout, 1848, mr of the *Bristol.*   S. (Wm), 1846, of the Mormon colony, with wife and child. v. 547. He was one of the founders of New Hope in the San Joaquin Val. v. 550; but left the Mormons, and in '47 was in the lumber business with Sirrine and Meder at Sta Cruz. In '48 had a store at the mines, perhaps of the firm of Brannan & Co.   S. (Wm C.), 1836 (?), agent of P. M. S. S. Co. from '48; died in N.Y. '70 at the age of 69; said to have visited Mont. in '36. iv. 118.   Stow (Aaron), 1847, Co. K, N.Y.Vol. (v. 499); at Davenport, Ia, '82.

Stradspeth, 1845, one of Frémont's men. iv. 583. *Kern.*   Strange (John), 1847, Co. C, N.Y.Vol. (v. 499).   Strauss (Fred.), 1846, sailor on the *Portsmouth,* killed at the S. Gabriel Jan. '47. v. 395; perhaps 'Stearns.'   Streeter (David), 1846, Co. C, 1st U.S. dragoons (v. 336); severely wounded at S. Pascual. v. 346, 355; later a barber at Sta B., where he died in '63.   S. (Wm A.), 1843, nat. of N.Y. and cousin of David; dentist and mechanic, who came from Peru with Stephen Smith as engineer to superintend the construction and running of the Bodega mill. iv. 396, 400. He soon left Smith and went south as dentist or physician till '48. iv. 651, 501. Went to the mines, was in partnership with Weber at Stockton, and leased the S. Buen. mission. Lived at S. Luis Ob. '51–5, and after '55 at Sta B., holding some local offices in both counties. In '78 he gave me his *Recollections of Early Events*. Prob. still living in '85 at the age of '74.　　Stribling (C. K.), 1836, com. of the U.S. *Cyane* '42 –3, and '45, and of the *Peacock* in '36. iv. 105, 308, 311, 321, 564–5.　　String-fellow (Jesse A), 1846, nat. of Pa and memb. of the Mormon colony. v. 547. He worked as a carpenter at S.F. (where he owned a lot), Napa, and S. José, going to the mines in '48–9. Later a farmer at S. José, where he died in '78, leaving a widow and 3 grown children.　　Stroms (John A.), 1846, Co. C, 1st U.S. dragoons (v. 336).　　Strong (Demas), 1848, Amer. trader at Big Bar and Sutter's mill; alderman and mayor of Sac.; returned to N.Y. '50; in N.Y. senate '64.　　S. (James H.), 1847, lieut on the U.S. *Columbus*.　　S. (John M.), 1847, Co. F, 3d U.S. artill. (v. 518).　　S. (Wm), 1847, Co. E, Morm. Bat. (v. 469).

Stuart (Chauncey), 1848, in S.F. letter-list.　　S. (María Ant.) 1813, mistress of Capt. Ayers. ii. 269.　　S. (W. K.), 1848, nat. of Md and overl. im-mig.; in Nevada co. '51 to his death in '73; widow living in '82.　　Study (David), 1847, Co. B, Morm. Bat. (v. 469).　　Stump (David), 1848, miner from Or. at Grass Valley and Placerville '48–9.　　Stupplebeen (Jacob), 1848, passp. from Hon.　　Sturgis (Thos), 1831, mr of the *Crusader* '31–2. iii. 382. Sturt (F.), 1848, passp. from Hon.　　Stuurtzenegger (John), 1846, Co. G, Cal. Bat. (v. 358); owner of S.F. lots '47–8; d. at Oakland about '60–5.

Suarez (Simon), 1797, sub-lieut of the compañía franca at Mont. i. 540–1, 544.　　S. (Vicente), juez de campo at S. José '44. iv. 685.　　Sublette (Wm), 1845, came overland with a party of 15 men whose names are not known; at S.F. Jan. '46; went east with Clyman and Hastings. iv. 577–8; v. 526.　　Suc-cara, chief of the Sotoyomes '37. iv. 72.　　Suckert (Leon), 1847, Co. D, N.Y. Vol. (v. 499); d. S. F. '71.　　Sugert, Ind. chief at Sta Cruz 1791. i. 494. Suhr (Albert), 1847, owner of S.F. lot.

Sullivan (Cornelius), 1847, Co. I, N.Y.Vol. (v. 499); locksmith at Mont. '47–8; Sta Clara '71–4; at Lompoc '82.　　S. (C. G.), 1839, doubtful date in a newspaper sketch. iv. 119; d. in '64, at or near Gold Hill.　　S. (James), see 'O'Sullivan.'　　S. (John), 1844, nat. of Ireland, and overl. immig. of the Stevens party with his sister Mary and two brothers. iv. 446, 453. He had come to Canada at the age of 6, and had worked as a stevedore there and as a logger in Me, going to Mo. in '42. After serving under Sutter in the Michel-torena campaign (iv. 476), he settled at S.F., v. 682, where he was teamster, trader, lot-owner, and later capitalist, being founder and president of the Hibernia Bank. He had also kept a store in '48 on Sullivan Cr., Tuolumne. He was a man of upright character, charitable, and well known for his gifts to the church. He died in '82 at the age of 58. His 1st wife was Catherine Farrely in '50, who died in '54; and the 2d was Ada E. Kenna of '60, by whom he had 10 children. There were 2 sons by the 1st marriage, one of whom, Robert, died in '82. The other, Frank J., b. in '52, was educated at St Igna-tius College of S.F., in England, and at Columbia law school, N.Y. In '78–85 he practised law at S.F., having been State senator in '82 and a candidate for congress in '84. His wife is Alice, daughter of James Phelan. He has fur-nished for my use a narrative of his father's life. John Sullivan's sister married Peter Sherreback.　　S. (John), 1847, Co. G, N.Y.Vol. (v. 499); d. S. Luis Rey '48.　　S. (Michael), 1844, brother of John, and immig. of the Stevens party. iv. 446, 453; owner of S. F. lot '47.　　S. (Richard), 1847, owner of S.F. lot.　　S. (Robert), 1844, brother of John, who came as a boy in the Stevens party. iv. 446, 453.

Sumedor (Wm), 1840, permitted to remain in Cal.　　Summers (W. F.), 1848, at S. Diego.　　Sumner (N.), 1847, Amer. at N. Helv.　　S. (Owen), 1845, immig. from Or. in the McM.-Clyman party with his family, including Mrs Payne. He went east with Clyman in '46. iv. 572–3; v. 526.　　S. (Owen Jr), 1843, son of Owen, who came from Or. with the Hastings party, perhaps with a family. His sister Lizzie married Geo. Davis at Sutter's fort. He prob. went east in '46 with his father. iv. 390–2, 400.　　S. (Wm), 1826, mr of the

Zamora, and in '32 of the *Waverly*. iii. 149,317, 364, 384, 652.   Suñer (Francisco), 1808, Span. friar who served at 5 different missions, and died at S. Buenaventura in '31. Biog. iii. 658–9; ment. ii. 90, 110, 147, 159–60, 265, 346, 348, 364, 394, 490, 576, 578, 655; iii. 96, 310, 351.

Suñol (Antonio María), 1817, nat. of Spain, who had been a sailor in the French naval service, coming to Cal. on the *Bordelais*, and deserting on her return from the north in '18. ii. 289. He settled at S. José, where he apparently kept a shop and sold liquor in '23. ii. 605; married about '24–5; was postmaster '26, '29. ii. 605; and in '28–30 was the object of some investigation on account of his Span. birth, but was not sent away. iii. 51–2. From about '39 he was owner of the rancho of S. José del Valle, and from about '37 of Los Coches, Alameda Co., selling live-stock to Sutter on credit and having no little trouble to collect the debt. iv. 134, 237; being síndico in '39–40, iii. 731, and sub-prefect '41–4. iv. 274, 684–6. He is mentioned by Mofras in '41 as 'very devoted' to France, and blunderingly by Wilkes; and in the padron of '41 is named as a Span. trader, age 41, wife María Dolores Bernal, child. José b. '26, Paula (later Mrs Sainsevain) '28, Narciso '36 ('35?), and Francisca '38. In '43 he was suplente of the junta. iv. 361; is ment. in the annals of '45–6. iv. 485–6; v. 4, 45; being the purchaser of S. Rafael mission, and a memb. of the S. José council. v. 561, 664, 670. He engaged in mining in '48; was the claimant for his two ranchos in '52. iv. 671, 713; and died in '65, leaving an excellent reputation. His son, José, was probably the man killed in '55 by a squatter on his rancho. He had been juez de policía in '49. Another son, Narciso, was educated in France, and still lives in Suñol Valley, '85, with wife, Rosario Palomares, and 6 child., Margarita, Virginia, Francesca, Eulalia, Josephine, and Juanita. Portrait in *Alam. Co. Hist.*, 176. Other children of Don Antonio María surviving in '83 were Encarnacion (Mrs Etchebarne), Antoneta (Mrs Murphy), and José Dolores.   Suria (Tomás), 1791, artist in Malaspina's exped. i. 490.   Suriano (Juan Fran.), 1602, alférez in Vizcaino's exped. i. 98.   Surok (Francisco), 1845, doubtful name of an applicant for land.   Sutphen (Wm), 1847, Co. A, N.Y.Vol. (v. 499).

Sutter (John Augustus), 1839, German-Swiss trader impelled by bankruptcy in '34 to become an adventurer in America, where, after an unsuccessful career in N. Mex. '35–7, he came to Cal. by way of Or., the Sandwich Isl., and Alaska, and established a trading and trapping post at New Helvetia, obtaining a land grant of 11 leagues, and in '41 the Russian improvements at Ross. Biog. matter relating to Sutter is given elsewhere in these volumes so fully and compactly as to require only reference here. For his early life and arrival in Cal. '39–40, see iv. 122–39, with ment. in iii. 670, 700; iv. 74, 93, 102, 117, 119. Progress of his estab. '41–2. iv. 226–40; also 211, 213, 219–20, 275, 283, 672–3, 679–80. Purchase of the Russian property in '41, with the Muldrow swindle, and efforts of the Russians '42–50 to collect the debt. iv. 177–89. Mention in '43 iv. 356, 366, 387–9, 396. Career in '44. iv. 439, 448–9, 453. Sutter's famous campaign of '44–5 undertaken against the Californians purely as a land speculation. iv. 407, 472, 474, 477–517. Affairs of '45, particularly his efforts to sell his estab. to the Mex. govt. iv. 607–16. Policy and acts of '46 in connection with the Bear revolt, etc. v. 3, 22, 29, 65, 80, 102, 104, 122–5, 359, 538. Mention in '47, when S. had a 'Cal. claim,' served as sub-Ind. agent, and owned a S.F. lot. v. 452, 467, 568, 610, 678. For his experience of '48 and the following years, especially in connection with the gold discovery, see vol. vi. of this series. In '48–9 Sutter was regarded as being very rich, having at least what in the hands of an abler man would have been the basis of an immense fortune; but his wealth, won by good luck without business capacity, could not thus be kept under the new conditions of the flush times, and soon he was reduced to comparative poverty, the successive steps of his downfall being too complicated for presentment here. Doubtless in some instances he was the victim of rascality on the part of sharper adventurers than himself. His original land grant of '41 was confirmed after it had passed for the most part out of his possession; but the Micheltorena grant of '45 was very justly rejected by the supreme court. The end of his public career, in a sense, was in '49, when he was a member of the constitutional convention, and received some 2,000 votes for governor. From '50, being joined by his family from Switzerland, he lived at Hock Farm. From '64, by act of the Cal. legislature, he received a pension of $250 per month till '78, when the bill was defeated. Meanwhile, about '65, he went east, and lived from '71 at Litiz, Pa, making constant but vain efforts to obtain from congress compensation for alleged wrongs of the past; though it does not appear that in his old age and infirmity he ever suffered actual privations. In '76, at his home, he dictated to me his *Personal Recollections*, identical in outline with the story so often told by him, but fuller in most phases than any that has been printed, and most interesting. He died at Washington, D.C., in '80 at the age of 77, leaving a widow who still lives, I think, in '85, two sons, and a daughter. The family seem to have come to Cal. from '44–50 at different dates, though I find but slight information on the subject. Of the sons, Alphonse died some years before '80. One of them seems to have come as early as '44, when the capt. writes to complain of his not being regarded as a naturalized citizen. John A. Jr, to whom his father turned over all his property temporarily in '49, and who was a partner of Hensley, Reading, & Co., was for some years before and prob. after '80 U.S. consul at Acapulco. Emil Victor, identical, I suppose, with E. J., who was Kern's lieut at the fort in '46, v. 298, was for many years to '80 a well-known notary at S.F., and committed suicide in Belgium in '83. The daughter, Anna Eliza, was married in '52 to Geo. Engler, and in '80, as Mrs Dr Link, was living at Acapulco. The biog. matter referred to above contains much of comment on Sutter's character. None of the pioneers named in this register has received so much praise from so many sources; few have deserved so little. Yet it has been by no means a pleasing task, in view of the famous captain's kindly nature and his misfortunes of later years—especially for one who, like myself, has heard from his own lips the story of his wrongs—to reveal the man's true character, as I have deemed it a duty to do. He was but an adventurer from the first, entitled to no admiration or sympathy. His career in N. Mex. was, at the best, discreditable. He came to Cal. in the false character of an ex-capt. of the French army. He was great only in his wonderful personal magnetism and power of making friends for a time of all who could be useful to him; good only in the possession of kindly impulses. His energy was a phase of his visionary and reckless enthusiasm; his executive ability did not extend beyond the skilful control of Indians and the management of an isolated trading post. Of principle, of honor, of respect for the rights of others, we find but slight trace in him. There was no side of any controversy that he would not readily adopt at the call of interest; nationality, religion, friendship, obligation, consistency, counted for little or nothing. There were no classes of his associates, hardly an individual, with whom he did not quarrel, or whom in his anger he did not roundly abuse. For all the favors received at the hands of Californians, he did not hesitate to turn against them, or even to arm foreigners and Indians against them, when a personal advantage seemed within his reach. That his frequent plots and threats of vengeance and revolution and French intervention were for the most more amusing than dangerous does not much increase our respect for the angry plotter. His only capital was money borrowed on the way to Cal., or property obtained on credit from Californians and Russians after his arrival, all on pretences more or less false. He never hesitated to assume any obligation for the future without regard to his ability to meet it; he rarely if ever paid a debt when due; and a general, vague, and kindly purpose to fulfil all his promises in the brilliant future but imperfectly excuses his short-comings. His apparent success in '39–45 was in a sense wonderful, but it rested almost entirely on a fortunate combination of circumstances, and notably on Gov. Alvarado's unwise act—partly inspired by the idea of introducing in the north an element of opposition to Vallejo, with whom he had a temporary quarrel—in permitting a foreigner to found an isolated rendezvous for hostile and uncontrollable elements of a vagabond population in the far interior. Though Sutter's establishment did something to promote the influx of Amer. settlers, it was in no sense beneficial to the interests of the U.S., merely fomenting filibusterism with all its unhappy results. The discovery of gold, often mentioned in this connection, was purely accidental; but I cannot see that its postponement for a time would have done any harm; and I can imagine that its earlier occurrence—likely enough to result from Sutter's settlement—might have been decidedly detrimental to the U.S. in some respects. That the establishment, chiefly by reason of its situation at the foot of the mountains, was of benefit to the immigrants is true; also that Sutter treated them kindly, though not more so than a dozen others; but that he did so at a personal sacrifice, as has been so often claimed, is not true; for Sutter's letters of that time are full of self-gratulations on hisl ucky chance to exchange food and cattle for wagons and implements, to hire mechanics, and to have his land increased in value by the influx of settlers. Neither is it true that Sutter in '45-6 was friendly to the U.S. or to the immigrants as Americans. He did not, as has been claimed by himself and friends, refuse an offer of $100,000 for his property that the immig. might not be deprived of a refuge; on the contrary, he did his best to sell, and failed chiefly because the Mex. govt saw a cheaper way to get the property by buying the Russian mortgage. And as elsewhere stated, I have the captain's original letter, in which he warned Gen. Castro against Gillespie as a secret agent of the U.S., urged the govt to buy his fort, and advised the stationing of a garrison there against the immigrants! Perhaps had this been known pioneers in later times would have been less profuse in their praise of the noble-hearted old patriot.   Suwerkrop (E.A.), 1848, at Hon. from S.F. on the *Julian.*

Swab (Emmanuel), 1847, Co. G, N.Y. Vol. (v. 499).   Swain, 1848, from Hon. on the *Sagadahoc.*   S., 1829, mr of the *Susana.* iii. 149.   S. (Chas A.), 1829(?), nat. of Mass., said to have visited the coast in the whaler *American,* iii. 179, and again on the same vessel in '38, though I find no record of such a vessel in either year. He returned in '49 to stay as a farmer, miner, and contractor, dying at S.F. '84 at the age of 71, leaving a widow and son. S. (F. B.), 1848, passp. from Hon.   S. (Isaac), 1823(?), on the roll of the Soc. Cal. Pion.   S. (Josiah H.), 1847, at Mont. '47-8; perhaps came in '46 on a whaler, and one of Maddox's volunteers, said to be living at S.F. '84. *Swan.* Swaine, 1794, one of Vancouver's men. i. 526.

Swan (John A.), 1843, nat. of England of Scotch parentage, who came as a sailor on the *Soledad* from Mazatlan after 11 years of adventure as a sailor in many parts of the world. iv. 400, 568, 651. He made two trips with Capt. Cooper on the schr *California* in '43-4, then quitting the sea. He kept a little shop and sailors' boarding-house at Mont., his name appearing from '44 on Larkin's books and in other records; made a trip to the gold-mines in '48; went to Fraser River in '59-63; again visited British Columbia in '64-6; and has since resided at Mont. He has written many articles on the olden time for the newspapers, which, with others in MS., have place in my collection, some of them being named in my list of authorities; and he has furnished me besides from time to time many useful items for this register. Swan's writings are not only interesting, but remarkably accurate, his memory being rarely at fault, and the tendency to testify on matters beyond his personal knowledge—too prevalent among pioneer writers—being in his case reduced to a minimum. His work in this direction merits high praise. In the later years down to '85 this kind-hearted old sailor, 73 years old, burdened with poverty and deafness, lives in an old historic adobe at the former capital, delighting in the old ruins that keep alive his dreamy recollections of the past; and occasionally, with 'pioneer of '43' plainly inscribed as credentials on his hatband, he makes a trip to S. José and S.F. to look after the constantly lessening band of his old-time acquaintances.   S. (Lyman), 1848, passp. from Hon. S. (Thos M.), 1848(?), in Napa Valley acc. to testimony in later litigation. Swanich (James), 1845, Delaware Ind. of Frémont's party '45-7. iv. 583, 587; said by Martin to have been killed on the Or. frontier '46.   Swanson (Joseph), 1848, in S.F. letter list; cl. in '53 for land in Contra Costa.   Swartout (Hamilton), 1847, Co. A, Morm. Bat. (v. 469).   Swartz (John S.), 1847, Co. E, N.Y. Vol. (v. 499).   Swasden, 1847, doubtful name in a Mont. list.

Swasey (Wm F.), 1845, nat. of Maine and overl. immig. from St Louis in the party that I have called by his name, which was really a division of the Grigsby-Ide party. iv. 576, 587. For two months he was employed by Sutter as book-keeper, and at the beginning of '46 went by way of S.F. and S. José to Mont., where he worked for a short time as clerk for Wm H. Davis, and from June to Sept. was consular clerk for Larkin at $60 per month. v. 16, 60. In Oct. he joined the Cal. Bat., serving through the southern campaign as asst commissary (v. 358); and having a 'Cal. claim' of $40 (v. 462). In '47 he came to S.F., where he was owner of a town lot, clerk of election, and sec. of the council. v. 648, 650. From '48 he was engaged in trade in partnership with Leighton & Co. at S.F. and with Southard at Napa. v. 670, 678, 681; also visiting the mines, and in '49 being a member of the S.F. district legislature and taking some part in politics. In '51-61 Swasey was a notary public at S.F., being also a witness in some of the famous land cases; in '61-6 capt. of volunteers and asst quartermaster at Benicia. He has continued to reside at S.F., though I find that he was appointed in '75 U.S. marshal of Wyoming, and has been a somewhat prominent member of the Pioneer Society, being the author of many gracefully written eulogies of dead pioneers. In '85, at the age of 60 years or more, though about 45 in appearance, he has received a new appointment as notary public. Of his family I know nothing except that his mother died recently in Cal. at a very advanced age. His *View of S. F. in '47* is ment. in v. 676, et seq. Capt. Swasey has furnished me his recollections of *California in '45-6;* to him I am indebted for the invaluable *New Helvetia Diary,* of which, as Sutter's clerk, he was one of the authors; and in several other matters he has afforded me some assistance.

Sweet (Chas C.), 1847, Co. D, N.Y.Vol. (v. 499). S. (Paul), 1840(?), nat. of R.I., said to have landed at Mont. this year. iv. 120. In '43-5 a tanner near Sta Cruz, iv. 356, being named in the Branciforte padron of '45 as Engl., age 30, and single; perhaps served in Cal. Bat. '46-7 (v. 358), having a Cal. claim of $35 (v. 462); and still at Sta Cruz '49-80. Sweeting, 1848, doubtful name of a hotel-keeper at S.F. *Brooks.* Swift (Granville P.), 1844, nat. of Ky, and immig. from Or. in the Kelsey party, having crossed the plains in '43. iv. 444-5, 453. He served in Sutter's campaign of '45. iv. 486, 501; was a leading filibuster of the Bears in '46. v. 95, 104, 107, 110, 147, 153, 168, 172; and in '46-7 was capt. of Co. C, Cal. Bat. v. 184, 282, 289, 361; having a Cal. claim of about $2,000 (v. 462). He was a fine-looking man, over 6 ft in height, a crack shot, and of undoubted bravery, a bitter hater of the Mexicans. He settled on Stony Cr., Colusa, in '47; made a large fortune in mining on Feather Riv., with the aid of Ind., in '48-9; later a stock-raiser in Colusa and Tehama; from '54 ranchero in Sonoma; and from about '68 engaged in fruit-culture and quicksilver-mining in Solano, where he was accidentally killed in '75, at the age of about 54. He had a habit of burying his money on his rancho; several such deposits being accidentally found after he had forgotten them, and in one instance $24,000 having been stolen by an employee. S., 1807, mr of the *Derby* and *Hazard;* perhaps on the coast earlier. ii. 17, 78, 84. S. (Richard), 1846, Co. B, Cal. Bat., enlisting at Mont. in Oct. (v. 358).

Swinburn (Wm), 1839, Engl. mate of the schr *California,* who became a lumberman in the Mont. district, getting a pass in '41. iv. 119. In '44 in S. F. dist, age 35. Swinson (Dav.), 1848, at Mont. Swords (Allen J.), 1847, Co. A, N.Y.Vol. (v. 499); d. at La Paz '48. S. (Thomas), 1846, major U.S.A., who came from N. Mex. with Kearny as quartermaster, and returned east with him in '47, after having made a trip to Honolulu for supplies; witness in the Frémont court-martial. v. 336, 343-7, 356, 440, 452, 456. In the war of '61-5 he was chief quartermaster of the western dept, and in '79 lived in N.Y. as a retired brigadier. Sylvester (Anthony), 1845, one of the men lost '46 on the *Warren's* launch. iv. 587; v. 384. Syrec, 1848, named as having kept a store on the Moquelumne.

Tabeau (Baptiste), 1844, one of Frémont's men, killed by Ind. iv. 437, 440. Taber (J. D.), 1846, apparently an overl. immig.; of T. & Hoyt, hotel-keepers at Mont. '47-8; had a family in Contra Costa '60.   T., 1847, mr of the *Copia*. v. 577.   Tabor (Wm), 1846, in Sta Clara Val. with family. *Hall*. Taforó (José Ignacio), 1819, nat. of S. Amer., soldier of the S. Blas comp. at Mont.; disch. '24; regidor at Mont. '27. ii. 612.   Taggart (Geo. W.), 1847, musician Co. B, Morm. Bat. v. 469.   T. (Robert), 1848, nephew of Dr Isbel, who killed B. K. Thompson on the way east overland.   T. (Sam.), 1842, executed at Los Ang. for murder. iv. 296, 342, 633; called also 'Tagget' and 'Taggett.'   Tait (James A.), 1847, Co. A, N.Y.Vol. (v. 499); at Sta Cruz '71-83.   T. (Wm G.), 1847, Co. A, ditto.   Tajochi (Tomás), Ind. chief of S. Diego '33. iii. 327, 359.

Talamantes (Felipe), settler at Los Ang. 1794; grantee of Sta B. land 1819; at La Ballona '39-40, age 57. ii. 349, 354; iii. 633, 637.   T. (Tomás), prob. brother of Felipe, at La Ballona '39, age 47. He took an active part in the fight against Gov. Victoria in '31. iii. 196, 207; was juez de campo '44. iv. 633; and still at Los Ang. '46.   Talbot, 1847, of L. & Upham at Mont. '47-8.   T. (J. M.), 1846, witness to enlistment in Cal. Bat.   T. (Theodore), 1844, nat. of Ky who came with Frémont, and again in '45. iv. 437, 581, 583. He was a young man of good education, who was in a sense com. of that division of the company entering Cal. by the southern route; and in Cal. acted as Frémont's confidential agent. v. 3, 6, 22, 644. He was left in com. of the Sta B. garrison, and later served as lieut and adjutant in the Cal. Bat. v. 287, 304, 316-17, 358, 360, 630. Being sent east with despatches in Feb. '47, he was a witness in the Frémont court-martial. v. 430, 456. Died at Wash., D. C., '62.   Talmadge (Abijah D.), 1847, Co. A, N.Y.Vol. (v. 499); killed in '48 by Moquelumne Ind.   Tamam (Ig.), 1846, doubtful name, Cal. Bat. (v. 358).   Tamanin (Prokop), 1822, mr of the *Volga*. ii. 474.   Tamaree (Peter), 1834, at Mont.   Tambor (Juan), nickname; killed at Los Ang. 45. iv. 492.

Tanferan (Toribio), at S.F. mission from '40; witness in the Santillan case '55.   Tanner (Albert), 1847, Co. E, Morm. Bat. (v. 469).   T. (John L.), 1848, married at Sonoma to Mary, daughter of J. D. Taber of Mont.   Tansill (Robert), 1846, lieut of marines on the *Dale;* in Marston's Sta Clara campaign; com. of the S.F. garrison '47. v. 380, 659.

Tapia (Antonio), juez aux. at S. Cárlos '42. iv. 653.   T. (Bartolo), ranchero at Los Ang. 1791-1813. ii. 270, 350-3.   T. (Cárlos), at Los Ang. '46.   T. (Felipe), soldier at S. José and settler 1786-90. i. 350, 477-8.   T. (Fernando), at Los Ang. '48.   T. (Francisco), cadet of Sta B. comp. '25-6. ii. 572.   T. (Gregorio), grantee of Aguajito rancho '35. iii. 676; at Pilarcitos '36, age 22, wife Martina Vasquez, child María de los Angeles; perhaps at Sta Cruz '54. i. 524.   T. (José Ant.), at Los Ang. '46; arrested in '45. iv. 541. T. (José Bartolomé), majordomo of S. Luis Ob. 1789, wife María Lobo; grantee of Topanga Malibu rancho 1804. ii. 112; iii. 634.   T. (Mariano), 1792, potter-instructor from Mex. '92-6. i. 615, 715.   T. (Ramon), at S. Bern. '46, age 25.   T. (Tiburcio), son of José Bartolomé, b. at S. Luis Ob. 1789; later soldier and corporal of the Sta B. comp., being com. of the Purísima guard in '24 at the revolt. ii. 529; member of the diputacion '27, '33. iii. 36-7, 41, 63, 246; alcalde of Los Ang. '30-1, '36; ii. 561; iii. 634, 636; síndico '33, and encargado de Ind. '35. iii. 635; favored Alvarado '38. iii. 565; aux. alcalde '38. iii. 636. In '39 he was alcalde, acting prefect, and grantee of Cucamonga rancho. iii. 586, 589, 633, 636, 640. In '42 he was a supl. ministro of the sup. court; and in '44 2d alcalde. iv. 296, 633. Don Tiburcio was a man of good sense, good character, and some wealth, still at Los Ang. '48 at the age of about 60. A current tradition of later times represented the old man as having buried his treasure on Frémont's approach in '46, and as having died without revealing its exact location.   T. (Urcino), settler at Los Ang. 1809. ii. 350.   Tapin, 1846, lieut on the U.S. *Savannah*.   Tapinto (Mariano), 1792, tailor-instructor '92-5. i. 615.

Tapis (Estévan), 1790, Span. friar who toiled as missionary longest at Sta B. and S. Juan B., and was president of the missions in 1803-12. Biog. ii. 623-4; ment. i. 388, 492, 522, 573-4, 576, 588-90, 594, 640, 669, 672, 689; ii. 7, 9-10, 26, 28, 33-4, 42, 55, 85, 88-90, 108-9, 112-13, 120-1, 140, 148, 159, 161, 165,

168, 175, 182, 326, 346, 366, 369, 378, 383, 386–7, 394, 396, 461, 518, 655. Taplin (Charles), 1844, of Frémont's party; also in '45, returning east in '46 with Sublette. iv. 437, 583. He again joined F. in '48. Tarakánof (Boris), 1806, Russ. chief of Aleut. otter-hunters; captured at Sta B. in '15. ii. 40, 80, 210, 274, 307–13, 353. Tasìon (Manuel S.), grantee of a S. Gabriel lot '47. iv. 637. Taufer (Andrew), 1847, German memb. of the Soc. Cal. Pion.; d. at S.F. '79, age 71.

Taylor, 1848, in the mines from Mont. and S. José. T., 1848, at S.F. from the states. T. (Alex. S.), 1848, nat. of S.C., where his father—who had been a lieut on the privateer *Saucy Jack* in the war of 1812—died in '21. The son came to Cal. from China in Sept. '48, but beyond the facts that he was for some years clerk of the U.S. district court at Mont., and later settled at Sta B., marrying Josefa Ortega, and dying in '76, nothing of biog. proper appears in any record that I have seen. He was known as Dr Taylor, but I do not know whether he ever practised medicine. It is not, however, as a pioneer, but as an investigator and writer on the ethnography, bibliography, and history of Cal. that he deserves particular notice; and in these respects he was a remarkable man. Without having any special aptitude by nature or education for such work, he developed a fondness for it almost amounting to a mania. His zeal in face of the most discouraging obstacles is worthy of all praise, though it must be confessed that the result was wellnigh valueless. He was not content with being a collector or even translator and narrator, but had a most unfortunate passion for working the results of his observations and study into what he regarded as a scientific form, the result being too often an absurd jumble of bad Spanish, worse Latin, and unintelligible affectations. While at Monterey he obtained from the priest a valuable collection of old mission documents (later given to the archbishop, and cited by me as *Arch. del Obispado*) which he made the basis of numerous newspaper articles, in which, by reason of faulty translations, typographical blunders, unfounded additions, and the difficulty of locating the dividing line between record and comment, the value of the original was much impaired. His writings from about '53 for the *S.F. Herald, Bulletin, Cal. Farmer, Hutchings' Magazine, Hesperian, Sac. Union*, and other papers were very voluminous. The most extensive of his works and most valuable, being least injured by his peculiar methods, though containing very little original matter, is the *Indianology of Cal.*, published in the *Cal. Farmer* of '60–3, of which most of the linguistic portions are reprinted in *Lucy-Fossarieu, Langues Indiennes de la Cal.*, Paris '81; and which gave Dr T., very properly, an honorary membership in several learned societies of the east. Another of his most ambitious attempts, but least valuable by reason of his utter lack of facilties for bibliographic work, was the *Bibliografía Californica*, pub. in the *Sac. Union*, and noticed in i. 35 of this work. His *Historical Summary of Lower California*, pub. in Ross Browne's *Resources*, ed. of '69, and his *Precis India Californicus*, included by Wm H. Knight in *Bancroft's Hand-book* of '64, are very creditable works, being the only ones that had the advantages of careful editing and proof-reading. His *First Voyage to the Coast of Cal.*, of '53, was a translation of Navarrete's version of Cabrillo's voyage, with comments of little value. i. 69, 72, 77. In his later years Dr Taylor collected all his writings, with numerous MS. additions here and there, into a series of 7 scrap-books, under the titles *Bibliografía California, Indianology of the Californias, Animated Nature of Cal., Odds and Ends of Cal. Life*, and *Discoverers and Founders of Cal., Felix, and Cal. Petra* (the 1st 3 being in '85 in the library of the Soc. Cal. Pion. in S.F.), and issued a descriptive circular, 'The Storehouse of Cal., History and Life,' through which he tried in vain to find in America and Europe a publisher for his collected writings, without a suspicion of the truth that the work and time and ability and resources of data that would enable an editor to put the crude mass in such shape as to do justice to the author's reputation would produce an original work of much greater value. I visited him in '74 at his rancho at La Partera, near Sta B., and found him, though grievously oppressed by illness and poverty, as enthusiastic as ever in all that pertained to early Cal. annals. He pointed sadly but with pride to a wooden box that contained his life work—the 7 volumes mentioned above; and when I sought his advice respecting my own researches, he pointed again to the box as containing all that could ever be gleaned about early Cal.; and he was, I am sure, entirely honest in his belief. 'Test, if you like,' he said, 'the accuracy of my work by examining the documents I gave the archbishop, but I know from long years of earnest research that nowhere else, especially from mission and Spanish sources, will you find a scrap of new information.' Yet only 3 miles away from the rancho where he had lived for many years, at Sta B. mission, I took 6,000 pages of copies of most important missionary correspondence that he had never seen! All honor, nevertheless, to such men as Hayes and Taylor and Lancey, who have toiled under more or less unfavorable auspices to save from destruction the data for our history.

Taylor (Christopher), 1848, came from Or. in Sept. on the *Henry*, engaging in trade at Sutter's fort, as member of the firm of Priest, Lee, & Co.; finally settled at Dayton, Or., where he was in '78.   T. (Geo. W.), 1847, nat. of Va, who enlisted in Co. F, 3d artill., at Mont. (v. 518); in the mines '49, and later at Mont.; d. at Napa '84. *Lancey.*   T. (Hiram), 1841, Amer. musician in the Workman party from N. Mex. iv. 278-9. I have his original passport dated Sta Fé Aug. 24th. At Los Ang. and on the Cosumnes '42; went to Or. with Leese in '43, but came back in '48. He made money in the mines, and settled at Cloverdale, where he died at a date not given.   T. (John), 1846, Co. C, 1st U.S. dragoons (v. 336).   T. (John), 1847, Co. E, N.Y. Vol. (v. 499); d. in N.Y. '79.   T. (Joseph), 1847, Co. A, Morm. Bat. (v. 469).

Taylor (Nelson), 1847, nat. of Conn., and capt. of Co. E, N.Y. Vol. v. 504, 511. He was a dentist, and after a brief experience in the mines settled at Stockton as a trader, also running a ferry on the Stanislaus; memb. of 1st legislature; trustee of insane asylum from '50; sheriff from '54. In '56 he went to N.Y. and became a lawyer; brig.-gen. in war of '61-5; in '65 memb. of congress; in '71-85 resid. of South Norwalk, Conn.   T. (Walter), 1847, sergt Co. G, N.Y. Vol. v. 504.   T. (Wm), 1818, Amer. lieut of Bouchard's insurgents. ii. 227, 237.   T. (Wm), 1828, Scotch tailor at Mont. '28-32, joining the comp. extranjera; a married man, age 34 in '29. iii. 178, 221. T. (Wm), 1834, mr of the *Magruder.* iii. 412, 383.   T. (Wm), 1834, Engl. sailor who landed from the *Margarita* at S. Diego, where he still lived in '40, an unmarried carpenter, age 43. Perhaps the same who voted at S. D. in '48; name written Tela, Telen, and Thell.   T. (W. E.), 1847, daughter born to his wife at Sonoma; at S. José '50.   T. (W. H.), 1848, passp. from Hon.

Teal (Hiram), 1841, nat. of New England, who brought a stock of goods from Mazatlan, and kept a store at S.F. '41-3, with Titcomb as partner or clerk. iv. 279; v. 683. He went to Hon. in '43 on the *Diamond*, en route for Mex. Tebaca (Gabriel), settler at the Colorado pueblos 1780-1, killed by Ind. i. 359, 362.   Teforia (José), 1831, named by Dye as one of Young's party. iii. 388. Tego (Manuel), resid. of Branciforte '30. ii. 627.   Tejeda (Juan de A.), 1602, alférez of Vizcaino's exped. i. 98.   Tellez (Rafael), 1842, Mex. lieut-col and brevet-col in com. of Micheltorena's batallon fijo; somewhat prominent in Cal. affairs till sent to Mex. for aid in '44. iv. 289, 357, 367, 409, 439, 461, 471-2. In '46 he seems to have started for Cal. with troops, but in Sinaloa engaged in a revolution, v. 32-3, and became acting com. at Mazatlan, where he was when the Amer. took the town in Feb. '48. He seems to have died before the end of that year, and Californians, who did not like him, delight in the tradition that after a drunken debauch he drowned himself in a barrel of mescal!

Temple (Francis Pliny F.), 1841, nat. of Mass., who came on the *Tasso* at the age of 20, engaging in trade at Los Ang. with his brother John. iv. 279. Later he established a stock rancho at S. Emigdio, near Ft Tejon; was a member of the banking firm of Hellman, T., & Co. from '68, and from '72 of T. & Workman. He died in '80 at his rancho of La Merced. iv. 635; v. 320; leaving a widow—the daughter of Wm Workman—and several children. He took but slight part in politics, but was always prominent in business affairs. All his property was lost by the failure of the banking firm in '75. In '77 he gave me a brief narrative of his *Recollections*, and rendered me assistance in

·obtaining testimony from others.   T. (John), 1827, nat. of Mass., and brother of the preceding, who came from Hon. on the *Waverly*, and in the earliest years signed his name 'Jonathan.' iii. 149, 176-7. He was at once baptized at S. Diego, and after a few trading trips on the coast obtained naturalization and married Rafaela, daughter of Francisco Cota, in '30, engaging in trade at Los Ang., in partnership with Geo. Rice, till '32, and later alone, or with his brother from '41. ii. 558. I have some of his business corresp., but he does not figure in public affairs, except that the vigilantes of '36 met at his house. ii. 418, 539; iv. 117. In the sectional quarrels he took no part, but was glad in '39 to hear of Alvarado's final success; is named in the following years as creditor of southern missions; and in '45 was the purchaser of Purísima. iii. 595, 623; iv. 92, 553, 629, 648; v. 558. In the annals of '46-7 he is named in connection with financial matters, having Cal. claims to the amount of about $16,000. v. 49-50, 435, 467. From about '48, becoming owner of the Cerritos rancho, iii. 633, he gave his attention to stock-raising on a large scale; later he was the builder of the Temple block and other fine structures at Los Angeles; and in Maximilian's time obtained an immensely profitable lease of the Mexican mint. He died at S.F. in '66, at the age of 68. He had been an able and successful man of business, socially genial and well liked. His widow survived him, living in Paris with her daughter, Mrs Ajuria, the only child of whom I find any mention, born in '31.

Tenchman (Christian), 1846, Co. C, 1st U.S. dragoons (v. 336).   Ten Eck (Anthony), 1848, U.S. commissioner from Hon. on the *Humboldt*.   Tenid (Th.), 1846, doubtful name in a Los Ang. list.   Tennent (Archibald), 1848, passp. from Hon.   T. (Sam. J.), 1848, Engl. surgeon on a whaler, who left his vessel at the Islands and came to Cal. on hearing of the gold discovery. He married Rafaela Martinez and settled at Pinole rancho, Contra Costa, where he still lived in '82 with 5 children, his wife having died in '68. Portrait in *Contra Costa Co. Hist.*, 46.   Tenorio (Ignacio), nat. of S. Amer., who had been oidor of the audiencia of Quito, and a very rich man, but who, traditionally, had devoted his fortune to charitable and educational purposes, and came to Cal. about '15 to live with the friars. Not much is known of him except that he was buried at S. Juan Cap. in '31 by P. Zalvidea, who in the record spoke in high terms of his piety.

Teran (José M.), regidor at Branciforte '34. iii. 696; memb. of the S. Diego ayunt. '37, and in trouble. iii. 508; perhaps two men.   Termain (James Gilbert), 1843, recommended by the Engl. consul for a carta.   Terrill (Joel J.), 1847, sergt Co. C, Morm. Bat. v. 477; at Ogden, Utah, in '82.   Teschemacher (Fred. Henry), 1842, clerk and supercargo of Boston trading craft '42-8. iv. 341; v. 579; owner of S.F. lots '46-7; resid. of S.F. after '49; cl. of the Lupyomi rancho, Napa, '52. iv. 671; mayor of S.F.; still living in '85, when he visited S.F. Portrait and brief biog. notice in *North Pac. Review.* i. 223, 252. I have a few of his early letters; but for so prominent a pioneer there is a remarkable lack of information about him.   Tessau, 1837, officer of Petit-Thouars' exped., making a survey of S.F. bay. iv. 149.

Thaffer (Andrew), 1847, Co. E, N.Y.Vol. (v. 499); d. S.F. '79.   Thamen (Henry), 1847, owner of S.F. lot.   Theall (Hiram W.), 1847, lieut Co. D, N.Y.Vol. v. 504; an early settler of Sonora; d. at White Pine, Nev., before '82; prob. in '69.   Theyer (Geo.), 1848, from Or., a settler in S. Joaquin. Thing (Capt.), 1838, left S. Diego for Boston on the *Kent.* iv. 104.

Thomas, 1845, doubtful immig. of the Grigsby-Ide party. iv. 579.   T., 1846, at Sta Cruz, June; perhaps same as following.   T., 1847, mr of the *Laura Ann* '47-8. v. 579; perhaps L. H.   T., 1847, at Sutter's fort.   T. (Ambrose), 1836, at S. José Dec.; also Antonio at Los Ang. '35; both prob. 'Tomlinson,' q.v.   T. (Christian), 1847, owner of S.F. lot. v. 685.   T. (Elijah), 1847, Co. C, Morm. Bat. (v. 469); at Leeds, Utah, '82.   T. (Ignacio), 1818, Engl. sailor who left the *Bordelais*, ii. 393, and in '29 lived at S. José, age 41, and blind.   T. (John W.), 1847, Co. A, N.Y.Vol. (v. 499); at S. José '82.   T. (L. H.), 1848, sold piano to Larkin; conducted prayer at the S.F. school-house. v. 657.   T. (Thomas), 1840, one of the S. Blas exiles who did not return. iv. 18.   Thomen (Henry), 1846, overl. immig. who worked for Sutter, and owned S.F. lot '47; at Sac. '60, age 45; perhaps at S.F. '79.

Thomes (Robert Hasty), 1841, nat. of Me, and overl. immig. of the Bartleson party. iv. 270, 275, 279. With Albert G. Toomes he worked as carpenter and builder at S.F. in '41-2, and later at Mont., where the firm name of Thomes & Toomes appears often in Larkin's books and other records. In '44 he was naturalized, and obtained a grant of Los Saucos, Tehama. iv. 673; and may have put some cattle on the place in '45, but did not settle there till '47, being mentioned at Mont. in '45-7, especially as a member of the 1st jury. v. 289. He took no part in the war or in politics, but spent his life—with a brief interval of mining on Feather River—on his Tehama rancho, becoming a wealthy and highly respected and influential citizen. He died in '78, at the age of 61, leaving no family. A sister resides in Oakland '85 as the wife of Isaac Given, a pioneer of '41. Portrait in *Tehama Co. Hist.*, 108.   T. (Wm H.) 1843, nat. of Me, and distant relative of R. H., who came from Boston as a sailor-boy, age 16, on the *Admittance*, which he left in '45, and returned east in '46 on the schr *California* to Mazatlan, and thence via England to Boston. Again he came to Cal. in '49 on the *Edward Everett*, returning via Manilla, etc., on the *Alex. Humboldt*. In Boston he was a journalist on the daily papers, and from '62 a publisher on his own account, making a comfortable fortune, which was lost in the great fire of '72. In later years of the firm of Thomes & Talbot, publishers of *Ballou's Monthly;* also author of many romances of adventure for boys. *On Sea and Land*, one of his latest works, is a narrative of adventures in Cal. on the *Admittance* in '42-5, full of interest and bad Spanish, remarkably accurate in its foundation of names and dates; let us hope that the superstructure of the sailor-boy's personal experiences is equally reliable. A later story of Cal. life, covering the period of the conquest and now appearing in the *Monthly* is likely to be as fascinating if somewhat less historic. An excellent account of the trip and company of '49 was also written by Thomes for the magazine, reprinted in the *S.F. Alta* of Oct. 22, 29, '82. In '85 he revisited Cal. to revive old recollections, at which time he furnished me many useful items about early men and things, also permitting me to consult the original *Diary* of Capt. Peterson, his old master on the *Admittance*, and later his father-in-law.

Thompson, 1841, blacksmith at Los Ang. and Sta B.   T. (A.), 1839, passenger from Hon. on the *Clementine*. iv. 102, 127.   T. (Alpheus B.), 1823, nat. of Me, and sup. on the *Washington* '25-30, having possibly visited the coast earlier. iii. 29, 139, 149; sup. of the *Convoy* '31; in '33-5 sup. of the *Loriot*, being arrested for smuggling in '33, and in '35 carrying prisoners to Mex. iii. 288, 365, 383, 393. He considered Sta B. his home, and dated his residence from '34, that being the year in which he married Francisca, daughter of Cárlos Carrillo, by whom he had 3 children before June '36. I have much of his corresp. from year to year. In '36-7 he was sup. of the *Bolivar*, on which he went to Hon. and back in '37; from '38 had a hide-house in the Clark's Point region of S.F.; is named as mr of the *Union* in '40; and also as creditor of several missions. iii. 657, 660; iv. 101, 106, 117; v. 684-5. He went to Hon. on the *Julia Ann* '41; was naturalized in '43, being still sup. of the *Bolivar;* was owner of the *Oajaca* in '44-5, sub-prefect at Sta B. '46, grantee of a rancho in S. Joaquin Co., having a Cal. claim of some $2,000, and being in all these years engaged to some extent in otter-hunting. iv. 563, 566-7; v. 282, 330, 455, 675. His name frequently occurs in commercial records down to '48; and after that date continued to reside at Sta B., where, and throughout the country, he had an excellent reputation for honorable conduct. He died at Los Ang. in '69 at the age of 74. His wife had died in '41, but there were 2 daughters and 4 sons who survived. One of the sons, Francis, is a somewhat prominent citizen of Sta B., and in '78 rendered me assistance in my search of the mission archives.

Thompson (Bluford K.), 1846, overl. immig. and capt. Co. G, Cal. Bat., taking part in the fight at Natividad. v. 361, 364-72. He was a coarse, profane, reckless fellow, a gambler by profession, with some pretensions to gentlemanly manners when sober; known sometimes as 'Red-headed' or 'Hell Roaring' Thompson. After the war he settled at Stockton, being candidate for Ind. agent in '47. v. 662; where he soon killed James McKee. He was tried for murder at Sutter's fort in Feb.'48, being acquitted; but was obliged to quit the country, and on the way east was killed in a new quarrel with R. Taggart on the Sweetwater.   T. (Ch.), 1847, at Sutter's fort.   T. (Edward), 1844, Amer. sailor on the schr *California*, in trouble at Mont.   T. (Edwin), 1848, at S.F. as he testified in '65.   T. (Frank A.), 1832, mr of the *Roxana* '32-3. iii. 384; mr of the *Pilgrim* and *Alert* '35-6. iii. 381, 383; •iv. 100.   T. (Geo. A.), 1839, naturalist who came from Hon. on the *Clementine* with letters from John C. Jones to the gov. and Gen. Vallejo. He was in search of specimens; called also Gordon H. T.   T. (Henry), 1847, Co. D, Morm. Bat. (v. 469).   T. (James), 1828, Irish sailor, age 28, from Acapulco on the *Maria Ester* at S. Diego with a letter from Virmond, intending to settle. ii. 545; iii. 178; got a carta in '29; in his application seems to say he had lived 8 years in Cal., but prob. means in Mex.   T. (James), 1846, sergt-major of Fauntleroy's dragoons (v. 232, 247); perhaps the man at Benicia '47.   T. (James), 1847, Co. A, N.Y. Vol. (v. 499); perhaps the man who on July 4th read the declaration at S.F.; at Brooklyn, N.Y., '82.   T. (James L.), 1847, Co. C, Morm. Bat. (v. 469).

Thompson (John), 1832, joined the comp. extranjera at Mont. iii. 221, 408; perhaps still at Mont. '36.   T. (John), 1843 (?), said to have crossed the plains, to have built a mill on Napa Creek '45, and to have spent 7 years on the coast; revisited Cal. in '76 from Brooklyn, N.Y. iv. 393, 400.   T. (John), 1847, Co. A, Morm. Bat. (v. 469); at Riverdale, Utah, '81; perhaps the owner of a S.F. lot '47. v. 685.   T. (John?), 1847, partner of Finch, and perhaps later of Bennett, in a S.F. saloon '44-8. v. 683; thought to be at S.F. '85.   T. (Joseph P.), 1842, nat. of Mass. who came this year acc. to his own affidavit in '62. iv. 341; perhaps came in '39-40 as sup. on the *Joseph Peabody*. He came again in '44 from Hon. on the *Fama;* at Sta Clara '45; at S.F. '46-7, being owner of a lot and sec. of the council. v. 648, 650; at Napa '47-8, where he kept a store; cl. for Napa lands '52; lost a leg by a street-car accident at S.F. '84. He was a brother-in-law of Henry A. 'Peirce,' q.v.   T. (Josiah), 1836, brother of Joseph P., at Mont. '36; sup. of the *Rasselas* '37-8. iv. 105, 141.   T. (Miles), 1847, Co. D, Morm. Bat. (v. 469); reënl.   T. (Peter), 1847, Co. A, N.Y. Vol. (v. 499); d. Los Ang. '79.   T. (Sam.), 1847, lieut Co. C, Morm. Bat. v. 477, 488-9, 496; capt of returning Mormons in '48.   T. (Sam.), see 'Buckle.'   T. (S. S.), 1830, man who ordered a bottle of brandy.   T. (Stephen B.), 1824, doubtful name of Taylor's list.   T. (Wm), see 'Buckle.'   T. (Wm), 1840, at Sta B., May.   T. (Wm), 1845, Spear's miller at S.F. '45-6. iv. 587; of 3d Donner relief '47; killed by a bull at Hon. in '50 after 7 years' resid. in Cal. These may be 1, 2, or 3 men.   T. (Wm H.), 1846, mid. on the *Congress;* act. lieut of Stockton's Bat. 41-7. v. 386.   T. (W. T.), 1823(?), said to have been mr of a trader this year; came to reside in Cal. '49; in '69-70 U.S. gauger at S.F. *Call.*   Thoms (Adalberto), 1846, aux. de policía at Mont. v. 637.

Thorburn (Robert D.), 1847, lieut in com. of the U.S. *Southampton* '47-8. v. 580.   Thorne, 1846, killed at the Natividad fight. v. 371; perhaps an overl. immig., or he may have been the following.   T. (Wm), 1846, of Fauntleroy's dragoons.   Thorner (François), 1847, Co. C, N.Y. Vol. (v. 499); d. at Los Ang. '48.   Thornton (J. Quinn), 1847, a prominent pioneer of Or. who touched at S.F. in Nov. on his way east by sea. Author of *Oregon and Cal. in '48,* a work containing much information on the overl. immig. of '46 and the Donner party. v. 527, 535-6; see also *Hist. Or.*   Thorp (Dav.), 1837, at Mont. Dec.   T. (Lindy), 1845, immig. from Or. in the McMahon party. iv. 572, 587; apparently living in Polk Val. '79. *Yolo Co. Hist.,* 86.   T. (W. S.), 1847, constable at S.F. v. 648; prob. the man who in '48 married Mrs Caroline Warner of the Mormon colony.   Thurning (Henry), 1843, sailor on the *Admittance;* deserted in '44. *Peterson.*   Thursby (Lewis P.), 1847,

Co. A, N.Y.Vol. (v. 499); in Ga '71.   Thurston (Chas H.), 1847, Co. B, N.Y. Vol. (v. 499); at Marysville '82.   Thusum (Benj. F.), 1845, mr of the *Hannah* '45-6. *Lancey.*   Thybury, 1847, shepherd in Sutter's service.

Tibbetts, 1837, in the cattle exped. from Or. iv. 85.   Tibbey (W. H.), 1848, mr of the Hawaiian schr *Mary.*   Tibeau, 1841, Fr. Canadian gambler from N. Mex. in the Workman party. iv. 278; died on the return trip in '42. Tibian (Fran.), doubtful name of '46. vi. 162.   Tickner (B.), 1847, fleet surgeon on the U.S. *Columbus.*   Ticó (Fernando), son of Joaquin b. at S.F. 1798; settled at Sta B., where in '29 he is ment. as ex-alcalde. iii. 78; grantee of Ojai ranchó '37. iii. 655; juez de paz '41. iv. 641; purchaser of S. Buen. '45-6. iv. 643, 634. He was constable at S. Buen. '52 and supervisor '54.   T. (Joaquin), 1796, sergt of Catalan volunteers. i. 540; executor of Alberni's will 1801. ii. 5. His wife was Juana Carrera, and several children were born at S.F.   Tierney (John), 1839, Irish carpenter named in Larkin's accounts '40. iv. 119; naturalized '44, claiming 5 years' residence; at Mont. to '48. Tieroff (August), 1847, Co. G, N.Y.Vol. (v. 499); owner of S.F. lot '47. v. 685; at S.F. '71-82.   Tighe (John), 1847, Co. H, ditto; dead before '82.

Tilee (Dan. E.), 1847, Co. D, ditto; d. N.Y. before '80.   Tilghman (Richard L.), 1846, lieut on the U.S. *Congress;* act. capt. of artill. in Stockton's bat. '46-7. v. 281, 327, 386.   Tillett (James F.), 1847, artificer Co. F, 3d U.S. artill. v. 518.   Tillotson (John H.), 1845, mid. on the U.S. *Portsmouth.* Timeans (Charles), 1847, Co. C, N.Y.Vol. (v. 499).   Tindall (Israel C.), 1846, Co. C, 1st U.S. dragoons (v. 336).   T. (Wm), 1847, Co. F, N.Y. Vol. (v. 499); d. S.F. before '82.   Tinker (John), see 'Finch.'   Tinkerman (Michael), 1847, Co. G, N.Y.Vol. (v. 499).   Tinslar (B.R.), 1841, surgeon on the U.S. *St Louis.*   Tinson (John), 1847, Co. B, N.Y Vol. (v. 499).   Tipson (Wm H.), 1847, Co. A, ditto; a Canadian printer who died at S.F. '79.   Tise (Andrew), 1847, Co. F, 3d U.S. artill. (v. 518).

Titcomb (Amos A.), 1847, nat. of N.Y. and resid. of S.F. till his death in '70, having held the office of supervisor. Left a widow and one child.   T. (Rufus), 1841, nat. of New England, who came from Mazatlan with H. Teal, whose clerk or partner he was at S.F. '41-3. iv. 279.   Tittel (F. G. Augustus), 1847, Co. G, N.Y.Vol. (v. 499); d. at S.F. '64 (or '68); apparently father of the 2 following, but there is some confusion about the family; name often written Tittle.   T. (Fred. Gustavus Ernest), 1847, son of F. G. A., a German fifer of Co. F, 3d U.S. artill. (v. 518), married Miss Winterhalder and settled at Sta Cruz as a farmer. Later livery-stable keeper, ward politician, supervisor, militia colonel, memb. of the legislature ('61), and cigar-dealer at S.F. In '70-1 he was engaged in the Alaska fur trade; and died in '77, leaving a daughter.   T. (F. G. Wm), 1846(?), brother of the preceding, said to have come this year; a lieut in Mex. under Maximilian; d. at S.F. '70 at the age of 42, leaving a widow and 2 daughters. The latter are actresses, or danseuses, in '85 involved in interesting legal complications respecting a lot in S. F. which was owned by their grandfather, and on which the Maison Dorée, Kearny St, now stands.

Toba (Fernando), cadet of the Mont. comp. 1801. ii. 147, 150; in later years act. com. at Loreto.   Tobar, named as a sergt '21. ii. 575.   T. (Albino), settler at S. José 1791-5, sent away for bad conduct. i. 598, 636, 716. T. (José), 1779, piloto on the *Santiago;* and later com. of the *Favorita* and other transports and exploring craft on the coast down to 1800. i. 328-9, 378, 430, 444, 540.   T. (Juan José), 1838, Mex. capt. and brevet lieut-col, who had been somewhat prominent in Sonora as a mil. officer and revolutionist since '28, and who came to Cal. to support Gov. Carrillo, retiring in disgust after the campaign of Las Flores. iii. 557-61, 505, 555.   Tobias, chief in the Sonoma region. iv. 72.   Tobin (Robt J.), 1848, from Tahiti; at S.F. with wife; still at S.F. '54.   Toca (José M.), ship-boy and teacher at Sta B. 1795-7. i. 643.

Todd (James J.), 1845, Amer. sailor at Mont.   T. (John), 1848, at Sta B., May; also in '50.   T. (John J.), 1845, Amer. sailor at Mont., perhaps same as James J.   T. (Thos J.), 1844, Amer. sailor at Mont., aided by the consulate and shipped for Oahu in '45.   T. (Wm J.), 1844, Amer. sailor in consular care at Mont. Though the records seem clear, it would seem likely that James J., John J., Thos J., and Wm J. did not represent 4 dif. men. T. (Wm L.), 1845, nat of Ill., nephew of Mrs Abraham Lincoln, and overl. immig. of the Swasey-Todd party. iv. 576, 580, 587. Named in the *N. Helv. Diary* '45-7. Early in '46 he went to Sonoma, where he joined the Bears, gained imperishable fame as the artist who painted the Bear flag, was the messenger sent with the news of revolt to Capt. Montgomery at S.F., and was at one time a captive of the wicked Californians. v. 110, 131, 146-9, 154, 156, 167-8. He lived at Sonoma for several years after '46, not, apparently, serving in the Cal. Bat.; then went to El Dorado Co., where a valley bears his name; and in '78 was living in S. Bernardino, his death not being reported down to '85.

Tole (Thomas), 1836, sailor at Los Ang. from Lima, age 24.   Toler (Hopeful), 1847, came to Cal. with despatches, some official appointment, and 2 daughters, on the *Preble*. v. 584-5; worked as a clerk in settling the Leidesdorff estate; went with his family to the mines in '48; in '49 a notary public at S.F. I have no record of what became of him. One of his daughters, Charlotte Catherine, married L. W. Hastings in '48, and died at a date not recorded; the other daughter was still living about '80.   T. (Wm P.), 1842, son of Hopeful and mid. U.S.N. with Com. Jones at Mont.; also on the *Savannah* '45-7; returned as lieut on the *St Mary* in '49. He married a Peralta, and still lived at S. Leandro in '85.   Tolman (H.), 1848, passp. from Hon. Talmayr (Louis Auguste), 1836, Fr. carpenter from Peru; at Los Ang., age 22.

Tometty (Nicholas), 1845, Amer. citizen at Mont. from St Louis Sept. Tomlinson (Ambrose G.), 1832, trapper of Young's party from N. Mex., who remained in Cal. iii. 388, 408. He is also called Thomas L. and Thomason, and known as 'Tom the Trapper.' He had a passp. in '34; was interested from '35 with Job Dye in a distillery near Sta Cruz; signed the letter of thanks to Com. Kennedy at Mont. '36. iv. 141; and apppears on Larkin's books from '37. He was one of Graham's riflemen (iii. 457); was arrested but not exiled in '40, being supposed by some to be the man who, in fear of death, revealed Graham's plot to P. Real at the confessional. iv. 5, 17. In '41 he wrote to Com. Forrest a report on the murder of Anthony Campbell. v. 686. At this time he lived at S. José as a carpenter, age 38, wife María de Jesus Bernal, child Tomás. In '42 Dr Maxwell amputated his leg, and he died before the end of '44. He is called Engl. and Amer., and possibly there were two of the name, but if so I cannot disentangle the records.   T. (John J.), 1848, nat. of Md, who came from Or.; trader in Cal. and Ariz., and memb. of a Los Ang. firm; d. S. Bern. '67, age 41.   Tompkins (Amos), 1830, at Mont. bound for Guaymas.   T. (Christopher Q.), 1847, nat of Va and capt. Co. F, 3d U.S. artill. v. 414-15, 429, 518-20. He went east with Kearny the same year; was a col in the confederate army '61-5; and died in N.Y. '77.   T. (Thomas), 1846, of the Mormon colony, with wife and 2 child. v. v. 547; at Sutter's fort '47-8; did not go to Utah.

Tooms (Geo. W.), 1847, Co. D, N.Y. Vol. (v. 499); treasurer of Stanislaus Co.; at Modesto '82.   Toomes (Albert G.), 1841, nat. of Mo. and overl. immig. in the Workman-Rowland party from N. Mex. iv. 278-9. In partnership with R. H. Thomes he worked as carpenter and builder at S.F. for a short time and at Mont. from '43. In '44 he was married to María Isabel Lorenzana, was naturalized, and obtained a grant of the Rio de los Molinos rancho in Tehama Co. iv. 673. He visited the rancho to put cattle on it in '45 and again in '47, but did not settle there till '49, as the firm of T. & T. is ment. at Mont. down to the end of '48. From '49 he lived on the place, becoming a rich and respected citizen, and dying in '73 at the age of 56. His widow, without children, died at Oakland in '78, leaving her large property to a neighbor who had been friendly during her illness. The will was contested by cousins of the Ortega family, with results not known to me.

Toribio, ment. in '18, '33. ii. 383; iii. 323-4.   Torre (Estévan de la), son of José Joaquin, who in '36 lived at Mont. age 18; in '44 regidor; in '46 juez de campo. iv. 653; v. 363, 637. He never had much to do with politics; but has always been an industrious, hard-working man, as ranchero and miner. In '76, living on his rancho of Bolsa de las Escarpines—of which Salv. Espinosa, his father-in-law, was grantee and claimant—he gave me a most interesting and valuable dictation of his *Reminiscencias*, which has been frequently cited in these volumes. His narrative is particularly valuable as a picture of manners and customs in Mex. times, but is also a good record of the various public events in which his brothers—more devoted to war and politics than himself—took part. He is a man of excellent repute, and still living in '85 with wife and several children. T. (Gabriel), brother of Estévan, soldier of the Mont. comp. from '27, taking part in the revolts of '28-30. iii. 67, 69-70; sergt in '34-6, taking part in the movement against Chico. iii. 671, 429; but retired about this time, and in '39 grantee of Zanjones rancho, and agente de policía at Mont. '44. iii. 679; iv. 633, 653. From '45 he was a capt. of defensores, and was active in '45-6 against Micheltorena and the U.S. under Castro and Flores, down to the final treaty of '47. iv. 515, 652, 654-5; v. 41, 362-3; and in '48, during the rumors of intended revolution, was one of the Californians required to give bonds and commit no hostilities. v. 585-6. He was a brave and somewhat reckless man, devoted to the cause of his country. I have no record of the date of his death. T. (Joaquin), brother of Estévan and Gabriel, b. about '12, educ. at Mont. ii. 429; soon enlisted in the Mont. comp.; corporal in '36; alférez from '39. iii. 583, 671; iv. 13, 652. In '40 he took an active part in arresting the foreigners, and accompanied the exiles to S. Blas, being also grantee of Arroyo Seco rancho. iv. 19-21, 30; iii. 677. In '42-4 he was celador at the Mont. custom-house. iv. 339, 377, 431; and in '45 took a leading part in the revolution against Micheltorena, being made capt. of the Mont. comp., and acting alcalde for a time. iv. 462, 487, 507, 652, 654. In '46 he was in com. of the troops sent by Castro against the Bears, getting the worst of a skirmish at Olompali, but deceiving Frémont by a ruse, he succeeded in crossing the bay and accompanied Castro to the south. v. 41, 134-6, 165-8, 174-7. After the occupation by the U.S. he was paroled, but with the rest broke his parole and fought in the Natividad campaign. v. 289, 331, 362, 366, 370. Don Joaquin was a man of much energy and courage, like his brother Gabriel in many respects, and not friendly to the Amer. invaders. He was cl. for Arroyo Seco in '52, and in '55 was killed by Anastasio García, a murderer whom he was trying to arrest near Sta B. T. (José Joaquin), 1801, Span. cadet of the Mont. comp. to '22, serving much of the time as governor's sec. ii. 379, 438, 457, 463, 580, 676. In '22 he was grantee of the Bolsa del Potrero, sold to Capt. Cooper in '29. ii. 615, 664; iii. 13; in '23-5 sec. of the junta and diputacion. ii. 486-7, 513, 612; iii. 7, 20; in the lists of Span. of '28-30, but not sent away. iii. 51-2. In '36 he is named in the Mont. padron as 48 years old (prob. 52, as his birth is recorded in 1784 in one doc.), wife María de los Angeles Cota, child. Estévan b. '18, José Ant. '20, Encarnacion (who married Capt. Silva) '22, Rita (who married Florencio Serrano) '26, Pablo '31, José '33, and María de Alta Gracia '34. I find no later record of Don José Joaquin. His widow died at Mont. in '77 at the age of 87, leaving 3 sons, 3 daughters, and 43 grandchildren. T. (José María), soldier of the Mont. comp. '36, age 19; juez de campo '42. iv. 653. T. (Pablo), in Castro's force '46. v. 363; son of J. J. T. (Raimundo), son of J. J., at Mont. '26. ii. 612; soldier from '28; corporal of the escolta at S. Miguel '29; involved in the Solis revolt and sent to Mex. '30. iii. 67-85; served in Jalisco and Sonora; and returned to Cal. in '47, to be murdered a little later near Mont.

Torrens (Hilario), 1786, Span. friar who served at S. Diego to '98, when he retired, dying in '99. Biog. i. 651; ment. i. 388, 423, 455-6, 459, 576-7. Torres (Antonio), at Los Ang. '46. T. (Francisco), 1834, Mex. physician of the H. & P. colony, who was in '35 exiled to Mex. for complicity in the movement at Los Ang. against Gov. Figueroa. iii. 284-90. T., 1792, mr of the *Sta Gertrudis*. i. 506. T. (Manuel), 1802, surgeon of the Cal. forces at Mont. 1802-3; and apparently at Mont. again 1805. ii. 31, 140. T. (Manuel), 1843, nat. of Peru, who came with Stephen Smith, his brother-in-law.

iv. 396; and for some years was employed by Smith at his Bodega mill. In '45 he signed the bonds of Amer. immigrants, iv. 581, and was grantee of the Muniz rancho, Sonoma Co., which was finally confirmed to him. iv. 672, 679. In '48 he married Mariana, daughter of Capt. Wm A. Richardson. He took but slight part in the troubles of '46-7. In '75, residing at S.F., Don Manuel gave me his *Peripecias de la Vida Californiana*, a most interesting MS., devoted to manners and customs and observations on early men rather than to a narrative of events. In '85 he resides at Martinez. Torrey, 1845, doubtful member of Frémont's party. iv. 583. Tosta (Bonifacio), appointed gov. in '23, but did not come to Cal. ii. 484-5. Totten (Matthew), 1846, Co. C, 1st U.S. dragoons (v. 336). Tova (Antonio), 1791, lieut of Malaspina's exped. i. 490.

Towner (Loammi), 1847, Co. B, N.Y.Vol. (v. 499); d. at S. José after '50. Towns (Charles), 1844, one of Frémont's men, who left the party in Cal. iv. 437, 439, 453. Townsend (Alfred A.), 1847, from Valparaíso with letters from Atherton to Larkin; of firm T. & Robinson, bakers and saloon-keepers at Mont. '47-8; went to the mines '48. T. (John), 1844, nat. of Va, a physician and overl. immig. from Mo. in the Stevens party with his wife. iv. 446, 453. He served as Sutter's aid in the Micheltorena campaign. iv. 483, 485, 516; then practised medicine at Mont. for a time in '45. In Clyman's *Diary* he is described as 'much attached to his own opinions, as likewise to the climate and country of Cal. His pleasant wife does not enter into all her husband's chimerical speculations.' In '46-9 Dr T. practised medicine at S.F., visiting Sutter's fort in '46. v. 128; being at Benicia '47, and also prospecting the Marin Co. hills for minerals; the owner of several S. F. lots, on one of which he built a house and office. v. 678; in '48 taking some part in town politics, and serving as school trustee and alcalde, but making a trip to the mines. v. 648-9, 651-2, 656; and in '49 member of the council. Late in '50 he moved to a farm near S. José, where he and his wife (a sister of Moses Schallenberger) died of cholera in Dec. '50 or Jan. '51. Dr T. was a man of excellent character, and of genial, enthusiastic temperament. T. (John M.), 1848, Sta Clara fruit-grower '59-76. T. (J. S.), 1848, passp. from Hon.; perhaps same as preceding. Towson (Thomas), 1846, Co. F, Cal. Bat. (v. 358); enlisting at S. Juan Oct. Toye (H. H. F.), 1847, Co. G. N.Y.Vol. (v. 499); d. in Nicaragua '56.

Trail (G.), 1848, passp. from Hon. Trapin (R. S.), 1845, lieut on the U.S. *Savannah;* performed relig. service at S.F. '46. v. 225. Travers (John) 1847, owner of a S.F. lot. v. 676. T. (Wm B.), 1847, sergt Co. G, N.Y.Vol. v. 504; killed by the Los Ang. explosion. v. 625. Travis (W.), 1848, passp. from Hon. Treadway (P.), 1848, mr of the *Kekanonohi.* v. 579; went back to Hon. on the *Julian.* Treanor (D.), 1848, passp. from Hon. Treat (Thomas), 1847, Co. D, Morm. Bat. (v. 469). Trejo (Entimio), appointed celador at Mont.; perhaps did not come. iv. 557. Tremmels (Wm R.), 1847, lieut Co. C, N.Y.Vol.; died on the voy. to Cal. v. 504, 513.

Tresconi (Alberto), 1844, prob. Italian, named in Larkin's accounts and other records at Mont. from this year. iv. 453; at Sta Cruz '79, owning property in Mont. Co. Trevethan (Wm), 1826, Engl. sailor who came from the Islands on the *Rover,* iii. 176, and worked as boatman at Mont., afterwards becoming lumberman and carpenter, and for a time majordomo of S. Miguel. In '29 his age was 26; and from '33 his name appears in various records as a sawyer in the Mont. dist. In '40 he was arrested, but not exiled. iv. 17, 23; naturalized in '44, and married, perhaps earlier, to María Antonia Perez. In these years he lived in the S. Antonio redwoods, and was for a time sub-alcalde; later he moved to Sta Cruz Co., where he still lived in '70, with 10 children. Trigo (José R.), at Los Ang. '46. Triunfo (José Miguel), grantee of Cahuenga rancho '45. iv. 634. Troutman (James B.), 1857, Co. F, N.Y.Vol. (v. 499). T. (John), 1847, drummer in ditto. Trow (Henry), 1845, Engl. sailor in Sutter's employ '45-6. iv. 578, 587; v. 675; ment. in connection with Benicia affairs '47-8; later in the mines of Trinity or Shasta; and last seen by Bidwell between '56 and '60.

Trubody (John), 1847, nat. of Engl. and overl. immig. from Mo. with family, who, after a short stay at Sutter's fort, settled at S.F., though owning land at Napa. He and his wife were active memb. of the 1st methodist society in Cal.; the latter, Jane Palmer, dying in '77.   T. (Josiah P.), 1847, son of John, b. in Pa, who went from S. F. in '56 to Napa; married Sophronia Ament in '65; at Napa in '80 engaged with his brother in the cultivation of berries.   T. (Wm A.), 1847, son of John, b. in Mo.; educated in the east from '50; married a daughter of T. L. Grigsby '68; at Napa '80.   Truett, 1847, at Sutter's fort; doubtful name.   Truitte (S.), 1846, Co. F, Cal. Bat., enlisting at S. Juan Oct. (v. 358).   Trujillo, half a dozen of the name at Los Ang. '46.   T. (Lorenzo), 1841, chief of a N. Mex. colony settling at S. Bern., where he still lived '46, age 50. iv. 278, 638.   T. (Manuel), Mex. sec. of Cárlos Carrillo as gov. '37-8; perhaps the same who was admin. of S. Luis Ob. '35; left Cal. with Tobar '38. iii. 548-9, 565, 682-3.   Truman (Jacob M.), 1847, Co. C, Morm. Bat. (v. 469); one of the explorers of a new route over the mts '48.   Trusted (Gottfried), 1847, Co. F, 3d U.S. artill. (v. 518).

Tubb (Michael), 1846, Co. C, 1st U.S. dragoons (v. 336); an alcalde in Mormon camp '49; apparently a partner of J. W. Cassin in Tehama Co. in later years.   T. (Wm), 1846, Co. C, ditto; prob. brother of Michael. Tucker (Geo. W.), 1846, nat. of Ohio, son of R. P., memb. of 1st Donner relief. v. 539; miner in '48-9; settler in Napa '47-81; married in '58 to Angelina Kellogg, by whom he has 8 children.   T. (John W.), 1846, brother of G. W., and resid. of Napa '47-81; wife Mrs C. E. Weed '79.   T. (Reasin P.), 1846, overl. immig. with wife and several sons. v. 529; a member of the 1st and 4th Donner relief. v. 538, 541; settled in Napa with his sons, but in '79 living at Soleta, Sta B.; also called Daniel.   T. (S. J.), perhaps another son of R. P., in Napa '47.   T. (Thomas), 1845, in Sutter's employ.   T. (Wm), 1847, Co. I, N.Y.Vol. (v. 499); at Sonora '71; not in Clark's last list. Tuel (James), 1846, Fauntleroy's dragoons (v. 232, 247).

Turcote (François), 1830, Canadian trapper of Young's party; prob. returned to N. Mex. iii. 174.   Turincio (Manuel), 1841, mr of the *Columbine*. iv. 564.   Turkson (Paul), 1845, trader at S.F.   Turnbull (Thomas), 1841, Engl. sailor on the *Braganza*, who left the vessel and was at Sta Cruz '42-3. In '48 his relatives in London write for information about him.   Turner, 1848, from Hon. on the *Sagadahoc*.   T. (Chas C.), 1845, com. of the U.S. *Erie* '45-7. iv. 565.   T. (David), 1847, Co. D, N.Y. Vol. (v. 499).   T. (Henry S.), 1846, capt. 1st dragoons, who came with Kearny from N. Mex., fought at S. Pascual; com. of 2d bat. of Stockton's force '46-7; went east with Kearny '47; and was a witness at the Frémont court-martial. v. 336, 347, 385, 391-5, 437, 441, 444, 452, 456. He was again at S.F. '52-4, being a member of the banking firm of Lucas, T., & Co.   T. (James M.), capt. of Co. B, N.Y.Vol. v. 503, 511; did not come to Cal. v. 540.   T. (John S.), 1826, one of Jed. Smith's trappers in Cal. '26-7. iii. 153, 159-60, 176; came back with McLeod's party '28. iii. 161; and again before '35, when he went from Cal. to Or., revisiting Cal. with the Cattle party of '37. iv. 85. Bryant met him near Clear Lake in '46; he was one of the 2d Donner relief '47. v. 540; and died the same year in Yolo Co.   T. (Loammi), 1847, Co. B. N.Y. Vol. (v. 499).   T. (Sam.), 1845, one of the men lost on the *Warren's* launch '46. iv. 587; v. 384.   Turney, 1848, from Or., kept a restaurant at Sutter's fort.

Tustin (Fernando), 1845, son of Wm I., who came overl. as a child. iv. 579, 587; a blacksmith in S.F. '83.   T. (Wm Isaac), 1845, nat. of Va, and overl. immig. of the Grigsby-Ide party with wife and son. v. 579, 587. He worked for Sutter and remained in the upper Sac. Val. '45-6; iv. 580; and in '47 settled at Benicia, where he built the first adobe house. v. 672. Later he moved to S.F., where he engaged in the manufacture of windmills, and where he still lives in '85 at the age of 65. In '80 he wrote for my use his *Recollections*, a MS. which has furnished me not a few items of interest.   Tuttle (Elanson), 1847, Co. C, Morm. Bat. (v. 469).   T. (Luther T.), 1847, sergt Co. D, ditto. v. 477; at Manti, Utah, '81.

Twist (Hilary), 1846, Co. C, 1st U.S. dragoons (v. 336). T. (W.W.), 1847 (?), sheriff of Los Ang. '52–3; killed in Sonora, Mex.; accredited to the N.Y.Vol. by Bell. *Remin.*, 58, 288. Twitchell (Anciel), 1847, Co. D, Morm. Bat. (v. 469). Tylee (Dan. E.), 1847, doubtful name Co. D, N.Y.Vol. (v. 499); not in Clark's last list. Tyler (Daniel), 1847, sergt Co. C, Morm. Bat.; also elder in the church, capt. of 50 on the return, and author of an excellent *History of the Morm. Bat.* v. 477, 488, 491, 493; in Utah '85. T. (Henry B.), 1847, capt. of marines on the U.S. *Columbus.* T. (J.), 1846, Co. B, artill. Cal. Bat., enlisting at Sac. Oct. (v. 358).

Uber, 1843, German in charge of Sutter's distillery. *Yates;* iv. 229. Uhrbrook (Henry), 1847, Co. G, N. Y. Vol. (v. 499); in Nicaragua with Walker; d. Sta Clara '75. Ulibarri (Francisco Roman Fernandez), 1809, Span. friar who served chiefly at S. Juan B. and Sta Inés, dying at S. Gabriel, '21. Biog. ii. 569; ment. ii. 154, 159–60, 237, 357, 366, 369, 386, 394, 655. Ulloa (Gonzalo), 1819, com. of the *S. Cárlos.* ii. 253; com. S. Blas '21–2. ii. 441, 456–7. U. (Francisco), 1539, in his navigation of the gulf possibly looked upon Cal. territory. i. 64, 68; *Hist. North Mex. St.*, i. 78 et seq.

Unamano (Francisco), 1842, mr of the *Constante.* iv. 564. Underwood (G.L.), 1847, Co. I, N.Y.Vol. (v. 499); at Petaluma '74; d. Portland, Or., '81. Unzueta (José), sergt of artill. at Mont. 1803–4. Upham (Wm), 1847, of U. & Talbot at Mont. '47–8. Upson (Trueman), 1847, Co. G, N.Y.Vol. (v. 499). Uren (Thomas), 1848, d. at Dutch Flat '73. *Placer Co. Hist.*, 411. Urguides (Antonio, Dolores, Guillermo, Juan, and Tomás), at Los Ang. '46–8. U. (Encarnacion), settler at Los Ang. '12; alcalde in '24. ii. 349, 354–5, 359. Uría (Francisco Javier de la Concepcion), 1797, Span. friar, whose longest service was at Sta Inés. He died at Sta B. in '34. Biog. iii. 659; ment. i. 562, 577; ii. 29, 115, 155, 159–60, 236, 368, 394, 526, 528–9, 579, 581, 620, 622, 655; iii. 92, 96, 118, 350–1, 657. U. (José Antonio), 1799, Span. friar, who served chiefly at S. José mission, retiring in 1808. Biog. ii. 115; ment. i. 556, 557; ii. 46, 68, 130, 137–8, 155, 159–60.

Uribe (Francisco, José M., and Pedro), at Los Ang. '46. U. (Ricardo), soldier of Sta B. comp. before '37; at Los Ang. '45, being a leader in a revolt. iv. 523, 541, 632. Uribes (José Miguel), settler at Branciforte 1797. i. 569. U. (Tomás), regidor at Los Ang. '19. ii. 351, 354. Uriquides (María Magdalena), 1794, wife of Gov. Borica. i. 728. Urrea (José), interpreter at the Col. River pueblos 1780–2. i. 359, 362, 367. Urresti (José Antonio), 1804, Span. friar, who served for brief terms at several missions, and died at S. Fern. in '12. Biog. ii. 357; ment. ii. 109, 114–16, 121–2, 159, 355, 394. Urselino (José), carpenter at S. Diego, killed by Ind. 1775. i. 250, 253. Ursua (Julian), grantee of Panocha rancho '44. iv. 672; chosen alcalde at S. Juan B. '47. v. 640. Usson (Ramon), 1772, Span. friar who was intended for the mission of S. Buenaventura, but after being stationed as supernumerary at S. Diego and S. Antonio, he went away sick as chaplain on the exploring transports in '74, retiring also from that service after one voyage. i. 192–3, 196, 227, 240–1, 455.

Vaca (Manuel), 1841, nat. of N. Mex., prob. of the prominent N. Mex. family of that name—descended from Capt. Vaca, one of the conquerors of 1600, and often absurdly connected with Cabeza de Vaca—who came with his family in the Workman party, settling in Solano Co., where with Peña he obtained a grant of the Putah rancho, where he spent the rest of his life, dying, I think, before '60. iv. 278, 516, 672; v. 119. Don Manuel was a hospitable man of good repute, whose name is borne by the valley and by the town of Vacaville. Of the family there is not much definite information. Juan was killed by Ind. on the Moquelumne in '45. Marcos is named in N. Helv. records from '45; had a Cal. claim of $4,967 (v. 462); and was perhaps grantee of a rancho. iv. 671; being 2d alcalde at Sonoma '45. iv. 678. Nepomuceno is named in a Sonoma list of '44; age 26; perhaps the same as Juan. Teófilo was 19 in '44, and died at the rancho in '77, leaving a family. These

I suppose were all sons of Manuel. In '30 José Ant. Vaca had visited Cal. from N. Mex. iii. 173.   Vail (James M.), 1847, Co. I, N.Y.Vol. (v. 499); killed by Ind. in El Dorado Co. '48.   Vaillant (Jean), 1830, trapper of Young's party from N. Mex. iii. 174.

Valdés (Antonio), settler at Los Ang. '15. ii. 350.   V. (Antonio María), at Los Ang. '36; age 25 in '39 (another Antonio '47); zanjero in '44. iv. 633. V. (Basilio), regidor at Los Ang. '36–7; síndico '40–1, '45. iii. 481, 509, 631–2, 634, 636, 638; still at Los Ang. '48.   V. (Cayetano), 1791, lieut of Malaspina's exped. i. 490; com. of the *Mexicana* 1792. i. 506–7; killed at Trafalgar. V. (Crescencio), soldier of Sta B. comp. before '37; at Los Ang. '39, age 40. V. (Dorotea), an old woman, aged 81, living at Mont. '74, who gave me her *Reminiscences* of very early times. ii. 232. She was a daughter of Juan B. Valdés, one of the early settlers of S. Diego, where she was born in 1793. V. (Eugenio), settler at Los Ang. 1800. ii. 349.   V. (Felix), 1843, Mex. officer of the batallon fijo, who seems to have come later than the main body; is named in several transactions of '43–5, and was the grantee of Temécula rancho in '44. iv. 406, 470, 509, 621, 639.   V. (Francisco), at S. Bern. '46, age 25.   V. (Gervasio), sub-deacon at the Sta Inés seminary '44. iv. 426. V. (Jesus), Sonoran killed at Sta B. '40. iii. 655.   V. (José), soldier of Sta B. comp. '32; at Los Ang. '46–8.   V. (José María), at Los Ang. and S. Bern. '39–46.   V. (José Ramon), b. at Los Ang. 1803; a soldier of '21–32; later ranchero and trader Sta B.; in '38 síndico. iii. 654; in '42–3 juez de paz. iv. 642; in '45 maj. at S. Buen., iv. 645, where in '78 he gave me his *Memorias.* ii. 240; wife Daría Ortega, 3 child. in '37.   V. (Juan B.), an old settler who left some hist. mem. i. 175.   V. (Julian), at Los Ang. '39–48.   V. (Luciano), teacher at Los Ang. '30. ii. 564.   V. (María Rita), grantee of S. Antonio rancho '31.   V. (Melecio), settler at Los Ang. 1789. i. 461.   V. (Miguel), at Los Ang. '48.   V. (Rafael), soldier of Sta B. comp. '32; wife Rafaela Pico; 5 child. in '37.   V. (Rodrigo), shoemaker at Mont. '41.   V. (Salvador), fifer of the S.F. comp. '39–42.   V. (Simplicio), arrested in '45 for conspiracy. iv. 522.   V. (Urita), in revolt at Los Ang. '46. v. 308.

Valencia (Antonio), soldier of S.F. comp. '19–28; hanged in '49 for murder of Pyle near S. José in '47; perhaps 2 men.   V. (Antonio), soldier of Sta B. comp. before '37; arrested in '37, and executed for murder at Los Ang. '42. iii. 638; iv. 632.   V. (Antonio), at Los Ang. '46.   V. (Ascencio), shot for murder at Los Ang. '41. iv.630.   V. (Bruno), soldier of the S.F. comp. '19– 27; in '41 at S. José, age 39, wife Bernarda Duarte, child. Francisco b. '31, María Concepcion '30, Meliton '35, José Ramon '38; owner of S.F. lot '43. iv. 669; v. 684; juez de campo '43. iv. 685. He apparently lived at S. Mateo. V. (Candelario), soldier of the S.F. comp. '23–33; in '34 grantee of Acalanes rancho, Contra Costa. iii. 711; S.F. elector '35. iii. 704; owner of lot at S.F. mission '40. iii. 706; juez de campo '42, iv. 665, being named on the S.F. padron as 38 years old, wife Paula Sanchez, child. Eustaquio b. '28, José Ramon '29, María '32, Lucía '43, Tomás '37, Josefa '41.   Sergt of defensores '44. iv. 667; juez de campo '46. v. 648; witness in the Santillan case '54. His wife was a cl. for Buri-buri rancho.   V. (Dolores), wife of Lieut Grijalva 1776. ii. 104.   V. (Eustaquio), son of Candelario, resid. at S.F. mission from '37, witness in the Santillan case '55. Grantee and cl. of a mission lot '45–52. iv. 673.   V. (Francisco), regidor at S. José 1802. ii. 134; still at S. José '41, age 68, nat. of Sonora, widower. He was perhaps the father of the S.F. Valencias. The family name is borne by a leading street in S.F.   V. (Gregorio), at S. Bern. '46.   V. (Guadalupe), at S. José '41, age 26, wife Ramona Martinez, child Miguel b. '40.   V. (Ignacio), settler at Los Ang. 1808. ii. 349; at S. Bern. '46, age 25, prob. a son.   V. (José de Jesus), soldier of the S.F. comp. '27–37; in '42 at S.F., age 35, wife Julia Sanchez, child. Catarina b. '35, Riso '37, and Francisco; corp. of defensores '44.   V. (J. M.), his wife the 1st person buried at S.F. '76. i. 296.   V. (José Ramon), b. at S.F. '28, grantee and cl. of mission lots. iv. 673; in Marin Co. '65–76.   V. (Julio), at S. José '41, age 35, wife Concepcion Alviso, child. Cirilo b. '28, Guadalupe '33, Magdalena '45, Manuel '39; in '44 of the S. José guard. iv. 685.   V. (Manuel), settler at S. José 1788, died. i. 477.   V. (Manuel), grantee of Cañada de Pinole, Contra Costa. iv. 672.   V. (Manuel), at Los Ang. '37 in jail; known as 'El Chino.'   V. (Miguel), 2d alcalde at Sta B. '29; soldier before '37, wife Prisca Olivera; alcalde '31–2, iii. 653, 212; maj. at Sta Inés '39. iii. 664.   V. (Ramon), grantee of land at S. Gabriel. iv. 637.   V. (Ritillo), arrested '38. iii. 638; a leader in Los Ang. tumult '45. iv. 523.   V. (Vicente), síndico at Sta B. '27, '39. ii. 572; iii. 52, 654; wife Margarita Valenzuela, 4 child. before '37. Valentin, at Soledad '26. ii. 623.   Valentino, at N. Helv. '47–8.   Valenzuela (Antonio), at Sta B. before '37, wife María Ant. Félix; grantee of land at S. Juan Cap. '41. iv. 626; land at S. Gabriel '43. iv. 637; at S. Gabriel '46. V. (Desiderio and Dolores), at Los Ang. '46–8.   V. (Estanislao), soldier of the S.F. comp. '27–31; at Los Ang. '46.   V. (Felipe and Francisco), at Los Ang. '46.   V. (Gaspar), zanjero at Los Ang. '44. iv. 633; resid. '39–48.   V. (Ignacio), inválido at Sta B, '32, wife Felipa Fernandez, child Juana.   V. (Ignacio), named in '46. v. 162.   V. (Joaquin), at Los Ang. '39, age 29; at S. Gab. '46–7 as juez de campo. v. 628; at Sta B. '50.   V. (José), at Los Ang. '46.   V. (José María), at Los Ang. '15. ii. 350; soldier at Sta B. '32; alcalde at Sta B. '35. iii. 654; maj. at Sta B. mission '38. iii. 656–7; admin. at Purísima '38–41. iii. 666; iv. 648; still at Sta B. '51. His wife was Josefa Cota, with 4 children before '37.   V. (José Sabas), at Los Ang. '46.   V. (Luis), soldier at Sta B. '32, wife Josefa Rocha; at Los Ang. '46–8.   V. (Manuel), soldier of Sta B. 1799; settled at Los Ang. 1800. ii. 349.   V. (Manuel), corp. at Mont. '36, age 22.   V. (Máximo), juez de campo at Los Ang. '38. iii. 636; still there '48.   V. (Pedro), settler at Los Ang. 1798. ii. 350; at Los Ang. '46; d. S. Juan Cap. '68.   V. (Próspero), owner of land at S. Gab. '43. iv. 637.   V. (Ramon), at Los Ang. '46–8.   V. (Salvador), ranchero at Sta B. '45.   V. (Secundino), at Los Ang. '39–46.   V. (Segundo), settler at Los Ang. 1800–19. ii. 349, 354

Valle (Antonio del), 1819, Mex. lieut of the S. Blas infantry comp., stationed at S.F. for a few years. ii. 253, 265, 371; in '22 accompanied the canónigo to Ross, ii. 464, and from that year was in com. of the inf. comp. at Mont. ii. 534, 536, 583, 609, 675, 549; iii. 26. In '23–4 he was in trouble, was tried by a military court for breaches of discipline, and once ordered to S. Blas, but was finally permitted to remain. His troubles seem to have sprung from the hostility of Gov. Argüello, against whom he made many complaints; and he was not released from arrest till '26. Robinson describes him in '31 as 'a little dried-up piece of vanity.' In '32 he supported Zamorano, going to Los Ang. with Ibarra. iii. 227; ment. in '34. iii. 271; in '34–5 he was comisionado for the secularization of S. Fern., where he served also as majordomo to '37. iii. 346, 353, 646–7. He opposed Alvarado in '36, was arrested in '37, and supported Cárlos Carrillo in '38. iii. 488, 504, 545. In '39 he was grantee of S. Francisco rancho, iii. 633, where he died in '41, the same year that gold was discovered on his place.   V. (Antonio), soldier of the Hidalgo batallon at Mont. '36, age 14; juez de paz at Sonoma '46. v. 668.   V. (Ignacio), 1825, son of the lieut and nat. of Jalisco, who came to Cal. with Echeandía, and in '28 became a cadet in the Sta B. comp., going to S. Diego with the gov. and serving as ayudante de plaza. ii. 572, 549. In '31–2 he joined the pronunciados against Victoria and Zamorano, though his father served on the other side, being made alférez in '31, and attached to the Mont. comp. from '32. iii. 201, 204, 227, 671. He was comisionado to secularize S. Gabriel '33, Sta Cruz '34, and S.F. '35. iii. 289, 326, 346, 354, 644, 694–5, 714–15. Don Ignacio supported Gutierrez against Alvarado in '36, going south after G.'s downfall, supporting Carrillo, and being sent to Sonoma as a prisoner in '38. iii. 463, 545, 449, 555, 566, 578. In '39 he is named as alf., habilitado, and supl. vocal of the junta; but was mustered out of the mil. service the same year, iii. 583, 590, 592, 641, 651, though still ment. as habil. in '40–1. On the death of his father in '41 he settled on the S. Francisco rancho, where in '42 he was appointed juez of the new mining district. iv. 297, 315, 630–1; in '43 elector, suplente of the junta, and grantee of Tejon. iv. 361, 635; in 45–6 still memb. and sec. of the junta, memb. elect of the consejo, and treasurer of the civil govt by Pico's appointment. iv. 519, 521, 547, 558, 631; v. 35. He was alcalde at Los Ang. in '50, recorder in '50-1, member of the council and of the legisl. '52. His record throughout his career is that of a faithful officer and excellent citizen. In '77, living at his rancho of Camulos, he dictated for me his recollections of *Lo Pasado de California*, and gave me a col. of *Doc. Hist. Cal.*, which contains some important papers. He died in '80 at the age of 72. Of his family I know only that a son, R. F., is in '85 prominent in Cal. politics, having been member of the assembly and state senator. V. (Luis), 1834, com. of the *Morelos*. iii. 269, 383. V. (Rafael), teacher at S. José '21. ii. 379.

Vallejo (Ignacio Vicente Ferrer), 1774, nat. of Jalisco, Mex., son of Gerónimo V. and Antonia Gomez, b. in 1748, of pure Span. blood, and of a family which included many persons of education, especially several priests, friars, and nuns of some prominence, as is proved by a certificate of limpieza de sangre founded on testimony taken in Jalisco 1806 at the petition of Juan José V., a priest and brother of Ignacio. The latter, however, had no inclination for education or the church; nothing definite is known of his early life; but in '73, at the age of 25, he enlisted at Compostela under Rivera for Cal. service, and arrived at S. Diego in Sept. '74 with Lieut Ortega. He was a somewhat unmanageable soldier, often in trouble; but was praised for bravery in connection with the Ind. rising at S. D. in '75. i. 255; and in '76 was given leave of absence from mil. service to become an employé at S. Luis Ob. i. 299, 428; being formally discharged, I suppose, at the expiration of his enlistment term. From '81 he was employed at S. Cárlos, having, it seems, much skill and energy in directing agric. and irrigation works, though by no means a model of regular conduct, as is shown by occasional charges and reprimands. In '85 he was appointed comisionado of S. José; reënlisted in '87 for 10 years in the Mont. comp.; was promoted to corporal '89; and in '95 was removed from his position at S.José on complaint of the citizens; being corp. of the escolta at Soledad in '93-5; returning to S. José as superintendent of flax culture '95-6, and holding again the post of comisionado, or perhaps corp. of the guard, in '97-9. i. 439, 478-9, 499, 543, 552, 587, 620, 710-11, 716-19, 725. In 1799 he was made comisionado at Branciforte, holding that place for several years, or more than once, the records not being quite clear. i. 571; ii. 156; in 1805 was promoted to sergt, and in 1807—having obtained the certificate of gentle blood in 1806, as mentioned above—was declared sargento distinguido. ii. 140-1, 182; iii. 451. I have his hojas de servicio of dif. dates, showing him to have been engaged in several Ind. campaigns, and to have been recommended for promotion, which—prob. on account of his intractability and early irregularities—he did not get. In '18 he is ment. in connection with the Bouchard affair, subsequently being employed on certain public works at Mont. ii. 230-1, 339, 379, 381, 609. In '24 he was sent to S. Luis Ob. on service connected with the Ind. revolt of that year; asking the same year for retirement, which was apparently not granted, though he got a grant of the Bolsa de S. Cayetano rancho, on which his cattle had been for some years. ii. 536-7, 615-16, 619, 664; iii. 43, 678; ment. in '30. iii. 83. He died at Mont. in '31 at the age of 83. Don Ignacio is described in his enlistment papers as 5 ft 5½ in. in height, with brown hair, gray eyes, short nose, full beard, and fair complexion. He was a rough, coarse-grained, uneducated man; proud of his Spanish blood and family; haughty in manner, insubordinate and unmanageable as a soldier, and often in trouble with his superiors; careless in his morals; but endowed with considerable force and executive ability, and honorable and straightforward, I think, in his dealings with other men. His wife was María Antonia, daughter of Francisco Lugo, married in 1790, who died in '53. There were 13 children, 5 sons—4 of whom survived their father, and are named in this register—and 8 daughters—3 of whom, including Magdalena b. 1833, Isidora, and the wife of Mariano Soberanes, died before 31. The survivors were Prudenciana, who married José Amesti, and died after '77. Encarnacion, who married Capt. J. B. R. Cooper, and still lives in '85; Rosalía, Mrs J. P. Leese, living in '85;

Josefa, wife of Alvarado (ii. 141), Estrada, and Madariaga successively; and María de Jesus, still living in '53.

Vallejo (José de Jesus), son of Ignacio, b. at S. José in 1798; 1st named in records of the Bouchard affair of 1818, when he perhaps commanded a battery at Mont. ii. 229–32, 234. From about '24 he seems to have lived at the Bolsa de S. Cayetano, belonging to his father and after '31 to himself, till '36, being suplente of the diputacion in '33, regidor at Mont. in '35, and capt. of militia artill. under Alvarado in '36–8. ii. 615; iii. 82, 246, 430, 457, 474, 511, 525, 567, 673, 678, 732. From '36 he was comisionado and admin. of S. José mission. iii. 725; iv. 47, 194; in '39 suplente of the junta. iii. 590; in '40 engaged in an Ind. campaign. iv. 76, 138; and in '40–2 grantee of the Arroyo de la Alameda, for which in later years he was the successful claimant. iii. 711; iv. 670. He was mil. com. at S. José '41–2, and is ment. in '44. iv. 201, 465, 684, 686; delegate to the consejo general '46. v. 45; Cal. claim of $2,825 '46–7 (v. 462). He spent the rest of his life at Mission S. José, where he was postmaster in '52, and in '75 dictated for my use his *Reminiscencias Históricas*. He died in '82 at the age of '84. His wife was Soledad Sanchez, and two daughters, Teresa and Guadalupe, survived him. V. (Juan Antonio), son of Ignacio, owner of S.F. lot '40. iii. 706; v. 681; suplente juez at Mont. '43. iv. 653; aux. de policía '46. v. 637. He was later a ranchero in the Pájaro Valley, having but little to do with public affairs at any time. Died at Mont. '57. Larkin describes him as the most popular of the brothers.

Vallejo (Mariano Guadalupe), son of Ignacio, b. at Mont. in 1808, and educated at the same town. ii. 429; see a sketch of his life to '36 in iii. 471–3. He entered the mil. service in '23 (or from Jan. 1, '24) as cadet of the Mont. comp., and in '27 was promoted to alférez of the S.F. comp., though remaining at Mont. till '30 as habilitado and sometimes acting com., being in '27 a suplente of the dip., and in '29 a prisoner of the Solis revolters, besides making a somewhat famous exped. against the Ind. ii. 583–4, 608; iii. 36, 65, 69, 73, 89, 112–14. From '30 he served at S.F., being com. from '31; but as memb. of the dip. during the revolution against Victoria, of which he was an active promoter, and the Zamorano-Echeandía régime of '32, he was absent in the south much of the time. iii. 50, 99, 187, 189, 192–3, 200, 212, 216–19, 365, 399, 701. In '33, though denied a place in the dip. on account of his mil. rank, V. was sent to the northern frontier to select a presidio site and to inspect the Russian establishment, on which he made a report; and was also occupied by troubles with his soldiers and with the missionaries. iii. 245–8, 254–5, 321–4, 393, 631, 699, 716; iv. 161–2. In '34 he was promoted to lieut, sent as comisionado to secularize Solano mission, and was grantee of the Petaluma rancho, besides being intrusted with the preliminary steps toward establishing a civil govt at S.F., and being elected a substitute member of congress. iii. 256–8, 279, 292, 712, 719–20. In '35 he was the founder of Sonoma, being made com. mil. and director of colonization on the northern frontier, engaging also in Ind. campaigns. iii. 286–7, 294, 354, 360, 363, 721–3; and from this time was indefatigable in his efforts to promote the settlement and development of the north, efforts that were none the less praiseworthy because they tended to advance his own personal interests. From '35 he was the most independent and in some respects the most powerful man in Cal. The year '36 brought new advancement, for though Lieut V. took no active part in the revolution, yet after the first success had been achieved, such was the weight of his name, that under Alvarado's new govt he was made comandante general of Cal., taking the office on Nov. 29th, and was advanced to the rank of colonel by the Cal. authorities; and in the sectional strife of '37–9, though not personally taking part in mil. operations, he had more influence than any other man in sustaining Alvarado, being advanced by the Mex. govt in '38 to the rank of capt. of the comp. and colonel of defensores, his position as comandante militar being recognized by Mex. from '39. iii. 423, 429–30, 440–3, 456–7, 471–4, 488–9, 511–14, 523–5, 531–4, 541–4, 546–7, 561–2, 567, 570,–4, 579–83, 590–2, 594, 670, 718; iv. 47, 67, 70–4, 86–7, 145. The new admin.

being fully established, Gen. V. gave his attention not only to the development of his frontera del norte, but to an attempted reorganization of the presidial companies in anticipation of foreign invasion, and to the commercial interests of Cal.; but insuperable obstacles were encountered, the general's views being in some respects extravagant, the powers at Mont. not being in sympathy with his reforms, and a quarrel with Alvarado being the result. Meanwhile no man's name is more prominent in the annals of '39–42, space permitting special reference here only to his relations with Sutter and with the Russians. iii. 595–604; iv. 11–12, 61, 92, 121, 128–9, 133–4, 165, 171–8, 196, 198–206, 208, 213–14, 218–20, 237–9, 249–52, 273–5. After several years of controversy with the gov., and large sacrifices of private means in fruitless efforts to serve his country, the general induced the Mex. govt to unite over his mil. and civil commands in one officer from abroad, and turned over his command to Micheltorena in '42. There is no foundation for the current charge that he sought the governorship and overreached himself. Under the new admin. he was promoted to lieut-colonel and made com. mil. of the linea del norte, his jurisdiction extending south to Sta Inés. iv. 281–93, 312–17, 338. In '43 he was granted the Soscol rancho for supplies furnished the govt, his grant of Petaluma being extended; and was engaged in '43–4 not only in his routine duties and efforts for progress, but in minor controversies with Micheltorena, Mercado, and Sutter. iv. 351–3, 356–7, 373, 386–8, 396, 402, 407–8, 423, 444–5, 672, 674. From this time the general clearly foresaw the fate of his country, and became more and more satisfied with the prospects, though still conscientiously performing his duties as a Mex. officer. In the movement against Micheltorena in '44–5 he decided to remain neutral, unwilling and believing it unnecessary to act against a ruler appointed through his influence, and still less disposed to engage in a campaign, the expense of which he would have to bear, in support of a treacherous governor; but he discharged his soldiers to take sides as they chose, and warmly protested against Sutter's villany in arming foreigners and Ind. against his country, the only phase of the affair likely to give a serious aspect to the expulsion of the cholos. Meanwhile he was a faithful friend to the immigrants. iv. 459–60, 462–5, 481–2, 486, 516, 519, 530, 561, 603, 608. In the spring of '46 he was an open friend of the U.S. as against the schemes for an English protectorate, though his famous speech on that subject must be regarded as purely imaginary. v. 17, 28, 36, 41, 43, 46, 59–63, 66, 105–6; and in June-Aug., perhaps because of his devotion to the cause of the U.S. in its more legitimate form, he was cast into prison at Sutter's fort by the Bears, being rather tardily released by the U.S. authorities, and even awarded some slight honors, and a considerable amount of his 'Cal. claim' being later allowed as partial recompense for his losses. v. 111–21, 123–6, 157, 297–300, 467–8. Commissions of brevet colonel and colonel were issued to him in Mex. in July and Sept. Still mindful of the interests of his section, he gave the site on which Benicia was founded, the town being named for his wife. v. 670–1; and in '47 he received the appointments of legislative councillor and Ind. agent. v. 433, 539, 568, 610, 667–8. In '49 Vallejo was a member of the constit. convention, in '50 a member of the 1st state senate; from that time he was engaged in brilliant and financially disastrous schemes to make Benicia the permanent capital of Cal., of which more will be found in vol. vi. of this work; and in '52 et seq. the claimant for several ranchos, with varying success. In later years Gen. V. has continued to reside at Sonoma to '85, often called upon to take part in public affairs, though reduced financially to what, in comparison with the wealth that once seemed secure in his grasp, must seem like poverty. That he has been from 1830 one of the leading figures in Cal. annals is clearly shown in the records to which I have referred above; and in connection with the narrative thus referred to will be found much of comment on his acts and character. Here it must suffice to say that without by any means having approved his course in every case, I have found none among the Californians whose public record in respect of honorable conduct, patriotic zeal, executive ability, and freedom from petty prejudices of race, religion, or sectional politics is more evenly favorable than his. As a private citizen he was always generous and kind-hearted, maintaining his self-respect as a gentleman and commanding the respect of others, never a gambler or addicted to strong drink, though by no means strict in his relations with women. In the earlier times he was not in all respects a popular man by reason of his haughty, aristocratic, overbearing ways that resulted from pride of race, of wealth, and of military rank. Experience, however, and long before the time of his comparative adversity, effected a gradual disappearance of his least pleasing characteristics, though the general still retained a pompous air and grandiloquence of speech that unfavorably impress those who know him but slightly. He is in a sense the last survivor of old-time Californians of his class; and none will begrudge him the honor that is popularly accorded, even if praise sometimes degenerates into flattery. He is a man of some literary culture, and has always taken a deep interest in his country's history. Many of his writings are named in my list of authorities. His services to me in this connection have been often and most gladly acknowledged. His collection of *Doc. Hist. Cal.* is a contribution of original data that has never been equalled in this or any other state. His MS. *Historia de Cal.*, while of course not to be compared with the original documents, is not only the most extensive but the most fascinating of its class; and while, like the works of Bandini, Osio, Alvarado, Pico, and the rest, it is a strange mixture of fact and fancy, yet to a student who has the key to its cipher, it is a most useful aid; and moreover it should be stated that its defects are not all fairly attributable to the author. In '32 Vallejo married Francisca, daughter of Joaquin Carrillo of S. Diego, who still lives in '85. They had 13 children. None of the sons has ever been prominent in public life; one of them, Platon, is a well-known physician of Vallejo—a town that, like a street in S.F., bears his father's name; and two others still reside in Cal. Two of the daughters married the Frisbie brothers and two others the Haraszthys all well-known men, and four or five I think still live in Cal.

Vallejo (Salvador), son of Ignacio, b. in '14. His early years were passed as a ranchero, but in '36 his brother established him at Sonoma, where he ranked as capt. of militia, was often in com. of the post, engaged in many Ind. campaigns, went south to serve Alvarado in the Las Flores campaign of '38, served as juez de paz in '39, when he also had an appointment as admin. of Solano mission; was capt. of defensores from '44. iii. 511–12, 522, 547, 552, 529, 561, 591, 720–3, 71–2, 163, 197, 252, 355, 362–3, 407, 444, 465, 678. He was grantee of the Napa rancho in '38, of Salvador's rancho in '39, and of Lupyomi in '44. iii. 705, 712; iv. 671. In '46 he was a prisoner of the Bears. v. 112–21, 298–9; is named in connection with the Walla Walla affair. v. 302; and had a Cal. claim, $11,000 of which was paid. v. 467. He is said to have made a large amount of money in '48–9 by the aid of Ind. miners; but his lands passed gradually out of his possession, though he was a successful cl. for Llajome. iv. 671. In '63 he was commissioned major of the native Cal. cavalry, going to Ariz., but engaging in no active service. He died at Sonoma, where he had long lived with the general, in '76. Don Salvador was a rough, hard-d.inking, unprincipled fellow; recklessly brave, and often inhumanly cruel in his Ind. warfare; very popular among his countrymen, though easily provoked to quarrel; generous and hospitable to the early immigrants, though hostile to Americans and to all foreigners as a rule. He dictated some *Notas Históricas* for my use, but his good qualities as a historian did not include truthfulness. His wife was María de la Luz Carrillo, but I have no further information about his family. Vallely (John), 1847, Co. G, N.Y.Vol. (v. 499). Vallivode (Stephen), 1839–40, doubtful name, mr of the *Elena.* iv. 103. Vallobodski (Stephen), 1837, mr of the *Sitka.* iv. 106; doubtful name, prob. same as preceding. Valois (Antoine), 1846, Frenchman at Los Ang. Valverde (Agustin), tailor at Los Ang. '39, age 27. V. (José M.), Mex. tailor at Los Ang. '36, age 29, wife Francisca, child José.

Vanallen (John), at Sta Cruz. Vanaken (Paul), 1846, Co. C, 1st U.S. dragoons (v. 336). Vanauken (Philander), 1847, Co. D, N.Y.Vol. (v. 499). Vanbussum (J.V.), 1847, Co. B, ditto; d. before '82. Vance (Robert), 1847,

Co. F, 3d U.S. artill. (v. 518); living in '64.　Vancoeur (Francis), 1846, from N. Mex. with Kearny. *Lancey*.　Vancouver (Geo.), **1792**, English navigator who accompanied Capt. Cook in his famous voyages; and in 1792–4 three times visited Cal. in com. of an exploring exped. to the N.W. coast and round the world. His *Voyage* contains much of interest on Cal., and is a standard work on the regions farther north. Capt. V. died in 1798. For his visits to Cal. and his book, see i. 510–29; ment. i. 503, 506, 533, 538, 602, 619, 623, 645–6, 649, 653, 658–9, 667–9, 674–5, 681–2, 685–6, 696, 698, 702–5, 714, 724; ii. 23, 121–2, 206; see also *Hist N.W. Coast*, i., this series.　Vanderbeck (J), 1847, owner of a S.F. lot.　Vandussey, 1847, at Sutter's fort.　Vanegas (Cosme), inválido at Sta B. '32, wife Bernardina Álvarez, child Estefana; ranchero at Sta B. '45.　V. (José), Ind. settler at Los Ang. 1781; alcalde '88, '96. i. 345, 348, 461, 661.　V. (Pablo), at Sta B. before '37, wife Rita Rodriguez, and 4 children.　Vanhorn (Barnett), 1847, Co. F, 3d U.S. artill. (v. 518); d. before '64.　Vankensen (Jeremiah), 1847, Co. I, N.Y. Vol. (v. 499); d. Aroca, N.Y., '55.　Vanness (Henry), 1848, nat. of N.J., who came from the Society Isl., became a pilot on S.F. Bay, and was lost in '67 on the pilot-boat *Caleb Curtis*, age 47, leaving a widow and 3 children.　Vanpelt (Jacob), 1847, Co. E, N. Y. Vol. (v. 499); owner of S.F. lot; d. at S.F. '49.　Vanriper (Abraham), 1847, sergt Co. E, N.Y. Vol. (v. 499); d. on the Mokelumne '48–9.　Vanvechten (Geo.), 1847, Co. H, ditto; at New Brunswick, N.J., '74–82.　Vanzandt (R. H.), 1847, mid. on the U.S. *Columbus*.

Varela, 1818, mr of the *S. Ruperto*. ii. 291–2.　V. (Casimiro), one of the 1st settlers at S.F. 1777. i. 297.　V. (Hilario), ringleader with his brother in a Los Ang. revolt. '44–5; also in '46. iv. 476, 538, 540–1; v. 308.　V. (Manuel), killed by Pomponio before '24. ii. 537.　V. (Sérbulo), brother of Hilario, a turbulent character at Los Ang. '38–9, age 26; engaged in revolts of '45–6; and taking part in the last campaigns against the U.S. iii. 564, 589; iv. 540–1; v. 307–14, 325.　Varelas (Casimiro), settler at Los Ang. 1790; d. before 1816.　V. (Cayetano), settler at Los Ang. 1809–19; still there in '46. ii. 349, 354.　V. (Ignacio), settler at Los Ang. '15. ii. 349.　Vargas (Francisco), Los Ang. trader '39, age 37; alférez of Mont. comp. '43, and appointed instructor of the S. Juan comp. of defensores '44. iv. 652, 407.　V. (Josefa Rodriguez de), wife of Capt. Soler. i. 398.　V. (José Manuel), 1828, Mex. convict, liberated in '34.　V. (Julian), 1831, perhaps of Young's party from N. Mex. iii. 388.　V. (Manuel), 1781, soldier of the Mont. comp.; cabo distinguido in 1787; sergt of the comp. from about '87 to '94, being generally employed by Gov. Fages as a clerk. On retiring from the service he taught school at S. José, S. Diego, and Sta B. down to 1800 or later. i. 468, 484, 642–4, 680, 688. His wife, married at S.F. 1783, was María Gertrudis Linares, and in '95 there was a daughter named Micaela.　V. (Mariano), friar named for Cal. 1801; did not come. ii. 159.　Vargas Machuca, 1834, named by Janssens as a Mex. alférez who came with the colony.　Varney, 1841, mr of the *Thos Perkins*. iv. 569.　V. (Sam.), 1846, mr of the *Angola*. v. 576; and trader at S.F. '46–8.

Vasquez, at Mont. '28. ii. 615.　V., at S.F. '44, age 48.　V., mr of the *Flecha* '48.　V. (Antonio), soldier of the Mont. comp. '36, age 20; perhaps the man killed at Los Ang. '45. iv. 492.　V. (Atanasio), settler at S. José 1786. i. 477.　V. (Felipe), of the Mont. policía '33. iii. 673; grantee of Chamizal '35. iii. 677; in '36 at Pilarcitos, age 54, wife María Nicanor Lugo, child. José Ant. b. '20, Pedro '22, Dionisio '24, Sinforosa '26, and Manuel '32.　V. (Hermenegildo), soldier at Mont. 1809; regidor at S. José '27. ii. 605; grantee of land '35.　V. (José), soldier of S.F. comp. '19–24; at Mont. '48; S. Luis Ob. '51.　V. (José Ign.), settler at S. José 1777. i. 312.　V. (José María), 1829, Mex. convict set a liberty '33; at S. José '41, age 31, wife Andrea García, child Susana b. '36.　V. (Julio), at Mont. '36, nat. of Cal., age 40, wife of Brigida German, child. Ambrosía b. '16, Apolonia '18, Ramon '23, Gregorio '26, Domingo '28, María Guad. '30, Altagracia '32, Perseverancia '33, Juan '34, Marcos '35.　V. (Pedro), applic. for land '45. iv. 656; cl. for Sonlajule '52. iv. 674; Cal. claim $3,375 '46–7 (v. 462).　Vasquez (Tiburcio),

Mex. settler at S.F. 1777, and at S. José '83. i. 297, 350 (another named as a convict of '98. i. 606); named in the S. José padron of '93, wife María Bohorques, child. Felipe, María, Hermenegildo, Rosalía, Faustino, and Félix; alcalde 1802, 1807. ii. 134, 192; síndico '24. ii. 605. He seems to have died in '27. The famous bandit of later years was prob. his grandson.   V. (Tiburcio), prob. son of the preceding; soldier of the S.F. comp. '19–25; in '39 regidor at S.F., and grantee of Corral de Tierra rancho. iii. 705, 711; in '40–6 admin. and maj. of S.F. mission. iii. 715; iv. 675; v. 660; named in the padron of '42, b. at S. José, age 49, wife Alvira Hernandez, child. Juan José b. '25, Bárbara '27, Josefa '29, Siriaca '31, José María '32, Purificacion '33, Luciano '34, Francisco '36, Francisca '38, and Pablo '40. He was still at S.F., a witness in the Santillan case, '55.   V. (Timoteo), at Branciforte 1803. ii. 156.   Vassilief, 1820, com. of Russ. vessels. ii. 319.

Vealy (John), 1829, Amer. cooper, age 34, who landed at S. Pedro ill from a Hon. vessel.   Vedder (Peter G.), 1847, Co. H, N.Y.Vol. (v. 499); d. in Nicaragua '56.   Vega (José), sergt killed by Ind. at the Colorado Riv. pueblos. i. 359–62.   V. (Matías), soldier at S. Juan Cap. 1776; killed at Colorado Riv. pueblos 1781. i. 303, 359–62.   V. (Victoriano), 1834, came from Mex. in the H. & P. colony at the age of 24; in '77 at S. Gabriel gaining a living by making cigarettes. He gave me a MS. dictation of 62 p. on *Vida Californiana.* His real name was Esparza.   V. (José M.), 1769, Span. arriero killed by Ind. at S. Diego. i. 138.   V. (Emigdio), juez de campo at Los Ang. '38; juez de paz at S. Juan '44–5; grantee of Boca de la Playa '46. iii. 636; iv. 627. In '46 living at S. Juan Cap. He was 35 years old, wife Rafaela Ávila, child. María de Jesus b. '38, Jesus '43, Ramon '45.   V. (Emilio), aided in taking Los Ang. '37. iii. 519.   V. (Enrique), juez de campo at Los Ang. '40. ii. 637.   V. (Francisco), settler at S. José 1791–5. i. 716–17; man of same name, son of Ricardo, at Los Ang. '46–77.   V. (Juan Crisóstomo), regidor at Los Ang. '39, age 25. iii. 636; member of the council '65–70.   V. (Lázaro and Manuel), at Los Ang. '46.   V. (Pablo), son of Salvador, b. at S. Diego in 1802; soldier of the S. D. comp. from '21, but soon sent to Mont. for an attempt to desert. In '28–9 he was a leader in the revolt, and was sent to Mex. in '30, but returned in '33. iii. 66–7, 69, 74, 85; again ment. in '37. iii. 519; and in a revolt of '46, being taken prisoner at S. Pascual. v. 308, 347. His wife was a daughter of Juan M. Félix and Isabel Cota. In '77, living near Spadra with his brother Ricardo, with a large family and in great poverty, he dictated 90 pages of the *Recuerdos de un Viejo* for my use.   V. (Ramon), at Los Ang. '46.   V. (Ricardo), son of Salvador; in '33 juez de campo Los Ang. iii. 635; grantee of S. José, or Azuza, '37–40. iii. 633; age 28 in '39. He became a rich man, but was reduced to poverty, and in '77 lived near Spadra with a large family.   V. (Salvador), 1792, Mex. carpenter-instructor at S. Diego '92–5; at Mont. '96. i. 615, 684. His wife was María Josefa Lopez.

Vela (Martin), at Branciforte '28–30. ii. 627; wife María de la Luz Fuentes. Velarde (Baltasar), at S. Bern. '46, age 34.   V. (Desiderio), Los Ang. hatter, age 38, in '39.   V. (Jacobo), settler at S. José 1791–1800. i. 716; alcalde in '98.   Velasquez (José), 1781, alférez of the S. Diego comp., engaged in explorations to the Colorado Riv. and in other directions; d. at S. Gabriel 1785. i. 340, 367, 451, 454–5; ii. 44.   V. (José), 1798, convict settler at Branciforte 1798–1803. i. 606; ii. 156.   V. (José), corporal of the S. Diego comp. 1803. ii. 14, 103.   Velez (Miguel), sirviente at S.F. 1777. i. 297.   V. (Rafael), appointed sec. of the com. gen. '29; did not come. iii. 54.   Velsor (Stephen), 1847, Co. A, N.Y.Vol. (v. 499); d. before '82.   Vendurm, 1846, doubtful name in a Los Ang. list.

Verdia (José), died in '16, leaving his property to the mission fund. ii. 407; iv. 338.   Verdugo (Crisóstomo), at Los Ang. 46.   V. (Francisco), at Los Ang. '39, age 38.   V. (José Antonio), at S. Bern. '46, age 20.   V. (José María), retired corp. of the S. Diego comp. and S. Gabriel escolta, who was grantee of the S. Rafael rancho in 1784, '98, and is often named down to 1816 in connection with farming operations. i. 553, 609, 612, 661, 664; ii. 111, 185, 350, 353, 663; iii. 634.   V. (Juan Diego), at S. Diego 1776; wife María Ign.

de la Concepcion Carrillo, who in '50 was cl. for the Félix rancho, granted in '43. iv. 634; daughter Rosalía, married to Sergt Góngora. V. (Julio), son of José María; aux. alcalde at S. Rafael rancho '31, '33, '36, and juez de campo '40. iii. 635–7; cl. for the rancho '52. V. (Manuel), juez de campo at S. Diego '41. iv. 619; soldier, retired with rank of lieut '44. iv. 408. V. (Mariano), 1769, soldier of the 1st exped., serving in the S. Diego comp.; sergt at Mont. '81–7; settler at Los Ang. 1787–1819 or later, being alcalde in 1790–3, 1802; grantee of Portezuelo rancho 1795. i. 252–3, 461, 468, 661–2; ii. 110, 350, 353–4, 663. V. (Miguel), at Sta Ana rancho Los Ang. '39, age 26; at S. Juan Cap. '41. iv. 626. V. (Pedro and Teodoro), at Los Ang. '46. Verduzco (Francisco), 1834, Mex. ex-capt., who was connected with the H. & P. colony; but being implicated in the alleged revolt of '35 was sent to Mex. as a prisoner. iii. 281, 286, 288. Vergara (Quirino), 1842, cornet in the batallon fijo '42–5. iv. 289.

Vermeule (Thomas L.), 1847, lieut Co. E, N.Y. Vol. v. 504, 511; nat. of N.J.; memb. of the constit. convention '49; lawyer, politician, and writer for the newspapers. He died at S. José before '67. Vermilion (John), 1840, one of the exiles not known to have returned. iv. 18. Vernon (Richard), 1848, overl. immig. with Allsopp. Verrot (Joseph), 1844, Canadian of Frémont's party, remaining in Cal. iv. 437, 439, 453; named in the N. Helv. Diary, '46 –8; an early settler of Yuba Co.; connected with the Donner relief. v. 537; married Mary Luther in '48, and a son, Charles, was born in '50. Usually called 'Vero' or 'Varro.' Vevis (Joseph), 1847, chief musician of N.Y. Vol. v. 503; d. before '82. Vhor (Christopher), 1836, Arabian, age 49, at Mont.

Viader (José), 1796, Span. friar who served for 37 years at Sta Clara, leaving Cal. in '33. Biog. iii. 726–7; ment. i. 577, 719–20, 723; ii. 56–7, 135, 137, 153, 159, 168, 218, 387, 394, 577, 585, 600, 623, 655; iii. 20, 88–9, 96, 318, 338, 365, 727. Viana (Francisco), 1791, lieut in Malaspina's exped. i. 490. Vice (James), 1846, sailor on the Dale. Vicente, corp. at Sta B. '38. iii. 656. Vich (Chris.), 1845, Amer. at Branciforte, age 20; doubtful name. Vichilman, 1823, mr of the Buldakof. ii. 492. Victoria (Manuel), 1830, Mex. lieut-colonel, who came in '30 as gov. and com. gen. of Cal.—appointment March 8th, arrival Dec.—and held that office from Jan. 31, '31, to Dec. 9th, when he yielded to a successful revolutionary movement, and sailed for Mex. Jan. 17, '32. He was an honest and energetic officer, who as general forgot that he was also governor; ignored the diputacion and all civil authorities and precedents; and by his well-meant short cuts to justice by military methods soon provoked a revolution that overwhelmed him. All that is known of the man is contained in the narrative of his rule and downfall. iii. 181–212. See also ment. in ii. 549, 551, 594; iii. 26, 54, 216–17, 233, 306–8, 364, 367–8, 374–6, 647, 652, 669–70; iv. 160. Vidal (Francisco), 1602, corp. in Vizcaino's exped. i. 98. V. (John A.), 1847, Co. F, N.Y. Vol. (v. 499); settled at Sta B., where in '53 he was killed in a fight over the possession of a rancho. See Sta B. Co. Hist., 82. V. (Mariano), 1776, purveyor of Anza's exped. to Cal. i. 258, 266.

Vigil (Francisco Estévan), 1841, in com. of a trading caravan from N. Mex. '41–2, and again in '48. iv. 207, 343; v. 625. Vignes (Jean), 1834, nephew of Louis, age 22, who came from Hon. on the D. Quixote to join his relatives at Los Ang. V. (Jean Louis), 1831, Fr. cooper and distiller, who came from Hon. on the Louisa at the age of 48. iii. 405. His Fr. passp. was dated Bordeaux '26. He at once applied for naturalization; in '32 joined the comp. extranjera at Mont. iii. 221; but soon settled at Los Ang., where he was in a sense the pioneer vineyardist and wine-maker, being joined by his nephew in '34. His name is occasionally mentioned in '36 et seq., he being one of the vigilantes in '36, an applicant for Sta Catalina Isl. in '40, and riding in the campaign against Micheltorena '45. iii. 417, 634; iv. 117, 495, 629; v. 49, 283, 365; had a Cal. claim of about $1,000 '46–7 (v. 462). He was founder of the wine-making firm of Sainsevain & Co.; was the cl. for Temécula—of which he had been in reality the grantee in '45, and of Pauba; and died at Los Ang. '62 at the age of 79 (or 82). He had no family in Cal., was an excellent and popular citizen, and was familiarly known as Don Luis del Aliso, from an immense sycamore, or cottonwood, on his land at Los Ang. V. (Pierre E.), Fr. at Branciforte '45, age 50; at S. José '47.

Vila (Vicente), 1769, com. of the *S. Cárlos* in the 1st exped. '69-70. i. 116, 128-9, 136, 165-8. Villa (Antonio M.), prob. son of Joaquin; cl. for Tequepis rancho, Sta B. iv. 643. V. (Buenaventura), soldier of the Mont. comp. '36, age 26. V. (Demetrio). at Los Ang. 39-48. V. (Diego), colegial at Sta Inés '44. iv. 426. V. (Eleuterio), inválido soldier '44-5. iv. 408. V. (Francisco), at Los Ang. 19. ii. 354; in charge of S. José del Valle '36. iii. 612; zanjero at S. Gabriel '47. v. 628; juez de campo at S. Luis Ob. '49; still at S. Luis '51. V. (Joaquin), soldier at Sta B. before '37; maj. at Sta. Inés '39. iii. 664; grantee of Tequepis '45. iv. 643. V. (José), settler at Los Ang. 1790. i. 461. V. (Luis), at Los Ang. '46. V. (María del Rosario), executed by vigilantes at Los Ang. '36. iii. 417-19. V. (Manuel), soldier of S.F. comp. '32-3. V. (Mariano), at Los Ang. '39, age 22; also in '46. V. (Mariano), 1842, Mex. lieut of the batallon fijo '42-5; remained in Cal. '46. iv. 289, 513; v. 41. V. (Miguel), settler for Los Ang., who deserted before reaching Cal. i. 345. V. (Rafael), cabo invál. 1793 at S. José, wife Ildefonsa, child. Pascual, Eleuterio, Rafael Gertrudis, María Ign., and Juana. The full name was prob. 'Villavicencio,' q.v. V. (Rafael), son of preceding, at S. Luis Ob. '42-60. V. (Vicente), at Los Ang. '19; regidor in '27. ii 354, 560.

Villagrana (José Félix), Mex. at S. José '41, age 52, wife Bernardina Martinez, child. Guadalupe b. '26, Juana '31, Lucia '36, Dolores '38; d. in '47. V. (Manuel), regidor at Branciforte '32. iii. 696. V. (Miguel), Mex. resid. of Branciforte from '28, alcalde '36, grantee of Aguagito '37, juez de campo '38. ii. 637; iii. 676, 697. In the padron of '45 named as 66 years old, wife Francisca Juarez, child. Carpio b. '25, Eugenio '27, Dorotea '29, Ignacia '31, Leandro '31, José Ign. '34, Andrés '38, Ponciana '40. V. (Miguel), at Branciforte '45, age 23, wife Concepcion, child. Julian b. '40, José '44. Villalba (Nicolas), settler of the Colorado Riv. pueblos, killed by Ind. 1781. i. 359-62. Villalobos (José), at Los Ang. '48. Villapando (Juan de J), mule-thief '33. iii. 396. Villarasa (Francis S.), 1848, said to have preached at Stockton. Villaroel (Francisco), 1777, com. of the *S. Antonio.* i. 310. Villaverde (Alonso), lieut for Cal. 1779; did not come. i. 340. V. (José), 1782, chaplain on the *Favorita.* i. 378. Villavicencio (Félix), Span. settler of Los Ang. 1781-6. i. 345, 348. V. (José María), resid. of Mont. '36, age 36, wife Rafaela Rodriguez, child. José Ant. b. '34, José Ramon '35; being at the time juez de campo. iii. 675. As capt. in Alvarado's force, and at times com. at Sta B., he was prominent in the operations of '36-8. iii. 460, 481, 505, 524-5, 546, 550, 552-3, 561, 565, 651, 672; also admin. of S. Antonio and S. Fernando '37-8, '40-3. iii. 647-8, 688; iv. 61, 638; acting prefect at Mont. '40. iii. 675; grantee of Corral de Piedra, S. Luis Ob., '41, '46. iv. 655; in '44 juez de paz at S. Luis Ob., and capt of defensores. iv. 407, 462, 658-9; also serving against the U.S. at S. Diego '46. v. 267. Still at S. Luis '51-2, and later a prosperous ranchero. Often called by himself and others 'Villa.' V. (Rafael), weaver at S. José 1791-1811. i. 716, 718; ii. 378. V. (Rafael), grantee of S. Gerónimo, S. Luis Ob., in '42. iv. 655; and cl. in '52. Villela (Felipe), soldier at Sta B. before '37; at Los Ang. '39, age '35. V. (Juan M. M.), settler at S. José 1777; did not remain. i. 312. V. (Marcos), soldier at Soledad 1791 et seq.; invál. at Branciforte '99. i. 499, 511.

Viñals (José), 1798, Span. friar who served at S. Cárlos, retiring in 1804. Biog. ii. 146-7; ment. i. 577, 686; ii. 159-60, 166. Vincent, 1848, mr of the *Zach Taylor,* built at Sta Cruz. *Fresno Co. Hist.*, 51. V. (Calvin), 1846, came to Sta Clara. *Hall.* V. (E. C.), 1848, passp. from Hon. V. (Geo. W.), 1826, nat. of Mass. and mate of the *Courier.* He came back as mr of the *Monsoon* '39-40; and in '44-6 com. the *Sterling;* owner of a S.F. lot and of a Cal. claim '46-7. In '48 he was mr of the *Sabine,* and remained at S.F., where he was killed in the fire of '51. iii. 146, 176; iv. 105, 568; v. 296, 580. A son, Geo. W., lives, I think, in S.F. '85. V. (Joshua S.), 1847, sergt Co. I,

N.Y.Vol. v. 504; at Linn Creek, Mo., '82. Vincenthaler (L. C.), 1846, in Cal. during the war of '46-7; prob. went east with Frémont or Stockton. v. 454; one of Frémont's men '48. Vines (Bartlett), 1843, overl. immig. of the Walker-Chiles party with his wife, who was a daughter of Geo. Yount. iv. 393, 400, 448. He settled in Napa Val., and still lived there in '81. A daughter was born in '45. Vinson (Wm), 1847, Co. E, N.Y. Vol. (v. 499). Vioget (Jean Jacques), 1837, Swiss sailor and surveyor who came as mr of the *Delmira* '37-9. iv. 103, 117-18. He settled at S.F., where he made the 1st town survey, owned a lot, and built a house in '39-40. iii. 706, 710; v. 679. In '40 he was naturalized, and from that time appears in various records as a trader, keeping also a billiard-saloon, and being employed by Sutter in '41 to make a survey of his N. Helvetia grant, having of course much trouble to collect his pay. iv. 179, 229-30, 237, 668. In '44-5, renting his saloon or hiring a man to keep it, he was mr of the *Clarita;* was employed to carry Micheltorena to Mex., and was grantee of the Blucher rancho, Sonoma Co. iv. 480, 564, 670. In '46-7 he made a trip to Hon. and back on the *Don Quixote;* and in '47-8 was mr of the *Euphemia,* running to the Islands, being judge of election, and advertising his hotel—The Portsmouth House—for sale. v. 578, 650, 680. He lived at S. José '49, and in '54 at S.F., age 55. I find no later record of him. His wife was apparently a Benavides. Vioget was a jolly, musical sort of fellow, speaking several languages, a sailor and surveyor and hotel-keeper of some skill. Virgen (Leonardo), soldier at Sta B. '24. ii. 532. Virgin (Thomas), 1827, Amer. at S. Diego.

Virmond (Henry), 1828, German merchant of Acapulco and the city of Mex., who did a large business with Cal., where he was well known to nearly everybody before he visited the country in '28-30. He was a skilful intriguer, had extraordinary facilities for obtaining the ear of Mex. officials, and was always the man first sought to solicit any favor, commercial, military, civil, or ecclesiastical, for his many Cal. friends. He owned the *Leonor, María Ester, Catalina, Clarita,* and many other vessels well known in the Cal. trade. He was the tallest man ever seen here till the coming of Dr Semple; was a business man of great enterprise; had many accomplishments and a Mex. wife; and had, also, his leg broken by the kick of a mule while in Cal. ii. 594; iii. 58, 141-3, 147, 149, 233, 313, 398, 572; iv. 249, 285. Vischer (Edward), 1842, Ger. clerk in Virmond's employ at Acapulco, who came to Cal. on the schr *California.* iv. 341, 349. After '49 he became a resident, being an artist, and his *Pictorial of Cal.* was a series of photographs from pencil sketches, with descriptive matter, published under the title of *Missions of Upper Cal.* His drawings, however, were all made after '65. He died at S.F. after '70.

Victoria (Marcos Antonio Saizar de), 1805, nat. of the province of Álava, Spain, b. in 1760; became a Franciscan in '76; came to Mex. in 1804. His missionary service was at Sta B. 1805-6, S. Buen. 1805-17 and '20-24, S. Fernando '18-20, Purísima '24-35, and Sta Inés '35-6. His death occurred on July 25, '36, at Sta Inés. Padre Vitoria was a most virtuous and exemplary man, always in feeble health, not accredited by his superiors with great ability, but beloved by his neophytes. *Autobig. Autog. de los Padres,* MS.; *Arch. Sta B.* iii. 48-50, 128; *Sta Inés Lib. Mis.,* 19-21. See mention in ii. 109, 121-2, 357, 490, 530, 578-9; iii. 96, 661-2, 664; iv. 63. Vivaldo (Feliciano), 1842, sublieut of the batallon fijo '42-5. iv. 289. Vivero, 1800, com. of the *Princesa.* i. 546. Vizcaino (Juan), 1769, Span. friar who served for a brief term at S. Diego; was wounded by the Ind. in Aug.; and retired on account of illness in '70. i. 127, 136, 138, 164-5. V. (Sebastian), 1602, Span. navigator in com. of an exped. that explored the Cal. coast 1602-3. See complete record of his visit, and mention of a later one of 1613, in i. 97-105, 111, 151-2, 158, 169; ii. 1. Vizcarra (José), soldier at Sta Cruz 1795. i. 496.

Vonks (Stephen), 1837, doubtful name of mr of the *Baical.* iv. 101. Vorhees (John), 1847, Co. E, N.Y.Vol. (v. 499). Vorhies (Wm Van), 1848 (?), postal agent for the govt; memb. of the 1st senate, and sec. of state under Gov. Burnett and his successors; prominent in later years as politician, law-year, **and** editor, residing many years in Oakland. He died at Eureka in '84. Vrandenburg (Adna), 1847, Co. A, Morm. Bat. (v. 469). Vyer (John), 1846, Co. C, 1st U.S. dragoons (v. 336).

Waccodzy, or Wacoocky (Basil), 1835, doubtful name of **mr** of the *Sitka* '35–6. iii. 384; iv. 106. Waddell (Archibald), 1847, Co. E, N.Y. Vol. (v. 499). Wade, 1847, at Sutter's fort '47–8, prob. one of the Mormons. W. (Edward W.), 1847, Co. C, Morm. Bat. (v. 469); at Ogden, Utah, '82. W. (Isaac), 1847, Co. F, 3d U.S. artill. (v. 518); d. before '64. W. (Moses), 1847, Co. C, Morm. Bat. (v. 469). W. (Wm), 1844, deserter from the U.S. *Warren.* Wadleigh (Joseph), 1848, maker of pans at Sutter's fort '48–9; went east with a fortune '49. *Grimshaw.* Wadsworth (James C. L.), 1847, came from N.Y. on the *Whiton;* became sutler's clerk of N.Y. Vol. v. 503; alcalde at Stockton '49; a resident of S.F. in later years to '85, being a well-known mining man. He gave me his testimony on matters connected with the *Vigilance Committee.* W. (Samuel), 1847, nat. of N.Y. and settler at Sta Clara; d. at Pleasanton '82 at the age of 62. Waggoner (P. W.), 1846, Cal. Bat., Co. B, artill. (v. 358); enlisting at Sta Cruz Oct. Wagner (Thomas), 1848, nat. of Va, who died at Snelling '77. Waine, 1846, lieut on the *Levant.* Wainwright (John), 1826, lieut on H. B. M. S. *Blossom* '26–7. iii. 121. W. (J. M.), 1847, acting mr of the U.S. *Columbus;* perhaps J. W. Wakefield (Benj.), 1847, act. boatswain on the *Preble.*

Walcott (Ephraim), 1844, Amer. deserter from a vessel who worked at S. F. for Fink, going into business for himself as a blacksmith in '47. iv. 453, 683; also at Sutter's fort '46–7. Wald (Wm), 1840, arrested at Los Ang. iv. 14. Waldo (Geo.), 1846, officer of the Cal. Bat. (v. 361). W. (Giles), 1848, passp. from Hon. Waldron, 1846, at Sutter's fort from S.F. June. W. (J. W. and R. R.), 1841, brothers and officers on the U.S. *Vincennes.* Walker, 1843, mate of the *Admittance* discharged at S. Diego; in '45 mr of the *John and Elizabeth;* perhaps two men. W. (Edwin), 1847, Co. D, Morm. Bat. (v. 469); reënl. W. (Henry D.), 1846, Co. C, 1st U.S. dragoons (v. 336).

Walker (James T.), 1848, nat. of Tenn. and nephew of Capt. Joe W., who came overland, starting in '47, but being obliged to winter on the way, through having, with the true family instinct, sought a new route. v. 556–7. Working as teamster, cattle-trader, and miner in '48–9, he went east by sea and came back across the plains in '50. The next year he went to Mo. via N. Mex., and in '52 made his 3d overl. trip to Cal. In '53 he settled in Contra Costa, where he still lived in '82, at the age of 57, with wife and 3 children. Portrait in *Contra Costa Co. Hist.*, 88. W. (Joel P.), 1841, nat. of Va, brother of Joseph, Ind. fighter from '14 in the Seminole and other wars, later in the Sta Fé trade, overl. immig. to Or. '40, who came to Cal. with his family from Or., accompanying a detachment of the U.S. Ex. Ex. After working for Sutter, and later for Yount, he returned to Or. with a drove of cattle, remaining there for 5 years, though he appears as owner of a S.F. lot in '45. iv. 233, 278–9, 347, 377, 390. He came back to Cal. in '48, lived at Napa till '53, being a member of the constit. convention in '49, and 1st assessor of Napa Co. In '53 he moved to Sonoma Co., where he still lived in '78 at the age of 81. His wife, Mary Young of Mo., was the 1st white woman to arrive in Cal. by land or to settle north of the bay. They had a daughter Louisa born in Or. '41; and the other children who came to Cal. in '41 were John, Joseph, Newton, and Isabella. The 1st was living at Sebastopol in '77. A MS. *Narrative* furnished by Joel P. to Robt A. Thompson is in my collection.

Walker (Joseph Reddeford), 1833, nat. of Tenn. who went to Mo. in '19, where he served as sheriff, and became one of the most skilful and famous of the guides, mountaineers, Ind.-fighters, and trappers of the far west. His 1st visit to Cal. was as com. of a party of Bonneville's trappers, spending the winter of '33–4 at Mont. Walker's lake, river, and pass were named for his discoveries on this trip. iii. 389–92, 409, 669; iv. 264, 434. In '41, unless there is an error in archive records, he came to Los Ang., prob. from N. Mex., to buy horses. iv. 278. In '43 he guided a division of Chiles' immig. party by a southern route to Cal., going back in '44. iv. 393–5, 679. His next visit was in '45–6 as guide to Frémont's party, a portion of which he brought through his original Walker pass. iv. 582–5; v. 3, 6. In July '46 he was met by Bryant at Ft Bridger on his return from Cal. Capt. W. continued his wanderings, with intervals of ranchero life and stock-trading experience in Cal., for 20 years, making extensive explorations in Arizona as well as in other sections; and then in '66–7 he settled in Contra Costa Co., living with his nephew James T., and dying in '76 at the age of 78. Capt. Joe Walker was one of the bravest and most skilful of the mountain men; none was better acquainted than he with the geography or the native tribes of the great basin; and he was withal less boastful and pretentious than most of his class. In his old age he was moved by the absurd praise accorded to a 'pathfinder' who had merely followed the tracks of himself and his trapper associates, to say many bitter and doubtless unjust things against Frémont, but his prejudice on this point was natural and merits but slight censure.   W. (R.), 1848, passp. from Hon.   W. (W. M.), 1841, lieut in U.S. Ex. Ex. iv. 241.   W. (Wm), 1846, sailor on the *Dale.*   W. (Wm), 1847, Co. B, Morm. Bat. (v. 469). Walkinshaw (Robert), 1847, nat. of Scotland and long resid. of Mex., who came as sup. of the *William,* and took charge of the N. Almaden quicksilver mine; cl. for Sta Clara lands '52. iv. 673; left Cal. in '58 and died in Scotland '59. A man of the same name and apparently of the same family resided at S.F. in '85.

Wall (Richard), 1847, Co. B, N.Y.Vol. (v. 499); d. in S. Joaq. Co. after '50.   W. (Wm), 1847, owner of a S. F. lot.   Wallace (Geo.), 1845, Amer. at Mont.; in prison '47. iv. 587.   Wallen (Edward), 1846, Co. A, Cal. Bat. (v. 358).   Wallis (Wm), 1846, Co. F, ditto, enlisting at S. Juan Oct.   Walpole (Fred.), 1846, lieut on the *Collingwood,* and author of *Four Years in the Pacific.* v. 213–14.   Walsh (James), 1847, Co. A, N.Y.Vol. (v. 499).   W. (John), 1818 (?), resident of Benicia '78–84, said to have visited S.F. in '18; prob. an error.   W. (Robert A.), 1838 (?), priest at Hon. '39, who had apparently visited Cal. with his associate, Murphy.

Walter, see 'Wolter.'   W. (Geo.), 1846, one of the Chino prisoners. v. 314; Co. A, Cal. Bat. (v. 358).   W. (John), 1847, perhaps of N.Y.Vol.; not on roll.   W. (Philip J.), 1832, Engl. carpenter and naturalized citizen at Mont. '32–6. iii. 408; perhaps 'Watson.'   Waltham (Henry), 1848, passp. from Hon.   Walther (Geo.), 1847, Co. K, N.Y.Vol. (v. 499); at Los Ang. '71–4.   Walton (Ambrose), 1841, overl. immig. of the Bartleson party, who prob. returned east in '42. iv. 270, 275, 342.   W. (Major), 1841, ditto; or, acc. to some sketches, was drowned in the Sac. Riv.; also named as one of the Chiles party of '43. iv. 393.   Walz (Geo.), 1847, Co. D, N.Y.Vol. (v. 499).

Wambough (M. M.), 1846, apparently from Or. in June. v. 526; enlisting at S. Juan Oct. in Co. F, Cal. Bat., of which he became lieut. v. 361. In '47 he became the owner of land in Sta Clara Co.; and in July, while on his way to Stockton's camp, was robbed and perhaps wounded near Altgeier's place in the Sac. Val.; though in later years, when he attempted to get relief from the govt, some doubt was thrown on the robbery. I do not know if he was the senator to whom Wm B. Ide directed his famous letter on the Bear revolt. Wanec (Wm), 1845, doubtful name of an Irish resid. of Branciforte, age 45, single.   Warbas (Thos A.), 1840 (?), on roll of Soc. Cal. Pion. iv. 120; in '42, acc. to list in the *Herald* of '51; at S. F. '54.   Warbeck (Henry K.), 1847, Co. I, N.Y.Vol. (v. 499); d. at S.F. after '50.   Warburton (Henry H.), 1847, Engl. physician who came as surgeon on the *Corea* (?), and settled at Sta Clara, where he still lived in '81, with wife, Catherine Pennell, and 5 child., Caroline, Ellen, John, Charles, and Henry.

Ward, 1848, of the ship *Confederacion* at S.F.   W. (Andrew J.), 1847, Co. I, N.Y.Vol. (v. 499); a physician at Sutter's fort '47–8; at Madison, Wis., '82.   W. (C. L.), 1848, at S.F. in August.   W. (Edward C.), 1847, officer on the U.S. *Preble.*   W. (Frank), 1846, came from N. Y. on the *Brooklyn,* though not a Mormon, and opened a store at S.F. as a member of the firm W. & Smith, which became prominent for several years; owner of town lots, inspector of election, marshal at the public reception of Com. Stockton, acting alcalde, etc. v. 295-6, 455, 539, 546-7, 648, 679, 681, 685. In '48 he testified on the Cal. claims at Wash., D.C., but came back to Cal. with his wife, Henrietta Zimmerman, who died at S.F. in '49. A little later, in business reverses, he shot himself, but not fatally; went east about '53; came back soon after '70, married the widow of Dr Bale, and some years later started east by sea, drowning himself on the way. He was not a very dissipated man, but stylish and extravagant. W. (Geo. R.), 1839, owner of a S.F. lot (?). W. (Henry), 1847, gunner on the *Preble*. W. (James C.), 1847, brother of Frank, who came in March with letters to Larkin; owner of lots at S.F., and member of the firm W. & Wells; inspector of election; lieut of S. F. guard, somewhat prominent in politics '47-8. v. 650-2. It was perhaps he instead of his brother who shot himself. He lived in Mass. '55-78, then returning to S.F., where he was a notary, and published his *Diary* of earlier times in the *Argonaut*. He had a shock of paralysis, and was taken back to Mass., where he died in '83, leaving a widow. W. (John), 1832 (?), nat. of Va, said to have been at Los Ang. '32-3. iii. 408; again in Cal. '43-6, returning in '49, and dying at Los Ang. '59. *Los Ang. Co. Hist.*, 35. The only original record that I find is a pass. for Sonora in '45. W. (John B.), 1840, nat. of Ireland, who came as a boy on the U.S. *St Louis*, visiting Mont. and S. F. He came back in '49 on the steamer *California;* married Arcadia Concepcion Estudillo; was one of the founders of S. Leandro; and still lives at S.F. in '85. W. (O. R.), 1847, at Mont. from Hon. on the *D. Quixote.* Wardell (Geo. S.), 1847, left S.F. on the *Chas Drew.* Warden (Wm), 1829, mr of the *Dhaulle*, or *Dolly.* iii. 146. Wardlow (Joseph), 1846, overl. immig. with family. v. 328; owner of Sonoma Co. lands in '47.

Ware, 1847, blacksmith at S. Buen. W. (T. H.), 1845, purser of the *Warren* '45-8. W. (Wm), 1832 (?), Irishman, who prob. came this year from N. Mex., but possibly with Walker in '33. iii. 388, 391, 408. He worked as distiller, tanner, and lumberman in the Sta Cruz region, his name often appearing on Larkin's books and other records from '34. In '40 he was arrested. iv. 17; but got a license to remain; and in '44 was naturalized. Wm H. Ware testified in Alameda Co. '68 that he had been in Cal. since '32; and acc. to the newspapers, Uncle Billy lived at his Zayante farm till his death in Feb. '68. Warfield, 1841, one of Lieut Emmons' guides from Or., with wife and child; perhaps remained. Waring (Richard), 1837, perhaps at Mont. Warley (Alex. F.), 1847, mid. on the U.S. *Independence.* Warner (Caroline), 1846, of the Mormon colony, with 3 children. v. 547; she married at S.F. a man named Thorp, and died some years before '84. W. (Cornelius), 1834, Amer. in a Mont. list. W. (John), 1840, Engl. exile, who returned from S. Blas in '41. iv. 18, 33, 120.

Warner (Jonathan Trumbull, known in Cal. as Juan José, or John J.), 1831, nat. of Conn., who went to St Louis and N. Mex. in '30, was a clerk for Jed. Smith at the time of the latter's death, and came to Cal. in Jackson's party of trappers. iii. 387, 405; iv. 264. He continued his occupation as a trapper in the Cal. valleys during '31-3, iii. 357, 393, and settled, '34, at Los Ang., where he is occasionally named in records of the following years, taking part with the vigilantes in '36, obtaining from the ayunt. a certificate of long residence the same year, and in '38 having an arm broken in resisting a search of his house during the political wars. iii. 566. In '39 he went east via Acapulco, and thence overland to V. Cruz; and during his stay he delivered at Rochester, N.Y., an interesting lecture on the far west, with special reference to a Pacific railroad, returning to Cal. in '41 on the *Julia Ann.* iv. 37, 223, 280, 566. In '43 he got a license to hunt goats and seals on the Sta B. islands. iv. 642; and in '44, being naturalized, he was grantee of the Agua Caliente rancho, S. Diego district, where he lived with his family from '45 to '57, the place being known as Warner's rancho, and another, Camajal y el Palomar. being perhaps granted in '46. iii. 611, 620; v. 619. Here Gen.

Kearny's force camped in '46 just before the fight of S. Pascual. v. 339; also the Mormon battalion in '47. v. 486; and here W. had much trouble with the Ind., notably at the time of the Pauma massacre. To a certain extent Warner was a confidential agent of Larkin for the U.S. in '46. v. 63. In his *Notes* of '45, Larkin described W. as a man of good information, addicted to politics, with some influence likely to increase. Since '57 he has resided at Los Ang., holding at times the positions of federal assessor and notary public, but much reduced financially. He has written much for the papers on topics of early history, respecting some phases of which, involving the trappers' explorations, he is recognized as one of the best authorities. He was selected to write the earliest annals for the centennial *Los Ang. Hist.;* and he has furnished for my use a brief *Biog. Sketch*, and a more extended book of *Reminiscences*, which I have often had occasion to cite. He still lives at Los Ang. in '85, age 78. About '37 he married Anita, daughter of Wm A. Gale, who died in '59, leaving a son.   W. (Richard), 1836, one of the Los Ang. vigilantes.   W. (Wm H.), 1846, capt. U.S. top. engineers, who came from N. Mex. with Kearny, and was wounded at S. Pascual. v. 336, 343-7. In '47 he came to Mont. and S.F., where he obtained a lot; and then engaged in trade with Sherman and Bestor at Coloma in '48, having previously made a survey of Sacramento City. He was killed in '49 by the Pit River Ind.

Warre (John), 1843, Sutter writes that he is not at N.Helv., but prob. at Sonoma.   Warren (James), 1847, Co. G, N.Y.Vol. (v. 499).   Warren (Wm), 1828 (?), negro known as 'Uncle Billy,' who died at S. José '75; said in newspaper sketches to have come in '28. iii. 178.   W. (Wm R.), 1836, nat. of Mass. who had lived at Hon. some 10 years or more, being known as 'Major.' iv. 118. He signed the memorial to Com. Kennedy at Mont. in Oct., unless Wm M. may have been another man. iv. 141; his name appears on Larkin's books in '37-42; and he was for some years in charge of Spear's store at Mont. In '40-1 he made a trip to Hon. and back. iv. 100, 567; and his daughter Mary, a quarter-breed Hawaiian, coming to Cal. about that time, married W. D. M. 'Howard,' q. v. Warren went back to Hon. and apparently died before '48.   Warrington, 1846 (?), connected with the legislature of '55. W. (John), 1847, Co. D, N.Y.Vol. (v. 499); at S. José '50; d. in Mendocino before '82.   W. (John H.), 1848, porter in U.S. naval store at Mont. '48-9.

Wasden (Stephen J.), 1844, Amer. who got a pass.   Washburn (Benjamin), 1844 (?), nat. of N.Y. who had lived in Ill. and Iowa, signed the call to foreigners at S. José in March '45, and prob. came overland in '43 or '44. iv. 453, 599. In April occurred the death of his wife, Elizabeth Woodred, at S. José; and in Nov. W. was ill at Perry's farm near N. Helv. In April '46 he was at S. José; and in July is named as one of the prisoners carried south by Castro. v. 136. I have no later record, but W. is thought by Given to have died at S. José.   W. (J.), 1845, at Sutter's fort; also at S. José. *Hall;* perhaps an error. iv. 578, 587.   W. (Lysander E.), 1847, Co. C, N.Y.Vol. (v. 499); at N. Helv. and Sonoma '47, taking part in a dramatic performance at Sonoma; capt. of Cal. volunteers in the war of '61-5; at S.F. '71-82.   Washington (Geo.), 1844, sailor on the *Monmouth.*

Watawha, or Wetowah, 1845, Delaware Ind. of Frémont's party; died in the service. iv. 583.   Waterfall (Christian), 1847, Co. F, 3d U.S. artill. (v. 518).   Waterman, 1841, mr of the *Braganza.* iv. 563; perhaps same as the following.   W. (Robert H.), 1848, nat. of N.Y., and for many years a sea-captain; founder of Fairfield, Solano Co., where he still lived in '79. His wife was Cordelia Sterling.   Waters (C.), 1848, from Hon.; clerk for Ross, Benton, & Co. at S.F.   W. (James), 1844, nat. of N.Y. and Rocky Mt trapper, who settled in S. Bern. Co., where he lived in '76.   Watkins (Adolphus), 1846, came from Hon. on the *Elizabeth;* owner of a S.F. lot '47.   W. (B. F.), 1847, from N.Y.; a fruit-grower at Sta Clara '76.   W. (Francis D.), 1847, owner of a S. F. lot; d. at Mission S. José '48, age 33.   W. (James T.), 1832 (?), com. of steamers from about '55, said to have touched at S. Diego in '32; died in China '67; a nat. of Md age 59. Also called James W., and accredited to '44. iv. 453.   W. (Richard), 1846, one of the party captured with

Alcalde Bartlett by Sanchez; in '82 a judge in Mono Co. Watmough (James H.), 1846, purser on the U.S. *Portsmouth*, who was com. of the Sta Clara garrison in Aug. and made a successful campaign against the Ind. on the Stanislaus. v. 102, 239–40, 294, 378, 567, 661. He was owner of a S.F. lot. v. 685; and in '47 bought land in Sonoma Co. from Vallejo, being in '53 an unsuccessful cl. for part of the Petaluma rancho. In later years he was a paymaster in the U.S.N., and in '77 chief of the dept of provisions and clothing. W. (Pendleton G.), 1846, mid. on the *Portsmouth*, who served in the S. José garrison under Lieut Pinckney.

Watson (Andrew), 1834, Engl. sailor named in several Mont. records, age 34; at S. José '36; on Larkin's books '39–41, and said by Farnham to have been arrested in '40. iii. 412; iv. 17. W. (Edward), 1828, Engl. carpenter who joined the comp. extranjera at Mont. in '32, and in '33 was baptized as José Eduardo María. iii. 178, 221. His name appears in various records from '34, and in '36 he is named in the Mont. padron as 31 years old, with a wife María Guadalupe Castillo, age 16; in '37 bought land of John Rainsford; in '40 was arrested but not exiled. iv. 17, 23; in '41 naturalized, being a trader and memb. of the ayunt. After the discov. of gold he went to the mines, and died at Dry Creek, near the Cosumnes in '48. W. (Francis), son of James, b. at Mont. about '30; educated at Hon. from '40. iii. 180; iv. 103. In the mines '48; married a daughter of Santiago Estrada; and in '75 still lived in Mont. Co. with 8 children. I have a brief *Narrative* from him. W. (Henry), 1846, Co. G, Cal. Bat. (v. 358), enlisting at S. José Nov. W. (Henry B.), 1846, lieut of marines on the U.S. *Portsmouth*, in com. of S.F. garrison; also with Stockton in the southern campaign of '46–7. v. 239–40, 295, 392, 436, 659.

Watson (James or David), 1824(?), Engl. sailor who left a whaler at Sta B. or S.F. about this time and settled as a trader at Mont. His original name seems to have been David, but was prob. called Santiago at baptism; also called Felipe Santiago, and in one record James Peter. ii. 495, 526. The 1st original record is in '30; in '32 he joined the comp. extranjera. iii. 221–2; and in '34 he had a wife, Mariana Escamilla, and 2 children—a number increased to 4 in '36, when he was a naturalized citizen, age 33. A lot was granted him in '35, and in '36 he bought a house of Luis Beltran, afterwards sold to Fuller and bought back. He was often a memb. of the ayunt. from '36, being a respected citizen and merchant frequently named in the records down to '48. iii. 675; iv. 117, 136, 218, 403, 653. Sir Geo. Simpson describes him as a Londoner from Redriff, whose father had been 'in the public line,' keeping the 'Noah's Hark between Globe Stairs and the 'Orse Ferry;' and Larkin, in his *Notes* of '45, as an uneducated, unambitious, honest man, who did not meddle in politics. He acquired a fortune, and is named by Willey and others in '49 as a very generous man. About '50 he bought the S. Benito rancho, for which he was successful claimant. iv. 655; but he was ruined by the drought of '63, and died the same year. His children were Francis b. abt '30; Catalina in '33; Tomás in '35 (later sheriff of Mont. where he still lived in '75); and Santiago Jr, born in '36. W. (J. B.), 1848, passp. from Hon. W. (J. M.), 1847, lieut U.S.N., who brought despatches to Gen. Kearny; later in com. of the *Erie;* d. at Vallejo '73, age 66. W. (Wm), 1836, Engl. lumberman in Mont. dist, age 30. W. (Wm), 1847, at Benicia. v. 673; at Napa '48. Watt (James), 1836, juez de campo at Mont. iii. 675; 'Santiago Guat,' prob. 'Watson,' q.v.; and Felipe Guati, an Engl. catholic mariner, at Mont. in '29, age 25, was also prob. the same 'Watson.' Watts (John), 1847, Co. B, Morm. Bat. (v. 469); reënl.; a man of the same name at S. José '50. W. (Wm), 1827, doubtful name of sup. of the *Karimoko*. iii. 147. W. (Wm), 1841, doubtful name at Mont. *Toomes.* Watty, 1845, at Larkin's soap-factory. Wayne (W.A.), 1845, lieut on the U.S. *Savannah*.

Weaitz (John), 1846, Co. B, Cal. Bat. (v. 358), enlisting at Mont. Oct. Weaver, 1831, a trapper, said by Nidever to have been in Young's party; called Powell W. by Dye. iii. 388; perhaps Pauline W., a noted mountain man of Ariz. later. He was also possibly the man who served as guide to the

Morm. Bat. v. 483; and a Paulino W. is named at S. Bern. in '46, age 40. W. (Daniel), 1846, Co. C, 1st U.S. dragoons (v. 336).   W. (Franklin), 1847, Co. A, Morm. Bat. (v. 469); in Utah '81; married Miss R. Reed at S.F. '48. W. (M.), 1846, doubtful name in a Los Ang. list.   W. (Miles), 1847, Co. A, Morm. Bat. (v. 469).   W. (Vance), 1846, Co. E, Cal. Bat. (v. 358), enlisting at Sonoma in Oct.; Cal. claim (v. 462).   W. (Wm E.), 1848, part owner of the S.F. *Californian;* perhaps same as the following.   W. (Wm J.), 1847, Co. C, N.Y.Vol. (v. 499); a printer.   Webb (Chas Y.), 1847, Co. A, Morm. Bat. (v. 469); at Parowan, Utah, '81.   W. (Wm), 1832, memb. of the comp. extranjera. iii. 221; still at Mont. '33-4.

Weber (Charles M.), 1841, nat. of Germany, who came to N. Orleans in '36, and in '41 was an overl. immig. of the Bartleson party from St Louis. He worked through the winter for Sutter, who had signed his bond on arrival. iv. 270, 275, 279; and in '42 settled at S. José as trader, miller, baker, and a little later salt-producer and shoemaker, also acquiring land and livestock, all in partnership with Wm Gulnac. In '43 they obtained, in G.'s name, as W. was not naturalized till '44, a grant of the Campo de los Franceses rancho, G.'s share of which was bought by W. in '45. Weber was an active business man, and well liked at this time by the Californians, to whom he afforded valuable support in their movement of '44 against Micheltorena's cholos, raising a comp. of foreign volunteers, being imprisoned at Sutter's fort on account of his efforts for his country without regard to the Swiss adventurer's personal schemes, being made capt. of militia in '45, and taking a prominent part in issuing the call for an assembly of foreign residents. iv. 462, 468-9, 483, 599, 604-5. His position in all these matters was consistent and praiseworthy, though his influence at this time and his prominence in events of the next year have been grossly exaggerated in the newspapers and county histories of late years. In '46 Weber was in sympathy with Larkin's plans rather than with those of the filibusters; but on hearing of the Bear rising he seems to have taken some steps for the protection of the settlers south of the bay, and on the discovery of his plans was arrested by Castro, who carried him south as a prisoner, but released him on leaving Cal. for Mex. I am inclined to think, however, that Castro did this at the request of W., who, having made enemies on both sides of the pending troubles, deemed it wise to absent himself for a time. v. 16, 136-7, 245, 277. He returned in Oct. in time to engage actively, to the great displeasure of many Californians, in the work of collecting horses and supplies for the Cal. Bat., in which he declined to serve on account of hostility to Frémont; but was made capt. of volunteers and took part in the final campaign against Sanchez, being ordered to discharge his men and thanked for past services in Feb. '47. v. 294-5, 377-8, 380, 382, 661. In '47 he settled on his French Camp rancho, and founded a settlement which he afterwards had laid out as a town and named Stockton. v. 674-5. In '48-9 he added to his wealth by successful gold-mining, with the aid of Ind., at Weber Creek and elsewhere; and his lands were vastly increased in value during the flush times. He was claimant for Campo de los Franceses and Cañada de S. Felipe. iii. 677, 711; iv. 671. He spent the rest of his life at Stockton, where he died in '81 at the age of 67, leaving a widow, the daughter of Martin Murphy, and 3 children. Weber was an intelligent, energetic, and honorable man of business; generous in his many gifts to his town and to his friends; but in his later life eccentric to the verge of insanity, morbidly sensitive, avoiding his fellow-men. There is nothing apparent in his record, that of a successful man, who was neither the author nor victim of any great wrongs, to account for his peculiarities. *Tinkham's Hist. of Stockton* contains a portrait, and is the best source of information outside of original records. An early MS. copy of *Halleck's Land Laws,* to which were appended some of Weber's correspondence of considerable interest, was for a short time in my possession.   W. (John), 1847, of N.Y. Vol.(?); at S.F. '74.   Webster (Charles A.), 1847, Co. G, N.Y. Vol. (v. 499); d. at Los Ang. '47.   W. (Ed. C.), 1848, at Mont.   W. (John H.) 1847, Co. F, N.Y. Vol. (v. 499); notary at Stockton, where he died in '81, leaving a family.

Weed (John W.), 1841, Amer. passenger on the *Julia Ann*, who came from N.Y. for his health, and went back in '42. iv. 566.　　Weeks (Elbert), 1847, Co. B, N.Y. Vol. (v. 499); d. before '82.　　Weeks (James W.), 1831, Engl. sailor who deserted from the whaler *Fanny*, at S.F. in Oct., while the crew were occupied in cutting wood at Pt Quintin. iii. 405. Spending some time at Read's, and then working for the Castros at S. Pablo, he lived for some months on the beach at S.F. trying with others to repair an old boat, tried a ranchero's life with Narvaez in Sta Clara Valley, cooked for a while in the Pulgas redwoods, joined Ewing Young's trappers, and returned via Ross to the redwoods. In '40 he was arrested but not exiled, having married a native wife. iv. 9, 17, 23; in '41-5 lived at Sta Cruz, iv. 280, 356, 663, being named in the padron of '45, age 32, wife Ramona Pinto, child. María Ana b. '41, Blas Antonio '43, Teodoro '44. He signed the S. José call to foreigners. iv. 599; in '46 was coroner in the Naile case. v. 641; was clerk for Alcalde Stokes and in charge of the archives, and later member of the council. v. 664; and in '47-8 alcalde of S. José. v. 662; went to the mines in '48; was sec. of the prefecture in '49; and continued to live in Sta Clara Co., being cl. for a part of S. Antonio rancho. In '77 he wrote for me his *Reminiscences*, a detailed narrative of his career in early times; and having fulfilled this part of his destiny, he died in '81, leaving 4 sons. He was an intelligent man with but slight education, of good character, though at times addicted to intemperance.　　Wehler (Edward), 1847, musician of N.Y. Vol. (v. 499).

Weidney (Anthony), 1847, Co. K, N.Y. Vol. (v. 499).　　Weifenback (Philip), 1847, Co. E, ditto.　Weimar, see 'Wimmer.'　Weir (James), 1847, Co. F, 3d U.S. artill. (v. 518).　　W. (Thomas), 1847, Co. A, Morm. Bat. (v. 469); employed by Sutter as a tanner.　Weirick (Wm H.), 1847, lieut Co. F, G, N.Y. Vol. v. 504.　　Weirgen (Christian), 1847, Co. A, ditto.　Weiss (Wm), 1847, Co. B, ditto; at S.F. '83.　Weit (John), 1847, Co. F, 3d U.S. artill. v. 518.

Welburn (Benj.), see 'Washburn,' signer of the S. José call to foreigners of '45, the name being incorrectly given in several county histories.　Welch, see 'Welsh.'　Welder (Anthony), 1847, Co. C, N.Y. Vol. (v. 499).　Weldon (Peter), 1835, Amer. carpenter, age 24, who came on the *Framen* (?); an anabaptist who joined Russell in his exped. from S. Diego to the Colorado in '36. iii. 613.　Weller (C. M.), 1846, Cal. claim $297 (v. 462); prob. an error for 'Weber.'　W. (Edward H.), 1847, Co. A, N.Y. Vol. (v. 499); at S.F. '71-4.　Wells, 1847, married by Sutter and remarried at Sta Clara. *Alexander;* prob. 'West.'　W., 1848, on the *Sagadahoc* from Hon.; perhaps Robert. W. (Benj. F.), 1846, mid. on the U.S. *Congress;* acting lieut in Stockton's Bat. '46-7. v. 386.　W. (David), 1848, came from Or. and settled in S. Joaq. Co.　W. (Robert), 1847, from N.Y. by sea; owner of S.F. lot; of firm W. & Co., merchants at S.F.; still here in '54.　W. (Thos J.), 1847, Co. G, N.Y. Vol. (v. 499); in N.Y. '71-82.　W. (Wm M.), 1847, Co. G, ditto.　Welsh, 1847, doubtful name or date of a justice at S. Buen.　W. (Charles), 1848, Amer. sea capt. said to have been educated in Spain and to have served in the Span. mail service; d. at S.F. '83. He married a sister of Philip A. Roach. W. (John H.), 1847, Co. E, N.Y. Vol. (v. 499); in N.Y. '71-84.　W. (Wm), 1821, Scotch sailor on the *Lady Blackwood* discharged at Bodega. ii. 478. He was at Los Ang. '29-30. ii. 558; is often named in northern records from '30. ii. 616; lived at S. José from '32, and in '44 was grantee of Las Juntas, Contra Costa. iv. 671. He seems to have been a brother-in-law of James A. Forbes, and to have been living in the S. José district '47; but died before '52, when the rancho was claimed by the admin. of his estate. He left a wife and 8 children.

Wescott (Joseph F. R.), 1836, nat. of Conn., baptized at S. Rafael in Oct. iv. 118. In '42 Francis Wescott is named as gunsmith of the S.F. comp.; and in '48 Conway & W. were proprietors of the Colonnade House at S.F., W. leaving his debtors in the lurch; perhaps not he of '36. v. 683.　Wesley, 1847, visitor at Sutter's fort.　West (Benj.), 1847, Co. E, Morm. Bat., reënl. (v. 469).　W. (Henry S.), 1843, mr of the *Rafak*. iv. 568.　W. (T.), 1846,

Fauntleroy's dragoons (v. 232, 247), enlisting at Mont. July.   W. (Thomas), 1846, overl. immig. with Bryant, sometime capt. of the party, accompanied by his wife and 4 sons. v. 528. He settled at S. José, and acc. to Hittell became wealthy and went east before '60. His sons Francis T. and Thomas M. kept a livery-stable at S. José in '47. Another, Wm T., served in Co. B, artill. Cal. Bat. (v. 358); and the 4th was Geo. R. The grave of Ann W. was passed on the overl. route by Bigler in '47.   W. (Thos J.), 1847, Co. G, N. Y. Vol. (v. 499); d. before '82.   W. (Wm C.), 1846, Co. C, 1st U.S. dragoons (v. 336); killed at S. Pascual. v. 346.

West (Wm Mark), 1832, Engl. carpenter, lumberman, and farmer, who had lived 7 years in Mex. territory before coming to Cal. iii. 408. In '34 he obtained naturalization, having been baptized at Sta Cruz, and owning property to the value of $1,500. From '33 he appears on Larkin's books, generally as a lumberman working with Trevethan in the redwoods. In the Mont. padron of '36 he is named as 40 years old, wife Guadalupe Vasquez, child María Luisa b. '33. In '40, being arrested but not exiled, he was grantee of the S. Miguel rancho, Sonoma, and of Llano de Sta Rosa in '44. iii. 713; iv. 17, 23, 673. I have no record of him after '48, but he died before '52, when his widow appears as cl. for the rancho, on which a stream still bears the name of Mark West Creek.   Westfall (Jacob), 1846, Co. C, 1st U.S. dragoons (v. 336).   Westgate (Francis J.), 1839, blacksmith and carpenter at Sonoma and S.F. '39–42, working for Spear & Hinckley and Salv. Vallejo. iv. 119; perhaps the man named as having lived at Pt Reyes in '46.   W. (Obadiah), 1833, gunsmith at S.F.; perhaps same as preceding.   Westlake (Richard), 1840, one of the exiles to S. Blas who did not return. iv. 18.   Weston, 1846, mr of the *Wm Neilson*. v. 581.   Wetmarsh, see 'Whitmarsh.'   Wetmore (C. E.), 1848, S.F. merchant of firm W. & Gilman. v. 680; member of the council '49; settled at Benicia with his wife.   Wetowah, see 'Watawha.' Wettermark (Chas P.), 1847, Co. A, N.Y.Vol. (v. 499).   Weyland (John), 1848, at S.F., advertising tents for sale.

Whalen (John), 1847, musician of N.Y.Vol. (v. 499); d. at Los Ang. '53. Whally (Scotch), 1840(?), a man known only by this name, who lived for several years in the redwoods near Mont., engaged in making shingles. iv. 120. About '45 he was killed by the Tulare Ind.   Wheeler (Alfred), 1847(?), nat. of N.Y., and memb. of 1st Cal. legislature. *Anaheim Gazette*, Oct. 16, '75. W. (Geo.), 1848, on roll of Soc. Cal. Pion.   W. (Henry), 1847, Co. C, Morm. Bat. (v. 469); reënl.   W. (John), 1847, Co. K, N. Y. Vol. (v. 499).   W. (John L.), 1847, Co. B, Morm. Bat. (v. 469); reënl.   W. (Merrill W.), 1847, Co. A, ditto.   W. (Wm), 1845, boy on the *Warren*, living at S. José '77, when he gave me a narrative on the *Loss of the Warren's Launch* in '46. iv. 587; v. 384.   W. (Wm H. H.), 1847, Co. D, N.Y.Vol. (v. 499); d. in L. Cal. '48. Wheelock (Lyman), 1847, Co. K, ditto.

Whisman (Andrew), 1847, nat. of Mo., who came overl. with his father, John W. (?), and in '47–8 kept an inn bet. S. José and S.F.; later a farmer in Sta Clara and Alameda counties. He died at Harrisburg '79. His 1st wife was Serelda Lynn, by whom he had 11 children; the 2d Catherine Smith '72.   W. (John), 1848, cousin of J. W. at Sta Clara.   W. (John W.), 1847, nat. of Va and overl. immig. with wife and son, settling in Sta Clara.   Whistler (Geo. R.), 1846(?), said to have come as a soldier; later in the mines; murdered in Ariz. '74; known as Geo. Reese.   Whitaker, 1845, doubtful name of an overl. immig. iv. 578.   W. (Amison), 1847, Co. F, N.Y.Vol. (v. 499); at Sac. '82.   W. (John Geo.), 1845, mid. on the U.S. *Savannah, Columbus,* and *Warren* '45–8.   Whitcomb (Wm N.), 1847(?), said to have come with Capt. Brackett's comp. in '46; committed suicide at Napa in '71. *N. Register.*

White, 1845, named as having come with McDowell and also with Frémont. iv. 578, 583.   W., 1847, at Stockton '47–8.   W. (Arthur F.), 1845, at Mont. from R.I.; bought goods from the wreck of the *Star of the West.* W. (Charles), 1846, overl. immig. who settled with his wife at S. José, where he was councilman in '46 and alcalde in '48–9, becoming the owner of a large estate and cl. for Arroyo de S.Antonio. He was killed in the *Jenny Lind* explosion in '53; his widow married Gen. C. Allen, and was the cl. for several ranchos. iii. 678, 711-12; iv. 655; v. 529, 662, 664. His son, Chas E., was a lawyer at S. José '81.   W. (Chris. S.), 1847, Co. B, N.Y.Vol. (v. 499).   W. (Henry), 1847, Co. F, 3d U.S. artill. (v. 518); d. before '82.   W. (J.), 1846, Co. F, Cal. Bat. (v. 358), enlisting at S. Juan in Oct.   W. (J.), 1848, passp. from Hon.   W. (John), 1846, Co. C, 1st U.S. dragoons (v. 336).   W. (John C.), 1847, Co. C, Morm. Bat. (v. 469).   W. (Joseph), 1847, Co. A, ditto. W. (Joseph), 1848 (?), trapper in the mines with Brooks who claimed to have come with Capt. Weber '41 (?).

White (Michael), 1829, Engl. or Irish sailor who came from Hon. on the *Dolly* or *Dhaulle*. iii. 179; having touched on the L. Cal. coast in '17, and sailed, sometimes as mate and mr, on Mex. and Hawaiian vessels from that date according to his own statement. He settled at Sta B., where he built a schooner in '30. ii. 573; iii. 140. Except from his own testimony nothing is known of him till '36, when his name appears in a Los Ang. list as an Irishman aged 30; though he may have been the White accused of smuggling at S.F. in '33. iii. 393. He says he made a trip to Mazatlan in the schr *Guadalupe*, which he had built for S.Gabriel mission, returning in '32, marrying María del Rosario Guillen, daughter of the famous old woman Eulalia Perez, opening a little store at Los Nietos, and keeping aloof from politics. In '38 he signed a petition against Carrillo. iii. 565; and in '39 went to N. Mex., but returned with the Workman party in '41. iv. 278. In '43 he was grantee of Muscupiabe rancho and a S. Gabriel lot. iv. 635, 637; served in the foreign comp. against Micheltorena '45. iv. 495, 595; and was one of the Chino prisoners in '46. v. 314. In later years he continued to live at S. Gabriel; was the successful cl. for his lands, which, however, in one way or another he finally lost; and occasionally indulged in a sea voyage. In '77, at the age of 75, somewhat feeble in health and very poor, having a large family of children and grandchildren, Miguel Blanco gave me his interesting reminiscences of *Cal. All the Way Back to '28*. His memory was good, and he seemed to be a truthful man. He died in or before '85.   W. (Milton), 1840, one of the exiles to S. Blas, arrested in the south; did not return. iv. 14, 18.   W. (Moses), 1847, Co. E, N.Y. Vol. (v. 499).   W. (Philander), 1847, Co. K, ditto.   W. (Sam. S.), 1847, Co. A, Morm. Bat. (v. 469); in Sutter's employ '47-8; at Pleasant Grove, Utah, '81.   W. (Thomas), 1840, deserter from the *St Louis*, who became a lumberman, married, and in '48 lived on the Salinas. He died about '50. iv. 120.   W. (Wm), 1836, named in Larkin's books.   W. (Wm), 1847, shoemaker in Sutter's employ.   W. (W.), 1846, Co. F, Cal. Bat. (v. 358), enlisting at S. Juan Nov.; perhaps same as one or both of the preceding.

Whitehouse (Benj.), 1847, Co. B, N.Y.Vol. (v. 499); perhaps the 'Dad' W. at Stockton '48-9; d. at S.F. after '50.   W. (Geo. W.), 1846, Co. C, 1st U.S. dragoons (v. 336); at Los Ang. '79.   W. (Joseph), 1840, one of the exiles to S. Blas who did not return. iv. 18.   Whitehurst, 1846, sergt, killed at S. Pascual (?). *Frémont Court-martial*, 169. See 'Whitness.'   Whiteman (Wm), 1846, overl. immig. who settled at S. José with his family; drowned in the S. Joaq. River '48. His widow lived at S. José '77, in the house built by W. in '46. A daughter was the wife of Waldo Lowe. A son, John T., who came as a child in '46, was a farmer in Sta Clara Co., and died at S. Luis Ob. in '77, leaving a widow. Whiting (Wm J.), 1830, trader on the coast '30-1.   Whitlock (Geo. W.), 1847, clerk for Wm H. Davis '47-9. v. 651; sergt of S.F. guard '48; at Sac. about '74-5.   W. (Jacob H.), 1847, Co. A, N.Y.Vol. (v. 499); d. at S.F. '49.   W. (Mervin R.), 1847, ditto; drowned in S. Joaq. River '49.   Whitmarsh (James), 1833, Amer. sailor who came from Mazatlan on the *Sta Bárbara*. iii. 409. In '37 a lumberman near S. Rafael; passp. in '40. Called 'Wetmarsh' and 'Webmarch,' but I have his autograph.   Whitness (Wm), 1846, sergt Co. K, 1st U.S. dragoons, killed at S. Pascual. v. 346; perhaps his name was 'Whitress;' also called 'Whitehurst.'   Whitney (Francis T.), 1847, Co. B, Morm. Bat. (v. 469).   W. (Wm), 1848, nat. of Engl., who came from Or. to the mines, and went back; died at Butterville, Or., '78.   Whittaker (Robert), 1845, boatswain on the

U.S. *Portsmouth;* owner of a S.F. lot '46. v. 685.   Whittemore, 1810, mr of the *Avon* and *Charon* '10–14; trader and fur-hunter. ii. 96, 267, 282, 328. Whittle, 1846, named as a physician at the Mont. hospital.   W. (W.), 1815 (?), said to be mentioned in a doc. of '35, in the Los Ang. arch., as a resid. for 20 years, doubtless an error. My copy makes the name 'Wittle,' and the time 25 years, perhaps another error.   Whittmer (L. C.), 1847, at Sutter's fort from Sonoma, Sept.   Whitton (1845), one of Frémont's men, who perhaps did not come to Cal. iv. 583.   W. (Ezekiel or Jerry), 1834, Amer. named on Larkin's books at Mont. '34–6. iii. 412.   Whitworth (Wm), 1847, Co. E, Morm. Bat. (v. 469).

Widger (Benj.), 1847, Co. I, N.Y. Vol. (v. 499).   Wierzbicki (Felix P.), 1847, Co. H, ditto; a Polish physician and author; owner of lots and participant in a political meeting at S.F. '47. v. 455. In '48 he sends Gen. Vallejo a copy of his work entitled *The Ideal Man.* He was also the author of *California as It is and as It may be, or A Guide to the Gold Region,* S.F., 1849, 8vo, 60 pp., published in 2 editions by Washington Bartlett (mayor of S.F. as I write, in '85), and the 1st book ever printed in this city. Dr W. died at S. F. in '60.   Wiggins (Wm), 1840, nat. of N.Y., who crossed the plains from Mo. to Or. in '39 and come to Cal. on the *Lausanne,* landing at Bodega and proceeding to Sutter's fort, and thence to Marsh's rancho. iv. 120–1, 136, 173. In '42–4 he was with Graham at Sta Cruz; served in Gantt's comp. to support Micheltorena in '45. iv. 486; is named in the Branciforte padron of '45 as 29 years old and single; went east overland in '46; returned at the head of an immig. party in '47, but taking a cut-off was obliged, after great dangers, to go to Or. v. 556; and came down to Cal. on the *Henry* in '48. He was perhaps the man who is named at Benicia in '48. v. 673; is said to have owned at one time part of the Capitancillos rancho, Sta Clara Co.; lived at S. Juan B. '53–68, and later at Mont., where in '77 he gave me his *Reminiscences.* He died at S. José in '80, at the age of 63. He was called 'doctor,' had no family, and was a man of somewhat eccentric ways.   Wight (David), 1847, carpenter and lumberman at Mont. '47–8.   W. (Randolph H.), 1848, nat. of N.Y., who came from Or. on the *Sterling,* working in the mines, and going east in '49. He came back in '52 to settle in Contra Costa, where he lived in '82 with wife and two daughters.   Wigman (Lewis), 1845, blacksmith and trader at Mont., S.F., and Sutter's fort '45–8, serving also in Fauntleroy's dragoons '48. iv. 578, 587; (v. 232, 247).

Wilber (James H.), 1847, Methodist preacher, touching at S.F. on his way to Or. on the *Whiton,* who organized a Sunday-school at S. F. v. 657. W. (Jacob), 1846, Co. C, 1st U.S. dragoons (v. 336).   Wilbur, 1846, mr of the *Magnet.* v. 579.   W., 1848, in charge of Sutter's launch.   W. (Jeremiah P.), 1846 (?), nat. of Conn.; owner of S. F. lots '48; married in '48 to Amanda Hoit; died at S.F. '64.   Wilcox (Edward), 1847, Co. B, Morm. Bat. (v. 469); nat. of Pa who went to the mines, and in '52–81 was a farmer in Mont. Co.   W. (Frank), 1846, Co. F, Cal. Bat. (v. 358), enlisting at S. Juan Oct.   W. (Henry), 1847, Co. B, Morm. Bat. (v. 469).   W. (James Smith), 1816, Amer. mr of the *Caminante,* or *Traveller,* '16–17, who was suspected of revolutionary designs, and wished to marry Concepcion Argüello. ii. 78, 216–17, 285–7, 291, 310, 362, 365, 382, 389.   W. (Matthew), 1847, Co. C, Morm. Bat. (v. 469).   Wilder (Peter), 1848, voter at S. Diego, and perhaps the P. Wilde of '44 at S.D., hired by Capt. Peterson of the *Admittance* to look for deserters.   Wiley (James), 1848, lieut of marines at Mont.; passp. from Hon.   Wilkes (Charles), 1841, lieut U.S.N. and com. of the U.S. ex. ex., and author of the *Narrative* of that exped., a work that, as far as Cal. is concerned, cannot be very highly praised. iv. 241–8; also iv. 2, 6, 20, 191, 208–9, 214, 227, 434, 569, 665.   W. (E. P.), 1847, owner of S.F. lot.   W. (James), 1846, came to S. José. *Hall;* also J.P.W., named at S. José '47.   W. (John), 1847, Co. K, N.Y. Vol. (v. 499).

Wilkin (David), 1847, sergt Co. C, Morm. Bat. v. 477; at Pioche, Nev., '82.   Wilkins (C. P.), 1848, in Q. M. dept Los Ang.; prob. same as preceding.   W. (Edward), 1847, at Sutter's fort.   Wilkinson, 1848, went from

Mont. to the mines with Colton; said to be a son of a U.S. minister to Russia.
W. (James), 1831, named by Dye and Nidever as one of Young's trappers;
perhaps did not come to Cal. iii. 388.   W. (John), 1845, act. mr of the U.S.
Portsmouth.   Willard, 1843, nat. of Mass. and mate under Capt. Cooper,
who had been naturalized and got a land grant in the Sac. Val. Doubtful
mention by Thomes.   W. (Fannie), 1846 (?), nat. of Mass. Married later to
Alfred Baldwin of Sta Cruz.   W. (Henry or Isaac), 1847, Co, A, N.Y.Vol.
(v. 499); miner in '48–9; farmer and trader in Marin Co. to '56; and later a
farmer in Mendocino, living at Sanel in '80 with wife and 10 children.
Willey (Jeremiah), 1847, Co. A, Morm. Bat. (v. 469).   Willhart (Louis),
1847, Co. C, N.Y.Vol. (v. 499).
        William, 1845, Chinook Ind. of Frémont's party; in Sta B. garrison. v.
316.   Williams, 1846, with Kearny from N. Mex. (v. 337); perhaps Geo. N.
W., 1846, Amer. at S. Luis Ob. v. 639.   W., 1848, arrested at S. José. v.
663.   W. (Aaron W.), 1828, mr of the *Clio*. iii. 146, 165.   W. (Albert),
1840, one of the exiles to S.Blas, who did not return. iv. 14, 18.   W. (Alonzo),
1846, applicant for land at S. José. *Sta Clara Co. Hist.*, 331.   W. (Alex.),
1836, Engl. sailor who landed at Sta B. from a whaler.   W. (B.), 1837, said
to have been one of the party driving cattle to Or. iv. 85.   W. (Baylis),
1846, one of the Donner party from Ill., who died in the Sierra. His half-
sister, Eliza, survived, and in '49 was living at S. José, married, but I do not
know what became of her. v. 530, 533–4.   W. (Benj.), 1847, owner of a S.
F. lot, perhaps at Sutter's fort '48, and on the first jury at S. José '48.   W.
(Charles), 1839, at Mont.; one of the exiles of '40 who did not return. v. 18.
W. (Edward), 1847, lieut of Co. E, N.Y.Vol. v. 504; in '82 a resid. of Oakland.   W. (Elonzo), 1846, came from N. Helv. to S. Juan B. in Jan.; served
in Fauntleroy dragoons (v. 232, 247); prob. same as Alonzo above.   W.
(Geo.), 1829 (?), Engl. sawyer named in Mont. lists of '34, who in '41 claimed a
resid. of 12 years; at S.F. '42, age 39. iii. 179; possibly same as the following.   W. (Geo.), 1832, nat. of Demerara, naturalized in '41, claiming a resid.
of 9 years. iii. 408.   W. (Geo.), 1845, overl. immig., perhaps of the Grigsby-
Ide party. iv. 579; settled at Sta Cruz and served in the Cal. Bat. '46. (v.
358).   W. (Geo. N.), 1846, Co. C, 1st. U.S. dragoons (v. 336).   W. (Henry
E.), 1846, Fauntleroy's dragoons (v. 232, 247).
        Williams (Isaac), 1832, nat. of N.Y. and one of Young's trappers from
N. Mex., where he had lived several years. iii. 388, 408. He settled at Los
Ang. as a trader, though occupied for some years as a hunter; built a house
in '34; aided in '35 in removing the Ind. from S. Nicolás Isl. iii. 361, 652; is
named in lists of '36 as 25, 38, and 50 years of age, obtaining that year a
certificate of residence from the ayunt. and joining the vigilance com. (iii.
430). He was generally known in Cal. as Julian W., often signing in that
way. In '39 he was naturalized, and about this time married María de Jesus,
daughter of Antonio M. Lugo, becoming the owner of the Chino rancho
granted to Lugo in '41, and being himself the grantee of an addition to the
rancho in '43. iv. 634, 117. His house in town was sold to the city govt. In
'46 he proposed to build a fort at the Cajon. v. 37; on the fight at Chino,
when W. was taken prisoner, see v. 312–14. He had a Cal. claim for property
destroyed for $133,000, which was not allowed (v. 462). In '47 he advertised
in the *Californian* for a large no. of men to build an adobe fence round his
rancho; and Col. Coutts says that the men all ran away to the mines in '48
just before the work was completed. He died in '56 at the age of '57, leaving
as heiresses of his large estate two daughters, María Merced, wife of John
Rains, and Francisca, wife of Robert Carlisle. His wife had died in '42, leaving the 2 daughters and apparently a son. Col. Williams was one of the typi-
cal rancheros of southern Cal., enterprising, hospitable, and generally of good
repute.   W. (Isaac), 1843, overl. imming. of the Chiles-Walker party, iv.
393–4, 400, who settled at Sta Cruz and later moved to Los Ang., where he
died about '70.   W. (James), 1843, brother of Isaac and memb. of the same
party. iv. 393–4, 400. He also settled at Sta Cruz as a lumberman and blacksmith, being naturalized in '45, and married by Larkin in Aug. to Mary Pat-

terson. In '46 he killed Henry Naile. v. 641; and is often named in records of '47-8, being a miner in the latter year. In '52 he was cl. for ranchos in Sta Cruz and the Sac. Val. iii. 677; iv. 670; and he died at Sta Cruz in '58 at the age of 45. W. (James V.), 1847, Co. E, Morm. Bat. (v. 469); reënl.; in Utah '82. W. (J. H.), 1848, passp. from Hon. W. (John), 1826, sailor on the *Rover*. W. (John), 1846, doubtful name of an overl. immig. v. 529.

Williams (John S.), 1843, brother of Isaac and James, and overl. immig. of the Chiles party. iv. 393-4, 400. He was a tanner by trade, and I find no original record of his presence till '45, when he is named in the Branciforte padron as 26 years old (Isabel and Esculla Williams living with him—prob. the Cal. rendering of Isaac and Squire!), and is mentioned at Sutter's fort. In Feb. '46 he asked for naturalization, continuing to work for Sutter, but travelling much up and down the valley, visiting Mont. and Sta Cruz, and perhaps serving with the Bears. v. 167. In '47, besides buying lots and building at Benicia, v. 672, he took charge of Larkin's rancho in Colusa, and was married in June to María Louisa, daughter of Joseph Gordon, at Wm Gordon's place on Cache Creek, by Alcalde Ide. I have many of his original letters. He went to the mines in '48; moved to Butte Co. in '49; and died in May of that year. His widow married Lindsay Carson in '50, was one of the cl. for the Arroyo Chico rancho '52, and still lived in Sonoma Co. '80. A son, John S., Jr, was born in Cal. '48, and was also one of the claimants. He went east, and in '70-80 lived in Texas. W. (N. L.), 1848, passp. from Hon. W. (Richard), 1846, sergt Co. C, 1st U.S. dragoons (v. 336), 341. W. (Robert), 1844, doubtful name of a man who came with his family. *Ariz. Hist.*, 268. W. (Squire), 1843, brother of John S. and James. v. 393-4, 400; Co. F, Cal. Bat. (v. 358); died at the Yuba mines '48; yet named as a cl. for Arroyo de la Laguna in '52. iii. 677. W. (S. H.), 1848, of S. H. W. & Co. at S.F. v. 678. W. (Thomas), 1847, sergt Co. D, Morm. Bat. v. 477, 481; perhaps did not come to Cal. W. (Wm), 1838, Engl. sailor who landed at S. Diego. iv. 119; in charge of Capt. Fitch's house '40; sub-Ind. agent at S. Luis Rey '48. v. 621-2; claimant for Valle de las Viejas '52. v. 619. W. (Wm H.), 1847, Co. A, N.Y.Vol. (v. 499); at Nyack, N.Y., '74-84.

Williamson (Benj.), 1846, Co. B, Cal. Bat. (v. 358), enlisting at Mont. Nov. W. (Daniel or David), 1846, Co. F, ditto, enlisting at S. Juan Oct.; at S. José '48; d. in '49. *Swan*. W. (James), 1826, on the *Rover*. W. (J. C.), 1838 (?), nat. of Mass., said to have come via N. Mex. in '38, iv. 119, and, returning, to have started in '41 with his family, killed by Ind. on the way. Then he turned Ind.-fighter; was with Frémont in '46 (?); was a sharpshooter in the war of '61-5; a scout under Custer later; then a hunter in Cal. known as Grizzly Dan; at Oroville '80. *Sac. Union*, July 3, '80. How much truth there may be in all this I do not know. W. (Thomas), 1833, at Mont. '33-4. W. (Thomas D.), 1847, Co. K, N.Y.Vol. (v. 499); at Sta Rosa '71-4; d. before '80. Willie (Henry), 1847, Co. H, ditto.

Willis (Ira), 1847, Co. B, Morm. Bat. (v. 469); later in Sutter's service, and at the Coloma mill when gold was found. W. (Otis W.), 1847, Co. F, N.Y.Vol. (v. 499); at S. Andrés '74. W. (Wm), 1827 (?), Englishman, owning cattle and applying for land at S. José in '28. ii. 595, 605; iii. 178. In '30 Wm With got permission to keep cattle at Mt Diablo. ii. 602. As Wilk and Villa he is named in '34, age 31, with wife and 3 children. In '41 Guillermo Wil is named in the S. José padron as an Amer., age 46, wife María Ant. Galindo, child. Guillermo b. '33, Concepcion '28, and Anastasio '30. There is also a Julian Wil named as a militiaman of S.F. in '37. There is a strange lack of definite information about this Wm Willis. W. (W. S. S.), 1847, known as Sidney W.; Co. B, Morm. Bat. (v. 469); in Sutter's employ '47-8, and at the Coloma mill when gold was discovered. Wilmot (James), 1845, perhaps overl. immig. of the Grigsby-Ide party. iv. 579; named at Sutter's fort '46. W. (Lewis), 1846, Cal. Bat. (v. 358); also Lewis A. W., sailor on the *Elizabeth* '48. Wilmoth (Geo.), 1845, boatswain on the U.S. *Savannah*. Wilson, 1845, in Sutter's employ; went east with Clyman in '46. v. 526. W., 1847, at S.F. from Hon., with wife and 2 children, on the *Julia*.   W., 1847, owner of land at Benicia.   W., 1848, at S.F. from Tahiti.   W., 1848, of Hood & W., carpenters at S.F. v. 684. W. (A.), 1824, sailor on the *Rover*.   W. (Alfred G.), 1847, Co. A, Morm. Bat. (v. 469); at Moab, Utah, '81.   W. (Amariah), 1847, owner of S.F. lots. W. (Alvin), 1840, nat. of Conn., who landed from Capt. Hinckley's vessel and became a lumberman in the Sta Cruz district. He was arrested with the other foreigners, but not exiled; and in '42 signed an appeal to the U.S. govt. He was killed by Ind. near Gilroy in July '44.   W. (B.), 1848, at Hon. from S.F., on the *Julian*.

Wilson (Benj. Davis), 1841, known in Cal. as Benito, nat. of Tenn., and immig. of the Workman party from N. Mex., where he had resided for 8 years as trapper and trader. iv. 277-9. In '43 he purchased the Jurupa rancho, iv. 635, and from this frontier station in the following years engaged in several campaigns against hostile Indians. In '45 he was prominent among the southern foreigners who served against Micheltorena. iv. 495, 504, 506-7. In '46 he acted as juez for the district ranchos; commanded a comp. of citizen riflemen intended to resist Castro; was in com. of the foreigners at the Chino fight; and after the U.S. occupation served as lieut in the Cal. Bat. v. 50-1, 265, 312-14, 360, 625. He was the 1st county clerk and 1st mayor of Los Ang.; Ind. agent in '52, taking pride in having been the 1st to urge the settling of the Ind. on reservations at the old missions; cl. for S. José de Buenos Aires rancho. iv. 635; and was state senator for two terms. Don Benito was a prosperous ranchero and fruit-raiser, an influential and respected citizen. In '77 he dictated for my use his *Observations* on early Cal. events, a MS. of considerable value, though on some points I have found Wilson's testimony less accurate than I had deemed it at first. I notice that a copy, left with the family at their request, has been consulted by some of the county history and newspaper men. W. died at his rancho of Lake Vineyard in '78, at the age of 67, leaving a widow—a 2d wife, the 1st having been Ramona, daughter of Bernardo Yorba, married in '44—and 3 daughters.   W. (Charles), 1848, carpenter at S.F.   W. (Dorsey), 1847, owner of S.F. lot.   W. (Henry), 1847, purser on the U.S. *Preble*.   W. (Henry J.), 1847, sergt Co. D, N.Y. Vol. v. 504.   W. (James), 1824, Engl. trader at Mont.; age 25 in '29; also at Mont. '30-3. ii. 609.   W. (James), 1844 (?), Engl. soldier, veteran of Waterloo, said to have come to Sta Clara and to have died in '70. v. 453. W. (James), 1847, Co. A, N.Y.Vol. (v. 499).

Wilson (John), 1826, Scotch shipmaster and trader on the roll of the Soc. Cal. Pion. as having arrived in April '26, and who in '37 claimed a residence of 12 years; the 1st original record being '28, when he was master of the *Thos Nowlan*. iii. 149. In '31-7 he was mr of the *Ayacucho;* of the *Index* '38-9, '41-3; of the *Fly* '40; of the *Juanita* in '44-5. iii. 381; iv. 101, 104, 566. Before '36 he married Ramona Carrillo de Pacheco, and from that time considered Sta B. his home; naturalized in '37, and from '39 to '47 a partner of James Scott; about '41 engaged in otter-hunting. In '45 Capt. W. took some part in the troubles with Micheltorena. iv. 498; and with Scott was the purchaser of the S. Luis Ob. estate, and grantee of the ranchos Cañada del Chorro and Cañada de los Osos, where he spent the rest of his life. iv. 553, 655, 658-9; v. 375, 558, 566. He died in '60 at the age of 65, leaving a widow, still living in '85, a son John who settled in England, and a daughter. There were few of the old pioneers better known or more respected than Capt. John Wilson.   W. (John), 1826, Amer. trapper, apparently of Jed. Smith's party. iii. 155, 190, 176. Ment. in '27-30; on Larkin's books '38-9; in '41 permitted to marry María F. Mendoza of S. Cárlos.   W. (John), 1837, grantee of Guilicos rancho, Sonoma, for which he was cl. in 53. iii. 712; iv. 118; ment. at Sonoma '43.   W. (John), 1841, deserter from the U.S. Ex. Ex. at N. Helv. July.   W. (John), 1844, owner of a lighter on S.F. bay; perhaps John of '37, or the captain.   W. (John), 1847, wounded at the S. Gabriel fight. v. 395; prob. Joseph.   W. (John), 1847, Co. D, N.Y. Vol. (v. 499); perhaps at Stockton '48-9.   W. (J. B.), 1847, carpenter at Mont. '47-8; perhaps the initials were E. B. or O. B.   W. (John E.), 1846, on roll of Soc. Cal.

Pion.; nat. of Sweden; d. at S.F. '77, age 63.   W. (John Henry), 1826, negro who landed from a whaler, and was still at Los Ang. '29 and '37. iii. 196. W. (John K.), 1845, mid. on the U.S. *Savannah* '45-7; lieut, and later capt., of the artill. comp. of the Cal. Bat. v. 361, 434, 446; in '48 a witness at Wash. on the Cal. claims.   W. (J. T.), 1847, owner of a S.F. lot.

Wilson (Joseph), 1845, asst-surg. on the U.S. *Savannah* '45-7.   W. (Joseph), 1846, seaman wounded at the S. Gabriel fight '47.   W. (Joseph), 1847, purser on the U.S. *Lexington.*   W. (Julian), 1828, partner of Exter in a trapping project. iii. 172-3, 178; named in the Branciforte padron of '28, wife Josefa Arbito (?), child María. ii. 627.   W. (Lorenzo), 1830 (?), brother of Julian, said by Vallejo to have had personal encounters with Pliego and José Castro.   W. (Mariano), 1846, had a Cal. claim (v. 462).   W. (Oliver C.), 1846, Co. C, 1st U.S. dragoons (v. 336).   W. (Robert), 1847, Co. G, N.Y. Vol. (v. 499); at Vallejo '82.   W. (Thomas), 1832, at Purísima, a farmer.   W. (Thomas A.), 1848, overl. immig., son of Wm D., settler in S. Joaquin Co., where he still lived with a family in '84.   W. (Wm), 1822, Amer. carpenter at Mont. '29, aged 27, married; also at Mont. '34. ii. 478. There way be some confusion between him and Wm 'Willis,' q. v.   W. (Wm), 1847, at S.F. from Tahiti.   W. (Wm C.), 1845 (?), nat. of Tenn. said to have come from Sonora this year; a well-known horseman who died at S. José '82, leaving a widow and son. iv. 587.   W. (Wm D.), 1848, nat. of Ky and overl. immig. who settled on the Cosumnes, where he built a wire bridge. He was rich at one time, but lost his fortune by floods and other misfortunes. He died near Gilroy in '75 at the age of 65, leaving a widow and son.   Wilt (John), 1847, sergt Co. B, N.Y. Vol. v. 504; d. before '82.

Wimmer (Peter L.) 1846, nat. of Ohio and overl. immig. with his wife, Elizabeth J. Bays. He may have served in the Cal. Bat. (v. 358); and in '47 was owner of a S.F. lot. v. 685. He worked for Sutter as a millwright in '47-8, and was one of the men employed at the Coloma mill when gold was discovered, being perhaps with Marshall on the eventful morning when 'they' picked up the 1st nugget. At any rate, Mrs W., ranking as cook and laundress of the camp, tested that nugget by boiling it in her soap-kettle, and still claimed to have it in her possession in '85. After the discovery the family kept a boarding-house, having also a choice assortment of pigs. A child was born in Aug. '48; in '49 W. went to Calaveras; in '55 he had 10 children. In '78-85 be resided in Southern Cal.   W. (John M.), 1847 (?), perhaps a brother of Peter, teamster at N. Helv. and Coloma '47-8. G. W. and family are also ment. in the *N. Nelv. Diary;* prob. error.

Winckley (J. F.), 1848, passp. from Hon.   Winders (John), 1847, nat. of Va; d. at Stockton '72, age 67.   Windmeyer (Richard), 1847, Co. F, N.Y. Vol. (v. 499).   Wing, 1847, mr of the *Obed Mitchell.* v. 579; on the *Sagadahoc* '48.   Winkley, 1847, at S.F. from Or. on the *Henry;* at Benicia. Winkworth (Wm), 1836, mr of the *Europa* '36-7. iv. 103.   Winn (Dennis), 1847, Co. A, Morm. Bat. (v. 469); laborer at Mont. '48; at Richmond, Utah, '81.   Winner (Geo. K.), 1846, one of the Mormon colony, with wife and 6 children. v. 547; owner of S.F. lot '47. v. 679.   Winnie (James), 1847, sergt Co. H, N.Y. Vol. v. 504; sergt of S. José guard '48; d. before '82. W. (Wm), 1847, Co. E, N.Y. Vol. (v. 499); carpenter and miner in Calaveras Co. '48-56; at Portland, Or., to '74, and at Oakland, Cal., to '85.   Winship, 1848, trader in the mines and at S.F.   W. (Charles), 1850, mr of the *Betsey.* i. 546, 656.   W. (Jonathan), 1806, mr of the *O'Cain;* a famous trader and smuggler on the coast 1806-12. ii. 25, 39-40, 78-9, 82, 84-5, 92-4, 267, 633. W. (Nathan), 1806, brother of Jonathan, mate of the *O'Cain;* mr of the *Albatross* 1807-12. ii. 39, 82, 84, 92-5, 148, 199, 267, 296.   Winslow, 1848, from Hon. on the *Sagadahoc.*   Winter (Jacob), 1847, Co. B, Morm. Bat. (v. 469); reënl.   W. (John D.), 1848, hotel-keeper at Coloma, of firm W. & Cromwell, owning an interest in Sutter's mill; later a resid. of S. Joaquin.   W. (Wm H.), 1843 (?), nat. of Ind. and overl. immig. of the Walker-Chiles party. iv. 393-4, 400; or possibly came to Or. '43 and to Cal. '44. He is said to have gone east in '45 and returned in '49, but is named in N. Helv. in '47.   He made other trips east, but in '53 settled in Cal. with his family, living in Colusa and Lake to '55, in Napa to '71, and in Shasta until his death in '79 at the age of 60, leaving 5 sons, one of them a lawyer at Napa.   W., 1843, mr of the whaler *Ana Maria. Peterson.*

Wise (Henry A.), 1847, lieut on the U.S. *Independence*, and author of *Los Gringos*, pub. in N.Y. '49, in which his experience is described. v. 100. I have also some MS. *Notes on Cal.* by him, but cannot say how or when they were obtained.   W. (Marion), 1845, apparently one of Frémont's men. iv. 583; at N. Helv. '46, and perhaps one of the Bears. v. 110, 128, 453; a witness at Wash. in Feb. '48. He perished in Frémont's exped. of '48-9.   Wismon (John), 1846, in Hittell's list.   Wisner (Geo.), 1845, carpenter on the U.S. *Portsmouth* '45-7; owner of a S.F. lot. v. 683.   Wissell (Fred.), 1847, Co. H, N.Y. Vol. (v. 499).   Wiswell (James), 1846, a doctor who became rich and went east. *Hittell.*   Withrell (Adolphus), 1846, sailor on the *Dale.* Wittam (Isaac), 1847, Co. I, N.Y. Vol. (v. 499).   Wittmer (Jacob), 1847, Swiss in Sutter's employ '47-8, often named in the *N. Helv. Diary.* On Feb. 14, '48, he arrived at the fort with glowing reports from the gold mines.   Witmarsh (Benj. H.), 1845, Amer. at Mont.   Wittengstein (David), 1847, Co. F, 3d U.S. artill. (v. 518).

Wodwarck, 1815, mr of the *Lady.* ii. 307.   Wohler (Herman), 1848, German who married a daughter of Capt. Cooper, and was a member of the legislature of '55. He lived on Mark West Creek, and later at Sonoma, where he had a vineyard. An accomplished musician, famous as an entertainer. He died in '77.   Vohlgemouth (Henry J.), 1847, Co. E, N.Y. Vol. (v. 499); at S.F. '82.   Wolcott (?), d. at Hon. '50; said to have lived 5 years in Cal.; prob. 'Walcott.'   Wolfe (James), 1826, mate of the *Blossom* '26-7. iii. 121.   W. (John), 1847, Co. D, N.Y. Vol. (v. 499); trader at Mont., Stockton, and in the mines; in N.Y. '71-82.   Wolfinger, 1846, German of the Donner party, who died before reaching the Sierra. His wife survived and was married in '47 at Sutter's fort to Geo. Zinns. v. 531-2, 534.

Wolfskill (John R.), 1838, nat. of Ky, who came from N. Mex., after some years residence in Mex. iv. 117, 119. After working for several years for his brother Wm in the south, he came north in '42 and settled on a rancho on Putah Creek—granted to Francisco Guerrero and owned by Wm Wolfskill. Here he has lived down to '85, his name rarely appearing in any early records that I have seen, possibly serving with the Bears and Cal. Bat., but not tempted away from his rancho and cattle by the gold excitement of '48-9. In the later years he has been one of the best known fruit-growers of Yolo and Solano, a man of wealth, and a citizen of the most excellent reputation, now 81 years of age. Portrait in *Yolo Co. Hist.*, 26. By his first wife, whose name I have not found, he had a son, Edward, who in later years was his business manager. In '58 he married Susan, daughter of Stephen Cooper, by whom he had 3 daughters living in '80. I have a brief *Biog. Sketch* of 'Uncle John,' taken by G. W. Boggs in '83.   W. (Sarchel), 1838(?), nat. of Mo., brother of John R., who may have come from N. Mex. '38-41; in Solano Co. '80. W. (Wm), 1831, brother of John R., nat. of Ky, and for several years a trapper and trader in N. Mex., coming to Cal. in com. of a trapping party by a new route. iii. 386, 405, 630; iv. 263-4. He had been naturalized in N. Mex. '30; and in Cal. for several years was engaged in hunting otter on the coast, building a schooner for that purpose. iii. 363, 393. In '36 he settled at Los Ang. as a carpenter, getting a lot, being named as one of the vigilantes, giving much attention to the raising of vines, and from '38 devoting himself wholly to the vineyards which were to make him rich and famous. iv. 117. He married in '41; in '42 became the owner of the Putah Creek rancho occupied from that time by his brother. iv. 673; in '44 was regidor at Los Ang. iv. 633; and is hardly mentioned in the political troubles of '45-7 or in public matters of later years. He died in '66 at the age of 68, leaving an enviable reputation as an honest, enterprising, generous, unassuming, intelligent man. He and Louis Vignes may be regarded as the pioneers of California's greatest industry, the production of wine and fruit. His wife Magdalena, daughter of

José Ign. Lugo, died in '62; a daughter Juana, Mrs Henry D. Barrows, died in '63, and another daughter in '55. The surviving children and heirs of his large estate were Joseph W. born in '44, Luis, Madelina (wife of Matias Sabici), and Francisca, apparently Mrs Cardwell. Wm had 3 brothers, perhaps including Sarchel, who came after '48.   Wolter (Charles), 1833, German mr of a Mex. vessel, who in Dec. obtained a certificate of Mex. citizenship, having been for 2 years a citizen of Peru. iii. 409. It is not unlikely that he visited Cal. before '33. He was mr of the *Leonor* '36–8, of the *Clara* or *Clarita* '40–3, of the *Julia* '44–5, and of *El Placer* '48. iii. 383; iv. 102, 104, 403, 563–4; v. 577. Capt. Wolter married an Estrada, settled at Mont., and was cl. for the Toro rancho. iii. 679. He died in '56 at the age of 65.

Wood, 1841, with Douglas. iv. 212; named at Sutter's fort.   W. 1846, at Sutter's fort from Or. in June. v. 526.   W., 1846, mr of the *Pandora*. v. 579.   W., 1847, juryman and constable at Sutter's fort. v. 542.   W., 1848, in the mines; discov. of Wood Creek; perhaps the man who came from Or. with Capt. Martin, and was killed by Ind.   W., 1848, builder at Benicia. v. 673.   W. (Geo.), 1831, mr of the *Louisa*. iii. 383.   W. (Geo. T.), 1844, deserter from the U.S. *Warren* at S.F., who lived among the Ind. of Marin Co. near Tomales, where Wood Point bears his name. iv. 453. The ex-sailor became an expert horseman, widely known as Tom Vaquero. He died at S. Rafael in '79.   W. (Henry), 1833, Amer. named in Larkin's books '33–7, known as the 'deacon.' iii. 409; in the Or. cattle party of '37. iv. 85; served in Cal. Bat. '46 (v. 358), and had a Cal. claim of $30 (v. 462); owner of S.F. lot '47; a carpenter at S.F. '51–4; perhaps several different men.   W. (John), 1847, Co. I, N.Y.Vol. (v. 499); at Hanford, Tulare Co., '82.   W. (Joseph), 1845, overl. immig. of the Grigsby-Ide party, who probably returned east in '46. iv. 579; but may have been one of the Woods named at Sutter's fort at the beginning of this paragraph.   W. (O. R.), 1848, at Hon. from Mont.; seems to have married a daughter of W. H. Merrill at S.F.   W. (Paul D.), 1846, Co. C, 1st U. S. dragoons (v. 336).   W. (Wm), 1840, sup. of the *Columbia* '40–1. iv. 102–3, 564.   W. (Wm), 1846, Co. E, Cal. Bat., enlisting at Sutter's fort Oct. (v. 358).   W. (Wm), 1847, Co. C, Morm. Bat. (v. 469). W. (Wm A.), 1847, Co. F, 3d U.S. artill. (v. 518).   W. (Wm Maxwell), 1844, fleet-surgeon of the Pacific squadron U.S.N. '44–6, who, on his way overland across Mex. in '46, sent to Com. Sloat at Mazatlan news of the outbreak of war. He published a narrative of his adventures under the title of *Wandering Sketches*. iv. 452–3, 460, 479, 661.

Woodard (John), 1832, witness at Mont.   Wooden (John), 1843, doubtful name of the Chiles-Walker immig. party. iv. 393–4.   Woodruff (Wilford), 1848, Mormon, and one of the discov. of gold at Mormon Isl.; perhaps 'Wilford.'   Woods (Henry), 1838, in Sta Clara; perhaps 'Wood.'   W. (Isaiah C.), 1848, nat. of Me, who came as sup. of a trader, and from '49 was prominent as manager of Adams & Co.'s express and banking business. He went east after the failure of that comp. in '55; among other enterprises established an overland mail from Texas to S. Diego; served as commissary of transportation in the war of '61–5; and returned to Cal. about '68. He died in '80, leaving a widow and 3 children.   W. (John), 1848, at Sta Cruz '81.   Woodside (Preston K.), 1847, Co. D, N.Y.Vol. (v. 499); clerk of the naval agency at Mont. '48; later clerk of supreme court. In '81 at Tucson, Ariz.   Woodward (E.), 1840, steward of the schr *California*.   W. (Francis), 1847, Co. C, Morm. Bat. (v. 469).   Woodworth, 1847, a Mormon in Sutter's employ '47–8, teaming between the fort and mill.   W. (John), 1834, Engl. at Mont. '34–5.

Woodworth (Selim E.), 1847, nat. of N.Y., and lieut U.S.N., who came overland to Or. in '46, and to Cal. in the winter of '46–7, taking some part in an exped. for the relief of the Donner party. v. 539; owning S.F. lots, joining the *Warren*, and in '48 acting as mr of the transport *Anita*. v. 576. In '49 he resigned his commission, engaged in trade in comp. with P. A. Roach, and was a member of the 1st state senate. Later he became a business man at S. F., being prominent in the vigilance com. of '51. In the war of '61–5 he rejoined the navy, reaching the rank of commodore, resigning about '67, and residing for the most part at S.F., where he died in '71, at the age of 55, leaving a widow and 5 children. Portrait in *Annals of S.F.*   Woolard (Henry), 1847, Co. K, N.Y.Vol. (v. 499); 58 lashes and a month in jail at S. José '48 for attempted murder.   Wooldridge, 1846, com. of the *Spy.* v. 580. Wooley (Wm), 1847, Co. A, N. Y. Vol. (v. 499); at Campo Seco '71–82. Wooster (Charles W.), 1847, nat. of N.Y., who came as sup. of the *Confederacion*, having been admiral in the Chilean navy. He presided at the 1st thanksgiving dinner at S.F. '47, being owner of lots here and at Benicia. v. 646, 672, 678. Partner of Ward and Fourgeaud in the Yuba mines; dying at Hock farm Aug. '48.

Worden (John L.), 1847, lieut on the *Southampton.*   W. (Stephen), 1844, doubtful name of an Amer. at S.F., age 25.   Work (John), 1833, a trapper applying for supplies. iii. 392.   Workman (Andrew J.), 1847, Co. B, Morm. Bat. (v. 469); at Virgin City, Utah, '82.   W., 1809, doubtful record of a hunter. ii. 89.   W. (Oliver G.), 1847, Co. B, Morm. Bat. (v. 469); reënl.; at Salt Lake City '82.   W. (Wm), 1841, nat. of England, who came from N. Mex. in com. of an immig. party with his family. iv. 276–9, 637. He had long been a trader at Taos, and at the time of his coming to Cal. was somewhat compromised in the eyes of the Mex. govt by his supposed connection with Texan political or revolutionary schemes. He obtained, with John Roland, the Puente rancho, confirmed in '45. iv. 331, 635; was a leader of the foreigners against Micheltorena in '45. iv. 495, 505; took some part in '46–7 in the direction of preventing warfare. v. 50–1, 332–3, 387, 396; and was the purchaser of S. Gabriel mission. v. 561, 627–9. In '52 he was cl. for the Cajon de los Negros and La Puente ranchos. From about '68 he was a banker in company with Temple at Los Ang., and in '76, on the failure of the bank, he committed suicide, at the age of 76. I know nothing of his family, except that a brother David died at La Puente in '55.   Wort (Geo.), 1847, Co. G, N.Y.Vol. (v. 499); d. at S.F. '47.   Worth (Caroline), 1848, nat. of Ind., resid. of Sonoma Co. '74–7.

Wrangell (Baron F. von), 1833, gov. of the Russian colonies in Alaska, at Ross in '33, and at Mont '35 on his way to Mex. iv. 160–9. See also *Hist. Alaska.*   Wright, 1845, doubtful member of the Grigsby-Ide party. iv. 579. W., 1847, had a hospital on Cooper St., Mont.   W., 1848, from Hon. on the *Sagadahoc.*   W., 1848, at Sta Cruz, buying C. C. Smith's interest in a store, which was perhaps in the mines.   W., 1848, partner of Dav. Ray in the Yuba mines.   W., 1848, of W. & Owen, liquor dealers at S.F.   W. (Chas), 1847, Co. B, Morm. Bat. (v. 469).   W. (David), 1847, carpenter at Mont.; cl. in '52 for Roblar de la Miseria rancho. iv. 673.   W. (Harry), 1846, Co. G, Cal. Bat., enlisting at S. José Nov. (v. 358).   W. (J.), 1840, passenger on the *Lausanne* perhaps, who went to Hon. iv. 104, 121.   W. (Jonathan), 1846, at Mont. '74, said by McPherson to have come this year.   W. (J. H.), 1848, passp. from Hon.   W. (Phineas R.), 1847, sergt Co. A, Morm. Bat. v. 477.   W. (Stephen A.), 1847, prob. overl. immig., perhaps of '46; at Mont. '47–8, of W. & Dickenson, lumber dealers; owner of S.F. lot '49. v. 685; and member of S.F. council '49; later a banker who failed and went to Ariz. before '60.   W. (Tiery), 1844 (?), perhaps one of Frémont's men. iv. 437.

Wümsen (John), 1823, appears as a witness at Sta B.; prob. a sailor. ii. 495.   Wunderlich (F. H.), 1848 (?), biog. in *Eureka Humboldt Times*, June 25, '79.   Wybourn (Robert), 1847, Co. I, N. Y.Vol. (v. 499); in Calaveras '71–4.   Wylie (John), 1847, Co. E, ditto.   Wylis (Richard), 1845, doubtful name of an overl. immig. iv. 578.   Wyman (Gardner), 1847, at Mont. '47–8. W. (Geo. F.), 1844 (?), sent by Sutter to raise recruits for the Micheltorena campaign in Dec. iv. 453, 486, 501; often named in the *N. Helv. Diary* '45–8; His wife, ment. in '47, was America, daughter of David Kelsey, still living in '85. In '78–84 W. was living at Spanishtown, S. Mateo Co., and in newspaper sketches and county histories is said to have left a whaler in '36.   W. (T.W.), 1847, capt. on the U.S. *Columbus.* v. 577.

Yame (Blas), 1806, sailor on the *Peacock.* ii. 38.   Yanonalit, Ind. chief at Sta B. 1782. i. 377.   Yard (Edward M.), 1846, lieut on the U.S. *Dale;*

at Trenton, N.J., '78.　　Yarnall (Mordecai), 1847, prof. of mathematics on the *Columbus.*　　Yates (John), 1842, Engl. sailor who came from Mazatlan and was employed by Sutter as mr of his launch. iv. 229, 341. In '43 he was in some trouble at Sonoma, Sutter furnishing bail; in Nov. '44 his launch was wrecked at Ross; he is named in the *N. Helv. Diary* '45-7, and seems to have been the owner of land in the Chico region '46-7, having also a Cal. claim of $50 (v. 462). In '51 he went to the Sandwich Isl., where he was living in '72, in which year he sent me his *Sketch of a Journey to the Sacramento Valley in '42,* including a narrative of earlier adventures. It is a most interesting and useful MS., though there are indications that the valley trip may have been antedated by a year or two.　　Y. (John D.), 1847, Co. H, N.Y.Vol. (v. 499); in '82 at Albany, N.Y.; a printer.　　Ybarra, etc., see 'Ibarra,' etc.

　　Yeamans (Edward), 1847, Co. E, N. Y. Vol. (v. 499).　　Yellow Serpent, Or. Ind. at Sutter's fort '44-6. v. 300-2.　　Yems, 1817, sailor at Sta B., doubtful name. ii. 286.　　Yergeens (Fred.), 1847, Co. F, 3d U. S. artill. (v. 518); living in '64.　　Yetch (August), 1847, perhaps of N. Y. Vol. under another name.　　Yim (James), 1828, Amer. pilot at Mont. '28-9, age 23; name doubtful; prob. 'Jim.'　　Yndarte (J. D.), 1845, mr of the *Farici.* iv. 565.　　Ynitia (Camilo), grantee of Olompali '43.　　Yonkins (Wm), 1847, Co. F, 3d U. S. artill. (v. 528); in the S. José hospital '64, suffering from an incurable cancer.

　　Yorba (Antonio), 1769, one of Fages' original Catalan volunteers; in 1777 corp. of the S. F. comp.; in 1782 corp. of the Mont. comp.; and in 1789 of the S. Diego comp. In 1797 he was retired as inválido sergt; and in 1809-10 grantee of the Santiago de Sta Ana rancho, Los Ang., which he or a son of the same name occupied down to '30, and the family later. i. 647, 663; ii. 104, 112, 172, 353, 565, 664; iii. 634. His wife, from 1782, was María Josefa, daughter of Alférez Grijalva; and the children named in early years were Isabel María, Cecilia, Raimunda (who married J. B. Alvarado), Francisca, and José Domingo who died in 1796.　　Y. (Bernardo), son of Antonio, age 35 in '39, aux. alcalde or juez de campo at St Ana '33, '36, '40, '44. iii. 635-7; iv. 633; grantee of Cañada de Sta Ana '34 and of Sierra '46. iii. 633; v. 628. His daughter Ramona married B. D. Wilson.　　Y. (Isabel), grantee of Guadalasca '46, and cl. in '52. iii. 655.　　Y. (José Ant.), son of Antonio, age 27 in '39; aux. alcalde and juez de campo at Sta Ana Abajo '36, '40. iii. 636-7; in '41 at S. Juan Cap. iv. 626, 628; in '47 regidor at Los Ang. v. 626. Y. (José Domingo), son of José Ant., b. at S. Diego 1795; cl. of S. Vicente Cañada '52. v. 629.　　Y. (Ramon), cl. for Las Bolsas '52. iii. 633.　　Y. (Teodosio), son of José Ant., age 22 in '39, aux. alcalde at Sta Ana '36 and '47. iii. 636; v. 626; a prisoner in '38. iii. 554-5; grantee of Arroyo Seco '40. iii. 711; at S. Juan Cap. '41. iv. 626; grantee of Lomas de Santiago '46. v. 627.　　Y. (Tomás Ant.), son of José Ant., age 55 in '39, supl. of the diputacion '30, '32. iii. 50, 216-18; aux. alcalde at Sta Ana '31-2, '35. iii. 635; ment. in '39, '40, '43. iii. 589, 629, 637.

　　Yorgens (Joseph), 1828, Amer. trapper of Pattie's party. iii. 163, 168; age 24 in '29. Either Y. and Ferguson were the same, or one of them could not have belonged to this party.　　York, 1834, Engl. sailor, age 23, in a Mont. list.　　Y. (John), 1845, nat. of Tenn. and overl. immig. of the Grigsby-Ide party, with his wife Lucinda Hudson and 2 sons, Wm E. and David, the latter being apparently born on the trip. iv. 579, 587. He settled at the head of Napa Valley; was at Sonoma during the Bear revolt; went to the mines in '48-9; and in '49-82 lived on his farm in Napa. There were 9 surviving children in '82, including those named above. Portrait in *Napa Co. Hist.,* 62. Y. (Wm), 1846, Co. F, Cal. Bat. v. 358; at S. José '48-50.

　　Young, 1833, at S. Diego '33-4, in Ebbetts' service, called capt.　　Y., 1647, mr of the *Com. Stockton,* at S.F. and Bodega. v. 577.　　Y. (Alpheus), 1847, Co. D, N.Y.Vol. (v. 499); at S.F. '82.　　Y. (Charles B.), 1847, lieut Co. A, ditto. v. 503.　　Y. (Chas D.), 1847, musician, ditto.　　Y. (Ewing), 1830, capt. of trappers, who came to Cal. from N. Mex., and again in '31-2, going to Or. in '34, returning in '37, to purchase cattle, and dying in Or. '41. ii. 600; iii. 174-5, 180, 357, 387-8, 393-4, 410, 630; iv. 85-7, 263-4; see also

Hist. Or., i. 90 et seq.   Y. (Francis), 1837, lumberman in the Mont. dist. '37-44. iv. 118. He failed in business '44; and nothing more is known of him unless he was with Ford at Olompali '46. v. 166.   Y. (John), 1844, on roll of Soc. Cal. Pion.; nat. of Scotland, and nephew of Capt. John Wilson; perhaps did not come from Valparaíso till '45. He was a trader and mr of vessels on the coast; and later superintendent of the N. Almaden mine. Died at S.F. '64.   Y. (Jonathan), 1847, mid. on the *Columbus*.   Y. (J. E.), 1848, miner at Mormon Isl., etc.; later a farmer in Placer Co. to '68.   Y. (Lewis or Levi), 1833, mr of the *Enriqueta*. iii. 382.   Y. (Nathan), 1847, of Morm. Bat. (v. 469); reënl. at Los Ang.   Y. (Romº), Mex. citizen at N. Helv.   Y. (Sam. C.), 1846, nat. of Tenn., and overl. immig. with his family. v. 528-30. He settled as a farmer at Sta Clara, where he died in '78, leaving 3 sons—Leander C., who died in '82, M. D., at S. José '81, and R. J., ditto.

Yount (George C.), 1831, nat. of N.C. who came as a trapper in Wolfskill's party from N. Mex. iii. 386, 405, 166, 363. For several years he hunted otter chiefly on S.F. bay and its tributaries, also making shingles at odd jobs. His name appears on Larkin's books in '33. In '35 he was baptized at S. Rafael as Jorge Concepcion, and worked for Vallejo at Sonoma. In '36 he obtained a grant of the Caymus rancho in Napa Valley, where he built a cabin, or block-house, and for years was the only representative of the gente de razon in the valley. iii. 711; iv. 117. He still spent much of his time in hunting, and had many encounters with the Ind., though by his long experience with the natives, his fearless character, and by his tact in forming alliances with the strongest rancherías, he managed to keep all under good control. In '43 he was grantee of the La Jota rancho, an extension of Caymus, iv. 671, where he soon built a saw-mill, having also a flour-mill on his place; and the same year he was joined by two daughters who came overland with Chiles, the latter having in his visit of '41 brought news from the family and been commissioned to bring them. iv. 393. In several of the old trapper's experiences, as related by him and embellished by others, a trace of faith in dreams and omens is shown; but the oft-repeated story that a dream of his led to the relief of the Donner party has no foundation in fact. In later years the old pioneer found the squatters and land-lawyers somewhat more formidable foes than had been the Ind. and grizzlies of earlier times; but he saved a portion of his land, and died at his Napa home—called Yountville in his honor—in '65 at the age of 71. Portraits in *Hesperian*, ii.; *Napa Co. Hist.*, 54; *Menefee's Sketch-book*, 160.   Y. (Lot G.), 1844, ranchero named in Larkin's papers; prob. error for Geo. C.   Youin (Juan), 1846, owner of S.F. lot. v. 684.

Zabriskie (Jerome), 1847, Co. B, Morm. Bat. (v. 469); reënl.; in Utah '82. Zaldíbar (Pedro), 1818, deserter from Bouchard's insurgents. ii. 241.   Zalvidea (José María), 1805, Span. friar whose missionary service was chiefly at S. Gabriel and S. Juan Cap. He died at S. Luis Rey in '46. Biog. v. 620-1; ment. ii. 48-50, 109, 114-15, 159-60, 352, 355-6, 394, 555, 567-8, 655; iii. 91, 96, 102, 317, 358, 625, 627; iv. 371, 422, 622-4.   Zamora (Ignacio), soldier at the Colorado pueblos 1780-1; killed by Ind. i. 359, 362.   Z. (Juan), capt. appointed for Cal.; did not come. iii. 54.   Z. (Manuel), Mex. soldier of the Hidalgo piquete at Mont. '30, age 26.   Z. (Nicanor), supl. com. de policía at Mont. '36. iii. 675.   Zamorano (Agustin Vicente), 1825, Mex. alférez who came with Echeandía; nat. of Florida, of Spanish parentage; capt. of the Mont. comp. from '31, and of the S. Diego comp. from '35. He left Cal. in '38, but returned in '42 as lieut-col, and died in that year at S. Diego. He is named in the Mont. padron of '36 as 36 years old, wife Luisa Argüello, child. Dolores b. '27 (married J. M. Flores), Luis '29, Gonzalo '32, Guadalupe '33 (married Henry Dalton), Josefa '34, and Agustin '36. An Eulalia is also named by Hayes as having married Vicente Estudillo. Of the sons I have no record. Biog. of the capt. iii. 559-61; ment. ii. 543-4, 549, 608, 669, 676; iii. 13-14, 33, 44, 47, 50, 61-2, 81, 84, 91, 99, 102, 205, 214, 220-32, 239, 243, 347, 364, 441, 445, 463, 515-20, 533, 549, 556, 568-9, 608, 614, 669-71; iv. 68, 290, 408, 619; v. 365.   Zampay, chief of the Yolo Ind. '36. iv. 72.

Zarembo (Dionisio), 1827, mr of the *Okhotsk* '27–9. iii. 148; and of the *Urup* '31–2. iii. 213, 384; again in Cal.' 45 as Russian agent. iv. 187–8. Zavaleta (Aniceto María), Mex. artilleryman at S. Diego '21 and earlier, a somewhat unmanageable fellow, though a good soldier. He became sergt, and about '28 was retired as teniente de premio; serious charges against him in '31; had much trouble in collecting his pay in later years; sec. of the ayunt. at S. D. '41. iv. 619; ment. in '45. iv. 508.   Zavalishin (W.), 1824, Russ. agent who visited Cal.; author of a work on the Russ. colony, *Delo o Koloniy Ross.* ii. 641, 647.   Zeballos (Areaco), 1791, Span. lieut in Malaspina's exped. i. 490.   Zeilin (Jacob), 1846, lieut of marines on the *Congress;* acting capt. in Stockton's Bat. '46–7. v. 281, 385, 391–5; perhaps 'Zielin.'   Zenon, Ind. leader of a plot at S. José '42. iv. 338.   Zerman (John Napoleon), 1846 (?), Fr. lieut at Waterloo; veteran of many campaigns; in Mex. war; in Cal. '49 et seq. and in '74; possibly in '46.   Zertaje, 1821, mr or sup. of the *S. F. Javier.* ii. 440, 202.   Zetch (August), 1847, gen. accredited to N.Y. Vol. (v. 499); settled at Petaluma; d. at S. F. '79; prob. the following.   Zetschsky (Charles), 1847, Co. C, N.Y. Vol. (v. 499); at Petaluma '83. *Clark.*

Zimmerman (Bernard), 1847, Co. F, 3d U.S. artill. (v. 518).   Z. (W.), 1847, ditto; in Cal. '64.   Zindel (Louis), 1844, one of Frémont's party; prob. did not come to Cal. iv. 437.   Zinky (D.), 1846, doubtful name of the Cal. Bat. (v. 358).   Zinns (Geo.), 1846, nat. of Lorraine, and overl. immig.; Cal. Bat. (v. 358); married Mrs Wolfinger at Sutter's fort '47, and is said to have built the first brick house at Sac. He was later a brewer and fruit-grower, but being ruined by fire and again by slickens, he lived on a chicken ranch from '72, and died at Oakland in '85 at the age of '86.   Zittle (Michael), 1847, Co. I, N.Y. Vol. (v. 499).   Zorrilla (Francisco), 1842, named as in charge of the Los Ang. gold mines. iv. 630.   Zúñiga (José), 1781, lieut of the S. Diego comp., acting as habilitado and com. to 1793. Later capt. at Tucson, Sonora; lieut-col 1810. He was one of the most efficient of the old presidio officers. Biog. i. 645–6; ment. i. 335, 340, 343, 372, 396, 398, 400, 441, 454, 461–3, 467, 484, 502, 522, 653; ii. 78.   Z. (Guillermo), land-owner at Los Ang. '39, age 48.   Z. (Nicolás), soldier of the Mont. comp. '36, age '21.   Z. (Pio Quinto), soldier of the S. Juan Cap. escolta 1776–9. i. 303. Z. (Ramon), soldier at Mont. '36, age 25.   Z. (Valentin), at Los Ang. '39, age 42.   Z. (Ventura), boy at Los Ang. 1802; soldier in '10. ii. 91.   Zurri-llaga 1824, mr of the *Constancia.* ii. 519.   Zurita (José), murderer at S. Juan B. '44. iv. 662.

END OF PIONEER REGISTER.